THE LAW
OF GOVERNANCE,
RISK MANAGEMENT,
AND COMPLIANCE

ASPEN CASEBOOK SERIES

THE LAW OF GOVERNANCE, RISK MANAGEMENT, AND COMPLIANCE

Second Edition

Geoffrey Parsons Miller

Stuyvesant P. Comfort Professor of Law
Director, Center for Financial Institutions
Co-Director, Program on Corporate Compliance and Enforcement
New York University Law School

. Wolters Kluwer

Published by Wolters Kluwer in New York.

Wolters Kluwer Legal & Regulatory U.S. serves customers worldwide with CCH, Aspen Publishers, and Kluwer Law International products. (www.WKLegaledu.com)

To contact Customer Service, e-mail customer.service@wolterskluwer.com, call 1-800-234-1660, fax 1-800-901-9075, or mail correspondence to:

Wolters Kluwer
Attn: Order Department
PO Box 990
Frederick, MD 21705

Printed in the United States of America.

2 3 4 5 6 7 8 9 0

ISBN 978-1-4548-8198-8

Names: Miller, Geoffrey P., author.
  Title: The law of governance, risk management, and compliance / Geoffrey Parsons Miller, Stuyvesant P. Comfort Professor of Law Director, Center for Financial Institutions Co-Director, Program on Corporate Compliance and Enforcement, New York University Law School.
  Description: Second edition. | New York : Wolters Kluwer, [2016] |
    Series: Aspen casebook series
  Identifiers: LCCN 2016044848 | ISBN 9781454881988
  Subjects: LCSH: Corporate governance–Law and legislation–United States. | Risk management–Law and legislation–United States. | Compliance. | LCGFT: Casebooks
  Classification: LCC KF1422 .M55 2016 | DDC 346.73/0662–dc23
  LC record available at https://lccn.loc.gov/2016044848

About Wolters Kluwer Legal & Regulatory U.S.

Wolters Kluwer Legal & Regulatory U.S. delivers expert content and solutions in the areas of law, corporate compliance, health compliance, reimbursement, and legal education. Its practical solutions help customers successfully navigate the demands of a changing environment to drive their daily activities, enhance decision quality and inspire confident outcomes.

Serving customers worldwide, its legal and regulatory portfolio includes products under the Aspen Publishers, CCH Incorporated, Kluwer Law International, ftwilliam.com and MediRegs names. They are regarded as exceptional and trusted resources for general legal and practice-specific knowledge, compliance and risk management, dynamic workflow solutions, and expert commentary.

To my parents

Summary of Contents

Contents

Chapter 3
Executives   **121**

Part II Compliance   155

Chapter 4
Introduction to Compliance   157

Chapter 7
Prosecutors   305

Chapter 10
Plaintiffs' Attorneys   **471**

Chapter 11
Information Security   **495**

Chapter 12
Off-Label Drugs

Chapter 13
Foreign Corrupt Practices   569

Chapter 14
Anti-Money Laundering, the Bank Secrecy Act, and OFAC   603

Part III Risk Management   707

Chapter 18
Introduction to Risk Management   709

Preface

This book is born out of concern and conviction. As a professor specializing in corporate and financial law, I have long nurtured an interest in governance, risk management, and compliance — topics that seemed to be incompletely conceptualized and imperfectly understood either individually or in relationship to each other. As an observer of business practices and financial markets, I am convinced that governance, risk management, and compliance are important today and will only increase in significance over the coming decades. As an independent director of a financial institution, I am impressed by the subtlety and breadth of the governance issues facing business organizations in a rapidly changing world. Added together, these considerations — coupled with the dearth of materials covering these topics on a systematic basis from a legal point of view — led me to write this book.

A word is in order about terminology. The world of governance, risk management, and compliance is populated by an exotic zoo of acronyms, technical terms, and metaphors, often used without much attempt to offer a precise definition or to explain the background of their use. I have attempted to avoid most of these terms, preferring instead to write in a simple and nontechnical way. However, the reader will observe that technical language does find its way into the pages that follow. Where arcane terminology is used, it is usually for one of two purposes. Sometimes the words usefully capture ideas or nuances of meaning that would not be embodied in more familiar language (for example, the notion of a "risk appetite"). At other times, I use unusual language because the terms are ubiquitous among people working in the field of governance, risk management, and compliance (e.g., the "three lines of defense" or "enterprise risk management"). Anyone who wants to become active in this field needs to know how to use these terms; you may as well start now. To aid the reader in this journey, I include text boxes containing definitions of many of the key concepts.

I have used the following conventions in excerpting materials. From time to time I have presented documents or problem sets involving fictional organizations. No connection with any actual organization is intended or should be assumed. In the interest of brevity I have limited the excerpted material to text that is most pertinent to the question at hand; although I provide background needed for a full understanding, some context is necessarily lost. I have included ellipses when substantive text is omitted but have not indicated the omission of citations, paragraph numbers, or other non-substantive material. In order to increase readability I have occasionally, and without alerting the reader, made stylistic alterations: breaking longish sections of text into separate paragraphs or joining shorter sections together, revising or eliminating headings, or changing the case of text. Readers should refer to the original texts for more information.

One cannot spend many years in the world of law and law practice without coming into contact with the leading problems of the day. I am grateful for having been a witness to some of the events recounted in this book. Those experiences have stimulated my interest in the topic of governance, risk management, and compliance, and enriched my understanding of the events and underlying social policies. Although I don't believe these experiences have biased the ideas presented in this book, in the interest of full disclosure I note that I have been involved in numerous class actions and shareholders derivative suits as a lawyer, adviser, or expert witness. I served as an expert in cases arising out of the failure of Bank of Credit and Commerce International, the Enron scandal, and the Deepwater Horizon oil spill. I am a member of the board of directors and the risk and compensation committees, and serve as chair of the audit committee of State Farm Bank, a thrift institution that is a wholly-owned subsidiary of State Farm Mutual Automobile Insurance Company.

Many people assisted in the preparation of this volume. Lauren Citrome, Colin S. Huston-Liter, and Adam Karman provided excellent research assistance. My extraordinarily capable assistant, Jerome Miller, helped keep me organized and facilitated the process in innumerable ways. Many colleagues and friends provided advice, counsel, and feedback: Jennifer Arlen, Colleen Baker, Stephen Bainbridge, Carole Basri, Karen Brenner, Theodore Eisenberg, Howell Jackson, Bruce McClure, Gerald Rosenfeld, Roberta Romano, and Helen Scott among many others. I have been fortunate to learn about governance from some exceptionally able business leaders including Charles Brummel, Carolyn Chin, Gerald Czarnecki, Steve Jones, Eric Malcholdi, Ed Rust, Marilyn Seymann, Mike Smith, Paul Smith, Michael Tipsord, Howard Thomas, and Astrid von Baillou. I am grateful to my publisher, Wolters Kluwer, for their professional production operation and for their confidence in producing a course book for a topic with no established market. My wife, Allison Brown, tolerated prolonged periods of distraction and research; she also provided generous input into many questions both of structure and detail. She taught me a lot about governance, risk management, and compliance! While each of these people or institutions provided invaluable input, none is responsible for errors or shortcomings. The field of governance, risk management, and compliance is developing with dizzying speed. Regulators, prosecutors, courts, and the regulated firms themselves generate new rules, new cases, new initiatives, and new ideas nearly every week. In the few years since the first edition of this book appeared, many law schools have instituted courses in compliance and several have started full-scale graduate programs in the field. Compliance is also becoming a recognizable topic of legal scholarship — still in its infancy, but showing potential for enlightening and imaginative thought and analysis. It has, accordingly, been necessary to prepare this second edition in a faster time track than is typical for law school books. This new edition both fleshes out topics greater detail and also incorporates treatments of many new and exciting developments. I hope that everyone who reads this book can experience some of the fascination and excitement that I have felt when writing the volume. It is truly a privilege to observe, comment, and teach about this important and growing area of law and policy.

Geoffrey Parsons Miller
November 2016

THE LAW
OF GOVERNANCE,
RISK MANAGEMENT,
AND COMPLIANCE

Introduction

A. WHAT ARE GOVERNANCE, RISK MANAGEMENT, AND COMPLIANCE?

Governance, risk management, and compliance are in vogue. Activist shareholders, institutional investors, and policymakers look to these activities as crucial means for improving business ethics, enhancing compliance with legal norms, and deterring firms from engaging in unsafe or unsound practices. Regulators encourage companies to upgrade their activities in these areas; if companies do not comply, the regulators find ways to force them to do so. Companies large and small seem to have "got it"; during the first and second decades of the twenty-first century they have greatly upgraded the role of governance, risk management, and compliance in their decision processes — and massively increased spending on these functions as well. These developments, moreover, are hardly limited to the United States; similar expansions in governance, risk management, and compliance can be observed throughout the world.

What are governance, risk management, and compliance, and why are they important? Why has their significance grown so rapidly in recent years? Will GRC achieve the goals that its proponents have set for it? What is the future of GRC: Is it a fad, with only passing significance, or is it a sea-change in how businesses and other organizations are managed? What is the role of attorneys in the area, and what should it be?

This book explores these and other issues raised by the explosion of GRC. Our focus will principally be on the business corporation, but we will attend also to other organizations where GRC plays a role: nonprofit firms, charities, religious organizations, and governments (among others). In these respects the coverage of the book is broad. But we will also examine GRC from a specific perspective: that of law, the legal system, and the legal profession. We will not be considering the topic from the standpoint of accountants, auditors, information technology experts, or people involved in specific lines of business. We will not examine GRC as an aspect of business strategy. These limitations on scope are needed, not only to make the

1

book manageable, but also because of the intended audience. This book is designed for two purposes: first for use as a textbook or resource in law school classes; and second as an introduction to the topic that can be useful for attorneys in governments, organizations, and private law firms who find themselves swept up in the GRC phenomenon.

Before launching into the substance of our topic, it is useful to define terms. At the outset, we can see that the term "governance, risk management, and compliance" suggests two things. The combination of words in a single phrase, and especially the use of an acronym ("GRC"), indicate that the topic has an internal unity: Governance, risk management, and compliance are not simply three things that companies do that are grouped together in arbitrary fashion; rather they have something fundamental in common. But the use of separate words, each with its own history and connotations, indicates that despite the overlap, there are also differences between these functions. Let's consider what is different about the key terms, as used in this book, and then turn to what they have in common.

First, what do we mean by "governance"? The term has to do with the structure of control within an organization. The governance of organizations is often complex, involving layers of responsibility and a variety of different offices and positions, with lines of authority projecting in many different ways. The formal structure of governance, moreover, may not present a full picture of how the process actually works. Creating an office and endowing it with formal authority does not necessarily mean that the authority will actually be exercised or that the office will perform its job competently. Power and decision making in an organization may sometimes have more to do with history, personality, and interpersonal relationships than with job descriptions. Unless one is inside an organization, however, these subtle ebbs and flows are not readily observable. For the student of governance, risk management, and compliance, there is often no realistic option but to go by organizational charts, committee charters, and job descriptions — recognizing that the structure of authority presented in these documents may only partially reflect the actual distribution of power and influence within the organization.

> "Governance" refers to the processes by which decisions relative to risk management and compliance are made within an organization.

Risk management takes account of the risks facing an organization. Unlike governance, risk management has a significant technical component. Organizations, especially these days, often attempt to quantify risk in precise ways, using where appropriate (and sometimes where not appropriate) complex mathematical formulas and analytical methods. The goal of risk management is not to eliminate risk but rather to manage it: The risk management function recognizes that the activities of the enterprise necessarily involve uncertain outcomes with different consequences for the success of the organization's mission.

> "Risk management" refers to the processes by which risk is identified, analyzed, included in strategic planning, and either reduced through risk control and mitigation tactics or accepted as inherent in activities that the organization wishes to conduct.

We will use the term "compliance" in a somewhat specialized way. In normal usage, the term means that a person conforms to some set of norms. Here we mean something more particular: the *processes* by which an organization seeks to ensure that employees and other constituents conform to applicable norms — norms that can include either the requirements of laws and regulations or the internal rules of

> "Compliance" refers to the processes by which an organization polices its own behavior to ensure that it conforms to applicable rules.

the organization. The compliance function usually does not create or establish these norms; it accepts them as given and seeks only to ensure that they are observed.

As we will see repeatedly in the pages that follow, the functions of governance, risk management, and compliance are not hermetically separated. Much of the law pertinent to compliance has to do with governance; it dictates how responsibility for enforcing applicable norms is allocated within an organization. The same goes for risk management, although to a lesser extent: Much of the law governing risk management requires that the regulated entity act through defined offices and institutions. Thus governance has a close relationship with both risk-management and compliance. Compliance and risk management also obviously have much in common: Non-compliance is itself a risk — and a significant one — that organizations must evaluate and attempt to control.

These overlaps are more than simply matters of definition. They arise out of a deep structural similarity between the three GRC functions. Considered from the most general perspective, governance, risk management, and compliance serve a common purpose: ensuring that organizations are managed well (effectively and in such a way as to enhance social welfare). The law of governance, risk management, and compliance is the body of rules, regulations, and best practices that, individually

> The law of governance, risk management, and compliance is the body of rules, regulations, and best practices that, individually and collectively, are intended to ensure that organizations are managed effectively and in such a way as to enhance social welfare.

and collectively, are intended to ensure that organizations achieve this goal.

The law of governance, risk management, and compliance includes, not only conventional rules and regulations, but also "soft law" recommendations from non-governmental organizations. Among the most important of these is the Committee of Sponsoring Organizations of the Treadway Commission (COSO), an umbrella organization of trade groups involved with GRC. COSO promotes the idea of "internal controls" to capture the essence of the GRC process. As set forth in the most recent iteration of its integrated framework, COSO defines internal control as "a process, implemented by an entity's board of directors, management, and other personnel, designed to provide reasonable assurance regarding the achievement of objectives relating to operations, reporting, and compliance." The COSO framework identifies the following key elements of internal control:

- Control environment: the general tone of the organization: its culture, attitudes, values, philosophy, human development procedures, and operating style. COSO views the control environment as the most important element of internal control.

- Risk assessment: the process by which the organization identifies and evaluates material risks to its operations, both internal (e.g., a fraud committed by senior officers) or external (e.g., changes in market prices).
- Control activities: the procedures and policies that an organization employs to ensure that decisions made by the board of directors and senior management are faithfully and competently executed throughout the organization.
- Information and communication: the means by which agents of the organization are supplied with the information needed to perform their duties.
- Monitoring: a process of quality assurance, both on an ongoing basis as operations are performed, and separate evaluations conducted after the fact.

What value can an effective system of internal controls add to an organization? According to COSO, internal controls help an organization achieve its objectives while reducing risk. The objectives of the organization include not only meeting profitability targets and reducing costs, but also ensuring compliance with applicable laws and regulations. At the same time, COSO warns that internal controls are no panacea or guarantee. They do not ensure success, are unable to predict adverse events, and cannot perform the alchemy of transforming a bad manager into a good one.

Questions and Comments

1. COSO is an umbrella organization of five organizations: the American Accounting Association, the American Institute of CPAs, Financial Executives International, the Association of Accountants and Financial Professionals in Business, and the Institute of Internal Auditors. Its mission is to improve and modernize practices for corporate directors and managers in the areas of internal controls, enterprise risk management, and fraud prevention. Together, COSO's sponsoring organizations carry considerable clout as spokespeople for authoritative opinion in the worlds of accounting, auditing, and corporate finance.

2. Do you see any logic inherent in the order of COSO's list of key internal control functions?

3. Is there anything in the report, as described above, that could not be divined through the exercise of common sense?

4. Why was the COSO report so influential? Does it offer something for everyone, without goring anyone's ox?

5. How, if at all, does the concept of internal controls serve the interests of COSO's sponsoring organizations?

Those who think about governance, risk management, and compliance display a nearly preternatural affection for metaphors. A leading metaphor in the field is that of the "three lines of defense." In conventional usage, the lines are the following:

The Three Lines of Defense

Line One: operating executives have initial responsibility for implementing internal controls within their own areas.
Line Two: risk-management and compliance operations catch problems that are not weeded out at the front line.
Line Three: internal audit checks up on everyone, including risk management and compliance, in an attempt to make sure that no problems remain.

Questions and Comments

1. Consider the image of the "three lines of defense." What human activity does it refer to?

2. What attitudes are invoked by this metaphor? Lines of defense are needed when a country is threatened by an external foe; the threat is to the institution as a whole and everyone in it. The enemy seeks to invade the organization's territory if given an opportunity. Everyone in the organization shares an interest in keeping the lines of defense as strong and as effective as possible.

3. The lines of defense metaphor seems to convey a mixed message about the organization's state of preparedness. The fact that three lines of defense are in place is reassuring; multiple backups minimize the chance that the destructive agent will penetrate to the organization's core. Yet the fact that three lines of defense are needed also warns that the threat is powerful and dangerous and that, if the worst case happens and the lines are penetrated, the consequences for the organization are likely to be grave.

4. Why is external audit not included in the lines of defense? Should it be considered a fourth line of defense?

5. What about regulators?

6. What purposes does the "lines of defense" metaphor serve?

7. Why is metaphoric language so powerful, and apparently so useful, in this supposedly scientific and rational enterprise?

8. The metaphor of the three lines of defense has tended to focus attention on the second and third lines — risk management and compliance, and internal audit. Is there a danger that the emphasis on the second and third lines will distract attention away from the place where the problems can most easily be avoided — the day-to-day business operations where appropriate diligence can prevent problems from arising in the first place?

B. THE ROLE OF ATTORNEYS

A distinctive feature of governance, risk management, and compliance is that these functions are inherently cross-disciplinary. Governance, for example, has a significant legal element: The rules allocating responsibility and authority for compliance and risk management are contained in formal legal documents such as charters, bylaws, and board resolutions — not to mention laws, regulations, letter rulings, judicial opinions, consent decrees, deferred prosecution agreements, and administrative orders. But governance also has important non-legal elements: Many decisions are made within the discretion of the board of directors or senior managers, without significant legal input.

The same holds for compliance. Many of the underlying norms and rules that are administered through the compliance function are legal in nature; but some are internal institutional policies or procedures not mandated by law. Lawyers are often used for investigations into allegations of misconduct by corporate employees; but investigations are also carried out by private investigators, computer technicians, forensic accountants, and other people. Much of the compliance function today, moreover, is outsourced to non-lawyer vendors who provide software systems that operate automatically and outside the direct control of lawyers.

Risk management, likewise, involves a combination of legal and non-legal considerations. Some of the most important risks an organization faces are explicitly legal in nature — for example, the risk that the institution will face onerous new regulations, or that it be required to pay a legal judgment or be subjected to punitive governmental sanctions. Yet other risks facing an organization have less to do with law: Examples are the risk that a financial institution will lose money in its trading operations, or the risk that private customer information will be stolen from a company's computerized records. Even these latter risks have a legal dimension, however: For example, most financial institutions are required to operate in a safe and sound manner, so that very large trading losses could represent a violation of legal obligations.

Lawyers thus play an important role in the area of governance, risk management, and compliance, but far from the only role. People specializing in other fields — management, accounting, investigation, finance, and information technology, among others — play major roles. Moreover, new professional roles have been developing at an astonishing pace. Many educational institutions offer certificates or degrees in the GRC area; Stanford University's Center for Professional Development, for example, awards a certificate in risk management. The Wharton School of the University of Pennsylvania, in cooperation with the Financial Industry Regulatory Authority (FINRA), offers a program of instruction whose graduates earn designation as Certified Regulatory and Compliance Professionals (CRCPs). An organization called "GRC Certify™" offers a menu of certifications in the combined field of governance, risk management, and compliance. And these are only a sample of dozens of programs offering instruction or certification in the area. We may in fact be witnessing the birth of two new professions — compliance and risk management — that combine elements of law, accounting, human resources, business, ethics, and more.

Questions and Comments

1. Notably missing from the list of COSO sponsors is any representation by lawyers. Neither the American Bar Association nor any other organization representing the legal profession sponsors this initiative. Given that one of the principal objectives of internal controls is "compliance with applicable laws and regulations," why are lawyers not represented?

2. Aware that GRC is a growth area for professional practice, law firms are now vigorously pursuing this line of work. The websites of many large law firms contain sections touting services in the area of compliance — services that range from specialized representations when a client gets into trouble to audits of compliance areas to full-scale outsourcing of tasks and responsibilities. Law firms are more tentative about offering risk management advice; but many clearly imply that their services will be valuable in controlling or mitigating legal, regulatory, and operational risks.

3. The growth of governance, risk management, and compliance as a discrete field of professional service, including important legal elements, raises the question whether professional service providers may offer a comprehensive and integrated package of services that includes both legal and non-legal expertise. Could one of the big accounting or consulting firms hire lawyers and put them to work providing

legal services to clients in engagements that also involve accountants, economists, marketing consultants, finance advisers, and other trained professionals?

4. Do attorneys perform their jobs differently than other compliance professionals? One might think so, given the special features of legal training — socialization into how to "think like a lawyer," sensitivity to legal rights and duties, awareness of the responsibility of zealous representation of clients, and immersion in an adversarial system of justice. A study of Australian firms concludes, however, that in general, lawyers don't perform their compliance jobs in a distinctive way. Robert Posen, Christine Parker & Vibeke Lehmann Nielsen, *The Framing Effects of Professionalism: Is There a Lawyer Cast of Mind? Lessons from Compliance Programs*, 40 Fordham Urb. L.J. 297 (2012).

C. SUBJECT AREAS

Our definitions of governance, risk management, and compliance are formulated at an abstract level that does not depend on any specific subject matter. Appropriately so: The functions served by governance, risk management, and compliance are quite general. All organizations — for-profit corporations, not-for-profit corporations, religious institutions, governments, and many others — must perform these functions. Thus the law in this area is not the law *of* any particular field of activity or area of commerce; it is a topic that pertains to all complex organizations.

At the same time, other elements of governance, risk management, and compliance are specific to particular subject matters. The ways in which governance, risk management, and compliance play out across areas of human endeavor is partially a function of the specific field. The rules pertaining to hospitals differ from the rules that apply to commercial airlines; those rules, in turn, differ from the rules that apply to securities broker-dealers. Each field has its own underlying policies and its own political environment that shapes the rules we observe. History also plays a role: We will see that rules often change in response to large and stressful events that are deemed, in one way or another, to have resulted from a breakdown in governance, risk management, or compliance.

This feature of governance, risk management, and compliance law — that it has a common structure but also includes specific and sometimes idiosyncratic rules — influences how this book is organized. We deal with issues in their general and abstract form, but also provide a "deep dive" into specific areas.

Part I of this book looks at the topic of governance from a general perspective. This part introduces the cast of characters within the organization: shareholders (Chapter 1), the board of directors and board committees (Chapter 2), and internal management (Chapter 3).

Part II turns to compliance. We take this up before reaching the topic of risk management — and thus deviate from the conventional order — because it is an area of particular pertinence to lawyers. Here, we examine in more detail what the compliance function is (Chapter 4). We then turn to the technology of compliance, examining the role of internal enforcement (Chapter 5), regulators (Chapter 6), prosecutors (Chapter 7), whistleblowers (Chapter 8), gatekeepers (Chapter 9), and plaintiffs' attorneys (Chapter 10). Next, we focus on specific topics where compliance plays a role: information security (Chapter 11), off-label drugs (Chapter 12), foreign corrupt practices (Chapter 13), money laundering and bank secrecy (Chapter 14), and sexual harassment (Chapter 15). These specific topics are important in their own right and also illustrative of general issues that arise in the compliance space. We end the unit on compliance by examining activities beyond compliance such as charitable gifts, code of ethics, corporate social responsibility, sustainability, and institutional culture (Chapter 16), and instances where compliance fails (Chapter 17).

Part III takes up the topic of risk management. After examining what risk management is (Chapter 18), we evaluate different approaches to risk management (Chapter 19). The book concludes with an examination of cases where risk management fails (Chapter 20).

Part I

Governance

Consider a company like Citigroup. In 2015, this vast financial firm serviced approximately 200 million customer accounts and did business in more than 160 countries and jurisdictions. With more than $76 billion in annual revenues, Citigroup would rank in the top 100 countries in the world by gross national product. Its quarter million employees could represent the workforce of a substantial city. Even more staggering is the amount of assets under its control — $1.9 trillion and counting. And Citigroup is not even the largest financial institution in the United States; JPMorgan Chase, Bank of America, and Wells Fargo are larger still.

Given the size and influence of complex organizations, it is obvious that decisions made by their managers have an impact on social welfare. If a company is well managed, it will tend to generate profits that enrich its shareholders and employees, who then are more willing to spend money and contribute to the health of the economy. Well-managed companies also represent efficient allocations of resources, since the assets under the control of the managers of these companies will be devoted to profitable uses. If a company is poorly managed, the opposite happens: People become poorer, spend less, and invest less; and the assets controlled by these companies are not put to their highest and best use. In the worst case, bad decisions can have systematic consequences: Poor investment policies by financial firms contributed to the financial crisis of 2007-2009. The question of governance — who decides what a complex organization will and will not do — is therefore one of considerable public importance.

For large organizations, the problem of governance is often conceptualized as that of the "separation of ownership and control" — a phrase that traces back to an influential book published in 1932 by Adolph Berle and Gardiner Means entitled *The Modern Corporation and Private Property*. Almost no one reads the book any more, but the concept of the separation of ownership and control remains a defining issue for corporate governance. The basic idea is this: Large corporations have thousands or millions of shareholders; even the largest of these owners has only a small percentage interest in the firm. The sheer number of shareholders makes it virtually impossible for them to exercise effective governance. Rather, managers control what happens in big companies, subject to only minimal checks from shareholders or other constituencies. But managers, if not controlled from without, will too often give in to the temptation to expropriate the benefits of control for themselves. Managerial misconduct of this sort is given various names — "abuse" by those (such as Berle and Means) who were steeped in the political values of the Progressive Era; and "agency costs" by later scholars who work in the framework of law and economics. No matter what the conduct is called, its consequences are the same: Corporations will not be managed so as to serve the best interests either of shareholders or of society as a whole. This concern about managerial incompetence or misconduct is the essential problem of corporate governance.

The issue of corporate governance has long been at the front burner of policy debate, both in the United States and around the world. A host of white papers, best practice manifestos, and official government policies purport to define how companies ought to be managed. Prestigious institutes, think tanks, politicians, and scholarly organizations offer their opinions on a regular basis.

Over time, the focus of enthusiasm on the part of these experts has shifted. Beginning with an emphasis on the importance of independent boards of directors, the outer edge of policy has moved successively toward an emphasis on the "market for corporate control" (the corporate takeover market); to reliance on institutional investors with large ownership stakes; to a focus on board committees; and to the governance reforms *de jour* of the 2010s: revamping compensation practices and enhancing shareholder power.

Do these or other corporate governance reforms improve the welfare of society? Definitely yes, in the judgment of advocates. Empirical researchers tend to be more cautious. Some studies find benefits of reforms; others do not. In general, it may be fair to say that some corporate governance reforms improve how large institutions are managed and others observe the Hippocratic principle of "do no harm." Still, skeptics question whether the plethora of corporate governance reforms is worth the candle in terms of results obtained.

Consider in this respect the following excerpts, one from the Organization for Economic Cooperation and Development (OECD), and the other from the author of a treatise on the law of corporate governance.

OECD Principles of Corporate Governance

2004

... In today's economies, interest in corporate governance goes beyond that of shareholders in the performance of individual companies. As companies play a pivotal role in our economies and we rely increasingly on private sector institutions to manage personal savings and secure retirement incomes, good corporate governance is important to broad and growing segments of the population.... The [OECD's] Principles [of Corporate Governance] are a living instrument offering non-binding standards and good practices as well as guidance on implementation, which can be adapted to the specific circumstances of individual countries and regions.... To stay abreast of constantly changing circumstances, the OECD will closely follow developments in corporate governance, identifying trends and seeking remedies to new challenges.

Douglas M. Branson, Proposals for Corporate Governance Reform: Six Decades of Ineptitude and Counting

48 Wake Forest L. Rev. 673 (2013)

This article is a retrospective of corporate governance reforms various academics have authored over the last 60 years or so. . . . The first finding is as to periodicity: even casual inspection reveals that the reformer group which controls the "reform" agenda has authored a new and different reform proposal every five years, with clock-like regularity. The second finding flows from the first, namely, that not one of these proposals has made so much as a dent in the problems that are perceived to exist. The third inquiry is to ask why this is so? Possible answers include the top down nature of scholarship and reform proposals in corporate governance; the closed nature of the group controlling the agenda, confined as it is to 8-10 academics at elite institutions; the lack of any attempt to rethink or redefine the challenges which governance may or may not face; and the continued adhesion to the problem as the separation of ownership from control as Adolph Berle and Gardiner Means perceived it more than 80 years ago.

Questions and Comments

1. The OECD is a respected good-governance organization. According to its website, its mission is to "promote policies that will improve the economic and social well-being of people around the world. . . . We set international standards on a wide range of things, from agriculture and tax to the safety of chemicals."

2. The OECD Principles of Corporate Governance are not law. No country is obligated to adopt these principles as a matter of internal law. Yet recommended "best practices" such as these can be influential. Why? Consider the following possibilities:

   a. The OECD's standards are good ideas, and when they are understood by others, they are adopted because they are recognized as a better way to govern.
   b. The OECD's standards provide a focal point around which a consensus of regulators and policy makers can coalesce. Once many people get behind a proposed reform, it has greater prospects for success than, say, if the idea is being promoted by a solitary academic.
   c. The OECD's standards make it easier for governments to adopt internal reforms because domestic political interests find it hard to resist proposals that have the backing of prestigious international organizations.
   d. The OECD's standards serve the interests of organizations and individuals who pursue agendas that do not necessarily align with the public interest.

Which of these possibilities seems most plausible to you?

3. Notice the difference in tone between the two excerpts. Implicit in the OECD statement is an optimistic view about the potential for progress in improving corporate governance. Standards would not be necessary if all companies were already following the OECD's recommendations. The OECD's approach carries with it an idea that working together, governments and private organizations can genuinely improve corporate behavior and that the result will be beneficial for everyone.

4. The OECD seems confident that its recommendations are wise and appropriate. What is the basis for this confidence? The OECD's opinions about corporate governance seem to be grounded, not on controlled studies but, rather, on the consensus of government officials. Is this a reliable source of information? What shapes the opinions of the government officials who take part in the OECD's councils? Could it be that these officials rely on the views of prestigious organizations such as the OECD? Is the process circular?

5. Branson's analysis displays a markedly different tone. He wonders whether governance reforms do much good at all and doubts that much has been learned over the years.

6. What, in Branson's view, drives changes in corporate governance recommendations? He suggests that a handful of academics have shaped opinions for everyone else. Is this plausible?

7. On what basis does Branson conclude that corporate governance reforms haven't worked? One of his key exhibits is evidence that these reforms are creatures of fashion — every five years or so another proposal becomes popular and flourishes for a while, only to be supplanted by a newcomer. If governance reforms are so fickle, Branson suggests, perhaps they are not grounded in real benefits. Do you agree?

8. For other critiques of fashionable corporate governance requirements, see Roberta Romano, *Quack Corporate Governance*, 28 Reg. 36 (2005); Stephen Bainbridge, Dodd-Frank: Quack Federal Corporate Governance Round II, UCLA School of Law Law-Econ Research Paper No. 10-12 (2010); Luigi Zingales & Dirk A. Zetzsche, Quack Corporate Governance, Round III? Bank Board Regulation Under the New European Capital Requirement Directive, European Corporate Governance Institute Law Working Paper No. 249/2014 (2014).

9. Even though at this point you may not yet have a well-developed opinion about the value of governance reforms, whose view seems more persuasive?

Corporate governance was once largely within the discretion of the regulated entity—subject, perhaps, to the gentle pressure of "best practice" principles but not otherwise within the purview of outside influences. No more. At least in the area of financial institutions, and increasingly in other industries, regulators are taking a close look at corporate governance practices and, at times, imposing the heavy hand of compulsory rules. Consider in this regard the following excerpt from the Basel Committee on Banking Supervision's "Core Principles of Banking Supervision," a document that purports to identify minimum acceptable standards for supervision of banks around the world.

Basel Committee on Banking Supervision
Consultative Document — Core Principles
for Effective Banking Supervision

December 2011

Principle 14: Corporate Governance

The supervisor determines that banks and banking groups have robust corporate governance policies and processes covering, for example, strategic direction, group and organizational structure, control environment, responsibilities of the banks' boards and senior management, and compensation. These policies and processes are commensurate with the risk profile and systemic importance of the bank.

Essential Criteria

- Laws, regulations, or the supervisor establish the responsibilities of the bank's board and senior management with respect to corporate governance to ensure there is effective control over the bank's entire business. The supervisor provides guidance to banks and banking groups on expectations for sound corporate governance.
- The supervisor regularly assesses a bank's corporate governance policies and practices, and their implementation, and determines that the bank has robust corporate governance policies and processes commensurate with its risk profile and systemic importance. The supervisor requires banks and banking groups to correct deficiencies in a timely manner.
- The supervisor determines that governance structures and processes for nominating and appointing a board member are appropriate for the bank and across the banking group. Board membership includes experienced non-executive members, where appropriate. Commensurate with the risk profile and systemic importance, board structures include audit, risk oversight, and remuneration committees with experienced non-executive members.
- Board members are suitably qualified, effective, and exercise their "duty of care" and "duty of loyalty."
- The supervisor determines that the bank's board approves and oversees implementation of the bank's strategic direction, risk appetite and strategy, and related policies, establishes and communicates corporate culture and values (e.g. through a code of conduct), and establishes conflicts of interest policies and a strong control environment.
- The supervisor determines that the bank's board, except where required otherwise by laws or regulations, has established fit and proper standards in selecting senior management, plans for succession, and actively and critically oversees senior management's execution of board strategies, including monitoring senior management's performance against standards established for them.
- The supervisor determines that the bank's board actively oversees the design and operation of the bank's and banking group's compensation system, and that it has appropriate incentives, which are aligned with prudent risk taking. The compensation system, and related performance standards, are consistent with long term objectives and financial soundness of the bank and is rectified if there are deficiencies.
- The supervisor determines that the bank's board and senior management know and understand the bank's and banking group's operational structure and its risks, including those arising from the use of structures that impede transparency (e.g. special-purpose or related structures). The supervisor determines that risks are effectively managed and mitigated, where appropriate.
- The supervisor has the power to require changes in the composition of the bank's board if it believes that any individuals are not fulfilling their duties related to the satisfaction of these criteria.

Questions and Comments

1. Should regulators be dictating corporate governance of banks?

2. Is there a danger of abuse, if the regulators are self-interested or vindictive?

3. These are set forth as minimum requirements. What else would you recommend, if anything?

1

Shareholders

A. PROS AND CONS OF SHAREHOLDER POWER

Shareholders have economic interests in the success or failure of corporations in which they hold shares. If the company does well, shareholders get a portion of the income (net of expenses, including the cost of debt service). If the company does poorly, they share in the loss. In the case of profits, shareholders gain in either of two ways: The company may declare a dividend distributing some of the surplus back to its owners; or the share price may rise to reflect the value of profits that have not been distributed. Shareholders incur losses when the value of their interest falls. If the company becomes insolvent, they forfeit the entire value of their investments. If the company winds up its business — say, by voluntary dissolution (rare) or by being acquired by another firm (common) — they get a distribution reflecting some measure of the value of their ownership interests.

One might think that shareholders would control the management of their firms for several reasons:

- Giving shareholders control rights can reduce the "agency costs" of management — the fact that executives, if not closely monitored, may expropriate for themselves an excessive share of the company's value, or may simply be lazy or incompetent.
- Because shareholders get the first portion of profits and losses, they want companies they own to make a profit, and therefore have an incentive to make profit-maximizing decisions about how the firm is run.

A little thought, however, reveals several reasons why shareholders cannot be the managers of the companies they officially own. The following are especially salient:

- It is not practical to ask shareholders to make most management decisions. These decisions must be made quickly. A business opportunity arises, and the company must decide *now* whether to take it or not. If all decisions had to be given to shareholders for a vote, the company would never "strike while the iron is hot."

- In addition to being time consuming, it is costly to ascertain shareholder preferences. The company must communicate the information necessary for an informed decision; the shareholders must consider how to vote; they must actually vote; and the votes must be collected and tabulated. This may not be too burdensome in small companies with only a few dozen shareholders; but for public firms with millions of shareholders, the costs are substantial. Proxy solicitation firms make a living doing nothing other than helping large companies manage the process of shareholder voting.

- Shareholders may not be well informed about decisions that they do make. Most shareholders don't have a lot invested in any particular company. Suppose you have inherited 20 shares in General Motors from Grandma. You might spend the time needed to research the condition of General Motors, to study the company's proxy materials, and to find out what analysts and others are saying about the company's prospects. Probably you won't do so, however. While your shares in General Motors are not irrelevant to your welfare, you aren't going to stay up at night worrying about them. If you have not examined the issue under consideration, your vote will not be an informed one, and will not contribute to the efficient management of the company.

- Most shareholders hold diversified portfolios of equity securities. Diversified shareholders are unlikely to care deeply about the fortunes of any particular company, simply because their ownership of many different companies effectively gives them a hedge: If the fortunes of one company go down, that bad result is likely to be offset by an improvement in the fortunes of another company also held by the shareholder. The feature of diversification reduces the shareholder's interest in monitoring the management of any particular company.

- If the company is publicly traded, shareholders have an easy option if they are not happy with how the company is performing. Rather than exercise "voice" by voting to throw out the incumbent board of directors, the simpler solution is just to sell one's stock. Then any shortcomings at the company become someone else's problem.

- Even if no issues with the company arise, shareholders often sell their interests for reasons such as rebalancing their portfolios or liquidating investments in order to raise cash for expenses. If the shareholder anticipates selling her stock, she has a reduced interest in tracking what is going on at the company.

- Of course, some shareholders are better informed. Institutional investors, such as pension funds, hire people to analyze the performance of companies in which they invest; broker-dealers such as Merrill Lynch employ experts who investigate company performance and make buy-sell recommendations; and professional proxy advisors make recommendations about how shareholders should vote. If informed shareholders control the outcome of shareholder votes, then arguably the fact that many shareholders are uninformed should not make a difference from the standpoint of social policy. However, informed shareholders do not possess the judgment needed to make day-to-day management decisions. Informed shareholders may not even be able to make accurate judgments about the most fundamental issues facing the company, such as what its stock is worth. Among the many painful lessons of the financial crisis of 2007-2009 was the fact that the stock market (along with nearly everyone else) appeared to have miscalculated the risks posed by subprime mortgage-backed securities.

- Even if shareholders could effectively exercise control on an informed basis, it is not clear that we would want them to do so. Shareholders' interests do not, in fact, align optimally with what society would prefer. They capture all the upside of a risky venture if the activity turns out well, but if the activity turns out poorly and the company becomes insolvent, some of the downside is borne by the creditors. In a sense, creditors provide a policy of insurance to shareholders protecting them against the costs of bankruptcy: If the company fails, the shareholder loses the deductible (the value of her share interest) but all the remaining costs are incurred by the creditors (the policy guarantee). All insurance policies create a problem of moral hazard — when you are insured against a risk you lose much of your incentive to prevent the loss from coming to pass. The "insurance" policy provided to shareholders by creditors is no different: When a company has debt in its balance sheet (and almost all do), then, and to that extent, the equity holders have an incentive to take on too much risk — not only more risk than creditors would prefer, but also more risk than would be socially optimal. Although creditors can limit this problem to some extent — for example, by insisting that borrowers agree to risk-controlling terms in their loan agreements — their control over shareholder risk taking can never be perfect. Accordingly, giving shareholders power to manage a company carries with it the risk that shareholders will make socially inefficient decisions.

It is evident, therefore, that the decision about what role shareholders should play in management presents a subtle problem of legal engineering. Shareholders should not be given control over all decisions a company has to make — this would be unworkable and not in anyone's best interests. On the other hand, if shareholders were cut out of any role in management, the result would be equally undesirable: People whose interests do not necessarily align with those of the firm will make all the decisions, and, not being subject to checks and balances, will often serve their own interests rather than the interests of the company or of society as a whole.

The law's answer to the problem is that shareholders get to make *fundamental* decisions and the board of directors and senior managers get to make the others. Four decisions are treated as fundamental in this sense:

- Election of the board of directors: While shareholders don't make managerial decisions, they do select who, at the highest level, does make these decisions: the members of the board of directors.
- Changes in the company charter: Shareholders vote on changes in the company's charter. Shareholder power over charter amendments, however, is generally an up-or-down vote on proposals placed on the ballot by the board of directors; they don't draft or propose amendments on their own.
- Fundamental corporate changes: Shareholders vote on fundamental corporate changes: mergers, sales of substantially all the assets, or dissolutions.
- Selection of the company's independent auditor: The law doesn't usually require a shareholder vote on the selection of a company's independent auditor. However, many large companies allow shareholders to vote on whether to ratify the selection of the independent auditor.

Questions and Comments

1. In general, shareholders have a right of approval when substantially all the assets of their firm are sold to another company, but not when their company acquires substantially all the assets of another company. The reason is that big companies often acquire substantially all the assets of smaller firms; it would not make sense if shareholders of the acquiring firm had to vote on each such acquisition. However, clever lawyers can structure a transaction such that — in form if not in substance — a big company sells substantially all its assets to a smaller firm. The result will be that the shareholders of the smaller company may lose certain legal protections, including the right to vote on the deal or the right to obtain a judicial appraisal of the consideration they receive. State courts disagree over whether the form of the transaction should prevail over the substance in this circumstance. *Compare* Farris v. Glen Alden Corp., 143 A.2d 25 (Pa. 1958) (giving shareholders the same rights as they would receive in a statutory merger) *with* Hariton v. Arco Electronics, Inc., 182 A.2d 22 (Del. Ch. 1962), *aff'd,* 188 A.2d 123 (Del. 1963) (privileging form over substance).

2. Several studies find that audit fees tend to be higher in companies that allow shareholders to vote on auditor selection; on the other hand, companies that submit the auditor's selection for shareholder ratification also have a lower likelihood of experiencing a restatement of earnings. How do you interpret these findings?

3. Should shareholder votes to ratify the selection of a company's independent auditor be mandatory, rather than in the discretion of the company's managers?

4. Although shareholders have the right to vote on charter amendments, managers can make important changes in a company's governance through board actions that do not require shareholder vote. Examples include "poison pill" shareholder rights plans, which can reduce the chance that a company will be acquired in a hostile takeover, see Moran v. Household International, Inc., 500 A.2d 1346 (Del. 1985); and bylaw amendments designating Delaware courts as the sole forums for lawsuits alleging breach of fiduciary duty in Delaware corporations, see Boilermakers Local 154 Retirement Fund v. Chevron Corp., 73 A.3d 934 (Del. Ch. 2013).

5. A shareholder vote isn't necessarily the end of the story. Consider the case of Big Lots, a Fortune 500 retailing company. In 2013, shareholders unhappy with the company's executive compensation policies obtained a "no" vote against the re-election of independent board member Russell Solt. It was then up to the remaining board members to fill the resulting vacancy; they deliberated and decided to appoint — Solt! A spokesman for the company explained that the board had interpreted the "no" vote on Solt as an expression of dissatisfaction with the company's governance in general rather than as a referendum on Solt. Because the board had taken substantive actions to address the governance concerns, including revamping its executive compensation policies, it deemed it best for the company to retain Solt in his position — and made him the chairman of its compensation committee to boot.

The traditional topics for shareholder vote — election of directors, charter amendments, fundamental corporate changes, and ratification of independent auditors — can all be understood as efforts to draw the line between cases where shareholder voting is desirable and when it is not. However, critics of American corporate governance have long complained that these powers mean little. For reasons already mentioned, most shareholders are rationally indifferent about the affairs of their corporations; they will usually go along with management's recommendations unless something is much amiss. Moreover, many shares were traditionally voted by institutional investors who abided by the "Wall Street Rule": Either vote with management, or if you don't like what management is doing, sell your shares. The result, in the view of many critics, was that shareholders had little control over management even in the limited areas where they officially enjoyed rights to express their opinion. Do you agree with the critics? Consider in this regard the following excerpts, which take different positions about the value of shareholder power.

Lucian Bebchuk, The Case for Increasing Shareholder Power

118 Harv. L. Rev. 833 (2005)*

This article reconsiders the basic allocation of power between boards and shareholders in publicly traded companies with dispersed ownership. U.S. corporate law has long precluded shareholders from initiating any changes in the company's basic governance arrangements. Professor Bebchuk's analysis and his empirical evidence indicate that shareholders' existing power to replace directors is insufficient to secure the adoption of value-increasing governance arrangements that management disfavors. He puts forward an alternative regime that would allow shareholders to initiate and adopt rules-of-the-game decisions to change the company's charter or state of incorporation. Providing shareholders with such power would operate over time to improve all corporate governance arrangements.

Furthermore, Professor Bebchuk argues that, as part of their power to amend governance arrangements, shareholders should be able to adopt provisions that would give them subsequently a specified power to intervene in additional corporate decisions. Power to intervene in game-ending decisions (to merge, sell all assets, or dissolve) could address management's bias in favor of the company's continued existence. Power to intervene in scaling-down decisions (to make cash or in-kind distributions) could address management's tendency to retain excessive funds and engage in empire-building. Shareholders' ability to adopt, when necessary, provisions that give themselves a specified additional power to intervene could thus produce benefits in many companies.

A regime with shareholder power to intervene, Professor Bebchuk shows, would address governance problems that have long troubled legal scholars and financial economists. These benefits would result largely from inducing management to act in shareholder interests without shareholders having to exercise their power to intervene. Professor Bebchuk also discusses how such a regime could best be designed to address concerns that supporters of management insulation could raise; for example, shareholder-initiated changes in governance arrangements could be adopted only if they enjoy shareholder support in two consecutive annual meetings. Finally, examining a wide range of possible objections, Professor Bebchuk concludes that they do not provide a good basis for opposing the proposed increase in shareholder power.

*The following is excerpted from an abstract of Professor Bebchuk's article.

Stephen M. Bainbridge, The Case for Limited Shareholder Voting Rights

53 UCLA L. Rev. 601 (2006)

... [I]n large corporations, authority-based decision making structures are desirable because of the potential for division and specialization of labor. Bounded rationality and complexity, as well as the practical costs of losing time when one shifts jobs, make it efficient for corporate constituents to specialize. Directors and managers specialize in the efficient coordination of other specialists. In order to reap the benefits of specialization, all other corporate constituents should prefer to specialize in functions unrelated to decision making, such as risk-bearing (shareholders) or labor (employees), delegating decision making to the board and senior management. This natural division of labor, however, requires that the chosen directors and officers be vested with discretion to make binding decisions. Separating ownership and control by vesting decision making authority in a centralized nexus distinct from the shareholders and all other constituents is what makes the large public corporation feasible.

Even if one could overcome the seemingly intractable collective action problems plaguing shareholder decision making, active shareholder participation in corporate decision making would still be precluded by the shareholders' widely divergent interests and distinctly different levels of information. Although neoclassical economics assumes that shareholders come to the corporation with wealth maximization as their goal, and most presumably do, once uncertainty is introduced it would be surprising if shareholder opinions did not differ on which course would maximize share value. ... Shareholder investment time horizons are likely to vary from short-term speculation to long-term buy-and-hold strategies, for example, which in turn is likely to result in disagreements about corporate strategy. Even more prosaically, shareholders in different tax brackets are likely to disagree about such matters as dividend policy, as are shareholders who disagree about the merits of allowing management to invest the firm's free cash flow in new projects. ...

Overcoming the collective action problems that prevent meaningful shareholder involvement would be difficult and costly, of course. Even if one could do so, moreover, shareholders lack both the information and the incentives necessary to make sound decisions on either operational or policy questions. ... Accordingly, shareholders will prefer to irrevocably delegate decision making authority to some smaller group, as, in the long run, this will maximize shareholder wealth.

What is that group? The Delaware Code, like the corporate law of virtually every other state, gives us a clear answer: The corporation's "business and affairs . . . shall be managed by or under the direction of a board of directors." ...

Questions and Comments

1. If corporations are democracies, then why shouldn't shareholders exercise genuine power to guide the decisions corporations make? Are there significant differences between shareholder voting and voting in political elections?

2. Does Bebchuk address the problem that the interests of shareholders don't fully align with the interests of society, because shareholders have an incentive to cause their companies to take on more risk than society would prefer?

3. Bainbridge, in support of the traditional allocation of authority between shareholders and managers, argues that the separation of ownership and control is not a problem but rather a solution to a problem. Corporations can't be run effectively by shareholders as a whole; they need to delegate responsibility to specialists who will make decisions on a timely and informed basis. How does Bainbridge deal with the problem that, given free rein, managers will be tempted to favor their own interests over the interests of the firms they are charged with managing?

4. Bainbridge objects to shareholder power on the ground that shareholders often disagree about what to do. Is this really a problem? Why not let the shareholders decide by majority vote?

5. In a part of his article not excerpted above, Bainbridge argues that shareholders are not well equipped to make sensible decisions about management because they rely on the market price. If the price of a company's stock is low — indicating that management is not performing well — the shareholder can simply sell rather than take the trouble of becoming informed about how and why management is falling down on the job. Do you agree?

6. What is the proper role of the board of directors in interacting with shareholders? Should board members be passive and allow the company's senior managers and investor relations department to take the leading oar, or should they take a more active role? For an analysis favoring the latter, see Lisa M. Fairfax, *Mandating Board-Shareholder Engagement?*, 2013 U. Ill. L. Rev. 821.

7. For a further response to Bebchuk's call for increased shareholder power, written by the Chief Justice of the Delaware Supreme Court, see Leo Strine Jr., *Can We Do Better by Ordinary Investors? A Pragmatic Reaction to the Dueling Ideological Mythologists of Corporate Law*, 114 Colum. L. Rev. 449 (2014).

8. Even when shareholders combine forces, their powers may be limited in the face of determined resistance by the incumbent managers. In 2014, shareholders of oil company Nabors Industries Ltd. rejected all three members of the board's compensation committee. No matter: The board of directors simply reappointed them (although it moved two of them off its compensation committee). The company issued an announcement praising the rejected directors and explaining the steps it had undertaken to improve governance and reform its executive pay practices.

B. SHAREHOLDER PROPOSALS

Dissatisfaction with management's power vis-à-vis shareholders is one motivation for the Security and Exchange Commission's (SEC) rule on shareholder proposals. Notice in the following excerpt that the rule is not phrased in classic "legalese." Instead it is set forth in a question-and-answer format and written, so far as possible, in "plain language" that ordinary people can understand.

Security and Exchange Commission Rule 14a-8

17 C.F.R. §240.14a-8

This section addresses when a company must include a shareholder's proposal in its proxy statement and identify the proposal in its form of proxy when the company holds an annual or special meeting of shareholders. In summary, in order to have your shareholder proposal included on a company's proxy card, and included along with any supporting statement in its proxy statement, you must be eligible and follow certain procedures. Under a few specific circumstances, the company is permitted to exclude your proposal, but only after submitting its reasons to the Commission. We structured this section in a question-and-answer format so that it is easier to understand. The references to "you" are to a shareholder seeking to submit the proposal.

WHAT IS A PROPOSAL?

A shareholder proposal is your recommendation or requirement that the company and/or its board of directors take action, which you intend to present at a meeting of the company's shareholders. Your proposal should state as clearly as possible the course of action that you believe the company should follow. If your proposal is placed on the company's proxy card, the company must also provide in the form of proxy means for shareholders to specify by boxes a choice between approval or disapproval, or abstention. Unless otherwise indicated, the word "proposal" as used in this section refers both to your proposal, and to your corresponding statement in support of your proposal (if any).

WHO IS ELIGIBLE TO SUBMIT A PROPOSAL, AND HOW DO I DEMONSTRATE TO THE COMPANY THAT I AM ELIGIBLE?

In order to be eligible to submit a proposal, you must have continuously held at least $2,000 in market value, or 1%, of the company's securities entitled to be voted on the proposal at the meeting for at least one year by the date you submit the proposal. You must continue to hold those securities through the date of the meeting. . . .

WHO HAS THE BURDEN OF PERSUADING THE COMMISSION OR ITS STAFF THAT MY PROPOSAL CAN BE EXCLUDED?

Except as otherwise noted, the burden is on the company to demonstrate that it is entitled to exclude a proposal. . . .

IF I HAVE COMPLIED WITH THE PROCEDURAL REQUIREMENTS, ON WHAT OTHER BASES MAY A COMPANY RELY TO EXCLUDE MY PROPOSAL?

(1) Improper under state law: If the proposal is not a proper subject for action by shareholders under the laws of the jurisdiction of the company's organization; . . . Depending on the subject matter, some proposals are not considered proper under state law if they would be binding on the company if approved by shareholders. In our experience, most proposals that are cast as recommendations or requests that the board of directors take specified action are proper under state law. Accordingly, we will assume that a proposal drafted as a recommendation or suggestion is proper unless the company demonstrates otherwise.

(2) Violation of law: If the proposal would, if implemented, cause the company to violate any state, federal, or foreign law to which it is subject; . . .

(3) Violation of proxy rules: If the proposal or supporting statement is contrary to any of the Commission's proxy rules . . . ;

(4) Personal grievance; special interest: If the proposal relates to the redress of a personal claim or grievance against the company or any other person, or if it is designed to result in a benefit to you, or to further a personal interest, which is not shared by the other shareholders at large;

(5) Relevance: If the proposal relates to operations which account for less than 5 percent of the company's total assets at the end of its most recent fiscal year, and for less than 5 percent of its net earnings and gross sales for its most recent fiscal year, and is not otherwise significantly related to the company's business;

(6) Absence of power/authority: If the company would lack the power or authority to implement the proposal;

(7) Management functions: If the proposal deals with a matter relating to the company's ordinary business operations;

(8) Director elections: If the proposal:

    (i) Would disqualify a nominee who is standing for election;

    (ii) Would remove a director from office before his or her term expired;

    (iii) Questions the competence, business judgment, or character of one or more nominees or directors;

    (iv) Seeks to include a specific individual in the company's proxy materials for election to the board of directors; or

    (v) Otherwise could affect the outcome of the upcoming election of directors.

(9) Conflicts with company's proposal: If the proposal directly conflicts with one of the company's own proposals to be submitted to shareholders at the same meeting; . . .

(10) Substantially implemented: If the company has already substantially implemented the proposal; . . .

(11) Duplication: If the proposal substantially duplicates another proposal previously submitted to the company by another proponent that will be included in the company's proxy materials for the same meeting;

(12) Resubmissions: If the proposal deals with substantially the same subject matter as another proposal or proposals that has or have been previously included in the company's proxy materials within the preceding 5 calendar years, a company may exclude it from its proxy materials for any meeting held within 3 calendar years of the last time it was included if the proposal received [a specified low percentages of the vote].

(13) Specific amount of dividends: If the proposal relates to specific amounts of cash or stock dividends. . . .

Questions and Comments

1. What do you think of the SEC's catechism-style of regulation?

2. The rule, in form, gives proponents broad rights to include proposals on the company's proxy statement, but also gives companies broad and vaguely defined justifications for excluding the proposals. Litigation over the rule tends to turn on the interpretation given to one or another of the exclusions.

3. Exclusion (1) covers proposals that are "improper under state law." In general, as noted above, state laws restrict the scope of shareholder authority. Thus, any proposal that purported to impose mandatory duties on a company's managers would potentially run afoul of this provision. In practice, advocates avoid this hurdle by phrasing their proposals as recommendations, suggestions, or requests — thus purporting to make the votes advisory only. In addition to surmounting a potentially fatal legal objection, the softening of proposals into requests or recommendations has the advantage of making them appear more

reasonable, and therefore potentially swinging undecided votes. You can see that the SEC is receptive to this strategy: It assumes that proposals couched as requests for management action are proper unless the company can demonstrate that they are not.

4. The fourth ground for exclusion concerns proposals that relate to a "personal grievance" or a "special interest." In theory, the SEC could have interpreted this exclusion broadly to apply to proposals, regardless of the topic, which are put forward by individuals or institutions for purposes of advancing a particular political or social agenda. Unions, for example, tend to dislike Wal-Mart because they view its policies as being hostile to the cause of unionization in its stores. Suppose that a labor union, for the apparent purpose of embarrassing or pressuring Wal-Mart, makes a proposal for shareholder vote at Wal-Mart that doesn't have anything in particular to do with union interests. The SEC has consistently taken the position in such cases that it will not look behind the proposal to the possible motivations of the proponent: If the proposal itself doesn't relate to a special interest of the proponent, the proponent's underlying strategy is not considered.

5. Proponents who wish to influence a company would obtain leverage if they could put their own director candidates on the ballot. Since voting on directors is a proper subject for shareholder action, such a proposal is probably not excludable on the ground that it is not authorized by law. However, exclusion (8) allows a company to reject any attempt to nominate a director and even any proposal that "could affect the outcome of the upcoming election of directors." This rule seems to interpose a significant obstacle to shareholder proposals that affect voting for directors. What is the purpose of excluding such proposals? If the selection of directors is truly fundamental to shareholder welfare, why not expand the shareholder franchise in this respect?

6. Does exclusion (8) completely bar attempts to influence shareholder elections? In American Federation of State, County & Municipal Employees v. American International Group, Inc., 462 F.3d 121 (2d Cir. 2006), a union submitted a proposal that would amend AIG's bylaws to require the company to publish the names of shareholder-nominated candidates for director positions. The union argued that the proposal survived exclusion (8) because it did not relate to any particular election but rather sought to establish a procedure to govern elections generally. Rejecting the interpretation offered by the SEC, the court agreed with the union. The text of Rule 14a-8 excerpted above reflects the court's interpretation.

7. What about exclusion (5), allowing management to reject a proposal if it "relates to operations which account for less than 5 percent of the company's total assets at the end of its most recent fiscal year, and for less than 5 percent of its net earnings and gross sales for its most recent fiscal year, and is not otherwise significantly related to the company's business"? This seems to provide broad authority to exclude proposals that don't relate to core company activities. However, the exclusion has proven to be less effective than managers of targeted companies might wish. Proposals for reforming corporate governance, for example, are often allowed on the ballot even though the proponent cannot demonstrate that, if implemented, they would have a material impact on the company's financial results; the SEC's theory is that, whether or not the results can be quantified, anything having to do with governance is probably important and therefore qualifies as a matter "significantly related to the company's business." Proposals on matters of current political debate are also often allowed, even though they relate to a small portion of the company's business; here the theory is that if the company gets swept up in

controversy the result could be bad for its financial position. *See* Lovenheim v. Iroquois Brands, Ltd., 618 F. Supp. 554 (D.D.C. 1985) (the term "otherwise significantly related" includes matters of ethical and social significance).

8. Rule 14a-8(i)(9) allows management to exclude shareholder proposals that directly conflict with one of the company's own proposals to be submitted to shareholders at the same meeting. This opens the possibility that management will repetitively submit proposals for action that are inconsistent with a proposal that management knows or suspects will be forthcoming by shareholder activists, and then use the management proposal as a rationale for excluding the shareholder proposal.

For example, on September 13, 2013, a shareholder submitted a proposal to the board of The Walt Disney Company requesting that the board take the steps necessary to allow holders of 10 percent of Disney stock to call a special shareholders meeting. Disney's board responded on October 4, 2013 by voting to submit its own proposal, which would authorize a special meeting only if called by 25 percent of the shareholders. Disney then sought and obtained a no-action letter from the SEC allowing the company to exclude the shareholder's proposal on the ground that it directly conflicted with the company's version. Since the chance that 25 percent of the shareholders would call for a special meeting is extremely low, the effect was to nullify the shareholder's initiative.

The days of this potential defense may be numbered, however. Early in 2015, SEC Chair Mary Jo White directed the agency staff to review the proper scope and application of the rule, and the Division of Corporation Finance announced that it would refrain from issuing no-action letters on this provision during the pendency of the review.

9. Section 971 of the Dodd-Frank Act, 15 U.S.C. §78n(a)(2), provides that the SEC may adopt a rule requiring that "a solicitation of proxy, consent, or authorization by (or on behalf of) an issuer include a nominee submitted by a shareholder to serve on the board of directors of the issuer"; and "a requirement that an issuer follow a certain procedure in relation to a solicitation. . . ." In other words, the SEC may allow shareholders to nominate directors.

In 2010, the SEC adopted Rule 14a-11, which required reporting companies to include in proxy materials the name of persons nominated by qualifying shareholders for election to the board of directors. The rule provided that, to qualify, a shareholder or group of shareholders must have continuously held at least 3 percent of the voting power of the company's securities for at least three years prior to the date the nominating shareholder or group submits notice of its intent to use the rule, and must continue to own those securities through the date of the annual meeting. However, business interests successfully challenged the rule on the ground that the SEC had failed to conduct a statutorily required cost-benefit analysis. Business Roundtable v. SEC, 647 F.3d 1144 (D.C. Cir. 2011). As a result, the rule never became effective. Is Rule 14a-11 a good idea? What are the pros and cons?

C. SAY ON PAY

Section 951 of the Dodd-Frank Act, 15 U.S.C. §78n-1, requires that "[n]ot less frequently than once every 3 years, a proxy or consent or authorization for an annual or other meeting of the shareholders for which the proxy solicitation rules of the

Commission require compensation disclosure shall include a separate resolution subject to shareholder vote to approve the compensation of executives. . . ."

Congress thus mandated shareholder votes on management compensation in firms subject to the proxy rules. Shareholders can by resolution determine whether these votes must occur more frequently than once every three years. These "say on pay" votes are advisory only; management is legally permitted to ignore them. However, if a pay package is disapproved by shareholders, it could be unwise for a company's managers to flout the shareholders' express wishes.

Questions and Comments

1. Although SEC-reporting companies are required to hold say-on-pay votes only every three years (subject to shareholder override), most have elected to hold these votes every year. This decision may reflect a change of heart on the part of management in favor of giving shareholders more power in the compensation process. Other factors may enter the calculation as well: the concern that anything less frequent than annual say-on-pay votes would appear uncharitable and defensive, or possibly the hope that annual voting will lose its novelty value and therefore its salience to many shareholders.

2. In general, shareholders have approved management pay packages. Of 2,215 companies in the Russell 3000 index that held say-on-pay votes in 2012, only 57 failed to gain approval. Seventy-three percent of companies received more than 90 percent approval votes on their pay packages in 2012.

3. A *Wall Street Journal* study in 2013 found that compensation of senior managers had remained relatively flat for the previous three years — suggesting that the say-on-pay rules that went into effect in 2011 may have had some effect (although it is difficult to disentangle the effect of say on pay from the lingering influence of the financial crisis of 2007-2009). Regardless, managers are hardly suffering. According to Fortune Magazine, every one of the 100 highest paid CEOs in the United States made more than $15 million in 2012; the highest paid was John H. Hammergren of McKessen, who brought in a cool $131 million (and change).

4. The following factors appear to influence a "no" vote:

    a. Poor performance: Companies that are performing badly relative to comparable institutions are more likely to experience negative say-on-pay votes.

    b. Generous packages: Pay packages that appear significantly more generous than the packages at peer group institutions are more likely to be rejected.

    c. Prior "no" votes: Pay packages appear more likely to be rejected if shareholders rejected a package in a previous vote.

    d. Negative recommendations from proxy advisory firms: An important factor in say on pay is the view of proxy advisory firms. Two firms — ISS and Glass, Lewis & Co. — dominate proxy advisory services. Together, they counsel clients that control 25 to 50 percent of the voting shares of large U.S. firms. In 2012, 94 percent of say-on-pay votes passed when ISS recommended a vote to approve the package but only 64 percent received shareholder endorsement where ISS recommended disapproval.

5. Arguably, the say-on-pay process will result in greater uniformity of management compensation practices — the theory being that companies wishing to avoid a "no" vote will structure their pay packages so as to be justifiable in light of what

everyone else is doing. Would this be a constructive development? Is there a value in experimentation or in providing exceptional pay for exceptional results? Could management compensation consultants engineer a gradual change in pay practices that "raises all the ships" — thus effectively increasing executive pay over what it had been before say on pay?

6. Say on pay represented a victory for activists who had long promoted the idea as a counterweight to exorbitant executive compensation. Yet, could the success boomerang? In the past, companies that enriched their executives were vulnerable to criticism for flouting shareholder interests. Now, if a pay package survives a say-on-pay vote, the company has a built-in defense to criticism: The package was submitted to shareholders, with full disclosure, and they approved.

7. The United States is far from the only country to experiment with shareholder votes on compensation. Much of the impetus for say on pay came from other countries: a 2004 recommendation by the European Commission and a G-20 declaration in 2009. In 2013, the United Kingdom revised its company law to split the report to shareholders on remuneration into two parts: (a) an "implementation report" that discloses how the company's policy has been implemented in the previous year, and (b) a "policy report" that discloses the company's current remuneration policies for executives. The implementation report is subject to a non-binding shareholders' vote every year. The policy report, however, is subject to a binding shareholder vote at least once every three years — a significant change as compared with prior practice. Perhaps surprisingly, stodgy Switzerland has gone even further: In March 2013, Swiss voters required public companies to give shareholders a binding (not advisory) annual vote on senior executive pay.

8. Voting on pay packages is only as good as the information available to shareholders. The SEC has long required reporting companies to disclose information about executive compensation, but has upgraded the requirements in recent years. Item 402 of the SEC's regulation S-K requires "clear, concise and understandable disclosure of all plan and non-plan compensation awarded to, earned by, or paid to [officers and directors] by any person for all services rendered in all capacities to the registrant and its subsidiaries, unless otherwise specifically excluded from disclosure." Supplementing this Rule, §953(b) of the Dodd-Frank Act instructs the SEC to mandate disclosure of "(A) the median of the annual total compensation of all employees of the issuer, except the chief executive officer . . . ; (B) the annual total compensation of the chief executive officer . . . ; and (C) the ratio of the amount described in subparagraph (A) to the amount described in subparagraph (B)." The SEC adopted a final rule implementing this requirement in 2015, scheduled to become effective in 2017.

9. In practice, reporting firms tend to offer even more fulsome disclosures about executive compensation than the SEC requires. Open the proxy statement of any major company and you are likely to find pages devoted to an elaborate analysis of the firm's compensation philosophy and practices. Why are firms so forthcoming? Is it because they wish to provide all the information shareholders need in order to make an informed vote on compensation? To demonstrate their commitment to the say-on-pay process, and thus dissuade activists or proxy advisory firms from targeting them? To overwhelm shareholders with detail in hopes that they will throw up their hands and vote "yes"?

10. What is the purpose of requiring disclosure of the ratio between the chief executive officer's pay and that of the median employee? Is this information required for the purpose of informing investors, to shame companies who pay

unusually large compensation to their chief executive officers, to raise salaries for lower-paid workers, to call public attention to the issue of executive compensation generally, or for some other reason?

11. How informative will this ratio be? Consider two companies: one, a publicly traded management consultant employing many highly compensated professionals; and the other, a tobacco company with its principal operations in Zimbabwe and Malawi. The ratio will be different for these companies because workers in Zimbabwe and Malawi don't get paid much by American standards. Will the differences in the ratios provide a reliable comparative measure of the reasonableness of chief executive officer compensation?

12. How easy will it be for large, global companies to compute the median compensation of their employees?

D. INVESTOR ACTIVISTS

We now consider the exercise of pressure by "activist" investors — people who, individually or by virtue of managing a pool of capital, attempt to influence the exercise of business judgment by corporate managers. Investor "activism" comes in various types and flavors. One form is aggressive and proactive; it seeks to organize shareholders in support of a proposal to force a company to undertake some action (spinning off a division, declaring a dividend or repurchasing stock, refocusing business strategy on particular products or services, or the like). Activists of this type are often hedge funds under the control of powerful money managers (William Ackman's Pershing Square Capital and Paul Singer's Elliott Management are examples). Another form of activism is more defensive; it focuses on structural reforms that purport to encourage the board of directors and senior managers to work hard and effectively to enhance the value of the company (e.g., proposals to eliminate staggered boards). The distinction is not clear-cut, however: Often activist campaigns have elements of both types of demands.

A notable example of shareholder activism occurred during the 2015 proxy season, when Nelson Peltz's activist $11 billion Trian Fund Management LLP demanded a wide variety of reforms at DuPont, including a proposal to split the company into several smaller firms. After attempts to negotiate with DuPont management failed, Peltz's fund launched a proxy fight. Trian alleged that the DuPont board was insular, out of touch, and committed to unprofitable long-term investment strategies. DuPont's management responded that the company had returned good value to its investors (its share value climbed 266 percent between 2009 and 2015, outperforming the S&P 500, which rose 165 percent during the same period). DuPont claimed that Peltz and his allies intended to cut research, eliminate jobs, and add unhealthy amounts of debt to the balance sheet, all with the goal of improving short-term financial results at the expense of the company's long-term interests. Peltz's fund posed a large threat to DuPont and to its CEO, Ellen Kullman: The fund had control over a large bloc of voting shares and it persuaded the two most influential proxy advisory firms, Institutional Shareholder Services Inc. and Glass-Lewis, to support its campaign. In the end, the incumbents retained their seats, but by an uncomfortably small margin of victory. DuPont disclosed that it had spent more than $15 million on the proxy battle; some analysts believe its true costs were higher. Kullman, meanwhile, had little time to savor her victory: She resigned under pressure less than a year later amid worsening profits and plummeting stock prices. And despite DuPont's efforts to maintain its corporate identity, it soon agreed to merge with Dow Chemical.

Questions and Comments

1. Do you believe that activist investors contribute to improving the quality and performance of public corporations?

2. Which type of activism offers the greatest benefits or risks for the public at large?

3. These days, sovereign wealth funds control enormous pools of assets (examples are Singapore's Temasek, with more than $220 billion under management, and the Kuwait Investment Authority, estimated to hold more than $300 billion). Entities this large have the potential to exercise considerable influence over businesses around the world. To date, however, sovereign wealth funds have mostly stayed on the sidelines in disputes over corporate policy. Should they become more active? What are the advantages or disadvantages?

E. PROXY ADVISERS

In the discussion above we have several times mentioned the role played by proxy advisory services. Institutional Shareholder Services (ISS), Glass Lewis, and other similar firms provide advice on corporate governance issues to pension funds, mutual funds, and asset managers. Their clients rely on the advice to inform how they vote on proxy issues.

In recent years, proxy advisers have gained a great deal of influence over institutional investor voting behavior. Admirers praise this development on the ground that it magnifies shareholder power and provides an effective check against incompetence and greed. Critics claim that proxy advisers have acquired too much power and that their recommendations on contested governance issues are informed more by ideology than by evidence. Critics also claim that these firms are subject to conflicts of interest. For example, in addition to offering proxy advice on matters that come before the shareholders, ISS operates a consulting division that provides services to companies it advises. Do you perceive a conflict of interest?

Questions and Comments

1. Efforts to regulate proxy advisory firms have progressed further in Europe than in the United States. In 2014, the European Commission proposed that the European Parliament and EU Council revise existing corporate governance directives. The proposal would require proxy advisors to disclose, on an annual basis:

- The essential features of the methodologies and models they apply;
- The main information sources they use;
- Whether and, if so, how they take national market, legal, and regulatory conditions into account;

- Whether they have dialogues with the companies that are the object of their voting recommendations, and, if so, the extent and nature thereof;
- The total number of staff involved in the preparation of the voting recommendations;
- The total number of voting recommendations provided in the last year.

Further, proxy advisors would be required to "identify and disclose without undue delay to their clients and the company concerned any actual or potential conflict of interest or business relationships that may influence the preparation of the voting recommendations and the actions they have undertaken to eliminate or mitigate the actual or potential conflict of interest." Would you favor such a reform for the United States?

2. The SEC's proxy rule makes it increasingly difficult for proponents to resubmit proposals dealing with "substantially the same subject matter" as another proposal submitted within the previous five years. Duplicative proposals must receive at least 3 percent of the total vote the first year, 6 percent in the second year, and 10 percent in the third year. An initiative may not be resubmitted for at least three years if it fails to satisfy these minimum requirements. At the time the SEC promulgated its rule, proposals that had been rejected once rarely met these requirements. Later, however, ISS and Glass Lewis became so influential with institutional investors that they can often, by recommending a "yes" vote, effectively guarantee that a proposal continues on the proxy materials indefinitely, even if it is voted down each time. In 2014, the U.S. Chamber of Commerce and other business groups petitioned the SEC to increase the thresholds in order to counteract what they described as the "tyranny of the minority," aided "by two proxy advisory firms that operate outside any internal or external oversight vis-à-vis shareholder proposals, and . . . function as de facto standard setters of U.S. corporate governance." Do you agree with the concerns expressed by these business groups?

3. Do proxy advisers offer good counsel about what pay package is best for a company? A study by three business school professors, examining a large number of say-on-pay votes in 2011, concluded that in order to avoid a negative recommendation, corporations frequently adjusted their pay proposals to include features favored by proxy advisers. The researchers also found that the stock market reaction to these compensation program changes was statistically *negative.* The market reacted badly when companies changed their compensation packages in ways favored by proxy advisers. The authors conclude that "the outsourcing of voting to proxy advisory firms appears to have the unintended economic consequence that boards of directors are induced to make choices that decrease shareholder value." David F. Larker, Allan L. McCall & Gaizka Ormazabal, *Outsourcing Shareholder Voting to Proxy Advisory Firms* (May 2013).

2

The Board of Directors

We now turn to the highest management authority in the organization. In corporations, this authority is the board of directors; in nonprofit organizations the equivalent authority may be called a "board of trustees" or some related term. Religious organizations are variously organized: The Catholic Church recognizes the authority of the Pope as supreme governor; Episcopalians look to the authority of bishops; other churches, temples, and mosques have different governance structures. Organizations in the public sector can be structured hierarchically (the President is chief executive of the United States), but may also be organized in multi-member boards (e.g., the Federal Reserve Board or the Securities and Exchange Commission). Here we will focus on the corporate board of directors, keeping in mind that the ultimate authority may be allocated differently in other organizations.

A. THE FULL BOARD

1. Powers

The board of directors is ultimately responsible for governing a corporation. Delaware General Corporation Law §141(a) phrases the matter as follows: "The business and affairs of every corporation . . . shall be *managed by or under the direction of a board of directors. . . .*" Other corporate codes contain similar language. New York's General Business Corporation Law, for example, states that "the business of a corporation shall be *managed under the direction of its board of directors.*"

To what extent may parties other than the board of directors exercise the power to manage? Responsibility can be shifted from the board in three ways. First, *board committees* may be established, either by action of the full board or in the corporation's governing documents. All state corporation laws authorize the establishment of board committees; they are ubiquitous in large corporations. Typically, but not always, everyone on a board committee must also be a member of the full board of directors. The committee may exercise an advisory role, in that it reports to the full board of directors on particular topics; but depending on the provisions of the governing documents, it can also exercise powers of the full board within the area of its competence. Delaware General Corporation Law §141(c)(2), states that a board committee, if duly authorized, may "exercise all the powers and authority of the board of directors in the management of the business and affairs of the corporation" (exceptions are that the committee may not amend the bylaws or act on a matter requiring shareholder approval). We will discuss some of the most important board committees in the pages that follow.

Second, fundamental management decisions are sometimes given to *persons outside the board.* For example, shareholders agreements or voting trusts may require shareholders or trustees to vote shares so as to accomplish defined outcomes (for example, so as to retain someone in office as the chief executive officer). A company's governing documents might also purport to vest management responsibility in persons other than the members of the board of directors.

At one time arrangements like these were problematic; courts resisted them on the theory that only the board could exercise the fundamental power of management. More recently, however, the law has developed a large degree of tolerance for such agreements. Section 141(a) of the Delaware General Corporation Law, provides that a company may vest management powers outside the board by including a provision in its charter. In general, the organizations within our field of study — those with significant risk management and compliance functions — are not organized under this sort of arrangement; basic management decisions are made by the board (although often with input from outside parties such as consultants or regulators).

The third way in which management responsibility can be exercised by parties other than the board is that the board can *delegate these tasks to senior officers.* Notice that Delaware General Corporation Law §141(a) recognizes two functions for the board: (a) managing a company, and (b) directing the management of a company. What is the difference between these? "Managing" refers to the direct performance of executive tasks, as when a board of directors hires or fires a chief executive officer or selects an auditor. "Directing the management" refers to the activity of supervising others — executive officers — who carry out day-to-day operations.

The boards of directors of large organizations perform both activities, but the largest share of their time is spent on supervision. This is so by necessity, since the myriad tasks facing such organizations are too burdensome to be carried out by a board of directors alone. The board's supervisory role allows a central decision maker to exercise overall control over the company's operations without becoming involved in the nitty-gritty details.

But this function of delegating responsibility subject to oversight also carries risk: Often the "devil is in the details." If boards delegate responsibility too comprehensively, they may miss issues that are crucial to a firm's welfare. Worse yet, if senior executives do not provide accurate information to the board, boards of directors will be disabled from making the best decisions on behalf of shareholders. Board "oversight" thus has a double edge: The board oversees management — a good thing — but sometimes the consequence is that it commits "oversights" — a bad thing. This problem of obtaining needed information from management is sometimes referred to as "asymmetric information risk" (for a discussion of how this sort of risk led to a serious corporate blunder, see the discussion of the "London Whale" fiasco in Chapter 20).

The problem of asymmetric information cannot be eliminated, but it can be mitigated if board members are active and involved: if they ask questions, refuse to accept pat answers, and pose a credible challenge to management on important issues. This does not mean that the board members should micro-manage, but rather that they should satisfy themselves that the company's executives are implementing the company's strategic vision in a reasonable fashion. In the jargon of governance, risk management, and compliance, the proper stance of a board when supervising a company's managers is "NIFO"—noses in, fingers out.

One approach to the problem of asymmetric information risk is the use of "deep dives" by board committees. A deep dive is simply a meeting at which a board committee is briefed in depth on a particular topic. Ideally, the meeting is scheduled for long enough to allow committee members to ask probing questions and, if they wish, to request additional briefings by responsible executives. To what extent do you think the "deep dive" approach will ameliorate the problem of information asymmetry?

> Inherent in the board function is "asymmetric information risk": the problem that the board of directors must make strategic decisions on behalf of the company in reliance on information provided by managers.

While an active and demanding board of directors is helpful, the fact remains that no board of directors, even the most capable, can fully track everything a company does. The two other substantive topics of this book—compliance and risk management—refer to the principal mitigation techniques that supplement the board's role in supervision and oversight and thus reduce asymmetric information risk. The compliance function addresses the risk that directors will miss violations of laws or other norms committed by others in the organization; the risk management function deals with the problem that directors will miss threats to the company's welfare that are inherent in its business. Thus, risk management and compliance can be understood as instruments designed to enhance and improve the management function in complex organizations.

2. Size

How large should a board of directors be? The answer involves tradeoffs of benefits and costs. Each new board member brings new insights and a new perspective to the table, and thus may improve board functioning to the extent these insights add value.

On the other hand, as the size of a board increases, individual responsibility for decisions may decrease: Each board member may find it convenient to fade into the background and let decisions be made by others. As board size grows, moreover, the difficulty of organizing a coalition increases as well. These organizational difficulties, in turn, might make it difficult for a large board to resist the wishes of the chief executive officer or other senior managers.

Empirical studies suggest that boards of directors become less effective once they cross a certain threshold of size. Economist David Yermack, for example, finds a significant negative relationship between board size and Tobin's Q (a measure of performance). *See* David Yermack, *Higher Market Valuation of Companies with a Small Board of Directors*, 40 J. Fin. Econ. 185 (1996). In other words, as boards grow large, the market has a less favorable view of the company's prospects.

Questions and Comments

1. The average publicly traded company has about nine directors, but there is considerable variation across firms. Boards of companies going public for the first time tend to be smaller and to increase in size after the company's initial public offering. What, if anything, does this information tell us about how large a board of directors should be?

2. Why would companies have large boards if doing so decreases performance?

3. Board size is sometimes regulated by law. For example, a national bank must have at least 5 and no more than 25 members. Cutting-edge corporation statutes, however, have abandoned the attempt to regulate board size, on the theory that the company itself is the best judge of how large its board should be. Delaware General Corporation Law §141(b) places no maximum limit on board size and allows a corporation to operate with a board of one person (who must, however, be a member of the species *homo sapiens*).

4. What if an organization sees the value of having senior advisers on call but does not want to appoint these people to the board of directors, perhaps because the board is already full or for other reasons? In such a case, the organization might create a paid senior advisory position with titles such as "advisory director," "associate director," "honorary director," or "emeritus director." These individuals perform some of the functions of board members and may even sit in on board meetings, but do not have the right to vote.

5. What are the advantages of advisory board members? They can bring new or broader perspectives to the organization and have those views heard at the highest strategic level. They may represent political accommodations that smooth out difficult transitions, as when the company has acquired another firm and keeps the former firm's former managers or board members on retainer in an advisory capacity. They may represent means for providing a voice, if not a vote, to constituencies other than shareholders.

6. What are the disadvantages of advisory boards? Consider the following: They are not vetted or elected by shareholders but may play an important role in decision making. They may bring conflicts of interest into play. Their commitment to the company may be limited by the restricted nature of their appointments. They may create external confusion if their titles sound too much like regular board positions.

7. The Comptroller of the Currency approves of using advisory boards for national banks in the following situations:

   a. When the operations of the bank are geographically dispersed and the board wants input from more segments of the communities served by the bank.
   b. When the board itself is small and the directors want direct involvement with a broader array of community leaders.
   c. To assist in business development.
   d. To gain access to special expertise.
   e. To help identify likely candidates for future board openings.

Do these guidelines impose significant limitation on when such people can be appointed?

8. To what extent should advisory board members be subject to the legal and regulatory exposure that applies to full-scale members? On the one hand, because they do not vote, perhaps they should have no exposure at all. On the other hand, if

they play a significant role in decision making, they might be considered to be de facto board members and required to answer under the law if something goes wrong. How should the law deal with these competing considerations?

9. An example of how not to use an advisory board might be the 2013 appointment of 15-year-old Andrew Zucker to the advisory board of Waywire, an Internet video sharing site founded by then-Newark Mayor Cory Booker. Waywire explained that Zucker was appointed because of his reputation for "being able to identify technologies that would be popular with teenagers and which ones wouldn't be." When the news leaked into the social media, critics wondered whether Zucker's appointment might have had to do with the fact he is the son of CNN President Jeff Zucker; they also pointed to the potential conflict of interest arising from the fact that CNN reported on Mayor Booker's official activities. The company quickly announced that the younger Zucker had resigned from the position "in order to avoid even the perception of a conflict."

3. Tenure in Office

Board members are typically appointed for a term of office defined in the organization's fundamental organizing document (for corporations, the charter). In many cases, all board members are elected annually. Sometimes, however, a longer term of office is defined. When this happens, the board is usually "staggered." A staggered board is one in which the directors serve for multi-year terms and only a minority (usually one-third) are elected each year. The classic example of a staggered board is the United States Senate: Senators serve for six-year terms and only one-third of them are elected in each biannual election.

Staggered boards have been around for a long time. They have obvious benefits, the most important of which is continuity in office. The staggered board structure ensures that no more than a fraction (less than half) of the board will be replaced in any given year. The directors who remain in office are able to bring their collective experience of managing the company to bear in its challenges going forward, and can instruct newly elected directors on the fine points of their jobs.

These benefits of staggered boards are also a problem. Because less than half the board can be replaced in any given year, it is impossible for someone who takes over the company to gain immediate control over the board of directors unless either (a) incumbent members voluntarily leave office, or (b) the dissident who takes over a majority of the company's stock is able to use existing corporate powers to remove incumbent directors involuntarily. The latter is usually very difficult, often requiring a finding of incapacity or misconduct in office. The former may be impossible if the takeover is hostile and the incumbent board members remain loyal to the former managers.

A considerable body of scholarship argues that staggered boards, because they are impossible to replace in a single year, represent an effective defense against hostile corporate takeovers. Harvard Law School professors Lucian Bebchuk, John Coates, and Guhan Subramanian study these effects in an influential paper, *The Powerful Antitakeover Force of Staggered Boards: Theory, Evidence, and Policy*, 54 Stan. L. Rev. 887 (2002). Examining hostile bids from 1996-2000, they find no bidders who won a proxy fight against an effective staggered board. Such a board nearly doubled the likelihood that the target firm will remain independent, cut by more than half the odds that a first bidder will be successful, and significantly reduced the chance of a sale to a white knight (a firm willing to carry out a friendly acquisition).

Shareholders of targets that remained independent after a hostile bid were worse off than shareholders of firms that eventually accepted the hostile bid or were acquired by a white knight.

This and other studies sparked a campaign to eliminate staggered boards, spearheaded by Harvard Law School's Shareholder Rights Project and other corporate governance activists. The following excerpt is from the 2013 proxy statement of Sally Beauty Holdings, Inc., a supplier of products to the hair salon industry:

Sally Beauty Holdings, Inc. 2013 Proxy Statement

... PROPOSAL TO REPEAL CLASSIFIED BOARD

Resolved, that shareholders of Sally Beauty Holdings, Inc. urge the Board of Directors to take all necessary steps (other than any steps that must be taken by shareholders) to eliminate the classification of the Board of Directors and to require that all directors elected at or after the annual meeting held in 2014 be elected on an annual basis. Implementation of this proposal should not prevent any director elected prior to the annual meeting held in 2014 from completing the term for which such director was elected.

Supporting Statement

This resolution was submitted on behalf of the Pension Reserves Investment Trust Fund by its trustee, the Pension Reserves Investment Management Board. The Shareholder Rights Project represented and advised the Pension Reserves Investment Management Board in connection with this resolution.

The resolution urges the board of directors to facilitate a declassification of the board. Such a change would enable shareholders to register their views on the performance of all directors at each annual meeting. Having directors stand for elections annually makes directors more accountable to shareholders, and could thereby contribute to improving performance and increasing firm value.

According to data from FactSet Research Systems, the number of S&P 500 companies with classified boards declined by more than 60% since 2000, and the average percentage of votes cast in favor of shareholder proposals to declassify the boards of S&P 500 companies during 2010 and 2011 exceeded 75%.

The significant shareholder support for declassification proposals is consistent with empirical studies reporting that:

- Classified boards are associated with lower firm valuation (Bebchuk and Cohen, 2005; confirmed by Faleye (2007) and Frakes (2007));
- Takeover targets with classified boards are associated with lower gains to shareholders (Bebchuk, Coates, and Subramanian, 2002);
- Firms with classified boards are more likely to be associated with value-decreasing acquisition decisions (Masulis, Wang, and Xie, 2007); and
- Classified boards are associated with lower sensitivity of compensation to performance and lower sensitivity of CEO turnover to firm performance (Falaye, 2007).

Although one study (Bates, Becher and Lemmon, 2008) reports that classified boards are associated with higher takeover premiums, this study also reports that classified boards are associated with a lower likelihood of an acquisition and that classified boards are associated with lower firm valuation.

Please vote for this proposal to make directors more accountable to shareholders.

Board of Directors' Statement in Opposition

. . . The Board is committed to strong corporate governance policies. The Board's Nominating and Corporate Governance Committee, comprised entirely of independent directors, regularly considers and evaluates a broad range of corporate governance issues affecting the Corporation, including board structure. As a result, the Nominating and Corporate Governance Committee and the Board have, both before and after receipt of the stockholder proposal, carefully considered the arguments that have been set forth for and against a classified board structure, including those arguments against that are raised in the proponent's supporting statement.

The Board believes that there is no "one size fits all" approach that suits all companies and that the appropriate standard by which to judge a classified board structure is whether it promotes stockholder interests in the circumstances of the company in question. For the following reasons, which we discuss in greater detail below, the Board disagrees with the proponent's assertions in the supporting statement and continues to believe that its classified structure provides important advantages to the Corporation and is in the best interests of the Corporation and our stockholders. . . .

CONSISTENTLY STRONG FINANCIAL PERFORMANCE

The proponent's assertions that declassifying the Board "could . . . contribute to improving performance and increasing firm value," and that classified boards are associated with "lower firm valuation," "lower gains to shareholders," "value-decreasing acquisition decisions," "lower sensitivity of compensation to performance" and "lower sensitivity of CEO turnover to firm performance," are quite inconsistent with the Corporation's sustained record of strong financial performance. . . . Over the past five fiscal years, the Corporation has delivered an average annual return to stockholders of 24.3%, compared to 1.1% for the S&P 500 Index and 5.5% for the Dow Jones U.S. Specialty Retailers Index (comprised of companies which are primarily in the retail sector in the U.S., including the Corporation). . . .

As a rationale for declassifying the Board, the proponent states that over the past decade, "many S&P 500 companies have declassified their board of directors" and "the number of S&P 500 companies with classified boards declined by more than 50%," suggesting that stockholder value would be enhanced if the Corporation followed the trend of these S&P 500 firms. However, given that the Corporation has significantly outperformed the S&P 500 Index in recent years, we believe that changing the Corporation's long-standing governance structure simply to "fall in line" with S&P 500 firms would be a considerable disservice to our stockholders. The fact that many large companies have taken steps to remove their classified boards is not, in the Board's judgment, a persuasive reason for the Corporation to undertake the same initiative.

MAXIMIZATION OF STOCKHOLDER VALUE IN CHANGE OF CONTROL TRANSACTIONS

Our classified board structure protects our stockholders by encouraging persons or firms making unsolicited takeover bids for the Corporation to negotiate directly with the Board and better positions the Board to negotiate effectively on behalf of stockholders to realize the greatest possible stockholder value. The classified board structure is designed to safeguard against a hostile purchaser replacing a majority or all of our directors with its own nominees at a single annual meeting, thereby gaining control of the Corporation and its assets without paying fair value to our stockholders. Because under a classified board structure only approximately one-third of the directors are elected at any annual meeting of stockholders, at least two annual meetings are required for an acquiror to be able to change a majority of the directors on our Board. As a result, most acquirors will elect to attempt to negotiate a transaction with the Board rather than wait this extended period of time to gain control of the Board.

A classified board does not, and is not intended to, preclude a takeover, and it does not alter the fiduciary responsibilities of our directors in responding to any such efforts. Instead, by simply eliminating the threat of imminent removal of a majority or all of our directors, a classified board causes potential acquirors to attempt to negotiate the terms of a transaction with the Board. As a result, the Board gains the time and flexibility necessary to be in the best position to evaluate the adequacy and fairness of proposed offers, protect all stockholders against abusive tactics during a takeover process, consider alternative methods of maximizing stockholder value and, as appropriate, negotiate the best possible return for all stockholders. As noted above, the Board has a fiduciary duty under the law to act in a manner that it believes to be in the best interests of the Corporation and its stockholders. Elimination of the classified board structure would make it more difficult for our independent, stockholder-elected Board to preserve and maximize value for all stockholders in the event of an unsolicited takeover bid.

OTHER EMPIRICAL RESEARCH

There are a couple of studies that reach a different conclusion, which could support the view that classified boards may benefit stockholders. This is a complicated issue with well-qualified experts on both sides, and the outcomes of studies can change depending on the attributes of the companies being analyzed.

One study has questioned the studies cited by the proponent, finding that classified boards can be value enhancing for some firms. While the study cited by the proponent reports that classified boards are associated with lower firm valuation and that board classification does reduce the likelihood of receiving a takeover bid, the study also finds that the economic effect of bid deterrence on firm valuation is "quite small." We encourage you to consider all the relevant research on this complex issue.

ACCOUNTABILITY TO STOCKHOLDERS

The proponent's assertion that the classified board structure diminishes director accountability to stockholders is, in our view, debatable. Directors elected to three-year terms are equally as accountable to stockholders as directors elected annually because all directors are required by law to fulfill their fiduciary duties to the Company and its stockholders, regardless of the length of their term of office. Further, even with a classified Board, stockholders have the opportunity to provide direct feedback to the Board at each annual meeting, as stockholders have the ability to elect a majority of the Board within two consecutive annual meetings, which could occur within as little as twelve months. This ability to vote directors off the Board holds the directors accountable for their actions and provides stockholders with considerable influence over the affairs of the Company.

Notably, nothing in the proponent's proposal alleges any lack of accountability by the Corporation's Board; the proposal is defended by reference to five general studies rather than anything specific at the Corporation. We believe that the Corporation's classified board structure has in no way diminished the Board's accountability to the stockholders.

BOARD STABILITY AND CONTINUITY

Our classified board structure is designed to provide stability and continuity of leadership, prevent sudden disruptive changes to our Board composition, enhance long-term planning and ensure that at any given time a majority of our directors will have served for multiple years. Three-year terms provide our directors an appropriate amount of time to develop a deeper and more thorough understanding of the Corporation's business, competitive environment and strategic goals. Experienced directors are better positioned to provide effective oversight and advice consistent with the best interests of the stockholders. Declassification of the Board could result in higher turnover of Board members and have an adverse impact on the effectiveness of the Board. Furthermore, given the current corporate governance climate in which many qualified directors are declining to serve on public company boards, the Corporation could be placed at a competitive disadvantage in recruiting qualified director candidates if such candidates are concerned that their service could potentially be cut short after only one year.

DIRECTOR INDEPENDENCE

Electing a director to a three-year term enhances the independence of a non-employee director by providing him or her with a longer term of office. This longer term provides enhanced independence from management and from special interest groups that may have an agenda contrary to the long-term interests of the Corporation's stockholders generally. Indeed, we believe that it is the multi-year terms of our classified Board members that encourage them to take on long-term initiatives for the substantial benefit of our stockholders, rather than to remain locked into the status quo for fear of short-term reprisal from stockholders.

PROCEDURAL MATTERS

Stockholders should be aware that this stockholder proposal is simply a non-binding request that the Board take the steps necessary to eliminate our classified board structure. Approval of this proposal may not result in the requested action being taken by the Board, and therefore approval of the proposal by the stockholders would not in itself declassify the Board.

To declassify the Board, a formal amendment of our Certificate of Incorporation would need to be recommended by the Board and submitted to our stockholders for approval at a future stockholders meeting. Approval of such an amendment would require the affirmative vote of the holders of a majority of the outstanding shares of each class of our stock then entitled to vote on the amendment. In addition, the Board or the stockholders would have to approve a conforming amendment to our By-Laws.

The Board of Directors recommends a vote "against" the stockholder proposal to repeal our classified board.

Questions and Comments

1. Who has the better of the argument on staggered boards?

2. Sally Beauty Holdings' managers point to the fact that the firm had displayed a strong financial performance under the staggered board structure. Is this a convincing argument, if true? Perhaps the company could have done even better if the staggered board had been abandoned earlier. Perhaps not. Should past performance be a guide?

3. The proponent of the proposal highlights the fact that many companies have abandoned staggered boards. How persuasive is this argument? Is slavishly conforming to current fashion better than holding out as an anachronistic throwback to a bygone era?

4. The proponent of the proposal admits that staggered boards are associated with higher takeover premiums, but argues that this effect is counterbalanced by the reduced chance that a takeover will occur. Why would staggered boards increase takeover premiums? Assuming they do increase premiums, is this good for shareholders in the long run? For society?

5. The opponent of the proposal touts the virtues of staggered boards as a means for ensuring continuity of management. Are you convinced? Notice that the lack of a staggered board does not mean that board members will turn over more quickly; they may remain in place for just as long without a staggered board as with one. The only difference is that they are up for election more frequently and that they can be more easily ousted in the event of a takeover.

6. To the extent that elimination of staggered boards increases director turnover, is this a bad thing? Is there a danger that during an extended period of board service a director will become complacent, or bored, or simply run out of ideas? That a director will become too friendly with the company's senior executives and lose some of her ability to act as an independent challenge to management? Would eliminating staggered boards reduce these risks?

7. Will the prospect of having to earn re-election each year keep board members on their toes, and also create greater opportunities for replacing them if they don't perform?

8. What about the argument that staggered boards create greater independence? Will a board member who knows that she can serve out a three-year term, unless replaced for cause, be more vocal at posing a credible challenge to managers in year one?

9. Why does the management of Sally Beauty warn the shareholders that an affirmative vote on the proposal will not automatically declassify the board? Are they subtly threatening not to implement the shareholder vote unless it is definitive? Would it be wise for the managers of a company to flout the will of the shareholders in a manner like this, even if they can do so as a matter of law?

10. It is often difficult, for personal reasons, to remove or fail to reappoint a director before they reach mandatory retirement age (if the company has such a policy). Would it be a good idea to impose term limits on directors, requiring that they leave the board, say, after a maximum of ten years? What about the lesser

remedy of term-limiting service as a committee chair, thus requiring board members to rotate across committees over time?

11. QuickScore, the governance rating system operated by proxy adviser Institutional Shareholder Services, defines tenure of more than nine years as an "excessive" length that potentially compromises director independence. Do you agree?

12. CalPERS, the California State Pension Fund, promotes "global governance principles," which include a "comply-or-explain" approach to long-serving directors. Under this approach, for directors who have served for more than 12 years, companies must either classify the director as non-independent or annually disclose the reasons why the company considers the long-serving director to be independent. Would you favor such a rule?

PROBLEM 2-1

You are an independent director of Bettyco, a high-end manufacturer of cosmetics, with two years left to serve on your three-year term. Bettyco's board of directors has been approached by Ogre, an aggressive hedge fund that owns 4.9 percent of the company's stock. Ogre wants Bettyco to introduce a line of inexpensive branded cosmetics for sale on television shopping channels. You believe that although Ogre's plan might increase profits in the short run, it will come at the expense of destroying Bettyco's reputation as a quality brand. Ogre has made it clear that if Bettyco doesn't give in to its demands it will launch a proxy fight for control of the company. Meanwhile, Governance Watch, a shareholder rights group, makes a request to declassify the board of directors, which is placed on the company's proxy statement. You believe that Governance Watch is acting in league with Ogre and that the purpose is intended to help Ogre win control of the company. Should you encourage Bettyco to resist the proposal? If the proposal passes, should you vote to ignore it?

4. Qualifications

Conscientious board members must digest enormous amounts of information, attend long and tiring meetings, and participate in anxiety-producing decisions affecting the fate of the company. If things go badly, board members can face public criticism and scrutiny, and may find themselves sued for damages in a lawsuit. Even if they don't have to pay damages — and they rarely do — being a defendant in a lawsuit arising out of board service can be stressful, time-consuming, and embarrassing.

Despite these downsides, many people wish to serve on boards of directors, simply because the advantages of doing so outweigh the costs. Members of boards of public companies are often paid several hundred thousand dollars a year for part-time jobs; they also may receive perks such as stays in four-star hotels, excellent meals, and travel on company jets. Service on a board can generate valuable business contacts. There are also the psychological benefits of performing an important responsibility, contributing to the community, dealing with interesting issues, and receiving public recognition as a person of distinction.

Who, among those willing to serve, should be selected? The answer is complicated because many factors play a role. Consider the following possible qualifications:

- The candidate is a senior executive at the firm.
- The candidate has a distinguished background in some other field of activity requiring leadership skills (for example, she is a retired four-star general).
- The candidate is a successful executive in some other industry.
- The candidate is politically or socially connected with people who might be of service to the organization.
- The candidate is a woman or a member of a racial or ethnic minority.
- The candidate has expertise about the industry or aspects of a firm's operations.
- The candidate owns a lot of the company's stock.
- The candidate is an attorney, accountant, or other professional service provider.
- The candidate is a representative of some important constituency in the firm.

Weaknesses also need to be considered. Consider the following:

- The candidate previously served on the board of another company that went bankrupt.
- The candidate is undergoing a contentious divorce.
- The candidate is living with a chronic medical condition that could disable her from further service on short notice.
- The candidate was expelled from college for cheating on an examination.
- The candidate is on bad terms with the person who heads up the company's government supervisor.
- The candidate publicly espouses unpopular views on matters of public controversy.

Which of these qualities, in your opinion, ought to be considered when selecting board members? Which (if any) should be out of bounds? How would you weigh them vis-à-vis one another—which is the most important and which is the least important? Are there any considerations you would add to this list? Is it valuable, in your opinion, to have a diversified set of skills, backgrounds, and endowments on the board?

This section examines qualifications for board membership, examining in particular the following attributes: (a) independence, (b) skills, and (c) diversity.

a. Independence

A key distinction among board members is whether or not they are independent. An inside director is someone employed by or otherwise linked to the company for reasons other than his or her service as a director; an independent director is someone without these connections. Many corporate boards—and all or nearly all boards of publicly traded companies—include both independent and inside directors.

Why do companies have both independent and inside directors? The conventional answer is that these two sorts of directors each bring something to the table. Senior executives offer important benefits:

- They are intimately involved in the management of the company. They understand the company's business, its operations, and its competitive and regulatory environment. They know the personalities, strengths, and weaknesses of other senior managers and are equipped to assess the best use of the available human resources.

- Above all, they have a commitment to the enterprise that is both financial (their compensation depends on the success or failure of the firm) and reputational (if the company does well, they will gain a name that can earn them other opportunities; if it does poorly they may find themselves scratching for work).

But inside directors also bring deficits to the table:

- Because they are insiders, they are likely to think along lines that are set within the organization. They may have spent their entire careers at the firm and thus may lack the perspective that comes with broader experience. Even if they have moved about, their work experience is likely to have been focused in a single industry.
- If they are not the chief executive officer, they may find themselves limited in what they can say on the board because of fear that the CEO, who controls their possibilities for promotion, may not approve.
- Insiders usually want to be paid more rather than less for their full-time service to the company; but every dollar paid to senior managers is a dollar not available to the company for useful projects or for dividends.
- Insiders tend to value the powers and perquisites of their jobs; they may wish to entrench themselves in office rather than allow the company to be acquired by an outside bidder who might push them over the transom, even if the bidder is offering superior value to shareholders.
- Insiders may be incompetent or unmotivated, and thus may prefer that the board of directors not closely scrutinize their job performance.

Independent directors offer a partial solution to these limitations:

- An independent director often comes from a different background and brings a different perspective to bear on strategic issues.
- Not being employed at the firm, the independent director is (presumably) less concerned about offending the chief executive officer.
- Independent directors are compensated for their work, but only on a part-time basis; their conflict of interest over the matter of compensation is less severe than in the case of inside directors.
- Independent directors value the benefits that come from board service, and thus, like inside directors, have an incentive to entrench themselves in office; but because the work is only part-time and is rarely the principal source of an independent director's income, the entrenchment motivation is likely to be less problematic.
- Independent directors have no incentive to allow the company's executive officers to behave in an incompetent or unmotivated way, and so are more likely to insist on good job performance.
- Independent directors have a public-relations function: A company with a majority of outside directors can rebut the charge that it is dominated by a small cadre of top officers. If some of the independent directors bring reputations to the job that shine a favorable light on the firm — for example, if they are well-known leaders in public service, social activism, the military, or other occupations held in high public esteem — this is all to the good.

Yet independent directors are also limited in their capacity to manage:

- Because they are only part-time servants of the enterprise, they can never have the knowledge base that an insider director brings to the table.
- Their partial involvement with the company is a strength but also a weakness: Having only a fraction of their personal wealth and reputational capital tied up in the firm, they have less to lose if it does poorly.
- The independence of independent directors is sometimes in question. As a practical matter, it is often the case that the independent director is selected by the chief executive officer or other inside directors; at the very least, it is unlikely that an independent director will be nominated against the wishes of senior management (unless the company is in the midst of a proxy fight). Independent directors are often connected to senior management by myriad ties of acquaintance, friendship, and shared interests. For these reasons, independent directors may find it difficult to raise hard or challenging questions in the collegial atmosphere of the board room.

The mix of independent and inside directors observed in large companies reflects a balancing of these factors. Both types of director have strengths and weaknesses, but they tend to offset each other: The strengths of inside directors are the weaknesses of outside directors, and vice versa. Overall—in theory—the company is better off with a mix of both.

Questions and Comments

1. What do you think of the arguments in favor of independent directors? Do independent directors play a constructive role? Is their ability to contribute to the firm's welfare greater in some circumstances than others?

2. Researchers have studied how companies perform with and without independent directors. One study reviewing the literature concluded that board composition, as measured by the ratio of inside to independent directors, is not correlated with standard measures of performance. *See* Benjamin Hermalin & Michael Weisbach, *Boards of Directors as an Endogenously Determined Institution: A Survey of the Economic Literature*, 9 Fed. Reserve Bank of N.Y. Econ. Pol'y Rev. 7 (2003). Given these findings, should we care whether a company has independent directors?

3. On the other hand, there is evidence that independent board members may improve a company's share price, as measured by the positive response of a company's stock price to the announcement that an independent director has been added to the board—indicating that the market, at least, seems to believe that they have value. The effect is not clear-cut, however, and is also relatively weak. In any event, how reliable are the market's estimates? The financial crisis of 2007-2009 demonstrated that the market is capable of misjudgments. Could a positive market response represent herd mentality or groupthink rather than a genuine measure of value?

4. There is some evidence that audit committees comprised of independent directors discourage companies from engaging in "earnings management" (manipulating financial operations and reporting so as to show steady growth of profits over time). If we view earnings management as a bad thing—not fraudulent, but at least designed to create an impression that doesn't fully comport with the facts—then

perhaps independent directors improve the quality of corporate disclosure, contribute to more informed and more efficient markets, and act as a check on managerial proclivities to be deceptive in their presentation of the company's results. On the other hand, could earnings management sometimes be beneficial? Markets can overreact and are subject to irrationalities of their own. If the company is fundamentally sound, is it deceptive to manage reported earnings to soothe over short-term losses?

5. The presence of independent directors also seems to increase the likelihood that companies will face a hostile takeover bid. The theory is that because independent directors are not as entrenched in office as inside directors, they will be less likely to resist a takeover which will result in the ousting of the current management. If we favor hostile bids — because, for example, they result in premiums for the target company's shareholders — this finding might be taken as supporting the case for independent directors. But do you favor hostile bids? Even though they benefit shareholders of the target company, hostile bids may also result in layoffs, plant closings, break-ups of firms, a more adversarial relationship with labor unions, or other consequences that some might oppose. Hostile bids, moreover, have become uncommon in recent years, so even if you favor independent directors on this ground, the effect may not be very significant. Also, once a hostile bid is made, is it possible that a board dominated by inside directors will be more effective at bargaining for a better price than a board dominated by independent directors? How do you assess the conflicting inferences?

6. Consider the role independent directors play in ordinary times and in crisis situations. Perhaps in ordinary times independent directors contribute principally by watching over managers to make sure there are no serious shortcomings; but in crisis times they take a more active role. Several studies suggest that boards of directors dominated by independent directors are more likely than boards dominated by insiders to fire the chief executive officer when firms are performing poorly. Assuming that replacing senior managers when things go poorly is, in general, a good strategic move, these studies may suggest that independent board members can be useful as a resource that is held in reserve in good times, but becomes important in bad times.

7. A word of caution is in order about the empirical research described above (and elsewhere in this book): It is dangerous to interpret correlation as establishing causation. For example, if earnings management is more common in boards dominated by inside directors, we may infer that inside directors cause a company to engage in more earnings management and independent directors cause companies to engage in less earnings management. This inference is not necessarily wrong; it may well be correct. But correlation and causation are two different things. Given observed relationships, it might be that independent directors are causing good things to happen and inside directors are causing bad things to happen; but it also might be that some other factor caused the observed results. For example, perhaps companies with certain institutional cultures select independent board members and also dislike earnings management; in such a case the institutional culture rather than the independent board members could be driving the observed results.

8. Should companies be allowed to retain companies to act as corporate directors? What are the potential advantages and disadvantages? *See* Stephen M. Bainbridge & M. Todd Henderson, *Boards-R-Us: Reconceptualizing Corporate Boards,* 166 Stan. L. Rev. 1051 (2014).

The distinction between inside and independent directors is important for a number of reasons beyond their respective contributions to firm performance. Companies whose shares are listed for trading on national securities exchanges, such as the New York Stock Exchange or the NASDAQ, must satisfy listing standards promulgated by those organizations. Both NYSE and NASDAQ require that the majority of directors of a listed company be independent. All members of the audit, compensation, and nominating committees of the board — if established — must be independent. NYSE and NASDAQ also require listed companies to disclose the identity of independent directors in their proxy statements and 10-K forms.

The SEC, for its part, requires listed companies to disclose the identity of directors determined to be independent under applicable stock exchange listing criteria as well as the identity of any member of the company's audit, nominating or compensation committee who is determined to not be independent under applicable stock exchange listing criteria. *See* Regulation S-K, item 407.

Independent directors are popular in other countries. The European Commission recommends that there be a "sufficient" number of independent directors on the board and that there be a "strong presence" of independent directors on committees. Commission Recommendation 2005/162/EC of 15 February 2005. Most EU member states impose requirements consistent with these recommendations. Even Japan — long criticized for its lax rules on corporate governance — has upgraded independence requirements; the Tokyo Stock Exchange now requires that listed companies must have at least one independent director. In 2012, the Japanese government proposed a revision to the general corporate law which would increase the role of independent directors still further.

Here is an excerpt from the definition of "independent" director under the New York Stock Exchange's listing standards:

New York Stock Exchange Listed Company Manual §303A.02

In order to tighten the definition of "independent director" for purposes of these standards:

(a)(i) No director qualifies as "independent" unless the board of directors affirmatively determines that the director has no material relationship with the listed company (either directly or as a partner, shareholder or officer of an organization that has a relationship with the company).

(ii) In addition, in affirmatively determining the independence of any director who will serve on the compensation committee of the listed company's board of directors, the board of directors must consider all factors specifically relevant to determining whether a director has a relationship to the listed company which is material to that director's ability to be independent from management in connection with the duties of a compensation committee member, including, but not limited to:

(A) the source of compensation of such director, including any consulting, advisory or other compensatory fee paid by the listed company to such director; and

(B) whether such director is affiliated with the listed company, a subsidiary of the listed company or an affiliate of a subsidiary of the listed company.

(b) In addition, a director is not independent if:

(i) The director is, or has been within the last three years, an employee of the listed company, or an immediate family member is, or has been within the last three years, an executive officer, of the listed company.

(ii) The director has received, or has an immediate family member who has received, during any twelve-month period within the last three years, more than $120,000 in direct compensation from the listed company, other than director and committee fees and pension or other forms of deferred compensation for prior service. . . .

(iii) (A) The director is a current partner or employee of a firm that is the listed company's internal or external auditor; (B) the director has an immediate family member who is a current partner of such a firm; (C) the director has an immediate family member who is a current employee of such a firm and personally works on the listed company's audit; or (D) the director or an immediate family member was within the last three years a partner or employee of such a firm and personally worked on the listed company's audit within that time.

(iv) The director or an immediate family member is, or has been with the last three years, employed as an executive officer of another company where any of the listed company's present executive officers at the same time serves or served on that company's compensation committee.

(v) The director is a current employee, or an immediate family member is a current executive officer, of a company that has made payments to, or received payments from, the listed company for property or services in an amount which, in any of the last three fiscal years, exceeds the greater of $1 million, or 2% of such other company's consolidated gross revenues.

Questions and Comments

1. This standard vests some of the decision as to whether a director is "independent" in the board of directors itself. Is this the equivalent of the fox guarding the henhouse? If not the board of directors, who is going to make this decision? Should it be given to the relevant regulatory body (the SEC, or the securities exchange where the company's stock is listed)?

2. Suppose that a director has no financial relationship with the company, other than her compensation for service as a director, but that she happens to be the cousin of the CEO? What if the director and CEO are best friends? What if they serve together on the board of a charity? The NYSE Listed Company Manual has this to say: "It is not possible to anticipate, or explicitly to provide for, all circumstances that might signal potential conflicts of interest, or that might bear on the materiality of a director's relationship to a listed company. . . . Accordingly, it is best that boards making 'independence' determinations broadly consider all relevant facts and circumstances. In particular, when assessing the materiality of a director's relationship with the listed company, the board should consider the issue not merely from the standpoint of the director, but also from that of persons or organizations with which the director has an affiliation. Material relationships can include commercial, industrial, banking, consulting, legal, accounting, charitable and familial relationships, among others." NYSE Listed Company Manual §303A. Do you find this advice helpful?

3. Does owning a large amount of stock in a company imply that a director is not independent? Certainly a director who has her personal assets invested in a company's stock has a financial interest in seeing that the stock does well. Could this lead to a temptation to wink at financial shenanigans by management designed to artificially pump up share value? Despite the potential cogency of this argument, owning a large amount of a company's stock, in itself, does not deprive a director of independence. According to the NYSE, the reason is that "the concern is independence from management." Do you agree?

4. The excerpt from the NYSE Listed Company Manual makes special rules for the independence of directors who serve on compensation committees. How are these special rules different from the rules applying to other directors? Why should the considerations pertinent to the independence of board members who serve on compensation committees be different from the considerations applicable to board service in general?

5. Independence can have a different meaning in the context of special committees set up to assess the merits of shareholders derivative litigation. As we will see in Chapter 10, even directors who are formally independent for other purposes may not be considered independent for the purposes of these special committees, if their other contacts with senior managers or other interested parties raise questions about their ability to act in the best interests of the company and its shareholders.

PROBLEM 2-2

You are recruited by an executive search firm to serve as an independent director of Middlesex Co., a mid-size apparel manufacturer whose stock is listed on the New York Stock Exchange. You have no prior involvement with Middlesex or any of its officers or directors. After you arrive you discover that Sam Smith, whom Middlesex lists as another independent director, is dating the company's chief financial officer. Another purportedly independent director, Wendy Williams, was the college roommate of the chief executive officer and remains one of his closest friends. You understand that the company has made a deliberate decision to declare these directors to be independent notwithstanding their connections with the company. You want very much to remain on the board. What should you do?

b. Skills

We don't let people practice law unless they have met educational requirements, passed a bar examination, and been deemed to possess the character and fitness necessary for the profession. Doctors, barbers, and massage therapists all need a license to practice their trades.

The task of corporate directors can be just as demanding and just as important as these occupations. Yet there is no general requirement that corporate directors undergo professional training, obtain specialized degrees, pass examinations, or participate in continuing professional education programs. State corporate codes typically impose no competency or educational requirements on directors, beyond perhaps a minimum age threshold (directors of New York corporations must be at least 18 years old).

Even in the case of bank directors — often thought to be the most crucial because of the systemic risk posed by bank failures — the regulators tend to content themselves with pabulum. In describing the skills that are requisite to a bank director, the Comptroller of the Currency's Director's Book offers the following: "When searching for new directors, boards should seek individuals who exercise independent judgment and who actively participate in decision making. The principal qualities of an effective bank director include strength of character, an inquiring and independent mind, practical wisdom, and sound judgment." The Comptroller supplements this helpful advice with some more specific considerations: Directors ought to have "basic knowledge of the banking industry, the financial regulatory system, and the laws and regulations that govern the operation of the institution; willingness to put the interests of the bank ahead of personal interests; willingness to avoid conflicts of interests; knowledge of the communities served by the bank; background, knowledge, and experience in business or another discipline to facilitate oversight of the bank; and willingness and ability to commit the time necessary to prepare for and regularly attend board and committee meetings." Office of Comptroller of the Currency, The Director's Book: The Role of a National Bank Director 3 (2010). These recommendations are not hard to satisfy, and in any event have no legal force.

There are, however, certain areas where particular skills are specified by law. Audit committee members may have to display a minimum level of competence about finance; and at least one of them may need to have more substantial skills in finance, accounting, or related matters. When companies get into trouble, the regulators may become more demanding. In the case of national banks, the Comptroller of the Currency can exercise plenary control over the selection (or removal) of directors when a bank under its supervision becomes undercapitalized. Even if the bank is not undercapitalized, regulators conduct examinations in which all aspects of management are evaluated; if in the opinion of the examiner-in-charge the board of directors of a particular bank lacks the requisite skills to manage it effectively, she will not hesitate to let that fact be known.

Aside from regulatory action, companies may impose requirements for directors voluntarily. Delaware General Corporation Law §141(b) recognizes that a company's governing documents "may prescribe other qualifications for directors." Activist shareholders, who are assuming an increasingly important role in public companies, are stepping up demands that candidates for board positions have qualifications for the positions. A number of private initiatives also seek to enhance director professionalism and skills. The National Association of Corporate Directors, among other groups, offers its members a set of skills training seminars and conferences, interface opportunities, and information about current developments in the areas of governance, risk management, and compliance.

Questions and Comments

1. Should the law require professional training for board members? Would you require Facebook chief executive officer Mark Zuckerberg to attend such training? If he gets a pass, why not others?

2. Would professional training, licensure, or continuing education requirements improve board performance? If, as the Comptroller of the Currency says, the most important qualifications for board service are integrity and strength of character, can these be taught?

3. Would board members tolerate training requirements that impose a large burden on their time?

4. Given that boards can benefit from the application of many different skill sets, is there one single curriculum that would serve for all?

5. Should companies train directors "in-house"? On the one hand, homemade director training can be fitted both to the particular features of the company and to the areas where the particular director needs to supplement her knowledge base. On the other hand, devising a program for only a few people, especially on a tailor-made basis, can be costly. Directors may also find it a bit undignified to be instructed by people they are supposed to manage. Still, some regulators endorse the idea. The Comptroller of the Currency has this to say: "A board should conduct orientation programs for new directors. While these programs vary based on the bank's size and complexity, at a minimum these programs should explain the operation of the bank and the banking industry and clearly outline the responsibilities of board members, individually and as a group. Ongoing education programs that describe local and overall economic conditions, emerging industry developments, opportunities, and risks also are important tools for maintaining director expertise and board effectiveness." Office of Comptroller of the Currency, The Director's Book: The Role of a National Bank Director 2 (2010).

6. Some people cap off distinguished careers by serving on multiple boards of directors. Often the age limit for board membership (generally around 70) is higher than the age limit for service as a corporate executive, so that people who are still vigorous can find useful — and well-compensated — work as directors after retiring from their day jobs. How should one assess the qualifications of a candidate who serves on other boards?

A person who serves on other boards will probably know something about how to be an effective board member. Moreover, prior board service may equip a candidate with information about how things are done elsewhere, which can be of value in their next position. On the other hand, too much of a good thing may be undesirable. Corporate governance advocates sometimes criticize board members for being "over-boarded." This doesn't mean that they have been tortured or thrown over the side of a boat. "Over-boarded" simply means that an individual, in the view of a critic, serves on too many boards. How many boards are too many?

7. Should companies value the skills that an attorney can bring to the board? The testimony of the market is "yes": As of 2013, nearly half of public company boards included at least one attorney. Attorneys may add value because they understand hot-button issues such as compliance, regulation, governance, or litigation. Rightly or wrongly, moreover, attorneys are sometimes said to bring interpersonal skills to their board service, including communication abilities and expertise in dispute resolution. The value of an attorney on the board, moreover, may be increasing as the government ratchets up compliance demands and increases the stringency of regulations. A survey by Legal Week Intelligence Corporate Risk Benchmarker, published in association with Deloitte, found that 43 percent of corporate boards discussed regulatory and legal risk at every one of their board meetings in 2013, up from 23 percent in 2012. Legal risk was especially prominent at boards of larger firms. Benchmarker Legal Week: Handling Risk in the Global Corporate Market, available at http://www.legalweek.com/digital_assets/6053/Deloitte_benchmarker_final_Email.pdf. Do you agree that legal training is a *desideratum* for board service? If so, can attorneys be most helpful in particular industries (e.g., finance or health

care) or when a company is facing special problems (e.g., regulatory enforcement actions or financial distress)?

c. Diversity

Women and minorities are under-represented on corporate boards relative to their share of the population. According to one study, as of 2006 women held 17 percent of seats on Fortune 100 boards and minorities held 15 percent; the combined percentage was 28 percent. A 2013 survey of public companies conducted by the National Association of Corporate Directors reported that 27.4 percent of responding companies had no female members. Disparities are even greater in Europe: As of 2011, only 10 percent of board seats on big European firms were held by women.

Consider possible reasons why a company might deem it desirable to include on the board people from groups that have traditionally been excluded from board membership. Including people from historically disadvantaged groups may:

- Introduce a valuable perspective on the issues facing the board and thus contribute to effective decision making.
- Signal to the company's employees that the firm has an inclusive corporate culture.
- Foster mentoring relationships that can groom talented women and minorities for promotion within the firm.
- Generate a favorable view of the firm in the public or in particular market segments.
- Reassure investors that the company is not tone-deaf on important public issues.
- Convince activists that the company has progressive views on social issues, and therefore that it should not be signaled out for criticism.
- Reassure regulators that the firm is eager to implement good governance practices and that it is compliant with changing social norms, thus deflecting potential enforcement scrutiny.

Questions and Comments

1. In your opinion, to what extent should an organization take diversity considerations into account in selecting board members?

2. Should women be given a preference?

3. Should ethnic or racial minorities be given a preference?

4. Should people from lower socio-economic backgrounds be given a preference?

5. Are the diversity arguments stronger for publicly traded companies than for companies held in private ownership?

6. The United States does not require companies to appoint a set percentage of women or minorities to their boards, but rules of this sort do exist elsewhere. France, Norway, and Spain, among other countries, require companies to work toward equalizing the number of woman on corporate boards. As of 2013, 10 countries had established explicit quotas for female representation on public company boards and 15 countries had included non-binding quotas in their corporate governance codes, requiring companies that fail to meet the quotas to disclose that fact and

explain why they have not complied. Siri A. Terjesen, Ruth V. Aguilera & Ruth Lorenz, *Legislating a Woman's Seat on the Board: Institutional Factors Driving Gender Quotas for Boards of Directors*, 128 J. Bus. Ethics 233 (2015). In 2011, the European Parliament issued a non-binding call for legislation at the European Union level that would require 40 percent of seats on listed companies' supervisory boards to be held by women as of 2020. Would you favor a quota approach for the United States?

7. Section 342 of the Dodd-Frank Act requires the SEC to establish an "Office of Minority and Women Inclusion," which is tasked, among other things, with "develop[ing] standards" for "assessing diversity policies and practices of regulated entities." Since the SEC has no power to mandate diversity policies for firms it regulates, what is the purpose of this provision?

8. For an empirical study finding that gender diversity on corporate boards increases firm value, see Thomas Schmid & Daniel Urban, Does It Matter Where You Work? International Evidence on Female Board Representation, available at http://papers.ssrn.com/sol3/papers.cfm?abstract_id=2344786 (examining data from 35,000 firms in 53 countries). For an argument that advocates of board diversity have over-stressed the potential economic benefits, to the exclusion of social or moral rationales, see Lisa M. Fairfax, *Board Diversity Revisited: New Rationale, Same Old Story?*, 89 N.C. L. Rev. 855 (2011).

9. Female representation on corporate boards around the world has been increasing gradually. A 2013 survey of British firms found that 20 percent of board members of the 100 largest listed companies in the U.K. were female — an increase over previous years and one possibly sparked by a voluntary commitment many companies made to increase female representation to 25 percent. According to a 2014 study published by Corporate Women Directors International, Europe has begun to change the ratio of women on corporate boards, accounting for 16 of the 25 Global 200 companies with the highest percentage of board members. One Norwegian company, Statoil, had more than 50 percent female representation as of 2014. In the United States, Procter & Gamble was the top big company in terms of female representation, with 45.5 percent in 2014.

5. Fiduciary Duties

The responsibilities conferred on the board of directors are large. We trust that boards will perform their jobs faithfully and well. But boards of directors, being composed of human beings, are also fallible. They make mistakes — sometimes enormous ones. Worse yet, they sometimes fail to display the degree of loyalty and good faith that one would expect from people charged with such important obligations.

Should board members be held legally responsible when they fall down on the job? The law's answer is a mixture of "yes" and "no." Directors are indeed subject to a legal duty to perform their responsibilities faithfully and well. But that duty is only sporadically enforced, and sometimes not enforced at all.

The director's legal responsibility is captured in the idea that directors are "fiduciaries" and that they owe companies and shareholders a "fiduciary duty." Directors of corporations are fiduciaries because they make decisions that affect many others: not only the company itself but also people such as shareholders who have an ownership interest in the firm. The directors' fiduciary duty is the duty they owe to their firms and, indirectly, to the firm's shareholders (and possibly other constituents).

PROBLEM 2-3

Underhill Co., a publicly traded company, publishes books and journals in the fields of Medicine, Dentistry, and Life Sciences. The company has recently endured a scandal in which account executives for several of its professional journals were shown to have received payments from authors in exchange for publishing their papers. Underhill Co. is actively exploring a restructuring that would seek to develop Asian markets and to move from print media to an online distribution system.

The company's nominating committee has two board vacancies to fill and five candidates. Of the five board members who will continue in office, four are men and one is a woman; two are employees of the company (including its current chief executive officer) and three are independent; one is African-American, one is an English citizen of European extraction, and the remainder are European-Americans. The continuing inside board members have spent their careers in business; the continuing outside directors include a former member of Congress, an architect who is the son of the company's founder and holder of 25 percent of its stock, and a professor of Chemistry at Massachusetts Institute of Technology.

The five candidates' qualifications are as follows:

Alan Able: Age 68. European-American. Retired CEO of Underhill Co. Graduate of Harvard (AB) and Stanford University (MBA in Marketing). He spent his career at Underhill, starting in the stock room and returning after completing his education. Improper payments for publications were received by company officers under his tenure but he was not personally involved. Under his leadership, Underhill Co. doubled in size and saw its profits grow by an average of 7 percent per year. Able's candidacy is favored by the son of the company's founder.

Janice James: Age 57. African-American. Graduate of Middlebury College (AB). She is a renowned poet and novelist and winner of the Pulitzer Prize in Fiction. Member of the Board of Directors of Placing Kids First, a charitable organization dedicated to improving educational opportunities for underprivileged children.

Betty Brown: Age 43. European-American. Graduate of University of Illinois (AB and JD). A specialist in trademark and intellectual property law, she currently serves as the company's in-house general counsel. Formerly a partner of Smith & Wallis, a law firm with 450 attorneys around the country. She is being groomed as a possible successor to Underhill Co.'s current chief executive officer.

Samuel Chin: Age 58. Chinese-American born in Hong Kong. Graduate of the Hong Kong University of Science and Technology (Bachelor of Accounting) and Singapore Management University (MBA in Accounting). Fluent in Chinese, English, and Malay. A former partner at a "big four" accounting firm, he now runs a successful hedge fund focusing on emerging markets in Asia.

David Drake: Age 73. European-American. Retired five-star general and former chairman of the Joint Chiefs of Staff, the highest military office in the United States. He is a graduate of West Point and a member of three other boards of directors in the defense, manufacturing, and pharmaceutical industries.

Which of these candidates should the company select to fill the vacancies?

The term "fiduciary duty" has a hoary lineage in the law, and often evokes a misty sense of gravity and importance. In Meinhard v. Salmon, 164 N.E. 545 (N.Y. 1928), Judge Cardozo delivered a classic peroration on the topic: "A trustee is held to something stricter than the morals of the market place. Not honesty alone, but the punctilio of an honor the most sensitive, is then the standard of behavior . . . the level of conduct for fiduciaries [has] been kept at a level higher than that trodden by the crowd." Id. at 546. Although Meinhard v. Salmon involved the duty partners owe to one another, Cardozo's encomium is sometimes carried over to the corporate law context to describe the duty of corporate directors.

> A "fiduciary" is a person charged under the law with making decisions fundamental to the welfare of someone else.

> A "fiduciary duty" is the legal duty that a fiduciary owes to the person on whose behalf she is acting.

The problem is that these flights of eloquence do not describe reality very well. Corporate directors are not, in fact, held under the law to anything like the duties that might be inferred from the concept of fiduciary duty as traditionally understood. In only one area — the duty of loyalty — is the fiduciary duty strictly enforced; and even there, a director blessed with good legal advice and an ability not to be too greedy can avoid most liability exposure. In other respects, the fiduciary duty of corporate directors is hardly enforced at all. We will examine the fiduciary duty of corporate directors in three contexts: (a) the duty of care; (b) the duty of loyalty; and (c) the duty of oversight.

a. The Duty of Care

In re Citigroup Inc. Shareholder Derivative Litigation
964 A.2d 106 (Del. Ch. 2009)

[This was a shareholders derivative action claiming that the board of directors of Citigroup breached their fiduciary responsibility to the company by (among other things) making improvident investments in subprime mortgage securities. The Delaware Chancery Court rejected the theory in definitive terms:]

[P]laintiffs' theory essentially amounts to a claim that the director defendants should be personally liable to the Company because they failed to fully recognize the risk posed by subprime securities. When one looks past the lofty allegations of duties of oversight and red flags used to dress up these claims, what is left appears to be plaintiff shareholders attempting to hold the director defendants personally liable for making (or allowing to be made) business decisions that, in hindsight, turned out poorly for the Company. Delaware Courts have faced these types of claims many times and have developed doctrines to deal with them — the fiduciary duty of care and the business judgment rule. These doctrines properly focus on the decision-making process rather than on a substantive evaluation of the merits of the decision. This follows from the inadequacy of the Court, due in part to a concept known as hindsight bias, to properly evaluate whether corporate decision-makers made a "right" or "wrong" decision. [In a footnote, the court defined hindsight bias as "the tendency for people with knowledge of an outcome to exaggerate the extent to which they believe that outcome could have been predicted."]

The business judgment rule "is a presumption that in making a business decision the directors of a corporation acted on an informed basis, in good faith and in the honest belief that the action taken was in the best interests of the company." The burden is on plaintiffs, the party challenging the directors' decision, to rebut this presumption. Thus, absent an allegation of interestedness or disloyalty to the corporation, the business judgment rule prevents a judge or jury from second guessing director decisions if they were the product of a rational process and the directors availed themselves of all material and reasonably available information.

Questions and Comments

1. The business judgment rule, referred to in the excerpt, is one of the fundamental tenets of modern corporate law. Although variously formulated, the definition offered in the excerpted opinion is about as good as it gets.

2. If the presumption of the business judgment rule is not overcome, the plaintiff has essentially no chance of winning a lawsuit against a director based on a claim of breach of fiduciary duty. Can this be reconciled with the idea of fiduciary duty put forth by Judge Cardozo in Meinhard v. Salmon?

3. Are all good faith exercises of business judgment protected against liability, no matter how reckless? What if the directors voted to pay $100 million for an asset they knew was worth only $50 million — in essence, gave away $50 million? Assume the vote was made in good faith: The directors were not venal, just stupid. The excerpted opinion implies that the substance of a decision is completely protected. Is it sensible to protect directors from liability for decisions that are breathtakingly misguided?

> The business judgment rule is a presumption that in making a business decision the directors of a corporation acted on an informed basis, in good faith, and in the honest belief that the action taken was in the best interests of the company.

4. While the business judgment rule shields directors from liability for bad judgments, it does not foreclose judicial inquiry into the *procedure* that the board used to reach the bad decision: The decision must result from a "rational process" in which the directors availed themselves of "all material and reasonably available information." What is the purpose of this distinction between the decision itself (substance) and the means by which the decision was reached (procedure)?

5. To what extent does procedural scrutiny protect shareholders? If—as is usually true in sophisticated companies—a board discusses the matter at length, reviews fat briefing books, and listens to presentations from highly paid advisers, does the court have much choice but to conclude that the procedure passes muster?

6. Can the line between substance and procedure hold in the business judgment context? In the example above, if the directors paid $100 million for an asset they knew to be worth only $50 million, could a court conclude, regardless of how witnesses testified at trial, that the directors could not have engaged in a rational process that utilized all material and reasonably available information? If the line does not hold, does this eliminate or reduce concerns about a rule that seemingly protects directors against liability for catastrophic decisions?

7. Delaware General Corporation Law §102(b)(7) allows a Delaware corporation to include in its certificate of incorporation a provision that eliminates liability of

directors for money damages in lawsuits based on violations of the duty of care. Section 102(b)(7) is sort of a "super business judgment rule." For companies that adopt the charter provision (and a large number of Delaware companies have done so), the statute makes it clear that, absent special circumstances, directors face no exposure for money damages in lawsuits claiming violations of the duty of care.

8. What is the rationale for the business judgment rule and other director-protecting principles such as §102(b)(7)? At least two theories can be teased out of the opinion excerpted above:

   a. The first idea is that directors of corporations know more than courts know about the business decisions they have to make. Directors are experts about what goes on in their companies; courts are dilettantes. Because directors know much more than judges, it makes sense, absent unusual circumstances, for the courts to defer to the business judgments of directors.

   b. The second idea has to do with timing. The "hindsight bias" referred to in the excerpted opinion refers to the fact that we often evaluate decisions in light of how they turned out. Often this is appropriate: Decisions that turn out badly are more likely to have been bad decisions than decisions that turn out well. However, this is not necessarily the case. Decisions that are well considered at the time they are made sometimes turn out badly and decisions that are poorly considered may turn out well. Hindsight bias is the tendency of people, after the fact, to give too much weight to how a decision turned out. The court in the excerpted case thinks judges are prone to hindsight bias and therefore may tend to be overly harsh in their evaluation of managerial decisions that have bad outcomes. The business judgment rule counteracts this tendency by requiring judges to credit the good faith and reasonableness of managerial decisions unless the contrary is shown.

9. Does it make sense to limit the authority of judges on the ground that they know less than managers about the conditions and business environment facing the company at the time of the events giving rise to the lawsuit? The problem with this idea is that courts are *never* experts. They are generalists who are asked in nearly every case — corporate or not — to rule on issues where the litigants themselves have more information and expertise. Consider a medical malpractice action. Judges are not doctors. They typically know far less about treatment options and medical techniques than the defendant. Yet judges (and juries, who probably know even less) routinely decide whether a defendant lived up to the standard of care expected of physicians in the community. Why are the decisions by corporate directors different? If differences exist, moreover, might judges of the Delaware Chancery Court have *more* expertise than in other types of cases? After all, the Delaware Chancery Court is one of the nation's leading business courts; it decides many corporate matters every year. Does a judge of the Delaware Chancery Court have less expertise about corporate matters than a director who serves on a part-time basis and attends four or six directors' meetings a year?

10. Consider the second rationale for the business judgment rule, namely that hindsight bias will skew the judge's evaluation of the facts. Is this persuasive? Once again, the theory doesn't really distinguish between corporate and other cases. Most decisions judges make are subject to hindsight bias, simply because the events that form the basis of a lawsuit occurred in the past. In an action for personal injuries, the fact that the car got into an accident may influence the judge to consider it more

likely that the driver was not exercising due care. Can you see anything that distinguishes corporate fiduciary duty cases?

11. Most people are not experts at evaluating past actions. It is natural that they fall prey to hindsight bias. Judges, however, are experienced at evaluating past actions: This is one of their central responsibilities. Given that evaluating the past is their stock in trade, is hindsight bias a serious problem for judges? Even if judges are subject to hindsight bias, moreover, is the business judgment rule the best solution to the problem? Instead of corrective lenses, the business judgment rule puts blinders on judges by requiring them to assume that directors acted reasonably and in good faith. Is this sensible?

12. Can you think of any explanations for the business judgment rule other than the ones provided by the court? Consider:

a. Shareholders tend to hold diversified portfolios of securities, and thus are insulated from the consequences of mistakes by the managers of any given corporation. Given that most shareholders are protected against catastrophic loss, there is less reason for the law to intervene.

b. Corporate managers are subject to market discipline that doesn't exist for other fiduciaries. If a company does poorly, its stock price will plummet, institutional investors will become restive, shareholder activists will complain, and corporate raiders will smell blood in the water. To avoid these and other bad consequences of poor decisions, corporate managers have strong incentives to perform their responsibilities well even in the absence of an enforceable duty of care.

c. In the case of public corporations, imposing personal liability on directors would do little to rectify the harm since the amount of damages will far exceed their resources.

d. If responsible people feared having to pay damages for violations of the duty of care, they would not want to serve on corporate boards. Companies would have to appoint less qualified candidates, with the result that the quality of governance would decrease, not increase.

e. States compete to attract corporate charters because of the tax revenue and other benefits that this business brings in. If a state imposed a duty of care with any significant threat of liability, companies would simply re-charter in a more accommodating jurisdiction.

Do any of these theories offer a better explanation of the business judgment rule than the one offered by the court?

b. The Duty of Loyalty

The business judgment rule is a presumption — an assumption that holds unless the contrary is established. The principal way that the presumption can be rebutted, under modern corporate law principles, is to show that the defendant director or controlling shareholder had a conflict of interest in the transaction in question. Where a conflict of interest is shown, the protections of the business judgment rule evaporate and the defendant is left in the unpleasant position of having to justify the transaction as being in the best interests of the corporation. In the following case, concerns about conflicts of interest with a controlling shareholder seem to have influenced the judge to reject a transaction, even though the deal had been blessed by a committee of independent directors in consultation with highly qualified legal and financial advisors.

In re Southern Peru Copper Corp. Shareholder Derivative Litigation

30 A.3d 60 (Del. Ch. 2011)

. . . The controlling stockholder of an NYSE-listed mining company came to the corporation's independent directors with a proposition. How about you buy my non-publicly traded Mexican mining company for approximately $3.1 billion of your NYSE-listed stock? A special committee was set up to "evaluate" this proposal · and it retained well-respected legal and financial advisors.

The financial advisor did a great deal of preliminary due diligence, and generated valuations showing that the Mexican mining company, when valued under a discounted cash flow and other measures, was not worth anything close to $3.1 billion. The $3.1 billion was a real number in the crucial business sense that everyone believed that the NYSE-listed company could in fact get cash equivalent to its stock market price for its shares. That is, the cash value of the "give" was known. And the financial advisor told the special committee that the value of the "get" was more than $1 billion less.

Rather than tell the controller to go mine himself, the special committee and its advisors instead did something that is indicative of the mindset that too often afflicts even good faith fiduciaries trying to address a controller. Having been empowered only to evaluate what the controller put on the table and perceiving that other options were off the menu because of the controller's own objectives, the special committee put itself in a world where there was only one strategic option to consider, the one proposed by the controller, and thus entered a dynamic where at best it had two options, either figure out a way to do the deal the controller wanted or say no. Abandoning a focus on whether the NYSE-listed mining company would get $3.1 billion in value in the exchange, the special committee embarked on a "relative valuation" approach. Apparently perceiving that its own company was overvalued and had a fundamental value less than its stock market trading price, the special committee assured itself that a deal could be fair so long as the "relative value" of the two companies was measured on the same metrics. Thus, its financial advisor generated complicated scenarios pegging the relative value of the companies and obscuring the fundamental fact that the NYSE-listed company had a proven cash value. These scenarios all suggest that the special committee believed that the standalone value of the Mexican company (the "get") was worth far less than the controller's consistent demand for $3.1 billion (the "give"). Rather than reacting to these realities by suggesting that the controller make an offer for the NYSE-listed company at a premium to what the special committee apparently viewed as a plush market price, or making the controller do a deal based on the Mexican company's standalone value, the special committee and its financial advisor instead took strenuous efforts to justify a transaction at the level originally demanded by the controller. . . .

I am left with the firm conclusion that this transaction was unfair however one allocates the burden of persuasion under a preponderance of the evidence standard. A focused, aggressive controller extracted a deal that was far better than market, and got real, market-tested value of over $3 billion for something that no member of the special committee, none of its advisors, and no trial expert was willing to say was worth that amount of actual cash. Although directors are free in some situations to act on the belief that the market is wrong, they are not free to believe that they can in fact get $3.1 billion in cash for their own stock but then use that stock to acquire something that they know is worth far less than $3.1 billion in cash or in "fundamental" or "intrinsic" value terms because they believe the market is overvaluing their own stock and that on real "fundamental" or "intrinsic" terms the deal is therefore fair. In plain terms, the special committee turned the "gold" it was holding in trust into "silver" and did an exchange with "silver" on that basis, ignoring that in the real world the gold they held had a much higher market price in cash than silver. That non-adroit act of commercial charity toward the controller resulted in a manifestly unfair transaction.

I remedy that unfairness by ordering the controller to return to the NYSE-listed company a number of shares necessary to remedy the harm. I apply a conservative metric because of the plaintiff's delay, which occasioned some evidentiary uncertainties and which subjected the controller to lengthy market risk. The resulting award is still large, but the record could justify a much larger award. [The court awarded damages of $1.263 billion plus pre-judgment and post-judgment interest.]

Questions and Comments

1. The damages awarded in this case were among the largest ever granted in a breach of fiduciary duty case.

2. What does this case suggest about the value of independent directors? The members of the committee that approved the deal on behalf of the public company appeared to have sterling credentials: one was a graduate of Columbia Law School who had worked at one of the country's leading corporate law firms and then in a major corporate group; another had a PhD in finance from the Wharton School at the University of Pennsylvania; still another had both an MBA and a law degree and had managed billion-dollar companies. The plaintiff did not question their independence. These directors don't sound like pushovers. But as the court describes the facts they seemed awfully willing to cater to the wishes of the controlling shareholder. Why?

3. The special committee's financial adviser was Goldman Sachs, one of the most powerful financial firms in the world. Should Goldman have done more to resist the committee's efforts to make the deal appear fair from a financial point of view?

4. Can this opinion be reconciled with the Citigroup opinion excerpted earlier in this chapter?

c. *Caremark* and the Duty of Oversight

What is the board's responsibility for ensuring that the companies they serve comply with applicable laws and regulations? A simple answer is that the responsibility is complete. Given that the board is charged with overseeing the management of the corporation, and that compliance is a key part of management, it would seem straightforward to say that the board is responsible for compliance.

The statement is true, of course, and also important. Board members who take their responsibilities seriously — as the vast majority of board members undoubtedly do — will view compliance as one of their primary responsibilities and will seek in good faith to fulfill their duty to ensure compliance. Yet, if not backed by some sort of legal sanctions, the requirement to ensure compliance may, in some cases, go unfulfilled. What *legally enforceable* compliance requirements are imposed on directors?

In re Caremark International Inc. Derivative Litigation

698 A.2d 959 (Del. Ch. 1996)

ALLEN, Chancellor:

... Caremark, a Delaware corporation with its headquarters in Northbrook, Illinois, was created in November 1992 when it was spun-off from Baxter International, Inc. ("Baxter") and became a publicly held company listed on the New York Stock Exchange. The business practices that created the problem pre-dated the spin-off. During the relevant period Caremark was involved in two main health care business segments, providing patient care and managed care services. As part of its patient care business, which accounted for the majority of Caremark's revenues, Caremark provided alternative site health care services, including infusion therapy, growth hormone therapy, HIV/AIDS-related treatments and hemophilia therapy. Caremark's managed care services included prescription drug programs and the operation of multi-specialty group practices.

A substantial part of the revenues generated by Caremark's businesses is derived from third party payments, insurers, and Medicare and Medicaid reimbursement programs. The latter source of payments are subject to the terms of the Anti-Referral Payments Law ("ARPL") which prohibits health care providers from paying any form of remuneration to induce the referral of Medicare or Medicaid patients. ...

As early as 1989, Caremark's predecessor issued an internal "Guide to Contractual Relationships" ("Guide") to govern its employees in entering into contracts with physicians and hospitals. The Guide tended to be reviewed annually by lawyers and updated. Each version of the Guide stated as Caremark's and its predecessor's policy that no payments would be made in exchange for or to induce patient referrals. ...

In August 1991, the HHS Office of the Inspector General ("OIG") initiated an investigation of Caremark's predecessor. ... In March 1992, the Department of Justice ("DOJ") joined the OIG investigation and separate investigations were commenced by several additional federal and state agencies. ...

The first action taken by management, as a result of the initiation of the OIG investigation, was an announcement that as of October 1, 1991, Caremark's predecessor would no longer pay management fees to physicians for services to Medicare and Medicaid patients. Despite this decision, Caremark asserts that its management, pursuant to advice, did not believe that such payments were illegal under the existing laws and regulations.

During this period, Caremark's Board took several additional steps consistent with an effort to assure compliance with company policies concerning the ARPL and the contractual forms in the Guide. In April 1992, Caremark published a fourth revised version of its Guide apparently designed to assure that its agreements either complied with the ARPL and regulations or excluded Medicare and Medicaid patients altogether. In addition, in September 1992, Caremark instituted a policy requiring its regional officers, Zone Presidents, to approve each contractual relationship entered into by Caremark with a physician. . . .

Throughout the period of the government investigations, Caremark had an internal audit plan designed to assure compliance with business and ethics policies. In addition, Caremark employed Price Waterhouse as its outside auditor. On February 8, 1993, the Ethics Committee of Caremark's Board received and reviewed an outside auditors report by Price Waterhouse which concluded that there were no material weaknesses in Caremark's control structure. Despite the positive findings of Price Waterhouse, however, on April 20, 1993, the Audit & Ethics Committee adopted a new internal audit charter requiring a comprehensive review of compliance policies and the compilation of an employee ethics handbook concerning such policies. . . .

During 1993, Caremark took several additional steps which appear to have been aimed at increasing management supervision. These steps included new policies requiring local branch managers to secure home office approval for all disbursements under agreements with health care providers and to certify compliance with the ethics program. In addition, the chief financial officer was appointed to serve as Caremark's compliance officer. In 1994, a fifth revised Guide was published.

On August 4, 1994, a federal grand jury in Minnesota issued a 47-page indictment charging Caremark, two of its officers (not the firm's chief officer), an individual who had been a sales employee of Genentech, Inc., and David R. Brown, a physician practicing in Minneapolis, with violating the ARPL over a lengthy period. According to the indictment, over $1.1 million had been paid to Brown to induce him to distribute Protropin, a human growth hormone drug marketed by Caremark. The substantial payments involved started, according to the allegations of the indictment, in 1986 and continued through 1993. Some payments were "in the guise of research grants," and others were "consulting agreements". . . .

Subsequently, five stockholder derivative actions were filed in this court and consolidated into this action. The original complaint, dated August 5, 1994, alleged, in relevant part, that Caremark's directors breached their duty of care by failing adequately to supervise the conduct of Caremark employees, or institute corrective measures, thereby exposing Caremark to fines and liability.

On September 21, 1994, a federal grand jury in Columbus, Ohio issued another indictment alleging that an Ohio physician had defrauded the Medicare program by requesting and receiving $134,600 in exchange for referrals of patients whose medical costs were in part reimbursed by Medicare in violation of the ARPL. Although unidentified at that time, Caremark was the health care provider who allegedly made such payments. The indictment also charged that the physician, Elliot Neufeld, D.O., was provided with the services of a registered nurse to work in his office at the expense of the infusion company, in addition to free office equipment.

An October 28, 1994 amended complaint in this action added allegations concerning the Ohio indictment as well as new allegations of over billing and inappropriate referral payments in connection with an action brought in Atlanta. . . .

Caremark began settlement negotiations with federal and state government entities in May 1995. In return for a guilty plea to a single count of mail fraud by the corporation, the payment of a criminal fine, the payment of substantial civil damages, and cooperation with further federal investigations on matters relating to the OIG investigation, the government entities agreed to negotiate a settlement that would permit Caremark to continue participating in Medicare and Medicaid programs. . . .

Settlement negotiations [in the present case] resulted in a memorandum of understanding ("MOU"), dated June 7, 1995, and the execution of the Stipulation and Agreement of Compromise and Settlement on June 28, 1995, which is the subject of this action. . . . In relevant part the terms upon which these claims asserted are proposed to be settled are as follows:

That Caremark, undertakes that it and its employees, and agents not pay any form of compensation to a third party in exchange for the referral of a patient to a Caremark facility or service or the prescription of drugs marketed or distributed by Caremark for which reimbursement may be sought from Medicare, Medicaid, or a similar state reimbursement program;

That Caremark, undertakes for itself and its employees, and agents not to pay to or split fees with physicians, joint ventures, any business combination in which Caremark maintains a direct financial interest, or other health care providers with whom Caremark has a financial relationship or interest, in exchange for the referral of a patient to a Caremark facility or service or the prescription of drugs marketed or distributed by Caremark for which reimbursement may be sought from Medicare, Medicaid, or a similar state reimbursement program;

That the full Board shall discuss all relevant material changes in government health care regulations and their effect on relationships with health care providers on a semi-annual basis;

That Caremark's officers will remove all personnel from health care facilities or hospitals who have been placed in such facility for the purpose of providing remuneration in exchange for a patient referral for which reimbursement may be sought from Medicare, Medicaid, or a similar state reimbursement program;

That every patient will receive written disclosure of any financial relationship between Caremark and the health care professional or provider who made the referral;

That the Board will establish a Compliance and Ethics Committee of four directors, two of which will be non-management directors, to meet at least four times a year to effectuate these policies and monitor business segment compliance with the ARPL, and to report to the Board semi-annually concerning compliance by each business segment; and

That corporate officers responsible for business segments shall serve as compliance officers who must report semi-annually to the Compliance and Ethics Committee and, with the assistance of outside counsel, review existing contracts and get advanced approval of any new contract forms.

[T]his Court is now required to exercise an informed judgment whether the proposed settlement is fair and reasonable in the light of all relevant factors. On an application of this kind, this Court attempts to protect the best interests of the corporation and its absent shareholders all of whom will be barred from future litigation on these claims if the settlement is approved. The parties proposing the settlement bear the burden of persuading the court that it is in fact fair and reasonable.

The complaint charges the director defendants with breach of their duty of attention or care in connection with the on-going operation of the corporation's business. The claim is that the directors allowed a situation to develop and continue which exposed the corporation to enormous legal liability and that in so doing they violated a duty to be active monitors of corporate performance. The complaint thus does not charge either director self-dealing or the more difficult loyalty-type problems arising from cases of suspect director motivation, such as entrenchment or sale of control contexts. The theory here advanced is possibly the most difficult theory in corporation law upon which a plaintiff might hope to win a judgment. . . .

Director liability for a breach of the duty to exercise appropriate attention may, in theory, arise in two distinct contexts. First, such liability may be said to follow from a board decision that results in a loss because that decision was ill advised or "negligent." Second, liability to the corporation for a loss may be said to arise from an unconsidered failure of the board to act in circumstances in which due attention would, arguably, have prevented the loss. The first class of cases will typically be subject to review under the director-protective business judgment rule, assuming the decision made was the product of a process that was either deliberately considered in good faith or was otherwise rational. What should be understood, but may not widely be understood by courts or commentators who are not often required to face such questions, is that compliance with a director's duty of care can never appropriately be judicially determined by reference to the content of the board decision that leads to a corporate loss, apart from consideration of the good faith or rationality of the process employed. That is, whether a judge or jury considering the matter after the fact, believes a decision substantively wrong, or degrees of wrong extending through "stupid" to "egregious" or "irrational," provides no ground for director liability, so long as the court determines that the process employed was either rational or employed in a good faith effort to advance corporate interests. To employ a different rule — one that permitted an "objective" evaluation of the decision — would expose directors to substantive second guessing by ill-equipped judges or juries, which would, in the long-run, be injurious to investor interests. Thus, the business judgment rule is process oriented and informed by a deep respect for all good faith board decisions.

Indeed, one wonders on what moral basis might shareholders attack a good faith business decision of a director as "unreasonable" or "irrational." Where a director in fact exercises a good faith effort to be informed and to exercise appropriate judgment, he or she should be deemed to satisfy fully the duty of attention. If the shareholders thought themselves entitled to some other quality of judgment than such a director produces in the good faith exercise of the powers of office, then the shareholders should have elected other directors. . . . [T]he core element of any corporate law duty of care inquiry [is] whether there was good faith effort to be informed and exercise judgment.

The second class of cases in which director liability for inattention is theoretically possible entail circumstances in which a loss eventuates not from a decision but, from unconsidered inaction. Most of the decisions that a corporation, acting through its human agents, makes are, of course, not the subject of director attention. Legally, the board itself will be required only to authorize the most significant corporate acts or transactions: mergers, changes in capital structure, fundamental changes in business, appointment and compensation of the CEO, etc. As the facts of this case graphically demonstrate, ordinary business decisions that are made by officers and employees deeper in the interior of the organization can, however, vitally affect the welfare of the corporation and its ability to achieve its various strategic and financial goals. If this case did not prove the point itself, recent business history would. . . . Financial and organizational disasters such as these raise the question, what is the board's responsibility with respect to the organization and monitoring of the enterprise to assure that the corporation functions within the law to achieve its purposes?

Modernly this question has been given special importance by an increasing tendency, especially under federal law, to employ the criminal law to assure corporate compliance with external legal requirements, including environmental, financial, employee and product safety as well as assorted other health and safety regulations. . . .

Can it be said today that, absent some ground giving rise to suspicion of violation of law, that corporate directors have no duty to assure that a corporate information gathering and reporting systems exists which represents a good faith attempt to provide senior management and the Board with information respecting material acts, events or conditions within the corporation, including compliance with applicable statutes and regulations? I certainly do not believe so. . . .

[I]t would, in my opinion, be a mistake to conclude that . . . corporate boards may satisfy their obligation to be reasonably informed concerning the corporation, without assuring themselves that information and reporting systems exist in the organization that are reasonably designed to provide to senior management and to the board itself timely, accurate information sufficient to allow management and the board, each within its scope, to reach informed judgments concerning both the corporation's compliance with law and its business performance.

Obviously the level of detail that is appropriate for such an information system is a question of business judgment. And obviously too, no rationally designed information and reporting system will remove the possibility that the corporation will violate laws or regulations, or that senior officers or directors may nevertheless sometimes be misled or otherwise fail reasonably to detect acts material to the corporation's compliance with the law. But it is important that the board exercise a good faith judgment that the corporation's information and reporting system is in concept and design adequate to assure the board that appropriate information will come to its attention in a timely manner as a matter of ordinary operations, so that it may satisfy its responsibility.

Thus, I am of the view that a director's obligation includes a duty to attempt in good faith to assure that a corporate information and reporting system, which the board concludes is adequate, exists, and that failure to do so under some circumstances may, in theory at least, render a director liable for losses caused by noncompliance with applicable legal standards. I now turn to an analysis of the claims asserted with this concept of the directors duty of care, as a duty satisfied in part by assurance of adequate information flows to the board, in mind. . . .

Here the record supplies essentially no evidence that the director defendants were guilty of a sustained failure to exercise their oversight function. To the contrary, insofar as I am able to tell on this record, the corporation's information systems appear to have represented a good faith attempt to be informed of relevant facts. If the directors did not know the specifics of the activities that lead to the indictments, they cannot be faulted.

The liability that eventuated in this instance was huge. But the fact that it resulted from a violation of criminal law alone does not create a breach of fiduciary duty by directors. The record at this stage does not support the conclusion that the defendants either lacked good faith in the exercise of their monitoring responsibilities or consciously permitted a known violation of law by the corporation to occur. The claims asserted against them must be viewed at this stage as extremely weak.

[The court concluded that although the settlement had not achieved much of value to the company, the settlement was fair and reasonable in light of the weakness of the underlying claims.]

Questions and Comments

1. Notice that this case is specifically about compliance. The plaintiffs alleged that Caremark's board of directors had violated their fiduciary duty by failing to ensure that the company did not violate rules governing its relationships with physicians.

2. Chancellor Allen derives a compliance duty from the traditional rule that, although decisions made in the exercise of business judgment are protected against liability, the rule does not protect directors if they fail to exercise judgment at all. To exercise judgment, directors must inform themselves, at least to some extent, about the problems they are addressing. This implied that a board has a duty to ensure itself that compliance systems are in place.

3. Was there any evidence in this case that the directors of Caremark acted in bad faith or in conscious disregard of their obligations? If not, how could the court conclude that the claims against the directors had any chance at all?

4. Does the compliance duty recognized in *Caremark* make sense in light of the rationale for the business judgment duty set forth in the case? It may be that Delaware court judges are not businesspeople and cannot constructively substitute their judgment for that of corporate directors. But neither are Delaware court judges compliance experts. Why does Chancellor Allen think that judges are any more equipped to judge whether a company has an effective compliance system in place than they are to judge any other business decision?

5. Chancellor Allen indicated that Caremark's board had satisfied its compliance duty. What steps did the board take to avoid the violations of law uncovered in the government's investigations, or the devastating fines that ensued? Do you agree that the board did enough to warrant protection against liability?

6. Is *Caremark* limited to compliance matters? Suppose the company had gone belly-up due to excessive spending, and the evidence showed that the directors had failed to ensure that an effective system of financial controls was in place to prevent the failure. Would this default be the basis for *Caremark*-style liability, or should the directors' behavior be entirely shielded by the business judgment rule?

7. Why did the Delaware courts become involved in the issue of compliance? The evidence showed that many federal and state agencies regulated different aspects of Caremark's business; they demonstrated the effectiveness of their regulatory activities by investigating Caremark and imposing sanctions for the violations which those investigations uncovered. Was it necessary for a state court to load a fiduciary duty on top?

8. Consider the relief that the derivative plaintiff's attorney negotiated in this settlement. To what extent (if any) were the governance changes mandated by the settlement likely to improve the effectiveness of Caremark's compliance operations? Do these changes represent reforms that Caremark would have likely adopted even without the spur of a lawsuit? Should the derivative plaintiff's attorneys have been paid by the company for their services? See Chapter 10 for more on compliance-related settlements of shareholders derivative suits.

9. For more on *Caremark*, see Stephen Bainbridge, Caremark *and Enterprise Risk Management*, 34 J. Corp. L. Summer 967 (2009); Jennifer Arlen, *The Story of* Allis-Chalmers, Caremark, *and* Stone: *Directors' Evolving Duty to Monitor*, Chapter 11 in *Corporate Stories* (J. Mark Ramseyer ed., 2009); Charles M. Elson & Christopher J. Gyves, *In re Caremark: Good Intentions, Unintended Consequences*, 39 Wake Forest L. Rev. 691 (2004).

Stone v. Ritter

911 A.2d 362 (Del. 2006)

HOLLAND, J.

[This case grew out of allegations that, in providing banking services to customers who turned out to be operating a Ponzi scheme, AmSouth Bank had failed to comply with the requirements of the Bank Secrecy Act (BSA) and federal anti-money laundering (AML) regulations. Numerous enforcement actions against the bank followed: The United States Attorney launched a criminal investigation which culminated in a deferred prosecution agreement and a $40 million fine; the Federal Reserve and the Alabama Banking Department jointly issued a cease-and-desist order; and the Federal Reserve and FinCEN (the office in the Department of the Treasury that enforces money laundering rules) imposed a $10 million civil money penalty. FinCEN explained that the penalty was based, in part, on the finding that "AmSouth's [AML compliance] program lacked adequate board and management oversight," and that "reporting to management for the purposes of monitoring and oversight of compliance activities was materially deficient."

[Shareholders brought a derivative lawsuit against the bank's directors for breach of fiduciary duty. They acknowledged that the directors neither knew nor should have known that violations of law were occurring, but argued that their case should proceed because the defendants had failed to implement monitoring, reporting, or information controls that would have enabled them to learn of problems requiring their attention.]

[T]he *Caremark* standard for so-called "oversight" liability draws heavily upon the concept of director failure to act in good faith. [The following are] examples of conduct that would establish a failure to act in good faith:

> A failure to act in good faith may be shown, for instance, where the fiduciary intentionally acts with a purpose other than that of advancing the best interests of the corporation, where the fiduciary acts with the intent to violate applicable positive law, or where the fiduciary intentionally fails to act in the face of a known duty to act, demonstrating a conscious disregard for his duties. There may be other examples of bad faith yet to be proven or alleged, but these three are the most salient.

The third of these examples describes, and is fully consistent with, the lack of good faith conduct that the *Caremark* court held was a "necessary condition" for director oversight liability, i.e., "a sustained or systematic failure of the board to exercise oversight—such as an utter failure to attempt to assure a reasonable information and reporting system exists. . . ."

It is important, in this context, to clarify a doctrinal issue that is critical to understanding fiduciary liability under *Caremark* as we construe that case. The phraseology used in *Caremark* and that we employ here—describing the lack of good faith as a "necessary condition to liability"—is deliberate. The purpose of that formulation is to communicate that a failure to act in good faith is not conduct that results, ipso facto, in the direct imposition of fiduciary liability. The failure to act in good faith may result in liability because the requirement to act in good faith "is a subsidiary element[,]" i.e., a condition, "of the fundamental duty of loyalty." It follows that because a showing of bad faith conduct, in the sense described in . . . *Caremark*, is essential to establish director oversight liability, the fiduciary duty violated by that conduct is the duty of loyalty.

This view of a failure to act in good faith results in two additional doctrinal consequences. First, although good faith may be described colloquially as part of a "triad" of fiduciary duties that includes the duties of care and loyalty, the obligation to act in good faith does not establish an independent fiduciary duty that stands on the same footing as the duties of care and loyalty. Only the latter two duties, where violated, may directly result in liability, whereas a failure to act in good faith may do so, but indirectly. The second doctrinal consequence is that the fiduciary duty of loyalty is not limited to cases involving a financial or other cognizable fiduciary conflict of interest. It also encompasses cases where the fiduciary fails to act in good faith. . . . "[A] director cannot act loyally towards the corporation unless she acts in the good faith belief that her actions are in the corporation's best interest."

We hold that *Caremark* articulates the necessary conditions predicate for director oversight liability: (a) the directors utterly failed to implement any reporting or information system or controls; or (b) having implemented such a system or controls, consciously failed to monitor or oversee its operations thus disabling themselves from being informed of risks or problems requiring their attention. In either case, imposition of liability requires a showing that the directors knew that they were not discharging their fiduciary obligations. Where directors fail to act in the face of a known duty to act, thereby demonstrating a conscious disregard for their responsibilities, they breach their duty of loyalty by failing to discharge that fiduciary obligation in good faith.

[The court ruled that the allegations in the complaint failed to create a reasonable inference of director liability.] The Board received and approved relevant policies and procedures, delegated to certain employees and departments the responsibility for filing [suspicious activity reports] and monitoring compliance, and exercised oversight by relying on periodic reports from them. Although there ultimately may have been failures by employees to report deficiencies to the Board, there is no basis for an oversight claim seeking to hold the directors personally liable for such failures by the employees.

With the benefit of hindsight, the plaintiffs' complaint seeks to equate a bad outcome with bad faith. The lacuna in the plaintiffs' argument is a failure to recognize that the directors' good faith exercise of oversight responsibility may not invariably prevent employees from violating criminal laws, or from causing the corporation to incur significant financial liability, or both. . . .

Questions and Comments

1. *Caremark* was a decision by the Delaware Chancery Court, not the Delaware Supreme Court, and one that arose in the somewhat unusual context of a decision evaluating the fairness and adequacy of a settlement in a shareholders derivative case. Thus, although the opinion was influential, its scope and precedential effect were not clearly established for a considerable period of time. The excerpted case, a decision by the Delaware Supreme Court, confirms the validity of *Caremark* liability under Delaware law, recognizes the generality of its application, and provides information about the scope of the duty.

2. Note the somewhat confusing discussion in the excerpted case of whether the category of actions not undertaken in good faith is itself an independent basis of liability, or rather a species of more traditional fiduciary duties of care or loyalty. The court concludes that *Caremark* liability is not a third branch of fiduciary duty, but

rather part of the duty of loyalty. Does this make sense? Is a director being disloyal when she fails to ensure that a company has a compliance system in place — or just negligent? Why did the court conclude that failing to exercise oversight over compliance was a breach of the duty of loyalty and not a violation of the duty of care or of an independent duty of good faith? Was it relevant that breaches of the duty of loyalty cannot be immunized from damages liability under Delaware Corporation Code §102(b)(7)? For general discussion, see Leo E. Strine Jr., et al., *Loyalty's Core Demand: The Defining Role of Good Faith in Corporation Law*, 93 Geo. L.J. 629 (2010); Claire A. Hill & Brett H. McDonnell, *Stone v. Ritter and the Expanding Duty of Loyalty*, 76 Fordham L. Rev. 1769 (2007).

3. While recognizing *Caremark* liability, the supreme court also imposes limitations on its use. Consider the two circumstances in which the court said *Caremark* liability would be appropriate. The first is where the directors "utterly fail" to implement any reporting or information system or controls. The second is where directors "consciously fail" to monitor or oversee the operation of a compliance system once it is in place. Going forward, how hard will it be for boards of directors to avoid *Caremark* liability under these tests?

4. In the excerpted case, the court held that the allegations in the complaint did not establish a plausible case for director liability. The court pointed to a KPMG report that, while critical of the bank's AML/BSA compliance efforts, nevertheless pointed to a variety of initiatives and steps that the board had undertaken in this area. Should these have been enough to immunize the board from *Caremark* liability, given that multiple government investigations had uncovered severe shortcomings in the bank's compliance program, resulting in onerous enforcement actions and $40 million in fines? If this was not enough to establish liability, what is?

5. Regulations applicable to particular industries may impose potential liability on board members when the institution they serve commits compliance violations. In the case of national banks, for example, the Comptroller of the Currency issues MRAs (matters requiring attention) when a bank examination detects deficiencies in internal controls. Once an MRA is issued, the regulator "expects the bank's board of directors to ensure timely and effective correction of the practices described in an MRA. Those expectations include holding management accountable for the deficient practices; directing management to develop and implement corrective actions; approving the necessary changes to the bank's policies, processes, procedures, and controls; and establishing processes to monitor progress and verify and validate the effectiveness of management's corrective actions." OCC Bulletin 2014-52, "Matters Requiring Attention."

Rich ex rel. Fuqi Int'l, Inc. v. Yu Kwai Chong

(Del. Ch. 2013)

[Fuqi is engaged in selling high quality, precious metal jewelry. Originally a Chinese corporation, it reinvented itself as a Delaware company by means of a reverse merger with a bankrupt U.S. firm, but kept its principal place of business in the People's Republic of China. Fuqi thereafter gained access to U.S. capital markets and raised more than $120 million from investors in a public offering in 2009. Its initial reports of operations were glowing, driving its stock price up to nearly $30/share. Problems surfaced in 2010, when the company disclosed significant deficiencies in its financial controls and restated earnings. Worse yet, it turned out that Chong, Fuqi's Chairman, had distributed approximately $130 million to unnamed parties in China. The stock was delisted from NASDAQ and, at the time of the opinion, traded in the "pink sheets" at approximately $1/share.]

. . . The [derivative] Plaintiff alleges that Fuqi's directors are liable for failure to oversee the operations of the corporation. Fuqi argues that the Complaint fails to plead facts that show that the directors "consciously and in bad faith failed to implement any reporting or accounting system or controls." . . .

The essence of a *Caremark* claim is a breach of the duty of loyalty arising from a director's bad-faith failure to exercise oversight over the company. A *Caremark* claim is "possibly the most difficult theory in corporation law upon which a plaintiff might hope to win a judgment." I am conscious of the need to prevent hindsight from dictating the result of a *Caremark* action; a bad outcome, without more, does not equate to bad faith. To survive a motion to dismiss, the plaintiff must plead facts that allow a reasonable inference that the defendants . . . knew they were not fulfilling their fiduciary duties. . . . Examples of directors' "disabling themselves from being informed" include a corporation's lacking an audit committee, or a corporation's not utilizing its audit committee.

One way a plaintiff may successfully plead a *Caremark* claim is to plead facts showing that a corporation had no internal controls in place. Fuqi had some sort of compliance system in place. For example, it had an Audit Committee and submitted financial statements to the SEC in 2009. However, accepting the Plaintiff's allegations as true, the mechanisms Fuqi had in place appear to have been woefully inadequate. In its press releases, Fuqi has detailed its extensive problems with internal controls. For example, Fuqi disclosed its "incorrect and untimely recordkeeping of inventory movements of retail operation." Problems with inventory are particularly troubling here, because Fuqi is a jewelry company, specializing in precious metals and gemstones which are valuable and easily stolen. Nonetheless, the Fuqi directors allowed the corporation to operate few to no controls over these vulnerable assets. Fuqi's self-disclosed accounting inadequacies include: (i) incorrect carve-out of the retail segment from the general ledger; (ii) unrecorded purchases and accounts payable; (iii) inadvertent inclusion of consigned inventory; (iv) incorrect and untimely recordkeeping of inventory movements of retail operation; and (v) incorrect diamond inventory costing, unrecorded purchases and unrecorded accounts payable.

These disclosures lead me to believe that Fuqi had no meaningful controls in place. The board of directors may have had regular meetings, and an Audit Committee may have existed, but there does not seem to have been any regulation of the company's operations in China. Nonetheless, even if I were to find that Fuqi had some system of internal controls in place, I may infer that the board's failure to monitor that system was a breach of fiduciary duty.

As the Supreme Court held in Stone v. Ritter, if the directors have implemented a system of controls, a finding of liability is predicated on the directors' having "consciously failed to monitor or oversee [the system's] operations thus disabling themselves from being informed of risks or problems requiring their attention." One way that the plaintiff may plead such a conscious failure to monitor is to identify "red flags," obvious and problematic occurrences, that support an inference that the Fuqi directors knew that there were material weaknesses in Fuqi's internal controls and failed to correct such weaknesses. It is unclear how far back in time Fuqi's internal controls have been inadequate. At the very least, the Fuqi board had several "warnings" that all was not well with the internal controls as far back as March 2010.

First, Fuqi was a preexisting Chinese company that gained access to the U.S. capital markets through the Reverse Merger. Thus, Fuqi's directors were aware that there may be challenges in bringing Fuqi's internal controls into harmony with the U.S. securities reporting systems. Notwithstanding that fact, according to the Complaint, the directors did nothing to ensure that its reporting mechanisms were accurate. Second, the board knew that it had problems with its accounting and inventory processes by March 2010 at the latest, because it announced that the 2009 financial statements would need restatement at that time. In the same press release, Fuqi also acknowledged the likelihood of material weaknesses in its internal controls. Third, Fuqi received a letter from NASDAQ in April 2010 warning Fuqi that it would face delisting if Fuqi did not bring its reporting requirements up to date with the SEC.

It seems reasonable to infer that, because of these "red flags," the directors knew that there were deficiencies in Fuqi's internal controls. Furthermore, NASDAQ's letter to Fuqi put the board on notice that these deficiencies risked serious adverse consequences. The directors acknowledged as much in their March 2010 press release. An analysis of the dates of Fuqi's disclosures demonstrates that it is reasonable, based on the facts pled, to infer that the directors knew that the internal controls were inadequate and failed to act in the face of a known duty. . . .

That Chong was able to transfer $130 million out of the company's coffers, without the directors knowing about it for over a year, strains credulity. Either the directors knew about the cash transfers and were complicit, or they had zero controls in place and did not know about them. If the directors had even the barest framework of appropriate controls in place, they would have prevented the cash transfers.

When faced with knowledge that the company controls are inadequate, the directors must act, i.e., they must prevent further wrongdoing from occurring. A conscious failure to act, in the face of a known duty, is a breach of the duty of loyalty. At the very least, it is inferable that even if the Defendants were not complicit in these money transfers, they were aware of the pervasive, fundamental weaknesses in Fuqi's controls and knowingly failed to stop further problems from occurring. This knowing failure, as alleged by the Plaintiff, states a claim for breach of the duty of good faith under *Caremark*.

Finally, . . . Fuqi management's failure to pay the fees of the Audit Committee's advisors is a deliberate failure to utilize the Audit Committee. Therefore, I may infer that the board has disabled itself from being informed.

For the reasons above, I find that the Plaintiff has stated a claim under *Caremark* upon which relief can be granted.

Questions and Comments

1. Why didn't the actions of the directors satisfy the *Caremark* standard? The company did have an audit committee, and made efforts to disclose material weaknesses in the system of financial controls when these were discovered. As to the cash transfer to China, it is clear that Fuqi's chairman, Chong, knew of the deal, but the court had no evidence that other directors knew. Do the facts alleged in the complaint establish a "conscious failure" to monitor?

2. Two Fuqi directors — Eileen B. Brody and Victor A. Hollander — appeared to be U.S. citizens. Brody held an MBA from Harvard Business School and was a former manager at KPMG Peat Marwick and an executive at several retailing firms; Hollander earned his accountancy certificate in 1958, had been a partner at a public accounting firm, and served as chief financial officer of a public company. Why might Chong have asked them to serve on the board of Fuqi? Why might they have accepted?

3. U.S. citizens serving on the boards of foreign companies face challenges in carrying out their oversight roles. How could Brody and Hollander know what was going on in Fuqi, a company with its principal place of business in China? On the other hand, if U.S. citizens do not serve on boards of companies like Fuqi, the incumbent managers might be less constrained from engaging in questionable activities.

4. Should the *Caremark* standard be applied in more lenient fashion when used against U.S. directors of foreign companies? In a more stringent fashion?

5. Brody and Hollander served on Fuqi's board for five years, including several years after its initial financial control deficiencies had come to light. They eventually resigned when Fuqi refused to pay the expenses of outside advisers to the audit committee. Should their resignation exonerate them from liability? If resignation could achieve this effect, then would the law simply encourage directors to abandon troubled companies to the control of those who are harming it? On the other hand, if resignation is not an option, then what are the independent directors supposed to do if the company does not cooperate with their efforts to improve the control environment?

PROBLEM 2-4

You are appointed as an independent director and chair of the audit committee of Gordito, a Delaware company with its principal place of business in Colombia. Gordito is in the business of importing vegetables from South America for use in gourmet snack foods. The management and board chairman of Gordito are Colombian nationals and the board meetings are conducted in Spanish, with simultaneous translation into English. You learned a little Spanish in college but have forgotten everything you knew. During your service on the audit committee you notice references to large cash transfers being made to a bank you have never heard of in Columbia. You ask the company's internal audit department (located in Colombia) to check into the matter and are informed that the practice is perfectly normal for that part of the world. A little while later an investigative reporter calls you at home and asks if you know anything about Gordito being a front for drug cartels. What should you do?

In re Pfizer Inc. Shareholder Derivative Litigation

722 F. Supp. 2d 453 (S.D.N.Y. 2010)

JED S. RAKOFF, District Judge.

On September 2, 2009, the United States Department of Justice announced that Pfizer, Inc. had agreed to pay $2.3 billion in fines and penalties arising from the illegal "off-label" marketing by Pfizer and one of its subsidiaries of various regulated drugs. Immediately thereafter, several derivative actions were commenced, mostly by institutional investors, seeking recovery on behalf of the company from various senior executives and present and former board members who were alleged to be responsible for the misconduct that resulted in these very large fines and penalties . . . .

The Complaint alleges, in pertinent part, the following: Pfizer's core business rests on the marketing of its drugs, not just to consumers, but also, importantly, to physicians and other health care professionals. The Federal Food, Drug, and Cosmetics Act, 21 U.S.C. §301 et seq., prohibits pharmaceutical companies from marketing or promoting their drugs for "off label" uses or dosages — i.e., uses or dosages that have not specifically been approved by the Food and Drug Administration. Various federal laws also prohibit paying "kickbacks" (i.e., concealed commercial bribes) to health care professionals to get them to prescribe or promote a company's drugs.

Pfizer was acutely aware of the need to prevent such illegal practices on the part of itself and its subsidiaries because of prior settlements with the Government attributing just such misconduct to various Pfizer subsidiaries shortly prior to their acquisition by Pfizer. For example, in 2002, Pfizer subsidiary Warner-Lambert settled charges brought by the Government under the False Claims Act alleging that Warner-Lambert, prior to its acquisition by Pfizer, had given concealed kickbacks to a managed care organization in exchange for that organization's agreement to give preferred status to Lipitor, an anti-cholesterol drug. Pursuant to this settlement, Pfizer paid $49 million in fines and entered into a five-year corporate integrity agreement (the "2002 CIA") to guarantee that Pfizer and Warner-Lambert would not pay illegal kickbacks in the future. The 2002 CIA required, among other things, that Pfizer's board would create and implement a compliance mechanism that would bring information about illegal marketing activities to the board's attention.

Similarly, in 2004, Pfizer entered into a settlement with the Government regarding Warner-Lambert's illegal off-label marketing (prior to Warner-Lambert's acquisition by Pfizer) of Neurontin, an anticonvulsant medication with dangerous side effects. In connection with this settlement, Warner-Lambert pleaded guilty to criminal and civil charges that it fraudulently promoted Neurontin for unapproved uses. The Government's sentencing memorandum noted that the marketing scheme, implemented "with knowledge and approval of senior management," included a variety of tactics to promote off-label use, ranging from direct solicitations by Warner-Lambert's sales representatives to sponsoring promotional meetings and "independent" medical education events to encourage off-label prescriptions. To settle these charges, Pfizer paid a $240 million criminal fine and an additional $190 million penalty. Additionally, Pfizer entered into another, more extensive CIA (the "2004 CIA") that required even more stringent steps to bring any such misconduct to the Board's attention.

Finally, in 2007, Pfizer paid another $34.6 million in criminal fines relating to the illegal off-label marketing by Pharmacia & Upjohn Company, Inc. ("Pharmacia"), another of Pfizer's wholly-owned subsidiaries, of Genotropin, a human growth hormone with dangerous side effects that were promoted by Pharmacia (prior to its acquisition by Pfizer) for its alleged use as an anti-aging agent. To settle these charges, Pharmacia pleaded guilty to illegally promoting and selling Genotropin and to intentionally violating the federal anti-kickback statute.

In the face of all these prior violations by its subsequently-acquired subsidiaries, and despite its promises to take significant steps to monitor and prevent any further violations, Pfizer itself engaged in the same misconduct. Using sophisticated "prescription data mining" and "influence mapping" analyses, Pfizer targeted specific physicians for visits by Pfizer sales representatives to promote off-label uses of Pfizer drugs. Sales representatives were given financial incentives and assigned quotas to encourage such off-label promotion, and these representatives were urged to make false claims regarding the safety and efficacy of off-label uses of Pfizer drugs. Pfizer also developed a "Scientific Ambassador Program" that used medical liaisons to promote off-label uses. Further, Pfizer commissioned articles published in medical journals that promoted certain off-label uses for "blockbuster" drugs based on skewed and inaccurate data, and then instructed its sales representatives and medical liaisons to use these studies to market the drugs to physicians. Doctors who were identified as marketing targets would be invited to "consultant meetings" in luxury hotels, where they were encouraged to make off-label prescriptions. Pfizer also designated certain doctors as "opinion leaders" and paid them to promote off-label prescriptions at purportedly independent continuing medical education meetings.

Pfizer kept careful track of how well their illegal activities were succeeding. For example, according to the Government, Pfizer's own records showed that such activities generated an estimated $664 million in off-label prescriptions for the Pfizer drug Bextra (discussed below). And, as alleged (among other places) in recently unsealed qui tam complaints filed by Pfizer employees, Pfizer's board and senior management, rather than attempting to stop this off-label promotional activity, retaliated against employees who reported internally that Pfizer's marketing practices were illegal.

It was thus activity by Pfizer itself, as well as by its subsidiary Pharmacia, that gave rise to the 2009 settlement. Among other things, Pfizer and Pharmacia engaged in the illegal marketing of Bextra, a painkiller known as a "COX-2 inhibitor." Beginning in October 2001, Pfizer entered into an alliance with Pharmacia to market Bextra jointly with Celebrex, a similar drug. Pharmacia applied for FDA approval of Bextra with respect to certain specific uses, but the FDA denied that application in several respects because of concerns about serious adverse health consequences. Nonetheless, Pfizer and Pharmacia immediately created plans to market Bextra for unapproved uses by, among other things, promoting the drug with false and misleading safety indications, distributing samples to doctors who had no FDA-approved use for the drug, creating sham doctor requests for information about unapproved uses, and funding purportedly independent continuing educational programs to promote the drug for off-label purposes. This marketing continued after Pfizer's acquisition of Pharmacia was completed in 2003 and after the 2002 and 2004 CIAs went into effect.

The 2009 settlement, however, covered not only the marketing of Bextra, but also a variety of other illegal marking activities undertaken by Pfizer between January 1, 2001 and October 31, 2008 with respect to thirteen different drugs, including seven of Pfizer's nine so-called "blockbuster" drugs, which generated over $1 billion of revenue per year. In the settlement agreement, Pfizer not only admitted that the illegal promotion of Bextra continued beyond 2003, when Pfizer's acquisition of Pharmacia was completed, but also that the illegal marketing of Zyvox, an antibacterial agent, continued past the time when the 2004 CIA went into effect and even after the FDA issued a warning letter with respect to Pfizer's misbranding of that drug in 2005.

The $2.3 billion amount of the 2009 settlement consisted of a criminal fine of $1.195 billion (the largest criminal fine ever imposed in the United States); criminal forfeitures of $105 million; and a $1 billion civil settlement — "the largest civil fraud settlement in history against a pharmaceutical company" — with respect to violations of the False Claims Act and the federal anti-kickback statute. Additionally, the settlement required Pfizer to enter into yet another CIA (the "2009 CIA") with still further compliance requirements.

In short, the Complaint, seemingly corroborated in material respects by the Government's own charges that led to the 2009 settlement, alleges a rather blatant pattern of misconduct by Pfizer, undertaken with the knowledge, approval, or, at the very least, conscious disregard, of Pfizer's board and senior management . . . .

The Court turns first to the argument made by all defendants — including nominal defendant Pfizer — that the Complaint must be dismissed, in its entirety, pursuant to Rule 23.1 of the Federal Rules of Civil Procedure, because plaintiffs have failed to plead with particularity facts that would warrant excusing plaintiffs' failure to issue a demand upon Pfizer's board of directors. Plaintiffs concede that they issued no such demand on the board, but assert that such a demand is excused, both because the directors' misconduct here alleged could not have been a valid exercise of business judgment and also because a majority of the current board is charged with the alleged misconduct and therefore would be conflicted from assessing the demand . . . .

Delaware law provides alternative tests for determining whether demand would have been futile, one applicable to situations where the board's business judgment is being challenged and one where it is not. Under either test, however, the Court, in evaluating a motion to dismiss for failure to make a demand, is required to accept the truth of all facts pleaded in the Complaint, and "plaintiffs are entitled to all reasonable factual inferences that logically flow from the particularized facts alleged." . . .

Plaintiffs cite the Seventh Circuit's decision in In re Abbott Laboratories Derivative Shareholders Litigation ("Abbott Labs"), 325 F.3d 795 (7th Cir. 2003) . . . . The derivative plaintiffs in *Abbott Labs* alleged that the company's directors knew of but disregarded numerous FDA warning letters and other alerts that the company was disobeying FDA regulations . . . . By pleading that the directors were aware of the noncompliance, *Abbott Labs* distinguished the plaintiffs' claim from the typical *Caremark* theory, which is predicated on the directors' ignorance of the illegality. [T]he *Abbott Labs* court found that the plaintiffs had pleaded a breach of the duty of good faith sufficiently to establish that demand was futile:

> Given the extensive paper trail . . . concerning the violations and the inferred awareness of the problems, the facts support a reasonable assumption that there was a "sustained and systematic failure of the board to exercise oversight," in this case intentional in that the directors knew of the violations of law, took no steps in an effort to prevent or remedy the situation, and that failure to take any action for such an inordinate amount of time resulted in substantial corporate losses, establishing a lack of good faith. We find that six years of noncompliance, inspections . . . , [FDA] Warning Letters, and notice in the press, all of which then resulted in the largest civil fine ever imposed by the FDA and the destruction and suspension of products which accounted for approximately $250 million in corporate assets, indicate that the

directors' decision to not act was not made in good faith and was contrary to the best interests of the company.

Other cases involving similar allegations that the directors knowingly or recklessly disregarded illegal activity have likewise held demand to be futile, especially when the alleged wrongdoing is of substantial "magnitude and duration."

[T]he Complaint details at great length a large number of reports made to members of the board from which it may reasonably be inferred that they all knew of Pfizer's continued misconduct and chose to disregard it. These include, for example, the reports to the board of the Neurontin and Genotropin settlements, a large number of FDA violation notices and warning letters, several reports to Pfizer's compliance personnel and senior executives of continuing kickbacks and off-label marketing, and the allegations of the qui tam lawsuits. Many of these disturbing reports were received during the same time that the board was obligated by the 2002 and 2004 CIAs to pay special attention to these very problems. Moreover, plaintiffs allege that a majority of the director defendants served on the board for a period that covers the dates of every "red flag" alleged to have been brought to the Board's attention.

Defendants maintain that these purported "red flags" cannot sustain plaintiffs' burden of proving futility . . . because the Complaint fails to detail what each individual director knew and did in response to such information. [T]here may be situations where the absence of particularized allegations as to what each director knew and what he or she did about that knowledge would not support excusing demand. However, demand futility is to be evaluated based on the facts of each particular case rather than through the invocation of rigid rules. Under the unique facts of this case, defendants have demonstrated a substantial likelihood that a majority of the board faces personal liability.

As illustrated by the sheer size of the 2009 fines, the wrongdoing here alleged was not only pervasive throughout Pfizer but also was committed in the face of the board's repeated promises to closely monitor and prevent such misconduct, as required by the 2002 and 2004 CIAs. These CIAs, which were part of larger settlements approved by the Pfizer board, imposed affirmative obligations on Pfizer's board that went well beyond the basic fiduciary duties required by Delaware law. Among other things, these agreements obligated Pfizer's chief Compliance Officer to report directly to the board the allegations of misconduct here at issue so that the board could deal with them directly, rather than relying on management. There is no reason to believe this reporting requirement was not fully complied with, thus guaranteeing that each member of the board was bombarded with allegations of continuing misconduct of the very kind that the prior settlements looked to the board to prevent. In such circumstances, nothing in either federal or Delaware law holds it insufficient for individual directors' knowledge and liability to be pleaded inferentially. For the foregoing reasons, the Court finds that plaintiffs have pleaded with sufficient particularity that a majority of directors face a substantial likelihood of personal liability because they deliberately disregarded reports of the illegal marketing practices eventually resulting in the 2009 settlement.

Questions and Comments

1. Was Judge Rakoff's decision based on a conclusion that Pfizer had engaged in substantial acts of misconduct leading up to the 2009 fines?

2. How are the facts of this case materially different from those in *Caremark* and related cases?

3. Why did Pfizer continue to purchase companies that turned out to have very large unpaid compliance liabilities?

4. How did the history of compliance problems at Pfizer contribute to the potential liability of Pfizer's board for breaching their fiduciary duty?

5. How will potential personal liability for breach of fiduciary duty impact a corporation's propensity to commit continuing compliance violations? Its willingness to enter to a settlement agreement? To enter into an agreement that acknowledges wrongdoing by the company?

6. What would you have done differently if you had been a member of Pfizer's board of directors at the time of the alleged breaches of fiduciary duty?

7. Do a board's *Caremark* duties change if the matter in question concerns the settlement of a prior enforcement action? Barovic v. Ballmer, 2014 WL 7011840 (W.D. Wash. 2014), involved a 2009 deal between Microsoft and European antitrust regulators in which Microsoft agreed to display a "browser choice screen" — thus eliminating the previous built-in preference for Microsoft Explorer. Subsequently, due to an engineering mistake, more than 15 million installations in Europe omitted the required screen — a default that wound up costing Microsoft more than $700 million in fines. Follow-on shareholder suits claimed that Microsoft's board of directors violated their fiduciary duty by failing to prevent the violations. A committee of disinterested directors investigated the allegations and recommended that the suits be dismissed.

This seemed like an easy case. There were no allegations of conflict of interest. A committee of disinterested directors, assisted by outside counsel, investigated the charges and found them lacking. The committee's recommendation was protected by the business judgment rule. There was no evidence that Microsoft intended to violate the prior settlement. When notified, Microsoft acknowledged responsibility and took corrective action. The company, moreover, had in place a suite of internal controls including reporting and monitoring systems of the sort called for in *Caremark*. Conventional analysis suggested that the lawsuits would be dismissed.

Nevertheless, the court allowed the cases to continue. The court observed that the lack of a browser choice screen could be detected easily on any one of more than 15 million installations. Microsoft's commitment to installing the screen was the key to settling one of the most highly publicized antitrust actions in history. Microsoft not only assumed a legal duty to install the screen, but had also agreed to monitor its compliance with this commitment. Given these considerations, the trial court concluded that the plaintiffs alleged sufficient facts to support the inference that board consciously failed to monitor or oversee the company's compliance obligations.

Do you agree with this decision? Between 2010 and 2012, Microsoft sold more than 630 million Windows 7 licenses, of which only about 15 million omitted the browser choice screen in violation of the European settlement. The problem was due to an engineering mistake. Apparently, no one on Microsoft's board or senior management knew of the issue until they were alerted by the European antitrust regulators. In 2012, Microsoft had a market capitalization of more than $235 billion; its board had many responsibilities other than ensuring compliance with the European settlement. Given these facts, is it reasonable to expect the board would have prevented the problem? To infer that they consciously failed to monitor the company's compliance operations? If you had served on Microsoft's board at the time, would you have done better?

B. CHAIRMEN

The board of directors is led by an individual known as the "chairman" (the term "man" is anachronistic; board chairmen these days may be women!). The chairman gets only one vote, same as every other board member; her principal official power is to lead meetings of the board. Even that authority is limited when the board operates through committees, because the chairman of the board rarely heads up committees.

It would be a mistake, however, to conclude that the chairman of the board is merely first among equals. Usually, the chairman's position is one of considerable power and influence — much greater than that exercised by other board members. There are several reasons for the chairman's authority.

- The chairman sets the agenda of board meetings.
- Under a company's bylaws, the chairman is often elected by the other directors; the fact the chairman won the election evidences that other directors hold her in esteem.
- The chairman is seen from without as the leader of the company; and in corporations as in government, the appearance of power is often a basis for its reality.
- Tradition may also play a role: The chairman has historically exercised disproportionate power in American companies; and companies have their own cultures which preserve memories across time.

The chairman is powerful even when she is not also a senior executive officer. When she also serves as the chief executive officer, her power is multiplied. For this reason, corporate governance advocates have campaigned to split these offices by prohibiting the chairman from also serving as CEO. Shareholder proposals to this effect are frequently included for vote at annual meetings; and unlike many proposals that advance ideological objectives and receive only a small percentage of the vote, these proposals enjoy relatively wide support from institutional investors and other constituents.

The following excerpt from Hess Corporation's 2013 proxy statement sets forth the case for and against separating the offices of board chairman and chief executive officer.

Hess Corporation 2013 Proxy Statement

. . . Resolved: that the stockholders of Hess Corporation, ("Hess" or "the Company") ask the Board of directors to adopt a policy that, whenever possible, the board's chairman should be an independent director who has not previously served as an executive officer of the company. The policy should be implemented so as not to violate any contractual obligation. The policy should also specify (A) how to select a new independent chairman if a current chairman ceases to be independent during the time between annual meetings of shareholders; and, (B) that compliance with the policy is excused if no independent director is available and willing to serve as chairman.

SUPPORTING STATEMENT FROM STOCKHOLDER PROPONENT

It is the responsibility of the Board of Directors to protect shareholders' long-term interests by providing independent oversight of management, including the Chief Executive Officer (CEO), in directing the corporation's business and affairs. Currently Mr. John Hess is Chairman of the Board and CEO. We believe that the practice of combining the two positions may not adequately protect shareholders.

We believe that an independent Chairman who sets agendas, priorities and procedures for the board can enhance board oversight of management and help ensure the objective functioning of an effective board. We also believe that having an independent Chairman (in practice as well as appearance) can improve accountability to shareowners, and we view the alternative of having a lead outside director, even one with a robust set of duties, as not adequate to fulfill these functions.

A number of respected institutions recommend such separation. CalPERS' Corporate Core Principles and Guidelines state that "the independence of a majority of the Board is not enough"; "the leadership of the board must embrace independence, and it must ultimately change the way in which directors interact with management." In 2009 the Milstein Center at Yale School of Management issued a report, endorsed by a number of investors and board members, that recommended splitting the two positions as the default provision for U.S. companies. A commission of The Conference Board stated in a 2003 report: "Each corporation should give careful consideration to separating the offices of Chairman of the Board and CEO, with those two roles being performed by separate individuals. The Chairman would be one of the independent directors. We believe that the recent economic crisis demonstrates that no matter how many independent directors there are on the Board, that Board is less able to provide independent oversight of the officers if the Chairman of that Board is also the CEO of the Company.

We, therefore, urge shareholders to vote for this proposal.

BOARD OF DIRECTORS STATEMENT

For the reasons discussed below the board of directors recommends a vote against the stockholder proposal.

The board of directors believes that stockholders are best served by giving the board the organizational flexibility to select the best person to serve as chairman. Effective corporate governance requires more than a "one size fits all" approach, and it is unwise to place unnecessary constraints on the board's ability to determine the leadership structure that it believes will work best given the dynamics of the board and senior management and other factors at any particular time. Although the board currently believes it is in the best interests of the company and its stockholders to combine the positions of chief executive officer and chairman of the board, the board is aware that in the future, there may be circumstances under which an independent chairman is appropriate. Therefore, while the board does not believe it is appropriate to have a policy requiring the separation of chairman and chief executive officer roles, it also believes it should not have a policy requiring that they always be combined.

At present, the board has chosen to combine the positions of chief executive officer and chairman of the board. The board believes this structure promotes better alignment of strategic development and execution, more effective implementation of strategic initiatives, and clearer accountability for their success or failure. In addition, the company's chief executive officer has the necessary experience, commitment and support of the other board members to also effectively carry out the role of chairman. His in-depth knowledge of the company and its historical development, his extensive industry expertise and his significant leadership experience make him particularly qualified to lead discussions on important matters affecting the company. Having the chief executive officer both lead management and chair the board has allowed the company to obtain the benefit of his strategic and operational insights and strong leadership skills across the full range of responsibilities of the company's leadership, from long-term strategic direction to day-to-day operational execution.

The board regularly reviews this leadership structure and believes that combining the chairman and chief executive officer positions at this time does not impede independent oversight. The board has taken several steps to create a balanced governance structure in which independent directors exercise substantial oversight over management. The board is currently composed of 14 individuals, 12 of whom are independent under the New York Stock Exchange rules and 13 of whom will be independent if the company's nominees are elected to the board at the 2013 annual meeting, and the members of each of the key board committees (the audit, compensation and management development, and corporate governance and nominating committees) are independent. Furthermore, the committees have unrestrained access to management and the authority to retain independent advisors as they deem appropriate. This means that oversight of key matters — such as the integrity of the company's financial statements, executive compensation, the nomination of directors and evaluation of the board and its committees — is entrusted to independent directors. In addition, the board has a lead independent director who is elected by the independent members of the board. Mr. Nicholas Brady, former chairman of the corporate governance and nominating committee, was acting as the previous lead independent director, and the current lead independent director is Mr. John H. Mullin III.

As set forth in the company's corporate governance guidelines, the responsibilities of the lead independent director include:

- presiding at all meetings of the board at which the chairman is not present, including executive sessions of the independent directors;
- serving as liaison between the chairman and the independent directors;
- approving board meeting schedules to assure that there is sufficient time for discussion of all agenda items, as well as meeting agendas and information sent to the board;
- having authority to call meetings of the independent directors; and
- if requested by major stockholders, ensuring that he or she is available for consultation and direct communication.

These responsibilities are substantially similar to many of the functions typically fulfilled by a board chairman and the board believes that such responsibilities provide an opportunity for the independent directors to frankly discuss management performance and other issues.

Based on the foregoing, the board believes that adopting a policy that requires an independent chairman would not be in the best interests of the company and its stockholders.

For these reasons, the board urges stockholders to vote against this proposal.

Questions and Comments

1. Do you agree with the proponents of this proposal that shareholder interests are best served by splitting the offices of CEO and chairman? Or do you find the arguments of the management more compelling?

2. Much depends on personalities: Some individuals might function well in both positions; others less so. In the case of Hess, both offices were filled by John Hess, the son of the founder of the company. Does that fact affect your judgment about the wisdom of splitting the positions? What about the fact that Mr. Hess had a distinguished educational background, with an undergraduate degree from Harvard College and an MBA from Harvard Business School? That he had managed the company since 1995? That Hess's stock had appreciated approximately 400 percent over the previous ten years?

3. Less than a week before the annual meeting, Hess Corporation did a *volte-face* and announced that it would separate the positions of chairman and CEO. A press release quoted Hess's lead independent director, John Mullin, as follows: "As we continue our transformation to a pure play E&P company, we have heard from shareholders who approve of our strategy while also expressing a desire for better accountability, increased board oversight, and the adoption of best-in-class corporate governance practices. We understand our shareholders' views, and recognize that our corporate governance structure should have been improved sooner. Separating the roles of Chairman and CEO and declassifying our Board reflects our commitment to shareholders."

4. What changed the board's mind? You probably will not be surprised to learn that there were factors at play other than the merits of splitting the position of CEO and chairman of the board. Hess was involved in a proxy battle with a large institutional investor, Elliott Management Corporation, controlled by billionaire Paul Singer, which held 4.5 percent of the company's stock. Elliott disagreed with the strategic direction being followed by the incumbent managers, which was to exit refining, gasoline retail, and other businesses to become a pure oil exploration and production company. Elliott nominated its own slate of directors and solicited proxies for their election instead of the directors favored by management. Could Hess's agreement to separate the chairman and the CEO positions have been an attempt to appease swing votes in the proxy contest?

5. Hess's strategy wasn't enough to deter Elliott from continuing the proxy fight. The shareholder meeting went ahead as planned, with Elliott's proposed slate of directors still on the ballot. Hours before the results were announced, however, the parties settled: Elliott agreed to support five of the company's board nominees in exchange for three seats of its own.

6. The campaign by corporate governance activists to split the positions of chairman and chief executive officer suffered a setback in 2013, when shareholders rejected a proposal to clip the wings of Jamie Dimon, JPMorgan Chase's powerful chairman and CEO. However, later that year the bank did institute other governance changes, including upgrading the power of the independent lead director in certain (minor) respects.

7. A 2011 study of the impact of splitting the CEO and chairman positions concluded that the reform was not associated with improved performance; companies that were forced to make this change due to pressure from investors performed more poorly, on average, than companies that switched for other reasons. Aiyesha Dey, Ellen Engel & Xiaohui Liu, *To Split or Not To Split?*, 17 J. Corp. Fin. 1595 (2011).

How do you read this study? Does it imply that it is a bad idea to split the offices of chairman and CEO? Might it imply rather something specific, and negative, about firms that split the offices: that they are poorly managed, that they are likely to come under attack by activists, or that they lack the backbone to stand up to pressure?

8. For more on splitting the CEO and chairman positions, see Nicola Faith Sharpe, *Informational Autonomy in the Boardroom*, 2013 U. Ill. L. Rev. 1089.

PROBLEM 2-5

Greenco is a manufacturer of environmentally friendly products for the agriculture industry. Its founder, board chairman and chief executive officer is Carolyn Crabb, a dedicated environmentalist and, by her own admission, a "hands-on" administrator. You are an independent board member and chair of the company's audit committee. Over the years, you have come to respect Crabb as a person, but also to see her management style as problematic: She dictates policy without listening to others and frequently makes decisions solely on the basis of environmental considerations, even though they reduce the company's profits. A shareholder places a proposal to split the offices of CEO and chairman on the company's annual proxy statement. You believe that if the proposal were adopted it would benefit the company because it would require Crabb to listen to others; you also believe that you would probably be named chairman if Crabb had to give up that title. You think that if the proposal is not adopted, it will be a black eye with institutional investors, who are likely to bail out of its stock. Crabb, however, hates the proposal and, because she owns 30 percent of the company's stock, can probably prevent it from passing if the company opposes it. What do you say at the directors' meeting where the company's response is debated?

C. LEAD DIRECTORS

As a partial corrective for the concentration of power in the hands of an inside chairman of the board, some companies appoint a "lead" independent director, whose role is to play a leadership role among the independent directors and also to act in the chairman's role when the chairman is unable to perform that responsibility. The following excerpt describes the duties of the lead independent director of Carlon Corporation, a (fictional) provider of long-term lodging for corporate travelers.

Carlon Corporation Charter of the Lead Independent Director

Carlon Corporation (the "Company") shall have a Lead Independent Director who shall be an independent director as defined by applicable NASDAQ rules. The Lead Independent Director shall be elected annually by the independent directors of the Company (the "Board"). The specific responsibilities of the Lead Independent Director are as follows:

- act as the principal liaison between the independent directors of the Board and the Chairman of the Board;

- develop the agenda for and preside at executive sessions of the Board's independent directors;
- advise the Chairman of the Board as to an appropriate schedule for Board meetings, seeking to ensure that the independent directors can perform their duties responsibly while not interfering with the flow of Company operations;
- approve with the Chairman of the Board the agenda for Board and Board Committee meetings and the need for special meetings of the Board;
- advise the Chairman of the Board as to the quality, quantity and timeliness of the information submitted by the Company's management that is necessary or appropriate for the independent directors to effectively and responsibly perform their duties;
- recommend to the Board the retention of advisors and consultants who report directly to the Board;
- interview, along with the chair of the Nominating Committee, all Board candidates, and make recommendations to the Nominating Committee;
- serve as Chairman of the Board when the Chairman is not present; and
- serve as a liaison for consultation and communication with shareholders.

Questions and Comments

1. What is the purpose of the lead independent director? Is it to provide better governance? To provide a smokescreen for a company's refusal to separate the function of the chairman and the CEO? Something else entirely?

2. Do you think lead independent directors will exercise real power in the company? How important is the authority to set the agenda for meetings of the independent directors? To advise the chairman about the quality of information being provided to the board by the company's management? To fill in when the chairman is absent?

3. Who should appoint the lead independent director? Would it make sense for the chairman to participate in the selection process? What are the pros and cons?

PROBLEM 2-6

Thirty years ago, James Smith founded Smith Corp., a manufacturer of software-based systems for extrusion plastic molding factories. From the begining, Smith has served as majority shareholder, chairman of the board, and chief executive officer and, effectively, has been the sole authority in running the company. Three years ago, Smith Corp. went public, resulting in members of the public, including various hedge funds and institutional investors, owning 66 percent of the stock. Smith retains the remaining 34 percent. Responding to pressure from institutional investors, Smith decides that the board should create the position of lead director. You are currently the relationship partner for Smith Corp. at Markup and Billem, a 400-person corporate law firm. Smith calls you up and asks if you would care to join the board as lead independent director, at an annual compensation of $200,000 per year (which you won't have to share with your law firm). The job will require about 12 days a year of your time. Should you accept? Before doing so, would you ask for anything to be included in the company's description of the lead director position?

D. AUDIT COMMITTEES

Boards of directors meet as full boards, but they are also authorized to delegate specific functions to committees composed of only some board members. For purposes of compliance, the most important such committee is usually the audit committee.

Audit committees were originally formed to supervise the company's finances and to manage its relationship with its outside auditor (the outside auditor is the independent accounting firm that reviews the company's reports of financial condition). The rationale for assigning financial matters to a specialized committee was twofold. Because the supervision of the company's financial management involves technical accounting issues, greater focus and clarity of action could be obtained by appointing to the audit committee board members who had familiarity with that subject. Moreover, because financial reporting is crucial to the company's share price, the full board might be somewhat suspect on this issue because of the presence of management directors, who have an interest in maximizing the company's stock price. Assigning the task to an audit committee composed entirely, or mostly, of independent directors addressed that problem.

Once the audit committee was in place, however, it was available to take on new responsibilities as they evolved. Supervision of compliance fit naturally in the audit committee's mandate. The audit function is one of checking — making sure that procedures are followed and items are properly recorded. Compliance is also a process of checking — ensuring that applicable norms of conduct are being followed by employees. When compliance became recognized as an independent function of the board of directors, therefore, it was naturally assigned to the audit committee. In many companies that is where the compliance function remains, although in others the function has emigrated to specialized board compliance or risk committees.

Audit committees exist in every public company and the vast majority of substantial private companies. The Sarbanes-Oxley Act, the implementing SEC regulations (SEC Rule 10a-3), and the listing requirements of national securities exchanges all require that the audit committee of a public company must be staffed entirely by independent directors. SEC Rule 10a-3 requires that each audit committee must have the authority to engage independent counsel and other advisers, as it deems necessary to carry out its duties. The audit committee also operates under guarantees of financial independence: For public companies, the SEC requires that the audit committee must be given "appropriate funding" for payment of the expenses of accountants and advisers as well as the committee's ordinary administrative expenses. The audit committee, not the full board, has the authority to determine what these expenses should be.

As mentioned above, unless there is some other specialized committee in place, the audit committee is ordinarily responsible for overseeing the company's compliance operation. In this capacity, the audit committee receives regular reports from the company's chief compliance officer. In order to ensure the free flow of information, the audit committee typically has discretion to meet with the compliance officer in private time, outside the presence of other executives. Audit committees of public companies are also required to establish channels of communication that circumvent senior managers: The Sarbanes-Oxley Act and implementing SEC regulations require that such committees establish procedures for the receipt, retention, and treatment of complaints regarding accounting, internal accounting controls, or auditing matters; and the confidential, anonymous submission employees of concerns regarding questionable accounting or auditing matters.

Audit committee members must satisfy competence qualifications. Each public company must disclose whether it has a "financial expert" on its audit committee and, if not, why not. Although this is not quite the same as requiring that listed companies appoint a financial expert to the audit committee, it is a requirement in all but name. NASDAQ goes further: Audit committees of NASDAQ-listed companies must include at least one member who has past experience in finance or accounting, professional accounting certifications, or comparable experience. Beyond this, the NYSE and NASDAQ listing standards require that all audit committee members possess minimum levels of financial literacy.

Questions and Comments

1. The audit committee is historically the most important board committee, and is a key mechanism for ensuring that the company remains compliant with applicable rules and regulations.

2. Why do the regulators require members of the audit committee to possess minimum levels of financial literacy? Presumably, committee members need a certain amount of expertise to understand a company's financial statements and to competently supervise the external auditors. The level of financial literacy required is not very demanding, however; a director could probably satisfy the standard if she has taken some college or graduate courses in accounting or if she has been exposed on a regular basis to accounting issues while serving in a management capacity. Will the regulations described above guarantee that audit committee members can perform their responsibilities competently?

3. An important function of the audit committee is to supervise the activities of the internal audit department, which checks to ensure that a company's policies and procedures are being carried out in a reliable and effective way. We will discuss the role of internal audit in Chapter 3.

4. What information about the audit committee should be disclosed to investors? The SEC requires that public company proxy materials must include a report of the audit committee disclosing whether the audit committee has reviewed and discussed the audited financial statements with management, discussed the financial statements with the company's outside auditor, and reviewed the auditors' independence. The report must also state whether the audit committee recommended to the board of directors that the audited financial statements be included in the company's annual report. In addition, the company must disclose information about the independence of the audit committee members and must periodically disclose its audit committee charter. See SEC, Audit Committee Disclosure, Release No. 34-42266 (effective 2000). How helpful are these requirements? Given that the role of audit committees has expanded well beyond the responsibilities exercised by such committees in 2000, is it time for the SEC to revise its requirements, perhaps by requiring enhanced disclosures about the committee's role in risk management, in supervising internal audit, or in overseeing the company's compliance operations?

PROBLEM 2-7

You serve as an outside director on the audit committee of SpaceTech, a company that supplies guidance systems for military and civilian spacecraft. A recent internal audit uncovers instances where required protocols for safeguarding government secrets were not followed. Sally Sanders, the company's chief of internal audit, decides that these problems are minor and easily corrected, and therefore are not a matter that needs to be brought to the committee. You find out about the issue only by asking probing questions at the audit committee meeting. In your opinion, the issue poses a risk to the company's reputation and certainly should have been disclosed proactively. This is not the first time that Sally, in your opinion, has minimized the seriousness of audit findings; past remonstrations have not changed her behavior. Although you are upset, you also know that Sally is being groomed by the chief executive officer as his successor when he retires next year. What should you do?

PROBLEM 2-8

You are an independent director and head of your company's audit committee. At the most recent audit committee meeting, you notice that Bob Blanchard, the head of internal audit, seems uncomfortable when describing the results of an audit of supply chain management. During private time, Blanchard tells the committee that the vice president in charge of the business line had demanded that the audit findings be revised to downplay the significance of the problems discovered during the audit. Blanchard admits that because this executive is a powerful figure in the organization, internal audit had softened the finding from "critical" to "significant." What problems does this present to you and to the committee?

E. RISK COMMITTEES

The responsibilities of audit committees have grown by accretion over the years. As new tasks and new responsibilities evolved for the board of directors to manage, it was convenient to vest many of these in a committee. Often the audit committee was the most suitable candidate, either because the new responsibilities resembled things the audit committee was already doing, or simply because the audit committee was there. However, the accumulation of tasks has tended to deflect the focus of the audit committee away from its core function of financial control, and has also overburdened audit committees to the point where their ability to perform their tasks responsibly might be in jeopardy. Accordingly, new committees have been created to take over some of the burden and to focus on tasks that are deemed to be discrete, important, and outside the central competence of the audit committee.

One such task is risk management. Many companies — especially in the financial services industry but increasingly in firms of all types — assign responsibility for risk management to a special committee of the board of directors. For ease of reference, we call these "risk committees." Today, nearly all large banks operate a board-level risk committee. Risk committees are also beginning to turn up in the non-financial sector, although at a lower rate; as of 2013, approximately 4 percent of non-financial service firms and 2 percent of manufacturing firms had a board-level risk committee. *See* Matteo Tonello, *Risk in the Boardroom*, Conf. Bd. Dir. Notes, (May 2013), https://www.conference-board.org/retrievefile.cfm?filename=TCB-DN-V5N9-13.pdf&type=subsite. However, that level is sure to rise in the years ahead.

Establishing a board-level risk committee may appear to be a matter of good governance which firms might adopt on their own, without the spur of regulation. But there are also pressures from without. Item 407(h) of SEC Regulation S-K requires public companies to disclose the extent of their board's role in overseeing the organization's risk exposure, including how the board administers its risk over-sight function and how the leadership structure accommodates such a role. The SEC explains the rationale for the disclosure requirement as follows: "Companies face a variety of risks, including credit risk, liquidity risk, and operational risk. [D]isclosure about the board's involvement in the oversight of the risk management process should provide important information to investors about how a company perceives the role of its board and the relationship between the board and senior management in managing the material risks facing the company. This disclosure requirement gives companies the flexibility to describe how the board administers its risk oversight function, such as through the whole board, or through a separate risk committee or the audit committee, for example. Where relevant, companies may want to address whether the individuals who supervise the day-to-day risk man-agement responsibilities report directly to the board as a whole or to a board com-mittee or how the board or committee otherwise receives information from such individuals." SEC, Proxy Disclosure Enhancements Final Rule, 74 Fed. Reg. 68,334 (Dec. 23, 2009). The SEC also facilitated the growth of risk committees by ruling in 2009 that shareholder proposals regarding risk could not be excluded from a com-pany's proxy materials on the ground that they related to the day-to-day operations of the firm.

Additional pressure to establish risk committees came from §165(h) of the Dodd-Frank Act, enacted in 2010, which directs the Federal Reserve Board to require certain large bank holding companies and systemically important nonbank finan-cial companies to establish a board risk committee that is responsible for oversight of enterprise-wide risk management, is comprised of an appropriate number of independent directors, and includes at least one risk management expert. The Fed implemented this instruction by requiring companies subject to the regulation to implement robust enterprise-wide risk management practices. These practices must be overseen by a risk committee of the board of directors and chief risk officer with appropriate levels of independence, expertise and stature. In proposing the regulation, the Fed stated that "[s]ound, enterprise-wide risk management by cov-ered companies reduces the likelihood of their material distress or failure and thus promotes financial stability." Federal Reserve System, Enhanced Prudential Stan-dards and Early Remediation Requirements For Covered Companies, 77 Fed. Reg. 594 (Jan. 5, 2012).

In Europe, legislation implementing the Basel III capital standards now requires that the management of European banks must "ensure that the management body devotes sufficient time to consideration of risk issues. The management body shall be actively involved in and ensure that adequate resources are allocated to the management of material risks addressed in [the Directive] as well as in the valuation of assets, the use of external credit ratings and internal models relating to those risks. The institution shall establish reporting lines to the management body that cover all material risks and risk management policies and changes thereof." European Union, Capital Requirements Directive IV Art. 76 ¶ 2. Larger European banks are required to establish risk committees "composed of members of the management body who do not perform any executive function in the institution concerned. Members of the risk committee shall have appropriate knowledge, skills, and expertise to fully understand and monitor the risk strategy and the risk appetite of the institution. The risk committee shall advise the management body on the institution's overall current and future risk appetite and strategy and assist the management body in overseeing the implementation of that strategy by senior management. The management body shall retain overall responsibility for risks." Id. ¶ 3. Less significant institutions are permitted to combine the risk and audit committees.

Questions and Comments

1. In general, the SEC only has power to order public companies to make disclosures to the market; it cannot instruct them how to manage their affairs. Nevertheless, some SEC disclosure requirements are more "regulatory" than others, in that they subtly (or not so subtly) encourage an issuer to engage or not engage in the action being disclosed. How much "bite" does the SEC's regulation on risk management have?

2. Should the SEC have gone further and required, for example, that public companies disclose any formal policies pertinent to risk that have been adopted by the board of directors? Instances where risk metrics are outside limits set by the board or board risk committee? Risks deemed to pose a material threat to the achievement of the company's financial goals in the upcoming quarter or fiscal year?

3. The Fed's proposed regulation would apply only to large companies, even though the Dodd-Frank Act gave it discretion to apply the regulation to all publicly traded bank holding companies. Should the Fed have cast the regulatory net wider?

4. The Fed's statement accompanying its proposed regulation announces that sound, enterprise-wide risk management reduces the probability of financial distress and promotes financial stability. In one sense this is a tautology: If a company manages risk well, it is less likely to experience financial distress. But the Fed means to do more than state the obvious. The suggestion is that a board-level risk committee that meets the Fed's specifications will materially enhance risk management. Aside from the Fed's *ipse dixit*, is there hard evidence that that this will be the case?

5. A so-called Shareholder Bill of Rights, introduced by New York Senator Charles Schumer, would have required the creation of board-level risk management committees for all SEC-reporting firms. S.B. 1074, 111th Cong. (1st Sess. 2009), available at http://www.gpo.gov/fdsys/pkg/BILLS-111s1074is/pdf/BILLS-111s 1074is.pdf. Do you favor this proposal?

6. Deloitte Touche Tohmatsu Limited examined risk committee practices in large companies in Australia, Brazil, China, Mexico, the Netherlands, Singapore, the United States, and the United Kingdom as of 2014. The analysis found that

about a quarter of the 400 companies analyzed had established board-level risk committees, with Singapore having the highest percentage (42 percent). Among financial services companies, 67 percent had free-standing board-level risk committees and 21 percent had hybrid board-level committees involved in risk. Risk committees were less common outside the financial services sector, but still were increasing in prevalence: 11 percent of non-financial companies had board-level risk committees and 15 percent had hybrid committees. *See* Deloitte, A Global View of Risk Committees, available at http://www2.deloitte.com/global/en/pages/governance-risk-and-compliance/articles/a-global-view-of-risk-committees.html.

Risk committees operate under charters approved by the full board of directors. The following is the risk committee charter for Greenbrier Corporation, a (fictional) manufacturer of telecommunications equipment.

Greenbrier Corporation Risk Committee Charter

The Risk Committee of the board of directors of Greenbrier Corporation shall consist of a minimum of three directors. Members of the committee shall be appointed by the board upon the recommendation of the Nominating Committee and may be removed by the board in its discretion. All members of the committee shall be independent directors under the NASDAQ's listing requirements.

The purpose of the Risk Committee shall be to assist the board in its oversight of the Company's management of key risks well as the guidelines, policies, and processes for monitoring and mitigating such risks.

The committee shall have the following responsibilities:

1. To review and discuss with management the Company's risk governance structure, risk assessment and risk management practices and the guidelines, policies and processes for risk assessment and risk management.
2. To review and discuss with management the Company's risk appetite and strategy relating to key risks, including credit risk, liquidity and funding risk, market risk, product risk and reputational risk, as well as the guidelines, policies and processes for monitoring and mitigating such risks.
3. To discuss with the Company's chief risk officer the Company's risk assessment and risk management guidelines, policies and processes, as the case may be.
4. To coordinate with the Company's Audit Committee with respect to risk-related issues within the scope of that committee's responsibilities.
5. To receive reports from the Company's corporate audit staff on the results of risk management reviews and assessments.
6. To approve the appointment and, when and if appropriate, replacement of the Company's chief risk officer, who shall have a reporting relationship with the committee.
7. To review disclosure regarding risk contained in the Company's Annual Report on Form 10-K and Quarterly Reports on Form 10-Q.
8. To review reports on selected risk topics as the committee deems appropriate from time to time.
9. To discharge any other duties or responsibilities delegated to the committee by the board.

The committee shall have the authority to delegate any of its responsibilities to subcommittees as the committee may deem appropriate. The committee shall have authority to retain such outside counsel, experts and other advisors as the committee may deem appropriate in its sole discretion. The committee shall have sole authority to approve related fees and retention terms.

The committee shall report its actions and any recommendations to the board and shall conduct and present to the board an annual performance evaluation of the committee. The committee shall review at least annually the adequacy of this Charter and recommend any proposed changes to the board for approval.

Questions and Comments

1. An advantage of a board-level risk committee is that it focuses exclusively on risk, and therefore doesn't get distracted by other responsibilities as could happen, for example, if the responsibility for assessing and managing risk were given to the audit committee. The risk committee, moreover, has the capacity to manage risk on an enterprise-wide basis, rather than by individual business lines as had often been the case in earlier years.

2. On the other hand, risk committees pose certain challenges for institutional design. Given that risk is fundamental to all strategic decisions the company makes, vesting responsibility to a committee of the board threatens to cut the other board members out of the loop. How should a board deal with the dilemma of achieving focus while not losing perspective? How does Greenbrier deal with the need to involve the whole board in the risk management process?

3. Another option is to have the risk committee be a committee of the whole — that is, to have all members of the board sit on the risk committee. Essentially, this is functionally similar to devoting part of the full board's agenda to a discussion of risk; but it has the potential advantage of segregating the risk analysis from other board responsibilities and also of designating one director, who can be independent, with ownership of the board-level risk management process. Is this a better approach?

4. How should board-level committees of holding companies deal with risks in subsidiaries? A subsidiary, even if wholly-owned, is a separate firm with its own board of directors. It is the subsidiary's board, not the board of the holding company, which is technically charged with managing that company's operations, including its response to risk. Nevertheless, the parent effectively controls the subsidiary and, as sole shareholder, is directly exposed to the consequences if risks undertaken at the subsidiary level go south. Given this fact, how should the company manage risk at the subsidiary?

5. Do you think that risk committees could have played a constructive role in preventing financial institutions from taking on high levels of leverage, investing in subprime mortgage-backed securities, and participating in potentially unstable derivative financial products during the period leading up to the financial crisis of 2007-2009? Could anyone have foreseen the crisis?

6. How should the risk committee relate to the compensation committee? Can you see why compensation of senior executive officers has a bearing on risk? If the company's leaders are compensated highly for taking risks, then they will be likely to take on more risk. To what extent should compensation packages be adjusted specifically with an eye towards managing the risk incentives of senior managers?

7. How should the risk committee interact with the audit committee? Given the overlap in functions, it seems that they should interact frequently and coordinate their supervisory activities. Among proposed best practices in this regard are (a) appointing common directors to both committees and (b) facilitating occasional joint meetings of both committees. What does Greenbrier's Risk Committee Charter say about this issue?

Should there be competency requirements for service on risk committees along the lines of requirements that apply to audit committees? Board risk committees under the Dodd-Frank Act must include "at least one risk management expert." Aside from this special case applicable to publicly traded bank holding companies with $10 billion or more in consolidated assets, there are no competency requirements for board risk committees. Should there be? Consider in this regard the makeup of JPMorgan Chase's three-member risk committee at the time of the "London Whale" trading fiasco of 2012, taken from the company's 2013 proxy statement:

- David Cote: Mr. Cote is Chairman and Chief Executive Officer of Honeywell International Inc., a diversified technology and manufacturing leader, serving customers worldwide with aerospace products and services; control technologies for buildings, homes and industry; turbochargers; and specialty materials. He was elected President and Chief Executive Officer in February 2002, and was named Chairman of the Board in July 2002. Prior to joining Honeywell, he served as Chairman, President and Chief Executive Officer of TRW Inc., which he joined in 1999 after a 25-year career with General Electric. Mr. Cote is a director of Honeywell International Inc. (since 2002).

  Mr. Cote graduated from the University of New Hampshire in 1976. In 2010, he was named by President Obama to serve on the bipartisan National Commission on Fiscal Responsibility and Reform. Mr. Cote was named co-chair of the U.S.-India CEO Forum by President Obama in 2009, and has served on the Forum since July 2005. Mr. Cote is a member of The Business Roundtable and serves on an advisory panel to Kohlberg Kravis Roberts & Co.

  At Honeywell and TRW, Mr. Cote gained experience dealing with a variety of issues relevant to the Firm's business, including audit and financial reporting, risk management, executive compensation, sales and marketing of industrial and consumer goods and services, and technology matters. He also has extensive experience in international business issues and public policy matters. His record of public service further enhances his value to the Board.

- Ellen Futter, a corporate lawyer who heads the Museum of Natural History in New York City. Ms. Futter became President of the American Museum of Natural History in 1993, prior to which she had been President of Barnard College since 1981. The Museum is one of the world's preeminent scientific, educational and cultural institutions. Her career began at Milbank, Tweed, Hadley & McCloy where she practiced corporate law. Ms. Futter is a director of Consolidated Edison, Inc. (since 1997) and was previously a director of American International Group Inc. (1999-2008) and Viacom (2006-2007). She was a director of the Federal Reserve Bank of New York (1988-1993) and served as its Chairman (1992-1993).

Ms. Futter graduated from Barnard College in 1971 and earned a law degree from Columbia Law School in 1974. She is a member of the Board of Overseers and Managers of Memorial Sloan-Kettering Cancer Center, a Fellow of the American Academy of Arts and Sciences and a member of the Council on Foreign Relations. Ms. Futter is also a trustee of the Brookings Institution, and a director of The American Ditchley Foundation and NYC & Company.

Ms. Futter has managed large educational and not-for-profit organizations, Barnard College and the American Museum of Natural History, and in that capacity, she has dealt with many complex organizational issues. Such work and her service on public company boards and the board of the Federal Reserve Bank of New York have given her experience with regulated enterprises, in particular the financial services industry, and with risk management, executive compensation, and audit and financial reporting. In her role at the Federal Reserve Bank of New York she also acquired valuable experience dealing with government officials and agencies. Her years of practicing corporate law give her enhanced perspective on legal and regulatory issues. Her extensive experience with philanthropic organizations provides her with insights that are relevant to the Firm's corporate responsibility initiatives.

- James Crown: Mr. Crown joined Henry Crown and Company, a privately owned investment company which invests in public and private securities, real estate and operating companies, in 1985 as Vice President and became President in 2002. Mr. Crown is a director of General Dynamics Corporation (since 1987). He is also a director of JPMorgan Chase Bank, N.A., a wholly-owned subsidiary of the Firm (since 2010). He previously served as a director of Sara Lee Corporation (1998-2012).

Mr. Crown graduated from Hampshire College in 1976 and received his law degree from Stanford University Law School in 1980. Following law school, Mr. Crown joined Salomon Brothers Inc. and became a vice president of the Capital Markets Service Group in 1983. In 1985 he joined his family's investment firm. He is a Trustee of the University of Chicago Medical Center, the Museum of Science and Industry, The Aspen Institute, the University of Chicago, and the Chicago Symphony Orchestra. He is a member of the American Academy of Arts and Sciences.

Mr. Crown's position with Henry Crown and Company and his service on other public company boards have given him exposure to many issues encountered by the Firm's Board, including audit and financial reporting, investment management, risk management, and executive compensation. His legal training gives him enhanced perspective on legal and regulatory issues. He is experienced in investment banking and capital markets matters through his prior work experience and subsequent responsibilities. The broad range of his philanthropic activities, in the Chicago area in particular, gives him important insight into the community concerns of one of the Firm's largest markets.

Questions and Comments

1. The "London Whale" was a trader located in the United Kingdom, Bruno Iksil, who had substantial discretionary authority to trade on JPMorgan Chase's behalf. For a number of years Iksil's trades had proven profitable for the bank — and for Iksil, who was taking home six or seven million dollars a year in compensation.

In 2012, however, Iksil's trading strategy backfired. The result, by some estimates, was more than six billion dollars in losses to the bank (see Chapter 20).

2. In the wake of the London Whale fiasco, JPMorgan Chase's risk committee and senior management came under fire for having failed to identify the risk that Iksil's activities posed for the bank and for having failed to properly limit his trading authority. A number of activist shareholders and opinion-shapers opposed the re-election of the three directors mentioned above on the ground that they lacked the capacity to serve on the risk committee of an institution as large and complex as JPMorgan Chase. Prominent among the opponents was ISS, an organization that billed itself as "the leading provider of corporate governance solutions to the global financial community."

3. Do you think these directors were qualified? Mr. Cote was chairman and CEO of Honeywell International, a Fortune 100 company with approximately 132,000 employees worldwide (with compensation of more than $55 million in 2012, he was also the fifth highest-paid CEO in the country, according to Fortune Magazine). He had previously been chairman, president, and CEO of TRW Inc., a conglomerate active in the aerospace, automotive, and credit reporting industries with 122,000 employees; and he was a top candidate for CEO at General Electric, where he spent the early years of his career. Those are impressive achievements. On the other hand, although as a chief executive officer Cote was necessarily concerned with risk management at his companies, it appears that he never specialized in that topic. His career was mostly in the areas of technology, manufacturing, and credit reporting. Did this experience qualify him to manage the risks of losses at one of the world's largest banks? Moreover, the job of serving as chairman and CEO of a Fortune 100 company is pretty demanding. Do you think Cote had the time to faithfully carry out his job on JPMorgan Chase's risk committee?

4. What about Ellen Futter? The Museum of Natural History is an important cultural institution, and one that no doubt poses many complex management challenges. But its mission has little to do with the banking industry or even with finance more generally defined. She previously served, however, as a director (not a manager) of the Federal Reserve Bank of New York, an agency of the U.S. central bank and an institution that carries out banking operations and acts as a regulator of banking firms. Was this enough exposure to the banking industry to qualify her as a member of JPMorgan Chase's risk committee? She was also, apparently, a successful corporate lawyer with a background at one of the finest law firms in the United States. Corporate lawyers are not unfamiliar with risk; one could argue that their principal role is to manage risk on behalf of their clients. However, the qualitative, judgment-based risk management that a lawyer undertakes is different from the technical and quantitative risk management undertaken by a bank. Futter had experience as a director of AIG, one of the largest insurance firms in the world, but that assignment went belly-up when AIG imploded during the financial crisis of 2007-2009 and required a multi-billion-dollar government bailout. Should her experience at AIG be considered a plus or a minus? Overall, did Futter have adequate qualifications to serve on JPMorgan Chase's risk committee?

5. James Crown was also a lawyer—a graduate of Stanford Law School—who spent most of his career in the area of finance, first at Salomon Brothers and then managing his family's money (estimated at more than $4 billion). Certainly Crown is knowledgeable about financial matters; and you probably have to be smart to get into Stanford Law School. What about his commendable record of public service in charitable and civic organizations in and around Chicago? JPMorgan Chase

advertises that these activities are qualifications for board service because they provide Crown with "important insight into the community concerns of one of the Firm's largest markets." Maybe so; but do these insights help much in managing the risk of a global bank with more than $2 trillion in assets? Overall did Crown have adequate qualifications to serve on JPMorgan Chase's risk committee?

6. Should these individuals be evaluated only in isolation, or is it also necessary to consider them in the context of a committee comprised of all three? Viewed as a group, did the three directors qualify as an effective risk committee even if any one of them individually would be inadequate for the job?

7. How independent were the members of the risk committee? They qualified as independent directors for regulatory purposes, but the bank reported a number of connections. It made charitable contributions to the American Museum of Natural History, Futter's institution. It leased office space from a company controlled by Crown. It purchased equipment from Honeywell International, Inc., where Cote was CEO. Do these connections make you suspicious of the committee's autonomy? Or are they simply what is to be expected when a bank of the size of JPMorgan Chase utilizes distinguished and well-connected people as directors?

8. What weight should you give to the fact that the risk committee did not succeed at placing appropriate limits on Iksil's trading authority, or preventing the bank from incurring a staggering loss? On the one hand, the failure seems to be a cause for concern. On the other hand, Iksil had generated spectacular profits for the bank in the past. Was the risk committee justified in light of his past success in giving him more trading leeway than would otherwise be appropriate? In any event, even good risk committees experience bad outcomes; their job is not to guarantee results but rather to make sure that the risk an organization takes on stays within the organization's tolerances and risk appetite. Should the risk committee be blamed because things turned out poorly?

9. In the 2013 proxy election, several institutional investors and proxy advisers recommended that shareholders vote against the re-election of Futter, Crown, and Cote. The three directors were re-elected, but not by the huge margins typical of proxy votes: Crown and Cote received 57 percent of the votes, while Futter squeaked by with 53 percent. Would you reappoint them to the risk committee? Would you re-

PROBLEM 2-9

You are an attorney and an independent member of the board risk committee of Fincorp, a consumer lending firm. You were appointed because the governance and nominating committee believed your legal skills would be helpful in managing risks of government regulation and class action lawsuits. Terry Thomas, Fincorp's chief risk officer and a graduate of MIT, makes a presentation to your committee describing a new computerized risk-management system that involves "state of the art" modeling under different economic scenarios. The presentation is mostly in the form of math that is so far over your head you don't even know how to ask a question. You are comforted by the fact that Jenny Jones, the chair of the risk committee and a professor at Harvard Business School, is smiling and nodding in agreement — especially when Thomas makes it clear that the financial models he is proposing to use are derived from Jones' own research papers. Is there anything here that should keep you up at night?

nominate them for board positions when their terms expire? In July 2013, both Futter and Cote resigned from the board—presumably after a face-saving period of continued service in the wake of the shareholder vote.

PROBLEM 2-10

The risk committee of Fidelity Insurance Company operates under a "risk appetite" approved by the full board that allows the company to acquire a portfolio of fixed-rate mortgage-backed securities. As a member of the risk committee, you are convinced that the portfolio does not pose a risk to safety and soundness. The insurance regulator, however, has a different view about the risk posed by un-hedged fixed-rate securities, and communicates that concern in no uncertain terms to the board of directors. Although there is nothing illegal about the company's investment strategy, it is likely to irritate the regulators unless it is changed. As a member of Fidelity Insurance's risk committee, how would you evaluate this situation?

F. COMPLIANCE COMMITTEES

Some companies—typically in industries with intensive regulation and high potential liability for infractions—maintain a specialized compliance committee that operates separately from the audit committee. These companies split the audit committee's traditional responsibilities in two, leaving financially related tasks with audit and allocating the compliance function to a different committee, which, like audit, is usually composed of a majority of independent directors.

Drafting a compliance committee charter is an important task, and one with long-range consequences for the governance of the organization. Following is an excerpt from the compliance committee charter of Applied Bosonics, a (fictional) supplier of high-tech telecommunications systems:

Applied Bosonics Compliance Committee Charter

The Compliance Committee (the "Committee") shall consist of five or more directors the majority of whom, in the judgment of the Board of Directors, shall be independent in accordance with NASDAQ listing standards and the Company's director qualification standards. At least one member of the Committee shall in the judgment of the Board of Directors have a background in telecommunications law and policy. The Committee's membership should, unless the Board of Directors determines otherwise, include at least one member of the Audit Committee, but the majority of the Committee shall not be members of the Audit Committee. The Chair of the Committee shall be an independent member of the Board of Directors who has experience in law, corporate compliance, regulatory or governmental affairs, academia or service on the Board of a highly regulated company.

The Committee shall assist the Board of Directors with the oversight of significant telecommunications-related regulatory and compliance issues. The Committee shall prepare a yearly overview of its activities generally for inclusion in the Company's annual report or proxy statement. The report shall be signed by the Committee chairperson and all Committee members.

The Committee's responsibilities include:

- Review and oversee the Company's Compliance Program, including but not limited to, evaluating its effectiveness and receiving updates about the activities of the Chief Compliance Officer and other compliance personnel.
- Review the status of the Company's compliance with relevant laws, regulations, and internal procedures.
- Review and evaluate internal reports and external data, based on criteria to be developed by the Committee, to assess whether there are significant concerns regarding the Company's regulatory and/or compliance practices.
- At least annually, receive a report from the Chief Compliance Officer regarding significant compliance investigations.
- At least annually, receive a report on retaliation claims, lawsuits alleging retaliation, settlements of retaliation claims, and reports of alleged retaliation to the Compliance Division and/or any Ombudsman program established by the Company.
- At least annually, receive a report on compliance audits undertaken by Internal Audit.
- Receive reports from management on internal communications to employees regarding the Company's commitment to behavior and practices that comply with law, as well as the Company's efforts to promote a compliant culture.
- Review reporting chains that seek to provide a protected channel for reporting compliance related concerns to the appropriate Board committee.
- Receive reports from management with respect to any significant disciplinary action against any of the Company's compliance personnel or internal audit personnel, including the nature of the conduct that led to the disciplinary action, the disciplinary action and the reason for it, and an analysis of whether the underlying conduct reflects any compliance or regulatory concerns or issues.
- Interface as appropriate with the Company's Executive Compliance Committee.

The Committee in consultation with the Compensation Committee will discuss with management an evaluation of whether compensation practices are aligned with the Company's compliance obligations. Any compensation practices evaluation prepared as a result may either be reported first to the Committee, or the Compensation Committee, which will then report the results to the Committee.

If there is a government or regulatory action that, in the judgment of the Committee, has caused significant financial or reputational damage to the Company or otherwise indicates a significant compliance or regulatory issue within the Company, then the Committee shall make a written recommendation to the Compensation Committee concerning the extent, if any, to which the incentive-based compensation of any executive, senior manager, compliance personnel and/or attorney involved in the conduct at issue or with direct supervision over an employee that engaged in the conduct at issue should be reduced or extinguished.

- The incentive-based compensation of any executive, senior manager, compliance personnel and/or attorney will not be impacted if they were not involved in the misconduct or not engaged in the direct or indirect supervision of the employee involved in the misconduct.
- If, prior to any regulatory or government investigation of the conduct that is the subject of the government or regulatory action described above, any person engaged in the supervision of the employee involved in the misconduct discovers and reports the misconduct through the appropriate Company

procedures (including, if required, one or more committees of the Board of Directors), in furtherance of having the matter properly investigated and remedied, then the Committee may in its discretion recommend to the Compensation Committee that no reduction of compensation is required for anyone not involved in the misconduct. . . .

- Nothing in this section is designed to limit or restrict management or the Board from taking any disciplinary action they deem appropriate.

The Committee shall report at least annually to the Board of Directors on the state of the Company's compliance functions, relevant compliance issues involving the Company of which the Committee has been made aware, including a summary of the results of any compliance investigations conducted by the Company, any potential patterns of non-compliance identified within the Company, any significant disciplinary actions against any compliance or internal audit personnel, and any other issues that may reflect any systemic or widespread problems in compliance or regulatory matters exposing the Company to substantial compliance risk. In advance of such report, the Committee and the Audit Committee, either through their respective Chairs or otherwise, shall confer on any matters of mutual interest in light of their respective responsibilities.

The Committee is authorized in its discretion to retain outside independent counsel with appropriate expertise, and may also, at its discretion, retain experts and consultants in the discharge of its responsibilities.

The Committee is authorized, in its discretion, to require management to conduct audits on compliance, regulatory and/or legal concerns. The Committee may also, in its discretion, direct whether or not the Committee should be the direct recipient of the results of such an audit.

Questions and Comments

1. Applied Bosonics' compliance committee charter requires that a majority of the members be independent. Why not require all members of the compliance committee to be independent, as is done for the audit committee?

2. Applied Bosonics' compliance committee is required to interface with an "Executive Compliance Committee." These are committees of senior executives — including but not limited to the chief compliance officer — who have responsibility for, or management overlaps with, the compliance function. What do you think is the purpose of an executive compliance committee, given that the company already has a chief compliance officer?

3. How should the compliance committee interface with the board risk committee? In one sense, compliance appears to be simply another risk that a company takes on: the risk that someone in the company will violate applicable legal norms or standards. Should compliance committees be folded into risk committees, or is there enough distinction of function to warrant separate treatment?

4. What about internal audit? Compliance committees are supposed to monitor the institution's activities to ensure that applicable legal norms are being followed; in this sense their responsibility overlaps substantially with those of the audit committee. At the same time, the compliance function is itself one of the key internal safeguards at an organization, and therefore is a candidate for monitoring by the internal auditors. How would you draw the line? The Basel Committee on Banking

Supervision (an international group of regulators who prescribe best practices for banks) has this to say:

> Compliance risk should be included in the risk assessment methodology of the internal audit function, and an audit programme that covers the adequacy and effectiveness of the bank's compliance function should be established, including testing of controls commensurate with the perceived level of risk. This principle implies that the compliance function and the audit function should be separate, to ensure that the activities of the compliance function are subject to independent review. It is important, therefore, that there is a clear understanding within the bank as to how risk assessment and testing activities are divided between the two functions, and that this is documented (e.g. in the bank's compliance policy or in a related document such as a protocol). The audit function should, of course, keep the head of compliance informed of any audit findings relating to compliance.

Basel Committee on Banking Supervision, *Compliance and the Compliance Function in Banks* ¶¶ 44-45 (April 2005).

5. What about the compensation committee? Note that the Applied Bosonics compliance committee charter has a rather elaborate border treaty setting forth the respective powers of the compliance and compensation committees. What is the company seeking to achieve by this?

6. For general discussion of the legal consequences of establishing (or not establishing) compliance committees, see Jill E. Fisch & Caroline M. Gentile, *The Qualified Legal Compliance Committee: Using the Attorney Conduct Rules to Restructure the Board of Directors*, 53 Duke L.J. 517 (2003).

PROBLEM 2-11

The compliance committee of a pharmaceutical company learns that salespeople in the marketing department have been pushing doctors to prescribe a particular medication for the treatment of heart palpitations, a use not approved by the Food and Drug Administration (FDA). Such conduct would constitute a violation of "off-label" marketing rules under federal law. The practice appears to be widespread and to have been coordinated by the vice president in charge of heart medications. As chair of the committee, you discuss these findings with the chief executive officer, who expresses the concern that if these activities are made public, the company will be sued for millions of dollars. He asks if the matter can be handled internally, without informing the FDA. What should you do?

PROBLEM 2-12

You are head of the compliance committee of the Covington Hospital. At a social dinner the night before the quarterly committee meeting, the chief compliance officer tells you in confidence that she has heard that a glitch in the hospital's billing software has resulted in the hospital being overpaid by several million dollars in Medicaid reimbursements. "I hear rumors like this all the time," she says, "and if nothing more substantial comes to our attention our policy is to let them go." You know that if the report is true, having to repay the overcharges and penalties could drive the hospital into bankruptcy. The next day, at the committee meeting, you see nothing in the chief compliance officer's report addressing the possible Medicaid overcharges. What should you do?

G. GOVERNANCE AND NOMINATING COMMITTEES

We have seen that the independence of directors can sometimes be challenged on the ground that even if a director is formally "independent" of management under applicable definitions of the term, the intricate network of friendship, family, business, and social ties makes it possible for a company's chief executive officer to exercise substantial control over the selection of independent board members and to influence, in some cases, the decisions these board members make once they join the firm. It is nearly impossible to police against these connections; most of the members of the board of directors of any substantial firm are linked to one another and to the company's senior managers by only a few degrees of separation. But the exercise of cronyism and "old boy" or "old school" connections can be reduced if the job of nominating new directors is taken away from the company's managers and given to unrelated parties. This is where a governance and nominating committee comes in.

New York Stock Exchange Listed Company Manual, ¶ 303A.04: Nominating/Corporate Governance Committee

    (a) Listed companies must have a nominating/corporate governance committee composed entirely of independent directors.

    (b) The nominating/corporate governance committee must have a written charter that addresses:

        (i) the committee's purpose and responsibilities—which, at minimum, must be to: identify individuals qualified to become board members, consistent with criteria approved by the board, and to select, or to recommend that the board select, the director nominees for the next annual meeting of shareholders; develop and recommend to the board a set of corporate governance guidelines applicable to the corporation; and oversee the evaluation of the board and management; and

        (ii) an annual performance evaluation of the committee.

    Commentary: A nominating/corporate governance committee is central to the effective functioning of the board. New director and board committee nominations are among a board's most important functions. Placing this responsibility in the hands of an independent nominating/corporate governance committee can enhance the independence and quality of nominees. The committee is also responsible for taking a leadership role in shaping the corporate governance of a corporation.

    If a listed company is legally required by contract or otherwise to provide third parties with the ability to nominate directors (for example, preferred stock rights to elect directors upon a dividend default, shareholder agreements, and management agreements), the selection and nomination of such directors need not be subject to the nominating committee process.

    The nominating/corporate governance committee charter should also address the following items: committee member qualifications; committee member appointment and removal; committee structure and operations (including authority to delegate to subcommittees); and committee reporting to the board. In addition, the charter should give the nominating/corporate governance committee sole authority to retain and terminate any search firm to be used to identify director candidates, including sole authority to approve the search firm's fees and other retention terms.

Boards may allocate the responsibilities of the nominating/corporate governance committee to committees of their own denomination, provided that the committees are composed entirely of independent directors. Any such committee must have a committee charter.

Questions and Comments

1. Do you agree that a nominating/corporate governance committee is "central to the effective functioning of the board"?

2. A principal purpose of a nominating/governance committee is to reduce the risk of hidden influences in the selection of board members. In theory, because all members of the nominating/governance committee are independent, they will not pick board members on the basis of personal connections. Do you think they will achieve this goal?

3. It is increasingly common for nominating/governance committees to seek input from professional placement consultants who have access to information about a larger pool of candidates than would be available to the committee members acting alone. The NYSE listing requirement explicitly refers to these firms and requires that the nominating/governance committee be provided with the resources to retain them. Reuters reported in 2013 that nine of the ten largest U.S. banks use executive search firms to find new directors; the lone holdout was JPMorgan Chase, where directors were identified by referrals from management.

4. These consultants are not cheap. Do they add value? If used, do they insulate the company from the charge that board members are selected on the basis of cronyism rather than their intrinsic merit?

5. An obvious question, when it comes to nominating/governance committees, is who nominates the committee members. If they nominate themselves, are they subject to the same risk of cronyism that exists in the traditional system of board selection?

6. The NYSE listing requirement says that the committee's charter must address "an annual performance evaluation of the committee." What does this mean? By what metric can the committee's performance be evaluated, and who is to do the evaluation? The listing requirement is vague enough to allow the committee to evaluate itself; but what will this achieve other than self-congratulation?

PROBLEM 2-13

You are an independent director and chair of the nominating and governance committee of a publicly traded company involved in supplying electronics for defense contractors. After the unexpected death of one of your colleagues, you are charged with identifying a successor. You get a call from the company's CEO, your friend Melanie Matthews. "Could you take a close look at Latoya Lamb for the new board position? I've known her since we were roommates in college and she's first rate." You look up Lamb's bio and discover that she has a PhD in electrical engineering, is an African American, and is a chaired professor in the engineering department of Rice University. What should you do? Would it make a difference if the company is owned by a private equity firm?

PROBLEM 2-14

You are an independent director and chair of the governance and nominating committee of Agritemp, a firm that leases harvesters and other equipment to farmers. The company's business model has been profitable for many years and, in your opinion, the senior executive team is competent. The company has no age limit for directors. Everett Evans, a renowned former U.S. Senator, has served on the board for the ten years since his retirement from public service at age 70. You notice that recently he has been falling asleep at board meetings and seems to be increasingly forgetful. You mention this in confidence to the chief executive officer, who responds, "I know Everett's lost a step or two, but he's famous and besides, I don't want to hurt his feelings." What should you do? Would it matter how many people serve on the board?

PROBLEM 2-15

You are an independent director and chair of the nominating and governance committee of Zbot Corporation, a company engaged in manufacturing industrial robots. Last year Alan Acton, an activist investor, launched a proxy fight seeking to unseat the incumbent board members (including you). After a long and bruising battle, Acton dropped his proxy challenge in exchange for the company's agreement that he could name two directors (subject to the technical requirement of approval by your committee). One of Acton's nominees is Tiffany Thomas, a celebrity chef who served time in prison ten years ago for insider trading; you also suspect that she is Acton's girlfriend. The chief executive officer instructs you to approve Thomas' nomination. You firmly believe that Thomas is unqualified for the position. What should you do?

PROBLEM 2-16

You are the general counsel of Spillways, a company engaged in providing filtration equipment and services to public water utilities. One of the independent directors of Spillways is Tommy Travis, a retired four-star general in the U.S. Army. The chairman of the board of Spillways comes to you one day with a problem. General Travis has been publicly accused by one of his senior aides of sexual harassment during his time in office, resulting in sensational coverage in the tabloid media. The Army announces that it is initiating an investigation into the charges. Based on your experience in government service, you predict that the investigation will take at least a year. In the meantime Travis will continue to serve as a director of Spillways unless some action is taken to remove him from the position. What do you advise?

PROBLEM 2-17

Bob Brown, the longtime CEO of Guardian Industries, a provider of home security systems, announces that he is taking six-week vacation and that, while he is gone, he will not be reachable. He explains that he wants to "retool and refresh" and that to do this, he intends to get away from the stresses of the job. Brown designates the company's COO to act as interim CEO in his absence. Brown has never before behaved this way. You are an independent director and chair of the nominating and governance committee at Guardian Industries. The day after Brown's announcement, as you are considering what steps to take in response, you receive a call from Brown's executive assistant. Asking for confidentiality, the assistant tells you that he saw some paperwork on Brown's desk referring to procedures for voluntary admission to a well-known drug and alcohol rehabilitation facility. You have not personally observed any indication that Brown might have a problem with substance abuse. What should you do?

PROBLEM 2-18

Veronica Jones, the 42-year old CEO of Fashion First, a discount women's clothing chain, announces that she is expecting her first child. Jones is unmarried and plans to raise the baby alone. She proposes to come to the office for two and a half days a week and to work the rest of the time from home for a period of three years after the baby is born. As a member of the nominating and governance committee, you have high respect for Jones' talent, initiative, and integrity, and you appreciate and understand her wish to be a present parent for her child. Nevertheless, you also believe that she will be less effective as a leader of the company if she is only around on a part-time basis. What should you do?

How should the governance and nominating committee — or other responsible board entity — handle the situation when a CEO runs into trouble or experiences difficulty handling the job? This is one of the most difficult problems a board of directors can face. Because the CEO is so central to the success or failure of any company, any factors that impair her effectiveness should be matters of concern. The issues involved are sensitive and the risks of mistake are significant.

First, the board may not have full information about the nature of the problem or the extent of the impairment. Most CEOs devoutly wish to keep their jobs. They do not wish others to know information that reflects badly on their fitness for office. Moreover, in some cases the information involved is embarrassing, creating another reason for the CEO to keep it secret. Yet this is often information that the board needs to faithfully carry out their responsibilities. How can the board find out the necessary facts without intruding unduly into the privacy of the CEO or exacerbating problems of lack of trust between the board and senior managers?

Even when the board is fully informed, the question of what to do with the information can be daunting. Significant reputational concerns are present — both the CEO's personal reputation and the reputation of the organization, which may be besmirched if the matter is not handled delicately. Any decision to sideline or dismiss the CEO also implicates legal questions regarding, for example, the executive's rights to severance payments, the vesting of options, or the continuation of benefits. CEOs may fight back if dismissed, claiming that they were not afforded an opportunity to defend themselves or that they suffered some form of illegal discrimination. The situation, in short, is volatile and dangerous, and one that requires wisdom and judgment on the part of the board members.

Consider in this regard the following opinion from the Supreme Court of Delaware, dealing with a board that faced exactly these sorts of problems:

Klaassen v. Allegro Development Corporation

106 A.3d 1035 (Del. 2014)

JACOBS, Justice.

. . . Allegro, a Delaware corporation headquartered in Dallas, Texas, is a provider of energy trading and risk management software. From the time that [Eldon] Klaassen founded Allegro in 1984, he has been Allegro's CEO, and until 2007, owned nearly all of Allegro's outstanding shares . . . . [In 2008 certain] investors received Series A Preferred Stock of Allegro in exchange for an investment of $40 million. Currently, the Series A Investors own all of Allegro's Series A Preferred Stock, and Klaassen holds the majority of Allegro's Common Stock . . . . From 2010 until November 1, 2012, [the] Board consisted of Michael Pehl and Robert Forlenza (the "Series A Directors"), George Patrick Simpkins, Jr. and Raymond Hood (the "Outside Directors"), and Klaassen (as the CEO director) . . . .

Not long after the Series A Investors became shareholders, Allegro began falling short of its financial performance projections. A 2007 private placement memorandum circulated by Allegro had projected revenues of $61 million in 2008, $75 million in 2009, and $85 million in 2010. In fact, Allegro generated only $46 million in revenue in 2008, $37.5 million in 2009, and less than $35 million in 2010. Although Allegro met its targets for the first three quarters of 2011, the company's fourth quarter performance was a "disaster," and the first quarter of 2012 was similarly disappointing.

Not surprisingly, the Series A Directors, and later the Outside Directors, became discontented with Klaassen's performance as a manager. After the Series A investment transaction, Allegro hired Chris Larsen as chief operating officer to address the Series A Investors' concerns about Klaassen's management. Ten months later, Mr. Larsen resigned, citing difficulty working with Klaassen. While Allegro's financial performance continued to falter, the Series A Directors became particularly frustrated with Klaassen's inability to provide the Board with accurate information. In 2012, only four days before the end of Allegro's best sales quarter to date, Klaassen fired Allegro's senior vice president of sales — disregarding the Board's request to wait until after the quarter's end, and acting without any succession plan in place. Finally, in September 2012, Allegro's chief marketing officer resigned, citing Klaassen's leadership style as the reason.

As frustration with Klaassen mounted, in 2012 the Board began exploring ways to address the Series A Investors' redemption right. At some point before the July 19, 2012 Board meeting, Klaassen proposed that Allegro buy out the Series A Investors'

Preferred Stock investment for $60 million. Initially the Series A Investors had demanded $92 million — the approximate value of their initial liquidation preference — but at a July 31, 2012 Board meeting they reduced their demand to $80 million. At that same meeting, Klaassen made a presentation about Allegro's financial performance, apparently hoping to make his $60 million offer to the Series A Investors appear more attractive. Instead, all that Klaassen accomplished was to highlight Allegro's poor performance as compared to its industry peers. As a result, Mr. Forlenza (a Series A Director) concluded that the only viable path for the Series A Investors to achieve a profitable exit was to "grow" the company before exiting.

In late summer 2012, the Board began seriously to consider replacing Klaassen as CEO. After the July 19 Board meeting, the Outside Directors discussed (with Klaassen), Klaassen's unwillingness to compromise with the Series A Investors. Mr. Hood pointedly told Klaassen that with three director votes, the Board could remove him as CEO. After Klaassen's July 31 Board meeting presentation, Messrs. Pehl and Forlenza (the Series A Directors) became more convinced that Klaassen had to be replaced. In an August 7, 2012 conference call, Messrs. Pehl, Forlenza, Hood, and Simpkins discussed the possibility of replacing Klaassen. Shortly after that call, Mr. Hood asked Baker Botts LLP (legal counsel for the Outside Directors) for advice about the ramifications of replacing Klaassen. On August 17, 2012, the Director Defendants spoke once again.

In mid-September 2012, Messrs. Simpkins and Hood met with Klaassen. Both warned Klaassen that his tenure as CEO was "in jeopardy." At some point, most likely in September, Mr. Pehl asked Mr. Hood whether he (Hood) would consider replacing Klaassen as CEO. Eventually, Hood agreed, and by mid-October, the four Director Defendants (Pehl, Forlenza, Hood, and Simpkins) decided to replace Klaassen at the next regularly scheduled Board meeting on November 1, 2012. Those four directors held two preparatory conference calls — on October 19 and October 26 — and asked Baker Botts to prepare a draft resolution removing Klaassen as CEO. The Director Defendants decided not to forewarn Klaassen that they planned to terminate him, because they were concerned about how Klaassen would react while still having access to Allegro's intellectual property, bank accounts, and employees.

On November 1, 2012, before the Board meeting, Mr. Hood emailed Klaassen, asking if Chris Ducanes, Allegro's general counsel, could attend the Board meeting to discuss the Series A redemption issue. Klaassen agreed. Mr. Hood later admitted that that email was "false" because, in fact, Mr. Ducanes' presence was needed to implement Klaassen's termination immediately after Klaassen was informed.

All five directors attended the November 1, 2012 Board meeting. Also attending were Messrs. Ducanes, and Jarett Janik, Allegro's chief financial officer. Toward the end of the meeting, the Director Defendants asked Messrs. Ducanes, Janik, and Klaassen to leave the room to allow the Director Defendants to meet in executive session. During the executive session, the Director Defendants confirmed their decision to remove and replace Klaassen. They then recalled Messrs. Ducanes and Janik, and informed them that Mr. Hood would be replacing Klaassen as CEO. Thereafter, Klaassen returned to the meeting, at which point Mr. Pehl informed Klaassen that the Board was removing him as CEO. The Board then voted on the resolution (prepared by Baker Botts) that removed Klaassen and appointed Hood as interim CEO, with the Director Defendants voting in favor and Klaassen abstaining.

After his removal as CEO, Klaassen initially offered to help Mr. Hood learn about the industry and Allegro's operations. In early to mid-November 2012, Klaassen also began negotiating the terms of a consulting agreement, under which he would serve as an "Executive Consultant" to Allegro, reporting to Allegro's CEO. The draft consulting agreement expressly precluded Klaassen from holding himself out to third parties as an Allegro employee or agent. In early December 2012, Klaassen communicated to Mr. Simpkins, that he (Klaassen), in his capacity as a director and common shareholder, would hold Hood "accountable" as CEO for Allegro's performance, and that if Allegro's performance did not improve, the "management change should be judged a failure."

At a Board meeting held in early December, Klaassen raised the issue of Hood's continued membership on the audit committee, given the bylaw requirement that Allegro employees could not serve on the audit committee. Thereafter, Klaassen circulated a written consent that would remove Hood from the audit committee and appoint Klaassen to the audit and compensation committees. On December 29, 2012, all five directors executed a revised written consent removing Mr. Hood from the audit committee and appointing Klaassen to the audit and compensation committees. As a member of the compensation committee, Klaassen provided feedback on Mr. Hood's employment agreement, and also participated in vetting candidates for Hood's future management team.

In late 2012, Klaassen began expressing displeasure about his termination as CEO. In an email Hood sent in late November 2012, Hood remarked that "Eldon has not accepted his fate." On November 29, 2012, Klaassen emailed Exxon-Mobil (a major Allegro client), informing Exxon that Allegro was in the midst of a "bitter" shareholder dispute and that the company had become "dysfunctional." Klaassen also began hosting events for Allegro employees, at which he criticized Allegro management and spread rumors of other employee terminations.

On June 5, 2013, Klaassen sent a letter to Messrs. Ducanes, Pehl, and Forlenza, claiming that his (Klaassen's) removal as CEO was invalid. Klaassen also delivered two written consents (in his capacity as majority shareholder) that purported to: (i) remove Messrs. Simpkins and Hood as outside directors; (ii) elect John Brown as the common director; and (iii) elect Dave Stritzinger and Ram Velidi as outside directors.

On June 5, 2013, Klaassen filed an action in the Court of Chancery . . . for a declaration that: (i) Klaassen was the lawful CEO of Allegro; (ii) Messrs. Simpkins and Hood had been effectively removed as Allegro directors; and that (iii) Messrs. Brown, Stritzinger and Velidi had been validly elected as Allegro directors. Klaassen challenged his removal as CEO on two separate grounds. First, he claimed that a majority of the Director Defendants had breached their fiduciary duty of loyalty by firing him. Second, Klaassen claimed that his November 1, 2012 termination was invalid, because the Director Defendants did not give him advance notice of (and employed deception in carrying out) their plan to terminate him before holding the November 1 Board meeting . . . .

[The Court of Chancery held] that because Klaassen's challenge to his removal as CEO was grounded in equity, that challenge was subject to the Director Defendants' equitable defenses. The court further found that Klaassen's challenge was barred by the equitable doctrines of laches and acquiescence. Finally, the court determined that Klaassen had validly removed Mr. Simpkins and had validly elected Mr. Brown, but that his removal of Mr. Hood and the election of Messrs. Stritzinger and Velidi were legally invalid.

On October 23, 2013 Klaassen appealed to this Court from that judgment, and moved for expedited scheduling, which this Court granted on October 24, 2013. On November 7, 2013, the Court of Chancery issued a "Status Quo Opinion," continuing in effect part of the pre-trial status quo order in force during the pendency of the Chancery litigation . . . .

Klaassen claims [here] that the Board action removing him as CEO at the November 1 meeting was invalid, because the Director Defendants employed deceptive tactics — namely, offering false reasons for rescheduling that meeting, and providing a false explanation for Mr. Ducanes' presence at that meeting. Our courts do not approve the use of deception as a means by which to conduct a Delaware corporation's affairs, and nothing in this Opinion should be read to suggest otherwise. Here, however, we need not address the merits of Klaassen's deception claim, because we find, as did the Court of Chancery, that Klaassen acquiesced in his removal as CEO.

Klaassen challenges his removal as a violation of "generally accepted notions of fairness." A claim of that kind is equitable in character. A fundamental principle of our law is that "he who seeks equity must do equity." Consequently, a plaintiff's equitable claim against a defendant may be defeated, in a proper case, by the plaintiff's inequitable conduct towards that defendant. It follows that board action taken in violation of equitable principles is voidable, not void, because "[o]nly voidable acts are susceptible to . . . equitable defenses." . . .

Finally, having determined that Klaassen's deception claim is voidable and properly subject to equitable defenses, we address whether the Court of Chancery correctly found that Klaassen's claim was barred by the doctrine of acquiescence. We conclude that the court correctly so found. A claimant is deemed to have acquiesced in a complained-of act where he: has full knowledge of his rights and the material facts and (1) remains inactive for a considerable time; or (2) freely does what amounts to recognition of the complained of act; or (3) acts in a manner inconsistent with the subsequent repudiation, which leads the other party to believe the act has been approved. For the defense of acquiescence to apply, conscious intent to approve the act is not required, nor is a change of position or resulting prejudice.

Klaassen does not claim that he lacked full knowledge of either his rights or the material facts. Accordingly, the narrow question is whether Klaassen's conduct amounted, in the eyes of the law, to recognition and acceptance of his removal as Allegro's CEO. We hold that it did . . . . Whatever may have been Klaassen's subjective intent, his conduct objectively evidenced that he recognized and accepted the fact that he was no longer Allegro's CEO . . . .

For the foregoing reasons, the Court of Chancery judgment is affirmed.

Questions and Comments

1. Can you see why Klaassen may have acted in a high-handed and preemptory way in managing the company? He was the founder and, for nearly 20 years, the unchallenged leader of the firm. Once the outside investors came in, he had to take their interests into account — something that he seemed unwilling or unable to do. Perhaps, also, Klaassen had an unjustified confidence in his own invulnerability. It appears that as the owner of a majority of the common stock, he had the power to

elect two of the five directors; and he appears to have been entitled to a board position for himself as CEO. He may have thought that he had three reliable votes in hand, and therefore didn't need to cater to the outside investors who controlled only two board seats.

2. Although it appears that the board of directors did make some efforts to address the issue of Klaassen's management problems, these gestures seem to have rather sporadic and ineffectual. Did the board do enough to address the problems with Klaassen's management style before the issues got out of hand?

3. To whom did the board members owe a fiduciary duty?

4. Klaassen challenged his removal from office on the ground that the board acted deceptively — by not informing him of the real agenda of the directors' meeting and offering a false pretense for why the general counsel had to be at the meeting, when the real reason was that the general counsel's presence was necessary to make Klaassen's removal immediately effective. Justice Jacobs acknowledges that such deception is generally disfavored under Delaware law: "Our courts do not approve the use of deception as a means by which to conduct a Delaware corporation's affairs, and nothing in this Opinion should be read to suggest otherwise." But because it finds that Klaassen initially acquiesced in his removal, it didn't need to decide whether the deception would be a basis for overturning the board's decision. How do you think the court would have ruled if it had been required to reach this issue?

5. Can you see why the board employed the deception? One of the director defendants testified that "if we told him we were terminating [him], that would give him an opportunity to take actions in the company that could be detrimental to the company. The last thing we wanted was an irate CEO with access to code, with access to cash and most importantly with access to employees to poison the well for the change that was coming." Was this a valid reason?

6. Klaassen's actions, once he decided to fight his ouster, suggest another reason for the board's decision to act surreptitiously. Claiming that he had been improperly removed, he filed documents purporting, in his capacity as CEO, to remove the remaining two independent directors and replace them with his own nominees — an action that, if successful, would have placed him in the position to regain control over the company. These actions failed, but had he done the same thing before the board removed him from office, the outcome could have been different. Why didn't the defendants acknowledge that this was an important reason for the secrecy?

7. In retrospect, did Klaassen make a tactical error when he purported to go along with his termination? What would have happened if he had rejected the decision from the start?

H. COMPENSATION COMMITTEES

Compensation of decision makers in firms — senior executives and boards of directors — is a central task of governance. But what does it have to do with the other topics of this book, compliance and risk management? Those topics concern what boards and managers do, not how much they are paid. In fact, the topics are closely connected.

1. General Considerations

Over the past decades, executive compensation has risen to the forefront of the corporate governance debate. The enhanced focus on compensation is due to a confluence of factors, including the following:

- Some companies paid what appears — to the general public at least — to be ludicrously high compensation to senior managers. Outrage at perceived excesses became widespread. The situation was not improved by the corporate scandals of the 1990s and early 2000s. Epitomizing the excesses of that era was the figure of Dennis Kozlowski, former chair and CEO of Tyco International, whose extravagant ways became the stuff of legend (he reportedly had Tyco pay $1 million toward the cost of a birthday party for his wife, which featured a private concert by Jimmy Buffett and an ice sculpture of Michelangelo's David urinating vodka).

- The financial crisis of 2007-2009 convinced many that corporate chief executive officers were not all they had been cracked up to be. Was Kenneth Lewis, the former chairman and chief executive officer of Bank of America, worth the $20 million he received in 2007, given that his business strategy led to a near-collapse of the company over the next few years? In light of subsequent events, critics might argue he was overpaid.

- Shareholder activists have become much more powerful in recent years, and a principal focus of their activism has been a campaign to curb excessive compensation of corporate managers.

Questions and Comments

1. Did CEO compensation really get out of hand over the past decades? One study found that during the period 1934 through 1938, during the depths of the Great Depression, the average salary and bonus for CEOs of leading companies on the New York Stock Exchange was $882,000 (in 1988 dollars), compared with $843,000 for 1982 through 1988. *Plus ça change, plus c'est la même chose?*

2. How much is an executive worth? Few would dispute that the chief executive officer can have an impact on a company's fortunes. When Steve Jobs returned to Apple in 1996, it was in a perilous financial condition; under his leadership and inspired sense of product development, he grew the business into one of the most valuable companies in the world. What about Warren Buffett of Berkshire Hathaway? Many credit Buffett for being the most brilliant investor of all time — skills that are reflected in the spectacular run-up of Berkshire Hathaway stock over many years. These executives were arguably worth far more than they were paid (even though both Jobs and Buffett became rich as a result of increases in the value of their companies' stock).

3. On the other hand, not all chief executives are as talented as Buffett and Jobs. Some can be affirmatively harmful. A few have even wound up as guests of the federal government after being convicted of crimes committed while in office; Bernard Ebbers of WorldCom, Dennis Kozlowski of Tyco International, and Charles Keating of Lincoln Savings & Loan come to mind.

4. Ideally, great executives like Jobs and Buffett should be paid a lot (or at least enough to keep them on the job); less able executives should be paid less; and executives such as Ebbers, Kozlowski, and Keating should never be appointed.

The problem is that it is difficult to tell a good CEO from a bad one just by looking at them. Impressive appearances can mask poor judgment, incompetence, or dishonesty. Even after the results are in, it is not always possible to tell the good from the bad: Bad CEOs get lucky and good CEOs are blamed for events beyond their control.

5. Are CEOs as valuable as sports stars? Successful athletes earn prizes, salaries, and endorsements. According to Forbes Magazine, boxer Floyd Mayweather earned $85 million between June 1011 and June 2012; golfer Tiger Woods was third with $59 million. The highest paid team athlete was basketball player LeBron James ($55 million). What about entertainment figures? According to Forbes, Oprah Winfrey earned $165 million between May 2011 and May 2012; film director Michael Bay of "The Transformers" earned an estimated $160 million.

6. What sorts of compensation would encourage an executive to manage the company in too risky a fashion? What sorts of compensation would discourage an executive from doing so?

2. Structure and Function

One obvious problem with CEO compensation is that of the "fox guarding the henhouse." Although the decision on how much to pay the CEO is officially reserved for the board of directors, this allocation of responsibility may be a smokescreen when the CEO dominates the board. Essentially, in such a case, the CEO is asked to set her own compensation — not necessarily a good state of affairs. Accordingly, policymakers have sought means to insulate the compensation decision from the self-interest of the managers who may be receiving the benefits. One of the principal mechanisms for enhancing the independence of the compensation function is to establish compensation committees staffed by independent directors.

Board-level compensation committees are ubiquitous in large companies. Such committees are mandated by listing standards of the national securities exchanges. *See, e.g.*, New York Stock Exchange Listed Company Manual §303A.05. Listing standards as well as the Dodd-Frank Act require that the compensation committees so established must be composed of independent directors.

How does a compensation committee do its job? Usually, these committees function within the "black box" of the firm, so that it is impossible to observe their performance from without. The following excerpt, however, reveals something of how the compensation committee functioned at the Walt Disney Company in the 1990s. References to this case seem to spark an irrepressible desire to make bad puns (judicial opinions are full of them); we will content ourselves with asking whether you feel that the compensation committee's activities in connection with Michael Ovitz's employment agreement were "Mickey Mouse."

In re The Walt Disney Company Derivative Litigation

906 A.2d 27 (Del. 1998)

Jacobs, Justice:

In August 1995, Michael Ovitz ("Ovitz") and The Walt Disney Company ("Disney" or the "Company") entered into an employment agreement under which

Ovitz would serve as President of Disney for five years. In December 1996, only fourteen months after he commenced employment, Ovitz was terminated without cause, resulting in a severance payout to Ovitz valued at approximately $130 million. . . . .

In 1994 Disney lost in a tragic helicopter crash its President and Chief Operating Officer, Frank Wells, who together with Michael Eisner, Disney's Chairman and Chief Executive Officer, had enjoyed remarkable success at the Company's helm. Eisner temporarily assumed Disney's presidency, but only three months later, heart disease required Eisner to undergo quadruple bypass surgery. Those two events persuaded Eisner and Disney's board of directors that the time had come to identify a successor to Eisner.

Eisner's prime candidate for the position was Michael Ovitz, who was the leading partner and one of the founders of Creative Artists Agency ("CAA"), the premier talent agency whose business model had reshaped the entire industry. By 1995, CAA had 550 employees and a roster of about 1400 of Hollywood's top actors, directors, writers, and musicians. That roster generated about $150 million in annual revenues and an annual income of over $20 million for Ovitz, who was regarded as one of the most powerful figures in Hollywood.

Eisner and Ovitz had enjoyed a social and professional relationship that spanned nearly 25 years. Although in the past the two men had casually discussed possibly working together, in 1995, when Ovitz began negotiations to leave CAA and join Music Corporation of America ("MCA"), Eisner became seriously interested in recruiting Ovitz to join Disney. Eisner shared that desire with Disney's board members on an individual basis. . . .

Eisner and Irwin Russell, who was a Disney director and chairman of the compensation committee, first approached Ovitz about joining Disney. Their initial negotiations were unproductive, however, because at that time MCA had made Ovitz an offer that Disney could not match. The MCA-Ovitz negotiations eventually fell apart, and Ovitz returned to CAA in mid-1995. Business continued as usual, until Ovitz discovered that Ron Meyer, his close friend and the number two executive at CAA, was leaving CAA to join MCA. That news devastated Ovitz, who concluded that to remain with the company he and Meyer had built together was no longer palatable. At that point Ovitz became receptive to the idea of joining Disney. Eisner learned of these developments and re-commenced negotiations with Ovitz in earnest. By mid-July 1995, those negotiations were in full swing.

Both Russell and Eisner negotiated with Ovitz, over separate issues and concerns. From his talks with Eisner, Ovitz gathered that Disney needed his skills and experience to remedy Disney's current weaknesses, which Ovitz identified as poor talent relationships and stagnant foreign growth. Seeking assurances from Eisner that Ovitz's vision for Disney was shared, at some point during the negotiations Ovitz came to believe that he and Eisner would run Disney, and would work together in a relation akin to that of junior and senior partner. Unfortunately, Ovitz's belief was mistaken, as Eisner had a radically different view of what their respective roles at Disney should be.

Russell assumed the lead in negotiating the financial terms of the Ovitz employment contract. In the course of negotiations, Russell learned from Ovitz's attorney, Bob Goldman, that Ovitz owned 55% of CAA and earned approximately $20 to $25 million a year from that company. From the beginning Ovitz made it clear that he would not give up his 55% interest in CAA without "downside protection."

Considerable negotiation then ensued over downside protection issues. During the summer of 1995, the parties agreed to a draft version of Ovitz's employment agreement (the "OEA") modeled after Eisner's and the late Mr. Wells' employment contracts. . . .

To assist in evaluating the financial terms of the OEA, Russell recruited Graef Crystal, an executive compensation consultant, and Raymond Watson, a member of Disney's compensation committee and a past Disney board chairman who had helped structure Wells' and Eisner's compensation packages. Before the three met, Crystal prepared a comprehensive executive compensation database to accept various inputs and to conduct Black-Scholes analyses to output a range of values for the options. Watson also prepared similar computations on spreadsheets, but without using the Black-Scholes method. [The Black-Scholes method is a formula for option valuation that is widely used and accepted in the industry and by regulators.]

On August 10, Russell, Watson and Crystal met. They discussed and generated a set of values using different and various inputs and assumptions, accounting for different numbers of options, vesting periods, and potential proceeds of option exercises at various times and prices. After discussing their conclusions, they agreed that Crystal would memorialize his findings and fax them to Russell. Two days later, Crystal faxed to Russell a memorandum concluding that the OEA would provide Ovitz with approximately $23.6 million per year for the first five years, or $23.9 million a year over seven years if Ovitz exercised a two-year renewal option. Those sums, Crystal opined, would approximate Ovitz's current annual compensation at CAA.

During a telephone conference that same evening, Russell, Watson and Crystal discussed Crystal's memorandum and its assumptions. Their discussion generated additional questions that prompted Russell to ask Crystal to revise his memorandum to resolve certain ambiguities in the current draft of the employment agreement. . . . Up to that point, only three Disney directors — Eisner, Russell and Watson — knew the status of the negotiations with Ovitz and the terms of the draft OEA.

While Russell, Watson and Crystal were finalizing their analysis of the OEA, Eisner and Ovitz reached a separate agreement. Eisner told Ovitz that: (1) the number of options would be reduced from a single grant of five million to two separate grants, the first being three million options for the first five years and the second consisting of two million more options if the contract was renewed; and (2) Ovitz would join Disney only as President, not as a co-CEO with Eisner. After deliberating, Ovitz accepted those terms, and that evening Ovitz, Eisner, Sid Bass [one of Disney's largest individual shareholders] and their families celebrated Ovitz's decision to join Disney.

Unfortunately, the celebratory mood was premature. The next day, August 13, Eisner met with Ovitz, Russell, Sanford Litvack (Executive Vice President and Disney's General Counsel), and Stephen Bollenbach (Disney's Chief Financial Officer) to discuss the decision to hire Ovitz. Litvack and Bollenbach were unhappy with that decision, and voiced concerns that Ovitz would disrupt the cohesion that existed between Eisner, Litvack and Bollenbach. Litvack and Bollenbach were emphatic that they would not report to Ovitz, but would continue to report to Eisner. Despite Ovitz's concern about his "shrinking authority" as Disney's future President, Eisner was able to provide sufficient reassurance so that ultimately Ovitz acceded to Litvack's and Bollenbach's terms.

On August 14, Eisner and Ovitz signed a letter agreement (the "OLA"), which outlined the basic terms of Ovitz's employment, and stated that the agreement (which would ultimately be embodied in a formal contract) was subject to approval by Disney's compensation committee and board of directors. Russell called Sidney Poitier, a Disney director and compensation committee member, to inform Poitier of the OLA and its terms. Poitier believed that hiring Ovitz was a good idea because of Ovitz's reputation and experience. Watson called Ignacio Lozano, another Disney director and compensation committee member, who felt that Ovitz would successfully adapt from a private company environment to Disney's public company culture. Eisner also contacted each of the other board members by phone to inform them of the impending new hire, and to explain his friendship with Ovitz and Ovitz's qualifications.

That same day, a press release made the news of Ovitz's hiring public. The reaction was extremely positive: Disney was applauded for the decision, and Disney's stock price rose 4.4% in a single day, thereby increasing Disney's market capitalization by over $1 billion.

[The final proposed Ovitz employment agreement had the following terms regarding the consequences if Ovitz were to leave the company: If Disney terminated Ovitz's employment without good cause or if Ovitz resigned from Disney with the consent of the Company (referred to in the Employment Agreement as a "Non-Fault Termination"), three million of Ovitz's options would vest immediately upon his separation from the Company, and Ovitz would be entitled to wait until the later of September 30, 2002, or 24 months after the date of separation to exercise these options. The Employment Agreement also provided for Ovitz to receive a lump sum payment of $10 million if he were terminated without cause prior to September 30, 2002. In addition, if Ovitz were terminated without cause, he would receive an additional payment equal to the present value of the remaining salary payments due under the Agreement through September 30, 2000, as well as the product of $7.5 million times the number of fiscal years remaining under the Agreement (i.e., Ovitz's approximate forgone bonuses).

[Once the terms of the proposed Ovitz agreement were finalized, the matter was presented to the compensation committee for approval. The committee consisted of the following members:

[Ignacio Lozano: publisher and editor of La Opinión, a Spanish language newspaper based in Los Angeles, and former United States Ambassador to El Salvador.

[Sydney Poitier: actor and movie director, winner of an Academy Award for Best Actor, and Bahamian ambassador to Japan.

[Irwin Russell, Chairman: entertainment lawyer, entrepreneur, and graduate of the Harvard Law School.

[Raymond Watson: architect and urban planner in Orange County, California.]

On September 26, 1995, the Disney compensation committee . . . met for one hour to consider, among other agenda items, the proposed terms of the OEA. A term sheet was distributed at the meeting, although a draft of the OEA was not. The topics discussed were historical comparables, such as Eisner's and Wells' option grants, and also the factors that Russell, Watson and Crystal had considered in setting the size of the option grants and the termination provisions of the contract. Watson testified that he provided the compensation committee with the spreadsheet analysis that he had performed in August, and discussed his findings with the committee. Crystal did not attend the meeting, although he was available by telephone to respond to questions if needed, but no one from the committee called. After Russell's and Watson's presentations, Litvack also responded to substantive questions. At trial Poitier and Lozano testified that they believed they had received sufficient information from Russell's and Watson's presentations to exercise their judgment in the best interests of the Company. The committee voted unanimously to approve the OEA terms, subject to "reasonable further negotiations within the framework of the terms and conditions" described in the OEA.

Immediately after the compensation committee meeting, the Disney board met in executive session. The board was told about the reporting structure to which Ovitz had agreed, but the initial negative reaction of Litvack and Bollenbach to the hiring was not recounted. Eisner led the discussion relating to Ovitz, and Watson then explained his analysis, and both Watson and Russell responded to questions from the board. After further deliberation, the board voted unanimously to elect Ovitz as President. . . .

Ovitz's tenure as President of the Walt Disney Company officially began on October 1, 1995, the date that the OEA was executed. When Ovitz took office, the initial reaction was optimistic, and Ovitz did make some positive contributions while serving as President of the Company. By the fall of 1996, however, it had become clear that Ovitz was "a poor fit with his fellow executives." By then the Disney directors were discussing that the disconnect between Ovitz and the Company was likely irreparable and that Ovitz would have to be terminated. . . .

By [November 25, 1996] the board knew Ovitz was going to be fired, yet the only action recorded in the minutes concerning Ovitz was his re-nomination to a new three-year term on the board. Although that action was somewhat bizarre given the circumstances, Stanley Gold, a Disney director, testified that because Ovitz was present at that meeting, it would have been a "public hanging" not to re-nominate him. An executive session took place after the board meeting, from which Ovitz was excluded. At that session, Eisner informed the directors who were present that he intended to fire Ovitz by year's end, and that he had asked Gary Wilson, a board member and friend of Ovitz, to speak with Ovitz while Wilson and Ovitz were together on vacation during the upcoming Thanksgiving holiday.

Shortly after the November 25 board meeting and executive session, the Ovitz and Wilson families left on their yacht for a Thanksgiving trip to the British Virgin Islands. Ovitz hoped that if he could manage to survive at Disney until Christmas, he could fix everything with Disney and make his problems go away. Wilson quickly dispelled that illusion, informing Ovitz that Eisner wanted Ovitz out of the Company. At that point Ovitz first began to realize how serious his situation at Disney had become. Reporting back his conversation with Ovitz, Wilson told Eisner that Ovitz was a "loyal friend and devastating enemy," and he advised Eisner to "be reasonable and magnanimous, both financially and publicly, so Ovitz could save face."

After returning from the Thanksgiving trip, Ovitz met with Eisner on December 3, [1996] to discuss his termination. Ovitz asked for several concessions, all of which Eisner ultimately rejected. Eisner told Ovitz that all he would receive was what he had contracted for in the OEA. . . . On December 11, Eisner met with Ovitz to agree on the wording of a press release to announce the termination, and to inform Ovitz that he would not receive any of the additional items that he requested. By that time it had already been decided that Ovitz would be terminated without cause and that he would receive his contractual NFT payment, but nothing more. Eisner and Ovitz agreed that neither Ovitz nor Disney would disparage each other in the press, and that the separation was to be undertaken with dignity and respect for both sides. After his December 11 meeting with Eisner, Ovitz never returned to Disney.

Questions and Comments

1. Ovitz worked at Disney for approximately 14 months. Although he arrived with good intentions, his relationships with other senior managers at Disney were rocky from the start and only deteriorated over time. Some have conjectured that the reason for the failure was that Ovitz never was given the power he believed he had been promised: Eisner didn't show any signs of retiring and other senior executives refused to be displaced. Others speculate that the problem had to do with the fact that Ovitz was unfamiliar with the norms and practices of managers at a public company. What does appear obvious is that his personality clashed with Disney's corporate culture, and that overall his tenure at the firm was unsuccessful and disruptive.

2. This case concerns the compensation due to Ovitz under his employment agreement after he was terminated. Although Disney might have claimed that his termination was for cause, the company refrained from making this argument. In consequence, Ovitz was due to the compensation promised under his employment agreement for non-cause termination — which, when added up, came to approximately $130 million.

3. What do you think of the qualifications of the compensation committee? They were no doubt distinguished people, but did any of them have financial expertise? Given the importance of executive compensation to the financial success of the company, did it make sense to staff the committee with a lawyer, an architect, a publisher, and an actor?

4. Plaintiffs in the excerpted case argued that two of the four members of the compensation committee were not independent. Russell served as Eisner's personal counsel and had a long history of personal and business ties to Eisner; his law office was listed as the mailing address for Eisner's primary residence; he was the registered agent for several entities in which Eisner was involved; and he represented Eisner in connection with Eisner's negotiation of his compensation agreement with Disney. Plaintiffs alleged that Russell practiced in a small firm for which the fees derived from Eisner represented a large portion of the total fees received. Given these connections, should Russell have served on a committee charged with setting the compensation for Eisner's hand-picked lieutenant?

5. As to Poitier, the allegation was that he was a longtime client of Creative Artists Agency — the talent agency that Ovitz founded. Even though Ovitz was proposing to leave Hollywood, he wasn't leaving the entertainment world. Did Poitier have an interest in pleasing Ovitz with respect to his compensation at Disney?

6. Did the compensation committee make an informed decision about the Ovitz compensation package? How could they give reasoned attention to this matter given that Ovitz's appointment had already been publicly announced — and that the other members of the board were waiting in another room, prepared to bless the transaction at the conclusion of the compensation committee meeting? Realistically, did the compensation committee have any choice but to go along?

7. The committee didn't have a copy of the compensation package before them—just a term sheet. A consultant was available by telephone, but no one called. It appears that the committee was never provided with the key information about Ovitz's termination package—namely that if he was fired after a year, he would walk away with as much as $130 million. Did the committee have enough information on which to make an informed decision?

8. Did the committee engage in sufficient deliberation? Their meeting lasted only an hour; and the committee had other business in addition to Ovitz's employment contract. Is less than an hour sufficient time for a board committee to consider a matter so fundamental to the welfare of the company?

9. The excerpted case illustrates a challenge facing compensation committees in the context of hiring senior managers from outside. Once a manager is on board, her compensation can be based on factors such as performance on the job and "comparables" received by officers of other companies who serve in similar positions. When a senior manager is being *hired*, however, those factors cannot be brought to bear in the same manner. As to performance, the candidate can only be judged on the basis of how they performed in jobs at other companies. Disney's compensation committee could not evaluate how Ovitz performed at Disney; they could only look to his record at the talent agency he headed. Good performance in one job does not necessarily translate into good performance in a new and different job—as apparently turned out to be the case with Ovitz.

10. As to comparables, the compensation committee could (and purportedly did) examine how much people at other firms were making in jobs similar to the one contemplated for Ovitz. But this information was not very useful, for two reasons. At the same time Ovitz's compensation was being negotiated by Russell, his job description was also changing as a result of negotiations with Eisner. Ovitz's authority was downgraded: He would not, as originally contemplated, be co-CEO, but only president; and other senior executives would report directly to Eisner rather than through Ovitz. The compensation decision, which was progressing on a different track, did not take account of Ovitz's reduced responsibilities. The second reason that comparables are not fully reliable for hiring decisions is that, once a candidate for a position has been identified, the objective is to persuade that person to join the company. When the decision has already been made to hire someone, whatever the cost, as was arguably the case with Ovitz, the baseline for compensation becomes what the person is making at her current position rather than what people make who are in similar positions to the one for which the candidate is being recruited. In Ovitz's case, these were different, simply because Ovitz was working in a different job in a different segment of the industry. Disney's compensation negotiations focused, not on what others were making in positions similar to the one for which Ovitz was being hired, but rather what Ovitz was making at his talent agency. That amount was huge—approximately $25 million a year.

11. In parts of the case not excerpted above, the Delaware Supreme Court upheld the Chancellor's decision that the Disney board of directors, including its compensation committee, had not acted in bad faith, had not wasted corporate assets, and did not violate their duty of care to the company. Do you agree?

3. Consultants

Disney's compensation committee had access to (but did not use) the advice of a compensation consultant, Graef Crystal, who had also been involved in the preliminary negotiations of Ovitz's compensation package. Nearly every large company today uses compensation consultants to advise them on the right way to pay senior executives. The Dodd-Frank Act and SEC regulations implicitly encourage firms to employ consultants, by requiring that the compensation committee be authorized to employ such consultants "in its sole discretion" and mandating that the issuer provide "appropriate funding," as determined by the compensation committee, for payment of these service providers.

Compensation consultants offer three potential benefits to the firms they advise. First, they provide expertise on laws and practices. Second, they have an extensive database of non-public information about compensation practices, which allows them to compare proposed compensation packages with those of other similar firms. Third, compensation consultants offer protection against attack: A company can answer critics of its executive pay practices by stating that the policies and amounts were determined with the help of an independent compensation consultant.

Despite the benefits, compensation consultants have come under criticism. The problem is that they are paid by their clients, and their clients may be under the control of the very executives whose salaries and benefits they are evaluating. They therefore have an incentive to provide a justification for inflated pay packages in order to get work in the future. The problem is particularly severe when the compensation consultant not only advises on executive compensation packages but also provides other services to the client. When the income for related services is a large part of the compensation consultant's remuneration, they have an incentive to cater to the executives who decide whether to award these contracts. Compensation consultants adamantly deny, however, that their advice is infected by any conflicts of interest.

Should compensation consultants be required to be "independent"? On the one hand, the case for independence seems overwhelming: If the compensation consultant has ties with the executive under review, or other connections that might impair the consultant's independent judgment, the result of her analysis might be skewed to the disadvantage of the firm that hires her. Given that compensation committees are entitled to rely on the expertise of the compensation consultant, the danger of non-independent consultants seems significant. On the other hand, since the compensation committee must be independent, they can (in theory) act as a check on potential consultant bias. Further, formulating independence standards for compensation consultants can be tricky because they typically provide services and receive fees from many companies. Standards for independence should not be so strict as to stamp out effective competition in the industry or unfairly favor some consultants (e.g., "boutique" firms) over others (e.g., large, multi-service companies).

Compensation consultants for public companies are regulated by §952 of the Dodd-Frank Act and implementing SEC regulations. Neither of these rules imposes formal independence requirements on compensation consultants. Instead, the rules provide a set of factors which the compensation committee must take into account when selecting a consultant. These include: (a) whether the consultant's company provides other services to the company; (b) the amount of fees received from the company by the consultant's company, as a percentage of total revenue; (c) the consultant's company's conflict of interest policies and procedures; (d) business or personal relationships between the consultant and a member of the compensation committee; (e) whether the consultant owns stock in the company; and (f) whether there are business or personal relationships between the consultant and an executive officer of the company. The Dodd-Frank Act requires public companies to disclose whether their compensation committee retained or obtained the advice of a compensation consultant, whether the work of the consultant raised any conflict of interest and, if so, the nature of the conflict and how the conflict is being addressed.

Questions and Comments

1. Do you find the critique of compensation consultants persuasive? For a powerful articulation of the objection, see Lucian Bebchuk & Jesse Fried, *Pay Without Performance: Overview of the Issues*, 20 Acad. Mgmt. Persp. 5 (2006).

2. Do you agree with the decision not to impose formal independence requirements on compensation consultants?

3. Note that three somewhat different concepts of independence are involved in the case of compensation consultants: (a) independence from the client (as measured, for example, by the amount of work that the compensation consultant's company receives from that particular firm); (b) independence from the compensation committee and its members (as measured by the presence or absence of business or personal relationships between the consultant and a member of the committee); and (c) independence from the executive whose compensation is being reviewed (as measured by the presence or absence of business or personal relationships between the consultant and the executive officer). Are the dangers of non-independence the same for these three categories? If different, which form of non-independence is the most worrisome?

4. None of the independence factors identified in the SEC's regulation addresses the biggest potential limitation on the compensation consultant's independence: the fact that the consultant and her company wish to gain a reputation in the industry as a firm that will not create surprises. Is there any way to deal with this issue?

5. In addition to utilizing the services of consultants, compensation committees are authorized to retain independent counsel to assist them in their work. When do you think outside counsel's services might be required?

PROBLEM 2-19

As head of the compensation committee of a public company, you are responsible for selecting a compensation consultant. One of two finalists for the job is Moran & Moran, a two-person boutique headed by James Moran, former chief of research at the Institutional Research Council, a proxy advisory firm. Moran & Moran has only been operating for a year and is hungry for your business. James Moran is recommended to you by your company's chief financial officer, who has developed a high opinion of his capabilities during their time together as board members of the city's opera company. The other finalist is Bigger & Best, a large management consulting firm. Compensation advice is one of many services offered by this latter firm. Bigger & Best has just completed a project advising your company how to position some of its brands in emerging markets. Four junior executives at your company started their careers at Bigger & Best; in your judgment they are some of the most promising officers at the firm. Moran & Moran's bid is about 10 percent below that of Bigger & Best. Which firm should you select?

PROBLEM 2-20

As chair of the compensation committee, you review the recommendations of the compensation consultant regarding the pay package for your chief executive officer and friend, Janice Jain. The proposed compensation package comes to $6 million when all elements are included. The table of comps demonstrates that $6 million is at the median of all CEOs at companies in your industry with gross revenues of at least $1 billion. Your firm has gross revenues of $1.05 billion. You know that Jain wants the $6 million. Is there anything you should be concerned about in the consultant's report? Is there anything you should do?

4. The Role of Shareholders in Compensation

These days the job of a compensation committee is complicated and also enriched by the presence of shareholder input. Traditionally, shareholders were quiescent on the matter of compensation; they voted with management and basically left the issue of how senior executives were paid up to the discretion of those inside the company. No longer. A potent combination of activists, institutional shareholders, and legal changes has significantly altered the balance of power over the issue of executive compensation, trimming the discretion of management and increasing the impact of shareholder voice.

Four provisions in the Dodd-Frank Act are significant:

- Section 953(a), discussed in the previous chapter, requires the SEC to promulgate rules covering the following required disclosures: (a) the relation of executive compensation actually paid and the financial performance of the issuer; (b) the total annual compensation of the chief executive officer; (c) the median annual compensation of all employees of the issuer excluding the chief executive officer; and (d) the ratio of chief executive officer compensation to the median annual compensation of all employees of the issuer excluding the chief executive officer. The SEC promulgated a rule implementing this requirement in September 2013.
- Section 951, also discussed in the previous chapter, imposes a "say-on-pay" requirement for public companies, under which shareholders are given non-binding votes on executive compensation packages.
- Section 954 provides for "clawbacks" — recovery of compensation previously paid to the chief executive officer — in the case of financial restatements.
- Section 956 imposes standards and limitations on executive pay at certain financial institutions.

Questions and Comments

1. Are clawbacks a good idea? Is there a concern that a candidate for the CEO position would be deterred from taking the job because of fear that if things go badly she will face a clawback even though she has done nothing wrong?

2. How should the compensation committee respond when the shareholders have voted "no" on a proposed pay package? The vote is advisory only; the company

need not follow the shareholders' recommendations. What factors might a compensation committee take into account when deciding what to do in the wake of a negative shareholder vote?

PROBLEM 2-21

Shareholders Collective, a proxy advisory firm, approaches your company to discuss executive compensation. Garry Good, the Shareholders Collective associate assigned to your company, announces that in his judgment the chief executive officer of your company is overpaid. He informs you that his firm will recommend a "no" vote on the next say-on-pay resolution unless you trim the sails. On further discussion, he says he will drop the demand for reduced executive compensation if your company agrees to separate the positions of chairman and chief executive officer. As chair of the compensation committee, you believe that your CEO is performing well and is appropriately compensated. You also believe that if Shareholders Collective issues a "no" recommendation, the pay package will pass but only by a slim majority. What should you do?

PROBLEM 2-22

At the last meeting the shareholders approved the chief executive's pay package by a 53 percent vote. You believe that if her pay isn't cut, the shareholders will reject it the next time around. Your CEO, however, refuses to accept any cut. "If the shareholders want to gripe, let them," she says, "it's not binding." She lets you know that if you do cut her pay, she will leave for other opportunities. Your company is in the midst of a major transformation of its product distribution system and you believe that a change at the top at this point would be catastrophic. You also believe that despite her rigidity on pay, the CEO is doing an excellent job and could not easily be replaced. What should you do?

5. Compensation of Independent Directors

What about compensation for independent directors? If the compensation committee sets the policy, then because they are also members of the board of directors they will be determining their own remuneration — a direct conflict of interest. On the other hand, someone has to determine how much they and the other directors earn. In practice, compensation committees rely heavily on compensation consultants in approving their own and their fellow directors' fees.

How much do independent directors make for their services? A 2012 study examined 240 publicly traded companies in the financial services, industrial, retail, and technology sectors. The report found that median annual compensation for a typical independent director ranged from $134,000 for firms in the financial sector to $200,000 for firms in the technology sector. Directors of large companies received about twice as much as directors of small companies. Typical compensation packages for independent directors included a combination of cash, stock awards, and stock options. Frederick W. Cook & Co., 2012 Director Compensation Report.

Should independent directors be compensated for performance? On the one hand, it makes sense to incentivize directors to supervize the management of their organizations effectively. That way they have an interest in attending closely to the issues and intervening more forcefully when the company's executives propose to do things that the independent directors believe are inadvisable. Some empirical research suggests that independent directors are more aggressive when they are compensated by stock options: Turnover of CEOs tends to be more common when directors are compensated in this fashion. On the other hand, performance-based compensation may incentivize independent directors to focus heavily on the company's share price — especially around the time they are allowed to exercise their options. Too intense a focus on share price is not necessarily desirable. Further, independent directors are valued, in part, because of their independence. If their compensation turned on the company's performance, would this compromise their capacity to make well-considered judgments on the company's behalf?

3

Executives

A. INTRODUCTION

The board of directors and the relevant board committees are charged in law and policy with the task of overseeing management of the organization, including managing risk and ensuring that the firm complies with all applicable laws and regulations. Yet, by necessity, the board's oversight must be conducted at a high level of generality. Board members meet only a few times a year—rarely more than once a month and often only once every two months or every quarter year. A few dozen hours of meetings is not enough to direct the affairs of a company at any level of detail. Board members do receive briefing materials that they are expected to review in advance of meetings, but the amount of information is necessarily limited by their capacity to absorb and understand it. Supplying too much information to the board threatens to create information overload, which impairs rather than enhances a board member's ability to make informed judgments.

Accordingly, the board can decide on broad issues of strategy and can oversee the operations of the company at a general level, but board members necessarily rely on the company's senior employees to carry out the practical tasks of management. Further, senior employees are also the board's eyes and ears: Independent board members only see and hear information provided to them by company employees.

The senior executive team as a whole is sometimes referred to as the "management" of a company. This usage can be confusing because, under the law, the board of directors is ultimately responsible for how the company is managed. In practice, however, as we have seen, the vast majority of decisions regarding the company's organization and strategies are made by senior executives rather than the board. The term "management" is an appropriate word for this group of employees.

This chapter examines the function of the management team and of the principal offices and departments that carry out the compliance and risk-management functions in-house: the chief executive officer, chief financial officer, head of

121

internal audit, chief compliance officer, corporate counsel, chief risk officer, and director of human resources.

Questions and Comments

1. These offices are headed, often, by someone with a "chief" in their title. The people holding the title "chief," and others with jobs of similar seniority, are sometimes referred to collectively as the "C-Suite."

2. Corporate governance these days has been chief-heavy: a form of title inflation. Companies employ all sorts of chief officers in addition to the ones just mentioned — e.g., chief technology officer, chief innovation officer, chief shareholder relations officer, and so on — and the list seems to expand every year.

3. Is it healthy, in terms of corporate governance, to increase the number of executives with reporting lines to the chief executive officer? At some point are there too many chiefs? How should a company decide what functions are important enough to warrant elevating the responsible officer to the C-Suite?

4. The offices and executive positions we will discuss in this chapter each deal, in different ways, with the problem of internal control. How is the responsibility allocated, and who has ultimate authority for a particular function or risk? As we will see, different firms answer these questions in different ways. The lack of consistency in this area, however, can leave outside observers guessing about how the company manages its internal control operations. The United Kingdom has addressed this problem in the case of financial institutions. Banks must maintain and disclose a "management responsibilities map" describing how control functions are allocated across the firm, outlining reporting lines and lines of responsibility, and providing detailed information about senior managers and their responsibilities. *See* Bank of England Prudential Regulation Authority, Strengthening Accountability in Banking: A New Regulatory Framework (July 2014). Should similar legislation be enacted in the United States? Should it apply to public companies generally? If such legislation were to be adopted, would it impact how companies manage their internal control responsibilities?

5. For analysis of the role of the C-Suite in compliance matters, see Michael D. Greenberg, Culture, Compliance and the C-Suite: How Executives, Boards, and Policymakers Can Better Safeguard Against Misconduct at the Top (Rand 2013).

B. THE MANAGEMENT TEAM

We start with the responsibilities of the management team as a whole. In the case of publicly traded firms, one of the management team's most important compliance responsibilities is contained in §404(a) of the Sarbanes-Oxley Act (SOX) — the corporate governance statute enacted in 2002 in the wake of Enron and other scandals. Section 404(a) requires that a reporting company's annual report must contain an "internal control report" which states "the responsibility of management for establishing and maintaining an adequate internal control structure and procedures for financial reporting." The report must also "contain an assessment . . . of the effectiveness of the internal control structure and procedures of the issuer for financial reporting." Fleshing out the congressional requirement, the SEC requires reporting firms to "maintain disclosure controls and procedures" and "internal control over financial reporting." *See* 17 C.F.R. §240.13a-15(a).

For purposes of the SEC's rules, "disclosure controls or procedures" are controls and procedures that are "designed to ensure that information required to be disclosed [under the securities laws] is recorded, processed, summarized and reported" within the [specified] time periods. Included are controls and procedures designed to ensure that the necessary information "is accumulated and communicated to the issuer's management, including its principal executive and principal financial officers, or persons performing similar functions, as appropriate to allow timely decisions regarding required disclosure." Id. §240.13a-15(e). In other words, there must be mechanisms in place to ensure that all necessary information is communicated to the people who make the key decisions.

An "internal control over financial reporting" is "a process designed by, or under the supervision of, the issuer's principal executive and principal financial officers, or persons performing similar functions, and effected by the issuer's board of directors, management and other personnel, to provide reasonable assurance regarding the reliability of financial reporting and the preparation of financial statements for external purposes in accordance with generally accepted accounting principles. Internal controls include those policies and procedures that: (1) pertain to the maintenance of records that in reasonable detail accurately and fairly reflect the transactions and dispositions of the assets of the issuer; (2) provide reasonable assurance that transactions are recorded as necessary to permit preparation of financial statements in accordance with generally accepted accounting principles, and that receipts and expenditures of the issuer are being made only in accordance with authorizations of management and directors of the issuer; and (3) provide reasonable assurance regarding prevention or timely detection of unauthorized acquisition, use or disposition of the issuer's assets that could have a material effect on the financial statements." Id. §240.13a-15(f).

Management is required to base its assessment of the effectiveness of internal control over financial reporting on a "suitable, recognized control framework established by a body of experts that followed due-process procedures, including the broad distribution of the framework for public comment." Id. §240.13a-15(c). The SEC does not require management to use any particular control framework but has indicated that to be considered suitable, a framework must be free from bias; must permit reasonably consistent qualitative and quantitative measurements of a company's internal control over financial reporting; must be sufficiently complete so that relevant factors are not omitted; and must be relevant to an evaluation of internal control over financial reporting. The SEC has issued interpretive guidance to aid management in designing an appropriate evaluation framework. *See* SEC Release No. 34-55929. Firms often use the "Integrated Framework" for internal control established by the Committee of Sponsoring Organizations of the Treadway Commission (COSO). A 2013 COSO revision to this framework identifies five components of internal control: (1) control environment; (2) risk assessment; (3) control activities; (4) information and communication; and (5) monitoring activities. These components are fleshed out in 17 "principles" (for example, in the case of the control environment: "commitment to integrity and ethical values," "oversight responsibility," "commitment to competence," and "accountability").

Questions and Comments

1. The requirements of §404(a) may seem simple, but in fact they are complex, demanding, and potentially expensive. Opponents claimed that the compliance costs for this section alone would exceed the cost of complying with the rest of the statute combined, and would be unaffordable for many small and mid-sized companies. In the years since §404(a) became effective, many researchers have attempted to assess the validity of these claims.

"Event studies," which examine the effect of a change on a company's stock price, reach ambiguous conclusions about whether SOX adversely impacted the market's assessment of firm value; those that find an effect generally conclude that the losses in value were concentrated on smaller firms. Other studies have examined decisions by firms to "go dark" — that is, to cease to be public companies. It appears that a substantial number of smaller firms did exit the public market in the wake of SOX, but the effect of the statute on these decisions is hard to disentangle from broader market conditions; the rate of exit also slowed after a few years.

Overall it appears that SOX probably did increase compliance costs, especially for smaller firms — a result that is hardly surprising given that the statute creates a new and demanding obligation requiring the services of highly compensated public accounting firms. The size of the effect is less clear, however. Moreover, note that a conclusion that SOX increased compliance costs is not tantamount to a criticism of the statute from the standpoint of public policy. Most new regulations increase compliance costs; the question is whether the increased costs are worth it in terms of the public benefit conferred.

2. Do you think §404(a) is a constructive and socially beneficial requirement, even if it does increase compliance costs? Does it go far enough?

3. Section 404(b) of the Sarbanes-Oxley Act requires that public company auditors must attest to and report on the management's assessment of the effectiveness of the company's internal control over financial reporting. We will discuss this audit responsibility when we come to the role of external auditors in Chapter 9.

General Electric Company Annual Report to Shareholders for the Fiscal Year Ended December 31, 2012

Management's Annual Report on Internal Control over Financial Reporting

Management is responsible for establishing and maintaining adequate internal control over financial reporting for the Company. With our participation, an evaluation of the effectiveness of our internal control over financial reporting was conducted as of December 31, 2012, based on the framework and criteria established in Internal Control–Integrated Framework issued by the Committee of Sponsoring Organizations of the Treadway Commission. Based on this evaluation, our management has concluded that our internal control over financial reporting was effective as of December 31, 2012. Our independent registered public accounting firm has issued an audit report on our internal control over financial reporting. Their report follows.

/s/ Jeffrey R. Immelt
Chairman of the Board and
Chief Executive Officer

/s/ Keith S. Sherin
Vice Chairman and
Chief Financial Officer
February 26, 2013

Questions and Comments

1. In practice, as the above excerpt illustrates, management reports on internal controls over financial reporting are not fulsome. One does not find an elaborate description of the controls, how they are designed, how they work and do not work, and so on. Rather, certifications simply recite the language required by the statute or SEC regulations, without elaboration.

2. How much information do these documents provide to an investor beyond the fact that the CEO and CFO have signed pieces of paper put in front of them by a lawyer? Should the SEC require more? What are the pros and cons?

What if the CEO and CFO sign the required certifications under §404 of SOX and the issuing firm's internal controls turn out to be inadequate — but all disclosures are otherwise accurate? Do the signers face securities fraud liability merely for false certifications about internal controls?

Technically, the answer is clearly "yes." But as a matter of practice and common understanding, the answer has long been "no": The SEC and private parties do not usually bring lawsuits solely because certifications of the adequacy of internal controls are inaccurate.

That understanding is breaking down. In In the Matter of Edward L. Cummings, CPA, SEC Administrative Proceeding No. 3-15991 (2014), the SEC alleged that on numerous occasions Cummings, an accountant and chief financial officer of a failed reporting firm, had improperly accelerated, for periods of up to a week, the company's recognition of accounts receivable and inventory received with a view toward improving the firm's access to credit markets.

The SEC did not allege that Cummings was aware that this practice would have materially affected the accuracy of the company's financial statements. Nor did the SEC allege that the practice had caused the company's financial statements to be misleading. Nevertheless, the SEC alleged that Cummings had (a) falsely represented that he and the other certifying officer had been responsible for establishing and maintaining the company's internal controls over financial reporting, when in fact the other officer had played no role; and (b) had falsely certified that he and the other officer had disclosed all significant deficiencies in internal controls to the company's independent auditor, when in fact he knew of deficiencies in internal controls — having exploited them on numerous occasions — and had failed to disclose these deficiencies to the company's auditor. In settlement of the charges, Cummings agreed not to practice before the SEC as an accountant for a period of at least five years and paid a fine of $23,000.

The CFO's liability in this case appears clear-cut: He certified matters that he knew to be false. Yet notice that the offenses were arguably not very severe. Cummings manipulated the books of the company, but only in minor ways, accelerating recognition of certain items by no more than one week. No material misstatements in the company's financial statements resulted from the conduct. Arguably, neither the company nor its public investors suffered harm. Yet Cummings was given a significant penalty and a sanction that impugned his reputation as well as lightened his wallet.

Did the punishment fit the offense? Commentators have speculated that the SEC, in this action, intended to signal to the broader community that even small offenses would not be tolerated—the so-called broken windows theory of policing—and also that the SEC takes seriously the SOX requirement of management certifications, quite apart from whether investors have been harmed in a given case. Stay tuned.

C. CHIEF EXECUTIVE OFFICER

The chief executive officer is the senior-most official in a firm. At one time the conventional name for this position was "president," but that title has been substantially downgraded. If a company has both a president and a chief executive officer, the former will usually report to the latter. Many companies have dispensed with the title of president altogether; the job has merged with that of the chief operating officer—the person who makes the trains run on time.

Technically, the CEO is an employee of the organization, working under a contract, reporting to the board of directors, and subject to many of the rules that apply to other employees. In practice, however, the CEO is more than that. She has many important responsibilities, and exercises the power that attends those duties:

- The CEO is the "public face" of a firm. She is the person who is "at the helm" and the one who is praised if the firm does well or blamed if it does not. Often the CEO is also the chairman of the board. But increasingly these days, as we saw in the previous chapter, the positions of CEO and board chairman are split. In such a case, the public face of the firm is still the CEO. Many people would know that Tim Cook was (in 2013) the CEO of Apple; fewer would be able to supply the name of the company's non-executive board chairman (Arthur D. Levinson).
- The CEO is ultimately responsible for making decisions at the management level. Traditionally, and still to a substantial extent, reporting lines will converge on the CEO with the same inevitable force as roads in the ancient world led to Rome. Today this hierarchical principle is somewhat modified by rules or practices that require officials for whom independence is considered important to report to the board of directors or a board committee—as is often the case with the head of internal audit. Nevertheless, the CEO remains the one at the top of the pyramid; good CEOs make sure they stay there.
- The CEO is a leader in the way other executives are not. She is not only the head of an organization; she is also head of a team of senior managers who must be led to cooperate with one another (often not an easy task) and to work jointly for the good of the enterprise.
- Most importantly, from the standpoint of compliance, the CEO is responsible for setting the "tone at the top." No one else can be as effective in communicating to everyone in the organization the crucial importance of scrupulous adherence to applicable laws and standards. Beyond this, no one else in the organization is in a position to establish and maintain a firm ethos that goes beyond compliance

and that encourages everyone associated with the firm to display ethical behavior that exceeds the formal requirements. For this reason the CEO, even if only a relatively small percentage of her time is spent on compliance matters, is in a real sense the most important compliance officer in the organization.

For public companies, CEOs also have one other important compliance responsibility. Section 302 of the Sarbanes-Oxley Act requires the CEO and chief financial officer (CFO) to certify in each annual and each quarterly report, based on their knowledge, that the report does not contain any untrue statement of a material fact or omit to state a material fact necessary in order to make the statements made, in light of the circumstances under which such statements were made, not misleading, and that the financial statements and other financial information included in the report fairly present in all material respects the financial condition and results of operations of the issuer for the reporting period.

In addition, these officers are required to certify the following with respect to the issuer's internal controls, that they "are responsible for establishing and maintaining internal controls"; have "designed such internal controls to ensure that material information relating to the issuer and its consolidated subsidiaries is made known to such officers by others within those entities"; have "evaluated the effectiveness of the issuer's internal controls as of a date within 90 days prior to the report"; and have "presented in the report their conclusions about the effectiveness of their internal controls based on their evaluation as of that date."

The CEO and CFO must certify that they have disclosed to the issuer's auditors and the board audit committee: "all significant deficiencies in the design or operation of internal controls which could adversely affect the issuer's ability to record, process, summarize, and report financial data and have identified for the issuer's auditors any material weaknesses in internal controls"; and "any fraud, whether or not material, that involves management or other employees who have a significant role in the issuer's internal controls." The signing officers must also indicate "whether or not there were significant changes in internal controls or in other factors that could significantly affect internal controls subsequent to the date of their evaluation, including any corrective actions with regard to significant deficiencies and material weaknesses."

A related provision, §906, requires that an issuer's periodic reports to the SEC be "accompanied" by a written statement of the CEO and CFO certifying that the information contained in the reports "fairly presents, in all material respects, the financial condition and results of operations of the issuer." Anyone who certifies a financial statement that does not "comport with" this requirement is subject to criminal penalties: up to 10 years' imprisonment if the officer acted "knowing that the periodic report accompanying the statement does not comport with all the requirements," and up to 20 years if the officer acted "willfully." 18 U.S.C. §1350.

Sections 302 and 906 have somewhat different coverage. Section 302 is a civil provision enforced by the SEC. Section 906 is backed by criminal penalties and is enforceable by the Department of Justice. Because §906 does not require that the issuer to "file" the certification with the SEC, the securities act liabilities that attach to items filed or incorporated by reference in SEC filings do not apply to violations of this statute.

General Electric Company Annual Report to Shareholders for the Fiscal Year Ended December 31, 2012

Certification Pursuant to Rules 13a-14(a) or 15d-14(a) Under the Securities Exchange Act of 1934, as Amended

I, Jeffrey R. Immelt, certify that:

1. I have reviewed this annual report on Form 10-K of General Electric Company;
2. Based on my knowledge, this report does not contain any untrue statement of a material fact or omit to state a material fact necessary to make the statements made, in light of the circumstances under which such statements were made, not misleading with respect to the period covered by this report;
3. Based on my knowledge, the financial statements, and other financial information included in this report, fairly present in all material respects the financial condition, results of operations and cash flows of the registrant as of, and for, the periods presented in this report;
4. The registrant's other certifying officer and I are responsible for establishing and maintaining disclosure controls and procedures (as defined in Exchange Act Rules 13a-15(e) and 15d-15(e)) and internal control over financial reporting (as defined in Exchange Act Rules 13a-15(f) and 15d-15(f)) for the registrant and have:
   (a) Designed such disclosure controls and procedures, or caused such disclosure controls and procedures to be designed under our supervision, to ensure that material information relating to the registrant, including its consolidated subsidiaries, is made known to us by others within those entities, particularly during the period in which this report is being prepared;
   (b) Designed such internal control over financial reporting, or caused such internal control over financial reporting to be designed under our supervision, to provide reasonable assurance regarding the reliability of financial reporting and the preparation of financial statements for external purposes in accordance with generally accepted accounting principles;
   (c) Evaluated the effectiveness of the registrant's disclosure controls and procedures and presented in this report our conclusions about the effectiveness of the disclosure controls and procedures, as of the end of the period covered by this report based on such evaluation; and
   (d) Disclosed in this report any change in the registrant's internal control over financial reporting that occurred during the registrant's most recent fiscal quarter (the registrant's fourth fiscal quarter in the case of an annual report) that has materially affected, or is reasonably likely to materially affect, the registrant's internal control over financial reporting; and
5. The registrant's other certifying officer and I have disclosed, based on our most recent evaluation of internal control over financial reporting, to the registrant's auditors and the audit committee of the registrant's board of directors (or persons performing the equivalent functions):
   (a) All significant deficiencies and material weaknesses in the design or operation of internal control over financial reporting which are

reasonably likely to adversely affect the registrant's ability to record, process, summarize and report financial information; and

(b) Any fraud, whether or not material, that involves management or other employees who have a significant role in the registrant's internal control over financial reporting.

/s/ Jeffrey R. Immelt
Chairman of the Board and
Chief Executive Officer

Questions and Comments

1. What is the objective of the certification requirements of §§302 and 906? What purpose is served by bringing the CEO and chief financial officer into the process in so direct a manner?

2. Section 302 requires the officers to certify that they have "designed" the system of disclosure and internal controls. Does this mean that the CEO and CFO must personally design the controls? That would not seem like a very sensible requirement since the CEO and CFO may have no special expertise at designing internal controls. The SEC's regulations make it clear that this requirement is satisfied if the officers certify that they have caused such disclosure controls and procedures to be designed under their supervision.

3. Section 906 imposes two levels of criminal penalty: one for cases where an officer acts "knowingly" and another, more serious penalty for officers who act "willfully." What do these terms mean, and what is the difference between them? Although the statute doesn't provide much help, it probably refers us to general concepts of knowledge and willfulness in the law. In general, knowledge doesn't require the sort of absolute certainty that some philosophers demand; it means, roughly, that a reasonable person in similar circumstances would have a high degree of conviction in the truth of the proposition. The "knowledge" in question is not knowledge of the law — and accordingly a person can be liable for violating §906 even if she did not understand the nature of their legal obligations. Rather, it appears that the knowledge required is knowledge of the facts and circumstances. As for "willfully," however, some understanding of the law seems to be required: In other contexts, the Supreme Court has held that a person acts willfully when she not only knows the facts but also knows that her conduct is unlawful. *See* Ratzlaf v. United States, 510 U.S. 135 (1994).

4. In the excerpted text, Mr. Immelt certifies that he has "evaluated the effectiveness of the registrant's disclosure controls and procedure." How much time do you think he spent on this evaluation?

5. Does Mr. Immelt certify that he knows that the financial reports are accurate, or that to the best of his knowledge, the financial reports are accurate? What is the difference?

6. The "Volcker Rule," a provision of the Dodd-Frank Act that regulates and limits proprietary trading by banks, contains a CEO certification analogous to the one under SOX. As originally proposed, the rule would have required that the CEO attest that the bank was in compliance with the rule; but the final rule watered this down to an attestation that the compliance program "is reasonably designed to achieve compliance with the rule." What is the difference?

PROBLEM 3-1

You are CEO of Rattlesnake Brewing Co., an owner of a national chain of brew pubs. The company is listed for trading on the NASDAQ. Two weeks before the company's quarterly report is due to be filed with the SEC, you receive a visit from a junior member of the accounting department. Describing herself as a "whistleblower," she informs you that the company's draft financial statement significantly understates the cost of hops (an important ingredient of beer), which have been recorded at the contractual cost even though the supplier has gone out of business and the company has had to purchase hops at a higher cost on the market. The employee says that she reported the discrepancy to her supervisor, who told her to focus on her assigned responsibilities and not to worry about how costs are reported. You immediately consult your CFO, who says she knows nothing about this and describes the "whistleblower" as mentally unstable. However, you notice that the CFO seems a little evasive. She promises to look into the matter. A few hours later she calls you back and tells you that there is nothing to the story: The purported whistleblower just misunderstood the company's system for cost accounting. What should you do?

D. CHIEF FINANCIAL OFFICER

The CFO is the officer principally responsible for financial controls and reporting. In her "controller" function, the CFO ensures that financial information about the company is compiled, processed, and presented to the appropriate decision makers in a timely and accurate fashion. The CFO also has an important role in risk management. She is responsible for monitoring the company's financial condition — and therefore for identifying when key items present a risk of moving outside accepted tolerances. She acts as an economic forecaster, assessing how the company is likely to respond to future events or conditions. The CFO also manages the treasury function, investing the company's extra cash (in the case of industrial firms) and making sure that the firm has sufficient liquidity on hand to pay its debts as they come due. As noted above, in the case of public companies, the CFO, together with the CEO, is responsible for signing the certifications required under §§302 and 906 of the Sarbanes-Oxley Act.

E. CHIEF AUDIT EXECUTIVE

1. What Is Internal Audit?

The internal audit function is carried out by a department within a firm. Internal audit departments are led by people with titles such as "Chief Audit Executive." This person, however titled, heads up the internal audit department; she or

> "Internal audit" is the function of monitoring the actions of employees, processes, and systems to verify their effectiveness and compliance with internal or external norms.

he may also have an input into broader management functions.

The head of internal audit reports to someone else in the company. Often, these days, she or he has a direct reporting line to the chief executive officer — a formal acknowledgment that the audit function is not subject to the control of any other department in the company and also a recognition that the head of internal audit has rights of access to the company's senior leadership. At the board level, the head of internal audit reports principally to the board audit committee. Typically, audit committees receive a report from internal audit at every regular meeting, which will discuss audit priorities, review the status of the audit plan, and probe into any audit findings requiring board attention.

To what extent should the internal audit department operate independently from the rest of the company? The tension here is that the internal audit department is there for the purpose of checking up on everyone in the company — including even the senior managers — to ensure that procedures are being followed and policies are being implemented effectively. Internal audit needs a degree of independence in order to assure that this process of investigation and validation is as impartial and objective as possible. On the other hand, internal audit is part of the company. It is not the external auditor. Thus the degree of independence expected of the external auditor is neither feasible nor desirable for the internal audit department.

What is the relationship between internal audit and a company's external auditor? On the one hand, the two operate at "arm's length." The external auditor reviews all aspects of a company's financial controls, including internal audit. In this respect the company's internal auditors are being reviewed by an independent and potentially exacting critic. On the other hand, internal audit typically cooperates in the performance of the external audit. Given that internal audit may have obtained information that will also be of relevance to the external audit, time and expense can be saved if external audit can use that information for its own purposes. The relationship between internal audit and external audit may also be beneficial in situations where the internal audit department is encountering resistance from other parts of the organization; internal audit can sometimes find a way to get its needs met through the (more powerful) voice of the external auditor.

What about the relationship between internal audit and the regulators? Once again, there are tensions. To the degree internal audit is part of the regulated entity, the regulator's approach is similar to its approach to all aspects of the company's operations — respectful but not chummy, with an inescapable potential for frostiness if the regulator detects resistance, deception, or non-compliance. On the other hand, internal audit is also performing part of the regulator's job. It is charged with insuring that the company's policies and procedures are being followed, including those that are required by law. Because regulators are busy and understaffed, they have an obvious interest in relying on internal audit to act as a line of defense against problems. In fact regulators do rely on internal audit departments, and to a substantial extent. But if the regulators' reliance is to be justified, they need assurance that internal audit is capable, vigorous, and unflinching in the performance of its responsibilities. Hence regulators push hard for companies to maintain robust and empowered internal audit departments.

2. How Does Internal Audit Work?

The first priority in the internal audit task is to define what will be audited. Internal audit deals with two sorts of auditable components: (a) functions, such as, say, the company's customer rewards program, and (b) entities, such as, say, the Atlanta distribution center. The sum of all auditable components is referred to as the "audit universe."

The term audit "universe" accurately defines its function. The physical universe is all there is. The audit universe is all there is *for purposes of internal audit.* If something is not included in the audit universe it doesn't exist as far as internal audit is concerned. It will not be audited

> The "audit universe" is the scope of functions and entities that will be audited by internal audit.

and any problems with the function or entity that could have been detected through the audit function will not be brought to light.

What components should be in the audit universe? There is no hard-and-fast answer to this question, but the principle is clear: The audit universe should include everything that can have a tangible effect on the company's fortunes, but should not include topics that do not have such a tangible effect. For internal audit to be effective, it must focus on things that really make a difference; for it to be efficient, it should not waste time on things that don't really matter.

Once the audit universe is identified, the audit department must determine how to fit any particular audit within the overall program. It must decide (a) how frequently the audit will occur, and (b) how many resources (usually measured in staff time) will be required when it occurs. This leads to the preparation of an audit plan.

> The "audit plan" is the schedule for the timing and anticipated resource requirements for all audits within the audit universe.

The audit plan serves as a strategic document that can guide the internal audit department in its budgeting and personnel decisions; it is also a control device by which the managers of internal audit and their supervisors, along with the board audit committee, can determine whether the department is completing its responsibilities in a timely fashion. Typically, the audit plan will be developed after a risk assessment by the internal audit department intended to identify those areas of the audit universe that pose the greatest risk to the company—and therefore that warrant the most intensive scrutiny during the audit process.

Once the audit plan is in place, a manager in the internal audit department assigns staff to each audit. The staff member responsible for the audit will contact the managers of the line of business being audited in order to coordinate the auditing tasks. Internal audit will also request that the business line provide it with information—reports, data, software, access to policies and procedures, and whatever else will facilitate the audit. The internal audit staff will meet with people from the line department and also examine the relevant documentation. If appropriate, they will conduct random testing or statistical analysis.

The internal audit process assesses whether, and to what extent, the audited component is performing according to the audit criteria—the expectations set by senior managers or external authorities. Internal audit does not ordinarily determine these criteria: Its job is not to make policy but rather to ascertain that policy is being followed and that systems of internal control are effective. In practice, however, the internal audit does have an impact on how policy is carried out at the ground level because the rigor of the audit will impact how carefully the line employees do their job.

As the audit progresses, internal auditors assess whether their review and investigation have uncovered any significant failures to satisfy the audit criteria. When such failures are identified, internal audit brings these to the attention to the line managers for discussion. If the line managers fail to provide a satisfactory explanation, internal audit makes audit findings that the criteria are not being met.

A finding of nonconformance with an audit criterion can be contentious because it might be taken by the line manager as a criticism of how she is performing her job. From the standpoint of internal audit, the point is not to praise or blame but rather to ascertain whether processes can usefully be improved. However, line officials don't always understand the distinction. It is internal audit's job to withstand pushback from the business units if the conclusions of the audit stand up after review.

> Audit findings are internal audit's determinations about whether the relevant audit criteria are being met. The term is typically used to mean that the criteria are not being met.

What is done when internal audit finds that audit criteria are not being met? The responsible decision maker ordinarily will agree to undertake prompt remediation to correct the discrepancy. Internal audit then schedules a follow-up to confirm that the undertakings are being honored.

Internal audit's report usually contains (a) a statement of any problem identified in the audit, or a statement that no problems were encountered; (b) a statement of the audit criterion or criteria; (c) an analysis of the cause of any negative findings; (d) a description of the consequences of the problem so identified; and (e) a statement of what is being done to remediate the problem or accept the risk, or a recommendation about what should be done.

If negative, audit findings are sorted according to severity. Some findings may be so minor that they are only brought to the attention of the line managers involved. More serious findings are raised to the level of senior managers. Critical findings are brought to the attention of the board audit committee.

Questions and Comments

1. Internal audit has become a profession in its own right, with qualifications and standards somewhat different from those associated with external audit. The Institute of Internal Auditors (IIA) is recognized as an international standard setting body for the internal audit profession. Several states have codified the IIA's professional standards in statutes regulating the internal audit function. As demonstrated by the excerpt below, the IIA's standards for internal audit are also endorsed by federal regulators.

3. Best Practices

How should internal audit function? The following description of internal audit best practices is from two policy statements by the bank regulators. Although directed to bank internal audit departments, the descriptions are representative of accepted best practices across a range of industries.

Board of Governors of the Federal Reserve System
Federal Deposit Insurance Corporation
Office of the Comptroller of the Currency
Office of Thrift Supervision, Interagency Policy Statement
on the Internal Audit Function and Its Outsourcing

Mar. 17, 2003

. . . When properly structured and conducted, internal audit provides directors and senior management with vital information about weaknesses in the system of internal control so that management can take prompt, remedial action . . . . [E]ach institution should have an internal audit function that is appropriate to its size and the nature and scope of its activities . . . .

The board of directors and senior management are responsible for having an effective system of internal control and an effective internal audit function in place at their institution. They are also responsible for ensuring that the importance of internal control is understood and respected throughout the institution. This overall responsibility cannot be delegated to anyone else. They may, however, delegate the design, implementation and monitoring of specific internal controls to lower-level management and the testing and assessment of internal controls to others.

Accordingly, directors and senior management should have reasonable assurance that the system of internal control prevents or detects significant inaccurate, incomplete, or unauthorized transactions; deficiencies in the safeguarding of assets; unreliable financial reporting (which includes regulatory reporting); and deviations from laws, regulations, and the institution's policies.

Some institutions have chosen to rely on so-called "management self-assessments" or "control self-assessments," wherein business line managers and their staff evaluate the performance of internal controls within their purview. Such reviews help to underscore management's responsibility for internal control, but they are not impartial. Directors and members of senior management who rely too much on these reviews may not learn of control weaknesses until they have become costly problems, particularly if directors are not intimately familiar with the institution's operations. Therefore, institutions generally should also have their internal controls tested and evaluated by units without business-line responsibilities, such as internal audit groups.

Directors should be confident that the internal audit function addresses the risks and meets the demands posed by the institution's current and planned activities. To accomplish this objective, directors should consider whether their institution's internal audit activities are conducted in accordance with professional standards, such as the Institute of Internal Auditors' (IIA) Standards for the Professional Practice of Internal Auditing. These standards address independence, professional proficiency, scope of work, performance of audit work, management of internal audit, and quality assurance reviews . . . .

Careful thought should be given to the placement of the audit function in the institution's management structure. The internal audit function should be positioned so that the board has confidence that the internal audit function will perform its duties with impartiality and not be unduly influenced by managers of day-to-day operations. The audit committee, using objective criteria it has established, should oversee the internal audit function and evaluate its performance. The audit committee should assign responsibility for the internal audit function to a member of management (hereafter referred to as the manager of internal audit or internal audit manager) who understands the function and has no responsibility for operating the system of internal control. The ideal organizational arrangement is for this manager to report directly and solely to the audit committee regarding both audit issues and administrative matters, e.g., resources, budget, appraisals, and compensation . . . .

Many institutions place the manager of internal audit under a dual reporting arrangement: functionally accountable to the audit committee on issues discovered by the internal audit function, while reporting to another senior manager on administrative matters. Under a dual reporting relationship, the board should consider the potential for diminished objectivity on the part of the internal audit manager with respect to audits concerning the executive to whom he or she reports. For example, a manager of internal audit who reports to the chief financial officer (CFO) for performance appraisal, salary, and approval of department budgets may approach audits of the accounting and treasury operations controlled by the CFO with less objectivity than if the manager were to report to the chief executive officer. Thus, the chief financial officer, controller, or other similar officer should ideally be excluded from overseeing the internal audit activities even in a dual role. The objectivity and organizational stature of the internal audit function are best served under such a dual arrangement if the internal audit manager reports administratively to the CEO.

Some institutions seek to coordinate the internal audit function with several risk monitoring functions (e.g., loan review, market risk assessment, and legal compliance departments) by establishing an administrative arrangement under one senior executive. Coordination of these other monitoring activities with the internal audit function can facilitate the reporting of material risk and control issues to the audit committee, increase the overall effectiveness of these monitoring functions, better utilize available resources, and enhance the institution's ability to comprehensively manage risk. Such an administrative reporting relationship should be designed so as to not interfere with or hinder the manager of internal audit's functional reporting to and ability to directly communicate with the institution's audit committee. In addition, the audit committee should ensure that efforts to coordinate these monitoring functions do not result in the manager of internal audit conducting control activities nor diminish his or her independence with respect to the other risk monitoring functions. Furthermore, the internal audit manager should have the ability to independently audit these other monitoring functions.

In structuring the reporting hierarchy, the board should weigh the risk of diminished independence against the benefit of reduced administrative burden in adopting a dual reporting organizational structure. The audit committee should document its consideration of this risk and mitigating controls . . . .

In managing the internal audit function, the manager of internal audit is responsible for control risk assessments, audit plans, audit programs, and audit reports. A control risk assessment (or risk assessment methodology) documents the internal auditor's understanding of the institution's significant business activities and their associated risks. These assessments typically analyze the risks inherent in a given business line, the mitigating control processes, and the resulting residual risk exposure of the institution. They should be updated regularly to reflect changes to the system of internal control or work processes, and to incorporate new lines of business.

An internal audit plan is based on the control risk assessment and typically includes a summary of key internal controls within each significant business activity, the timing and frequency of planned internal audit work, and a resource budget. An internal audit program describes the objectives of the audit work and lists the procedures that will be performed during each internal audit review.

An audit report generally presents the purpose, scope, and results of the audit, including findings, conclusions, and recommendations. Workpapers that document the work performed and support the audit report should be maintained.

Ideally, the internal audit function's only role should be to independently and objectively evaluate and report on the effectiveness of an institution's risk management, control, and governance processes. Internal auditors increasingly have taken a consulting role within institutions on new products and services and on mergers, acquisitions, and other corporate reorganizations. This role typically includes helping design controls and participating in the implementation of changes to the institution's control activities. The audit committee, in its oversight of the internal audit staff, should ensure that the function's consulting activities do not interfere or conflict with the objectivity it should have with respect to monitoring the institution's system of internal control. In order to maintain its independence, the internal audit function should not assume a business-line management role over control activities, such as approving or implementing operating policies or procedures, including those it has helped design in connection with its consulting activities . . . .

The internal audit function should be competently supervised and staffed by people with sufficient expertise and resources to identify the risks inherent in the institution's operations and assess whether internal controls are effective. The manager of internal audit should oversee the staff assigned to perform the internal audit work and should establish policies and procedures to guide the audit staff. The form and content of these policies and procedures should be consistent with the size and complexity of the department and the institution. Many policies and procedures may be communicated informally in small internal audit departments, while larger departments would normally require more formal and comprehensive written guidance.

The frequency and extent of internal audit review and testing should be consistent with the nature, complexity, and risk of the institution's on- and off-balance-sheet activities. At least annually, the audit committee should review and approve internal audit's control risk assessment and the scope of the audit plan, including how much the manager relies on the work of an outsourcing vendor. It should also periodically review internal audit's adherence to the audit plan. The audit committee should consider requests for expansion of basic internal audit work when significant issues arise or when significant changes occur in the institution's environment, structure, activities, risk exposures, or systems.

To properly carry out their responsibility for internal control, directors and senior management should foster forthright communications and critical examination of issues to better understand the importance and severity of internal control weaknesses identified by the internal auditor and operating management's solutions to these weaknesses. Internal auditors should report internal control deficiencies to the appropriate level of management as soon as they are identified. Significant matters should be promptly reported directly to the board of directors (or its audit committee) and senior management. In periodic meetings with management and the manager of internal audit, the audit committee should assess whether management is expeditiously resolving internal control weaknesses and other exceptions. Moreover, the audit committee should give the manager of internal audit the opportunity to discuss his or her findings without management being present.

Furthermore, each audit committee should establish and maintain procedures for employees of their institution to submit confidentially and anonymously concerns to the committee about questionable accounting, internal accounting control, or auditing matters . . . .

The global financial crisis that peaked in 2008 raised concerns that the message of the excerpted text had not been received: If internal audit had been more independent, more capable, or more assertive, perhaps some of the mistakes and abuses that came to light during and after the crisis would never have happened. Part of the regulators' response to the crisis, therefore, was a push to upgrade and empower internal audit. A particular area of concern was the shortcomings displayed by the largest institutions, whose size and activities made them systemically important to the health of the financial sector as a whole. The following excerpt reflects the post-crisis thinking of the Federal Reserve Board as it applies to the internal audit function in large banking institutions.

Board of Governors of the Federal Reserve System, Supplemental Policy Statement on the Internal Audit Function and Its Outsourcing

Jan. 23, 2013

. . . As a result of the supervisory experience during and following the recent financial crisis, Federal Reserve staff identified areas for improving regulated institutions' internal audit functions. This supplemental policy statement addresses the characteristics, governance, and operational effectiveness of an institution's internal audit function . . . .

An institution's internal audit function should incorporate the following enhanced practices into their overall processes:

Internal audit should analyze the effectiveness of all critical risk management functions both with respect to individual risk dimensions (for example, credit risk), and an institution's overall risk management function. The analysis should focus on the nature and extent of monitoring compliance with established policies and processes and applicable laws and regulations within the institution as well as whether monitoring processes are appropriate for the institution's business activities and the associated risks.

Internal audit should identify thematic macro control issues as part of its risk-assessment processes and determine the overall impact of such issues on the institution's risk profile.

Additional audit coverage would be expected in business activities that present the highest risk to the institution. Internal audit coverage should reflect the identification of thematic macro control issues across the firm in all auditable areas.

Internal audit should communicate thematic macro control issues to senior management and the audit committee.

In addition, internal audit should identify patterns of thematic macro control issues, determine whether additional audit coverage is required, communicate such control deficiencies to senior management and the audit committee, and ensure management establishes effective remediation mechanisms.

Internal audit should challenge management to adopt appropriate policies and procedures and effective controls. If policies, procedures, and internal controls are ineffective or insufficient in a particular line of business or activity, internal audit should report specific deficiencies to senior management and the audit committee with recommended remediation. Such recommendations may include restricting business activity in affected lines of business until effective policies, procedures, and controls are designed and implemented. Internal audit should monitor management's corrective action and conduct a follow-up review to confirm that the recommendations of both internal audit and the audit committee have been addressed.

When an institution designs and implements infrastructure enhancements, internal audit should review significant changes and notify management of potential internal control issues. In particular, internal audit should ensure that existing, effective internal controls (for example, software applications and management information system reporting) are not rendered ineffective as a result of infrastructure changes unless those controls are compensated for by other improvements to internal controls.

Internal audit should understand risks faced by the institution and confirm that the board of directors and senior management are actively involved in setting and monitoring compliance with the institution's risk tolerance limits. Internal audit should evaluate the reasonableness of established limits and perform sufficient testing to ensure that management is operating within these limits and other restrictions.

Internal audit should evaluate governance at all management levels within the institution, including at the senior management level, and within all significant business lines. Internal audit should also evaluate the adequacy and effectiveness of controls to respond to risks within the organization's governance, operations, and information systems in achieving the organization's strategic objectives. Any concerns should be communicated by internal audit to the board of directors and senior management . . . .

When an adverse event occurs at an institution (for example, fraud or a significant loss), management should conduct a post-mortem and "lessons learned" analysis. In these situations, internal audit should ensure that such a review takes place and appropriate action is taken to remediate identified issues. The internal audit function should evaluate management's analysis of the reasons for the event and whether the adverse event was the result of a control breakdown or failure, and identify the measures that should be put in place to prevent a similar event from occurring in the future. In certain situations, the internal audit function should conduct its own post-mortem and a "lessons learned" analysis outlining the remediation procedures necessary to detect, correct, and/or prevent future internal control breakdowns (including improvements in internal audit processes) . . . .

Questions and Comments

1. What features of an effective internal audit department are stressed in these policy statements?

2. The 2003 policy statement notes that some institutions had chosen to rely on documents called "management self-assessments," which basically are surveys of senior managers asking them to assess for themselves the efficacy of internal controls within their departments. The policy statement notes advantages and disadvantages of this strategy. What are they?

3. The 2003 policy statement stresses the importance of independence and impartiality in the performance of internal audit's responsibilities. Why are these qualities so important? Can they really be achieved given that internal audit is a department of an organization and not an independent institution?

4. To whom should the head of internal audit report? The tradeoff here is between control and autonomy. It might make sense, for example, for the head of internal audit to report to the chief financial officer, on the theory that the CFO has overall responsibility for the financial affairs of the company and that testing the efficacy of financial controls is one of the internal audit department's principal jobs. But subordinating internal audit to the CFO threatens to compromise its independence: What happens if internal audit discovers shortcomings — or worse — in the company's system of financial controls and reporting? An alternative is for the head of internal audit to report to the chief executive officer; a direct reporting line to the head of the organization both confers stature within the organization and insulates the person from internal pressures. Even so, the chief executive officer may have reasons to influence internal audit's activities or findings.

5. A common solution is for the head of internal audit to report to the board-level audit committee on matters of substance, thus bypassing all executive officials. This approach gives the internal audit function a degree of independence even from the chief executive officer. At the same time, however, the internal audit department, including its head, is part of the organization and accordingly must be subject to general administrative controls. Internal audit cannot report administratively to the board audit committee because the audit committee does not deal with administration. This leads to the dual reporting structure under which the chief audit officer reports substantively to the audit committee and administratively to someone else in the organization. Here again a question of independence arises. Ordinarily, it makes sense for the administrative reporting line to lead to the chief financial officer; but subordinating internal audit to the CFO even on administrative matters might compromise independence (what if the CFO implicitly threatened to cut the audit department's budget if it displayed too much independent judgment on audit findings?). What does the Federal Reserve Board recommend in such cases? If they have strong opinions on the matter, why don't they simply require banks under their supervision to make the head of internal audit report functionally to the audit committee and administratively to the CEO?

6. What changes of tone or substance do you detect between the 2003 and 2013 policy statements on internal audit? The dark shadow of the financial crisis of 2007-2009 looms over the later pronouncement. It is manifested principally in a heightened emphasis on risk-based auditing. Instead of "check the box" or "cookie-cutter" audits that run mechanically through a series of checks, internal audit is supposed to devise an audit plan that focuses attention (in terms of frequency of audits and amount of resources devoted) on the areas that pose the greatest risk to

the institution — both taken individually and considered in light of the overall risk to the enterprise.

7. In this respect, the 2013 policy statement refers to "thematic macro control issues." What does this mean? The term is not defined in the policy statement. Perhaps the Federal Reserve Board meant to refer to policies and procedures that can be adversely affected by turmoil in financial markets such as that which occurred in 2008; but if so why couldn't the statement have said this directly?

8. The new emphasis on risk has implications for internal audit beyond its role in structuring the audit plan. There is also the question of what internal audit does when risks are identified. It is not internal audit's job to eliminate risk, or even to determine the amount of risk that is acceptable. Determining the amount of risk that the enterprise is willing to accept is beyond internal audit's pay grade; it is a job for the risk committee or the full board of directors. Should internal audit be the enforcer and monitor of the company's risk appetite?

9. Traditionally, internal audit was not responsible for developing a company's internal controls; its job was to test whether those controls were rigorously followed and whether they were effective at achieving their purpose. This passive role arguably created a degree of inefficiency because internal audit was intimately familiar with the control systems in place and also well positioned to evaluate their design, efficacy, and interaction with control systems used elsewhere in the organization. The 2013 policy statement reflects a push by bank regulators to enhance internal audit's role in the process, not only in testing controls, but also participating in their design in order to achieve maximum effectiveness.

10. Suppose internal audit concludes that a particular system of controls is inadequate, and the head of the business unit refuses to implement changes that internal audit believe are needed to correct the problem? What is internal audit's recourse? The 2013 policy statement has an answer: The head of internal audit should take the issue up to the level of the audit committee. The policy also suggests a sanction for non-compliance: The audit committee should consider restricting activity in affected lines of business until the problem is remediated to the satisfaction of internal audit and the audit committee. Do you think this approach gives the right amount of authority to internal audit, too much authority, or too little?

11. As noted in the Introduction, internal audit is often referred to as the "third line of defense," a metaphor suggesting that it performs a "gotcha!" role: It catches mistakes, shortcomings, and failures of people or processes and then brings them to the attention of management (and potentially the board audit committee) in the form of audit findings. Is this the best way to conceive of internal audit? Internal audit certainly does function as a backup to other control systems, but the metaphor of the third line of defense may create an impression that it is there only to highlight mistakes and embarrass line officers. Arguably, there are two problems with this connotation. First, if business line officials consider that internal audit is only there to show them up, they may be less than fully cooperative with the internal audit process, and may push back when hit with audit findings rather than welcoming the feedback as an opportunity for improvement. Second, internal audit is not necessarily limited to an after-the-fact role. When an organization is instituting a new business line or process, for example, it may make sense to involve internal audit from the start in a consulting role, in order to "bake in" controls that, if they receive "buy in" from the operations people at the outset, may reduce the risk of audit findings in the future.

12. Should companies be required to host an internal audit function? For large firms, this question is largely theoretical because all or nearly all major companies

would establish an internal audit department even in the absence of regulatory requirements. Smaller firms, however, may find it inconvenient to create a department of internal audit. The recent trend has been to require public companies to operate an internal audit function regardless of size. In 2013, for example, NASDAQ proposed a rule requiring NASDAQ-listed firms to establish and maintain such a function:

> Each Company must establish and maintain an internal audit function to provide management and the audit committee with ongoing assessments of the Company's risk management processes and system of internal control. The Company may choose to outsource this function to a third party service provider other than its independent auditor. The audit committee must meet periodically with the internal auditors (or other personnel responsible for this function) and assist the Board in its oversight of the performance of this function. The audit committee should also discuss with the outside auditor the responsibilities, budget and staffing of the internal audit function.

SEC Release No. 34-69030 (Mar. 4, 2013). The NYSE had previously done the same thing. Do you agree with these rules? What are the pros and cons? Would you permit a company to comply with the rules by outsourcing the internal audit function to a third-party service provider?

PROBLEM 3-2

FidelityCorp, a bank holding company with $200 billion in assets, owns all the stock in Fidelity Securities, a mutual fund adviser, and also all the stock in Fidelity National Bank. After reviewing a cost-benefit analysis, FidelityCorp's chief executive officer concludes that the enterprise as a whole could achieve savings by combining the internal audit departments of the bank and the mutual fund adviser into a single enterprise-wide internal audit department. She believes that a unified internal audit function will be more comprehensive — and thus will allow fewer matters to fall in the cracks between firms — and also more responsive to the enterprise's overall risk appetite. You are an outside legal consultant commissioned by the holding company's board of directors to evaluate this proposal. What would you recommend? Would you make the same recommendation if you were commissioned by the board of directors of the mutual fund adviser?

---

4. Vendors

The tasks of internal audit have increased dramatically in recent years, both in magnitude and in complexity. The job gets more difficult every year. To manage their increased responsibilities, and to keep costs under control, internal audit departments have turned to the use of outside vendors. Vendors are useful for most firms, but they can be particularly helpful for smaller institutions. While larger firms can realize economies of scale by performing the audit function in-house, smaller firms cannot. Vendors help reduce this disparity. Vendors provide two general types of services to internal audit departments: (a) they provide help in performing actual audits, up to and including "turnkey" arrangements in which particular audits are delegated in their entirety to an outside vendor (subject to supervision by internal audit); and (b) they offer vendor-created audit software.

Vendor-provided internal audit software is particularly useful in five key areas:

- It provides controls that managers can use to make sure that applicable rules and standards are being followed. The software typically contains built-in controls but also allows managers to customize their own control applications.
- It can organize work-flow by assigning audit tasks to particular members of the internal audit team, providing instructions for how to complete the job, and tracking to ensure that the task is completed on time.
- It can maintain documentation of audit activities for internal and regulatory purposes.
- It can provide templates and other assistance in the preparation of required reports.
- As periodically updated, it can track changing audit requirements and integrate them into the audit plan.

Accordingly, vendors provide a valuable service to aid in the internal audit function. But they also pose risks. The vendor's product may not perform as represented, or may require access to proprietary or non-public information maintained by the client, creating a risk of data breaches (see Chapter 11 on information security). Consider the banking agencies' advice on how internal audit should manage vendors:

Board of Governors of the Federal Reserve System, Interagency Policy Statement on the Internal Audit Function and Its Outsourcing

Mar. 17, 2003

. . . In addressing various quality and resource issues, many institutions have been engaging independent public accounting firms and other outside professionals (outsourcing vendors) in recent years to perform work that traditionally has been done by internal auditors . . . .

Outsourcing may be beneficial to an institution if it is properly structured, carefully conducted, and prudently managed. However, the agencies have concerns that the structure, scope, and management of some internal audit outsourcing arrangements do not contribute to the institution's safety and soundness. Furthermore, the agencies want to ensure that these arrangements with outsourcing vendors do not leave directors and senior management with the erroneous impression that they have been relieved of their responsibility for maintaining an effective system of internal control and for overseeing the internal audit function . . . .

An outsourcing arrangement is a contract between an institution and an outsourcing vendor to provide internal audit services. Outsourcing arrangements take many forms and are used by institutions of all sizes. Some institutions consider entering into these arrangements to enhance the quality of their control environment by obtaining the services of a vendor with the knowledge and skills to critically assess, and recommend improvements to, their internal control systems. The internal audit services under contract can be limited to helping internal audit staff in an assignment for which they lack expertise. Such an arrangement is typically under the control of the institution's manager of internal audit, and the outsourcing vendor reports to him or her.

Institutions often use outsourcing vendors for audits of areas requiring more technical expertise, such as electronic data processing and capital markets activities. Such uses are often referred to as "internal audit assistance" or "audit co-sourcing."

Some outsourcing arrangements are structured so that an outsourcing vendor performs virtually all the procedures or tests of the system of internal control. Under such an arrangement, a designated manager of internal audit oversees the activities of the outsourcing vendor and typically is supported by internal audit staff. The outsourcing vendor may assist the audit staff in determining risks to be reviewed and may recommend testing procedures, but the internal audit manager is responsible for approving the audit scope, plan, and procedures to be performed.

Furthermore, the internal audit manager is responsible for the results of the outsourced audit work, including findings, conclusions, and recommendations. The outsourcing vendor may report these results jointly with the internal audit manager to the audit committee.

Even when outsourcing vendors provide internal audit services, the board of directors and senior management of an institution are responsible for ensuring that both the system of internal control and the internal audit function operate effectively. In any outsourced internal audit arrangement, the institution's board of directors and senior management must maintain ownership of the internal audit function and provide active oversight of outsourced activities. When negotiating the outsourcing arrangement with an outsourcing vendor, an institution should carefully consider its current and anticipated business risks in setting each party's internal audit responsibilities.

The outsourcing arrangement should not increase the risk that a breakdown of internal control will go undetected.

To clearly distinguish its duties from those of the outsourcing vendor, the institution should have a written contract, often taking the form of an engagement letter.

Contracts between the institution and the vendor typically include provisions that:

- Define the expectations and responsibilities under the contract for both parties;
- Set the scope and frequency of, and the fees to be paid for, the work to be performed by the vendor;
- Set the responsibilities for providing and receiving information, such as the type and frequency of reporting to senior management and directors about the status of contract work;
- Establish the process for changing the terms of the service contract, especially for expansion of audit work if significant issues are found, and stipulations for default and termination of the contract;
- State that internal audit reports are the property of the institution, that the institution will be provided with any copies of the related workpapers it deems necessary, and that employees authorized by the institution will have reasonable and timely access to the workpapers prepared by the outsourcing vendor;
- Specify the locations of internal audit reports and the related workpapers;

- Specify the period of time (for example, seven years) that vendors must maintain the workpapers;
- State that outsourced internal audit services provided by the vendor are subject to regulatory review and that examiners will be granted full and timely access to the internal audit reports and related workpapers prepared by the outsourcing vendor;
- Prescribe a process (arbitration, mediation, or other means) for resolving disputes and for determining who bears the cost of consequential damages arising from errors, omissions, and negligence; and
- State that the outsourcing vendor will not perform management functions, make management decisions, or act or appear to act in a capacity equivalent to that of a member of management or an employee and, if applicable, will comply with AICPA, U.S. Securities and Exchange Commission (SEC), Public Company Accounting Oversight Board (PCAOB), or regulatory independence guidance.

VENDOR COMPETENCE

Before entering an outsourcing arrangement, the institution should perform due diligence to satisfy itself that the outsourcing vendor has sufficient staff qualified to perform the contracted work. The staff's qualifications may be demonstrated, for example, through prior experience with financial institutions. Because the outsourcing arrangement is a personal services contract, the institution's internal audit manager should have confidence in the competence of the staff assigned by the outsourcing vendor and receive timely notice of key staffing changes. Throughout the outsourcing arrangement, management should ensure that the outsourcing vendor maintains sufficient expertise to effectively perform its contractual obligations.

MANAGEMENT

Directors and senior management should ensure that the outsourced internal audit function is competently managed. For example, larger institutions should employ sufficient competent staff members in the internal audit department to assist the manager of internal audit in overseeing the outsourcing vendor. Small institutions that do not employ a full-time audit manager should appoint a competent employee who ideally has no managerial responsibility for the areas being audited to oversee the outsourcing vendor's performance under the contract. This person should report directly to the audit committee for purposes of communicating internal audit issues.

COMMUNICATION

Communication between the internal audit function and the audit committee and senior management should not diminish because the institution engages an outsourcing vendor. All work by the outsourcing vendor should be well documented and all findings of control weaknesses should be promptly reported to the institution's manager of internal audit.

Decisions not to report the outsourcing vendor's findings to directors and senior management should be the mutual decision of the internal audit manager and the outsourcing vendor. In deciding what issues should be brought to the board's attention, the concept of "materiality," as the term is used in financial statement audits, is generally not a good indicator of which control weakness to report. For example, when evaluating an institution's compliance with laws and regulations, any exception may be important.

CONTINGENCY PLANNING

When an institution enters into an outsourcing arrangement (or significantly changes the mix of internal and external resources used by internal audit), it may increase its operational risk. Because the arrangement may be terminated suddenly, the institution should have a contingency plan to mitigate any significant discontinuity in audit coverage, particularly for high-risk areas.

Board of Governors of the Federal Reserve System, Supplemental Policy Statement on the Internal Audit Function and Its Outsourcing

Jan. 23, 2013

. . . As stated in the 2003 Policy Statement, an institution's board of directors and senior management are charged with the overall responsibility for maintaining an effective system of internal controls. Responsibility for maintaining an effective system of internal controls cannot be delegated to a third party. An institution that chooses to outsource audit work should ensure that the audit committee maintains ownership of the internal audit function. The institution's audit committee and CAE [chief audit executive] should provide active and effective oversight of outsourced activities. Institutions should carefully consider the oversight responsibilities that are consequential to these types of arrangements in determining appropriate staffing levels.

To distinguish its duties from those of the outsourcing vendor, the institution should have a written contract, which may take the form of an engagement letter or similar services agreement. Contracts between the institution and the vendor should include a provision stating that work papers and any related non-public confidential information and personal information must be handled by the vendor in accordance with applicable laws and regulations. An institution should periodically confirm that the vendor continues to comply with the agreed-upon confidentiality requirements, especially for long-term contracts. The audit committee should approve all significant aspects of outsourcing arrangements and should receive information on audit deficiencies in a manner consistent with that provided by the in-house audit department.

An institution should have appropriate policies and procedures governing the selection and oversight of internal audit vendors, including whether to continue with an existing outsourced arrangement. The audit committee and the CAE are responsible for the selection and retention of internal audit vendors and should be aware of factors that may impact vendors' competence and ability to deliver high-quality audit services.

Questions and Comments

1. The Federal Reserve Board endorses the use of vendors for internal audit services, but also cautions that responsibility for maintaining an effective system of internal controls cannot be delegated. Can these two propositions go together?

Can the audit committee and senior management retain the full range of authority and responsibility for internal audit while simultaneously outsourcing large amounts of the work?

2. Much depends on the quality of the vendor. The policy statement indicates that the audit committee and the chief audit executive are jointly responsible for the selection and retention of internal audit vendors. Given that internal audit vendors are offering a complex suite of services that are probably beyond the technical capacity of either internal audit or the audit committee, how can they carry out their oversight obligations responsibly?

3. At one time outsourced internal audit tasks were largely performed by the firm's external auditor. Despite the efficiencies that can be obtained by combining the internal and external audit functions, the combination of these functions creates an obvious tension between the auditor's role as independent monitor of the company's financial operations and its role as a paid provider of services (for more on this conflict, see Chapter 9). For public companies, this practice was ended by the Sarbanes-Oxley Act, which prohibits a company's external auditor from simultaneously providing outsourced services to internal audit.

4. The policy statements note that in deciding which issues should be brought to the board's attention, the concept of "materiality," as the term is used in financial statement audits, is generally not a good indicator of which control weakness to report. What is wrong with using the concept of materiality as the filter for what should and should not be reported to senior management?

PROBLEM 3-3

You are head of the board audit committee at Lancer, a medical device supplier. Over the past several years your costs have skyrocketed due to ever-increasing complexity in the regulations governing the health care industry. The head of internal audit announces at a meeting of the board audit committee that the company has entered into a contract with SoftMed, a company specializing in providing computerized compliance and internal audit monitoring in the health care industry. The head of internal audit estimates that the SoftMed product will allow Lancer to save nearly a million dollars a year. How should you respond?

PROBLEM 3-4

You are head of the board audit committee at Pharmex, a manufacturer of generic drugs. Internal audit at Pharmex is using the services of Informics, a large provider of outsourced services to internal audit departments. The chief audit officer of Pharmex tells you that the services provided by Informics are first-rate. One day the chief technology officer and chief operating officer at Informics are indicted for insider trading on confidential information they obtained from files that Informics maintains on its internal audit customers. The chief executive officer of Informics issues a statement denying that anyone in that company has engaged in violations of the law, but also announcing that the indicted officials have been placed on paid administrative leave pending resolution of the charges. What should you do?

F. CHIEF COMPLIANCE OFFICER

Some companies vest the compliance function in a special office headed by a senior executive officer sometimes referred to as the chief compliance officer (CCO). The following is a (fictional) job description for a chief compliance officer in the health care field:

Chief Compliance Officer

The Chief Compliance Officer oversees the corporate compliance program, functioning as an independent and objective body that reviews and evaluates compliance issues/concerns within the organization. The position ensures the board of directors, management, and associates are in compliance with the rules and regulations of regulatory agencies, that company policies and procedures are being followed, and that behavior in the organization meets the company's standards of conduct.

The Chief Compliance Officer acts as staff to the CEO and board of directors corporate compliance committee by monitoring and reporting results of the compliance/ethics efforts of the company and in providing guidance for the Board and senior management team on matters relating to compliance. The Chief Compliance Officer, together with the corporate compliance committee, is authorized to implement all necessary actions to ensure achievement of the objectives of an effective compliance program . . . .

Qualifications: Bachelor's degree required; Master's desired. JD preferred.

Questions and Comments

1. To what degree should the CCO be insulated from others in the organization in order to confer a form of effective job independence? What institutional protections could be implemented to establish the requisite level of independence? Consider in this regard the following options (individually or in combination):

   a. A functional reporting line directly to the audit committee of the board of directors rather than to the chief executive officer or other management-level official;
   b. An official job description that expressly recognizes the authority of the CCO to act independently of direction from senior executive officials;
   c. Explicit guarantees of being invited to high-level meetings where matters pertinent to compliance are discussed;
   d. Guarantees of adequate resources, enforced, for example, by assurances that the compliance department will have its own budget line rather than sharing one with the general counsel or internal audit;
   e. Protections of tenure in office — for example, a requirement that the COO can only be fired by the audit committee or full board of directors.

Would you favor any of these arrangements? All of them? Which of these are included in the job description reported above?

2. A widely implemented practice is that the independent members of the audit committee or the independent directors as a whole have the opportunity for "alone time" with the CCO, without other senior executive officers being present. To what extent do you think this requirement will be effective at enhancing the position and independence of the CCO?

3. How should the role of the CCO be conceptualized? Is she a technician who "checks the boxes" to ensure that everyone is following the rules? Does she, or should she, have the more substantive function of promoting the development of pro-compliance norms within an organization? For an endorsement of the latter role, see James A. Fanto, *Surveillant and Counselor: A Reorientation in Compliance for Financial Firms*, Brooklyn L. Sch., Legal Studies Paper No. 358 (Sept. 5, 2013), available at SSRN: http://ssrn.com/abstract=2321317 at p.1 or http://dx.doi.org/10.2139/ssrn.2321317 ("[R]ather than being only a transcriber of rules and monitor of their enforcement, a compliance officer would be an educator about policies, standards and the appropriate firm and industry culture and an adviser and counselor concerning how they should inform daily employee decisions.") Do you agree?

4. A Deloitte survey conducted in 2013 found that reporting lines for CCOs were quite varied: CEO (34%), the board of directors (17%), the CFO (7%), the general counsel (20%), the chief risk officer (2%), and "other" (19%).

5. For a skeptical view of separating out the compliance function and placing it in a new "C-Suite" executive, rather than allowing the general counsel to perform that task, see Michele Beardslee DeStefano, *Creating a Culture of Compliance: Why Departmentalization May Not Be the Answer*, 10 Hastings Bus. L.J. 71 (2014). Professor DeStefano argues that such departmentalization "may not increase transparency into compliance transgressions at corporations, actual compliance by corporations, or the commitment by corporations to a culture of compliance and ethics. Further, such structural reorganization of the compliance function may generate consequences that offset the potential benefits of departmentalization and create a sense of false complacency that distracts from substantive cultural change that is integrated throughout the organization." Do you agree?

G. GENERAL COUNSEL

Traditionally, the general counsel was, in effect, the company's compliance officer. In some companies, general counsels continue to perform that function. In many firms, however, their responsibility for compliance has been curtailed, although they continue to play an important role in other respects. The compliance obligations once given to the general counsel are exercised, instead, by the chief compliance officer.

Why has the compliance role of corporate general counsels been curtailed in some companies? A number of answers might be proposed. In the first place, the job of compliance, as it has evolved, is no longer exclusively a legal task. The job does retain important legal aspects, but other aspects do not require the services of lawyers. For example, the compliance operation tests for conformity not only with external legal norms, but also with internal codes of conduct that may not be binding in a strict legal sense. Testing for compliance, moreover, is not a specifically legal task; it has more in common with internal audit. Cost considerations are also relevant: A modern compliance operation cannot be staffed exclusively by lawyers because doing so would be cost prohibitive.

In addition to the fact that the compliance function has morphed into an enterprise with significant non-legal elements, the function of compliance is in tension with the legal role of the corporate general counsel. As the company's lawyer, the general counsel owes strong obligations of loyalty to her client. The general counsel is not a regulator or an agent of regulators; her relationship with the regulator is potentially adversarial. These professional duties of loyalty and zeal sit uncomfortably with the compliance operation, which is in a sense a form of privatized law enforcement. Given this implicit conflict of roles, some companies have clarified that the general counsel is the company's lawyer. The general counsel is not expected to act as a beat cop walking the corridors of the company's organization chart to ensure that rules and regulations are being followed.

This doesn't mean that the general counsel is squeezed completely out of the compliance function, even in companies that host a specialized compliance office. If legal violations are detected, the general counsel will usually have input in devising the company's response. If outside counsel is retained to perform an investigation, the general counsel will usually be responsible for interfacing with the private law firm — retaining them, monitoring their work, and attempting (sometimes ineffectually) to keep their bills under control. If the company sues or is sued by regulator, the general counsel will usually supervise the litigation.

At the same time as it has shrunk in some respects, the role of the general counsel has expanded in others. Especially when relieved of the role as principal overseer of compliance within the company, the general counsel can play an increased role in strategic management. Perhaps most importantly, the general counsel is likely to have significant input into the company's assessment of reputational risks. A lawsuit against the company, whether by the government or by class action plaintiffs, can have significant repercussions for how the company is perceived by its customers, suppliers, shareholders, and creditors. The general counsel can play a constructive role in strategic planning to minimize reputational risk before adverse events occur, and to manage the harmful impact afterward.

Questions and Comments

1. What qualities are required for the job of corporate general counsel? Former Delaware Supreme Court Chief Justice E. Norman Veasey and co-author Christine T. Di Guglielmo identify the following fundamental characteristics: (a) great technical skills as a lawyer, (b) wisdom and judgment as a counselor, (c) strong leadership ability, (d) independence, and (e) an unwavering moral compass. Norman Veasey & Christine T. Di Guglielmo, *The Indispensable Counsel: The Chief Legal Officer in the New Reality* (2012). Other than King Solomon, who is blessed with all these virtues?

2. Veasey and Guglielmo use the term "CLO" (chief legal officer) to refer to the position of corporate general counsel. Was this accidental? What might they be trying to accomplish by the subtle change of the terms of reference?

3. Veasey and Guglielmo suggest that the CLO should seek to manage tensions within the organization as they arise, including disagreements between the chief executive officer and the board of directors. Does this mean that the CLO should function as some sort of go-between, or facilitator, or even quasi-therapist?

4. Is a model of the CLO as mediator consistent with the traditional concept of the attorney as a zealous advocate?

5. Why not split the role of CLO? One attorney could represent the board of directors; the other could represent the CEO and her team. Does the problem of conflict of interest disappear, or would such an arrangement create even more problems?

6. What, if anything, does the Veasey-Guglielmo approach suggest about the tension between the attorney's role as zealous advocate and her role as servant of the public interest?

7. For discussion of ethical problems that can arise when the roles of chief legal officer and chief compliance officer are merged, see John B. McNeece IV, *The Ethical Conflicts of the Hybrid General Counsel and Chief Compliance Officer*, 25 Geo. J. Legal Ethics 677 (2012).

PROBLEM 3-5

You are in-house general counsel of Coulomb Co., a manufacturer of electrical equipment. In the ordinary course of business you are copied on emails regarding a purchase contract for several million dollars of low-coolant shut-down valves for the company's line of industrial generators. You observe in one email that Coulomb's engineers have raised concerns about these valves: They sometimes shut the generator down when coolant levels are normal and at other times fail to shut down the generator when coolant levels are low. You understand that without proper coolant functioning, the equipment can suffer breakdowns or catch fire. You review the purchase contract and approve it for legal form. In a private meeting with the CEO, you ask about the engineers' concerns. "Don't worry about that," the CEO replies dismissively, "these parts are much cheaper than what we have been using and we are confident they are good enough to meet our customers' needs." At the board meeting, the CEO touts the cost reductions achieved by the purchase of new shut-down valves but doesn't mention anything about the concerns raised by the engineers. Should you speak up?

PROBLEM 3-6

As general counsel for Slimco, a retailer of exercise equipment, you have come to know and like the members of the board of directors over the years. One day the chair of the audit committee calls you and says: "I have to talk with you about a confidential matter that involves Mary." You know he is referring to Mary Malani, the company's chief executive officer. The audit committee chair continues, "You have to promise me first that nothing I say or even the fact I contacted you will ever get back to her." What should you say?

PROBLEM 3-7

Jack Jones is the chairman and chief executive officer of Jones Corporation, a Denver-based importer of children's clothing with $1.2 billion in annual sales. Jones Corporation is 80 percent owned by Jack Jones and his children. You are general counsel; your job description requires you to devote essentially all of your professional time to Jones Corporation business. One day Jack Jones pops into your office with a request. "Hey, I know you used to practice real estate law. My wife and I are buying a vacation home in Aspen. I want you to represent us!" Jones makes it clear that you will be in line for a big annual bonus if you do what he asks, *gratis*. What do you say?

H. THE CHIEF RISK OFFICER

Many companies host a chief risk officer (CRO) in a senior management position. The CRO, where one exists, is charged with designing and implementing risk management policies and procedures across the organization. She may report to the chief executive officer, the chief financial officer, another senior executive, or to the board or the board risk committee.

At one time the role of the CRO was relatively low in the status hierarchy of firms. Former Treasury Secretary Timothy Geithner famously reported an incident in which John Thain, then chief executive officer of Merrill Lynch, admitted he did not know the name of his chief risk officer — who at the time was sitting next to him.

It is fair to say that the status and influence of CROs has grown exponentially since then — sparked in no small measure by the perception among regulators and industry leaders that the disaster of the financial crisis of 2007-2009 could have been mitigated if banks and other financial firms had implemented better risk management strategies in the preceding years. The position of CRO has grown up along with the increasing importance of enterprise risk management strategies that seek to coordinate risk across the entire organization. As of 2013, according to one survey, CROs operated in more than half of financial services firms and about a quarter of non-financial firms. Matteo Tonello, *Risk in the Boardroom*, Conf. Bd. Dir. Notes, (May 2013), https://www.conference-board.org/retrievefile.cfm? Filename=TCB-DN-V5N9-13.pdf&type=subsite.

Questions and Comments

1. To whom should the chief risk officer report? The chief executive officer? The board risk committee (or other committee performing similar functions)? Someone else?

2. Consider the following:

   a. The company is considering acquiring or merging with another company.
   b. The company is considering entering the market in Canada, where it has not previously done business.
   c. The company is changing vendors of software for its sales force.
   d. The company has been sued in a class action lawsuit seeking $10 million in damages.
   e. The company is looking to hire a new chief technology officer.
   f. The company is assessing the implications for its business of an upcoming presidential election.

On which of these issues should the CRO be consulted? On which, if any, should she be excluded?

3. Some companies have created management-level risk committees that replicate, at the executive level, some of the functions of the board risk committee. In addition to the chief risk officer, members of the management risk committee may include the chief executive officer, chief operating officer, general counsel, and the heads of any departments deemed especially critical to risk management (e.g., in a financial institution, the head of the credit committee). The function of the management risk committee is to coordinate risk management activities at the level

of implementation, leaving to the board risk committee or the full board the formulation of general policies relating to risk.

4. The reporting requirements for the management risk committee are not well understood. Should the management risk committee report to the chief risk officer — or should the chief risk officer report to the management risk committee? Should the management risk committee report to the board risk committee, the full board of directors, the chief executive officer, some combination of the above, or no one in particular? There appears to be no consistent pattern.

5. CROs often rely heavily on vendors to assist them in compiling and analyzing information pertinent to risk and in crafting tables, heat maps, and other graphic tools that assist in the risk management task. Do you see any problems with relying on an outside vendor for help with a function as fundamental as risk management?

6. What qualities of character or judgment qualify someone to be a chief risk officer? What conditions facilitate success for the CRO, and what are likely to induce failure? Best practices are increasingly favoring policies that provide a degree of independence to the CRO and empower that official within the organization. In the words of the Group of Thirty, a CRO should be someone who is "independent, has stature within the management structure and unfettered access to the board risk committee, and has the authority to find the appropriate balance between constraint and support of risk taking. The CRO must have the independence, skills, and stature to influence the firm's risk-taking activities." Beyond this, CROs "need courage and conviction, and they should be willing to walk away from their job if their judgment on major issues is ignored." Group of Thirty, Toward Effective Governance of Financial Institutions (2012), pp. 21, 48. Do you agree?

7. As in the case of compliance, compensation for risk management officers has skyrocketed as market demand has increased. In some cases, salaries have doubled in the space of just a few years. As of 2014, CROs at mid-size regional banks were making as much as $1 million per year in salary; for the largest banks, the compensation is even larger.

8. For more on the role of the CRO, see Anette Mikes, *Chief Risk Officers at Crunch Time: Compliance Champions or Business Partners?*, J. Risk Mgmt. in Fin. Institutions 2, no. 1 (November-December 2008); Robert S. Kaplan et al., *Managing Risk in the New World*, 87 Harv. Bus. Rev., 68 (October 2009).

9. Banks in the European Union are now required to "have a risk management function independent from the operational functions and which shall have sufficient authority, stature, resources and access to the management body" — in other words, an executive risk management operation. The risk management function must be "actively involved in elaborating the institution's risk strategy and in all material risk management decisions and [must be able to] deliver a complete view of the whole range of risks of the institution." Executive risk management is granted substantial independence from business line executives: "The head of the risk management function shall be an independent senior manager with distinct responsibility for the risk management function, . . . shall not be removed without prior approval of the management body in its supervisory function and shall be able to have direct access to the management body in its supervisory function where necessary." European Union Capital Requirements Directive IV, Art. 76 ¶5. Would you recommend a similar degree of independence for CROs of American banks? For CROs of other companies?

10. Should government agencies appoint their own risk officers to manage the risks to their effective functioning? If they do not, how can they in good conscience

insist that the entities that they regulate do so? In 2015, the Office of the Comptroller of the Currency established a precedent by appointing a chief risk officer to head up a new Office of Enterprise Risk Management. The CRO is responsible for developing an agency-wide view of risks and evaluating adherence to the agency's risk appetite statement.

I. DIRECTOR OF HUMAN RESOURCES

The human resources department plays an important role in managing employment-related compliance and risk management issues. The HR department becomes involved in these issues at the very earliest stage of a person's contact with a company: when the person is hired. By establishing priorities, values, and "tone," the director of human resources can exercise an important influence on who comes to the company. Her influence is particularly important for junior people, who may not be on the "radar screen" of senior management. Those junior people become a resource of the company; if they stick around, they may eventually be promoted into the ranks of senior managers where they participate in strategic decisions pertinent to risk and compliance.

Human resources also plays a role when problems arise. Suppose, for example, that a manager in the purchasing department is suspected of accepting bribes from suppliers. The human resources department must determine what to do with the suspect while the matter is being investigated. Should the person be re-assigned pending the outcome of the investigation? Placed on administrative leave? Fired? If she is fired, should she receive a severance package? What happens if after an investigation the employee is determined to have engaged in misconduct? Can the company recoup any of the salary it has paid out? Is the employee entitled to continuation of benefits, such as health insurance? What if the employee is fired and the investigation eventually concludes she has done nothing wrong—does the former employee have any rights against the company?

Human resources departments are lodged at different places in different firms. In some, the head of HR (usually designated as an "director of human resources," "executive vice president for human resources," or an equivalent) reports directly to the chief executive officer; in others the reporting line passes through another senior officer such as the chief operating officer.

Part II

Compliance

4

Introduction to Compliance

A. WHAT IS COMPLIANCE?

We briefly defined the term "compliance" in the Introduction. Now let's examine the idea in more detail. The term "compliance," as commonly understood, has the following elements: (a) an actor is conforming her behavior to some standard or norm; (b) the standard or norm is external — not set by the actor, but rather by some other authority; and (c) the actor would not necessarily act in accordance with the standard on her own — some effort of will, incentive, or compulsion is involved.

This everyday understanding of "compliance" is part of what we mean when we use the term in this book. But for present purposes, we mean something more specific. The key additional elements are these: (a) the actor in question is a complex organization, not an individual; and (b) we refer, not only to the organization's behavior in conforming to the norm, but also — and more importantly — to the actions that the organization undertakes to ensure that the norm is obeyed.

At the most general level, compliance can be seen to involve a tradeoff of costs and benefits. On the one hand, if compliance functions well, it is a cheaper and more effective means to ensure that complex organizations obey applicable norms. The reason is that an external norm enforcer does not

> The compliance function is a form of internalized norm enforcement within organizations.

have the resources or the ability either to effectively monitor what happens inside a complex organization or to devise an effective system of sanctions. The organization has the knowledge and the ability to perform these tasks much more effectively than any outside party. It therefore makes sense for institutions to police themselves — to carry out a compliance operation.

On the other hand, because compliance delegates responsibility for norm enforcement to the organization, the external enforcer (regulator, prosecutor, etc.) loses some degree of control over the situation: It may be perilous to rely on an institution to police itself when the institution wants to flout the norm or to cover up violations after they have occurred. Accordingly, the external enforcer needs to monitor the compliance function to ensure that it is faithfully and effectively carried out. There is also a problem of costs. When the external enforcer operates directly, rather than through a compliance operation, the enforcer bears all the costs of the enforcement activity. It therefore has an incentive to perform the enforcement in a cost-effective way. When, however, the external enforcer relies on internal compliance to enforce norms, the enforcer doesn't bear the costs of enforcement; these are imposed on the organization. There is, accordingly, a danger of overkill: Since the external enforcer doesn't internalize the costs of compliance, it may demand that the organization implement compliance operations that are costly but not particularly effective or necessary.

The job of policymakers is to devise a compliance system that minimizes the total costs of norm enforcement and norm violations. This task cannot be performed scientifically. Lawmakers are not structural engineers. When it comes to designing a compliance system much is done by intuition and guesswork. Nevertheless, in examining any given compliance system, we can still ask the basic questions: Does it draw the right line between internal and external enforcement; are the requirements for compliance operations appropriate, insufficient, or excessive; are there sufficient back-up lines of defense; and overall, does the chosen structure represent a reasonable tradeoff of costs and benefits?

B. LANDMARKS IN THE HISTORY OF COMPLIANCE

To understand the modern compliance function, it is useful to know something about its background and origins. The following list identifies some of the key points in the development of this institution.

- The Interstate Commerce Commission: Although history has no beginning (other than the Big Bang), we can usually identify a provisional starting point. In the case of the compliance function, that point might be the Interstate Commerce Act of 1887, which created a federal administrative agency, the Interstate Commerce Commission (ICC), to regulate the railroads. Establishing a model that many would follow, the statute empowered the ICC to investigate and adjudicate on complaints against railroads and to issue cease-and-desist orders to stop illegal practices.
- The Progressive Movement of the 1890s through 1920s: This period of American history reflected concern for eliminating corruption and enhancing the efficiency of government. Among its achievements were Pure Food and Drug Act (1906), the Federal Reserve Act (1913), and the Clayton Antitrust Law (1914).
- The Depression and the New Deal of the 1930s: The collapse of financial markets and the Depression of the 1930s led to fundamental reforms of the American financial system. Among the key statutes to emerge from this period were the Banking Act of 1933 and the Securities Acts of 1933 and 1934. More generally, this period witnessed a change in attitude on the Supreme Court, from one that generally resisted regulation of business to one that enthusiastically embraced it.

- Environmental awareness: The rise of environmental concerns in the 1960s sparked a series of important federal statutes, including the Clean Water Act and the Clean Air Act, as well as the birth of a new federal administrative agency, the Environmental Protection Agency.

- Foreign corrupt practices: In the mid-1970s, many American companies were exposed for paying bribes to foreign government officials. Public outrage led to the enactment of the Foreign Corrupt Practices Act of 1977 (see Chapter 13).

- The savings and loan debacle: In 1979, to curb inflation, the Federal Reserve Board adopted tight monetary policies that greatly increased interest rates. An unintended consequence was severe financial distress for savings and loan (S&L) institutions. These banks specialized in making fixed rate mortgage loans with funds obtained on savings accounts with interest rates capped by law. As interest rates skyrocketed, the value of S&L mortgage loan portfolios fell sharply; meanwhile they lost billions from their traditional funding base as depositors withdrew funds in order to invest in higher-yielding assets. To overcome the distress, many S&Ls resorted to risky nontraditional investments (such as junk bonds) and began to seek alternative but more expensive sources of funding. Eventually, a substantial portion of the industry collapsed, bankrupting the deposit insurance fund for these institutions and costing the American taxpayers more than $100 billion. The manifold failures of the regulators and the greed displayed by some S&L operators shook America's confidence in the integrity and honesty of the financial system, leading to significant legislation that upgraded banking regulation in many respects.

- The corporate scandals of the early 2000s: Enron, one of America's largest energy companies, went bankrupt in 2001 after it was revealed that several of the company's complex financing transactions were fraudulent. In the wake of the disclosures, the government indicted Arthur Andersen, one of the nation's biggest public accounting firms, which had served as Enron's auditor during the period in which the frauds were perpetrated (see Chapter 9). Although the indictment charged only a relatively minor offense (the government claimed that Andersen had obstructed justice when it destroyed Enron-related records), the firm could not withstand the reputational effects of the indictment and quickly closed its doors. Enron was only one of several spectacular corporate failures during this period; others included WorldCom, Global Crossing, and Adelphia. These scandals led to the enactment of the Sarbanes-Oxley Act (2002), one of the most important governance and compliance statutes in American history.

- Terror and rogue states: The attacks of September 2001 focused the nation's attention on a new threat to its security. In order to choke off terror financing and also to identify terrorist activity before an attack occurs, the government enhanced the obligation of financial institutions to report suspicious activities (see Chapter 14). Meanwhile, an ever-increasing set of sanctions were imposed on governments deemed not to be in compliance with the obligations of international law. The resulting complex of regulations is one of the more troublesome areas for compliance today.

- The financial crisis of 2007-2009: A sustained period of low interest rates sparked a "bubble" in housing markets in the early to mid-2000s, with home prices rising far above their historical trend line. Financial institutions made or refinanced mortgage loans, often to "subprime" borrowers with poor credit histories, and packaged those loans into mortgage-backed securities which were then sold on public credit markets. After the housing bubble burst in 2007, millions of homeowners went into foreclosure because they had invested in homes they could not afford; and some of the world's largest financial institutions faced severe distress as a result of the rapid deterioration in the value of their holdings of mortgage-backed securities. The cataclysmic events of that period — the failures of Bear Stearns, Lehman Brothers, Indymac, and AIG (among others); the distress sale of Merrill Lynch to Bank of America; government takeovers of Fannie Mae and Freddy Mac; a massive run on the money market fund industry; distress conversions of Goldman Sachs and Morgan Stanley into bank holding companies; the bankruptcies and bailouts of General Motors and Chrysler; sovereign debt problems in Europe; bailouts of Greece, Portugal, Ireland, Cyprus, and Spain; and the effective bankruptcy of an entire country (Iceland) — will form a chapter in business history for hundreds of years to come. Among other consequences, the crisis gave birth to the Dodd-Frank Act (2010), the most significant piece of financial regulation since the Great Depression, which contains many provisions pertinent to compliance.

C. THE RISE OF THE ADMINISTRATIVE STATE

These and other events punctuated a much broader, deeper, and more fundamental development in American law: the rise of the administrative state. The authority of government to regulate private organizations in the nineteenth century followed what might be termed a *judicial model* of regulation. Under this model, the government and the regulated organization were seen as parties on essentially equal footing. True, the government was a particularly powerful party with many resources at its disposal; but the government also faced special disadvantages, including the need to comply with constitutional norms. To obtain relief under the judicial model, the government needed to go to court and establish its case under the applicable standard of proof. Complex regulatory statutes didn't exist. The governing rules were often those of the common law. If the applicable principles were statutory, it was the courts, not the government, that gave meaning and content to ambiguous provisions. Criminal enforcement against organizations was unknown. Penalties, where enforced, were not exorbitant.

Compare this with the situation today, and you will find that the judicial model, while not yet extinct, is definitely an endangered species. Its habitat has been invaded by a different model of enforcement, which we might call the *administrative model* of regulation. The key to the administrative model is that legal norms governing complex organizations are defined, adjudicated, and enforced by administrative agencies rather than courts. Judges are not absent from the process, but play a decidedly less important role than they did in years past.

This section examines three important aspects of the transition from the judicial model to the administrative model: (a) increases in the extent and complexity of regulation; (b) displacement of courts from their traditional role in defining and adjudicating legal rights; and (c) increases in the government's enforcement powers.

1. Increases in the Scope and Complexity of Regulation

The most obvious feature of the modern administrative state, as compared with its predecessor, is the extraordinary growth in the scope and complexity of regulation. Congress has increased the intensity of regulation in three general phases: first, in the Progressive Era when it imposed federal regulations on anticompetitive conduct, foods and drugs, and the railroad industry; second, in the New Deal, when it regulated banks, securities firms, and financial markets; and third, a period starting in the 1960s and continuing today when the government became more or less continuously active in many different settings. Although this most recent period also saw sporadic episodes of deregulation (airline pricing and bank affiliations with other financial services firms being examples), the general trend has been for Congress and state legislatures to impose ever more complicated and more comprehensive regulations over an ever-increasing domain of private activity.

2. From Judging to Administration

a. The Power to Establish Norms of Conduct

Judges once occupied a preeminent position in establishing the norms of conduct that regulated the behavior of complex institutions. Suppose, for example, that a factory was emitting smoke and vibrations. Not too long ago, protection of environmental quality was left to the judge-made law of nuisance, which provided a means by which the government or an aggrieved landowner could obtain an order "abating" the problem.

Today, in contrast, the legal landscape has transformed from one where substantive rules were provided largely by judges to one where substantive rules are provided largely by legislatures and administrative agencies. The problem of the polluting factory would be addressed by an administrative agency — the EPA or state officials — and would be resolved on the basis of standards of conduct promulgated by the legislature or the agency.

The process has not been easy, and at the beginning was fiercely resisted by many judges. They applied a maxim that statutes in derogation of the common law would be strictly construed — in other words, they were as uncharitable as possible to legislative challenges to judicial lawmaking. When unfriendly rules of interpretation didn't work, courts resorted to higher authority: Statutes were invalidated on the ground that they invaded rights to contract, delegated too much power to administrators, were beyond congressional authority under the Constitution, or ran afoul of constitutional rights. Those efforts at judicial resistance largely ended during the New Deal of the 1930s.

SEC v. Chenery Corp.

332 U.S. 194 (1947)

[Citing judicial precedent, the SEC held that managers of a public utility in reorganization could not convert preferred stock they owned in the company into stock of the reorganized company. In 1943, the Supreme Court rejected the agency's decision on the ground that it was not supported by the cited judicial authority. On remand, the SEC reached the same decision, but supported it this time with public policy arguments rather than case law. Five years after its initial decision, the Court upheld the agency's decision.]

Mr. Justice MURPHY delivered the opinion of the Court:

. . . There is . . . a reasonable basis for a value judgment that the benefits and profits accruing to the management from the stock purchases should be prohibited, regardless of the good faith involved. And it is a judgment that can justifiably be reached in terms of fairness and equitableness, to the end that the interests of the public, the investors and the consumers might be protected. But it is a judgment based upon public policy, a judgment which Congress has indicated is of the type for the Commission to make . . . . Whether we agree or disagree with the result reached, it is an allowable judgment which we cannot disturb.

Mr. Justice JACKSON, dissenting:

The Court by this present decision sustains the identical administrative order which only recently it held invalid. There being no change in the order, no additional evidence in the record, and no amendment of relevant legislation, it is clear that there has been a shift in attitude between that of the controlling membership of the Court when the case was first here and that of those who have the power of decision on this second review.

I feel constrained to disagree with the reasoning offered to rationalize this shift. It makes judicial review of administrative orders a hopeless formality for the litigant, even where granted to him by Congress. It reduces the judicial process in such cases to a mere feint . . . .

If it is of no consequence that no rule of law be existent to support an administrative order, and the Court of Appeals is obliged to defer to administrative experience and to sustain a Commission's power merely because it has been asserted and exercised, of what use is it to print a record or briefs in the case, or to hear argument? Administrative experience always is present, at least to the degree that it is here, and would always dictate a like deference by this Court to an assertion of administrative power . . . .

Questions and Comments

1. Consider the lessons of the *Chenery* case for administrative agencies. The SEC originally followed a version of the judicial model. Even though it decided the rights of the parties on its own, without going into court, at least it supported its decision by reference to judicial precedents. When this didn't fly, the SEC simply gave up on citing judicial precedents and supported exactly the same decision with free-floating policy rationales. *Presto!* The alchemy of expertise transformed the decision from one outside the agency's authority into one inside its authority. Given *Chenery*, what agency would elect to rely on case law when it can accomplish more, and with greater ease, by supporting its decision on policy grounds?

2. One issue in the case was whether the agency could impose a new standard of conduct on private parties to govern actions already taken. Justice Murphy, writing for the Court, had no problem with this: "The absence of a general rule or regulation . . . did not affect the Commission's duties in relation to the particular proposal before it." Justice Jackson, in dissent, argued that the SEC's "administrative authoritarianism" undervalued the rule of law. Who has the better of the argument?

3. Have common law courts always decided legal questions on a case-by-case basis and imposed the results retroactively? Is it different when the decision is made by an administrative agency?

4. *Chenery* is a landmark in the transition from the judicial to the administrative model of enforcement. The excerpted opinions demonstrate that the Justices understood this fact. Justice Jackson, in dissent, bemoans the loss of judicial power implied by the move to the administrative model of regulation: ". . . what action is, and what is not, within the law must be determined by courts, . . . no matter how much deference is due to the agency's fact finding. Surely an administrative agency is not a law unto itself . . . ." Justice Murphy, on the other hand, is comfortable with ceding judicial authority: "The Commission's conclusion here rests squarely in that area where administrative judgments are entitled to the greatest amount of weight by appellate courts. It is the product of administrative experience, appreciation of the complexities of the problem, realization of the statutory policies, and responsible treatment of the uncontested facts. It is the type of judgment which administrative agencies are best equipped to make and which justifies the use of the administrative process." Who has the better of the argument?

5. Granting that an agency can elect to establish law through case-by-case adjudication, rather than through rulemaking, are there limits to the degree it can innovate when developing the law through the enforcement process? Are there due process limits to the ability of an agency to spring a totally unexpected requirement on an unsuspecting citizen, and then impose sanctions on the regulated party for failing to predict what the agency would do? The answer is clearly "yes": It would be fundamentally unfair to punish people out of the blue. *See* Christopher v. SmithKline Beecham Corp., 132 S. Ct. 2156, 2168 (2012) ("It is one thing to expect regulated parties to conform their conduct to an agency's interpretations once the agency announces them; it is quite another to require regulated parties to divine the agency's interpretations in advance or else be held liable when the agency announces its interpretations for the first time in an enforcement proceeding and demands deference."); FCC v. Fox Television Stations, Inc., 132 S. Ct. 2307 (2012) (setting aside FCC indecency policy on the ground that it failed to provide sufficient notice to broadcasters of what was and was not permissible). But it is far from clear how far an agency can go before it crosses the line.

Justice Murphy's view in the *Chenery* case prevailed. Over time courts came to accept that not only legislatures, but also administrative agencies could establish norms of conduct that differed substantially from the norms traditionally enforced under principles of equity or the common law. Those norms, moreover, did not have to be announced in a formal rule before they were applied; an agency could invent them on the fly and apply them retroactively even when there was no particular reason to anticipate they would be adopted. The Administrative Procedure Act, enacted in 1946, recognized and confirmed that federal agencies can determine private rights and obligations, and can do so either by way of a formal rulemaking procedure or through case-by-case determinations.

Agencies also came to enjoy substantial powers vis-à-vis courts in the *interpretation* of governing norms. Traditionally, courts asserted the power to "say what the law is." But in administrative contexts, the judicial role in interpretation is trumped by the *Chevron* doctrine, which requires courts to defer to agency interpretations: "When a court reviews an agency's construction of the statute which it administers, it is confronted with two questions. First, always, is the question whether Congress has directly spoken to the precise question at issue. If the intent of Congress is clear, that is the end of the matter; for the court as well as the agency, must give effect to the unambiguously expressed intent of Congress. If, however, the court determines Congress has not directly addressed the precise question at issue, the court does not simply impose its own construction on the statute, as would be necessary in the absence of an administrative interpretation. Rather, if the statute is silent or ambiguous with respect to the specific issue, the question for the court is whether the agency's answer is based on a permissible construction of the statute." Chevron v. Natural Resources Defense Council, 467 U.S. 837, 843 (1984). In other words, if the statute is reasonably susceptible to several meanings, one of which is adopted by the agency charged with its implementation, the court should defer to the agency's interpretation even if the court, on its own, might prefer a different interpretation.

The following case explores the outer reaches of the *Chevron* doctrine.

National Cable & Telecommunications Association v. Brand X Internet Services

545 U.S. 967 (2005)

[Petitioners challenged the Federal Communications Commission's (FCC) ruling that cable companies offering broadband Internet access did not provide a "telecommunications service," and hence were exempt from mandatory regulation under the Communications Act.]

Justice THOMAS delivered the opinion of the Court.

. . . At issue in these cases is the proper regulatory classification under the Communications Act of broadband cable Internet service. The Act defines two categories of regulated entities relevant to these cases: telecommunications carriers and information-service providers. The Act regulates telecommunications carriers, but not information-service providers, as common carriers . . . .

In September 2000, the Commission initiated a rulemaking proceeding to, among other things, apply these classifications to cable companies that offer broadband Internet service directly to consumers . . . . In the Declaratory Ruling, the Commission concluded that broadband Internet service provided by cable companies is an "information service" but not a "telecommunications service" under the Act, and therefore not subject to mandatory . . . common-carrier regulation . . . .

The Court of Appeals . . . held that the Commission could not permissibly construe the Communications Act to exempt cable companies providing Internet service from . . . regulation. Rather than analyzing the permissibility of that construction under the deferential framework of Chevron, however, the Court of Appeals grounded its holding in the stare decisis effect of AT & T Corp. v. Portland, 216 F.3d 871 (9th Cir. 2000). Portland held that cable modem service was a "telecommunications service," though the court in that case was not reviewing an administrative proceeding and the Commission was not a party to the case. Nevertheless, Portland's holding, the Court of Appeals reasoned, overrode the contrary interpretation reached by the Commission in the Declaratory Ruling . . . .

The *Chevron* framework governs our review of the Commission's construction. Congress has delegated to the Commission the authority to "execute and enforce" the Communications Act, and to "prescribe such rules and regulations as may be necessary in the public interest to carry out the provisions" of the Act. These provisions give the Commission the authority to promulgate binding legal rules; the Commission issued the order under review in the exercise of that authority; and no one questions that the order is within the Commission's jurisdiction. Hence, as we have in the past, we apply the *Chevron* framework to the Commission's interpretation of the Communications Act . . . .

The Court of Appeals declined to apply *Chevron* because it thought the Commission's interpretation of the Communications Act foreclosed by the conflicting construction of the Act it had adopted in Portland. It based that holding on the assumption that Portland's construction overrode the Commission's, regardless of whether Portland had held the statute to be unambiguous. That reasoning was incorrect.

A court's prior judicial construction of a statute trumps an agency construction otherwise entitled to *Chevron* deference only if the prior court decision holds that its construction follows from the unambiguous terms of the statute and thus leaves no room for agency discretion. This principle follows from *Chevron* itself. *Chevron* established a "presumption that Congress, when it left ambiguity in a statute meant for implementation by an agency, understood that the ambiguity would be resolved, first and foremost, by the agency, and desired the agency (rather than the courts) to possess whatever degree of discretion the ambiguity allows." Yet allowing a judicial precedent to foreclose an agency from interpreting an ambiguous statute, as the Court of Appeals assumed it could, would allow a court's interpretation to override an agency's. *Chevron*'s premise is that it is for agencies, not courts, to fill statutory gaps. The better rule is to hold judicial interpretations contained in precedents to the same demanding *Chevron* step one standard that applies if the court is reviewing the agency's construction on a blank slate: Only a judicial precedent holding that the statute unambiguously forecloses the agency's interpretation, and therefore contains no gap for the agency to fill, displaces a conflicting agency construction.

A contrary rule would produce anomalous results. It would mean that whether an agency's interpretation of an ambiguous statute is entitled to *Chevron* deference would turn on the order in which the interpretations issue: If the court's construction came first, its construction would prevail, whereas if the agency's came first, the agency's construction would command *Chevron* deference. Yet whether Congress has delegated to an agency the authority to interpret a statute does not depend on the order in which the judicial and administrative constructions occur. The Court of Appeals' rule, moreover, would "lead to the ossification of large portions of our statutory law," by precluding agencies from revising unwise judicial constructions of ambiguous statutes. Neither *Chevron* nor the doctrine of stare decisis requires these haphazard results.

The dissent answers that allowing an agency to override what a court believes to be the best interpretation of a statute makes "judicial decisions subject to reversal by executive officers." It does not. Since *Chevron* teaches that a court's opinion as to the best reading of an ambiguous statute an agency is charged with administering is not authoritative, the agency's decision to construe that statute differently from a court does not say that the court's holding was legally wrong. Instead, the agency may, consistent with the court's holding, choose a different construction, since the agency remains the authoritative interpreter (within the limits of reason) of such statutes. In all other respects, the court's prior ruling remains binding law (for example, as to agency interpretations to which *Chevron* is inapplicable). The precedent has not been "reversed" by the agency, any more than a federal court's interpretation of a State's law can be said to have been "reversed" by a state court that adopts a conflicting (yet authoritative) interpretation of state law.

[Applying *Chevron* deference, the Court upheld the FCC's interpretation.]

Justice SCALIA, dissenting.

. . . Article III courts do not sit to render decisions that can be reversed or ignored by executive officers . . . . That is what today's decision effectively allows. Even when the agency itself is party to the case in which the Court construes a statute, the agency will be able to disregard that construction and seek Chevron deference for its contrary construction the next time around . . . .

I would adhere to what has been the rule in the past: When a court interprets a statute without Chevron deference to agency views, its interpretation (whether or not asserted to rest upon an unambiguous text) is the law . . . . It is a sadness that the Court should go so far out of its way to make bad law.

I respectfully dissent.

Questions and Comments

1. Can you see how the *Chevron* rule undermines the judicial model of enforcement and supports the administrative model?

2. How does the principal case extend the *Chevron* rule and further restrict the authority of federal courts to interpret statutes in ways inconsistent with interpretations favored by an administrative agency?

3. How does the majority opinion see the authority of courts to interpret administrative statutes? How does it conceptualize the interpretive powers of agencies charged with enforcing these statutes? Do you agree?

4. What policy rationale does the Court offer for the *Chevron* rule? Do you agree that agencies are better equipped than courts to make "difficult policy choices"? Do courts make difficult policy choices in other contexts? Is an administrative agency likely to make a better policy choice, or one that is politically more expedient?

5. Given that statutory interpretation is a key judicial power, why are the courts apparently so willing to give that authority away?

Should the rule of deference be different when the statutory provision in question goes to the extent of the agency's jurisdiction rather than to some substantive matter within the scope of the agency's jurisdiction? Consider the following:

City of Arlington v. F.C.C.

133 S. Ct. 1863 (2013)

Justice SCALIA delivered the opinion of the Court:

. . . *Chevron* is rooted in a background presumption of congressional intent: namely, "that Congress, when it left ambiguity in a statute" administered by an agency, "understood that the ambiguity would be resolved, first and foremost, by the agency, and desired the agency (rather than the courts) to possess whatever degree of discretion the ambiguity allows." *Chevron* thus provides a stable background rule against which Congress can legislate: Statutory ambiguities will be resolved, within the bounds of reasonable interpretation, not by the courts but by the administering agency. Congress knows to speak in plain terms when it wishes to circumscribe, and in capacious terms when it wishes to enlarge, agency discretion.

The question here is whether a court must defer under *Chevron* to an agency's interpretation of a statutory ambiguity that concerns the scope of the agency's statutory authority (that is, its jurisdiction). The argument against deference rests on the premise that there exist two distinct classes of agency interpretations: Some interpretations — the big, important ones, presumably — define the agency's "jurisdiction." Others — humdrum, run-of-the-mill stuff — are simply applications of jurisdiction the agency plainly has. That premise is false, because the distinction between "jurisdictional" and "non-jurisdictional" interpretations is a mirage. No matter how it is framed, the question a court faces when confronted with an agency's interpretation of a statute it administers is always, simply, whether the agency has stayed within the bounds of its statutory authority . . . .

The false dichotomy between "jurisdictional" and "non-jurisdictional" agency interpretations may be no more than a bogeyman, but it is dangerous all the same. Like the Hound of the Baskervilles, it is conjured by those with greater quarry in sight: Make no mistake — the ultimate target here is *Chevron* itself. Savvy challengers of agency action would play the "jurisdictional" card in every case. Some judges would be deceived by the specious, but scary-sounding, "jurisdictional"-"non-jurisdictional" line; others tempted by the prospect of making public policy by prescribing the meaning of ambiguous statutory commands. The effect would be to transfer any number of interpretive decisions — archetypal *Chevron* questions, about how best to construe an ambiguous term in light of competing policy interests — from the agencies that administer the statutes to federal courts.

[Note 4: The Chief Justice's discomfort with the growth of agency power is perhaps understandable. But the dissent overstates when it claims that agencies exercise "legislative power" and "judicial power." The former is vested exclusively in Congress, the latter in the "one supreme Court" and "such inferior Courts as the Congress may from time to time ordain and establish," Art. III, §1. Agencies make rules . . . and conduct adjudications . . . and have done so since the beginning of the Republic. These activities take "legislative" and "judicial" forms, but they are exercises of — indeed, under our constitutional structure they must be exercises of — the "executive Power."]

[The majority held that *Chevron* deference applied.]

Chief Justice ROBERTS, dissenting:

One of the principal authors of the Constitution famously wrote that the "accumulation of all powers, legislative, executive, and judiciary, in the same hands, . . . may justly be pronounced the very definition of tyranny." The Federalist No. 47, p. 324 (J. Cooke ed. 1961) (J. Madison). Although modern administrative agencies fit most comfortably within the Executive Branch, as a practical matter they exercise legislative power, by promulgating regulations with the force of law; executive power, by policing compliance with those regulations; and judicial power, by adjudicating enforcement actions and imposing sanctions on those found to have violated their rules. The accumulation of these powers in the same hands is not an occasional or isolated exception to the constitutional plan; it is a central feature of modern American government.

The administrative state "wields vast power and touches almost every aspect of daily life." The Framers could hardly have envisioned today's "vast and varied federal bureaucracy" and the authority administrative agencies now hold over our economic, social, and political activities. And the federal bureaucracy continues to grow; in the last 15 years, Congress has launched more than 50 new agencies. And more are on the way.

Although the Constitution empowers the President to keep federal officers accountable, administrative agencies enjoy in practice a significant degree of independence. As scholars have noted, "no President (or his executive office staff) could, and presumably none would wish to, supervise so broad a swath of regulatory activity." Kagan, Presidential Administration, 114 Harv. L. Rev. 2245, 2250 (2001); see also S. Breyer, Making Our Democracy Work 110 (2010) ("the president may not have the time or willingness to review [agency] decisions"). President Truman colorfully described his power over the administrative state by complaining, "I thought I was the president, but when it comes to these bureaucrats, I can't do a damn thing." President Kennedy once told a constituent, "I agree with you, but I don't know if the government will." The collection of agencies housed outside the traditional executive departments, including the Federal Communications Commission, is routinely described as the "headless fourth branch of government," reflecting not only the scope of their authority but their practical independence.

As for judicial oversight, agencies enjoy broad power to construe statutory provisions over which they have been given interpretive authority . . . . When it applies, Chevron is a powerful weapon in an agency's regulatory arsenal. Congressional delegations to agencies are often ambiguous — expressing "a mood rather than a message." By design or default, Congress often fails to speak to "the precise question" before an agency. In the absence of such an answer, an agency's interpretation has the full force and effect of law, unless it "exceeds the bounds of the permissible."

It would be a bit much to describe the result as "the very definition of tyranny," but the danger posed by the growing power of the administrative state cannot be dismissed.

What the Court says in footnote 4 of its opinion is good, and true (except of course for the "dissent overstates" part). The Framers did divide governmental power in the manner the Court describes, for the purpose of safeguarding liberty. And yet . . . the citizen confronting thousands of pages of regulations — promulgated by an agency directed by Congress to regulate, say, "in the public interest" — can perhaps be excused for thinking that it is the agency really doing the legislating. And with hundreds of federal agencies poking into every nook and cranny of daily life, that citizen might also understandably question whether Presidential oversight — a critical part of the Constitutional plan — is always an effective safeguard against agency overreaching.

It is against this background that we consider whether the authority of administrative agencies should be augmented even further, to include not only broad power to give definitive answers to questions left to them by Congress, but also the same power to decide when Congress has given them that power.

Questions and Comments

1. Do you see a difference between administrative interpretations of governing statutes in cases where the agency's authority to act is not in question and interpretations that establish the agency's right to act? Is there a reason why a court might be more suspicious of the reliability of an agency's judgment with respect to the latter?

2. The majority and dissent disagree over whether the line between "jurisdictional" and "non-jurisdictional" interpretations can hold up to scrutiny. Why is the majority so keen on denying the viability of the distinction? Why is the dissent so keen on establishing it?

3. Notice the scholars whom Chief Justice Roberts, writing in dissent, cites in support of his critique of the administrative state. Is it a coincidence that both happen to be the Chief Justice's colleagues, and that both joined the majority opinion? *J'en doute.*

4. Do you understand what the majority opinion is getting at in footnote 4? Does the dissenting opinion agree with these points, or disagree — or a little of both?

5. It is pretty unusual for the Chief Justice of the United States to say in a published opinion that "the danger posed by the growing power of the administrative state cannot be dismissed." The Court, after all, has the power to declare the administrative state unconstitutional — an action that would have profound consequences for the entire American system of government. Three Justices joined Chief Justice Roberts' dissent, thus indicating their agreement with this statement. Moreover, the majority opinion doesn't really disagree, does it? Justice Scalia doesn't offer a stout defense of the administrative state — in fact he admits that the dissent's "discomfort with the growth of agency power is perhaps understandable." Do you think any of the Justices would consider creating constitutional limits on the administrative state, or is the criticism merely complaining about something that cannot be changed?

6. Any Justice who thought about trimming the powers of the administrative state would need to consider the Court's experience during the New Deal. A conservative majority on the Court originally resisted President Roosevelt's attempts to increase government control over the private sector. In fact the Court invalidated Roosevelt's initial effort in this respect, the First New Deal. The President's response was to seek to "pack" the Court by increasing its size and appointing friendly Justices. The Court-packing plan failed but Roosevelt prevailed in the long run: Eventually, he was able to gain majority support for his programs; the result was to establish the constitutional charter for the administrative state we have today.

7. Do you agree with Chief Justice Roberts' critique of the administrative state?

8. Many legal scholars believe that, despite its shortcomings, the administrative state has improved the lives of citizens. The classic justification is James M. Landis, *The Administrative Process* (1938); more recent contributions include Jeremy Waldron, *The Rule of Law and the Measure of Property* (2012); and Bruce Ackerman, *We the People* (1991). For dissenting opinions, see, e.g., Gary Lawson, *The Rise and Rise of the Administrative State*, 107 Harv. L. Rev. 1221 (1994); Richard A. Epstein, *Design for Liberty: Private Property, Public Administration, and the Rule of Law* (2011).

Administrative agencies, like courts, can change their interpretations of governing law. Is the same judicial deference owed to an agency's interpretation if it runs counter to a previous interpretation by the same agency? Arguably, if the agency is so uncertain of its position as to reverse course on an important statutory issue, the courts should not be as strictly constrained to follow the agency in its new view. But generally courts give agencies substantial leeway to reverse or modify their interpretations, so long as the agency can demonstrate that the new interpretation is a reasonable construction of the law.

On the other hand, the courts may require agencies to allow the public an opportunity to comment on interpretations that significantly change prior law. In Paralyzed Veterans of America v. D.C. Arena Limited Partnership, 117 F.3d 579 (D.C. Cir. 1997), the D.C. Circuit held that the Administrative Procedure Act requires agencies to provide notice and to receive and evaluate public comments before adopting new interpretations that significantly change existing rules. That doctrine received a mixed reaction in other federal circuits, with some accepting the D.C. Circuit's approach and others rejecting it.

The validity of the *Paralyzed Veterans* rule came before the Supreme Court in Perez v. Mortgage Bankers Association, 135 S. Ct. 1199 (2015). The Labor Department had to decide whether bank loan officers are entitled to overtime pay. Until 2006, the agency had declared that officers were entitled to this benefit if they worked at the bank's office. Then, in 2006, during a Republican administration, the Department issued an interpretive ruling declaring that such officers qualified for an administrative exemption and were not entitled to overtime. In 2010, under a Democratic administration, the agency declared that loan officers should not receive an administrative exemption, thus reinstating the original policy. Mortgage bankers challenged the 2010 decision on the ground that it had not been issued with notice and comment, as required under the *Paralyzed Veterans* case.

Writing for the Court, Justice Sotomayor held that a notice and comment rule-making was not required when the agency changed its position — a victory for the administrative state. Other Justices voiced critiques of expansive administrative power. Justice Alito joined in the result but was troubled by "the aggrandizement of the power of administrative agencies as a result of the combined effect of (1) the effective delegation to agencies by Congress of huge swaths of lawmaking authority, (2) the exploitation by agencies of the uncertain boundary between legislative and interpretive rules, and (3) this Court's cases holding that courts must ordinarily defer to an agency's interpretation of its own ambiguous regulations." Justice Scalia, concurring in the judgment, highlighted the potential for overreaching that arises when courts defer to informal administrative interpretations: "By supplementing the APA with judge-made doctrines of deference, we have revolutionized the import of interpretive rules' exemption from notice-and-comment rulemaking. Agencies may now use these rules not just to advise the public, but also to bind them. After all, if an interpretive rule gets deference, the people are bound to obey it on pain of sanction, no less surely than they are bound to obey substantive rules, which are accorded similar deference. Interpretive rules that command deference do have the force of law." And Justice Thomas, also concurring in the judgment, highlighted the potential unconstitutionality of a doctrine that gives the force of law to informal agency interpretations of statutes: "Because this doctrine effects a transfer of the judicial power to an executive agency, it raises constitutional concerns. This line of precedents undermines our obligation to provide a judicial check on the other branches, and it subjects regulated parties to precisely the abuses that the Framers sought to prevent."

Who has the better of the argument?

b. The Power to Determine Legal Rights

With the growth of the administrative state, it became increasingly difficult for regulators to carry out their responsibilities through judicial proceedings. Courts were slow and overloaded, and the vast scope of administrative responsibilities would overburden them still more, further delaying matters and adding to backlogs in other cases. During the early days of the administrative state, moreover, some judges were resistant to the fact that many administrative schemes displaced the common law. These and other considerations provided potent reasons for limiting the role of courts and for redirecting to administrative agencies themselves the power to issue binding compliance orders. There were, however, significant obstacles to the accomplishment of this objective, among them the following:

- The Due Process Clauses of the Fifth and Fourteenth Amendments guarantee that parties who are subjected to the compulsory power of government have a right to fair procedures — which traditionally meant that they were guaranteed their day in court. Is due process satisfied if a party is brought before an administrative agency rather than a court? Can due process be satisfied if the party is required to defend herself in front of the very bureaucratic agency that is seeking to impose sanctions against her?

- Juries are not empanelled in administrative proceedings. How can this be reconciled with the Seventh Amendment, which guarantees federal court litigants the right to a trial by jury in suits at common law?

- Article III of the Constitution provides that federal judges serve during good behavior (i.e., they cannot be term-limited), and that their salaries may not be reduced during their time in office. Federal judges are nominated by the President and confirmed in office by the Senate, thus ensuring that the selection of federal judges is subject to political checks and balances. How can administrative adjudications be reconciled with these structural requirements for federal judges?

- The Appointments Clause of the Constitution, art. II, §2, cl. 2, provides that "[the President] shall nominate, and, by and with the Advice and Consent of the Senate, shall appoint Ambassadors, other public Ministers and Consuls, Judges of the supreme Court, and all other Officers of the United States, whose Appointments are not herein otherwise provided for, and which shall be established by Law: but the Congress may by Law vest the Appointment of such inferior Officers, as they think proper, in the President alone, in the Courts of Law, or in the Heads of Departments." If federal administrative officials are not appointed in conformity with this clause, do they lack the power to adjudicate individual rights?

The following case deals with the first and third of these problems. It is a basic precedent authorizing administrative agencies to adjudicate legal rights in compliance cases.

Crowell v. Benson

285 U.S. 22 (1932)

[The Longshoremen's and Harbor Workers' Compensation Act of 1927 created a scheme of workers' compensation for injuries occurring on the navigable waters of the United States. An administrative agency, the United States Employees' Compensation Commission, administered the statute. Claims for compensation were filed with a deputy commissioner who had "full authority to hear and determine all questions in respect to the claim." The deputy commissioner was required to investigate claims, and upon application of any interested party was required to conduct a hearing at which the claimant and the employer could present evidence. The deputy commissioner was not bound by conventional rules of evidence or formal procedures, but rather was required to "ascertain the rights of the parties." If a compensation order was "not in accordance with law," it could be suspended or set aside through injunction proceedings brought in federal district court.]

The contention under the due process clause of the Fifth Amendment relates to the determination of questions of fact . . . . Apart from cases involving constitutional rights to be appropriately enforced by proceedings in court, there can be no doubt that the act contemplates that as to questions of fact, arising with respect to injuries to employees within the purview of the act, the findings of the deputy commissioner, supported by evidence and within the scope of his authority, shall be final. To hold otherwise would be to defeat the obvious purpose of the legislation to furnish a prompt, continuous, expert, and inexpensive method for dealing with a class of questions of fact which are peculiarly suited to examination and determination by an administrative agency specially assigned to that task. The object is to secure within the prescribed limits of the employer's liability an immediate investigation and a sound practical judgment, and the efficacy of the plan depends upon the finality of the determinations of fact with respect to the circumstances, nature, extent, and consequences of the employee's injuries and the amount of compensation that should be awarded . . . . The use of the administrative method for these purposes, assuming due notice, proper opportunity to be heard, and that findings are based upon evidence, falls easily within the principle of the decisions sustaining similar procedure against objections under the due process clauses of the Fifth and Fourteenth Amendments . . . .

The contention based upon the judicial power of the United States . . . presents a distinct question. As to determinations of fact, the distinction is at once apparent between cases of private right and those which arise between the government and persons subject to its authority in connection with the performance of the constitutional functions of the executive or legislative departments. The Court referred to this distinction in Murray's Lessee v. Hoboken Land & Improvement Company, pointing out that "there are matters, involving public rights, which may be presented in such form that the judicial power is capable of acting on them, and which are susceptible of judicial determination, but which Congress may or may not bring within the cognizance of the courts of the United States, as it may deem proper." Thus the Congress, in exercising the powers confided to it, may establish "legislative" courts (as distinguished from "constitutional courts in which the judicial power conferred by the Constitution can be deposited") which are to form part of the government of territories or of the District of Columbia, or to serve as special tribunals "to examine and determine various matters, arising between the government and others, which from their nature do not require judicial determination and yet are susceptible of it." But "the mode of determining matters of this class is completely within congressional control. Congress may reserve to itself the power to decide, may delegate that power to executive officers, or may commit it to judicial tribunals." Familiar illustrations of administrative agencies created for the determination of such matters are found in connection with the exercise of the congressional power as to interstate and foreign commerce, taxation, immigration, the public lands, public health, the facilities of the post office, pensions, and payments to veterans . . . .

The present case does not fall within the categories just described, but is one of private right, that is, of the liability of one individual to another under the law as defined. But, in cases of that sort, there is no requirement that, in order to maintain the essential attributes of the judicial power, all determinations of fact in constitutional courts shall be made by judges . . . . In cases of equity and admiralty, it is historic practice to call to the assistance of the courts, without the consent of the parties, masters, and commissioners or assessors, to pass upon certain classes of questions, as, for example, to take and state an account or to find the amount of damages. While the reports of masters and commissioners in such cases are essentially of an advisory nature, it has not been the practice to disturb their findings when they are properly based upon evidence, in the absence of errors of law, and the parties have no right to demand that the court shall re-determine the facts thus found . . . .

The recognition of the utility and convenience of administrative agencies for the investigation and finding of facts within their proper province, and the support of their authorized action, does not require the conclusion that there is no limitation of their use, and that the Congress could completely oust the courts of all determinations of fact by vesting the authority to make them with finality in its own instrumentalities or in the executive department. That would be to sap the judicial power as it exists under the federal Constitution, and to establish a government of a bureaucratic character alien to our system, wherever fundamental rights depend, as not infrequently they do depend, upon the facts, and finality as to facts becomes in effect finality in law . . . . Even where the subject lies within the general authority of the Congress, the propriety of a challenge by judicial proceedings of the determinations of fact deemed to be jurisdictional, as underlying the authority of executive officers, has been recognized . . . . In cases brought to enforce constitutional rights, the judicial power of the United States necessarily extends to the independent determination of all questions, both of fact and law, necessary to the performance of that supreme function.

Questions and Comments

1. Murray's Lessee v. Hoboken Land & Improvement Co., 59 U.S. 272 (1856), cited in the excerpted case, held that in general, Congress may not "withdraw from judicial cognizance any matter which, from its nature, is the subject of a suit at the common law, or in equity, or admiralty." This sounds like a broad protection of judicial prerogatives. However, that case went on to articulate an exception that provides the fundamental charter for today's administrative tribunals: "At the same time there are matters, involving public rights, . . . which are susceptible of judicial determination, but which Congress may or may not bring within the cognizance of the courts of the United States, as it may deem proper."

2. Crowell v. Benson and later cases give broad scope to this "public rights" exception — so broad that at times it might have seemed that no scope was left for the basic rule. The Court has made it clear, however, that there remains an essential core of common law authority that cannot be divested by congressional action. See Stern v. Marshall, 564 U.S. 462 (2011), involving a common law counterclaim in bankruptcy court (the case is also interesting for the backstory it provides on the life and death of the late celebrity Anna Nicole Smith).

3. What·rationale does the Court identify for administrative courts? It says that such tribunals can offer a "prompt, continuous, expert, and inexpensive method for dealing with a class of questions of fact which are peculiarly suited to examination and determination by an administrative agency specially assigned to that task." Do you agree?

4. Are there downsides, from the policy perspective, from vesting authority of this type in an administrative tribunal?

5. In the excerpted case, the administrator was judging between claims of rights asserted by private parties. However, such tribunals often adjudicate claims by the agencies themselves against private parties. Are the due process considerations different in the latter sort of cases?

6. While recognizing Congress' broad authority to create administrative tribunals, the Court also identifies certain limitations. The same due process protections that would apply in court proceedings apply in the administrative tribunal — thus there must be notice and an opportunity to be heard, and decisions must be reasonably based on evidence of record. Agency findings of jurisdictional fact are subject to de novo review in federal court. The same goes for findings in cases involving constitutional rights.

7. How must judges of administrative courts be appointed? Art. II, §2, cl. 2 of the Constitution requires that "officers of the United States" must be appointed by the President, but that Congress may delegate appointment of "inferior officers" to the "heads of departments." "Inferior officers" are officers whose work is directed and supervised by superiors appointed by the President with the Senate's consent. Edmond v. United States, 520 U.S. 651, 662-663 (1997). "Heads of departments" include both individuals (such as cabinet secretaries), and governors or commissioners of multi-member administrative bodies acting as a group. *See* Free Enterprise Fund v. Public Company Accounting Oversight Board, 561 U.S. 477 (2010). What if an administrative law judge is appointed, not by the head of a department, but rather by a subordinate official? This has been the case with SEC administrative law judges, who are selected by bureaucratic procedures and not appointed by members of the Commission. In two cases from 2015, federal district court judges held that SEC administrative judges are "inferior officers" of the United States who cannot be validly appointed by subordinate officials; but the courts of appeals remitted the constitutional issues for adjudication in the first instance. Duka v. SEC, No. 15-cv-357 (S.D.N.Y. 2015), *abrogated by* Tilton v. SEC, 2016 WL 3084795 (2d Cir. 2016); Hill v. SEC, 2015 WL 4307088 (N.D. Ga. 2015), *vacated and remanded*, 2016 WL 3361478 (11th Cir. 2016). These cases set up a constitutional confrontation that could define the appointment requirements for federal administrative law judges. Even if the complaining parties prevail in those cases, however, it appears that the SEC could solve the problem going forward by having the Commission's members "rubber stamp" the appointments of all existing and future administrative law judges.

8. What about state regulators? International Shoe Co. v. Washington, 326 U.S. 310 (1945), familiar from classes in Civil Procedure, upheld broad authority for state regulators to issue binding legal judgments. The result was to empower state administrative agencies to adjudicate claims in favorable tribunals and to avoid the need to bring their cases in the courts of other states.

Crowell v. Benson dealt with two constitutional objections to administrative tribunals—the Due Process Clause and the requirements for federal courts under Article III. The following case deals with the jury trial right under the Seventh Amendment.

Atlas Roofing Co., Inc. v. Occupational Safety and Health Review Commission

430 U.S. 442 (1977)

[The Occupational Safety and Health Act of 1970 empowered the Occupational Safety and Health Review Commission (Commission) to impose civil penalties and abatement orders on employers who fail to provide safe working conditions. If an employer contests a penalty or abatement order, an administrative law judge of the Commission conducts a hearing and is empowered to affirm, modify, or vacate the proposed abatement order and penalty. The judge's decision becomes the Commission's final, appealable order, subject to review by the full Commission. If such review is granted, the Commission's subsequent order directing abatement and payment of a penalty becomes final unless the employer petitions for judicial review in the appropriate court of appeals, but the Commission's findings of fact, if supported by substantial evidence, are conclusive. Employers who were subject to penalties and abatement orders under this scheme complained that they were deprived of their Seventh Amendment right to trial by jury.]

[W]hen Congress creates new statutory "public rights," it may assign their adjudication to an administrative agency with which a jury trial would be incompatible, without violating the Seventh Amendment's injunction that jury trial is to be "preserved" in "suits at common law." Congress is not required by the Seventh Amendment to choke the already crowded federal courts with new types of litigation or prevented from committing some new types of litigation to administrative agencies with special competence in the relevant field. This is the case even if the Seventh Amendment would have required a jury where the adjudication of those rights is assigned instead to a federal court of law instead of an administrative agency . . . .

The Seventh Amendment was never intended to establish the jury as the exclusive mechanism for fact finding in civil cases. It took the existing legal order as it found it, and there is little or no basis for concluding that the Amendment should now be interpreted to provide an impenetrable barrier to administrative fact finding under otherwise valid federal regulatory statutes. We cannot conclude that the Amendment rendered Congress powerless when it concluded that remedies available in courts of law were inadequate to cope with a problem within Congress' power to regulate to create new public rights and remedies by statute and commit their enforcement, if it chose, to a tribunal other than a court of law such as an administrative agency in which facts are not found by juries.

Questions and Comments

1. What policy arguments does the Court provide for dispensing with the jury trial right in administrative proceedings? Is it sufficient to argue that "already crowded" federal courts should not be "choke[d]" by new administrative remedies?

Could Congress deal with docket overcrowding by increasing the number of federal judges?

2. The Court suggests that a recognizing a jury trial right in administrative tribunals would create "an impenetrable barrier to administrative fact finding under otherwise valid federal regulatory statutes." Could Congress authorize the empanelling of juries in administrative proceedings? In any event is the practical management of administrative proceedings a sufficiently compelling reason to overcome a constitutional right?

3. Does the outcome of this case reflect the federal courts' distaste for dealing with mundane and repetitive cases with little overarching public policy significance?

4. The Seventh Amendment problem does not arise in state administrative cases because, unlike other provisions of the Bill of Rights, the right to jury trial has never been incorporated against the states. State constitutions, however, may confer analogous rights to jury trial.

Even when the initial authority to adjudicate legal rights is vested in an administrative agency, disappointed parties typically have a right to challenge the administrative action in court. To what extent do rights of judicial review maintain a realistic role for courts in administrative cases?

Administrative agencies often bring enforcement actions against suspected violations in their own tribunals rather than in court. This practice is well entrenched and longstanding; but it does raise basic questions of fairness and due process. How can a suspected lawbreaker expect to receive a fair hearing before a tribunal staffed by persons who are employed by the very agency who is making the accusations? In such a case, is the government acting as prosecutor, judge, and jury at the same time? How can such an administrative tribunal be expected to administer fair and even-handed justice?

A long string of judicial decisions stemming back at least to the New Deal era has endorsed the legality of administrative tribunals over the objection that they violate the target's right to due process. Recall the case of Crowell v. Benson, excerpted above, which upheld against a due process challenge a procedure for the administrative determination of claims for unemployment compensation. Because the tribunal afforded due process protections similar to those that could be obtained before a judge, the Court saw no constitutional defect, and recognized the utility of these non-judicial forums in providing for the "utility and convenience of administrative agencies for the investigation and finding of facts within their proper province, and the support of their authorized action." Crowell v. Benson, 285 U.S. 22 (1932).

An issue that has arisen more recently concerns how administrative law judges are appointed:

Gray Financial Group, Inc. v. SEC

1:15-CV-0492-LMM (N.D. Ga. 2015)

[Gray Financial Group is an investment adviser registered with the SEC. In May 2015, the SEC charged the adviser with violating federal securities laws by selling its clients an investment that did not comply with Georgia law. The charges contemplated that the proceedings would be adjudicated before an administrative law judge (ALJ) on the staff of the SEC. Gray Financial responded by filing suit in federal district court seeking to enjoin the administrative proceeding on the ground that the ALJ did not have the constitutional authority to preside over the proceedings. The following excerpt is from the court's opinion granting a preliminary injunction against the SEC's enforcement action.]

SEC ALJs, including ALJ Elliot who presides over Plaintiffs' case, are "not hired through a process involving the approval of the individual members of the Commission." An ALJ's salary is set by statute. Congress has authorized the SEC to delegate its functions to an ALJ. Pursuant to that authority, the SEC has promulgated regulations which set out its ALJ's powers. 17 C.F.R. §200.14 makes ALJs responsible for the "fair and orderly conduct of [administrative] proceedings" and gives them the authority to: "(1) Administer oaths and affirmations; (2) Issue subpoenas; (3) Rule on offers of proof; (4) Examine witnesses; (5) Regulate the course of a hearing; (6) Hold pre-hearing conferences; (7) Rule upon motions; and (8) Unless waived by the parties, prepare an initial decision containing the conclusions as to the factual and legal issues presented, and issue an appropriate order."

The SEC's website also describes SEC ALJs in the following manner:

> Administrative Law Judges are independent judicial officers who in most cases conduct hearings and rule on allegations of securities law violations initiated by the Commission's Division of Enforcement. They conduct public hearings at locations throughout the United States in a manner similar to non-jury trials in the federal district courts. Among other actions, they issue subpoenas, conduct prehearing conferences, issue defaults, and rule on motions and the admissibility of evidence. At the conclusion of the public hearing, the parties submit proposed findings of fact and conclusions of law. The Administrative Law Judge prepares an Initial Decision that includes factual findings, legal conclusions, and, where appropriate, orders relief. . . . An Administrative Law Judge may order sanctions that include suspending or revoking the registrations of registered securities, as well as the registrations of brokers, dealers, investment companies, investment advisers, municipal securities dealers, municipal advisors, transfer agents, and nationally recognized statistical rating organizations. In addition, Commission Administrative Law Judges can order disgorgement of ill-gotten gains, civil penalties, censures, and cease-and-desist orders against these entities, as well as individuals, and can suspend or bar persons from association with these entities or from participating in an offering of a penny stock.

Plaintiffs [claim, inter alia,] that the ALJ's appointment violates the Appointments Clause of Article II because he was not appointed by the President, a court of law, or a department head[.] Plaintiffs' arguments depend on this Court finding that the ALJ is an inferior officer who would trigger these constitutional protections. Therefore, the Court will consider this threshold issue first.

The issue of whether the SEC ALJ is an inferior officer or employee for purposes of the Appointments Clause depends on the authority he has in conducting administrative proceedings. The Appointments Clause of Article II of the Constitution provides: "[The President] shall nominate, and by and with the Advice and Consent of the Senate, shall appoint Ambassadors, other public Ministers and Consuls, Judges of the supreme Court, and all other Officers of the United States, whose Appointments are not herein otherwise provided for, and which shall be established by Law: but the Congress may by Law vest the Appointment of such inferior Officers, as they think proper, in the President alone, in the Courts of Law, or in the Heads of Departments." U.S. Const. art. II, §2, cl. 2.

The Appointments Clause thus creates two classes of officers: principal officers, who are selected by the President with the advice and consent of the Senate, and inferior officers, whom "Congress may allow to be appointed by the President alone, by the heads of departments, or by the Judiciary." The Appointments Clause applies to all agency officers including those whose functions are "predominately quasi-judicial and quasi-legislative" and regardless of whether the agency officers are "independent of the Executive in their day-to-day operations." "[A]ny appointee exercising significant authority pursuant to the laws of the United States is an 'Officer of the United States,' and must, therefore, be appointed in the manner prescribed by §2, cl. 2, of [Article II]."

By way of example, the Supreme Court has held that "district-court clerks, thousands of clerks within the Treasury and Interior Departments, an assistant surgeon, a cadet-engineer, election monitors, federal marshals, military judges, Article I [Tax Court special trial] judges, and the general counsel for the Transportation Department are inferior officers."

Plaintiffs claim that SEC ALJs are inferior officers because they exercise "significant authority pursuant to the laws of the United States" while the SEC contends ALJs are "mere employees" based upon Congress's treatment of them and the fact that they cannot issue final orders, cannot grant "certain injunctive relief," and do not have contempt power. The Court finds that . . . SEC ALJs are inferior officers.

In [Freytag v. Commissioner, 501 U.S. 868 (1991)], the Supreme Court was asked to decide whether special trial judges ("STJ") in the Tax Court were inferior officers under Article II. The Government argued, much as the SEC does here, that STJs do "no more than assist the Tax Court judge in taking the evidence and preparing the proposed findings and opinion," id., and they "lack authority to enter a final decision." The Supreme Court rejected that argument, stating that the Government's argument

> ignores the significance of the duties and discretion that special trial judges possess. The office of special trial judge is "established by Law," and the duties, salary, and means of appointment for that office are specified by statute. These characteristics distinguish special trial judges from special masters, who are hired by Article III courts on a temporary, episodic basis, whose positions are not established by law, and whose duties and functions are not delineated in a statute. Furthermore, special trial judges perform more than ministerial tasks. They take testimony, conduct trials, rule on the admissibility of evidence, and have the power to enforce compliance with discovery orders. In the course of carrying out these important functions, the special trial judges exercise significant discretion.

Freytag, 501 U.S. at 881-82.

The Court finds that like the STJs in *Freytag*, SEC ALJs exercise "significant authority." The office of an SEC ALJ is established by law, and the "duties, salary, and means of appointment for that office are specified by statute." ALJs are permanent employees — unlike special masters — and they take testimony, conduct trial, rule on the admissibility of evidence, and can issue sanctions, up to and including excluding people (including attorneys) from hearings and entering default. The SEC argues that unlike the STJs who were inferior officers in *Freytag*, SEC ALJs do not have contempt power and cannot issue final orders, as the STJs could in limited circumstances. . . .

The Court concludes that the Supreme Court in *Freytag* found that the STJ's powers — which are nearly identical to the SEC ALJs here — were independently sufficient to find that STJs were inferior officers. Only after it concluded STJs were inferior officers did *Freytag* address the STJ's ability to issue a final order; the STJ's limited authority to issue final orders was only an additional reason, not the reason. Therefore, the Court finds that *Freytag* mandates a finding that the SEC ALJs exercise "significant authority" and are thus inferior officers. . . .

Because SEC ALJs are inferior officers, the Court finds Plaintiffs have established a likelihood of success on the merits of their Appointments Clause claim. Inferior officers must be appointed by the President, department heads, or courts of law. Otherwise, their appointment violates the Appointments Clause. The SEC concedes that Plaintiffs' ALJ, ALJ Elliot, was not appointed by an SEC Commissioner. The SEC ALJ was not appointed by the President, a department head, or the Judiciary. Because he was not appropriately appointed pursuant to Article II, his appointment is likely unconstitutional in violation of the Appointments Clause. . . .

Questions and Comments

1. What is the purpose of the Appointments Clause? Would that purpose be frustrated if SEC ALJs were allowed to carry out the tasks assigned to them by statute and administrative regulation?

2. This is one of several court decisions addressing the question of whether SEC administrative law judges are constitutionally authorized to carry out their assigned powers. The courts have split on the issue. *See, e.g.,* Raymond Lucia Companies, Inc. v. SEC, ___ F.3d ___ (D.C. Cir. 2016) (rejecting an Appointments Clause challenge to the constitutionality of SEC administrative law judges). It appears likely that the issue will eventually need to be determined by the United States Supreme Court.

3. Would it have made a difference if the ALJ had been appointed by an order of the SEC commissioners? Does this suggest that, going forward, the SEC has an easy way around the constitutional difficulty?

4. In the meantime, however, an order declaring that SEC administrative law judges are invalidly appointed could lead to chaos because it threatens to upend hundreds or thousands of already decided cases. Should preserving the finality of SEC decisions be a relevant consideration when constitutional rights are involved?

Camp v. Pitts

411 U.S. 138 (1973)

In 1967, respondents submitted an application to the Comptroller of the Currency for a certificate authorizing them to organize a new bank in Hartsville, South Carolina. On the basis of information received from a national bank examiner and from various interested parties, the Comptroller denied the application and notified respondents of his decision through a brief letter, which stated in part: "[W]e have concluded that the factors in support of the establishment of a new National Bank in this area are not favorable." No formal hearings were required by the controlling statute or guaranteed by the applicable regulations, although the latter provided for hearings when requested and when granted at the discretion of the Comptroller.

Respondents did not request a formal hearing but asked for reconsideration. That request was granted and a supplemental field examination was conducted, whereupon the Comptroller again denied the application, this time stating in a letter that "we were unable to reach a favorable conclusion as to the need factor," and explaining that conclusion to some extent. [The letter reads in part: "On each application we endeavor to develop the need and convenience factors in conjunction with all other banking factors and in this case we were unable to reach a favorable conclusion as to the need factor. The record reflects that this market area is now served by the Peoples Bank with deposits of $7.2MM, The Bank of Hartsville with deposits of $12.8MM, The First Federal Savings and Loan Association with deposits of $5.4MM, The Mutual Savings and Loan Association with deposits of $8.2MM and the Sonoco Employees Credit Union with deposits of $6.5MM. The aforementioned are as of December 31, 1968."]

Respondents then brought an action in federal district court seeking review of the Comptroller's decision. The entire administrative record was placed before the court, and, upon an examination of that record and of the two letters of explanation, the court granted summary judgment against respondents, holding that de novo review was not warranted in the circumstances and finding that "although the Comptroller may have erred, there is substantial basis for his determination, and . . . it was neither capricious nor arbitrary." On appeal, the Court of Appeals did not reach the merits. Rather, it held that the Comptroller's ruling was "unacceptable" because "its basis" was not stated with sufficient clarity to permit judicial review.

For the present, the Comptroller does not challenge this aspect of the court's decision. He does, however, seek review here of the procedures that the Court of Appeals specifically ordered to be followed in the District Court on remand. The court held that the case should be remanded "for a trial de novo before the District Court" because "the Comptroller has twice inadequately and inarticulately resolved the (respondents') presentation." The court further specified that in the District Court, respondents "will open the trial with proof of their application and compliance with the statutory inquiries, and proffer of any other relevant evidence." Then, "[t]estimony may . . . be adduced by the Comptroller or intervenors manifesting opposition, if any, to the new bank." On the basis of the record thus made, the District Court was instructed to make its own findings of fact and conclusions of law in order to determine "whether the (respondents) have shown by a preponderance of evidence that the Comptroller's ruling is capricious or an abuse of discretion."

We agree with the Comptroller that the trial procedures thus outlined by the Court of Appeals for the remand in this case are unwarranted under present law.

Unquestionably, the Comptroller's action is subject to judicial review under the Administrative Procedure Act (APA), 5 U.S.C. §701. But it is also clear that neither the National Bank Act nor the APA requires the Comptroller to hold a hearing or to make formal findings on the hearing record when passing on applications for new banking authorities . . . .

The appropriate standard for review was . . . whether the Comptroller's adjudication was "arbitrary, capricious, an abuse of discretion, or otherwise not in accordance with law," as specified in 5 U.S.C. §706(2)(A). In applying that standard, the focal point for judicial review should be the administrative record already in existence, not some new record made initially in the reviewing court . . . .

If, as the Court of Appeals held and as the Comptroller does not now contest, there was such failure to explain administrative action as to frustrate effective judicial review, the remedy was not to hold a de novo hearing but . . . to obtain from the agency, either through affidavits or testimony, such additional explanation of the reasons for the agency decision as may prove necessary. We add a caveat, however. [I]n the present case there was contemporaneous explanation of the agency decision. The explanation may have been curt, but it surely indicated the determinative reason for the final action taken: the finding that a new bank was an uneconomic venture in light of the banking needs and the banking services already available in the surrounding community. The validity of the Comptroller's action must, therefore, stand or fall on the propriety of that finding, judged, of course, by the appropriate standard of review. If that finding is not sustainable on the administrative record made, then the Comptroller's decision must be vacated and the matter remanded to him for further consideration. It is in this context that the Court of Appeals should determine whether and to what extent, in the light of the administrative record, further explanation is necessary to a proper assessment of the agency's decision.

Questions and Comments

1. This remedy ordered by the court of appeals was essentially a hybrid procedure. The agency got two chances to provide a reasoned explanation for its determination to deny a new bank charter. The first time around, the agency provided virtually no reason at all; the second, it offered up an explanation that the appeals court viewed as pathetically inadequate. Faced with what appeared to be congenital incompetence, the appeals court kicked the agency out and instructed the district court to decide the controversy based on traditional judicial procedures. The Supreme Court would have none of it: The power of a reviewing court is limited to determining whether the agency's decision is "arbitrary, capricious, an abuse of discretion, or otherwise not in accordance with law," and doesn't extend to conducting a de novo trial, no matter how feckless the administrative agency appears to be.

2. The district court and the court of appeals disagreed as to the sufficiency of the Comptroller's explanation. The trial court found that even though the agency's decision may have been erroneous, it was supported by a substantial basis. The appeals court held that the Comptroller had not stated the basis for its decision with sufficient clarity to permit judicial review. Who has the better of this argument? Review the administrator's explanation. What, if anything, is missing from the Comptroller's analysis?

3. If on remand the trial court concludes that the Comptroller's explanation is inadequate to permit judicial review, what is the remedy? The Supreme Court indicates that the remedy is to ask the Comptroller to provide further explanation. Can the Comptroller, with little more than the cursory effort it displayed in the case so far, simply supply a longer and more detailed justification for its decision and thereby persuade the court that its decision was neither arbitrary nor capricious?

4. The Supreme Court makes it clear that the Comptroller is not allowed, after the fact, to supplement the administrative record in an effort to bolster its decision. This constraint might give the applicant some degree of hope. But what if the Comptroller is unable to provide an adequate explanation based on the record it had before it at the time? The Supreme Court's answer is that the district court must remand to the agency. The agency's response would probably be to reopen the

administrative record and compile further evidence. How likely is it that, at the conclusion of the supplemental investigation, the Comptroller would reverse course and decide to grant the new bank charter after all?

5. In spite of the obstacles created by Camp v. Pitts and other decisions, regulated entities can still challenge government enforcement actions in court—and sometimes they win. Yet the costs of fighting can be high. Consider the case of Nelson Obus, a partner in an investment firm who was subpoenaed by the SEC on suspicion of insider trading in 2002. Four years later, when Obus refused to settle, the SEC filed a lawsuit against him seeking disgorgement and civil money penalties. The litigation followed a long and winding road culminating in a trial in 2014, capped by a jury verdict in favor of the defendant. *See* Joel Cohen et al., *SEC v. Obus: A Case Study on Taking the Government to Trial and Winning*, 47 Rev. Sec. & Commodities Reg. 247 (2014). Mr. Obus was vindicated, but at what cost? He had to endure the anxiety, expense, and cloud on reputation that came with 13 years of litigation. How many people in his position would have the fortitude or the resources to do the same?

Even when the right to judicial review offers a realistic hope for success on the merits, it may mean little if the regulated party, in order to obtain a judicial determination of its rights, risks devastating sanctions if she is ultimately adjudged to have committed a violation. The risks of incurring large penalties and then losing the subsequent court case may deter people from challenging the agency's action in the first place. More than a century ago the United States Supreme Court addressed this question and imposed limits.

Ex parte Young

209 U.S. 123 (1908)

[Minnesota laws and administrative regulations slashed the rates that railroads could charge customers in the state. Violators were subject to heavy civil and criminal penalties.]

Coming to the inquiry regarding the alleged invalidity of these acts, we take up the contention that they are invalid on their face on account of the penalties. For disobedience to the freight act the officers, directors, agents, and employees of the company are made guilty of a misdemeanor, and upon conviction each may be punished by imprisonment in the county jail for a period not exceeding ninety days. Each violation would be a separate offense, and, therefore, might result in imprisonment of the various agents of the company who would dare disobey for a term of ninety days each for each offense. Disobedience to the passenger-rate act renders the party guilty of a felony and subject to a fine not exceeding $5,000 or imprisonment in the state prison for a period not exceeding five years, or both fine and imprisonment. The sale of each ticket above the price permitted by the act would be a violation thereof. It would be difficult, if not impossible, for the company to obtain officers, agents, or employees willing to carry on its affairs except in obedience to the act and orders in question. The company itself would also, in case of disobedience, be liable to the immense fines provided for in violating orders of the commission. The company, in order to test the validity of the acts, must find some agent or employee to disobey them at the risk stated.

The necessary effect and result of such legislation must be to preclude a resort to the courts (either state or Federal) for the purpose of testing its validity. The officers and employees could not be expected to disobey any of the provisions of the acts or orders at the risk of such fines and penalties being imposed upon them, in case the court should decide that the law was valid. The result would be a denial of any hearing to the company . . . . [W]hen the penalties for disobedience are by fines so enormous and imprisonment so severe as to intimidate the company and its officers from resorting to the courts to test the validity of the legislation, the result is the same as if the law in terms prohibited the company from seeking judicial construction of laws which deeply affect its rights . . . .

We hold, therefore, that the provisions of the acts relating to the enforcement of the rates, either for freight or passengers, by imposing such enormous fines and possible imprisonment as a result of an unsuccessful effort to test the validity of the laws themselves, are unconstitutional on their face, without regard to the question of the insufficiency of those rates . . . .

Questions and Comments

1. The problem, from the perspective of the regulated party, is that even if it believes in good faith that the conduct in question is entirely legal, it may avoid engaging in the behavior out of fear of the devastating liability that would ensue if it is wrong. But because the regulated party doesn't undertake the action in question, the legality of the action is never tested. The regulated organization, in short, finds itself between a rock and a hard place: It can engage in the behavior and face exorbitant liability if its conduct is ultimately found to be blameworthy; or it can refrain from engaging in the questioned behavior and forfeit any opportunity to vindicate its claim of right.

2. What was unconstitutional about the Minnesota rules? Was the problem that the state imposed the penalties for non-compliance without prior notice or hearing? That the penalties were progressive — growing larger with every violation? That the penalties for violations were large? That the statutes and orders in question threatened to interfere with the free flow of passengers and freight traffic over the interstate railroad system?

3. What impact would the rule of the excerpted case have on the ability of government agencies to enforce compliance with the law? If fines could not start to run until after a judicial determination that they were justified, then private parties might be able to put off the day when they must obey the law until the conclusion of the proceedings — potentially a very long time. Would this make sense?

4. Although the rule of the excerpted case has not been repudiated, it has been narrowed. It only applies when the penalties in question are severe. Moreover, the rule may not apply if the party can avoid the sanction by interposing a good faith challenge to the enforcement action. Reisman v. Caplin, 375 U.S. 440 (1964).

The problem that troubled the Court in *Ex parte Young* can be avoided if the regulated party is afforded some means to obtain a determination of its rights prior to engaging in the potentially forbidden conduct. For example, the regulated party might be able to obtain a temporary restraining order or preliminary injunction barring the agency from enforcing the sanction pending determination of the case on the merits. Neither of these strategies will work, however, if the relevant statutes specifically deny the right to pre-enforcement review, or deny rights to any judicial review at all, because then there is no basis to go into court to obtain either preliminary or permanent relief.

In the following case, an agency argued that the regulated party had no right to pre-enforcement judicial review of the agency's action, and therefore had to incur the risk of severe sanctions if it chose to disobey the agency's order.

Sackett v. Environmental Protection Agency

132 S. Ct. 1367 (2012)

Justice SCALIA delivered the opinion of the Court.

We consider whether Michael and Chantell Sackett may bring a civil action under the Administrative Procedure Act to challenge the issuance by the Environmental Protection Agency (EPA) of an administrative compliance order under . . . the Clean Water Act. The order asserts that the Sacketts' property is subject to the Act, and that they have violated its provisions by placing fill material on the property; and on this basis it directs them immediately to restore the property pursuant to an EPA work plan.

The Clean Water Act prohibits, among other things, "the discharge of any pollutant by any person," without a permit, into the "navigable waters," which the Act defines as "the waters of the United States." If the EPA determines that any person is in violation of this restriction, the Act directs the agency either to issue a compliance order or to initiate a civil enforcement action. When the EPA prevails in a civil action, the Act provides for "a civil penalty not to exceed [$37,500] per day for each violation." And according to the Government, when the EPA prevails against any person who has been issued a compliance order but has failed to comply, that amount is increased to $75,000 — up to $37,500 for the statutory violation and up to an additional $37,500 for violating the compliance order.

The particulars of this case flow from a dispute about the scope of "the navigable waters" subject to this enforcement regime. Today we consider only whether the dispute may be brought to court by challenging the compliance order — we do not resolve the dispute on the merits . . . .

The Sacketts . . . own a 2/3-acre residential lot in Bonner County, Idaho. Their property lies just north of Priest Lake, but is separated from the lake by several lots containing permanent structures. In preparation for constructing a house, the Sacketts filled in part of their lot with dirt and rock. Some months later, they received from the EPA a compliance order. The order contained a number of "Findings and Conclusions," including [findings that the Sacketts had violated the Clean Water Act].

On the basis of these findings and conclusions, the order directs the Sacketts, among other things, "immediately [to] undertake activities to restore the Site in accordance with [an EPA-created] Restoration Work Plan" and to "provide and/or obtain access to the Site . . . [and] access to all records and documentation related to the conditions at the Site . . . to EPA employees and/or their designated representatives."

The Sacketts, who do not believe that their property is subject to the Act, asked the EPA for a hearing, but that request was denied. They then brought this action in the United States District Court for the District of Idaho, seeking declaratory and injunctive relief. Their complaint contended that the EPA's issuance of the compliance order was "arbitrary [and] capricious" under the Administrative Procedure Act, and that it deprived them of "life, liberty, or property, without due process of law," in violation of the Fifth Amendment . . . .

The Sacketts brought suit under Chapter 7 of the APA, which provides for judicial review of "final agency action for which there is no other adequate remedy in a court." 5 U.S.C. §704 . . . . In Clean Water Act enforcement cases, judicial review ordinarily comes by way of a civil action brought by the EPA . . . . But the Sacketts cannot initiate that process, and each day they wait for the agency to drop the hammer, they accrue, by the Government's telling, an additional $75,000 in potential liability.

[The Government argues that, notwithstanding §704, review under the APA was unavailable. It] relies on §701(a)(1) of the APA, which excludes APA review "to the extent that [other] statutes preclude judicial review." The Clean Water Act, it says, is such a statute . . . .

Nothing in the Clean Water Act expressly precludes judicial review under the APA or otherwise. But in determining "[w]hether and to what extent a particular statute precludes judicial review," we do not look "only [to] its express language." The APA, we have said, creates a "presumption favoring judicial review of administrative action," but as with most presumptions, this one "may be overcome by inferences of intent drawn from the statutory scheme as a whole." The Government offers several reasons why the statutory scheme of the Clean Water Act precludes review . . . .

[Among those arguments were certain policy-based considerations. The] Government notes that Congress passed the Clean Water Act in large part to respond to the inefficiency of then-existing remedies for water pollution. Compliance orders, as noted above, can obtain quick remediation through voluntary compliance. The Government warns that the EPA is less likely to use the orders if they are subject to judicial review. That may be true — but it will be true for all agency actions subjected to judicial review. The APA's presumption of judicial review is a repudiation of the principle that efficiency of regulation conquers all. And there is no reason to think that the Clean Water Act was uniquely designed to enable the strong-arming of regulated parties into "voluntary compliance" without the opportunity for judicial review — even judicial review of the question whether the regulated party is within the EPA's jurisdiction. Compliance orders will remain an effective means of securing prompt voluntary compliance in those many cases where there is no substantial basis to question their validity.

We conclude that the compliance order in this case is final agency action for which there is no adequate remedy other than APA review, and that the Clean Water Act does not preclude that review. We therefore reverse the judgment of the Court of Appeals and remand the case for further proceedings consistent with this opinion.

It is so ordered.

Justice GINSBURG, concurring.

. . . The Court holds that the Sacketts may immediately litigate their jurisdictional challenge in federal court. I agree, for the Agency has ruled definitively on that question. Whether the Sacketts could challenge not only the EPA's authority to regulate their land under the Clean Water Act, but also, at this pre-enforcement stage, the terms and conditions of the compliance order, is a question today's opinion does not reach out to resolve. Not raised by the Sacketts here, the question remains open for another day and case. On that understanding, I join the Court's opinion.

Justice ALITO, concurring.

The position taken in this case by the Federal Government — a position that the Court now squarely rejects — would have put the property rights of ordinary Americans entirely at the mercy of EPA employees.

The reach of the Clean Water Act is notoriously unclear. Any piece of land that is wet at least part of the year is in danger of being classified by EPA employees as wetlands covered by the Act, and according to the Federal Government, if property owners begin to construct a home on a lot that the agency thinks possesses the requisite wetness, the property owners are at the agency's mercy. The EPA may issue a compliance order demanding that the owners cease construction, engage in expensive remedial measures, and abandon any use of the property. If the owners do not do the EPA's bidding, they may be fined up to $75,000 per day ($37,500 for violating the Act and another $37,500 for violating the compliance order). And if the owners want their day in court to show that their lot does not include covered wetlands, well, as a practical matter, that is just too bad. Until the EPA sues them, they are blocked from access to the courts, and the EPA may wait as long as it wants before deciding to sue. By that time, the potential fines may easily have reached the millions. In a nation that values due process, not to mention private property, such treatment is unthinkable.

The Court's decision provides a modest measure of relief. At least, property owners like petitioners will have the right to challenge the EPA's jurisdictional determination under the Administrative Procedure Act. But the combination of the uncertain reach of the Clean Water Act and the draconian penalties imposed for the sort of violations alleged in this case still leaves most property owners with little practical alternative but to dance to the EPA's tune.

Real relief requires Congress to do what it should have done in the first place: provide a reasonably clear rule regarding the reach of the Clean Water Act . . . . Allowing aggrieved property owners to sue under the Administrative Procedure Act is better than nothing, but only clarification of the reach of the Clean Water Act can rectify the underlying problem.

Questions and Comments

1. The Sacketts complained that they were being unfairly treated by the EPA because they had no right to initiate a judicial challenge. Were they denied all rights of judicial review?

2. Do you agree with the Court that the Clean Water Act (CWA) did not foreclose judicial review? The CWA establishes a detailed administrative scheme — one that does explicitly provide for judicial review in some situations — but doesn't provide for judicial review prior to the initiation of an agency enforcement proceeding.

Given that Congress evidently intended to comprehensively regulate the environmental quality of the nation's waters, is the best reading of the statute that it nevertheless allows a form of judicial review under general administrative law?

3. Do you agree that the agency action was final and that there was no other adequate remedy in a court?

4. The excerpted case involved an action against an agency of the United States subject to the federal Administrative Procedure Act (APA). The APA, however, will not be available to provide an avenue for pre-enforcement judicial review of compliance orders issued by *state* regulators. Is there a federal remedy in such a case? Federal courts may sometimes grant declaratory or injunctive relief in the case of threatened state prosecutions which chill fundamental rights. *See* Steffel v. Thompson, 415 U.S. 452 (1974); 414 Theater Corp. v. Murphy, 499 F.2d 1155, 1162 (2d Cir. 1974). It is not clear, however, that this authority extends so far as to include threatened state *civil* enforcement proceedings or a proceeding that, if successful, would impose only monetary penalties. Attempts to enlist federal courts as shields against state compliance orders could also face potential challenge under the Eleventh Amendment, which provides that federal courts may not exercise jurisdiction over lawsuits brought against a state by citizens of another state.

5. Who do you feel was in the right in this case — the Sacketts, who were summarily told not to develop their land on pain of ruinous penalties if they disobeyed; or the EPA, a federal agency charged with the vital task of protecting the environment, include fragile wetlands?

6. What if the Court had come out the other way and concluded that there was no expeditious means for obtaining judicial review? Would the application of sanctions against the Sacketts have violated the constitutional principle announced in *Ex parte Young*?

7. Does due process require that aggrieved parties always be given a right to challenge agency action in federal court, even under the deferential review standard of the APA, or is it permissible for Congress to foreclose all rights to judicial review? The cases make it clear that Congress may entirely foreclose rights to judicial review of agency action in ordinary cases — although, as illustrated by the excerpted case, courts will struggle to avoid this result if they can. *See* Thunder Basin Coal Co. v. Reich, 510 U.S. 200, 212-213 (1994). The rule may be otherwise, however, where constitutional rights are involved. *See* Webster v. Doe, 486 U.S. 592, 603 (1988) (a "serious constitutional question" would arise if a federal statute denied any judicial forum for constitutional claims).

8. The Court's determination that the Clean Water Act did not preclude judicial review did not fully resolve the legal issues surrounding the reviewability of Clean Water Act determinations. Review under the Administrative Procedure Act is available only if the challenge is to a "final agency action for which there is no other adequate remedy in a court." In United States Army Corps of Engineers v. Hawkes Co., Inc., 136 S. Ct. 1807 (2016), the Court addressed a challenge to a jurisdictional determination by the Corps of Engineers that certain mining properties contained "waters of the United States." Upholding the availability of judicial review under the APA, the Court stressed the significant civil and criminal penalties the private parties faced if they turned out to be mistaken in their view that the statute did not apply. The concurring opinion of Justices Kennedy, Thomas, and Alito expressed concern that the Clean Water Act "continues to raise troubling questions regarding the Government's power to cast doubt on the full use and enjoyment of private property throughout the Nation."

9. Another obstacle to judicial relief is the fact that the defendant may fear that the agency will take it amiss if its determinations are challenged in court. The regulated entity has to deal with its regulator on a repeat basis; and if the regulator is irritated, it has many ways large and small to make the entity's life miserable. Even if the organization were to prevail in court, the victory could be pyrrhic because the retribution after the fact would be harsh.

10. Often, before a regulated entity can exercise a right of judicial review, it must exhaust internal remedies within the agency. This requirement can be a deterrent against seeking judicial relief because the organization may fear that, in order to deter recourse to judicial review that may undercut the agency's authority, the head of the agency may impose a punitive increase in the sanction. Financial institutions took note in 2015 when PHH Corporation challenged a Consumer Financial Protection Bureau administrative law judge's ruling imposing a $6 million fine for violations of the Real Estate Settlement Procedures Act. This was the first appeal of a contested administrative adjudication to arise within the agency. The CFPB's director, Richard Cordray, not only rejected the appeal but also increased the fine — by 1,700 percent! Consumer Financial Protection Bureau, In the Matter of PHH Corporation, Administrative Proceeding File No. 2014-CFPB-0002 (June 4, 2015). Given this apparently punitive response, what organization would dare to challenge the CFPB's authority in the future? Perhaps reviewing courts will provide a safety net: In August 2015, the United States Court of Appeals for the District of Columbia Circuit granted PHH's motion for a stay pending appeal, finding that the appellant had satisfied the "stringent requirements" for such relief. PHH Corporation v. Consumer Financial Protection Bureau, No. 15-1177 (D.C. Cir. Aug. 3, 2015). On October 11, 2016, the Court of Appeals for the District of Columbia Circuit upheld PHH's challenge. In a major defeat for the CFPB, the appeals court ruled that the CFPB had violated the company's due process rights — and added for good measure a holding that the CFPB is unconstitutionally structured because too much power is vested in a single Director of a putatively independent agency. PHH Corp. v. Consumer Financial Protection Bureau, No. 15-1177 (D.C. Cir., October 11, 2016).

3. Enforcement Powers

a. Power to Obtain Information

Government regulators enjoy broad rights of access to information about the affairs of business firms. Consider the following:

- Any company that wants to list its securities on a public exchange must make fulsome disclosure of its operations, financial performance, and governance arrangements.
- Companies that need government licenses must provide the licensing agency with information as a precondition to obtaining the authority in question.
- Industries such as banking, insurance, mining, pharmaceuticals, or nuclear power must submit to inspections in which agents of the government come onto the company's premises to examine its compliance with applicable norms.
- Tax authorities require elaborate disclosure of a company's income and expenses.
- Armed with warrants or subpoenas, agents of the government can break down walls, rifle through papers, eavesdrop on conversations, and confiscate evidence.

Despite these rather awesome powers of obtaining information, there is still some scope of privacy left for corporations and other complex organizations. Among other things, companies, being legal persons, are protected by the Bill of Rights. Government investigations that probe too deeply may run afoul of the Fourth Amendment, which prohibits unreasonable searches and seizures. The following excerpt explores the scope of a company's Fourth Amendment rights in the context of federal mine safety law.

Donovan v. Dewey

452 U.S. 594 (1981)

. . . The Federal Mine Safety and Health Act of 1977 requires the Secretary of Labor to develop detailed mandatory health and safety standards to govern the operation of the Nation's mines. Section 103(a) of the Act, provides that federal mine inspectors are to inspect underground mines at least four times per year and surface mines at least twice a year to insure compliance with these standards, and to make follow-up inspections to determine whether previously discovered violations have been corrected. This section also grants mine inspectors "a right of entry to, upon, or through any coal or other mine" and states that "no advance notice of an inspection shall be provided to any person." If a mine operator refuses to allow a warrantless inspection conducted pursuant to §103(a), the Secretary is authorized to institute a civil action to obtain injunctive or other appropriate relief.

In July 1978, a federal mine inspector attempted to inspect quarries owned by appellee Waukesha Lime and Stone Co. in order to determine whether all 25 safety and health violations uncovered during a prior inspection had been corrected. After the inspector had been on the site for about an hour, Waukesha's president, appellee Douglas Dewey, refused to allow the inspection to continue unless the inspector first obtained a search warrant. The inspector issued a citation to Waukesha for terminating the inspection, and the Secretary subsequently filed this civil action in the District Court for the Eastern District of Wisconsin seeking to enjoin appellees from refusing to permit warrantless searches of the Waukesha facility . . . .

Our prior cases have established that the Fourth Amendment's prohibition against unreasonable searches applies to administrative inspections of private commercial property. However, unlike searches of private homes, which generally must be conducted pursuant to a warrant in order to be reasonable under the Fourth Amendment, legislative schemes authorizing warrantless administrative searches of commercial property do not necessarily violate the Fourth Amendment. The greater latitude to conduct warrantless inspections of commercial property reflects the fact that the expectation of privacy that the owner of commercial property enjoys in such property differs significantly from the sanctity accorded an individual's home, and that this privacy interest may, in certain circumstances, be adequately protected by regulatory schemes authorizing warrantless inspections . . . .

The interest of the owner of commercial property is not one in being free from any inspections. Congress has broad authority to regulate commercial enterprises engaged in or affecting interstate commerce, and an inspection program may in some cases be a necessary component of federal regulation. Rather, the Fourth Amendment protects the interest of the owner of property in being free from unreasonable intrusions onto his property by agents of the government. Inspections of commercial property may be unreasonable if they are not authorized by law or are unnecessary for the furtherance of federal interests. Similarly, warrantless inspections of commercial property may be constitutionally objectionable if their occurrence is so random, infrequent, or unpredictable that the owner, for all practical purposes, has no real expectation that his property will from time to time be inspected by government officials .... In such cases, a warrant may be necessary to protect the owner from the "unbridled discretion [of] executive and administrative officers," by assuring him that "reasonable legislative or administrative standards for conducting an ... inspection are satisfied with respect to a particular [establishment]." ... [However, a] warrant may not be constitutionally required when Congress has reasonably determined that warrantless searches are necessary to further a regulatory scheme and the federal regulatory presence is sufficiently comprehensive and defined that the owner of commercial property cannot help but be aware that his property will be subject to periodic inspections undertaken for specific purposes ....

Applying this analysis to the case before us, we conclude that the warrantless inspections required by the Mine Safety and Health Act do not offend the Fourth Amendment. As an initial matter, it is undisputed that there is a substantial federal interest in improving the health and safety conditions in the Nation's underground and surface mines. In enacting the statute, Congress was plainly aware that the mining industry is among the most hazardous in the country and that the poor health and safety record of this industry has significant deleterious effects on interstate commerce. Nor is it seriously contested that Congress in this case could reasonably determine ... that a system of warrantless inspections was necessary "if the law is to be properly enforced and inspection made effective." ...

These congressional findings were based on extensive evidence showing that the mining industry was among the most hazardous of the Nation's industries .... "[I]n [light] of the notorious ease with which many safety or health hazards may be concealed if advance warning of inspection is obtained, a warrant requirement would seriously undercut this Act's objectives." We see no reason not to defer to this legislative determination ....

Finally, the Act provides a specific mechanism for accommodating any special privacy concerns that a specific mine operator might have. The Act prohibits forcible entries, and instead requires the Secretary, when refused entry onto a mining facility, to file a civil action in federal court to obtain an injunction against future refusals. This proceeding provides an adequate forum for the mine owner to show that a specific search is outside the federal regulatory authority, or to seek from the district court an order accommodating any unusual privacy interests that the mine owner might have. Under these circumstances, it is difficult to see what additional protection a warrant requirement would provide.

Questions and Comments

1. What policy tradeoff is articulated in the excerpted case?

2. The excerpted opinion notes that the government has a compelling interest in ensuring safety of workers in mines. Why does this justify the result in the case, namely that the regulators don't need to obtain a warrant before conducting an inspection? Imposing a warrant requirement would not disable the government from obtaining the necessary information; the officials would only have to get a

warrant first. One rationale suggested by the Court is that if the mine operator is tipped off, it can disguise evidence of infractions and thereby frustrate the purposes of the program. But warrants are usually obtained ex parte without the participation of the party being searched. Accordingly, a warrant requirement would not alert the mine operator that inspectors are coming. If so, why would a warrant requirement interfere with the effectiveness of inspections?

3. Is the Court concerned about relieving the courts of the burden of having to approve warrants for routine administrative inspections? How burdensome would such a requirement be? Is reducing the burden on the judiciary an adequate reason for restricting constitutional rights?

4. Is the basis for the decision that mine operators have a low expectation of privacy in their workplace? The opinion indicates as much. Yet it also acknowledges that the Fourth Amendment applies to commercial premises and that sometimes a warrant is required. Is anything different about mines?

5. Is the rationale for the decision the conclusion that the Mine Safety and Health Act is such a comprehensive regulatory scheme that mine operators have no expectation they won't be searched? Does it make sense to say that if the government intrudes on privacy only sporadically a warrant is required, but if it does so all the time the constitutional protection disappears?

6. Notice that — as happened in this case — the mine inspectors could not force the owner to submit to a search at the time that they show up without a warrant. If the owner refuses to allow them to enter, they have to leave and then file a civil action prohibiting further refusals. Does this procedure provide equivalent protections to what a warrant would confer? If so, then why didn't the Court rely more explicitly on this basis in their decision?

b. The Power to Impose Penalties

Another key aspect of agency enforcement powers is the array of sanctions they can threaten against regulated entities who violate applicable norms or resist enforcement efforts. In the case of civil penalties, consider the following:

- Under CERCLA (the statute enacted to clean up toxic waste sites), violators are subject to penalties of up to $25,000 a day for serious misconduct. 42 U.S.C. §9609. The EPA can also perform its own cleanup and then may recover three times its costs from a responsible party who fails to comply with a cleanup order. Cleanup costs can run to millions of dollars.
- Civil money penalties for violations of federal banking regulations can run up to $5,500 a day, for ordinary violations; up to $27,500 a day for more serious violations; and up to $1,100,000 or 1 percent of the violator's total assets for violations that are knowingly committed and cause a substantial loss to the institution or a substantial pecuniary gain to the violator.
- Controlling persons who violate insider trading rules can be liable for penalties of up to the greater of $1,000,000 or three times the violator's profits. 15 U.S.C. §78u-1(a)(3).
- Violators of the Bank Secrecy Act can be assessed penalties of up to $25,000 per violation. 31 U.S.C. §5321(a). This may not sound like that much, but penalties can multiply quickly because in a given case there may be thousands of transactions that constitute violations, and for each of these transactions the statute provides that a separate violation occurs for each day and at each office, branch, or place of business at which the violation occurs.

- Violators of the Resource Conservation and Recovery Act may be assessed civil penalties of up to $27,500 for each day of non-compliance. 42 U.S.C. §6928(a), 28 U.S.C. §2461.

Supplementing these civil sanctions is a dazzling array of criminal penalties. Criminal prosecutions of institutions and individuals for failure of compliance were rare before the late 1980s — in part reflecting other law enforcement priorities (such as narcotics), and in part due to the perceived difficulty of explaining complex regulatory crimes to juries. But by the 1990s, however, the Department of Justice was vigorously pursuing hundreds of criminal investigations and prosecutions based on alleged compliance violations. Reasons for the enhanced vigor of enforcement included increased appropriations, the creation of specialized task forces, rewards and protections for whistleblowers and informants, and heightened public appetite to see harsh punishments meted out for violations. The trend continues today.

Two types of criminal statutes are most relevant. First are laws specific to the industry in question. In the case of banks, for example, possible criminal violations include prohibitions on bribing bank examiners, 18 U.S.C. §212; taking kickbacks for loans, id. §215; acting as a "financial kingpin" by operating a continuing financial crimes enterprise, id. §225; embezzling or misapplying money from a federally insured institution, id. §§656-657; falsifying bank books, records, or reports, id. §§1005-1007; making a false statement to influence a federally insured institution's credit decisions, id. §1014; concealing assets from the FDIC, id. §1032; bank fraud, id. §1344; obstructing a criminal investigation of a banking institution or its customers, id. §1510(b); obstructing the examination of a financial institution, id. §1517; violating removal or suspension orders, 12 U.S.C. §1818(j); and participating in an insured depository institution's affairs after conviction of a crime involving dishonesty or breach of trust, id. §1829. Penalties for some of these crimes can run up to $1 million in fines and 30 years in prison for each violation (in the case of the financial kingpin statute, life imprisonment). Knowing violations of bank regulatory statutes, such as the Bank Holding Company Act, 12 U.S.C. §1847(a), and the Savings and Loan Holding Company Act, id. §1467a(i), also carry criminal penalties, although at more modest levels.

In addition to industry-specific crimes, prosecutors may charge a variety of general federal offenses. These include conspiracy, 18 U.S.C. §371; making false statements to federal officials, id. §1001; mail fraud, id. §1341; wire fraud, id. §1343; criminal RICO, id. §§1962-1963; obstruction of justice, id. §1503, and interstate transportation of property obtained by fraud, id. §2314.

Sentences can be harsh. The U.S. Sentencing Guidelines, for example, prescribe severe sentences if the crime "substantially jeopardized the safety and soundness of a financial institution," or if the crime affected a financial institution and the defendant derived more than $1 million in gross receipts from the crime. U.S. Sentencing Guidelines Manual §§2B1.1(b)(15)(A)-(B)(i), 2B4.1(b)(2) (2012).

Questions and Comments

1. Some protections are available to shield a regulated party against these threats of civil or criminal liability.

a. If the penalty scheme is simply irrational — if it bears no credible relationship with any of the statutory purposes — a court might declare that imposing a sanction would violate principles of substantive due process. To win a substantive due process challenge, however, the aggrieved party must do more than show that the rule in question is "unwise, improvident, or out of harmony with a particular school of thought," Williamson v. Lee Optical of Oklahoma, 348 U.S. 483, 487-488 (1955). Rather, the party must demonstrate that the challenged rule is not rationally related to a legitimate government purpose. Usery v. Turner Elkhorn Mining Co., 428 U.S. 1, 15 (1976). Nearly any statute, no matter how poorly conceived or incompetently drafted, can be construed to have a minimal core of rationality sufficient to survive this lenient standard.

b. A court might declare that the penalty violates the "excessive fines" clause of the Eighth Amendment. To prevail on this theory, however, a party must establish that the regulatory action was punitive and that the penalties are grossly disproportionate to the gravity of the alleged offense. United States v. Bajakajian, 524 U.S. 321 (1998). Most criminal statutes applicable to compliance violations would pass this test.

c. A court might elect to interpret an ambiguous statute in an effort to avoid constitutional issues. This possibility depends on the statute being ambiguous and the constitutional issue being difficult or substantial. These are demanding conditions. Accordingly, attempts to avoid regulatory sanctions through statutory interpretation will often be unavailing.

d. In criminal cases, the defendant is entitled to have a jury determine beyond a reasonable doubt any fact (other than a prior conviction) that increases the penalty for a crime beyond the statutory minimum. Apprendi v. New Jersey, 530 U.S. 466, 490 (2000). In Southern Union Co. v. United States, 132 S. Ct. 2344 (2012), a judge imposed a $6 million fine on a company convicted of violating the Resource Conservation and Recovery Act. The judge set the fine based on the probation office's conclusion that the violation had lasted for 762 days. The jury, however, had not determined the number of days that the violation continued. The Supreme Court held that Apprendi applied and that the defendant could not be fined for more than one day of violation. The regulated party won in this case, but in later cases, prosecutors will be more careful to ensure that the jury decides all the required elements of the penalty determination.

The arguments presented above offer only faint solace to a defendant charged with civil or criminal violations of regulatory statutes. In the vast majority of cases, the penalties can legally be imposed. Defendants are well advised to recognize the extent of their exposure at the time they decide on a course of conduct.

This awesome array of potential sanctions might seem like a desirable response to the problem of non-compliance by corporations and other organizations. After all, if the organization has engaged in misconduct, why worry about the size of the fine? Yet there are also countervailing considerations that counsel for mitigating the size of the penalty.

In the first place, policymakers worry about over-deterrence. Society sometimes would prefer an actor to violate a rule. It may be illegal to drive faster than 65 miles per hour, but if the passenger in the car is being rushed to the hospital after suffering a heart attack, we might not want to enforce the speed limit at the cost of a person's life. Over-deterrence can also be a problem when the scope of a rule is uncertain. If penalties for violation are very large, people may refrain from engaging in legal behavior if there is even a remote change that their conduct will subsequently be declared to have been illegal.

There is also the problem of inaccuracy: Regulators and prosecutors don't always get it right. They make errors; and when they do, the erroneous imposition of a sanction on an innocent party represents a cost society would prefer to avoid. Moreover, regulators (being human) may have other objectives than merely serving the public interest. Consider the following:

- Ideology: Perhaps a regulator is motivated by an enforcement zeal that causes her to exceed the level of enforcement contemplated or desired by the Congress that enacted the statute in question.
- Political ambition: Perhaps a regulator wants to get headlines and favorable publicity that will help in a future run for public office.
- Ego: Perhaps a regulator wants to be or feel powerful, to have people cater to her, to be able to lord it over powerful industry leaders with threats of enforcement actions.
- Turf: Perhaps a regulator wants, by vigorously pursuing her enforcement authority, to expand the "turf" — the jurisdiction and power — of the agency which she is leading.
- Money: Given the enormous fines available in enforcement actions today, perhaps the regulator wishes to capture money for the public treasury, and to gain whatever personal or institutional benefits flow from doing so.

Questions and Comments

1. We will see in the pages that follow that regulators routinely issue press releases in connection with major enforcement actions and settlements. Are these motivated solely by a wish to inform the public, or is there a degree of self-promotion involved?

2. For a discussion of pecuniary considerations underlying regulatory enforcement actions, see Margaret H. Lemos & Max Minzner, *For-Profit Public Enforcement*, 127 Harv. L. Rev. 853 (2014) (arguing that "public enforcers often seek large monetary awards for self-interested reasons divorced from the public interest in deterrence").

3. Given the competing considerations noted above, how would you think about devising an appropriate sanctioning regime for compliance violations?

Most observers would agree that the vigor of enforcement and the severity of penalties has increased markedly over the past decades. Why might this be so? Consider the following theories:

- The public once held a degree of confidence that firms and organizations could be trusted to do the right thing. Not everyone would have gone so far as General Motors CEO Charlie Wilson, who believed that "what was good for our country is good for General Motors, and vice versa," but many would have endorsed the general tenor of that remark. People today are more suspicious of complex organizations. Although in general the public continues to believe that most businesses behave ethically, there appears to be less faith that firms will, without careful regulation, act in accordance with the public interest. In 1965, according to Gallup polling, 35 percent of respondents listed "big business" as the greatest threat to the country; by 1998, 64 percent listed big business as the greatest threat. A Harris poll conducted near the height of the financial crisis in 2008 found that only 11 percent of respondents reported a "great deal" of confidence in business leaders; 35 percent had "hardly any." Aware of these changing attitudes, politicians and regulators have piled ever more onerous obligations and penalties on American business enterprises.

- Business enterprises today represent increased threats to the public welfare. As businesses have grown larger, more sophisticated, and more interconnected, the systematic risk they create has increased apace. Meanwhile events such as the corporate frauds of the early 2000s and the financial crisis of 2007-2009 have revealed that businesses cannot always be trusted to manage these threats on their own. Because the danger of corporate harm is large, the penalties are appropriately large as well.

- Regulators have limited budgets and large responsibilities. Acting on their own, they cannot possibly detect and punish more than a tiny fraction of the violations that might occur. The move from the judicial to the administrative model is a rational response to this problem. By increasing their access to information and substituting administrative for judicial enforcement, the regulators reduce their costs of administering the law because it is easier for them to detect violations and, if they detect a violation, it is cheaper for them to enforce the rules. Regulators also reduce the costs of enforcement by increasing the severity of sanctions. If penalties are set very high, then the regulators don't have to catch and sanction more than a small percentage of violators to achieve optimal deterrence. To give a simple example, suppose that the public harm from a particular regulatory violation is $10,000, the fine is also set at $10,000, and that the probability of detection given the regulator's budget constraints is 10 percent. Then the level of violations will be too high because the expected penalty for a violator is only $1,000 (10% of $10,000). Anyone who gets more than $1,000 in benefit from committing a violation will do so (assuming that they are rational, self-interested, and not responsive to risk). If, however, the penalty is increased to $100,000, then optimal deterrence can be achieved with the same level of enforcement since the violator's expected penalty is now identical to the social harm ($10,000). *See* Gary Becker, *Crime and Punishment: An Economic Approach*, 76 J. Pol. Econ. 169 (1968).

Which of these theories appeals to you (if any)? What are their respective pros and cons?

D. THE COMPLIANCE RESPONSE

Taken as a whole, the foregoing materials demonstrate a spectacular increase in the government's power to impose its will on private actors. In some respects, regulators might be said to occupy the role of de facto dictators vis-à-vis regulated parties—benevolent dictators, in the vast majority of cases, but dictators nonetheless. The trend shows no signs of slowing; indeed, as this book is written, the pace of enforcement is accelerating, with billion-dollar-plus settlements becoming a normal part of the news cycle and with regulators proclaiming ever more ambitious enforcement agendas.

When the regulators fix unfriendly eyes on someone they suspect to have flouted the rules, the question is sometimes not how the case will turn out but rather how much the regulated party will have to give up to induce the regulator to relent. The transformation of enforcement from the judicial to the administrative model described above, and the enormous upgrade in regulatory power that accompanied that transformation, is a fundamental reason for the growth of the compliance function over the past decades.

Questions and Comments

1. For a valuable introduction to the growth of the modern compliance function, see Miriam Hechler Baer, *Governing Corporate Compliance*, 50 B.C. L. Rev. 949 (2009).

E. THE COMPLIANCE INDUSTRY

The developments discussed in this chapter have sparked an enormous increase in the size and importance of compliance departments. Particular growth areas include banks, securities firms, health care companies, energy companies, and educational institutions; but growth of compliance departments is observed across all sorts of companies.

The Bureau of Labor Statistics reports that there were approximately 210,000 compliance officers in the United States in 2011, a number that is expected to grow by 15 percent by 2020, generating 32,000 new jobs and 26,000 replacement jobs. The top 10 percent of compliance officers earned an average of $96,000 per year in 2011. The compliance industry, moreover, is not limited to compliance departments of regulated firms. Governments at both the state and federal level employ compliance specialists to assist in carrying out their regulatory function. Legal, accounting/auditing, and consulting firms offer compliance-based services that employ thousands of people. Vendors of compliance software employ hundreds more — people who develop and service software, interact with organization customers, analyze trends and developments, and seek to enlarge and develop markets for their products.

Often, senior people in compliance departments are attorneys. However, there is no requirement that compliance executives be attorneys. Accountants, holders of MBAs, and other professionals are often found in compliance departments; and increasingly, these offices are staffed by people whose professional training is specifically in the area of compliance. The developments described above have also led to the birth of what may come to be seen as a new profession — the compliance officer — which combines elements of existing professions (law, accounting, business, management science), but adds something of its own.

5

Internal Enforcement

A. INTRODUCTION

Having defined compliance, explored its costs and benefits, and examined the phenomenal growth of compliance obligations over the past few decades, we are now in a position to consider ways in which the compliance function is carried out. This chapter begins that process by examining compliance within an organization.

B. COMPLIANCE POLICIES

The fundamental charter of an organization's compliance operation is its compliance policy.

Compliance policies are usually phrased in aspirational terms. But it is easy to *say* you are committed to compliance. Words alone are necessary but not sufficient: The management of the company must find a way to demonstrate to the workforce and others

> A compliance policy is a statement approved by the highest authority in an organization that sets forth the organization's philosophy and general approach to compliance issues.

that the company is truly committed to the compliance enterprise at the highest level. An attitude of receptivity and support for compliance values is often referred to as "tone at the top." The phrase recognizes that much of what happens in a company — its "corporate culture" — is influenced by the attitudes of its leaders. If the leaders are genuinely committed to compliance, and if they effectively communicate their commitment throughout the organization, then others in the organization are more likely to take seriously the obligation to obey governing norms.

How can an organization's leaders convey a genuine commitment to compliance values? Any set of actions can be feigned, but some signals are more credible than others. A company can signal its commitment to compliance, for example, by appointing a high-level officer to head up a compliance office and giving that person both the resources necessary to conduct her job effectively and access to decision makers such as the chief executive officer or the board audit committee. Swift and thoroughgoing responses to compliance violations also signal tone at the top: If a com-

> "Tone at the top" refers to a set of values and standards that is subscribed to by an organization's leaders and effectively communicated throughout the organization.

pany launches an investigation, conducts it with integrity, and administers punishments as warranted by the facts, these actions will become known throughout the firm.

Although actions speak louder than words, rhetoric is not unimportant. Many companies find that a colloquial tone is more effective than forbidding and off-putting legalese. Google, a corporate leader in so many ways, is at the forefront of rhetorical innovation in this space. Consider the following excerpt from that company's Code of Conduct:

> "Don't be evil." Googlers generally apply those words to how we serve our users. But "Don't be evil" is much more than that. Yes, it's about providing our users unbiased access to information, focusing on their needs and giving them the best products and services that we can. But it's also about doing the right thing more generally — following the law, acting honorably and treating each other with respect . . . . The Google Code of Conduct is one of the ways we put "Don't be evil" into practice.

Questions and Comments

1. Compliance can seem a bit of a bore, especially to young computer geeks who are more interested in programming than in following some externally created set of rules. How does the Google Code of Conduct address this problem?

2. Who is speaking here? It seems to be a corporate Google — a body composed of everyone in the Google community. The message doesn't come from on high, but rather purports to represent the collective judgment of everyone involved.

3. Does the slightly light-hearted tone detract from or add to the seriousness of the underlying message?

4. Although the rhetoric is informal and colloquial, do you detect a subtle hint of compulsion? If you want to be a true "Googler," you need to endorse and abide by the values expressed in the document. If you fail to live up to the standard, well then — you are not part of the Google family.

5. The argot of governance, risk management, and compliance has a term for effective culture change: "getting it." It is easy to talk the talk without really understanding or internalizing the values being communicated. "Getting it" means that a light bulb goes off in someone's head — she develops a perspective on issues that reorients how she thinks. There is no litmus test for whether or not someone has "gotten it," but careful observation of how people act, communicate, and present themselves to others can provide cues to a careful observer.

6. How can one shape an organization's culture? The task is difficult because culture is so deep-seated. Cultural values are often so internalized that they are unspoken; they are communicated pervasively and absorbed by osmosis rather than intellectual effort. For this reason, the culture can't be changed by a single

"retreat" or by flowery statements of organizational ethics and values. Changing culture is a process, usually an extended one. If culture can be changed, the initiative must come from the top; but the changes must occur throughout the organization. To effectively change a culture, the leader must not only communicate values verbally, but must also "live" them — demonstrate by her behavior in matters great and small that she is committed to a particular set of values and behaviors and that she expects others to follow suit.

7. A study by Biggerstaff, Cicero, and Puckett found that firms whose CEOs had personally benefited from backdated options were more likely to engage in other corporate misbehaviors such as financial fraud. The authors take this as evidence that culture matters and that firms with an unethical culture are more likely than other firms to engage in compliance violations. Lee Biggerstaff, David C. Cicero & Andy Puckett, *Suspect CEOs, Unethical Culture, and Corporate Misbehavior*, ___ J. Fin. Econ. ___ (2015). Do you agree?

8. If Biggerstaff, Cicero, and Puckett are correct that culture can predict conduct, should auditors or regulators explicitly take this factor into account when performing a risk assessment to determine the intensity and scope of their examinations? The U.K. Financial Conduct Authority assesses compliance culture and uses it as a basis for enforcement actions. Should U.S. regulators do the same?

Let's consider a bit more deeply the idea that "culture" is a major determinant of compliance. A compliant organization is one that has a significant internal commitment, backed by genuine norms and standards, to obey the law for its own sake and not merely as a means to avoid penalties. A non-compliant organization is one that may adopt the forms and language of compliance but which treats the commitments so made as a form of lip service, not reflecting any genuine belief in the value of obeying governing norms or in following the rules when self-interest counsels otherwise. The difference between these organizations is said to lie in "culture" — one organization has a culture of compliance and the other does not.

Implicit in the idea of organizational culture is a concept of the costs of enforcing norms. Culture is a set of social practices that defines social roles and assigns those roles to individuals. Rituals and other cultural practices encourage people to accept the legitimacy of social roles and to identify personally with the roles assigned to them. If the process of acceptance and identification works properly, people will act in role-appropriate ways simply because they experience such roles as consistent with their own identities. Because people experience role-inappropriate behaviors as violations of their identity and sense of proper social order, they refrain from engaging in such conduct and willingly join in efforts to sanction others who do violate the norms. Thus culture itself reduces the need for external norm enforcement mechanisms such as police or regulators.

Translated to the arena of compliance, the idea is that an organization with a compliant culture is one in which people are socialized to accept the legitimacy of the norms being enforced and to identify personally with a social role — that of employee — which includes as one of its important dimensions a commitment to obeying applicable laws and norms. Such an organization is likely to display a substantially higher level of voluntary compliance than is an organization that is outwardly similar but which does not encourage employees to adopt these attitudes and beliefs.

While the idea that culture is important for compliance is easily understood, it is obviously also problematic. It is one thing to speak of the culture of a larger society, but does the idea make sense when it comes to an organization functioning within such a setting? People who work in organizations are creatures of a broader culture that they share with many others. Rules forbidding employment discrimination and encouraging diversity suppress — for good reasons — practices that might facilitate the development of distinctive cultures. People do not inhabit organizations in the same way they inhabit the broader society: It may be costly to find another job, but it is often far more difficult to become a citizen of a different country. Accordingly, it is not clear that organizations such as corporations will be effective at causing employees to internalize social roles in a way that significantly alters behavior.

Even if organizations do display cultures that have important impacts on compliance, the problem remains as to how one can distinguish a compliant culture from a non-compliant one. All organizations proclaim that they are committed to compliance; if they did not do so, they would quickly be crushed by negative public opinion and harsh regulatory action. If an organization doesn't have a compliant culture, moreover, how can this defect be addressed? Culture is notoriously durable and resistant to attempts to change it from without. Strategies for effecting genuine change, as opposed to mere verbal assurances, are difficult to devise and hard to administer. And strategies that hold promise to be effective might also require wrenching change that can only be accomplished with significant collateral costs. Thus, even if other problems can be solved, the challenge of moving from a non-compliant to a compliant culture can be daunting. The problem of identifying, instituting, and managing a culture of compliance is at the cutting edge of modern compliance theory.

Questions and Comments

1. Regulators are increasingly focusing on the concept of culture as a key to improving compliance with applicable norms. In a 2014 speech to executives from big banks, New York Federal Reserve Bank President William Dudley warned them to improve their compliance management or face compelled downsizing by the government. And he specifically identified bad compliance culture as the root cause of much misconduct at financial institutions: "I reject the narrative that the current state of affairs is simply the result of actions of isolated rogue traders or a few bad actors within these firms." Dudley's remarks were widely circulated in banking and compliance circles, and appeared to reflect a change in the priorities of at least one important regulator, with others likely to follow suit. *See* Victoria McGrane, *Fed's Dudley: Bad Bank Behavior Could Drive Break Up: New York Fed President Suggests Putting Senior Management on Hook for Regulatory Fines*, Wall St. J., Oct. 24, 2014.

2. In the same speech, Dudley proposed that banks should defer bonuses for top executives for a ten-year period, with the money being held essentially as a bond that the manager would forfeit if the company is later shown to have committed serious compliance violations during the period when the executive was in a leadership position. What do you think of this idea as a means for preventing executives from behaving unethically and then moving on before their misdeeds are discovered?

3. Dudley proposed, further, that financial institutions should create a database to track lower-level employees who are sanctioned for ethical or compliance lapses, so that other firms would have access to this information when considering whether to hire the employee. Is this a good idea?

4. People who work in an industry often report that they know which companies are clean and which are not. They learn this information from reputation channels that derive ultimately either from within a firm or from counterparties who have experience working with the firm. Would surveys of people in the industry, asking about the compliance reputations of different firms, be useful tools for encouraging the development of compliant corporate cultures?

C. COMPLIANCE PROGRAMS

Because compliance policies are typically framed at a high level of generality, they are often fleshed out in a more detailed document known as a compliance program, which may or may not be part of the same document as the compliance policy.

The law does not generally require organizations to adopt and implement compliance programs, although specific regulatory statues do sometimes impose such requirements. Thus a firm's failure to adopt a compliance program is not, in general, an independent basis for legal liability. Even when not required to do so, however, organizations frequently adopt compliance programs voluntarily. The idea of "voluntary" compliance programs must be qualified by the fact that such programs are often adopted in the shadow of enforcement actions, and serve, in part, the purpose of mitigating that exposure.

> A compliance program consists of the mechanisms that an organization uses to ensure compliance, and the procedures that it employs when possible instances of non-compliance are discovered.

What does a compliance program look like? Consider the following excerpt from the compliance program of a fictional firm, Zambac Co.

Zambac Co. Compliance Program

Zambac Co. ("Zambac" or the "Company") administers a Compliance Program that reflects its longstanding commitment to compliance with applicable laws and regulations. The goal of Zambac's Compliance Program is to maintain a culture that promotes the prevention, detection, and resolution of potential violations of law or Company policy.

- Zambac has a Compliance Officer dedicated to support Zambac's culture of compliance. The Compliance Officer reports to the Chief Executive Officer and periodically to the Company's Board of Directors.
- The Compliance Officer manages a department of compliance professionals who provide guidance and oversight for the processes, training, and implementation needed to ensure full compliance with applicable laws, regulations, and policies.
- Zambac is committed to ensuring that its Compliance Officer has the ability to effectuate change within the organization as necessary and to exercise

independent judgment. The compliance function has unrestricted access to information, executives, and meetings related to business operations.

The development and distribution of written standards of conduct, as well as written policies, procedures, and guidelines has long been a key element of Zambac's Compliance Program.

- Zambac's Code of Conduct is our statement of the values, standards, and ethical principles that guide our daily operations. The Code of Conduct is available to all employees on the Company's intranet and applies to everyone conducting business on behalf of Zambac.
- In addition to its Code of Conduct, Zambac maintains corporate policies, procedures, and guidelines that outline the specific behaviors required for day-to-day operations and outline how Zambac employees are expected to conduct their activities.

Another critical element of our Compliance Program is the education and annual training of our employees on their legal and ethical obligations under Zambac policy and the laws, regulations, and guidelines.

- Zambac is committed to taking all necessary steps to effectively communicate our standards and procedures to all affected personnel. Zambac's Code of Conduct, corporate policies, procedures, and guidelines are available to employees at all times through the Zambac intranet.
- All Zambac employees are required to participate in annual training as a condition of their employment. In addition, these employees will undergo periodic re-training and remedial training programs as necessary.

As a matter of policy, employees are required to bring workplace issues of any type to the attention of management. Zambac strives to provide a work environment that encourages employees to communicate openly with management about all types of workplace issues without fear of retaliation or recrimination. To support this concept, Zambac has established the following resources:

- Zambac encourages employees, as a first step, to seek out an immediate supervisor or manager to discuss workplace issues. If the matter is not successfully resolved, the employee is encouraged to pursue the issue with his or her next level of management or Human Resources.
- The Zambac Ombudsman Program, managed by the Chief Ethics and Compliance Officer, complements Zambac's primary resolution mechanisms by providing an alternative channel for employees to address work-related concerns, including conduct inconsistent with Zambac's policies, practices, values, and standards. The Program is available to all employees and is designed to provide a "safe haven" where concerns can be addressed in confidence and without fear of reprisal. All conversations with the Ombudsman are kept confidential unless they raise issues of potential harm to an individual or the Company. The Ombudsman is a neutral party who will listen to and review concerns as an advocate for the Company's values and standards. The Ombudsman has a stand-alone office that is part of the Office of Ethics.
- Zambac also has a confidential outside telephone line made available to all employees who wish to anonymously raise concerns about potential unethical or illegal behavior or violations of Zambac policies. This telephone line is

operated by an independent firm that will forward reported concerns to Zambac's Office of Ethics for response or investigation. The telephone line is available 24 hours a day, 7 days a week.

- The Office of Ethics is accountable for ensuring appropriate review and follow-up with respect to issues raised to the Ombudsman or via the confidential telephone line.

Zambac's Compliance Program includes monitoring, auditing, and ongoing evaluation regarding compliance with the company's policies and procedures. The nature of review as well as the extent and frequency of our compliance monitoring and auditing varies according to a variety of factors, including new regulatory requirements, changes in business practices, and other considerations. Results of auditing, monitoring, and evaluation are, as appropriate, followed up on specifically, incorporated in training and communications strategies, and considered when making choices in connection with ongoing general management of the business.

The primary responsibility for oversight is with management. To assist managers with this responsibility, Zambac provides them with reports from tracking and oversight systems that capture key compliance indicators to aid them in monitoring compliance with company policy and investigating any potential violations of policy. Management oversight is supplemented by audits.

Zambac is committed to hiring a workforce whose actions will reflect a high degree of integrity and ethics, recognizing that the ability to excel depends on the integrity, knowledge, and skills of our people. Accordingly, the Company invests significant resources in identifying and hiring highly qualified and skilled individuals. In addition, prior to allowing an individual to commence employment with the Company, Zambac performs a drug screening and background investigation of the individual. The background investigation includes verification of employment history and education. Zambac also performs a criminal background investigation that searches for any felony or misdemeanor on both a county and federal level. If deemed appropriate to the position, checks also will be conducted of professional certifications and licenses, motor vehicle records, and credit history.

Our Compliance Program requires employees to report and the company to respond promptly to potential violations of law or company policy, and take appropriate disciplinary action. Specifically, Zambac's Compliance Program includes a clearly defined violations process that sets out the potential consequences of violating the law or company policy. Although each situation is considered on a case-by-case basis, Zambac policy requires that consistent and appropriate disciplinary action be taken to address inappropriate conduct and deter future violations. Zambac also assesses whether identified violations are in part due to gaps in our policies, practices, or internal controls, and if so, takes appropriate action to prevent future violations.

Questions and Comments

1. What rules does the Zambac compliance program seek to enforce? Notice that the program is officially intended to cover both laws and "company policy." Is there any difference, in terms of compliance, between externally created norms (laws) and internally created norms (company policy)?

2. What do you make of the reporting arrangement under which the chief compliance officer reports to the chief executive officer and "periodically" to the board of directors?

3. The program refers to a department staffed with "compliance professionals." Why does the company use the term "compliance professionals" as opposed to something more prosaic, such as "staff"? This statement seems to take as given something that would only a few years ago have been disputable: that there exists a compliance "profession" distinct from other professions such as law, accounting, engineering, and the like.

4. What guarantees of independence does this program provide to the chief compliance officer? She is assured the right to "effectuate change within the organization as necessary." This sounds impressive, but what does it mean in practice? Could the chief compliance officer fire the executive vice president in charge of marketing?

5. The chief compliance officer is assured of the ability to "exercise independent judgment." What does this mean in practice?

6. The chief compliance officer also is assured of the ability to attend meetings — an important power in an organization, since those who are not at the meeting cannot influence the outcome. But as a practical matter, how likely is the chief compliance officer to butt in on a meeting to which she is not invited?

7. Notice that the Zambac compliance program goes beyond merely providing a safe means for employees to communicate compliance-related concerns to senior management: Employees are *required* to "bring workplace issues of any type to the attention of management." What, however, is a "workplace issue"? Are employees required to report to management that the water cooler is broken?

8. To what degree does the Zambac compliance program seek to define and also reinforce the organization's attitude toward compliance by setting a "tone at the top" that can serve as a model for others in the organization?

9. To what degree does the Zambac compliance program incorporate considerations of risk management? Is the organization's appetite for risk brought to bear in the structuring of the program? In the analysis of responses when instances of noncompliance are uncovered?

10. A compliance program will not work well unless it contains training and educational programs designed to instruct employees on the requirements applicable to their jobs and to update them on regulatory changes. To what extent does the excerpted program ensure adequate staff training in compliance issues?

11. The Zambac compliance program is, officially, an internal document prepared for and used by people within the organization. Do you detect a different audience as well? The compliance program is also an external document designed to demonstrate to regulators, shareholders, and the public at large that the company is serious about compliance. Might the company hope that by promoting itself as a "good guy" in the compliance arena, it will avoid criticism by activists or ward off potential regulatory action?

12. In addition to the obligations set forth in an organization's compliance program, the compliance function increasingly involves a host of representations, commitments, rights, and obligations contained in contractual agreements with counterparties, in areas as diverse as vendor risk management and supply chain due diligence. *See* Scott Killingsworth, The Privatization of Compliance, RAND Center for Corporate Ethics and Governance Symposium White Paper Series,

Symposium on Transforming Compliance: Emerging Paradigms for Boards, Management, Compliance Officers, and Government (2014).

D. HIRING

Compliance is only as good as the people who work in an organization. Even the best-designed compliance program will fail if the people are unreliable or unethical; and even poorly conceived compliance programs will succeed if the people are outstanding. Thus a key step in any compliance program — as recognized in the Zambac Compliance Program reproduced above — is the selection of the people who work in an organization.

Most important among these are senior staff, especially those involved in the three lines of defense. But employees well below the senior-most level can impact compliance. In financial institutions, traders can make excessive bets on price movements. Barings Bank, one of the oldest investment houses in the world, went out of business after a trader named Nicholas Leeson embarked on a course of ruinous speculation; many other institutions have learned hard lessons about the harms that "rogue" traders can inflict. Lower-level employees pose even more of a threat when it comes to information security (see Chapter 11), since a tech-savvy person with access to non-public information can sometimes misappropriate or disclose sensitive matters.

1. Background Investigations

Prior to hiring a new employee — especially one brought into a sensitive position — many companies conduct a background investigation. It is much better, from the perspective of a potential employer, to know about problems before the employee joins the company. Afterwards, if skeletons rattle in the closet, the situation can get messy: The employee may commit compliance violations that expose the employer to regulatory sanctions; she may steal from the employer; she may, while on company business, cause harm to third parties. The employer may face lawsuits based on a theory of *respondeat superior* or claiming that the employer was negligent in hiring an unqualified person (the latter are often seen when an employee commits an act of violence at the workplace against a fellow employee).

An amazing amount of information is available about every one of us if we dig deep enough. Our marriages and divorces, home purchases and sales, arrests and convictions, lawsuits (subject to state rules), foreclosures, driving records, status as registered sex offenders, and bankruptcies are all public knowledge. With the candidate's consent, the employer may seek to verify the existence of claimed educational degrees and obtain the candidate's credit history compiled by credit rating agencies. An investigator might snoop around the Internet, scanning our Facebook page (watch out what you put on it!), our blogs, our writings, our appearances in the press, our photographs, and much else besides. If assiduous, the investigator might make discreet personal contacts with people who are able to supply even more information on a confidential basis. Employers need not conduct investigations on their own; there are hundreds of companies that specialize in providing background checks on potential hires.

All this may be legal, at least so long as no deception is used and the investigation does not intrude on information deemed to be private under the law. Nevertheless, there are limits on what a potential employer may do. Some types of information may not be requested at all, even with the candidate's consent; medical records are an example (the employer may, however, inquire whether the employee has any medical condition or disability that could interfere with the successful performance of the job). An employer should refrain from asking information about a candidate's race, age, gender, disability, or other protected category. Reference to sources such as Facebook should be used with caution because they may reveal protected information (such as someone's race or gender). Some information requires the candidate's consent before it is provided (credit history is an example). And an employer is well advised to conduct the same kind of background checks for all similarly situated candidates; otherwise it may face claims of illegal discrimination.

2. Use of Information

Background checks and other sources provide potential employers with lots of information. But what use can the employer make of information once obtained? In particular, what sorts of compliance-related information may a potential employer use when determining whether to hire an applicant?

a. Arrests and Convictions

Consider the case where a job applicant has previously been arrested or convicted of a crime. On the one hand, it appears obvious that actions a person has performed in the past are predictive, at least to some extent, of things they may do in the future. If a person has perpetrated frauds, engaged in sexual misconduct, or committed other wrongful acts, this appears to be a legitimate factor for a potential employer to take into account. Knowing a candidate's criminal history, accordingly, is potentially important information an organization should consider in order to make good compliance-related hiring decisions.

On the other hand, the use of this sort of information as a negative factor in job applications is problematic. Society benefits when people with the greatest skills are matched with jobs: If someone has an arrest or conviction on their record but also has significant skills, society could be better off if that person is hired notwithstanding their history. Also important are policies against discrimination in employment. If it turns out that people in certain protected categories have a greater propensity for problems under the criminal law, then the use of these problems as a basis for negative employment decisions would have the effect of screening out a disproportionately large number of people in the protected group. Finally, there may be privacy concerns at play: People often, and for good reason, don't want others looking into their prior acts of criminal misconduct.

Current federal law doesn't bar an employer from asking about arrest and conviction records. The Equal Employment Opportunity Commission (EEOC), however, takes the position that "using such records as an absolute measure to prevent an individual from being hired could limit the employment opportunities of some protected groups and thus cannot be used in this way." Instead, arrest and conviction records can be used, in the EEOC's view, "only to the extent that it is evident that the applicant cannot be trusted to perform the duties of the position when considering the nature of the job, the nature and seriousness of the offense, and the length of time since it occurred." Some states or cities have stricter rules, which may prohibit the potential employer from asking about arrest records at all during job interviews or restrict the use of conviction data in making employment decisions.

In June 2013 the EEOC filed an important test case against two employers that allegedly used criminal histories to discriminate against African-American applicants:

Equal Employment Opportunity Commission, EEOC Files Suit Against Two Employers for Use of Criminal Background Checks

June 11, 2013

A BMW manufacturing facility in South Carolina, and the largest small-box discount retailer in the United States violated Title VII of the Civil Rights Act by implementing and utilizing a criminal background policy that resulted in employees being fired and others being screened out for employment, the U.S. Equal Employment Opportunity Commission alleged in two lawsuits filed today . . . .

The EEOC alleges that BMW disproportionately screened out African Americans from jobs, and that the policy is not job related and consistent with business necessity. The claimants were employees of UTi Integrated Logistics, Inc. ("UTi"), which provided logistic services to BMW at the South Carolina facility. The logistics services included warehouse and distribution assistance, transportation services and manufacturing support.

Since 1994, BMW has had a criminal conviction policy that denies facility access to BMW employees and employees of contractors with certain criminal convictions. However, when UTi assigned the claimants to work at the BMW facility, UTi screened the employees according to UTi's criminal conviction policy. UTi's criminal background check limited review to convictions within the prior seven years. BMW's policy has no time limit with regard to convictions. The policy is a blanket exclusion without any individualized assessment of the nature and gravity of the crimes, the ages of the convictions, or the nature of the claimants' respective positions.

In 2008, UTi ended its contract with BMW. During a transitional period, UTi employees were informed of the need to re-apply with the new contractor to retain their positions in the BMW warehouse. As part of the application process, BMW directed the new contractor to perform new criminal background checks on every current UTi employee applying for transition of employment. The new contractor subsequently discovered that several UTi employees had criminal convictions in violation of BMW's criminal conviction policy. As a result, those employees were told that they no longer met the criteria for working at the BMW facility and were subsequently terminated and denied rehire as employees of the new contractor, despite the fact that many of the employees had worked at the BMW facility for years.

In Illinois, the Chicago office of the EEOC filed a nationwide lawsuit [against Dollar General] based on discrimination charges filed by two rejected black applicants. That lawsuit charges that Dollar General conditions all of its job offers on criminal background checks, which results in a disparate impact against blacks.

Dollar General operates 10,000 stores in 40 states, plus 11 distribution centers. Ninety percent of all Dollar General employees are store clerks who are both stockers and cashiers at the stores.

According to the EEOC, one of the applicants who had filed a charge with EEOC was given a conditional employment offer, although she had disclosed a six-year-old conviction for possession of a controlled substance. Her application also showed that she had previously worked for another discount retailer as a cashier-stocker for four years. Nevertheless, her job offer was allegedly revoked because Dollar General's practice was to use her type of conviction as a disqualification factor for 10 years.

The other applicant who filed an EEOC charge was fired by Dollar General although, according to the EEOC, the conviction records check report about her was wrong—she did not have the felony conviction attributed to her. The EEOC said that although she advised the Dollar General store manager of the mistake in the report, the company did not reverse its decision and her firing stood.

"Title VII of the Civil Rights Act of 1964 prohibits discrimination against job applicants and employees on account of their race," said EEOC Chair Jacqueline A. Berrien. "Since issuing its first written policy guidance in the 1980s regarding the use of arrest and conviction records in employment decisions, the EEOC has advised employers that under certain circumstances, their use of that information to deny employment opportunities could be at odds with Title VII."

"The Commission is committed to using public education and informal resolution to address discriminatory hiring practices," said David Lopez, EEOC General Counsel. "When these methods are unsuccessful, the Commission will, if necessary, seek redress from the federal courts and ensure equal opportunity for all. This is the latest in a series of systemic cases the Commission has filed to challenge unlawful hiring practices."

Both lawsuits were brought under Title VII of the Civil Rights Act of 1964, which prohibits discrimination on the basis of race and national origin as well as retaliation. The EEOC will assert claims of disparate impact, in both cases, against African Americans. The EEOC filed suit in each instance after attempting to resolve the matter through settlement. In all, the Commission will seek back pay, as well as injunctive relief to prevent future discrimination of employees and applicants.

Questions and Comments

1. Could *any* criterion—even legitimate factors such as education or experience in the industry—differentially affect the employment opportunities of a protected group? If so, does this mean that an employer subject to EEOC regulations simply cannot have any hard-and-fast criteria for hiring, such as BMW's rule that categorically excluded people who had been convicted of certain crimes?

2. As to arrest records, the EEOC takes the position that "since an arrest alone does not necessarily mean that an applicant has committed a crime, the employer should not assume that the applicant committed the offense. Instead, the employer should allow him or her the opportunity to explain the circumstances of the arrest(s) and should make a reasonable effort to determine whether the explanation is reliable." EEOC, Pre-Employment Inquiries and Arrest & Conviction, available at http://www.eeoc.gov/laws/practices/inquiries_arrest_conviction.cfm, p.1.

Given that people are presumed innocent until the contrary is proven, should arrests be considered at all?

3. The charge against BMW alleges that the defendant required the new contractor to apply more exacting criminal history standards only when those people were rehired by a new contractor for the same job. What is the relevance of this? Is an employer forbidden to change the rules?

4. What may an employer do with regard to job candidates' past criminal records, in the view of the EEOC?

b. Credit History

To what extent should an employer be allowed to use a job applicant's credit history as a basis for an adverse employment decision? Here, again, we see a conflict of policy. On the one hand, the fact that a person has experienced or is currently experiencing financial distress is potentially relevant to her performance on the job, especially with respect to compliance issues. Financial distress can create pressures to engage in conduct that a person would ordinarily avoid. If a purchasing officer of a company is undergoing a bankruptcy, for example, she might be more open to accepting gratuities from a supplier in exchange for buying that supplier's product. Credit problems can also be a proxy for problems other than financial distress that bear on an employee's propensity to abide by an organization's compliance policy. Sometimes people run into credit problems because of other underlying issues that could also adversely affect their job performance.

On the other hand, any inquiry into a person's financial history is intrusive on her privacy. Further, social policy favors giving people second chances in their financial affairs. A fundamental purpose of bankruptcy law, in fact, is to allow people to put their financial distress behind them and make a fresh start in life. If a poor credit history were to be used as a basis for denying employment, people would have a much harder time recovering from their problems. Anyone with a bad credit history can attest to the misery that past mistakes can impose on the future.

The law seeks to balance these conflicting policies. Employers are permitted to ask for a job candidate's credit report, and credit rating agencies are permitted to provide the report (provided the agency has reason to believe that the requester intends to use the information for employment purposes and receives a certification that the employer will not use the information in violation of any law or regulation governing equal opportunity in employment). However, the report may not be provided unless the applicant provides written authorization. Before finalizing a decision not to hire the applicant based on the credit report, a potential employer must provide the candidate with a copy of her credit report and a statement of her right to challenge information contained in the report.

Questions and Comments

1. How relevant, in your opinion, is a person's credit history to his job performance? Does the answer depend in part on the nature of the job?

2. In general, an employer doesn't have to explain what factors about an applicant's credit history resulted in an adverse job action. Should employers be required to justify their decisions?

3. How effective is the requirement that the applicant provide authorization before the employer examines his credit history? What inference would an employer draw if the applicant refused to consent?

E. TRAINING

Training is an important part of many companies' compliance programs. The nature of the training will depend in large measure on the type of job involved. Senior executive positions tend to be staffed by people with relatively high educational levels; even if they are no smarter than ordinary employees, they may be capable of digesting information in more abstract form. The types of training given to senior officials also should reflect the nature of their jobs: If the official is a back-office person, she may not need training on compliance issues surrounding customer relations (unless she supervises people who do become involved with customers). But the person may need specialized training relating to what she does in other respects. Lower-level employees may require a different type of training.

Companies may not be particularly good at setting up in-house training programs. Many vendors offer to fill this gap. Through a vendor, a company may purchase an online training package that employees can review in front of a computer at work (obviously, with suitable assurances that they actually complete the task!). Vendors will also send instructors to a company's facility in order to conduct in-person training sessions.

Training is particularly important in the case of companies that employ many lower-level workers whose activities may implicate compliance concerns. Drug companies, for example, employ legions of salespeople who call on doctors' offices in an attempt to persuade the physicians to prescribe the company's mediations. These salespeople are incentivized by compensation schemes that reward them for results. Under current law drug companies must be scrupulous to ensure that these salespeople don't exceed the limits on items of value that can be given to doctors in order to cultivate their good will. Training programs for newly hired sales staff are one part of the process for managing the compliance risk posed by these employees.

Securities broker-dealers, likewise, employ traders who are compensated, in part, by the profits they generate for the firm from their trades. These traders can expose the company to compliance problems if they violate applicable regulations with respect to their trading activities; an obvious example is the case where they trade on the basis of material non-public information. Training programs for new traders, coupled with mandatory refresher classes, can mitigate, although not eliminate, the risk that they will let greed override good judgment in the performance of their jobs.

Training programs are often included in compliance programs established in settlements of enforcement proceedings. An excellent example is reproduced in Chapter 15, involving an EEOC consent decree against Carrols Corporation (the world's largest Burger King franchise) covering sexual harassment in the workplace.

Questions and Comments

1. Consider three effects a training program might have:

    a. It might make someone aware that certain forms of conduct are prohibited.
    b. It might make someone aware of the serious penalties she can expect if she violates a rule.
    c. It might influence how a person thinks about certain forms of conduct — to cause a change in values so that conduct that once appeared attractive is now avoided.

Of these three, which is a training program most likely to accomplish? Least likely? Best for society?

2. Compliance training programs are sometimes viewed negatively by the people required to take them — much as instruction in legal ethics is sometimes resisted by third-year law students. The idea of "sensitivity" training, in particular, has come in for more than its fair share of derision. A negative attitude on the part of employees towards training programs can be counterproductive, because it may convey the message that the values being inculcated are not taken seriously by the company, which is forced to provide the instruction, or by the workforce, which is forced to undergo it. The resulting cynicism can be detrimental to morale as well as destructive to the effectiveness of the program. How can this problem be addressed, if at all?

F. MONITORING

A key part of internal enforcement is the job of monitoring employees. Here too we find a policy tradeoff between efficacy and privacy. Unless they monitor employees' compliance with governing norms, firms will detect fewer violations; and because they detect fewer violations, more violations will occur. On the other hand, the monitoring function raises obvious concerns of employee privacy. How intensively can an employer scrutinize its employees? Can an employer, in the guise of monitoring its employees, act as "big brother," watching their staff on an ongoing basis?

1. Drug and Alcohol Testing

Substance abuse can lead to poor performance on the job and, sometimes, to illegal conduct. Organizations have an obvious interest in monitoring employees in order to guard against these problems. One form of monitoring is to impose mandatory drug or alcohol testing.

Drug testing by public officials is regulated by law, including the Fourth Amendment's prohibition of unreasonable searches and seizures. Given that some organizations are very large, and to some extent occupy the role of a government with respect to their employees, one might think that analogous protections would be available in the employment relationship. This, however, is not the case. Unless the employment agreement or union contract specifically regulates what the employer can do as regards drug and alcohol testing, there is almost no limit under the law on the employer's conduct in this regard.

The following model drug testing policy is promulgated by the Texas Workforce Commission, an agency of the state of Texas:

Texas Workforce Commission, Model Drug-Free Workplace Policy

XYZ Corporation, Inc. (the Company) intends to help provide a safe and drug-free work environment for our clients and our employees. With this goal in mind and because of the serious drug abuse problem in today's workplace, we are establishing the following policy for existing and future employees of XYZ Corporation, Inc.

The Company explicitly prohibits:

- The use, possession, solicitation for, or sale of narcotics or other illegal drugs, alcohol, or prescription medication without a prescription on Company or customer premises or while performing an assignment.
- Being impaired or under the influence of legal or illegal drugs or alcohol away from the Company or customer premises, if such impairment or influence adversely affects the employee's work performance, the safety of the employee or of others, or puts at risk the Company's reputation.
- Possession, use, solicitation for, or sale of legal or illegal drugs or alcohol away from the Company or customer premises, if such activity or involvement adversely affects the employee's work performance, the safety of the employee or of others, or puts at risk the Company's reputation.
- The presence of any detectable amount of prohibited substances in the employee's system while at work, while on the premises of the company or its customers, or while on company business. "Prohibited substances" include illegal drugs, alcohol, or prescription drugs not taken in accordance with a prescription given to the employee.

The Company will conduct drug and/or alcohol testing under any of the following circumstances:

Random Testing: Employees may be selected at random for drug and/or alcohol testing at any interval determined by the Company.

For-Cause Testing: The Company may ask an employee to submit to a drug and/or alcohol test at any time it feels that the employee may be under the influence of drugs or alcohol, including, but not limited to, the following circumstances: evidence of drugs or alcohol on or about the employee's person or in the employee's vicinity, unusual conduct on the employee's part that suggests impairment or influence of drugs or alcohol, negative performance patterns, or excessive and unexplained absenteeism or tardiness.

Post-Accident Testing: Any employee involved in an on-the-job accident or injury under circumstances that suggest possible use or influence of drugs or alcohol in the accident or injury event may be asked to submit to a drug and/or alcohol test. "Involved in an on-the-job accident or injury" means not only the one who was or could have been injured, but also any employee who potentially contributed to the accident or injury event in any way.

If an employee is tested for drugs or alcohol outside of the employment context and the results indicate a violation of this policy, or if an employee refuses a request to submit to testing under this policy, the employee may be subject to appropriate disciplinary action, up to and possibly including discharge from employment.

In such a case, the employee will be given an opportunity to explain the circumstances prior to any final employment action becoming effective.

Questions and Comments

1. This model policy prohibits being impaired or under the influence of legal or illegal drugs or alcohol away from the company or customer premises, if such impairment or influence "adversely affects the . . . safety of the employee or of others." How far does this go? If you get drunk at a New Year's Eve party and rupture your Achilles tendon falling down the stairs, requiring several days' absence from work, does this constitute grounds for discipline?

2. The policy does not prohibit the possession, use, or sale of illegal drugs unless the conduct in question impairs the employee's job performance, endangers safety, or puts the employer's reputation at risk. Given that the possession, use, or sale of illegal drugs is by definition illegal, why not state that *any* illegal drug-related activity is a violation of the policy? Is this a bow to the reality that large numbers of people (probably including some of the company's managers) occasionally smoke pot?

3. Could a company adopt a policy that it will only hire people who abstain from alcohol at all times?

PROBLEM 5-1

Jamal Jones, an account executive at Wren Industries, has a back problem inherited from his days as a college lacrosse player. Recently, the problem has flared up badly, causing him intense pain. Following his physician's advice, Jones begins to take prescription pain killers, which make it possible for him to sit at his desk. Unfortunately, the medication also makes him groggy. His supervisor is aware of the situation and concludes that Jones is unable to perform his job. The supervisor asks the HR department what to do. What should HR say?

PROBLEM 5-2

Guardco, a corporation with its principal place of business in Denver, Colorado, manufactures equipment for law enforcement officers such as batons, Tasers, and handcuffs. Assume it has adopted the drug-free workplace policy described in the text excerpted above. As you probably know, the citizens of Colorado voted in 2012 to legalize the recreational use of marijuana. Recreational use of the drug is still banned under federal law, even though the U.S. government has refrained from prosecuting users in Colorado after the passage of the referendum. Guardco's president believes that the company's customers oppose the recreational use of marijuana, and that it would impair the company's reputation if it appeared to be "soft" on this issue. The company learns that one of its employees owns a marijuana shop on Federal Boulevard, one of Denver's major thoroughfares. You're the general counsel of Guardco. The president asks you what the company should do with respect to this employee. What do you recommend?

PROBLEM 5-3

Smith Co., a manufacturer of specialty parts for factories, employs Stan Sims as a machine operator. The machines Sims works on are safe so long as the user exercises caution, but can cause injuries if the safety procedures are not followed. Sims has never before displayed any problems around alcohol but one Monday morning he shows up on the job with a pint flask of whiskey in his pocket, obviously at the tail end of a bender. His supervisor sends him home and tells him to return when he has sobered up. Several days later Sims returns to work sober and has not displayed alcohol problems since. The company's employee manual states that it has a "zero tolerance" for alcohol at the workplace, and also says that, except in cases of misconduct, employees will be given two months of severance pay if they are terminated. In practice, the company has routinely helped employees with alcohol problems, even sending them to clinics at the company's expense and not firing them until the third or fourth episode of drinking on the job. However, in this case, Smith Co.'s human resources manager, hearing about the incident with Sims, decides that he should be fired immediately. The executive's reasons are two-fold: First, unlike other employees who have been given second or third chances, Sims works at a dangerous machine. Second, Sims was never good at his job and the executive wants an excuse to let him go. Can the company fire Sims and refuse to give him severance pay?

2. Surveillance

To what extent may an employer snoop on employees by reviewing logs of their phone calls, analyzing keystrokes on their computer, reviewing videos from surveillance cameras, checking the websites the employee has visited while at work, or reading emails sent from her work computer? The answer is: to a very large extent indeed.

Employers monitor workers' use of computers at the workplace. "Packet sniffers" allow the employer to check, for example, on what websites the employee has visited, what material she has reviewed on the site, what emails she has sent, whom the email was sent to, and what the employee has downloaded. Other programs allow the employer to delve deeper, viewing whatever is on the employee's screen or even tracking every keystroke she makes on a work computer. The employer may not even need to monitor the employees' activities in "real time." And the employee's efforts to delete the information are probably going to be unsuccessful because the information is retained somewhere.

Can an employer record your telephone calls made to or from a work phone? Voice mail messages stored on the company's system are fair game. What about recording other conversations? In general, the law prohibits this practice unless the party consents (or the monitoring is done for a legitimate law enforcement purpose). But this protection of privacy doesn't necessarily apply in the workplace: Employers sometimes listen in on "job-related" phone conversations (in practice, this can mean every conversation when the recording is being done automatically).

The employer may install video surveillance cameras and may monitor them at all times. However, these generally may not be used in places where employees have a high expectation of privacy, such as toilets or gym locker rooms.

Can an employer rifle through an employee's possessions stored at her work desk? Generally yes, if the work desk is in a public space. If the employer provides lockers for employees to store their possessions, this is likely to be considered a private space that the employer may not enter.

In short, employees have few legal protections for their privacy at the workplace. This doesn't mean, however, that all employers act like "big brother." An employer must trade off its interest in ensuring compliance and preventing employee misconduct, on the one hand, and its interest in having a happy and satisfied workforce, on the other. People who fear that their every word is being overheard by someone in a back room are not likely to be joyful as they go about their appointed tasks. Accordingly, most employers refrain, as a general matter, from exercising the full rights of surveillance to which they are entitled under the law. If, as is sometimes the case, an employer elects to embed protections of employee privacy in a formal policy or manual, the employer must respect the rights so conferred.

Questions and Comments

1. Many companies archive employees' instant messages in "write-once, read-many" storage, which can be reviewed for compliance but cannot be altered. Vendors provide software that automatically checks on employees' electronic communications to identify potentially problematic conduct. These tools review instant messages and chat room discussions for suspect words and phrases. Software of this type is useful, but its effectiveness is limited by the fact that employees intent on committing misconduct are likely to use code words or slang to circumvent the monitoring system.

2. Suppose a company's internal control operation discovers from a review of an employee's phone records that she is engaging in illegal sports gambling — an activity with no connection to her work responsibilities. The employee is in all respects a model worker who has never caused problems in her ten years at the firm. Should the company take any action? What if the employee was engaged in viewing pornography from a work computer, but does so only during breaks?

G. INVESTIGATIONS

1. Types of Investigations

Internal investigations sort into two general types. First are small-scale inquiries into minor misconduct. Typically, these investigations are performed in-house by the company's human resources department. It may be a good idea, however, to place the overall supervision of the investigation under the company's general counsel in order to create a claim of privilege for the investigation and its work papers.

Many companies have standardized procedures in place to deal with small-scale investigations. The procedures involve stepped-up surveillance, including reading the employee's emails, recovering logs of telephone conversations, removing and copying hard drives, and speaking with others who may know information. Typically, the company will call the suspected employee to a meeting only after it has uncovered enough facts to warrant a conclusion as to what to do. If the decision is to terminate the employee, the company will usually insist that she vacate the work space immediately, taking only enough time to clear out her personal possessions.

If the company has uncovered evidence of criminal behavior, should it alert the authorities? There appears to be no formal requirement that it do so; the company might prefer to let the matter drop after the problematic employee has departed, on the theory that a referral to prosecutors will only cause further disruption. However, if the employee has stolen money from the company, it may make the referral in hopes of recouping some of the losses or supporting a claim on an insurance policy. If the misconduct involves acts of violence, the company may consider whether it faces liability if it refrains from alerting the authorities and then the employee harms someone else.

Different considerations come into play when a company faces a problem involving widespread or high-level misconduct. Here, the reputational and strategic risks can be large, and a suitably comprehensive response is indicated. Large-scale investigations have three principal differences from small-scale investigations:

- As a practical matter, large-scale investigations cannot be performed in-house. Where there is pervasive misconduct being committed by lower-level employees, the company is likely to lack the resources to manage the problem on its own. When the alleged misconduct has occurred at a high corporate level, the officials charged with conducting investigations — typically the head of human resources and the company's general counsel — will often lack the clout within the organization to make an in-house investigation effective. Attempts to manage a large-scale investigation in-house can lead to the perception that the company is attempting to minimize the problem rather than get to the bottom of things. For these and other reasons, outside help is usually needed. When outside investigators are brought into a company, the costs can be high. To make the investigation credible, the company has to hire experts such as law firms that have earned a reputation in the field. These firms are not cheap. Further, to establish the credibility of the investigation, the company usually has to agree that there are no limits on the topics that the outside investigator can evaluate. An internal investigation of possible Foreign Corrupt Practices Act violations cost Avon Products $93 million in 2011, $95 million in 2010, and $59 million in 2009. In six months during 2011, News Corporation spent $104 million in investigation costs and private settlements stemming from a scandal involving phone hacking and payments to government officials.
- The second major difference between large-scale and small-scale investigations concerns disclosure. Small-scale investigations are usually kept confidential and never disclosed. In the case of large-scale investigations, it is often expected that they will be disclosed, at least after they are concluded. The question is whether they should be disclosed earlier. Here the company must balance potential harms. If the investigation is impossible to conceal in the long run, as is usually true for large-scale investigations, a firm may decide to disclose the fact that an investigation is ongoing in order to head off damaging rumors and demonstrate the firm's commitment to transparency. On the other hand, early disclosure of an investigation has drawbacks. Witnesses may become adversarial if the person being contacted

knows that the company has launched a formal investigation. If the existence of an investigation is known, moreover, participants in misconduct may take the opportunity to rehearse their stories, making it more difficult to get to the bottom of things. Further, unlike the government, firms do not have subpoena or arrest powers; they need to rely on the witness' agreement to answer questions. If the existence of an investigation is known, that cooperation may disappear.

- A third difference between large-scale and small-scale investigations is that large-scale investigations of compliance breaches are conducted under the shadow of government enforcement actions. Organizations know that everything they do during the investigation is likely to be reviewed with a skeptical eye by government officials. For this reason, in many cases, companies conducting large-scale investigations inform the government of the nature of the problem and of the fact that they are performing an investigation, and make an effort to cooperate with any parallel government investigation in hopes of receiving credit when and if sanctions are administered.

Questions and Comments

1. What factors should play a role in an organization's decision to launch (or not to launch) an internal investigation, and, if so, what sort of investigation to conduct? Consider the following:

   a. The likely expense of an investigation;
   b. The anticipated drain on managerial time;
   c. The effect on morale;
   d. The nature of the alleged wrongdoing;
   e. The credibility of the source that brought the problem to management's attention;
   f. The potential for the allegation to "go viral" on social media if word leaks out;
   g. The extent of potential misconduct within the organization;
   h. The potential problems that might arise if the company fails to launch an investigation (e.g., a reduced likelihood of leniency in a subsequent administrative enforcement action);
   i. The degree to which the alleged wrongdoing occurred at vendors or contractors rather than at the company itself;
   j. Whether the alleged wrongdoing occurred at an independent company that was subsequently acquired;
   k. The extent to which the alleged wrongdoing occurred abroad, and the possible consequences within other countries of launching or not launching an investigation.

2. For an excellent practical guide to internal investigations, see Mayer Brown, *Current Issues in Internal Corporate Investigations.*

How far can a company go in an internal investigation without trenching on other important values? Consider the following discussion of Hewlett-Packard

Corporation's use of "pretexting" to identify a member of the board of directors who had been leaking confidential information to the press.

Miriam Hechler Baer, Corporate Policing and Corporate Governance: What Can We Learn from Hewlett-Packard's Pretexting Scandal?

77 U. Cin. L. Rev. 523 (2008)

[HP had previously investigated leaks of confidential board deliberations but had failed to identify the source. When the leaks continued, Patricia Dunn, HP's non-executive chairman, initiated a new investigation now known as "Project Kona II."]

Among other things, the investigation featured the following techniques:

- Reviewing the company email accounts, company phone records, and computer hard drives of every member of HP's "Executive Council";
- Hiring a private investigation firm, which subcontracted out the job of obtaining private telephone records of select Board members and nine journalists, including Dawn Kawamoto, the . . . reporter who had written the . . . article;
- Surreptitiously following Kawamoto and suspected Board members in public (and apparently searching through their trash);
- Setting up a "sting" in which investigators sent Kawamoto an email containing fake tips about HP and an attachment whose tracking software would trace the email's path after it reached Kawamoto's computer.

The investigation was monitored and supervised by HP's chief compliance officer and attorney, Kevin Hunsaker. Hunsaker reported to Baskins [HP's general counsel], who, with Hunsaker, periodically advised Dunn of the progress of the investigation. Dunn would later contend that as a non-executive chairwoman, she exercised no control over the investigation that she initiated.

After investigators identified George Keyworth as the source of the . . . leak, Dunn and Baskins sought outside counsel from Wilson Sonsini, on how they should handle the matter and whether it should go before the governance sub-committee or the entire Board. Prior to the Board's May 18, 2006 meeting, the chair of the Board's Audit Committee, Robert Ryan, asked Keyworth if he was the source of the [leak]; Keyworth admitted that he was. Ryan then disclosed that Keyworth was the leak during the Board's subsequent meeting. After Keyworth addressed the Board, it met separately to consider whether to ask for Keyworth's resignation. During the deliberations, another of the Board's members, the well-known venture capitalist Thomas Perkins, stormed out of the meeting and announced his resignation from the Board. Over the next six weeks, Perkins and HP's outside counsel, Larry Sonsini, debated (a) the manner by which HP had conducted the investigation, (b) the investigator's attempts to obtain information regarding Perkins' personal phone line, and (c) HP's obligation to disclose Perkins' reasons for leaving HP.

As a result of Perkins's protests, HP's pretexting investigation became public in early September 2006. On September 12, 2006 Keyworth resigned; he admitted that he had been the . . . source, but contended that he had HP's best interests in mind . . . . Almost immediately after the investigation became public, HP's tactics triggered inquiries by Congress, the SEC, and simultaneous state and federal criminal investigations.

Questions and Comments

1. Most of the people involved in this imbroglio wound up with little or no sanctions. The article excerpted above reports as follows: "The California Attorney General's (AG's) office initially indicted on felony charges Dunn, Hunsaker, and the investigators who either approved or engaged in pretexting. Eventually, the AG's office reduced the felony charges to misdemeanors, and a court ultimately dismissed Dunn's charge. Hunsaker and two former investigators pled no-contest and the court hearing their case agreed to dismiss their charges in exchange for ninety-six hours of community service."

2. Was it legitimate and appropriate for HP to investigate the source of the leaks?

3. At the time of the events in question, the legality of "pretexting" was unclear. How should the company have evaluated its legal rights and obligations in this respect? HP did not request a legal opinion from its outside counsel, Wilson Sonsini, regarding the legality of its investigative techniques, relying instead on the opinion of Hunsaker, its chief compliance officer. On an issue this sensitive, should Wilson Sonsini or some other outside expert have been consulted?

4. The HP pretexting imbroglio raises the issue of "who chaperones the chaperone." The board of directors is charged with exercising oversight to ensure compliance with legal norms, and with monitoring the activities of corporate executives to ensure that they do not cross legal lines. But what happens when a member of the board of directors has herself potentially violated the law? Likewise the chief compliance officer is charged with monitoring from the stockroom to the boardroom to ensure that everyone associated with the company complies with her legal obligations; but what happens when the chief compliance officer is or may be one of the wrongdoers?

5. The author of the excerpted article observes that the HP scandal illustrates a troubling feature of modern corporate law: the fact that compliance operations, designed to enforce legal norms, can sometimes result in their being violated. "[M]onitoring and surveillance have not merely migrated upward within the corporate food chain, but by necessity, have become more complex and, as HP reveals, more deceptive. With complexity and deception, ironically, comes the very result that the post-Enron response sought to prevent: the breaking of laws. It is hardly news that law enforcers sometimes break laws in the course of their jobs. The prevalence of internal affairs units in large police departments across the country aptly demonstrates the maxim that those who enforce laws are not immune from the urge to break them. However steeped in common sense this problem may appear, it is one that has been largely ignored by the proponents of corporate compliance." Is there a way out of this dilemma?

6. Many companies do a substantial amount of overseas business. What if a company's internal investigation requires an analysis of overseas transactions? A problem here is that many countries provide greater protections for privacy than are afforded under U.S. law. The organization must be cautious about engaging in American-style investigative techniques abroad if these involve discovery of personal employee data.

7. Europe operates under a directive that gives wide privacy protections, but which also provides permission for reasonable investigative needs. Other countries pose greater difficulties. China, for example, has made it a crime for a professional to misappropriate personal information, including electronic information. In 2013, two fraud investigators, at least one an American citizen, were arrested for allegedly violating this law, reportedly in connection with a bribery investigation involving the pharmaceutical industry. The investigators had apparently accessed public records showing ownership of automobiles and real property (among other information), and had packaged the information into reports they sold to clients. The government of China accused them of trafficking in personal information in violation of China's privacy statute — a move that raised alarms for many who offer investigative services in the Chinese market.

8. If a company conducts an internal investigation overseas, should it import data back to the United States? It is often more convenient and effective to do so. A potential downside, however, is that data located in the United States are subject to American rules on discovery in litigation or administrative actions, which are more far-reaching than the rules that apply in many other countries. If the organization wishes to protect the information against compelled disclosure in an American forum, it may be well advised to leave it where it is.

PROBLEM 5-4

You are general counsel at AirSolutions, a freight forwarder in the air cargo industry. A senior account manager visits you in your office and alleges that her boss has been secretly meeting with competitors and that the result of those meetings has been to fix rates in certain routes. You know from past experience that this particular employee is excitable and tends to see problems that aren't actually there. Still, her story is not completely implausible. You thank her for the information and tell her you will get back to her shortly. You bring the matter to the CEO, who instructs you that if illegal conduct has occurred it must be stopped and the responsible officials must be fired. But she also expresses the hope that the matter will not come to the attention of the authorities. You begin a confidential investigation of the allegation. One of your first interviews is with the purported whistleblower. Taking the CEO's instructions into account, what considerations would you bring to bear in conducting the interview?

2. Comparison of Internal Investigations and Government Investigations

At least ostensibly, both internal investigations and government investigations seek the same objective: to ferret out evidence of legal violations within the organization. The two are, in a sense, substitutes for each another. At the same time, there are significant differences between them along a number of dimensions.

One important consideration is the effectiveness of the investigation, as measured by its likelihood of uncovering the true facts in a cost-effective manner. Here each type of investigation has advantages and disadvantages.

Government investigations have access to the formidable powers of the compulsory process. The subpoena power allows government agencies to compel the production of evidence. Armed with a search warrant or other authorization, government agents can enter a workplace or an employee's home, rifle through her possessions, and take away evidence. The government also benefits from the law making it a crime to lie to a federal official. Private firms have no access to these means for compelling the production of information.

On the other hand, private firms have certain advantages over the government when it comes to obtaining information. As noted above, employees have low expectations of privacy in the workplace vis-à-vis their employers. Employers do not need a subpoena or warrant to investigate an employee's activities. Private companies also enjoy potential advantages when it comes to interrogations. The Fifth Amendment privilege against self-incrimination protects suspects against having to admit criminal wrongdoing when questioned by the government. If the government interrogates a suspect in custody it must provide *Miranda* warnings and the right to counsel. These protections are absent in the case of interrogations in internal investigations. Private companies can interview suspected employees (or others) and they do not need to inform the employee of the reasons for their inquiries. The employee has no right to counsel and no Fifth Amendment privilege against compelled self-incrimination; and although the employee cannot be required to answer, his failure to answer can be used against him — for example, he could be fired.

Considered from the standpoint of the employee who is a target of an investigation, the situation appears different. No one wants to be pursued by the government, with its enormous reservoir of penalties and sanctions and its power to compel the production of evidence. The most the employer can do to you directly is to fire you and harm your chances of getting another job — you might be poor, but the employer can't put you in prison. Your employer, however, can and often will turn over to the government information it has developed during its investigation. Now the government can pursue you, equipped with inculpatory information that it has not developed on its own. In the meantime, your employer doesn't have to afford you the constitutional protections that would apply if the government was asking the questions. In some respects, accordingly, the employee gets the worst of both worlds.

Questions and Comments

1. For more on the comparison between internal investigations and government investigations, see Bruce A. Green & Ellen S. Podgor, *Unregulated Internal Investigations: Achieving Fairness for Corporate Constituents*, 54 B.C. L. Rev. 73 (2013).

2. Should organizations provide the equivalent of *Miranda* warnings to employees they target in internal investigations?

3. Often, investigations result in a report that is then disclosed either to government regulators or more generally to constituencies such as contractual counterparties, shareholders, the press, or by web publication to the general public (an example is the UBS "Transparency Report" to shareholders, excerpted in Chapter 20). These reports gain credibility if they "name names" — if they identify the persons whose activities resulted in the breaches of norms. If such a report is published, what recourse does the accused person have to clear her name? One option is a lawsuit for defamation of character. The problem here is that a company faced with such a lawsuit is likely to defend on the ground that the report of investigation is protected by a privilege.

The law in this area is poorly developed. It is generally accepted that communications made during judicial and quasi-judicial proceedings are protected by an absolute privilege, precluding any possibility of defamation liability. But reports of internal investigation do not satisfy the traditional requirements since they are not communications made during official proceedings. Some courts recognize a qualified or conditional privilege for communications made in the public interest. Arguably, an internal investigation report satisfies this standard; but a qualified privilege might add little in the case of a defamation action, since if the plaintiff is able to establish the intent required to establish liability for defamation the same proof would also likely defeat the privilege. What approach would you favor — an absolute privilege, a qualified privilege, or no privilege at all? *See* Writt v. Shell Oil Co., 409 S.W.3d 59 (Tex. App. 2013) (recognizing a qualified privilege).

4. In 2015, T-Mobile required employees who were being interviewed in internal investigations to agree to the following policy:

> You have been asked to provide information in connection with an investigation being conducted by T-Mobile Human Resources. We are meeting with you because an allegation of inappropriate conduct has been received by our team and we believe you have information that is relevant to the investigation. We are required to investigate this allegation, and it may be reportable to the Compliance Committee, the TMUS Audit Committee, the VP of Legal Affairs and Compliance, and/or TMUS management. . . .
>
> Employees must fully cooperate in internal investigations, including providing complete, truthful, and accurate information and written statements upon request. An employee's refusal to cooperate in any investigation may result in forfeiture of good standing, and/or may result in performance improvement action up to and including dismissal.
>
> Employees should maintain the confidentiality of the names of the employees involved in the investigations, whether as complainants, subjects or witnesses, throughout the pendency of the investigation, and you should only disclose such information to T-Mobile Corporate Investigators, Human Resources personnel or counsel for T-Mobile, unless permitted by law. You should keep confidential all communications between you and the investigator(s) concerning this matter throughout the pendency of this investigation unless permitted by law. This includes all questions and answers during this interview, any written statement that you provide to the investigator(s), and all other information or documents provided to the investigator(s) in connection with this matter. Conduct that interferes with, undermines, impedes or is otherwise detrimental to any internal investigation is prohibited.

Do you see a problem? A union challenged the policy on the ground that it prohibited employees from discussing the terms and conditions of employment with other employees, in violation of §7 of the National Labor Relations Act, which protects the right of employees to engage in "concerted activities for the purpose of collective bargaining or other mutual aid or protection." 29 U.S.C. §157. An NLRB administrative law judge agreed and declared that T-Mobile's policy amounted to an unfair practice under federal labor law. Mobile USA, Inc. and Communications Workers of America, AFL-CIO, Cases 01-CA-142030 10-CA-133833 (NLRB, New York Branch Office 2015). Do you agree? What about the fact that the policy explicitly allowed disclosure if "permitted by law"? In light of this decision, what options are open to employers such as T-Mobile who wish to maintain confidentiality of internal investigations?

3. The Role of Counsel

Internal investigations are usually spearheaded by counsel. Attorneys have three key advantages that make them suitable choices to lead these activities.

- Placing the investigation under the leadership of an attorney allows the organization to claim the attorney's privileges. Notes, mental impressions, drafts, and legal theories prepared or developed by or under the direction of an attorney are likely to be protected against compelled disclosure under work product protection; communications between people in the company and attorneys in connection with the investigation may qualify for the attorney-client privilege (for more on the role of these privileges in compliance matters, see Chapter 9).

- The attorney's professional training and expertise may make her a good candidate to head up the investigation. Since the investigation is looking into whether legal norms have been violated, understanding the precise contours of the rules in question is a vital step in the process. Attorneys are professionally trained in this skill. Attorneys are also trained in understanding the forensic relevance of facts and in organizing facts according to legal significance — another key skill for conducting an effective investigation.

- The status of being an attorney carries a degree of *gravitas* within organizations. Employees who are asked to supply information to the organization's attorney may provide a quicker and more comprehensive response than if the request comes from some other source.

PROBLEM 5-5

You have just signed on as general counsel for Mogesta, Inc, a manufacturer of dietary supplements that has just "gone public." Your previous career has been spent at a corporate law firm writing securities disclosure statements; you were hired because Mogesta Inc., having become a public company, needs someone with expertise in securities law. After you have been on the job for a few weeks, the company receives a notice from the FDA inquiring about claims that several of the company's products have been adulterated with a dangerous chemical. Your boss, the chief executive officer, instructs you to conduct a "comprehensive" internal investigation. Where do you even start?

PROBLEM 5-6

You are outside securities counsel for Bonbon Inc., a publicly traded manufacturer of chocolates, candies, and confectioneries. You get an urgent call from Sybil Sweet, the company's general counsel. She tells you that the company has just received a Wells notice from the SEC (a Wells notice is a warning that the SEC is likely to bring an enforcement proceeding). Sweet asks if federal securities law requires the company to report the Wells notice at this point in time. "We would much rather not report this right away," she says, "because we believe we can convince the SEC we did nothing wrong, and if we report now our investors are going to overreact." Your company's quarterly "10-Q" report is due in three weeks. What do you advise?

4. Disclosure

What duty, if any, does a firm have to report the results of its investigations? Often in such cases the facts or law are not clear: The company might have committed a violation, but also might not. What should the firm do in case of uncertainty?

This problem can pose difficulties in the area of securities law. Item 303(a)(3)(ii) of SEC Regulation S-K requires management of reporting companies to inform investors about a reporting firm's financial condition and results of operations, including "any known . . . uncertainties that . . . the registrant reasonably expects will have a material . . . impact on net sales or revenues or income from continuing operations." SEC Rule 10b-5, likewise, makes it illegal, in connection with the purchase or sale of a security, to "omit to state a material fact necessary in order to make the statements made, in the light of the circumstances under which they were made, not misleading." These considerations suggest that companies must report the existence of compliance problems even if a violation has not been established.

On the other hand, requiring a company to disclose potential violations has downsides. Because the violations have not been established, disclosure of problems might confuse investors or lead them to overestimate the risks facing the firm. Meanwhile such disclosures are nearly certain to trigger plaintiffs' class action lawsuits, which can impose costs on firms and courts while undermining the government's enforcement discretion. For these and other reasons, courts tend to view the existence of potential but unproven violations as "soft information" that need not be disclosed to investors. *See, e.g.*, In re Sofamor Danek Group, Inc., 123 F.3d 394 (6th Cir. 1997).

But what if the company, although not required to do so, *voluntarily* announces that it complies with legal requirements? Here, the company has not kept silent, but rather has made a disclosure; and having made a disclosure, it is required, under the securities laws, to speak truthfully. Even so, liability exposure under Rule 10b-5 will be limited. That rule requires a showing of "scienter" — knowledge or recklessness. If a firm announces that it has not committed any violation, and that statement is not reckless or knowingly false, then the declarant will be shielded from Rule 10b-5 liability even if the company is later found to have committed violations.

The same is not necessarily true for lawsuits based on §11 of the Securities Act of 1933, which imposes strict liability for material misstatements or omissions in registration statements. In Omnicare, Inc. v. Laborers District Council Construction Industry Pension Fund, 135 S. Ct. 1318 (2015), a pharmaceutical service provider's registration statement, filed in connection with its initial public offering, asserted that the company's contracts with drug manufacturers were "legally and economically valid." Plaintiffs alleged that this statement was materially misleading because the company was engaging in illegal activities in connection with those contracts. The defendant argued that the statements were merely expressions of opinion not subject to liability under the securities acts. The Supreme Court agreed with the defendant in holding that liability attaches only for false statements of fact. But it went on to note that every statement of opinion carries an implicit statement of fact—namely that the speaker actually believes the opinion being expressed. Because the company's sincerity was not in question, it was not liable insofar as it merely expressed an opinion. This wasn't the end of the story, however. Section 11 liability extends, not only to statements, but also to *omissions*—failures to disclose facts that would be considered material to a reasonable investor. For example, liability might attach if, although the company reasonably believed it had not engaged in illegal conduct that would invalidate its contracts with drug manufacturers, it nevertheless knew of and failed to disclose red flags of potential violations. The Supreme Court remanded the case for an analysis of whether the complaint adequately alleged material omissions of this sort.

PROBLEM 5-7

In its recent comprehensive bank examination, the First National Bank of Sleepy Hollow received a grade of "needs to improve" for its compliance program. The Comptroller of the Currency noted numerous weaknesses in the bank's system of internal controls over money laundering and fair lending practices. The report of examination did not point to any specific instances of violations, and the bank's managers disagree with the regulators' opinion: They think the compliance program is robust and effective. The bank is about to "go public" by issuing securities registered with the SEC. The draft registration statement states that "the Bank's systems of internal controls are well designed and scalable to account for future anticipated growth." As outside securities counsel, you are aware of the "needs to improve" rating. You are also aware that the bank is legally prohibited from disclosing information about its examination reports. Your client and its investment bank insist that the statement about internal controls is essential in order to assure the success of the public offering. What do you do?

---

5. Enforcement Credit

Government regulators and prosecutors often take the quality of an organization's internal investigation into account when determining whether to bring charges or how much to demand in settlement. Assistant Attorney General Leslie Caldwell had this to say in a speech delivered on May 19, 2015:

Assistant Attorney General Leslie R. Caldwell Remarks at the Compliance Week Conference

May 19, 2015

While we in the Criminal Division will not tell a company how it should conduct an investigation, we evaluate the quality of a company's internal investigation, both through our own investigation and in considering what if any charges to bring against a company. In that regard, we have seen some "best practices" with regard to internal investigations.

Good internal investigations uncover the facts. They don't promote corporate talking points or whitewash the truth. The investigation should be focused on rooting out the relevant facts, identifying and interviewing the knowledgeable actors and capturing and preserving relevant documents and other evidence. The investigation should seek to identify responsible individuals, even if those individuals hold senior positions at the company.

It is reasonable to take resources—time and money—into account. If an internal investigation unearths criminal conduct, the inquiry should be thorough enough to identify the relevant facts, players, documents and other evidence, and to get a sense of the pervasiveness of the misconduct. But, we do not believe that it is necessary or productive for a company to employ its internal investigators to look under every rock and pebble — particularly when a company has offices or personnel around the globe that do not appear to be involved in the misconduct at issue. In fact, doing so will cost companies much more in the end, both in fees but also because it ultimately will delay our investigation and delay resolution and closure for the company. For example, if a multi-national corporation discovers [a Foreign Corrupt Practices Act] violation in one country, and has no basis to suspect that the misconduct is occurring elsewhere, the Criminal Division would not expect that the internal investigation would extend beyond the country in which the violation was discovered. By contrast, if the known offenders operated in multiple countries, we would expect that the internal investigation would extend into those locations as well.

Once your company learns of potential criminal conduct and confirms it through a reasonable internal investigation, the company then must choose whether to disclose the conduct to the government, and whether to cooperate in the government's investigation. These are the company's choices, and very few companies have a legal obligation to disclose criminal misconduct to the department. Likewise, there is no obligation to cooperate beyond compliance with lawful process. But if a company chooses to cooperate with the government in its investigation — particularly at an early stage — the company likely will receive significant credit for such efforts when the government is contemplating what prosecutorial action to take.

In conducting an investigation, determining whether to bring charges and negotiating plea or other agreements, federal prosecutors take into account, among other factors, the corporation's timely and voluntary disclosure of wrongdoing and its willingness to cooperate in the investigation of its agents. Prosecutors also consider the availability of alternative or supplemental remedies such as civil or regulatory enforcement action.

To receive cooperation credit, a company must do more than comply with subpoenas or other compulsory process. Companies must provide a full accounting of the known facts about the conduct or events under review, and affirmatively must identify responsible individuals (and provide evidence supporting their culpability), including corporate executives and officers — and they must do so in a timely way.

A company's cooperation may be particularly helpful where the criminal conduct continued over an extended period of time, and the knowledgeable or culpable individuals and/or the relevant documents are dispersed or located abroad. Under these circumstances, cooperation includes helping to circumvent barriers to the investigation by making knowledgeable personnel available for interviews or testimony, and by producing documents and other evidence that otherwise may not be readily accessible to the government.

We recognize that some foreign data privacy laws may limit or prohibit the disclosure of certain types of data or information. Over the years, the Criminal Division has developed an understanding of certain oft-cited data privacy laws, and we will challenge what we perceive to be unfounded reliance on these laws to justify withholding requested information. Companies should avoid this by giving careful consideration to the government's requests for information, refraining from making broad "knee jerk" claims that large categories of information are protected from disclosure and producing what can be disclosed.

The consequences of refusing to cooperate in an ongoing investigation are evident in department's recent, landmark criminal resolution with BNP Paribas (BNPP) — the fourth largest bank in the world. Between 2004 and 2012, BNPP knowingly violated the [International Emergency Economic Powers Act (IEEPA)] and the Trading with the Enemy Act (TWEA) by moving more than $8.8 billion through the U.S. financial system on behalf of Sudanese, Iranian and Cuban entities subject to U.S. economic sanctions. The majority of the transactions facilitated by BNPP were on behalf of entities in Sudan, which is subject to a U.S. embargo due to the Sudanese government's role in facilitating terrorism and committing human rights abuses. BNPP's criminal conduct took place despite repeated warnings expressed by the bank's own compliance officers and its outside counsel. In response to the concerns identified by compliance personnel, high-ranking BNPP officials explained that the questioned transactions had the "full support" of BNPP management in Paris. In short, BNPP expressly elected to favor profits over compliance. BNPP refused to cooperate with our investigation. In fact, the bank hindered the investigation by dragging its feet and making exaggerated assertions that certain information was precluded from disclosure by foreign data privacy laws. BNPP's intransigence thwarted the government's ability to prosecute responsible individuals or satellite banks. Ultimately, BNPP pleaded guilty to conspiracy to violate the IEEPA and the TWEA, and agreed to pay record-setting penalties of over $8.9 billion. And the company admitted its misconduct — including its disregard of compliance advice — in a detailed statement of facts that was made public. BNPP's refusal to cooperate was a key factor in the department's decision to seek a parent-level guilty plea.

Questions and Comments

1. Assistant Attorney General Caldwell acknowledges that the Justice Department doesn't want companies to spend money unnecessarily on internal investigations. How much comfort will this give to a company that is in the midst of such an experience? When the outside law firm demands the right to inquire into new topics, will the company be able to resist by showing counsel a copy of the excerpted speech? Resisting an investigator's request to expand the scope of an inquiry is perilous because it can easily be interpreted as an effort to shut down the inquiry.

2. Caldwell says that a good investigation focuses on uncovering facts rather than promoting "talking points." How realistic is it to demand that a company that is a target or potential target of a government enforcement action will not also look for evidence that exonerates or mitigates its potential liability? Whether a company is "whitewashing the truth" may be a matter of judgment: What the target sees as a legitimate interpretation of corporate actions may seem to prosecutors like evasion. Ultimately, it is the Department of Justice that decides whether the investigation is a genuine inquiry or a whitewash. In light of this power imbalance, how much leeway does a company enjoy to interpret facts in a light favorable to its interests?

3. In another speech, Caldwell outlined the following minimum expectations that the Department of Justice has for any internal investigation:

- "We expect you to learn the relevant facts, assuming they are learnable."
- "If you choose to cooperate with us, we expect that you will provide us with those facts, be they good or bad."

- "Importantly, that includes facts about individuals responsible for the misconduct, no matter how high their rank may be."
- "We expect timely provision of evidence. What does that mean? That doesn't mean you need to call us on day one. In most cases it is in everyone's interest for there to be an orderly internal investigation. Exact timing varies with the facts, but once companies know the facts, we do not expect them to delay providing them to us."

4. Caldwell says that the Department of Justice won't instruct companies how to conduct an internal investigation. But then she offers opinions about "best practices." Would you advise your company to ignore her recommendations?

5. What if the internal investigation uncovers "facts" during the course of a privileged attorney-client communication? Must the company still turn those facts over to the Department of Justice in order to avoid catastrophic penalties? Would turning over such facts waive attorney-client privilege?

6. Caldwell acknowledges that "few companies have a legal obligation to disclose criminal misconduct to the department" and that "there is no obligation to cooperate beyond compliance with lawful process." Given the tenor of her remarks, would you advise a company to withhold evidence of criminality it has uncovered in an internal investigation, even if the company has no formal obligation to do so?

7. What was the point of Caldwell's description of the catastrophic $8.9 billion fine imposed on BNP Paribas, other than to terrorize companies into cooperating with the government, even if they have no legal obligation to do so?

8. Where do you draw the line between prosecutorial conduct that is reasonable, effective, and vigorous, and conduct that is abusive and unwarranted?

9. At what point must the company inform the Department of Justice if it wishes to receive credit for its internal investigation? Assistant Attorney General Caldwell indicates that the company doesn't need to inform the government until it has confirmed the existence of a violation; thus it seems that early-stage investigations need not be shared. Once the company has confirmed that a violation has occurred, the options change. At this point, as Caldwell acknowledges, the company is not obligated to tell the government about what it has found. But if it does not inform the government, it risks losing access to the "significant credit" that is held out as inducement for cooperation.

6

Regulators

In this chapter we examine the role of civil regulators in compliance. The chapter follows from the previous two chapters in the following sense. Chapter 4 explored the growth of the regulatory state and associated increases in exposure to regulatory sanctions. Chapter 5 examined the compliance response: actions that organizations voluntarily undertake to meet increased regulatory demands. In this chapter we deal with civil enforcement by government regulators; in the next chapter we deal with criminal enforcement by prosecutors.

We start with an issue that cuts across both civil and criminal enforcement: the degree to which the government should seek to impose penalties on corporations or other entity defendants as opposed to penalizing individuals who commit wrongful acts in the course of their employment at the entity.

A. INDIVIDUAL OR CORPORATE LIABILITY?

The legal background of this issue is the law of agency. In general, agents—such as employees of corporations—remain individually liable for their wrongful acts even when they are acting in the service of an employer. A delivery truck driver who negligently causes harm to another motorist is personally responsible for the damages caused, even if the accident occurs while she is delivering items on behalf of her employer. On the other hand, the employer is also liable in this circumstance. The injured plaintiff can sue both the employer and the employee for the same harm.

The same principles hold when translated to the arena of compliance and enforcement. Usually, a corporate employee who commits a legal violation during the course of her employment is subject to liability in an action by a regulator or a prosecutor. A salesperson who bribes a purchasing manager has committed a crime, and also a civil violation, and can be held to account for both. But if the bribe is paid in furtherance of the salesperson's employer's business, the employer can also be subject to enforcement actions and required to answer for the employee's misconduct.

Accordingly, just like tort victims, government enforcement officials — whether they be civil regulators or prosecutors — have a choice in most cases about whether to pursue the individual, the corporation, or both. Over time, in the compliance space, the pattern of enforcement shifted toward going after the corporation, with less attention paid to pursuing individual wrongdoers. The corporation usually had much deeper pockets than the employee; and corporations were often more willing to settle cases and thus reduce the burden on the government enforcement staff.

But the preference for pursuing the entity rather than the individual ran into criticism, which heightened in the aftermath of the financial crisis of 2007-2009. Commentators argued that poorly aligned individual incentives contributed materially to excessive risk taking by the managers of financial institutions in the years preceding the crisis — a point that logically led to the idea that, if these individuals had feared being made to pay personally for their poor decisions, they would have behaved more responsibly with investor funds. At the same time, commentators questioned the efficacy of pursuing corporations for compliance violations. Corporations, being abstract entities, cannot feel pain or shame; and the incidence of penalties imposed on corporations falls largely on public shareholders who are innocent of wrongdoing.

Politicians, for their part, looked for people (other than themselves) to blame for the disaster. Proceedings against corporations, even if they resulted in billion-dollar fines, did not have the same public resonance as the satisfying knowledge that a malefactor has been brought to justice. In Iceland, the government vigorously prosecuted many bankers whose reckless conduct had contributed to the financial disaster there; but in the United States, precious few bankers heard the "clang" of prison doors shutting behind them.

The following excerpt reflects an evolving consensus that prosecutors and regulators had, in past years, been overly lenient toward the individuals whose misconduct led to their companies getting into compliance trouble. It is an important statement by a senior Justice Department official mandating a shift in enforcement priorities in the direction of more vigorous enforcement against individuals whose wrongful acts contributed to corporate violations.

Individual Accountability for Corporate Wrongdoing
Deputy Attorney General Sally Quillian Yates

Sept. 9, 2015

. . . One of the most effective ways to combat corporate misconduct is by seeking accountability from the individuals who perpetrated the wrongdoing. Such accountability is important for several reasons: it deters future illegal activity, it incentivizes changes in corporate behavior, it ensures that the proper parties are held responsible for their actions, and it promotes the public's confidence in our justice system.

There are, however, many substantial challenges unique to pursuing individuals for corporate misdeeds. In large corporations, where responsibility can be diffuse and decisions are made at various levels, it can be difficult to determine if someone possessed the knowledge and criminal intent necessary to establish their guilt beyond a reasonable doubt. This is particularly true when determining the culpability of high-level executives, who may be insulated from the day-to-day activity in which the misconduct occurs. As a result, investigators often must reconstruct what happened based on a painstaking review of corporate documents, which can number in the millions, and which may be difficult to collect due to legal restrictions.

These challenges make it all the more important that the Department fully leverage its resources to identify culpable individuals at all levels in corporate cases. To address these challenges, the Department convened a working group of senior attorneys from Department components and the United States Attorney community with significant experience in this area.

The working group examined how the Department approaches corporate investigations, and identified areas in which it can amend its policies and practices in order to most effectively pursue the individuals responsible for corporate wrongs. This memo is a product of the working group's discussions. The measures described in this memo are steps that should be taken in any investigation of corporate misconduct. Some of these measures are new, while others reflect best practices that are already employed by many federal prosecutors. Fundamentally, this memo is designed to ensure that all attorneys across the Department are consistent in our best efforts to hold to account the individuals responsible for illegal corporate conduct.

The guidance in this memo will also apply to civil corporate matters. In addition to recovering assets, civil enforcement actions serve to redress misconduct and deter future wrongdoing. Thus, civil attorneys investigating corporate wrongdoing should maintain a focus on the responsible individuals, recognizing that holding them to account is an important part of protecting the public fisc in the long term.

The guidance in this memo reflects six key steps to strengthen our pursuit of individual corporate wrongdoing, some of which reflect policy shifts and each of which is described in greater detail below: (1) in order to qualify for any cooperation credit, corporations must provide to the Department all relevant facts relating to the individuals responsible for the misconduct; (2) criminal and civil corporate investigations should focus on individuals from the inception of the investigation; (3) criminal and civil attorneys handling corporate investigations should be in routine communication with one another; (4) absent extraordinary circumstances or approved departmental policy, the Department will not release culpable individuals from civil or criminal liability when resolving a matter with a corporation; (5) Department attorneys should not resolve matters with a corporation without a clear plan to resolve related individual cases, and should memorialize any declinations as to individuals in such cases; and (6) civil attorneys should consistently focus on individuals as well as the company and evaluate whether to bring suit against an individual based on considerations beyond that individual's ability to pay . . . .

1. In order for a company to receive any consideration for cooperation under the Principles of Federal Prosecution of Business Organizations, the company must completely disclose to the Department all relevant facts about individual misconduct. Companies cannot pick and choose what facts to disclose. That is, to be eligible for any credit for cooperation, the company must identify all individuals involved in or responsible for the misconduct at issue, regardless of their position, status or seniority, and provide to the Department all facts relating to that misconduct. If a company seeking cooperation credit declines to learn of such facts or to provide the Department with complete factual information about individual wrongdoers, its cooperation will not be considered a mitigating factor . . . . Once a company

meets the threshold requirement of providing all relevant facts with respect to individuals, it will be eligible for consideration for cooperation credit. The extent of that cooperation credit will depend on all the various factors that have traditionally applied in making this assessment (e.g., the timeliness of the cooperation, the diligence, thoroughness, and speed of the internal investigation, the proactive nature of the cooperation, etc.). This condition of cooperation applies equally to corporations seeking to cooperate in civil matters; a company under civil investigation must provide to the Department all relevant facts about individual misconduct in order to receive any consideration in the negotiation.

The requirement that companies cooperate completely as to individuals, within the bounds of the law and legal privileges, does not mean that Department attorneys should wait for the company to deliver the information about individual wrongdoers and then merely accept what companies provide. To the contrary, Department attorneys should be proactively investigating individuals at every step of the process — before, during, and after any corporate cooperation. Department attorneys should vigorously review any information provided by companies and compare it to the results of their own investigation, in order to best ensure that the information provided is indeed complete and does not seek to minimize the behavior or role of any individual or group of individuals.

Department attorneys should strive to obtain from the company as much information as possible about responsible individuals before resolving the corporate case. But there may be instances where the company's continued cooperation with respect to individuals will be necessary post-resolution. In these circumstances, the plea or settlement agreement should include a provision that requires the company to provide information about all culpable individuals and that is explicit enough so that a failure to provide the information results in specific consequences, such as stipulated penalties and/or a material breach.

2. Both criminal and civil attorneys should focus on individual wrongdoing from the very beginning of any investigation of corporate misconduct. By focusing on building cases against individual wrongdoers from the inception of an investigation, we accomplish multiple goals. First, we maximize our ability to ferret out the full extent of corporate misconduct. Because a corporation only acts through individuals, investigating the conduct of individuals is the most efficient and effective way to determine the facts and extent of any corporate misconduct. Second, by focusing our investigation on individuals, we can increase the likelihood that individuals with knowledge of the corporate misconduct will cooperate with the investigation and provide information against individuals higher up the corporate hierarchy. Third, by focusing on individuals from the very beginning of an investigation, we maximize the chances that the final resolution of an investigation uncovering the misconduct will include civil or criminal charges against not just the corporation but against culpable individuals as well.

3. Early and regular communication between civil attorneys and criminal prosecutors handling corporate investigations can be crucial to our ability to effectively pursue individuals in these matters. Consultation between the Department's civil and criminal attorneys, together with agency attorneys, permits consideration of the full range of the government's potential remedies (including incarceration, fines, penalties, damages, restitution to victims, asset seizure, civil and criminal forfeiture, and exclusion, suspension and debarment) and promotes the most thorough and appropriate resolution in every case . . . . Criminal attorneys handling corporate investigations should notify civil attorneys as early as permissible of conduct that

might give rise to potential individual civil liability, even if criminal liability continues to be sought. Further, if there is a decision not to pursue a criminal action against an individual — due to questions of intent or burden of proof, for example — criminal attorneys should confer with their civil counterparts so that they may make an assessment under applicable civil statutes and consistent with this guidance. Likewise, if civil attorneys believe that an individual identified in the course of their corporate investigation should be subject to a criminal inquiry, that matter should promptly be referred to criminal prosecutors, regardless of the current status of the civil corporate investigation. Department attorneys should be alert for circumstances where concurrent criminal and civil investigations of individual misconduct should be pursued. Coordination in this regard should happen early, even if it is not certain that a civil or criminal disposition will be the end result for the individuals or the company.

4. There may be instances where the Department reaches a resolution with the company before resolving matters with responsible individuals. In these circumstances, Department attorneys should take care to preserve the ability to pursue these individuals. Because of the importance of holding responsible individuals to account, absent extraordinary circumstances or approved departmental policy such as the Antitrust Division's Corporate Leniency Policy, Department lawyers should not agree to a corporate resolution that includes an agreement to dismiss charges against, or provide immunity for, individual officers or employees. The same principle holds true in civil corporate matters; absent extraordinary circumstances, the United States should not release claims related to the liability of individuals based on corporate settlement releases. Any such release of criminal or civil liability clue to extraordinary circumstances must be personally approved in writing by the relevant Assistant Attorney General or United States Attorney.

5. Corporate cases should not be resolved without a clear plan to resolve related individual cases before the statute of limitations expires and declinations as to individuals in such cases must be memorialized. If the investigation of individual misconduct has not concluded by the time authorization is sought to resolve the case against the corporation, the prosecution or corporate authorization memorandum should include a discussion of the potentially liable individuals, a description of the current status of the investigation regarding their conduct and the investigative work that remains to be done, and an investigative plan to bring the matter to resolution prior to the end of any statute of limitations period. If a decision is made at the conclusion of the investigation not to bring civil claims or criminal charges against the individuals who committed the misconduct, the reasons for that determination must be memorialized and approved by the United States Attorney or Assistant Attorney General whose office handled the investigation, or their designees.

Delays in the corporate investigation should not affect the Department's ability to pursue potentially culpable individuals. While every effort should be made to resolve a corporate matter within the statutorily allotted time, and tolling agreements should be the rare exception, in situations where it is anticipated that a tolling agreement is nevertheless unavoidable and necessary, all efforts should be made either to resolve the matter against culpable individuals before the limitations period expires or to preserve the ability to charge individuals by tolling the limitations period by agreement or court order.

6. The Department's civil enforcement efforts are designed not only to return government money to the public fisc, but also to hold the wrongdoers accountable

and to deter future wrongdoing. These twin aims — of recovering as much money as possible, on the one hand, and of accountability for and deterrence of individual misconduct, on the other — are equally important. In certain circumstances, though, these dual goals can be in apparent tension with one another, for example, when it comes to the question of whether to pursue civil actions against individual corporate wrongdoers who may not have the necessary financial resources to pay a significant judgment.

Pursuit of civil actions against culpable individuals should not be governed solely by those individuals' ability to pay. In other words, the fact that an individual may not have sufficient resources to satisfy a significant judgment should not control the decision on whether to bring suit. Rather, in deciding whether to file a civil action against an individual, Department attorneys should consider factors such as whether the person's misconduct was serious, whether it is actionable, whether the admissible evidence will probably be sufficient to obtain and sustain a judgment, and whether pursuing the action reflects an important federal interest. Just as our prosecutors do when making charging decisions, civil attorneys should make individualized assessments in deciding whether to bring a case, taking into account numerous factors, such as the individual's misconduct and past history and the circumstances relating to the commission of the misconduct, the needs of the communities we serve, and federal resources and priorities.

Although in the short term certain cases against individuals may not provide as robust a monetary return on the Department's investment, pursuing individual actions in civil corporate matters will result in significant long-term deterrence. Only by seeking to hold individuals accountable in view of all of the factors above can the Department ensure that it is doing everything in its power to minimize corporate fraud, and, over the course of time, minimize losses to the public fisc through fraud.

Questions and Comments

1. Although the Yates Memorandum reflects a shift in enforcement priorities at the Department of Justice, it doesn't represent a sea-change. The Department has traditionally proceeded against individuals who engage in misconduct. The Department's Antitrust Division has been a leader in the field. As early as 1961, the Antitrust Division set a precedent by prosecuting a price-fixing cartel in the electrical equipment manufacturing business in which seven senior executives were sent to prison. The Antitrust Division's pursuit of individuals continued in more recent times. During the 1990s, the division prosecuted 476 individuals and 480 corporations, and in the decade of the 2000s, it prosecuted twice as many individuals as corporations. Commenting on the Yates Memorandum, a high-level official in the Division remarked in 2016 that "the Yates memo emphasizes what the division already expects." Individual Accountability for Antitrust Crimes, Remarks of Deputy Assistant Attorney General Brent Snyder at the Yale Global Antitrust Enforcement Conference (Feb. 19, 2016).

2. Do you agree with the policy behind the Yates Memo? On the one hand, the rationale for imposing liability on culpable individuals seems unassailable. If the people responsible for wrongdoing are actually required to pay for their misconduct, they are less likely to engage in bad behavior in the first place. On the other hand, if senior managers fear individual liability, is there a concern that companies will fight

enforcement actions more vigorously—thus straining official resources and, potentially, generating precedents that ultimately weaken enforcement powers? Will senior managers, fearing possible personal liability, refrain from engaging in socially valuable innovations? Could fear of individual liability deter capable people from serving as corporate managers? Are there concerns about fairness or due process when principles of prosecution developed in the context of actions against corporations are applied without modification to actions against individual defendants?

B. REGULATION OF THE COMPLIANCE PROGRAM

Regulators employ several strategies to push organizations to implement robust compliance policies and programs. We will explore these strategies in the pages that follow.

1. General Considerations

Why do regulators encourage or require private parties to adopt compliance programs?

The answer to this question may seem obvious: Compliance programs reduce the incidence of violations. Since we want to deter violations, compliance programs should be encouraged. But on reflection, the question becomes more intriguing. Given that adopting a compliance program is often advisable as a matter of self-interest, why does the government need to nudge the private sector to do so? Even if government intervention would be useful, moreover, policies that encourage or require compliance programs have costs as well as benefits. Presumably, it would not be a good idea for the government to promote compliance programs if the costs of doing so exceed the benefits.

Consider the following downsides to government policies that encourage or require compliance programs:

- Knowing that a compliance program will earn them credit if they are caught, organizations might create "Potemkin villages"—pretend compliance programs that have the appearance of being an effective and robust operation but that, in fact, accomplish little. Instead of deterring misconduct, giving credit for compliance programs might encourage bad behavior by affording organizations a built-in defense to liability.
- Giving credit for a compliance program eliminates or reduces the company's liability. As a result, organizations will engage in more of the activity than they would engage in if they did not receive credit for a compliance program. If the activity in question creates a risk of socially costly outcomes (e.g., environmental harm), then a credit for compliance will tend to generate undesirable levels of harm-producing activity.
- The government may need to expend resources to monitor the organization's compliance operation to satisfy itself that the operation is robust and effective.
- The government may make mistakes in specifying the criteria for an acceptable program since it lacks information about the regulated entity.
- When the government does make errors, it is likely to require that regulated parties expend too many rather than too few resources on its compliance function. The reason is that the government officials fear being criticized if

violations occur, but do not fear (or fear as much) being criticized for imposing excessive regulatory burdens.

Offsetting these costs are certain benefits that can be achieved when the government encourages organizations to institute compliance programs. Consider the
following:

- When penalties are imposed on an organization for violations committed by
  its employee or agent, the incidence falls principally on people who have little
  direct control over the organization's policies — shareholders, other employees, trading partners, and even the public at large. Accordingly, the threat of
  penalties against organizations may not translate into effective compliance
  programs. Regulators can potentially manage incentives more effectively by
  punishing senior officers. But the penalties meted out against top managers
  are usually not very severe. If penalties for violations are not effective at inducing organizations to create optimal compliance programs, there may be a
  need for other types of intervention.
- Companies don't always behave rationally. Even though it would be in their
  interest to adopt compliance programs, they may not do so. They may fail to
  act because of internal turf battles. The company's managers may be focused
  on other things, or may lack the vision to understand that upgrading their
  compliance operations would serve the company and its shareholders.
  In such cases, some might argue that regulators do a favor to an organization
  when they encourage the firm to institute a robust compliance program.
- When the government provides a defense or mitigation of liability for firms
  that maintain robust compliance programs, the effect is to reduce the risk a
  firm faces as compared with the traditional rule that firms are strictly liable for
  the misconduct of their agents. If firms are risk-averse, there could be an
  advantage to allowing them, in effect, to purchase an insurance policy against
  the risk of liability by expending the resources to create a robust compliance
  operation.
- Government encouragement of compliance programs may reflect perceptions of blameworthiness. Companies that implement bona fide compliance
  programs demonstrate by their actions that they wish to avoid violating legal
  norms. It might seem unfair or unjust to penalize these actors — the good
  guys — as severely we penalize those who don't even try.
- Compliance programs can arguably provide external benefits that go beyond
  the particular rules being enforced. Companies that upgrade the vigor and
  profile of their compliance operations signal to others — employees, their
  shareholders, others in the industry, and the public at large — that they
  take their compliance obligations seriously. As more and more companies
  get on board the compliance bandwagon, the general values of the industry as
  a whole are likely to shift in favor of more public-regarding conduct.

Questions and Comments

1. Which (if any) of the foregoing do you find persuasive as explanations for why
regulators encourage firms under their supervision to implement vigorous compliance operations? Are these justifications powerful enough to overcome the costs of
encouraging compliance programs?

2. Are there costs or benefits not included in the list?

3. For economic analysis of the choice between compliance-based standards and strict corporate liability, see Jennifer Arlen & Reinier Kraakman, *Controlling Corporate Misconduct: An Analysis of Corporate Liability Regimes*, 72 N.Y.U. L. Rev. 687 (1997).

4. For an analysis of the optimal amount companies should be required to spend on compliance, see Geoffrey P. Miller, An Economic Analysis of Effective Compliance Programs, forthcoming in Jennifer Arlen ed., *Research Handbook on Corporate Crime and Financial Misdealing* (Edward Elgar 2016).

2. "Best Practice" Recommendations

A company that maintains a program that the regulators find acceptable is likely to receive favorable treatment when violations occur. Accordingly, the recommendations of regulators on adequate compliance programs carry a great deal of weight. Consider in this regard the following comments by a high-ranking Justice Department official:

Remarks by Assistant Attorney General for the Criminal Division Leslie R. Caldwell

(Oct. 1, 2014)

[T]here is . . . no "off the rack" compliance program that can be installed at every company. Effective compliance programs must be tailored to the unique needs and risks faced by each company. But there are hallmarks of good compliance programs. The [Department of Justice] includes many of these in our non-prosecution agreements and deferred prosecution agreements, and I'd like to discuss them with you. [The following are guideposts that we consider important to the success of a strong program]:

1. High-level commitment. A company must ensure that its directors and senior management provide strong, explicit, and visible commitment to its corporate compliance policy. Stated differently, and again, "tone from the top." This means that the importance of compliance should be communicated from the very top of the company. I once heard of a large company whose prominent CEO refused to put his signature on a company-wide communication announcing the company's new compliance program. When asked why not, he replied: "Because we don't hire those kinds of people." Well, he could not have been more wrong. Every company hires "those kinds of people." . . .

2. Written Policies. A company should have a clearly articulated and visible corporate compliance policy memorialized in a written compliance code. Again, employees need to know what to do — or not do — when faced with a tough judgment call involving business ethics. Companies need to make that as easy as possible for their employees.

3. Periodic Risk-Based Review. A company should periodically evaluate these compliance codes on the basis of a risk assessment addressing the individual circumstances of the company. Companies change over time through natural growth, mergers, and acquisitions . . . .

4. Proper Oversight and Independence. A company should assign responsibility to senior executives for the implementation and oversight of the compliance program. Those executives should have the authority to report directly to independent monitoring bodies, including internal audit and the Board of Directors, and should have autonomy from management. Compliance programs needed to be funded; they need to have resources. And they need to have teeth and respect within the company. For years, Wall Street banks housed their compliance programs across the Hudson River, in New Jersey. They were out of sight, out of mind. They were underpaid. And nobody paid much attention to them. Compliance programs need to have an appropriate stature within the company, or compliance will be the last thing on the mind of an employee tempted to engage in wrongdoing.

5. Training and Guidance. A company should implement mechanisms designed to ensure that its compliance code is effectively communicated to all directors, officers, employees. This means repeated communication, frequent and effective training, and an ability to provide guidance when issues arise. And as I said before, employees should see that the importance of compliance is being communicated from the top — whether the CEO, the Board, the General Counsel, or some other very highly respected senior-level figure within the company.

6. Internal Reporting. A company should have an effective system for confidential, internal reporting of compliance violations. I know that many companies have multiple mechanisms, which is good.

7. Investigation. A company should establish an effective process with sufficient resources for responding to, investigating, and documenting allegations of violations. What this means on the ground will depend on the company. A sophisticated multi-national corporation obviously will be expected to have more resources devoted to compliance than a small regional company.

8. Enforcement and Discipline. A company should implement mechanisms designed to enforce its compliance code, including appropriately incentivizing compliance and disciplining violations. And the response to a violation must be even-handed. Too often, we see situations where low level employees who may have implemented the bad conduct are fired, but their boss, who saw what they were doing and did nothing — and maybe even the directed the conduct — is left in place. This should not happen . . . . Leaving in place senior managers who sanction bad behavior sends a very wrong message about the company's true commitment to compliance and ethics. People watch what people do much more carefully than what they say. When it comes to compliance, you must both say and do.

9. Third-Party Relationships. A company should institute compliance requirements pertaining to the oversight of all agents and business partners. I cannot emphasize strongly enough the need to sensitize third parties, like vendors, agents, and consultants, to the importance of . . . compliance. And these partners need to understand that the company really expects its partners to be compliant. This often means more than just including a boilerplate paragraph in a contract in which the partner promises to comply with the law and company policies. It means warning, and even terminating, relationships with partners who fail to behave in a compliant manner.

10. Monitoring and Testing. A company should conduct periodic reviews and testing of its compliance code to improve its effectiveness in preventing and detecting violations. Kick the tires regularly. As I said, compliance programs must evolve with changes in the law, business practices, technology and culture.

Questions and Comments

1. What do career prosecutors know about designing an effective compliance program?

2. Assistant Attorney General Caldwell states that "leaving in place senior managers who sanction bad behavior sends a very wrong message about the company's true commitment to compliance and ethics." Obviously, a company needs to take decisive action when it learns that one of its managers has participated actively in illegal behavior. But the statement carries broader implications. First, what is "bad" behavior? Caldwell doesn't limit her comments to illegal conduct. Does the category include, say, a persistent failure to observe internal compliance controls, even if the employee in question doesn't actually commit violations? Second, what does it mean to "sanction" bad behavior? Is it necessary for the senior manager to gain some personal benefit for a subordinate's bad conduct? What if a manager recommends a bonus for an employee even though the manager knows that the employee has violated a rule? What if the manager cuts the bonus but doesn't fire or reassign the employee? What if the manager doesn't know about the bad behavior, but does know of "yellow flags" that might prompt a diligent manager to inquire further? Finally, note that Caldwell recommends that a senior manager who sanctions bad behavior must not be "left in place." Does this mean that the senior manager must be fired? What about if she is demoted or denied a bonus?

3. Caldwell states that "I cannot emphasize strongly enough the need to sensitize third parties, like vendors, agents, and consultants, to the importance of . . . compliance." The stress placed on this criterion apparently reflects the perception that compliance programs have not done enough in monitoring of agents and business partners—and signals that this will be an important focus of DOJ enforcement in the future. Again, the rhetoric is susceptible to broader and narrower interpretations. When a company employs an agent or business partner to evade legal requirements, the justification for imposing controls is clear. For example, suppose a company wants to bribe a foreign official in order to get a lucrative construction contract. Directly bribing the official would violate the Foreign Corrupt Practices Act, but so would employing an agent to do the same thing. Compliance programs need to police against such conduct. And, because business agents in foreign countries rarely inform their clients of what they intend to do, the compliance program must also extend to implicit understandings for corrupt behavior. This much is obvious. But Caldwell's comments carry potentially broader implications. Does a company have responsibility, not only to police and prevent activities by third parties that can directly implicate the company in illegal conduct, but also conduct that, while illegal, cannot be attributed to the company? In other words, must corporate compliance programs act as de facto deputies to the government in its general law enforcement function? This broader function of compliance programs—acting as de facto partners with the government in the general project of law enforcement—is controversial and, as yet, largely undeveloped. To what extent do you think corporate compliance programs should serve in this role?

3. Legislative and Regulatory Mandates

Sometimes the government requires organizations to maintain compliance operations. An example of a government-mandated compliance function is the rule on money laundering. This statute provides as follows in pertinent part:

Bank Secrecy Act

31 U.S.C. §5318(h)

(1) In general. — In order to guard against money laundering through financial institutions, each financial institution shall establish anti-money laundering programs, including, at a minimum —

(A) the development of internal policies, procedures, and controls;

(B) the designation of a compliance officer;

(C) an ongoing employee training program; and

(D) an independent audit function to test programs.

Questions and Comments

1. Consider the four requirements that Congress considered to be the irreducible minima of a money laundering compliance program. These are sometimes referred to as the "four pillars" of compliance because they describe key features of any internal compliance program: internal policies, a senior official specially tasked with the compliance function, training of line employees, and the backstop of internal audit.

2. How would you relate the four required aspects of money laundering compliance functions to the "three lines of defense" discussed in the Introduction to this book?

3. The language quoted above was adopted by Congress in the USA PATRIOT Act in 2001. Previously, the law had authorized the Secretary of the Treasury to mandate that banks adopt money laundering compliance programs, but did not directly require that banks do so. Why were the requirements upgraded in 2001? During debate on the measure, Senator Levin explained the change as follows: "The antiterrorism bill we have before us today would be very incomplete — only half of a toolbox — without a strong anti-money-laundering title to prevent foreign terrorists and other criminals from using our financial institutions against us. With the anti-money laundering provisions in this bill, the antiterrorism bill gives our enforcement authorities a valuable set of additional tools to fight those who are attempting to terrorize this country. Osama bin Laden has boasted that his modern new recruits know, in his words, the 'cracks' in 'Western financial systems' like they know the 'lines in their own hands.' Enactment of this bill with these provisions will help seal those cracks that allow terrorists and other criminals to use our own financial systems against us." 147 Cong. Rec. S10990-02 (daily ed. Oct. 25, 2001). Are government-mandated anti-money laundering compliance programs at U.S. financial institutions essential tools in the fight against global terrorism?

4. Another law mandating the establishment of a compliance department is found in the Dodd-Frank Act's provisions on swap dealers and futures commission merchants. The statute requires swap dealers and major swap participants to designate a chief compliance officer who reports directly to the board of directors or to the senior officer of the registrant. The CCO is required to review and ensure the registrant's compliance with the Commodities Exchange Act (CEA), resolve conflicts of interest, and establish procedures for procedures for the remediation of non-compliance issues. The CCO must prepare and sign an annual report describing the registrant's compliance with the CEA and implementing regulations as well as company codes of ethics and conflict of interest policies. 7 U.S.C. §§6d(d), 6s(k).

Sometimes government-mandated compliance programs are adopted in regulations rather than legislation. An example is found in the following excerpt:

Securities and Exchange Commission Final Rule: Compliance Programs of Investment Companies and Investment Advisers

Dec. 17, 2003

The Commission is adopting new rule 206(4)-7 under the Advisers Act and new rule 38a-1 under the Investment Company Act. The new rules require each registered investment adviser and each fund to adopt and implement compliance programs that conform to the new rules. Failure of an adviser or fund to have adequate compliance policies and procedures in place will constitute a violation of our rules independent of any other securities law violation. The new rules will thus permit the Commission to address the failure of an adviser or fund to have in place adequate compliance controls, before that failure has a chance to harm clients or investors.

INVESTMENT ADVISERS

Under rule 206(4)-7, it is unlawful for an investment adviser registered with the Commission to provide investment advice unless the adviser has adopted and implemented written policies and procedures reasonably designed to prevent violation of the Advisers Act by the adviser or any of its supervised persons. The rule requires advisers to consider their fiduciary and regulatory obligations under the Advisers Act and to formalize policies and procedures to address them . . . .

Each adviser, in designing its policies and procedures, should first identify conflicts and other compliance factors creating risk exposure for the firm and its clients in light of the firm's particular operations, and then design policies and procedures that address those risks. We expect that an adviser's policies and procedures, at a minimum, should address the following issues to the extent that they are relevant to that adviser:

- Portfolio management processes, including allocation of investment opportunities among clients and consistency of portfolios with clients' investment objectives, disclosures by the adviser, and applicable regulatory restrictions;
- Trading practices, including procedures by which the adviser satisfies its best execution obligation, uses client brokerage to obtain research and other services ("soft dollar arrangements"), and allocates aggregated trades among clients;
- Proprietary trading of the adviser and personal trading activities of supervised persons;
- The accuracy of disclosures made to investors, clients, and regulators, including account statements and advertisements;
- Safeguarding of client assets from conversion or inappropriate use by advisory personnel;
- The accurate creation of required records and their maintenance in a manner that secures them from unauthorized alteration or use and protects them from untimely destruction;
- Marketing advisory services, including the use of solicitors;

- Processes to value client holdings and assess fees based on those valuations;
- Safeguards for the privacy protection of client records and information; and
- Business continuity plans.

Rule 206(4)-7 does not require advisers to consolidate all compliance policies and procedures into a single document. Nor does it require advisers to memorialize every action that must be taken in order to remain in compliance with the Advisers Act. In some cases, it may be enough for the compliance policies and procedures to allocate responsibility within the organization for the timely performance of many obligations, such as the filing or updating of required forms.

INVESTMENT COMPANIES

Rule 38a-1 requires fund boards to adopt written policies and procedures reasonably designed to prevent the fund from violating the federal securities laws. The procedures must provide for the oversight of compliance by the fund's advisers, principal underwriters, administrators, and transfer agent (collectively, "service providers") through which the fund conducts its activities . . . . The final rule requires fund boards to approve the policies and procedures of fund service providers, and requires the fund's policies and procedures to include provisions for the fund to oversee compliance by its service providers . . . .

Policies and Procedures

Funds' or their advisers' policies and procedures should address the issues we identified for investment advisers above. In addition, we expect policies and procedures of funds (or fund service providers) to cover certain other critical areas. In light of our recent enforcement actions against a number of fund managers and service providers, we are taking this opportunity to review the application of these policies and procedures to several important areas of compliance with the federal securities laws by funds and their service providers.

The Commission understands that, in some cases, the fund may employ the services of a service provider that is not an affiliated person of the fund, such as a transfer agent or administrator, and that provides similar services to a large number of funds. In such cases, it may be impractical for the fund or its compliance officer to directly review all of the service provider's policies and procedures. In such cases, we will consider a fund's policies and procedures to have satisfied the requirements of this rule if the fund uses a third-party report on the service provider's procedures instead of the procedures themselves when the board is evaluating whether to approve the service provider's compliance program. The third-party report must describe the service provider's compliance program as it relates to the types of services provided to the fund, discuss the types of compliance risks material to the fund, and assess the adequacy of the service provider's compliance controls . . . .

Questions and Comments

1. This action by the SEC governs compliance obligations in the investment company industry, including both investment companies ("funds") and investment advisers. Rule 206(4)-7 deals with advisers and Rule 38a-1 deals with funds. Some background on this industry: An investment company pools funds contributed by investors and invests them in a portfolio of assets. Approximately 10,000 such funds

operated in the United States as of 2012. Investment companies are organized as business entities (corporations or business trusts) and are officially governed by a board of directors or board of trustees. Typically, these entities have few if any employees. They rely almost wholly on third-party service providers. Most investment companies are organized, managed, and controlled by their investment advisers. An investment adviser is an entity that provides investment advice and other services. The investment adviser typically sponsors and advises the investment company. It creates the company, promotes it, brands it (alone or in affiliation with a "family" of funds), arranges for the sale of its securities to the public, selects its investment strategy, and makes day-to-day investment decisions. In some cases, if allowed by SEC regulations, the investment adviser might provide other services to the investment company, such as brokerage. Investment advisers are regulated at the federal level by the Investment Advisers Act; investment companies are regulated by the Investment Company Act. Both of these statutes are administered by the SEC and implemented through regulations promulgated by that agency.

2. Prior to the adoption of the amendments described in the excerpt above, investment companies typically relied on the compliance operations of their service providers for assurance that the rules were being followed. The SEC believes that this practice was ineffective and provided insufficient protections for investors, for two reasons: The compliance function was balkanized into silos representing different service providers, and the assurance provided by the service provider was only as good as the compliance operation at that firm—which the SEC suggests was often not very good. The requirements of the rule that relate to investment companies were intended to rectify these problems. Do they?

3. Given that the boards of an investment company are typically composed of a majority of independent directors who serve on a part-time basis and who have no staff to assist them, how can they responsibly fulfill the obligations imposed on them by this rule?

4. The rule discussed in the excerpted text requires the board of an investment company to oversee compliance activities by service providers. Some of these companies will be in the business of providing services to hundreds of funds. Does each fund need to fully vet the compliance policies of these firms? The release says that in such cases the board may be entitled to rely on a "third party report." Who would prepare such a report?

5. The rule encourages regulated entities to engage in a two-step process in designing a compliance program: First, identify compliance factors creating risk exposure for the firm; and second, design a compliance program that takes account of these risk factors. This "risk-based" approach is nearly universal in the compliance world today (and we will study several other examples of the approach in the pages that follow). What are the advantages of performing a risk assessment before designing a compliance program? Can you identify any potential disadvantages?

6. Many of the matters addressed in the excerpted text fall squarely in the traditional area of "business judgment," where decisions are traditionally committed to the sound discretion of management and the board of directors. Do the regulations discussed above go too far in decreeing what funds and fund advisers must do in the area of compliance?

7. Should the SEC rules described above be adopted as models for other industries? Should all firms with substantial compliance operations be required to create compliance departments headed by a chief compliance officer who reports directly to the board of directors or a board committee?

8. Consider possible alternatives to the creation of a robust in-house compliance function at investment companies. What about a rule requiring regulated firms to undergo third-party compliance reviews similar to the review process that is already provided by external auditors with respect to financial statements and systems of internal controls? Major accounting firms would be delighted to add this to their portfolio of services. Would this be a good idea for the investment company industry, or more generally for regulated industries across the board? The SEC considered and rejected this option, but noted that "compliance audits could be a useful supplement to our examination program and would assure the frequent examination of advisers and funds."

9. What about the idea, also floated during the SEC's consideration of these rules, that regulated industries should be required to obtain fidelity bonds from insurance companies to protect against losses resulting from legal violations?

10. Compliance activities are sometimes required by self-regulatory organizations. Rule 3130 of the Financial Industry Regulatory Authority (FINRA) requires that each member firm must designate a chief compliance officer and further requires the chief executive officer to certify that the member "has in place processes to establish, maintain, review, test and modify written compliance policies and written supervisory procedures reasonably designed to achieve compliance" with applicable rules, laws, and regulations. Likewise, Rule 3012 of the National Association of Securities Dealers (NASD) requires members to designate an officer responsible for establishing, maintaining and enforcing a "supervisory control system." Among other things, this system must test and verify that the member's supervisory practices are reasonably designed to comply with applicable rules, laws, and regulations. What about creating a self-regulatory organization for investment companies and empowering that organization to conduct compliance examinations?

In 2011, the SEC rolled out a new policy, the Compliance Program Initiative, designed to further incentivize firms to comply with the compliance program requirements of its investment company/investment advisers rule. This program targets firms that have been warned by the SEC about deficiencies in their compliance programs and that subsequently are found to have committed regulatory violations. Essentially, the program encourages firms to adopt robust compliance programs because if they do not do so and are warned about the problem, they will receive especially harsh treatment in the event of a subsequent violation.

In In re Modern Portfolio Management, Inc., File No. 3-15583, the SEC issued a cease-and-desist order against an investment adviser and its senior executives, requiring the defendants to pay fines and to upgrade their compliance operations. Among the deficiencies in compliance noted by the SEC were the fact that the company's designated CCO had virtually no experience or training and repeatedly failed to complete required annual compliance reviews; and that when this person left office one of the individual defendants stepped in as CCO, despite an obvious lack of qualifications. These failures, coupled with alleged repeated misrepresentations in marketing materials, was the basis for the SEC's action.

Questions and Comments

1. The SEC did not put this investment adviser out of business, despite what appears to have been a persistent pattern of paying lip service to compliance obligations. Should it have taken stronger action?

2. Although some investment adviser firms are large and well funded, others are quite small; the company involved in the *MPM* case appears to have had only a handful of employees. What sort of compliance program can be expected from such an outfit?

3. The SEC criticizes the defendants for putting one of the adviser's principal officers in charge of compliance when the CCO departed. Yet this is not, in itself, charged as a violation. Should the SEC allow investment advisers to designate a principal owner and manager as the CCO? Are there obvious conflicts of interest here that might bespeak caution about such an arrangement?

One controversial feature of the Dodd-Frank financial reform law is the so-called Volcker Rule, which prohibits banks and their affiliates from engaging in proprietary trading and from acquiring or retaining ownership interests in or sponsoring a hedge fund or private equity fund. Implementation of the rule proved to be contentious as banks, regulators, consumer groups, and others bickered about what should be in the regulations. The final rule, a joint project of the Federal Deposit Insurance Corporation, the Federal Reserve Board, the Office of the Comptroller of the Currency, the Securities and Exchange Commission, and the Commodity Futures Trading Commission, is a complex compromise containing an elaborate set of detailed and technical requirements as well as numerous exceptions. Office of the Comptroller of the Currency, Board of Governors of the Federal Reserve System, Federal Deposit Insurance Corporation, and Securities and Exchange Commission, Prohibitions and Restrictions on Proprietary Trading and Certain Interests in, and Relationships with, Hedge Funds and Private Equity Funds (Jan. 31, 2014).

Of particular interest here is the compliance section of the rule. Subpart D requires a banking entity engaged in covered activities to develop and implement a program reasonably designed to ensure and monitor compliance with the prohibitions and restrictions on covered activities and investments.

A banking entity with total consolidated assets of $10 billion or less that engages in covered activities or investments may satisfy the requirements of the final rule by including in its existing compliance policies and procedures appropriate references to the requirements of the Dodd-Frank Act and the final rule and adjustments as appropriate given the activities, size, scope, and complexity of the company.

For banking entities with total assets greater than $10 billion and less than $50 billion, the final rule specifies six elements that each compliance program must include:

- Written policies and procedures reasonably designed to document, describe, monitor, and limit trading activities and covered fund activities and investments conducted by the banking entity;
- A system of internal controls reasonably designed to monitor compliance;
- A management framework that clearly delineates responsibility and accountability for compliance and includes appropriate management review of trading limits, strategies, hedging activities, investments, incentive compensation, and other matters identified in the rule or by management as requiring attention;
- Independent testing and audit of the effectiveness of the compliance program conducted periodically by qualified personnel of the banking entity or by a qualified outside party;
- Training for trading personnel and managers, as well as other appropriate personnel, to effectively implement and enforce the compliance program; and

- Making and keeping records sufficient to demonstrate compliance, which a banking entity must promptly provide to the relevant supervisory agency upon request and retain for a period of no less than five years.

A banking entity with $50 billion or more total consolidated assets is required to adopt an enhanced compliance program with more detailed policies, limits, governance processes, independent testing, and reporting. In addition, the chief executive officer of these larger banking entities must attest that the banking entity has in place a program reasonably designed to achieve compliance.

Questions and Comments

1. Why might an effective compliance function be of special importance in assuring that a large and complex financial institution adheres to a technical set of obligations such as those contained in the Volcker Rule?

2. Why might the regulators have determined it was necessary to impose "enhanced" compliance requirements on mega-banks?

3. Note the provision requiring establishment of a management framework that clearly delineates responsibility and accountability for compliance. This sort of responsibility map is considered state of the art in the design of compliance programs. What purpose does it serve? What is the difference between "responsibility" and "accountability," and why are they separately specified?

Federally chartered banks regulated by the Comptroller of the Currency are assigned "CAMELS" ratings as part of the supervision process. Among other things, banks are rated for "consumer compliance" — compliance with consumer protection and civil rights statutes and regulations — and the adequacy of their operating systems designed to ensure continuing compliance. Factors to be considered include (1) the nature and extent of present compliance with consumer protection and civil rights statutes and regulations; (2) the commitment of management to compliance and their ability and willingness to assure continuing compliance; and (3) the adequacy of operating systems, including internal procedures, controls, and audit activities, designed to ensure compliance on a routine and consistent basis. Banks need to maintain good CAMELS ratings in order to reduce their deposit insurance premiums, receive permission to engage in business developments, and avoid unwanted regulatory scrutiny.

Banks receive consumer compliance ratings ranging from "1" (very desirable) to "5" (very undesirable). To receive the highest rating, a bank must convince the regulators that there is "no cause for supervisory concern." Specifically, the regulators must conclude the following:

- Management is capable of and staff is sufficient for effectuating compliance.
- An effective compliance program, including an efficient system of internal procedures and controls, has been established.
- Changes in consumer statutes and regulations are promptly reflected in the institution's policies, procedures, and compliance training.
- The institution provides adequate training for its employees.
- If any violations are noted, they are relatively minor deficiencies in forms or practices and are easily corrected.
- There is no evidence of discriminatory acts or practices, reimbursable violations, or practices resulting in repeat violations.
- Violations and deficiencies are promptly corrected by management.

Effectively, the consumer compliance rating system requires banks to support a robust compliance operation; if they do not do so, the regulators will conclude that internal controls are lacking and that management has not displayed the requite commitment to achieving a culture of compliance at the bank. The result will be a markdown on the CAMELS rating, with unpleasant consequences to follow.

4. Compliance Terms in Settlements

In many cases, the government demands during settlement negotiations over civil or criminal enforcement actions that companies implement or upgrade compliance programs. The following excerpt provides an example of such a compliance-based settlement agreement.

United States of America
Department of the Treasury
Comptroller of the Currency

In the Matter of:	)
RBS Citizens, N.A.	)
Providence, Rhode Island	)

CONSENT ORDER

[The Office of the Comptroller of the Currency concluded, after an examination, that RBS Citizens (part of the Royal Bank of Scotland group) had engaged in deceptive practices in violation of the Federal Trade Commission Act. The pertinent part of the cease and desist order follows:]

. . . (1) Within ten (10) days, the Board shall appoint a Compliance Committee of at least three (3) independent directors, which may not be employees or officers of the Bank or any of its subsidiaries or affiliates. The Compliance Committee shall be responsible for monitoring and coordinating the Bank's adherence to the provisions of the Order. The Compliance Committee shall maintain minutes of its meetings at which compliance with this Order is discussed.

(2) The Compliance Committee shall meet at least monthly.

(3) Within sixty (60) days of the date of this Order and within thirty (30) days of each calendar quarter thereafter, the Compliance Committee shall submit a written progress report to the Board setting forth in detail:

(a) actions taken since the prior report (if any) to comply with each Article of this Order;

(b) the results of those actions; and

(c) a description of the actions needed and the anticipated time frame to achieve full compliance with each Article of this Order;

(4) The Board shall forward a copy of the Compliance Committee's report, with any additional comments by the Board, to the Examiner-in-Charge within thirty (30) days of receiving such report. These reports shall:

(a) include the Compliance Committee's report to the Board for the applicable quarter, with any additional comments by the Board; and

(b) describe any actions initiated by the Board or the Bank to comply with each Article of this Order.

Questions and Comments

1. Based on this order, what can one infer about the attitude of the bank regulators regarding compliance committees? If you were representing a bank, would you recommend that it establish such a committee, even if the regulator was not currently demanding one?

2. The consent decree requires that the compliance committee meet "at least monthly." For independent directors, it might be quite a burden to travel to 12 meetings a year. It is likely that the bank's charter allows directors to meet by telephone. Would you recommend telephonic meetings? How long should the meetings last?

3. What is the compliance committee's mandate? The decree says only that the committee is "responsible for monitoring and coordinating the Bank's adherence to the provisions of the Order." Is that all the compliance committee is likely to do? Why was the decree limited in this way?

4. At some point, the regulator may conclude that the bank is in compliance with the law and lift the obligations of the decree. If it does so, would you advise the bank to dissolve the compliance committee, given that it has no further work to do?

Department of the Treasury
Comptroller of the Currency

In the Matter of:	)
HSBC Bank USA, N.A.	)
McLean, Virginia	)

CONSENT ORDER

The Comptroller [of the Currency] has identified certain unsafe or unsound practices related to enterprise-wide compliance [at HSBC Bank USA, N.A., ("Bank")] . . . . By this Stipulation and Consent, which is incorporated by reference, the Bank has consented to the issuance of this Consent Order ("Order") by the Comptroller.

The Comptroller finds, and the Bank neither admits nor denies, the following:

The Bank has a supervisory history of non-compliance with banking laws and regulations, as well as non-conformance with policies, procedures, and prescribed practices in the compliance area that have occurred over a multi-year period. During the past year, additional deficiencies have surfaced from internal and external reviews that evidence broad and serious weaknesses in the Bank's compliance program. The robustness of the compliance program has not kept pace with the bank's size, complexity, and risk profile.

The Comptroller's examination findings establish that the Bank has engaged in unsafe or unsound practices with respect to enterprise-wide compliance. Specifically, the Bank's compliance program has historically shown deficiencies in adequate, proactive leadership, risk reporting, and policies and procedures. Pursuant to the authority invested in him by the Federal Deposit Insurance Act, as amended, 12 U.S.C. §1818(b), the Comptroller hereby orders that:

The Board shall maintain a Compliance Committee of at least three (3) directors, of which at least two (2) may not be employees or officers of the Bank or any of its subsidiaries or affiliates . . . .

The Compliance Committee shall meet at least monthly.

Within ninety (90) days of this Order and quarterly thereafter, the Compliance Committee shall submit a written progress report to the Board setting forth in detail:

- a description of the actions needed to achieve full compliance with each Article of this Order;
- actions taken to comply with each Article of this Order; and
- the results and status of those actions.

The Board shall forward a copy of the Compliance Committee's report, with any additional comments by the Board, to the Deputy Comptroller and Examiner-in-Charge within ten (10) days of receiving such report.

Within ninety (90) days of the date of this Order, the Board, or a designated committee of the Board, shall adopt, implement, and thereafter ensure adherence to a written enterprise-wide compliance program designed to ensure that the Bank is operating in compliance with applicable laws, rules, regulations, regulatory guidance, and supervisory findings. This program shall include, but not be limited to:

- written description of the duties, responsibilities, and authority of the chief compliance officer and a requirement that this position be staffed by a qualified individual;
- written descriptions of the duties, responsibilities, and reporting lines of other compliance management officers and compliance personnel, and requirements that these positions be staffed with qualified personnel;
- performance objectives and compensation plans that align with written descriptions of duties and responsibilities of compliance personnel;
- written compliance values statement, to be communicated across the Bank;
- annual written analysis of the products and services offered by the Bank that fully assesses risk presented by applicable laws, rules, regulations, regulatory guidance, and supervisory findings;
- the preparation of a policies and procedures manual covering applicable laws, rules, regulations, regulatory guidance, and supervisory findings for use by appropriate Bank personnel in the performance of their duties and responsibilities;
- at least semi-annual review of the written policies and procedures manual to update it, as appropriate, to ensure it remains current;
- a control environment maintained by business lines and risk functions ("second lines of defense") that ensures compliance with applicable laws, rules, regulations, regulatory guidance, and supervisory findings;
- integration of compliance risk into the enterprise-wide risk management framework;
- an audit program that tests compliance with applicable laws, rules, regulations, regulatory guidance, and supervisory findings;
- at least semi-annual independent evaluation of the effectiveness of the enterprise-wide compliance program, including but not limited to management, management information systems, staffing, and training;
- at least semi-annual independent reporting of the results of the evaluation of the enterprise-wide compliance program to the Board or a committee thereof;
- procedures to ensure that exceptions noted in testing and validation reports are corrected and responded to by the appropriate Bank personnel in a timely manner; and

- the education and training of all appropriate Bank personnel to ensure their awareness of applicable laws, rules, regulations, regulatory guidance, and Bank policies and procedure.

Upon completion of the program, the Board shall submit the program to the Deputy Comptroller and the Examiner-in-Charge for prior written determination of no supervisory objection. In the event the Deputy Comptroller recommends changes to the program, the Board shall incorporate those changes into the program. Upon receiving a written determination of no supervisory objection from the Deputy Comptroller, the Bank shall immediately implement and adhere to the program.

The Board shall direct management to undertake and complete all steps necessary to correct the circumstances and conditions, as noted in the Bank's most recent Report of Examination, which prompted the need for the enterprise-wide compliance program required by this Order.

Within ninety (90) days of this Order, the Board shall develop and adopt a written plan that:

- explains the specific actions that Bank management will take to achieve full implementation of the enterprise-wide compliance program, . . . including personnel resource requirements and the associated on boarding timeline;
- specifies how the Board will ensure Bank management's implementation of the plan; and
- sets forth a timetable for the implementation of each action specified in the plan.

Upon completion of the plan, the Board shall submit the plan to the Deputy Comptroller and Examiner-in-Charge for a prior written determination of no supervisory objection. Upon receiving a written determination of no supervisory objection from the Deputy Comptroller, the Bank shall immediately implement and adhere to the plan.

The plan shall be implemented pursuant to the time frames set forth within the plan unless events dictate modifications to the plan. Where the Board considers modifications appropriate, those modifications shall be submitted to the Deputy Comptroller and Examiner-in-Charge for prior written determination of no supervisory objection. Upon receiving a written determination of no supervisory objection from the Deputy Comptroller, the Bank shall implement and adhere to the revised plan.

Questions and Comments

1. HSBC Bank USA is an affiliate of HSBC Group, a giant international bank headquartered in London, and operating more than 6,000 offices in more than 80 countries and territories. HSBC Group describes its corporate objective as to "be acknowledged as the world's leading international bank." Did the OCC's enforcement proceeding impact the realization of that goal?

2. Do you detect a tone in the consent decree suggesting that HSBC was an outlier as far as compliance was concerned — that is, that it displayed an unusual degree of indifference to its obligations to comply with U.S. banking rules? Could the fact that HSBC is a foreign bank have influenced its attitudes and behavior in

this respect? Could its foreign status have been a factor that the OCC took into account in imposing this agreement?

3. Why did HSBC consent to this order? Should the board of directors have done more to resist the OCC's demands that it comprehensively revamp its compliance program? As a practical matter, was there anything that the bank could have done to resist?

4. Notice that the bank neither admitted nor denied misconduct. It was pretty clear, however, that the agency believed the bank was a persistent abuser. Should the OCC have insisted that the bank admit some culpability? Why didn't it do so?

5. What does the OCC think caused the problems at HSBC? Part of the problem appears to have been lack of "tone at the top" in which the bank's leaders nurture a culture of compliance. What aspects of the consent decree appear directed at improving the tone at the top?

6. Another root cause of the deficiencies, in the OCC's opinion, appears to have been the failure on the part of the bank's senior officers and board of directors to manage change as the bank grew in size and complexity. What aspects of the consent decree appear designed to remediate this problem?

7. The OCC also implies that the bank had displayed a persistent habit of secrecy and non-reporting of problems. To what extent do the obligations imposed under this consent order address these deficiencies?

8. The subject of this consent order—HSBC Bank USA—is wholly owned by HSBC Group. As a practical matter, HSBC Group has the power to select HSBC Bank USA's directors and to dictate much of its activity. To what extent, if any, do the obligations of this order apply to the larger enterprise as opposed to the American chartered bank? If the broader enterprise is not affected, how effective is the relief imposed by this decree likely to be?

9. The excerpted order was one of several actions that the Comptroller issued against HSBC in 2012. In a different action, the Comptroller imposed a $500 million civil money penalty against HSBC for failing to fully implement a previous order that had required the bank to take actions to improve its Bank Secrecy Act compliance program. The fine was the largest ever imposed by the agency.

10. HSBC Bank's willingness to implement a compliance program was part of the consideration that it provided to the OCC in exchange for the agency dropping its effort to obtain even more onerous remedies. Would you recommend that firms not adopt compliance programs voluntarily, in order to hold back a "bargaining chip" to use in settlement negotiations after the firm is subject to an enforcement proceeding? What are the downsides to delay?

11. In general, when a company agrees to implement compliance reforms in the face of government civil enforcement actions, the quid pro quo is that the government will go easier on the company in terms of the penalty it demands. What if the company then engages in new, similar misconduct? How many times can it go to the well before the well runs dry—or, worse yet, becomes poisoned? Each agency has its own practices in this respect; the SEC's is that "remedial steps counsel in favor of a . . . reduced monetary sanction," but that "recidivism is taken into account."

12. When a defendant agrees to undertake governance changes, what resources does an agency have available to ensure that the defendant complies with the promise and that the compliance continues during the entire period of the remedy? Some agreements contain regular reporting requirements intended to update the agency on the defendant's performance of its promises; other agreements require the regulated entity to retain (and pay for) an independent private monitor. If these

are absent, the agency's principal source of information is its continuing oversight power.

13. What is the agency's remedy if it discovers that the defendant is not complying? Since the governance changes are typically embodied in an injunction issued by the court at the time it approves the agreement, the usual remedy if the defendant defaults on its governance and compliance promises is for the agency to bring proceedings for contempt of court. These proceedings, however, appear to be rare. Why do you think there are so few contempt proceedings?

14. The excerpted case involved a proceeding by a regulator against a bank. The use of enforcement proceedings as levers to induce firms to adopt compliance programs is not limited to the banking context, however. Far from it: Similar strategies are observed across the entire compliance landscape. We will encounter examples elsewhere in this book.

United States v. International Brotherhood of Teamsters, Chauffeurs, Warehousemen and Helpers of America, AFL-CIO

No. 988 Civ. 4486 (S.D.N.Y. Mar. 14, 1989)

. . . Whereas, the union defendants acknowledge that there have been allegations, sworn testimony and judicial findings of past problems with La Cosa Nostra corruption of various elements of the IBT; and

Whereas, the union defendants agree that it is imperative that the IBT, as the largest trade union in the free world, be maintained democratically, with integrity and for the sole benefit of its members and without unlawful outside influence;

It is hereby ordered and decreed that: . . .

PERMANENT INJUNCTION

[Defendant IBT Executive Board members] are hereby permanently enjoined from committing any acts of racketeering activity, as defined in 18 U.S.C. §1961 et seq., and from knowingly associating with any member or associate of the Colombo Organized Crime Family of La Cosa Nostra, the Genovese Organized Crime Family of La Cosa Nostra, the Gambino Organized Crime Family of La Cosa Nostra, the Lucchese Organized Crime Family of La Cosa Nostra, the Bonnano Organized Crime Family of La Cosa Nostra, any other Organized Crime Families of La Cosa Nostra or any other criminal group, or any person otherwise enjoined from participating in union affairs, and from obstructing or otherwise interfering with the work of the court-appointed officers or the Independent Review Board described herein . . . .

COURT-APPOINTED OFFICERS

The Court shall appoint three (3) officers—an Independent Administrator, an Investigations Officer and an Election Officer—to be identified and proposed by the Government and the union defendants, to oversee certain operations of the IBT as described herein. The parties shall jointly propose to the Court at least two persons for each of these three positions. Such proposal shall be presented to the Court within four weeks of the date of the entry of this Order, except that for good cause shown such period may be extended by the Court. Except as otherwise provided herein, the duties of those three officers shall be the following:

Disciplinary Authority — From the date of the Administrator's appointment until the termination of the Administrator's authority as set forth . . . herein, the Administrator shall have the same rights and powers as the IBT's General President and/or General Executive Board under the IBT's Constitution . . . to discharge those duties which relate to: disciplining corrupt or dishonest officers, agents, employees or members of the IBT or any of its affiliated entities (such as IBT Locals, Joint Councils and Area Conferences), and appointing temporary trustees to run the affairs of any such affiliated entities. The Investigations Officer shall have the authority to investigate the operation of the IBT or any of its affiliates and, with cause,

- To initiate disciplinary charges against any officer, member or employee of the IBT or any of its affiliates in the manner specified for members under the IBT Constitution and,
- To institute trusteeship proceedings for the purpose and in the manner specified in the IBT Constitution . . . .

Review Authority — From the date of the Administrator's appointment until the certification of the IBT elections to be conducted in 1991, the Administrator shall have the authority to veto whenever the Administrator reasonably believes that any of the actions or proposed actions listed below constitutes or furthers an act of racketeering activity within the definition of Title 18 U.S.C. §1961, or furthers or contributes to the association directly, or indirectly, of the IBT or any of its members with the LCN or elements thereof:

- any expenditures or proposed expenditure of International Union funds or transfer of International Union property approved by any officers, agents, representatives or employees of the IBT,
- any contract or proposed contract on behalf of the International Union, other than collective bargaining agreements, and
- any appointment or proposed appointments to International Union office of any officer, agent, representative or employee of the IBT . . . .

Access to Information — (i) The Investigations Officer shall have the authority to take such reasonable steps that are lawful and necessary in order to be fully informed about the activities of the IBT in accordance with the procedures as herein established. The Investigations Officer shall have the right:

- To examine books and records of the IBT and its affiliated, provided the entity to be examined receives three (3) business days advance notice in writing, and said entity has the right to have its representatives present during said examination.
- To attend meetings or portions of meetings of the General Executive Board relating in any way to any of the officer's rights or duties as set forth in this Order, provided that prior to any such meeting, the officer shall receive an agenda for the meeting and then give notice to the General President of the officer's anticipated attendance.
- To take and require sworn statements or sworn in-person examinations of any officer, member, or employee of the IBT provided the Investigations Officer has reasonable cause to take such a statement and provided further that the person to be examined receives at least ten (10) days advance notice in writing

and also has the right to be represented by an IBT member or legal counsel of his or her own choosing, during the course of said examination.

- To take, upon notice and application for cause made to this Court, which shall include affidavits in support thereto, and the opportunity for rebuttal affidavits, the sworn statements or sworn in person examination of persons who are agents of the IBT (and not covered in subparagraph (c) above).
- To retain an independent auditor to perform audits upon the books and records of the IBT or any of its affiliated entities (not including benefit funds subject to ERISA), provided said entity receives three (3) business days advance notice in writing and said entity has the right to have its representatives present during the conduct of said audit . . . .

The Independent Administrator, Investigations Officer and Election Officer shall each be provided with suitable office space at the IBT headquarters in Washington, D.C.

IBT Election — The IBT Constitution shall be deemed amended, and is hereby amended, to provide for the following new election procedures. . . .

The Election Officer shall supervise the IBT election described above to be conducted in 1991 and any special IBT elections that occur prior to the IBT elections to be conducted in 1991. In advance of each election, the Election Officer shall have the right to distribute materials about the election to the IBT membership. The Election Officer shall supervise the balloting process and certify the election results for each of these elections as promptly as possible after the balloting. Any disputes about the conduct and/or results of elections shall be resolved after hearing by the Administrator.

The union defendants consent to the Election Officer, at Government expense, to supervise the 1996 IBT elections. The union defendants further consent to the U.S. Department of Labor supervising any IBT elections or special elections to be conducted after 1991 for the office of the IBT General President, IBT General Secretary-Treasurer, IBT Vice President, and IBT Trustee . . . .

Reports to Membership — The Administrator shall have the authority to distribute materials at reasonable times to the membership of the IBT about the Administrator's activities. The reasonable cost of distribution of these materials shall be borne by the IBT. Moreover, the Administrator shall have the authority to publish a report in each issue of the International Teamster concerning the activities of the Administrator, Investigations Officer and Election Officer.

Reports to the Court — The Administrator shall report to the Court whenever the Administrator sees fit but, in any event, shall file with the Court a written report every three (3) months about the activities of the Administrator, Investigations Officer and Election Officer. A copy of all reports to the Court by the Administrator shall be served on plaintiff United States of America, the IBT's General President and duly designated IBT counsel.

Hiring Authority — The Administrator, the Investigations Officer and the Election Officer shall have the authority to employ accountants, consultants, experts, investigators or any other personnel necessary to assist in the proper discharge of their duties. Moreover, they shall have the authority to designate persons of their choosing to act on their behalf in performing any of their duties, as outlined in subparagraphs above. Whenever any of them wish to designate a person to act on their behalf, they shall give prior written notice of the designation to plaintiff United States of America, and the IBT's General President; and those parties shall then have the right, within fourteen (14) days of receipt of notice, to seek review by this Court of the designation, which shall otherwise take effect fourteen (14) days after receipt of notice.

Compensation and Expenses — The compensation and expenses of the Administrator, the Investigations Officer and the Election Officer (and any designee or persons hired by them) shall be paid by the IBT. Moreover, all costs associated with the activities of these three officials (and any designee or persons hired by them) shall be paid by the IBT . . . .

INDEPENDENT REVIEW BOARD

Following the certification of the 1991 election results, there shall be established and Independent Review Board, (hereinafter, referred to as the "Review Board"). Said Board shall consist of three members, one chosen by the Attorney General of the United States, one chosen by the IBT and a third person chosen by the Attorney General's designee and the IBT's designee. In the event of a vacancy, the replacement shall be selected in the same manner as the person who is being replaced was selected.

The Independent Review Board shall be authorized to hire a sufficient staff of investigators and attorneys to investigate adequately (1) any allegations of corruption, including bribery, embezzlement, extortion, loan sharking, [etc.], or (2) any allegations of domination or control or influence of any IBT affiliated, member or representative by La Cosa Nostra or any other organized crime entity or group, or (3) any failure to cooperate fully with the Independent Review Board in any investigation of the foregoing.

The Independent Review Board shall exercise such investigative authority as the General President and General Secretary-Treasurer are presently authorized and empowered to exercise pursuant to the IBT Constitution, as well as any and all applicable provisions of law.

All officers, members, employees and representatives of the IBT and its affiliated bodies shall cooperate fully with the Independent Review Board in the course of any investigation or proceeding undertaken by it. Unreasonable failure to cooperate with the Independent Review Board shall be deemed to be conduct which brings reproach upon the IBT and which is thereby within the Independent Review Board's investigatory and decisional authority.

Upon completion of an investigation, the Independent Review Board shall issue a written report detailing its findings, charges, and recommendations concerning the discipline of union officers, members, employees, and representatives and concerning the placing in trusteeship of any IBT subordinate body. Such written reports shall be available during business hours for public inspection at the IBT office in Washington, D.C.

Any findings, charges, or recommendations of the Independent Review Board regarding discipline or trusteeship matters shall be submitted in writing to an appropriate IBT entity (including designating a matter as an original jurisdiction case for General Executive Board review), with a copy sent to the General President and General Executive Board. The IBT entity to which a matter is referred shall thereupon promptly take whatever action is appropriate under the circumstances, as provided by the IBT Constitution and applicable law. Within 90 days of the referral, that IBT entity must make written findings setting forth the specific action taken and the reasons for that action.

The Independent Review Board shall monitor all matters which it has referred for action if, in its sole judgment, a matter has not been pursued and decided by the IBT entity to which the matter has been referred in a lawful, responsible, or timely matter, or that the resolution proposed by the relevant IBT entity is inadequate under the circumstances, the Independent Review Board shall notify the IBT affiliate involved of its view, and the reasons therefore. A copy of said notice shall be sent by the Independent Review Board, to the General President and the General Executive Board.

Within 10 days of the notice described in paragraph (f) above, the IBT entity involved shall set forth in writing any and all additional actions it has taken and/or will take to correct the defects set forth in said notice and a deadline by which said action may be completed. Immediately thereafter, the Independent Review Board shall issue a written determination concerning the adequacy of the additional action taken and/or proposed by the IBT entity involved. If the Independent Review Board concludes that the IBT entity involved has failed to take or propose satisfactory action to remedy the defects specified by the Independent Review Board's notice, the Independent Review Board shall promptly convene a hearing, after notice to all affected parties. All parties shall be permitted to present any facts, evidence, or testimony which is relevant to the issue before the Independent Review Board. Any such hearing shall be conducted under the rules and procedures generally applicable to labor arbitration hearings.

After a fair hearing has been conducted, the Independent Review Board shall issue a written decision which shall be sent to the General President, each member of the General Executive Board, and all affected parties.

The decision of the Independent Review Board shall be final and binding, and the General Executive Board shall take all action which is necessary to implement said decision, consistent with the IBT Constitution and applicable Federal laws.

The Independent Review Board shall have the right to examine and review the General Executive Board's implementation of the Independent Review Board's decisions; in the event the Independent Review Board is dissatisfied with the General Executive Board's implementation of any of its decisions, the Independent Review Board shall have the authority to take whatever steps are appropriate to insure proper implementation of any such decision.

The Independent Review Board shall be apprised of and have the authority to review any disciplinary or trusteeship decision of the General Executive Board, and shall have the right to affirm, modify, or reverse any such decision. The Independent Review Board's affirmance, modification, or reversal of any such General Executive Board decision shall be in writing and final and binding.

The IBT shall pay all costs and expenses of the Independent Review Board and its staff (including all salaries of Review Board members and staff). Invoices for all such costs and expense shall be directed to the General President for payment . . . .

APPLICATION TO COURT

This Court shall retain jurisdiction to supervise the activities of the Administrator and to entertain any future applications by the Administrator or the parties. This Court shall have exclusive jurisdiction to decide any and all issues relating to the Administrator's actions or authority pursuant to this order. In reviewing actions of the Administrator, the Court shall apply the same standard of review applicable to review of final federal agency action under the Administrative Procedure Act . . . .

NON-ADMISSION CLAUSE

Nothing herein shall be construed as an admission by any of the individual union defendants of any wrongdoing or breach of any legal or fiduciary duty or obligation in the discharge of their duties as IBT officers and members of the IBT General Executive Board . . . .

Questions and Comments

1. This settlement arose out of an action by the United States alleging that senior officials of the Teamsters, the largest labor union in the United States, was effectively under the control of the Mafia (referred to in the settlement document as ''La Cosa Nostra'' or ''LCN'').

2. The lawsuit was based on the ''RICO'' law, Racketeer Influenced and Corrupt Organizations Act, 18 U.S.C. §§1961-1968, an important statute designed to eliminate mob influence in legitimate business operations. RICO applies when there is shown to be a ''pattern of racketeering activity,'' defined to mean at least two of a laundry list of criminal activities commonly associated with organized crime. The Act prohibits anyone from investing proceeds of such activity in an enterprise, obtaining an interest in an enterprise through such activity, running an enterprise through such activity, or conspiring to commit any of the foregoing offenses. RICO is enforceable both through criminal prosecutions and civil lawsuits, including lawsuits by the government to prohibit or restrain a defendant from violating the statute. The settlement excerpted above is the result of a civil RICO lawsuit initiated by the United States Department of Justice.

3. It is one thing to obtain a consent decree; it is another to enforce it. The IBT initially resisted the decree at nearly every turn both at the national level and at the level of many locals. Over time the national union seems to have moderated its opposition, although frictions remain. For a fascinating account, see James B. Jacobs & Kerry T. Cooperman, *Breaking the Devil's Pact: The Battle to Free the Teamsters from the Mob* (2011).

4. Notice in the excerpt above the details on who pays for enforcing the decree. These were important because if the government had paid, the union's leaders could have conducted a scorched earth campaign to wear down the government's resistance. Even with the requirement that the union pay most of these costs, the decree has been expensive to administer: Jacobs and Cooperman estimate that total remediation costs through 2010 have exceeded $100 million.

5. More than 500 IBT officers have been removed or resigned on account of the efforts of the court-appointed disciplinary monitor; and the elections monitor and staff have developed and implemented election rules that arguably make the IBT one of the most democratic unions in the country. Nevertheless, there is always the threat that mob influence could return. At what point would proof of genuine and lasting reforms be sufficient to warrant terminating the decree?

6. Notice that none of the individual defendants admitted to any wrongful actions. Should the government have agreed to this provision, given that it appeared fairly clear that someone in the union was involved?

7. The *IBT* case is not unique: The government has used its power under civil RICO to seek equitable relief against ongoing or future violations in actions against more than 20 local, regional, and international unions across the country. *See* James

B. Jacobs, *Mobsters, Unions and Feds: The Mafia and the American Labor Movement* (2007).

C. REGULATION OF COMPLIANCE OFFICERS

The chief compliance officer is a key part of an organization's compliance program. Lawmakers, regulators, and prosecutors understandably take a strong interest in this office and its functioning.

1. Requirements to Establish and Empower Compliance Officers

Securities and Exchange Commission Final Rule: Compliance Programs of Investment Companies and Investment Advisers

Dec. 17, 2003

CHIEF COMPLIANCE OFFICER

Investment Advisers

Rule 206(4)-7 requires each adviser registered with the Commission to designate a chief compliance officer to administer its compliance policies and procedures. An adviser's chief compliance officer should be competent and knowledgeable regarding the Advisers Act and should be empowered with full responsibility and authority to develop and enforce appropriate policies and procedures for the firm. Thus, the compliance officer should have a position of sufficient seniority and authority within the organization to compel others to adhere to the compliance policies and procedures.

Investment Companies

Rule 38a-1 requires each fund to appoint a chief compliance officer who is responsible for administering the fund's policies and procedures approved by the board under the rule. A fund's chief compliance officer should be competent and knowledgeable regarding the federal securities laws and should be empowered with full responsibility and authority to develop and enforce appropriate policies and procedures for the fund. The chief compliance officer of a fund, like the chief compliance officer of an investment adviser, should have sufficient seniority and authority to compel others to adhere to the compliance policies and procedures.

The rule contains several provisions . . . designed to promote the independence of the chief compliance officer from the management of the fund. First, the chief compliance officer will serve in her position at the pleasure of the fund's board of directors, which can remove her if it loses confidence in her effectiveness. The fund board (including a majority of independent directors) must approve the designation of the chief compliance officer, and must approve her compensation (or any changes in her compensation). The board (including a majority of the independent directors) can remove the chief compliance officer from her responsibilities at any time, and can prevent the adviser or another service provider from doing so.

Second, the chief compliance officer will report directly to the board of directors. She must annually furnish the board with a written report on the operation of the fund's policies and procedures and those of its service providers. The report must address, at a minimum: (i) the operation of the policies and procedures of the fund and each service provider since the last report, (ii) any material changes to the policies and procedures since the last report, (iii) any recommendations for material changes to the policies and procedures as a result of the annual review, and (iv) any material compliance matters since the date of the last report. We have added a definition of the term "material compliance matter" to the rule, to clarify that the report should inform the board of those compliance matters about which the fund's board reasonably needs to know in order to oversee fund compliance.

Third, we are requiring that the chief compliance officer meet in executive session with the independent directors at least once each year, without anyone else (such as fund management or interested directors) present. The executive session creates an opportunity for the chief compliance officer and the independent directors to speak freely about any sensitive compliance issues of concern to any of them, including any reservations about the cooperativeness or compliance practices of fund management.

Fourth, we have added a provision to protect the chief compliance officer from undue influence by fund service providers seeking to conceal their or others' non-compliance with the federal securities laws. Rule 38a-1 prohibits the fund's officers, directors, employees or its adviser, principal underwriter, or any person acting under the direction of these persons, from directly or indirectly taking any action to coerce, manipulate, mislead or fraudulently influence the fund's chief compliance officer in the performance of her responsibilities under the rule.

The appointment of a chief compliance officer with overall responsibility for management of a fund complex's compliance program is a key element of the investor protections we are today adopting. Some commenters representing fund management companies urged us to permit funds to continue to use multiple compliance managers employed by different service providers, rely on the policies of the fund service providers, and omit the requirement that fund boards approve the compliance officer. These commenters would have us maintain funds' current approach to compliance management. Current practices, however, balkanize responsibility for fund compliance and isolate fund boards from compliance personnel, thus impeding boards' abilities to exercise their oversight responsibilities effectively. We decline to accept current practices, which we believe have contributed to the serious compliance lapses that are now the subject of our enforcement actions.

We have observed that executives at service providers have overruled their own compliance personnel because of business considerations. For example, some fund advisers have continued to permit investors with whom they had other business relationships to engage in harmful market timing in fund shares after compliance personnel and portfolio managers brought the market timing activity to their attention. These compliance personnel may not have had access to fund directors or, having been overruled by their own management, may have felt they were not in a position to approach the board.

To address these concerns, rule 38a-1 provides fund boards with direct access to a single person with overall compliance responsibility for the fund who answers directly to the board. The rule provides the board with a powerful tool to exercise its oversight responsibilities over fund compliance matters. The new rule also strengthens the hand of compliance personnel by establishing a direct line of reporting to fund boards that is not controlled by management. We have observed that compliance failures have occurred when a fund service provider has denied information to the fund's board, or has been less than forthright, because the service provider viewed full disclosure as detrimental to its own interests. Under the new rule, the chief compliance officer will be responsible for keeping the board apprised of significant compliance events at the fund or its service providers and for advising the board of needed changes in the fund's compliance program.

We expect that a fund's chief compliance officer will often be employed by the fund's investment adviser or administrator. We are not adopting a requirement that the chief compliance officer be employed by only the fund because we believe that such a provision would actually weaken her effectiveness. Funds today typically have no employees, and delegate management and administrative functions, including the compliance function, to one or more service providers. If we were to preclude the chief compliance officer from being an employee of an adviser or any other service provider, she would be divorced from all fund operations. The adviser's chief compliance officer would continue to administer the adviser's compliance programs, and the role of the fund's chief compliance officer would be limited to oversight of the service providers' compliance policies and providing advice to the board on their operation. As a result, the fund's chief compliance officer would be almost entirely dependent on information filtered through the senior management of the fund's adviser rather than, for example, information received directly from a trading desk. Moreover, fund management would be unlikely to consult with an "outside" compliance officer on a prospective business decision to ascertain the compliance implications.

We recognize, however, that a chief compliance officer who is an employee of the fund's investment adviser might be conflicted in her duties, and that the investment adviser's business interests might discourage the adviser from making forthright disclosure to fund directors of its compliance failures. The rule, as adopted, is designed to address these concerns by requiring a fund's chief compliance officer to report directly to the board. The board, and the board alone, can discharge the officer if she fails to live up to the position. Thus, a chief compliance officer who fails to fully inform the board of a material compliance failure, or who fails to aggressively pursue non-compliance within the service provider, would risk her position. She would also risk her career, because it would be unlikely for another board of directors to approve such a person as chief compliance officer.

The chief compliance officer, in exercising her responsibilities under the rule, will oversee the fund's service providers, which will have their own compliance officials. A chief compliance officer should diligently administer this oversight responsibility by taking steps to assure herself that each service provider has implemented effective compliance policies and procedures administered by competent personnel. The chief compliance officer should be familiar with each service provider's operations and understand those aspects of their operations that expose the fund to compliance risks. She should maintain an active working relationship with each service provider's compliance personnel. Arrangements with the service provider should provide the fund's chief compliance officer with direct access to these personnel, and should provide the compliance officer with periodic reports and special reports in the event of compliance problems. In addition, the fund's contracts with its service providers might also require service providers to certify periodically that they are in compliance with applicable federal securities laws, or could provide for third-party audits arranged by the fund to evaluate the effectiveness of the service provider's compliance controls. The chief compliance officer could conduct (or hire third parties to conduct) statistical analyses of a service provider's performance of its duties to detect potential compliance failures.

The SEC's amended rule prohibits lying to or impeding an investment company's chief compliance officer. Violation of this requirement could lead to severe sanctions, including fines and an order barring an offender from working in the securities industry. The following excerpt provides an example.

Questions and Comments

1. Note the provisions designed to protect a fund's chief compliance officer against possible interference by fund management. Why were these considered necessary? How effective will this removal power be if the fund's board of directors, even if formally independent, is actually dominated by the adviser?

2. The SEC says that it is acceptable — even desirable — for an investment company's chief compliance officer to be employed by the investment adviser rather than the fund. How can a chief compliance officer carry out a duty of undivided loyalty to the fund when she is employed by the fund's investment adviser?

2. Obligations to Compliance Officers

Securities and Exchange Commission, In the Matter of Carl D. Johns

Release No. 3655, Aug. 27, 2013

Respondent Carl D. Johns, 49 years old, is a resident of Louisville, Colorado. From January 1999 to January 2011, Johns was employed in various capacities by Boulder Investment Advisers, LLC ("BIA"), including assistant portfolio manager. Johns, on behalf of BIA and an affiliated adviser, Rocky Mountain Advisers, LLC ("RMA," together with BIA, the "Advisers"), assisted in the management of the portfolios for, and served as an officer of, several registered investment companies. On January 9, 2011, Johns was placed on administrative leave and, on January 12, 2011, he resigned from his positions with the Advisers and the Boulder Funds . . . .

While employed by the Advisers, Johns engaged in active personal trading in securities, including securities of companies held or to be acquired by the Boulder Funds. From 2006 through 2010, Johns executed approximately 850 personal securities transactions. In many instances, Johns held the securities for only a few days. Rule 17j-1(d) under the Investment Company Act required Johns to submit quarterly reports of his personal securities transactions and annual reports of his securities holdings. In addition, the Advisers' and the Boulder Funds' joint Code of Ethics ("Code of Ethics"), applicable to Johns, contained further restrictions on when and how Johns could trade in securities. The Code of Ethics (i) required that all securities transactions be pre-cleared by the chief compliance officer, subject to certain limited exceptions, (ii) restricted trading in securities that the Boulder Funds were buying or selling, and (iii) required annual certification of compliance with the Code of Ethics. During the relevant period, Johns certified annually that he received, read, and understood the Code of Ethics.

From 2006 through 2010, Johns failed to comply with the Commission's reporting requirements and the Code of Ethics. Johns did not pre-clear or report approximately 640 of his trades, including at least 91 trades in securities held or to be acquired by the fund, . . . and 14 trades that did not comply with the Code of Ethics' restrictions on trading in securities that the Boulder Funds were buying or selling.

To conceal his personal securities trading, Johns submitted false quarterly and annual reports and falsely certified his annual compliance with the Code of Ethics. Johns' efforts to conceal his trading from the Advisers also included physically altering brokerage statements, trade confirmations, and pre-clearance approvals that were then submitted to the Advisers. For example:

- Johns created several documents that purported to be pre-clearance requests approved by the Advisers' and the Boulder Funds' chief compliance officer ("CCO"), but that were not actually reviewed or approved by the CCO. Johns created these false pre-clearance approvals to cover-up instances in which his year-end annual report contained securities transactions that were not pre-cleared.
- Johns altered trade confirmations submitted to the Advisers by backdating the dates of the securities transactions. Johns backdated the trade confirmations to make it falsely appear as though pre-clearances were granted in advance of the transactions.
- Johns manually deleted securities holdings listed on his brokerage statements before submitting them to the Advisers. Johns did this to avoid disclosing securities purchases that were not pre-cleared.

In late 2010, the CCO identified certain irregularities in the documents Johns submitted to the Advisers detailing his personal securities transactions. Based on those irregularities, the CCO made certain inquiries of Johns to ascertain his full compliance with the Code of Ethics.

In response, Johns misled the CCO. Johns falsely told the CCO that certain of his brokerage accounts were closed, when in fact they remained open and reflected trades that were not pre-cleared as required by the Code of Ethics. Johns also accessed the hard copy file of his previously submitted brokerage statements and physically altered them to create the false impression that Johns' trading was in compliance with the Code of Ethics . . . .

Rule 38a-1(c) under the Investment Company Act prohibits an officer, director, or employee of a fund, or its investment adviser, from, directly or indirectly, taking any action to coerce, manipulate, mislead, or fraudulently influence the fund's chief compliance officer in the performance of his or her duties under the Investment Company Act.

As a result of the conduct described above, Johns willfully violated Rule 38a-1(c) under the Investment Company Act. Johns misled the Advisers' and Boulder Funds' CCO in the performance of her duties by misrepresenting the status of certain of his brokerage accounts and tampering with the Boulder Funds' compliance files.

In view of the foregoing, the Commission deems it appropriate and in the public interest to impose the sanctions agreed to in Respondent's Offer. Accordingly, . . . it is hereby Ordered that:

- Respondent cease and desist from committing or causing any violations and any future violations of Section 17(j) of the Investment Company Act and Rules 17j-1 and 38a-1 promulgated thereunder.

- Respondent be, and hereby is: barred from association with any broker, dealer, investment adviser, municipal securities dealer, municipal advisor, transfer agent, or nationally recognized statistical rating organization; and prohibited from serving or acting as an employee, officer, director, member of an advisory board, investment adviser or depositor of, or principal underwriter for, a registered investment company or affiliated person of such investment adviser, depositor, or principal underwriter, with the right to apply for reentry after five (5) years to the appropriate self-regulatory organization, or if there is none, to the Commission.
- Any reapplication for association by the Respondent will be subject to the applicable laws and regulations governing the reentry process, and reentry may be conditioned upon a number of factors . . . .
- Respondent shall, within 20 days of the entry of this Order, pay disgorgement of $231,169, prejudgment interest of $23,889, and a civil money penalty in the amount of $100,000 to the United States Treasury . . . .

Questions and Comments

1. What are the pros and cons of making it an independent offense to deceive or interfere with a compliance officer?

2. Would you recommend that a requirement like this be adopted for compliance programs across the board?

3. Liability of Compliance Officers

Compliance officers face significant and increasing potential liability in the performance of their jobs. Their exposure comes in three main forms. First, a compliance officer faces sanctions if she actively and knowingly engages in illegal conduct. This form of liability is not problematic since, if the compliance officer is a knowing participant, she can be held liable or sanctioned like any other employee.

The amount of the appropriate sanction against a compliance officer for misconduct in office can be a delicate issue. On the one hand, because compliance officers are a key line of defense in protecting their companies against illegal conduct, there is a strong public interest in deterring illegal behavior by such individuals. The problem is not only that if they behave improperly they won't catch violations; it is also that the behavior of compliance officers sends a signal to the rest of the organization about expected standards of behavior. These considerations counsel for particularly harsh sanctions for proven violations. On the other hand, it is also easy for a company to make a compliance officer a scapegoat and thereby deflect responsibility away from others who may have had a greater role in the misconduct. Compliance officers, moreover, have not always exercised authority commensurate with the importance of their jobs; they may find themselves being pushed around by more powerful figures within the organization. Extremely high sanctions against compliance officers, moreover, may deter even good people from desiring to work in the compliance space, since even people who do their best can get caught up in allegations of systematic wrongdoing.

Regulators are increasingly focusing on the CCO as a key control officer inside complex organizations—and imposing regulatory requirements that reflect this perception. The following excerpts illustrate the trend.

In the Matter of Judy K. Wolf
SEC Administrative Proceeding File No. 3-16195

Aug. 5, 2015

. . . Wolf is sixty-two years old and resides in St. Louis, Missouri. She holds a degree in finance from Washington University in St. Louis and began working in the securities industry in 1979 . . . . From 2004 to June 13, 2013, Wolf worked at Wells Fargo and its predecessor entities as a compliance consultant in the Retail Control Group of the compliance department, where she eventually earned approximately $61,000 per year. During her time at Wells Fargo, Wolf worked in a cubicle and was supervised by Roseann St John (St John) and Modesto Moya (Moya), St John's supervisor . . . . Wolf has been unemployed since June 2013.

In 2010, Prado was a registered representative and associated person of Wells Fargo in a branch office in Miami . . . . The Commission filed a complaint against Prado on September 20, 2012, in the United States District Court for Southern District of New York, charging him with insider trading in Burger King securities . . . . The Commission accused Prado and his tippees of reaping over $2 million in total insider trading profits. The Commission obtained a final judgment by default against Prado on January 7, 2014. The final judgment permanently enjoined Prado from violating [securities laws] and ordered him to disgorge $397,110.01 plus prejudgment interest of $41,622.90, and imposed civil penalties of $5,195,500.

Wells Fargo was a dually registered broker-dealer and investment adviser at all relevant times . . . . Wells Fargo consented to: a cease-and-desist order finding that it had willfully violated [securities laws]; a censure; a $5 million civil penalty; and an order directing it to comply with certain undertakings . . . .Wells Fargo also admitted . . . that it failed to adequately maintain or enforce its policies and procedures (Policies) and that it had produced an altered document to the Commission in January 2013 . . . .

Wolf was the Wells Fargo compliance department employee responsible for conducting its insider trading reviews . . . . Although Wells Fargo's Policies required contacting the relevant branch involved and discussing the situation with the branch manager if any red flags were found, Wolf had the discretion to close a file without further escalation if she felt no further action was required. To initiate reviews, Wolf relied primarily on news stories. Wolf would typically print the Yahoo! Finance webpage for the security at issue in each review she conducted, because the page showed both the stock movement and the news headlines . . . .

On September 2, 2010, it was publicly announced that 3G Capital would acquire Burger King and take it private. [Burger King stock opened 24 percent higher on the day of the announcement.] That same day, Wolf began her review of pre-acquisition announcement trading in Burger King securities at Wells Fargo by Prado and three of his customers. In that review, Wolf determined: (a) Prado and his customers represented the top four positions in Burger King securities firm-wide; (b) Prado and his customers bought Burger King securities within ten days prior to the announcement, including on the same days; (c) the profits by Prado and his customers each exceeded the $5,000 threshold specified in the Policies; (d) both Prado and Burger King were located in Miami; and (e) Prado, one or more of his customers, and 3G Capital were Brazilian. Wolf conducted an "enhanced review," which included determining if any of Prado's clients were board members or officers of Burger King. Wolf determined there were no "red flags" requiring follow-up and that none of the trading was out of character . . . . Wolf did not: follow up with Prado or his branch manager about Prado's trading; contact the branch; escalate the review to her manager; or take any further steps. Wolf closed the review with "no findings."

In 2012, the Commission initiated an investigation into Prado's insider trading. On June 13, 2012, as part of that investigation, Commission staff requested . . . that Wells Fargo produce, among other things, "[a]ll documents concerning any inquiry made by any representative of [Wells Fargo], including but not limited to the compliance department, relating to trades in Burger King securities made by [Prado] and his response to any such inquiry." . . .

On September 28, 2012, with St John's permission, Wolf had her Burger King insider trading review file retrieved from Iron Mountain [a document storage facility]. Once retrieved, Wolf kept her Burger King review file in her cubicle . . . .

On December 28, 2012, at 8:41 A.M., Wolf added two sentences (the Two Sentences) to the "Contacts and Notes" section of her Log pertaining to Burger King, which read: "Rumors of acquisition by a private equity group had been circulating for several weeks prior to the announcement. The stock price was up 15% on 9/1/*12*, the day prior to the announcement." (emphasis added). Prior iterations of the Log, dated before December 28, 2012, do not show the Two Sentences, and the metadata associated with the Log shows that Wolf was the last person to update the Log . . . .

On January 11, 2013, Wells Fargo produced documents relating to Wolf's Burger King insider trading review, including the cover page containing the Two Sentences. Prior to Wells Fargo's production on January 11, 2013, Wolf did not tell anyone at Wells Fargo that she had added the Two Sentences to the Log, or that she had created the cover page from the altered Log.

After the Commission staff requested Wolf's testimony, Wells Fargo advised Wolf that she would be provided with counsel, namely, Toben, who represented Wells Fargo and other individuals in the investigation, and Stephen Young (Young), who had previously represented Prado in the investigation and continued to represent Wells Fargo. Wolf signed engagement letters with Young and Toben on March 8, 2013, and March 11, 2013, respectively. On March 11, 2013, Wolf met with Toben (with Young participating by telephone) to prepare for her testimony on March 13, 2013 . . . . Wolf did not tell Toben or Young that she had added the Two Sentences to the Log or cover page approximately ten weeks earlier.

Wolf testified on March 13, 2013, via video conference, and was the first Wells Fargo individual to testify regarding her September 2010 Burger King insider trading review . . . . Wolf denied altering the Log used to create the cover page after September 2010. When questioned about the discrepancy in the years referenced in the Log entry—i.e., "09/02/10" compared to "9/1/12"—Wolf testified that "9/1/12" was a typographical error she made in September 2010. The interview was "a little bit traumatic" for Wolf because the Division attorneys were "pretty agitated," in particular when talking about the cover sheet, which Wolf had not expected.

The next day, on March 14, 2013, Commission staff requested production of the metadata for the Log, as well as any version of the Log that existed prior to January 14, 2013. On March 25, 2013, Wells Fargo advised the Commission staff that the Log had been altered on December 28, 2012, prior to its production to the Commission.

Wolf was not aware at that time that Wells Fargo had produced documents to the Commission showing her prior testimony had been false.

On March 27, 2013, Commission staff sent a subpoena to Toben, requiring Wolf to produce, among other things, documents relating to her Burger King insider trading review by April 19, 2013, and to personally appear again for testimony in the investigation on April 30, 2013. Toben and Young subsequently informed Wolf that they could no longer represent her because Wells Fargo's interests and Wolf's were "no longer aligned." Wells Fargo placed Wolf on administrative leave in late March 2013. Wolf engaged her present counsel on April 10, 2013. On June 13, 2013, Wells Fargo terminated Wolf, citing "significant concern [regarding] alteration of documents." . . .

Wolf testified before the Commission staff again on April 10, 2014, and explained that she had "made a mistake" in her March 13, 2013, testimony. She testified that she left the March 13, 2013, interview feeling very poorly and decided to check the September 2010 month-end report "snapshot" to verify "whether or not [she] really had put [the Two Sentences] in 2010 or if it was some other time." Upon doing so, Wolf testified that she realized that the Two Sentences were not in the Log in September 2010. Wolf then checked the other 2010 insider trading review files stored in the box retrieved from Iron Mountain and noticed that they did not contain cover sheets, also contrary to her March 13, 2013, testimony . . . .

The evidence showed that Wolf, a seasoned compliance consultant who had been in the securities industry for over thirty years and held four securities licenses, was well trained and aware of the importance of keeping scrupulously accurate records for Wells Fargo, a regulated entity. Although Wolf's $61,000 salary is not indicative of a high-level employee, in practice Wolf exercised a key compliance function, having sole responsibility for conducting insider trading reviews and discretion on whether to escalate such reviews or not. Thus, Wells Fargo relied on Wolf to serve as the gatekeeper for detecting insider trading, a crucial role within the compliance department . . . .

Given Wolf's nearly decade-long experience as a compliance professional and her knowledge of the importance of maintaining meticulous records, Wolf "must have been aware" that adding the Two Sentences to her Log, without indicating when the addition had been made, was misleading because it gave the impression that the Two Sentences had been present in the Log in 2010 . . . . The record similarly belies Wolf's assertion that when she first testified in 2012 she did not remember having altered the Log ten weeks prior, and therefore assumed she must have added the Two Sentences in 2010 . . . . Thus, Wolf's assertion that she did not realize her testimony had been incorrect until she retrieved the 2010 month-end report and saw that the Two Sentences were not present is simply not credible. The more plausible explanation is that upon seeing how aggressive the Division attorneys were during her testimony with regard to the date she added the Two Sentences, Wolf panicked and sought to verify if there was a way her alteration would be uncovered. Upon realizing that it would, she then claimed it had been a "mistake." . . .

Wolf's failure to inform the Division during her initial testimony that the Log was a document routinely updated, her unequivocal testimony at that time that she had not altered the Log after 2010, and her admission to altering the Log only after she realized the Commission was focusing on it, demonstrate that Wolf must have understood the wrongfulness of her actions. Moreover, although Wolf conceded at the hearing that falsification of records is wrong, that "there are things that [she] could have done better," and that she wished she had not closed her Burger King review with "no findings" in 2010, Wolf continues to maintain that she is not culpable because she "[did] not alter[] documents for purposes of misleading anyone or for purposes of falsifying documentation." While Wolf sincerely regrets the consequences resulting from her alteration of the Log, and the profound effect it has had on her life, she does not recognize the wrongful nature of her misconduct.

On the other hand, Wolf's alteration of the Log was an isolated event. Although Wolf was not initially forthcoming about having altered the Log, and thereby prolonged the period that the truth was hidden, her violation was limited to the addition of the Two Sentences to the Log and cover sheet, and was thus neither a recurrent nor widespread offense. Nor does her hearing testimony transform her misconduct, which surely took no more than a few minutes to complete, into a recurrent infraction. Wolf also provided assurances against future violations. Wolf credibly testified that she has no desire to ever work in the securities industry again, and that she does not believe she would even be able to because of the allegations in this proceeding. Since her termination by Wells Fargo, Wolf has been unable to find employment, and at age sixty-two, is functionally retired. For these same reasons, Wolf is not, and is unlikely to ever be, in an occupation presenting opportunities for committing securities violations . . . .

I do not condone Wolf's misconduct, or her deceit in attempting to cover it up. As an experienced compliance professional, Wolf knew of the importance of ensuring the integrity of records, and nevertheless purposefully altered the Log after the fact to make it appear that her past review had been more thorough than it was. Wolf must have known there was a strong likelihood that her altered documents would end up in the hands of the Commission, which would be misled into thinking that the produced Log was the same as the Log that existed in 2010. She knew that it is wrong to mislead Commission staff while testifying under oath.

But overall, Wolf's violation was not egregious and it caused no proven harm to investors or the marketplace. [T]here is literally no evidence that Wolf's alteration of the Log materially impeded the Division's investigation of Prado . . . . [N]o documents were destroyed, Wolf timely produced all documents requested of her, Wolf's Log alteration was minimal and the cover sheet simply duplicated what was already in the file, and, most importantly, there is no evidence that Wolf's misconduct made any material difference to the investigation of Prado. Nor did her violation have any effect on investors or the marketplace. Wolf may have violated the law, but she did not do so egregiously.

The weightiest public interest consideration, however, is deterrence. To be sure, remedial sanctions "provide specific deterrence even where respondents may no longer work in the industry." But Wolf has persuasively shown that she believes she has no realistic chance of ever working in the securities industry again, even without the imposition of remedial sanctions. On the facts of this case, the incremental specific deterrent effect of a sanction is vanishingly small. As for general deterrence, there is, of course, a "need to deter . . . other persons." On the facts of this case, however, I am satisfied that any remedial sanction, no matter how small, will not be an effective general deterrent. This is principally because of Wolf's status at Wells Fargo. She was low-ranking, relatively low-paid, supervised no one, and worked in a cubicle. Of all the individuals at Wells Fargo who contributed to its compliance failures, the only one charged individually was notably low-ranking.

By sanctioning only Wolf — who, to her credit, does not blame anyone else for her misconduct, but whose testimony suggests that at least St John and possibly

Moya could have been charged with the same misconduct—the rest of the securities industry could view this proceeding as proof that Wolf's violation was isolated and non-systemic. That is, if Wolf is sanctioned, there is a likelihood that others in the industry will perceive Wolf as simply a bad apple, a low status worker who unilaterally caused Wells Fargo to violate the law, and will see no need to examine their own practices and corporate cultures. In fact, this would be a misperception, as the settled proceeding against Wells Fargo amply demonstrates. Wells Fargo clearly had much deeper and more systemic problems than one bad apple . . . . [T]here is a likelihood that others in the securities industry will focus on the superficial aspects of this proceeding, rather than on the details of Wolf's misconduct in the context of Wells Fargo's overall practices. Thus, any sanction here will not only fail to have the desired general deterrent effect, but may actually be counterproductive.

There is one additional consideration: the fact that Wolf worked in compliance. Obviously, compliance professionals are subject to the securities laws like everyone else. But Wolf is correct to complain that in compliance, "the risk is much too high for the compensation." In my experience, firms tend to compensate compliance personnel relatively poorly, especially compared to other associated persons possessing the supervisory securities licenses compliance personnel typically have, likely because their work does not generate profits directly. But because of their responsibilities, compliance personnel receive a great deal of attention in investigations, and every time a violation is detected there is, quite naturally, a tendency for investigators to inquire into the reasons that compliance did not detect the violation first, or prevent it from happening at all. The temptation to look to compliance for the "low hanging fruit," however, should be resisted. There is a real risk that excessive focus on violations by compliance personnel will discourage competent persons from going into compliance, and thereby undermine the purpose of compliance programs in general. That is, "we should strive to avoid the perverse incentives that will naturally flow from targeting compliance personnel who are willing to run into the fires that so often occur at regulated entities." . . .

Again, I do not condone Wolf's misconduct. Neither the Division nor the Commission as a whole should tolerate falsified records or knowingly false testimony, and the Division was quite right to at least investigate Wolf. But now that the evidence has been fully aired, it is clear that sanctioning Wolf in any fashion would be overkill. Accordingly, no sanction will be imposed.

Questions and Comments

1. What do you think of Wolf's initial investigation? Were there red flags of potential violations? Was she right to close the review without escalating the matter?

2. Why did Wolf add the two extra sentences to her log? What did she hope to gain?

3. Do you agree with the judge's determination not to impose any penalty, given his conclusion that Wolf had altered the file and then repeatedly lied about having done so in testimony to the SEC?

4. The judge distinguishes between specific and general deterrence. What is the difference, and how did it play a role in the analysis of an appropriate sanction for Ms. Wolf? What benefit is achieved by not punishing a compliance officer who knowingly violated the law in the performance of her duties? What message was the judge seeking to convey—and to whom?

5. This case reflects a stereotype of the status of compliance departments that is rapidly becoming obsolete — as sleepy backwaters inhabited by unimaginative, underpaid, overstressed, and demoralized functionaries who are playing out the years until retirement. Today, compliance department personnel in many institutions have much more exciting and responsible jobs than the one assigned to Wolf, exercise substantially greater power and authority, and participate to a larger extent in strategic decisions affecting the organizations in which they work. But they are still overstressed!

6. Did Toben and Young behave ethically in representing Wolf, or in casting her aside when the alteration of documents came to light? The record is not clear as to what warnings, if any, the attorneys gave to Wolf regarding the scope and limits of their representation. What would you have done if you had been assigned by Wells to represent her in connection with her testimony to the SEC?

7. What do you think of Wells Fargo's compliance program? Was it wise to vest so much responsibility in a low-level official who "worked in cubicle" and made $61,000 a year, as compared with the millions per year earned by some of the brokers she was overseeing? The SEC didn't think much of the company's program; in fact this was a principal basis for its actions against Wells Fargo that resulted in censure and a $5 million fine. The SEC had this to say:

> One of the ways Wells Fargo Advisors sought to prevent the misuse of material nonpublic information received by registered representatives and advisory personnel from firm customers and advisory clients was by conducting "look back" reviews of trading in employee accounts and in customer and client accounts after market-moving announcements to detect whether trades may have been based on material nonpublic information . . . . Wells Fargo Advisors' policies and procedures with respect to conducting "lookback" reviews were not reasonably designed because the Retail Control Group ("RCG"), a unit in the firm's compliance department, was designated as having primary, if not sole, responsibility for conducting the look back reviews even though other departments within the firm often had relevant information. No other units had a designated role or were mentioned in the firm's policies and procedures.
>
> The manner in which the policies and procedures were designed affected the Burger King review. Multiple units within the firm received indications suggesting that the registered representative was misusing material nonpublic information obtained from a customer to trade in Burger King securities. Because of a lack of assigned responsibility or coordination, each of these units failed to: (a) recognize the significance of those indications; (b) properly consider them; and (c) elevate those indications within their own group or communicate with other groups responsible for conducting surveillance. As a result, the way in which the policies and procedures were designed caused Wells Fargo Advisors not to recognize several red flags that its representative was engaging in insider trading in Burger King securities.
>
> In addition to the inadequate design of the policies and procedures, Wells Fargo Advisors did not effectively maintain and enforce them. Wells Fargo Advisors' failure to implement the policies and procedures occurred in myriad ways. For example, although the policies and procedures required the RCG to contact the branch manager if an employee's trading raised red flags, sometimes the RCG contacted the branch manager and other times, such as the Burger King review, it did not. Additionally, although the policies and procedures required "daily review to identify situations when profit or avoidance of loss could most likely result from trading prior to the public release of information," for a ten month period the RCG failed to perform reviews in a timely manner of at least 40 instances of possible insider trading flagged for review.

During an investigation, Commission staff formally requested that Wells Fargo Advisors produce all documents relating to reviews of trading by the registered representative who traded in Burger King securities. When Wells Fargo Advisors produced documents in response to the staff's request, documents relating to the RCG review of the Burger King trading were not produced. Wells Fargo Advisors unreasonably delayed for six months producing documents relating to the RCG review without any explanation why they were not produced previously.

When the documents were produced, the firm failed to produce an accurate record of the review as it existed at the time of the staff's request. Instead, the firm produced a document that had been altered by an employee after the Commission staff issued its follow up request. When questions arose surrounding the altered document, Wells Fargo Advisors placed the employee on administrative leave and eventually terminated this employee.

Securities and Exchange Commission Release No. 73175, In the Matter of Wells Fargo Advisors LLC (Sept. 22, 2014). How would you reform Wells Fargo Advisors' insider trading compliance operation, if you were in charge?

8. In 2013, the New York Department of Financial Services (NYDFS) imposed a $250 million penalty on Bank of Tokyo-Mitsubishi UFJ (BTMU), a Japanese institution, in connection with violations of U.S. sanctions legislation. That order was premised in part on findings of an independent consultant, PricewaterhouseCoopers, which had examined the transaction records. Later the regulator learned that a senior compliance manager at the bank had persuaded PwC to water down its findings. The result was a new round of charges that resulted in another fine of $315 million. The settlement included the bank's agreement to fire the senior compliance manager and to remove two other senior compliance officials from involvement in United States matters. Even more significantly, the bank agreed to relocate its anti-money laundering and sanctions-related activities to New York, and further agreed that these programs would have U.S. compliance oversight over all transactions affecting the bank's New York branch, including transactions performed outside the United States that "affect" the New York branch. As a practical matter, most foreign banks, presumably including BTMU, clear dollar transactions through their New York branches. The apparent result of the agreement, therefore, was that the New York State regulator and the Federal Reserve Board assumed regulatory authority over a large segment of the bank's worldwide compliance function. *See* New York Department of Financial Services, In the Matter of the Bank of Tokyo-Mitsubishi UFJ Ltd. New York Branch, November 18, 2014, available at http://www.dfs.ny.gov/about/press2014/pr1411181-consent.pdf.

9. The U.K. Financial Conduct Authority has also taken actions against compliance officers working at financial services firms. *See, e.g.*, U.K. Financial Conduct Authority, In re Anthony Rendell Boyd Wills (March 4, 2015) (settling administrative proceedings against a former compliance officer of the Bank of Beirut, upon a finding that the officer had failed to keep the authority informed of shortcomings in the bank's compliance monitoring processes and falsely indicated to the authority that the bank had completed a required upgrade in its compliance program).

10. The subject of the U.K. action, Mr. Wills, was alleged to have violated a requirement that compliance officers and other control personnel must deal with the regulators "in an open and cooperative way and must disclose appropriately any information of which the [regulators] would reasonably expect notice." Is this a wise obligation to impose on compliance officers? What are the pros and cons?

Even though she was not penalized for her infractions, the SEC's action against Ms. Wolf illustrates an apparent trend on the part of this agency to hold compliance officials accountable when they fail to display proper diligence or care in carrying out their responsibilities. In 2015, SEC Commissioner Daniel M. Gallagher issued a public protest against what he viewed as an unfortunate development:

Statement of Commissioner Daniel M. Gallagher on Recent SEC Settlements Charging Chief Compliance Officers with Violations of Investment Advisers Act Rule 206(4)-7

June 18, 2015

I recently voted against two settled SEC enforcement actions involving alleged violations of Investment Advisers Act Rule 206(4)-7 by chief compliance officers ("CCOs"): In the Matter of Blackrock Advisors, LLC (April 20, 2015) and In the Matter of SFX Financial Advisory Management Enterprises, Inc. (June 15, 2015). I have long called on the Commission to tread carefully when bringing enforcement actions against compliance personnel. These recent actions fly in the face of my admonition, and I feel compelled to explain my rationale for dissenting.

In Blackrock, the Commission charged a CCO with causing the firm's [regulatory] violations in connection with his alleged failure to ensure that the firm had compliance policies and procedures to assess and monitor the outside activities of employees and disclose conflicts of interest to fund boards and advisory clients. In SFX, the Commission alleged that a CCO failed to implement compliance policies and procedures that, if carried out appropriately, would have detected an alleged multi-year theft of client assets by the president of the firm. In both instances, the Commission's order states that the CCO was responsible for the implementation of the firms' policies and procedures.

Both settlements illustrate a Commission trend toward strict liability for CCOs under Rule 206(4)-7. Actions like these are undoubtedly sending a troubling message that CCOs should not take ownership of their firm's compliance policies and procedures, lest they be held accountable for conduct that, under Rule 206(4)-7, is the responsibility of the adviser itself. Or worse, that CCOs should opt for less comprehensive policies and procedures with fewer specified compliance duties and responsibilities to avoid liability when the government plays Monday morning quarterback.

I am especially worried about the potential impact of this trend on small advisers, as it appears that many such advisers have just one set of policies and procedures covering both compliance and business functions. At these firms, there is a significant risk that by taking ownership of the implementation of the policies and procedures, CCOs could unwittingly also be taking ownership of business functions, subjecting them to strict liability whenever there is a violation of the securities laws.

Much of the blame, of course, can be laid at the feet of Rule 206(4)-7 itself, which is not a model of clarity. The rule merely states that registered investment advisers are required to "[a]dopt and implement written policies and procedures reasonably designed to prevent violation[s]" of the Advisers Act and its rules, but offers no guidance as to the distinction between the role of CCOs and management in carrying out the compliance function. And in the eleven years since the rule was adopted, the Commission has not issued any guidance about how to comply with the rule.

Unfortunately, the only guidance market participants have at their disposal are enforcement actions, which in some cases have unfairly contorted the rule to treat the compliance function as a new business line, with compliance officers assuming the role of business heads. On its face, Rule 206(4)-7 speaks directly to the responsibility of the adviser, but all too often, the Commission interprets the rule as being directed at CCOs. The rule expressly states that the firm must designate a CCO to administer its compliance policies and procedures. At the end of the day, ultimate responsibility for implementation of policies and procedures rests with the adviser itself.

The Commission needs to be especially cognizant of the messages it sends to the compliance community, and in particular to CCOs of investment advisers. To put it bluntly, for the vast majority of advisers, CCOs are all we have. They are not only the first line of defense, they are the only line of defense. There are nearly three times as many investment advisers registered with the SEC than there are broker dealers — approximately 11,700 investment advisers versus about 4,200 broker-dealers — yet the SEC devotes roughly the same amount of resources to examining broker-dealers as it does to investment advisers. And unlike the brokerage industry, there is no SRO interposed between the SEC and advisers. Given the vitally important role played by compliance personnel, I am very concerned that continuing uncertainty as to the contours of liability under Rule 206(4)-7 will dis-incentivize a vigorous compliance function at investment advisers.

One thing is certain: we should not be resolving this uncertainty through enforcement actions. There are, of course, situations where CCOs should be held accountable for violations of the securities laws. However, as regulators, we should strive to avoid the perverse incentives that will naturally flow from targeting compliance personnel who are willing to run into the fires that so often occur at regulated entities. This includes exercising restraint and discretion even at the investigation stage. The psychological impact, and in many cases reputational damage, that can come with months or years of testimony, the Wells process, and settlement negotiations can be just as chilling as the scarlet letter of an enforcement violation.

The Commission must take a hard look at Rule 206(4)-7 and consider whether amendments, or at a minimum staff or Commission-level guidance, are needed to clarify the roles and responsibilities of compliance personnel under the rule so that these individuals are not improperly held accountable for the misconduct of others. The status quo simply will not do. As it stands, the Commission seems to be cutting off the noses of CCOs to spite its face.

Questions and Comments

1. Do you agree with Commissioner Gallagher that the SEC should "tread carefully" when considering whether to investigate or impose sanctions on compliance officers at investment advisory firms?

2. What is the problem, in Commissioner Gallagher's view, with establishing rules of liability through enforcement actions? Do you agree?

3. Why would cutting off the noses of CCOs spite the SEC's face?

4. What standard of culpability do you think should be appropriate in SEC enforcement actions against CCOs of investment advisory firms?

PROBLEM 6-1

As chief compliance officer of Granite Co., the nation's leading manufacturer of high-end kitchen countertops, you uncover that the company's head of marketing has been secretly meeting with her counterparts in the other four largest firms in the industry. You know that added together the five firms control 80 percent of the market. You raise your concerns with the chief executive officer. She thanks you for your input and says she will look into the matter. Several weeks later, you are called to a meeting with the CEO and the head of human resources and informed that your services are no longer required. You are handed a legal agreement that provides you with three months' severance pay and requires you to maintain the confidentiality of all information obtained in the performance of your job. You are given two hours to clear out your desk. What should you do?

Even if a compliance officer has not knowingly engaged in misconduct, she may face sanctions for failing to do her job well enough. The SEC has pursued compliance officers who failed to prevent violations if it concludes that, when confronted with multiple red flags, the officer did nothing or essentially nothing to investigate or correct the situation. E.g., Matter of Rizzo, Exchange Act Release No. 67479 (July 20, 2012). The issue here is the degree of fault the SEC will require. For example, does a compliance officer face potentially career-ending sanctions if she did respond to the red flags, but did not do so effectually? If her actions were arguably negligent, but not grossly so? There are no definitive answers.

A compliance officer may also face liability for failing to supervise others who work at the organization. The issue is difficult because compliance officers rarely have direct line authority over traders and other line officers; their official supervisory power extends only to people in the compliance department itself. Yet compliance officers are charged with ensuring that the organizations they serve comply with the law, and thus could be said to exercise a form of supervisory authority over everyone in the organization. This issue came to the forefront in a 2010 SEC enforcement proceeding:

In the Matter of Theodore W. Urban
SEC Administrative Proceeding File No. 3-13655 (2010)

https://www.sec.gov/litigation/aljdec/2010/id402bpm.pdf

[Theodore Urban served as general counsel and member of the board of directors of FBW, a registered securities broker-dealer. As general counsel Urban had overall responsibility for FBW's compliance department. Over a three-year period, Stephen Glantz, a broker at FBW, engaged in acts of fraud, manipulation, and unauthorized and self-serving behavior. Glantz circumvented FBW's internal controls by persistently misclassifying accounts, lying on internal disclosure documents, and otherwise disguising his pattern of illegal conduct. The SEC brought an enforcement proceeding against Urban, charging him with failing to supervise the broker.

[Urban argued that he could not be held liable because he was not Glantz's supervisor. He claimed, and the hearing examiner agreed, that he "was not responsible and had no authority for hiring, assessing performance, assigning activities, promoting, or terminating employment of anyone, outside of the people in the departments he directly supervised." Specifically, Urban "did not have any of the traditional powers associated with a person supervising brokers." Nevertheless, the hearing examiner concluded that Urban was Glantz's supervisor. Urban's opinions on legal and compliance issues were "viewed as authoritative and his recommendations were generally followed by people in FBW's business units . . . ." And although Urban did not direct the firm's response when allegations of improper behavior surfaced against Glantz, he did serve on the board credit committee and dealt with Glantz on behalf of that committee. That was enough, in the hearing examiner's view, to expose Urban to liability for negligent failure to supervise.

[On the merits, SEC enforcement officials claimed that Urban had failed to act on numerous "red flags" indicating possible misconduct by Glantz. After being placed on notice that something was amiss, Urban's duty was "to take concerns about Glantz's conduct to FBW's Board or Executive Committee, and, if they did not act, . . . to resign and report the matter to regulatory authorities."

[Urban responded that his actions were reasonable under the circumstances. He had encouraged the firm's compliance department to investigate the fund for which Glantz was trading; brought potential problems in that fund to the attention of the board credit committee; recommended that the credit committee limit the supply of credit to the fund in question; urged line officials to increase their vigilance over Glantz's trading activities; reported Glantz's unauthorized trading to the SEC, as required by SEC regulations; advocated that Glantz be fired when his problematic actions came to light; and advocated that Glantz be placed under special supervision when senior business managers refused to fire Glantz. Urban also pointed out that he had no personal interest in Glantz's trading and gained no benefit from the lenient treatment shown to Glantz within the firm.]

[The hearing examiner defined the standard of liability as follows:] Even where knowledge of supervisors is limited to "red flags" or "suggestions" of irregularity, they cannot discharge their supervisory obligations simply by relying on the unverified representations of employees. Instead, . . . "[t]here must be adequate follow-up and review when a firm's own procedures detect irregularities or unusual trading activity . . . ." [Applying this standard, the hearing examiner concluded that Urban had behaved reasonably under the circumstances and, accordingly, could not be held liable for failing to supervise Glantz.]

[The hearing examiner concluded that Urban had reasonably relied on assurances he had received from line officials that the appropriate steps would be undertaken to rein in Glantz's unauthorized trades.] Urban received assurances from Glantz's top supervisors, Akers and Vaughan, more than once, that they would take measures to improve supervision of Glantz, but they did not do so. Urban did not just simply rely on the unverified representations of employees. He relied on continuous representations by multiple individuals in high level managerial roles, some of whom he had known for years, and had no reason to distrust and he followed up with Compliance oversight of Glantz. The evidence is that none of Glantz's direct supervisors did what he was required to do and what he represented he was doing.

[The hearing examiner concluded that, even if Urban could not rely on representations he received from Glantz's supervisors, he was not to be faulted for failing to go "up the ladder" by raising the matter with Calvert, FBW's chief executive officer.] If Urban could not rely on Akers's commitment to exercise special supervision, he had few, if any, options for further action. Urban knew that it would have been futile to go to Calvert, on paper Akers's superior, and seek to terminate Glantz despite Akers's refusal to do so. The evidence is overwhelming that Calvert deferred to Akers on matters involving retail Sales. Calvert knew that there were supervisory concerns about Glantz, and he did absolutely nothing to support Compliance or Urban's efforts to assure that Glantz was supervised, despite being the CEO with ultimate responsibility for supervision.

[Finally, the hearing examiner concluded that Urban could not be faulted for failing to raise the problem with the board of directors.] Assuming that relying on Akers's commitment to exercise special supervision is considered unreasonable, the issue becomes whether Urban should have gone to the Board or Executive Committee with his recommendation to terminate Glantz. I believe that it was reasonable for Urban not to attempt to raise the issue with the Board because the unanimous evidence is that he would not have succeeded. It is undisputed that Calvert deferred to Akers on matters involving Retail Sales. Without Calvert's support going to the Board would have been futile. Excluding Akers, four of the twelve remaining members worked for Akers (Gordon, Winslow, and the two brokers). Finally, Urban's belief that the Board did not consider this type of issue is confirmed by the evidence. I reject [an expert witness's] position that Urban was required to do what his best judgment told him was futile.

Questions and Comments

1. When problems with Glantz's trades came to light, Urban urged that he be fired, but executives in the retail sales department refused. They kept Glantz at the firm and continued to pay him generous bonuses. They may well have benefited financially from Glantz's trades. Given these considerations, was it reasonable for Urban to rely on their assurances — later shown to be false — that they would rein in Glantz's trading behavior going forward?

2. Calvert, the CEO, deferred to the managers in the retail sales department, even on matters of ethics and compliance; he did not back up Urban's recommendation that Glantz be fired in light of the latter's deceptive behavior and unauthorized trades. What can you infer about the "culture" at FBW? About the "tone at the top"?

3. If you had been in Urban's position, what would you have done after the line officers rejected your position to fire Glantz?

4. Do you agree with the hearing examiner that Urban was not to be faulted for failing to go to the CEO? Calvert's previous actions didn't give much reason to believe he would be responsive to such an overture, but what was the cost of trying? Likewise, do you agree with the hearing officer that Urban was not to be faulted for failing to go to the board of directors? Perhaps, as the hearing officer implied, the board was dominated by traders who didn't want to be bothered with those sorts of concerns. But, again, what was the harm in trying?

5. Had Urban gone to the CEO or the board, would his own position at the firm have been jeopardized? Could this concern have influenced the hearing examiner's judgment?

6. The Enforcement Division argued that, if reporting the matter "up the ladder" was ineffective, Urban's responsibility was to resign and report the matter to the SEC. As an attorney, could Urban have reported the matter to the SEC without violating his ethical duty to preserve client confidences?

7. What role did the SEC envisage for compliance officers at registered broker-dealers? What role did the hearing officer envisage? What is best from the standpoint of social policy?

8. Urban, the defendant in this case, graduated with a degree in electrical engineering from Cornell University and a law degree from Catholic University. He worked at the SEC as a staff attorney, branch chief, and assistant director in the Division of Market Regulation. He then moved to the Commodity Futures Trading Commission, where he served as Deputy Director of Trading and Markets. He joined FBW's predecessor firm in 1984 and remained there until he retired. He was a member of the Board of Directors of the Maryland Chamber of Commerce and Vice Chairman of the Board of Investment Trustees for the Montgomery County Public Schools Employee Pension and Retirement System. Witnesses were unanimous in describing Urban as a person of honesty and integrity. Will persons with this sort of distinction be willing to serve as compliance officials at broker-dealers if they fear being haled before the Commission to answer for the misconduct of rogue traders?

9. The full SEC failed to act in this case, thus leaving the hearing examiner's opinion undisturbed. The SEC has, however, issued more general guidance on the question of when compliance officials become supervisors. *See* SEC Division of Trading and Markets, Frequently Asked Questions About Liability of Compliance and Legal Personnel at Broker Dealers Under Sections 15(b)(4) and 15(b)6) of the Exchange Act, available at www.sec.gov/divisions/marketreg/faq-cco-supervision-093013.htm (opining that compliance and legal personnel are not per se supervisors, but that this status "depends on whether, under the facts and circumstances of a particular case, that person has the requisite degree of responsibility, ability or authority to affect the conduct of the employee whose behavior is in issue").

10. The common law recognizes a tort of negligent supervision. Section 213 of the Restatement (Second) of Agency provides: "A person conducting an activity through servants or other agents is subject to liability for harm resulting from his conduct if he is negligent or reckless: . . . [b] in the employment of improper persons or instrumentalities in work involving risk of harm to others; or [c] in the supervision of the activity; or [d] in permitting, or failing to prevent, negligent or other tortious conduct, by persons, whether or not his servants or agents, upon premises or with instrumentalities under his control." Section 317 of the Restatement (Second) of Torts provides: "A master is under a duty to exercise reasonable care so to control his servant while acting outside the scope of his employment as to prevent him from intentionally harming others . . . if (a) the servant (i) is upon the premises in possession of the master or upon which the servant is privileged to enter only as his servant, or (ii) is using a chattel of the master, and (b) the master (i) knows or has reason to know that he has the ability to control his servant, and (ii) knows or should know the necessity and opportunity for exercising such control. Should these common law principles carry over when the question is a compliance officer's regulatory liability for failing to prevent employee misconduct? Why or why not?

D. OVERSIGHT LIABILITY

We saw in Chapter 2 that members of the board of directors of a Delaware corporation owe a duty to shareholders to exercise oversight of the company's compliance programs. Governments do not ordinarily sue for violation of this duty, unless they stand in the shoes of shareholders for some reason (for example, bank regulators who have taken over a failed bank). But other provisions of law may provide the government with a basis to allege a similar failure of oversight. Consider the following:

Securities and Exchange Commission, In the Matter of Steven A. Cohen

Administrative Proceeding, File No. 3-15382 (2013)

. . . After an investigation, the Division of Enforcement (the "Division") alleges that:

[Steven A.] Cohen — the founder and owner of hedge fund investment advisers that bear his initials (S.A.C.) and that until recently managed portfolios of over $15 billion — failed reasonably to supervise two of his senior employees, who engaged in insider trading under his watch.

On at least two separate occasions in 2008, two portfolio managers who reported to Cohen obtained material nonpublic information about three different publicly traded companies. Both portfolio managers provided information to Cohen indicating that they may have had access to inside information to support their trading. Based on that information, both portfolio managers engaged in unlawful insider trading.

In each case, Cohen received highly suspicious information that should have caused any reasonable hedge fund manager in Cohen's position to take prompt action to determine whether employees under his supervision were engaged in unlawful conduct and to prevent violations of the federal securities laws. Cohen failed to take reasonable steps to investigate and prevent such violations. Instead, faced with red flags of potentially unlawful conduct by employees under his supervision, Cohen allowed his traders to execute the recommended trades and stood by while the portfolio managers traded in the portfolios they managed.

Based on these trades, and Cohen's failure reasonably to supervise his portfolio managers who executed the trades, Cohen's hedge funds earned profits and avoided losses totaling more than $275 million.

Cohen later praised one of the portfolio managers for his role in one of the trades and rewarded the other with a $9 million bonus for his work.

Both portfolio managers have been criminally charged with insider trading. An analyst who reported to one of those portfolio managers has pleaded guilty to criminal insider trading charges . . . .

In view of the allegations made by the Division of Enforcement, the Commission deems it necessary and appropriate in the public interest that public administrative proceedings be instituted to determine:

Whether the allegations set forth [above] are true and, in connection therewith, to afford Respondent an opportunity to establish any defenses to such allegations;

What, if any, remedial action is appropriate in the public interest against Respondent . . . including, but not limited to, civil penalties pursuant to Section 203(i) of the Advisers Act . . . .

Questions and Comments

1. Steven A. Cohen was a giant in the hedge fund industry at the time the SEC brought this proceeding. His company, S.A.C. Capital Advisors (S.A.C.), enjoyed spectacular returns for many years, and Cohen profited handsomely from its success. In March 2013, Forbes listed him as the 106th richest man in the world (and the 35th richest in the United States) with a net wealth of $9.3 billion.

2. The SEC's lawsuit grew out of an insider trading scandal that erupted at S.A.C. Capital in 2012. Several senior employees at companies controlled by S.A.C. were indicted or pleaded guilty to criminal offenses. In March 2013, S.A.C. settled civil charges with the SEC for $616 million. The SEC, however, was apparently unable to obtain sufficient evidence to obtain an indictment of Cohen himself. The SEC filed its civil case against Cohen just before the statute of limitations was due to expire on some of the underlying conduct.

3. Section 203(f) of the Investment Advisors Act, 15 U.S.C. §80b-3(f), allows the SEC to bring a civil action to bar or suspend someone from being associated with an investment adviser if he is found to have committed certain wrongful acts. Because S.A.C. Capital Advisors was an investment adviser, the SEC's action essentially sought to bar Cohen from the securities industry, and also to impose substantial civil penalties against him.

4. To prove failure of oversight, the SEC needed to establish that Cohen acted with some sort of bad intent — mere negligent failure of oversight was probably not enough to support the government's theory. Although not mentioned in the complaint, S.A.C. Capital Advisors apparently did operate a compliance program. Its website once declared that the company's "strong culture of compliance" was intended to "deter insider trading" and that its compliance program, staffed by "no fewer than 38 full-time compliance personnel," was at the "cutting edge" of the hedge fund industry. If true, how do these facts affect your judgment about the government's allegations?

5. The SEC settled the administrative action against Cohen early in 2016. In the Matter of Steven A. Cohen, Administrative Proceeding No. 3-15382, Investment Advisers Act of 1940 Release No. 4307 (Jan. 8, 2016). Cohen agreed that he had "failed reasonably to supervise" Matthew Martoma, one of S.A.C.'s portfolio managers who had been convicted in 2014 of securities fraud in connection with trades made on behalf of S.A.C. The relief the SEC obtained against Cohen, however, fell short of expectations. Cohen agreed to retain, at least through year-end 2017, the services of an "independent consultant" (commonly referred to as a "monitor"), who is responsible for conducting a review of Cohen's entities' compliance with the securities laws and with recommending additional practices and procedures to ensure such compliance. Cohen also agreed to conduct an internal review of profitable trades identified by the SEC and to cooperate with any investigation into such trades conducted by the SEC. He also agreed, at least through year-end 2017, to refrain from associating in a supervisory capacity with any securities broker, dealer, or investment adviser. No fines were assessed; and if Cohen complies with the terms

of the agreement, he will be free to return to managing the funds of public investors within a few years.

United States v. S.A.C. Capital Advisors, LLP

Sealed Indictment

[T]his Indictment charges the corporate entities responsible for the management of a major hedge fund with criminal responsibility for insider trading offenses committed by numerous employees and made possible by institutional practices that encouraged the widespread solicitation and use of illegal inside information. Unlawful conduct by individual employees and an institutional indifference to that unlawful conduct resulted in insider trading that was substantial, pervasive and on a scale without known precedent in the hedge fund industry . . . .

The [defendants] committed the insider trading scheme through the acts of, among others, numerous portfolio managers ("S.A.C. PMs") and research analysts ("S.A.C. RAs") who engaged in a pattern of obtaining Inside Information from dozens of publicly-traded companies across multiple industry sectors. Employees of the [defendants] traded on Inside Information themselves and, at times, recommended trades to [Cohen] based on Inside Information.

The [defendants] enabled and promoted the Insider Trading scheme through several means detailed herein. First, the [defendants] sought to hire S.A.C. PMs and S.A.C. RAs with proven access to public company contacts likely to possess Inside Information. Second, the [defendants'] employees were financially incentivized to recommend to the S.A.C. Owner "high conviction" trading ideas in which the S.A.C. PM had an "edge" over other investors, but repeatedly were not questioned when making trading recommendations that appeared to be based on Inside Information. Third, on numerous occasions the [defendants] failed to employ effective compliance procedures or practices to prevent S.A.C. PMs and S.A.C. RAs from engaging in insider trading.

At bottom, the encouragement by the [defendants] of S.A.C. PMs and S.A.C. RAs to pursue aggressively an information "edge" overwhelmed limited S.A.C. compliance systems. Further, the relentless pursuit of an information "edge" fostered a business culture within S.A.C. in which there was no meaningful commitment to ensure that such "edge" came from legitimate research and not Inside Information. The predictable and foreseeable result, as charged herein, was systematic insider trading by the [defendants] resulting in hundreds of millions of dollars of illegal profits and avoided losses at the expense of members of the investing public . . . .

As a result of committing the [charged offenses], the [defendants] shall forfeit to the United States . . . all property, real and personal, which constitutes or is derived from proceeds traceable to the commission of those offenses.

Questions and Comments

1. This indictment followed hard on the heels of the civil action against Cohen excerpted above. It is not based on a theory of oversight liability, but rather the claim that the corporate entities were themselves guilty of insider trading.

2. Given a grand jury indictment, what was the chance that S.A.C. Capital or its affiliates could remain in business with capital from outside investors—even if it is ultimately acquitted of the charges?

3. The indictment takes account of S.A.C. Capital Advisor's compliance operation, charging that the defendants failed to "employ effective compliance procedures or practices." What does it suggest about how that operation functioned? Could the compliance department have been given "make-work" responsibilities—checking off boxes—while being cut out of any real access to S.A.C. Capital Advisor's operations? Could the department have been unaware of the institutional culture described in the government's indictment, if such a culture existed?

4. Can a compliance department exacerbate rather than reduce the risk of violations? For example, if the department presents the appearance of being vigorous and competent, it might induce an atmosphere of complacency within the organization or unwarranted trust on the part of regulators, making illegal acts easier to commit. Worse yet, the department might signal to others in the organization as to the areas where they must be careful to disguise their activities—thus making it more difficult for regulators to uncover the misconduct. How realistic are these concerns?

5. Suppose that S.A.C. Capital Advisors did operate a "state-of-the-art" compliance operation. If true, what does this say about the benefits of compliance departments in general?

6. In November 2013, S.A.C. Capital agreed to plead guilty to the criminal charges, pay $1.8 billion in fines, and cease providing investment advice to public clients.

E. MITIGATION OF PENALTIES

Another way that regulators can induce organizations to institute compliance programs or conduct internal investigations is to offer opportunities to mitigate penalties for violations if the organization has manifested good faith efforts to comply with the law and to report and remediate instances of non-compliance. One of the earliest and still most important of these mitigation strategies is outlined in the following excerpt.

Environmental Protection Agency, Incentives for Self-Policing: Discovery, Disclosure, Correction and Prevention of Violations

65 Fed. Reg. 19,618 (April 11, 2000)

... EPA's enforcement program provides a strong incentive for compliance by imposing stiff sanctions for noncompliance. Enforcement has contributed to the dramatic expansion of environmental auditing as measured in numerous recent surveys. For example, in a 1995 survey by Price Waterhouse LLP, more than 90% of corporate respondents who conduct audits identified one of the reasons for doing so as the desire to find and correct violations before government inspectors discover them . . . .

At the same time, because government resources are limited, universal compliance cannot be achieved without active efforts by the regulated community to police themselves. More than half of the respondents to the same 1995 Price Waterhouse survey said that they would expand environmental auditing in exchange for reduced penalties for violations discovered and corrected. While many companies already audit or have compliance management programs in place, EPA believes that the incentives offered in this Policy will improve the frequency and quality of these self-policing efforts.

INCENTIVES FOR SELF-POLICING

[T]he Audit Policy identifies the major incentives that EPA provides to encourage to encourage self-policing, self-disclosure, and prompt self-correction. For entities that meet the conditions of the Policy, the available incentives include waiving or reducing gravity-based civil penalties, declining to recommend criminal prosecution for regulated entities that self-police, and refraining from routine requests for audits. [The conditions are (1) systematic discovery of the violation; (2) voluntary discovery; (3) prompt disclosure; (4) discovery and disclosure independent of government or third party plaintiff; (5) correction and remediation; (6) steps to prevent recurrence; (7) no repeat violation; (8) other violations excluded; and (9) cooperation.] . . .

- Eliminating Gravity-Based Penalties

In general, civil penalties that EPA assesses are comprised of two elements: the economic benefit component and the gravity-based component. The economic benefit component reflects the economic gain derived from a violator's illegal competitive advantage. Gravity-based penalties are that portion of the penalty over and above the economic benefit. They reflect the egregiousness of the violator's behavior and constitute the punitive portion of the penalty . . . .

Under the Audit Policy, EPA will not seek gravity-based penalties for disclosing entities that meet all nine Policy conditions, including systematic discovery. ("Systematic discovery" means the detection of a potential violation through an environmental audit or a compliance management system that reflects the entity's due diligence in preventing, detecting and correcting violations.) EPA has elected to waive gravity-based penalties for violations discovered systematically, recognizing that environmental auditing and compliance management systems play a critical role in protecting human health and the environment by identifying, correcting and ultimately preventing violations . . . .

- 75% Reduction of Gravity-Based Penalties

Gravity-based penalties will be reduced by 75% where the disclosing entity does not detect the violation through systematic discovery but otherwise meets all other Policy conditions. The Policy appropriately limits the complete waiver of gravity-based civil penalties to companies that conduct environmental auditing or have in place a compliance management system. However, to encourage disclosure and correction of violations even in the absence of systematic discovery, EPA will reduce gravity-based penalties by 75% for entities that meet [the other conditions] of the Policy. EPA expects that a disclosure under this provision will encourage the entity to work with the Agency to resolve environmental problems and begin to develop an effective auditing program or compliance management system.

- No Recommendations for Criminal Prosecution

... EPA generally does not focus its criminal enforcement resources on entities that voluntarily discover, promptly disclose and expeditiously correct violations, unless there is potentially culpable behavior that merits criminal investigation. When a disclosure that meets the terms and conditions of this Policy results in a criminal investigation, EPA will generally not recommend criminal prosecution for the disclosing entity, although the Agency may recommend prosecution for culpable individuals and other entities . . . .

The "no recommendation for criminal prosecution" incentive is available for entities that meet [the last eight conditions] of the Policy. [The condition] "systematic discovery" is not required to be eligible for this incentive, although the entity must be acting in good faith and must adopt a systematic approach to preventing recurring violations . . . .

- No Routine Requests for Audit Reports

EPA reaffirms its Policy . . . to refrain from routine requests for audit reports. That is, EPA has not and will not routinely request copies of audit reports to trigger enforcement investigations . . . . In general, an audit that results in expeditious correction will reduce liability, not expand it. However, if the Agency has independent evidence of a violation, it may seek the information it needs to establish the extent and nature of the violation and the degree of culpability . . . .

CONDITIONS . . .

- Systematic Discovery of the Violation

[T]he violation must have been discovered through either (a) an environmental audit, or (b) a compliance management system that reflects due diligence in preventing, detecting and correcting violations . . . . [A compliance management system is] a systematic management plan or systematic efforts to achieve and maintain compliance . . . .

Compliance management programs that train and motivate employees to prevent, detect and correct violations on a daily basis are a valuable complement to periodic auditing. Where the violation is discovered through a compliance management system and not through an audit, the disclosing entity should be prepared to document how its program reflects the due diligence criteria defined in [this] Policy statement. These criteria, which are adapted from existing codes of practice — such as Chapter Eight of the U.S. Sentencing Guidelines for organizational defendants, effective since 1991 — are flexible enough to accommodate different types and sizes of businesses and other regulated entities. The Agency recognizes that a variety of compliance management programs are feasible, and it will determine whether basic due diligence criteria have been met in deciding whether to grant Audit Policy credit.

As a condition of penalty mitigation, EPA may require that a description of the regulated entity's compliance management system be made publicly available. The Agency believes that the availability of such information will allow the public to judge the adequacy of compliance management systems, lead to enhanced compliance, and foster greater public trust in the integrity of compliance management systems.

- Voluntary Discovery

[T]he violation must have been identified voluntarily, and not through a monitoring, sampling, or auditing procedure that is required by statute, regulation, permit, judicial or administrative order, or consent agreement . . . .

- Prompt Disclosure

[The entity must] disclose the violation in writing to EPA within 21 calendar days after discovery . . . . The trigger for discovery is when any officer, director, employee or agent of the facility has an objectively reasonable basis for believing that a violation has, or may have, occurred. The "objectively reasonable basis" standard is measured against what a prudent person, having the same information as was available to the individual in question, would have believed. It is not measured against what the individual in question thought was reasonable at the time the situation was encountered. If an entity has some doubt as to the existence of a violation, the recommended course is for the entity to proceed with the disclosure and allow the regulatory authorities to make a definitive determination . . . .

- Discovery and Disclosure Independent of Government or Third Party Plaintiff

[T]he entity must discover the violation independently. That is, the violation must be discovered and identified before EPA or another government agency likely would have identified the problem either through its own investigative work or from information received through a third party. This condition requires regulated entities to take the initiative to find violations on their own and disclose them promptly instead of waiting for an indication of a pending enforcement action or third-party complaint . . . .

- Correction and Remediation

[T]he entity must remedy any harm caused by the violation and expeditiously certify in writing to appropriate Federal, State, and local authorities that it has corrected the violation. Correction and remediation in this context include responding to spills and carrying out any removal or remedial actions required by law. The certification requirement enables EPA to ensure that the regulated entity will be publicly accountable for its commitments through binding written agreements, orders or consent decrees where necessary.

Under the Policy, the entity must correct the violation within 60 calendar days from the date of discovery, or as expeditiously as possible. EPA recognizes that some violations can and should be corrected immediately, while others may take longer than 60 days to correct . . . .

- Prevent Recurrence

[T]he regulated entity must agree to take steps to prevent a recurrence of the violation after it has been disclosed. Preventive steps may include, but are not limited to, improvements to the entity's environmental auditing efforts or compliance management system.

- No Repeat Violations

[Repeat offenders are barred] from receiving Audit Policy credit.

The repeat violation exclusion benefits both the public and law-abiding entities by ensuring that penalties are not waived for those entities that have previously been notified of violations and fail to prevent repeat violations . . . .

• Other Violations Excluded

[This provision] excludes violations that result in serious actual harm to the environment or which may have presented an imminent and substantial endangerment to public health or the environment. When events of such a consequential nature occur, violators are ineligible for penalty relief and other incentives under the Audit Policy . . . . [The provision also excludes] excludes violations of the specific terms of any order, consent agreement, or plea agreement . . . .

• Cooperation

[T]he regulated entity must cooperate as required by EPA and provide the Agency with the information it needs to determine Policy applicability. The entity must not hide, destroy or tamper with possible evidence following discovery of potential environmental violations . . . .

Entities that disclose potential criminal violations may expect a more thorough review by the Agency. In criminal cases, entities will be expected to provide, at a minimum, the following: access to all requested documents; access to all employees of the disclosing entity; assistance in investigating the violation, any noncompliance problems related to the disclosure, and any environmental consequences related to the violations; access to all information relevant to the violations disclosed, including that portion of the environmental audit report or documentation from the compliance management system that revealed the violation; and access to the individuals who conducted the audit or review . . . .

Questions and Comments

1. The EPA notes that its enforcement policies had already resulted in a significant increase in voluntary environmental auditing procedures by regulated firms. Given this fact, how does the EPA explain the need to offer the "carrot" of leniency to companies that adopt such policies?

2. The EPA points to a survey indicating that companies would upgrade their environmental audit activities if they could receive leniency for doing so. Are these survey responses surprising?

3. Is a premise of the EPA's policy the idea that if some environmental auditing by companies is good, more must be better? Is there a point where a company is expending too many resources on environmental compliance?

4. One of the EPA's incentives for self-policing is that the agency will not "routinely request copies of audit reports." What concern is the EPA addressing here? Is this really an incentive for self-policing, or is it more properly classified as a promise not to penalize companies for doing so?

5. There are two components to EPA monetary penalties: (a) the "economic gain" that the company accrues by not complying with the law, and (b) a "gravity-based" element, over and above the economic component, that reflects the agency's evaluation of the blameworthiness of the conduct. What is the rationale for dividing the penalties this way? If the only penalty a violator expects is having to disgorge its illegal profits if it gets caught, the violator will not have sufficient incentives to obey

the law — it will be as well off violating the law as obeying it. Arguably, the "gravity-based" sanction, among other things, addresses the problem that not all violators will be caught. Does this help explain why the EPA waives the gravity-based sanction if the company catches a violation through its internal compliance processes?

6. One of the conditions for receiving leniency is that the offender demonstrate cooperation with the EPA's investigation of the violation. Would this, or should this, include the company's agreement to waive attorney-client privilege as to pertinent communications?

7. Sometimes the idea of giving credit for compliance activities is embodied in a statute. The Securities and Exchange Act of 1934, for example, authorizes the SEC to impose sanctions on securities brokers or dealers, and their supervisors, for committing violations of the securities law. Section 15(b)(4)(E) of that statute, however, contains a safe harbor protecting against supervisory liability if "there have been established procedures, and a system for applying such procedures, which would reasonably be expected to prevent and detect, insofar as practicable, any such violation by such other person, and such person has reasonably discharged the duties and obligations incumbent upon him [sic] by reason of such procedures and system without reasonable cause to believe that such procedures and system were not being complied with." 15 U.S.C. §78o(b)(4)(E). Effectively, this provision allows supervisors to avoid liability for failing to supervise if the company is shown to have a robust compliance program in place.

8. Even if a government agency decides it will give credit for compliance activities, how can it know where a compliance program is effective? Mere "paper" programs that do not prevent misconduct should not receive credit. But it can be dauntingly difficult to distinguish a paper program from a genuine one. The government's response to this issue has tended to be haphazard, with evaluations of the credibility and effectiveness of programs being made in the first instance by whichever official was in charge of the enforcement action. In 2015, the Department of Justice's Criminal Division attempted to rationalize this inquiry by hiring a compliance expert — a sort of in-house consultant responsible for evaluating whether the government should bring charges against companies that fail to detect or prevent wrongdoing by employees. How effective do you think this step will be? Can such an official reliably distinguish robust compliance programs from bogus ones? Will the official have the resources, the independence, and the credibility within the Department to carry out her responsibility in an accurate and impartial manner?

Securities and Exchange Commission, Report of Investigation Pursuant to Section 21(a) of the Securities Exchange Act of 1934 and Commission Statement on the Relationship of Cooperation to Agency Enforcement Decisions

Exchange Act Release No. 44969 (Oct. 23, 2001)

Today, we commence and settle a cease-and-desist proceeding against Gisela de Leon-Meredith, former controller of a public company's subsidiary. Our order finds that Meredith caused the parent company's books and records to be inaccurate and its periodic reports misstated, and then covered up those facts.

We are not taking action against the parent company, given the nature of the conduct and the company's responses. Within a week of learning about the apparent misconduct, the company's internal auditors had conducted a preliminary review and had advised company management who, in turn, advised the Board's audit committee, that Meredith had caused the company's books and records to be inaccurate and its financial reports to be misstated. The full Board was advised and authorized the company to hire an outside law firm to conduct a thorough inquiry. Four days later, Meredith was dismissed, as were two other employees who, in the company's view, had inadequately supervised Meredith; a day later, the company disclosed publicly and to us that its financial statements would be restated. The price of the company's shares did not decline after the announcement or after the restatement was published. The company pledged and gave complete cooperation to our staff. It provided the staff with all information relevant to the underlying violations. Among other things, the company produced the details of its internal investigation, including notes and transcripts of interviews of Meredith and others; and it did not invoke the attorney-client privilege, work product protection or other privileges or protections with respect to any facts uncovered in the investigation.

The company also strengthened its financial reporting processes to address Meredith's conduct — developing a detailed closing process for the subsidiary's accounting personnel, consolidating subsidiary accounting functions under a parent company CPA, hiring three new CPAs for the accounting department responsible for preparing the subsidiary's financial statements, redesigning the subsidiary's minimum annual audit requirements, and requiring the parent company's controller to interview and approve all senior accounting personnel in its subsidiaries' reporting processes.

Our willingness to credit such behavior in deciding whether and how to take enforcement action benefits investors as well as our enforcement program. When businesses seek out, self-report and rectify illegal conduct, and otherwise cooperate with Commission staff, large expenditures of government and shareholder resources can be avoided and investors can benefit more promptly. In setting forth the criteria listed below, we think a few caveats are in order:

First, the paramount issue in every enforcement judgment is, and must be, what best protects investors. There is no single, or constant, answer to that question. Self-policing, self-reporting, remediation and cooperation with law enforcement authorities, among other things, are unquestionably important in promoting investors' best interests. But, so too are vigorous enforcement and the imposition of appropriate sanctions where the law has been violated. Indeed, there may be circumstances where conduct is so egregious, and harm so great, that no amount of cooperation or other mitigating conduct can justify a decision not to bring any enforcement action at all. In the end, no set of criteria can, or should, be strictly applied in every situation to which they may be applicable.

Second, we are not adopting any rule or making any commitment or promise about any specific case; nor are we in any way limiting our broad discretion to evaluate every case individually, on its own particular facts and circumstances. Conversely, we are not conferring any "rights" on any person or entity. We seek only to convey an understanding of the factors that may influence our decisions.

Third, we do not limit ourselves to the criteria we discuss below. By definition, enforcement judgments are just that — judgments. Our failure to mention a specific criterion in one context does not preclude us from relying on that criterion in another. Further, the fact that a company has satisfied all the criteria we list below will not foreclose us from bringing enforcement proceedings that we believe are necessary or appropriate, for the benefit of investors.

In brief form, we set forth below some of the criteria we will consider in determining whether, and how much, to credit self-policing, self-reporting, remediation and cooperation — from the extraordinary step of taking no enforcement action to bringing reduced charges, seeking lighter sanctions, or including mitigating language in documents we use to announce and resolve enforcement actions.

- What is the nature of the misconduct involved? Did it result from inadvertence, honest mistake, simple negligence, reckless or deliberate indifference to indicia of wrongful conduct, willful misconduct or unadorned venality? Were the company's auditors misled?
- How did the misconduct arise? Is it the result of pressure placed on employees to achieve specific results, or a tone of lawlessness set by those in control of the company? What compliance procedures were in place to prevent the misconduct now uncovered? Why did those procedures fail to stop or inhibit the wrongful conduct?
- Where in the organization did the misconduct occur? How high up in the chain of command was knowledge of, or participation in, the misconduct? Did senior personnel participate in, or turn a blind eye toward, obvious indicia of misconduct? How systemic was the behavior? Is it symptomatic of the way the entity does business, or was it isolated?
- How long did the misconduct last? Was it a one-quarter, or one-time, event, or did it last several years? In the case of a public company, did the misconduct occur before the company went public? Did it facilitate the company's ability to go public?
- How much harm has the misconduct inflicted upon investors and other corporate constituencies? Did the share price of the company's stock drop significantly upon its discovery and disclosure?
- How was the misconduct detected and who uncovered it?
- How long after discovery of the misconduct did it take to implement an effective response?
- What steps did the company take upon learning of the misconduct? Did the company immediately stop the misconduct? Are persons responsible for any misconduct still with the company? If so, are they still in the same positions? Did the company promptly, completely and effectively disclose the existence of the misconduct to the public, to regulators and to self-regulators? Did the company cooperate completely with appropriate regulatory and law enforcement bodies? Did the company identify what additional related misconduct is likely to have occurred? Did the company take steps to identify the extent of damage to investors and other corporate constituencies? Did the company appropriately recompense those adversely affected by the conduct?
- What processes did the company follow to resolve many of these issues and ferret out necessary information? Were the Audit Committee and the Board of Directors fully informed? If so, when?
- Did the company commit to learn the truth, fully and expeditiously? Did it do a thorough review of the nature, extent, origins and consequences of the conduct and related behavior? Did management, the Board or committees consisting solely of outside directors oversee the review? Did company employees or outside persons perform the review? If outside persons, had they done other work for the company? Where the review was conducted by

outside counsel, had management previously engaged such counsel? Were scope limitations placed on the review? If so, what were they?

- Did the company promptly make available to our staff the results of its review and provide sufficient documentation reflecting its response to the situation? Did the company identify possible violative conduct and evidence with sufficient precision to facilitate prompt enforcement actions against those who violated the law? Did the company produce a thorough and probing written report detailing the findings of its review? Did the company voluntarily disclose information our staff did not directly request and otherwise might not have uncovered? Did the company ask its employees to cooperate with our staff and make all reasonable efforts to secure such cooperation?

- What assurances are there that the conduct is unlikely to recur? Did the company adopt and ensure enforcement of new and more effective internal controls and procedures designed to prevent a recurrence of the misconduct? Did the company provide our staff with sufficient information for it to evaluate the company's measures to correct the situation and ensure that the conduct does not recur?

- Is the company the same company in which the misconduct occurred, or has it changed through a merger or bankruptcy reorganization?

Questions and Comments

1. Agencies often administer significant penalties in highly publicized cases in an effort to send a message to the industry about what not to do. In this case, the opposite occurred: The SEC conspicuously refrained from administering a sanction against a company in order to send a message to the industry about what should be done. Do you believe it is appropriate for an agency to use enforcement proceedings as a vehicle for this type of communication? Should it instead focus on the conduct before it in the case, without shaping its response with reference to the incentive effects in other cases? If the agency does focus on incentive effects, is there a difference between administering especially harsh penalties in order to deter misconduct and exercising unusual leniency in order to encourage good conduct?

2. What did the issuer do that induced the SEC to be merciful?

3. While encouraging self-policing, the SEC is careful not to indicate that cooperation of this sort will automatically be a shield against liability. What are the concerns? Is the agency worried that if misconduct occurred, this is evidence that the defendant did not take effective steps to prevent the compliance breakdown? That if potential defendants know they can avoid sanctions *ex post* by fully cooperating once a violation has occurred, they will be less eager to prevent violations from occurring? That there will be a public outcry if companies get a free pass for demonstrated acts of misconduct?

4. One step that the agency applauds is the fact that the company promptly fired the responsible officials. Is there a downside to encouraging this sort of quick job action? What if it turns out after an investigation that the official was not personally responsible? A career will have been compromised, and whatever the company does after the fact to make amends — if anything — will probably not repair the damage.

5. The SEC notes that the issuer's shares didn't decline after the company publicly disclosed its problem. What is the relevance?

6. For another leniency protocol, see U.S. Department of Health & Human Services, Office of the Inspector General, *Updated OIG's Provider Self-Disclosure Protocol* (2013), available at https://oig.hhs.gov/compliance/self-disclosure-info/files/ Provider-Self-Disclosure-Protocol.pdf.

PROBLEM 6-2

Lionheart, Inc., a public company, manufactures electric batteries used in golf carts and similar vehicles. In the third quarter of the fiscal year, the company lost a major contract to a competitor. Jane Jones, Lionheart's chief executive officer, met with her senior managers and exhorted them to redouble their sales efforts so that the company would not show a loss for the year. Mark McCarthy, head of the golf division, responded by arranging for a company-paid Seychelles Islands vacation for the purchasing manager of a golf cart producer. The customer tripled its order for the fourth quarter, on the understanding that it would reduce orders by a like amount in future quarters. The result was that Lionheart reported a profit for the year, just as the CEO wished. The company's share price soared when the profit figure came out. Soon thereafter, however, the company's internal audit department pointed out that accounting regulations do not allow a company to book current profits for orders that relate to future purchases, and also raised questions about the Seychelles Islands vacation. The matter is referred to you as General Counsel of Lionheart. What will you suggest (or insist) the company do to respond to the problem?

PROBLEM 6-3

Quadrivium College, an undergraduate institution of higher education, maintains student records on a server operated by its information technology department. Due to a programming mistake, the system made it possible for anybody, with a little effort, to access and tamper with student grades from the school's website. As far as anyone knows, no one actually exploited the vulnerability. Nevertheless, recognizing that disclosure of grades to inappropriate persons could violate the Family Education Rights and Privacy Act of 1974 (FERPA), the college's president retained an outside consultant to investigate. Her hope was that by launching an investigation before news came out about any breach, the school might receive leniency in any subsequent enforcement action by the U.S. Department of Education. Unfortunately, the consultant accidentally deleted the information that would have made it possible to determine whether grades had been disclosed. What do you recommend?

F. ADVICE

Regulated organizations have a host of resources to which they can turn for advice regarding how to structure or administer their compliance operations — accounting firms, law firms, compliance consultants, and many others are active in this space. The most informative and reliable source of advice, however, is probably the regulators themselves—since these are the people who will have to determine whether the organization has committed a violation and—often—whether it has an effective compliance program in place.

Regulators do, in fact, offer extensive advice about various elements of compliance. These can take the form of written "guidance," which is widely distributed in the industry and often publicly available on government websites. We will have the opportunity to review examples of such advice in this book. Regulators also offer more particularized advice as part of their supervisory responsibilities. A report of examination, for example, may contain a section detailing deficiencies noted in the regulated firm's compliance operations. That report will be vetted with management before it is finalized, and will be made available to the board of directors afterward.

Regulators also convey compliance-related advice on a more informal basis. Highly regulated industries have extensive contact with their regulators; in some cases (large banks are an example), the regulator maintains permanent staff and offices within the organization. The frequent interactions that these contacts make possible are fruitful opportunities for conveying information—not only advice about formal policies and procedures, but also suggestions for best practices and hints about the regulator's overall enforcement priorities and philosophy.

Questions and Comments

1. Are any dangers inherent in this process? The advice that regulators offer about compliance may technically be only that—advice—but the identity of the party giving the advice cannot help but have an impact. An organization should think long and hard before flouting the recommendations of the regulator who holds the keys to its survival. Thus advice, although technically discretionary, can be mandatory in all but name. Yet such advice is often adopted without the formal protections of notice-and-comment rulemaking or other avenues for public vetting. Is this problematic from the standpoint of public policy?

2. The line between "advice" and "threats" is sometimes attenuated. If a regulator provides recommendations about how an organization should structure its compliance operation, there may be an unspoken sanction at the back end if the advice is not heeded—the agency will take some action to punish the organization. Should regulators be required to be more transparent when seeking to bend organizations to their will?

3. Can the provision of informal advice lead to a too-cozy relationship between the regulator and its regulated industry? Bragg v. United States, 230 W. Va. 532, 741 S.E.2d 90 (2013), was a lawsuit arising out of a horrific coal mine accident. The federal Mine Safety and Health Administration determined that the accident had resulted, in part, from negligence of its own inspectors, who had failed to identify or demand correction of numerous safety violations. The investigation report surmised that the inspector's failures could have been caused by a conflict of interest: "[S]ome of the identified deficiencies may have stemmed from the relationship that MSHA developed with [company] representatives . . . . [U]sing enforcement personnel in this manner to assist the [company] with its compliance efforts may have created a conflict of interest that, over time, may have affected the level of scrutiny MSHA provided at [the mine] during subsequent mine inspections . . . ."

G. ADMISSIONS

If an enforcement proceeding goes to a litigated judgment, the determination could be used against the defendant in a subsequent lawsuit: The facts and conclusions necessary to the judgment might give rise to an estoppel that would bar the defendant from denying them in a subsequent case.

In the case of a settlement, the effect is more ambiguous: Since there is no litigated judgment, the settlement might be seen as purely a private compromise that establishes no facts at all. Nevertheless, defendants worry that if they agree to settlements — especially ones imposing substantial obligations — their compromise of government actions will be held against them in subsequent cases. The concern is that the settlement itself will be taken as an admission of culpability that can be used against the defendant in later legal proceedings, such as private class actions or shareholders derivative lawsuits.

Even if not creating an estoppel, defendants might worry that the settlement will be admissible in evidence as probative of liability. If the settlement involves an agreement to upgrade the defendant's compliance operation, there is the added concern that the agreement will be admitted as evidence that the defendant's system of internal controls was previously inadequate. The general rule in tort law is that subsequent repairs are not admissible to establish negligence; the obvious reason is that otherwise defendants would not undertake the socially beneficial activities of correcting dangerous conditions. When a company institutes a compliance program in response to a government enforcement proceeding, the effect is similar to a subsequent repair: The party is correcting a potentially dangerous condition, namely its failure to have an effective compliance program in place. In general, therefore, a company's agreement to upgrade its compliance operations in response to a government lawsuit may be deemed inadmissible as evidence bearing on liability in a subsequent private lawsuit. Notwithstanding this protection, defendants worry that their agreement to enter a consent decree will buy trouble in the form of subsequent lawsuits.

To avoid these risks, defendants generally insist that settlement agreements with the government recite that they do not admit misconduct. The government's willingness to agree to such stipulations is often of material assistance in smoothing the way to a settlement. But should the government agree to such terms?

The following excerpts, which record a testy exchange between a defensive SEC and an irascible judge, explore this issue in fascinating detail. The first excerpt contains the SEC's answers to questions posed by the judge in connection with the parties' motion for a judgment approving the settlement; the succeeding excerpts record the judge's response and the reaction of an appellate court.

SEC's Memorandum of Law in Response to Questions Posed by the Court Regarding Proposed Settlement

SEC v. Citigroup Global Markets Inc., 11 Civ. 7387 (JSR) (S.D.N.Y. 2011)

[The SEC alleged that Citigroup Global Markets had engaged in misrepresentations in connection with the marketing of collateralized debt obligation securities. The consent decree required Citigroup to (a) pay the SEC a fine of $95 million; (b) disgorge $160 million of profits and $30 million of interest; and (c) undertake a series of measures for a period of three years designed to prevent the repeat of this conduct by Citigroup in the future. The latter undertakings included the following provisions:]

- [The role of the Capital Markets Approval Committee or Commitment Committee would be expanded and processes put in place to ensure that written marketing materials for mortgage securities do not include any material misstatement or omissions.]
- [In-house legal or compliance personnel would review all marketing materials and certain other written materials used by Citigroup in connection with mortgage securities offerings.]
- [For all mortgage securities offerings where Citigroup retained outside counsel, such outside counsel would be required to review all written marketing materials and offering circulars/prospectuses and be provided with documents sufficient to reflect all material terms of the transaction.]
- [Citigroup would be required to conduct annual internal compliance audits and certify annually, in writing, compliance in all material respects with the undertakings.]

The Court has posed a number of questions to the parties regarding the proposed settlement. The Commission's responses to those questions are set forth below:

> *Why should the Court impose a judgment in a case in which the S.E.C. alleges a serious securities fraud but the defendant neither admits nor denies wrongdoing?*

[T]he use and entry of consent judgments has long been endorsed by the Supreme Court. "[T]he central characteristic of a consent judgment is that the court has not actually resolved the substance of the issues presented." Rather, a consent decree is a "judgment entered by consent of the parties whereby the defendant agrees to stop alleged illegal activity without admitting guilt or wrongdoing." "[A] disclaimer of liability is, of course, a standard feature in consent decrees." Indeed, the Supreme Court expressly has endorsed the entry of consent decrees notwithstanding a defendant's explicit denial of material allegations of the complaint. Accordingly, there is nothing unusual or untoward about a consent decree entered without an admission of wrongdoing by the defendant, and criticism of consent decrees for not including such an admission is "unjustified."

Consistent with this standard practice, the SEC has long utilized consent decrees in which defendants admit no wrongdoing. While such consent decrees are entirely appropriate, the SEC became troubled by defendants' subsequent public denials of wrongdoing. Thus, in 1972, the Commission issued the following policy statement regarding its settlements:

> The Commission has adopted the policy that in any civil lawsuit brought by it or in any administrative proceeding of an accusatory nature pending before it, it is important to avoid creating, or permitting to be created, an impression that a decree is being entered or a sanction imposed, when the conduct alleged did not, in fact, occur. Accordingly, it hereby announces its policy not to permit a defendant or respondent to consent to a judgment or order that imposes a sanction while denying the allegations in the complaint or order for proceedings. In this regard, the Commission believes that a refusal to

admit the allegations is equivalent to a denial, unless the defendant or respondent states that he neither admits nor denies the allegations.

In other words, while consent decrees often allow defendants to deny wrongdoing, the SEC sought to preclude denials both in the consent decree itself and elsewhere. While the Commission does not require express admissions (given their collateral estoppel effects), the Commission has prohibited the denials that consent decrees often contain. Since this policy was announced, the Commission has, as a general matter, included in its proposed consent judgments a provision that the defendant neither admits nor denies the Commission's allegations.

Consistent with this policy, Citigroup and the Commission have entered into a no admit/deny settlement here. It appears that this approach has succeeded in clearly conveying that the conduct alleged did in fact occur. The Complaint lays out in detail the alleged facts, Citigroup has paid nearly $300 million as a result, Citigroup has not denied the allegations, and Citigroup's public statement regarding the settlement focused on the fact that the company has "overhauled the risk management function, significantly reduced risk on the balance sheet, and returned to the basics of banking."

Obviously, there are advantages and disadvantages to both parties in a no admit/deny consent judgment. The defendant is not subject to collateral estoppel with regard to the claims asserted, but at the same time investors are able to pursue any available private remedies in addition to the relief obtained by the SEC. On the other hand, the Commission is able to bring the matter to a speedy resolution, obtain compensation for victims in a timely manner, and allocate its limited resources to bringing additional enforcement actions for the protection of still more investors. Courts repeatedly have recognized the balance of advantages and disadvantages in settlements entered pursuant to the no admit/deny policy and expressed a reluctance to upset that balance. The Commission respectfully submits that this Court should do the same.

This Court previously has questioned whether the SEC's no admit/deny policy is consistent with the position taken by the Justice Department when "[c]onfronted with the same choice." In particular, the Court referenced the policy of the Justice Department not to accept nolo contendere pleas in criminal cases. But that is not the proper comparison and does not present the "same choice." The Justice Department is confronted with the "same choice"—that is, whether to accept a consent judgment in the absence of an admission of liability—when it settles civil enforcement actions, not criminal prosecutions.

And in the civil enforcement context, the Justice Department makes the "same choice" as the SEC, namely not to require admissions of liability by settling defendants. Guilty pleas in criminal cases do not present the Justice Department with the "same choice" as is presented in civil enforcement cases because the Federal Rules of Criminal Procedure and constitutional law limit the conditions under which criminal punishment can be imposed. Federal Rule of Criminal Procedure 11(b)(3) requires that judgment be entered on a guilty plea only after a district court finds a "factual basis" for the plea, and even a nolo contendere plea can be accepted only if there is a factual basis for the defendant's guilt.

In fact, the Justice Department often obtains consent decrees in civil enforcement actions in which the defendant expressly and repeatedly denies liability. Other federal agencies similarly obtain consent decrees that contain no admission of wrongdoing. Thus, the SEC's policy with regard to no admit/deny consent decrees reflects the Commission's effort to go beyond its fellow federal agencies to "avoid creating, or permitting to be created," confusion over the factual accuracy of the Commission's allegations. . . .

This Court should not upset the balance that the SEC has attempted to strike in its no admit/deny approach to settlements . . . .

Questions and Comments

1. Why do defendants resist making any admissions of misconduct when settling civil complaints? The following reasons are most salient:

   a. Admissions of wrongdoing would be embarrassing and could lead to long-term reputational harm for the organization.

   b. Admissions of wrongdoing might be followed by removal from office of any officials of the defendant organization who had anything to do with the misconduct — including senior officers such as the chief executive officer who had general oversight responsibility for the conduct in question.

   c. Admissions of wrongdoing could have "collateral estoppel" effect, in that the defendant might thereafter be precluded from denying the facts so admitted in subsequent civil or criminal litigation brought against the organization or its officers.

   d. Admissions of wrongdoing might result in problems under the organization's liability insurance policy, which will typically exclude coverage for particular types of wrongful acts.

2. Are the foregoing reasons, individually or as a group, a sufficient reason for the SEC to refrain from insisting on admissions of wrongdoing in civil settlements?

3. The SEC points out that "neither admit nor deny" consent decrees have been used for many years. Does a long history of agency use indicate that these types of settlements serve the public interest?

4. At one time, the typical settlement acknowledged that the defendants denied the allegations. After the settlement was announced, and the judgment releasing the defendant from liability became final, defendants would publicly state that they had done nothing wrong. In 1972, the SEC modified its policy and required that the defendant "neither admit nor deny" the allegations. That way the defendant could not subsequently claim that it had denied the allegations in the consent decree. Do you see a substantial difference between denying an allegation of misconduct and neither admitting nor denying it?

5. The SEC interpreted its post-1972 policy as also precluding a defendant from making post-settlement statements which deny the allegations (the SEC indirectly alludes to this aspect of the policy when it says that the new approach would preclude denials both in the consent decree itself "and elsewhere"). Is it constitutionally proper for an agency of the government to pressure a defendant to muzzle its freedom of speech in this fashion?

6. What happens if a defendant, after agreeing to a "neither admit nor deny" settlement, is subsequently sued privately for the same conduct that formed the basis of the government action (for example, in a shareholders derivative lawsuit or a securities class action)? Federal Rule of Civil Procedure 8(b)(1)(B) requires a defendant, in its answer to the complaint, to "admit or deny the allegations asserted against it by an opposing party." There is no option to neither admit nor deny:

Rule 8(b)(6) states that "[a]n allegation . . . is admitted if . . . the allegation is not denied." If a defendant were precluded from denying the truth of the allegations in the new forum, the consequences would likely be that the defendant would be held to admit them. In recognition of this problem, the SEC did not object when a defendant denied the allegations in court pleadings.

7. The SEC claims that even though Citigroup Global Markets neither admitted nor denied wrongdoing, the settlement in question "has succeeded in clearly conveying that the conduct alleged did in fact occur." The reasons given are that the allegations in the complaint were very detailed, that the defendant didn't deny the allegations, that the defendant paid a substantial monetary penalty, and that the defendant subsequently overhauled its risk-management process. Do these facts persuade you that the conduct complained of occurred as alleged and was illegal? Would it affect your opinion to know that in 2012, after a two-week trial, a jury found that Brian Stoker, the Citigroup employee primarily responsible for structuring the CDO transaction, was not liable for securities law violations in connection with the challenged scheme?

8. If it was so certain that the illegal conduct occurred, why did the SEC settle this case for $95 million, given its claim that "a reasonable calculation of the maximum penalty available under the Securities Act is $190 million."

9. How robust are the governance, risk-management, and compliance measures contemplated by this settlement? Is internal auditing of marketing activities something the bank would not do on its own, especially in the wake of the financial crisis of 2007-2009? Are the other measures anything more than requirements that marketing materials be vetted more widely in the organization?

SEC v. Citigroup Global Markets, Inc.

No. 11-Civ-7387, (S.D.N.Y. Nov. 28, 2011)

JED S. RAKOFF, U.S.D.J.:

[T]he Court concludes, regretfully, that the proposed Consent Judgment is neither fair, nor reasonable, nor adequate, nor in the public interest. Most fundamentally, this is because it does not provide the court with a sufficient evidentiary basis to know whether the requested relief is justified under any of these standards. Purely private parties can settle a case without ever agreeing on the facts, for all that is required is that a plaintiff dismiss his complaint. But when a public agency asks a court to become its partner in enforcement by imposing wide-ranging injunctive remedies on a defendant, enforced by the formidable judicial power of contempt, the court, and the public, need some knowledge of what the underlying facts are: for otherwise, the court becomes a mere handmaiden to a settlement privately negotiated on the basis of unknown facts, while the public is deprived of ever knowing the truth in a matter of obvious public importance.

Here, the SEC's long-standing policy — hallowed by history, but not by reason — of allowing defendants to enter in to Consent Judgments without admitting or denying the underlying allegations — deprives the Court of even the most minimal assurance that the substantial injunctive relief it is being asked to impose has any basis in fact. There is little real doubt that Citigroup contests the factual allegations in the Complaint. In colloquy with the Court, counsel for Citigroup expressly reconfirmed that his client was not admitting the allegations of the complaint. He also noted, correctly, that he was free — notwithstanding the SEC's gag order precluding Citigroup from contesting the SEC's allegations in the media — to fully contest the facts in any parallel litigation; and he strongly hinted that Citigroup would do just that.

The SEC, by contrast, took the position that, because Citigroup did not expressly deny the allegations, the Court, and the public, somehow knew the truth of the allegations. This is wrong as a matter of law and unpersuasive as a matter of fact. As a matter of law, an allegation that is neither admitted nor denied is simply that, an allegation. It has no evidentiary value and no collateral estoppel effect . . . . As for common experience, a consent judgment that does not involve any admissions and that results in only very modest penalties is just as frequently viewed, particular in the business community, as a cost of doing business imposed by having to maintain a working relationship with a regulatory agency, rather than as any indication of where the real truth lies. This, indeed, is Citigroup's position in this very case.

Of course, the policy of accepting settlements without any admissions serves various narrow interests *of the parties.* In this case, for example, Citigroup was able, without admitting anything, to negotiate a settlement that (a) charges it only with negligence, (b) results in a very modest penalty, (c) imposes the kind of injunctive relief that Citigroup (a recidivist) knew that the SEC had not sought to enforce against any financial institution for at least the last 10 years, and (d) imposes relatively inexpensive prophylactic measures for the next three years. In exchange, Citigroup not only settles what it states was a broad-ranging four-year investigation by the SEC of Citigroup's mortgage-backed securities offerings, but also avoids any investors' relying in any respect on the SEC Consent Judgment in seeking return of their losses. If the allegations of the Complaint are true, this is a very good deal for Citigroup; and, even if they are untrue, it is a mild and modest cost of doing business.

It is harder to discern from the limited information before the Court what the SEC is getting from this settlement other than a quick headline. By the SEC's own account, Citigroup is a recidivist, and yet, in terms of deterrence, the $95 million civil penalty that the Consent Judgment proposes is pocket change to any entity as large as Citigroup. While the SEC claims that it is devoted not just to the protection of investors but also to helping them recover their losses, the proposed Consent Judgment, in the form submitted to the Court, does not commit the SEC to returning any of the total of $285 million obtained from Citigroup to the defrauded investors but only suggests that the SEC "may" do so. In any event, this still leaves the defrauded investors substantially short-changed. To be sure, at oral argument, the SEC reaffirmed its long-standing purported support for private civil actions designed to recoup investors' losses. But in actuality, the combination of charging Citigroup only with negligence and then permitting Citigroup to settle without either admitting or denying the allegations deals a double blow to any assistance the defrauded investors might seek to derive from the SEC litigation in attempting to recoup their losses through private litigation, since private investors not only cannot bring securities claims based on negligence, but also cannot derive any collateral estoppel assistance from Citigroup's non-admission/non-denial of the SEC's allegations. Nor, as noted, does the public, especially the business public, have any reason to credit those allegations, which remain entirely unproven.

The point, however, is . . . that the parties' successful resolution of their competing interests cannot be automatically equated with the public interest, especially in the absence of a factual basis on which to assess whether the resolution was fair, adequate and reasonable. Even after giving the fullest deference to the SEC's views — which have more than once persuaded this Court to approve an SEC Consent Judgment it found dubious on the merits — the Court is forced to conclude that a proposed Consent Judgment that asks the Court to impose substantial injunctive relief, enforced by the Court's own contempt power, on the basis of allegations unsupported by any proven or acknowledged facts whatsoever is neither reasonable, nor fair, nor adequate, nor in the public interest.

It is not reasonable, because how can it ever be reasonable to impose substantial relief on the basis of mere allegations? It is not fair, because, despite Citigroup's nominal consent, the potential for abuse in imposing penalties on the basis of facts that are neither proven nor acknowledged is patent. It is not adequate, because, in the absence of any facts, the Court lacks a framework for determining adequacy. And, most obviously, the proposed Consent Judgment does not serve the public interest, because it asks the Court to employ its power and assert its authority when it does not know the facts.

An application of judicial power that does not rest on facts is worse than mindless, it is inherently dangerous. The injunctive power of the judiciary is not a free-roving remedy to be invoked at the whim of a regulatory agency, even with the consent of the regulated. If its deployment does not rest on facts — cold, hard solid facts, established either by admissions or by trials — it serves no lawful or moral purpose and is simply an engine of oppression.

Finally, in any case like this that touches on the transparency of financial markets whose gyrations have so depressed our economy and debilitated our lives, there is an overriding public interest in knowing the truth. In much of the world, propaganda reigns, and truth is confined to secretive, fearful whispers. Even in our nation, apologists for suppressing or obscuring the truth may always be found. But the SEC, of all agencies, has a duty, inherent it its statutory mission, to see that the truth emerges; and if it fails to do so, this Court must not, in the name of deference or convenience, grant judicial enforcement to the agency's contrivances.

Accordingly, the Court refuses to approve the proposed Consent Judgment. Instead, the Court . . . directs the parties to be ready to try this case . . . .

Questions and Comments

1. Much of Judge Rakoff's opinion addresses separation-of-powers concerns about the role of federal courts in the consent decree process. As he describes it, he was essentially given the agreement as a *fait accompli*, instructed to rubber stamp it, and then expected to provide the contempt powers of the federal court in enforcing it — all without any real independent authority or even information necessary to perform his statutory function. If accurate, does this description of the role of federal courts in consent decrees give you a basis for concern?

2. Judge Rakoff suggests that the procedure described above violates the constitutional guarantee of judicial independence. Does it?

3. Judge Rakoff complains that he doesn't have enough information to determine whether the settlement is fair, adequate, and reasonable. Is he right? What information did he have before him at the time he rendered this judgment? What additional information would, in his opinion, have cured the defect?

4. Judge Rakoff suggests that the proposed settlement, while it doesn't serve the interest of the public, does serve the interest of the parties. He provides reasons for why Citigroup benefited from the deal. But when it comes to the SEC, he comments

that the SEC's private motivation is "harder to discern." Was the SEC only interested in a "quick headline"?

5. As a jurist in the Southern District of New York (located in Manhattan), Judge Rakoff and his fellow judges see many securities cases and have frequent interaction with the SEC. Do you get the idea from the language of this opinion that the judge is fed up with the agency? He notes that he has "more than once" deferred to the SEC's recommendation that he approve a settlement that he found to be dubious; and at the close of the opinion he characterizes the SEC's actions as "contrivances." Should a judge let his prior experience with an agency in other cases influence his opinion in a new and different case? Has the judge lost track of the impartiality that jurists need to bring to all their judicial functions?

6. The day the consent decree was announced, the SEC issued a press release touting the event. The document quoted Robert Khuzami, Director of the SEC's Division of Enforcement, as follows: "The securities laws demand that investors receive more care and candor than Citigroup provided to these CDO investors. . . . Investors were not informed that Citigroup had decided to bet against them and had helped choose the assets that would determine who won or lost." Does this support Judge Rakoff's suggestion that part of the SEC's motivation in settling this case was to catch a quick headline?

7. Could politics have played a role in the SEC's actions here? Certainly, the meltdown in global financial markets associated with collateralized debt obligation and other mortgage-backed securities did not create a favorable public impression of the SEC; its failure for more than a decade to catch Bernard Madoff's colossal Ponzi scheme didn't help either. Were these settlements a bid for redemption? If so, does this cast a different light on the controversy?

SEC v. Citicorp Global Markets, Inc.

752 F.3d 285 (2d Cir. 2014)

The United States Securities and Exchange Commission ("S.E.C.") in conjunction with Citigroup Global Markets, Inc. ("Citigroup") appeals from the November 28, 2011 order of the United States District Court for the Southern District of New York (Rakoff, J.) refusing to approve a consent decree entered into by the parties and instead setting a trial date. Our Court stayed that order and referred the matter to a merits panel for consideration of the underlying questions. We now hold that the district court abused its discretion by applying an incorrect legal standard in assessing the consent decree and setting a date for trial . . . . As both parties before us advocated for approving the consent order, we ordered counsel appointed to advocate for the district court's order. Before us now is the merits appeal.

We review the district court's denial of a settlement agreement under an abuse of discretion standard. A district court abuses its discretion if it "(1) based its ruling on an erroneous view of the law," (2) made a "clearly erroneous assessment of the evidence," or (3) "rendered a decision that cannot be located within the range of permissible decisions." . . .

[T]o bring an interlocutory appeal from a district court's denial of settlement approval, a party must demonstrate "that (1) the district court, by refusing to approve a settlement, effectively denied a party injunctive relief and (2) in the absence of an interlocutory appeal, a party will suffer irreparable harm." That standard is satisfied here. The rejected consent decree provided for two types of injunctive relief: (1) enjoining Citigroup from violating provisions of the Act in the future, and (2) requiring Citigroup to undertake steps aimed at preventing future occurrences of securities fraud, and periodically demonstrate compliance to the S.E.C. The S.E.C. also demonstrated irreparable harm: . . . the district court expressed no willingness to revisit the settlement agreement with the parties, instead setting a trial date. We are satisfied that our Court may exercise jurisdiction over this interlocutory appeal.

We quickly dispense with the argument that the district court abused its discretion by requiring Citigroup to admit liability as a condition for approving the consent decree. In both the briefing and at oral argument, the district court's *pro bono* counsel stated that the district court did not seek an admission of liability before approving the consent decree. With good reason — there is no basis in the law for the district court to require an admission of liability as a condition for approving a settlement between the parties. The decision to require an admission of liability before entering into a consent decree rests squarely with the S.E.C. As the district court did not condition its approval of the consent decree on an admission of liability, we need not address the issue further.

We turn, then, to the far thornier question of what deference the district court owes an agency seeking a consent decree. Our Court recognizes a "strong federal policy favoring the approval and enforcement of consent decrees." "To be sure, when the district judge is presented with a proposed consent judgment, he is not merely a 'rubber stamp.'" The district court here found it was "required, even after giving substantial deference to the views of the administrative agency, to be satisfied that it is not being used as a tool to enforce an agreement that is unfair, unreasonable, inadequate, or in contravention of the public interest." Other district courts in our Circuit view "[t]he role of the Court in reviewing and approving proposed consent judgments in S.E.C. enforcement actions [as] 'restricted to assessing whether the settlement is fair, reasonable and adequate within the limitations Congress has imposed on the S.E.C. to recover investor losses.'"

The "fair, reasonable, adequate and in the public interest" standard invoked by the district court finds its origins in a variety of cases. Our Court previously held, in the context of assessing a plan for distributing the proceeds of a proposed disgorgement order, that "once the district court satisfies itself that the distribution of proceeds in a proposed S.E.C. disgorgement plan is fair and reasonable, its review is at an end." The Ninth Circuit — in circumstances similar to those presented here, a proposed consent decree aimed at settling an S.E.C. enforcement action — noted that "[u]nless a consent decree is unfair, inadequate, or unreasonable, it ought to be approved."

Today we clarify that the proper standard for reviewing a proposed consent judgment involving an enforcement agency requires that the district court determine whether the proposed consent decree is fair and reasonable, with the additional requirement that the "public interest would not be disserved," in the event that the consent decree includes injunctive relief. Absent a substantial basis in the record for concluding that the proposed consent decree does not meet these requirements, the district court is required to enter the order.

We omit "adequacy" from the standard. Scrutinizing a proposed consent decree for "adequacy" appears borrowed from the review applied to class action settlements, and strikes us as particularly inapt in the context of a proposed S.E.C. consent decree. The adequacy requirement makes perfect sense in the context of a class action settlement—a class action settlement typically precludes future claims, and a court is rightly concerned that the settlement achieved be adequate. By the same token, a consent decree does not pose the same concerns regarding adequacy—if there are potential plaintiffs with a private right of action, those plaintiffs are free to bring their own actions. If there is no private right of action, then the S.E.C. is the entity charged with representing the victims, and is politically liable if it fails to adequately perform its duties.

A court evaluating a proposed S.E.C. consent decree for fairness and reasonableness should, at a minimum, assess (1) the basic legality of the decree; (2) whether the terms of the decree, including its enforcement mechanism, are clear; (3) whether the consent decree reflects a resolution of the actual claims in the complaint; and (4) whether the consent decree is tainted by improper collusion or corruption of some kind. Consent decrees vary, and depending on the decree a district court may need to make additional inquiry to ensure that the consent decree is fair and reasonable. The primary focus of the inquiry, however, should be on ensuring the consent decree is procedurally proper, using objective measures similar to the factors set out above, taking care not to infringe on the S.E.C.'s discretionary authority to settle on a particular set of terms.

It is an abuse of discretion to require, as the district court did here, that the S.E.C. establish the "truth" of the allegations against a settling party as a condition for approving the consent decrees. Trials are primarily about the truth. Consent decrees are primarily about pragmatism. "[C]onsent decrees are normally compromises in which the parties give up something they might have won in litigation and waive their rights to litigation." Thus, a consent decree "must be construed as . . . written, and not as it might have been written had the plaintiff established his factual claims and legal theories in litigation." Consent decrees provide parties with a means to manage risk. "The numerous factors that affect a litigant's decision whether to compromise a case or litigate it to the end include the value of the particular proposed compromise, the perceived likelihood of obtaining a still better settlement, the prospects of coming out better, or worse, after a full trial, and the resources that would need to be expended in the attempt." These assessments are uniquely for the litigants to make. It is not within the district court's purview to demand "cold, hard, solid facts, established either by admissions or by trials," as to the truth of the allegations in the complaint as a condition for approving a consent decree.

As part of its review, the district court will necessarily establish that a factual basis exists for the proposed decree. In many cases, setting out the colorable claims, supported by factual averments by the S.E.C., neither admitted nor denied by the wrongdoer, will suffice to allow the district court to conduct its review. Other cases may require more of a showing, for example, if the district court's initial review of the record raises a suspicion that the consent decree was entered into as a result of improper collusion between the S.E.C. and the settling party. We need not, and do not, delineate the precise contours of the factual basis required to obtain approval for each consent decree that may pass before the court. It is enough to state that the district court here, with the benefit of copious submissions by the parties, likely had a sufficient record before it on which to determine if the proposed decree was fair and reasonable. On remand, if the district court finds it necessary, it may ask the S.E.C. and Citigroup to provide additional information sufficient to allay any concerns the district court may have regarding improper collusion between the parties.

As noted earlier, when a proposed consent decree contains injunctive relief, a district court must also consider the public interest in deciding whether to grant the injunction. . . . A plaintiff must demonstrate: (1) that it has suffered an irreparable injury; (2) that remedies available at law, such as monetary damages, are inadequate to compensate for that injury; (3) that, considering the balance of hardships between the plaintiff and defendant, a remedy in equity is warranted; and (4) that the public interest would not be disserved by a permanent injunction.

Our analysis focuses on the issue reached by the district court: that the district court must assure itself the "public interest would not be disserved" by the issuance of a permanent injunction.

The job of determining whether the proposed S.E.C. consent decree best serves the public interest, however, rests squarely with the S.E.C., and its decision merits significant deference: [F]ederal judges — who have no constituency — have a duty to respect legitimate policy choices made by those who do. The responsibilities for assessing the wisdom of such policy choices and resolving the struggle between competing views of the public interest are not judicial ones: "Our Constitution vests such responsibilities in the public branches."

The district court correctly recognized that it was required to consider the public interest in deciding whether to grant the injunctive relief in the proposed injunction. However, the district court made no findings that the injunctive relief proposed in the consent decree would disserve the public interest, in part because it defined the public interest as "an overriding interest in knowing the truth." The district court's failure to make the proper inquiry constitutes legal error. On remand, the district court should consider whether the public interest would be disserved by entry of the consent decree. For example, a consent decree may disserve the public interest if it barred private litigants from pursuing their own claims independent of the relief obtained under the consent decree. What the district court may not do is find the public interest disserved based on its disagreement with the S.E.C.'s decisions on discretionary matters of policy, such as deciding to settle without requiring an admission of liability.

To the extent the district court withheld approval of the consent decree on the ground that it believed the S.E.C. failed to bring the proper charges against Citigroup, that constituted an abuse of discretion. The exclusive right to choose which charges to levy against a defendant rests with the S.E.C. Nor can the district court reject a consent decree on the ground that it fails to provide collateral estoppel assistance to private litigants — that simply is not the job of the courts.

Finally, we note that to the extent that the S.E.C. does not wish to engage with the courts, it is free to eschew the involvement of the courts and employ its own arsenal of remedies instead. Admittedly, these remedies may not be on par with the relief afforded by a so-ordered consent decree and federal court injunctions. But if the S.E.C. prefers to call upon the power of the courts in ordering a consent decree and issuing an injunction, then the S.E.C. must be willing to assure the court that the settlement proposed is fair and reasonable. "Consent decrees are a hybrid in the sense that they are at once both contracts and orders; they are construed largely as contracts, but are enforced as orders." For the courts to simply accept a proposed S.E.C. consent decree without any review would be a dereliction of the court's duty to ensure the orders it enters are proper.

For the reasons given above, we vacate the November 28, 2011 order of the district court and remand this case for further proceedings in accordance with this opinion . . . .

LOHIER, Circuit Judge, concurring:

I thank my panel colleagues for addressing many of my concerns in this case. In particular, today's majority opinion makes clear that district courts assessing a proposed consent decree should consider principally four factors: "(1) the basic legality of the decree; (2) whether the terms of the decree, including its enforcement mechanism, are clear; (3) whether the consent decree reflects a resolution of the actual claims in the complaint; and (4) whether the consent decree is tainted by improper collusion or corruption of some kind." I write separately to make two more observations.

First, in my view, the "fair and reasonable" standard for assessing the appropriateness of monetary relief (as opposed to injunctive relief) involves a straightforward analysis of *only* the four factors identified by the majority and described above. If all four factors are satisfied, the perceived modesty of monetary penalties proposed in a consent decree is not a reason to reject the decree.

Second, I would be inclined to reverse on the factual record before us and direct the District Court to enter the consent decree. It does not appear that any additional facts are needed to determine that the proposed decree is "fair and reasonable" and does not disserve the public interest. Nor, to use the words of the majority opinion's holding, is there a "substantial basis . . . for concluding" that further development of the record will show that the proposed terms of this decree are not fair, reasonable, and in the public interest. Under the circumstances, though, it does no harm to vacate and remand to permit the very able and distinguished District Judge to make that determination in the first instance.

Questions and Comments

1. Why is a federal court any less able to evaluate the fairness and reasonableness of a settlement than it is, say, to assess whether a physician committed malpractice or the defendants fixed prices in a relevant market?

2. The appeals court judges observe that federal courts "have no constituency" and suggest that the lack of a constituency impairs their ability to assess a settlement as compared, for example, with an administrative agency. Why does the lack of a constituency disable a court from deciding the issue presented here? Could you argue that what should be disabling is not lacking a constituency but *having one*? If an official represents a constituency, might she be more likely to read the facts and law in a biased or slanted way?

3. The appeals panel suggests that Judge Rakoff did not give proper deference to the SEC. Why does it say this, given that Judge Rakoff explicitly stated that he *was* giving deference to the agency?

4. In August 2014, Judge Rakoff bowed to the inevitable and approved the proposed settlement—but not without getting in a parting shot both at the SEC and at the Court of Appeals: "Upon review of the underlying record in this case, the Court cannot say that the proposed Consent Judgment is procedurally improper or in any material respect fails to comport with the very modest standard imposed by the Court of Appeals. Accordingly, in an Order that will be filed separately today, the Consent Judgment will be approved.

Nonetheless, this Court fears that, as a result of the Court of Appeals' decision, the settlements reached by governmental regulatory bodies and enforced by the judiciary's contempt powers will in practice be subject to no meaningful oversight whatsoever. But it would be a dereliction of duty for this Court to seek to evade the dictates of the Court of Appeals. That Court has now fixed the menu, leaving this Court with nothing but sour grapes." SEC v. Citigroup Global Mkts. Inc., No. 1:11-cv-07387-JSR (S.D.N.Y. Aug. 5, 2014).

5. In a footnote, Judge Rakoff criticized the appeals court's suggestion that the SEC could resolve the matter without obtaining court approval at all: "[T]he Court of Appeals invites the SEC to avoid even the extremely modest review it leaves to the district court by proceeding on a solely administrative basis. ('Finally, we note that to the extent that the S.E.C. does not wish to engage with the courts, it is free to eschew the involvement of the courts and employ its own arsenal of remedies instead.')" One might wonder: From where does the constitutional warrant for such unchecked and unbalanced administrative power derive? How would you answer that question?

6. In spite of the arguments it made in the excerpted case, the SEC has gradually moved away from a uniform policy of negotiating "neither admit nor deny" settlement agreements. Since 2012, it has generally required some concession of wrongdoing in settlements involving a parallel criminal case in which admissions or convictions have been obtained. In 2013, it informally announced that it would also refuse to enter into "neither admit nor deny" settlements in cases of egregious conduct or widespread shareholder harm. For discussion, see Lynndon Groff, *Is Too Big to Fail Too Big to Confess? Scrutinizing the SEC's "No-Admit" Consent Judgment Proposals*, 54 B.C. L. Rev. 1727 (2013); Sanuel W. Buell, *Liability and Admissions of Wrongdoing in Public Enforcement of the Law*, 82 U. Cin. L. Rev. 505 (2013).

7. The SEC's new policy quickly bore fruit. In SEC v. Falcone, the SEC entered a consent decree with an investment fund (Harbinger) and its principal officer (Falcone) to settle charges that Falcone improperly used $113 million in fund assets to pay his personal taxes, secretly favored certain customer redemption requests at the expense of other investors, and conducted an improper "short squeeze" in bonds issued by a Canadian manufacturing company. As part of the consent decree, Falcone and Harbinger admitted to multiple acts of misconduct. The settlement required Falcone to pay $6,507,574 in disgorgement, $1,013,140 in prejudgment interest, and a $4,000,000 penalty. The Harbinger entities were required to pay a $6,500,000 million penalty. As regards the admissions policy, the settlement required the defendants to acknowledge that they engaged in specific improper actions and that their behavior was reckless. Although the SEC extracted admissions of fault, the defendants only admitted to having acted recklessly. They did not admit to intentionally violating the law. Should the SEC have sought this stronger admission? Why might the defendants have resisted an admission of intentional misconduct? Why did the SEC settle for less? One reason Falcone may have resisted a stronger admission was that he also occupied a lucrative position as chairman and CEO of a publicly traded company, Harbinger Group, which owns two life insurance companies. The consent decree did not require him to give up these positions. S.E.C. v. Philip A. Falcone et al., No 12-Civ-5027 (S.D.N.Y. 2013). In 2013, after settling his case with the SEC, Falcone received compensation of nearly $20 million from the public company. Does this place the severity of the SEC's penalty in a somewhat different light?

8. Perhaps the most highly publicized application of the new SEC policy was its $200 million settlement agreement with JPMorgan Chase in connection with the "London Whale" trading fiasco (see Chapter 20). As part of the settlement, JPMorgan Chase admitted that "its conduct violated the federal securities laws." In the Matter of JPMorgan Chase & Co., SEC Release No. 70458 (Sept. 19, 2013).

7

Prosecutors

The previous chapter discussed the role of civil authorities in the compliance process. Now we turn to an increasingly important, and much feared, means for inducing compliance by the private sector: criminal enforcement against companies and managers who allegedly cause the company to violate legal obligations.

A. THE PROBLEM OF CORPORATE CRIMINAL LIABILITY

The idea of criminal prosecutions of companies may seem odd. Consider the following:

- Companies are not human beings. They are fictional persons. They cannot feel emotions or have evil intent; everything they do is simply the result of actions undertaken by their employees or other agents. How can a company have the *mens rea* required for criminal liability?
- Companies cannot be imprisoned or executed (except metaphorically, in the form of penalties that cause them to cease doing business). The most effective — and essentially the only — criminal penalty against a corporation is a fine; but fines or their equivalents can be enforced through civil actions as well, and civil actions don't come with the disadvantages (from the government's point of view) of high burdens of proof and the constitutional protections afforded to criminal defendants.
- Given that the only effective penalty against a company is a fine, the incidence of the penalty will fall principally on the company's shareholders who will take a loss when the fine — and any losses associated with the damage to the company's reputation — appear on the bottom line. Yet shareholders are not culpable actors; they rarely cause the company to engage in illegal conduct. Shareholders, moreover, are not particularly effective monitors of corporate misconduct because they hold diversified portfolios and because they have

little authority in any event (see Chapter 1). Do criminal prosecutions of corporations assign the costs of violations to the wrong parties?

- Companies can only act through agents, and agents can be prosecuted if they cause their employers to violate the law. Unlike corporations, company managers and other agents can act out of evil intent; they can also feel remorse or contrition for their misconduct. Unlike corporations, they can be sent to prison or even executed for particularly egregious conduct. Because corporations only act through their agents, moreover, deterrence of human beings associated with a corporation is the only way that a corporation itself can be deterred from engaging in misconduct. Accordingly, if criminal prosecution is warranted for corporate misconduct, would it be more appropriately directed at the company's managers rather than at the company itself?
- Prosecutors have responsibilities other than enforcing corporate compliance obligations — they need to deal with murderers, terrorists, and drug lords, among others. Since other public officials — regulators — are available to enforce compliance obligations, why are prosecutors even needed?

Samuel W. Buell, The Blaming Function of Entity Criminal Liability

81 Ind. L.J. 473 (2006)

Despite sustained and deep attention, the criminal form of enterprise liability remains of puzzling legitimacy. This puzzle is well worth solving. The law and practice of entity criminal liability have grown increasingly salient, in tandem with the growth of the criminal law's regulatory role and the relative expansion of federal law and enforcement in the field of criminal law. . . .

The law in this area had a weak start nearly a century ago when common law courts, looking to expand available means for regulating business enterprises, imported respondeat superior liability from tort law into the criminal law, but without serious theoretical analysis. At least as a matter of federal law — the law that governs most cases of criminal enterprise liability — if a master were an entity, the master could be convicted for virtually any crime the master's agent committed within the scope of agency. Inquiry into an entity's criminal responsibility would proceed no further. The only slight modification to this rule has been to add a requirement that the agent have acted, in some part, to benefit the master.

Since its inception, this form of liability has faced steady criticism. Criminal law scholars have doubted the doctrine's theoretical soundness, pointing to illogic in retribution toward objects and the impossibility of fitting liberal concepts about responsibility with nonhuman actors. Entity criminal liability, these arguments go, is a purely imputed form of fault that has little or nothing to do with blameworthiness. And the doctrine is concerned with the fault of something without free will or character — that is, an apparition with "no soul to be damned and no body to be kicked."

Neoclassical economic analysis has propelled the critique further by leading scholars to question even the simple regulatory rationale that first gave rise to the doctrine. If the only pain that the state can inflict on a legal entity is fiscal, there is said to be little point, and perhaps waste, in maintaining a dual structure of civil and criminal enterprise liability. In response to this argument, a few have reached, not yet entirely successfully, to find some utility in a separate criminal practice of institutional liability.

Yet criminal enterprise liability has flourished in the legal system; if not, persistent interest in the doctrine would be inexplicable. Respondeat superior has become firmly entrenched as, more or less, the across-the-board rule of enterprise liability for all manner of crimes. The use of the tool against business enterprises and other organizations has become a prominent, perhaps central, feature of the criminal justice system, particularly at the federal level and in matters of white-collar crime. Most interesting, in the shadow of a strikingly broad de jure rule of liability that is nearly indistinguishable from its civil counterparts, the criminal system's actors gradually have developed a practice of imposing enterprise liability that looks much narrower and is tied to a form of heightened criminal law responsibility.

At the same time, organizations are ubiquitous, and worries about their production of unwanted events have increased. Institutions — our businesses, employers, schools, nonprofits, and so on — determine the course of much of our lives and even our identities. No matter what the law might have to say, we find ourselves continually wondering what to do about harmful human behavior, including behavior legally defined as criminal, that is explicable (even describable) only with reference to the institutional settings where it arises.

Treatments of this problem have run in one of three directions: toward the conclusions that retribution against nonhuman legal forms is nonsensical and pointless, and that therefore the legal slip-up of recognizing criminal liability for entities should be reversed; toward at least doubt, and sometimes deep skepticism, that criminal law could add anything useful to the project of regulating firms, which can suffer only financial consequences from legal action; or toward embrace of a popular impulse to condemn entities criminally for the harms they visit upon people.

Only the third (and newest) of these currents in the literature has begun to explain fully what is involved in the modern practice of imposing criminal liability on organizations, and why the practice has been so persistent. So far, however, the accounts have only scratched the surface of a genuine social account of entity criminal liability. This Article delves deeper, offering the thesis that the blaming function of entity criminal liability is linked closely to the utility of the doctrine. I will claim that the existence of institutional influence on an individual offender explains both the impulse to blame an entity and why such blaming can beneficially alter group behavior to make wrongdoing in organizations less likely. These features of blaming institutions look to be inseparable, potent, and dependent upon criminal process. . . .

Reassessing entity criminal liability in light of its contemporary social function will yield several helpful conclusions, some of them novel. In modern life, an organization can be blamed for wrongdoing with a kind of moral assessment characteristic of judgments of criminality and on the basis of the organization's relationship to the wrong. Unlike present law, social practice discriminates among cases of wrongdoing in organizations and, in determining where to ascribe blame, considers what a given case says about an organization and its tendency to produce unwanted individual behavior.

Effects of this kind of evaluation and condemnation can include altering an organization's reputation. Conducting such assessments through legal process gives them a clarity and authority that strengthens reputational effects. Such reputational sanctions can flow through to affiliated individuals in ways that can alter behavior, cause re-evaluation and reform of institutional arrangements, and reduce wrongdoing in organizational settings. Because of its communicative force and preference-shaping authority, only criminal process fully produces these effects of legally imposed entity blame. . . .

Questions and Comments

1. The author of this except, Samuel Buell, was one of the principal prosecutors of Arthur Andersen in the Enron scandal, discussed at length in Chapter 17.

2. Buell argues that the conventional justifications for corporate criminal liability are problematic. What justification does he propose instead?

3. As Buell notes, the scope of corporate criminal liability is potentially very large. Corporations are strictly liable for acts of their agents that cause the corporation to engage in criminal behavior — even if the corporation has done everything possible to prevent this from happening. It is true that the agent must have acted, in some sense, to serve the interests of the corporation, but nearly everything an agent does in some sense serves the interest of the principal. In what way does Buell recommend restricting the scope of corporate criminal liability?

4. Corporations, not being human, cannot feel shame. What point is there in blaming someone who is shameless?

5. Buell argues that even though corporations can't feel shame, the people who work in a corporation do experience negative reactions when their companies are prosecuted; fear of experiencing these feelings can deter people from participating in corporate wrongdoing. Do you agree?

6. Is there a social utility to allowing people a means to channel and discharge angry or judgmental feelings by observing corporations being criminally sanctioned for serious acts of misconduct?

7. If there is a social utility to blaming corporations for compliance violations, is criminal prosecution the best way to achieve this result? Why might criminal prosecutions have certain superior features over other blaming devices?

8. Are there other reasons for imposing criminal liability on a company rather than its agents? Often a company manager or agent acts out of mixed motivations; their conduct doesn't seem to be as blameworthy as that, say, of someone who hires a hit man. Because of the devastating reputational and personal impact of criminal liability, moreover, there can be a concern that the threat of criminal sanctions will over-deter — that is, that managers will be so fearful of incurring criminal liability that they shy away from committing the corporation to conduct that is not only legal, but also socially desirable. If the corporation rather than the agent is held criminally responsible, perhaps the risk of over-deterrence could be reduced — but then would the result be under-deterrence?

9. The trend toward increased stringency and vigor of criminal enforcement is unmistakable. But is it a good idea? On the one hand, it seems desirable to deter organizational misconduct, and if criminal sanctions contribute to deterrence, why not impose them? On the other hand, deterrence is not cost-free. Where standards of culpability are ambiguous, high penalties may discourage private actors from engaging in legal, socially desirable activities because they fear the consequences if they wind up being accused of committing crimes. For some organizations, meanwhile, the prospect of an acquittal at trial offers little solace because, as a practical matter, they cannot stay in business if they are accused. "Over-criminalization" is therefore a legitimate concern. But does it occur? It is virtually impossible to measure the degree to which organizations refrain from legal activities out of fear of criminal liability; the most we can do, probably, is to make an informed guess. For analysis, see Lucian E. Dervan, *White Collar Over-Criminalization: Deterrence, Plea Bargaining, and the Loss of Innocence*, 101 Ky. L.J. 543 (2013); Ellen S. Podgor, *Over-Criminalization: The Politics of Crime*, 54 Am. U. L. Rev. 541 (2005); Sara Sun Beale,

The Many Faces of Over-Criminalization: From Morals and Mattress Tags to Over-Federaliza-tion, 54 Am. U. L. Rev. 747 (2005).

10. On the other hand, in the view of some commentators, the problem is not over-criminalization, but under-criminalization. Some commentators argue that prosecutors are too lenient with corporate defendants, possibly because of concerns about the effects that severe sanctions would impose on employees, shareholders, communities, and other constituencies. Do you agree? For discussion, see Brandon L. Garrett, *Too Big to Jail: How Prosecutors Compromise with Corporations* (2014).

11. Are some institutions "too big to jail"? That is, are some firms so big or so interconnected that an indictment would be unthinkable because of the collateral harm it would create? In March 2013, Attorney General Eric Holder, in testimony before the Senate Judiciary Committee, suggested that this was the case: "[T]he size of some of these institutions becomes so large that it does become difficult for us to prosecute them when we are hit with indications that if we do prosecute — if we do bring a criminal charge — it will have a negative impact on the national economy, perhaps even the world economy." The remarks caused a firestorm. In May 2013 testimony before the House Judiciary Committee, Holder seemed to back off these comments, remarking, "Let me be very clear, there's no bank, there's no institution, there's no individual that cannot be prosecuted by the U.S. Department of Justice." Later, his deputy, in an attempt to clarify his remarks, said that while size is no bar to prosecution, the Department of Justice faces certain "complexities" when consider-ing whether to prosecute a mega-bank. What do you think?

12. Are there less costly alternatives to corporate criminal liability? For an ana-lysis of corporate regulation as an alternative to criminal sanctions, see Lisa M. Fairfax, *On the Sufficiency of Corporate Regulation as Alternative to Corporate Criminal Liability*, 41 Stetson L. Rev. 117 (2011). What if the incentives of the private sector could be enlisted to incentivize companies to better police their employees? Miriam Hechler Baer offers an interesting suggestion along these lines: She recommends that the law should abolish entity-wide criminal liability but require instead that companies take out policies of insurance against the costs of civil sanctions. In theory, the insurance company could price the policy based on its assessment of the effectiveness of the company's compliance system, and thus would penalize companies that fell short in their compliance programs. How effective would this market-based solution be as a substitute for corporate criminal liability? Would insurance policies written under this proposal be subject to moral hazard, in the sense that a company that is insured against monetary sanctions for compliance violations might become less diligent at preventing them? Could insurance compa-nies devise effective strategies to combat this problem? *See* Miriam Hechler Baer, *Insuring Corporate Crime*, 83 Ind. L.J. 1035 (2008).

B. THE DECISION TO PROSECUTE

Prosecutors do not seek indictments for every potential crime that comes to their attention. They examine the facts and circumstances to ascertain if there is sufficient evidence to establish guilt under the applicable standard of proof. Even if they conclude that a conviction is reasonably possible, they often refrain from charging an offender, applying "prosecutorial discretion." The term "discretion" in this phrase is meaningful: Prosecutors have considerable freedom to charge or not to charge an offender based on the application of relatively unconstrained judgment.

Prosecutorial discretion reflects several considerations. The resources of the prosecutor's offices are limited. As a practical matter, no prosecutor can charge and prosecute every crime that comes to her attention. Some degree of triage is necessary. Equally important, prosecutors are aware of the devastating consequences of an indictment for the person being charged. Even if someone may have committed an offense, the prosecutor may decide that the facts and circumstances are such that it would be better that the person not be charged.

On the other hand, while there are good reasons for prosecutorial discretion, there are also reasons for limiting that discretion in appropriate cases. Untrammeled discretion facilitates abuse of the prosecutor's office for political purposes and raises concerns in the public about the rule of law. Too much discretion can also impair the deterrence objectives of the criminal law. Taken to the extreme, discretion can convert the prosecutor into some version of the Queen of Hearts in *Alice's Adventures in Wonderland*, who orders capital punishment at random, with the result that no one pays any attention. Constraints on prosecutorial discretion give citizens notice about what conduct is likely to be punished and how severe the punishment will be, enhancing compliance with those rules that the prosecutor takes most seriously. Constraints on prosecutorial discretion also facilitate the effective management of the prosecutor's office by giving clear indications to staff attorneys about enforcement priorities.

The following excerpt is a statement of how the U.S. Department of Justice exercises prosecutorial discretion in deciding whether or not to charge corporations with criminal offenses.

United States Attorneys Manual, Principles of Federal Prosecution of Business Organizations

2015

9-28.100 Corporate directors and officers owe a fiduciary duty to a corporation's shareholders (the corporation's true owners) and they owe duties of honest dealing to the investing public and consumers in connection with the corporation's regulatory filings and public statements. A prosecutor's duty to enforce the law requires the investigation and prosecution of criminal wrongdoing if it is discovered. In carrying out this mission with the diligence and resolve necessary to vindicate the important public interests discussed above, prosecutors should be mindful of the common cause we share with responsible corporate leaders who seek to promote trust and confidence . . . .

9-28.200 General Principle: Corporations should not be treated leniently because of their artificial nature nor should they be subject to harsher treatment. Vigorous enforcement of the criminal laws against corporate wrongdoers, where appropriate, results in great benefits for law enforcement and the public, particularly in the area of white collar crime. Indicting corporations for wrongdoing enables the government to be a force for positive change of corporate culture, and a force to prevent, discover, and punish serious crimes. . . .

9-28.210 Focus on Individual Wrongdoers: General Principle: Prosecution of a corporation is not a substitute for the prosecution of criminally culpable individuals within or without the corporation. Because a corporation can act only through individuals, imposition of individual criminal liability may provide the strongest deterrent against future corporate wrongdoing. Provable individual culpability should be pursued, particularly if it relates to high-level corporate officers, even in the face of an offer of a corporate guilty plea or some other disposition of the charges against the corporation, including a deferred prosecution or non-prosecution agreement, or a civil resolution. In other words, regardless of the ultimate corporate disposition, a separate evaluation must be made with respect to potentially liable individuals.

9-28.300 Factors to Be Considered: General Principle: Generally, prosecutors apply the same factors in determining whether to charge a corporation as they do with respect to individuals. Thus, the prosecutor must weigh all of the factors normally considered in the sound exercise of prosecutorial judgment: the sufficiency of the evidence; the likelihood of success at trial; the probable deterrent, rehabilitative, and other consequences of conviction; and the adequacy of noncriminal approaches. However, due to the nature of the corporate "person," some additional factors are present. In conducting an investigation, determining whether to bring charges, and negotiating plea or other agreements, prosecutors should consider the following factors in reaching a decision as to the proper treatment of a corporate target:

- the nature and seriousness of the offense, including the risk of harm to the public, and applicable policies and priorities, if any, governing the prosecution of corporations for particular categories of crime;
- the pervasiveness of wrongdoing within the corporation, including the complicity in, or the condoning of, the wrongdoing by corporate management;
- the corporation's history of similar misconduct, including prior criminal, civil, and regulatory enforcement actions against it;
- the corporation's willingness to cooperate in the investigation of its agents;
- the existence and effectiveness of the corporation's pre-existing compliance program;
- the corporation's timely and voluntary disclosure of wrongdoing;
- the corporation's remedial actions, including any efforts to implement an effective corporate compliance program or to improve an existing one, to replace responsible management, to discipline or terminate wrongdoers, to pay restitution, and to cooperate with the relevant government agencies;
- collateral consequences, including whether there is disproportionate harm to shareholders, pension holders, employees, and others not proven personally culpable, as well as impact on the public arising from the prosecution;
- the adequacy of remedies such as civil or regulatory enforcement actions; and
- the adequacy of the prosecution of individuals responsible for the corporation's malfeasance.

9-28.400 Special Policy Concerns: General Principle: The nature and seriousness of the crime, including the risk of harm to the public from the criminal misconduct, are obviously primary factors in determining whether to charge a corporation. In addition, corporate conduct, particularly that of national and multi-national corporations, necessarily intersects with federal economic, tax, and criminal law enforcement policies. In applying these Principles, prosecutors must consider the practices and policies of the appropriate Division of the Department, and must comply with those policies to the extent required by the facts presented. . . .

9-28.500 Pervasiveness of Wrongdoing Within the Corporation: General Principle: A corporation can only act through natural persons, and it is therefore held responsible for the acts of such persons fairly attributable to it. Charging a corporation for even minor misconduct may be appropriate where the wrongdoing was pervasive and was undertaken by a large number of employees, or by all the employees in a particular role within the corporation, or was condoned by upper management. On the other hand, it may not be appropriate to impose liability upon a corporation, particularly one with a robust compliance program in place, under a strict *respondeat superior* theory for the single isolated act of a rogue employee. There is, of course, a wide spectrum between these two extremes, and a prosecutor should exercise sound discretion in evaluating the pervasiveness of wrongdoing within a corporation. . . .

9-28.600 The Corporation's Past History: General Principle: Prosecutors may consider a corporation's history of similar conduct, including prior criminal, civil, and regulatory enforcement actions against it, in determining whether to bring criminal charges and how best to resolve cases. . . .

9-28.700 The Value of Cooperation: General Principle: In order for a company to receive any consideration for cooperation under this section, the company must identify all individuals involved in or responsible for the misconduct at issue, regardless of their position, status or seniority, and provide to the Department all facts relating to that misconduct. If a company seeking cooperation credit declines to learn of such facts or to provide the Department with complete factual information about the individuals involved, its cooperation will not be considered a mitigating factor under this section. Nor, if a company is prosecuted, will the Department support a cooperation-related reduction at sentencing. If a company meets the threshold requirement of providing all relevant facts with respect to individuals, it will be eligible for consideration for cooperation credit. To be clear, a company is not required to waive its attorney-client privilege and attorney work product protection in order to satisfy this threshold. The extent of the cooperation credit earned will depend on all the various factors that have traditionally applied in making this assessment (e.g., the timeliness of the cooperation, the diligence, thoroughness and speed of the internal investigation, and the proactive nature of the cooperation).

9-28.720 Cooperation: Disclosing the Relevant Facts: Eligibility for cooperation credit is not predicated upon the waiver of attorney-client privilege or work product protection. Instead, the sort of cooperation that is most valuable to resolving allegations of misconduct by a corporation and its officers, directors, employees, or agents is disclosure of the relevant *facts* concerning such misconduct. In this regard, the analysis parallels that for a non-corporate defendant, where cooperation typically requires disclosure of relevant factual knowledge and not of discussions between an individual and his attorneys.

Thus, when the government investigates potential corporate wrongdoing, it seeks the relevant facts. For example, how and when did the alleged misconduct occur? Who promoted or approved it? Who was responsible for committing it? In this respect, the investigation of a corporation differs little from the investigation of an individual. In both cases, the government needs to know the facts to achieve a just and fair outcome. The party under investigation may choose to cooperate by disclosing the facts, and the government may give credit for the party's disclosures. If a corporation wishes to receive credit for such cooperation, which then can be considered with all other cooperative efforts and circumstances in evaluating how fairly to proceed, then the corporation, like any person, must disclose the relevant facts of which it has knowledge.

Individuals and corporations often obtain knowledge of facts in different ways. An individual knows the facts of his or others' misconduct through his own experience and perceptions. A corporation is an artificial construct that cannot, by definition, have personal knowledge of the facts. Some of those facts may be reflected in documentary or electronic media like emails, transaction or accounting documents, and other records. Often, the corporation gathers facts through an internal investigation. Exactly how and by whom the facts are gathered is for the corporation to decide. Many corporations choose to collect information about potential misconduct through lawyers, a process that may confer attorney-client privilege or attorney work product protection on at least some of the information collected. Other corporations may choose a method of fact-gathering that does not have that effect — for example, having employee or other witness statements collected after interviews by non-attorney personnel. Whichever process the corporation selects, the government's key measure of cooperation must remain the same as it does for an individual: has the party timely disclosed the relevant facts about the putative misconduct? That is the operative question in assigning cooperation credit for the disclosure of information — *not* whether the corporation discloses attorney-client or work product materials. Accordingly, a corporation should receive the same credit for disclosing facts contained in materials that are not protected by the attorney-client privilege or attorney work product as it would for disclosing identical facts contained in materials that are so protected. . . .

In short, the company may be eligible for cooperation credit regardless of whether it chooses to waive privilege or work product protection in the process, if it provides all relevant facts about the individuals who were involved in the misconduct. But if the corporation does not disclose such facts, it will not be entitled to receive any credit for cooperation.

Two final and related points bear noting about the disclosure of facts, although they should be obvious. First, the government cannot compel, and the corporation has no obligation to make, such disclosures (although the government can obviously compel the disclosure of certain records and witness testimony through subpoenas). Second, a corporation's failure to provide relevant information about individual misconduct alone does not mean the corporation will be indicted. It simply means that the corporation will not be entitled to mitigating credit for that cooperation. Whether the corporation faces charges will turn, as it does in any case, on the sufficiency of the evidence, the likelihood of success at trial, and all of the other [relevant] factors. . . . If there is insufficient evidence to warrant indictment, after appropriate investigation has been completed, or if the other factors weigh against indictment, then the corporation should not be indicted, irrespective of whether it has earned cooperation credit. The converse is also true: The government may charge even the most cooperative corporation pursuant to these Principles if, in weighing and balancing the factors described herein, the prosecutor determines that a charge is required in the interests of justice. Put differently, even the most sincere and thorough effort to cooperate cannot necessarily absolve a corporation that has, for example, engaged in an egregious, orchestrated, and widespread fraud. Cooperation is a potential mitigating factor, but it alone is not dispositive. . . .

9-28.730 Obstructing the Investigation: Another factor to be weighed by the prosecutor is whether the corporation has engaged in conduct intended to impede the investigation. Examples of such conduct could include: inappropriate directions to employees or their counsel, such as directions not to be truthful or to conceal relevant facts; making representations or submissions that contain misleading assertions or material omissions; and incomplete or delayed production of records. . . .

9-28.740 Offering Cooperation: No Entitlement to Immunity: A corporation's offer of cooperation or cooperation itself does not automatically entitle it to immunity from prosecution or a favorable resolution of its case. A corporation should not be able to escape liability merely by offering up its directors, officers, employees, or agents. Thus, a corporation's willingness to cooperate is not determinative; that factor, while relevant, needs to be considered in conjunction with all other factors.

9-28.750 Oversight Concerning Demands for Waivers of Attorney-Client Privilege or Work Product Protection by Corporations Contrary to This Policy: The Department underscores the attorney practices that are consistent with Department policies like those set forth herein concerning cooperation credit and due respect for the attorney-client privilege and work product protection. Counsel for corporations who believe that prosecutors are violating such guidance are encouraged to raise their concerns with supervisors, including the appropriate United States Attorney or Assistant Attorney General. Like any other allegation of attorney misconduct, such allegations are subject to potential investigation through established mechanisms.

9-28.800 Corporate Compliance Programs: General Principle: Compliance programs are established by corporate management to prevent and detect misconduct and to ensure that corporate activities are conducted in accordance with applicable criminal and civil laws, regulations, and rules. The Department encourages such corporate self-policing, including voluntary disclosures to the government of any problems that a corporation discovers on its own. However, the existence of a compliance program is not sufficient, in and of itself, to justify not charging a corporation for criminal misconduct undertaken by its officers, directors, employees, or agents. In addition, the nature of some crimes, e.g., antitrust violations, may be such that national law enforcement policies mandate prosecutions of corporations notwithstanding the existence of a compliance program.

The existence of a corporate compliance program, even one that specifically prohibited the very conduct in question, does not absolve the corporation from criminal liability under the doctrine of *respondeat superior.*

While the Department recognizes that no compliance program can ever prevent all criminal activity by a corporation's employees, the critical factors in evaluating any program are whether the program is adequately designed for maximum effectiveness in preventing and detecting wrongdoing by employees and whether corporate management is enforcing the program or is tacitly encouraging or pressuring employees to engage in misconduct to achieve business objectives. The Department has no formulaic requirements regarding corporate compliance programs. The fundamental questions any prosecutor should ask are: Is the corporation's compliance program well designed? Is the program being applied earnestly and in good faith? Does the corporation's compliance program work? In answering these questions, the prosecutor should consider the comprehensiveness of the compliance program; the extent and pervasiveness of the criminal misconduct; the number and level of the corporate employees involved; the seriousness, duration, and frequency of the misconduct; and any remedial actions taken by the corporation, including, for example, disciplinary action against past violators uncovered by the prior compliance program, and revisions to corporate compliance programs in light of lessons learned. Prosecutors should also consider the promptness of any disclosure of wrongdoing to the government. In evaluating compliance programs, prosecutors may consider whether the corporation has established corporate governance mechanisms that can effectively detect and prevent misconduct. For example, do the corporation's directors exercise independent review over proposed corporate actions rather than unquestioningly ratifying officers' recommendations; are internal audit functions conducted at a level sufficient to ensure their independence and accuracy; and have the directors established an information and reporting system in the organization reasonably designed to provide management and directors with timely and accurate information sufficient to allow them to reach an informed decision regarding the organization's compliance with the law.

Prosecutors should therefore attempt to determine whether a corporation's compliance program is merely a "paper program" or whether it was designed, implemented, reviewed, and revised, as appropriate, in an effective manner. In addition, prosecutors should determine whether the corporation has provided for a staff sufficient to audit, document, analyze, and utilize the results of the corporation's compliance efforts. Prosecutors also should determine whether the corporation's employees are adequately informed about the compliance program and are convinced of the corporation's commitment to it. This will enable the prosecutor to make an informed decision as to whether the corporation has adopted and implemented a truly effective compliance program that, when consistent with other federal law enforcement policies, may result in a decision to charge only the corporation's employees and agents or to mitigate charges or sanctions against the corporation.

Compliance programs should be designed to detect the particular types of misconduct most likely to occur in a particular corporation's line of business. Many corporations operate in complex regulatory environments outside the normal experience of criminal prosecutors. Accordingly, prosecutors should consult with relevant federal and state agencies with the expertise to evaluate the adequacy of a program's design and implementation. . . .

9-28.900 Voluntary Disclosures: In conjunction with regulatory agencies and other executive branch departments, the Department encourages corporations, as part of their compliance programs, to conduct internal investigations and to disclose the relevant facts to the appropriate authorities. Some agencies, such as the Securities and Exchange Commission and the Environmental Protection Agency, as well as the Department's Environmental and Natural Resources Division, have formal voluntary disclosure programs in which self-reporting, coupled with remediation and additional criteria, may qualify the corporation for amnesty or reduced sanctions. The Antitrust Division has a policy of offering amnesty to the first corporation that self-discloses and agrees to cooperate.

Even in the absence of a formal program, prosecutors may consider a corporation's timely and voluntary disclosure, both as an independent factor and in evaluating the company's overall cooperation and the adequacy of the corporation's compliance program and its management's commitment to the compliance program. However, prosecution may be appropriate notwithstanding a corporation's voluntary disclosure. Such a determination should be based on a consideration of all the factors set forth in these Principles.

9-28.1000 Restitution and Remediation: General Principle: Although neither a corporation nor an individual target may avoid prosecution merely by paying a sum of money, a prosecutor may consider the corporation's willingness to make restitution and steps already taken to do so. A prosecutor may also consider other remedial actions, such as improving an existing compliance program or disciplining wrongdoers, in determining whether to charge the corporation and how to resolve corporate criminal cases.

In determining whether or not to prosecute a corporation, the government may consider whether the corporation has taken meaningful remedial measures. A corporation's response to misconduct says much about its willingness to ensure that such misconduct does not recur. Thus, corporations that fully recognize the seriousness of their misconduct and accept responsibility for it should be taking steps to implement the personnel, operational, and organizational changes necessary to establish an awareness among employees that criminal conduct will not be tolerated.

Among the factors prosecutors should consider and weigh are whether the corporation appropriately disciplined wrongdoers, once those employees are identified by the corporation as culpable for the misconduct. Employee discipline is a difficult task for many corporations because of the human element involved and sometimes because of the seniority of the employees concerned. Although corporations need to be fair to their employees, they must also be committed, at all levels of the corporation, to the highest standards of legal and ethical behavior. Effective internal discipline can be a powerful deterrent against improper behavior by a corporation's employees. Prosecutors should be satisfied that the corporation's focus is on the integrity and credibility of its remedial and disciplinary measures rather than on the protection of the wrongdoers.

In addition to employee discipline, two other factors used in evaluating a corporation's remedial efforts are restitution and reform. As with natural persons, the decision whether or not to prosecute should not depend upon the target's ability to pay restitution. A corporation's efforts to pay restitution even in advance of any court order is, however, evidence of its acceptance of responsibility and, consistent with the practices and policies of the appropriate Division of the Department entrusted with enforcing specific criminal laws, may be considered in determining whether to bring criminal charges. Similarly, although the inadequacy of a corporate compliance program is a factor to consider when deciding whether to charge a corporation, that corporation's quick recognition of the flaws in the program and its efforts to improve the program are also factors to consider as to the appropriate disposition of a case.

9-28.1100 Collateral Consequences: General Principle: Prosecutors may consider the collateral consequences of a corporate criminal conviction or indictment in determining whether to charge the corporation with a criminal offense and how to resolve corporate criminal cases.

One of the factors in determining whether to charge a natural person or a corporation is whether the likely punishment is appropriate given the nature and seriousness of the crime. In the corporate context, prosecutors may take into account the possibly substantial consequences to a corporation's employees, investors, pensioners, and customers, many of whom may, depending on the size and nature of the corporation and their role in its operations, have played no role in the criminal conduct, have been unaware of it, or have been unable to prevent it. Prosecutors should also be aware of non-penal sanctions that may accompany a criminal charge, such as potential suspension or debarment from eligibility for government contracts or federally funded programs such as health care programs. Determining whether or not such non-penal sanctions are appropriate or required in a particular case is the responsibility of the relevant agency, and is a decision that will be made based on the applicable statutes, regulations, and policies.

Almost every conviction of a corporation, like almost every conviction of an individual, will have an impact on innocent third parties, and the mere existence of such an effect is not sufficient to preclude prosecution of the corporation. There-fore, in evaluating the relevance of collateral consequences, various factors already discussed, such as the pervasiveness of the criminal conduct and the adequacy of the corporation's compliance programs, should be considered in determining the weight to be given to this factor. For instance, the balance may tip in favor of prosecuting corporations in situations where the scope of the misconduct in a case is widespread and sustained within a corporate division (or spread throughout pockets of the corporate organization). In such cases, the possible unfairness of visiting punishment for the corporation's crimes upon shareholders may be of much less concern where those shareholders have substantially profited, even unknowingly, from widespread or pervasive criminal activity. Similarly, where the top layers of the corporation's management or the shareholders of a closely-held corporation were engaged in or aware of the wrongdoing, and the conduct at issue was accepted as a way of doing business for an extended period, debarment may be deemed not collateral, but a direct and entirely appropriate consequence of the corporation's wrongdoing . . . .

9-28.1200 Civil or Regulatory Alternatives: General Principle: Prosecutors should consider whether non-criminal alternatives would adequately deter, punish, and rehabilitate a corporation that has engaged in wrongful conduct. In evaluating the adequacy of non-criminal alternatives to prosecution — *e.g.*, civil or regulatory enforcement actions — the prosecutor should consider all relevant factors, including:

- the sanctions available under the alternative means of disposition;
- the likelihood that an effective sanction will be imposed; and
- the effect of non-criminal disposition on federal law enforcement interests.

While non-criminal sanctions may not be appropriate where a serious violation, pattern of wrongdoing, or prior non-criminal sanctions without proper remediation have occurred, there may be other instances where the goals of punishment, deter-rence, and rehabilitation may be satisfied through civil or regulatory actions against the corporation. In determining whether the most appropriate resolution for a corporation is a criminal resolution or a civil or regulatory resolution, prosecutors and their civil counterparts should confer and consider factors similar to those considered when determining whether to leave prosecution of a natural person to another jurisdiction or to seek civil or other regulatory alternatives. These factors include: the strength of the civil or regulatory authority's interest; the civil or reg-ulatory authority's ability and willingness to take effective enforcement action; the probable sanction if the civil or regulatory authority's enforcement action is upheld; and the effect of a non-criminal disposition on criminal law enforcement interests. In order to make possible a consideration of the full range of the government's remedies and promote the most thorough and appropriate resolution in every case, criminal prosecutors handling corporate investigations should maintain early and regular communication with their civil counterparts and regulatory attorneys, to the extent permitted by law, and even if it is not certain whether the end result will be a civil or criminal disposition.

9-28.1300 Adequacy of the Prosecution of Individuals: General Principle: In deciding whether to charge a corporation, prosecutors should consider whether charges against the individuals responsible for the corporation's malfeasance will adequately satisfy the goals of federal prosecution.

Assessing the adequacy of individual prosecutions for corporate misconduct should be made on a case-by-case basis and in light of the factors discussed in these Principles. Thus, in deciding the most appropriate course of action for the corporation — i.e., a corporate indictment, a deferred prosecution or non-prosecution agreement, or another alternative — a prosecutor should consider the impact of the prosecution of responsible individuals, along with the other factors . . . .

Questions and Comments

1. The Manual claims that "corporate directors and officers owe a fiduciary duty to a corporation's shareholders (the corporation's true owners)." Corporate attorneys might quibble with this comment. Technically, managers owe fiduciary duties to the *companies* — not to the shareholders. The distinction might be subtle, but a purist would be inclined to point it out. Further, what does the document mean when it says that shareholders are the "true" owners of a company? Who else could be the owner?

2. The Manual was revised in 2015 to reflect the Department's new focus on pursuing individual malefactors, discussed in Chapter 6 in connection with the Yates Memo. Does it draw the right balance in this regard?

3. The Manual acknowledges that certain types of crime can be given special treatment. As an example, it cites the Antitrust Division's policy that that amnesty is available only to the first corporation to come clean. What is different about criminal violations of the antitrust laws? Is the exception for antitrust cases an example of ceding turf to a competing division with the Department of Justice?

4. How does the Manual deal with the potential breadth of corporate criminal liability? Under the theory of *respondeat superior*, any act of any corporate employee may be the basis for corporate criminal liability, so long as it is committed with an intent to serve the company. If the Justice Department indicted all such cases there would be no end to corporate criminal prosecutions. The Manual addresses this issue, in part, with the concept of "pervasiveness": Conduct of low-level employees will be the basis for charging the corporation, but only if it is widespread. The idea seems to be that prosecutors will overlook isolated or sporadic cases where low-level employees commit federal crimes; but if many such employees commit crimes, the company can face an indictment. Does this make sense as a principle of prosecutorial discretion?

5. What if the criminal behavior is isolated, but the employee or employees involved are high-level corporate officials? The Manual indicates that in such cases the government may well seek an indictment, even though the offenses are committed only by a few people. Is this a sensible approach?

6. Large companies are complex organizations, often operating many divisions conducting different forms of business in different locations. What if a company has an excellent enterprise-level compliance program adopted at its home office in Minneapolis, but one rogue division in Dallas commits a crime? Should the entire company be indicted? What if the crime is committed by a wholly-owned subsidiary?

7. Among the factors federal prosecutors should consider in deciding whether to charge a corporation with criminal misconduct is the presence of "collateral consequences, including whether there is disproportionate harm to shareholders, pension holders, employees, and others not proven personally culpable, as well as

impact on the public arising from the prosecution." Do innocent shareholders always suffer disproportionate harm when a corporation is indicted?

8. The Manual provides a powerful incentive for corporations to adopt compliance programs, by indicating that the existence of such programs is a factor the Department of Justice will consider in deciding whether to prosecute a corporation. At the same time, it warns that the program in question must not be merely a "paper" program but instead must be bona fide and effective. Of course, no program will announce that it is intended to be ineffective. Do prosecutors possess the training and experience needed to distinguish between effective and ineffective programs? What guidance does the Manual provide?

9. In cases where prosecution of a corporation is contemplated, we may infer that the compliance program has not succeeded in preventing employees from engaging in misconduct. What weight should prosecutors give to the evident failure of the program when they assess whether it is effective?

10. What steps should a corporation take once the Department of Justice starts a criminal investigation? Is it then too late to qualify for leniency if the company has no compliance program or has failed to identify or disclose the criminal conduct on its own? The Department's answer is no. The company will get credit for undertaking certain actions: cooperating with the authorities and implementing remedial actions designed to ensure that the problems do not recur. How much credit should a company receive for cleaning up its act after the fact?

11. The Manual indicates that a corporation may receive credit if it takes appropriate disciplinary actions against the employees who participated in the wrongdoing. What sorts of disciplinary actions should qualify?

12. At various points in the excerpt the Manual disclaims any intent to intrude on attorney-client privilege or work-product protection. These disclaimers reflect a long and tortuous process within the agency, which at one time explicitly considered waivers of privilege to be a mitigating factor. Do you think the Manual goes far enough in protecting the privilege?

13. It appears clear that the Department of Justice does not consider the attorney-client privilege to extend to facts — even if those facts are discovered by the company during the course of an investigation conducted by counsel. Many attorneys representing private clients would disagree with this interpretation of the scope of privilege, since it appears to limit the protection to the narrow category of communications between lawyer and client specifically involving the provision of legal advice — a position that appears to be in implicit tension with the arguably broader scope of privilege recognized in Upjohn v. United States, 449 U.S. 383 (1981). Having pared the privilege to the quick, the Department can proclaim adherence to its sanctity without sacrificing much in the way of investigatory power.

C. PLEA BARGAINS, DEFERRED PROSECUTION AGREEMENTS, AND NON-PROSECUTION AGREEMENTS

Corporate criminal cases rarely go to trial. Much more commonly, the prosecutor's charges will be resolved by some sort of pretrial disposition. Three forms of pretrial disposition are important: plea bargains, deferred prosecution agreements, and non-prosecution agreements.

1. Plea Bargains

United States Attorneys Manual, Principles of Federal Prosecution of Business Organizations

2015

9-28.1500 Plea Agreements with Corporations: General Principle: In negotiating plea agreements with corporations, as with individuals, prosecutors should generally seek a plea to an appropriate offense. In addition, the terms of the plea agreement should contain appropriate provisions to ensure punishment, deterrence, rehabilitation, and compliance with the plea agreement in the corporate context. Absent extraordinary circumstances or approved departmental policy such as the Antitrust Division's Corporate Leniency Policy, no corporate resolution should provide protection from criminal or civil liability for any individuals.

Prosecutors may enter into plea agreements with corporations for the same reasons and under the same constraints as apply to plea agreements with natural persons. This means, inter alia, that the corporation should generally be required to plead guilty to the most serious, readily provable offense charged . . . . A corporation should be made to realize that pleading guilty to criminal charges constitutes an admission of guilt and not merely a resolution of an inconvenient distraction from its business. As with natural persons, pleas should be structured so that the corporation may not later "proclaim lack of culpability or even complete innocence." Thus, for instance, there should be placed upon the record a sufficient factual basis for the plea to prevent later corporate assertions of innocence.

A corporate plea agreement should also contain provisions that recognize the nature of the corporate "person" and that ensure that the principles of punishment, deterrence, and rehabilitation are met. In the corporate context, punishment and deterrence are generally accomplished by substantial fines, mandatory restitution, and institution of appropriate compliance measures, including, if necessary, continued judicial oversight or the use of special masters or corporate monitors. In addition, where the corporation is a government contractor, permanent or temporary debarment may be appropriate. Where the corporation was engaged in fraud against the government (e.g., contracting fraud), a prosecutor may not negotiate away an agency's right to debar or delist the corporate defendant.

Questions and Comments

1. Sometimes defendants plead guilty, in exchange for a reduced sentence, but then deny their guilt when questioned by the court. The problem presented is whether to accept the plea, given that the defendant now asserts his innocence. In North Carolina v. Alford, 400 U.S. 25 (1970), the Supreme Court held that a court may accept the defendant's guilty plea, notwithstanding later protestations of innocence, if the plea is knowingly and deliberately made and the record contains sufficient evidence of guilt. The Alford case allows courts, in appropriate circumstances, to refuse to give effect to the defendant's claims of innocence when reviewing plea bargain agreements.

2. What if, after a plea agreement is finalized, the defendant subsequently proclaims her innocence or seeks to minimize her guilt? Such behavior is problematic because it detracts from the perceived gravity of the offense and reduces the deterrent effect of the prosecution on other companies; it also indicates that the defendant is likely to commit future offenses. The Manual disapproves of such conduct, warning that "[a] corporation should be made to realize that pleading guilty to criminal charges constitutes an admission of guilt and not merely a resolution of an inconvenient distraction from its business." But how can the prosecutors prevent such behavior? Several factors work together to discourage defendants from disavowing or minimizing responsibility for their crimes:

a. Some jurisdictions require that the defendant make a statement at the time the plea is presented that admits guilt (an "allocution"). Having made the statement, the defendant will be hard-pressed to disavow it.

b. As indicated in the document excerpted above, the prosecutors are advised to place evidence of guilt on the record, which can be used to refute subsequent protestations of innocence.

c. If, despite the foregoing, a defendant acts in such a way as to indicate it doesn't take the guilty plea seriously, the prosecutors or civil regulators are likely to view this conduct in a negative light the next time the defendant gets into trouble.

3. Some jurisdictions allow a plea of *nolo contendere* (no contest), which neither admits nor denies guilt but which can have the same effect as a guilty plea for purposes of plea bargaining. When the defendant enters a *nolo* plea, she may be relieved from the need to allocute the plea by formally admitting to wrongful acts. Although the rules vary across jurisdictions, this procedure can limit the degree to which the plea bargain can be used against the defendant in subsequent civil, criminal, or administrative proceedings. Does this use of the *nolo contendere* plea represent sound public policy for corporate defendants?

4. Although federal courts do not prohibit *nolo* pleas, see Hudson v. United States, 272 U.S. 451 (1926), the U.S. Department of Justice generally refuses to negotiate them. If the defendant is adamant, the DOJ might in some cases "wink" at the *nolo* plea by simply allowing the defendant to make the plea in court, without the department's approval, and then cooperating with the defendant in a joint sentencing recommendation. A risk to the defendant from this approach, even if the prosecutors agree to go along, is that the recommendation is not binding and therefore might be ignored by the sentencing judge.

5. Corporate defendants often resist entering into plea agreements because of the potential collateral consequences. The admission of guilt that is required in a plea agreement may deprive a corporate defendant of the protections of its insurance coverage, which may exclude indemnification for criminal misconduct. The guilty plea may come back to haunt the company or its directors in civil litigation brought by shareholders or others. The company may forfeit the right to bid on government contracts. The reputational costs of a plea agreement are also high, particularly in certain areas of commerce such as the service or government contracting sectors. How does the Manual deal with these collateral consequences? Does it provide sufficient guidance to prosecutors as to how to exercise discretion with respect to this consideration?

2. Deferred Prosecution and Non-Prosecution Agreements

Deferred prosecution agreements (DPAs) or non-prosecution agreements (NPAs) offer alternative avenues to dispose of corporate criminal cases without the inconveniences and risks of a formal guilty plea.

a. Nature and Rationale

In the DPA, the target complies with the government's investigation and agrees to implement remedial measures; in exchange the government agrees to defer the filing of charges. If the target satisfies the government that it has fully complied with its promises, the government never brings the prosecution. An NPA is similar except that the government is satisfied with the target's compliance and therefore agrees to drop the case at the time of the agreement. NPAs, being more definitive, are typically seen only when the target has made a prompt self-report of the violation and provided the government with extensive cooperation in its investigation.

These sorts of agreements have grown greatly in importance over the past decade. According to one estimate, the Department of Justice entered into 35 corporate DPAs or NPAs in 2012, with total recoveries of $9 billion.

United States Attorneys Manual, Principles of Federal Prosecution of Business Organizations

2015

9-28.1100 Collateral Consequences

. . . [W]here the collateral consequences of a corporate conviction for innocent third parties would be significant, it may be appropriate to consider a non-prosecution or deferred prosecution agreement with conditions designed, among other things, to promote compliance with applicable law and to prevent recidivism. Such agreements are a third option, besides a criminal indictment, on the one hand, and a declination, on the other. Declining prosecution may allow a corporate criminal to escape without consequences. Obtaining a conviction may produce a result that seriously harms innocent third parties who played no role in the criminal conduct. Under appropriate circumstances, a deferred prosecution or non-prosecution agreement can help restore the integrity of a company's operations and preserve the financial viability of a corporation that has engaged in criminal conduct, while preserving the government's ability to prosecute a recalcitrant corporation that materially breaches the agreement. Such agreements achieve other important objectives as well, like prompt restitution for victims. The appropriateness of a criminal charge against a corporation, or some lesser alternative, must be evaluated in a pragmatic and reasoned way that produces a fair outcome, taking into consideration, among other things, the Department's need to promote and ensure respect for the law.

Questions and Comments

1. DPAs and NPAs conserve on the prosecutor's resources and generate reasonably credible guarantees of compliance going forward — all good things. But are there any downsides? Note that unlike a plea agreement, a DPA or NPA doesn't have

to be presented to a court for review. This means that, at least for the particular case, there will be no judicial evaluation of the credibility of the government's case or the reasonableness of its legal theories. Is it possible that, armed with the formidable threat of prosecution, the government may be able to enforce stretched or exorbitant interpretations of the law?

2. Companies ordinarily do not admit guilt when entering into a DPA or NPA. Should they be required to do so? What stops them from subsequently proclaiming their innocence?

3. Do victims of wrongdoing have any standing to object to the terms of a DPA or NPA? Can they appeal the trial court's decision to approve one of these agreements? Should they be entitled to restitution for the harms they suffered? In general, the answer is no to each. Should victims be given greater rights in this setting? What are the pros and cons?

4. Targets often agree to adopt enhanced compliance programs and activities as consideration for the government's agreement to a DPA or NPA. Do such agreements represent a genuine sanction, or are they a face-saving way that the government and the target can both put the matter behind them without admitting failure or fault?

5. For an empirically based analysis of the effects of DPAs and NPAs on corporate governance, see Wulf A. Kaal & Timothy A. Lane, *The Effect of Deferred and Non-Prosecution Agreements on Corporate Governance: Evidence from 1993-2013*, 70 Bus. Law. 6 (Winter 2014-2015).

b. Contents

The following excerpt provides an example of what the government expects in a DPA:

United States District Court for the Southern District of Texas

United States of America	:	
	:	**NO: CR H-07-05(LNH)**
v.	:	
	:	
Aibel Group Limited	:	

Deferred Prosecution Agreement

Defendant Aibel Group Limited ("Aibel Group"), a United Kingdom corporation, by its undersigned attorneys, pursuant to authority granted by its Board of Directors, and the United States Department of Justice, Criminal Division, Fraud Section ("Department of Justice" or the "Department") enter into this Deferred Prosecution Agreement ("Agreement") which shall apply to Aibel Group, its subsidiaries, including Vetco Aibel AS, Vetco Aibel Holding Limited and Drilling Controls Inc., (all three hereinafter referred to as "Principal Subsidiaries") and all affiliates and subsidiaries thereof (hereinafter jointly referred to as the "Vetco Aibel Entities"). The terms and conditions of this Agreement are as follows:

Aibel Group accepts and acknowledges that the United States will file a criminal Information in the United States District Court for the Southern District of Texas charging Aibel Group with violating the Foreign Corrupt Practices Act ("FCPA").

In so doing, Aibel Group knowingly waives its right to indictment on these charges, as well as all rights to a speedy trial pursuant to the Sixth Amendment to the United States Constitution, Title 18, United States Code Section 3161, Federal Rule of Criminal Procedure 48(b), and all applicable Local Rules of the United States District Court for the Southern District of Texas for the period during which this Agreement is in effect.

Aibel Group accepts and acknowledges that it is responsible for the acts of its officers and employees as set forth in the Statement of Facts annexed hereto as "Attachment A." Should the Department . . . initiate the prosecution that is deferred by this Agreement, Aibel Group agrees that it will neither contest the admissibility of, nor contradict, in any such proceeding, the facts contained in the Statement of Facts. Aibel Group does not endorse, ratify or condone criminal conduct and, as set forth below, has taken and commits to continue to take significant steps to prevent such conduct from occurring in the future.

This Agreement is agreed to by the Department based upon the fact that Aibel Group had voluntarily disclosed the misconduct referenced in the Statement of Facts; conducted a thorough investigation of that misconduct; regularly reported all its findings to the Department; cooperated in the Department's subsequent investigation of this matter; agreed to implement remedial measures to ensure that this conduct will not recur and to continue to cooperate with the Department in its ongoing investigation of the conduct of Aibel Group, the Vetco Aibel Entities, and the officers, directors and employees thereof; and, proposed and agreed to the compliance structure set forth . . . herein, including the duties and obligations of the Executive Chairperson, Compliance Committee and Compliance Counsel as more fully set out herein.

During the three (3) year term of this Agreement, Aibel Group agrees to cooperate fully with the Department, and any other authority or agency, domestic or foreign, designated by the Department investigating Aibel Group and the Vetco Aibel Entities, or any of its present and former directors, officers, employees, agents, consultants, contractors and subcontractors, or any other party, in any and all matters relating to corrupt payments in connection with its operations. Aibel Group agrees that its cooperation shall include, but is not limited to, the following:

- Aibel Group and the Vetco Aibel Entities shall continue to cooperate fully with the Department, and with all other authorities and agencies designated by the Department, and shall truthfully disclose all information with respect to the activities of Aibel Group and the Vetco Aibel Entities and its present and former subsidiaries and affiliates, and the directors, officers, employees, agents, consultants, contractors and subcontractors thereof, concerning all matters relating to corrupt payments in connection with their operations, related false books and records, and inadequate internal controls about which Aibel Group and the Vetco Aibel Entities has any knowledge or about which the Department shall require. This obligation of truthful disclosure includes the obligation of Aibel Group and the Vetco Aibel Entities to provide to the Department, upon request, any document, record, or other tangible evidence relating to such corrupt payments, books and records, and internal controls about which the Department shall inquire of Aibel Group and the Vetco Aibel Entities. If specifically requested by the Department, this obligation of truthful disclosure also includes an obligation to provide access to the information, documents, records, facilities and employees of Aibel Group and the Vetco Aibel Entities that may be subject to the attorney-client and/or work product privileges. The parties also agree that the disclosure of information to the Compliance Counsel retained by Aibel Group and the Vetco Aibel Entities and the Compliance Committee, referenced below, concerning corrupt payments and related books and records, shall not relieve Aibel Group or the Vetco Aibel Entities of its obligation to truthfully disclose such matters to the Department.

- Upon request of the Department, with respect to any issue relevant to its investigation of corrupt payments in connection with the operations of Aibel Group and the Vetco Aibel Entities, or any of their former subsidiaries or affiliates, related books and records, and inadequate internal controls, these entities shall designate knowledgeable employees, agents, or attorneys to provide to the Department the information and materials described . . . above, on behalf of Aibel Group and the Vetco Aibel Entities. It is further understood that Aibel Group and the Vetco Aibel Entities must at all times provide complete, truthful, and accurate information.

- With respect to any issue relevant to the Department's investigation of corrupt payments in connection with the operations of Aibel Group and the Vetco Aibel Entities, or any of their former subsidiaries or affiliates, these entities shall use their best efforts to make their directors, officers, employees, agents and consultants available to provide information and testimony as requested by the Department, including sworn testimony before a federal grand jury or in federal trials, as well as interviews with federal law enforcement authorities. Cooperation under this Paragraph will include identification of witnesses who, to the knowledge of Aibel Group and the Vetco Aibel Entities, may have material information regarding the matters under investigation.

- With respect to any issue relevant to the Department's investigation of corrupt payments in connection with the operations of Aibel Group and the Vetco Aibel Entities, or any of their former subsidiaries or affiliates, these entities shall use their best efforts to make available, for interviews or for testimony, such present and former Aibel Group and Vetco Aibel Entities officers, directors, agents, consultants, and employees, and the officers, directors, employees, agents and consultants of contractors and sub-contractors, as may be requested by the Department.

- With respect to any information, testimony, document, record, or other tangible evidence provided to the Department pursuant to this Agreement, Aibel Group and the Vetco Aibel Entities consent to any and all disclosures to other Government agencies, whether agencies of the United States or a foreign government, of such materials as the Department, in its sole discretion, shall deem appropriate.

In return for the full and truthful cooperation of Aibel Group and the Vetco Aibel Entities, and compliance with all the terms and conditions of this Agreement, the Department agrees not to use any information related to the conduct described in the attached Statement of Facts against Aibel Group or the Vetco Aibel Entities in any criminal or civil case, except in a prosecution for perjury or obstruction of justice; in a prosecution for making a false statement after the date of this

Agreement; in a prosecution or other proceeding relating to any crime of violence; or in a prosecution or other proceeding relating to a violation of any provision of Title 26 of the United States Code. In addition, the Department agrees, except as provided herein, that it will not bring any criminal or civil case against Aibel Group or the Vetco Aibel Entities related to the conduct of present and former employees of these entities as described in the attached Statement of Facts. This Paragraph does not provide any protection against prosecution for any corrupt payments, if any, made in the future by Aibel Group or the Vetco Aibel Entities, or any of their officers, directors, employees, agents or consultants, whether or not disclosed by Aibel Group or the Vetco Aibel Entities, pursuant to the terms of this Agreement, nor does it apply to any such payments, made in the past, which are not described in the attached Statement of Facts. In addition, this Paragraph does not provide any protection against criminal prosecution of any present or former officer, employee, director, shareholder, agent or consultant of Aibel Group or the Vetco Aibel Entities for any violations committed by them.

Questions and Comments

1. The misconduct charged in this case was a violation of the Foreign Corrupt Practices Act. For more on the compliance implications of this statute, see Chapter 13.

2. Note that this DPA requires the defendant (Aibel) to waive its right to a speedy trial. Such waivers are, or should be, parts of every DPA because otherwise the target could claim, after a suitable period of time, that the government had waited too long to bring it to trial, and thus could avoid further compliance with its obligations under the agreement.

3. Does Aibel admit guilt?

4. Notice that this agreement requires the target to waive the attorney-client and/or work-product privileges. Should the government demand this sort of information? Does the requirement that the waiver be made only in response to a "specific request" provide much protection?

5. Does this agreement provide any protections to Aibel's officers, agents, or employees? Did Aibel throw them under the bus to protect its own interests? Given what you see in this agreement, would you trust that your employer will stand by you when the going gets rough?

6. The DPA in the *Aibel* case recites that the company had agreed to institute "remedial measures" to ensure that the conduct did not recur. Presumably, these measures involved some sort of corporate governance changes related to compliance. In other DPAs, the prosecutors become much more deeply involved, and the agreement itself specifies in detail the changes that are required as a condition of the government not proceeding. Among the governance provisions commonly observed in DPAs are the following:

- Commitments to fire specified employees (or recitations that these individuals had already been terminated).
- Creation of specified managerial positions, such as that of a chief compliance officer or a chief risk officer.
- Guarantees of reporting lines for these or other officers to the chief executive officer, the board audit committee, or other senior corporate body.

- Splitting of the positions of board chairman and chief executive officer.
- The addition of directors.
- Additional guarantees of director independence.
- The creation of new board committees or the vesting of new powers in existing committees.
- Retention of a consultant, paid by the defendant, to recommend additional governance changes.
- Appointment of outside monitors to evaluate continuing compliance.

Should prosecutors obtain corporate governance changes as a condition for not proceeding with criminal charges?

7. Are the corporate governance changes listed above closely tailored to rectifying or preventing criminal acts by corporations or their employees?

8. What do prosecutors know about corporate governance? Are they qualified to understand what will and will not be effective?

9. A DPA is not the product of an informed judgment on the merits made by a judge or jury. Is there a danger of overreaching or abuse by prosecutors who can threaten to impose devastating sanctions on any company that doesn't agree to the prosecutor's settlement demands?

10. Because criminal cases against corporations rarely go to trial, the role of the judge and jury in such matters is attenuated. Is this a healthy development? Are prosecutors equipped to perform the tasks traditionally assigned to the judge and the jury — for example, the impartial administration of the law, or the application of community norms and values? Consider in this regard the comments of Justice Breyer in a 2012 case: "[T]he prosecutor in such a system, perhaps armed with statutes providing for mandatory minimum sentences, can become the ultimate adjudicator. The prosecutor/adjudicator plays an important role in many 'European inquisitorial' systems. But those prosecutors, unlike ours, typically are trained formally to be more like neutral adjudicators than advocates." *Southern Union Co. v. United States*, 132 S. Ct. 2344, 2371 (2012) (Breyer, J., dissenting). Do you agree with this concern?

11. For more on corporate governance provisions in DPAs and other criminal prosecutions, see *Prosecutors in the Boardroom: Using Criminal Law to Regulate Corporate Conduct* (Anthony Barkow & Rachel Barkow eds., 2011); Brandon L. Garrett, *Structural Reform Prosecution*, 93 Va. L. Rev. 853 (2007); Leonard Orland, *The Transformation of Corporate Criminal Law*, 1 Brook. J. Corp., Fin. & Com. Law. 45 (2006). For criticism of corporate governance changes effected through criminal prosecutions, see, e.g., Jennifer Arlen, *Removing Prosecutors from the Boardroom: Deterring Crime Without Prosecutor Interference in Corporate Governance*, in *Prosecutors in the Boardroom* (2011). For an explanation by prosecutors of their reasons for seeking corporate governance changes, see Christopher J. Christie & Robert M. Hanna, *A Push Down the Road of Good Corporate Citizenship: The Deferred Prosecution Agreement Between the U.S. Attorney for the District of New Jersey and Bristol-Myers Squibb Co.*, 43 Am. Crim. L. Rev. 1042 (2006). For an interesting recommendation that prosecutors should consider corporate governance reforms early in the process, rather than at the time of settlement, see Lawrence A. Cunningham, *Deferred Prosecutions and Corporate Governance: An Integrated Approach to Investigation and Reform*, 65 Fla. L. Rev. 1 (2013).

c. Judicial Review

United States v. Fokker Services B.V.

818 F.3d 733 (D.C. Cir. 2016)

SRINIVASAN, Circuit Judge:

The Constitution allocates primacy in criminal charging decisions to the Executive Branch. The Executive's charging authority embraces decisions about whether to initiate charges, whom to prosecute, which charges to bring, and whether to dismiss charges once brought. It has long been settled that the Judiciary generally lacks authority to second-guess those Executive determinations, much less to impose its own charging preferences. The courts instead take the prosecution's charging decisions largely as a given, and assume a more active role in administering adjudication of a defendant's guilt and determining the appropriate sentence.

In certain situations, rather than choose between the opposing poles of pursuing a criminal conviction or forgoing any criminal charges altogether, the Executive may conclude that the public interest warrants the intermediate option of a deferred prosecution agreement (DPA). Under a DPA, the government formally initiates prosecution but agrees to dismiss all charges if the defendant abides by negotiated conditions over a prescribed period of time. Adherence to the conditions enables the defendant to demonstrate compliance with the law. If the defendant fails to satisfy the conditions, the government can then pursue the charges based on facts admitted in the agreement.

This case arises from the interplay between the operation of a DPA and the running of time limitations under the Speedy Trial Act. Because a DPA involves the formal initiation of criminal charges, the agreement triggers the Speedy Trial Act's time limits for the commencement of a criminal trial. In order to enable the government to assess the defendant's satisfaction of the DPA's conditions over the time period of the agreement—with an eye towards potential dismissal of the charges—the Speedy Trial Act specifically allows for a court to suspend the running of the time within which to commence a trial for any period during which the government defers prosecution under a DPA.

In this case, appellant Fokker Services voluntarily disclosed its potential violation of federal sanctions and export control laws. After extensive negotiations, the company and the government entered into an 18-month DPA, during which Fokker would continue cooperation with federal authorities and implementation of a substantial compliance program. In accordance with the DPA, the government filed criminal charges against the company, together with a joint motion to suspend the running of time under the Speedy Trial Act pending assessment of the company's adherence to the agreement's conditions. The district court denied the motion because, in the court's view, the prosecution had been too lenient in agreeing to, and structuring, the DPA. Among other objections, the court disagreed with prosecutors' decision to forgo bringing any criminal charges against individual company officers.

We vacate the district court's denial of the joint motion to exclude time under the Speedy Trial Act. We hold that the Act confers no authority in a court to withhold exclusion of time pursuant to a DPA based on concerns that the government should bring different charges or should charge different defendants. Congress, in providing for courts to approve the exclusion of time pursuant to a DPA, acted against the backdrop of long-settled understandings about the independence of the Executive with regard to charging decisions. Nothing in the statute's terms or structure suggests any intention to subvert those constitutionally rooted principles so as to enable the Judiciary to second-guess the Executive's exercise of discretion over the initiation and dismissal of criminal charges.

In vacating the district court order, we have no occasion to disagree (or agree) with that court's concerns about the government's charging decisions in this case. Rather, the fundamental point is that those determinations are for the Executive — not the courts — to make. We therefore grant the government's petition for a writ of mandamus and remand for further proceedings consistent with this opinion.

I.

A.

The Speedy Trial Act establishes time limits for the completion of various stages of a criminal prosecution. See 18 U.S.C. §§3161-3174. For instance, the Act requires the commencement of trial within seventy days of the filing of an information or indictment by the government. Id. §3161(c)(1). The Act also excludes various pretrial periods from the running of that seventy-day time clock. Of particular relevance, the Act excludes "[a]ny period of delay during which prosecution is deferred by the attorney for the Government pursuant to written agreement with the defendant, with the approval of the court, for the purpose of allowing the defendant to demonstrate his good conduct." Id. §3161(h)(2).

That exemption exists to enable prosecutors to resolve cases through DPAs. DPAs, along with their out-of-court analogues, non-prosecution agreements (NPAs), afford a middle-ground option to the prosecution when, for example, it believes that a criminal conviction may be difficult to obtain or may result in unwanted collateral consequences for a defendant or third parties, but also believes that the defendant should not evade accountability altogether. Both DPAs and NPAs generally include an admitted statement of facts, require adherence to "conditions designed . . . to promote compliance with applicable law and to prevent recidivism," and remain in effect for a period of one to three years. During that period, if the defendant fails to abide by the terms of the agreement, the government can prosecute based on the admitted facts. While prosecutors at one time seldom relied on NPAs and DPAs, their use has grown significantly in recent years.

DPAs differ from NPAs primarily with regard to the filing of criminal charges. With an NPA, "formal charges are not filed and the agreement is maintained by the parties rather than being filed with a court." A DPA, by contrast, "is typically predicated upon the filing of a formal charging document by the government."

For that reason, a DPA's viability depends on the specific exclusion of time for such agreements set forth in the Speedy Trial Act. The filing of an information or indictment would ordinarily trigger the Act's seventy-day clock within which trial must commence. But in the case of a DPA, if the defendant were to fulfill the agreement's conditions, the prosecution would move to dismiss all charges with prejudice at the end of the specified time period, ordinarily one to three years. Without the statutory exclusion of time for DPAs, the government would relinquish its ability to prosecute based on the conceded facts if the defendant were to violate the agreement after seventy days. That would largely eliminate the leverage that engenders the defendant's compliance with a DPA's conditions. The statutory exclusion of time for DPAs therefore is essential to the agreements' effective operation.

B.

Fokker Services, a Dutch aerospace services company, provides technical and logistical support to owners of aircraft manufactured by its predecessor company. In 2010, Fokker voluntarily disclosed to the United States Departments of Treasury and Commerce that it had potentially violated federal sanctions and export control laws concerning Iran, Sudan, and Burma. At the time Fokker came forward, no government agency had initiated any investigation focused on the company.

Over the course of the next four years, Fokker cooperated in the wide-ranging investigation conducted by federal authorities. The company facilitated interviews of relevant witnesses, expedited the government's requests to Dutch authorities for documents under the Mutual Legal Assistance Treaty, and initiated its own internal investigation. Fokker's internal investigation revealed that, from 2005 to 2010, the company had participated in 1,147 illicit transactions through which it earned some $21 million in gross revenue. The company instituted remedial measures to improve its sanctions compliance program, adopting a set of procedures to track parts and bolstering its employee training requirements. It also fired its president and demoted or reassigned other employees who had been involved in the violations. The company's compliance efforts have been described by government officials as "a model to be followed by other corporations."

In light of Fokker's cooperation, remediation efforts, and other mitigating factors, federal agencies negotiated a global settlement with the company. The settlement included, as an integral component, an 18-month DPA. During the DPA's 18-month period, Fokker was to: continue full cooperation with the government, implement its new compliance policy, and pay fines and penalties totaling $21 million (a sum equaling the gross revenues gained by the company from the illicit transactions). Fokker also accepted responsibility for the acts described in the stipulated factual statement accompanying the DPA.

On June 5, 2014, pursuant to the agreement, the government filed with the district court a one-count information against Fokker, together with the DPA. The information charged Fokker with conspiracy to violate the International Emergency Economic Powers Act. The same day, the government and Fokker filed a joint motion for the exclusion of time under the Speedy Trial Act, in order to "allow [the company] to demonstrate its good conduct and implement certain remedial measures."

The district court then held a series of status conferences, during which it repeatedly emphasized its concerns about the absence of any criminal prosecution of individual company officers. The court requested several additional written submissions from the government. The government was asked to explain why the interests of justice supported the court's approval of the deal embodied by the DPA, and also to address whether Fokker's initial disclosures to the government had in fact been voluntary.

In response, the government described why the "proposed resolution with Fokker Services is fair and is an appropriate exercise of the government's discretion," and affirmed the absence of any indication "that Fokker Services was motivated to make its disclosures out of fear about a nonexistent U.S. government investigation." The district court later expressed that it might still reject the DPA because it was "too good a deal for the defendant."

On February 5, 2015, the district court denied the joint motion for the exclusion of time. In explaining the reasons for its decision, the court criticized the government for failing to prosecute any "individuals . . . for their conduct." According to the court, approval of an agreement in which the defendant had been "prosecuted so anemically for engaging in such egregious conduct for such a sustained period of time and for the benefit of one of our country's worst enemies" would "promote disrespect for the law." The court further noted that certain employees had been permitted to remain with the company; that the DPA contained no requirement for an independent monitor; and that the amount of the fine failed to exceed the revenues Fokker gained from the illegal transactions. Based on those considerations, the court rejected the DPA as an "[in]appropriate exercise of prosecutorial discretion."

The district court's order marks the first time any federal court has denied a joint request by the parties to exclude time pursuant to a DPA. Both parties filed a timely notice of appeal. Because both parties seek to overturn the district court's denial of their joint motion to exclude time, we appointed an amicus curiae to present arguments defending the district court's action.

II.

Although we face a threshold question concerning our jurisdiction to review the district court's interlocutory order, our assessment of the jurisdictional issue is substantially informed by our consideration of the merits of the parties' challenge to the district court's action. Consequently, we first consider whether the district court legally erred in its denial of the joint motion to exclude time pursuant to the DPA. We conclude that it did.

By rejecting the DPA based primarily on concerns about the prosecution's charging choices, the district court exceeded its authority under the Speedy Trial Act. The Act excludes any period of time "during which prosecution is deferred by the attorney for the Government pursuant to written agreement with the defendant, with the approval of the court, for the purpose of allowing the defendant to demonstrate his good conduct." While the exclusion of time is subject to "the approval of the court," there is no ground for reading that provision to confer free-ranging authority in district courts to scrutinize the prosecution's discretionary charging decisions. Rather, we read the statute against the background of settled constitutional understandings under which authority over criminal charging decisions resides fundamentally with the Executive, without the involvement of—and without oversight power in—the Judiciary. So understood, the statute's "approval of the court" requirement did not empower the district court to disapprove the DPA based on the court's view that the prosecution had been too lenient.

A.

The Executive's primacy in criminal charging decisions is long settled. That authority stems from the Constitution's delegation of "take Care" duties, U.S. Const. art. II, §3, and the pardon power, id. §2, to the Executive Branch. Decisions to initiate charges, or to dismiss charges once brought, "lie[ ] at the core of the Executive's duty to see to the faithful execution of the laws." The Supreme Court thus has repeatedly emphasized that "[w]hether to prosecute and what charge to file or bring before a grand jury are decisions that generally rest in the prosecutor's discretion."

Correspondingly, "judicial authority is . . . at its most limited" when reviewing the Executive's exercise of discretion over charging determinations. The decision whether to prosecute turns on factors such as "the strength of the case, the prosecution's general deterrence value, the [g]overnment's enforcement priorities, and the case's relationship to the [g]overnment's overall enforcement plan." The Executive routinely undertakes those assessments and is well equipped to do so. By contrast, the Judiciary, as the Supreme Court has explained, generally is not "competent to undertake" that sort of inquiry. Indeed, "[f]ew subjects are less adapted to judicial review than the exercise by the Executive of his discretion in deciding when and whether to institute criminal proceedings, or what precise charge shall be made, or whether to dismiss a proceeding once brought." "Judicial supervision in this area" would also "entail[ ] systemic costs." It could "chill law enforcement," cause delay, and "impair the performance of a core executive constitutional function." As a result, "the presumption of regularity" applies to "prosecutorial decisions and, in the absence of clear evidence to the contrary, courts presume that [prosecutors] have properly discharged their official duties."

B.

Those settled principles counsel against interpreting statutes and rules in a manner that would impinge on the Executive's constitutionally rooted primacy over criminal charging decisions. Of particular salience, Rule 48(a) of the Federal Rules of Criminal Procedure requires a prosecutor to obtain "leave of court" before dismissing charges against a criminal defendant. That language could conceivably be read to allow for considerable judicial involvement in the determination to dismiss criminal charges. But decisions to dismiss pending criminal charges—no less than decisions to initiate charges and to identify which charges to bring—lie squarely within the ken of prosecutorial discretion. To that end, the Supreme Court has declined to construe Rule 48(a)'s "leave of court" requirement to confer any substantial role for courts in the determination whether to dismiss charges. Rather, the "principal object of the 'leave of court' requirement" has been understood to be a narrow one—"to protect a defendant against prosecutorial harassment . . . when the [g]overnment moves to dismiss an indictment over the defendant's objection." A court thus reviews the prosecution's motion under Rule 48(a) primarily to guard against the prospect that dismissal is part of a scheme of "prosecutorial harassment" of the defendant through repeated efforts to bring—and then dismiss—charges.

So understood, the "leave of court" authority gives no power to a district court to deny a prosecutor's Rule 48(a) motion to dismiss charges based on a disagreement with the prosecution's exercise of charging authority. For instance, a court cannot deny leave of court because of a view that the defendant should stand trial notwithstanding the prosecution's desire to dismiss the charges, or a view that any remaining charges fail adequately to redress the gravity of the defendant's alleged conduct. The authority to make such determinations remains with the Executive . . . .

C.

The same considerations govern our interpretation of the Speedy Trial Act provision at issue here. That provision, as noted, allows for excluding "[a]ny period of delay during which prosecution is deferred by the attorney for the Government pursuant to [a DPA], with the approval of the court, for the purpose of allowing the defendant to demonstrate his good conduct." As with the "leave of court" language in Rule 48(a) . . . , we construe the "approval of the court" language in

§3161(h)(2) in a manner that preserves the Executive's long-settled primacy over charging decisions and that denies courts substantial power to impose their own charging preferences.

As an initial matter, the context of a DPA, like that of Rule 48(a), concerns the prosecution's core prerogative to dismiss criminal charges. While dismissal under a DPA follows from the defendant's adherence to agreed-upon conditions over a specified period, the decision to seek dismissal pursuant to a DPA—as under Rule 48(a)—ultimately stems from a conclusion that additional prosecution or punishment would not serve the public interest. Dismissal in either situation thereby fulfills the Executive's duty under Article II to see that the laws are faithfully executed.

We see no reason to recognize a substantially broader authority for courts to scrutinize prosecutorial charging choices in the context of a DPA than in the context of Rule 48(a). Just as Rule 48(a)'s "leave of court" authority does not allow a court to withhold approval of a motion to dismiss charges based on a belief that more serious charges should be brought against the defendant (or against a third party), §3161(h)(2)'s "approval of the court" authority does not permit a court to withhold approval of a motion to exclude time under a DPA based on that same belief. In either situation, the court's withholding of approval would amount to a substantial and unwarranted intrusion on the Executive Branch's fundamental prerogatives. And the Judiciary's lack of competence to review the prosecution's initiation and dismissal of charges equally applies to review of the prosecution's decision to pursue a DPA and the choices reflected in the agreement's terms. As with conventional charging decisions, a DPA's provisions manifest the Executive's consideration of factors such as the strength of the government's evidence, the deterrence value of a prosecution, and the enforcement priorities of an agency, subjects that are ill-suited to substantial judicial oversight.

To be sure, the criminal charges filed as part of a DPA remain on the court's docket throughout the time of the agreement (i.e., pending assessment of whether the defendant has satisfied the agreement's conditions, upon which the prosecution seeks dismissal of the charges). But the existence of charges on the court's docket suggests no greater power on the part of the court to second-guess the underlying charging decisions than under Rule 48(a): there, too, criminal charges remain on the court's docket until dismissed. The key point is that, although charges remain pending on the court's docket under a DPA, the court plays no role in monitoring the defendant's compliance with the DPA's conditions. For instance, defendants who violate the conditions of their DPA face no court-ordered repercussions. Rather, the prosecution—and the prosecution alone—monitors a defendant's compliance with the agreement's conditions and determines whether the defendant's conduct warrants dismissal of the pending charges. Just as is the case under Rule 48(a), the prosecution, after taking stock of the circumstances, concludes that continued pursuit of a criminal conviction is unwarranted . . . .

E.

Judged by those principles, the district court in this case erred in denying the parties' motion for exclusion of time under §3161(h)(2). There is no indication that the parties entered into the DPA to evade speedy trial limits rather than to enable Fokker to demonstrate its good conduct and compliance with law. Rather, the district court denied the exclusion of time based on its view that the prosecution should have brought different charges or sought different remedies. In doing so, the court exceeded its authority under §3161(h)(2) . . . .

Questions and Comments

1. The court's decision is grounded in principles of separation of judicial and executive powers. And the court is certainly right that, in general, charging decisions fall within the authority of the executive. However, it is also clear that there must be some judicial check on executive discretion in this regard. Suppose, for example, that a prosecutor had a policy of never charging people of a particular race or religion. Clearly, the courts would have power to correct this sort of abuse. The issue as regards DPAs, accordingly, is one of degree: Are the circumstances such that courts should be disabled from intervening? On this issue, the district court and court of appeals disagreed. Where do you come down on the debate?

2. The court of appeals' opinion draws on the practice under Federal Rule of Criminal Procedure 48, which requires leave of the court when the government wishes to dismiss an indictment. The jurisprudence around Rule 48 allows the court very little substantive role in this process: A court cannot refuse to allow dismissal, for example, even if the judge strongly believes that the defendant should be prosecuted. Likewise, the court of appeals argues, judicial involvement in approving DPAs should also be minimal. Is the analogy to Rule 48 valid? What about the fact that a DPA contemplates that the matter will remain on the court's docket during the period of the DPA, subject to potential re-opening if the defendant fails to comply with its terms? Is there more scope for discretion in the decision about whether to enter a DPA and what terms to impose than there is when the only issue is whether to dismiss an indictment? Rule 48, moreover, doesn't entirely displace substantive judicial scrutiny; leave of court can be denied, for example, if the dismissal is "clearly contrary to manifest public interest." United States v. Pimentel, 932 F.2d 1029, 1033 n.5 (2d Cir. 1991). Even if the analogy holds, does the jurisprudence under Rule 48 provide authority for a court to exercise similar substantive scrutiny over a DPA?

3. What policies underlie the court's platitudes about separation of powers? Consider how you would weigh the value of judicial oversight (keeping prosecutors competent and honest, enforcing adherence to the rule of law, for example) against the downsides of judicial involvement (burden on the courts, uncertainty in outcomes, lack of judicial expertise, need to empower prosecutors in order to facilitate settlement bargaining, etc.).

4. United States v. HSBC Bank USA, No. 12-cr-763, 2013 WL 3306161 (E.D.N.Y. July 1, 2013), involved a DPA entered into in connection with charges that HSBC had failed to maintain an effective anti-money laundering program and had facilitated transactions on behalf of sanctioned entities. Judge Gleeson identified two possible sources of authority for judicial review: the Speedy Trial Act, discussed in the excerpted opinion, and the court's supervisory power. Judge Gleeson found that the Speedy Trial Act unequivocally contemplates a district court's participation in the process to approve a deferred-prosecution agreement and that this approval requirement "is grounded in a concern . . . that parties will collude to circumvent the speedy trial clock" — meaning that courts must "consider whether a deferred prosecution agreement is truly about diversion and not simply a vehicle for fending off a looming trial date." The court's supervisory power provides additional

authority, Judge Gleeson concluded, because "[b]y placing a criminal matter on the docket of a federal court, the parties have subjected their DPA to the legitimate exercise of that court's authority." Judge Gleeson approved the deferred prosecution agreement pursuant to the court's supervisory power. Judge Gleeson observed that "[a]s long as the government asks the Court to keep this criminal case on its docket, the Court retains the authority to ensure that the implementation of the DPA remains within the bounds of lawfulness and respects the integrity of this Court." Pursuant to this authority, Judge Gleeson directed the parties to file quarterly reports "with the Court to keep it apprised of all significant developments in the implementation of the DPA. Doubts about whether a development is significant should be resolved in favor of inclusion."

5. What if, after executing a DPA, the prosecutors discover that the potential defendant has not been straightforward about the scope of its past misconduct? What if there turn out to be errors or shortcomings in an independent consultant's report that forms part of the basis of the government's agreement not to prosecute? Can the government tear up the old agreement and insist on additional penalties — or institute a prosecution?

6. For a critique of DPAs and NPAs based on rule of law considerations, see Jennifer Arlen, *Prosecuting Beyond the Rule of Law: Corporate Mandates Imposed Through Pretrial Diversion Agreements*, ___ J. Legal Analysis ___ (2017).

D. SENTENCING

The sentencing of corporations convicted of federal crimes is heavily influenced by the Federal Sentencing Guidelines for Organizations, first promulgated by the United States Sentencing Commission in 1991. The guidelines provide that in some circumstances a corporate defendant may receive a more lenient sentence if it has in place an "effective compliance and ethics program."

Federal Sentencing Guidelines, §8B2.1 Effective Compliance and Ethics Program

(a) To have an effective compliance and ethics program, . . . an organization shall —

(1) exercise due diligence to prevent and detect criminal conduct; and

(2) otherwise promote an organizational culture that encourages ethical conduct and a commitment to compliance with the law.

Such compliance and ethics program shall be reasonably designed, implemented, and enforced so that the program is generally effective in preventing and detecting criminal conduct. The failure to prevent or detect the instant offense does not necessarily mean that the program is not generally effective in preventing and detecting criminal conduct.

(b) Due diligence and the promotion of an organizational culture that encourages ethical conduct and a commitment to compliance with the law within the meaning of subsection (a) minimally require the following:

(1) The organization shall establish standards and procedures to prevent and detect criminal conduct.

(2) (A) The organization's governing authority shall be knowledgeable about the content and operation of the compliance and ethics program and shall exercise reasonable oversight with respect to the implementation and effectiveness of the compliance and ethics program.

(B) High-level personnel of the organization shall ensure that the organization has an effective compliance and ethics program, as described in this guideline. Specific individual(s) within high-level personnel shall be assigned overall responsibility for the compliance and ethics program.

(C) Specific individual(s) within the organization shall be delegated day-to-day operational responsibility for the compliance and ethics program. Individual(s) with operational responsibility shall report periodically to high-level personnel and, as appropriate, to the governing authority, or an appropriate subgroup of the governing authority, on the effectiveness of the compliance and ethics program. To carry out such operational responsibility, such individual(s) shall be given adequate resources, appropriate authority, and direct access to the governing authority or an appropriate subgroup of the governing authority.

(3) The organization shall use reasonable efforts not to include within the substantial authority personnel of the organization any individual whom the organization knew, or should have known through the exercise of due diligence, has engaged in illegal activities or other conduct inconsistent with an effective compliance and ethics program.

(4) (A) The organization shall take reasonable steps to communicate periodically and in a practical manner its standards and procedures, and other aspects of the compliance and ethics program, to the individuals referred to in subparagraph (B) by conducting effective training programs and otherwise disseminating information appropriate to such individuals' respective roles and responsibilities.

(B) The individuals referred to in subparagraph (A) are the members of the governing authority, high-level personnel, substantial authority personnel, the organization's employees, and, as appropriate, the organization's agents.

(5) The organization shall take reasonable steps—

(A) to ensure that the organization's compliance and ethics program is followed, including monitoring and auditing to detect criminal conduct;

(B) to evaluate periodically the effectiveness of the organization's compliance and ethics program; and

(C) to have and publicize a system, which may include mechanisms that allow for anonymity or confidentiality, whereby the organization's employees and agents may report or seek guidance regarding potential or actual criminal conduct without fear of retaliation.

(6) The organization's compliance and ethics program shall be promoted and enforced consistently throughout the organization through (A) appropriate incentives to perform in accordance with the compliance and ethics program; and (B) appropriate disciplinary measures for engaging in criminal conduct and for failing to take reasonable steps to prevent or detect criminal conduct.

(7) After criminal conduct has been detected, the organization shall take reasonable steps to respond appropriately to the criminal conduct and to

prevent further similar criminal conduct, including making any necessary modifications to the organization's compliance and ethics program.

(c) In implementing subsection (b), the organization shall periodically assess the risk of criminal conduct and shall take appropriate steps to design, implement, or modify each requirement set forth in subsection (b) to reduce the risk of criminal conduct identified through this process.

Questions and Comments

1. The adoption of the sentencing guidelines for organizations in 1991 was an important step in the development of the modern law of compliance; it provided an incentive to firms to adopt compliance programs in order to mitigate the severity of their sentences if they were subsequently convicted of federal crimes, and also served as a model for compliance programs outside the criminal justice sphere.

2. What are the seven elements of an "effective" compliance and ethics program?

3. Notice that the guidelines require the company to have in place an effective "compliance and *ethics*" program. The reference to compliance is clear: Companies should not violate the law. But why is it any business of federal criminal law to encourage companies to have ethics programs in place?

4. Professor Jennifer Arlen criticizes the sentencing guidelines for organizations on the ground that they offer too little credit for organizations' self-policing activity:

> To deter corporate crime, corporate sanctions must be structured to induce large corporations to help federal prosecutors detect and punish corporate crime. Specifically, firms must be encouraged to detect and report wrongdoing, and to cooperate with the government's effort to identify and sanction the individuals responsible for the crime. Firms will not engage in these activities unless they face lower expected sanctions if they detect, report, and cooperate than if they do not. . . . Although the Organizational Sentencing Guidelines offer sanction mitigation to firms that adopt effective compliance programs, self-report, and cooperate, . . . these provisions offer too little mitigation to encourage firms to detect, report, and cooperate. Indeed, the Guidelines' mitigation provisions are particularly inadequate in the very circumstances where corporate detection and investigation is most important: in cases involving crimes committed by managers of large firms.

Jennifer Arlen, *The Failure of the Organizational Sentencing Guidelines*, 66 U. Miami L. Rev. 321 (2012). Do you agree?

8

Whistleblowers

We turn now to an increasingly important mechanism for enhancing an organization's compliance with legal norms: the phenomenon of the whistleblower.

A. WHISTLEBLOWERS

1. Who Is a Whistleblower?

First, let's define terms. We can start with what a whistleblower is not. A whistleblower is not a law enforcement agent. Detectives and professional investigators are not whistleblowers because it is part of their jobs to ferret out and report violations. Nor is the whistleblower someone like an internal or external auditor, who also has a formal responsibility to check for shortcomings and to report them when they are found. The whistleblower is a volunteer who has personal knowledge of misconduct within an organization and who comes forward on her own.

The term "whistleblower" appears to derive from the image of a policeman with a whistle — thus alluding to the law enforcement function of whistleblowing. The term also resonates with the world of sports. Referees and similar officials are part of the game. When they observe a foul, they blow the whistle. The whistle stops play and allows the referee to explain the nature of the foul and assess a penalty.

Translated to the area of compliance, the term retains some of its original connotations. A compliance whistleblower, like a cop or a referee, is an observer: She watches what happens within an organization. Like a cop or referee, she is positioned "on the field": She is actually involved, in one respect or another, with the activities at issue. Also like a cop or a referee, the whistleblower enforces rules or norms; she blows the whistle when she sees something that she considers to be a violation of the rules. If the process works well, the organization takes the appropriate steps in response to her information, which could

> The term "whistleblower" refers to a person who, without being required to do so, reports on misconduct within an organization.

include ceasing to engage in the problematic action or administering a sanction against employees found to have committed violations.

What's it like to be a whistleblower? Consider Sherron Watkins' description of her experience blowing the whistle at Enron.

Testimony of Sherron Watkins Before the Oversight and Investigations Subcommittee of the House Energy and Commerce Committee

Feb. 14, 2002

I began my career in 1982 at Arthur Andersen as an auditor. I spent eight years at Andersen in both the Houston and New York offices. I joined New York-based MG Trade Finance in 1990 to manage their portfolio of commodity-backed finance assets. I held that position until October of 1993.

In October of 1993, I was hired by Mr. Andrew Fastow [Enron's Chief Financial Officer] and moved back to Houston to manage Enron's newly-formed partnership with CALPERS, the California Public Employee Retirement System. The partnership was the Joint Energy Development Investments Limited Partnership, or JEDI. I held the JEDI management portfolio position until the end of 1996.

From 1997 until early 2000, I worked for Enron International, primarily in the Mergers & Acquisitions Group, which is also known as the Corporate Development Group. In early 2000, I transferred to Enron Broad-Band Services. I worked there until June of 2000 in a variety of roles.

In mid to late June of 2001, I went to work directly for Mr. Fastow, assisting in the corporate development work that had been put under his supervision after Cliff Baxter resigned in May of 2001. I worked for Mr. Fastow in this new role into late August 2001. I have since been reassigned into the Human Resources Group, with a variety of assignments.

While working for Mr. Fastow in 2001, I was charged with reviewing all assets that Enron considered for sale and determining the likely economic impact of sale. As part of the sale analysis, I reviewed the estimated book values and market values of each asset.

A number of assets were hedged with an entity called Raptor. Any asset that was hedged should, for the most part, have a locked-in sales value for Enron, meaning that despite current market prices, Enron should realize the hedged price of the Raptor.

It was my understanding that the Raptor special-purpose entities were owned by LJM, a partnership run by Mr. Fastow. In completing my work, certain Enron business units provided me with analyses that showed certain of the hedged losses that had been incurred by Raptor were actually coming back to Enron. The general explanation was that the . . . Raptor hedge had declined in value such that Raptor would have a shortfall and would be unable to fully cover the hedge price that it owed Enron.

I was highly alarmed by the information I was receiving. My understanding as an accountant is that a company could never use its own stock to generate a gain or avoid a loss on its income statement. I continued to ask questions and seek answers, primarily from former co-workers in the Global Finance Group or in the business units that had hedged assets with Raptor. I never heard reassuring explanations.

I was not comfortable confronting either Mr. [Jeffrey] Skilling [Enron's Chief Executive Officer] or Mr. Fastow with my concerns. To do so, I believe, would have been a job-terminating move.

On August 14th, 2001, I was informed of Mr. Skilling's sudden resignation, and felt compelled to inform Mr. [Kenneth] Lay [Enron's Chairman] of the accounting problems that faced Enron. I sent Mr. Lay an anonymous letter on August 14th, 2001, in response to a request for questions for an upcoming all-employee meeting to be held August 16th, to address Mr. Skilling's departure.

At the all-employee meeting, Mr. Lay commented that our visions and values had slipped, and that if any employee was troubled by anything at Enron, please bring those concerns to him or any member of the top management, including Cindy Olson, Steve Kane and others.

On August 16th I met with Ms. Olson to show her a copy of the letter and discuss it with her. She encouraged me to meet with Mr. Lay personally. Since Mr. Lay was traveling through the rest of the week, she said the meeting would probably take place the week of August 20th. I was concerned that Mr. Lay was planning to fill the Office of the Chair over the weekend, and that he might choose Mr. Fastow or Rick Causey, the chief accounting officer. To voice my concerns, I met with Rex Rogers, Enron's associate general counsel on Friday, August 17th, 2001. I provided Mr. Rogers with a version of the anonymous letter, as well as two additional memos, all of which are part of the seven pages that this committee discovered in . . . January 2002. On Monday, August 20th, 2001, Mr. Lay's assistant scheduled a meeting for me to meet with Mr. Lay that following Wednesday, August 22nd, 2001. I subsequently held discussions with a former mentor at Andersen . . . and a long-time friend and co-worker . . . to vet my concerns before my meeting with Mr. Lay.

I met with Mr. Lay on the afternoon of Wednesday, August 22nd, 2001. The meeting lasted just over one half hour. I provided him with five memos I had drafted to help explain the problems facing the company. These five memos constitute the seven pages this committee discovered and subsequently disclosed on January 14th, 2002. Additionally, I provided Mr. Lay an analysis of the Raptor entity economics and a presentation prepared by Enron's risk assessment and control group.

I primarily used the memo titled "Summary of Raptor Oddities" as talking points with Mr. Lay. My main point to Mr. Lay was that by this time Raptor owed Enron in excess of $700 million under certain hedging agreements. My understanding was that the Raptor entities basically had no other business aside from these hedges; therefore, they had collectively lost over $700 million. I urged Mr. Lay to find out who lost that money. If he discovered that this loss would be borne by Enron shareholders, via an issuance of stock in the future, then I thought we had a very large problem on our hands. I gave Mr. Lay my opinion that it is never appropriate for a company to use its stock to affect its income statement.

At the conclusion of the meeting, Mr. Lay assured me that he would look into my concerns. I also requested a transfer, as I was uncomfortable remaining as a direct report to Mr. Fastow.

Questions and Comments

1. Although the events recounted in this report are now some time in the past, the name "Enron" still evokes reactions of fear and loathing; it has become nearly

synonymous with the idea of big business, aided and abetted by high-paid advisers, abusing the public trust and unjustifiably enriching senior executives.

2. Watkins is an accountant, and in this testimony she sounds like one. She provides a matter-of-fact, serious, and careful summary of the events that gave rise to her conversation with Mr. Lay, without glorifying her own role or seeking to allocate blame beyond the facts that she could verify.

3. What was it about the Raptor entities that so alarmed Watkins? The possibility that Enron obtained favorable accounting treatment by dealing with an entity that Enron itself had created and still controlled? The fact that Raptor was owned by Fastow, Enron's Chief Financial Officer — a clear conflict of interest? The fact that Raptor had lost hundreds of millions of dollars? All of the above?

4. Watkins originally reported on her findings by sending an anonymous letter to Lay; later she revealed her identity in a face-to-face meeting. Why do you think she opened up?

5. Watkins indicated that she distrusted Fastow, someone she had known for most of a decade; she asked to be removed from his supervision during her conversation with Lay. Can you discern why she distrusted him so much?

6. On the other hand, Watkins appears to have trusted Lay, Enron's chairman. Lay was a huge figure in the energy business at the time — a dynamic and visionary executive who was widely credited with transforming Enron from a stodgy natural gas pipeline company to a cutting edge leader in energy trading and other business lines. Perhaps his reputation gave her comfort. On the other hand, she had just uncovered a massive fraud at the company — a transaction of such magnitude that Lay must have been aware of it in some respects. And Lay had empowered Fastow and others who appeared to have perpetrated the fraud. Was Watkins wise to trust him?

7. Watkins seemed satisfied that Lay had heard her out in good faith and that he would look into her concerns. Lay did, in fact, commission an investigation by Enron's outside counsel, Vinson & Elkins. However, as discussed in Chapter 17, the investigation was hedged by so many limitations that it failed to uncover the truth.

8. After the fraud at Enron came to light, several of the figures in Watkins' narrative were convicted of crimes: Fastow, Skilling, Causey, and Lay himself were all sentenced to prison for their roles in the scandal (Lay died before serving his sentence).

9. For another interesting account of a whistleblower's experience, see Cynthia Cooper, *Extraordinary Circumstances: The Journey of a Corporate Whistleblower* (2008). For a first-person description of an unusual case where the President and CEO blew the whistle on serious corporate fraud in his own organization, see Michael Woodford, *Exposure* (2012).

10. In 2014, Keith Edwards, a former JPMorgan Chase employee, received a whistleblower award of $63.9 million for providing the government with information indicating that the bank had been falsely certifying FHA and VA mortgage loans. JPMorgan Chase eventually settled the case for $614 million and admitted that it had approved thousands of loans that didn't meet the government's underwriting requirements. The settlement agreement included the bank's commitment to enhance its quality control program for loans submitted for government insurance.

11. One of the more colorful whistleblowers of recent times is Jim Marchese, better known for his role on the reality TV show, "The Real Housewives of New

Jersey." When not appearing on camera, Marchese has made a lucrative business in whistleblowing, receiving awards of $1.6 million for reporting a former employer for Medicare fraud and $8.5 million for alerting the Department of Justice to problems with Bank of America's home mortgage business (the government eventually entered into a $16.6 billion settlement). Explaining his penchant for whistleblowing, Marchese was quoted as saying: "I'm trained as an attorney. I'm Sicilian. And I'm from New Jersey. If I see you kick a puppy, I'm going to say something. It's not within me to not say something."

12. For characteristics of whistleblowers in fraud cases, see Alexander Dyck, Adair Morse & Luigi Zingales, *Who Blows the Whistle on Corporate Fraud?*, 65 J. Fin. 2213 (2010).

13. Life after whistleblowing is not necessarily comfortable. J. Fred Alford's book *Whistleblowers: Broken Lives and Organizational Power* (2002) documents the fate of 36 whistleblowers. Many lost their jobs and never worked in the industry again; several divorced; most experienced episodes of depression; alcoholism was common; and about half declared bankruptcy. How do you interpret this information?

14. Whistleblower laws and policies are not unique to the United States. Many countries have hopped onto the bandwagon by adopting comprehensive whistleblower laws, including, in the developed world, Australia, Canada, Japan, South Korea, New Zealand, and the United Kingdom. Emerging or developing markets have also been active in this space. The Indian Companies Act requires listed companies to establish reporting and whistleblower protection mechanisms, and the Chinese Basic Internal Control Norms for Enterprises require Chinese-listed companies to set up whistleblower protection systems.

2. Encouraging Whistleblowing

Possibly because of its association with sports, the term "whistleblower" has generally favorable connotations. Especially in recent years, being known as a whistleblower is often seen as a mark of pride. Whistleblowers are sometimes lionized for their courage in coming forward. Cynthia Cooper, then a junior executive at WorldCom, reported evidence of fraud to the company's board audit committee in 2002, leading to Cooper being named one of Time Magazine's Persons of the Year. Enron whistleblower Sherron Watkins received similar tributes.

Yet more often, whistleblowers are not thanked for their services. Sometimes they are punished and often they are shunned. The same underlying conduct that is lauded as whistleblowing is also known by other names with less favorable associations: "leaker," "tattle-tale," "snitch," "fink," and "rat," to name a few. This ambiguity in the social meaning of the whistleblower has an important impact on public policy. Despite occasional instances where whistleblowers are lauded, the more common pattern is that they are disliked. The distaste for whistleblowers seems to be deeply rooted in the human psyche.

Many communities operate under powerful norms against reporting others. These include criminal enterprises—ranging from youth gangs who operate under the principle "snitches get stitches" to the Mafia's *omerta*, the code of silence that has traditionally been one of that organization's most important rules. Even politicians sometimes operate under these norms: After hearing that a colleague had secretly recorded conversations to aid a corruption probe, one New York leader candidly remarked, "There are few among us who can stand up to 20, 30, 40 years [in jail] without, as the streets call [it], snitching."

Why do we observe these norms against telling on others?

Part of the answer is straightforward: People who are engaged in wrongdoing don't want their behavior to become known, so they intimidate anyone who might blow the whistle.

Another consideration is the factor of identification. Nearly everyone has done something wrong at one time or another — or at least has thought about doing something wrong. Even if the person is not telling on *you*, you may identify with the target of the tattling: "There but for the grace of God go I."

Still another explanation for the norm against snitching is that communities often prefer to manage their own problems rather than have someone come in from without. Perhaps the concern is that whoever comes in from outside may be even worse than the people within the group. Better the "devil you know" than one you don't.

None of these seems fully satisfactory as an explanation for the norm against snitching. Regardless, the norm exists. And its existence is a powerful deterrent to whistleblowing. Someone who has internalized the norm — who identifies with it and considers it to be binding on her behavior — is unlikely to blow the whistle simply because she considers it wrong to do so. Even if she doesn't consider it wrong to tell, others probably will and, in consequence, the tattletale faces retribution for transgressing the community norm.

Questions and Comments

1. For further discussion of the norm against snitching, see Ethan Brown, *Snitch: Informants, Cooperators, and the Corruption of Justice* (2007); Bret D. Asbury, *Anti-Snitching Norms and Community Loyalty*, 89 Or. L. Rev. 1257 (2011); Yuval Feldman & Orly Lobel, *The Incentives Matrix: The Comparative Effectiveness of Rewards, Liabilities, Duties, and Protections for Reporting Illegality*, 88 Tex. L. Rev. 1151 (2010); Shannon Kay Quigley, Comment, *Whistleblower Tug-of-War: Corporate Attempts to Secure Internal Reporting Procedures in the Face of External Monetary Incentives Provided by the Dodd-Frank Act*, 52 Santa Clara L. Rev. 256 (2012).

How can the anti-snitching norm be counteracted so as to encourage people to come forward with evidence of violations? Four strategies are most commonly observed: cultural reforms to encourage whistleblowing, whistleblower protection rules, rewards and bounties, and mandatory reporting obligations.

a. Tone at the Top

We discussed the important topic of tone at the top in Chapter 5. Setting the right tone is especially crucial where whistleblowers are concerned. Many employees will be deterred from coming forward by two concerns: Their complaints will not be heard or acted on, and they will suffer retaliation from management or others. Senior managers need to counter the natural skittishness of potential whistleblowers by credibly reassuring them on both fronts: Their reports are valued and will be carefully investigated; and the organization will neither retaliate against them nor will it tolerate others doing so.

b. Protections for Whistleblowers

Numerous state and federal statutes protect whistleblowers against retaliation by employers for actions informing the authorities of potential misconduct. The Sarbanes-Oxley Act, for example, prohibits publicly traded companies from retaliating against people who provide information in connection with an investigation into potential violations of the securities laws. 18 U.S.C. §1514A(a). Remedies for proven violations include reinstatement, back pay, and "compensation for any special damages sustained as a result of the discrimination, including litigation costs, expert witness fees, and reasonable attorney fees."

Whistleblower protections are also a common feature of organizational codes of ethics. Typically, the organization will commit in writing not to retaliate against people who in good faith bring potential misconduct to the attention of senior managers; organizations may also promise to protect the whistleblower against retaliation by anyone within the organization (for example, people against whom the whistleblower has informed). The following, from Apple Computer's *Principles of Business Conduct*, is illustrative: "Apple will not retaliate — and will not tolerate retaliation — against any individual for filing a good-faith complaint with management, HR, Legal, Internal Audit, Finance, or the Business Conduct Helpline, or for participating in the investigation of any such complaint."

The following case examines the scope of whistleblower protections under the Sarbanes-Oxley Act:

Lawson v. FMR LLC

134 S. Ct. 1158 (2014)

GINSBURG, J.

. . . The Sarbanes—Oxley Act aims to "prevent and punish corporate and criminal fraud, protect the victims of such fraud, preserve evidence of such fraud, and hold wrongdoers accountable for their actions." Of particular concern to Congress was abundant evidence that Enron had succeeded in perpetuating its massive shareholder fraud in large part due to a "corporate code of silence"; that code, Congress found, "discourage[d] employees from reporting fraudulent behavior not only to the proper authorities, such as the FBI and the SEC, but even internally." When employees of Enron and its accounting firm, Arthur Andersen, attempted to report corporate misconduct, Congress learned, they faced retaliation, including discharge. As outside counsel advised company officials at the time, Enron's efforts to "quiet" whistleblowers generally were not proscribed under then-existing law. Congress identified the lack of whistleblower protection as "a significant deficiency" in the law, for in complex securities fraud investigations, employees "are [often] the only firsthand witnesses to the fraud."

Section 806 of Sarbanes—Oxley addresses this concern. 18 U.S.C. §1514A . . . reads in relevant part:

"Civil action to protect against retaliation in fraud cases
"(a) WHISTLEBLOWER PROTECTION FOR EMPLOYEES OF PUBLICLY TRADED COMPANIES. — No [public] company, or any officer, employee, contractor, subcontractor, or agent of such company, may discharge, demote, suspend, threaten,

harass, or in any other manner discriminate against an employee in the terms and conditions of employment because of any lawful act done by the employee—

"(1) to provide information, cause information to be provided, or otherwise assist in an investigation regarding any conduct which the employee reasonably believes constitutes a violation of section 1341 [mail fraud], 1343 [wire fraud], 1344 [bank fraud], or 1348 [securities or commodities fraud], any rule or regulation of the Securities and Exchange Commission, or any provision of Federal law relating to fraud against shareholders, when the information or assistance is provided to or the investigation is conducted by [a federal agency, Congress, or supervisor]. . . . "

Congress has assigned whistleblower protection largely to the Department of Labor (DOL), which administers some 20 United States Code incorporated whistleblower protection provisions. The Secretary has delegated investigatory and initial adjudicatory responsibility over claims under a number of these provisions, including §1514A, to DOL's Occupational Safety and Health Administration (OSHA). OSHA's order may be appealed to an administrative law judge, and then to DOL's Administrative Review Board (ARB). . . . An employee prevailing in a proceeding under §1514A is entitled to "all relief necessary to make the employee whole," including "reinstatement with the same seniority status that the employee would have had, but for the discrimination," backpay with interest, and compensation for litigation costs. . . .

Petitioners Jackie Hosang Lawson and Jonathan M. Zang (plaintiffs) separately initiated proceedings under §1514A against their former employers, privately held companies that provide advisory and management services to the Fidelity family of mutual funds. The Fidelity funds are not parties to either case; as is common in the mutual fund industry, the Fidelity funds themselves have no employees. Instead, they contract with investment advisers like respondents to handle their day-to-day operations, which include making investment decisions, preparing reports for shareholders, and filing reports with the Securities and Exchange Commission (SEC). Lawson was employed by Fidelity Brokerage Services, LLC, a subsidiary of FMR Corp., which was succeeded by FMR LLC. Zang was employed by a different FMR LLC subsidiary, Fidelity Management & Research Co., and later by one of that company's subsidiaries, FMR Co., Inc. For convenience, we refer to respondents collectively as FMR.

Lawson worked for FMR for 14 years, eventually serving as a Senior Director of Finance. She alleges that, after she raised concerns about certain cost accounting methodologies, believing that they overstated expenses associated with operating the mutual funds, she suffered a series of adverse actions, ultimately amounting to constructive discharge. Zang was employed by FMR for eight years, most recently as a portfolio manager for several of the funds. He alleges that he was fired in retaliation for raising concerns about inaccuracies in a draft SEC registration statement concerning certain Fidelity funds. Lawson and Zang separately filed administrative complaints alleging retaliation proscribed by §1514A. After expiration of the 180-day period specified in §1514A(b)(1), Lawson and Zang each filed suit in the U.S. District Court for the District of Massachusetts.

FMR moved to dismiss the suits, arguing, as relevant, that neither plaintiff has a claim for relief under §1514A. FMR is privately held, and maintained that §1514A protects only employees of public companies—i.e., companies that either have "a class of securities registered under section 12 of the Securities Exchange Act of 1934," or that are "required to file reports under section 15(d)" of that Act. In a joint order, the District Court rejected FMR's interpretation of §1514A and denied the dismissal motions in both suits. . . .

We granted certiorari to resolve the division of opinion on whether §1514A extends whistleblower protection to employees of privately held contractors who perform work for public companies.

In determining the meaning of a statutory provision, "we look first to its language, giving the words used their ordinary meaning." . . . The ordinary meaning of "an employee" in this proscription is the contractor's own employee.

FMR's interpretation of the text requires insertion of "of a public company" after "an employee." But where Congress meant "an employee of a public company," it said so: With respect to the actors governed by §1514A, the provision's interdictions run to the officers, employees, contractors, subcontractors, and agents "of such company," i.e., a public company. Another anti-retaliation provision in Sarbanes-Oxley provides: "[A] broker or dealer and persons employed by a broker or dealer who are involved with investment banking activities may not, directly or indirectly, retaliate against or threaten to retaliate against any securities analyst employed by that broker or dealer or its affiliates. . . . " In contrast, nothing in §1514A's language confines the class of employees protected to those of a designated employer. Absent any textual qualification, we presume the operative language means what it appears to mean: A contractor may not retaliate against its own employee for engaging in protected whistleblowing activity.

Section 1514A's application to contractor employees is confirmed when we enlarge our view from the term "an employee" to the provision as a whole. The prohibited retaliatory measures enumerated in §1514A(a) — discharge, demotion, suspension, threats, harassment, or discrimination in the terms and conditions of employment — are commonly actions an employer takes against its own employees. Contractors are not ordinarily positioned to take adverse actions against employees of the public company with whom they contract. FMR's interpretation of §1514A, therefore, would shrink to insignificance the provision's ban on retaliation by contractors. The dissent embraces FMR's "narrower" construction.

FMR urges that Congress included contractors in §1514A's list of governed actors simply to prevent public companies from avoiding liability by employing contractors to effectuate retaliatory discharges. FMR describes such a contractor as an "ax-wielding specialist," illustrated by George Clooney's character in the movie *Up in the Air*. As portrayed by Clooney, an ax-wielding specialist is a contractor engaged only as the bearer of the bad news that the employee has been fired; he plays no role in deciding who to terminate. If the company employing the ax-wielder chose the recipients of the bad tidings for retaliatory reasons, the §1514A claim would properly be directed at the company. Hiring the ax-wielder would not insulate the company from liability. Moreover, we see no indication that retaliatory ax-wielding specialists are the real-world problem that prompted Congress to add contractors to §1514A.

Moving further through §1514A to the protected activity described in subsection (a)(1), we find further reason to believe that Congress presumed an employer-employee relationship between the retaliator and the whistleblower. Employees gain protection for furnishing information to a federal agency, Congress, or "a person with supervisory authority over the employee (or such other person working for the employer who has the authority to investigate, discover, or terminate misconduct)." And under §1514A(a)(2), employees are protected from retaliation for assisting "in a proceeding filed or about to be filed (with any knowledge of the employer) relating to an alleged violation" of any of the enumerated fraud provisions, securities regulations, or other federal law relating to shareholder fraud. The reference to employer knowledge is an additional indicator of Congress' expectation that the retaliator typically will be the employee's employer, not another entity less likely to know of whistleblower complaints filed or about to be filed. . . .

Our textual analysis of §1514A fits the provision's purpose. It is common ground that Congress installed whistleblower protection in the Sarbanes-Oxley Act as one means to ward off another Enron debacle. And, as the ARB observed in *Spinner*, "Congress plainly recognized that outside professionals — accountants, law firms, contractors, agents, and the like — were complicit in, if not integral to, the shareholder fraud and subsequent cover-up [Enron] officers . . . perpetrated." Indeed, the Senate Report demonstrates that Congress was as focused on the role of Enron's outside contractors in facilitating the fraud as it was on the actions of Enron's own officers. . . .

Also clear from the legislative record is Congress' understanding that outside professionals bear significant responsibility for reporting fraud by the public companies with whom they contract, and that fear of retaliation was the primary deterrent to such reporting by the employees of Enron's contractors. Congressional investigators discovered ample evidence of contractors demoting or discharging employees they have engaged who jeopardized the contractor's business relationship with Enron by objecting to Enron's financial practices. . . .

Our reading of §1514A avoids insulating the entire mutual fund industry from §1514A, as FMR's and the dissent's "narrower construction" would do. . . . Virtually all mutual funds are structured so that they have no employees of their own; they are managed, instead, by independent investment advisers. The United States investment advising industry manages $14.7 trillion on behalf of nearly 94 million investors. These investment advisers, under our reading of §1514A, are contractors prohibited from retaliating against their own employees for engaging in whistleblowing activity. This construction protects the "insiders [who] are the only firsthand witnesses to the [shareholder] fraud." Under FMR's and the dissent's reading, in contrast, §1514A has no application to mutual funds, for all of the potential whistleblowers are employed by the privately held investment management companies, not by the mutual funds themselves. . . .

Indeed, affording whistleblower protection to mutual fund investment advisers is crucial to Sarbanes-Oxley's endeavor to "protect investors by improving the accuracy and reliability of corporate disclosures made pursuant to the securities laws." As plaintiffs observe, these disclosures are written, not by anyone at the mutual funds themselves, but by employees of the investment advisers. "Under FMR's [and the dissent's] proposed interpretation of section 1514A, FMR could dismiss any FMR employee who disclosed to the directors of or lawyers for the Fidelity funds that there were material falsehoods in the documents being filed by FMR with the SEC in the name of those funds." It is implausible that Congress intended to leave such an employee remediless.

Unable credibly to contest the glaring under-inclusiveness of the "narrower reading" FMR urges, the dissent emphasizes instead FMR's claim that the reading of §1514A we adopt is all too inclusive. . . . There is scant evidence, however, that these floodgate-opening concerns are more than hypothetical. [It] would thwart Congress' dominant aim if contractors were taken off the hook for retaliating against their whistleblowing employees, just to avoid the unlikely prospect that babysitters, nannies, gardeners, and the like will flood OSHA with §1514A complaints.

Plaintiffs and the Solicitor General observe that overbreadth problems may be resolved by various limiting principles. They point specifically to the word "contractor." Plaintiffs note that in "common parlance," "contractor" does not extend to every fleeting business relationship. Instead, the word "refers to a party whose performance of a contract will take place over a significant period of time." The Solicitor General further maintains that §1514A protects contractor employees only to the extent that their whistleblowing relates to "the contractor . . . fulfilling its role as a contractor for the public company, not the contractor in some other capacity." Finally, the Solicitor General suggests that we need not determine the bounds of §1514A today, because plaintiffs seek only a "mainstream application" of the provision's protections. We agree. . . .

For the reasons stated, we hold that 18 U.S.C. §1514A whistleblower protection extends to employees of contractors and subcontractors. The judgment of the U.S. Court of Appeals for the First Circuit is therefore reversed, and the case is remanded for further proceedings consistent with this opinion.

[Opinion of Justices Scalia and Thomas omitted.]

Justice SOTOMAYOR, with whom Justice KENNEDY and Justice ALITO join, dissenting.

Section 806 forbids any public company, or any "officer, employee, contractor, subcontractor, or agent of such company," to retaliate against "an employee" who reports a potential fraud. The Court recognizes that the core purpose of the Act is to "safeguard investors in public companies." And the Court points out that Congress entitled the whistleblower provision, "Protection for Employees of Publicly Traded Companies Who Provide Evidence of Fraud." Despite these clear markers of intent, the Court does not construe §1514A to apply only to public company employees who blow the whistle on fraud relating to their public company employers. The Court instead holds that the law encompasses any household employee of the millions of people who work for a public company and any employee of the hundreds of thousands of private businesses that contract to perform work for a public company.

The Court's interpretation gives §1514A a stunning reach. As interpreted today, the Sarbanes-Oxley Act authorizes a babysitter to bring a federal case against his employer—a parent who happens to work at the local Walmart (a public company)—if the parent stops employing the babysitter after he expresses concern that the parent's teenage son may have participated in an Internet purchase fraud. And it opens the door to a cause of action against a small business that contracts to clean the local Starbucks (a public company) if an employee is demoted after reporting that another nonpublic company client has mailed the cleaning company a fraudulent invoice.

Congress was of course free to create this kind of sweeping regime that subjects a multitude of individuals and private businesses to litigation over fraud reports that have no connection to, or impact on, the interests of public company shareholders. . . . The Court's decision upsets the balance struck by Congress. Fortunately, just as Congress has added further protections to the system it originally designed when necessary, so too may Congress now respond to limit the far-reaching implications of the Court's interpretation. But because that interpretation relies on a debatable view of §1514A's text, is inconsistent with the statute's titles and its context, and leads to absurd results that Congress did not intend, I respectfully dissent.

Questions and Comments

1. Note that this case involved employees of a mutual fund's investment adviser. As we have noted already, mutual funds typically have no employees: They contract out all or nearly all their work, most commonly to their investment adviser. Thus, in this special context, the narrowing interpretation favored by the dissent would effectively eliminate whistleblower protection for publicly traded mutual funds. This was surely an important consideration underlying the majority's analysis of the statutory language.

2. On the other hand, the majority's opinion, while providing a sensible rule for mutual funds, might open a Pandora's Box of potential liability for firms that provide services to other public companies. Consider the examples highlighted by the dissent:

   a. A babysitter brings a federal case against his employer — a parent who happens to work at the local Walmart (a public company) — if the parent stops employing the babysitter after he expresses concern that the parent's teenage son may have participated in an Internet purchase fraud.

   b. A small business, which among other clients contracts to clean the local Starbucks (a public company), demotes an employee after the latter reports that another non-public company client has mailed the cleaning company a fraudulent invoice.

Do these scenarios satisfy the elements of §1514A as interpreted in the majority opinion?

3. The Dodd-Frank Act contains a whistleblower protection rule similar in many respects to §1514A. 15 U.S.C. §78u-6(h)(1)(A) provides that "[n]o employer may discharge, demote, suspend, threaten, harass, directly or indirectly, or in any other manner discriminate against, a whistleblower in the terms and conditions of employment because of any lawful act done by the whistleblower — (i) in providing information to the Commission in accordance with this section; (ii) in initiating, testifying in, or assisting in any investigation or judicial or administrative action of the Commission based upon or related to such information; or (iii) in making disclosures that are required or protected under the Sarbanes-Oxley Act of 2002 (15 U.S.C. 7201 et seq.), the Securities Exchange Act of 1934 (15 U.S.C. 78a et seq.), including section 10A(m) of such Act (15 U.S.C. 78f(m)), section 1513(e) of Title 18, and any other law, rule, or regulation subject to the jurisdiction of the Commission."

4. To bring a viable claim under the Dodd-Frank Act, does the employee have to report the problem to the SEC before the adverse action? The definitional section of the statute might imply as much, since it defines "whistleblower" as "any individual who provides . . . information relating to a violation of the securities laws to the Commission." 15 U.S.C. §78u-6(a)(6). Under this interpretation, the Dodd-Frank whistleblower protections would not apply to an employee who suffered retaliation after raising the matter internally but who did not approach the SEC. Can you see how this is a significant limitation on the efficacy of the protection? The SEC disagrees with the above interpretation. 17 C.F.R. §240.21F-2. The case law is divided: *Compare* Liu v. Siemens AG, No. 13-4385 (2d Cir. 2014) and Berman v. Neo@Ogilvy LLC, No. 14-4626 (2d Cir. 2015) *with* Asadi v. G.E. Energy (USA), LLC, No. 12-20522, 2013 WL 3742492 (5th Cir. July 17, 2013). Stay tuned: The Supreme Court may be addressing another whistleblower case soon.

PROBLEM 8-1

John Jones is an internal auditor at Dyetech, a NYSE-listed company engaged in the business of manufacturing fabric dying and printing equipment. During one internal audit Jones uncovered what he believed to be evidence that a Dyetech sales official had provided an improper gratuity to a foreign official in exchange for an import license. Jones' team reported the problem in an internal audit report, but the head of internal audit, Connie Choi, refused to identify the matter as a "critical audit finding" that would be referred to the audit committee of the board of directors. Choi informed Jones that his concerns had been investigated by an outside law firm and found to be unsubstantiated. Jones then approached Choi's boss, general counsel Mustafa Muhammad, and complained that Choi was refusing to act on information, which, if substantiated, could result in SEC or DOJ enforcement actions or in shareholder lawsuits for failing to disclose material information in SEC filings. Mustafa said he would look into the matter. An hour later Jones received an angry phone call from Choi, who accused him of undercutting her authority. These and other problems caused Jones to experience sleeplessness, anxiety, and depression, requiring psychotherapy and mood-enhancing medication. His frustration came to a head in connection with the internal audit department's annual summer outing, which Jones was responsible for organizing. Two weeks before the event, Jones discovered that his personal secretary had neglected to book a venue for the event. He exploded in rage, cursing and berating his secretary for her incompetence and unreliability. Five or six other employees observed this event and confirmed that Jones had behaved in an abusive and unprofessional fashion. Jones had never acted this way before. Dyetech's director of human resources commenced an investigation into the matter and, having concluded that Jones committed a breach of the company's code of employee conduct, recommended that he be terminated. Jones was fired with two month's severance pay. Jones files a whistleblower lawsuit under the Sarbanes-Oxley Act. What result?

PROBLEM 8-2

Anne Able is a fifth year associate at Tyrone and Rex, a 1,000-lawyer firm specializing in corporate and securities work. She was assigned to work on an initial public offering of the common stock of Marintech, a company supplying software applications in Internet commerce. Anne became concerned that the draft registration statement did not fully disclose the details of a contract between Marintech and its founder and chief executive officer that entitled the latter, after the date of the IPO, to repurchase certain items of intellectual property from the company at what Able believed was a below-market price. She raised these concerns with the engagement partner at her law firm, who dismissed them on the ground that the contracts were not material. Anne wasn't satisfied with this explanation and brought the matter to the head of the securities group, who told her he would look into the matter. Anne then rotated off the Marintech engagement and went to work on other matters. The IPO went forward without any change in the language about the CEO's repurchase rights. Several months later, Anne received her annual review and was informed that her prospects of being promoted to partner were not strong. Anne was very upset at this news since her prior evaluations had adopted a more positive tone. She comes to see you in your capacity as an employment law attorney at another firm, and asks about her rights. What would you advise regarding her prospects for a lawsuit under §806 of the Sarbanes-Oxley Act?

PROBLEM 8-3

Dave Davis is a carpet installer employed by Reliable Carpets, a private company. He raises with his supervisor a concern that Reliable has been billing customers for carpets of a higher quality than what was actually installed. The supervisor tells Davis to mind his own business. A few days later, the supervisor reassigns Davis to performing maintenance work at the company's headquarters. Although the pay is the same, Davis prefers his former job. Reliable has only one public company customer, Bigco, which accounts for about 1 percent of Reliable's annual revenues. Does Davis have a claim against Reliable under §1514A? Would it matter if all of Reliable's bills to Bigco are accurate and honest?

PROBLEM 8-4

Dosas Unlimited, a public company in the ethnic foods business, requires all employees to sign a code of ethics that, inter alia, prohibits them from transmitting non-public personal information about customers to anyone outside the company, except as required by law. Jane Jones, an accountant at Dosas, violates this rule by sending an email to her roommate containing the names, Social Security numbers, and credit card numbers of several hundred Dosa employees. When Dosa discovered the data breach, it confronted Jones with its findings. Jones admitted that she had transmitted the information to a third party, but asserted that she had done so as part of a plan to retransmit the information to the Internal Revenue Service in support of a claim under the IRS's Whistleblower Rewards Program. Jones alleged that the employees in question had fraudulently received millions of dollars in reimbursement from Dosas for personal expenditures and failed to report these amounts to the IRS as income. Can Dosas penalize Jones for violating company policy?

c. Rewards and Bounties

The organization may reward the whistleblower financially, by offering bonuses or bounties for information or by promoting the person within the company. Most organizations have not gone this far, however, relying instead on the whistleblower's conscience and sense of justice to inspire them to come forward. Given the disincentives for whistleblowing noted above, should companies offer rewards for useful information?

Governments have never been quite so cautious about offering rewards. Criminal law enforcement has traditionally used a whistleblower device in the form of rewards offered for information leading to the arrest and conviction of wrongdoers. More recently, systems of rewards for civil whistleblowers have been institutionalized. The SEC's whistleblower bounty program, now codified as Regulation 21F, authorizes payments to individuals who voluntarily provide the SEC with "original information" that leads to an SEC enforcement action generating more than $1 million in sanctions. Qualifying individuals can receive between 10 and 30 percent of the sanctions—a bounty that could be exceptionally large in big cases.

Rewards for whistleblowing are also available in "off-label" marketing cases against pharmaceutical manufacturers (discussed in Chapter 12). In the 2009 Eli Lilly Zyprexa case, four whistleblowers shared approximately 20 percent of an $800 million settlement, or about $160 million. Many people would welcome being tagged as a snitch if doing so was associated with a $40 million payday!

The IRS also operates a whistleblower bounty program for tax compliance, the Informant Whistleblower Award Program. In 2012, Bradley C. Birkenfeld, a former UBS banker, received a $104 million whistleblower award from the IRS for revealing illegal actions by Swiss banks in facilitating tax fraud by U.S. citizens. Birkenfeld might have been particularly pleased with the award because his life had not been going so well: He had recently been released from prison where he was serving time for—conspiring to evade taxes!

Questions and Comments

1. To date, bounty programs have generally been restricted to cases of fraud. Commentators and law reform advocates, however, have discussed the utility of bounty programs for a variety of other possible contexts. *See, e.g.,* Jarold S. Gonzalez, *A Pot of Gold at the End of the Rainbow: An Economic Incentives-Based Approach to OSHA Whistleblowing,* 14 Emp. Rts. & Emp. Pol'y J. 325 (2010); Kevin R. Sullivan, Kate Ball & Sarah Klebolt, *The Potential Impact of Adding a Whistleblower Rewards Program to ACPERA,* 11 Antitrust Source 1 (2001); William E. Kovacic, *Bounties as Inducements to Identify Cartels,* in European Law Annual 2006: Enforcement or Prohibition of Cartels 571 (Claus-Dieter Ehlermann & Isabell Anansiu eds., 2007); Thomas C. Crumplar, *An Alternative to Public and Victim Enforcement of the Federal Securities and Antitrust Laws: Citizen Experiment,* 13 Harv. J. on Legis. 76 (1975); Aaron Petty, *How* Qui Tam *Actions Could Fight Public Corruption,* 39 U. Mich. J.L. Reform 851 (2006).

2. To what extent may a company limit the activities of potential whistleblowers by causing a counterparty to sign employee contracts or separation agreements containing confidentiality or non-disparagement provisions? The SEC's Rule 21F-17 provides: "No person may take any action to impede an individual from communicating directly with the Commission staff about a possible securities law violation, including enforcing, or threatening to enforce, a confidentiality agreement . . . with respect to such communications." In 2015, the SEC fined KBR, Inc., an engineering and construction company, for requiring witnesses in certain internal investigations to sign confidentiality agreements that appeared to prohibit communications with any third party unless authorized in advance by the legal department of the company. The settlement agreement imposed a $130,000 fine, even though the SEC found no instances in which a confidentiality agreement was used to prevent individuals from communicating with the agency about possible securities law violations. In re KBR Inc., SEC Admin. Proc. File No. 3-16466 (Apr. 1, 2015). KBR (parent company of Kellogg Brown & Root) had previously paid $579 million to settle allegations of serious FCPA violations involving the company's chief executive officer. *See* United States v. Kellogg Brown & Root LLC, No. H-09_071 (S.D. Tex. Feb. 11, 2009) (plea agreement); SEC Litigation Release No. 20897 (Feb.

11, 2009); SEC Accounting and Auditing Enforcement Release No. 2935 (Feb. 11, 2009).

3. Increasingly, SEC whistleblower awards are given to foreign informants; in 2014 tips came from individuals in 60 foreign countries, and the largest award ever—more than $30 million—went to a foreign national. For analysis of the SEC's recent approach to whistleblowing, see Amanda M. Rose, *Better Bounty Hunting: How the SEC's New Whistleblower Program Changes the Securities Fraud Class Action Debate*, 108 Nw. U. L. Rev. 1235 (2014).

4. Another important whistleblower provision is contained in the Federal Financial Institution Reform, Recovery and Enforcement Act of 1988 (FIRREA), a statute enacted in the wake of the savings and loan crisis of the 1980s, which involved numerous acts of misconduct by executives at savings institutions. Among other provisions, FIRREA makes it illegal to execute or attempt to execute a scheme to defraud a financial institution or to make false entries on the books of a financial institution. FIRREA further provides, in 12 U.S.C. §4205, that private individuals may submit confidential claims of FIRREA violations to the Department of Justice, which has 12 months to investigate. If the government responds by initiating enforcement proceedings, the whistleblower is entitled to between 20 and 30 percent of the first million recovered, 10 to 20 percent of the next $4 million, and 5 to 10 percent of the next $5 million—making the maximum award equal to $1.6 million. During the current decade, the Department of Justice has increasingly relied on the FIRREA whistleblower provision to obtain information leading to enforcement actions against banks in connection with their actions before and during the financial crisis of 2007-2009 (these claims were timely due to FIRREA's exceptionally generous ten-year statute of limitations).

5. Should internal control personnel such as compliance officers be entitled to a whistleblower bounty if they report corporate misconduct to the government? In general, this would seem perverse because the officials' job is to function as an internal control agent. However, bounties are awarded to these people in some cases, and sometimes these awards are substantial. An example is the case of John Slowik, who was appointed in 2009 as the first compliance officer for Olympus Corporation of the Americas, a manufacturer of endoscopy equipment. While working at Olympus, Slowik discovered evidence of massive illegality in the marketing of his company's products. Senior managers at Olympus fired Slowik in 2010. He responded by filing a False Claims Act against his former employer based on the information he had discovered. In 2015, three enforcement lawsuits that had grown out of Slowik's information settled for a total of $646 million. Slowik received a whistleblower award of $51 million for his role in bringing the illegal conduct to light. *See* Settlement Agreement, United States ex rel. John Slowik et al. v. Olympus Corporation of the Americas, et al., Civ. No. 10-cv-5994 (D.N.J. 2015).

6. The exceptions that allow bounties to control personnel are for situations where the informant had a reasonable basis to believe that reporting to the regulator was necessary to prevent the organization from engaging in conduct that was likely to cause substantial injury to the financial interest or property of the organization or its investors or serious bodily harm to anyone; the informant reasonably believed that reporting to the regulator was necessary to prevent the organization from materially impeding a government investigation; or, after reporting the matter to higher authority in the organization, the informant reasonably concluded that the organization would not remediate the wrongdoing. Do these exceptions draw the right line?

7. When, if at all, should attorneys be entitled to a whistleblower bounty? For discussion, see Jennifer M. Pacella, *Advocate or Adversary? When Attorneys Act as Whistleblowers*, 28 Geo. J. Legal Ethics 1027 (2015) (suggesting that lawyers who collect bounties violate state ethical rules governing attorney conflicts of interest). For an influential judicial opinion, see Fair Laboratory Practices Associates v. Quest Diagnostics, 734 F.3d 154 (2d Cir. 2013) (concluding that New York's ethical rules prohibited attorneys from acting as relators and receiving bounties under the False Claims Act by reporting on their client's fraudulent conduct).

8. For general analysis of the pros and cons of bounty programs, see David Freeman Engstrom, *Whither Whistleblowing? Bounty Regimes, Regulatory Context, and the Challenge of Optimal Design*, 15 J. Theoretical Inquiries 605 (2014); Geoffrey Christopher Rapp, *Beyond Protection: Invigorating Incentives for Sarbanes-Oxley Corporate and Securities Fraud Whistleblowers*, 87 B.U. L. Rev. 91 (2007). A useful history of recent whistleblower reforms is found in Geoffrey Christopher Rapp, *Four Signal Moments in Whistleblower Law: 1983-2013*, 30 Hofstra Lab. & Emp. L.J. 389 (2013).

d. Mandatory Reporting

The organization may require people with knowledge of compliance violations to report what they know, on penalty of being disciplined themselves if they keep silent. Again, Apple's policy is illustrative: "If you have knowledge of a possible violation of Apple's Business Conduct Policy or principles, other Apple policies, or legal or regulatory requirements, you must notify either your manager (provided your manager is not involved in the violation), Human Resources, Legal, Internal Audit, Finance, or the Business Conduct Helpline. . . . [F]ailure to report a violation may result in disciplinary action up to and including termination of employment or the end of your working relationship with Apple."

The legal profession is subject to an important "snitch" obligation. The American Bar Association's Model Rule 8.3, adopted in nearly all states, provides that "a lawyer who knows that another lawyer has committed a violation of the Rules of Professional Conduct that raises a substantial question as to that lawyer's honesty, trustworthiness or fitness as a lawyer in other respects, shall inform the appropriate professional authority."

Questions and Comments

1. Under the Model Rules of Professional Conduct, non-compliance with the duty to report on rule violations is itself a violation of a rule. Thus an attorney who observes another attorney failing to report on a violation by a third attorney is required (in theory) to report both the initial violator and the person who did not turn that person in. And if this attorney doesn't report and is observed by a fourth attorney, the fourth attorney is, in theory, required to report all the previous three. Is this workable?

2. Earlier iterations of Rule 8.3 purported to require reporting every violation of the rules, with the consequence that attorneys were technically required to inform on their fellow lawyers for even minor or technical infractions. The current rule doesn't require that attorneys report all violations — only those that raise a "substantial question" as to the other attorney's honesty, trustworthiness, or fitness.

Technical or minor violations of the rules do not trigger the potentially endless reporting loop described above.

3. On the other hand, neither the model rules nor the official commentary describes which violations are so serious as to require reporting. In leaving this up to the attorney herself, do the rules allow too much room for discretionary judgments that conveniently relieve the attorney of the obligation to disclose?

4. A careful reading of the text of Rule 8.3 reveals another loophole. The reporting obligation applies only when an attorney "knows" that another attorney has committed a violation. When does an attorney "know" something to be the case — as opposed, say, to merely believing or surmising that it may be so? The rules define the term "knows" as "actual knowledge of the fact in question," which may be inferred from the circumstances. Model Rule 1.0(f). But to say you know something when you have actual knowledge of it is hardly illuminating. To what extent can an attorney rationalize a failure to report on the ground that while she is pretty confident that another attorney has violated the rules, she doesn't actually know it?

3. Whistleblower Policies

An organization's whistleblower policy will contain some or all of the features outlined above. The following excerpt sets out a policy of a fictional company, OVB Inc., a mid-sized, publicly traded biotech firm located in California:

OVB Inc. Whistleblower Policy

It is the policy of OVB Inc., that its reported financial information be accurate and complete in all material respects. Illegal or unethical activity, including but not limited to corruption, fraud, criminal activity, abuse and conflict of interest, by the employees of OVB Inc., will not be permitted, tolerated or condoned. This policy shall encourage proper individual conduct, and provide a means for early detection of problematic situations before they have serious consequences. This policy is intended to ensure that OVB Inc. fulfills its responsibilities under the U.S. whistleblower laws, including the Sarbanes-Oxley Act of 2002, as amended, and California Law.

The Audit Committee has adopted the following practices and procedures in furtherance of this policy.

SCOPE

This policy provides a process for the anonymous submission of suspected wrongdoing (whistleblowing) by any employee of OVB Inc., or any subsidiary, vendor, customer, or other person who may have concerns about illegal or unethical behavior, internal controls or questionable accounting practices, and desires to report these concerns. These procedures relate to concerns and complaints relating to accounting, internal controls, or auditing matters of OVB Inc. ("complaints"), including without limitation, the following:

- Fraud or deliberate error in the preparation, evaluation, review or audit of any financial statement of OVB Inc.;
- Fraud or deliberate error in the recordkeeping and maintaining of financial records of OVB Inc.;

- Deficiencies in or noncompliance with OVB Inc.'s internal accounting controls;
- Misrepresentation or false statement to or by an officer of OVB Inc. or an accountant regarding a matter contained in the financial records, financial reports, or audit reports of OVB Inc.; or
- Any deviation from full and fair reporting of OVB Inc.'s financial condition as required by applicable laws.

REPORTING ILLEGAL OR UNETHICAL ACTIVITY

All Complaints will be kept confidential to the fullest extent reasonably practicable within the legitimate needs of law and any ensuing evaluation or investigation. The Complaint may, at the discretion of the person submitting the Complaint, be submitted anonymously and should be promptly reported directly to either the company's Chief Compliance Officer or Chief Executive Officer. Where appropriate, individuals may also report such activity to governmental authorities having jurisdiction over the illegal or unethical activity. An employee reporting such activity to OVB Inc. may do so orally or in writing, and may do so confidentially or anonymously. While OVB Inc. cannot ensure the confidentiality of such reporting, it will attempt to maintain confidentiality and anonymity as much as reasonably possible.

Each member of the Audit Committee is an independent third party who will coordinate delivery of complaints to the appropriate OVB Inc. personnel. In the event a Complaint includes an officer or senior management, an individual may submit their complaint to any member of the Audit Committee.

COMPLAINTS

To assist OVB Inc. in the response and/or investigation of a complaint, the complaint should be factual rather than speculative, and contain as much specific information as possible. It is less likely that OVB Inc. will be able to conduct an investigation based on a complaint that contains unspecified wrongdoing or broad allegations without verifiable evidentiary support. Without limiting the foregoing, the complaint should, to the extent possible, contain the following information:

- The alleged event, matter or issue that is the subject of the complaint;
- The name(s) of the person(s) involved;
- The approximate time and location of the specific events or events; and
- Any additional information, documentation or other supporting evidence available.

INVESTIGATION OF CLAIMS

A copy of all complaints shall be promptly forwarded to the Audit Committee and reviewed at the next regularly scheduled meeting. Unless otherwise directed by the Audit Committee, based on a finding of special circumstances, all investigations conducted by OVB Inc. in accordance with these practices and procedures shall be conducted under the direction and supervision of the Audit Committee or Chief Executive Officer. Generally, the Compliance Officer will conduct the investigations. However, the Audit Committee reserves the right to designate another individual to perform an investigation if deemed necessary.

The Compliance Officer shall gather such documents and materials and interview such individuals as is reasonably necessary to complete the investigation. The results of any investigation conducted pursuant to this policy shall be reported to the Audit Committee and the Chief Executive Officer of OVB Inc. The Audit Committee shall have the authority to request a briefing regarding any investigation and any findings as a result of that investigation. Upon completion of the investigation, the Audit Committee shall review the results and determine the corrective action, or direct further investigation, if necessary.

INVESTIGATION REPORTS

The findings of investigations conducted by OVB Inc. shall, as appropriate, be set forth in a written report which shall include findings of fact, conclusions and recommendations (the "Report"). The Compliance Officer shall provide the Audit Committee with a copy of the completed Report. All Reports prepared by outside third parties, including outside counsel, shall be directed to the Audit Committee as well. A copy of any response letter shall be filed with the complaint and, if possible, provided to the complainant.

DISPOSITION OF CLAIMS

Upon completion of an investigation, the Audit Committee shall take appropriate action pursuant to these practices and procedures. Appropriate action may include referral to the CEO or the appropriate California authorities for disciplinary or administrative action.

CONFIDENTIALITY

Concerns of illegal or unethical behavior may be reported anonymously, at the individual's option. OVB Inc. shall maintain the confidentiality or anonymity of the individual(s) making the complaint to the fullest extent reasonably practicable within the requirements of law. In some cases, it may not be possible to proceed with or properly conduct an investigation unless the complainant reveals their identity. Complainants should be cautioned that their identity might become known for reasons outside the control of OVB Inc. The identity of other individuals subject to or participating in any inquiry or investigation relating to a complaint shall be maintained in confidence subject to the same limitations.

PROHIBITION OF RETALIATION

It is the policy of OVB Inc. that an employee who, in good faith, has disclosed information relating to a complaint or otherwise participated in an investigation relating to a complaint concerning inappropriate behavior by another employee, or by OVB Inc. in general, shall not suffer reprisal, retaliation or punitive action by OVB Inc. or its employees. It is a violation of this policy and applicable law to retaliate or take punitive action against any employee for the reporting of such alleged activity. Retaliation and punitive action may include adverse employment actions such as termination of employment, demotion, and the creation of a hostile work environment. Employees who retaliate or take wrongful action against an employee for protected whistleblower reporting shall be subject to disciplinary action, up to and including termination from employment.

ABUSE OF PRACTICES AND PROCEDURES AND MERITLESS CLAIMS

It shall be a violation of this policy for any employee to report or disclose information covered by this procedure that the employee knows or reasonably should know to be untrue, unfounded or misleading or for which there is no basis for the claim reported in law, rule or regulation. OVB Inc. recognizes that, in some instances, it may not be possible to determine whether a report is warranted. Employees should not be reluctant to report information because they are uncertain or unable to determine the merits of their complaint.

Questions and Comments

1. What sort of tone at the top is conveyed by this policy?

2. How credible are the company's assurances that it will maintain the confidentiality of reports?

3. How credible is the company's commitment neither to retaliate nor to allow others to retaliate against a whistleblower?

4. Is the scope of the policy appropriate?

5. What do you think of the procedures set forth in the policy for making reports?

6. The policy cautions against employees making false or unsubstantiated reports. What are the pros and cons of including this language?

7. Does anything in this policy promise to reward whistleblowers for making complaints that turn out to be substantiated?

4. Responding to the Whistleblower

What should an organization do when a whistleblower comes forward? The problem is delicate. Sometimes the whistleblower's allegations are explosive. Prematurely disclosing them before the organization has all the facts could be destructive. On the other hand, when a whistleblower comes forward with allegations of misconduct, the company cannot sit idly by; it must respond. The first step in an organization's response — other than reassuring the whistleblower — is usually to launch an internal investigation. The following excerpt deals with two such investigations at Enron in the wake of Sherron Watkins' disclosures: one conducted soon after the whistleblower came forward, when the company was under its former management; the other conducted later, after the former managers had been replaced.

Report of Investigation by the Special Investigative Committee of the Board of Directors of Enron Corp. (Feb. 1, 2002)

. . . In light of considerable public attention to what has been described as a "whistleblower" letter to Lay by an Enron employee, Sherron Watkins, we set out the facts as we know them here. However, we were not asked to, and we have not, conducted an inquiry into the resulting investigation.

Shortly after Enron announced Skilling's unexpected resignation on August 14, 2001, Watkins sent a one-page anonymous letter to Lay. The letter stated that "Enron has been very aggressive in its accounting — most notably the Raptor transactions." The letter raised serious questions concerning the accounting treat-ment and economic substance of the Raptor transactions (and transactions between Enron and Condor Trust, a subsidiary of Whitewing Associates), identifying several of the matters discussed in this Report. It concluded that "I am incredibly nervous that we will implode in a wave of accounting scandals."

Lay told us that he viewed the letter as thoughtfully written and alarming. Lay gave a copy of the letter to James V. Derrick, Jr., Enron's General Counsel. Lay and Derrick agreed that Enron should retain an outside law firm to conduct an inves-tigation. Derrick told us he believed that Vinson & Elkins ("V&E") was the logical choice because, among other things, it was familiar with Enron and LJM matters. Both Lay and Derrick believed that V&E would be able to conduct an investigation more quickly than another firm, and would be able to follow the road map Watkins had provided. Derrick says that he and Lay both recognized there was a downside to retaining V&E because it had been involved in the Raptor and other LJM transac-tions. (Watkins subsequently made this point to Lay during the meeting described below and in a supplemental letter she gave to him.) But they concluded that the investigation should be a preliminary one, designed to determine whether there were new facts indicating that a full investigation — involving independent lawyers and accountants — should be performed.

Derrick contacted V&E to determine whether it could, under the legal ethics rules, handle the investigation. He says that V&E considered the issue, and told him that it could take on the matter. Two V&E partners, including the Enron relation-ship partner and a litigation partner who had not done any prior work for Enron, were assigned to handle the investigation. Derrick and V&E agreed that V&E's review would not include questioning the accounting treatment and advice from Andersen, or a detailed review of individual LJM transactions. Instead, V&E would conduct a "preliminary investigation," which was defined as determining whether the facts raised by Watkins warranted further independent legal or accounting review. Watkins subsequently identified herself as the author of the letter. On August 22, one week after she sent her letter, she met with Lay in his office for approximately one hour. She brought with her an expanded version of the letter and some supporting documents. Lay recalls that her major focus was Raptor, and she explained her concerns about the transaction to him. Lay believed that she was serious about her views and did not have any ulterior motives. He told her that Enron would investigate the issues she raised.

V&E began its investigation on August 23 or 24. Over the next two weeks, V&E reviewed documents and conducted interviews. V&E obtained the documents pri-marily from the General Counsel of Enron Global Finance. We were told that V&E, not Enron, selected the documents that were reviewed. V&E interviewed eight Enron officers, six of whom were at the Executive Vice President level or higher, and two Andersen partners. V&E also had informal discussions with lawyers in the firm who had worked on some of the LJM transactions, as well as in-house counsel at Enron. No former Enron officers or employees were interviewed. We were told that V&E selected the interviewees.

After completing this initial review, on September 10, V&E interviewed Watkins. In addition, V&E provided copies of Watkins' letters (both the original one-page letter and the supplemental letter that she gave to Lay at the meeting) to Andersen, and had a follow-up meeting with the Andersen partners to discuss their reactions. V&E also conducted follow-up interviews with Fastow and Causey.

On September 21, the V&E partners met with Lay and Derrick and made an oral presentation of their findings. That presentation closely tracked the substance of what V&E later reported in its October 15, 2001 letter to Derrick. At Lay's and Derrick's request, the V&E lawyers also briefed Robert Jaedicke, the Chairman of the Audit and Compliance Committee, on their findings. The lawyers made a similar presentation to the full Audit and Compliance Committee in early October 2001.

V&E reported in writing on its investigation in a letter to Derrick dated October 15, 2001. The letter described the scope of the undertaking and identified the documents reviewed and the witnesses interviewed. It then identified four primary areas of concern raised by Watkins: (1) the "apparent" conflict of interest due to Fastow's role in LJM; (2) the accounting treatment for the Raptor transactions; (3) the adequacy of the public disclosures of the transactions; and (4) the potential impact on Enron's financial statements. On these issues, V&E observed that Enron's procedures for monitoring LJM transactions "were generally adhered to," and the transactions "were uniformly approved by legal, technical and commercial professionals as well as the Chief Accounting and Risk Officers." V&E also noted the workplace "awkwardness" of having Enron employees working for LJM sitting next to Enron employees.

On the conflict issues, V&E . . . concluded that "none of the individuals interviewed could identify any transaction between Enron and LJM that was not reasonable from Enron's standpoint or that was contrary to Enron's best interests." On the accounting issues, V&E said that both Enron and Andersen acknowledge "that the accounting treatment on the Condor/Whitewing and Raptor transactions is creative and aggressive, but no one has reason to believe that it is inappropriate from a technical standpoint." V&E concluded that the facts revealed in its preliminary investigation did not warrant a "further widespread investigation by independent counsel or auditors," although they did note that the "bad cosmetics" of the Raptor related-party transactions, coupled with the poor performance of the assets placed in the Raptor vehicles, created "a serious risk of adverse publicity and litigation."

V&E provided a copy of its report to Andersen. V&E also met with Watkins to describe the investigation and go over the report. The lawyers asked Watkins whether she had any additional factual information to pass along, and were told that she did not.

With the benefit of hindsight, and the information set out in this Report, Watkins was right about several of the important concerns she raised. On certain points, she was right about the problem, but had the underlying facts wrong. In other areas, particularly her views about the public perception of the transactions, her predictions were strikingly accurate. Overall, her letter provided a road map to a number of the troubling issues presented by the Raptors.

The result of the V&E review was largely predetermined by the scope and nature of the investigation and the process employed. We identified the most serious problems in the Raptor transactions only after a detailed examination of the relevant transactions and, most importantly, discussions with our accounting advisors — both steps that Enron determined (and V&E accepted) would not be part of V&E's investigation. With the exception of Watkins, V&E spoke only with very senior people at Enron and Andersen. Those people, with few exceptions, had substantial professional and personal stakes in the matters under review. The scope and process of the investigation appear to have been structured with less skepticism than was needed to see through these particularly complex transactions.

Questions and Comments

1. The excerpt is from a document commonly known as the "Powers Report," after the committee chairman, William C. Powers, Jr. Powers, a distinguished Texas attorney and law school dean, was appointed to the Enron board in October 2001 — after the events giving rise to Enron's problems — for the purpose of chairing the investigative committee. He resigned five months later, explaining that, having completed his report, he needed to return to his full-time duties as a dean.

2. Ably assisting in the preparation of this report was the law firm, Wilmer Cutler & Pickering (now Wilmer Cutler Pickering Hale and Dorr). This firm has long been a leader in conducting internal investigations of allegations of corporate misconduct.

3. When the Powers Committee began work in October 2001, Enron was already in trouble: It had restated earnings, its stock price was plummeting, the SEC had commenced a preliminary investigation, and Andrew Fastow had been fired after he revealed to the board of directors that he had earned profits from self-dealing transactions. During the time the committee was working on the report (it was issued on February 1, 2002), more bad things happened: Enron's stock continued to tank; a buyout deal fell through; the SEC launched a formal investigation; the SEC brought a civil fraud case against Enron's public accountant; and in December 2002, Enron filed for bankruptcy — at the time, the largest insolvency in American history.

4. This excerpt illustrates two sorts of investigation: (a) the investigation engaged in by Vinson & Elkins, Enron's long-time outside law firm, and (b) the subsequent investigation engaged in by the special investigating committee, which in the excerpted text comments on the nature of the first investigation.

5. What do you think of the reason given for assigning the initial investigation to Vinson & Elkins — that, being familiar both with Enron and with the questioned transactions, it could conduct a preliminary review of the matter to determine whether a more fulsome investigation was warranted? Was this a sufficient reason to select this firm rather than another, in light of what was known at the time?

6. Vinson & Elkins concluded that it was not ethically precluded from conducting the investigation. Do you agree, given that Vinson & Elkins was Enron's outside counsel, had provided advice and prepared documentation in connection with questioned transactions, and had assisted Enron with the preparation of its disclosures of related-party transactions in SEC filings?

7. Was it appropriate for Enron to restrict the scope of Vinson & Elkins' investigation, by ruling out inquiries into the accounting treatment and advice from Andersen or a detailed review of individual financing transactions? Should Vinson & Elkins have accepted the assignment under these conditions?

8. Was it appropriate that one of the two Vinson & Elkins partners assigned to handle the investigation was the Enron chief relationship partner? Why or why not?

9. The intensive phase of Vinson & Elkins' initial investigation lasted for about two weeks. The firm reviewed documents, interviewed eight Enron employees and two Andersen partners, and discussed the questioned transactions with its own lawyers who had worked on the matter. Was this a sufficient investigation given the gravity of the whistleblower's allegations?

10. The Vinson & Elkins investigation, while critical of some aspects of the transactions, concluded that no further review was warranted. Subsequent events revealed that these and other transactions had been part of a massive criminal fraud, one that brought down both Enron and Arthur Andersen. Was Vinson &

Elkins justified in reaching this conclusion, based on the limitations imposed on the scope of its inquiry?

11. Only two members of the Powers Committee, Troubh and Winokur, signed the portions of the report excepted above. Powers recused himself from this portion "because of the relationship between Vinson & Elkins and the University of Texas School of Law." Powers happened to be the dean of University of Texas Law School at time. Vinson & Elkins was a major donor to the school, supplied attorneys to teach courses there, and was a significant employer of the school's graduates.

12. What do you make of Troubh and Winokur's assessment of Vinson & Elkins' performance? They conclude that the "result of the V&E review was largely predetermined by the scope and nature of the investigation and the process employed." Is this a criticism of the firm, or an excuse for the firm's failure to identify the deeper issues?

13. The Powers Report is widely credited as a model for what an independent investigation should be. Note, however, that at the time this report was issued, Enron's former managers were no longer in charge of the company: Enron had filed for bankruptcy and effective control had passed to its creditors, who had an interest in recovering damages from the company's former managers, advisers, and consultants. Would the report have been as hard-hitting if the former managers had remained in power?

B. *QUI TAM* ACTIONS

Qui tam litigation, a special type of whistleblower proceeding, has been around for many years but recently has exploded in importance. The term *"qui tam"* comes from *qui tam pro domino rege quam pro se ipso in hac parte sequitur:* "who pursues this action on our Lord the King's behalf as well as his own." As you can tell by the archaic language, *qui tam* actions have a hoary lineage; they are discussed in Blackstone's Commentaries on the Laws of England (first published in the 1760s). *Qui tam* actions are a traditional mechanism for encouraging whistleblowers to come forward by offering them bounties if they do so.

Several federal *qui tam* statutes were enacted in the nineteenth century; all are still on the statute books but only the False Claims Act (FCA) is in widespread use. The *qui tam* provision of that statute, 31 U.S.C. §3730, sets forth a procedure whereby a private party (called a "relator") can file a lawsuit on behalf of the government charging that a person has made a false claim on the government in violation of 31 U.S.C. §3729. The relator must deliver a copy of the complaint plus any supporting evidence to the government, which then has 60 days to decide whether to intervene. If the government intervenes, it takes principal responsibility for the litigation, although the relator retains the right to participate in the lawsuit. If the government doesn't intervene, the relator may continue on her own. Relators receive a bonus if the litigation generates a settlement or judgment on the merits, which ranges from 15 to 25 percent if the Government intervenes and from 25 to 30 percent if it does not. The relator is also entitled to attorneys' fees and costs.

Qui tam actions have similarities with other whistleblower programs discussed above, but they have one special feature that gives extraordinary power to the person providing the information. In many programs, the whistleblower may be incentivized by the promise of a bounty if the government acts on the information provided, but if the government does not act, the whistleblower may be out of luck. In the case of *qui tam* actions, in contrast, the relator is allowed to proceed on her own if the government refuses to act — giving the relator potentially larger benefits from coming forward.

Recoveries in *qui tam* actions can be large, and in some cases have enriched the relators who bring these actions and the attorneys who litigate them. Many states, moreover, are jumping on the *qui tam* bandwagon by enacting their own "mini-FCAs" to deal with false claims under state programs.

Questions and Comments

1. The relator in an FCA action seeks recovery on behalf of the government; her interest in the matter is that of a good citizen who wants to protect the public finances, coupled with the not-insubstantial interest in receiving a bounty at the end of the day. How, then, does a *qui tam* plaintiff have standing to bring the action? This issue, dormant for many years, was resolved in Vermont Agency of Natural Resources v. United States ex rel. Stevens, 529 U.S. 765 (2000), holding that the injury-in-fact sustained by the United States was sufficient to confer Article III standing on the *qui tam* plaintiff.

2. Is it enough under the FCA for the plaintiff to establish that the defendant made a false statement in connection with a claim for payment (for example, in its certification that it satisfies conditions of participation in the program), or must the false statement cause the government's harm in the sense that the claim would not have been paid if the government had known the true facts? *See* United States ex rel. Hobbs v. MedQuest Assocs., 711 F.3d 707, 709 (6th Cir. 2013) (endorsing the second, more demanding standard in the context of a Medicare reimbursement case).

3. Given that the *qui tam* relator is essentially a volunteer — and a potentially well-paid one at that — it can be expected that multiple suits will be filed when news of a potential FCA violation begins to leak out. Which relator gets the case? The FCA allocates the litigation to the first person to file the action. 31 U.S.C. §3730(b)(5). Is this sensible? It would seem to reward those who are fastest to the courthouse rather than those who are most capable of furthering the government's interest. Can you think of an alternative? What about holding a hearing to determine which relator is best qualified? What about conducting an auction to distribute the case to the qualified relator who is willing to accept the lowest bounty?

4. If the purpose of the FCA's *qui tam* provision is to encourage whistleblowers, it hardly seems necessary to reward a putative relator who brings to the government's attention information that is already known. The FCA deals with this issue in 31 U.S.C. §3730(e)(4), which bars a *qui tam* relator from bringing a case based upon allegations that already have been publicly disclosed, unless the relator is an "original source" of the information. "Original source" is defined to include an individual who either "[(1)] prior to a public disclosure under subsection (e)(4)(a), has voluntarily disclosed to the Government the information on which allegations or transactions in a claim are based, or (2) who has knowledge that is independent of and materially adds to the publicly disclosed allegations or transactions, and who has voluntarily provided the information to the Government before filing an action under this section."

5. Can a defendant can ward off a *qui tam* action by publicly self-disclosing its own FCA violations? Consider the competing policies. On the one hand, perhaps

defendants who have defrauded the government should not be allowed to avoid the consequences of their misconduct associated with *qui tam* litigation. On the other hand, if the purpose of the *qui tam* action is to smoke out information regarding frauds against the government, the law may not care much about where the information comes from. *See* United States ex rel. Estate of Cunningham v. Millennium Labs. of California, 713 F.3d 662 (1st Cir. 2013) (suggesting that disclosure by a defendant may be sufficient to preclude subsequent *qui tam* actions). Is this the right result?

6. The FCA allows a relator to pursue litigation even when the government doesn't want to pursue the case. Since the government is the injured party, should it be allowed to decide whether litigation proceeds against a particular defendant?

7. Underlying the FCA appear to be two policies that are not perfectly reconciled: (a) encouraging whistleblowers to bring evidence of fraudulent claims to the attention of the government, and (b) enlisting the *qui tam* relator as a participant — and to some degree as a monitor — in the government's conduct of litigation. Which of these statutory purposes is more important?

To get a feel for how the FCA process works, it is useful to examine an actual case. The following excerpt involves the C.R. Bard Company, a manufacturer of medical devices.

Darity v. C.R. Bard Inc.

No. 06-cv-0208 (N.D. Ga.) (2007)

COMPLAINT

. . . Plaintiff Darity's qui tam action to recover treble damages and civil penalties on behalf of the United States of America arises from Plaintiff-Relator's information and belief, set forth more specifically below, that Defendants have submitted and/or caused to be submitted false and fraudulent claims to the United States Government ("Government") for payment through the use of false records and false statements. . . .

Plaintiff was employed by Defendant C.R. Bard, Inc. as the Manager for Brachytherapy Contracts Administration at the time her employment with employment with Defendant terminated on November 18, 2005. In her capacity as Manager for Brachytherapy Contracts Administration, Plaintiff worked from her home in Macon, Georgia, as well as the offices of Bard Urological Division, 8195 Industrial Boulevard, Covington, GA 30014.

Defendant C.R. Bard, Inc. . . . represents itself to be "a leading multinational developer, manufacturer, and marketer of innovative, life-enhancing medical technologies in the fields of Vascular, Urology, and Oncology, and Surgical Specialty products" that "markets its products and services worldwide to hospitals, individual health care professionals, extended care facilities, and alternate site facilities." . . .

Since 2000, Defendant Bard has engaged in a variety of schemes designed to induce customers to purchase its brachytherapy seeds. Inducements provided by Bard to customers result in increased prices for brachytherapy seeds. These increased prices are subsequently paid for by the Medicare and Medicaid programs.

The Anti-Kickback Statute makes it a felony to offer kickbacks or other payments in exchange for referring patients "for the furnishing of any item or service for which payment has been made in whole or in part under a Federal health care program." 42 U.S.C. §1320a-7b(b)(2)(A). . . .

Bard's inducements for the customers' brachytherapy seed purchases included the provision of disposable products at no cost or below manufacturer's production cost, provision of equipment on loan for extended periods of time at no cost to the customer (for example, stabilization equipment), donation of capital equipment to customers, repairs or replacements of customer-owned equipment at no cost, and the sale of equipment below Bard's acquisition cost. The amount of business that Bard gained by offering these inducements is in excess of $2,000,000. These inducements were offered by multiple sales representatives of Bard at separate locations around the United States.

Bard uses rebates as inducements for the customer to purchase its brachytherapy seeds. The members of a group purchasing organization in Texas received rebates that were not disclosed on the individual invoices or in separately-provided disclosure statements. Through August 31, 2005, the rebates [exceeded] $82,000. In exchange for issuing these rebates, Defendant Bard was able to sell seeds at higher price per seed. Bard provides additional rebates to its customers in the form of Corporate incentive rebates. These rebates are not disclosed in individual invoices and are not linked such that the customer can link the rebates to specific claims made for pass through payments.

Bard provides additional services at no cost to its customers to induce the customers to purchase Bard's brachytherapy seeds. Examples include the provision of customized training at no cost, variable billing arrangements that allow the customer to profit from resale of the brachytherapy seeds, advertising grants, and unrestricted educational grants. The amount of business gained by Bard through these actions is in excess of $2,000,000.

Bard awarded research grants as inducements for the brachytherapy seed orders of Seattle Prostate Institute and Chicago Prostate Institute. These two practices are among the highest volume brachytherapy centers in the United States. Despite the high volume of seeds purchased, these customers were charged list price or significantly higher than average seed price for the seeds invoiced in order for the grants to be funded. In the case of one of the customers, the price of brachytherapy seeds was increased despite the overwhelming trend of price decrease in the United States. The combined volume of business for these practices was in excess of $4,000,000 through August 31, 2005.

Bard awarded a research grant as an inducement for brachytherapy seed purchases of Mt. Sinai Hospital in New York City, NY, a large teaching hospital. In a meeting held at Bard on December 17, 2001, the Sales Division Manager reported that a purchase order had been received from the institution. In response, the marketing department was directed to provide the institution with confirmation of the grant on December 17, 2001. Bard had invoiced this customer in excess of $3,500,000 from December 17, 2001 to August 31, 2005. . . .

Questions and Comments

1. Bard was allegedly able to engage in its illegal marketing strategy because under applicable regulations, payments for brachytherapy seeds were passed directly on to the Medicare and Medicaid programs. That meant that hospitals and other health care providers would not incur a loss if they overpaid. It would arguably have been easy to persuade health care providers to overpay because the government was picking up the tab.

2. Why might reputable health care providers such as Mt. Sinai Hospital have gone along with this alleged scheme? Could they have been unaware that they were overpaying and submitting inflated bills to the government?

3. The relator in this case worked as Manager for Bard's Brachytherapy Contracts Administration, and accordingly was in a position to observe the alleged misconduct. On the other hand, was she also in an excellent position to stop it? Would it make sense to reward her for blowing the whistle after the fact if she had done nothing to prevent the harm while it was occurring?

4. What does this complaint illustrate about the utility of *qui tam* actions? Would the government have ever been able to obtain the sort of detailed, inside information about what allegedly went on in C.R. Bard's marketing department if someone like this relator had not come along?

Department of Justice, Office of Public Affairs, C.R. Bard Inc. to Pay U.S. $48.26 Million to Resolve False Claims Act Claims

May 13, 2013

C.R. Bard Inc. has agreed to pay the United States $48.26 million to resolve claims that it knowingly caused false claims to be submitted to the Medicare program for brachytherapy seeds used to treat prostate cancer in violation of the False Claims Act. Bard is a New Jersey based corporation that develops, manufacturers, and markets medical products used for a variety of conditions, including prostate cancer.

The settlement requires that Bard pay $48.26 million and it resolves claims relating to Bard's sale of brachytherapy seeds, a form of radiation therapy, to hospitals. The United States alleged that from 1998 to 2006, Bard provided illegal remuneration to customers and physicians to induce them to purchase Bard's seeds, in violation of the Anti-Kickback Statute. The illegal remuneration allegedly took the form of certain grants, guaranteed minimum rebates, conference fees, marketing assistance and/or free medical equipment that Bard paid to customers and/or physicians who used the seeds to perform treatment for prostate cancer. Hospitals ultimately submitted bills to Medicare for these seeds, which the government alleged were rendered false by Bard's illegal kickback activity. The government alleged that Bard was liable under the False Claims Act for causing the submission of those false claims.

"This settlement is part of the United States' on-going effort to combat the payment of illegal kickbacks to health care providers," said Stuart F. Delery, Acting Assistant Attorney General for the Department of Justice's Civil Division. "Such illegal payments subvert the medical marketplace and provide an unfair advantage to those who break the law."

"Illegal kickbacks in any form pervert our health care system, which is designed to insure that health care providers make decisions based solely on what is best for the patient," said U.S. Attorney for the Northern District of Georgia Sally Quillian Yates.

"We will continue to work with our various law enforcement partners in the pursuit of those who abuse publicly funded health care programs such as Medicare and Medicaid, through criminal prosecutions or civil settlements under the False Claims Act," stated Mark F. Giuliano, Special Agent in Charge, FBI Atlanta Field Office. "Such abuses as we've seen in this case will not be tolerated."

"Medicare beneficiaries should never have to question whether treatment recommendations are based on their doctors' best financial interests rather than their best medical advice," said Daniel R. Levinson, Inspector General of the U.S. Department of Health and Human Services. "Companies paying these kickback bribes should expect aggressive investigation and prosecution."

The civil settlement resolves a lawsuit filed in the U.S. District Court for the Northern District of Georgia by Julie Darity, a former Bard manager for brachytherapy contracts administration under the qui tam, or whistleblower provisions, of the False Claims Act. Under the False Claims Act, private citizens may bring suit for false claims on behalf of the United States and share in any recovery obtained by the government. The former manager will receive $10,134,600 as her share of the civil settlement.

In addition, according to a non-prosecution agreement with the United States, Bard has agreed to pay an additional $2.2 million and to take numerous remedial steps, many of which the company identified and began to implement prior to the criminal investigation, to enhance its corporate compliance program to prevent similar illegal actions in the future. For example, Bard has agreed to refine its Code of Conduct and other written policies and procedures that promote Bard's commitment to full compliance with all Federal health care program requirements and to develop an effective program to monitor medical education grants provided by Bard to ensure compliance with those requirements. . . .

These settlements were the result of a coordinated effort by the U.S. Attorney's Office for the Northern District of Georgia; the Department of Justice, Civil Division, Commercial Litigation Branch; the FBI and HHS-OIG, in investigating the allegations in this case.

Questions and Comments

1. Did the Department of Justice obtain an admission of responsibility from the defendant as part of this settlement? What does the press release tell us about this?

2. The press release follows a canonical form, nearly always found in these documents, in which the agency touts its achievements and distributes quotations in order of seniority. When more than one office or agency is involved, each gets a quote. The lead agency's perception of the importance of the event is signaled by the level of responsibility of the first quoted official. Here, the first quote is from the Acting Assistant Attorney General for the Civil Division — a high-level officer (had this settlement been even more important, the first quote could been given to the Attorney General himself). We can infer that the Department of Justice considered this settlement to be a significant achievement. The other two quotes are allocated to less senior officers who have different reporting lines within the Department of Justice: the U.S. Attorney for the Northern District of Georgia and the Special Agent in Charge of the FBI Atlanta Field Office. Because the Department of Health and Human Services was also involved, it too gets a quote, from the Department's Inspector General — a high-level official in that agency, but one whose position last in the quotation chain signals that the Department of Justice was running the show.

3. The press release doesn't give a lot of credit to the relator, Julie Darity. As far as this document is concerned, this outstanding settlement appears to have been the result of the assiduous efforts and excellent cooperation displayed by the Department of Justice and the Department of Health and Human Services. The relator is

mentioned almost as an afterthought, with the remark that the settlement "resolves" her lawsuit. Do you think the release fairly allocates credit for the successful conclusion of this matter?

4. Darity may not have minded too much about being slighted in the press release, given that she took home a cool $10,134,600. Was she appropriately compensated for blowing the whistle and bringing this *qui tam* action?

5. The press release notes that even prior to the criminal investigation, the defendant had identified and began to implement "numerous remedial steps." Why does the press release mention Bard's remedial steps? Is the suggestion that the government exercised a degree of leniency and might have demanded even more had Bard not behaved responsibly? If so, should Bard be given credit for after-the-fact improvements in its compliance function? Did Bard suddenly get religion about compliance, or did it realize it was busted after the relator filed her *qui tam* action?

6. The press release emphasizes the concern for protecting public health. Is there any evidence that Bard's activities put patients in danger or impaired the quality of care? Was the government complaining about a threat to public health, or that it was overcharged for services? Why does the press release focus on the former concern?

7. This was not the first time Bard got in regulatory trouble. In 1994, it pleaded guilty to criminal charges that it had produced and distributed defective angioplasty catheters, and agreed, among other things, to pay more than $60 million in fines and civil penalties. United States v. C.R. Bard, Inc., 848 F. Supp. 287 (D. Mass. 1994). Should the Department of Justice have taken Bard's compliance rap sheet into consideration when it agreed to the settlement described above?

9

Gatekeepers

A. INTRODUCTION

We turn now to another group of actors who play an important role in the compliance function. We refer to these parties as "gatekeepers."

The term "gatekeeper" is widely used in compliance circles, but the specific meaning is not always precise. Accordingly, before examining gatekeepers' role in compliance, it is useful to define the term.

In ordinary usage a gatekeeper is someone who guards a gate. The "gate" in this metaphor separates the organization from some objective that the organization seeks to achieve. The gatekeeper has control over the gate, and accordingly can prevent or impede the organization from achieving its objective. The gatekeeper bars the gate when, in her professional opinion, the organization cannot achieve the objective without violating some applicable rule or standard.

This definition clarifies the nature of a gatekeeper's role, but leaves open an ambiguity as to the nature of the gatekeeper's duty. Whose interests does the gatekeeper take into account when deciding whether to bar the door or open it? Here two models of the gatekeeper's role compete for priority.

> A "gatekeeper" is someone whose certification or support is needed before an organization can reach a goal.

In one model, the gatekeeper acts as a *zealous advocate* on behalf of the organization. Her only concern in carrying out the gatekeeper function is to serve the best interests of her client within the bounds of the law.

In the other model, the gatekeeper serves the organization, but also, to a substantial extent, acts in the public interest. The gatekeeper as conceived in this second model is, at least in part, a *public servant* who carries out a broader responsibility by ensuring that the organization complies with governing norms.

The contrast between these two images of gatekeepers should not be taken too far. When a gatekeeper plays the second role—ensuring compliance with governing norms — she arguably also acts as a zealous advocate because the organization's best interests are served when the organization doesn't break the rules. The gatekeeper's actions in such cases may conflict with the interests of people who happen to be running the organization at any given time, but not with those of the organization itself.

Nevertheless, there is real content to the contrast between the two concepts of the gatekeeper's duty. Normative obligations are often not clear cut; and when gatekeepers have a choice of interpretations, they must decide whether to adopt ones that serve the organization's interests or ones that the regulators prefer or that, in their view, best serve the broader public. When representing an organization, moreover, a gatekeeper can elect to make the government's job easier or more difficult. In these and other situations, the two ideas of the gatekeeper's duty are in tension: The person may have to choose between helping the organization fend off the government and helping the government force the organization to comply with the government's wishes. As we will see in the pages that follow, that choice can be difficult, and risky.

Questions and Comments

1. When you hear the term "gatekeeper," what connotations does it bring to mind? Are they good or bad?

2. A case from outside the compliance context helps to illustrate the two concepts of a gatekeeper's duty. Automobile mechanics provide services to customers who wish them to repair or improve their vehicles. Because customers don't have the skill to do the job themselves, the mechanic acts in effect as a gatekeeper. When responding to the customer's request, the mechanic serve as a loyal fiduciary: to the best of her ability she seeks to achieve the customer's expressed wishes. If, however, a customer asks the mechanic to remove the vehicle's catalytic converter (equipment that reduces pollution by reducing harmful exhaust gasses), the mechanic is legally required to refuse to do so. Here the public interest in environmental quality trumps the customer's interest in specifying the configuration of her car. In such circumstances, the mechanic is asked to serve the broader interest and becomes a de facto public servant rather than an agent of the client.

3. The concept of "gatekeeper" also depends, in part, on the reason why the role is being defined. The definition offered above deals with the gatekeeper's role in the context of compliance. A somewhat different definition may be appropriate in other settings. Consider the following from law professor John C. Coffee, Jr., which uses the term in the context of ensuring the integrity and efficiency of securities markets: "A gatekeeper is an agent who acts as a reputational intermediary to assure investors as to the quality of the 'signal' sent by the corporate issuer." John C. Coffee, Jr., *Gatekeepers: The Professions and Corporate Governance* (2006).

4. For more on gatekeepers, see Reinier H. Kraakman, *Gatekeepers: The Anatomy of Third Party Enforcement Strategy*, 2 J.L. Econ. & Org. 53 (1986).

The two concepts of the gatekeeper's duty have both played a role in the self-concept of the professions. Historically, the concept of gatekeeper as zealous advocate was more important. Recently, however, the concept of gatekeeper as public servant has gained traction.

The change can be traced, in part, to the savings and loan fiasco of the 1980s, when many traditionally conservative housing finance institutions began to speculate in dubious commercial real estate deals and risky corporate bonds. When these institutions crashed and burned — costing taxpayers north of $100 billion — the public outrage raised fundamental questions about the role of the professionals who had failed to prevent the disaster.

Much of this outrage focused on Lincoln Savings & Loan, a once conservatively managed thrift institution that, under a charismatic leader named Charles Keating, experienced spectacular growth and an equally spectacular failure, followed by a raft of lawsuits and indictments. The following opinion famously critiqued the role that professional service providers played in facilitating Keating's machinations.

Lincoln Savings & Loan Ass'n v. Wall

743 F. Supp. 901 (D.D.C. 1990)

[Bank regulators took control of Lincoln Savings after concluding that it was insolvent. The former controlling parties sued to get it back. The trial judge concluded that Lincoln Savings' financial strategies were rife with fraud and misconduct. In the course of his opinion upholding the government's actions, the judge asked the following trenchant questions:]

Where were these professionals, a number of whom are now asserting their rights under the Fifth Amendment, when these clearly improper transactions were being consummated?

Why didn't any of them speak up or disassociate themselves from the transactions?

Where also were the outside accountants and attorneys when these transactions were effectuated?

What is difficult to understand is that with all the professional talent involved (both accounting and legal), why at least one professional would not have blown the whistle to stop the overreaching that took place in this case. . . .

While we in this nation have been trying to place blame for the savings and loan crisis on the various governmental participants in the crisis and on the government's fostering of deregulation within the thrift industry, this Court believes far too little scrutiny has been focused on the private sector. We are the world's greatest example of the success of the private enterprise system. It would thus seem that the private sector ought to be able to put in place a system that would prevent the kinds of excesses that took place in Lincoln from recurring. Here it is clear the private sector was not willing to cooperate with the public oversight regulators. Indeed, the private sector at times impeded the regulatory authorities from discharging their duties. All too often Keating and those individuals working with him adopted strategies to thwart and frustrate the regulatory process. Such tactics included making it difficult for the Board's examiners to obtain records and threats to institute lawsuits. These tactics were somewhat successful in that through their intimidating effect they delayed the Board from taking prompt action. . . .

One of the great attributes of this nation is it learns from its mistakes. It is clear that this case should provide all of us with a very valuable learning experience. If the lessons are learned well, we will have gone a long way in preventing these abusive activities from recurring in the future.

Questions and Comments

1. The judge in this case, Stanley Sporkin, had previously been Director of the Bureau of Enforcement of the SEC. Could that experience have influenced the views expressed in the excerpted text? Should a federal judge be using this sort of language?

2. Do you sense in the opinion a certain frustration at the fact that the professionals who assisted Lincoln Savings & Loan seem to have gotten away without suffering any consequences?

3. Later commentators often quote Sporkin as asking, "Where were the lawyers?" As far as appears from the opinion, the judge never used that phrase. No matter: The comment is just as universally attributed to Sporkin as "lead on Macduff" is to Shakespeare or "play it again Sam" to *Casablanca.*

4. Sporkin identifies two problems with the behavior of the professionals who provided services to Lincoln Savings & Loan: a cynical attitude of disrespect for the law, and a failure to do the right thing when confronted with evidence of misconduct. As evidence of the former, Sporkin cites a statement made by one of Lincoln's accountants (which turned out to be Arthur Andersen) when it resigned from the Lincoln audit:

> _____ confirmed to the Registrant that _____'s resignation was not the result of any concern by _____ with the Registrant's operations, recordkeeping, books and records, management cooperation, or asset/liability management; _____ expressed full confidence in the Registrant's financial disclosure. _____ advised the Registrant that the resignation was a result of _____'s concern over potential liability in representing certain savings and loan associations in view of the very litigious environment controlled to a large degree by regulators. In particular, _____ cited the regulators' criticism over thrift institutions' rate of growth and asset mix (although consistent with applicable statutes and regulations), and _____'s concern over the considerable publicity generated by the FHLBB's and its Chairman, Mr. Gray's, disagreements with the policies of the Registrant.

In other words, the accountant claims to have resigned, not because of any fault at Lincoln Savings & Loan, but rather because the regulators were litigious publicity hounds. Sporkin trashes the explanation on the ground that "the accounting firm was more concerned with attempts of conscientious regulators to deal with the savings and loans industry's severe crisis than the 'creative accounting' of its 'high flying' client." Do you share his evaluation?

5. As regards the failure to do the right thing, Sporkin asks why no one blew the whistle, spoke up, or dissociated themselves from the questionable transactions. How easy would that have been to do?

B. ATTORNEYS

We turn now to the role of attorneys. These are classic gatekeepers because their services are often needed if an organization is to achieve its objectives. We will explore the degree to which attorneys for clients in compliance matters are (or should be) zealous advocates or, alternatively, public servants serving a quasi-enforcement role; we will also examine three special advantages that the attorney brings to the gatekeeper role: the attorney-client privilege, the work-product protection, and the defense of reliance on counsel.

1. Zealous Advocates or Public Servants?

a. Lord Brougham, Dean Pound, and the Rules of Professional Conduct

The tension between the two concepts of a gatekeeper's duty is evidenced in authoritative expressions of the lawyer's professional role. In 1821, Lord Brougham, a distinguished British attorney, offered what is still the best-known justification of the lawyer's role as zealous advocate:

> [A]n advocate, in the discharge of his duty, knows but one person in all the world, and that person is his client. To save that client by all means and expedients, and at all hazards and costs to other persons, and, amongst them, to himself, is his first and only duty; and in performing this duty he must not regard the alarm, the torments, the destruction which he may bring upon others. Separating the duty of a patriot from that of an advocate, he must go on reckless of the consequences, though it should be his unhappy fate to involve his country in confusion.

2 Trial of Queen Caroline 3 (1821).

The quote is memorable in its own right. And it is especially meaningful given the context in which it was uttered. Lord Brougham's client, Queen Caroline, was being prosecuted for adultery on the complaint of her husband, King George IV, who wanted to justify a divorce. The matter was deeply political because the king was unpopular and Queen Caroline enjoyed the support of many British subjects. Small wonder, therefore, that Lord Brougham worried about involving his country in confusion.

Lord Brougham's encomium to the lawyer as zealous advocate also points to one of the principal justifications for a rule of undivided loyalty to the client. Throughout history attorneys have acted as bulwarks between the might of the state and the fortunes of individuals, resisting attempts at tyranny and helping to establish constitutional rights. Lord Brougham was doing just that: Arrayed against his client was the full force of the British monarchy — an institution that in his time was hardly the figurehead it is today. The attorney's duty of undivided loyalty to her client is arguably one of the foundations of a free society; without that duty, clients would have substantially less protection against oppression by their governments.

Questions and Comments

1. Lord Brougham prevailed in his case: The state dropped the prosecution and the king never got his divorce (although the queen died soon after from natural causes).

2. According to Lord Brougham, among those whose interests the attorney must disregard in the single-minded service of the client is the attorney himself. This comment was obviously self-referential. Lord Brougham might indeed have been risking his career and even his personal safety for his vigorous representation of the queen, which involved a potential challenge to the king's right to the crown. But the case made Brougham a superstar; he went on to become Lord Chancellor of Great Britain and lived to the age of 90.

3. The trial of Queen Caroline and Lord Brougham's conduct as her counsel has generated a vast literature. For a sampling, see Monroe H. Freeman, *Lord Brougham and Zeal*, 34 Hofstra L. Rev. 1319 (2006); Fred C. Zacharias & Bruce A. Green, *"Anything Rather Than a Deliberate and Well Considered Opinion"—Henry Lord Brougham, Written by Himself*, 19 Geo. J. Legal Ethics 1221 (2006).

The leading formulation of the competing vision of the lawyer's duty—the attorney as public servant—is that of Roscoe Pound, a noted legal scholar and teacher (and dean of the Harvard Law School from 1916 to 1936). In 1953, Pound wrote the following description of the term "profession"; although his definition applied to professions generally, he clearly had attorneys in mind:

> The term refers to a group . . . pursuing a learned art as a common calling in the spirit of public service—no less a public service because it may incidentally be a means of livelihood.

R. Pound, *The Lawyer from Antiquity to Modern Times* 5 (1953).

Questions and Comments

1. What contrasts can you discern between Pound's vision of the lawyer's role and Brougham's? Consider:

   a. Pound emphasizes the lawyer's role in a group; Brougham, the lawyer as a solitary champion of her client's rights.
   b. Brougham focuses exclusively on the client; clients are not even mentioned in Pound's formulation.
   c. Pound stresses the lawyer's duty to the public; Brougham, the lawyer's duty to ignore the public when doing so is necessary to serve the interests of her client.
   d. Pound draws on metaphors from monasticism and religion ("common calling," "spirit"); Brougham draws on metaphors from the hunt.

2. Pound's description of the lawyer as public servant resonated with changes in American society during the 1960s and 1970s, and achieved formal recognition at the highest levels of the profession in 1986 when a blue-ribbon commission of the American Bar Association published a manifesto on the future of the legal profession which directly drew on Pound and his vision. *See* ABA Commission on Professionalism, "In the Spirit of Public Service:" A Blueprint for the Rekindling of Lawyer Professionalism (1986).

3. While the ABA commission bowed to Pound and sought to claim some of his charisma, the recommendations contained in this report did not, in fact, move far in the direction of requiring lawyers to act as public servants. The commission contented itself with pabulum such as recommendations that attorneys should be less greedy, do more pro bono work, strive to meet higher standards of conduct, and behave with "integrity, competence, fairness, independence, courage, and a devotion to the public interest."

4. Part of the subtext of the ABA report may be found in its recommendation that "[t]he Bar should employ all its organizational resources necessary in order to

assure that the legal profession remains genuinely self-regulating." In other words, the authors of the report wished to stave off government regulation of attorneys.

5. Do you think the American Bar Association, or any self-regulatory professional organization, will ever consent voluntarily to defining themselves as public servants rather than zealous advocates for their clients' interests?

6. For general treatment, see Stephen M. Bainbridge, *Corporate Lawyers as Gatekeepers, in* S.M. Bainbridge, Corporate Governance After the Financial Crisis (2012).

7. In a 2014 speech to the Association of American Law Schools, SEC Chair Mary Jo White endorsed Pound's approach to the attorney's professional role: "As Roscoe Pound, the distinguished former Dean of Harvard Law School, so eloquently captured it, private sector lawyers also have an obligation to practice law 'in the spirit of public service.' For me, that means that we are obligated to ask our clients the 'should' or 'ought to' questions and include those considerations in the advice we give. Or, as Archibald Cox put it in terms we can all understand — lawyers should be willing to say to clients, 'Yes, the law lets you do that, but don't do it. It's a rotten thing to do.' Cox's point is obviously that our role as lawyers transcends the technical — it requires us to consider the public's welfare in addition to the interests of a private client. That is how it should be." Mary Jo White, Public Service: An Obligation and Opportunity for Lawyers, Jan. 3, 2015. (You may recall that Archibald Cox, among other public positions, served as Special Prosecutor during the Watergate scandal.) Is an attorney professionally obligated to communicate unsolicited moral objections to a client's proposed course of action? May the attorney bill for such advice?

The rules governing attorneys generally favor the model of the attorney as zealous advocate, but also refer at points to the model of the attorney as public servant.

The American Bar Association's Model Rules of Professional Conduct (adopted in large measure in all states other than California), state that "[a] lawyer, as a member of the legal profession, is a representative of clients, an officer of the legal system and a public citizen having special responsibility for the quality of justice." ABA Model Rules, Preamble [1]. Here we find references both to Brougham (the lawyer is a "representative of clients") and also to Pound (the lawyer is "an officer of the legal system" and a "public citizen").

The Model Rules go on to identify different roles an attorney plays, and to tie those to varying degrees of zeal in the representation of a client:

> As advisor, a lawyer provides a client with an informed understanding of the client's legal rights and obligations and explains their practical implications. As advocate, a lawyer zealously asserts the client's position under the rules of the adversary system. As negotiator, a lawyer seeks a result advantageous to the client but consistent with requirements of honest dealings with others. As an evaluator, a lawyer acts by examining a client's legal affairs and reporting about them to the client or to others.

ABA Model Rules, Preamble [2]. Which of these roles resonates with Brougham, and which move, at least to some extent, in the direction of Pound?

These general statements don't offer much help in dealing with real cases. How far can an attorney actually go in representing a client when doing so is arguably at odds with the interests of a regulator? The rules provide some guidance here. The lawyer may not lie to the regulator about a material fact. Model Rule 4.1(a). A lawyer may not knowingly fail to disclose material information to a government official if the information is not otherwise protected from disclosure by the ethical duty of confidentiality and if disclosing the matter is necessary to avoid assisting the client in a criminal or fraudulent act. Model Rule 4.1(b). Lawyers may generally not impede investigations by government agencies. Thus, in general, an attorney may not ask a person other than a client to refrain from voluntarily giving relevant information to a government agency conducting a compliance investigation.

What limits, if any, apply to the advice an attorney can give to a client? Model Rule 2.1 requires that the attorney exercise "independent professional judgment" and render "candid advice." Presumably, this means that the attorney should not be a "yes man" or simply tell the client what the client wants to hear. Can the lawyer attempt to dissuade the client from a course of conduct? Certainly, if the client intends to do something illegal. What if the client's intended course of action is not technically illegal, but nevertheless, in the attorney's opinion, creates unacceptable business risks or violates moral principles? The rule permits an attorney, when counseling a client, to refer to "other considerations such as moral, economic, social and political factors, that may be relevant to the client's situation."

Difficult questions arise when the attorney's advice can be used by the client as a means for avoiding getting caught rather than for complying with the client's legal obligations. In tax cases, for example, attorneys are often asked about the chances that the government will launch an audit—a legitimate question, in many cases, but also one that could assist the client in deciding whether to undertake an illegal course of action. Or suppose in a criminal case the attorney truthfully tells the client that, under the law, if the client planned to kill the victim, she will probably be convicted of first-degree murder, but if the client flew into an unplanned rage, she could well be acquitted or convicted on a lesser charge. Is this providing independent legal advice, or subtly counseling the client about how to testify?

Legislatures or administrative agencies may, in theory, impose obligations on attorneys that go beyond those contained in the bar's disciplinary rules, or even that contradict those rules. In general other authorities have deferred to the disciplinary rules and refrained from imposing extensive additional obligations on attorneys. But since the disciplinary rules are often themselves ambiguous, they may not protect attorneys who are caught up in the problem of vigorously representing their clients while also complying with broader obligations. The following cases illustrate the sorts of problems attorneys can experience in attempting to balance these responsibilities.

b. The Kaye Scholer Affair

Nineteen months after Judge Sporkin issued his 1990 opinion in the *Lincoln Savings & Loan* case excerpted above, officials at the Office of Thrift Supervision (OTS), then the regulator of savings and loan institutions, demonstrated that they had heard his complaints about professional service providers. The OTS and Department of Justice sued a leading corporate law firm, Kaye, Scholer, Fierman, Hays & Handler, and three Kaye Scholer partners who had worked on Lincoln Savings & Loan matters. The case was brought in an OTS administrative tribunal. The agency demanded $275 million in penalties and froze the defendants' assets pending resolution of the charges.

The OTS's action against Kaye Scholer raised fundamental questions regarding the role of attorneys as gatekeepers. The issue was whether Kaye Scholer's representation of Lincoln Savings & Loan was proper, or whether the firm had crossed over the line into illegality. In this regard consider the following description of the substantive charges against the law firm written by OTS's then-general counsel — keeping in mind that as one of the officials responsible for the agency's case, the author had an incentive to present the charges in the most persuasive fashion.

Harris Weinstein, Attorney Liability in the Savings and Loan Crisis

1993 U. Ill. L. Rev. 53

[T]he Notice of Charges against Kaye Scholer . . . contained ten claims. Eight were substantive, while two were essentially wrap up charges that synthesized the case in broader terms.

Five of the charges arose from Kaye Scholer's conduct in representing Lincoln during the bank examination process. Here I ought to describe what a bank examination is, because it has rules that are foreign to anyone unfamiliar with bank regulation. As part of the price of federal deposit insurance, a federally insured depository institution — a bank, a savings and loan, a credit union — submits to a regulatory regime. Statutes and regulations specifically and unequivocally require that the insured institution make available to its federal regulator every book, record, and individual. Bank examiners, often on an annual basis, come into the institution, review the books and records, and interview the personnel. They then try to make some hardheaded judgments about the quality of the investments on the books, what the institution's real financial position is, and whether the institution is well and honestly run.

In implementing its authority, the OTS has adopted a regulation that closely resembles in concept and is modeled in language upon Rule 10b-5 of the federal securities laws. That regulation, which applies to the examination process and every other process before the agency other than a formal investigation, requires that anyone making representations to the agency not make any false statements and, more importantly, not make any material omissions. This means that in making statements to the agency, one may not omit any factual matters the omission of which makes the statement misleading in context. Thus, one is forbidden to lie and to make material omissions, and in an examination one is required to provide the agency full access to the books, records, and people.

Kaye Scholer was retained during a bank examination of Lincoln in the middle of 1986. One of the first things Kaye Scholer did was write a letter to the regulators saying, in substance, "You may not ask Lincoln for any information. If you want any information, you must write a letter to our partner in New York City." Our position in the OTS case against Kaye Scholer was that by taking that step, by interposing itself between the Bank Board and the bank, Kaye Scholer assumed the bank's obligations for making the necessary disclosures required by the statute and by our rule.

This point is at the heart of the OTS charges against the firm. Five of the eight specific claims in the case allege that Kaye Scholer made factual representations to the Bank Board that contained either material omissions or misstatements of fact. If you go through our Notice of Charges, you will see that the Notice in these respects is constructed in a specific way. In several instances, the Notice first quotes statements from internal memoranda prepared by Kaye Scholer lawyers who had investigated Lincoln's operations and next quotes a statement made to the Bank Board by Kaye Scholer on behalf of Lincoln. The notice then alleges that Kaye Scholer had material information at odds with the statements that it made to the Bank Board and failed to disclose that material information when it made those statements to the Bank Board. As a result, the notice alleged, the statements made were misleading in context.

For example, the OTS alleged that Kaye Scholer systematically reviewed Lincoln's major loan files over an extended period of months and found a long laundry list of problems in Lincoln's credit risk assessment and loan underwriting. Internal Kaye Scholer files detailed loan by loan what Lincoln was required to do but had not done. Despite this investigation conducted by the firm, however, you will see quoted in the Notice of Charges a series of general statements made by Kaye Scholer to the Bank Board on behalf of Lincoln asserting that, for example, Lincoln "has always undertaken very careful and thorough procedures to analyze the collateral and the borrower." The OTS position was that Kaye Scholer could not make those broad general statements about Lincoln's business practices without at the same time revealing the specific information the law firm had collected from Lincoln's files that impeached those representations.

As I said, allegations of this sort accounted for five of the eight detailed charges in the case. A sixth charge was similar in concept. Kaye Scholer was asked to provide information on the reasons that Lincoln's auditor, Arthur Andersen and Co., had resigned. Kaye Scholer sent to the Bank Board, without comment, Lincoln's securities Form 8-K, which purported to give the reasons for the auditor's resignation. That form stated, among other things, that the auditors' resignation "was not the result of any concern by AA [Arthur Andersen] with [ACC/Lincoln's] operations . . . or asset/liability management." The OTS alleged that Kaye Scholer did not disclose, however, that one of its partners had interviewed an Arthur Andersen reviewing partner and had been told that Arthur Andersen had substantial concerns about Lincoln's viability. Those substantial concerns were that Lincoln had a so-called negative spread since its cost of funds and overhead exceeded its income from investments. As a result, Lincoln had to rely on a series of sales of appreciated assets to make up that negative spread.

Not only did a memorandum of that interview exist in Kaye Scholer's files, but about four days before sending the Bank Board the Form 8-K without any comment, that same Kaye Scholer memorandum had been sent to Charles Keating with a letter (also quoted in the Notice of Charges) that said, "[the memorandum] gives some insight into what may have motivated Andersen's decision." The same Kaye Scholer partner who sent that letter to Charles Keating sent the Form 8-K to the Bank Board. OTS charged that the failure to tell us about the interview with the Arthur Andersen partner rendered the law firm's transmission of the Form 8-K to the Bank Board misleading.

Another charge related to Kaye Scholer's retention in 1985 to provide Lincoln with a legal opinion that subsequently was given to the Bank Board and on which Lincoln relied to make many millions of dollars of so-called "direct investments." These . . . were direct investments by a savings and loan in the equity of a real estate project and thus much riskier than a mortgage loan. In 1985, the Home Loan Bank Board adopted a regulation curtailing the amount of those investments that could be made in the future. The regulation, however, contained a grandfather provision — investments that had been definitively committed as of December 10, 1984, could be made after that date.

Kaye Scholer was engaged to opine on whether certain investments had been committed definitively before that key date of December 10, 1984. One of the issues was whether the board of directors of Lincoln had finally approved those investments before December 10, 1984. Kaye Scholer relied on a series of documents that purported to demonstrate the unanimous consent of the board of directors of Lincoln and that bore dates before December 10, 1984. The Notice alleged that Kaye Scholer had learned those documents had been prepared in 1985 and were backdated. The OTS position was that Kaye Scholer properly was charged with malpractice for rendering an opinion based on factual assumptions that it knew were incorrect.

The eighth detailed charge against Kaye Scholer involved a mortgage loan that one of its partners had secured from Lincoln. She and her husband had purchased a multi-family building in Manhattan, in which they occupied an apartment. Kaye Scholer represented the partner as borrower at the same time the law firm was doing other work for Lincoln. OTS thought it was ambiguous whether the firm also was representing Lincoln on the specific loan transaction. The loan on its face failed to comply with Bank Board underwriting regulations. For example, OTS alleged that the appraisal showed on its face that the appraiser, who had appraised the property at more than the purchase price, never had visited the property. In addition to not calling that fact to the attention of Lincoln, the Notice alleged that Kaye Scholer failed to perfect Lincoln's security interest in securities that the borrower had posted as additional collateral. The Notice also alleged that the firm's and the partner's participation in that transaction constituted aiding and abetting the regulatory violation of improper underwriting by Lincoln.

Those were the substantive charges. The other two charges were general charges that sought to bring all of these together. In one OTS alleged, for example, that Kaye Scholer violated its fiduciary duty as lawyer to its client, Lincoln. OTS charged that Kaye Scholer had a professional obligation when it learned that officers and directors of Lincoln were engaged in certain unlawful conduct to bring that to the attention of Lincoln's board of directors. Kaye Scholer had not done that. . . .

Questions and Comments

1. Prior to the failure of his institution, Charles Keating was an outspoken critic of his institution's regulators. Was this a wise strategy for the leader of a bank?

2. Keating was convicted of crimes associated with the Lincoln Savings fiasco and served four years in federal prison. He was released in 1990 and died in 2014 at the age of 90.

3. OTS faulted Kaye Scholer for insisting that any communications with its client regarding the ongoing examination had to go through the law firm rather than directly to the client. Can you see why this demand would have made the agency apoplectic? Bank examiners routinely speak with officers at banks they are examining without having to go through counsel. If bank examiners had to route all requests for information through counsel — especially outside counsel like Kaye Scholer — the examination process would be hamstrung. Reading between the lines, it seems evident that the OTS decided that it could not afford to let Kaye Scholer's approach to bank examinations become a precedent that other banks

might want to follow — and decided to make an example of Kaye Scholar in order to prevent that from happening.

4. On the other hand, was there anything wrong, in itself, with Kaye Scholar inserting itself between the government and its client? It is standard practice for lawyers representing clients in litigation to insist that the adversary's counsel communicate only through them. In fact attorneys are prohibited from communicating directly with adverse parties who are represented by counsel unless they first obtain counsel's consent. Kaye Scholer might have taken the position that to the extent the bank examination was conducted under the supervision of counsel, it was the OTS attorneys, not Kaye Scholer, who would have violated ethical rules by communicating with the bank directly. That would be a stretch, but even Weinstein doesn't claim that Kaye Scholer's demand that communications flow through it was itself a violation of any rules.

5. The OTS argued that by interposing itself between the bank and its regulator, Kaye Scholer assumed the responsibility for fair and honest reporting that otherwise would have been the bank's burden alone. The agency argued that if it had no other source of information, then the attorney would have to take responsibility for the accuracy of what was reported. Does this make sense? Does an attorney representing a client in litigation warrant the accuracy of information obtained from the client and passed on to the adversary? Did the agency have other sources of information — for example, through the power to subpoena documents?

6. The notice of charges alleges that Kaye Scholer had gone through Lincoln Savings & Loan's loan files and found problems, but then had reported to the OTS that its client "has always undertaken very careful and thorough procedures to analyze the collateral and the borrower." Was this a deliberate falsehood? No bank "always" undertakes very careful and thorough procedures to analyze the collateral and the borrower; mistakes get made. Taken in context, could Kaye Scholer's representation have meant simply that the client used careful procedures to review the security of its loan portfolio?

7. The notice of charges accuses Kaye Scholer of engaging in misconduct when, in response to a query as to why Arthur Andersen had resigned as Lincoln Savings' auditor, the firm supplied the bank's Form 8-K report explaining the departure (the report is quoted in the notes and comments following Sporkin's opinion). OTS claimed this was deceptive because one Arthur Andersen auditor had remarked to a Kaye Scholer attorney that Andersen had concerns about Lincoln Savings' viability. Who was the law firm supposed to believe — a disgruntled partner or the firm's official statement of its reasons for terminating the engagement?

8. The notice charged that Kaye Scholer represented one of its own partners who had taken out a mortgage loan from Lincoln Savings & Loan in a situation where the OTS thought it was "ambiguous" whether the firm also was representing Lincoln in the same transaction. What do you think of this claim as a basis for the charges against Kaye Scholer?

9. Taken as a whole, are the charges as described by Weinstein sufficient to make out a claim of serious wrongdoing against the law firm, or do they merely show a form of aggressive advocacy that might in other settings be viewed as commendable?

10. How likely was Kaye Scholer to get a fair hearing in the forum where the OTS filed its charges? The charges were not brought in a court of law but rather in the OTS's own administrative tribunal. Was an OTS hearing officer likely to rule against the agency's general counsel on a case with this much riding on it?

11. In another part of the excerpted text, Weinstein notes that many firms had provided legal services to Lincoln Savings & Loan and had not received the treatment given to Kaye Scholer. Weinstein explains the difference as follows: "Why did some of those law firms become defendants while others did not? Future scholars may well conclude that the distinction between those who were sued and those who were not sued was the latter's attention to the established ethical principles of our profession." Did Kaye Scholer fail to pay attention to the established ethical principles of the profession?

The second, even more controversial part of the OTS's proceeding was its imposition of a freeze on Kaye Scholer's assets. The strategy employed here — freezing a defendant's assets — had previously been reserved for people accused of serious criminality who were viewed as flight risks. An asset freeze had never been employed against a defendant such as Kaye Scholer, which was reputable and which, due to the nature of its business, posed no flight risk. The government explained, without much evidence to back it up, that the freeze was necessary to prevent Kaye Scholer from hiding assets. Critics argued that the assertion was dubious because Kaye Scholer's assets effectively included the personal assets of its partners that could not be easily concealed.

Even if the OTS was justified in seeking to freeze the law firm's assets, the extent of the freeze it imposed — without obtaining prior court approval — was widely viewed as extraordinary:

- Kaye Scholer was prohibited from making capital expenditures in excess of $50,000;
- The three individually named partners and the firm as a whole were prohibited from transferring assets in excess of $5,000 without written notice to the OTS;
- Other partners were prohibited from transferring assets outside the United States or from leaving the firm without posting security;
- One quarter of the earnings of all partners were placed in escrow pending disposition of the OTS's charges;
- Individually named partners had even more of their earnings sequestered: 50 percent for Peter Fishbein and 33 percent for Karen Katzman.

Consider how devastating this freeze must have been to Kaye Scholer and its partners. One-fourth of every partner's income disappeared into an escrow overnight. That meant 25 percent less money to pay the mortgage, the rent, the kids' college tuitions, medical bills, or other expenses. Meanwhile, the spectacular publicity associated with the freeze imposed an immediate reputational loss. Clients began to wonder about whether they should continue to use the firm for their legal business, both because of the bad publicity and also because of questions about the continued viability of the firm if the OTS charges were not resolved. The firm's access to credit came into question for the same reason: It is one thing to lend money to a prosperous, elite law firm; it is another to lend to a firm that is scratching to survive. Kaye Scholer held out for six days. Then it capitulated and agreed to pay a $41 million fine in exchange for the government dropping the case and, with it, the asset freeze.

Questions and Comments

1. Even though it resulted in no judgments or findings of liability, the Kaye Scholer case was important, in part because of its implications for the role of attorneys representing clients in compliance matters. The case shocked many observers because of what it demonstrated about the respective powers of the government and private counsel. Kaye Scholer was a powerful law firm. It had rich and successful partners and a thriving practice representing premier clients. The OTS was a small government agency, overworked and understaffed, with little experience dealing with litigators in firms like Kaye Scholer. Most observers would have laid odds against the government. But when the confrontation came, it was no contest: The OTS flattened the firm's resistance in less time than it took Germany's Panzer divisions to level Poland. The case symbolized, to many, a sea-change in the respective powers of the government and private attorneys in compliance matters.

2. There are arguments for both sides of this case.

Consider the matter from the standpoint of the OTS. The agency, long a sleepy institution charged with overseeing conservatively managed thrift institutions, was unexpectedly faced with an enormous crisis that overwhelmed its resources and placed it in the crosshairs of public criticism. Lincoln Savings & Loan was emblematic of all that had gone wrong in the industry — irresponsible managers, inappropriate investments, deceptive financial reporting, accounting gimmicks, and the aggressive use of political influence. The last thing the OTS needed on top of all this was having to cope with a law firm that treated what should have been a routine bank examination as the equivalent of scorched earth litigation. From the agency's point of view, Kaye Scholer was little more than a co-conspirator with Charles Keating in a campaign to thwart and frustrate its attempts to safeguard the public interest. The OTS wanted to punish Kaye Scholer, not only for its perceived misconduct, but also to make an example of the firm so that others would not get the same idea.

On the other hand it is also easy to see the matter from Kaye Scholer's perspective. The firm acted with no intent to violate any law. Their representation of Lincoln Savings was vigorous, but vigorous representation is what clients in Lincoln Savings' position want and expect. At the time Kaye Scholer represented the bank, relations with its regulator had become adversarial; it was hardly a surprise, accordingly, that Kaye Scholer would treat the engagement along the model of contested litigation rather than friendly transaction.

Which of these points of view is more persuasive to you?

3. For contrasting views on the Kaye Scholer case, compare Geoffrey C. Hazard, Jr., *The Meaning of the Kaye Scholer Case*, 26 Akron L. Rev. 395 (1992-1993) with William Simon, *The Kaye Scholer Affair: The Lawyer's Duty of Candor and the Bar's Temptations of Evasion and Apology*, 23 Law & Soc. Inquiry 243 (1998). For other commentary, see, e.g., Howell Jackson, *Reflections on Kaye, Scholer: Enlisting Lawyers to Improve the Regulation of the Financial System*, 66 S. Cal. L. Rev. 1019 (1993); Jonathan R. Macey & Geoffrey P. Miller, *Kaye Scholer, FIRREA, and the Desirability of Early Closure: A View of the Kaye, Scholer Case from the Perspective of Bank Regulatory Policy*, 66 S. Cal. L. Rev. 1115 (1993); David B. Wilkins, *Making Context Count: Regulating Lawyers After Kaye, Scholer*, 66 S. Cal. L. Rev. 1145 (1993). *See also* James Fanto, *Advising Compliance in Financial Firms: A New Mission for the Legal Academy*, 8 Brook. J. Corp., Fin. & Com. L. 1 (2013).

4. Given the Kaye Scholer affair, how should attorneys representing clients facing regulatory examinations conceive of their professional roles? To what extent

should the concept of attorney as zealous advocate give way to one in which lawyers act as champions of the broader public interest?

c. Lauren Stevens

The Kaye Scholer case had devastating consequences for the law firm, but at least the potential liability there was civil in nature. The attorneys at Kaye Scholer stood to lose clients and a lot of money, but they were not going to prison. Sometimes, however, an attorney's vigorous representation of a client in a compliance matter can generate a risk of criminal penalties. The following materials describe the experience of Lauren Stevens, an in-house attorney at a pharmaceutical company. As you review these materials, consider the implications for the attorney's role as zealous advocate of the client's interests.

United States v. Stevens*

Criminal Action: RWT-10-694, D. Md. 2010

[Lauren Stevens was Vice President and Associate General Counsel of GlaxoSmithK line ("GSK"), a manufacturer of prescription drugs. The FDA launched an investigation into whether GSK had illegally promoted its depression medication Wellbutrin SR™ for weight loss, an unapproved use (see Chapter 12). The FDA asked GSK to turn over copies of materials presented at GSK programs related to Wellbutrin. Stevens led GSK's response to the FDA's inquiry, in consultation with GSK's outside counsel King & Spaulding. The government indicted Stevens and took the case to a jury trial. At the conclusion of the government's case-in-chief, the key facts appeared to be as follows:

- Stevens contacted 550 of 2,700 people who had spoken at GSK events and received slide decks from 40 of them. Twenty-eight of those decks contained discussions of unapproved uses for Wellbutrin. After consulting King & Spaulding, Stevens turned over three of these decks to the FDA.
- Stevens had her team prepare a spreadsheet about a GSK speakers program including information requested by the FDA on dates, locations, speakers, and the number of attendees. After consulting King & Spaulding, she deleted from the draft a column of information, which the FDA had not requested, which contained information about the entertainment provided at these events.
- Stevens informed the FDA that GSK had "national" and "local" advisory boards but failed to add that the company also had "special issue" advisory boards.
- In consultation with King & Spaulding, Stevens informed the FDA that "[a]ttendees were not paid, reimbursed, or otherwise compensated to attend these events." It turned out that speakers were allowed to participate in entertainment activities provided at the events and also were entitled to receive a "medically relevant" gift.
- In consultation with King & Spaulding, Stevens represented that "GSK has not developed, devised, established, or maintained any program or activity to promote, either directly or indirectly, the use of Wellbutrin SR to achieve

*The following is the author's synopsis of the case.

weight loss or treat obesity." She disclosed, however, that inappropriate off-label discussions had occurred at GSK events from time to time; that at several training sessions GSK had inadvertently provided speaker trainees with a slide deck discussing off-label uses; and that one speaker's standard presentation could be interpreted as indicating that weight loss was an approved use.

The indictment charged that Stevens had violated two statutes:

- 18 U.S.C. §1512(c)(2), providing for up to 20 years in prison for anyone who "corruptly . . . obstructs, influences, or impedes any official proceeding, or attempts to do so. . . . "
- 18 U.S.C. §1519, providing for up to 20 years in prison for anyone who "knowingly alters, destroys, mutilates, conceals, covers up, falsifies, or makes a false entry in any record, document, or tangible object with the intent to impede, obstruct, or influence the investigation or proper administration of any matter within the jurisdiction of any department or agency of the United States. . . . "

Stevens claimed that she had not violated either statute. She argued that she never represented to the FDA that the three slide decks she provided were all the decks in her possession, and she claimed that the FDA was aware that other decks existed. She asserted that there was nothing wrongful about deleting from the draft spreadsheet information about entertainment that the FDA had not requested; that her failure to disclose the existence of special issue advisory boards was an innocent oversight and in any event was not material to the FDA's investigation; that her statement that attendees were not compensated for attendance was true, since participation in entertainment or the receipt of a medically relevant gift were not compensation; and that her statement that GSK had not established any program or activity to promote Wellbutrin as an obesity treatment was reasonable based on facts known to her.

Stevens also advanced three more general defenses. She argued that she had not acted with wrongful intent; that her actions were undertaken in reliance on the advice of counsel; and that as to certain counts of the indictment, her actions were protected by 18 U.S.C. §1515(c), which provides that "[t]his chapter does not prohibit or punish the providing of lawful, bona fide, legal representation services in connection with or anticipation of an official proceeding."]

Questions and Comments

1. Why was the FDA so angry at this defendant?

2. A fair reading of the evidence suggests that the defendant was not eager to give the government what it wanted, and that she did not provide the government with all the information in her possession relevant to off-label marketing of Wellbutrin. Is this an obstruction of justice, or simply zealous representation?

3. Stevens argued that she should be acquitted because all her actions were undertaken in reliance on advice from King & Spaulding. As further discussed below, the "reliance on counsel" defense allows criminal defendants to show that they didn't have the requisite guilty mental state due to the fact that they were relying on the advice of an attorney.

4. In your opinion, do the facts summarized above indicate that Stevens provided only "lawful, bona fide, legal representation services" to GSK?

5. Based on the facts recited above, could a reasonable jury conclude that the government met its burden of showing beyond a reasonable doubt that the defendant was guilty of the offenses charged?

At the conclusion of the government's case-in-chief at trial, the defense moved to dismiss the indictment. An excerpt from the court's oral ruling on the motion follows:

Under Rule 29 [of the Federal Rules of Criminal Procedure, governing motions for judgment of acquittal], the standard is whether any rational trier of fact could find the defendant guilty beyond a reasonable doubt, viewing the evidence in the light most favorable to the government, which is the standard I must and will apply.

During the government's case, which is now concluded, the Court heard extensive testimony of both FDA and GSK officials and, to put it mildly, a large volume of documentary evidence. Very significant portions of the documents placed before the Court were what would otherwise be privileged attorney-client documents. They were obtained by the United States as a result, as I've learned, of an order of a magistrate judge in the District of Massachusetts who ordered them produced under what's known as the Crime Fraud Exception.

There are, of course, profound implications for the free flow of communications between a lawyer and client when the privilege is abrogated, as it was in this case. The Crime Fraud Exception is designed to overcome the privilege only when the evidence establishes that the client intended to perpetrate a crime or fraud and the communications at issue between the attorney and the client were made in furtherance of such crime or fraud. . . .

With the 20/20 vision of hindsight, and that's always the place to be in terms of wisdom, the Massachusetts Order was an unfortunate one, because I now have benefitted from a trial in which these documents that were ordered produced were paraded in front of me, and the prosecutors were permitted to forage through confidential files to support an argument for criminality of the conduct of the defendant.

What those records demonstrate to the Court is, first of all, that access should not have been granted to them in the first place. But that's not for me to decide. That's already been decided by a magistrate judge in Massachusetts. But they also show that this was a [lawyer] that was not engaged to assist a client to perpetrate a crime or fraud. Instead, the privileged documents in this case show a studied, thoughtful analysis of an extremely broad request from the Food and Drug Administration and an enormous effort to assemble information and respond on behalf of the client.

The responses that were given by the defendant in this case may not have been perfect; they may not have satisfied the FDA. They were, however, sent to the FDA in the course of her bona fide legal representation of a client and in good faith reliance of both external and internal lawyers for GlaxoSmithKline.

Now, what are the consequences of that? As to Counts One and Two, the Safe Harbor Provision of Section 1515(c) is an absolute bar. GlaxoSmithKline did not come to Ms. Stevens and say, assist us in committing a crime or fraud. It came to her for assistance in responding to a letter from the FDA. I conclude on the basis of this record that no reasonable juror could conclude otherwise beyond a reasonable doubt. . . .

As to all counts relating to the question of advice of counsel, the evidence in this case can only support one conclusion, and that is that the defendant sought and obtained the advice and counsel of numerous lawyers. She made full disclosure to them. Every decision that she made and every letter she wrote was done by a consensus. Now, even if some of these statements were not literally true, it is clear that they were made in good faith which would negate the requisite element required for all six of the crimes charged in this case.

The government contends that some statements were false. For example, they point to the statement made by Ms. Stevens in a letter to the FDA in which she states that GlaxoSmithKline is not engaged in the promotion of Wellbutrin SR for weight loss. They seek to take that statement, however, in isolation, and the Court simply cannot do that and cannot permit a jury to do that. It is clear that while that statement was made, the same or other communications clearly disclosed to the FDA that . . . approximately 75 speaker presentations had off-label topics; that Dr. Wolkowitz had used the presentation that contained phrases and information about the effect of the drug on body weight that some may consider as outside the product's approved indication. She also disclosed that the company became aware of certain activities that were inconsistent with the company's policies; took its responsibilities seriously and instituted appropriate and necessary corrective actions to address these activities. . . . So, this is not a statement that can be taken as being false when you consider it in the context in which it was given.

I conclude on the basis of the record before me that only with a jaundiced eye and with an inference of guilt that's inconsistent with the presumption of innocence could a reasonable jury ever convict this defendant. . . . In my seven and a half years as a jurist I have never granted [a Rule 29 motion]. There is, however, always a first. . . . I believe that it would be a miscarriage of justice to permit this case to go to the jury.

Moreover, there are serious implications for the practice of law generated by this prosecution. Lawyers can never assist a client in the commission of a crime or a fraud, and that's well established. . . . However, a lawyer should never fear prosecution because of advice that he or she has given to a client who consults him or her, and a client should never fear that its confidences will be divulged unless its purpose in consulting the lawyer was for the purpose of committing a crime or a fraud.

There is an enormous potential for abuse in allowing prosecution of an attorney for the giving of legal advice. I conclude that the defendant in this case should never have been prosecuted and she should be permitted to resume her career. . . .

Questions and Comments

1. This case was closely watched by lawyers who worked in the compliance area, many of whom must have thought "there but for the grace of God go I." The judgment of acquittal was widely hailed in those circles as a vindication of the rights of attorneys to provide a vigorous defense for their clients.

2. The result was a victory for Stevens. But the victory came at a price. She had to endure months of anxiety as the government sought and obtained attorney-client information pertinent to the case. She went through the nightmare of being

indicted and then had to prepare for and participate in a criminal trial. Her position at GSK may have been in jeopardy. She had to turn her passport over to the authorities. For seven months, between the time of the indictment in November 2010 and the judge's order dismissing the case in May 2011, she and her family had to endure the fear of 20 years in prison, possible fines, and loss of her law license. Would you want her job if you had to face this kind of risk?

3. Although the government lost this case, what would stop the FDA from doing the same thing the next time an attorney resisted its requests for information from the attorney's client?

4. Can you see how the FDA's position was implicitly premised on the model of the attorney-gatekeeper as public servant, whereas the defendant (and to some extent the trial judge) viewed the matter from the perspective of the attorney as zealous advocate?

5. New York Judiciary Law §487 provides that "[a]n attorney or counselor who [is] guilty of any deceit or collusion, or consents to any deceit or collusion, with intent to deceive the court or any party . . . [is] guilty of a misdemeanor, and in addition to the punishment prescribed therefor by the penal law, he forfeits to the party injured treble damages, to be recovered in a civil action." Suppose an attorney defending a client in a compliance action tells the counsel for the government that "my client intends to fight this case all the way to the Supreme Court!" — knowing that her client, in fact, is seriously considering whether to accept a consent judgment that the government has offered, if it cannot get any better deal. Could the attorney be prosecuted or required to pay treble damages?

d. Cahill Gordon

Williams v. BASF Catalysts LLC

765 F.3d 306 (3d Cir. 2014)

. . . Cahill Gordon & Reindel LLP represented BASF and its predecessors in asbestos litigation from 1983 to 2010. During that time, Howard G. Sloane, Scott A. Martin, and Ira J. Dembrow worked for BASF as lawyers at Cahill. We refer to these Cahill defendants as "Cahill."

From 1967 to 1983, Engelhard operated a talc mine in Johnson, Vermont. . . . Engelhard talc products "contained chrysotile asbestos fibers, as well as other asbestos forms including tremolite and serpentine asbestos." During the 1970s and 1980s, multiple laboratory tests indicated that Engelhard talc, including Emtal brand talc and talc from the Johnson Mine, contained asbestos. Engelhard, and later BASF, "had knowledge" of these tests and their results, and, in fact, maintained "[t]he tests and assay results" in their records.

Faced with unfavorable test results, Engelhard ignored them. According to the complaint, Engelhard "represented to its customers, industry trade groups and the Federal Government that the Emtal talc was asbestos free and even marketed the product as a viable asbestos substitute, thereby causing wide spread [sic] and unknowing exposure to asbestos to United States citizens, including workers and workers' spouses and children, nationwide."

In 1979, David Westfall sued Eastern Magnesia Talc Company, an Engelhard subsidiary, for exposing his deceased relative to asbestos. Cahill Gordon defended Eastern Magnesia in the suit. The lawsuit turned-up "test and assay results" confirming the presence of asbestos in Engelhard's talc.

Engelhard's personnel and records demonstrated that the talc had been contaminated. Glenn Hemstock, then an Engelhard scientist and executive, gave two days of deposition testimony in the *Westfall* case. Hemstock testified that Emtal talc contained asbestos fibers. He "admitted that various tests performed throughout the 1970s and 1980s, both by [Engelhard] employees and by third parties, indicated the presence of asbestos fibers in Emtal talc that was tested or assayed." Emil J. Triglia, an Engelhard employee, also testified that Emtal talc contained asbestos fibers. Peter Gale, an Engelhard researcher, testified that he had conducted analytical testing on talc ore samples obtained from the Johnson mine. He recorded his results in lab notebooks stored in Engelhard's library.

After these depositions, BASF, through Cahill, settled the *Westfall* case. The settlement included a confidentiality clause that prohibited the *Westfall* parties from discussing the case or sharing the evidence. Much of the *Westfall* evidence has yet to be seen again.

Engelhard anticipated that the *Westfall* action would be the first of many asbestos lawsuits. In March 1984, Hemstock circulated a memorandum entitled "DOCUMENT RETRIEVAL — DISCONTINUED OPERATIONS." The memorandum directed Engelhard employees to collect for discard documents relating to Emtal talc. It stated that "[i]t is the policy of Engelhard Corporation to avoid the undue accumulation of documents that are no longer likely to be needed in our business operations." The memorandum instructed employees to collect materials related to Engelhard Minerals Ltd. and Emtal, among other "discontinued operations." The employees complied. "All documentary evidence relating to Engelhard's asbestos-containing talc[ ] was thereafter gathered up, collected by the BASF Perpetrators or their agents, and subsequently was either destroyed or secreted away. . . . "

Next, the complaint alleges, Engelhard manufactured favorable evidence with Cahill's help. Together, they assembled "template and stock pleading, discovery and motions documents for use by local counsel in asbestos injury claim lawsuits" that contained false or misleading information about Emtal talc products. Engelhard and Cahill procured "false unsworn and sworn representations, including false affidavits, false and incorrect expert reports and discovery response verifications by [Engelhard] employees, [Engelhard] officers, and/or [Engelhard] consultants and experts."

Cahill and Engelhard, and later, BASF, used the absence of inculpating evidence and the existence of false exonerating evidence to frustrate asbestos injury suits. The complaint charges that, when lawsuits materialized, BASF and Cahill misled the claimants about the facts. "[W]henever an asbestos injury claim or lawsuit was filed or came to BASF's attention," BASF represented "systematically and uniformly . . . that Emtal talc ore and products did not contain asbestos and/or there was not any evidence that it did." Indeed, BASF's lawyers threatened claimants and their lawyers "with the possibility of sanctions or penalties if asbestos claims or suits were not discontinued by questioning counsels' good faith basis to continue the claims" in light of BASF's representations that its talc products did not contain asbestos. Further, because BASF and its lawyers made these misstatements "in correspondence, responses to discovery and/or pleadings or motion papers," they misled courts as well as adversaries.

The scheme worked against the named plaintiffs. Williams's husband, Charles, for example, developed asbestosis and lung cancer after a career at Goodyear Tire & Rubber. The Williams sued Engelhard in Ohio state court. Defendants told them that Engelhard's talc did not contain asbestos. In response, they voluntarily dismissed the claims against Engelhard. Similarly, the other plaintiffs discontinued, dismissed, or settled their asbestos-injury lawsuits against BASF based on Engelhard and Cahill Gordon's false representations.

The scheme collapsed a few years ago, during a New Jersey Superior Court action. In that case, Paduano v. Ace Scientific Supply Co., a former research chemist for Engelhard testified that he had discovered asbestos in Engelhard's talc while working for the company many years ago. He further testified that Engelhard closed the Johnson mine because it contained asbestos and that defendant Hemstock instructed him to turn over all of his talc-related records.

The chemist's testimony triggered discovery into what documents BASF had destroyed or concealed in the litigation. Many of these documents had been secretly kept in a Cahill storage facility. The *Paduano* case settled and the incriminating documents were placed in escrow pursuant to the terms of the settlement agreement. Among the documents are tests from 1972, 1977, 1978, and 1979 that establish the presence of asbestos fibers in Engelhard talc. None had ever been produced or disclosed in earlier litigation.

In the aftermath of the *Paduano* case, Williams and the other named plaintiffs commenced this action. . . . BASF, Cahill, and the individual defendants moved to dismiss the Amended Class Action Complaint. [T]he District Court . . . dismissed the complaint in its entirety with prejudice. Williams has appealed. . . .

We next address the District Court's dismissal of Williams's fraud claim on the basis of New Jersey's litigation privilege. The privilege often immunizes lawyers and parties from recrimination based on their statements in judicial proceedings, but the privilege has never applied to shield systematic fraud directed at the integrity of the judicial process. Nor should it be. Accordingly, we reverse the District Court's dismissal of this claim. . . .

Williams asserts that BASF and Cahill Gordon falsely represented that "BASF and its predecessor companies' talc ore and talc products did not contain asbestos fibers" and "that there was not any evidence BASF and its predecessor companies['] talc ore and talc products contained asbestos." The complaint pleads many of these statements precisely, quoting from various letters and faxes sent by Cahill attorneys on behalf of BASF. It alleges that BASF and Cahill offered these representations to Williams, for example, for the purpose of "obstructing, impeding, impairing, [or] terminating" asbestos-injury litigation. And Williams alleges that, after receiving these communications, she and the other plaintiffs each altered their litigation posture — settling, dismissing, or abandoning their claims against BASF.

Taken together, Williams has alleged that BASF and Cahill obtained "an undue advantage by means of some act or omission that is unconscientious or a violation of good faith," the essence of fraud.

Nonetheless, the District Court dismissed the claim on the ground that New Jersey's litigation privilege foreclosed liability for any statements made in the course of asbestos-injury litigation. New Jersey's so-called litigation privilege functions as a form of civil immunity: it "generally protects an attorney from civil liability arising from words he has uttered in the course of judicial proceedings." The privilege reflects "the need for unfettered expression" in adversarial proceedings. Cahill and BASF urge the Court to extend the privilege to the false statements and evidence given to Williams and the other plaintiffs.

We decline. New Jersey's Supreme Court has interpreted the privilege to "protect[ ] attorneys not only from defamation actions, but also from a host of other tort-related claims." But New Jersey's Supreme Court has never recognized the litigation privilege to immunize systematic fraud, let alone fraud calculated to thwart the judicial process. . . . We believe that New Jersey's Supreme Court would not extend the privilege to this claim.

First, the complaint describes conduct that impairs New Jersey's goals for the litigation privilege. "One purpose of the privilege is to encourage open channels of communication and the presentation of evidence in judicial proceedings." Another is to afford parties "an unqualified opportunity to explore the truth of a matter without fear of recrimination." Here, the claim is that lawyers and litigants actively frustrated the search for the truth and purposefully misled their adversaries. The purposes of the privilege are never served by allowing counsel to practice deceit and deception in the course of litigation, nor by permitting counsel to make false and misleading statements in the course of judicial proceedings. Indeed, when this kind of misconduct has occurred in the past, policy considerations have weighed against extending the privilege. . . .

Second, New Jersey's Supreme Court has admonished that "[t]he absolute privilege does not extend to statements made in situations for which there are no safeguards against abuse." For defamation and the like, judicial oversight or criminal or professional sanctions often adequately deter litigation misconduct. These deterrents prove inadequate for systematic fraud. For one thing, the misconduct occurred in and out of courtrooms from Ohio to Pennsylvania to New York. No single court had the perspective or authority to mitigate the fraud or the ability to detect it. For another, Williams has alleged that BASF — the client — was responsible for "verifying the truth of [its] discovery responses" and for "[s]uborning or otherwise procuring false unsworn and sworn representations from its employees, officers[,] consultants and experts." Professional sanctions have little deterrent value against clients. Finally, this alleged fraud apparently outlasted the careers of many of the perpetrators. However appropriate professional discipline may have been (or may still be), should the allegations be proven true, that discipline would be too little and too late to do any good for the plaintiffs or the courts.

Third, the allegations of this case place the offending conduct far from the core of the privilege. Although "[t]he litigation privilege protects attorneys not only from defamation actions, but also from a host of other tort-related claims," the privilege is "[t]ypically" invoked against defamatory remarks. Indeed, the Restatement of Torts identifies this type of privilege as a defense to a defamation action. See Restatement (Second) of Torts §§586 (defense for attorney at law), 587 (defense for parties to judicial proceedings). This case is not a situation where a witness, lawyer, or agent made hurtful or defamatory remarks about another, as in *Hawkins*. Rather, the allegations here describe conduct calculated to thwart the judicial process and, in that way, are more akin to malicious prosecution, perjury, and spoliation. The judicial privilege will not excuse malicious prosecution or criminal perjury. Nor will it apply to claims of spoliation, which concerns a party's conduct and not the party's statements. We conclude that it likewise would not apply here.

Fourth, even a broad reading of the privilege fails to fit the facts of this case. "The privilege shields any communication (1) made in judicial or quasi-judicial proceedings; (2) by litigants or other participants authorized by law; (3) to achieve the objects of the litigation; and (4) that have some connection or logical relation to the action." Here, the complaint alleges, BASF and Cahill engineered the false statements and evidence in advance of litigation. Then, either directly or through local counsel, BASF and Cahill deployed their prefabricated defense against claimants as they arose. They did not merely use a permissible procedural device in bad faith, as in *Loigman.* They rigged the game from the beginning. Thus, we cannot accept, as BASF contends, that its statements were made "to achieve the object of the defense" insofar as they "were made with the aim of defeating Plaintiffs' asbestos personal injury claims and shielding BASF from liability." The New Jersey Supreme Court has observed that "[s]eeking truthful, accurate, and non-tainted testimony certainly is the objective of every litigated case." How then can calculated false and misleading statements serve the truth-seeking function of the litigation? According to the complaint, BASF and Cahill were not mischaracterizing the facts; they were creating them.

Finally, the New Jersey Supreme Court has never immunized systematic fraud designed to prevent a fair proceeding. Neither have the trial or intermediate courts of New Jersey. . . .

Williams has pled a claim for fraud. The viability of that claim turns on whether New Jersey would extend its litigation privilege to a claim of fraud directed at the integrity of the judicial process. Based on the policies underlying the privilege and the New Jersey cases applying it, we conclude that New Jersey's Supreme Court would not extend the privilege to the fraud claim alleged here. Accordingly, we reverse the District Court's dismissal of this claim. . . .

Questions and Comments

1. Taking as true the material allegations in the complaint, do you agree that the plaintiffs sufficiently pleaded claims of fraud and fraudulent concealment?

2. Even if the complaint adequately pleaded fraud, the plaintiff had to surmount the argument that the defendants' conduct was protected by New Jersey's litigation privilege. The litigation privilege generally protects attorneys and clients against liability for statements made during the course of judicial proceedings. A classic example is the tort of defamation: One is allowed to assert things in court pleadings that might otherwise be considered defamatory. What is the reason for this privilege?

3. Should the litigation privilege apply differently to outside litigation attorneys, such as the lawyers from the Cahill firm, than it does to inside counsel such as Halket and Dornbusch?

4. Suppose Cahill was misled by its client into believing that there was in fact no asbestos in the company's talc. Should it escape fraud liability? What if — as was alleged — it was aware of damaging documents indicating the presence of asbestos, but was assured by officials in the company that those documents were in error? Did Cahill have a duty to inquire further once it became aware of the fact that the company's denials might not be entirely accurate?

5. Was it wrongful for Cahill to engineer "secret" settlements with asbestos plaintiffs, which precluded the parties from disclosing evidence of the company's wrongdoing to potential plaintiffs with similar claims?

6. If Cahill defends on the ground that its client misled it, can it reveal attorney-client information in order to establish its defense? The rules seem fairly clear: Model Rule 1.6(b)(5) provides that an attorney may reveal confidences "to establish a defense to a criminal charge or civil claim against the lawyer based upon conduct in which the client was involved, or to respond to allegations in any proceeding concerning the lawyer's representation of the client." Can the attorney break the attorney-client privilege, on the same theory?

7. Suppose, hypothetically, that while representing the client the Cahill attorneys discovered that witnesses intended to make false statements under oath in response to discovery requests. What must the attorneys do in such a case? *See* Model Rule 3.3(a)(3), providing that a lawyer shall not knowingly "offer evidence that the lawyer knows to be false." Does this provide an answer?

8. In the previous scenario, would Cahill have had a duty to report the intended course of conduct to the CEO or, if the CEO will not act, to the board of directors? *See* Model Rule 1.13.

9. What if the Cahill attorneys had learned of false deposition testimony by the client after the fact—would they have any duty to correct the record? *See* Model Rule 3.3(a)(3): "If . . . the lawyer's client . . . has offered material evidence and the lawyer comes to know of its falsity, the lawyer shall take reasonable remedial measures, including, if necessary, disclosure to the tribunal."

10. Federal Rule of Civil Procedure 11 authorizes federal district courts to impose sanctions against attorneys who sign pleadings containing false statements, in cases where the attorney has made an insufficient investigation. *See* Rule 11(b)(4). Could the Cahill attorneys be sanctioned if it turns out that they signed court pleadings falsely denying that the company's talc contained asbestos? Given the existence of Rule 11, is it necessary also to impose potential fraud liability on attorneys for false statements made in the course of litigation?

11. To what extent (if any) will the fraud liability recognized in the excerpted case deter inside or outside counsel from defending clients charged with wrongful conduct? Does the opinion encourage attorneys to act as guardians of the public interest rather than as zealous advocates for clients?

2. Organization Clients

a. Who Is the Client?

Consider the following problem:

PROBLEM 9-1

You are a junior counsel at Eastern Logistics, a manufacturer of aircraft navigation systems. A whistleblower in the firm alleges that the company is conspiring with its chief competitor to fix the prices of its products. Your boss, the chief counsel, tasks you with conducting an internal investigation of the allegations. Your preliminary investigation gives you reason to suspect that the CEO may have had personal involvement in criminal conduct. You know that the Justice Department's Antitrust Division will give leniency in price fixing cases to companies that are the first to come forward and provide help to the Department in prosecuting other conspirators. You believe that this may be the best option for your company. However, when you present the idea to the general counsel she emphatically vetoes the proposal on the ground that "we have not done anything wrong." You believe that the general counsel's response might be motivated more by a concern for protecting the CEO than a wish to serve the best interests of the company: If the company comes forward to admit involvement in a criminal antitrust conspiracy, the CEO is likely to lose her job and may not receive the same exemption from prosecution that the Division is likely to give to the company.

Who is your client in this situation, and what does your duty to the client require you to do? The answer to the first question is straightforward: Your client is the organization, not the CEO or any other individual. The answer to the second question is not so clear. Since organizations are not human beings, they can act only through agents. The CEO is the chief executive officer of the organization and, ordinarily, has the right to make decisions on its behalf (subject of course to overall supervision by the board of directors). Should you go with the formal organization chart, and defer to the CEO and general counsel, or take the dangerous course of going elsewhere with your suspicions?

The American Bar Association's Model Rule of Professional Conduct 1.13 provides a degree of guidance here. The rule provides as follows:

American Bar Association, Model Rule of Professional Conduct 1.13, Organization as Client

(a) A lawyer employed or retained by an organization represents the organization acting through its duly authorized constituents.

(b) If a lawyer for an organization knows that an officer, employee or other person associated with the organization is engaged in action, intends to act or refuses to act in a matter related to the representation that is a violation of a legal obligation to the organization, or a violation of law that reasonably might be imputed to the organization, and that is likely to result in substantial injury to the organization, then the lawyer shall proceed as is reasonably necessary in the best interest of the organization. Unless the lawyer reasonably believes that it is not necessary in the best interest of the organization to do so, the lawyer shall refer the matter to higher authority in the organization, including, if warranted by the circumstances to the highest authority that can act on behalf of the organization as determined by applicable law. . . .

Questions and Comments

1. Rule 1.13(a) makes it clear that your client is the organization — that is, Eastern Logistics. But Eastern Logistics is not a human being; it is a fictional person that has no voice, no judgment, and no soul other than what is animated through human beings. In the chain of command, the general counsel — and your boss — is charged with the initial responsibility for deciding what to do. Have you satisfied your obligation if you defer to the decision made by the general counsel?

2. Rule 1.13(b) addresses the case where an attorney believes that the person to whom she reports within the organization is not acting in the best interests of the company. It provides that in some circumstances the attorney has not only the permission, but also the professional obligation, to "refer the matter to higher authority in the organization." This is sometimes referred to as "up-the-ladder" reporting. When the rule applies, the attorney must go over the head of the officer to more senior people who have authority to act. If all else fails, the attorney must raise the issue with the "highest authority that can act on behalf of the organization" — ordinarily the board of directors.

3. While Rule 1.13(b) is couched in mandatory terms, how much discretion does it give to an attorney who doesn't want to rock the boat? The requirement to report

up the ladder doesn't apply unless the lawyer "knows" of illegal activity by someone in the organization. As philosophers have demonstrated since the time of Plato, the concept of knowledge is notoriously tricky: Can we really say we know anything at all, given that anything is possible? The Rules don't use the term "know" in a rigorous philosophical sense; Model Rule 1.10(f) speaks of "actual knowledge of the fact in question." Still, the term gives a lawyer "wiggle room" to avoid carrying out the procedure contemplated in Rule 1.13(b). What about under the facts of the hypothetical above — is the attorney obligated to go up the ladder?

4. Even if the attorney concludes that she knows of misconduct in the organization, are there other reasons not to act? The rule requires that the attorney must act as "reasonably necessary in the best interest of the organization." If, therefore, the attorney reasonably concludes that the best interests of the organization would not be served by further reporting, the attorney does not have to act.

5. What if the attorney acts under Rule 1.13(b) and, instead of being thanked for her efforts, gets a pink slip informing her that her services are no longer required? Rule 1.13(e) provides that "[a] lawyer who reasonably believes that he or she has been discharged because of the lawyer's actions taken pursuant to paragraphs (b) or (c), or who withdraws under circumstances that require or permit the lawyer to take action under either of those paragraphs, shall proceed as the lawyer reasonably believes necessary to assure that the organization's highest authority is informed of the lawyer's discharge or withdrawal." In other words, after being fired, the attorney may need to inform the board of directors. How much solace does this provide for a lawyer who is now searching for work?

6. Does Rule 1.13 draw the right balance between competing social policies?

7. For more on lawyers as gatekeepers for corporate clients, see Sung Hui Kim, *Gatekeepers Inside Out*, 21 Geo. J. Legal Ethics 411 (2008); Sung Hui Kim, *Naked Self-Interest? Why the Legal Profession Resists Gatekeeping*, 63 Fla. L. Rev. 129 (2011).

PROBLEM 9-2

As a new partner at your law firm, you are eager to bring in clients and to demonstrate your skills as a "rainmaker." One day you get a call from Bob Brown, a friend of your family who is the chief executive officer of Omniware, a manufacturer of non-stick cooking utensils. Brown says that his firm is being investigated by the Consumer Product Safety Commission on suspicion that it used a toxic chemical on its cooking surfaces. Brown says, "I can assure you that this was a problem with our Chinese supplier; we had nothing to do with it." He asks if you would be interested in conducting the company's investigation of what happened. He is delighted when you express interest in the job. "Great!," he says. "Just one more thing: For reasons of confidentiality, the results of your investigation are to be shared only with me personally; no one else needs to know about it." Should you accept the assignment? If so, on what terms?

b. Relations with Employees

Does an attorney who represents an organization in a compliance matter also represent individuals within the organization suspected of misconduct? The issue is important because if the attorney represents the individuals, then information obtained by the attorney from these people during the representation may be considered to be ethically protected and therefore not subject to disclosure without the individual's consent. This could constrain efforts by the organization to obtain leniency from prosecutors or regulators by bartering information about the employee.

The issue is complicated by the fact that in the early stages of a compliance matter, the interests of the organization and the individual are likely to be aligned. Neither the organization nor the individual wants the regulators or prosecutors to conclude that any violations of law have occurred. Given the alignment of interests, it is often easy for the individual to assume that counsel for the company is representing her interests as well. Believing this to be the case, the individual may make damaging admissions or entrust sensitive information to counsel in the belief that counsel will not use this information to the individual's disadvantage.

That assumption, however, may be misguided. Generally, if nothing has been said to clarify the relationship, the individual defendant must establish the following factors in order to prove that counsel for a corporation also represented her:

> First, they must show they approached [counsel] for the purpose of seeking legal advice. Second, they must demonstrate that when they approached [counsel] they made it clear that they were seeking legal advice in their individual rather than in their representative capacities. Third, they must demonstrate that the [counsel] saw fit to communicate with them in their individual capacities, knowing that a possible conflict could arise. Fourth, they must prove that their conversations with [counsel] were confidential. And, fifth, they must show that the substance of their conversations with [counsel] did not concern matters within the company or the general affairs of the company.

In re Bevill, Bresler & Schulman Asset Mgmt. Corp., 805 F.2d 120, 123-125 (3d Cir. 1986). How easy will it be to meet this test?

What happens when, as a result of an investigation, an employee retains separate counsel to represent her in the matter? Can the attorney for the organization communicate directly with the employee about the issue — for example by interviewing her? Absent an agreement to the contrary, the answer is "no": Model Rule 4.2 provides that "[i]n representing a client, a lawyer shall not communicate about the subject of the representation with a person the lawyer knows to be represented by another lawyer in the matter, unless the lawyer has the consent of the other lawyer or is authorized to do so by law or a court order." The organization's attorney may communicate directly with the employee, rather than going through counsel, only if the employee's counsel consents.

Suppose that during a government investigation an officer of an organization provides false statements to the organization's attorney who in good faith then passes these statements on to the government investigators. Lying to government investigators can be a crime. But in the example given above, who can be prosecuted? The attorney acted in good faith and accordingly lacks the requisite *mens rea*. The employee did not act in good faith, but prosecuting this person for obstruction of justice faces several obstacles. First, the statements are made to an attorney on the subject matter of the representation, and accordingly would ordinarily be protected by both the ethical rules on confidentiality and the attorney-client privilege. The government may need to demonstrate an exception to the privilege (such as the crime-fraud rule) in order to discover the substance of the communication, a challenging task. Even if the government does overcome the privilege, it must cope with the fact that the employee's statements are not made to the government but rather to counsel; proving intent to obstruct justice in this situation may be challenging. On the other hand, if the government cannot overcome these obstacles, guilty employees could shelter themselves behind counsel and essentially "white-wash" statements intended to deceive government investigators, a distinctly undesirable result.

Targets of prosecutorial investigations sometimes take actions with respect to their legal defense that could have the effect of limiting the government's access to information. Examples include paying the attorneys' fees of employees who are under investigation or facing charges, or entering into joint defense agreements containing confidentiality provisions. How should prosecutors deal with these sorts of behaviors, given that they are legal in their own right?

The Department of Justice has this to say:

United States Attorneys Manual, Principles of Federal Prosecution of Business Organizations

2013

9-28.730 Obstructing the Investigation: ... In evaluating cooperation ... prosecutors should not take into account whether a corporation is advancing or reimbursing attorneys' fees or providing counsel to employees, officers, or directors under investigation or indictment. Likewise, prosecutors may not request that a corporation refrain from taking such action. This prohibition is not meant to prevent a prosecutor from asking questions about an attorney's representation of a corporation or its employees, officers, or directors, where otherwise appropriate under the law. Neither is it intended to limit the otherwise applicable reach of criminal obstruction of justice statutes such as 18 U.S.C. §1503. If the payment of attorney fees were used in a manner that would otherwise constitute criminal obstruction of justice — for example, if fees were advanced on the condition that an employee adhere to a version of the facts that the corporation and the employee knew to be false — these Principles would not (and could not) render inapplicable such criminal prohibitions.

Similarly, the mere participation by a corporation in a joint defense agreement does not render the corporation ineligible to receive cooperation credit, and prosecutors may not request that a corporation refrain from entering into such agreements. Of course, the corporation may wish to avoid putting itself in the position of being disabled, by virtue of a particular joint defense or similar agreement, from providing some relevant facts to the government and thereby limiting its ability to seek such cooperation credit. Such might be the case if the corporation gathers facts from employees who have entered into a joint defense agreement with the corporation, and who may later seek to prevent the corporation from disclosing the facts it has acquired. Corporations may wish to address this situation by crafting or participating in joint defense agreements, to the extent they choose to enter them, that provide such flexibility as they deem appropriate.

Questions and Comments

1. Should it make a difference if the target company advances attorneys' fees or defense costs to an employee pursuant to a preexisting indemnification agreement—so that refusing to provide these funds would arguably be a breach of contract—as opposed to a situation where the target advances defense costs as a matter of discretion?

2. A joint defense agreement is an arrangement under which independent entities facing similar legal problems coordinate their legal strategy and share attorney-client information without waiving privilege. Prosecutors tend to dislike these agreements for the obvious reason that they facilitate the ability of defendants to put up a united front. What does the Manual say about how prosecutors should view these agreements?

3. The Manual notes that a joint defense agreement may limit a target's ability to receive credit for cooperation. Is this different than saying that the prosecutors can take reliance in a joint defense agreement as a negative factor in making a charging determination?

4. The Manual suggests that potential targets would be well advised, when drafting a joint defense agreement, to preserve leeway for cooperation by providing "such flexibility as they deem appropriate." What sorts of provisions do the authors of this document have in mind? Are these provisions in a potential target's interest at the time they are made?

3. Confidentiality

a. Scope of the Lawyer's Duty of Confidentiality

One of an attorney's most sacred responsibilities—as well, perhaps not coincidentally, as one of her principal claims to authority within an organization—is the professional obligation to maintain the confidences of clients. This obligation has an ancient lineage, extending back to pre-revolutionary English practice; it is alive and well today even if, occasionally, it comes under stress.

The core obligation of confidentiality is found in Rule 1.6(a) of the American Bar Association's Model Rules of Professional Conduct: A lawyer "shall not reveal information relating to the representation of a client unless the client gives informed consent, the disclosure is impliedly authorized in order to carry out the representation or the disclosure is permitted by paragraph (b)."

The general rule is one of non-disclosure: The attorney may not reveal the information. The scope of the non-disclosure obligation, moreover, is broad indeed. The obligation to maintain confidentiality is not limited to communications between lawyer and client that would be protected by the attorney-client privilege. It is not limited to information that would be embarrassing or harmful to the client if disclosed. It is not even limited to information about the client: Any information "relating to the representation" is included. If the information relates to the representation, it is protected.

Why cast the net of confidentially so wide? The answer has to do with a balance of costs. The framers of the rule believed that the cost of keeping the information confidential is usually slight, given the extensive rights of pretrial discovery afforded under modern rules of procedure. On the other hand, at least some information relating to the representation could be damaging to the client if disclosed. Rather than seek to distinguish between information that would harm the client if disclosed and information that would not, the rule makers included all such information within the scope of confidentiality and relied on exceptions to the rule to provide an escape valve for situations where the costs of non-disclosure exceed the costs of disclosure.

The consequence is to place a great deal of pressure on the exceptions. The rule lists three of these. First, disclosure is permitted if the client gives "informed consent." This provision respects the autonomy of the client and recognizes that the client herself is usually the best judge of her own interests. Much, obviously, will depend on the knowledge that the client must have in order for her consent to be "informed." In the case of the complex organizations, the sophistication of the client is often a basis for concluding that the consent is valid.

Second, disclosure is permitted if disclosure is impliedly authorized in order to carry out the representation. It doesn't make sense for the attorney to be pestering the client with requests for permission to reveal information which obviously must be revealed if the lawyer is to do her job. When the client retains the attorney's services, therefore, she implicitly consents to the attorney exercising professional judgment about what information should be revealed in order to represent the client most effectively (the implied consent can be canceled if the client specifically bars the attorney from disclosing specified information).

The third exception—and the one that is most relevant to the issue of compliance—is the provision referring for disclosures permitted under paragraph (b). This is not a single exception but rather a grab bag that has evolved over the years at American Bar Association meetings, sometimes in a contentious process. Let's examine cases where disclosure is permitted.

American Bar Association, Model Rule of Professional Conduct 1.6(b), Confidentiality of Information

(b) A lawyer may reveal information relating to the representation of a client to the extent the lawyer reasonably believes necessary:

(1) to prevent reasonably certain death or substantial bodily harm;

(2) to prevent the client from committing a crime or fraud that is reasonably certain to result in substantial injury to the financial interests or property of another and in furtherance of which the client has used or is using the lawyer's services;

(3) to prevent, mitigate or rectify substantial injury to the financial interests or property of another that is reasonably certain to result or has resulted from the client's commission of a crime or fraud in furtherance of which the client has used the lawyer's services;

(4) to secure legal advice about the lawyer's compliance with these Rules;

(5) to establish a claim or defense on behalf of the lawyer in a controversy between the lawyer and the client, to establish a defense to a criminal charge or civil claim against the lawyer based upon conduct in which the client was involved, or to respond to allegations in any proceeding concerning the lawyer's representation of the client;

(6) to comply with other law or a court order; or

(7) to detect and resolve conflicts of interest arising from the lawyer's change of employment or from changes in the composition or ownership of

a firm, but only if the revealed information would not compromise the attorney-client privilege or otherwise prejudice the client. . . .

———————

It might appear, on cursory review, that these exceptions allow disclosure in cases where the client is egregiously violating its compliance obligations. The extent of the lawyer's role in disclosing client information under this rule is, however, significantly narrower than might at first appear.

We can understand this point best through analysis of hypothetical cases.

PROBLEM 9-3

You are general counsel at a mining company. The company experiences a disaster in which three miners are killed in an explosion. During the course of an internal investigation you discover that in the weeks before the accident safety officials had reported dangerously high levels of explosive gas in the mine. Normal procedure would be to cease mining operations while the gas is vented out. However, you discover that the supervisor had overridden these procedures in order to keep production on track to meet an important contract. In your opinion the supervisor's actions manifested a depraved indifference to human life. Although the mine has been shut since the accident and safe working conditions are being restored, nothing can bring back the dead miners. May you report the supervisor's misconduct to the Mine Safety and Health Administration?

PROBLEM 9-4

You are an attorney at Draper & Clydesdale, a boutique tax firm. After advising your client, Smith Manufacturing Co., you discover that the client has deliberately reported certain items to you as current expenses when they are in fact long-term investments. The return you worked on improperly deducts the full amount of these costs in the tax year just ended, rather than amortizing them over time. The result is that the client underpaid the government by $50,000. The client refuses to rectify the mistake. Can you inform the IRS of the fraud?

PROBLEM 9-5

In your role as general counsel to Oregon Edison, an electric utility company, you discover that the firm has been deliberately emitting more carbon dioxide into the atmosphere from its generator than is permitted by a consent decree with the EPA. You are upset by the discovery, especially because you filed disclosure statements required by the consent decree that falsely represent that the company is in compliance. If caught, the company may face a substantial fine; but you believe that the emissions are not likely to be detected by the regulator. Can you disclose the violations to the regulator if the company refuses to change its practice?

PROBLEM 9-6

Same facts as above except that the client is secretly discharging a lethal chemical into the water system. You have reason to believe that people are likely to die as a result of the illegal behavior. Must you tell the authorities if your client refuses to cease the practice?

Questions and Comments

1. What is the social policy behind imposing strict duties of confidentiality on members of the legal profession?

2. Does Model Rule 1.6 draw the right balance between the client's interest in keeping confidences and the public's interest in knowing of regulatory violations?

3. How does Model Rule 1.6 enhance the attorney's value to the client in compliance matters?

4. What do you think of the rule that an attorney is not ethically required to reveal information about a client's intention to commit a crime that is reasonably certain to take an innocent life?

b. Special Confidentiality Rules for Organization Clients

Rule 1.6 applies to all forms of representation. However, in the case of organizational clients, a limited further exception to the rule of confidentiality applies. Review Rule 1.13, reproduced above. What happens if an attorney goes "up the ladder" and fails to get a satisfactory result from the client's highest authority? This situation is covered by Rules 1.13(c) and (d):

American Bar Association, Model Rule of Professional Conduct 1.13, Organization as Client

(c) Except as provided in paragraph (d), if

(1) despite the lawyer's efforts in accordance with paragraph (b) the highest authority that can act on behalf of the organization insists upon or fails to address in a timely and appropriate manner an action, or a refusal to act, that is clearly a violation of law, and

(2) the lawyer reasonably believes that the violation is reasonably certain to result in substantial injury to the organization, then the lawyer may reveal information relating to the representation whether or not Rule 1.6 permits such disclosure, but only if and to the extent the lawyer reasonably believes necessary to prevent substantial injury to the organization.

(d) Paragraph (c) shall not apply with respect to information relating to a lawyer's representation of an organization to investigate an alleged violation of law, or to defend the organization or an officer, employee or other constituent associated with the organization against a claim arising out of an alleged violation of law. . . .

Questions and Comments

1. This rule allows a lawyer to disclose client information in circumstances where disclosure would not otherwise be permitted under Rule 1.6. Notice, however, that the opening for disclosure is subject to stringent conditions: The lawyer must "reasonably believe" that the violation is "reasonably certain" to result in "substantial injury" to the organization. In such a case, the attorney may reveal the information "only and to the extent" that the lawyer reasonably believes necessary to prevent the injury. Even in this circumstance the attorney "may" reveal the information, implying that she is not required to do so.

2. Why were framers of the Model Rules so stingy? Surely if the highest authority in the organization refuses to act in a case where there is a clear violation threatening a substantial injury to the organization, this is a powerful reason for requiring the attorney to reveal the information. What are the policy reasons on the other side of the ledger?

Section 307 of the Sarbanes-Oxley Act requires the SEC to set forth "minimum standards of professional conduct for attorneys appearing and practicing before the Commission," including a rule:

(1) requiring an attorney to report evidence of a material violation of securities law or breach of fiduciary duty or similar violation by the company or any agent thereof, to the chief legal counsel or the chief executive officer of the company (or the equivalent thereof); and

(2) if the counsel or officer does not appropriately respond to the evidence (adopting, as necessary, appropriate remedial measures or sanctions with respect to the violation), requiring the attorney to report the evidence to the audit committee of the board of directors of the issuer or to another committee of the board of directors comprised solely of directors not employed directly or indirectly by the issuer, or to the board of directors.

In 2002, the SEC proposed rules to implement these requirements. One provision of the proposed rules — dubbed the "noisy withdrawal" provision — proved controversial because it appeared to compromise the attorney's duty of confidentiality. The rule dealt with the following situation:

- The attorney reports evidence of a material securities law violation up the ladder;
- The attorney fails to receive an appropriate response within a reasonable time;
- The attorney reasonably believes that the violation is ongoing or about to occur;
- The attorney believes the violation is likely to result in substantial injury to the financial interest of the company or investors.

In such cases, the rule would require the attorney to withdraw from representing the issuer based on "professional considerations," and, within one business day, to notify the Commission of the withdrawal and promptly disaffirm any materially false or misleading document or representation supplied or made by the attorney.

The proposal sparked intense opposition from bar leaders. Among the arguments put forth against the rule, the following were commonly heard:

- If an attorney informs the SEC that she is withdrawing from representing a client for "professional considerations," this is tantamount to disclosing a client confidence: It would effectively guarantee an SEC investigation that would reveal the nature of the attorney's concerns.
- Mandated attorney withdrawal would deprive firms from the benefit of legal representation at the time when they are most in need.
- The rule would encourage attorneys to withdraw before they were required to do so, in order to avoid the fatal "professional considerations" notice to the SEC.
- The rule would incentivize attorneys not to ask the hard questions needed to ensure compliance, out of concern for the answers they might receive.
- The rule would drive a wedge between lawyer and client and reduce the client's willingness to share sensitive information with the attorney.
- Companies faced with a threat of noisy withdrawal might feel compelled to disclose damaging information to the market even in situations where no wrongdoing had in fact occurred.

Questions and Comments

1. The metaphor of the "noisy" withdrawal is cleverly chosen, for two reasons. Noise is something that calls attention to itself; the lawyer's announcement that she is withdrawing for "professional considerations" would certainly have that effect. Noise is also something that obscures a message; here the metaphor suggests that although the lawyer is withdrawing and conveying information by doing so, the actual content of the message — the client confidences — are not disclosed.

2. Do you agree with the criticisms of the SEC's proposals?

3. The final rule published by the SEC contained an up-the-ladder reporting requirement for attorneys practicing before the SEC similar to the general approach of the Model Rules. The noisy withdrawal provision, however, was not included in the final rule; the SEC announced that it was delaying that proposal while it considered further comments. After more than ten years of delay, the SEC has yet to act, leaving a rusty sword of Damocles hanging over the heart of the securities bar.

4. Attorney-Client Privilege

a. Scope

Upjohn Co. v. United States

449 U.S. 383 (1981)

... Petitioner Upjohn Co. manufactures and sells pharmaceuticals here and abroad. In January 1976 independent accountants conducting an audit of one of Upjohn's foreign subsidiaries discovered that the subsidiary made payments to or for the benefit of foreign government officials in order to secure government business. The accountants so informed petitioner, Mr. Gerard Thomas, Upjohn's Vice President, Secretary, and General Counsel. Thomas is a member of the Michigan and New York Bars, and has been Upjohn's General Counsel for 20 years. He consulted with outside counsel and R. T. Parfet, Jr., Upjohn's Chairman of the Board. It was decided that the company would conduct an internal investigation of what were termed "questionable payments." As part of this investigation the attorneys prepared a letter containing a questionnaire which was sent to "All Foreign General and Area Managers" over the Chairman's signature. The letter began by noting recent disclosures that several American companies made "possibly illegal" payments to foreign government officials and emphasized that the management needed full information concerning any such payments made by Upjohn. The letter indicated that the Chairman had asked Thomas, identified as "the company's General Counsel," "to conduct an investigation for the purpose of determining the nature and magnitude of any payments made by the Upjohn Company or any of its subsidiaries to any employee or official of a foreign government." The questionnaire sought detailed information concerning such payments. Managers were instructed to treat the investigation as "highly confidential" and not to discuss it with anyone other than Upjohn employees who might be helpful in providing the requested information. Responses were to be sent directly to Thomas. Thomas and outside counsel also interviewed the recipients of the questionnaire and some 33 other Upjohn officers or employees as part of the investigation.

On March 26, 1976, the company voluntarily submitted a preliminary report to the Securities and Exchange Commission on Form 8-K disclosing certain questionable payments. A copy of the report was simultaneously submitted to the Internal Revenue Service, which immediately began an investigation to determine the tax consequences of the payments. Special agents conducting the investigation were given lists by Upjohn of all those interviewed and all who had responded to the questionnaire. On November 23, 1976, the Service issued a summons . . . demanding production of:

"All files relative to the investigation conducted under the supervision of Gerard Thomas to identify payments to employees of foreign governments and any political contributions made by the Upjohn Company or any of its affiliates since January 1, 1971 and to determine whether any funds of the Upjohn Company had been improperly accounted for on the corporate books during the same period. The records should include but not be limited to written questionnaires sent to managers of the Upjohn Company's foreign affiliates, and memorandums or notes of the interviews conducted in the United States and abroad with officers and employees of the Upjohn Company and its subsidiaries."

The company declined to produce the documents . . . on the grounds that they were protected from disclosure by the attorney-client privilege and constituted the work product of attorneys prepared in anticipation of litigation. On August 31, 1977, the United States filed a petition seeking enforcement of the summons. . . . That court adopted the recommendation of a Magistrate who concluded that the summons should be enforced. Petitioners appealed to the Court of Appeals for the Sixth Circuit which rejected the Magistrate's finding of a waiver of the attorney-client privilege, but agreed that the privilege did not apply "[t]o the extent that the communications were made by officers and agents not responsible for directing Upjohn's actions in response to legal advice . . . for the simple reason that the communications were not the 'client's.'" The court reasoned that accepting petitioners' claim for a broader application of the privilege would encourage upper-echelon management to ignore unpleasant facts and create too broad a "zone of silence." Noting that Upjohn's counsel had interviewed officials such as the Chairman and President, the Court of Appeals remanded to the District Court so that a determination of who was within the "control group" could be made. . . .

The attorney-client privilege is the oldest of the privileges for confidential communications known to the common law. Its purpose is to encourage full and frank communication between attorneys and their clients and thereby promote broader public interests in the observance of law and administration of justice. The privilege recognizes that sound legal advice or advocacy serves public ends and that such advice or advocacy depends upon the lawyer's being fully informed by the client. . . . Admittedly complications in the application of the privilege arise when the client is a corporation, which in theory is an artificial creature of the law, and not an individual; but this Court has assumed that the privilege applies when the client is a corporation, and the Government does not contest the general proposition.

The Court of Appeals, however, considered the application of the privilege in the corporate context to present a "different problem," since the client was an inanimate entity and "only the senior management, guiding and integrating the several operations, . . . can be said to possess an identity analogous to the corporation as a whole." . . . Such a view, we think, overlooks the fact that the privilege exists to protect not only the giving of professional advice to those who can act on it but also the giving of information to the lawyer to enable him to give sound and informed advice. The first step in the resolution of any legal problem is ascertaining the factual background and sifting through the facts with an eye to the legally relevant. . . .

In the case of the individual client the provider of information and the person who acts on the lawyer's advice are one and the same. In the corporate context, however, it will frequently be employees beyond the control group as defined by the court below — "officers and agents . . . responsible for directing [the company's] actions in response to legal advice" — who will possess the information needed by the corporation's lawyers. Middle-level — and indeed lower-level — employees can, by actions within the scope of their employment, embroil the corporation in serious legal difficulties, and it is only natural that these employees would have the relevant information needed by corporate counsel if he is adequately to advise the client with respect to such actual or potential difficulties.

The control group test adopted by the court below thus frustrates the very purpose of the privilege by discouraging the communication of relevant information by employees of the client to attorneys seeking to render legal advice to the client corporation. The attorney's advice will also frequently be more significant to non-control group members than to those who officially sanction the advice, and the control group test makes it more difficult to convey full and frank legal advice to the employees who will put into effect the client corporation's policy.

The narrow scope given the attorney-client privilege by the court below not only makes it difficult for corporate attorneys to formulate sound advice when their client is faced with a specific legal problem but also threatens to limit the valuable efforts of corporate counsel to ensure their client's compliance with the law. In light of the vast and complicated array of regulatory legislation confronting the modern corporation, corporations, unlike most individuals, "constantly go to lawyers to find out how to obey the law," particularly since compliance with the law in this area is hardly an instinctive matter.

The test adopted by the court below is difficult to apply in practice, though no abstractly formulated and unvarying "test" will necessarily enable courts to decide questions such as this with mathematical precision. But if the purpose of the attorney-client privilege is to be served, the attorney and client must be able to predict with some degree of certainty whether particular discussions will be protected. An uncertain privilege, or one which purports to be certain but results in widely varying applications by the courts, is little better than no privilege at all. The very terms of the test adopted by the court below suggest the unpredictability of its application. The test restricts the availability of the privilege to those officers who play a "substantial role" in deciding and directing a corporation's legal response. Disparate decisions in cases applying this test illustrate its unpredictability. . . .

The communications at issue were made by Upjohn employees to counsel for Upjohn acting as such, at the direction of corporate superiors in order to secure legal advice from counsel. As the Magistrate found, "Mr. Thomas consulted with the Chairman of the Board and outside counsel and thereafter conducted a factual investigation to determine the nature and extent of the questionable payments *and to be in a position to give legal advice to the company with respect to the payments.*" Information, not available from upper-echelon management, was needed to supply a basis for legal advice concerning compliance with securities and tax laws, foreign laws, currency regulations, duties to shareholders, and potential litigation in each of these areas. The communications concerned matters within the scope of the employees' corporate duties, and the employees themselves were sufficiently aware that they were being questioned in order that the corporation could obtain legal advice. The questionnaire identified Thomas as "the company's General Counsel" and referred in its opening sentence to the possible illegality of payments such as the ones on which information was sought. A statement of policy accompanying the questionnaire clearly indicated the legal implications of the investigation. The policy statement was issued "in order that there be no uncertainty in the future as to the policy with respect to the practices which are the subject of this investigation." It began "Upjohn will comply with all laws and regulations," and stated that commissions or payments "will not be used as a subterfuge for bribes or illegal payments" and that all payments must be "proper and legal." Any future agreements with foreign distributors or agents were to be approved "by a company attorney" and any questions concerning the policy were to be referred "to the company's General Counsel." This statement was issued to Upjohn employees worldwide, so that even those interviewees not receiving a questionnaire were aware of the legal implications of the interviews. Pursuant to explicit instructions from the Chairman of the Board, the communications were considered "highly confidential" when made, and have been kept confidential by the company. Consistent with the underlying purposes of the attorney-client privilege, these communications must be protected against compelled disclosure.

The Court of Appeals declined to extend the attorney-client privilege beyond the limits of the control group test for fear that doing so would entail severe burdens on discovery and create a broad "zone of silence" over corporate affairs. Application of the attorney-client privilege to communications such as those involved here, however, puts the adversary in no worse position than if the communications had never taken place. The privilege only protects disclosure of communications; it does not protect disclosure of the underlying facts by those who communicated with the attorney. Here the Government was free to question the employees who communicated with Thomas and outside counsel. Upjohn has provided the IRS with a list of such employees, and the IRS has already interviewed some 25 of them. While it would probably be more convenient for the Government to secure the results of petitioner's internal investigation by simply subpoenaing the questionnaires and notes taken by petitioner's attorneys, such considerations of convenience do not overcome the policies served by the attorney-client privilege.

Needless to say, we decide only the case before us, and do not undertake to draft a set of rules which should govern challenges to investigatory subpoenas. While such a "case-by-case" basis may to some slight extent undermine desirable certainty in the boundaries of the attorney-client privilege, it obeys the spirit of the Rules. At the same time we conclude that the narrow "control group test" sanctioned by the Court of Appeals, in this case cannot, consistent with "the principles of the common law as . . . interpreted . . . in the light of reason and experience," govern the development of the law in this area. . . .

Accordingly, the judgment of the Court of Appeals is reversed, and the case remanded for further proceedings.

Questions and Comments

1. *Upjohn* is a compliance case. The company received information about possible illegal payments — a compliance violation. It then commenced an internal investigation, spearheaded by counsel, in an attempt to determine the scope of the problem. The results of the investigation were then shared "voluntarily" with the SEC. All of these actions would now be considered conventional responses to a compliance crisis, with the possible exception that today the investigation might be outsourced to outside counsel.

2. What does the Court think of the Upjohn's internal investigation?

3. What does the Court think of the IRS's actions? Could the IRS have uncovered the information it needed without having access to the attorney-client information it sought?

4. Did the Court reach the right result from the standpoint of compliance policy?

5. What, exactly, was the scope of the attorney-client privilege recognized in the excerpted case? The Court was not very clear and in fact appeared deliberately to avoid setting forth any definitive test. Later cases have recognized the following elements:

- The privilege covers only communications, not facts.
- The communications must have been made for the purpose of obtaining legal advice.
- The employee who makes the communication must have been encouraged or requested to do so by a more senior officer.

6. What do you think of the "control group" test adopted by the lower court but rejected in Upjohn? What function does it imply for the attorney-client privilege? What function for the privilege is implied by the Supreme Court's analysis?

7. In a footnote, the Court declined to decide whether the privilege should apply to communications by former Upjohn employees concerning activities undertaken during their period of employment. Do you see any differences, so far as the scope of

the privilege is concerned, when the communications are with former rather than current employees?

8. Companies often make it a policy to copy in-house counsel on all sensitive information. Should internal emails that include corporate counsel among other recipients be automatically accorded the attorney-client privilege? If not, what should the standard be?

9. What if an attorney, in furtherance of the representation of a client in a compliance matter, shares attorney-client confidences with an outside consultant in order to gain a better understanding of the facts? Does this waive the privilege for the information that is shared? For other related information, even if not shared? Most courts recognize that the privilege extends to bona fide consultations needed to facilitate the representation or the formulation of competent legal advice.

In re Kellogg Brown & Root, Inc.

756 F.3d 754 (D.C. Cir. 2014), *cert. denied*, 135 S. Ct. 1163 (2015)

More than three decades ago, the Supreme Court held that the attorney-client privilege protects confidential employee communications made during a business's internal investigation led by company lawyers. . . . In this case, the District Court denied the protection of the privilege to a company that had conducted just such an internal investigation. The District Court's decision has generated substantial uncertainty about the scope of the attorney-client privilege in the business setting. We conclude that the District Court's decision is irreconcilable with *Upjohn*. We therefore grant KBR's petition for a writ of mandamus. . . .

Harry Barko worked for KBR, a defense contractor. In 2005, he filed a False Claims Act complaint against KBR and KBR-related corporate entities, whom we will collectively refer to as KBR. In essence, Barko alleged that KBR and certain subcontractors defrauded the U.S. Government by inflating costs and accepting kickbacks while administering military contracts in wartime Iraq. During discovery, Barko sought documents related to KBR's prior internal investigation into the alleged fraud. KBR had conducted that internal investigation pursuant to its Code of Business Conduct, which is overseen by the company's Law Department.

KBR argued that the internal investigation had been conducted for the purpose of obtaining legal advice and that the internal investigation documents therefore were protected by the attorney-client privilege. Barko responded that the internal investigation documents were unprivileged business records that he was entitled to discover. After reviewing the disputed documents in camera, the District Court determined that the attorney-client privilege protection did not apply because, among other reasons, KBR had not shown that "the communication would not have been made 'but for' the fact that legal advice was sought." KBR's internal investigation, the court concluded, was "undertaken pursuant to regulatory law and corporate policy rather than for the purpose of obtaining legal advice."

KBR vehemently opposed the ruling. The company asked the District Court to certify the privilege question to this Court for interlocutory appeal and to stay its order pending a petition for mandamus in this Court. The District Court denied those requests and ordered KBR to produce the disputed documents to Barko within a matter of days. KBR promptly filed a petition for a writ of mandamus in this Court. A number of business organizations and trade associations also objected to the District Court's decision and filed an amicus brief in support of KBR. We stayed the District Court's document production order and held oral argument on the mandamus petition. . . .

The attorney-client privilege is the "oldest of the privileges for confidential communications known to the common law." As relevant here, the privilege applies to a confidential communication between attorney and client if that communication was made for the purpose of obtaining or providing legal advice to the client. . . .

KBR's assertion of the privilege in this case is materially indistinguishable from Upjohn's assertion of the privilege in that case. As in *Upjohn*, KBR initiated an internal investigation to gather facts and ensure compliance with the law after being informed of potential misconduct. And as in *Upjohn*, KBR's investigation was conducted under the auspices of KBR's in-house legal department, acting in its legal capacity. The same considerations that led the Court in *Upjohn* to uphold the corporation's privilege claims apply here.

The District Court in this case initially distinguished *Upjohn* on a variety of grounds. But none of those purported distinctions takes this case out from under *Upjohn*'s umbrella.

First, the District Court stated that in *Upjohn* the internal investigation began after in-house counsel conferred with outside counsel, whereas here the investigation was conducted in-house without consultation with outside lawyers. But *Upjohn* does not hold or imply that the involvement of outside counsel is a necessary predicate for the privilege to apply. On the contrary, the general rule, which this Court has adopted, is that a lawyer's status as in-house counsel "does not dilute the privilege." . . .

Second, the District Court noted that in *Upjohn* the interviews were conducted by attorneys, whereas here many of the interviews in KBR's investigation were conducted by non-attorneys. But the investigation here was conducted at the direction of the attorneys in KBR's Law Department. And communications made by and to non-attorneys serving as agents of attorneys in internal investigations are routinely protected by the attorney-client privilege. So that fact, too, is not a basis on which to distinguish *Upjohn*.

Third, the District Court pointed out that in *Upjohn* the interviewed employees were expressly informed that the purpose of the interview was to assist the company in obtaining legal advice, whereas here they were not. The District Court further stated that the confidentiality agreements signed by KBR employees did not mention that the purpose of KBR's investigation was to obtain legal advice. Yet nothing in *Upjohn* requires a company to use magic words to its employees in order to gain the benefit of the privilege for an internal investigation. And in any event, here as in *Upjohn* employees knew that the company's legal department was conducting an investigation of a sensitive nature and that the information they disclosed would be protected. KBR employees were also told not to discuss their interviews "without the specific advance authorization of KBR General Counsel." In short, none of those three distinctions of *Upjohn* holds water as a basis for denying KBR's privilege claim.

More broadly and more importantly, the District Court also distinguished *Upjohn* on the ground that KBR's internal investigation was undertaken to comply with Department of Defense regulations that require defense contractors such as KBR to maintain compliance programs and conduct internal investigations into allegations of potential wrongdoing. The District Court therefore concluded that the purpose of KBR's internal investigation was to comply with those regulatory requirements rather than to obtain or provide legal advice. In our view, the District Court's analysis rested on a false dichotomy. So long as obtaining or providing legal advice was one of the significant purposes of the internal investigation, the attorney-client privilege applies, even if there were also other purposes for the investigation and even if the investigation was mandated by regulation rather than simply an exercise of company discretion.

The District Court began its analysis by reciting the "primary purpose" test, which many courts (including this one) have used to resolve privilege disputes when attorney-client communications may have had both legal and business purposes. But in a key move, the District Court then said that the primary purpose of a communication is to obtain or provide legal advice only if the communication would not have been made "but for" the fact that legal advice was sought. In other words, if there was any other purpose behind the communication, the attorney-client privilege apparently does not apply. The District Court went on to conclude that KBR's internal investigation was "undertaken pursuant to regulatory law and corporate policy rather than for the purpose of obtaining legal advice." Therefore, in the District Court's view, "the primary purpose of" the internal investigation "was to comply with federal defense contractor regulations, not to secure legal advice."

The District Court erred because it employed the wrong legal test. The but-for test articulated by the District Court is not appropriate for attorney-client privilege analysis. Under the District Court's approach, the attorney-client privilege apparently would not apply unless the sole purpose of the communication was to obtain or provide legal advice. That is not the law. We are aware of no Supreme Court or court of appeals decision that has adopted a test of this kind in this context. The District Court's novel approach to the attorney-client privilege would eliminate the attorney-client privilege for numerous communications that are made for both legal and business purposes and that heretofore have been covered by the attorney-client privilege. And the District Court's novel approach would eradicate the attorney-client privilege for internal investigations conducted by businesses that are required by law to maintain compliance programs, which is now the case in a significant swath of American industry. In turn, businesses would be less likely to disclose facts to their attorneys and to seek legal advice, which would "limit the valuable efforts of corporate counsel to ensure their client's compliance with the law." We reject the District Court's but-for test as inconsistent with the principle of *Upjohn* and longstanding attorney-client privilege law.

Given the evident confusion in some cases, we also think it important to underscore that the primary purpose test, sensibly and properly applied, cannot and does not draw a rigid distinction between a legal purpose on the one hand and a business purpose on the other. After all, trying to find the one primary purpose for a communication motivated by two sometimes overlapping purposes (one legal and one business, for example) can be an inherently impossible task. It is often not useful or even feasible to try to determine whether the purpose was A or B when the purpose was A and B. It is thus not correct for a court to presume that a communication can have only one primary purpose. It is likewise not correct for a court to try to find the one primary purpose in cases where a given communication plainly has multiple purposes.

Rather, it is clearer, more precise, and more predictable to articulate the test as follows: Was obtaining or providing legal advice a primary purpose of the communication, meaning one of the significant purposes of the communication? We agree with and adopt that formulation — "one of the significant purposes" — as an accurate and appropriate description of the primary purpose test. Sensibly and properly applied, the test boils down to whether obtaining or providing legal advice was one of the significant purposes of the attorney-client communication.

In the context of an organization's internal investigation, if one of the significant purposes of the internal investigation was to obtain or provide legal advice, the privilege will apply. That is true regardless of whether an internal investigation was conducted pursuant to a company compliance program required by statute or regulation, or was otherwise conducted pursuant to company policy.

In this case, there can be no serious dispute that one of the significant purposes of the KBR internal investigation was to obtain or provide legal advice. In denying KBR's privilege claim on the ground that the internal investigation was conducted in order to comply with regulatory requirements and corporate policy and not just to obtain or provide legal advice, the District Court applied the wrong legal test and clearly erred.

Questions and Comments

1. Can you see why the opinion of the district court set off alarm bells within corporations and for attorneys who advise them? What would the consequences have been had this opinion been allowed to stand?

2. Why do think the district court sought to dilute the privilege?

3. Was the appeals court's decision over-protective? How often will a company be unable to argue that at least one significant purpose of an investigation is to obtain legal advice?

4. Is there something of the tail wagging the dog when a company claims that an internal investigation is being undertaken for the purpose of obtaining legal advice? Are most investigations undertaken for that purpose, or for the purpose of finding out what happened and seeking clemency from regulators if something untoward occurred? Or are these latter functions also part of the job of providing legal advice to a client?

5. The appeals court sent the case back to the district court, undoubtedly expecting that would be the end of the matter. The trial judge, however, rebelled and declared that the privilege did not apply, offering ostensibly different rationales. KBR again sought a writ of mandamus to the D.C. Circuit, and again the result was the same: The appeals court declared that the documents in question were privileged. In re Kellogg Brown & Root, Inc., 796 F.3d 137 (D.C. Cir. 2015), *cert. denied*, 136 S. Ct. 823 (2016). The panel's opinion voiced strong support for maintaining the privilege in internal investigations:

> If allowed to stand, the District Court's rulings would ring alarm bells in corporate general counsel offices throughout the country about what kinds of descriptions of investigatory and disclosure practices could be used by an adversary to defeat all claims of privilege and protection of an internal investigation. These alarm bells would be well founded. If all it took to defeat the privilege and protection attaching to an internal investigation was to notice a deposition regarding the investigations (and the privilege and protection attaching them), we would expect to see such attempts to end-run these barriers to discovery in every lawsuit in which a prior internal investigation was

conducted relating to the claims. Accordingly, we think it is essential to act on this Petition in order to protect our privilege waiver jurisprudence.

b. The Crime-Fraud Exception

Even if information is otherwise protected by the attorney-client privilege, its production may still be compelled if the communications between attorney and client are in furtherance of a crime or fraud. The rationale for the crime-fraud exception is that the calculus of social costs and benefits flips when the communications between attorney and client are used by the client for purposes of committing an offense.

While the rationale for the crime-fraud exception is fairly clear, its administration is not. The problem is to determine whether the exception applies: It may be necessary for some third party to look to the documents themselves in order to determine whether the claim of privilege is appropriate. But looking at the document would potentially vitiate the purpose of the privilege. At one time, some courts required the party seeking information to demonstrate the availability of the exception by independent evidence outside the contested document. However, in United States v. Zolin, 491 U.S. 554 (1989), the Supreme Court held that the availability of the exception may be determined by appropriately structured review by the court. To invoke the exception, the party seeking to abrogate the privilege must present *prima facie* evidence showing that the claimed exception has some foundation in fact. If the party seeking production meets this burden, the proponent of the privilege is required to come forward with an explanation for the evidence offered against it. The trial court then reviews the materials *in camera*. The privilege will remain if the district court finds the proponent's explanation satisfactory; but if the district court finds the explanation unsatisfactory, it will order the document to be disclosed.

Questions and Comments

1. How should prosecutors treat the situation where the target of a criminal investigation asserts a privilege with respect to matters where the prosecutors believe the attorney has been a participant in misconduct?

2. The Department of Justice's United States Attorneys Manual states that communications between a corporation and corporate counsel that are made in furtherance of a crime or fraud are, under settled precedent, outside the scope and protection of the attorney-client privilege. As a result, the Department may properly request such communications if they in fact exist. Does this adequately respond to the policy dilemma? What if the prosecutor demands the communications on the ground that she believes them to have been in furtherance of a crime or fraud, and the target resists on the ground that they were not in furtherance of a crime or fraud? Could or should the prosecutor in such a case take the target's refusal to turn over the information as a factor counseling in favor of charging the target?

c. The Fiduciary Exception

We now consider an important but poorly understood threat to the sanctity of attorney-client communications in the compliance context: the "fiduciary" exception to the attorney-client privilege.

Garner v. Wolfinbarger

430 F.2d 1093 (5th Cir. 1970), *cert. denied*, 401 U.S. 974 (1971)

[This was a shareholder class action against First American Life Insurance Co. (FAL) and certain of its officers, directors, and controlling persons. The lawsuit alleged that the defendants had made falsely optimistic statements in connection with the sale of FAL stock. During pretrial discovery, an attorney for the plaintiffs took the deposition of FAL's former in-house counsel, Schweitzer, who had subsequently been elevated to the position of president. Schweitzer refused to answer questions that concerned communications between him and the corporation, made in his capacity as counsel, that fell within the scope of the attorney-client privilege.]

The problem before us concerns . . . a balancing of interests between injury resulting from disclosure and the benefit gained in the correct disposal of litigation. We consider it in a particularized context: where the client asserting the privilege is an entity which in the performance of its functions acts wholly or partly in the interests of others, and those others, or some of them, seek access to the subject matter of the communications.

It is urged that disclosure is injurious to both the corporation and the attorney. Corporate management must manage. It has the duty to do so and requires the tools to do so. Part of the managerial task is to seek legal counsel when desirable, and, obviously, management prefers that it confer with counsel without the risk of having the communications revealed at the instance of one or more dissatisfied stockholders. The managerial preference is a rational one, because it is difficult to envision the management of any sizeable corporation pleasing all of its stockholders all of the time, and management desires protection from those who might second-guess or even harass in matters purely of judgment.

But in assessing management assertions of injury to the corporation it must be borne in mind that management does not manage for itself and that the beneficiaries of its action are the stockholders. Conceptualistic phrases describing the corporation as an entity separate from its stockholders are not useful tools of analysis. They serve only to obscure the fact that management has duties which run to the benefit ultimately of the stockholders. For example, it is difficult to rationally defend the assertion of the privilege if all, or substantially all, stockholders desire to inquire into the attorney's communications with corporate representatives who have only nominal ownership interests, or even none at all. There may be reasonable differences over the manner of characterizing in legal terminology the duties of management, and over the extent to which corporate management is less of a fiduciary than the common law trustee. There may be many situations in which the corporate entity or its management, or both, have interests adverse to those of some or all stockholders. But when all is said and done management is not managing for itself.

The representative and the represented have a mutuality of interest in the representative's freely seeking advice when needed and putting it to use when received. This is not to say that management does not have allowable judgment in putting advice to use. But management judgment must stand on its merits, not behind an ironclad veil of secrecy which under all circumstances preserves it from being questioned by those for whom it is, at least in part, exercised. . . .

Apart from the conceptualism that surrounds the management-stockholder relationship, the ABA [as *amicus curiae*] alternatively contends . . . that the benefits of disclosure are outweighed by the harm done to both client and attorney. . . . The ABA urges that the privilege is most necessary where the corporation has sought advice about a prospective transaction, where counsel in good faith has stated his opinion that it is not lawful, but the corporation has proceeded in total or partial disregard of counsel's advice. The ABA urges that the cause of justice requires that counsel be free to state his opinion as fully and forthrightly as possible without fear of later disclosure to persons who might attack the transaction, and that without the cloak of the privilege counsel may be "required by the threat of future discovery to hedge or soften their opinions."

The ABA brief does not always distinguish clearly between the separate interests of the corporate client and of the attorney in freedom from disclosure, nor is it possible always to do so. The privilege's exemptions from the broad duty to divulge are designed not only to protect the individual client who may assert the privilege but also to promote free and open communication between clients and attorneys in all matters. All these interests should properly be taken into account in any decision on the privilege. However, we reject the idea that the prospective decision of the client on whether to abide by advice or disregard it, or the guarantee of a veil of secrecy, either establishes or narrows the attorney's obligation in the giving of advice. And to grant to corporate management plenary assurance of secrecy for opinions received is to encourage it to disregard with impunity the advice sought. . . .

In summary, we say this. The attorney-client privilege still has viability for the corporate client. The corporation is not barred from asserting it merely because those demanding information enjoy the status of stockholders. But where the corporation is in suit against its stockholders on charges of acting inimically to stockholder interests, protection of those interests as well as those of the corporation and of the public require that the availability of the privilege be subject to the right of the stockholders to show cause why it should not be invoked in the particular instance.

There are many indicia that may contribute to a decision of presence or absence of good cause, among them the number of shareholders and the percentage of stock they represent; the bona fides of the shareholders; the nature of the shareholders' claim and whether it is obviously colorable; the apparent necessity or desirability of the shareholders having the information and the availability of it from other sources; whether, if the shareholders' claim is of wrongful action by the corporation, it is of action criminal, or illegal but not criminal, or of doubtful legality; whether the communication related to past or to prospective actions; whether the communication is of advice concerning the litigation itself; the extent to which the communication is identified versus the extent to which the shareholders are blindly fishing; the risk of revelation of trade secrets or other information in whose confidentiality the corporation has an interest for independent reasons. The court can freely use *in camera* inspection or oral examination and freely avail itself of protective orders, a familiar device to preserve confidentiality in trade secret and other cases where the impact of revelation may be as great as in revealing a communication with counsel.

Questions and Comments

1. Given this opinion, can a company ever be confident that communications with counsel regarding compliance issues will be protected against compelled disclosure in court?

2. What factors, in the court's view, weigh in favor of respecting the privilege in a given case, and what weigh in favor of dispensing with it?

3. Do you find convincing the court's reason for rejecting the argument that, but for the privilege, lawyers would pull their punches when advising clients about the legal risks inherent in particular courses of action?

4. Does the fiduciary exception to the attorney-client privilege apply when documents are sought, not through civil discovery in court proceedings, but rather pursuant to the right of shareholders to inspect the books and records of corporations in which they invest? *See* Wal-Mart Stores, Inc. v. Indiana Electrical Workers Pension Trust Fund IBEW, 95 A.3d 1264 (Del. 2014) (applying the *Garner* doctrine to shareholder demands to inspect corporate books and records under §220 of the Delaware General Corporation Law, in connection with a shareholder inquiry into reports of corrupt practices at Walmart's Mexican subsidiary).

5. Work-Product Protection

Hickman v. Taylor

329 U.S. 495 (1947)

On February 7, 1943, the tug "J. M. Taylor" sank while engaged in helping to tow a car float of the Baltimore & Ohio Railroad across the Delaware River at Philadelphia. The accident was apparently unusual in nature, the cause of it still being unknown. Five of the nine crew members were drowned. Three days later the tug owners and the underwriters employed a law firm, of which respondent Fortenbaugh is a member, to defend them against potential suits by representatives of the deceased crew members and to sue the railroad for damages to the tug.

A public hearing was held on March 4, 1943, before the United States Steamboat Inspectors, at which the four survivors were examined. This testimony was recorded and made available to all interested parties. Shortly thereafter, Fortenbaugh privately interviewed the survivors and took statements from them with an eye toward the anticipated litigation; the survivors signed these statements on March 29. Fortenbaugh also interviewed other persons believed to have some information relating to the accident and in some cases he made memoranda of what they told him. At the time when Fortenbaugh secured the statements of the survivors, representatives of two of the deceased crew members had been in communication with him. Ultimately claims were presented by representatives of all five of the deceased; four of the claims, however, were settled without litigation. The fifth claimant, petitioner herein, brought suit in a federal court under the Jones Act on November 26, 1943, naming as defendants the two tug owners, individually and as partners, and the railroad.

One year later, petitioner filed 39 interrogatories directed to the tug owners. The 38th interrogatory read: "State whether any statements of the members of the crews of the Tugs 'J. M. Taylor' and 'Philadelphia' or of any other vessel were taken in connection with the towing of the car float and the sinking of the Tug 'John M. Taylor.' Attach hereto exact copies of all such statements if in writing, and if oral, set forth in detail the exact provisions of any such oral statements or reports."

Supplemental interrogatories asked whether any oral or written statements, records, reports or other memoranda had been made concerning any matter relative to the towing operation, the sinking of the tug, the salvaging and repair of the tug, and the death of the deceased. If the answer was in the affirmative, the tug owners were then requested to set forth the nature of all such records, reports, statements or other memoranda.

The tug owners, through Fortenbaugh, answered all of the interrogatories except No. 38 and the supplemental ones just described. While admitting that statements of the survivors had been taken, they declined to summarize or set forth the contents. They did so on the ground that such requests called "for privileged matter obtained in preparation for litigation" and constituted "an attempt to obtain indirectly counsel's private files." It was claimed that answering these requests "would involve practically turning over not only the complete files, but also the telephone records and, almost, the thoughts of counsel."

In connection with the hearing on these objections, Fortenbaugh made a written statement and gave an informal oral deposition explaining the circumstances under which he had taken the statements. But he was not expressly asked in the deposition to produce the statements. The District Court for the Eastern District of Pennsylvania, sitting en banc, held that the requested matters were not privileged. The court then decreed that the tug owners and Fortenbaugh, as counsel and agent for the tug owners forthwith "Answer Plaintiff's 38th interrogatory and supplemental interrogatories; produce all written statements of witnesses obtained by Mr. Fortenbaugh, as counsel and agent for Defendants; state in substance any fact concerning this case which Defendants learned through oral statements made by witnesses to Mr. Fortenbaugh whether or not included in his private memoranda and produce Mr. Fortenbaugh's memoranda containing statements of fact by witnesses or to submit these memoranda to the Court for determination of those portions which should be revealed to Plaintiff." Upon their refusal, the court adjudged them in contempt and ordered them imprisoned until they complied.

The Third Circuit Court of Appeals, also sitting en banc, reversed the judgment of the District Court. It held that the information here sought was part of the "work product of the lawyer" and hence privileged from discovery under the Federal Rules of Civil Procedure. The importance of the problem, which has engendered a great divergence of views among district courts, led us to grant certiorari. . . .

In urging that he has a right to inquire into the materials secured and prepared by Fortenbaugh, petitioner emphasizes that the deposition-discovery portions of the Federal Rules of Civil Procedure are designed to enable the parties to discover the true facts and to compel their disclosure wherever they may be found. It is said that inquiry may be made under these rules . . . as to any relevant matter which is not privileged; and since the discovery provisions are to be applied as broadly and liberally as possible, the privilege limitation must be restricted to its narrowest bounds. On the premise that the attorney-client privilege is the one involved in this case, petitioner argues that it must be strictly confined to confidential communications made by a client to his attorney. And since the materials here in issue were secured by Fortenbaugh from third persons rather than from his clients, the tug owners, the conclusion is reached that these materials are proper subjects for discovery. . . .

As additional support for this result, petitioner claims that to prohibit discovery under these circumstances would give a corporate defendant a tremendous advantage in a suit by an individual plaintiff. Thus in a suit by an injured employee against a railroad or in a suit by an insured person against an insurance company the corporate defendant could pull a dark veil of secrecy over all the pertinent facts it can collect after the claim arises merely on the assertion that such facts were gathered by its large staff of attorneys and claim agents. At the same time, the individual plaintiff, who often has direct knowledge of the matter in issue and has no counsel until some time after his claim arises could be compelled to disclose all the intimate details of his case. By endowing with immunity from disclosure all that a lawyer discovers in the course of his duties, it is said, the rights of individual litigants in such cases are drained of vitality and the lawsuit becomes more of a battle of deception than a search for truth.

But framing the problem in terms of assisting individual plaintiffs in their suits against corporate defendants is unsatisfactory. Discovery concededly may work to the disadvantage as well as to the advantage of individual plaintiffs. Discovery, in other words, is not a one-way proposition. It is available in all types of cases at the behest of any party, individual or corporate, plaintiff or defendant. The problem thus far transcends the situation confronting this petitioner. And we must view that problem in light of the limitless situations where the particular kind of discovery sought by petitioner might be used.

We agree, of course, that the deposition-discovery rules are to be accorded a broad and liberal treatment. No longer can the time-honored cry of "fishing expedition" serve to preclude a party from inquiring into the facts underlying his opponent's case. Mutual knowledge of all the relevant facts gathered by both parties is essential to proper litigation. To that end, either party may compel the other to disgorge whatever facts he has in his possession. . . .

We also agree that the memoranda, statements and mental impressions in issue in this case fall outside the scope of the attorney-client privilege and hence are not protected from discovery on that basis. It is unnecessary here to delineate the content and scope of that privilege as recognized in the federal courts. For present purposes, it suffices to note that the protective cloak of this privilege does not extend to information which an attorney secures from a witness while acting for his client in anticipation of litigation. Nor does this privilege concern the memoranda, briefs, communications and other writings prepared by counsel for his own use in prosecuting his client's case; and it is equally unrelated to writings which reflect an attorney's mental impressions, conclusions, opinions or legal theories.

But the impropriety of invoking that privilege does not provide an answer to the problem before us. Petitioner has made more than an ordinary request for relevant, non-privileged facts in the possession of his adversaries or their counsel. He has sought discovery as of right of oral and written statements of witnesses whose identity is well known and whose availability to petitioner appears unimpaired. He has sought production of these matters after making the most searching inquiries of his opponents as to the circumstances surrounding the fatal accident, which inquiries were sworn to have been answered to the best of their information and belief. Interrogatories were directed toward all the events prior to, during and subsequent to the sinking of the tug. Full and honest answers to such broad inquiries would necessarily have included all pertinent information gleaned by Fortenbaugh through his interviews with the witnesses. Petitioner makes no suggestion, and we cannot assume, that the tug owners or Fortenbaugh were incomplete or dishonest in the framing of their answers. In addition, petitioner was free to examine the public testimony of the witnesses taken before the United States Steamboat Inspectors. We are thus dealing with an attempt to secure the production of written statements and mental impressions contained in the files and the mind of the attorney Fortenbaugh without any showing of necessity or any indication or claim that denial of such production would unduly prejudice the preparation of petitioner's case or cause him any hardship or injustice. For aught that appears, the essence of what petitioner seeks either has been revealed to him already through the interrogatories or is readily available to him direct from the witnesses for the asking. . . .

In our opinion, [none of the federal rules] dealing with discovery contemplates production under such circumstances. That is not because the subject matter is privileged or irrelevant, as those concepts are used in these rules. Here is simply an attempt, without purported necessity or justification, to secure written statements, private memoranda and personal recollections prepared or formed by an adverse party's counsel in the course of his legal duties. As such, it falls outside the arena of discovery and contravenes the public policy underlying the orderly prosecution and defense of legal claims. Not even the most liberal of discovery theories can justify unwarranted inquiries into the files and the mental impressions of an attorney.

Historically, a lawyer is an officer of the court and is bound to work for the advancement of justice while faithfully protecting the rightful interests of his clients. In performing his various duties, however, it is essential that a lawyer work with a certain degree of privacy, free from unnecessary intrusion by opposing parties and their counsel. Proper preparation of a client's case demands that he assemble information, sift what he considers to be the relevant from the irrelevant facts, prepare his legal theories and plan his strategy without undue and needless interference. That is the historical and the necessary way in which lawyers act within the framework of our system of jurisprudence to promote justice and to protect their clients' interests. This work is reflected, of course, in interviews, statements, memoranda, correspondence, briefs, mental impressions, personal beliefs, and countless other tangible and intangible ways — aptly though roughly termed by the Circuit Court of Appeals in this case as the "Work product of the lawyer." Were such materials open to opposing counsel on mere demand, much of what is now put down in writing would remain unwritten. An attorney's thoughts, heretofore inviolate, would not be his own. Inefficiency, unfairness and sharp practices would inevitably develop in the giving of legal advice and in the preparation of cases for trial. The effect on the legal profession would be demoralizing. And the interests of the clients and the cause of justice would be poorly served.

We do not mean to say that all written materials obtained or prepared by an adversary's counsel with an eye toward litigation are necessarily free from discovery in all cases. Where relevant and non-privileged facts remain hidden in an attorney's file and where production of those facts is essential to the preparation of one's case, discovery may properly be had. Such written statements and documents might, under certain circumstances, be admissible in evidence or give clues as to the existence or location of relevant facts. Or they might be useful for purposes of impeachment or corroboration. And production might be justified where the witnesses are no longer available or can be reached only with difficulty. Were production of written statements and documents to be precluded under such circumstances, the liberal ideals of the deposition-discovery portions of the Federal Rules of Civil Procedure would be stripped of much of their meaning. But the general policy against invading the privacy of an attorney's course of preparation is so well recognized and so essential to an orderly working of our system of legal procedure that a burden rests on the one who would invade that privacy to establish adequate reasons to justify production through a subpoena or court order. That burden, we believe, is necessarily implicit in the rules as now constituted.

[The federal rules give] the trial judge the requisite discretion to make a judgment as to whether discovery should be allowed as to written statements secured from witnesses. But in the instant case there was no room for that discretion to operate in favor of the petitioner. No attempt was made to establish any reason why Fortenbaugh should be forced to produce the written statements. There was only a naked, general demand for these materials as of right and a finding by the District Court that no recognizable privilege was involved. That was insufficient to justify discovery under these circumstances and the court should have sustained the refusal of the tug owners and Fortenbaugh to produce.

But as to oral statements made by witnesses to Fortenbaugh, whether presently in the form of his mental impressions or memoranda, we do not believe that any showing of necessity can be made under the circumstances of this case so as to justify production. Under ordinary conditions, forcing an attorney to repeat or write out all that witnesses have told him and to deliver the account to his adversary gives rise to grave dangers of inaccuracy and untrustworthiness. No legitimate purpose is served by such production. The practice forces the attorney to testify as to what he remembers or what he saw fit to write down regarding witnesses' remarks. Such testimony could not qualify as evidence; and to use it for impeachment or corroborative purposes would make the attorney much less an officer of the court and much more an ordinary witness. The standards of the profession would thereby suffer. . . .

Petitioner's counsel frankly admits that he wants the oral statements only to help prepare himself to examine witnesses and to make sure that he has overlooked nothing. That is insufficient under the circumstances to permit him an exception to the policy underlying the privacy of Fortenbaugh's professional activities. If there should be a rare situation justifying production of these matters, petitioner's case is not of that type.

We fully appreciate the wide-spread controversy among the members of the legal profession over the problem raised by this case. It is a problem that rests on what has been one of the most hazy frontiers of the discovery process. But until some rule or statute definitely prescribes otherwise, we are not justified in permitting discovery in a situation of this nature as a matter of unqualified right. . . .

Questions and Comments

1. Like *Upjohn*, this case involves an internal investigation conducted under the auspices of counsel, and accordingly is an important precedent for compliance-related internal investigations today.

2. The Court notes that plaintiff's counsel had access to all of the facts at issue through sources other than the attorney's notes and mental impressions. If so, why was counsel attempting to discover this information from attorney Fortenbaugh?

3. Why wasn't the information in question protected by the attorney-client privilege?

4. This case presented a potential conflict between the discovery provisions of the Federal Rules of Civil Procedure — at the time relatively newly enacted — and the traditional role of attorneys in uncovering information essential to their client's case. Prior to the enactment of these rules, inquiries of the sort at issue in the excerpted case would usually be rejected on the theory that they ranged too far afield and constituted a "fishing expedition." The federal rules, however, endorsed broad rights of discovery into any relevant and non-privileged matter, based on the theory that justice was best served if all parties in litigation had full knowledge of the facts. Given the mandate of the federal rules, and the fact that witness statements fell outside the traditional scope of attorney-client privilege, how did the Court conclude that the rules did not require the defendant to turn over the requested information?

5. Is the work-product protection recognized in the excerpted case as absolute as the attorney-client privilege? Consider, in this regard, the Court's statement that "[w]here relevant and non-privileged facts remain hidden in an attorney's file and where production of those facts is essential to the preparation of one's case, discovery may properly be had."

6. The work-product protection for federal litigation is codified in Federal Rule of Civil Procedure 26(b)(3)(A), which provides in pertinent part: "Ordinarily, a party may not discover documents and tangible things that are prepared in anticipation of litigation or for trial by or for another party or its representative (including the other party's attorney, consultant, surety, indemnitor, insurer, or agent)." But those materials may be discovered if "the party shows that it has substantial need for the materials to prepare its case and cannot, without undue hardship, obtain their substantial equivalent by other means."

7. To what extent is an attorney's work on compliance matters protected by the work-product rule? As noted in Rule 26(b)(3)(A), the privilege covers matters prepared "in anticipation of litigation or for trial." Thus ordinary compliance work, where there is no expectation of an adversarial proceeding, probably is not protected. The privilege does apply however, if there is some reasonable prospect of an adversarial proceeding, even if no charges have yet been brought.

8. Often attorneys need to consult outside experts in preparing a case for litigation, either on a consulting basis or as potential expert witnesses. Communications with experts were once not protected by the work-product doctrine. This led to many inefficient techniques for equipping the witness with the necessary knowledge without revealing information for which attorney-client privilege or work-product protection might be claimed, as well as efforts to avoid the preparation of any draft reports that might subsequently be discovered by the adversary. The federal rules now provide work-product protection both for drafts of expert reports by witnesses as well as for communications with expert witnesses other than: those relating to the expert's compensation; facts or data that the party's attorney provided and that the expert considered in forming the opinions to be expressed; and assumptions that the party's attorney provided and that the expert relied on in forming her opinions. Federal Rule of Civil Procedure 26(b)(4).

9. As in the case of attorney-client privilege, the rules applicable to work-product protection may vary from jurisdiction to jurisdiction; the various states do not necessarily track the federal rules discussed above.

10. Like the attorney-client privilege, the work-product protection is subject to an exception for materials prepared in furtherance of a crime or fraud.

PROBLEM 9-7

Metalco operates smelters used in the production of iron, copper, and lead. The company learns that a TV reporter is producing an exposé of the company's alleged violations of environmental laws. Belinda Burke, Metalco's general counsel, hires an environmental consulting firm to perform an investigation of the smelting operations. Her purpose is to have data on hand to use in rebutting the story when it airs. Unfortunately, the consultant concludes that the journalist's allegations are substantially accurate. For obvious reasons, Burke decides not use the report. Within weeks the company is sued by an environmental organization. The plaintiff learns about report and files a discovery demand that Burke turn it over. Must she do so?

6. Waiver of Privilege

Although the attorney-client privilege is a matter of profound importance to clients and attorneys alike, it is easily lost. Perhaps the most common situation where communications otherwise privileged are subject to compelled production in legal proceedings is when the client waives her rights. As long as the waiver is voluntary, it will be enforced—the theory being that if the client elects to forgo the benefits of a privilege, the law should not stand in her way. The following excerpt sets forth the policy of the U.S. Department of Justice on privilege waivers in criminal prosecutions of business organizations.

United States Attorneys Manual, Principles of Federal Prosecution of Business Organizations

2015

9-28.710 Attorney-Client and Work Product Protections

The attorney-client privilege and the attorney work product protection serve an extremely important function in the American legal system. The attorney-client privilege is one of the oldest and most sacrosanct privileges under the law. *See Upjohn v. United States*, 449 U.S. 383, 389 (1981). As the Supreme Court has stated, "[i]ts purpose is to encourage full and frank communication between attorneys and their clients and thereby promote broader public interests in the observance of law and administration of justice." *Id.* The value of promoting a corporation's ability to seek frank and comprehensive legal advice is particularly important in the contemporary global business environment, where corporations often face complex and dynamic legal and regulatory obligations imposed by the federal government and also by states and foreign governments. The work product doctrine serves similarly important goals.

For these reasons, waiving the attorney-client and work product protections has never been a prerequisite under the Department's prosecution guidelines for a corporation to be viewed as cooperative. Nonetheless, a wide range of commentators and members of the American legal community and criminal justice system have asserted that the Department's policies have been used, either wittingly or unwittingly, to coerce business entities into waiving attorney-client privilege and work-product protection. Everyone agrees that a corporation may freely waive its own privileges if it chooses to do so; indeed, such waivers occur routinely when corporations are victimized by their employees or others, conduct an internal investigation, and then disclose the details of the investigation to law enforcement officials in an effort to seek prosecution of the offenders. However, the contention, from a broad array of voices, is that the Department's position on attorney-client privilege and work product protection waivers has promoted an environment in which those protections are being unfairly eroded to the detriment of all.

The Department understands that the attorney-client privilege and attorney work product protection are essential and long-recognized components of the American legal system. What the government seeks and needs to advance its legitimate (indeed, essential) law enforcement mission is not waiver of those protections, but rather the facts known to the corporation about the putative criminal misconduct under review. In addition, while a corporation remains free to convey nonfactual or "core" attorney-client communications or work product — if and only if the corporation voluntarily chooses to do so — prosecutors should not ask for such waivers and are directed not to do so. The critical factor is whether the corporation has provided the facts about the events, as explained further herein.

Questions and Comments

1. The policy excerpted above is the product of a contentious process in which law enforcement interests initially sought to erode the protections of the attorney-client and work-product privileges, and then softened their position in the face of opposition from lawyers, civil libertarians, and others.

2. What is wrong with a prosecutor demanding that a target waive attorney-client or work-product privileges as a condition for refraining from seeking an indictment or recommending leniency in sentencing? Prosecutors can and do play "hardball" with criminal defendants in other respects; they have no compunction, for example, about threatening to impose ruinous penalties on the target of a criminal investigation unless she cooperates by providing information on other suspects. What is different about seeking a waiver of attorney privileges?

3. The Sixth Amendment guarantees criminal suspects the effective assistance of counsel. Is someone denied the effective assistance of counsel when the prosecution threatens to bring the full force of the law against someone who refuses to waive attorney-client or work-product privileges?

4. The United States Attorneys Manual applies to criminal prosecutions. Should similar policies apply when the action is brought by a regulator seeking only civil fines or other sanctions?

5. For more on the Justice Department's policy on privilege waivers, see Lance Cole, *Revoking Our Privileges: Federal Law Enforcement's Multi-Front Assault on the Attorney-Client Privilege (and Why It Is Misguided)*, 48 Vill. L. Rev. 469 (2003); Christopher T. Hines, *Returning to First Principles of Privilege Law: Focusing on the Facts in Internal Corporate Investigations*, 60 U. Kan. L. Rev. 33 (2011); Gregory C. Sisk & Pamela J. Abbate, *The Dynamic Attorney-Client Privilege*, 23 Geo. J. Legal Ethics 201 (2010); Julie R. O'Sullivan, *Does DOJ's Privilege Waiver Policy Threaten the Rationales Underlying the Attorney-Client Privilege and Work Product Doctrine? A Preliminary "No,"* 45 Am. Crim. L. Rev. 1237 (2008).

6. A controversy that paralleled in some respects the debate over privilege waivers in prosecutions concerns the policies applied in sentencing. The federal Sentencing Guidelines once took waivers of privilege into account as a positive factor that could reduce the severity of a sentence. That statement was deleted from the guidelines in 2006. *See* USSG §8C2.5(g), comment, n.12. The guidelines continue, however, to reduce the corporation's offense level as a reward for voluntary disclosure of information. *See* USSG §8C2.5(g).

Attorneys are often brought into the picture when a client is suspected of wrongdoing. As *Upjohn* makes clear, communications with the attorney pursuant to the investigation will likely be privileged. Once the government has focused on a particular client as a potential target of enforcement actions, however, the company may wish to demonstrate a cooperative attitude towards the government by sharing the results of its internal investigation. The problem is that in sharing the results of its investigation the company may also be waiving the privilege. Can this tension be resolved?

The Department of Justice has this advice in connection with the decision whether to prosecute an organization:

United States Attorneys Manual, Principles of Federal Prosecution of Business Organizations

2015

9-28.720 Cooperation: Disclosing the Relevant Facts
  (b) Legal Advice and Attorney Work Product
Separate from (and usually preceding) the fact-gathering process in an internal investigation, a corporation, through its officers, employees, directors, or others, may have consulted with corporate counsel regarding or in a manner that concerns the legal implications of the putative misconduct at issue. Communications of this sort, which are both independent of the fact-gathering component of an internal investigation and made for the purpose of seeking or dispensing legal advice, lie at the core of the attorney-client privilege. Such communications can naturally have a salutary effect on corporate behavior — facilitating, for example, a corporation's effort to comply with complex and evolving legal and regulatory regimes. [A corporation generally] need not disclose and prosecutors may not request the disclosure of such communications as a condition for the corporation's eligibility to receive cooperation credit.

Likewise, non-factual or core attorney work product — for example, an attorney's mental impressions or legal theories — lies at the core of the attorney work product doctrine. A corporation need not disclose, and prosecutors may not request, the disclosure of such attorney work product as a condition for the corporation's eligibility to receive cooperation credit.

Questions and Comments

1. Did the Justice Department go too far in refraining from seeking voluntary disclosure of communications with counsel in connection with internal investigations?

2. The Manual does not prevent a target from volunteering attorney-client information, even if the prosecutors have not requested it. If a target volunteers the information, can the prosecutors accept the offer?

7. Reliance on Counsel

The attorney-client privilege and work-product protection provide significant advantages to attorneys as service providers in compliance matters. Communications between people in the organization and counsel to the organization will generally be protected if connected with the provision of legal advice; and the attorney's own notes, research, and memoranda will generally be protected if prepared in contemplation of legal proceedings. For these reasons, it may be advisable for organizations to include an attorney on all significant compliance-related communications and to place an attorney in charge of compliance-related internal investigations. The value of an attorney doesn't end there, however. Attorneys can also provide a potential shield against liability, under the "advice of counsel" theory.

The advice of counsel defense applies to allegations of misconduct that require the government to establish that the defendant acted with some sort of culpable mental state. Charged with an offense, the defendant can argue that she had sought the advice of counsel and counsel assured her that the contemplated actions were legally permissible. Because defendant's reliance on counsel's advice negates the culpable mental state that is an element of the offense, the advice-of-counsel theory is not technically an affirmative defense, but rather a refutation of an element of the government's case-in-chief.

Questions and Comments

1. If there are facts known to the defendant but not disclosed to the attorney, this circumstance will both tend to negate the defendant's good faith and also undermine the reliability of the attorney's advice. Thus, to obtain the benefit of the advice-of-counsel theory, the defendant must establish that she fully informed the attorney of all the facts material to the proposed course of action.

2. A downside of the advice-of-counsel theory is that it waives the client's attorney-client privilege at least for the advice given. If the client advances the theory, moreover, the government is likely to argue that the waiver extends beyond the specific circumstances.

3. What happens if the party raising an advice-of-counsel defense is an individually charged corporate employee, and the lawyer whose advice is involved is an attorney for the corporation? Can the individual defendant waive the corporation's attorney-client privilege?

4. How should prosecutors assess a target's claim of reliance on counsel at the time they make the charging decision? If they simply accept the claim at face value, they may allow wrongdoers to hide behind the defense and thereby get away with criminal misconduct. If they insist on documentation, they risk invading the privilege. The Justice Department's United States Attorneys Manual has this to say:

> Occasionally a corporation or one of its employees may assert an advice-of-counsel defense, based upon communications with in-house or outside counsel that took

place prior to or contemporaneously with the underlying conduct at issue. In such situations, the defendant must tender a legitimate factual basis to support the assertion of the advice-of-counsel defense. The Department cannot fairly be asked to discharge its responsibility to the public to investigate alleged corporate crime, or to temper what would otherwise be the appropriate course of prosecutive action, by simply accepting on faith an otherwise unproven assertion that an attorney — perhaps even an unnamed attorney — approved potentially unlawful practices. Accordingly, where an advice-of-counsel defense has been asserted, prosecutors may ask for the disclosure of the communications allegedly supporting it.

United States Attorneys Manual 9-28.720(b)(i).

Is this an appropriate resolution of the problem? If the prosecutors demand the production of the communications allegedly supporting the advice-of-counsel defense, is this tantamount to demanding a waiver of privilege? Would the prosecutors be entitled to demand such a waiver, given that the target is the one who is putting communications with counsel into the decision process?

C. ACCOUNTANTS

Accountants provide services to organizations in their internal financial management. Like lawyers, accountants are professionally obligated to exercise independence and objectivity in the performance of their responsibilities. One goal of professional independence and objectivity is to protect the public interest: The Code of Professional Conduct of the American Institute of Certified Public Accountants recognizes that "[a] distinguishing mark of a profession is acceptance of its responsibility to the public. The accounting profession's public consists of clients, credit grantors, governments, employers, investors, the business and financial community, and others who rely on the objectivity and integrity of certified public accountants to maintain the orderly functioning of commerce. This reliance imposes a public interest responsibility on certified public accountants. The public interest is defined as the collective well-being of the community of people and institutions the profession serves."

The line between the accountant's duty to the client and her duty to serve the public interest is sometimes difficult to draw. Accounting standards are not applied with mathematical precision; there is often room for judgment in how particular events or transactions should be characterized. In performing services for clients, an accountant is entitled and expected to advocate for a favorable reading of applicable rules. At some point, however, advocacy threatens the objectivity and independence of the accountant's judgment. Where that point lies is a difficult question.

Recent decades have witnessed a slow evolution in the concept of the accountant's duties, with a change in the direction of highlighting the accountant's duty to the public and downplaying the expectation that the accountant will serve as a zealous advocate of the client. In the United States, however, the zealous advocacy norm is still the prevailing approach to the professional duties of accountants.

The same may not be true in the United Kingdom. The Institute of Chartered Accountants in England and Wales requires accountants to consider the public interest when performing services for clients. In 2013, a dispute resolution tribunal considered charges against Deloitte LLP, an accounting and consulting firm, and Maghsoud Einollahi, a retired Deloitte partner. The defendants had provided professional services in connection with financing transactions involving MG Rover Group, a British carmaker which had come under the control of four investors (the "Phoenix Four") after it was split off from BMW. Several years after the Phoenix Four took over, Rover collapsed amid allegations the controllers had looted the company at the expense of public investors. Deloitte and Maghsoud were charged with having facilitated their improper behavior.

The tribunal found the following allegations (among others) to have been established:

In relation to a scheme to transfer MG Rover Group's tax losses to a company indirectly controlled by the "Phoenix Four" and enabling substantial payments to be made for the benefit of the Phoenix Four, Deloitte & Touche and Einollahi:

- Failed to consider the public interest as corporate advisers to the Phoenix Four.
- Failed to identify and consider conflicts of interest between the MG Rover Group, Phoenix Venture Holdings, and the Phoenix Four.
- Failed to make it clear to MG Rover Group that Deloitte did not represent them or act in their interests.
- Failed to put in place safeguards between MG Rover Group and the Phoenix Four, including advising MG Rover Group to seek independent advice.
- Wrongly used an old letter of engagement from another project.
- Failed to identify, consider, and safeguard against the self-interest threat of earning a large contingent fee.

Based on these findings, the tribunal fined Deloitte £14 million ($22 million). In justifying the sanction, the tribunal remarked that "[i]t has been put to us that in corporate finance work and tax work the only duty that a member owes is to his client, provided that he acts with integrity, and that the public interest is not a matter that needs to concern him. We do not accept this."

Should Congress or regulatory agencies in the United States require accountants to take greater account of the public interest when performing services for public companies? What are the pros or cons of imposing such a rule?

D. AUDITORS

1. Introduction

External auditors have long played a key role in compliance. Their job, traditionally, is to check up on a firm's financial reporting and to certify to investors and others that the books are up to snuff.

Auditors and accountants have similar background and training but perform different tasks as far as compliance is concerned. Accountants perform services for organizations in preparing financial statements, tax returns, and other financial documents and reports; auditors conduct an independent review of the company's financial statements and controls. Unlike accountants, who owe duties to their clients, auditors owe their principal duties to investors or other third parties who rely on the integrity of the financial statement that the auditor has reviewed.

The Supreme Court recognized the public role of the independent auditor in the following terms: "By certifying the public reports that collectively depict a corporation's financial status, the independent auditor assumes a public responsibility transcending any employment relationship with the client. The independent public accountant performing this special function owes ultimate allegiance to the corporation's creditors and stockholders, as well as to the investing public. This 'public watchdog' function demands that the accountant maintain total independence from the client at all times and requires complete fidelity to the public trust." United States v. Arthur Young & Co., 465 U.S. 805, 817-818 (1984).

The auditing profession was self-regulated for many years. The Sarbanes-Oxley Act ended that era in the case of public companies. This statute established a new agency, the Public Company Accounting Oversight Board (PCAOB), and empowered it to exercise regulatory authority over public company auditors. PCAOB's authority includes the power to establish auditing standards, to inspect public company auditors for quality and compliance purposes, to investigate allegations of misconduct, and to impose disciplinary sanctions on auditing firms found to have violated the rules. Sarbanes-Oxley changed the oversight of public company auditors in another way as well. By requiring that all public companies host audit committees composed entirely of independent board members, the statute empowered independent directors to select, compensate, and monitor their company's auditor.

PCAOB, Proposed Auditing Standards — The Auditor's Report on an Audit of Financial Statements When the Auditor Expresses an Unqualified Opinion

Release No. 2013-005 (Aug. 13, 2013)

The auditor's report is the primary means by which the auditor communicates with investors and other financial statement users information regarding his or her audit of the financial statements. As it exists today, the auditor's report identifies the financial statements that were audited, describes the nature of an audit, and presents the auditor's opinion as to whether the financial statements present fairly, in all material respects, the financial position, results of operations, and cash flows of the company in conformity with the applicable financial reporting framework. This type of auditor's report has been commonly described as a pass/fail model because the auditor opines on whether the financial statements are fairly presented (pass) or not (fail).

The auditor's report in the United States has changed very little since the 1940s. The existing pass/fail model is thought by many to be useful because it provides a clear indication of whether the financial statements are presented fairly. However, while the existing auditor's report provides important information about an audit in general, it does not provide information that is specific to a particular audit.

Academic research suggests that investors and other financial statement users refer to the existing auditor's report only to determine whether the opinion is unqualified because it does not provide any other informational value about the particular audit. During the Board's outreach activities over the last three years, many investors have expressed dissatisfaction that the content of the existing auditor's report provides little, if any, information specific to the audit of the company's financial statements to investors or other financial statement users. During a financial statement audit, auditors obtain and evaluate important information concerning the company, the company's environment, and the preparation of the company's financial statements. Many investors have indicated that they would benefit from additional auditor reporting because they do not have access to, or may not be aware of, much of this information. Additionally, many investors indicated that auditors have unique and relevant insight based on their audits and that auditors should provide information about their insights in the auditor's report to make the reports more relevant and useful. . . .

Briefly, the Board's proposed auditor reporting standard would retain the pass/fail model, including the basic elements of the current auditor's report, and would provide more information to investors and other financial statement users regarding the audit and the auditor. Most significantly, the proposed auditor reporting standard would require the auditor to communicate in the auditor's report "critical audit matters" that would be specific to each audit. The auditor's required communication would focus on those matters the auditor addressed during the audit of the financial statements that involved the most difficult, subjective, or complex auditor judgments or posed the most difficulty to the auditor in obtaining sufficient appropriate audit evidence or forming an opinion on the financial statements.

The auditor's report as currently designed, and as confirmed by academic research, conveys to investors and other financial statement users little of the information obtained and evaluated by the auditor. The proposed auditor reporting standard is intended to provide investors and other financial statement users with potentially valuable information that investors have expressed interest in receiving but have not had access to in the past.

Requiring auditors to communicate critical audit matters could help investors and other financial statement users focus on aspects of the company's financial statements that the auditor also found to be challenging. Communicating critical audit matters would provide investors and other financial statement users with previously unknown information about the audit that could enable them to analyze more closely any related financial statement accounts and disclosures. The communication of critical audit matters could help to alleviate the information asymmetry that exists between company management and investors. More specifically, company management is typically aware of the auditor's most challenging areas in the audit because of regular interactions with the auditor as part of the audit, but this information is not usually known to investors. Reducing the level of information asymmetry between company management and investors could result in more efficient capital allocation and, as academic research has shown, could lower the average cost of capital. . . .

Questions and Comments

1. Audit reports have long been criticized for being short on detail. When an external auditor issues an unqualified report, that document has typically been accompanied by little other than the disclosure that the audit firm did not uncover material weaknesses in the company's financial reporting or internal controls.

2. Do you agree with the decision to maintain a "pass/fail" reporting system, in which the auditor generally gives a thumbs-up or thumbs-down evaluation but doesn't provide extensive detail about its findings?

3. Although in general PCAOB proposes to keep the existing system in place, it does propose a significant upgrade to auditor reporting in connection with critical audit matters — subjects that involve difficult auditor judgments or pose problems

for the auditor in obtaining evidence sufficient to form an opinion. Is this desirable? Would the result be to better inform investors, or to confuse them by swamping them with technical and arcane detail about the audit process or the complex judgments an auditor may have made in evaluating the characterization of financial reporting matters?

4. The disclosures required under the proposed standard would place the auditor in the potentially uncomfortable position of making original disclosures of information internal to an audit client. This would represent a change from existing practice, where the audit client is the one expected (and sometimes required) to disclose details of its operations and financial condition. Should the rules allow the audit client to control disclosures of company-specific information?

5. Suppose the audit firm gives an unqualified opinion but includes extensive discussion of critical audit matters. To what extent will this undermine the credibility of the auditor's global judgment that the company's financial reporting and controls are adequate?

6. Could the new standard undermine the audit process by impairing the willingness of auditors to communicate frankly with management regarding concerns or difficulties encountered during the audit process?

7. The European Union has also expanded the scope of audit reports. Auditors are required to describe the most significant assessed risks of material misstatement, including assessed risks of material misstatement due to fraud; summarize their response to those risks; and, if relevant, offer observations or explanations. The report must also express an opinion on management's non-financial statements contained in the annual report: whether the report is consistent with the financial statements for the same financial year; whether the report has been prepared in accordance with the applicable legal requirements; and whether, in the light of the knowledge obtained in the course of the audit, the auditor has identified material misstatements in the report.

8. In the U.K., audit reports must describe how and why audit resources were allocated in the engagement; explain how the auditor applied the concept of materiality in planning and performing the audit; and explain the scope of the audit, including an explanation of how the scope addressed the risk and materiality considerations.

9. PCAOB reissued its proposal in 2016 after receiving a flood of comments; as this edition is being written, it is not clear when a final rule can be expected.

Modern regulation of the audit process has been shaped, in part, by the disaster that occurred to Arthur Andersen in connection with the auditing and other services it provided to Enron Corporation. The following excerpt reflects one of the key episodes that changed the concept of the relationship between auditors and their clients — at least if the clients are publicly traded firms.

United States District Court
Southern District of Texas

_____ X

United States of America
- against -   INDICTMENT
Arthur Andersen, LLP _____ X

ANDERSEN AND ENRON

Arthur Andersen, LLP ("Andersen"), is a partnership that performs, among other things, accounting and consulting services for clients that operate businesses throughout the United States and the world. Andersen is one of the so-called "Big Five" accounting firms in the United States. Andersen has its headquarters in Chicago, Illinois, and maintains offices throughout the world, including in Houston, Texas.

Enron Corp. ("Enron") was an Oregon corporation with its principal place of business in Houston, Texas. For most of 2001, Enron was considered the seventh largest corporation in the United States based on its reported revenues. In the previous ten years, Enron had evolved from a regional natural gas provider to, among other things, a trader of natural gas, electricity and other commodities, with retail operations in energy and other products.

For the past 16 years, up until it filed for bankruptcy in December 2001, Enron retained Andersen to be its auditor. Enron was one of Andersen's largest clients worldwide, and became Andersen's largest client in Andersen's Gulf Coast Region. Andersen earned tens of millions of dollars from Enron in annual auditing and other fees.

Andersen performed both internal and external auditing work for Enron mainly in Houston, Texas. Andersen established within Enron's offices in Houston a work space for the Andersen team that had primary responsibility for performing audit work for Enron. In addition to Houston, Andersen personnel performed work for Enron in, among other locations, Chicago, Illinois, Portland, Oregon, and London, England.

THE ANTICIPATION OF LITIGATION AGAINST ENRON AND ANDERSEN

In the summer and fall of 2001, a series of significant developments led to Andersen's foreseeing imminent civil litigation against, and government investigations of, Enron and Andersen.

On or about October 16, 2001, Enron issued a press release announcing a $618 million net loss for the third quarter of 2001. That same day, but not as part of the press release, Enron announced to analysts that it would reduce shareholder equity by approximately $1.2 billion. The market reacted immediately and the stock price of Enron shares plummeted.

The Securities and Exchange Commission ("SEC"), which investigates possible violation of the federal securities laws, opened an inquiry into Enron the very next day, requesting in writing information from Enron.

In addition to the negative financial information disclosed by Enron to the public and to analysts on October 16, 2001, Andersen was aware by this time of additional significant facts unknown to the public.

- The approximately $1.2 billion reduction on shareholder equity disclosed to analysts on October 16, 2001 was necessitated by Andersen and Enron having previously improperly categorized hundreds of millions of dollars as an *increase*, rather than a decrease, to Enron shareholder equity.
- The Enron October 16, 2001, press release characterized numerous charges against income for the third quarter as "non-recurring" even though Andersen believed the company did not have a fair basis for concluding that the charges would in fact be non-recurring. Indeed, Andersen advised Enron

against using that term, and documented its objections internally in the event of litigation, but did not report its objections or otherwise take steps to cure the public statement.

- Andersen was put on direct notice of the allegations of Sherron Watkins, a current Enron employee and former Andersen employee, regarding possible fraud and other improprieties at Enron, and in particular, Enron's use of off-balance-sheet "special purpose entities" that enabled the company to camouflage the true financial condition of the company. Watkins had reported her concerns to a partner at Andersen, who thereafter disseminated them within Andersen, including to the team working on the Enron audit. In addition the team had received warnings about possible undisclosed side-agreements at Enron.

- The Andersen team handling the Enron audit directly contravened the accounting methodology approved by Andersen's own specialists working in its Professional Standards Group. In opposition to the views of its own experts, the Andersen auditors had advised Enron in the spring of 2001 that it could use a favorable accounting method [for] its "special purpose entities."

- In 2000, an internal review conducted by senior management within Andersen evaluated the Andersen team assigned to audit Enron and rated the team only a "2" on a scale of five, with five being the highest rating.

- On or about October 9, 2001, correctly anticipating litigation and government investigations, Andersen, which had an internal department of lawyers for routine legal matters, retained an experienced New York law firm to handle future Enron-related litigation.

The Wholesale Destruction of Documents by Andersen

By Friday, October 19, 2001, Enron alerted the Andersen audit team that the SEC had begun an inquiry regarding the Enron "special purpose entities" and the involvement of Enron's Chief Financial Officer. The next morning, an emergency conference call among high-level Andersen management was convened to address the SEC inquiry. During the call, it was decided that documentation that could assist Enron in responding to the SEC was to be assembled by the Enron auditors.

After spending Monday, October 22, 2001 at Enron, Andersen partners assigned to the Enron engagement team launched on October 23, 2001, a wholesale destruction of documents at Andersen's offices in Houston, Texas. Andersen personnel were called to urgent and mandatory meetings. Instead of being advised to preserve documentation so as to assist Enron and the SEC, Andersen employees on the Enron engagement team were instructed by Andersen partners and others to destroy immediately documentation relating to Enron, and told to work overtime if necessary to accomplish the destruction. During the next few weeks, an unparalleled initiative was undertaken to shred physical documentation and delete computer files. Tons of paper relating to the Enron audit were promptly shredded as part of the orchestrated document destruction. The shredder at the Andersen office at the Enron building was used virtually constantly and, to handle the overload, dozens of large trunks filled with Enron documents were sent to Andersen's main Houston office to be shredded. A systematic effort was also undertaken and carried out to purge the computer hard-drives and E-mail system of Enron-related files.

In addition to shredding and deleting documents in Houston, Texas, instructions were given to Andersen personnel working on Enron audit matters in

Portland, Oregon, Chicago Illinois, and London, England, to make sure that Enron documents were destroyed there as well. Indeed, in London, a coordinated effort by Anderson partners and others, similar to the initiative undertaken in Houston, was put into place to destroy Enron-related documents within days of notice of the SEC inquiry. Enron-related documents were also destroyed by Andersen partners in Chicago.

On or about November 8, 2001, the SEC served Andersen with the anticipated subpoena relating to its work for Enron. In response, members of the Andersen team on the Enron audit were alerted finally that there could be "no more shredding" because the firm had been "officially served" for documents.

THE CHARGE: OBSTRUCTION OF JUSTICE

On or about and between October 10, 2001, and November 9, 2001, within the Southern District of Texas and elsewhere, including Chicago, Illinois, Portland, Oregon, and London, England, Andersen, through its partners and others, did knowingly, intentionally and corruptly persuade and attempt to persuade other persons, to wit: Andersen employees with intent to cause and induce such persons to (a) withhold records, documents and other objections from official proceedings namely: regulatory and criminal proceedings and investigations, and (b) alter, destroy, mutilate and conceal objects with intent to impair the objects' integrity and availability for use in such official proceedings.

(Title 18, United States Code, Sections 1512(b)(2) and 3551 et seq.)

A TRUE BILL
_____
Foreperson

Questions and Comments

1. Arthur Andersen, prior to these events, was one of the largest accounting and auditing companies in the world. After Enron collapsed in 2001, prosecutors took a hard look at the services Andersen had provided to its longtime audit client. Although they may have hoped to bring more serious charges, in the end the indictment alleged only that Andersen obstructed justice by destroying documents. A jury convicted the firm, and it quickly ceased to do business. Several years later the Supreme Court reversed the conviction, Arthur Andersen LLP v. United States, 544 U.S. 696 (2005), but the victory came too late to rescue the company. Further discussion of the Enron case can be found in Chapter 17.

2. When the relationship between an external auditor and an audited firm becomes too extensive, there is a danger that the close connection will erode the auditor's independence. Do you see anything in the indictment reproduced above that suggests a concern that Andersen had crossed the line? The indictment noted that Andersen's accountants had established a work space in Enron's offices; that Enron was one of Andersen's largest clients worldwide and its single largest client in the Gulf Coast Region; and that Andersen earned tens of millions of dollars from Enron in annual auditing and other fees. What is the relevance of these allegations to the charge that Andersen had engaged in an obstruction of justice?

3. Largely in response to the Enron scandal and perceptions that Arthur Andersen had some culpability in the events, the Sarbanes-Oxley Act prohibited an

accounting firm from acting as the external auditor of a public company during the same period that the firm provides internal audit outsourcing and certain other services to the company. Even for permitted services, the audit committee of the board must approve in advance if the auditing firm is retained to perform services other than the external audit.

4. Can you see the advantage of an auditor remaining on an account for a substantial period of time? Perhaps a longstanding relationship will give the auditor a deeper understanding of the client — its business, its practices, its history, and above all the character and predilections of its senior officers. On the other hand, are there disadvantages? Too much familiarity can generate cozy, overly familiar relations between an auditor and its client that could lead to suspicious conduct going unquestioned. In the worst case, the auditor might be in on a fraud: Here the lack of rotation in the auditing firms will prevent a new set of eyes checking out the books. How do you draw this tradeoff?

2. Independence Requirements

A major concern of the Sarbanes-Oxley Act was the perception that audit firms, although ostensibly independent, were in fact beholden to the clients who selected them and paid their fees. To address this concern, the Act and implementing PCAOB regulations contain several measures intended to enhance public company auditor independence:

- The audit committee (which must be composed of independent directors) is responsible for the selection, compensation, and oversight of the external auditor (SOX §301).
- Audit firms are prohibited from providing the following services to their audit clients during the course of their audit engagement: (1) bookkeeping or other services related to the accounting records or financial statements of the audit client; (2) financial information systems design and implementation; (3) appraisal or valuation services, fairness opinions, or contribution-in-kind reports; (4) actuarial services; (5) internal audit outsourcing services; (6) management or human resources functions; (7) broker or dealer, investment adviser, or investment banking services; (8) legal services and expert services unrelated to the audit; and (9) any other service that PCAOB determines to be impermissible (id. §201).
- The audit committee must pre-approve all auditing services as well as all non-auditing services provided by the independent auditor (id. §202).
- Lead audit partners must rotate off the engagement every five years (§203).
- The auditor must report the following information to the audit committee: (1) all critical accounting policies and practices to be used; (2) all alternative treatments of financial information within generally accepted accounting principles that have been discussed with management officials of the issuer, ramifications of the use of such alternative disclosures and treatments, and the treatment preferred by the auditor; and (3) other material written communications between the audit firm and the management of the issuer, such as any management letter or schedule of unadjusted differences (id. §204).
- An audit firm may not provide specified services if the client's chief executive officer, controller, chief financial officer, chief accounting officer, or other individual serving in an equivalent position, was employed by the audit firm

and worked on the company's audit during the one year before the start of the audit services (id. §206).

Questions and Comments

1. United States firms have tended to stick with the same auditor for many years. Goldman Sachs has used PwC as its auditor since 1926; Caterpillar has used PwC since 1925. And these are far from the longest auditor relationships: General Electric has used KPMG since 1909; Procter & Gamble has used Deloitte since 1890 — the year that shredded wheat entered the American diet and the fire alarm was invented. Long auditor tenures such as these have come under fire as compromising independence, but as yet few companies have replaced their long-standing auditors for this reason.

2. While U.S. law requires rotation of audit partners, it does not require rotation of audit firms. A company can comply with this statute simply by getting a new audit partner. How effective will partner rotation be at ensuring auditor independence?

3. Some corporate governance advocates have called for mandatory rotation of the audit firm. Do you favor such a reform? What are the pros and cons?

4. In 2011, PCAOB ramped up debate on this issue by issuing a concept release that noted that "the time has come to again explore mandatory auditor rotation." The initiative sparked resistance by audit firms and managers of large corporations, including efforts to enact a statute that would prohibit PCAOB from issuing a rule on the topic. So far the proposal has not been implemented.

5. Although the United States has resisted the idea, mandatory audit firm rotation is already a reality in parts of Europe. France and Italy have implemented auditor term limits of six and nine years, respectively, and the European Parliament has considered imposing a 14-year limit. In 2013, the United Kingdom's Corporate Governance Code, which applies to large listed companies, was revised to call for re-contracting with the external auditor every ten years. However, it is not clear whether this provision calls for mandatory rotation of auditors or only a re-tender of the contract, which could lead to the existing auditor being retained. In April 2014, the European Parliament voted to require all European companies to rotate auditors. Listed companies and banks ("public interest entities") will be required to replace their auditors every ten years, but can defer if they put the audit contract up for bid or if they retain a co-auditor. The new rules also limit the consulting services audit firms can provide for their European audit clients. The move cut back on the initial proposal, which would have required companies to rotate auditors every six years.

6. In 2015, the SEC announced that it was considering regulations to improve audit quality, including a proposal to require listed firms to disclose the length of their relationships with their existing auditors. In your opinion, would such disclosure be a good idea? Does it go far enough?

3. Attestation of Internal Controls

Section 404(b) of the Sarbanes-Oxley act requires the auditor to attest to, and report on, management's assessment of its internal controls over financial reporting required under §404(a) (see Chapter 3). In performing this function, the auditor must employ a framework for evaluation. In practice, American public accounting firms employ the framework for internal control promulgated by the Committee of Sponsoring Organizations of the Treadway Commission (COSO). PCAOB sets forth the standards for audits of internal controls in Auditing Standard No. 5, An Audit of Internal Control over Financial Reporting That Is Integrated with an Audit of Financial Statements.

Applying a suitable evaluative framework, the auditor is responsible for assessing whether there are "deficiencies" in internal control over financial reporting. A deficiency exists when "the design or operation of a control does not allow management or employees, in the normal course of performing their assigned functions, to prevent or detect misstatements on a timely basis." Auditing Standard No. 5, Appendix A3.

- Deficiencies can exist both in the design and in the operation of internal controls. A deficiency in design exists when "(a) a control necessary to meet the control objective is missing or (b) an existing control is not properly designed so that, even if the control operates as designed, the control objective is not always met."
- A deficiency in operation exists when "a properly designed control does not operate as designed, or when the person performing the control does not possess the necessary authority or qualifications to perform the control effectively."

If deficiencies of design or operation are found, the auditor must determine how serious the problem is. Some deficiencies are relatively minor and need not be elevated to senior management. More serious is a "significant" deficiency, which is a deficiency, or a combination of deficiencies, in internal control over financial reporting that is less severe than a material weakness, yet important enough to merit attention by those responsible for the company's financial reporting. PCAOB Auditing Standard No. 5, Appendix A11.

Even more serious deficiencies, or combinations of deficiencies, are deemed to constitute a "material weaknesses" in the system of internal controls. A "material weakness" is "a deficiency, or a combination of deficiencies, in internal control over financial reporting, such that there is a reasonable possibility that a material misstatement of the company's annual or interim financial statements will not be prevented or detected on a timely basis." Id. A7.

PCAOB provides helpful examples of situations that would call for a material weakness conclusion. One, involving controls over financial transactions between affiliated companies, is described as follows:

The company processes a significant number of intercompany transactions on a monthly basis. Intercompany transactions relate to a wide range of activities, including transfers of inventory with intercompany profit between business units, allocation of research and development costs to business units and corporate charges. Individual intercompany transactions are frequently material.

A formal management policy requires monthly reconciliation of intercompany accounts and confirmation of balances between business units. However, there is not a process in place to ensure that these procedures are performed on a consistent basis. As a result, reconciliations of intercompany accounts are not performed on a timely basis, and differences in intercompany accounts are frequent and significant. Management does not perform any alternative controls to investigate significant intercompany account differences.

Based only on these facts, the auditor should determine that this deficiency represents a material weakness for the following reasons: The magnitude of a financial statement misstatement resulting from this deficiency would reasonably be expected to be material, because individual intercompany transactions are frequently material and relate to a wide range of activities. Additionally, actual un-reconciled differences in intercompany accounts have been, and are, material. The likelihood of such a misstatement is more than remote because such misstatements have frequently occurred and compensating controls are not effective, either because they are not properly designed or not operating effectively. Taken together, the magnitude and likelihood of misstatement of the financial statements resulting from this internal control deficiency meet the definition of a material weakness.

PCAOB Auditing Standard No. 2, Appendix D (now superseded by Auditing Standard No. 5).

If all goes well, the auditor can issue an unqualified opinion—which is what management devoutly hopes will happen. But what if all does not go well? If management fails to provide a sufficient basis on which to perform the audit, the auditor must so inform management and the audit committee and disclaim an opinion on the ground that the audit cannot be successfully completed. Auditing Standard No. 5, ¶¶ C3-C7. If the audit can be completed but the audit determines that one or more material weaknesses in the system of controls exists, management is precluded from concluding that internal control over financial reporting is effective. In these circumstances, the auditor must express an adverse opinion on the company's internal controls. Id. ¶¶ 90-91.

What is involved in the audit process? The auditor is required to examine and evaluate all the company's internal controls over financial reporting. The auditor utilizes a "top down" approach to determining which controls to test. This approach "begins at the financial statement level and with the auditor's understanding of the overall risks to internal control over financial reporting. The auditor then focuses on entry-level controls and works down to significant accounts and disclosures and their relevant assertions. This approach directs the auditor's attention to accounts, disclosures, and assertions that present a reasonable possibility of material misstatement to the financial statements and related disclosures. The auditor then verifies his or her understanding of the risks in the company's processes and selects for testing those controls that sufficiently address the assessed risk of misstatement to each relevant assertion. Id. ¶ 21.

Management must also supply a variety of representations pertinent to internal controls, including (among other things) matters such as acknowledging management's responsibility for establishing and maintaining effective internal controls, stating that management has assessed the effectiveness of these controls, stating that the management assessment did not use the same procedures as the auditor uses (why is this important?), setting forth management's conclusion about the effectiveness of controls, describing any material frauds, and stating whether control deficiencies identified during previous audit engagements have been resolved. Id. ¶ 75.

Beyond obtaining information, the auditor has to perform a systematic, on-site evaluation of all of management's controls over financial reporting, including an assessment of the overall control environment, the company's risk assessment processes, the control activities in place, management's information and communication processes, and management's own monitoring of controls. The auditor must not only understand these issues, but must also test and evaluate the effectiveness of the controls, both individually and in combination. The testing of internal controls extends to the granular level of identifying and analyzing significant accounts, important processes, and major classes of transactions. The auditor is expected, in this regard, to perform "walkthroughs" that trace a transaction from its origination through the company's information systems until it is reflected in the company's financial reports. The auditor must also consider the effectiveness of the audit committee's oversight of the company's external financial reporting and internal control over financial reporting. In short, the auditor is expected to perform a comprehensive scrutiny of the reporting company's financial controls from "soup to nuts."

Questions and Comments

1. Many public companies—and especially smaller and mid-sized firms—complain about the expense and burden of §404(b) audits. They object that the audit process is time-consuming and expensive, not only because of the auditor fees involved, but also because of the time, energy, and focus that it demands of management.

2. How valid are these objections? There is evidence that audit fees for public companies rose after the enactment of the Sarbanes-Oxley Act, and that the increase in fees was disproportionately experienced by smaller issuers (the impact on small firms is due, presumably, to the economies of scale that can be achieved in SOX compliance as a firm grows in size). The fact that audit fees have increased, however, is not necessarily a valid objection to the §404(b) requirement; what matters is whether the increased costs are offset by corresponding benefits.

3. How much value do you think is conferred by the requirement of an external audit of management's assessment of internal controls?

4. PCAOB Enforcement Actions

PCAOB has the authority to examine public accounting firms and to impose supervisory sanctions if violations of laws or regulations are discovered. The following is an excerpt of a regulatory action taken by PCAOB against Ernst & Young, one of the nation's largest accounting firms.

In the Matter of Ernst & Young LLP

PCAOB Release No. 105-2012-001, Feb. 8, 2012

... E&Y is, and at all relevant times was, a public accounting firm organized as a limited liability partnership under the laws of the state of Delaware and headquartered in New York, New York. E&Y has offices in multiple locations, including Phoenix, Arizona, and is licensed by, among others, the Arizona State Board of Accountancy. . . . E&Y has been Medicis' independent auditor since 1990. . . .

Jeffrey S. Anderson, 56, of Paradise Valley, Arizona, . . . supervised E&Y's audit engagement teams and authorized the issuance of E&Y's audit reports. . . . Anderson also participated in the 2006 AQR [audit quality review] and the Product Returns Consultation.

Robert H. Thibault, 65, of Blaine, Washington, . . . exercised the responsibilities of a "concurring or reviewing partner." Prior to July 1, 2005, Thibault was E&Y's Professional Practice Director for the Pacific Southwest Sub-Area. . . .

Ronald Butler, Jr., 42, of Phoenix, Arizona, . . . was the second partner, supervised by Anderson, for E&Y's audits of Medicis' financial statements for the fiscal years ended June 30, 2004 and 2005, and the six months ended December 31, 2005. . . .

Thomas A. Christie, 50, of Phoenix, Arizona, . . . was the second partner, supervised by Anderson, for E&Y's audit of Medicis' financial statements for the year ended December 31, 2007. . . .

Medicis Pharmaceutical Corporation is a Delaware corporation with principal executive offices located in Scottsdale, Arizona. . . .

[At all relevant times, Medicis sold pharmaceutical products that were time-dated. Medicis primarily sold its products to wholesale distributors and retail chain drug stores, which resold Medicis' products to consumers. Medicis' standard "Return Goods Policy," in effect at all relevant times, gave the company's customers the right to return product within four or six months before expiration date or up to 12 months after expiration date (collectively, "expired product"). The majority of the Company's products had a shelf life of 18 to 24 months.

[When customers returned expired product, Medicis' Return Goods Policy provided that Medicis would give customers a full credit by issuing a credit memo in the amount of "the original purchase price or pricing one (1) year prior to the date the warehouse receives the return."

[The Return Goods Policy did not require customers to purchase the same or similar product as a condition of receiving or using a credit from Medicis for returning expired product. Medicis' customers, however, routinely applied return credits to purchases of the same or similar products as the products that were returned due to expiry. Moreover, most subsequent purchases occurred during the same quarter in which the return credit was issued.

[At all relevant times, Statement of Financial Accounting Standard 48 applied to Medicis' revenue recognition for its product sales because Medicis gave its customers the right to return expired product. Under SFAS 48, a company which sells product subject to a right to return may recognize revenue from those sales transactions at the time of sale only if certain conditions, including the ability to estimate the amount of future returns, are met. If those conditions are not met, revenue recognition must be postponed. If they are met, sales revenue and cost of sales reported in the income statement must be reduced to reflect estimated returns.

[At all relevant times, Medicis represented to E&Y that it recognized product revenue at the time of sale in accordance with SFAS 48. Because its customers had the right to return expired product, Medicis also recorded estimates of future product returns at the time of sale. Medicis used these estimates to establish a sales returns reserve that reduced revenue reported in its financial statements. . . .

[For its sales returns reserve, Medicis reserved for returns replaced at replacement cost and returns not replaced at gross sales price. Medicis' Return Goods Policy did not distinguish between returns replaced and returns not replaced.

[At all relevant times, 97 percent of all of Medicis' product returns were for expired products, and returns replaced were the predominant share of expired product returns. For example, in performing the 2006 audit, the E&Y engagement team determined that "approximately 72% of all expired products returned were replaced in the same quarter" during 2006.]

. . . Respondents failed to comply with PCAOB auditing standards in evaluating Medicis' sales returns reserve estimate, including evaluating Medicis' practice of reserving for most of its estimated product returns at the cost of replacing the product ("replacement cost"). The audit evidence available to Respondents indicated that, at all relevant times, SFAS 48 . . . applied to Medicis' product sales subject to a right of return due to expiration and required Medicis to reserve for all of those estimated returns at gross sales price. Reserving for most of its estimated returns at replacement cost, rather than gross sales price, resulted in Medicis' reported sales returns reserve being materially understated and its reported revenue being misstated. Overall, Respondents' approach to evaluating Medicis' sales returns reserve methodology and estimate was inconsistent with their obligations to exercise professional skepticism as the Company's independent auditor.

In connection with the December 31, 2005 audit, Anderson, Thibault, and Butler failed to obtain sufficient competent evidential matter supporting Medicis' conclusion that an "exchange" exception to SFAS 48's general rule of reserving at gross sales price supported Medicis' reserving for most of its product returns at replacement cost. They concurred with this conclusion notwithstanding contradictory audit evidence indicating that the product returns in question were not eligible for the exchange exception to SFAS 48. Therefore, they failed to identify and appropriately address a material departure from U.S. generally accepted accounting principles ("GAAP") resulting from Medicis' reliance on the exchange exception.

Merely two months after Anderson, Thibault, and Butler had concurred with the application of the SFAS 48 exchange exception, E&Y personnel responsible for the 2006 AQR questioned Medicis' reliance on the exchange exception and, with Anderson, Thibault and Butler, concluded that the exchange exception did not support Medicis' use of replacement cost. Rather than appropriately addressing this material departure from GAAP, Anderson, Thibault, and other E&Y personnel decided that a different accounting rationale supported Medicis' reserving at replacement cost for most of its estimated product returns. They concluded that Medicis' existing accounting result was supported by reference or analogy to warranty accounting under Statement of Financial Accounting Standards No. 5, Contingencies. . . . At all relevant times, however, Respondents understood that the product returns at issue were not returns of defective products pursuant to a warranty and that customers returning the products to Medicis were not relying on a warranty in making such returns. Instead, customers were returning products because Medicis provided them with a right to return expired products. After the Product Returns Consultation, Medicis, with E&Y's concurrence, relied on the flawed warranty accounting rationale to continue reserving for most of its product returns at replacement cost in 2005, 2006, and 2007. As a result, Anderson, Thibault, and Butler failed to identify and appropriately address a material departure from GAAP. . . .

In connection with a 2008 inspection of E&Y's audits of Medicis, the PCAOB inspection staff questioned E&Y's acceptance of Medicis' use of replacement cost to calculate its returns reserve. After the PCAOB staff questioning, E&Y's National Accounting Group determined that Medicis' use of replacement cost was not appropriate. Additionally, E&Y made internal inquiries of audit partners in relevant practice groups to determine whether any of its other audit clients or other pharmaceutical companies reserved for product returns at replacement cost. E&Y was unable to identify any other comparable companies that accounted for their returns reserve as Medicis did. Ultimately, E&Y concluded that Medicis' reserving at replacement cost was not in conformity with GAAP and the Company was required to restate its accounting for its returns reserve.

On November 10, 2008, Medicis filed with the Commission an amended annual report on Form 10-K/A, restating the Company's financial statements for the years ended December 31, 2007 and 2006, the six months ended December 31, 2005, and the fiscal year ended June 30, 2005. In the restatement, Medicis' returns reserve increased $94.6 million (585%) as of December 31, 2005, $52.1 million (148%) as of December 31, 2006, and $58.9 million (600%) as of December 31, 2007. E&Y audited Medicis' restated financial statements for the foregoing periods and issued an audit report dated November 6, 2008, in which E&Y expressed an unqualified opinion that the restated financial statements presented fairly, in all material respects, Medicis' financial position and results of operations in conformity with GAAP. . . .

In view of the foregoing, and to protect the interests of investors and further the public interest in the preparation of informative, accurate, and independent audit reports, the Board determines it appropriate to impose the sanctions agreed to in Respondents' Offers. [By this Order, the Board (1) censures Ernst & Young; (2) bars Jeffrey S. Anderson and Robert H. Thibault from being associated with a registered public accounting firm; (3) censures Ronald Butler, Jr., and Thomas A. Christie; and (4) imposes civil money penalties in the amounts of $2,000,000 as to E&Y, $50,000 as to Anderson, $25,000 as to Thibault, and $25,000 as to Butler.]

Questions and Comments

1. Medicis Pharmaceutical Corporation describes itself as "the leading independent specialty pharmaceutical company in the United States focusing primarily on the treatment of dermatological and aesthetic conditions." In 2011 and 2012, it was listed as "one of the world's most ethical companies," an award given to a "small select group of high-performing organizations that have achieved leadership positions in their respective industries through exemplary business practices and social responsibility."

2. The accounting principles at play in the excerpted order may sound esoteric, but they are basically simple. Medicis sells products to pharmacies, which resell to consumers. The products have an expiration date after which they cannot be sold. Medicis' contracts with its pharmacy customers allow them to return expired and unsold products. In exchange, the customer can elect to receive either a refund of the purchase price or new replacement product. Most customers choose the latter option. Accounting rules allow Medicis to book the initial sales but require it to also designate a reserve for expected returns. For returns that were expected to result in a request for a refund, Medicis reserved the purchase price; for returns that were expected to result in a request for replacement products, Medicis reserved its replacement cost. The replacement cost (as would be expected) was significantly lower than the purchase price.

This accounting treatment appeared to violate generally accepted accounting principles (GAAP). SFAS 48, interpreting GAAP, on its face required Medicis to reserve for all estimated returns at gross sales price rather than replacement cost. E&Ys audit engagement team, however, did not insist that Medicis follow this approach. When E&Y's audit quality review team questioned the accounting treatment, the engagement team simply ginned up another argument for maintaining the same accounting treatment by analogizing the product returns to returns of defective products under warranty. The incorrect accounting treatment continued for three years and only came to a halt when PCAOB challenged the practice in its own review. Senior people at E&Y then rejected the audit team's analysis and required that the company reserve for returns at gross sales price. The result was that the company's profits for 2005, 2006, and 2007 were materially overstated, requiring an embarrassing restatement of the company's financial statements for those years.

3. The restatement generated class action litigation, which settled in September 2011 for $18 million ($11 million from the company and $7 million from E&Y).

4. What do you think would have happened to E&Y's relationship with this client had E&Y refused to issue an unqualified opinion based on disagreements about the return reserve policy?

5. Aside from the apparent violation of GAAP, was the accounting treatment endorsed by the E&Y engagement team unreasonable? Medicis' treatment of returns appeared to align with economic reality: The company's cost of returns was lower if customers elected — as most did — to receive replacement products rather than a return of their purchase price. Perhaps the underlying problem was that the accounting standard was poorly conceived, at least as applied to this company's operations. Were the members of the engagement team behaving unethically when they endorsed the company's approach?

6. Once the initial problem was identified by E&Y's quality review process, why did the engagement team revert to an even less plausible interpretation of GAAP? Could they have been trying to cover their prior mistake, which would have required a restatement if the prior accounting treatment were reversed?

7. The penalties administered by PCAOB to the individuals on the team might seem harsh. Anderson and Thibault, the senior members of the team, were barred from the industry. At ages 56 and 65, this probably meant the end of their auditing careers (PCAOB did give them permission to apply for reinstatement after a year or two, but given their ages and the blot on their reputations, it seems unlikely they would have much prospect of revitalizing their careers in the auditing field). They retained their CPA qualifications and could work as accountants, but not in affiliation with any public company auditor. Were these penalties appropriate? What was PCAOB's motivation in administering such harsh sanctions?

8. E&Y, on the other hand, seems to have escaped the most severe penalties. True, it was censured and had to pay a $2 million civil money penalty, but the firm doesn't seem to have suffered any long-term consequences. Was E&Y's penalty appropriate? What actions by E&Y might PCAOB have taken into account in determining the sanction?

9. At the time of PCAOB's investigation, E&Y had been Medicis' outside auditor for 22 years. Was that too long?

In addition to bringing enforcement actions in connection with inspections of individual audits, PCAOB conducts annual inspections of auditor performance for registered public accounting firms that provide audit reports for more than 100 issuers. These annual inspections include analysis of selected audit-specific inspection reports. Deficiencies are commonly noted in compliance with the following standards (among others):

- AU 230, which requires the independent auditor to plan and perform his or her work with due professional care.

- AS No. 5, which requires the auditor to plan and perform the audit to obtain appropriate evidence that is sufficient to support the auditor's opinion on internal control over financial reporting.
- AS No. 13, which requires that, if the auditor plans to assess control risk at less than the maximum and to base the nature, timing, and extent of substantive audit procedures on that lower assessment, the auditor must obtain evidence that the controls tested were designed and operating effectively during the entire period for which the auditor plans to rely on controls to modify the substantive procedures.
- AS No. 15, which requires the auditor to plan and perform audit procedures to obtain sufficient appropriate audit evidence to provide a reasonable basis for the audit opinion.

Reports of annual examinations also include PCAOB's evaluation of the audit firm's policies and procedures for quality control in the areas of:

- Management structure and processes, including the tone at the top.
- Practices for partner management, including allocation of partner resources and partner evaluation, compensation, admission, and disciplinary actions.
- Policies and procedures for considering and addressing the risks involved in accepting and retaining clients, including the application of the firm's risk-rating system.
- Processes related to the firm's use of audit work that the firm's foreign affiliates perform on the foreign operations of the firm's U.S. issuer audit clients.
- The firm's processes for monitoring audit performance, including processes for identifying and assessing indicators of deficiencies in audit performance, independence policies and procedures, and processes for responding to weaknesses in quality control.

In general, when the PCAOB issues a report of an annual inspection, it will identify what it considers to be deficiencies in selected audits. This part of the report is made public (with the identities of the audit clients expunged). The report also contains analysis of the firm's quality control environment. Unlike the specific audit analyses, PCOAB's "criticisms of or potential defects in the quality control systems" are not made public unless the firm fails to address those criticisms to PCAOB's satisfaction within 12 months. Sarbanes-Oxley Act §104(g)(2).

In 2013, PCAOB released the confidential portions of two annual inspection reports for PricewaterhouseCoopers (PwC), one of the world's largest public accounting firms. Its public statement announcing this conclusion, and PwC's response, is contained in the following excerpt:

In the Matter of PricewaterhouseCoopers LLP's Quality Control Remediation Submissions

PCAOB Release No.104-2013-054, Mar. 7, 2013

[PCAOB] has evaluated the submissions of PricewaterhouseCoopers LLP ("the Firm") . . . for the remediation periods ended March 25, 2010 and August 12, 2011 concerning the Firm's efforts to address certain quality control criticisms included in the nonpublic portions of the Board's March 25, 2009 and August

12, 2010 inspection reports on the Firm ("the Reports"). The Board has determined that as of March 25, 2010 and August 12, 2011, respectively, the Firm had not addressed certain criticisms in the Reports to the Board's satisfaction. Accordingly, . . . the Board is making public the portions of the Reports that deal with those criticisms.

The Firm has notified the Board that it will not seek Securities and Exchange Commission review of the determination, which the Firm has a right to do under the Act and Commission rules. The Firm has requested that a related statement by the Firm be attached as an Appendix to this release, and the Board has granted that request. By allowing the Firm's statement to be attached as an Appendix to this release, however, the Board is not endorsing, confirming, or adopting as the Board's view any element of the Firm's statement.

The quality control remediation process is central to the Board's efforts to cause firms to improve the quality of their audits and thereby better protect investors. The Board therefore takes very seriously the importance of firms making sufficient progress on quality control issues identified in an inspection report in the 12 months following the report. Particularly with the largest firms, which are inspected annually, the Board devotes considerable time and resources to critically evaluating whether the firm did in fact make sufficient progress in that period. The Board makes the relevant criticisms public when a firm has failed to do so to the Board's satisfaction.

It is not unusual for an inspection report to include nonpublic criticisms of several aspects of a firm's system of quality control. Any Board judgment that results in later public disclosure is a judgment about whether the firm made sufficient effort and progress to address the particular criticisms articulated in the report on that firm in the 12 months immediately following the report date. It is not a broad judgment about the effectiveness of a firm's system of quality control compared to those of other firms, and it does not signify anything about the merits of any additional efforts a firm may have made to address the criticisms after the 12-month period.

[Among PCAOB's criticisms of PwC's quality control environment in the earlier inspection reports were the following:

- Failing to obtain sufficient support for estimates of an asset's fair value.
- Relying too heavily on an audited client's internal controls.
- Relying too heavily on work performed by an audit client's internal audit department.
- Failing to deal adequately with the implications of a finding that an audit client's internal controls had failed in some respect.
- Relying excessively on system-generated data.
- Failing to exercise sufficient skepticism over management's estimates of key audit numbers.]

Statement of PricewaterhouseCoopers LLP on the PCAOB's March 7, 2013, Release No. 104-2013-054

The execution of quality audits in full compliance with PCAOB standards is the top priority of our practice and something in which our professionals take a significant amount of personal and professional pride. We continue to support the mission of the Public Company Accounting Oversight Board.

The Board issued a Release today making public certain portions of Part II of our 2008 and 2009 Inspection Reports (the "Part II comments"). The Release is based on the Board's determination that we did not address the matters contained in the Part II comments to the Board's satisfaction during the 12 month period following issuance of the reports. We believe that our actions in response to the Part II comments were significant, but we acknowledge the Board's determination with a view toward continued cooperation with the Board and in furtherance of our commitment to audit quality.

The Part II comments relate to some of the most complex, judgmental and evolving areas of auditing. Our actions relating to those areas, during the 12 months following issuance of the comments and thereafter, have included providing our audit professionals with enhanced audit tools, training and additional technical guidance to promote more consistent audit execution. We believe that these efforts have been important positive contributors to audit quality at our firm. We are proud of our focus on continuous improvement and of the dedication and high quality audit work performed by our partners and other professionals.

As the Board has explained, "[i]t is not unusual for an inspection report to include nonpublic criticisms of several aspects of a firm's system of quality control. Any Board judgment that results in later public disclosure is a judgment about whether the firm made sufficient effort and progress to address the particular criticisms articulated in the report on that firm in the 12 months immediately following the report date. It is not a broad judgment about the effectiveness of a firm's system of quality control compared to those of other firms, and it does not signify anything about the merits of any additional efforts a firm may have made to address the criticisms after the 12-month period."

We are one of the world's largest audit practices and a leader in the profession, and we are committed to maintaining our leading role in promoting further improvements in auditing and financial reporting and delivering the highest quality audits in the profession. We look forward to continuing our dialogue with the Board in support of our commitment to audit quality.

Questions and Comments

1. How significant is PCAOB's conclusion that PwC had failed for a period of years to remediate deficiencies noted in annual reports of inspection?

2. What happens if, in PCAOB's opinion, PwC continues to fall short in its remediation efforts? In 2012, PwC's worldwide revenues were $31.5 billion; the company had 180,000 employees. Are there limits to the enforcement actions that PCAOB could realistically take against a firm this huge and this central to the world's financial system?

3. What explanation, if any, did PCAOB provide for its conclusion that PwC had failed to adequately remediate the deficiencies noted in the prior inspection reports?

4. What sort of response did PwC provide? Did it admit the validity of PCAOB's conclusion that it had failed to remediate the problems? Did it deny the validity of PCAOB's conclusions? Did it say anything of substance at all?

5. What recourse does an audit firm have when PCAOB publishes criticisms of its audit performance? It can file a response and, if no change is made to the PCAOB's report, can take an appeal to the Securities and Exchange Commission. However, what are the chances that such an appeal will succeed?

6. What is the rationale for withholding public disclosure of PCAOB's criticisms of an audit firm's quality control environment? For allowing such disclosure after one year if the firm has failed to remedy the problems to PCAOB's satisfaction?

7. Should PCAOB enforcement actions and inspection reports be relevant or admissible in an action against a public accounting firm for professional negligence? In an action for securities fraud based on false or misleading statements in an annual report or registration statement?

8. The PCAOB is not the only agency with enforcement authority over public accounting firms. In July 2013, the SEC announced the creation of a "Financial Reporting and Audit Task Force" dedicated to detecting fraudulent or improper financial reporting. In a widely reported speech on September 19, 2013, Andrew Ceresney, Co-Director of the SEC's Division of Enforcement, underscored the SEC's intention to heighten its scrutiny of auditing firms: "[W]e will continue to focus on auditors. . . . [It] is important that we carefully monitor their work and ensure that they fully comply with their professional obligations. If there is a significant restatement or if we learn about improper accounting from a whistleblower, our proactive efforts, or the media, then you can expect that we will scrutinize not only the CEO, CFO and Controller, but also the engagement partner, engagement quality reviewer, and the auditing firm as a whole. We are going to probe the quality of the audit and determine whether the auditors missed or ignored red flags, whether they have proper documentation, and whether they followed the professional standards."

PROBLEM 9-8

Alliedco, a NASDAQ-listed manufacturer of equipment for the restaurant industry, has long used Cheshire & Manx as its external auditor. Cheshire & Manx is a "second-tier" audit firm with 5,000 employees. It has developed an excellent working relationship with Alliedco's senior management, cemented both by a close personal friendship between Alliedco's chief executive officer and Cheshire & Manx's senior audit partner, and by the fact that Cheshire & Manx performs its audit services for a substantially lower fee than any of the "big four" auditors. To achieve these cost savings, Cheshire & Manx relies substantially on workpapers prepared by Alliedco's internal audit department. Over the 15 years of its engagement with Alliedco, Cheshire & Manx has always issued unqualified opinions on the company's financial statements and internal controls. This past year Cheshire & Manx paid $10 million to settle a securities fraud lawsuit brought against it by shareholders of one of Alliedco's competitors in the restaurant supply business. The allegation was that the company had engaged in "channel stuffing" — inflating profits by reporting sales that had not yet occurred — and that Cheshire & Manx was culpable in failing to uncover the fraud. PCAOB also issued an inspection report criticizing Cheshire & Manx's performance of that company's audit, noting in particular that the auditor had relied excessively on the services of internal audit and on management's estimates of key accounting numbers. PCAOB banned two of Cheshire & Manx's senior partners from the industry for life in connection with this investigation. You are an outside director and head of Alliedco's audit committee. The issue of Cheshire & Manx's renewal as the company's auditor is before you for decision. The chief executive officer has let it be known that she strongly favors retaining the auditor for the coming year. What do you do?

5. Compliance Audits

As is evident from the preceding discussion on audits of management attestation of internal controls, the concept of external audit goes beyond the specific topic of financial reporting narrowly defined. Over the past decades, the concept of external audit has expanded even further to include more general compliance-based audits. A compliance auditor may examine a firm's operations to assess whether they conform to a variety of different standards: legal requirements, codes of best practices promoted by standard-setting bodies, internal ethics codes, and more. These compliance audits may be conducted at the behest of the organization whose activities are being scrutinized; they may also be demanded by commercial counterparties.

Public company auditors were charged with certain compliance audit responsibilities as a result of new §10A of the Exchange Act, added in the Private Securities Litigation Reform Act of 1995, 15 U.S.C. §78j-1. Section 10A(a) requires, inter alia, that each public company audit must include "procedures designed to provide reasonable assurance of detecting illegal acts that would have a direct and material effect on the determination of financial statement amounts [and] procedures designed to identify related party transactions that are material to the financial statements or otherwise require disclosure therein."

Section 10A(b)(1) specifies what a public company auditor must do after becoming aware of information indicating that an illegal act has or may have occurred (an "illegal act," within the meaning of this statute, means an "act or omission that violates any law, or any rule or regulation having the force of law"). In such cases, the auditor must determine whether it is likely that an illegal act has occurred; if, so, determine and consider the possible effect of the illegal act on the financial statements of the issuer (including any contingent monetary effects, such as fines, penalties, and damages); and as soon as practicable, inform the appropriate level of management and assure that the audit committee or the board of directors of the issuer is adequately informed, unless such illegal act is clearly inconsequential.

What happens if the issuer fails to take appropriate remedial action after being notified by the auditor? If the auditor concludes that (1) the illegal act has a material effect on the financial statements of the issuer; (2) the senior management has not taken, and the board of directors has not caused senior management to take, timely and appropriate remedial actions with respect to the illegal act; and (3) the failure to take remedial action is reasonably expected to warrant departure from a standard report (e.g., an unqualified audit opinion) of the auditor, when made, or warrant resignation from the audit engagement, then the auditor is required to report the matter directly to the board of directors, and the issuer thereafter must promptly report the matter to the SEC. If the independent auditor resigns, it is required to provide the SEC with a copy of their report to the board of directors of the issuer. Violations of these requirements may result in SEC enforcement actions. Section 10A is a particularly potent weapon in the SEC's enforcement arsenal because an audit firm can be subjected to administrative sanctions for negligently failing to detect illegal activity at the reporting firm. *See* SEC v. Solucorp Indus., Ltd., 197 F. Supp. 2d 4 (S.D.N.Y. 2002).

An important area for compliance-based audits is the global supply chain. A variety of different standards apply to firms in the supply chain, including labor rules, environmental rules, human rights rules, product quality standards, and governance rules. Examples include ISO 14001, on environmental management; ISO 9001, on quality management; ISO 22000, on food safety; SA8000, on social practices at the workplace; government-imposed environmental and labor rules; and organization-specific codes on ethics or compliance.

Questions and Comments

1. For an empirical study of supply chain audits, see Jodi L. Short, Michael W. Toffel & Andrea R. Hugill, *What Shapes Gatekeepers? Evidence from Global Supply Chain Auditors*, Harvard Business School Working Paper 14-032 (2014), available at http://papers.ssrn.com/sol3/papers.cfm?abstract_id=2343802.

2. International standard-setting bodies sometimes issue standards for the certification of the audit firms that perform compliance-based audits. The International Organization for Standardization, based in Geneva, Switzerland, is particularly active in specifying requirements for firms that audit compliance using that organization's standards.

3. Attorneys have been some somewhat late in entering the field of compliance audit, but today a number of law firms advertise this area as one of their specialties.

4. Should the law require external compliance audits for publicly traded firms? For any organizations, public or not, whose activities have a potentially substantial impact on public health, safety or welfare? Should firms be required to disclose the results of these audits to regulators, or in their annual reports to shareholders?

E. MONITORS

Monitors — sometimes referred to as "independent private sector inspector general" (IPSIG) — play an important role in compliance and enforcement by providing an independent assessment of whether an organization is adhering to the law or to commitments it has made in consent agreements with regulators or prosecutors.

According to the website of an organization called the International Association of Independent Private Sector Attorneys General, an IPSIG is "an independent, private sector firm with legal, auditing, investigative, management and loss prevention skills, employed by an organization (voluntarily or by compulsory process) to ensure compliance with relevant law and regulations, and to deter, prevent, uncover and report unethical and illegal conduct by, within and against the organization. The IPSIG may, in addition, be a major participant with management in enhancing the economy, efficiency, and effectiveness of the organization." *See* http://www.iaipsig.org/ethics.html. The role of the monitor is crucial because government offices typically do not have the resources to engage in continuous checking on the performance of a regulated firm.

Monitorships are frequently established in agreements settling regulatory charges. The HSBC excerpt below considers the function of monitors in criminal cases, but the discussion could equally apply to many civil enforcement contexts.

Questions and Comments

1. Some might take issue with the characterization of monitors as gatekeepers, on the ground that they enter the picture only after violations have occurred,

whereas gatekeepers operate at the front end to prevent violations from happening in the first place. In a more general sense, however, monitors play a role similar to that performed by traditional gatekeepers: They have the capacity to stand in the way of an organization's achievement of an important strategic goal — dismissal of the charges or other favorable regulatory action. And, in performing that role, the monitor, like other gatekeepers, may (in fact must) take the interests of the broader public into account.

2. The role of monitors has become increasingly important over the past decades — so much so that the appointment of a monitor is a standard consideration in the negotiation of any enforcement proceeding against a complex organization for systematic compliance violations. Jacobs and Goldstock, two prominent commentators, see an equally bright future for monitorships in the context of criminal actions against organizations: "The market [for monitors and IPSIGs] will likely grow even more rapidly in the future because of prosecutors' recent use of IPSIG and IPSIG-like monitors in number of high profile deferred prosecutions and plea bargains including cases involving huge public corporations and partnerships like Computer Associates, Con Edison, Merrill Lynch, and KPMG as well as the boom in private sector firms' use of monitors to comply with the Federal Sentencing Organizational Guidelines. Moreover, prompted by widespread fraud in the administration of aid to victims of Hurricane Katrina, 50 members of Congress proposed a bill that would require the U.S. Department of Homeland Security to study the applicability of the IPSIG model to future disaster recovery efforts." *See* James B. Jacobs & Ronald Goldstock, *Monitors & IPSIGS: Emergence of a New Criminal Justice Role*, 43 Crim. L. Bull. 217 (2007).

3. For more on monitors, see Vikramaditya Khanna & Timothy L. Dickinson, *The Corporate Monitor: The New Corporate Czar?*, 105 Mich. L. Rev. 1713 (2007); Veronica Root, *The Monitor-"Client" Relationship*, 100 Va. L. Rev. 523 (2014).

United States v. HSBC Bank USA, N.A. and HSBC Holdings PLC

2016 WL 347670 (E.D.N.Y. 2016)

JOHN GLEESON, United States District Judge:

As part of a deferred prosecution agreement ("DPA"), HSBC agreed to the appointment of a corporate compliance monitor ("Monitor") to supervise HSBC's compliance with the law during the pendency of the DPA. Hubert Dean Moore, Jr. seeks access to the Monitor's First Annual Follow-Up Review Report ("Monitor's Report" or "Report") evaluating HSBC's performance. HSBC and DOJ do not want the public to have access to the Report. I find that the Report is a judicial record, and that the public has a First Amendment right to see the Report. Further, I have balanced the public's right to access with the government's and HSBC's concerns with unsealing the Report, and I order the parties to submit to me for review a redacted version of the Report, as detailed below.

In December 2012, the government charged HSBC Bank USA, N.A. with willfully failing to maintain an effective anti-money laundering ("AML") program, in violation of the Bank Secrecy Act, 31 U.S.C. §5311 et seq., and HSBC Holdings PLC with willfully facilitating financial transactions on behalf of sanctioned entities, in violation of the International Emergency Economic Powers Act and the Trading with the

Enemy Act. Simultaneously, the government publicly filed a DPA requesting that I hold the case in abeyance for five years in accordance with the terms of the DPA, a statement of facts describing HSBC's alleged misconduct, and a Corporate Compliance Monitor agreement. According to the DPA, if after five years HSBC has complied with the terms and provisions of the DPA, the government will seek to dismiss the Information with prejudice; if not, the government may prosecute HSBC "for any federal criminal violation of which [the government] has knowledge," including — but not limited to — the charges in the already-filed Information.

I preliminarily approved the DPA pursuant to my supervisory power on July 1, 2013 and granted the parties' request to hold the case in abeyance for five years pursuant to the Speedy Trial Act. I gave this tentative approval after reviewing the terms of the DPA, and — of particular relevance here — in reliance on the Monitor's supervision over HSBC's implementation of remedial measures and ongoing compliance with the laws under which it was charged. In giving this approval, I specifically stated that it is "subject to a continued monitoring of [the DPA's] execution and implementation." I retained my supervisory power over the implementation of the DPA and directed the government to file quarterly reports with me, as well as keep me apprised "of all significant developments in the implementation of the DPA," for as long as the open criminal case remained pending before me.

In January 2015, the Monitor issued the Report, which set forth his "findings and assessment of the then-current state of HSBC Group's AML and sanctions compliance program and of the Bank's progress over the course of the preceding year in improving its AML and sanctions compliance program." On April 1, 2015, the government filed a six-page status report purporting to summarize the Monitor's conclusions. On April 28, 2015, I ordered the government to file the Monitor's Report with the Court. On June 1, 2015, the government filed the Report under seal, and on November 3, 2015, Moore wrote a letter to the Court, which I construed to be a motion to unseal the Report. I heard oral argument on the application to unseal the Report on January 15, 2016, and now grant that application to the extent set forth below.

The inquiry in this case — whether to allow the public to see the Monitor's Report — explores the bounds of a court's duty to "ensure that ours is indeed a government of the people, by the people, and for the people." One of the ways this seemingly abstract principle of governance directly affects the job responsibilities of a federal judge is the duty it creates to uphold the public's right of access to judicial documents. Both the common law and the First Amendment give the public this right. See, e.g., United States v. Amodeo, 44 F.3d 141, 145 (2d Cir. 1995) ("Amodeo I") ("The common law right of public access to judicial documents is said to predate the Constitution."); Hartford Courant Co. v. Pellegrino, 380 F.3d 83, 91 (2d Cir. 2004) (members of the public have a "qualified First Amendment right to attend judicial proceedings and to access certain judicial documents").

Before I can analyze whether the public's right of access under the common law or the First Amendment compel me to unseal the Monitor's Report, I must determine whether the Report is a judicial document. I may consider the Monitor's Report a "judicial document" if it is "relevant to the performance of the judicial function and useful in the judicial process." I conclude that it is. . . .

There is an open criminal case before me. As the government puts it, my authority here "is to ensure that the DPA remains within the bounds of lawfulness and respects the integrity of this Court." I cannot perform that task without receiving at least some updates from the parties about HSBC's compliance with the DPA. Indeed, I specifically directed the parties to keep me "apprised of all significant developments in the implementation of the DPA." Believing the Monitor's Report to qualify as one of these "significant developments," I directed the government to file the Report with the Court in April 2015.

The government also argues that because the Monitor's Report had not been written when I approved the DPA, "the Report could have played no role" in my decision, and therefore, the argument continues, it is irrelevant to my judicial function. But as mentioned above, my approval of the DPA was preliminary; it was and remains contingent upon my "continued monitoring of its execution and implementation." . . . I care a great deal about the results of the Monitor's investigation; my review of those results is necessary to do my job properly.

The government argues that I am "charged neither with enforcing or granting relief from the Monitor's efforts nor with playing any role in the Monitor's work," but that argument misses the point. My job is to oversee the unfolding of the criminal case that the government chose to file in my court. The parties, in the DPA, made the Monitor's work a component of the case, and thus made the instant Report critical to the execution of my duties. If, for example, the Monitor's Report disclosed that HSBC were systematically and extensively laundering money for drug traffickers, it would demean this institution for me to sit by quietly while the government took no action. Indeed, my oversight of the DPA and the open criminal case goes to the heart of the public's right of access: federal courts must "have a measure of accountability," and the public must have "confidence in the administration of justice." Most tellingly, even a "[d]istrict [c]ourt's inaction is subject to public accountability." These are important interests that the government itself chose to implicate by resolving its investigation of HSBC in a manner that involved the filing of a pending criminal case.

The Monitor's Report will also be integral to the future resolution of the case. If the government determines that HSBC has breached the terms of the DPA, and presses forward to an adjudication of the four pending charges, this Court will oversee those proceedings. If the government determines that HSBC has complied with the terms of the DPA, it will seek to dismiss the charges against HSBC at the end of the DPA's term. But the parties can only effectuate such a dismissal "with leave of court." Fed. R. Crim. P. 48. Although Rule 48 gives the government "near-absolute power . . . to extinguish a case that it has brought," leave of court may be denied if the dismissal is "clearly contrary to manifest public interest." That determination cannot properly be made without judicial review of the Report. Thus, even if the government chooses to dismiss this case, that decision will invoke the Court's authority in a way that the government's decision not to prosecute in the first instance would not.

The Monitor's Report here is thus directly relevant to my judicial function, and as a result falls squarely within the definition of a judicial document. Having so concluded, I would ordinarily analyze the public's common law right of access. However, because I find "that the [Monitor's Report] [is] subject to a First Amendment right of access, which is stronger and can only be overcome under more stringent circumstances than the common law presumption," I turn directly to the protections given to the public by the First Amendment.

First Amendment right attaches to judicial documents for which "experience and logic" support public access. Under the "experience and logic" text, I "consider both whether the documents 'have historically been open to the press and general public' and whether 'public access plays a significant positive role in the functioning of the particular process in question.'"

The government argues that its decision "whether a defendant is abiding by the terms of a DPA" is akin to a charging decision, and that documents supporting that decision are typically non-public. But this argument skates over the fact that the government has already brought charges against HSBC. A DPA is not analogous to documents related to building a case; it provides for the undoing of an already-filed case. The government did not begin to employ DPAs with companies until the early 1990s, so there is scant historical evidence of public access to documents in the precise posture of the Monitor's Report at issue here.

Even so, "the notion of public access to judicial documents is a capacious one: the courts of this country have long recognized a 'general right to inspect and copy public records and documents, including judicial records and documents.'" And the First Amendment right of public access applies both to the trial as well as pretrial phases of a criminal proceeding. In extending the right of public access to pretrial proceedings — even though pretrial proceedings were not public at common law — the Second Circuit noted that "[t]here is a significant benefit to be gained from public observation of many aspects of a criminal proceeding."

When all goes well for the defendant, a DPA is, at its core, a substitute for a plea agreement or a trial — to both of which the public has historically had a First Amendment right of access. And the Monitor's Report is integral to the fulfilment of my continuing obligation to monitor the execution and implementation of the DPA. I conclude that the public's right of access extends to such documents. Accordingly, I find that "experience" supports unsealing the Monitor's Report.

I also find that "logic bears out this experience, since 'public access plays a significant positive role in the functioning of the particular process in question.'" This case implicates matters of great public concern, and is "therefore one[ ] which the public has an interest in overseeing." DOJ and the Court are public institutions. HSBC Bank USA, N.A. "serves 2.4 million customers through retail banking and wealth management, commercial banking, private banking, asset management, and global banking and markets segments" and "operates more than 230 bank branches throughout the United States." It is an indirect subsidiary of HSBC Holdings PLC, which has shares listed in London, Hong Kong, Paris, and Bermuda, and has an American Depositary Receipt ("ADR") program in the United States. HSBC Holdings PLC is self-described as "one of the world's largest banking and financial services organizations."

Given the institutions involved, and HSBC's structure and impact, it is no wonder that after the parties filed their DPA, I became aware of "heavy public criticism of the DPA," and "received unsolicited input from members of the public urging me to reject the DPA." It was appropriate and desirable for the public to view and comment on the widespread nature of the criminal conduct documented in the Statement of Facts, and to view and comment upon DOJ's decision to file a DPA in the public forum of this courthouse. It is equally appropriate and desirable for the public to be interested and informed now in the progress of the arrangement between DOJ and HSBC that the government chose to make the centerpiece of a federal criminal case, and in whether I am doing my job of monitoring the execution and implementation of that arrangement.

Thus, because of the historical practice of allowing public access to documents filed in connection with important criminal proceedings, and because the interests of transparency, accountability, and credibility remind me "of the logic of democratic monitoring of judicial processes," I find that the First Amendment right of access attaches to the Monitor's Report.

Even if the First Amendment right of access has attached to a judicial document, a court may still seal that document in whole or in part "if specific, on the record findings are made demonstrating that closure is essential to preserve higher values and is narrowly tailored to serve that interest." The government and HSBC advance four such interests.

First, the parties argue that the Monitor's (and thus the government's) ability to assess HSBC's compliance with the terms of the DPA will be negatively impacted by the potential chilling effect that making the Report public would have on HSBC employees in cooperating with the Monitor. The parties also contend that I should consider the privacy interests of the employees, because they are innocent third parties. I share these concerns, but conclude that targeted redactions will easily alleviate them. . . . I will redact any identifying information about HSBC employees. However, the non-identifying information that these employees have provided may be made public without implicating any of the government's and HSBC's raised concerns.

Second, the parties contend that publicizing the Report could give criminals a "road map" to exploit weaknesses in HSBC's AML and sanctions compliance programs. I have reviewed the Report, and much of the information is generalized or would likely be otherwise unhelpful to a would-be money launderer. Moreover, the Report "is, to a large extent, historical, as many of the shortcomings have been or are in the process of being rectified," alleviating the concern that individuals could feed upon HSBC's weaknesses. However, to the extent that information detailing the processes by which criminals could exploit HSBC exists in the Monitor's Report, that information will be redacted.

Third, the government argues that public disclosure will negatively impact the effectiveness of monitors in future cases, and specifically could "impact the relationship between the Department of Justice and financial regulators in the future when independent monitors are imposed." But this concern need not be true; the government did not have to file a DPA in this case. The decision to do so presumably benefitted the parties, but it also means that the government and HSBC are parties to a pending federal criminal case, which, "is not window dressing." This adage remains true three years into this DPA's term, and will remain true should the government choose to resolve future criminal conduct by way of a DPA. Thus, I find that the government's interest in prohibiting public access to the Report for the sake of its future law enforcement efforts is minimal.

Finally, the government and HSBC argue that disclosure of the Report would negatively affect the Monitor's relationship with foreign regulators, and thus would negatively affect the work product the Monitor could produce. Specifically, they contend that public release of the Report would: contravene assurances the Monitor has given foreign regulators; cause these regulators to "feel misled"; prompt them to withdraw their consent to the Monitor's site visits; and/or compel them to restrict the Monitor's access to confidential information. I credit these claims. Accordingly, five of the six appendices — all except the United States Country Review Report, which will be subject to redactions on the same terms as the Monitor's Report — will remain under seal. Further, country names and explicit references to confidential material, as identified by these foreign jurisdictions, will be redacted from the Monitor's Report and the United States Country Review Report. These blanket measures will ensure that "confidential materials [are] restricted to the FCA, DOJ and FRB [and HSBC]."

I disagree with the government and HSBC that the interests the parties have raised cannot be addressed through targeted redactions of the Monitor's Report. The Monitor warns that because "the report with all of its components is more than 1,000 pages long . . . if the sensitive factual content were to be redacted, the report likely would be materially changed." But withholding some of the factual support that gives the Report context and meaning will not render the Report either useless or incomprehensible.

In sum, I find that the parties have set forth several interests that warrant withholding or redacting portions of the Monitor's Report. But because my sealing order must be "narrowly tailored to achieve th[e] aim" of sealing only when "necessary to preserve higher values," I also find that the majority of the Report and the United States Country Review Report will be made public.

I am mindful of the Second Circuit's admonition that, though "it is proper for a district court, after weighing competing interests, to edit and redact a judicial document in order to allow access to appropriate portions of the document, we consider it improper for the district court to delegate its authority to do so." However, I will allow the government and HSBC to submit proposed redactions to the Report on or before February 12, 2016, which I will then review and consider in making the appropriate redactions. When making those redactions, I will be guided by the considerations set forth above, that is, the appropriateness of redacting: (1) identifying information about HSBC employees; (2) information detailing the processes by which criminals could exploit HSBC exists in the Monitor's Report; and (3) country names and explicit references to confidential material, as identified by these foreign jurisdictions.

For the reasons stated above, I grant the motion to unseal the Monitor's Report and the appended United States Country Report, subject to redactions made at the conclusion of the process described above. The government and HSBC shall submit proposed redactions to those two documents on or before February 12, 2016. The other five country reports shall remain under seal.

Questions and Comments

1. Judge Gleeson's opinion discusses two theories for making the monitor's report public. One is the right of access to judicial documents recognized under common law, a right that has been carried forward in federal court jurisprudence as a matter of federal common law. The other theory is grounded directly in the First Amendment, and concerns the public's right to know about their government and the functioning of the judicial branch. Judge Gleeson's opinion is based explicitly on the First Amendment consideration, but it seems pretty clear he would have reached the same result if he had decided the matter under the common law right of access.

2. In either case, the public's right of access is limited to documents that are "judicial" in character. The monitor's report in this case was not prepared by a judge and was not a required filing in court. The parties originally sought to keep the report out of court altogether, offering instead to provide the judge with a summary; it was only filed—and then filed under seal—when the judge so required. The monitor himself was not a magistrate, law clerk, or other judicial

official; he is a private party compensated and working under a contract with the defendant bank. In what sense is the report a judicial document?

3. Do you agree with Judge Gleeson that the public has a strong interest in reviewing the monitor's report — a more than 1,000-page-long document, undoubtedly filled with technical details? What do you think of the countervailing interests in non-disclosure? Why did the government and the bank fight so hard to keep this document away from prying eyes?

4. Do you agree with the scope of disclosure ordered in this case?

5. Do you detect in this opinion some of the judicial frustrations that motivated the district court opinions, discussed in Chapter 7, which attempted to claim for the judiciary a larger role in the review and approval of deferred prosecution agreements?

6. Professor Root recommends the creation of a statutory privilege that protects communications between the monitor, the corporation, and the government. Veronica Root, *The Monitor-"Client" Relationship,* 100 Va. L. Rev. 523 (2014). To what extent, if any, would such a privilege affect the First Amendment right of access recognized in Judge Gleeson's opinion? To what extent would it affect the common law right of access?

7. Does a court's supervisory power — the power to supervise and manage proceedings pending before the court — provide an alternative source of authority for disclosing information from monitor reports on compliance with pending DPAs?

F. CONSULTANTS

In addition to attorneys, accountants, and auditors, a variety of consultants advise or assist organizations in the performance of their compliance functions. The following excerpts illustrate the tension between the role of an external consultant as advocate for the client and servant of the public interest.

In re American Continental/Lincoln Savings & Loan Securities Litigation

884 F. Supp. 1388 (D. Ariz. 1995)

Plaintiff Lexecon is an economic consulting firm, some of whose employees, including Plaintiff Daniel Fischel, testify frequently as experts on certain economic issues. Fischel is a tenured professor at the University of Chicago Law School. Defendants Milberg Weiss Bershad Hynes & Lerach, Cotchett, Illston & Pitre, and Greenfield & Chimicles are law firms that specialize in securities class action litigation. As such, they were co-counsel for class plaintiffs in Shields v. Keating, a multi-district case litigated in the district of Arizona.

Shields was a class action brought on behalf of purchasers of securities issued by Keating's company, American Continental Corporation ("ACC" or "ACC/Lincoln"). The class sought over $360 million in pre-trebled damages and unspecified punitive damages against a variety of defendants claiming that they had conspired to violate securities and racketeering laws by misleading investors with respect to the safety of ACC securities. In September 1989, the accounting firm of Arthur

Young & Co., one of the Shields defendants, retained Lexecon and Fischel as experts to assist in preparing its defense.

In March 1990, defendants (as class counsel) sought leave to file a fifth amended complaint in order to add both Lexecon and Fischel as parties. Defendants based the class claim against Lexecon and Fischel on certain reports prepared by that organization on behalf of ACC/Lincoln for submission to federal regulators. The proposed Fifth Amended Complaint alleged that Lexecon and Fischel had learned the "true" nature of ACC/Lincoln's business practices, but nevertheless assisted the thrift in its efforts to keep regulators at bay while it continued to sell worthless debentures. The motion for leave to file an amended complaint was denied in May of 1990.

Approximately six months after this ruling, defendants renewed their efforts to bring Lexecon into the Shields litigation. Defendants created a purported "Sixth Amended Complaint" naming Lexecon and Fischel as defendants. This document was circulated to dozens of Lexecon's potential clients—individual lawyers, law firms, and corporations—not all of whom were prospective parties to the complaint. This pleading was never filed. A few days later, however, a different version of the proposed "Sixth Amended Complaint" was filed, this time deleting Fischel as a named defendant. On January 30, 1991, leave to file was granted.

According to Lexecon, defendants' purpose behind involving Lexecon and Fischel in the Shields litigation was threefold: (1) to extract false testimony implicating other Shields defendants, (2) prevent Arthur Young & Co. from using Lexecon as an expert in Shields, and (3) "to make Lexecon in general and Fischel in particular far less attractive to potential clients as expert witnesses." Lexecon claims that defendants were making good on Melvyn Weiss' threat to "destroy" Fischel because of his testimony widely believed to have produced several big victories against clients represented by Milberg Weiss. . . .

In November of 1992, Lexecon filed a complaint in the Northern District of Illinois alleging malicious prosecution, abuse of process, defamation, and other commercial disparagement torts. It is Lexecon's position that it had no choice but to sue due to defendants' improper collateral use of Lexecon's involvement in Shields. The case was thereafter referred to the multi-district litigation panel which determined that the matter was properly considered a part of the American Continental Corporation/Lincoln Savings and Loan Litigation. The case is now pending before this Court. . . .

Questions and Comments

1. This litigation represents an attempt by plaintiffs' attorneys to impose a form of gatekeeper liability on an economic consulting firm that had provided services to Lincoln Savings. The case turned into a grudge match between several of the most powerful (and wealthiest) firms on either side of the divide: prominent class action firms, on one side (including the best known plaintiffs' securities firm of the era, Milberg Weiss); and on the other side Lexecon, one of the most successful forensic consulting firms in the country.

2. The plaintiffs' attorneys' efforts to drag Lexecon into the case backfired badly. Lexecon and one of its principals, Daniel Fischel, sued them for defamation and malicious prosecution. The battle raged all the way to the Supreme Court of the United States, *see* Lexecon, Inc. v. Milberg Weiss Bershad Hynes & Lerach, 523 U.S.

26 (1998). Eventually, the case went to trial in federal district court in Illinois on Lexecon's claim for compensatory and punitive damages. The jury awarded Lexecon tens of millions of dollars in compensatory damages, whereupon the defendants settled the punitive claim for millions more in order to avoid a jury verdict on that part of the case. Milberg's travails were not over: In an unrelated matter, the firm and several of its partners, including a principal partner in the Lincoln Savings case, were convicted of crimes associated with paying clients to serve as representative plaintiffs. Meanwhile Daniel Fischel went on to become the dean of the University of Chicago Law School.

3. This case quieted efforts by plaintiffs' attorneys to use litigation as a vehicle for imposing a gatekeeper function on private economic and forensic consultants such as Lexecon. Putting aside the particular facts of the *Lexecon* case, do you think that the result was beneficial and appropriate?

New York State Department of Financial Services, In the Matter of Deloitte Financial Advisory Services LLP

June 18, 2013

[In 2004 and 2005 Deloitte FAS performed consulting work for the New York branch of Standard Chartered Bank (SCB) in connection with compliance with money laundering regulations and regulations restricting the provision of services to entities subject to U.S. economic sanctions.]

Now, having fully considered the evidence, the Department and Deloitte FAS agree that Deloitte FAS violated [New York Banking Law] and Deloitte FAS's own policies by knowingly disclosing confidential supervisory information to SCB regarding other Deloitte FAS client banks.

Furthermore, by removing a recommendation regarding "cover payments" from its final report during the SCB engagement, Deloitte FAS did not demonstrate the necessary autonomy and objectivity that is now required of consultants performing regulatory compliance work for entities supervised by the Department. . . .

The Department and Deloitte FAS wish to establish a constructive relationship focused on protecting investors and the capital markets.

The Department and Deloitte FAS will work together to develop enhanced procedures and safeguards applicable to independent consultants in Department engagements that will address the issues identified during the Department's investigation of the SCB matter, and that will become the "gold standard" in conducting engagements with the Department.

Accordingly, in order to resolve this matter without proceedings, the Parties agree upon the following facts and settlement provisions.

FACTUAL BACKGROUND

On October 7, 2004, SCB executed a joint written agreement with the Federal Reserve Bank of New York (the "Reserve") and the New York State Banking Department (which subsequently became the Department), which identified several compliance and risk management deficiencies in the anti-money laundering and Bank Secrecy Act controls at SCB's New York Branch. The agreement required SCB to complete certain remedial actions, among them retaining a qualified independent consulting firm acceptable to the Reserve and the Department to conduct an historical review of account and transaction activity. The purpose of the review was to determine whether suspicious activity involving accounts or transactions at, by, or through the New York Branch was properly identified and reported in accordance with applicable suspicious activity reporting regulations ("Transaction Review").

On October 27, 2004, SCB formally engaged with the predecessor entity of Deloitte FAS as its qualified independent consulting firm to conduct the Transaction Review.

On August 30, 2005, a senior member of the Deloitte FAS engagement team sent two consecutive emails to another Deloitte FAS engagement team member and an SCB employee. The SCB employee subsequently forwarded one of those emails to her SCB supervisor.

The emails attached copies of two transaction review reports that Deloitte FAS had previously performed for other client banks. One report contained an historical transaction review for suspicious activity — specifically, activity related to U.S. dollar clearing and possible money laundering at the bank's New York branch. The other report involved also contained an historical transaction review for suspicious activity, but addressed cash transactions, sales of monetary instruments and funds transfer activity in the retail operations of that bank.

The emails suggested that the two other bank reports be used as templates for drafting the SCB final report. The emails also directed the Deloitte FAS and SCB engagement managers to compare the draft SCB report against confidential supervisory information contained in one of the improperly disclosed reports. Specifically, the Deloitte FAS and SCB managers were directed to cross-check to "Bad guy/ bad bank" lists contained in each report in order to match up individuals and institutions "as to whom suspicious activity reports may have been previously filed" and, thus, "put on the bank's enhanced due diligence or watch list."

Both reports contained confidential supervisory information, which Deloitte FAS was legally barred by New York Banking Law from disclosing to any individual or entity without the Department's prior authorization. Deloitte FAS was not authorized by the Department to disclose those two reports to SCB.

In early October 2005, Deloitte FAS finalized the draft Transaction Review report. One or more drafts of the Transaction Review report included a recommendation generally explaining how certain [messages] used by the Society for Worldwide Interbank Financial Telecommunication message system could be manipulated by banks to evade money laundering controls on U.S. dollar clearing activities and suggesting the elimination or restriction of such payments.

Based primarily on SCB's objection, Deloitte FAS removed the recommendation from the written final report before the written report was submitted to the Department.

The Department has found no evidence that Deloitte FAS intentionally advanced SCB's unlawful conduct.

SETTLEMENT PROVISIONS

Monetary Payment

Within five (5) business days of executing this agreement, Deloitte FAS will pay to the Department ten million U.S. dollars ($10,000,000). This payment represents in the aggregate the approximate amount of fees and expenses received by Deloitte FAS for its work on the Transaction Review and reimbursement to the Department for the costs of its investigation and for the costs to be incurred by the Department in connection with the development and implementation of the procedures and safeguards required by the Agreement.

Practice Reforms

Deloitte FAS will establish and implement, as promptly as possible but in any event within twelve (12) months from the date of this Agreement, the procedures and safeguards for engagements set forth in Exhibit A, which are intended to raise the standards now generally viewed as applicable to independent financial services consultants. The specific design and implementation of these procedures are subject to such modification or refinement as may be agreed between Deloitte FAS and the Department on the basis of further analysis and experience. The Department and Deloitte FAS will meet at least monthly to discuss Deloitte FAS's progress in implementing these procedures and safeguards.

The Department intends to use these procedures and safeguards as the model for establishing the standards that will govern all independent consultants who seek to be retained or approved by the Department.

Voluntary Abstention from Department Engagements

For one year from the date of this Agreement, while it develops and implements the best practices described above, Deloitte FAS will not accept any new engagements that would require the Department to approve Deloitte FAS as an independent consultant or to authorize the disclosure of confidential information under New York Banking Law to Deloitte FAS, provided, however, that after at least six (6) months from the date of this Agreement, the Department (in its sole and unreviewable discretion) and Deloitte FAS may agree to an early termination of Deloitte FAS's voluntary practice abstention if Deloitte FAS has established and implemented the procedures and safeguards set forth in Exhibit A. . . .

Exhibit A
New York Department of Financial Services
Independent Consultant Practices for Departmental Engagements

- When a firm is engaged by a financial institution ("Financial Institution") as an independent consultant (a "Consultant") pursuant to a Written Agreement, Consent Order or other type of regulatory agreement ("Consent Order") with the New York Department of Financial Services ("DFS"), the Consultant, the Financial Institution and DFS will adhere to the practices set forth below in order to provide DFS with better transparency regarding the work performed by the Consultant during the course of an engagement.
- The process by which DFS determines whether a Consultant engaged by a Financial Institution pursuant to a Consent Order is acceptable to DFS shall include disclosure by the Financial Institution and the Consultant of all prior work by the Consultant (not including non-U.S. member firms or non-U.S. affiliates) for the Financial Institution in the previous 3 years, subject to privilege and confidentiality constraints.
- DFS shall directly contact the Consultant and the Financial Institution if it believes that any of the prior work may impair the Consultant's independence with respect to the services to be provided pursuant to the Consent Order.

- Resolution of the issue shall be discussed among the parties prior to a final determination by DFS.
- The engagement letter between the Consultant and the Financial Institution shall require that although the consultant may take into account the expressed views of the Financial Institution, the ultimate conclusions and judgment will be that of the Consultant based upon the exercise of its own independent judgment.
- The Consultant and the Financial Institution shall submit a work plan to DFS setting forth the proposed procedures to be followed during the course of the engagement and the proposed timeline for the completion of the work.
- The work plan submitted to DFS by the Financial Institution and the Consultant shall, among other components, confirm the location(s) from which the transaction and account data planned to be reviewed during the engagement will be obtained, as applicable.
- Any material modifications or additions to the work plan shall be submitted to DFS for approval prior to commencement of the modified or additional work.
- DFS and the Consultant will maintain an open line of communication during the course of the engagement.
- DFS will identify key personnel at DFS with whom the Consultant will have ongoing contact. The Consultant shall do the same. The Consultant will notify DFS and the Financial Institution in writing should there be a need to make a change in the identity of any key personnel at the Consultant.
- The Financial Institution will consent that contacts between the Consultant and DFS may occur outside the presence of the Financial Institution, during which information can be shared, including information regarding difficult or contentious judgments made in the course of the engagement. Such meetings shall take place on a monthly basis unless otherwise agreed among the parties.
- Should a disagreement about a material matter relating to the engagement arise between the Consultant and the Financial Institution during the course of an engagement relating to the work plan, a particular finding by the Consultant, the scope of the review, interpretation of the engagement letter, or the inclusion or exclusion of information from the final report, and the disagreement cannot be resolved through discussions between the Consultant and the Financial Institution, such disagreement shall be brought to the attention of DFS. Such a procedure should be memorialized in the Consent Order.
- The Consultant and Financial Institution shall maintain records of recommendations to the Financial Institution relating to Suspicious Activity Report filings that the Financial Institution did not adopt, and provide such records to DFS at DFS's request. The Financial Institution should consent to provision of such records to DFS in the engagement letter governing the project or such a requirement should be memorialized in the Consent Order.
- The Consent Order shall require that a final report be issued by the Consultant in an engagement. The Consultant may share drafts of the final report with the Financial Institution prior to submission. The Financial Institution shall be required by the Consent Order to disclose to the Consultant who within the Financial Institution has reviewed or commented on drafts of the findings, conclusions and recommendations to be included in the final report. The final report shall contain a listing of all the personnel from the

Financial Institution made known to the Consultant who substantively reviewed or commented on drafts of the findings, conclusions and recommendations to be included in the final report.

- The Consultant shall have in place policies and procedures designed specifically to maintain the confidentiality of bank supervisory material, which would provide, among other things, that such material would not be shared with anyone who was not authorized by law or regulation to receive such material.

- The Consultant shall develop a comprehensive training program regarding the requirements of New York Banking Law governing confidential supervisory information, and shall provide such training to all of its partners, principals and employees assigned to engagements in which it is expected that the Consultant will have access to materials covered by New York Banking Law.

- Deloitte FAS shall draft, in consultation with DFS, a handbook providing guidance as to what materials are covered by New York Banking Law governing confidential supervisory information and how such materials should be handled. DFS shall approve the final version of the handbook. The Consultant shall circulate copies of the handbook to its personnel assigned to an engagement in which it is expected that the Consultant will have access to materials covered by New York Banking Law.

Questions and Comments

1. Who was Deloitte's "client" in the initial engagement?

2. What sorts of fiduciary obligation, if any, did Deloitte owe to SCB when conducting this engagement?

3. How would the relationship between Deloitte and clients such as SCB change under the new DFS procedure?

4. Suppose under the new procedure the consultant has a disagreement with a bank about how to characterize certain transactions. Can the consultant "tell on" the bank by informing the regulator? Must it do so? Under what conditions?

5. Note that under the new procedure the consultant is allowed to share a draft of its report with the client before finalizing it in a form that the regulator can see. Must it inform DFS of material changes in the final report? Should it do so as a matter of prudence?

6. Deloitte shared confidential supervisory information in its possession about another bank — but did this warrant a $10 million fine and a year of banishment?

7. At the request of SCB, Deloitte dropped a recommendation from its final report. What was wrongful about this? Is an independent service provider entitled to listen to its client and to modify a report if the client makes a compelling case?

8. DFS is frank about its wish to use this case as a vehicle to establish "best practices" for consultants in Deloitte's situation. Did DFS seize on a weak case against Deloitte so it could have an excuse to promulgate its new rules in a way that generated media attention? If so, is it appropriate to use an enforcement proceeding for this purpose? Should the Department instead have simply promulgated and published a code of best practices in a rulemaking-type procedure?

9. The excerpted agreement was used by politicians — including New York's Governor — as an opportunity to promote the effectiveness of their administrations

at a time of widespread public distrust of financial institutions. An official press release issued contemporaneously with the agreement stated, in part:

> Governor Andrew M. Cuomo today announced that the Administration has reached an agreement with Deloitte Financial Advisory Services ("Deloitte") regarding the company's misconduct, violations of law, and lack of autonomy during its consulting work at Standard Chartered on anti-money laundering issues. . . . "The State's agreement with Deloitte will serve as a new model for reforming the financial services consulting industry in New York as well as across the country," Governor Cuomo said. "When tasked by government agencies to undertake regulatory work at financial institutions, it is critical for these consultants to remain autonomous and avoid conflicts of interest. Our homeowners, investors, and economy are protected when independent consultants are truly 'independent.'" . . . Benjamin M. Lawsky, Superintendent of Financial Services, said, "At times, the consulting industry has been infected by an 'I'll scratch your back if you scratch mine' culture and a stunning lack of independence. Today, we are taking an important step in helping ensure that consultants are independent voices — rather than beholden to the large institutions that pay their fees. Our aggressive work investigating and reforming the consulting industry is far from over and will continue in the days, weeks, and months ahead."

10. This case involved a consultant hired as part of an enforcement proceeding. Should the same standards apply to consultants who are retained by a bank to advise or assist in money laundering compliance when the bank is not subject to any enforcement action?

11. In 2013, the New York State financial services regulator issued subpoenas to two of the most important firms providing consulting services to the banking industry, Promontory Financial Group and PricewaterhouseCoopers, related to concerns about those firms' services to banks in connection with money laundering and money transfers to countries subject to U.S. sanctions. Press reports on the investigation suggested that the regulator was concerned that these consultants operated with severe conflicts of interest — while they are supposed to provide objective advice on compliance and risk-management issues, they are selected and compensated by the banks which they are advising.

12. Should the government strengthen the independence requirements for companies that provide consulting services to regulated industries in the areas of compliance and risk management?

In August 2014, the NYDFS policy of bringing enforcement actions against consultants bore more substantial fruit, when the agency settled charges with PricewaterhouseCoopers in connection with services provided by PwC to Bank of Tokyo Mitsubishi in connection with its compliance with anti-money laundering rules:

NYDFS Announces PricewaterhouseCoopers Regulatory Advisory Services Will Face 24-Month Consulting Suspension; Pay $25 Million; Implement Reforms After Misconduct During Work at Bank of Tokyo Mitsubishi

Aug. 18, 2014

Benjamin M. Lawsky, Superintendent of Financial Services, announced today that PricewaterhouseCoopers ("PwC") Regulatory Advisory Services will be suspended for 24 months from accepting consulting engagements at financial institutions regulated by the New York State Department of Financial Services (NYDFS); make a $25 million payment to the State of New York; and implement a series of reforms after improperly altering a report submitted to regulators regarding sanctions and anti-money laundering compliance at Bank of Tokyo Mitsubishi (BTMU). Under pressure from BTMU executives, PwC removed a warning in an ostensibly "objective" report to regulators surrounding the Bank's scheme to falsify wire transfer information for Iran, Sudan, and other sanctioned entities.

Superintendent Lawsky said: "We are continuing to find examples of improper influence and misconduct in the bank consulting industry. As a regulatory community, it may well be advisable for us to take a hard look in the mirror and ask whether we are doing enough to root out and investigate this troubling web of conflicts. When bank executives pressure a consultant to whitewash a supposedly 'objective' report to regulators — and the consultant goes along with it — that can strike at the very heart of our system of prudential oversight."

A more than year-long DFS investigation uncovered that PwC — under pressure from BTMU executives — improperly altered an "historical transaction review" (HTR) report submitted to regulators on wire transfers that the Bank performed on behalf of sanctioned countries and entities. During the 11th month (May 2008) of a 12-month engagement (June 2007 to June 2008), PwC found that BTMU had issued special instructions to Bank employees to strip wire messages of information that would have triggered sanctions compliance alerts — after the Bank denied having such a policy only weeks before in a meeting with regulators. PwC understood that this improper data manipulation could significantly compromise the HTR's integrity and PwC inserted into an earlier draft of the report an express acknowledgement informing regulators that "had PwC know[n] about these special instructions at the initial Phase of the HTR then we would have used a different approach in completing this project." Specifically, PwC would have conducted a more in-depth, forensic investigation into the Bank's scheme — rather than simply a more rote, mechanical review of the transactions provided to it by the Bank. In other words, the discovery of the Bank's scheme to falsify wire transfer information cast doubts on whether PwC had a complete set of data to review (among other issues).

However, at the Bank's request, PwC ultimately removed the original warning language from the final HTR Report the Bank submitted to regulators and, in fact, inserted a passage stating the exact opposite conclusion: "[W]e have concluded that the written instructions would not have impacted the completeness of the data available for the HTR and our methodology to process and search the HTR data was appropriate." Moreover, also at the Bank's request, PwC removed other key information from drafts of the HTR Report, including:

- deleting the English translation of BTMU's wire stripping instructions, which referenced the Bank doing business with "enemy countries" of the U.S.;
- deleting a regulatory term of art that PwC used throughout the report in describing BTMU's wire-stripping instructions ("Special Instruction") and replacing it with a nondescript reference that lacked regulatory significance ("Written Instruction");
- deleting most of PwC's discussion of BTMU's wire-stripping activities;
- deleting information concerning BTMU's potential misuse of OFAC screening software in connection with its wire-stripping activities;

- deleting several forensic questions that PwC identified as necessary for consideration in connection with the HTR Report; and
- deleting a section of the HTR Report that discussed the appearance of special characters (such as "#" "-" and ",") in wire transfer messages, which disabled PwC's filtering system from detecting at least several transactions involving Sudan and Myanmar (e.g. SUD#AN).

Questions and Comments

1. This case involves PwC, the global auditing, accounting, and consulting behemoth. The identity of the defendant was probably no accident: The entire financial market takes note when a firm such as PwC is sanctioned. What message was NYDFS attempting to convey?

2. What, exactly, did the PwC do that was wrong? What should a party in PwC's position do next time around?

3. How, if at all, will orders such as this affect clients' willingness to share all information with their consultants, even in cases stemming from regulatory violations? How will it affect the questions that consultants ask?

4. NYDFS followed up on this order with severe sanctions against the bank, including a fine of $315 million, the resignation of the compliance manager, and the relocation of the bank's New York–related compliance operations to its offices in New York. *See* http://www.dfs.ny.gov/about/press2014/pr1411181-consent.pdf.

More was to come. In August 2015, the NYDFS effectively barred one of the country's leading banking consultants, Promontory Financial Group, from doing business in New York State. Promontory had been engaged by Standard Chartered Bank to perform an investigation compliance with money laundering and sanctions regulations. In connection with that engagement, Promontory prepared reports and made presentations to Standard Chartered Bank's management and its regulators, including the predecessor of the NYDFS.

In 2012, relying in part on information obtained from Promontory, the NYDFS entered into a consent decree with the bank requiring it to pay $340 million in fines and to install an independent on-site monitor to examine and evaluate the Bank's BSA/AML compliance programs, policies, and procedures. Once installed, the monitor identified other, previously unreported failures in the bank's transaction monitoring systems. In August 2014, Standard Chartered and the Department entered into a second Consent Order, pursuant to which Standard Chartered suspended certain U.S. dollar clearing through its New York branch, paid an additional $300 million penalty, extended the term of the monitor for two years, and agreed to take additional remedial steps.

NYDFS then commenced an investigation of Promontory, the consultant. The Department concluded that although Promontory had touted its independence and credibility, it had on numerous occasions made changes to tone down language used in its reports, avoid additional questions from regulators, omit red flag terms, or otherwise make the reports more favorable to the Bank. The Department also apparently disbelieved the testimony of Promontory witnesses in the investigation, concluding that their statements "lacked credibility." As a sanction, the Department determined to deny Promontory access to confidential supervisory information. New York Department of Financial Services, Report of Investigation of Promontory Financial Group, LLC (August 2015).

Questions and Comments

1. The effect of the NYDFS decision was likely to be severe: A bank consultant such as Promontory cannot provide effective services to its clients if it lacks access to the kind of information denied to it by the Department's decision.

2. The vigor of the Department's actions against Promontory reflect the perception that regulators cannot do their job effectively if they cannot rely on the independency and credibility of consultants such as Promontory who guide regulated entities in shaping their response to regulatory enforcement actions. Do you get the sense that by going after the leading firm in the industry, NYDFS was seeking to send a message to all of its competitors that they had best avoid this sort of behavior when representing bank clients in regulatory matters involving the agency?

3. Granting the importance of the public policy being advanced by the NYDFS, was the sanction it imposed in this case appropriate? This decision by the Department did not come after a contested hearing where Promontory was allowed to present its case, call witnesses, or cross examine witnesses called by the government. It was not protected by rules of evidence designed to weed out unreliable testimony. The decision to deny it proprietary information was not made by an impartial official, but rather by an agency that was pursuing a pre-announced agenda to crack down on consultants such as Promontory. Because the decision to deny Promontory access to supervisory materials was within the discretion of the agency, it was far from clear that Promontory would have any effective means for obtaining judicial review of the agency's action. Even if Promontory could obtain such review, deferential principles of judicial review made it highly unlikely that such a recourse would provide any relief.

4. Is it healthy, in a democracy, for a government agency to possess — much less exercise — this sort of nearly unchecked power?

G. PROVIDERS OF FINANCIAL SERVICES

Financial service providers fit the definition of gatekeepers to the extent that their services are needed to allow a client to accomplish some goal (such as, for example, selling a new issue of securities or buying or selling another company or division). To what extent does such a party owe gatekeeper-type duties to the public when providing such a service to a client? To date, the answer has been: "only to a very limited extent." However, some rustlings in the wind suggest that these firms may someday soon be charged with more explicit responsibilities to the public, or at least to constituents such as shareholders. Consider the following excerpt in this regard:

In re Rural Metro Corporation Stockholders Litigation
88 A.3d 54 (Del. Ch.), *app. dismissed,* 105 A.3d 990 (Del. 2014)

On June 30, 2011, Rural/Metro Corporation ("Rural" or the "Company") merged with an affiliate of Warburg Pincus LLC ("Warburg" or "WP"). Each publicly held share of Rural common stock was converted into the right to receive $17.25 in cash.

The plaintiffs contend that the members of the Rural board of directors (the "Board") breached their fiduciary duties by approving the merger and by failing to disclose material information in the Company's definitive proxy statement (the "Proxy Statement"). The plaintiffs further contend that defendant RBC Capital Markets, LLC ("RBC") aided and abetted the directors' breaches of fiduciary duty. The directors settled before trial. . . . The case proceeded to trial against RBC.

This post-trial decision holds RBC liable for aiding and abetting breaches of fiduciary duty by the Board.

[Rural, a NASDAQ-listed Delaware corporation, is a leading provider of ambulance and fire protection services. RBC, which had recently helped the company in a financing deal, pitched its services as a "sell-side" adviser, hoping to earn fees (a) from Rural in any sale of that firm, (b) from retentions as a "buy-side" adviser in certain other ostensibly unrelated engagements, and (c) from arranging "staple financing" offered to potential bidders in a sale of Rural. Rural responded by empowering a special board committee to explore and recommend strategic alternatives. The special committee retained Rural as a sell-side adviser, even though it recognized that Rural had a conflict of interest due to its interest in arranging the financing. Rural thereupon began soliciting buyer interest, focusing on private equity firms from which it might expect buy-side engagements and giving a lower priority to other firms. Many firms declined to participate because they were also negotiating to acquire Rural's chief competitor — a fact known to Rural's board and to RBS, its adviser.

[A meeting of Rural's board of directors received a briefing on sales efforts from RBS that did not contain any valuation metrics. RBS explained that it had not pursued non-financial firms as possible buyers because they would probably not be interested. The board determined not to extend the bidding process to accommodate an interested buyer that was in the process of acquiring its chief competitor. Eventually, only Warburg submitted a bid. RBS continued to delay in offering a fairness opinion because it hoped to supply buy-side financing to Warburg. Eventually, after RBS offered a fairness opinion in a process that the court depicts as manipulated to support the deal, the full Rural board approved the sale to Warburg. Plaintiff shareholders filed a derivative suit against Rural's directors and its investment advisers.]

Directors are not expected to have the expertise to determine a corporation's value for themselves, or to have the time or ability to design and carry out a sale process. Financial advisors provide these expert services. In doing so, they function as gatekeepers. . . . The threat of liability helps incentivize gatekeepers to provide sound advice, monitor clients, and deter client wrongs. Framed for present purposes, the prospect of aiding and abetting liability for investment banks who induce boards of directors to breach their duty of care creates a powerful financial reason for the banks to provide meaningful fairness opinions and to advise boards in a manner that helps ensure that the directors carry out their fiduciary duties when exploring strategic alternatives and conducting a sale process, rather than in a manner that falls short of established fiduciary norms. . . .

[The court held that the board of directors had breached their fiduciary duties in numerous respects. It faulted the board on multiple counts, among them: failing to authorize the special committee to conduct a sale of the company; initiating a sale at a time when potential acquirers were preoccupied with negotiations to acquire the company's principal competitor; focusing on financial buyers and ignoring strategic acquirers; failing to properly supervise RBC as its sell-side adviser; failing to acquire credible valuation information in a timely fashion; and failing to fully consider alternatives to the Warburg deal. The court then held that RBS had knowingly aided and abetted the board's breach of fiduciary duty.]

RBC created the unreasonable process and informational gaps that led to the Board's breach of duty. At the outset, RBC knew that it was not disclosing its interest in obtaining a role financing the acquisition of EMS or how it intended to use the Rural process to capture the EMS financing business.

RBC similarly knew that the Board and the Special Committee were uninformed about Rural's value when making critical decisions. RBC had not provided any preliminary valuation analysis since December 23, 2010, and had only provided its December 23 book to the Special Committee.

Most egregiously, RBC never disclosed to the Board its continued interest in buy-side financing and plans to engage in last minute lobbying of Warburg. As a result, it was natural for the Board to assume that Warburg's fully financed bid left RBC out of the picture and to send RBCV to negotiate with Warburg. RBC knew and failed to disclose to the Board that on Saturday, March 26, 2011, senior bankers at RBC were engaged in a full-court press to convince Warburg to use RBC's staple financing or include RBC in the financing package. While those fevered efforts were underway, RBC was simultaneously revising its valuation of Rural downward. . . .

Contrary to RBC's argument, the fact that RBC ultimately did not provide staple financing and receive the buy-side fees it coveted does not mean that RBC did not act consciously to obtain them. Humans do not always achieve the ends we seek. Failure does not imply that we did not pursue the means. Elite athletes spend years training and sacrificing for a chance at an Olympic medal. To not qualify at the trials, or to fall short of the podium, does not negate the pursuit. RBC knowingly participated in the Board's breach of its duty of care by creating the informational vacuum that misled the board. . . .

[The court also concluded that RBC's machinations had damaged the company.] The evidence at trial demonstrated persuasively that the fair value of Rural's stock at the time of the sale exceeded the $17.25 per share that Warburg was willing to pay. . . . RBC's actions led to (i) an ill-timed sale of Rural that did not capture value attributable to its acquisition strategy; (ii) a mismanaged sale process that generated only one final bid by a bidder that knew it had the upper hand in bidding and price negotiations; and (iii) uninformed board approval based on manipulated valuation analyses. . . . [B]ut for RBC's actions, a fully-informed Board would have had numerous opportunities to achieve a superior result.

A disinterested board that benefitted from disinterested advice and actually obtained an analysis of potential alternatives [(a)] likely would have concluded that Rural should wait before conducting a sale process[; (b)] would not have sent a conflicted agent to negotiate with Warburg from a position of weakness [; (c)] would have received valuation materials periodically throughout the process, rather than getting a valuation deck for the first time after 9:30 P.M. on March 27 and then approving the merger shortly after midnight[; and (d)] would have understood Rural's going concern value and been able to evaluate whether to continue to pursue the Company's business plan and preserve the opportunity for a sale at a more opportune time in the future, rather than relying at the last minute on valuation materials that RBC manipulated while making a final push for a role in Warburg's buy-side financing. As a result of this faulty process, the merger did not generate for stockholders the best value reasonable attainable. . . .

Questions and Comments

1. A majority of the members of Rural's board who participated in this transaction were genuinely "outside," "disinterested" directors. Why did they allow such a flawed process? Why did they seem so willing to be manipulated by the investment bankers? How could they have considered it appropriate to approve a sale of the company without seeing a valuation analysis until hours before the sale was approved?

2. Although the plaintiffs in this case did not claim that the board members violated their duty of loyalty, the court does note that certain directors who played a key role in this process had an interest in the transaction. Most importantly, Shackelton, who chaired the special committee, was managing director of a hedge fund that held a large position in Rural's stock. Yet while this interest might have provided an inducement to support a cash sale of the company, it would not have encouraged Shackleton to sell the company for a bargain — which, boiled down to its essentials, is what the court claims the directors did.

3. We saw in Chapter 2 that Delaware's duty of care has hardly any teeth. Do you agree that the behavior of Rural's directors was so deficient as to breach that duty? Could most of the directors have reasonably deferred to Shackleton, knowing that he was leading the process and that he had a strong interest in getting the best price for the company? Would the deference have been further confirmed by the fact that the ultimate sale price ($17.25 per share) represented a 37 percent over the company's pre-announcement trading price? What about the fact that Rural's stock had increased nearly 400 percent in value over the previous two years, even before the company came into play as an acquisition candidate? What happened to the business judgment rule?

4. The members of the board did not face personal liability in this case, even though their conduct is severely criticized in the opinion. The reason is that the company had opted out of director liability for violations of the duty of care, as permitted under §102(b)(7) of the Delaware General Corporation Law. How, then, could the investment bank be liable to pay damages, if the directors were not? The court in the excerpted opinion held, in a case of first impression, that §102(b)(7) doesn't shield persons other than directors from damages liability for aiding and abetting breaches of fiduciary duty, even if the directors who actually breach the duty are not themselves subject to liability.

5. Can we understand this decision in light of its role in the compliance landscape? The court explicitly enlists investment banks to act in the role of gatekeepers: institutions charged, to some extent at least, with monitoring corporate directors to ensure that they don't stray too far from their assigned roles as fiduciaries of the company and its shareholders. The case illustrates that the duty of care — even if it is largely ineffective against public companies that have made a §102(b)(7) election — can still be indirectly enforced, in some cases, through this gatekeeping role.

6. How effective will this decision be at enlisting investment banks as champions of shareholder interests? The facts appear egregious: RBC apparently flagrantly manipulated its client, engaged in egregious conflicts of interest, made a mockery

of its commitment to offer an impartial fairness opinion, and displayed the type of callous greed that the public all too often associates with investment bankers (RBC undoubtedly has a different account of what transpired, but the court's interpretation is what counts for the development of the law). If the adviser's behavior was this bad, then perhaps conduct less deplorable would not support liability on an aiding and abetting theory. In short, is this opinion a genuine foray into the area of gatekeeper liability, or a warning shot to scare away the worst abuses, leaving a wide range of discretion for investment advisers to serve their own interest or the interest of corporate managers at the expense of companies and shareholders?

10

Plaintiffs' Attorneys

In the previous chapter we examined the role of attorneys as "gatekeepers" of the compliance function. There we examined how in-house counsel and outside lawyers hired by a regulated entity could (or could not) play a constructive role in enhancing compliance with applicable rules and standards. We now turn to a different role for attorneys: the entrepreneurial lawyer who brings lawsuits against organizations alleging violations of legal rules. We have encountered these figures before, most notably in the context of our discussion of *qui tam* litigation (Chapter 8). Here they take center stage.

Plaintiffs' attorneys play three related but somewhat different roles in compliance matters:

- They bring lawsuits based on alleged breaches of regulatory duties, and in that capacity act as direct instruments for enforcing compliance.
- They bring lawsuits against corporate boards of directors alleging breaches of the *Caremark* duty to ensure that compliance systems are in place (see Chapter 2).
- They obtain settlements of lawsuits that include among their provisions commitments by defendants to institute or to upgrade their compliance operations.

A. SHAREHOLDERS DERIVATIVE LITIGATION

The shareholders derivative remedy is a platypus of the law. A platypus, as you may recall, is a weird animal that shouldn't exist: a beaver-furred, otter-tailed, duck-billed mammal that hatches its young in eggs. The shareholders derivative remedy is also an odd amalgam of disparate and conflicting parts. It is brought on behalf of a corporation by shareholders who, in the usual scheme of things, have only a minimal role in day-to-day management (see Chapter 1). The defendants are (usually) senior officers and directors who, in every other respect, control the very company that is purportedly suing them. The company itself is in the bizarre position of being both a plaintiff (the lawsuit is brought in its name) and a defendant (the company is controlled by people who are hostile to the lawsuit).

The unusual features of the derivative remedy are a function of its purpose. A company's directors and senior managers owe duties to serve the company with loyalty and competence. If they default on those duties, however, who will bring a lawsuit to hold them to account? The company is the injured party, but the company is under the control of the potential defendants. To give meaning to the legal duties of corporate managers, the law long ago deemed it expedient to create a remedy under which a shareholder could bring a lawsuit in the name of a corporation against a person who has allegedly harmed the company, in situations where the company itself will not act. The shareholder in such a case does not bring the lawsuit in her own personal capacity; her claim "derives" from the rights of the corporation she claims to represent.

1. Procedural Hurdles

Because of their odd role in the legal system, shareholders derivative cases face obstacles that are absent in ordinary cases: the demand requirement; the risk of a special litigation committee; and problems of obtaining a favorable venue for litigation.

a. The Demand Requirement

Because the derivative plaintiff is a volunteer — and one, moreover, who may be a figurehead for an entrepreneurial plaintiffs' attorney bent on obtaining a fee — the courts don't simply accept at face value her assertion that she is seeking to further the best interests of the corporation. Instead, the law contains a "demand requirement," which purportedly ensures that the company's board of directors will have an opportunity to evaluate the case before the derivative plaintiff proceeds. The demand requirements under Federal Rule of Civil Procedure 23.1 and similar state rules require the derivative complaint to "state with particularity: (A) any effort by the plaintiff to obtain the desired action from the directors or comparable authority and, if necessary, from the shareholders or members; and (B) the reasons for not obtaining the action or not making the effort."

Grimes v. Donald

673 A.2d 1207 (Del. 1996)

[Grimes, the derivative plaintiff, complained that the Company had entered into an illegal contract with its chief executive officer that effectively nullified the board's authority to supervise the management of the company's affairs. Grimes alleged that he wrote to the Board on September 23, 1993 and demanded that the Board abrogate the contract. The Board refused the demand in a letter dated November 8, 1993, which stated in part:]

> The Compensation Committee of our Board of Directors, as well as the entire Board, have seriously considered the issues set forth in your letter of September 29. To assist in the review, the Board obtained reports analyzing the relevant issues from the Company's outside benefits consultant, Hirschfeld, Stern, Moyer & Ross, Inc. and from the

Company's outside legal counsel, Jones, Day, Reavis & Pogue. The Compensation Committee and the full Board of Directors believe that a thorough analysis of the applicable provisions of Delaware law necessarily leads to a conclusion that Mr. Donald's duties as described in the Employment Agreement do not constitute an impermissible delegation of the duties of the Board of Directors. . . . Consequently, the Board declines to take any action to abrogate any provision of the Employment Agreement or the 1990 Long-Term Incentive Compensation Plan as you have requested. . . .

[T]he Chancellor held that Grimes waived his right to argue that demand was excused with respect to these claims because he had already made demand that the agreements be abrogated as unlawful. We agree. . . .

A stockholder filing a derivative suit must allege either that the board rejected his pre-suit demand that the board assert the corporation's claim or allege with particularity why the stockholder was justified in not having made the effort to obtain board action. . . . [Aronson v. Lewis, 473 A.2d 805 (Del. 1984).]

One ground for alleging with particularity that demand would be futile is that a "reasonable doubt" exists that the board is capable of making an independent decision to assert the claim if demand were made. The basis for claiming excusal would normally be that: (1) a majority of the board has a material financial or familial interest; (2) a majority of the board is incapable of acting independently for some other reason such as domination or control; or (3) the underlying transaction is not the product of a valid exercise of business judgment. If the stockholder cannot plead such assertions . . . after using the "tools at hand" to obtain the necessary information before filing a derivative action, then the stockholder must make a pre-suit demand on the board.

The demand requirement serves a salutary purpose. First, by requiring exhaustion of intra-corporate remedies, the demand requirement invokes a species of alternative dispute resolution procedure which might avoid litigation altogether. Second, if litigation is beneficial, the corporation can control the proceedings. Third, if demand is excused or wrongfully refused, the stockholder will normally control the proceedings.

The jurisprudence of [the demand requirement] is designed to create a balanced environment which will: (1) on the one hand, deter costly, baseless suits by creating a screening mechanism to eliminate claims where there is only a suspicion expressed solely in conclusory terms; and (2) on the other hand, permit suit by a stockholder who is able to articulate particularized facts showing that there is a reasonable doubt either that (a) a majority of the board is independent for purposes of responding to the demand, or (b) the underlying transaction is protected by the business judgment rule.

Aronson introduced the term "reasonable doubt" into corporate derivative jurisprudence. Some courts and commentators have questioned why a concept normally present in criminal prosecution would find its way into derivative litigation. Yet the term is apt and achieves the proper balance. Reasonable doubt can be said to mean that there is a reason to doubt. This concept is sufficiently flexible and workable to provide the stockholder with "the keys to the courthouse" in an appropriate case where the claim is not based on mere suspicions or stated solely in conclusory terms.

WRONGFUL REFUSAL DISTINGUISHED FROM EXCUSAL

Demand has been excused in many cases in Delaware under the *Aronson* test. The law regarding wrongful refusal is not as well developed, however. Although

Delaware law does not require demand in every case because Delaware does have the mechanism of demand excusal, it is important that the demand process be meaningful. Therefore, a stockholder who makes a demand is entitled to know promptly what action the board has taken in response to the demand. A stockholder who makes a serious demand and receives only a peremptory refusal has the right to use the "tools at hand" to obtain the relevant corporate records, such as reports or minutes, reflecting the corporate action and related information in order to determine whether or not there is a basis to assert that demand was wrongfully refused. In no event may a corporation assume a position of neutrality and take no position in response to the demand.

If a demand is made, the stockholder has spent one — but only one — "arrow" in the "quiver." The spent "arrow" is the right to claim that demand is excused. The stockholder does not, by making demand, waive the right to claim that demand has been wrongfully refused. Simply because the composition of the board provides no basis ex ante for the stockholder to claim with particularity . . . that it is reasonable to doubt that a majority of the board is either interested or not independent, it does not necessarily follow ex post that the board in fact acted independently, disinterestedly or with due care in response to the demand. A board or a committee of the board may appear to be independent, but may not always act independently. If a demand is made and rejected, the board rejecting the demand is entitled to the presumption of the business judgment rule unless the stockholder can allege facts with particularity creating a reasonable doubt that the board is entitled to the benefit of the presumption. If there is reason to doubt that the board acted independently or with due care in responding to the demand, the stockholder may have the basis ex post to claim wrongful refusal. The stockholder then has the right to bring the underlying action with the same standing which the stockholder would have had, ex ante, if demand had been excused as futile.

APPLICATION TO THIS CASE

In the case before the Court, plaintiff made a pre-suit demand. Later, however, plaintiff contended that demand was excused. [P]laintiff, by making a demand, waived his right to contest the independence of the board. As the Court of Chancery properly held, plaintiff may not bifurcate his theories relating to the same claim. Thus, demand having been made as to the propriety of the Agreements, it cannot be excused as to the claim that the Agreements constituted waste, excessive compensation or was the product of a lack of due care. . . .

In this case, the Board of DSC considered and rejected the demand. After investing the time and resources to consider and decide whether or not to take action in response to the demand, the Board is entitled to have its decision analyzed under the business judgment rule unless the presumption of that rule can be rebutted. Grimes cannot avoid this result by holding back or bifurcating legal theories based on precisely the same set of facts alleged in the demand.

Since Grimes made a pre-suit demand with respect to all claims arising out of the Agreements, he was required . . . to plead with particularity why the Board's refusal to act on the derivative claims was wrongful. The complaint recites the Board's rejection of Grimes' demand and proceeds to assert why Grimes disagrees with the Board's conclusion. The complaint generally asserts that the refusal could not have been the result of an adequate, good faith investigation since the Board decided not to act on the demand. . . . The complaint fails to include particularized allegations which would raise a reasonable doubt that the Board's decision to reject the demand was the product of a valid business judgment.

Accordingly, the judgment of the Court of Chancery is affirmed.

Questions and Comments

1. In practice, derivative plaintiffs rarely make a demand on directors before filing suit. Instead, they argue that presenting a demand would be futile. The *Grimes* case illustrates why it is risky to make a demand. In the usual case, the demand will be referred to independent board members who, assisted by outside counsel, will review the request and then (predictably) reject it. The problem from the plaintiff's point of view is that once the demand has been reviewed by independent directors, their decision to reject the demand is likely to be reviewed under the deferential "business judgment" standard and upheld for that reason. Plaintiff then is out of luck. If, on the other hand, the board decides to accept the demand (unlikely), the company takes over the lawsuit and the plaintiff's counsel is again out of luck (other than retaining a potential claim for fees incurred prior to the board's action). Better, then, to claim that demand is excused and hope that the court agrees that the board is incapable of making an impartial decision.

2. The *Aronson* case, cited and endorsed in *Grimes*, held that demand could be excused if the plaintiff established that a "reasonable doubt" exists that the board is capable of making an independent decision to assert the claim if demand were made. The term "reasonable doubt" resonates with the prosecution's burden of proof in criminal law. If that were the standard for the demand requirement in Delaware, it would seem quite easy for a derivative plaintiff to establish demand futility. In practice, however, Delaware requires that the derivative plaintiff do more than establish a criminal law type of reasonable doubt in order to avoid the demand requirement.

3. What does the court mean by the "tools at hand" that a complaining stockholder can use to obtain relevant corporate records? Are those tools likely to be effective?

4. The court explains that the demand requirement helps to "deter costly, baseless suits by creating a screening mechanism to eliminate claims where there is only a suspicion expressed solely in conclusory terms." Does the requirement, in fact, function as a discretionary screen that allows the judges of the Delaware Chancery Court to throw out lawsuits that they consider, based on their judicial experience, to have a low chance of success?

5. If the demand requirement does operate as a discretionary pretrial screening mechanism, is there anything problematic about this device? Why doesn't the Delaware Supreme Court come out and say this is what the requirement is intended to do?

b. Special Litigation Committees

Zapata Corp. v. Maldonado

430 A.2d 779 (1981)

Quillen, Justice:

... Maldonado, a stockholder of Zapata, instituted a derivative action in the Court of Chancery on behalf of Zapata against ten officers and/or directors of Zapata, alleging, essentially, breaches of fiduciary duty. Maldonado did not first demand that the board bring this action, stating instead such demand's futility because all directors were named as defendants and allegedly participated in the acts specified. . . .

The board [of Zapata] created an "Independent Investigation Committee" composed solely of the two new directors [who had not been on the board at the time of the alleged misconduct] . . . to determine whether the corporation should continue any or all of the litigation. . . . Following an investigation, the Committee concluded . . . that each action should "be dismissed forthwith as their continued maintenance is inimical to the Company's best interests. . . ."

When, if at all, should an authorized board committee be permitted to cause litigation, properly initiated by a derivative stockholder in his own right, to be dismissed? . . . Even though demand was not made in this case and the initial decision of whether to litigate was not placed before the board, Zapata's board, it seems to us, retained all of its corporate power concerning litigation decisions. . . . The corporate power inquiry then focuses on whether the board, tainted by the self-interest of a majority of its members, can legally delegate its authority to a committee of two disinterested directors. We find our statute clearly requires an affirmative answer to this question.

Our focus now switches to the Court of Chancery which is faced with a stockholder assertion that a derivative suit, properly instituted, should continue for the benefit of the corporation and a corporate assertion, properly made by a board committee acting with board authority, that the same derivative suit should be dismissed as inimical to the best interests of the corporation.

At the risk of stating the obvious, the problem is relatively simple. If, on the one hand, corporations can consistently wrest bona fide derivative actions away from well-meaning derivative plaintiffs through the use of the committee mechanism, the derivative suit will lose much, if not all, of its generally-recognized effectiveness as an intra-corporate means of policing boards of directors. If, on the other hand, corporations are unable to rid themselves of meritless or harmful litigation and strike suits, the derivative action, created to benefit the corporation, will produce the opposite, unintended result. It thus appears desirable to us to find a balancing point where bona fide stockholder power to bring corporate causes of action cannot be unfairly trampled on by the board of directors, but the corporation can rid itself of detrimental litigation.

As we noted, the question has been treated by other courts as one of the "business judgment" of the board committee. . . . We are not satisfied, however, that acceptance of the "business judgment" rationale at this stage of derivative litigation is a proper balancing point. While we admit an analogy with a normal case respecting board judgment, it seems to us that there is sufficient risk in the realities of a situation like the one presented in this case to justify caution beyond adherence to the theory of business judgment.

The context here is a suit against directors where demand on the board is excused. We think some tribute must be paid to the fact that the lawsuit was properly initiated. It is not a board refusal case. Moreover, this complaint was filed in June of 1975 and, while the parties undoubtedly would take differing views on the degree of litigation activity, we have to be concerned about the creation of an "Independent Investigation Committee" four years later, after the election of two new outside directors. Situations could develop where such motions could be filed after years of vigorous litigation for reasons unconnected with the merits of the lawsuit.

Moreover, notwithstanding our conviction that Delaware law entrusts the corporate power to a properly authorized committee, we must be mindful that directors are passing judgment on fellow directors in the same corporation and fellow directors, in this instance, who designated them to serve both as directors and committee members. The question naturally arises whether a "there but for the grace of God go I" empathy might not play a role. And the further question arises whether inquiry as to independence, good faith and reasonable investigation is sufficient safeguard against abuse, perhaps subconscious abuse. . . .

Whether the Court of Chancery will be persuaded by the exercise of a committee power resulting in a summary motion for dismissal of a derivative action, where a demand has not been initially made, should rest, in our judgment, in the independent discretion of the Court of Chancery. We thus steer a middle course between those cases which yield to the independent business judgment of a board committee and this case as determined below which would yield to unbridled plaintiff stockholder control. In pursuit of the course, we recognize that "(t)he final substantive judgment whether a particular lawsuit should be maintained requires a balance of many factors ethical, commercial, promotional, public relations, employee relations, fiscal as well as legal." But we are content that such factors are not "beyond the judicial reach" of the Court of Chancery which regularly and competently deals with fiduciary relationships, disposition of trust property, approval of settlements and scores of similar problems. We recognize the danger of judicial overreaching but the alternatives seem to us to be outweighed by the fresh view of a judicial outsider. Moreover, if we failed to balance all the interests involved, we would in the name of practicality and judicial economy foreclose a judicial decision on the merits. At this point, we are not convinced that is necessary or desirable.

After an objective and thorough investigation of a derivative suit, an independent committee may cause its corporation to file a pretrial motion to dismiss in the Court of Chancery. The basis of the motion is the best interests of the corporation, as determined by the committee. The motion should include a thorough written record of the investigation and its findings and recommendations. Under appropriate Court supervision, akin to proceedings on summary judgment, each side should have an opportunity to make a record on the motion. As to the limited issues presented by the motion noted below, the moving party should be prepared to meet the normal burden . . . that there is no genuine issue as to any material fact and that the moving party is entitled to dismiss as a matter of law. The Court should apply a two-step test to the motion.

First, the Court should inquire into the independence and good faith of the committee and the bases supporting its conclusions. Limited discovery may be ordered to facilitate such inquiries. The corporation should have the burden of proving independence, good faith and a reasonable investigation, rather than presuming independence, good faith and reasonableness. If the Court determines either that the committee is not independent or has not shown reasonable bases for its conclusions, or, if the Court is not satisfied for other reasons relating to the process, including but not limited to the good faith of the committee, the Court shall deny the corporation's motion. If, however, the Court is satisfied . . . that the committee was independent and showed reasonable bases for good faith findings and recommendations, the Court may proceed, in its discretion, to the next step.

The second step provides, we believe, the essential key in striking the balance between legitimate corporate claims as expressed in a derivative stockholder suit and a corporation's best interests as expressed by an independent investigating committee. The Court should determine, applying its own independent business judgment, whether the motion should be granted. This means, of course, that instances could arise where a committee can establish its independence and sound bases for its good faith decisions and still have the corporation's motion denied. The second step is intended to thwart instances where corporate actions meet the criteria of step one, but the result does not appear to satisfy its spirit, or where corporate actions would simply prematurely terminate a stockholder grievance deserving of further consideration in the corporation's interest. The Court of Chancery of course must carefully consider and weigh how compelling the corporate interest in dismissal is when faced with a non-frivolous lawsuit. The Court of Chancery should, when appropriate, give special consideration to matters of law and public policy in addition to the corporation's best interests. If the Court's independent business judgment is satisfied, the Court may proceed to grant the motion, subject, of course, to any equitable terms or conditions the Court finds necessary or desirable.

Questions and Comments

1. The questions before the court in the excerpted case were fundamental. If in a demand excused case the representative shareholder can control the litigation from that time forward, without constraints from the board of directors, the result could compromise the basic principle that the board of directors is ultimately responsible for the management of the corporation. Moreover, because the representative shareholder has only a minor stake in the company, her interests don't necessarily align well with the interests of the company she purports to represent. Probably for those reasons, the court is unwilling to go so far as to say that the mere fact that demand is excused is sufficient to divest the board of directors of all managerial power.

2. On the other hand, if the board of directors — cleansed of the taint of interested directors — retains all the powers that it had prior to the institution of the litigation, then the shareholder would accomplish little by surviving the demand excused obstacle; the independent directors could simply take over the case at will and oust the representative shareholder of any further role. Moreover, even though the directors on the special litigation committee are — in theory — independent and untainted by the allegations in the derivative action, their sympathies are likely to be with the defendants, their colleagues on the board of directors, rather than on a representative shareholder whom they may view as an officious intermeddler.

3. Can you articulate how the court navigated between these two unacceptable outcomes — vesting complete power in the representative shareholder or in the special committee?

4. What does it mean to speak of the court's "own independent business judgment"? This concept might seem like a solecism. A principal justification for the business judgment rule is the perception that because courts lack the experience, knowledge base, and exposure to strategic issues that is possessed by corporate managers, they cannot readily second-guess business decisions made by those charged with running the company. In other words, courts do not have business judgment. Yet in Zapata v. Maldonado, courts suddenly *do* have business judgment — and a judgment that is "independent" of the judgments of corporate managers. What gives?

In re Oracle Corp. Derivative Litigation

824 A.2d 917 (Del. Ch. 2003)

STRINE, Vice Chancellor.

In this opinion, I address the motion of the special litigation committee ("SLC") of Oracle Corporation to terminate this action, "the Delaware Derivative Action," and other such actions pending in the name of Oracle against certain Oracle directors and officers. These actions allege that these Oracle directors engaged in insider trading while in possession of material, non-public information showing that Oracle would not meet the earnings guidance it gave to the market for the third quarter of Oracle's fiscal year 2001. The SLC bears the burden of persuasion on this motion and must convince me that there is no material issue of fact calling into doubt its independence. This requirement is set forth in Zapata Corp. v. Maldonado and its progeny. . . .

During discovery, it emerged that the two SLC members — both of whom are professors at Stanford University — are being asked to investigate fellow Oracle directors who have important ties to Stanford, too. Among the directors who are accused by the derivative plaintiffs of insider trading are: (1) another Stanford professor, who taught one of the SLC members when the SLC member was a Ph.D. candidate and who serves as a senior fellow and a steering committee member alongside that SLC member at the Stanford Institute for Economic Policy Research or "SIEPR"; (2) a Stanford alumnus who has directed millions of dollars of contributions to Stanford during recent years, serves as Chair of SIEPR's Advisory Board and has a conference center named for him at SIEPR's facility, and has contributed nearly $600,000 to SIEPR and the Stanford Law School, both parts of Stanford with which one of the SLC members is closely affiliated; and (3) Oracle's CEO, who has made millions of dollars in donations to Stanford through a personal foundation and large donations indirectly through Oracle, and who was considering making donations of his $100 million house and $170 million for a scholarship program as late as August 2001, at around the same time period the SLC members were added to the Oracle board. . . .

I begin with an important reminder: the SLC bears the burden of proving its independence. It must convince me. But of what? According to the SLC, its members are independent unless they are essentially subservient to the Trading Defendants — i.e., they are under the "domination and control" of the interested parties. If the SLC is correct and this is the central inquiry in the independence determination, they would win. Nothing in the record suggests to me that either Garcia-Molina or Grundfest [the Stanford professors who comprised the special committee] are dominated and controlled by any of the Trading Defendants, by Oracle, or even by Stanford.

But, in my view, an emphasis on "domination and control" would serve only to fetishize much-parroted language, at the cost of denuding the independence inquiry of its intellectual integrity. Take an easy example. Imagine if two brothers were on a corporate board, each successful in different businesses and not dependent in any way on the other's beneficence in order to be wealthy. The brothers are brothers, they stay in touch and consider each other family, but each is opinionated and strong-willed. A derivative action is filed targeting a transaction involving one of the brothers. The other brother is put on a special litigation committee to investigate the case. If the test is domination and control, then one brother could investigate the other. Does any sensible person think that is our law? I do not think it is.

And it should not be our law. Delaware law should not be based on a reductionist view of human nature that simplifies human motivations on the lines of the least sophisticated notions of the law and economics movement. Homo sapiens is not merely homo economicus. We may be thankful that an array of other motivations exist that influence human behavior; not all are any better than greed or avarice, think of envy, to name just one. But also think of motives like love, friendship, and collegiality, think of those among us who direct their behavior as best they can on a guiding creed or set of moral values.

Nor should our law ignore the social nature of humans. To be direct, corporate directors are generally the sort of people deeply enmeshed in social institutions. Such institutions have norms, expectations that, explicitly and implicitly, influence and channel the behavior of those who participate in their operation. Some things are "just not done," or only at a cost, which might not be so severe as a loss of position, but may involve a loss of standing in the institution. In being appropriately sensitive to this factor, our law also cannot assume—absent some proof of the point—that corporate directors are, as a general matter, persons of unusual social bravery, who operate heedless to the inhibitions that social norms generate for ordinary folk.

For all these reasons, this court has previously held that the Delaware Supreme Court's teachings on independence can be summarized thusly: "At bottom, the question of independence turns on whether a director is, for any substantial reason, incapable of making a decision with only the best interests of the corporation in mind. That is, the Supreme Court cases ultimately focus on impartiality and objectivity."

Without backtracking from these general propositions, it would be less than candid if I did not admit that Delaware courts have applied these general standards in a manner that has been less than wholly consistent. Different decisions take a different view about the bias-producing potential of family relationships, not all of which can be explained by mere degrees of consanguinity. Likewise, there is admittedly case law that gives little weight to ties of friendship in the independence inquiry. In this opinion, I will not venture to do what I believe to be impossible: attempt to rationalize all these cases in their specifics. Rather, I undertake what I understand to be my duty and what is possible: the application of the independence inquiry that our Supreme Court has articulated in a manner that is faithful to its essential spirit.

In examining whether the SLC has met its burden to demonstrate that there is no material dispute of fact regarding its independence, the court must bear in mind the function of special litigation committees under our jurisprudence. Under Delaware law, the primary means by which corporate defendants may obtain a dismissal of a derivative suit is by showing that the plaintiffs have not met their pleading burden under the test of Aronson v. Lewis. . . . In simple terms, these tests permit a corporation to terminate a derivative suit if its board is comprised of directors who can impartially consider a demand.

Special litigation committees are permitted as a last chance for a corporation to control a derivative claim in circumstances when a majority of its directors cannot impartially consider a demand. By vesting the power of the board to determine what to do with the suit in a committee of independent directors, a corporation may retain control over whether the suit will proceed, so long as the committee meets the standard set forth in Zapata.

In evaluating the independence of a special litigation committee, this court must take into account the extraordinary importance and difficulty of such a committee's responsibility. It is, I daresay, easier to say no to a friend, relative, colleague, or boss who seeks assent for an act (e.g., a transaction) that has not yet occurred than it would be to cause a corporation to sue that person. This is admittedly a determination of so-called "legislative fact," but one that can be rather safely made. Denying a fellow director the ability to proceed on a matter important to him may not be easy, but it must, as a general matter, be less difficult than finding that there is reason to believe that the fellow director has committed serious wrongdoing and that a derivative suit should proceed against him.

The difficulty of making this decision is compounded in the special litigation committee context because the weight of making the moral judgment necessarily falls on less than the full board. A small number of directors feels the moral gravity — and social pressures — of this duty alone. For all these reasons, the independence inquiry is critically important if the special litigation committee process is to retain its integrity, a quality that is, in turn, essential to the utility of that process. . . .

Using the contextual approach I have described, I conclude that the SLC has not met its burden to show the absence of a material factual question about its independence. I find this to be the case because the ties among the SLC, the Trading Defendants, and Stanford are so substantial that they cause reasonable doubt about the SLC's ability to impartially consider whether the Trading Defendants should face suit. . . .

Rather than form an SLC whose membership was free from bias-creating relationships, Oracle formed a committee fraught with them. As a result, the SLC has failed to meet its Zapata burden, and its motion to terminate must be denied. Because of this reality, I do not burden the reader with an examination of the other Zapata factors. In the absence of a finding that the SLC was independent, its subjective good faith and the reasonableness of its conclusions would not be sufficient to justify termination. Without confidence that the SLC was impartial, its findings do not provide the assurance our law requires for the dismissal of a derivative suit without a merits inquiry.

Questions and Comments

1. The case represented a victory for the plaintiffs' attorneys. However, the victory was short-lived. The following year Chancellor Strine granted summary judgment to the defendants on other grounds. In re Oracle Corp. Derivative Litigation, 867 A.2d 904 (Del. Ch. 2004).

2. What limits does Chancellor Strine place on the membership of special litigation committees?

3. Corporate boardrooms are filled with people, often of a certain age, who have had many experiences in life and who have many connections with others in the business, educational, and social arenas. Especially in the small world of Silicon Valley, it would be unusual if members of the special committee were not linked in many ways with the directors whose conduct they are asked to evaluate. To what extent should a court involve itself in teasing out this intricate web of connections when it evaluates the independence of a special litigation committee?

2. Compliance Remedies

In re Johnson & Johnson Derivative Litigation

900 F. Supp. 2d 467 (D.N.J. 2012)

... Presently before the Court is a motion to approve the final settlement reached between Plaintiffs-shareholders and nominal Defendant Johnson & Johnson Corporation ("J&J") in several consolidated shareholder derivative actions, as well as motions to intervene and dismiss by an objector to the settlement. Through the settlement, J&J agrees to institute corporate governance changes and pay up to $10 million in attorney's fees and $450,000 in costs, subject to this Court's approval. ...

Many corporate governance settlements include the following unremarkable list of reforms:

- A rule requiring a majority or more of the directors to meet existing or enhanced independence requirements;
- A requirement that the board or certain committees of the board meet regularly in executive sessions;
- An agreement to appoint, or enhance the duties of, a lead independent director;
- The addition of one or more independent directors to the board;
- A policy allowing the board and/or its committees to hire advisors;
- A limitation on the number of boards on which the directors can serve;
- A requirement that directors attend a certain percentage of board, committee, or shareholder meetings;
- A requirement or recommendation that the board adopt a "clawback" provision, or a provision requiring executive officers to repay bonuses or other monies in the event of a restatement of the company's financial statements; and
- A provision allowing major shareholders to nominate candidates for the corporation's board of directors.

For these sorts of reforms, corporations have usually agreed to maintain them for two to five years. ...

The settlement here includes more substantial and tailored terms than these. Specifically, they provide for J&J's adoption of the Q & C Core Objective, the creation and adoption of a more robust compliance committee than existed prior to the litigation (the RCGC), and the implementation of a PRM Standard. I address these specific reforms in detail.

Q & C Core Objective

The Q & C Core Objective is a Board commitment to create quality control and assurance systems that will prevent, timely detect, and correct noncompliance with drug marketing laws, CGMP [Current Good Manufacturing Practice] regulations, and the PRM [Product Risk Management] Standard. What I find significant about this objective is that, by creating company-wide control and assurance systems, it remedies the failings of J&J's decentralized management approach. ... Plaintiffs' experts, [former SEC Chairman Harvey Pitt] and Dr. [Michael] Glass, both conclude in their reports that the corporate governance reforms confer a substantial benefit upon J&J. In particular, I find compelling Chairman Pitt's reasoning that the objective sends a signal from the Board to all operating companies that they must conduct their business activities in conformity with applicable laws, regulations, and internal policies and, further, that the objective constitutes direction from the leaders of J&J that they expect instances of noncompliance to be reported. Pitt's reasoning is consistent with Dr. Glass's opinion that adoption of the objective sends an important message to the entire company regarding what the Board considers important.

In addition, the Settlement further provides that the objective must be communicated every year to each J&J employee, and that it will be considered in the evaluation and compensation of the employees, from low-level employees to senior management. As Dr. Glass notes, this feature underscores, for employees, how seriously the Board considers quality control and assurance, and legal compliance. Moreover, as Chairman Pitt notes, the objective also provides for oversight of resource allocations to quality control systems. This directly addresses another of Plaintiffs' allegations — that the quality control functions at various J&J subsidiaries were vastly underfunded.

In that regard, I reject Objector Petri's additional contention the Core Objective is merely a restatement of J&J's Credo, which was developed earlier in J&J's corporate existence, yet only recently posted on its website. That credo provides, in pertinent part: "We must provide competent management, and their actions must be just and ethical [and o]ur final responsibility is to our stockholders." It further states that, in meeting customer needs "everything we do must be of high quality." Unlike the Core Objective, the credo is aspirational in nature and is not tied to any objective criterion such as employee review and compensation.

In addition, as Dr. Glass notes, the objective helps ensure that critical information is reported upward to the Board. This is a key benefit of the objective that directly addresses the alleged lack of reporting to the Board of quality control issues at various J&J subsidiary plants. Moreover, this feature of the objective further distinguishes it from the J&J credo, which does not explicitly address upward reporting.

RCGC Charter and Operating Procedure

By agreeing to create and operate RCGC, the J&J Board will further cement its now centralized role in overseeing J&J's compliance with drug marketing laws and CGMP. As noted, the RCGC Charter and Operating Procedure ("C/OP") directs the Committee to assess the information it is receiving to support its oversight functions on an annual basis, and directs the Board to annually review and approve J&J's internal audit plans related to compliance and quality. Chairman Pitt opines that the creation of a standing committee designed to provide oversight over J&J's compliance with regulations and internal policies is historic and significant because the committee will unify the oversight of legal and regulatory compliance and quality control. I find that this reform is tailored to remedy the Plaintiffs' overarching allegation that the Board insulated itself from reporting on quality control issues. In addition, as Dr. Glass notes, the creation of the committee constitutes a best practice, which is tailored to remedy the Plaintiffs' allegation that J&J failed to institute good manufacturing practices in its subsidiaries.

PRM Standard

Like the Q & C Core Objective and the creation of the RCGC Committee, I find that the PRM Standard is tailored to remedy the alleged deficiencies in J&J's oversight structure as alleged in the Plaintiffs' complaints. The PRM standard is, essentially, J&J's own internal quality control framework. As noted, once in effect, the standard will "set forth the independence and role of Quality personnel in the PRM process, and provide that all quality issues subject to the PRM Standard will be managed in accordance with the escalation reporting line defined in the Quality Policy." I find it significant that the settlement also locates particular oversight responsibility with one individual — J&J's Chief Quality Officer. Designating one individual with ultimate responsibility will make it more difficult for officers and directors to "pass the blame" through the ranks should any quality control issue arise in the future. I also find it significant that the settlement provides that the independent Enterprise Regulatory Compliance Group will oversee the CQO. This adds an additional level of protection for the company.

Another critical component of the PRM Standard is the creation of a timeliness metric designed to evaluate whether quality assurance issues are promptly rectified. This metric, and other aspects of the PRM Standard too lengthy to recount here, will help ensure the early identification and timely resolution of quality control issues. According to Dr. Glass, if this sort of PRM Standard had been in place at the time of the alleged corporate misconduct, much of that conduct could have been avoided. In this connection, I note Objector Petri's argument that Plaintiffs have failed to explain how the PRM Standard improves upon J&J's pre-existing quality policy. In my view, it is implicit in Dr. Glass's aforesaid statement that a comparable standard was not in place at the time of the alleged corporate misconduct. Thus, I find Petri's criticism unwarranted.

Finally, and with respect to all of the corporate governance reforms, the settlement binds J&J for five years and requires J&J to fully fund the settlement's measures during that time frame. Chairman Pitt and Dr. Glass agree that such a funding commitment helps ensure J&J's compliance with the settlement's directives. Objector Petri assails the five-year time frame and the funding commitment, arguing that Plaintiffs have not demonstrated that a five-year restriction on management discretion and the funding requirement could ultimately harm shareholders "if J&J spends more money to implement cosmetic and superfluous changes than it would have spent in its normal business judgment in pursuit of [J&J's] Credo. . . . " Of course, his objection is based on the presumption that the corporate governance reforms are of no value. But, as I have explained, the Credo is merely aspirational while the reforms, in contrast, increase director and employee accountability, among the other benefits described above. Thus, in my view, the five-year time frame and the funding element of the settlement confer further value on J&J.

Questions and Comments

1. This derivative action followed a misbranding prosecution against a J&J subsidiary, Scios Inc., involving alleged off-label marketing of the congestive heart failure drug Natrecor to treat other chronic heart problems. In 2011, Scios pleaded guilty to misdemeanor charges and agreed to pay an $85 million fine. For more on off-label marketing, see Chapter 12.

2. Examine the court's list of "unremarkable" reforms. To what extent are these things that companies would be inclined to do on their own, even without the spur of a shareholder's derivative lawsuit?

3. The excerpted opinion distinguishes the settlement before the court from these common reforms — thus, presumably, classifying them as "remarkable." What is remarkable about them?

4. What weight do you give to the fact that both Harvey Pitt, a distinguished former SEC chairman and a witness for the plaintiffs, and the corporation's expert Dr. Michael Glass agreed that the governance reforms contemplated by the settlement provided real and substantial value to the corporation?

5. The court seemed impressed by the technical jargon and officious use of acronyms in the company's compliance commitments. Did these commitments confer real value, or were they merely hot air?

6. A substantial percentage of settlements in shareholders derivative lawsuits involve corporate governance changes rather than the payment of money damages. *See* Jessica Erickson, *Corporate Governance in the Courtroom: An Empirical Analysis*, 51 Wm. & Mary L. Rev. 1749 (2010). Why would this be so?

7. Some cases, usually involving mergers and takeovers, result in settlements in which the management agrees to make supplemental or corrective disclosures to shareholders. Do these disclosure-only settlements provide substantial value to shareholders? Do you agree with critics who see many such settlements as a last resort under which plaintiffs' lawyers can salvage some hope of getting a fee? For a catalog of fee awards in disclosure-only cases, see In re Sauer-Danfoss Inc. Shareholders Litigation, 65 A.3d 1116 (Del. Ch. 2011). Disclosure-only settlements are strictly reviewed in Delaware and will be upheld only under stringent conditions. *See* In re Trulia, Inc. Stockholder Litig., 2016 WL 270821 (Del. Ch. 2016).

8. In 2013, the year after this decision was handed down, J&J agreed to pay more than $2.2 billion to settle claims that it had improperly marketed its anti-psychotic drug Risperdal for off-label uses. The conduct in question occurred between 1999 and 2005, before the settlement of the excerpted case. Would the illegal conduct have occurred if the governance changes called for in the settlement had been in place?

B. CLASS ACTIONS

A class action is a device for joining multiple similar claims in a single proceeding. Most class actions are "opt out" actions, under which a person remains a member of the class unless she affirmatively determines to exclude herself. Class actions are officially brought by representative plaintiffs seeking to act as champions of a class of similarly situated plaintiffs. In fact, the driving force behind many class actions is often the plaintiffs' attorney who identifies the lawsuit, locates the plaintiff, and makes the key strategic decisions. Class actions can be brought in federal and state courts; however, as a result of the federal Class Action Fairness Act, most large cases now occur in a federal forum.

Class actions are brought to enforce "direct" claims against the defendants, in contrast with shareholders derivative lawsuits where the claims are brought derivatively on behalf of the corporation. While the distinction between direct and derivative claims may be clear in theory, in practice the two concepts are often muddied. In Grimes v. Donald, 673 A.2d 1207 (Del. 1996), the court tried to draw the line as follows: "The distinction depends upon 'the nature of the wrong alleged' and the relief, if any, which could result if plaintiff were to prevail." To pursue a direct action, the stockholder-plaintiff "must allege more than an injury resulting from a wrong to the corporation." The plaintiff must state a claim for "'an injury which is separate and distinct from that suffered by other shareholders,' . . . or a wrong involving a contractual right of a shareholder . . . which exists independently of any right of the corporation." Id. at 1213.

Class actions occasionally generate settlements that include governance reforms as an element of relief. The incidence of these settlements is lower than in the case of derivative litigation, for the obvious reason that derivative litigation is principally about governance failures: The derivative plaintiff argues that the defendants breached fiduciary duties to the company. Class actions are usually not about governance failures, except indirectly; they are about violations of substantive legal standards.

Nevertheless, governance type settlements do appear in class actions as well as derivative litigation, and often are approved as fair, adequate, and reasonable. However, if the settlement doesn't include a cash component, the proponent of the deal may have to work harder to convince the court that the proposal offers real and substantial benefits for shareholders. Consider the following case:

In re JPMorgan Chase & Co. Securities Litigation

2009 WL 537062 (N.D. Ill. 2009)

The [class action] complaints are premised on an allegation that the defendants failed to disclose in the proxy statement soliciting votes for the 2004 merger between JPMorgan Chase & Co. ("JPMC") and Bank One Corporation ("Bank One"), that William Harrison, the then-CEO of JPMC, rejected an offer from James Dimon, the then-CEO of Bank One, to structure the deal as a zero-premium, stock-for-stock transaction, with Dimon as CEO of the combined company upon consummation. That purported offer had been reported in a June 27, 2004 article in The New York Times entitled "The Yin, the Yang and the Deal," which cited as sources "two people close to the deal"; articles in The Financial Times and The Wall Street Journal reported similar accounts. In their complaint, the plaintiffs alleged that Harrison had rejected the offer and agreed instead to a deal with a 14% premium (worth approximately $7 billion) so that he could retain his position as CEO for two years.

Despite two years of discovery, including reviewing more than 445,800 pages of documents, issuing interrogatories, deposing multiple current and former JPMC executives, and subpoenaing numerous third parties, the lead plaintiffs' attorneys represent that they have not found evidence to corroborate independently the newspapers' accounts. Rather, the merger-related documents produced by defendants show that (1) Dimon sought a premium throughout the merger negotiations; (2) Harrison resisted paying a premium until the final stages of the negotiations; and (3) the two had reached an agreement on succession issues before their final negotiations on pricing.

That account is consistent with JPMC's response to an interrogatory that "[a]t no time did Dimon make an offer to proceed with the merger for no premium or a lower premium to Bank One shareholders in exchange for Dimon becoming CEO or Chairman of the merged company immediately." The director defendants, too, deny knowledge of any similar offer. As do four JPMC executives, including two senior executives from its media relations department who had the most contact with Landon Thomas, the author of the New York Times article, and who had arranged and/or attended Thomas's interviews with Dimon and Harrison. Walter Shipley, the former CEO of JPMC, whom Harrison had consulted about the merger, and Steven Black, one of two co-CEOs of J.P. Morgan Securities and a longtime close friend of Dimon, also denied knowledge of the offer.

Failing independently to uncover anyone with knowledge of the alleged offer, the plaintiffs attempted to obtain the names of the sources cited in the publications that had reported the offer. Although Blau's counsel subpoenaed the journalists, each newspaper refused to name their sources, and Thomas himself has not volunteered the names. The plaintiffs say it would be "nearly impossible" to override the journalists' assertions of privilege in court.

The lack of a "smoking gun" is not the plaintiffs' only trouble. They note that, even if the alleged offer was made, they would have the burden of showing that it was material. On this score, they've found no evidence to contradict the defendants' assertion that, even if Dimon had made the alleged proposal, it was not a viable offer. They say that no evidence suggests that the board of directors and the shareholders of JPMC and Bank One, respectively, would have approved a no-premium merger with Dimon as the immediate CEO.

The steepest hurdle, according to the plaintiffs, is proving damages. They argue that the Seventh Circuit's method for calculating damages . . . would not offer them much relief. They posit that damages would be awarded only if the merger was unfair, and they note that far higher premiums have been tendered in comparable mergers between large financial institutions, including Bank of America's payment of a 40% premium in favor of Fleet Boston when they merged. They add that JPMC's stock price did not drop significantly in the wake of the merger announcement, even though the stock price of an acquirer frequently falls after a stock-for-stock acquisition is announced.

As a result of these weaknesses, the plaintiffs attempted first to negotiate with defendants a monetary settlement. Defendants refused, so the Blau plaintiffs next considered a "corporate therapeutics" settlement. . . . JPMC was willing to agree to the proposed reforms, and so on December 7, 2007, Blau's counsel entered into a Stipulation of Settlement. . . .

In the Settlement, JPMC agrees that it will adopt the following corporate governance reforms, which will remain in effect for four years:

- the CEO of JPMC will inform JPMC's Presiding Director, appointed by JPMC's non-management directors, of discussions with any third party who expresses interest in a transaction that would require approval by JPMC's shareholders under Delaware law or the rules or regulations of any stock exchange on which JPMC has listed its stock;
- the Presiding Director and the CEO will review with the Board, or a committee thereof, the process for communicating with the Board, or a committee thereof, about the proposed transaction, including the method and frequency of communications;
- the Board will review any proxy statement issued in connection with a transaction requiring shareholder approval and will appoint a "Designated Committee" to help it in this process;

- the Designated Committee will review, with the assistance of management and financial and legal advisors, the "Background of the Merger" section of any such proxy statement, and will have the authority to recommend changes to the Board;
- in order to carry out the duties imposed by the reforms, the Board and the Designated Committee will have the discretion to seek paid assistance from outside consultants; and
- in the fourth year of the implementation of the reforms, the Board's Corporate Governance and Nominating Committee, which is comprised of non-management directors, shall determine whether to recommend to the Board that the reforms be continued.

The Stipulation further provides that any of these procedures may be altered or terminated if the Board, upon advice of counsel, determines that (a) the procedures conflict with any law, regulation or rule to which JPMC is subject; (b) a different corporate governance measure adopted by the Board would more appropriately effect the goals of the reforms; or (c) JPMC merges into another company and is not the surviving entity of such merger. . . .

As murky as the value of the plaintiffs' claims is, the benefits of the Settlement are even murkier. That the benefits are non-monetary is not necessarily problematic — courts have recognized that reforms, such as material changes in corporate governance, provide substantial benefits to corporations and their shareholders. Nevertheless, the non-monetary benefit must be "substantial," meaning that it "accomplishes a result which corrects or prevents an abuse which would be prejudicial to the rights and interests of the corporation or affect the enjoyment or protection of an essential right to the stockholder's interest."

As an initial matter, the court is persuaded that the reforms in the Settlement, even if they remain in place only for four years, could provide a substantial benefit to JPMC shareholders. Professor Gordon opined that the Board's early participation in acquisition negotiations may result in a better price and the shaping of a better management team. He estimates that "even small improvements in deal terms" could "add tens of millions to shareholder value" in JPMC. Another expert retained by Blau, Professor James L. Bicksler, Professor of Financial Economics at Rutgers University Graduate School of Management, is more optimistic: He estimates that the reforms could result in a deal's increased value of anywhere between $600 million and $4.4 billion. Meanwhile, Professor Gordon opines that the Designated Committee's review of proxy statements will increase management accountability in negotiations, increase public confidence in the accuracy of proxy statements, and ultimately reduce the company's exposure to potential litigation. Professor Bicksler has argued, based on empirical studies, that similarly meaningful oversight of management by independent board members generally results in improved stock performance of up to 8.5%. (Based on JPMC's current market capitalization of approximately $130 billion, even a 1% positive incremental effect on JPMC's equity as a result of the reforms would be worth $1.3 billion per year.)

But the court also shares [the objector's] concern that the substantial value of the reforms could be entirely ephemeral. The Settlement provides JPMC's board with virtually unfettered discretion to modify the reforms at any time, as long as the change "would more appropriately effect the goals of the reforms." Although that power is constrained by the board's fiduciary duties, at the fairness hearing the parties could not articulate how those duties would limit the board's discretion. Giving the board that flexibility is not necessarily problematic, but it should not be done in a way that limits the shareholders' ability to enforce their rights under the Settlement. As it stands, however, the board could make those changes without notifying shareholders before or after doing so — potentially rendering meaningless the clause giving shareholders the right to enforce the Settlement's terms. Because the Settlement does not, at the very least, obligate the board to give some notice to shareholders of any changes to the reforms (e.g., 30 days), its benefit may be insubstantial. . . .

Because the plaintiffs have not attempted to quantify the value of their claims, and because the proposed Settlement does not provide a substantial benefit to the class, the court denies the motion for settlement.

Questions and Comments

1. Plaintiffs' theory of the case was that JPMC should have taken Dimon up on his supposed offer of a no-premium deal in exchange for Dimon's immediate promotion to head of the combined firm; in their view the 14 percent premium JPMC paid was essentially compensation for allowing the existing CEO of JPMG, Harrison, to keep his job for an extra two years. The case may have looked great at the time it was filed, given the press accounts, but it turned out to be a bust: The plaintiffs' attorneys never discovered any evidence of the purported offer and, in any event, the 14 percent premium that JPMC paid for Bank One was low by industry standards, so it would have been nearly impossible to establish that it was unreasonable for JPMC's shareholders.

2. Normally, when a case goes belly-up, the lawyers simply agree to dismiss it. In this case the plaintiffs' attorneys did not abandon ship; they pressed on with a demand for governance reforms. Why did they do this?

3. The trial court rejected the settlement on the ground that the defendant could unilaterally walk away from the deal, constrained only by their fiduciary duty and the requirement that they explain why what they were substituting would more effectively accomplish the goals of the settlement. Is it true that JPMG could so easily escape this settlement? Would a unilateral change in previously-agreed-to reforms generate unfavorable publicity and impair the company's public image, at least to some extent? Would a change spark unhealthy market speculation about the reasons — for example, that JPMG was about to enter negotiations with a potential merger partner?

4. On the other hand, the trial court agreed that the reforms themselves might confer a substantial benefit on the company. Do you agree? Is it a good idea to constrain the freedom of a CEO to engage in private discussions with the CEO of a potential merger partner before others on the board are brought into the picture? What good can the full board accomplish at this stage other than to interfere with the deal by leaking?

5. If there was a corporate benefit from these reforms, was it "substantial"?

6. What value do these reforms confer on class members who sold their JPMC stock after the merger with Bank One but before the settlement agreement was finalized?

Chevron Corporation v. Donziger

2013 WL 1087236 (S.D.N.Y. 2013)

[This case arose out of a 1993 a class action lawsuit filed against Texaco in New York on behalf of indigenous people living in the Amazon rain forest of the Oriente region of Ecuador (the court refers to these people as the "Lago Agrio Plaintiffs" or "LAP"). The allegation was that Texaco's Ecuadorian operations had caused environmental damage to the plaintiffs' land and harmed their means of livelihood. Texaco obtained a dismissal on the ground that New York was not a convenient forum. Plaintiffs then re-filed their case in Ecuador. Texaco settled the controversy in 1998 and promised to engage in clean-up efforts. In 2002, Chevron acquired Texaco.

[Thereafter Attorney Donziger and others renewed the litigation in Ecuador, claiming that Texaco had failed to abide by its clean-up obligations. In 2011, a court in Ecuador awarded an $18.2 billion judgment against Texaco (now Chevron) — the largest environmental judgment in history. Chevron responded by filing a civil RICO lawsuit against Donziger and others involved on the plaintiffs' side of the litigation, claiming that they had procured the Ecuadorian judgment through fraud, corruption, and intimidation of judges. Chevron sought an injunction prohibiting the defendants from enforcing the Ecuadorian judgment. In one of many pretrial orders, the federal judge concluded as follows:]

There is probable cause to suspect, and often stronger evidence, that:

- Representatives of the LAPs bribed the Ecuadorian judge to obtain the result they wanted and, as part of the deal, wrote the Judgment to which the judge put his name. . . .
- At an earlier stage of the Lago Agrio litigation, representatives of the LAPs coerced the then-presiding Ecuadorian judge to terminate judicial inspections of alleged pollution sites, to replace that process with a global expert charged with making an independent evaluation, and to appoint the LAPs' candidate, Richard Stalin Cabrera Vega ("Cabrera"), to that position. They did so by threatening [the judge] with a judicial misconduct complaint if he did not accede to their wishes.
- The report that Cabrera ultimately submitted in fact was planned and written, at least in major part and quite possibly entirely, by lawyers and consultants retained on behalf of the LAPs though it was signed by Cabrera and filed as if it were his independent work. LAP representatives, moreover, took a number of steps to create or reinforce the entirely inaccurate contention that the Cabrera report was the unbiased work of an independent expert when, in fact, it had been the work of the LAPs' representatives themselves and was not independent in the slightest respect.
- Once the improprieties surrounding Cabrera began to come to light, the LAPs or their representatives then obstructed justice and committed fraud in at least one . . . proceeding in the United States by submitting . . . a deceptive account of the LAPs' relationship with Cabrera.
- At a still earlier stage of the lawsuit in Ecuador, the LAPs filed two site inspection reports with the trial court over the signature of one of their experts that

the expert neither adopted nor agreed with. The evidence readily gives rise to the inference that the LAP lawyers wrote the reports, affixed the expert's signature to them in the knowledge that they did not reflect his views, and filed them.

In March 2014, Judge Kaplan issued an opinion in the case, nearly 500 pages long, that confirmed his initial findings:

Chevron Corp. v. Donziger

974 F. Supp. 2d 362 (S.D.N.Y. 2014), aff'd, ___ F.3d ___ (2d Cir. 2016)

. . . The facts are many and sometimes complex. They include things that normally come only out of Hollywood — coded emails among Donziger and his colleagues describing their private interactions with and machinations directed at judges and a court appointed expert, their payments to a supposedly neutral expert out of a secret account, a lawyer who invited a film crew to innumerable private strategy meetings and even to ex parte meetings with judges, an Ecuadorian judge who claims to have written the multibillion dollar decision but who was so inexperienced and uncomfortable with civil cases that he had someone else (a former judge who had been removed from the bench) draft some civil decisions for him, an 18-year old typist who supposedly did Internet research in American, English, and French law for the same judge, who knew only Spanish, and much more. The evidence is voluminous. The transnational elements of the case make it sensitive and challenging. Nevertheless, the Court has had the benefit of a lengthy trial. It has heard 31 witnesses in person and considered deposition and/or other sworn or, in one instance, stipulated testimony of 37 others. It has considered thousands of exhibits. It has made its findings, which of necessity are lengthy and detailed.

Upon consideration of all of the evidence, including the credibility of the witnesses — though several of the most important declined to testify — the Court finds that Donziger began his involvement in this controversy with a desire to improve conditions in the area in which his Ecuadorian clients live. To be sure, he sought also to do well for himself while doing good for others, but there was nothing wrong with that. In the end, however, he and the Ecuadorian lawyers he led corrupted the Lago Agrio case. They submitted fraudulent evidence. They coerced one judge, first to use a court-appointed, supposedly impartial, "global expert" to make an overall damages assessment and, then, to appoint to that important role a man whom Donziger hand-picked and paid to "totally play ball" with the LAPs. They then paid a Colorado consulting firm secretly to write all or most of the global expert's report, falsely presented the report as the work of the court-appointed and supposedly impartial expert, and told half-truths or worse to U.S. courts in attempts to prevent exposure of that and other wrongdoing. Ultimately, the LAP team wrote the Lago Agrio court's Judgment themselves and promised $500,000 to the Ecuadorian judge to rule in their favor and sign their judgment. If ever there were a case warranting equitable relief with respect to a judgment procured by fraud, this is it.

Questions and Comments

1. Donziger's lawsuit alleged that over the course of several decades, Texaco, together with other oil companies, had ruthlessly degraded the environment around Lago Agrio, destroying rainforest habitat to make roads and airstrips, dumping 18 billion gallons of toxic waste, and filling hundreds of open pits with dangerous sludge. The lawsuit claimed that these activities caused cancers, birth defects, miscarriages, death of fish and livestock, and the near-eradication of several tribes.

2. Chevron is one of the largest energy companies in the world; it could afford the best legal representation money could buy, especially when faced with an $18 billion judgment. The plaintiffs, on the other hand, were strapped for cash from the beginning. But the attorneys had a potentially valuable asset — the expectation of receiving a legal fee if the case succeeded. Donziger obtained funding from a Philadelphia law firm, Kohn, Swift & Graf, which took a share of the contingency fee, and later from a litigation finance company, Burford Capital.

3. Part of Chevron's strategy was to impeach the conduct of the plaintiffs' principal attorney, Donziger. Chevron obtained outtakes from a documentary critical of Texaco's environmental activities in Lago Agrio that Donziger had solicited. Material cut from the film allegedly showed Donziger remarking that "this is how the game is played — dirty" and "this is something we would never do in the United States. This is out of bounds both in terms of judicial behavior and what a lawyer would do." Other outtakes allegedly showed Donziger commenting on the corruption in the Ecuadorian legal system, rejecting the opinion of his own expert regarding the extent of environmental damage, and expressing pleasure in the thought that the Ecuadorian judge might rule in his favor because he feared he would be killed if he did not. Chevron was eventually able to obtain even more information which raised questions about the conduct of the plaintiffs' attorneys, including what it claimed was evidence that plaintiffs' lawyers had paid an Ecuadorian judge $500,000 to allow them to write his opinion; that they had intimidated an Ecuadorian judge to appoint a biased expert; and that they had ghostwritten an expert report estimating damages at $27 billion.

4. How do you assess this case? Is Donziger, as his attorney portrayed him, a heroic figure in the mold of Thurgood Marshall or Ralph Nader — champions who bravely stood up to authority in order to seek justice for people who cannot protect themselves? Can Donziger's alleged misconduct, even if it occurred, be understood as a necessary adjustment to the realities of litigating in a country with different norms and different traditions? Was his behavior justified by the idea that he was acting in a noble cause? Was Chevron engaged in a campaign of harassment, intimidation, and character assassination? How effective can plaintiffs' attorneys be at enforcing compliance obligations if they fear retaliatory lawsuits brought against them by well-financed, sophisticated corporations?

5. On the other hand, if Chevron's allegations are substantiated, would that place this lawsuit in a different light? Did Chevron receive due process in the courts of Ecuador? Were Donziger's ethics impaired by a belief in the rightness of his cause? Was he, as Chevron suggested, really interested in the prospect of an attorneys' fee that could run to more than a hundred million dollars?

6. Putting aside the facts of this case, how can companies conduct legitimate international business operations if they face the danger of devastating judgments issued by corrupt foreign judges?

PROBLEM 10-1

Gaggle, Inc., a company located in Marin County, California, provides mapping services to firms and governments around the world. Part of its business involves sending a vehicle equipped with a camera to photograph the roads in as many countries as possible. One such country is Expropria, an impoverished nation in Latin America. A change in government in Expropria brings a populist leader into office. The new leader fires the country's judges and installs cronies in their place. She also breaks off diplomatic relations with the United States. The new public prosecutor, who is also the president's brother-in-law, brings an enforcement action against Gaggle claiming that the photography project and subsequent sale of images violates Expropria's privacy laws. Gaggle defends in the courts of Expropria, claiming that the privacy laws don't cover the conduct in question and that in any event these laws had never been enforced. No matter: the judge finds Gaggle guilty and imposes a fine of $10 billion. Expropria's president touts the judgment as a much-needed source of funds to alleviate the suffering of Expropria's poor. Expropria hires excellent attorneys who seek to enforce the judgment by attaching Gaggle's assets wherever they may be found. Gaggle has no evidence that the prosecutor or judge have been bribed, but believes that the judgment is based on political considerations and that, if paid, most of the money will line the pockets of the president and her friends. What can Gaggle do?

11

Information Security

A. INTRODUCTION

Organizations compile, maintain, and analyze stupendous amounts of information. Some of this data is in the public record. For example, a person's telephone number, if the customer has chosen to list it in a public source, is not private information. Anyone can find it out without engaging in extraordinary efforts.

Often, however, the subject of the information does wish to keep it from others. For example, a person might not want it known that she recently filed for bankruptcy or made a campaign contribution to an indicted politician. Whether or not the person wishes it to be disclosed, this information is in the public record and cannot be concealed.

A great deal of information is not public in this sense. We can define this as "non-public information": information about a person or entity that is not legitimately available from public sources. Non-public information comes in various types, with varying degrees of sensitivity. Consider the following:

- A person's net assets.
- The fact a person has been diagnosed with a sexually transmitted disease.
- A person's Social Security number.
- The secret formula for Coca-Cola™ syrup.
- The fact a company is about to make a takeover bid.
- The fact that someone is a CIA agent.

These (and many other) types of information have the feature that they are, to one extent or another, protected by law against their acquisition by unauthorized persons. What distinguishes these sorts of information from information that receives no protection under the law?

One feature is the harm that will or is likely to occur if the information is disclosed. In each of the above categories, the subjects would probably prefer that the information not be made available to the public. Still the level of harm varies among these examples: Disclosure of a person's net assets might be embarrassing or inconvenient, but possibly not as harmful to the person as disclosure of the fact that she is a CIA operative.

Another factor enters the calculus. It is not only the harm that would result if the information is disclosed that matters. The law also takes account of the harm to others if the information is *not* disclosed. Where the harm from not disclosing the information is large, even sensitive personal information may be forced into the public record. An example is sex offender registries: Even though sex offenders would usually prefer that their past offenses not be bruited about, the government places their names on a public registry.

The decision to protect information under the law — or alternatively to allow or require its production — is therefore a function of at least two considerations: the harm expected to occur if the information is disclosed, and the harm expected to occur if the information is not disclosed. The policies we discuss in this chapter represent instances in which policymakers have made this tradeoff in favor of protecting rather than disclosing private information.

The law has long been concerned with these questions — what information should be kept confidential, what may be revealed, and what must be revealed. Those issues, however, have increased greatly in importance over the past few decades. The reason has to do with the enormous growth of information storage, retrieval, and communication technologies. We live in an information world; and with ever-reducing costs of storing, analyzing, and retrieving information, the amount of information available for use is increasing at dizzying rates.

Anyone who has watched the development of personal computers (and now a host of other devices) can attest to this fact. A few decades ago data storage was limited and expensive; the first IBM PC hard drive, introduced in 1982, had a capacity of five megabytes (five million bytes) and cost more than $1,000. Large data sets could be maintained only on bulky mainframes operated by companies or educational institutions. Today the volume of data that would have taxed the capacity of one of the early mainframe computers is routinely available on laptops and PCs. A 2013, a hard drive with a capacity of one terabyte — a trillion bytes of data — fits in a desktop computer and costs less than $100. Storage capacity in large commercial servers, meanwhile, is measured in the petrabytes (one quadrillion bytes).

This exponential growth of memory capacity (and shrinkage of cost) has had profound consequences for the operations of businesses and other organizations. Even small firms maintain lots of information about their customers and others. Big organizations house truly staggering amounts (consider the fact that banks like JPMorgan Chase have millions of deposit customers; the bank maintains detailed current and historical transaction records for every one of them). What information a firm does not maintain in-house, moreover, can often be acquired from others: Large databases are on offer in many markets and business lines.

These phenomenal increases in storage capacity have been matched by equally amazing increases in the ease and speed of information transmission. The amount of data that can be transmitted over the Internet, and the speed of transmission, increases every year. In the early 1990s the only feasible mode of Internet access was dial-up, a technology that started with information transmission speeds of about .1 kilobytes per second. Dial-up connections increased to more than

50 kilobytes per second — a 500-fold increase. With the introduction of broadband, transmission speeds grew still more dramatically; broadband in the 2000s reached more than four megabytes (4,000 kilobytes) per second.

Astounding developments like this made it possible for organizations not only to store vast amounts of data internally, but also to make that data available to people located anywhere on the planet (or in orbit, for that matter). Building on these advances, the 2000s saw the rapid growth of cloud computing — distributed computing networks running many applications and devices. Cloud computing can achieve economies of scale by storing data on efficient centralized servers, providing applications from a centralized source, and offering computer power on an "as needed basis" (thus eliminating the need to maintain excess capacity to deal with surges in demand).

The rapid growth of data storage, analysis, and communications has revolutionized many aspects of contemporary life. But as with any technological development, the benefits conferred come with costs. One of the main costs has been an increased threat to privacy. When data were physically stored in paper files, they could be accessed by unauthorized persons, but such access would have been burdensome and difficult. Not so for information stored in computer memories. If someone has access to computer files, they can remove vast amounts of data very quickly, and then can use the data for whatever purpose suits them. The threat increases further when the data are made accessible remotely, since it then becomes easier for unauthorized persons to hack into storage facilities or to intercept data transfers. When vendors or other third parties enter the picture the risks increase still more.

Accompanying the growth of data storage and communications, therefore, has been an ever-growing series of threats. Among these are the following:

- Employee negligence: Modern information security systems are exceedingly complicated, and often involve demanding or confusing technical requirements. A leading cause of security breaches is simply negligence on the part of employees who fail to understand or neglect to follow the required procedures and safeguards.

- System glitches: Data security systems occasionally fail to perform as expected even when no definite cause for the breakdown can be assigned.

- Vandals: So-called hackavists attack an organization's information security systems, not because they hope to gain financially from doing so, but simply for the challenge of the thing, for the pleasure — however twisted — of doing harm to others, or for ideological reasons such as hostility to banks or big business.

- Domestic enemies: Organizations have enemies: competitors, disgruntled employees, dissatisfied customers. If these enemies are angry (or greedy) enough they may find it justifiable or convenient to attempt to breach information security defenses in order to obtain non-public information about the organization or its customers.

- Fraudsters: During the decade of the 2010s, Internet fraud grew by leaps and bounds. Readers of this book are probably familiar with the "Nigerian scam" — associated with fraudsters located in Nigeria, but by no means limited to that country — in which an unknown person contacts you to offer a business opportunity that seems too good to be true — because it is. Other common frauds include the "lonely hearts" scam, often targeted to middle-aged men, in which a beautiful young woman from another country promises romance or marriage — provided that the victim advances a small amount to help her through her current difficulties. Fraudsters have considerable Internet skills and a seemingly inexhaustible imagination for scenarios that are likely to deprive a target of her judgment and separate her from her money. Fraudsters also target institutions, constantly probing for weaknesses in the information security infrastructure that can help them obtain information on the institution or its customers.

- Hostile foreign governments: These days, among the biggest threats to information security are hostile foreign governments. In 2013, a former chairman of the Joint Chiefs of Staff described the situation as follows: "Cyber security is one of two existential threats to our nation; the other is nuclear weapons, which have been used once, thank God. But cyber weapons are used thousands of times every day." Cyber-attacks are anonymous and hard to trace, but it is no secret that, in the view of the U.S. government and many security consultants, many of these attacks come from China. A remarkable report issued in April 2013 by Mandiant, a cyber-security consulting firm, traced some of these attacks to a Chinese military facility known as "APT1" or "Unit 61398." The goal of this facility, apparently, was to misappropriate information from American businesses. Mandiant concluded that APT1 had been stealing "hundreds of terabytes of data from at least 141 organizations across a diverse set of industries beginning as early as 2006." These activities, according to Mandiant, were extensive and widespread: The operation targeted dozens of organizations at the same time. Once the intrusion was accomplished, moreover, the operation could milk it for months or years, acquiring "technology blueprints, proprietary manufacturing processes, test results, business plans, pricing documents, partnership agreements, emails and contact lists from victim organizations' leadership." Mandiant concluded that the activity it uncovered is only a "small fraction" of the total cyber espionage engaged in by this operation. Mandiant Intelligence Center Report, *APT1: Exposing One of China's Cyber Espionage Units*, available at http://intelreport.mandiant.com.

Many Americans were sensitized to the threat of data security by the massive breach experienced in 2013 by Target, one of the nation's largest retailers. Hackers stole approximately 40 million debit and credit card numbers as well as personal information, including names, home addresses, and telephone numbers, of an additional 70 million customers. The fallout at Target was significant. Numerous class action lawsuits were filed on behalf of cardholders whose information had been compromised. Target speeded up plans to enhance the security of its store-branded cards by moving to chip-and-pin–based cards. Meanwhile several very large heads rolled: CIO Beth Jacob and CEO Gregg Steinhafel both resigned within a matter of months.

The Target breach is only one of many incidents at American companies. Other companies reported similar (but smaller) attacks, including Michael's, the large craft store chain, and White Lodging Services, a hotel management firm. In March 2013, White House officials told industry executives that over the preceding year federal agents had notified 3,000 companies that their computer systems had been hacked — and acknowledged that these incidents of known breaches were only a fraction of the total. A survey conducted by Verizon Enterprise Solutions concluded that in seven out of ten cases, the victim learned of the hack through some external source such as law enforcement. The conventional wisdom is that regardless of its state of knowledge, a company can assume it has been hacked — leading to the following quip: "When it comes to information security, there are two kinds of companies: those that know they've been hacked, and those that don't know they've been hacked."

The government is vigorously attempting to combat the cyber threat. As of 2013, the FBI had more than 1,000 agents dedicated to cybercrime investigations. In November 2013, FBI Director James B. Comey testified to the Senate Homeland Security Committee that resources devoted to cyber-based threats are expected to eclipse resources devoted to terrorism. In April 2014, the SEC announced that it would greatly enhance its supervision of cyber-security risks at broker-dealers and registered investment advisers. Many other initiatives are underway.

But these efforts have had only limited success: Cybercrime is estimated to cost more than $100 billion per year for U.S. companies and individuals. While criminal and civil enforcement are necessary, the only truly effective response to the hacking threat is the adoption of expensive technological defenses such as end-to-end encryption, partition of sensitive data into separate networks, and the implementation of credit card technology that holds customer information on an embedded chip rather than the formerly dominant black magnetic strip.

Questions and Comments

1. The Mandiant report described above concluded that the APT1 was only the most prolific of nearly two dozen similar operations based in China.

2. The Mandiant report went viral in the information security world, with predictable consequences: The Chinese government reportedly took steps to hide the APT1 operation from further scrutiny, and hackers appended malicious code to emails distributing the report in an attempt to infect computers of people working in the information security field.

3. Although the report concluded only that the APT1 facility engages in espionage, its capacity to inflict operational damage on U.S. businesses is obvious. Some have accused the Chinese government of actually conducting such attacks. In January 2013, the Chinese Defense Ministry responded to the allegations as follows: "[I]t is unprofessional and groundless to accuse the Chinese military of launching cyber-attacks without any conclusive evidence." Is this a denial?

4. The threat of cyber-attacks is acknowledged at the highest levels of government. In his 2013 State of the Union Address, President Obama stated, "America must also face the rapidly growing threat from cyber-attacks. We know hackers steal people's identities and infiltrate private e-mail. We know foreign countries and companies swipe our corporate secrets. Now our enemies are also seeking the ability to sabotage our power grid, our financial institutions, and our air traffic control systems. We cannot look back years from now and wonder why we did nothing in the face of real threats to our security and our economy. That's why, earlier today, I signed a new executive order that will strengthen our cyber defenses by increasing information sharing, and developing standards to protect

our national security, our jobs, and our privacy. Now, Congress must act as well, by passing legislation to give our government a greater capacity to secure our networks and deter attacks."

5. Executive Order 13636, Improving Critical Infrastructure Cybersecurity (Feb. 12, 2013), referred to in the President's speech, established that "[i]t is the Policy of the United States to enhance the security and resilience" of the nation's data security infrastructure and calls for the development of a voluntary risk-based cybersecurity framework—a set of industry standards and best practices to help organizations manage cybersecurity risks. Elements of the framework are spelled out in U.S. Department of Commerce National Institute of Standards and Technology (NIST), Critical Infrastructure Cybersecurity (version 1.0) (Feb. 12, 2014).

6. One indication of the increasing gravity of the risk is the fact that governments and private institutions are now conducting "war game" scenarios involving worst-case scenarios of cyber-attacks. In 2013, dozens of American banks took part in a drill titled "Quantum Dawn 2," which simulated a coordinated cyber-attack on U.S. banking institutions. Also participating were a variety of government agencies including Treasury, the Department of Homeland Security, the Securities and Exchange Commission and the FBI. A similar exercise in Great Britain was called "Operation Waking Shark."

7. The costs of security breaches—or even of breakdowns of safeguards not accompanied by breach—can be significant. A 2013 study by the Ponemon Institute found that per capita costs of data breaches ranged from $78 for retail firms to $233 for the health care industry. These may not seem like large numbers, but remember that each data breach may involve thousands or millions of customers.

Based on the discussion above, it is obvious that the problem of data security, and the risks of potential data breaches, are endemic to modern commerce. They are, potentially, subject to a single regulatory scheme, enacted at the federal level with broad preemption of state authority, which would impose uniform standards and obligations on companies of all sorts that maintain, process or transmit sensitive personal data.

As yet, however, the idea of a unified national regulatory system is a pipe dream. Developments have been so rapid that there has not been time to formulate any regulatory system that would work across areas of commerce; it has been hard enough to define standards and obligations in discrete fields. Moreover, even if a single standard were feasible, regulatory competition would prove potentially intractable. Many agencies, at both the state and federal level, are competing to exercise authority over data security matters.

The upshot is that, for the time being at least, many different regulators and different bodies of regulation govern the field of data security. The resulting legal issues can be complex. For example, there is no single standard for how an organization must communicate the circumstances of a data breach to potentially affected parties. Instead, the organization must deal with a patchwork of state laws (46 states had enacted data breach notification statutes as of 2013), as well as federal laws applicable to discrete areas of commerce. In 2014, Attorney General Eric Holder called for enhanced federal regulation of cyber breaches in the form of "a strong, national standard for quickly alerting consumers whose information may be compromised . . . would empower the American people to protect themselves if they are at risk of identity theft. It would enable law enforcement to better investigate these crimes—and hold compromised entities accountable when they fail to keep sensitive information safe." As this edition goes to press, however, a general federal data breach notification standard has yet to be adopted.

Data breaches create overlapping legal and business problems that must be addressed in an atmosphere of crisis and uncertainty. The organization must become aware that a breach has occurred. This can be challenging because malefactors often insert code into an organization's systems that disguises the fact that information is being misappropriated. Once the institution becomes aware of a potential breach, it must then assess the magnitude and severity of the problem and must rapidly implement corrective measures. If the institution is supervised by a state or federal regulator, it must determine whether to notify the regulator of the problem and when to do so. The "when" question can be challenging because regulators like to be informed of problems early, but the organization may wish to hold off communicating with the government until it has a better handle on what happened. There is also the issue of notification to customers. When must customers be informed of a breach, what must they be told, and what remedial measures should the organization implement if customers have been or may be harmed? This latter issue involves complex legal and business considerations.

Viator, a worldwide provider of tours and other tourist services, sent the following notification to its customers after it experienced a data breach in 2014:

Viator Email to Customers

Sept. 19, 2014

Dear Viator Customer:

We want to make you aware that Viator has experienced a data compromise that could potentially affect payment card data used to make bookings through Viator's websites and mobile offerings. If you have created a Viator account, this compromise may also affect your email address, password and Viator "nickname." We deeply regret any inconvenience this may cause. The protection of our customers' personal information is of paramount concern. We are dedicating all the resources necessary to investigate and resolve this incident.

We have alerted the credit card companies and law enforcement, in addition to taking appropriate steps to secure our systems. We are writing to make you aware of the occurrence so that you can also monitor your accounts as a prudent measure, and take any other precautions you believe may be appropriate. We are offering our customers in the U.S. free identity protection services, including credit monitoring.

Meanwhile, we are continuously working to strengthen our security measures to help minimize the potential for incidents of this nature in the future. While our investigation is ongoing, here is some important information to be aware of.

On September 2, we were informed by our credit card service provider that unauthorized charges had been made on a number of our customers' credit cards. We have hired forensic experts, notified law enforcement and we have been working diligently and comprehensively to investigate the incident, identify how our systems may have been impacted, and secure our systems. Although our investigation is continuing, we currently believe that some forms of your data may be affected by the compromise. This information includes encrypted credit or debit card number, along with card expiration date, name, billing address, email address and, if you have created a Viator account, the associated email address, encrypted password and Viator "nickname." At this time, we have no reason to believe that the three or four digit value printed at the back or front of your card was compromised. Additionally, debit PIN numbers are not collected by Viator and could therefore not be compromised.

We recommend that all affected customers monitor their card activity and report any fraudulent charges to their credit card company. It is always a good practice to review your credit and debit card account statements regularly for suspicious activity. If you notice suspicious activity involving your account, please report it immediately to the appropriate financial institution or credit card company. You will not be responsible for fraudulent charges to your account if you report them in a timely manner.

To assist our customers in the U.S., we are offering free identity protection services, including credit monitoring. More information on that offer is below.

Additionally, we encourage you to reset your Viator password the next time you sign in to your Viator account, and change it on any other sites where you used the same password. To change passwords on the Viator site, [take the following actions]. If you have questions related to this situation, you can contact us anytime through our dedicated toll-free information helpline at 888-xxx-xxxx or at 702-xxx-xxxx.

Responding properly to this incident is our top priority, and we are committed to taking all appropriate steps to safeguard your personal information. For over 10 years, Viator's mission has been dedicated to offering travelers the best tours and activities worldwide, and to delivering a superior experience in all our customer interactions. That mission continues. We deeply regret any inconvenience or concern this may cause you and we thank you for your patience as we continue our investigation. We are focused on doing everything possible to maintain your trust so that we can continue to serve you in the future.

Sincerely,

Barrie Seidenberg
CEO, Viator

Questions and Comments

1. Did the letter provide the right amount of detail for customers? Was the tone appropriate? What would you do differently if you were drafting the message?

2. Why did the company provide free credit report and credit monitoring services to customers who signed up?

3. Does this letter increase or reduce the risk that Viator will face legal liability to customers or regulatory action by the FTC or other agency?

PROBLEM 11-1

You are CEO of Styx, a startup ride sharing company seeking to compete with Uber, Lyft, and similar firms. Your company is seeking to capture part of the corporate end of the market by offering volume discounts and other perks to companies that open an account and meet certain minimum usage requirements. The startup costs for the enterprise are significant, and you have already blown through most of your initial $50 million in venture capital funding. However, you are about to finalize contracts with several Fortune 50 companies that will position the company to go public, making you so rich that you will never have to hail a cab again in your life. A problem arises, however, when your internal audit department uncovers that a former employee has downloaded information on thousands of customer credit cards to a USB flash drive and is now attempting to sell the information on the "dark web." If you disclose this to your customers, you are pretty sure the pending deals will fall through and your company will fail. If you don't disclose, you believe it is likely that no one will learn where the stolen information came from. What should you do?

B. GRAMM-LEACH-BLILEY ACT

Financial information is often sensitive. People don't want others to know who they do business with, how much they take home in salary, or how much they spend at the local liquor store. When you entrust information to a financial institution, you do so on faith that they will not abuse your trust and use that information to your disadvantage. Even beyond these privacy concerns, there are real financial risks. Identity theft has become a serious problem in today's marketplace, especially with the advent of Internet-based commerce. Do you know or have you heard of anyone who has been a victim of identity theft? Many people do. The problems go beyond individuals. As noted above, these days financial institutions are attacked repeatedly by a malicious actors who seek to inflict mischief on banks and our banking system.

Information security became a central focus of compliance for the financial services sector with the enactment of the Gramm-Leach-Bliley Act in 1999.

Gramm-Leach-Bliley Act §501

15 U.S.C. §6801

(a) It is the policy of the Congress that each financial institution has an affirmative and continuing obligation to respect the privacy of its customers and to protect the security and confidentiality of those customers' nonpublic personal information.

(b) Financial institution safeguards

In furtherance of the policy in subsection (a) of this section, each [federal financial institution regulator], other than the Bureau of Consumer Financial Protection, shall establish appropriate standards for the financial institutions subject to their jurisdiction relating to administrative, technical and physical safeguards —

(1) to insure the security and confidentiality of customer records and information;

(2) to protect against any anticipated threats or hazards to the security or integrity of such records; and

(3) to protect against unauthorized access to or use of such records or information which could result in substantial harm or inconvenience to any customer.

Questions and Comments

1. The quoted language is part of the Gramm-Leach-Bliley Act, a statute that fundamentally altered the regulation of the American financial services industry by permitting affiliations between banks, insurance companies, and securities underwriters under the control of a common financial holding company. Congress realized that together with enhanced affiliations came increased threats to the privacy of consumer information. Section 501 of the Act, quoted above, deals with this problem. The House Committee Report on the Gramm-Leach-Bliley Act stated:

> As financial institutions become increasingly diversified and complex, they must rely upon databases and customer service mechanisms that require the sharing of information both within the institution itself, among its affiliates, and among various service providers, in order to provide consumers with competitive products. At the same time, consumers have become increasingly sensitive to the use of their personal information by financial institutions as a commodity to be sold to outside parties with which the consumer has no expectation or, necessarily, desire to do business, as well as the use of that personal information by the financial institution itself in ways that are unrelated to the transaction or product the consumer originally sought from the institution.

H.R. Rep. 106-74, p. 118 (1999). It is evident from this report that Congress in 1999 had little idea of the extent of the threats to consumer privacy that would come from malicious forces outside the financial institution.

2. Banking agencies may enforce the provisions of §501 with the same sanctions that they currently use to regulate financial institutions, including penalties ranging from $5,000 up to $1 million per day.

The Federal Financial Institution Examination Council — an umbrella organization of financial institution regulators — has established two general rules to implement §501 and related requirements. The Privacy Rule prohibits a financial institution from disclosing a consumer's non-public information to a non-affiliated third party unless certain notice requirements are met and the consumer does not opt out of the disclosure. You have probably seen the Privacy Rule in action, in the form of notices that financial institutions are required to provide to consumers which describe the institution's policies and practices designed to protect the confidentiality and security of financial information. The Privacy Rule doesn't impose obligations with respect to safeguarding information; that task is left to the Security Guidelines, which are intended to prevent or respond to unauthorized access or use of private information. The Security Guidelines establish standards relating to administrative, technical, and physical safeguards for customer information. An excerpt follows:

Federal Financial Institution Examination Council, Interagency Guidelines Establishing Information Security Standards

2005

[E]ach financial institution must:

- Develop and maintain an effective information security program tailored to the complexity of its operations, and
- Require, by contract, service providers that have access to its customer information to take appropriate steps to protect the security and confidentiality of this information. . . .

Each financial institution must identify and evaluate risks to its customer information, develop a plan to mitigate the risks, implement the plan, test the plan, and update the plan when necessary. If an Agency finds that a financial institution's performance is deficient under the Security Guidelines, the Agency may take action, such as requiring that the institution file a compliance plan.

The Security Guidelines require financial institutions to safeguard and properly dispose of customer information. Customer information is any record containing nonpublic personal information about an individual who has obtained a financial product or service from the institution that is to be used primarily for personal, family, or household purposes and who has an ongoing relationship with the institution. . . .

Implementing an information security program begins with conducting an assessment of reasonably foreseeable risks. Like other elements of an information security program, risk assessment procedures, analysis, and results must be written. Under the Security Guidelines, a risk assessment must include the following four steps:

- Identifying reasonably foreseeable internal and external threats that could result in unauthorized disclosure, misuse, alteration, or destruction of customer information or customer information systems;
- Assessing the likelihood and potential damage of identified threats, taking into consideration the sensitivity of the customer information;
- Assessing the sufficiency of the policies, procedures, customer information systems, and other arrangements in place to control the identified risks; and
- Applying each of the foregoing steps in connection with the disposal of customer information.

IDENTIFYING REASONABLY FORESEEABLE INTERNAL AND EXTERNAL THREATS

A risk assessment must be sufficient in scope to identify the reasonably foreseeable threats from within and outside a financial institution's operations that could result in unauthorized disclosure, misuse, alteration, or destruction of customer information or customer information systems, as well as the reasonably foreseeable threats due to the disposal of customer information. The scale and complexity of its operations and the scope and nature of an institution's activities will affect the nature of the threats an institution will face. . . .

ASSESSING THE LIKELIHOOD AND POTENTIAL DAMAGE OF IDENTIFIED THREATS

In addition to identifying reasonably foreseeable threats to customer information, customer information systems, and customer information that a financial institution disposes of, a risk assessment must evaluate the potential damage from these threats. The Security Guidelines allow latitude to determine the sensitivity of customer information in the course of assessing the likelihood of and potential damage from the identified threats. . . .

In the course of assessing the potential threats identified, an institution should consider its ability to identify unauthorized changes to customer records. In addition, it should take into consideration its ability to reconstruct the records from duplicate records or backup information systems.

Assessing the Sufficiency of Policies and Procedures

Evaluating the sufficiency of policies and procedures is a key element of a financial institution's risk assessment. The evaluation process includes identifying weaknesses or other deficiencies in existing security controls and assessing the extent to which customer information and customer information systems are at risk as a result of those weaknesses. It should also identify the extent to which customer information is at risk as a result of improper methods of disposal.

The risk assessment may include an automated analysis of the vulnerability of certain customer information systems. However, an automated analysis likely will not address manual processes and controls, detection of and response to intrusions into information systems, physical security, employee training, and other key controls. Accordingly, an automated analysis of vulnerabilities should be only one tool used in conducting a risk assessment. . . .

Hiring an Outside Consultant to Conduct the Risk Assessment

A financial institution may decide to hire an outside consultant to conduct the risk assessment of its information security program, but it nevertheless remains responsible for the adequacy of the assessment. Therefore, the institution must ensure that the assessment specifically examines the risks that relate to *its* customer information, customer information systems, and systems for disposal of customer information. . . .

If an outside consultant only examines a subset of the institution's risks, such as risks to computer systems, that is insufficient to meet the requirement of the Security Guidelines. The institution will need to supplement the outside consultant's assessment by examining other risks, such as risks to customer records maintained in paper form. . . .

Engaging in an Ongoing Risk Assessment Process

Risk assessment is an ongoing process. Financial institutions should continually review their current policies and procedures to make certain they are adequate to safeguard customer information and customer information systems. . . . The institution must also update the risk assessment, as necessary, to account for system changes before they are implemented, or new products or services before they are offered.

Designing Security Controls

The Security Guidelines require a financial institution to design an information security program to control the risks identified through its assessment, commensurate with the sensitivity of the information and the complexity and scope of its activities. Thus, an institution must consider a variety of policies, procedures, and technical controls and adopt those measures that it determines appropriately address the identified risks.

The Security Guidelines provide a list of measures that an institution must consider and, if appropriate, adopt. These are:

- Access controls on customer information systems, including controls to authenticate and permit access only to authorized individuals and controls to prevent employees from providing customer information to unauthorized individuals who may seek to obtain this information through fraudulent means;
- Access restrictions at physical locations containing customer information, such as buildings, computer facilities, and records storage facilities to permit access only to authorized individuals;
- Encryption of electronic customer information, including while in transit or in storage on networks or systems to which unauthorized individuals may have access;
- Procedures designed to ensure that customer information system modifications are consistent with the institution's information security program;
- Dual control procedures, segregation of duties, and employee background checks for employees with responsibilities for or access to customer information;
- Monitoring systems and procedures to detect actual and attempted attacks on or intrusions into customer information systems;
- Response programs that specify actions to be taken when the institution suspects or detects that unauthorized individuals have gained access to customer information systems, including appropriate reports to regulatory and law enforcement agencies; and
- Measures to protect against destruction, loss, or damage of customer information due to potential environmental hazards, such as fire and water damage or technological failures. . . .

An institution should:

- Ensure that paper records containing customer information are rendered unreadable as indicated by its risk assessment, such as by shredding or any other means; and
- Recognize that computer-based records present unique disposal problems. Residual data frequently remains on media after erasure. Since that data can be recovered, additional disposal techniques should be applied to sensitive electronic data.

In addition to considering the measures required by the Security Guidelines, each institution may need to implement additional procedures or controls specific to the nature of its operations. An institution may implement safeguards designed to provide the same level of protection to all customer information, provided that the level is appropriate for the most sensitive classes of information.

Insurance coverage is not a substitute for an information security program. Although insurance may protect an institution or its customers against certain losses associated with unauthorized disclosure, misuse, alteration, or destruction of customer information, the Security Guidelines require a financial institution to implement and maintain controls designed to prevent those acts from occurring.

DEVELOP AND IMPLEMENT A RESPONSE PROGRAM . . .

The components of an effective response program include:

- Assessment of the nature and scope of the incident and identification of what customer information has been accessed or misused;
- Prompt notification to its primary federal regulator once the institution becomes aware of an incident involving unauthorized access to or use of sensitive customer information;
- Notification to appropriate law enforcement authorities, in addition to filing a timely Suspicious Activity Report, in situations involving Federal criminal violations requiring immediate attention;
- Measures to contain and control the incident to prevent further unauthorized access to or misuse of customer information, while preserving records and other evidence; and
- Notification to customers when warranted.

CIRCUMSTANCES FOR CUSTOMER NOTICE

The Incident Response Guidance describes when and how a financial institution should provide notice to customers affected by unauthorized access or misuse of sensitive customer information. In particular, it indicates that:

- Once the institution becomes aware of an incident of unauthorized access to sensitive customer information, it should conduct a reasonable investigation to determine promptly the likelihood that the information has been or will be misused.
- If the institution determines that misuse of customer information has occurred or is reasonably possible, it should notify any affected customer as soon as possible.

Sensitive customer information means:

- A customer's name, address, or telephone number, in conjunction with the customer's social security number, driver's license number, account number, credit or debit card number, or a personal identification number or password that would permit access to the customer's account; or
- Any combination of components of customer information that would allow an unauthorized third party to access the customer's account electronically, such as user name and password or password and account number.

TRAINING STAFF

The Security Guidelines require a financial institution to train staff to prepare and implement its information security program. . . .

TESTING KEY CONTROLS

The Security Guidelines require a financial institution to test the key controls, systems, and procedures of its information security program. . . .

OVERSEEING SERVICE PROVIDERS

The Security Guidelines set forth specific requirements that apply to a financial institution's arrangements with service providers. An institution must:

- Exercise appropriate due diligence in selecting its service providers; Require its service providers by contract to implement appropriate measures designed to meet the objectives of the Security Guidelines; and
- Where indicated by its risk assessment, monitor its service providers to confirm that they have satisfied their obligations under the contract described above. . . .

CONTRACTS WITH SERVICE PROVIDERS

The contract provisions in the Security Guidelines apply to *all* of a financial institution's service providers. After exercising due diligence in selecting a company, the institution must enter into and enforce a contract with the company that requires it to implement appropriate measures designed to implement the *objectives* of the Security Guidelines.

In particular, financial institutions must require their service providers by contract to:

- Implement appropriate measures designed to protect against unauthorized access to or use of customer information maintained by the service provider that could result in substantial harm or inconvenience to any customer; and
- Properly dispose of customer information.

In addition, the Incident Response Guidance states that an institution's contract with its service provider should require the service provider to take appropriate actions to address incidents of unauthorized access to the financial institution's customer information, including notification to the institution as soon as possible following any such incident.

MONITORING SERVICE PROVIDERS

A financial institution must monitor each of its service providers in accordance with its risk assessment. However, the Security Guidelines do not impose any specific requirements regarding the methods or frequency of monitoring service providers to ensure that they are fulfilling their contractual obligations. Some service providers are financial institutions that are subject to the Security Guidelines, or to other standards for safeguarding information promulgated by their primary regulator, and therefore may have implemented their own information security programs.

To the extent that monitoring is warranted, a financial institution must confirm that the service provider is fulfilling its obligations under its contract. Institutions may review audits, summaries of test results, or equivalent evaluations of a service provider's work. These audits, tests, or evaluations should be conducted by a qualified party independent of management and personnel responsible for the development or maintenance of the service provider's security program.

The reports of test results may contain proprietary information about the service provider's systems or they may include non-public personal information about customers of another financial institution. Under certain circumstances it may be appropriate for service providers to redact confidential and sensitive information from audit reports or test results before giving the institution a copy. Where this is the case, an institution should make sure that the information is sufficient for it to conduct an accurate review, that all material deficiencies have been or are being corrected, and that the reports or test results are timely and relevant.

The institution should include reviews of its service providers in its written information security program.

ADJUSTING THE PROGRAM

A financial institution should adjust its information security program to reflect the results of its ongoing risk assessment and the key controls necessary to safeguard customer information and ensure the proper disposal of customer information. It should adjust the program to take into account changes in technology, the sensitivity of its customer information, internal or external threats to information, and the institution's own changing business arrangement such as mergers, acquisitions, alliances and joint ventures, outsourcing arrangements, and changes in customer information systems. . . .

RESPONSIBILITIES OF AND REPORTS TO THE BOARD OF THE DIRECTORS

Under the Security Guidelines, a financial institution's board of directors, or an appropriate committee of the board, must satisfy specific requirements designed to ensure that the institution's information security program is developed, implemented, and maintained under the supervision of those who are ultimately responsible. At the outset, the board, or appropriate committee, must approve the written information security program. Thereafter, the board or appropriate committee must oversee the implementation and maintenance of the program. These duties include assigning specific responsibility for implementing the program and reviewing management reports. . . .

Questions and Comments

1. The Federal Financial Institutions Examination Council consists of the Comptroller of the Currency, the Board of Governors of the Federal Reserve System, the Federal Deposit Insurance Corporation, the National Credit Union Administration, the Consumer Financial Protection Bureau, and representing representative of state financial institution supervisors.

2. One key to any information security compliance regime is to define the nature of the information protected against disclosure. In the case of financial institutions, the Security Guidelines define the class of protected information as "any record containing nonpublic personal information about an individual who has obtained a financial product or service from the institution that is to be used primarily for personal, family, or household purposes and who has an ongoing relationship with the institution." Why is the definition limited to customers who have an ongoing relationship with the institution?

3. This compliance regime is risk-based: "Implementing an information security program begins with conducting an assessment of reasonably foreseeable risks." In this respect, the Security Rule is similar to many other modern compliance programs that require the regulated entity to perform its own risk analysis and to tailor its compliance program accordingly.

4. The guidelines require institutions to identify "reasonably foreseeable threats" to information security. Why limit the threats to those that are reasonably foreseeable?

5. Information security is a dynamic area because the threats are constantly evolving. Each "patch" or "fix" to a security vulnerability seems to be followed by a report of another weakness which malefactors could exploit. Moreover,

technology and consumer behavior change rapidly in this space, requiring rapid introduction of new products and systems that may not be fully tested for data security weaknesses. How do the Security Guidelines address the protean nature of information security threats?

6. The guidelines set forth "measures that an institution must consider and, if appropriate, adopt." The implication is that an institution need not implement these measures if, after due consideration, it reasonably concludes that it is not appropriate to adopt them. Why do the bank regulators adopt such a weak requirement—why not mandate that institutions subject to their jurisdiction adopt the specified measures?

7. The guidelines recognize that financial institutions may use consultants and third-party service providers to assist in their information security program. The obvious benefits of bringing outsiders into the picture are to provide a "second set of eyes" which may be able to detect problems that the client has overlooked, and to provide expertise in a highly specialized and technologically sophisticated area of activity. But the use of outsiders also carries risks. Having retained a consultant, the institution may let its own guard down on the theory that someone else is minding the store; also the purported specialist may lack the necessary expertise or may be subject to its own information security issues. How do the Security Guidelines deal with the tradeoff?

What must be done if an information security breach has occurred at a financial institution?

An initial question is whether the organization must notify the people whose non-public information has been compromised. Disclosing a data breach carries multiple risks. Being exposed as vulnerable to cyber threats can be harmful to a firm's reputation and ability to raise capital. One survey found that 78 percent of investors were "somewhat or very unlikely" to invest in a company with a history of being targeted in cyber-attacks, while 69 percent were reluctant to invest in a company with a history of one or more data breaches. Regulators are likely to become alarmed when a company experiences a significant data security problem, and may decide to institute investigations or impose administrative sanctions. Class action attorneys, always on the lookout for new cases, may file claims against the company on behalf of thousands or millions of plaintiffs. For these and other reasons, organizations that have suffered a security breach are often reluctant to disclose this fact.

Where voluntary action is unlikely, the law steps in. The following excerpts describe some of the legal rules that require organizations to self-disclose significant compromises of their data security systems:

Federal Financial Institution Examination Council, Interagency Guidance on Response Programs for Unauthorized Access to Customer Information and Customer Notice

Apr. 1, 2005

The Federal Financial Institutions Examination Council (FFIEC) agencies are issuing the attached interpretive guidance stating that every financial institution should develop and implement a response program designed to address incidents of unauthorized access to sensitive customer information maintained by the financial institution or its service provider.

The agencies are issuing the interpretive guidance under the authority of section 501(b)(3) of the Gramm-Leach-Bliley Act (GLBA), which states the information security standards established by the agencies must include various safeguards to protect against not only "unauthorized access to" but also the "use of" customer information in a manner that could result in "substantial harm or inconvenience to any customer."

COMPONENTS OF A RESPONSE PROGRAM

At a minimum, an institution's response program should contain procedures for:

- Assessing the nature and scope of an incident and identifying what customer information systems and types of customer information have been accessed or misused;
- Notifying its primary federal regulator as soon as possible when the institution becomes aware of an incident involving unauthorized access to or use of sensitive customer information;
- Consistent with the agencies' Suspicious Activity Report (SAR) regulations, filing a timely SAR, and in situations involving federal criminal violations requiring immediate attention, such as when a reportable violation is ongoing, promptly notifying appropriate law enforcement authorities;
- Taking appropriate steps to contain and control the incident to prevent further unauthorized access to or use of customer information; and
- Notifying customers when warranted in a manner designed to ensure that a customer can reasonably be expected to receive it.

When an incident of unauthorized access to sensitive customer information involves customer information systems maintained by an institution's service provider, it is the financial institution's responsibility to notify its customers and regulator. However, an institution may authorize or contract with its service provider to notify the institution's customers or regulator on its behalf.

SENSITIVE CUSTOMER INFORMATION

For purposes of this guidance, sensitive customer information means a customer's name, address or telephone number in conjunction with the customer's Social Security number, driver's license number, account number, credit or debit card number, or a personal identification number or password that would permit access to the customer's account. It also includes any combination of components of customer information that would allow someone to log on to or access the customer's account, such as user name and password or password and account number.

WHEN CUSTOMER NOTICE SHOULD BE PROVIDED

The interpretive guidance states that a financial institution should provide a notice to its customers whenever it becomes aware of an incident of unauthorized access to customer information and, at the conclusion of a reasonable investigation, determines that misuse of the information has occurred or it is reasonably possible that misuse will occur.

CUSTOMER NOTICE

Customer notice should be given in a clear and conspicuous manner. The notice should include the following items:

- Description of the incident;
- Type of information subject to unauthorized access;
- Measures taken by the institution to protect customers from further unauthorized access;
- Telephone number customers can call for information and assistance; and
- Remind customers to remain vigilant over next twelve to twenty four months, and report suspected identity theft incidents to the institution.

The guidance encourages financial institutions to notify the nationwide consumer reporting agencies prior to sending notices to a large number of customers that include contact information for the reporting agencies.

DELIVERY OF CUSTOMER NOTICE

Customer notice should be delivered in a manner designed to ensure that a customer can reasonably be expected to receive it. For example, the institution may choose to contact all customers affected by telephone or by mail, or by electronic mail for those customers for whom it has a valid e-mail address and who have agreed to receive communications electronically.

Questions and Comments

1. The guidance excerpted above requires a financial institution to promptly inform its regulator when the institution learns of an incident involving unauthorized access to or use of sensitive customer information. What if the institution's own internal controls catch a security vulnerability before any breach occurs? Should the regulators be informed of potential breaches that were averted?

2. Although the institution is required to inform the regulator of a breach involving sensitive information, and also to inform customers of the same events, the guidance doesn't require that the institution clear the consumer notification with the regulator before it is distributed. Why not? If you were advising an institution facing a data breach situation, would you recommend that the regulator be informed in advance of the content of any proposed customer notice?

3. Why only notify consumers when misuse of the information has occurred or it is reasonably possible that misuse will occur? Does the consumer have a right to know of serious shortcomings in a service provider's information security program, even if no harm to the customer will occur from this particular breach?

4. What if — as is often the case — the breach occurs not at the financial institution itself, but at a company that provides services to the institution? In such a case, the financial institution doesn't want to be blamed for a problem it did not cause. On the other hand, the customer notification will necessarily name the financial institution; and customers are unlikely to draw a sharp distinction between the institution itself and an independent company to which it has outsourced information and security-related responsibilities. In such cases, the FFIEC guidance allows the notification to come from the service provider directly. What sorts of

negotiations are likely to occur behind the scenes between the service provider and its financial institution client regarding the language of this notice?

PROBLEM 11-2

You are the chief executive officer of Deposit Information Systems, a company that performs "back office" processing of checking account information for several thousand banks, savings and loan institutions, and credit unions. Your service requires you to hold personally identifying information for hundreds of thousands of depositors in your customer's accounts. One day your chief technology officer knocks on your office door and says, "We've got a problem." A routine security sweep has uncovered the fact that a hacker has inserted malware into your system that has the capacity for accessing and misappropriating any information your company has received from its financial institution customers. Your CTO doesn't yet know how much data may have been stolen, but she thinks it may be "a lot." As a provider of electronic data processing and back-office services to financial institutions, your company is subject to regulatory oversight and examination by federal banking regulators and various state regulatory authorities; your bank customers are subject to the requirements of the Gramm-Leach-Bliley Act. What should you do?

C. HIPAA

The Health Insurance Portability and Accountability Act (HIPAA) requires health care entities to protect the confidentiality of health-related information (protected health information or "PHI"). PHI is personal medical information, including name, address, Social Security number, and all medical information. "Covered entities" — health plans, health care providers, or health care clearinghouses — are subject to potential civil or criminal penalties if they improperly handle or disclose PHI.

It requires little imagination to see the enormous scope of HIPAA's data-related requirements. The vast majority of more than 300 million people in the United States have health care records on file somewhere — often in many places. Those records must be stored; they must also be accessible when needed — and accessed by many potential users including hundreds of insurance organizations and more than half a million physicians and other health care professionals. Protecting this information against intentional or inadvertent disclosure to the wrong people while ensuring that it is available to the right ones is a daunting task.

The Department of Health and Human Services (HHS) has implemented HIPAA's data protection provisions through two principal rules. The Privacy Rule, 45 C.F.R. §§164.500-164.534 (2013), deals with all media in which health-related information is stored. The Security Rule, 45 C.F.R. §§164.302-164.318 (2013), deals specifically with electronic medical information ("Electronic Protected Health Information" or "ePHI"). The following excerpt gives a flavor of the requirements contained in the Security Rule.

Health and Human Services, 45 C.F.R. §164.306 Security Standards: General Rules

(a) General requirements. Covered entities must do the following:

(1) Ensure the confidentiality, integrity, and availability of all electronic protected health information the covered entity creates, receives, maintains, or transmits.

(2) Protect against any reasonably anticipated threats or hazards to the security or integrity of such information.

(3) Protect against any reasonably anticipated uses or disclosures of such information that are not permitted or required under [this regulation].

(4) Ensure compliance . . . by its workforce.

(b) Flexibility of approach.

(1) Covered entities may use any security measures that allow the covered entity to reasonably and appropriately implement the standards and implementation specifications as specified in this subpart.

(2) In deciding which security measures to use, a covered entity must take into account the following factors:

(i) The size, complexity, and capabilities of the covered entity.

(ii) The covered entity's technical infrastructure, hardware, and software security capabilities.

(iii) The costs of security measures.

(iv) The probability and criticality of potential risks to electronic protected health information. . . .

(d) Implementation specifications. In this subpart:

(1) Implementation specifications are required or addressable. If an implementation specification is required, the word "Required" appears in parentheses after the title of the implementation specification. If an implementation specification is addressable, the word "Addressable" appears in parentheses after the title of the implementation specification.

(2) When a standard . . . includes required implementation specifications, a covered entity must implement the implementation specifications.

(3) When a standard . . . includes addressable implementation specifications, a covered entity must—

(i) Assess whether each implementation specification is a reasonable and appropriate safeguard in its environment, when analyzed with reference to the likely contribution to protecting the entity's electronic protected health information; and

(ii) As applicable to the entity—

(A) Implement the implementation specification if reasonable and appropriate; or

(B) If implementing the implementation specification is not reasonable and appropriate — [d]ocument why it would not be reasonable and appropriate to implement the implementation specification; and [i]mplement an equivalent alternative measure if reasonable and appropriate.

The Security Rule specifies administrative, physical, and technical security safeguards and sets forth implementation specifications for each.

Administrative Safeguards:

45 C.F.R. §164.308 requires covered entities to adopt the following eight administrative safeguards:

1. Implement policies and procedures to prevent, detect, contain, and correct security violations:

- Conduct an "accurate and thorough assessment of the potential risks and vulnerabilities to the confidentiality, integrity, and availability of electronic protected health information held by the covered entity."
- Implement security measures "sufficient to reduce risks and vulnerabilities to a reasonable and appropriate level."
- Apply "appropriate sanctions against workforce members who fail to comply with the security policies and procedures of the covered entity."
- Implement procedures to "regularly review records of information system activity, such as audit logs, access reports, and security incident tracking reports."

2. Identify the "security official who is responsible for the development and implementation of the policies and procedures required by this subpart for the entity."

3. Implement "policies and procedures to ensure that all members of its workforce have appropriate access to electronic protected health information, . . . and to prevent those workforce members who do not have access . . . from obtaining access to electronic protected health information." Addressable specifications here include the following:

- Implement procedures for the "authorization and/or supervision of workforce members who work with electronic protected health information or in locations where it might be accessed."
- Implement procedures to "determine that the access of a workforce member to electronic protected health information is appropriate."
- Implement procedures for "terminating access to electronic protected health information when the employment of a workforce member ends or as required. . . ."

4. Implement "policies and procedures for authorizing [appropriate] access to electronic protected health information." Specifications include:

- If a health care clearinghouse is part of a larger organization, the clearinghouse must "implement policies and procedures that protect the electronic protected health information of the clearinghouse from unauthorized access by the larger organization" (required).
- Implement "policies and procedures for granting access to electronic protected health information, for example, through access to a workstation, transaction, program, process, or other mechanism" (addressable).
- Implement "policies and procedures that, based upon the entity's access authorization policies, establish, document, review, and modify a user's right of access to a workstation, transaction, program, or process" (addressable).

5. Implement a security awareness and training program for all members of its workforce (including management). Addressable specifications include:

- Periodic security updates.
- Procedures for guarding against, detecting, and reporting malicious software.
- Procedures for monitoring log-in attempts and reporting discrepancies.
- Procedures for creating, changing, and safeguarding passwords.

6. "Identify and respond to suspected or known security incidents; mitigate, to the extent practicable, harmful effects of security incidents that are known to the covered entity; and document security incidents and their outcomes."

7. Establish "policies and procedures for responding to an emergency or other occurrence . . . that damages systems that contain electronic protected health information." Required implementation specifications include:

- Establish and implement "procedures to create and maintain retrievable exact copies of electronic protected health information."
- Establish "procedures to restore any loss of data."
- Establish "procedures to enable continuation of critical business processes for protection of the security of electronic protected health information while operating in emergency mode."

Addressable Specifications Include:

- "Implement procedures for periodic testing and revision of contingency plans."
- Assess "the relative criticality of specific applications and data in support of other contingency plan components."

8. Perform a "periodic technical and nontechnical evaluation, based initially upon the standards implemented under this rule and subsequently, in response to environmental or operational changes affecting the security of electronic protected health information. . . ."

In addition to these administrative requirements for covered organizations, 45 C.F.R. §164.308 contains requirements for vendors and other business associates: "[a] covered entity . . . may permit a business associate to create, receive, maintain, or transmit electronic protected health information on the covered entity's behalf only if the covered entity obtains satisfactory assurances . . . that the business associate will appropriately safeguard the information."

Questions and Comments

1. Why does the Security Rule distinguish between "required" and "addressable" implementation specifications?

2. Among the required implementation specifications are the duties to (a) conduct a risk evaluation and (b) implement measures to reduce risk to a reasonable level. This is essentially the technique of risk management, which we will study at length in Part III of this book. In adopting a risk-focused approach to information security, the Security Rule follows what is today an orthodox approach to compliance enforcement.

3. Notice the Security Rule's focus on ensuring compliance by the workforce. A particular feature of information security is that a breach can be caused by many different people — and often by people at a relatively low level of seniority in the organization. Effective compliance therefore requires that the applicable procedures and policies — as well as more the more general value of respecting and protecting patient privacy — be understood and internalized by everyone in the organization with substantive control over protected health information.

4. A difficulty of HIPAA enforcement is the wide variety of enterprises and individuals who are subject to the statute's requirements. These range from health maintenance organizations employing tens of thousands of people to physicians in solo practice assisted by one or two employees. Compliance procedures that may be perfectly appropriate for one may be entirely inappropriate for the other. How does the HHS Security Rule deal with this problem? Is this an effective approach?

5. A serious problem with information security is that of termination of access rights. It is all too easy for organizations, having given access rights to employees or others, to neglect to cut off those rights when the person moves to another position in the organization or leaves altogether. Somehow the minds of IT officers seem more focused on the dangers of granting access than on the (potentially equally significant) dangers of failing to restrict or eliminate it once granted. The Security Rule deals with this problem by including an addressable specification that the covered organization should implement procedures for terminating access to electronic protected health information when the employment of a workforce member ends. Is this a sufficient response?

6. Note the rule's application to vendors and other "business associates." This is also a recurring theme in much of modern compliance practice: recognition that third-party vendors can create nearly as much havoc as employees of the regulated entity, if they fail to follow appropriate compliance and risk management practices.

7. HHS could have enforced HIPAA by imposing significant *ex post* sanctions for unauthorized disclosures of protected health information, but elected not to follow that course. Instead, it seeks, through the detailed requirements of the Security Rule and its sibling, the Privacy Rule, to ensure that protected information is not disclosed in the first place. Was this a wise strategy, from the standpoint of the goals and purposes of HIPAA? In terms of the practical limitations on HHS's enforcement powers?

Several HIPAA requirements are at issue in the following agreement settling charges of administrative violations:

Resolution Agreement, U.S. Department of Health and Human Services and Wellpoint, Inc.

July 8, 2013

The Parties to this Resolution Agreement ("Agreement") are the United States Department of Health and Human Services, Office for Civil Rights ("HHS") . . . and WellPoint, Inc., an Indiana corporation, on behalf of the health plans under its common ownership or control that have been designated as a single Affiliated Covered Entity. . . .

On June 18, 2010, HHS received notification from WellPoint regarding a breach of certain of its unsecured electronic protected health information (ePHI). On

September 9, 2010, HHS notified WellPoint of HHS's investigation regarding Well-Point's compliance with the Privacy, Security, and Breach Notification Rules. . . .

Beginning on October 23, 2009, until March 7, 2010, WellPoint did not adequately implement policies and procedures for authorizing access to ePHI maintained in its web-based application database consistent with the applicable requirements of the Security Rule.

WellPoint did not perform an adequate technical evaluation in response to a software upgrade, an operational change affecting the security of ePHI maintained in its web-based application database that would establish the extent to which the configuration of the software providing authentication safeguards for its web-based application met the requirements of the Security Rule.

Beginning on October 23, 2009, until March 7, 2010, WellPoint did not adequately implement technology to verify that a person or entity seeking access to ePHI maintained in its web-based application database is the one claimed.

Beginning on October 23, 2009, until March 7, 2010, WellPoint impermissibly disclosed the ePHI, including the names, dates of birth, addresses, Social Security Numbers, telephone numbers and health information, of approximately 612,000 individuals whose ePHI was maintained in the web-based application database.

No Admission. This Agreement is not an admission of liability by WellPoint for actions arising out of the covered conduct.

No Concession. This Agreement is not a concession by HHS that WellPoint has not violated the Privacy or Security Rules or that WellPoint is not liable for civil money penalties. . . .

In consideration of the Parties' interest in avoiding the uncertainty, burden and expense of further investigation and formal proceedings, the Parties agree to resolve this matter according to the Terms and Conditions below.

WellPoint agrees to pay HHS the amount of $1,700,000.00 ("Resolution Amount") by electronic funds transfer on or before July 11, 2013, pursuant to written instructions to be provided by HHS.

In consideration of and conditioned upon WellPoint's performance of its obligations under this Agreement, HHS releases WellPoint from any actions it has or may have against WellPoint under the Privacy and Security Rules for the Covered Conduct. . . .

Agreement by Released Party. WellPoint shall not contest the validity of its obligation to pay, nor the amount of, the Resolution Agreement or any other obligations agreed to under this Agreement. . . .

Questions and Comments

1. WellPoint is the largest independent licensee of the Blue Cross and Blue Shield Association. In 2012, it had $61.7 billion in total revenues and net income of $2.65 billion. How much impact will a $1.7-million-dollar fine have on its financial position?

2. The HHS press release states that "OCR's investigation indicated that Well-Point did not implement appropriate administrative and technical safeguards as required under the HIPAA Security Rule. The investigation indicated WellPoint did

not: adequately implement policies and procedures for authorizing access to the on-line application database; perform an appropriate technical evaluation in response to a software upgrade to its information systems; [or] have technical safeguards in place to verify the person or entity seeking access to electronic protected health information maintained in its application database."

3. As we have seen, settlement agreements with government regulators typically include commitments by the regulated party to improve its compliance operations and procedures. No such agreements appear in the excerpted settlement. Why not? News reports indicated that after discovering the breach, WellPoint voluntarily notified all potentially affected individuals, enhanced the security of its database, and provided credit monitoring and identity theft insurance to affected persons.

4. The HHS press release stated that "[t]his case sends an important message to HIPAA-covered entities to take caution when implementing changes to their information systems, especially when those changes involve updates to Web-based applications or portals that are used to provide access to consumers' health data using the Internet." It appears that the breach at WellPoint occurred as that organization was upgrading its database; the government's action against the company was intended to mark out database upgrades as key points of vulnerability in information security and privacy programs.

5. The press release added the following comment: "Whether systems upgrades are conducted by covered entities or their business associates, HHS expects organizations to have in place reasonable and appropriate technical, administrative and physical safeguards to protect the confidentiality, integrity and availability of electronic protected health information — especially information that is accessible over the Internet. Beginning Sept. 23, 2013, liability for many of HIPAA's requirements will extend directly to business associates that receive or store protected health information, such as contractors and subcontractors." Reading between the lines, it seems that the problem was related to a contractor that the company had employed to assist with the process. The settlement appears intended, in part, to warn health care companies that they are responsible for potential violations caused by contractors as well.

Unlike some other compliance obligations, Congress elected not to provide a private right of action for HIPAA violations. Thus, when a violation occurs, it is up to the government, not victims or their attorneys, to hold a covered entity to account. However, the lack of a private right of action under HIPAA has not deterred creative attorneys from seeking to exploit that law in other respects.

Acosta v. Byrum

180 N.C. App. 562, 638 S.E.2d 246 (2006)

. . . Plaintiff was a patient of Psychiatric Associates, which is located in Ahoskie, North Carolina. She was also employed by Psychiatric Associates from September 2003 until early spring of 2004. Psychiatric Associates is owned by Dr. Faber, a citizen and resident of Alabama. Byrum was the office manager at Psychiatric Associates during the time period at issue. Plaintiff alleged that Byrum had severe personal animus towards plaintiff.

Plaintiff alleged that Dr. Faber improperly allowed Byrum to use his medical record access number. Numerous times between 31 December 2003 and 3 September 2004, Byrum used Dr. Faber's access code to retrieve plaintiff's confidential psychiatric and other medical and healthcare records. Byrum then provided information contained in those records to third parties without plaintiff's authorization or consent.

Plaintiff alleged in her complaint that by providing Byrum with his access code, Dr. Faber violated . . . the Health Insurance Portability and Accountability Act of 1996 ("HIPAA"). Plaintiff alleged that she experienced severe emotional distress, humiliation, and anguish from the exposure of her medical records to third parties. Plaintiff alleged that Dr. Faber knew or should have known that his negligence would cause severe emotional distress.

Responding to these claims, Dr. Faber filed a motion to dismiss pursuant to Rules 12(b)(2) and (6). After a hearing, the trial court granted Dr. Faber's motion to dismiss. Plaintiff appeals from that order. . . .

The substantive elements of negligent infliction of emotional distress are: "(1) the defendant negligently engaged in conduct, (2) it was reasonably foreseeable that such conduct would cause the plaintiff severe emotional distress . . . , and (3) the conduct did in fact cause the plaintiff severe emotional distress." Therefore, in analyzing the sufficiency of the complaint, the dispositive question becomes whether plaintiff sufficiently stated a claim for negligent infliction of emotional distress for which relief can be granted. . . .

Plaintiff first contends she sufficiently alleged defendant's negligence. Plaintiff alleged that defendant negligently engaged in conduct by permitting Byrum to use his access code in violation of [HIPAA]. . . . Plaintiff contends that no claim for an alleged HIPAA violation was made and therefore dismissal on the grounds that HIPAA does not grant an individual a private cause of action was improper. We agree. In her complaint, plaintiff states that when Dr. Faber provided his medical access code to Byrum, Dr. Faber violated the rules and regulations established by HIPAA. This allegation does not state a cause of action under HIPAA. Rather, plaintiff cites to HIPAA as evidence of the appropriate standard of care, a necessary element of negligence. Since plaintiff made no HIPAA claim, HIPAA is inapplicable beyond providing evidence of the duty of care owed by Dr. Faber with regards to the privacy of plaintiff's medical records. . . .

Questions and Comments

1. Do you see the difference between seeking a recovery for a HIPAA violation and what the plaintiff alleged in this case?

2. Do you agree that a violation of HIPAA should be considered to be evidence of negligence under state law?

3. Could a HIPAA violation ever be considered negligence per se — that is, not just as probative of a violation of a standard of care defined under state law, but as conclusively establishing such a default? In I.S. v. Washington University, 2011 WL 2433585 (E.D. Mo. 2011), plaintiff asked the defendant medical center to inform plaintiff's employer of the dates of plaintiff's colon cancer treatments. Defendant allegedly forwarded medical records including information regarding HIV status, mental health issues, and insomnia treatments. Plaintiff alleged that the unauthorized disclosure constituted negligence per se. The defendant argued that plaintiff's

claim of negligence per se was a thinly disguised attempt to circumvent the lack of a private right of action under HIPAA. The court, however, concluded that plaintiff had properly pleaded negligence per se under state law. The reference to HIPAA did not state an independent claim for relief, but did provide "the standard of care by which to adjudge the defendant's actions."

D. FTC ACT

The Federal Trade Commission, an independent federal regulatory agency, exercises authority under §5 of the Federal Trade Commission Act to punish unfair or deceptive practices directed against consumers. Does a company commit an unfair or deceptive consumer practice when it fails to maintain proper controls over nonpublic information about its customers? Consider the following:

Federal Trade Commission v. Wyndham Worldwide Corporation

799 F.3d 236 (3d Cir. 2015)

Wyndham Worldwide is a hospitality company that franchises and manages hotels and sells timeshares through three subsidiaries. Wyndham licensed its brand name to approximately 90 independently owned hotels. Each Wyndham-branded hotel has a property management system that processes consumer information that includes names, home addresses, email addresses, telephone numbers, payment card account numbers, expiration dates, and security codes. Wyndham "manage[s]" these systems and requires the hotels to "purchase and configure" them to its own specifications. It also operates a computer network in Phoenix, Arizona, that connects its data center with the property management systems of each of the Wyndham-branded hotels.

[On three occasions in 2008 and 2009, hackers accessed Wyndham's network and the property management systems of Wyndham-branded hotels. In April 2008, hackers first broke into the local network of a hotel in Phoenix, Arizona, which was connected to Wyndham's network and the Internet. They then used the brute-force method — repeatedly guessing users' login IDs and passwords — to access an administrator account on Wyndham's network. This enabled them to obtain consumer data on computers throughout the network. In total, the hackers obtained unencrypted information for over 500,000 accounts, which they sent to a domain in Russia.

[In March 2009, hackers attacked again, this time by accessing Wyndham's network through an administrative account. The FTC claims that Wyndham was unaware of the attack for two months until consumers filed complaints about fraudulent charges. Wyndham then discovered "memory-scraping malware" used in the previous attack on more than 30 hotels' computer systems. . . . In this second attack, the hackers obtained unencrypted payment card information for approximately 50,000 consumers from the property management systems of 39 hotels.

[Hackers in late 2009 breached Wyndham's cybersecurity a third time by accessing an administrator account on one of its networks. Because Wyndham "had still not adequately limited access between . . . the Wyndham-branded hotels' property management systems, [Wyndham's network], and the Internet," the hackers had access to the property management servers of multiple hotels. Wyndham only learned of the intrusion in January 2010 when a credit card company received complaints from cardholders. In this third attack, hackers obtained payment card information for approximately 69,000 customers from the property management systems of 28 hotels.]

The FTC alleges that, at least since April 2008, Wyndham engaged in unfair cybersecurity practices that, "taken together, unreasonably and unnecessarily exposed consumers' personal data to unauthorized access and theft." This claim is fleshed out as follows.

1. The company allowed Wyndham-branded hotels to store payment card information in clear readable text.

2. Wyndham allowed the use of easily guessed passwords to access the property management systems. For example, to gain "remote access to at least one hotel's system," which was developed by Micros Systems, Inc., the user ID and password were both "micros."

3. Wyndham failed to use "readily available security measures" — such as firewalls — to "limit access between [the] hotels' property management systems, . . . corporate network, and the Internet."

4. Wyndham allowed hotel property management systems to connect to its network without taking appropriate cybersecurity precautions. . . .

5. Wyndham failed to "adequately restrict" the access of third-party vendors to its network and the servers of Wyndham-branded hotels. . . .

6. It failed to employ "reasonable measures to detect and prevent unauthorized access" to its computer network or to "conduct security investigations."

7. It did not follow "proper incident response procedures.". . .

The FTC alleges that, in total, the hackers obtained payment card information from over 619,000 consumers, which . . . resulted in at least $10.6 million in fraud loss. It further states that consumers suffered financial injury through "unreimbursed fraudulent charges, increased costs, and lost access to funds or credit," and that they "expended time and money resolving fraudulent charges and mitigating subsequent harm.". . .

[The FTC argued that Wyndham's conduct constituted an unfair act or practice within the meaning of the Federal Trade Commission Act, 15 U.S.C. §45(a). According to the agency's prior decisions, the following three factors govern unfairness decisions: (1) whether the practice, without necessarily having been previously considered unlawful, offends public policy as it has been established by statutes, the common law, or otherwise — whether, in other words, it is within at least the penumbra of some common law, statutory, or other established concept of unfairness; (2) whether it is immoral, unethical, oppressive, or unscrupulous; and (3) whether it causes substantial injury to consumers (or competitors or other businesspersons). Almost a decade later, the Supreme Court implicitly approved these factors. The Court also held that, under the policy statement, the FTC could deem a practice unfair based on the third prong — substantial consumer injury — without finding that at least one of the other two prongs was also satisfied.]

We are . . . not persuaded by Wyndham's arguments that the alleged conduct falls outside the plain meaning of "unfair." . . . Having rejected Wyndham's arguments that its conduct cannot be unfair, we assume for the remainder of this opinion that it was. . . .

Questions and Comments

1. This is an important case in the data security area because it represents an assertion by the FTC of power to regulate in this area under the open-ended provisions of §5 of the FTC Act. The excerpted case is the first to reach a federal court of appeals.

2. The FTC began to bring administrative actions against companies with allegedly deficient cyber-security controls in 2005. Prior to this action against Wyndham, however, the FTC had not promulgated any general rule on data security, and had suggested in a number of congressional hearings that it would not engage in heavy-handed regulation in this space. Did Wyndham have sufficient warning that the FTC might treat the problems in its organization as a violation?

3. Why do poor cyber-security controls constitute an "unfair" consumer practice?

4. How inadequate do Wyndham's data security controls appear to have been? Could the FTC have proceeded against hundreds or thousands of other companies on the same theory over the past decade? Was Wyndham distinctive in that the data breach resulted in substantial consumer harm? Should the presence of consumer harm be a decisive criterion for when the FTC brings a cyber-security case?

5. What standard should the FTC apply to determine when a company's cyber-security controls are sufficient so as to make its conduct not "unfair"? Are there any limits to the FTC's ability, on a case-by-case basis, to impose sanctions on firms that have experienced data breaches involving non-public consumer information?

6. For a critique of the FTC's sudden entry into data security regulation, see Gerard M. Stegmaier & Wendell Bartnick, *Psychics, Russian Roulette, and Data Security: The FTC's Hidden Data-Security Requirements*, 20 Geo. Mason L. Rev. 673 (2013).

In the following case, we see the FTC's authority being exercised in the context of a company's failure to maintain the security of private consumer information:

Federal Trade Commission, In the Matter of Dave & Buster's, Inc.

File No. 0823153, Agreement Containing Consent Order

[Dave & Buster's owns and operates restaurant and entertainment complexes in the United States. In conducting its business, Dave & Buster's collects information from consumers to obtain authorization for payment card purchases, including the credit card account number, expiration date, and an electronic security code for payment authorization.

[The FTC alleged that "since at least April 2007, Dave & Buster's engaged in a number of practices that, taken together, failed to provide reasonable and appropriate security for personal information on its computer networks. Among other things, Dave & Buster's: (a) failed to employ sufficient measures to detect and prevent unauthorized access to computer networks or to conduct security investigations, such as by employing an intrusion detection system and monitoring system logs; (b) failed to adequately restrict third-party access to its networks, such as by restricting connections to specific IP addresses or granting temporary, limited access; (c) failed to monitor and filter outbound traffic from its networks to identify and block export of sensitive personal information without authorization; (d) failed to use readily available security measures to limit access between in-store networks, such as by using firewalls or isolating the payment card system from the rest of the corporate network; and (e) failed to use readily available security measures to limit access to its computer networks through wireless access points on the networks.

["[B]etween April 30, 2007 and August 28, 2007, an intruder, exploiting some of these vulnerabilities, connected to Dave & Buster's networks numerous times without authorization, installed unauthorized software, and intercepted personal information in transit from in-store networks to its credit card processing company. The breach compromised approximately 130,000 unique payment cards used by consumers in the United States."]

... This agreement is for settlement purposes only and does not constitute an admission by proposed respondent that the law has been violated as alleged in the draft complaint, or that the facts as alleged in the draft complaint, other than the jurisdictional facts, are true. ...

"Personal information" shall mean individually identifiable information from or about an individual consumer including, but not limited to: (a) a first and last name; (b) a home or other physical address, including street name and name of city or town; (c) an email address or other online contact information, such as an instant messaging user identifier or a screen name; (d) a telephone number; (e) a Social Security number; (f) a driver's license number; (g) a credit card or debit card account number; (h) a persistent identifier, such as a customer number held in "cookie" or processor serial number, that is combined with other available data that identifies an individual consumer; or (i) any information that is combined with any of (a) through (h) above. ...

It is ordered that respondent ... shall ... establish and implement, and thereafter maintain, a comprehensive information security program that is reasonably designed to protect the security, confidentiality, and integrity of personal information collected from or about consumers. Such program, the content and implementation of which must be fully documented in writing, shall contain administrative, technical, and physical safeguards appropriate to respondent's size and complexity, the nature and scope of respondent's activities, and the sensitivity of the personal information collected from or about consumers, including:

A. the designation of an employee or employees to coordinate and be accountable for the information security program;
B. the identification of material internal and external risks to the security, confidentiality, and integrity of personal information that could result in the unauthorized disclosure, misuse, loss, alteration, destruction, or other compromise of such information, and assessment of the sufficiency of any safeguards in place to control these risks. At a minimum, this risk assessment should include consideration of risks in each area of relevant operation, including, but not limited to: (1) employee training and management; (2) information systems, including network and software design, information processing, storage, transmission, and disposal; and (3) prevention, detection, and response to attacks, intrusions, or other systems failures;
C. the design and implementation of reasonable safeguards to control the risks identified through risk assessment and regular testing or monitoring of the effectiveness of the safeguards' key controls, systems, and procedures;
D. the development and use of reasonable steps to select and retain service providers capable of appropriately safeguarding personal information

they receive from respondent, and requiring service providers by contract to implement and maintain appropriate safeguards; and

E. the evaluation and adjustment of respondent's information security program in light of the results of the testing and monitoring required by [this agreement], any material changes to respondent's operations or business arrangements, or any other circumstances that respondent knows or has reason to know may have a material impact on the effectiveness of its information security program.

Respondent shall obtain initial and biennial assessments and reports ("Assessments") from a qualified, objective, independent third-party professional, who uses procedures and standards generally accepted in the profession. . . .

Each Assessment shall:

A. set forth the specific administrative, technical, and physical safeguards that respondent has implemented and maintained during the reporting period;

B. explain how such safeguards are appropriate to respondent's size and complexity, the nature and scope of respondent's activities, and the sensitivity of the personal information collected from or about consumers;

C. explain how the safeguards that have been implemented meet or exceed the protections required by . . . this order; and

D. certify that respondent's security program is operating with sufficient effectiveness to provide reasonable assurance that the security, confidentiality, and integrity of personal information is protected and has so operated throughout the reporting period.

Each Assessment shall be prepared and completed . . . by a person qualified as a Certified Information System Security Professional (CISSP) or as a Certified Information Systems Auditor (CISA); a person holding Global Information Assurance Certification (GIAC) from the SysAdmin, Audit, Network, Security (SANS) Institute; or a similarly qualified person or organization approved by the [FTC]. . . .

Questions and Comments

1. Most categories of "personal information" covered by this consent order are easy to understand — a person's name, home address, driver's license number, or Social Security number, for example. More mysterious is the reference to a "persistent identifier." This is a piece of information, such as an IP address or mobile device identifier, that is associated with some use that lasts over time. A persistent identifier, in this sense, need not be personally identifying: Someone who has access to the identifier may be able to associate information or activity with a particular device, but not necessarily a particular person. In the excerpted consent order, the FTC added the requirement that the persistent identifier be combined with other available data that identifies an individual consumer — thus ensuring that the information is personally identifying. In other cases, however, the FTC has claimed a broader mandate to protect persistent identifiers even when they are not personally identifying, on the ground that the traditional distinction between personally identifiable information and non-personally identifiable information is no longer very relevant.

2. Consider how the FTC deals with vendors in this consent order. It recognizes that vendors are a part of contemporary e-commerce, and that a company such as Dave & Buster's has little practical choice but to use them. But it imposes an obligation to select and retain "capable" service providers and to require these providers by contract "to implement and maintain appropriate safeguards." If you were the responsible executive at Dave & Buster's, how would you go about fulfilling these commitments?

3. A different part of the consent order, also excerpted above, requires Dave & Buster's to retain an independent third-party expert to assess its performance in the area, including its compliance with the order. Why doesn't the FTC do this job instead of indirectly outsourcing it to a third party? Given that the third-party expert will be selected and paid by Dave & Buster's, will its feedback be truly independent? How does the FTC seek to ensure that the expert will be capable? Do you think those measures will be effective?

4. Companies often make voluntary commitments to consumers to protect the privacy of their personal information. Is the company obligated to keep that promise if it turns out later on that it is inconvenient to do so? The answer, according to the Federal Trade Commission, is "yes." Any reneging on a privacy commitment to consumers is likely to be considered to be a deceptive or unfair practice under §5 of the FTC Act. Companies, accordingly, should be cautious about making privacy commitments that they may not be able to keep. Such promises, moreover, may travel with the company even if it is acquired by a separate firm that has not made an equivalent promise. Facebook discovered this fact to its chagrin in 2014 in connection with its acquisition of mobile messaging company WhatsApp. WhatsApp's privacy policy promises that, absent consent, user's personal information will not be used for advertising purposes or be sold to third parties for commercial or marketing purposes. Facebook's business practice is to use such information for advertising and marketing. The FTC sternly warned Facebook that it was obligated to continue the privacy protections for WhatsApp customers, and threatened that if Facebook did not do so, it could face charges of violating the FTC Act.

E. SECURITIES LAW

1. Disclosure Requirements

Publicly traded companies often face large data security risks, which they manage on an ongoing basis. What must or should such a company disclose about its risks in the data security area? What if anything should a company disclose when it uncovers a significant vulnerability in its data security operation? What must the company do when a security breach has actually occurred?

Securities and Exchange Commission, Cybersecurity

Oct. 13, 2011

For a number of years, registrants have migrated toward increasing dependence on digital technologies to conduct their operations. As this dependence has increased, the risks to registrants associated with cyber-security have also increased, resulting in more frequent and severe cyber incidents. Recently, there has been increased focus by registrants and members of the legal and accounting professions on how these risks and their related impact on the operations of a registrant should be described within the framework of the disclosure obligations imposed by the federal securities laws. As a result, we determined that it would be beneficial to provide guidance that assists registrants in assessing what, if any, disclosures should be provided about cyber-security matters in light of each registrant's specific facts and circumstances.

We prepared this guidance to be consistent with the relevant disclosure considerations that arise in connection with any business risk. We are mindful of potential concerns that detailed disclosures could compromise cyber-security efforts — for example, by providing a "roadmap" for those who seek to infiltrate a registrant's network security — and we emphasize that disclosures of that nature are not required under the federal securities laws.

In general, cyber incidents can result from deliberate attacks or unintentional events. We have observed an increased level of attention focused on cyber-attacks that include, but are not limited to, gaining unauthorized access to digital systems for purposes of misappropriating assets or sensitive information, corrupting data, or causing operational disruption. Cyber-attacks may also be carried out in a manner that does not require gaining unauthorized access, such as by causing denial-of-service attacks on websites. Cyber-attacks may be carried out by third parties or insiders using techniques that range from highly sophisticated efforts to electronically circumvent network security or overwhelm websites to more traditional intelligence gathering and social engineering aimed at obtaining information necessary to gain access.

The objectives of cyber-attacks vary widely and may include theft of financial assets, intellectual property, or other sensitive information belonging to registrants, their customers, or other business partners. Cyber-attacks may also be directed at disrupting the operations of registrants or their business partners. Registrants that fall victim to successful cyber-attacks may incur substantial costs and suffer other negative consequences, which may include, but are not limited to:

- Remediation costs that may include liability for stolen assets or information and repairing system damage that may have been caused. Remediation costs may also include incentives offered to customers or other business partners in an effort to maintain the business relationships after an attack;
- Increased cyber-security protection costs that may include organizational changes, deploying additional personnel and protection technologies, training employees, and engaging third party experts and consultants;
- Lost revenues resulting from unauthorized use of proprietary information or the failure to retain or attract customers following an attack;
- Litigation; and
- Reputational damage adversely affecting customer or investor confidence.

DISCLOSURE BY PUBLIC COMPANIES REGARDING CYBER-SECURITY RISKS AND CYBER INCIDENTS

The federal securities laws, in part, are designed to elicit disclosure of timely, comprehensive, and accurate information about risks and events that a reasonable investor would consider important to an investment decision. Although no existing disclosure requirement explicitly refers to cyber-security risks and cyber incidents, a number of disclosure requirements may impose an obligation on registrants to disclose such risks and incidents. In addition, material information regarding cyber-security risks and cyber incidents is required to be disclosed when necessary in order to make other required disclosures, in light of the circumstances under which they are made, not misleading. Therefore, as with other operational and financial risks, registrants should review, on an ongoing basis, the adequacy of their disclosure relating to cyber-security risks and cyber incidents.

The following sections provide an overview of specific disclosure obligations that may require a discussion of cyber-security risks and cyber incidents.

RISK FACTORS

Registrants should disclose the risk of cyber incidents if these issues are among the most significant factors that make an investment in the company speculative or risky. In determining whether risk factor disclosure is required, we expect registrants to evaluate their cyber-security risks and take into account all available relevant information, including prior cyber incidents and the severity and frequency of those incidents. As part of this evaluation, registrants should consider the probability of cyber incidents occurring and the quantitative and qualitative magnitude of those risks, including the potential costs and other consequences resulting from misappropriation of assets or sensitive information, corruption of data or operational disruption. In evaluating whether risk factor disclosure should be provided, registrants should also consider the adequacy of preventative actions taken to reduce cyber-security risks in the context of the industry in which they operate and risks to that security, including threatened attacks of which they are aware.

Consistent with the Regulation S-K Item 503(c) requirements for risk factor disclosures generally, cyber-security risk disclosure provided must adequately describe the nature of the material risks and specify how each risk affects the registrant. Registrants should not present risks that could apply to any issuer or any offering and should avoid generic risk factor disclosure. Depending on the registrant's particular facts and circumstances, and to the extent material, appropriate disclosures may include:

- Discussion of aspects of the registrant's business or operations that give rise to material cyber-security risks and the potential costs and consequences;
- To the extent the registrant outsources functions that have material cyber-security risks, description of those functions and how the registrant addresses those risks;
- Description of cyber incidents experienced by the registrant that are individually, or in the aggregate, material, including a description of the costs and other consequences;
- Risks related to cyber incidents that may remain undetected for an extended period; and
- Description of relevant insurance coverage.

A registrant may need to disclose known or threatened cyber incidents to place the discussion of cyber-security risks in context. For example, if a registrant experienced a material cyber-attack in which malware was embedded in its systems and customer data was compromised, it likely would not be sufficient for the registrant to disclose that there is a risk that such an attack may occur. Instead, as part of a broader discussion of malware or other similar attacks that pose a particular risk, the registrant may need to discuss the occurrence of the specific attack and its known and potential costs and other consequences.

While registrants should provide disclosure tailored to their particular circumstances and avoid generic "boilerplate" disclosure, we reiterate that the federal securities laws do not require disclosure that itself would compromise a registrant's cyber-security. Instead, registrants should provide sufficient disclosure to allow investors to appreciate the nature of the risks faced by the particular registrant in a manner that would not have that consequence.

MANAGEMENT'S DISCUSSION AND ANALYSIS OF FINANCIAL CONDITION AND RESULTS OF OPERATIONS (MD&A)

Registrants should address cyber-security risks and cyber incidents in their MD&A if the costs or other consequences associated with one or more known incidents or the risk of potential incidents represent a material event, trend, or uncertainty that is reasonably likely to have a material effect on the registrant's results of operations, liquidity, or financial condition or would cause reported financial information not to be necessarily indicative of future operating results or financial condition. For example, if material intellectual property is stolen in a cyber-attack, and the effects of the theft are reasonably likely to be material, the registrant should describe the property that was stolen and the effect of the attack on its results of operations, liquidity, and financial condition and whether the attack would cause reported financial information not to be indicative of future operating results or financial condition. If it is reasonably likely that the attack will lead to reduced revenues, [or] an increase in cyber-security protection costs, including related to litigation, the registrant should discuss these possible outcomes, including the amount and duration of the expected costs, if material. Alternatively, if the attack did not result in the loss of intellectual property, but it prompted the registrant to materially increase its cyber-security protection expenditures, the registrant should note those increased expenditures.

DESCRIPTION OF BUSINESS

If one or more cyber incidents materially affect a registrant's products, services, relationships with customers or suppliers, or competitive conditions, the registrant should provide disclosure in the registrant's "Description of Business." In determining whether to include disclosure, registrants should consider the impact on each of their reportable segments. As an example, if a registrant has a new product in development and learns of a cyber incident that could materially impair its future viability, the registrant should discuss the incident and the potential impact to the extent material.

LEGAL PROCEEDINGS

If a material pending legal proceeding to which a registrant or any of its subsidiaries is a party involves a cyber incident, the registrant may need to disclose information regarding this litigation in its "Legal Proceedings" disclosure. For example, if a significant amount of customer information is stolen, resulting in material litigation, the registrant should disclose the name of the court in which the proceedings are pending, the date instituted, the principal parties thereto, a description of the factual basis alleged to underlie the litigation, and the relief sought.

FINANCIAL STATEMENT DISCLOSURES

Cyber-security risks and cyber incidents may have a broad impact on a registrant's financial statements, depending on the nature and severity of the potential or actual incident.

PRIOR TO A CYBER INCIDENT

Registrants may incur substantial costs to prevent cyber incidents [which may have to be disclosed in the company's accounting for the capitalization of these costs].

DURING AND AFTER A CYBER INCIDENT

Registrants may seek to mitigate damages from a cyber incident by providing customers with incentives to maintain the business relationship. . . .

Cyber incidents may result in losses from asserted and un-asserted claims, including those related to warranties, breach of contract, product recall and replacement, and indemnification of counterparty losses from their remediation efforts. . . .

Cyber incidents may also result in diminished future cash flows, thereby requiring consideration of impairment of certain assets including goodwill, customer-related intangible assets, trademarks, patents, capitalized software or other long-lived assets associated with hardware or software, and inventory. Registrants may not immediately know the impact of a cyber incident and may be required to develop estimates to account for the various financial implications. Registrants should subsequently reassess the assumptions that underlie the estimates made in preparing the financial statements. A registrant must explain any risk or uncertainty of a reasonably possible change in its estimates in the near-term that would be material to the financial statements. Examples of estimates that may be affected by cyber incidents include estimates of warranty liability, allowances for product returns, capitalized software costs, inventory, litigation, and deferred revenue.

To the extent a cyber incident is discovered after the balance sheet date but before the issuance of financial statements, registrants should consider whether disclosure of a recognized or non-recognized subsequent event is necessary. If the incident constitutes a material non-recognized subsequent event, the financial statements should disclose the nature of the incident and an estimate of its financial effect, or a statement that such an estimate cannot be made.

DISCLOSURE CONTROLS AND PROCEDURES

Registrants are required to disclose conclusions on the effectiveness of disclosure controls and procedures. To the extent cyber incidents pose a risk to a registrant's ability to record, process, summarize, and report information that is required to be disclosed in Commission filings, management should also consider whether there are any deficiencies in its disclosure controls and procedures that would render them ineffective. For example, if it is reasonably possible that information would not be recorded properly due to a cyber incident affecting a registrant's information systems, a registrant may conclude that its disclosure controls and procedures are ineffective.

Questions and Comments

1. Two types of disclosure are covered in the excerpted guidance: disclosure of cyber *risks* and disclosure of cyber *breaches*. As to risks, some firms are probably willing and even eager to engage in fulsome disclosure. The rationale is that the more they disclose about risks *ex ante*, the less shareholders or the SEC can complain about inadequate disclosure *ex post* when a breach has occurred. As to breaches, the calculus is likely to be different. Companies do not like to disclose security breaches. As noted above, doing so is likely to trigger an inquiry from regulators, may cause investors to lose confidence in the company's management, and may spark class action lawsuits.

2. Given that cyber risks come in so many different forms, from so many sources, and that they result in such a range of possible harms, how can a reporting firm assess with any confidence whether a risk is material to its business? Even if it concludes that the risk is material and must be disclosed, how can it craft a disclosure that informs the investing public without creating a misleading impression about the severity of the risk or the degree of confidence the issuer has in its estimate?

3. The SEC counsels against "generic risk factor disclosure." How can an issuing firm engage in risk factor disclosure that isn't generic, at least to a substantial extent, given that the exact nature of the risk is intrinsically difficult to know before an incident occurs?

4. If the company gets down to the granular level of detail, the reporting may have the perverse effect of guiding hackers on how to breach the issuer's cyber defenses. The SEC says that federal securities laws "do not require disclosure that itself would compromise a registrant's cyber-security." This is easy to say; how easy is it to implement?

5. Reporting firms utilize the services of third-party vendors to help manage their cyber risks. How can an issuer know that the services of the vendor will be effective?

6. Utilizing a vendor for cyber security also creates risk, in that the vendor may suffer a breach that compromises data owned by the client. How should issuing firms handle disclosures about this sort of risk?

7. The SEC's approach in the excerpted guidance is to fold cyber threats into the existing disclosure rules. Given the growing importance of the topic, should the SEC require specific disclosure of cyber threats or incidents in a separate part of a reporting company's disclosure documents?

2. Regulated Entities

In addition to setting standards for disclosure and anti-fraud rules for issuers and sellers of securities, the SEC regulates securities companies and organizations such as broker-dealers, securities exchanges, and self-regulatory organizations.

In the Matter of R.T. Jones Capital Equities Management, Inc.
Securities and Exchange Commission Investment Advisers Act
Release No. 4204

Sept. 22, 2015

. . . R.T. Jones, located in St. Louis, Missouri, is an investment adviser registered with the Commission that has approximately 8400 client accounts and about $480

PROBLEM 11-3

Wish List Corp. is an Internet-based, publicly traded company that allows subscribers to make wishes and also to grant wishes made by other subscribers. The company has been surprisingly successful; in the past fiscal year it had $65 million in revenues and profits of $20 million. To accommodate its expansion, the company is moving to a new platform for storage of data and customer management. At present the move to the new platform is in test mode; the company has not yet gone live with this functionality. Due to a mistake by a vendor, however, access to the new platform is accidentally made available to third parties for a six-hour period before the error is detected and corrected. During that period, non-public personal information for about 20,000 of the company's 100,000 customers could have been obtained by anyone with access to the Internet. The company quickly investigates the incident and concludes that no non-public information was disclosed. The company is working on the problem and believes that it will soon be addressed. Until now the company has made no disclosure about cyber risks in its SEC disclosure documents, other than the statement that "like other Web-based firms, the Company is at risk of breaches or data losses that may have a material adverse effect on its financial position." If you were securities counsel to the company, what would you advise regarding its disclosure obligation in the wake of the incident?

million in regulatory assets under management. The firm does not have custody of client assets.

Through agreements with a retirement plan administrator and various retirement plan sponsors, R.T. Jones provides investment advice to individual plan participants using a managed account option called Artesys. Artesys offers a variety of model portfolios that range in investment objectives and risk profiles. Plan participants can access the Artesys program through R.T. Jones's public website. Plan participants who elect to enroll in the program are instructed to fill out a questionnaire on the website regarding their investment objectives and risk tolerance. Based on information provided in the questionnaire, R.T. Jones recommends a particular portfolio allocation from among the Artesys models to the client. If the client agrees to the recommended allocation, R.T. Jones provides trade instructions to the retirement plan administrator, which then effects the transactions. R.T. Jones does not control or maintain client accounts or client account information.

During the relevant period, in order to verify eligibility to enroll in Artesys, R.T. Jones required prospective clients to log on to its website by entering their name, date of birth and social security number. The login information was then compared against the PII of eligible plan participants, which was provided to R.T. Jones by its plan sponsor partners. R.T. Jones stored this PII, without modification or encryption, on its third party-hosted web server. To facilitate the verification process, the plan sponsors provided R.T. Jones with information about all of their plan participants. Thus, even though R.T. Jones had fewer than 8000 plan participant clients, its web server contained the PII of over 100,000 individuals.

R.T. Jones limited access to the PII stored on the server to two individuals who held administrator status. In July 2013, R.T. Jones discovered a potential cybersecurity breach at its third party-hosted web server. R.T. Jones promptly retained more than one cybersecurity consulting firm to confirm the attack and assess the scope of the breach. One of the forensic cybersecurity firms reported that the cyberattack had been launched from multiple IP addresses, all of which traced back to mainland China, and that the intruder had gained full access rights and copy rights to the data stored on the server. However, the cybersecurity firms could not determine the full nature or extent of the breach because the intruder had destroyed the log files surrounding the period of the intruder's activity.

Soon thereafter, R.T. Jones retained another cybersecurity firm to review the initial report and independently assess the scope of the breach. Ultimately, the cybersecurity firms could not determine whether the PII stored on the server had been accessed or compromised during the breach.

Shortly after the breach incident, R.T. Jones provided notice of the breach to all of the individuals whose PII may have been compromised and offered them free identity monitoring through a third-party provider. To date, the firm has not learned of any information indicating that a client has suffered any financial harm as a result of the cyber-attack.

The Safeguards Rule [Rule 30(a) of Regulation S-P, 17 C.F.R. §248.30(a)], which the Commission adopted in 2000, requires that every investment adviser registered with the Commission adopt policies and procedures reasonably designed to: (1) insure the security and confidentiality of customer records and information; (2) protect against any anticipated threats or hazards to the security or integrity of customer records and information; and (3) protect against unauthorized access to or use of customer records or information that could result in substantial harm or inconvenience to any customer. The Commission adopted amendments to the Safeguards Rule, effective January 2005, to require that the policies and procedures adopted thereunder be in writing.

During the relevant period, R.T. Jones maintained client PII on its third party-hosted web server. However, the firm failed to adopt any written policies and procedures reasonably designed to safeguard its clients' PII as required by the Safeguards Rule. R.T. Jones's policies and procedures for protecting its clients' information did not include, for example: conducting periodic risk assessments, employing a firewall to protect the web server containing client PII, encrypting client PII stored on that server, or establishing procedures for responding to a cybersecurity incident. Taken as a whole, R.T. Jones's policies and procedures for protecting customer records and information were not reasonable to safeguard customer information. As a result of the conduct described above, R.T. Jones willfully violated [the Safeguards Rule].

To mitigate against any future risk of cyber threats, R.T. Jones has appointed an information security manager to oversee data security and protection of PII, and adopted and implemented a written information security policy. Among other things, the firm no longer stores PII on its webserver and any PII stored on its internal network is encrypted. The firm has also installed a new firewall and logging system to prevent and detect malicious incursions.

Finally, R.T. Jones has retained a cybersecurity firm to provide ongoing reports and advice on the firm's information technology security.

In determining to accept R.T. Jones's Offer, the Commission considered the remedial acts promptly undertaken by R.T. Jones and the cooperation R.T. Jones afforded the Commission staff. [R.T. Jones was censured, required to pay a $75,000 fine, and ordered to cease and desist from further violations of the Safeguards Rule.]

Questions and Comments

1. In the special context of the securities law, a "willful" violation has been interpreted to mean that "the person charged with the duty knows what he is doing." Wonsover v. SEC, 205 F.3d 408, 414 (D.C. Cir. 2000). Were R.T. Jones' violations "willful" in this sense?

2. A censure and a $75,000 fine might be considered a slap on the wrist. Why was the SEC so lenient?

3. If you were advising a firm like R.T. Jones, what would you advise it to do in order to avoid the fate of this defendant?

4. The excerpted opinion references the Safeguards Rule, adopted in 2000. In addition, concerns about IT systems in the securities industry have skyrocketed as a result of alarming glitches and breakdowns on securities exchanges, including trading delays and halts, problems in reporting pricing data, and breakdowns in automated compliance operations. These incidents, together with a perception that the industry is subject to a significant cybersecurity risk, led the SEC in 2014 to adopt Regulation SCI (for "systems, compliance, and integrity"), governing IT practices and systems at securities exchanges and self-regulatory organizations (SCI Entities). Among other things, this regulation requires each SCI entity to establish, maintain, and enforce "written policies and procedures reasonably designed to ensure that its SCI systems . . . have levels of capacity, integrity, resiliency, availability, and security, adequate to maintain the SCI entity's operational capability and promote the maintenance of fair and orderly markets." A key element of this regulation is the obligation to maintain adequate data security.

F. FIDUCIARY DUTIES

What are the fiduciary duties of a board of directors when it comes to information security?

Consider in this regard the following quote from a 2014 speech by SEC Commissioner Luis A. Aguilar: "Boards of directors are already responsible for overseeing the management of all types of risk, including credit risk, liquidity risk, and operational risk — and there can be little doubt that cyber-risk also must be considered as part of board's overall risk oversight. . . . Board oversight of cyber-risk management is critical to ensuring that companies are taking adequate steps to prevent, and prepare for, the harms that can result from such attacks. . . . Effective board oversight of management's efforts to address these issues is critical to preventing and effectively responding to successful cyber-attacks and, ultimately, to protecting companies and their shareholders." Commissioner Luis A. Aguilar, Boards of Directors, Corporate Governance and Cyber-Risks: Sharpening the Focus (June 10, 2014), available at http://op.bna.com/car.nsf/id/rtuk9kyr8q/$File/6.10.14%20Aguilar%20Comments.pdf.

We saw in Chapter 2 that the board of directors has a responsibility to oversee the affairs of a business corporation in order to "assure themselves that information and reporting systems exist in the organization that are reasonably designed to provide to senior management and to the board itself timely, accurate information sufficient to allow management and the board, each within its scope, to reach informed judgments concerning both the corporation's compliance with the law and its business performance." In re Caremark International Inc. Derivative Litigation, 698 A.2d 959 (Del. Ch. 1996). How does the *Caremark* oversight duty apply in the case of information security?

The massive data breaches of recent times have sparked litigation that tests that issue. In general, these cases have not been successful, at least when the board of directors manifested a reasonable level of diligence and concern about the problem of information security and acted promptly to address breaches when they occurred. An example is Palkon v. Holmes, 2014 WL 5341880 (D.N.J. 2014). Derivative plaintiffs claimed that the board of directors of Wyndham Worldwide Corporation had violated their fiduciary duty in connection with the same data breaches that triggered the FTC's action in the Federal Trade Commission v. Wyndham Worldwide Corporation case discussed above.

The board of directors rejected the plaintiffs' demand that the company investigate and remedy the harm inflicted by the breach — actions that could have caused the company to sue the very board members who were voting to reject the demand. The trial court agreed that the demand was properly rejected and that the derivative lawsuit should not proceed. Central to the trial court's decision was the fact that the board of directors and senior management of Wyndham Worldwide had made concerted efforts to address the problem of cybersecurity: "[T]he Board discussed the cyber-attacks, WWC's security policies, and proposed security enhancements at fourteen meetings between October 2008 and August 2012. The Audit Committee reviewed the same matters in at least sixteen meetings during that period. WWC hired technology firms to investigate each breach and to issue recommendations on enhancing the company's security. Following the second and third breaches, WWC began to implement those recommendations."

Questions and Comments

1. Do cases like Palkon v. Holmes make it too easy for boards of directors to evade responsibility for cyber-security issues by merely going through the motions, rather than undertaking the hard actions required to establish robust protections against data breaches?

2. If you were representing a company faced with potential data security issues (as virtually all companies are), what measures would you recommend, either as a matter of avoiding *Caremark* liability, or simply as good corporate practice? Consider the following:

- Compiling an inventory of assets containing potentially sensitive information, and conducting a risk assessment to determine the potential that the information contained in a given asset would be lost or stolen;
- Drafting, testing, and validating written policies and procedures dealing with data security;
- Creating a new board committee tasked with oversight of information security issues, or re-tasking the audit committee or other board committee;

- Creating a high-level executive at the "C-Suite" level and assigning that individual with responsibility for information security;
- Retaining an external information security consultant to evaluate and test the organization's policies and systems;
- Drafting an incident response plan that sets forth actions the organization will undertake if faced with an information security problem, and assigning specific responsibilities to different corporate actors in the event the response plan is activated;
- Convening special meetings of the board of directors or the appropriate cyber-security committee in the event of a serious breach; and
- Conducting "war game" scenarios that test whether the organization will be able to respond adequately in the event of serious problems.

For what sorts of organizations might these measures be desirable? Do they go too far? Not far enough?

3. One limitation on potential liability for corporate directors (or others) for failing to manage cybersecurity is the lack of definitive standards or widely accepted industry practices. But this situation appears to be rapidly changing as good-governance institutions step up to the plate to offer recommendations on best practices. Would you favor a regime of tort liability against senior corporate officials who conspicuously fail to implement safeguards of the sorts recommended in these statements of best practices?

G. RULES OF PROFESSIONAL RESPONSIBILITY

We saw in Chapter 9 that attorneys have strong professional obligations not to disclose client information. The obligations we studied there applied principally to conduct that was intentional or nearly intentional: The attorney is generally prohibited from "revealing" client information, a term that implies some sort of deliberate action. Information security, however, is principally about conduct that is not deliberate. Organizations don't usually breach data security obligations intentionally; breaches happen as a result of accident, neglect, or malicious actions by others. What obligations does an attorney have to maintain the security of client information?

The problem of data security in law firms is in some respects more severe than the analogous problems in other organizations. The material maintained at law firms is among the most sensitive information in existence. Because of the attorney's duties of confidentiality and the attorney-client privilege, clients can and do share with counsel information they would never tell others; they do so with the implicit understanding that the attorney will keep it secret, keep it safe. If this information were to fall into the hands of antagonistic parties, the result could be catastrophic. These considerations suggest that attorneys should be held to exacting obligations for maintaining data security.

On the other hand, several considerations have — at least until recently — militated against imposing draconian requirements and ruinous sanctions on attorneys:

- Attorney-client information has not traditionally been held in computer-accessible, machine-readable form. It was held in paper files in credenzas near partners' offices, in back files lurking in the bowels of the law firm's offices, or in off-site document storage facilities. Paper documents can be stolen or copied, but the barriers to such defalcation are high. Attorneys therefore had less to worry about when it came to information security, than, say, a bank that had long maintained customer information in computerized form.

- Law firm files are filled with all sorts of information, much of it difficult to understand without context and much of it of no commercial value. Unlike a security breach in a credit card company, where the malefactor can abscond with easily accessed information with obvious commercial value, a data breach at a law firm would reveal copious files that themselves would need to be studied by sophisticated parties before valuable information could be extracted.
- Many law firms are small, even in the United States. It is probably not worth a malefactor's time to intrude on the client files of a small law firm.

These factors have, to some extent, insulated law practices from the plague of security breaches that have affected other industries. However, the vulnerability of the legal profession is obviously significant and is growing every day. More and more frequently, client files are stored electronically; attorneys access their computers and company files remotely; attorneys do business through mobile devices with different kinds of security configurations; and malefactors are becoming increasingly proficient and sophisticated at penetrating through firewalls and at analyzing complex information. Law practices cannot escape the threats to information security that afflict many other types of firm.

The framers of rules governing attorney conduct are aware of the growing cyber threat. ABA Model Rule of Professional Conduct 1.6(c), added in 2012, requires that "[a] lawyer shall make reasonable efforts to prevent the inadvertent or unauthorized disclosure of, or unauthorized access to, information relating to the representation of a client." Comment [18] to Rule 1.6 fleshes out this requirement as follows:

The unauthorized access to, or the inadvertent or unauthorized disclosure of, information relating to the representation of a client does not constitute a violation of paragraph (c) if the lawyer has made reasonable efforts to prevent the access or disclosure. Factors to be considered in determining the reasonableness of the lawyer's efforts include, but are not limited to, the sensitivity of the information, the likelihood of disclosure if additional safeguards are not employed, the cost of employing additional safeguards, the difficulty of implementing the safeguards, and the extent to which the safeguards adversely affect the lawyer's ability to represent clients (e.g., by making a device or important piece of software excessively difficult to use). . . .

Comment [19] continues on the subject of data transmission:

When transmitting a communication that includes information relating to the representation of a client, the lawyer must take reasonable precautions to prevent the information from coming into the hands of unintended recipients. This duty, however, does not require that the lawyer use special security measures if the method of communication affords a reasonable expectation of privacy. Special circumstances, however, may warrant special precautions. Factors to be considered in determining the reasonableness of the lawyer's expectation of confidentiality include the sensitivity of the information and the extent to which the privacy of the communication is protected by law or by a confidentiality agreement. A client may require the lawyer to implement special security measures not required by this Rule. . . .

Questions and Comments

1. Rule 1.6(c) imposes a duty on attorneys to safeguard the security of client information, but both the rule and the comments also stress that an attorney is protected if she undertakes precautions that are reasonable under the circumstances. Is this an appropriate standard?

2. The ABA's rules apply to all attorneys, whether in large firms or solo practitioners. Can you detect a sensitivity to the needs of lawyers in smaller firms in the way the rules and the comments are phrased? Should a different rule — or different factors in applying the same rule — be used in the case of large law firms?

3. Who enforces this rule?

4. Model Rule 1.1 Comment [8] provides: "To maintain the requisite knowledge and skill, a lawyer should keep abreast of changes in the law and its practice, *including the benefits and risks associated with relevant technology,* engage in continuing study and education and comply with all continuing legal education requirements to which the lawyer is subject." The italicized phrase was added by the House of Delegates in 2013. Evidently, one of the most important risks associated with the technology of law practice is the risk of cyber breach. This may sound like a new and somewhat ominous requirement, but the report accompanying the resolution substantially softened the obligation: "The proposed amendment, which appears in a Comment, does not impose any new obligations on lawyers. Rather, the amendment is intended to serve as a reminder to lawyers that they should remain aware of technology, including the benefits and risks associated with it, as part of a lawyer's general ethical duty to remain competent." What was the purpose of adding this language if it doesn't change anything?

5. In 2014, an ABA task force on cybersecurity issued a report that recognized the severity of the cyber threat faced by law firms:

> Law firms are businesses and should take special care to ensure that they have a strong security posture and a well-implemented security program. The data and information kept by law firms are largely protected by the attorney-client privilege and/or the work product doctrine, as well as by various legal ethics requirements.
>
> The threat of cyber-attacks against law firms is growing. Lawyers and law offices are facing unprecedented challenges from the widespread use of electronic records and mobile devices.
>
> There are many reasons for hackers to target the information being held by law firms. They collect and store large amounts of critical, highly valuable corporate records, including intellectual property, strategic business data, and litigation-related theories and records collected through e-discovery. . . . Lawyers and law offices have a responsibility to protect confidential records from unauthorized access and disclosure, whether malicious or unintentional, by both insiders and hackers.

American Bar Association Cybersecurity Legal Task Force Section of Science & Technology Law, Report to the House of Delegates (2014).

6. The task force proposed the following resolution:

> RESOLVED, That the American Bar Association encourages all private and public sector organizations to develop, implement, and maintain an appropriate security

program, including: (1) conducting regular assessments of the threats, vulnerabilities, and risks to their data, applications, networks, and operating platforms, including those associated with operational control systems; and (2) implementing appropriate security controls to address the identified threats, vulnerabilities, and risks, consistent with the types of data and systems to be protected and the nature and scope of the organization.

FURTHER RESOLVED, That the American Bar Association encourages these organizations to develop and test a response plan for possible cyber-attacks, including disclosure of data breaches, notification of affected individuals, and the recovery and restoration of disrupted operations; and

FURTHER RESOLVED, That the American Bar Association encourages these organizations to (1) engage in partnerships or cooperative relationships, where appropriate, to address the problem of cyber-attacks by sharing information on cyber threats, and (2) develop points of contact and protocols to enable such information sharing.

The House of Delegates balked at this proposal. In the end, the ABA endorsed only the following watered-down resolution:

RESOLVED, That the American Bar Association encourages all private and public sector organizations to develop, implement, and maintain an appropriate cybersecurity program that complies with applicable ethical and legal obligations and is tailored to the nature and scope of the organization and the data and systems to be protected.

What was objectionable about the original language?

7. In addition to ethical pressures for upgrading their controls over information security, law firms are facing increasing pressure from customers. Banks, in particular, are asking their law firms to provide assurances that they are providing adequate protections against cyber-security breaches. The banks themselves are under pressure because they are faced with nearly daily cyber-attacks and because their regulators, including most prominently the New York State Department of Financial Services, have pressured them to make sure their vendors, including their law firms, offer adequate security for sensitive information.

8. Meanwhile, law firms themselves are monitoring their own vendors for the same reason. For example, some firms outsource word processing jobs to third parties; because the documents to be processed often contain sensitive client information, the law firm must assure itself that the word processing vendor has adequate physical and technical cyber-security measures in place.

9. Further guidance on best practices for dealing with cyber-security issues at law firms is found in American Bar Association, Cybersecurity Handbook: A Resource for Attorneys, Law Firms, and Business Professionals (2013).

10. The 2015 Annual Security Report from Cisco Systems, Inc. concluded that among American industries, law firms were the seventh most vulnerable to malware. It has been estimated that at least 80 percent of the biggest 100 law firms have had some sort of breach. Bar leaders are increasingly concerned about the risk of cyber breaches at law firms. Consider the following 2015 statement by Harvey Rishikof, co-chairman of the American Bar Association Cybersecurity Legal Task Force, "Law firms are very attractive targets. They have information from clients on deal negotiations which adversaries have a keen interest in. They're a treasure trove that is extremely attractive to criminals, foreign governments, adversaries and intelligence entities."

11. Law firm files contain many drafts of contracts composed during negotiations. Counterparties would like to see these drafts because they can thereby learn

about the negotiation strategy of their potential business partners. Hackers have increasingly attempted to obtain this information from law firm files. The biggest threat may come from China. Richard Betjlich, chief security strategist of data-security company FireEye Inc., remarked in 2015, "If you're doing business in China or representing clients in China, you will get hacked. And they're not just stealing intellectual property for reproduction. They're interested in mergers and acquisitions as well. It's the way they conduct due diligence."

The following excerpt is one of the few official ethics opinions dealing with data security at law firms. Although this opinion was issued prior to the adoption of Model Rule 16(c), its conclusions are in line what that later provision:

State Bar of Arizona Ethics Opinion 05-04

July 2005

05-04: Electronic Storage; Confidentiality 7/2005

[Rules] 1.6 and 1.1 require that an attorney act competently to safeguard client information and confidences. It is not unethical to store such electronic information on computer systems whether or not those same systems are used to connect to the internet. However, to comply with these ethical rules as they relate to the client's electronic files or communications, an attorney or law firm is obligated to take competent and reasonable steps to assure that the client's confidences are not disclosed to third parties through theft or inadvertence. In addition, an attorney or law firm is obligated to take reasonable and competent steps to assure that the client's electronic information is not lost or destroyed. In order to do that, an attorney must be competent to evaluate the nature of the potential threat to client electronic files and to evaluate and deploy appropriate computer hardware and software to accomplish that end. An attorney who lacks or cannot reasonably obtain that competence is ethically required to retain an expert consultant who does have such competence.

FACTS

The Inquiring Attorney has sought guidance from the Committee regarding the steps the lawyer's firm must take to safeguard electronic client information from Internet hacking and viruses. The Inquiring Attorney's firm has, until recently, kept documents which include confidential client information in electronic form on a computer system which is accessible only from computers within the law firm itself. Although the law firm had access to the internet, that access was through a separate computer system. Neither the computer system on which the client information was stored nor any computer which could access that information was ever connected to the internet.

The Inquiring Attorney's firm now wishes to change that system and allow attorneys and staff to access the internet through the same computers they use to access the client information. Though the Inquiring Attorney does not specifically state this, it is assumed that firm attorneys and other employees will be able to access the client documents remotely. That is, an attorney or other employee may access this information from a computer outside the physical offices of the firm. Such access would be through the internet.

Question Presented

How do we protect the confidentiality and integrity of client information while continuing to increase reliance on internet for research, filings, communication, and storage of documents? . . .

Opinion

It is clear that a lawyer has an ethical obligation to protect the confidences entrusted by clients. . . . Thus, the short answer to the Inquiring Attorney's inquiry is that a lawyer must act in a competent and reasonable manner to assure that the information in the firm's computer system is not disclosed through inadvertence or unauthorized action. Of course, this syllogism does not really answer the question. . . .

The Inquiring Attorney's concerns focuses on what a lawyer must do to protect electronic files from being (1) stolen, (2) inadvertently disclosed to others, and (3) lost or destroyed. All of those scenarios have been extensively discussed by the courts in the context of waiver of the attorney-client or work product privilege.

Stolen Electronic Information — The Purloined Letter

The Inquiring Attorney's first concern was that electronic information stored on computers which are also used to access the internet may be subject to "hackers" who wish to steal the client's information. It does not matter whether the hacker's motive is to obtain information for sale or for the hacker's own mysteriously prurient interests.

The courts' treatment of document theft have changed in recent years. Until the late twentieth century, the common rule was that any document, otherwise protected from disclosure by the attorney-client or work product privilege, would lose that privilege if it was disclosed even when such disclosure was caused by theft. This rule, sometimes referred to by commentators as the "Wigmore Rule," has been largely abandoned. . . . [T]he modern rule is that precautions must be taken to prevent the theft of confidential communications to preserve the privilege.

Inadvertent Disclosure

Instances where privileged information has been stolen are relatively rare. More common is the predicament where a lawyer has inadvertently disclosed otherwise privileged information. . . . [A]n attorney must take [certain] precautions with regard to electronically stored communications. It is plain that some efforts must be undertaken. A panoply of electronic and other measures [is] available to assist an attorney in maintaining client confidences. "Firewalls" — electronic devices and programs which prevent unauthorized entry into a computer system from outside that system — are readily available. Recent upgrades in Microsoft operating systems incorporate such software systems automatically. A host of companies, including Microsoft, Symantec, McAfee and many others, provide security software that helps prevent both destructive intrusions (such as viruses and "worms") and the more malicious intrusions which allow outsiders access to computer files (sometimes call "adware" or "spyware").

Software systems are also readily available to protect individual electronic files. Passwords can be added to files which prevent viewing of such files unless a password is first known and entered. The files themselves can also be encrypted so that, even if the password protection is compromised, the file cannot be read without knowing the encryption key—something that is extremely difficult to break.

Precisely which of these software and hardware systems should be chosen—and the extent to which they must be employed—is beyond the scope and competence of the Committee. This is the kind of thing each attorney must assess. The expectation of the client that the client's records and communications will be held in confidence is significant. . . .

It is not surprising that few lawyers have the training or experience required to act competently with regard to computer security. Such competence is, however, readily available. Much information can be obtained through the internet by an attorney with sufficient time and energy to research and understand these systems. Alternatively, experts are readily available to assist an attorney in setting up the firm's computer systems to protect against theft of information and inadvertent disclosure of client confidences.

MALICIOUS DESTRUCTION OF CLIENT FILES

The Inquiring Attorney also expressed concern that allowing access to client files on computers which are also used to access the internet can lead to the malicious destruction of those files. The threat of such destructive viruses is well known.

As with the inadvertent disclosure analysis above, [the rules] require the lawyer to act competently in assuring that electronic information transmitted to the attorney is not lost or destroyed. Much of the security software and hardware discussed above provides protection against such destructive intrusions. Moreover, it is common practice to routinely back-up computer files. In that way, even if a computer system is entirely disabled through malicious attack, nearly all data can be retrieved from back-up files. Easy to use and inexpensive systems are available to make this kind of back-up an automatic process.

Once again, the extent to which such systems need to be employed and which systems best accomplish that goal is something which an individual attorney must determine. Doing so competently may require additional research or the employment of an expert consultant.

CONCLUSION

[The rules] require that an attorney act competently to safeguard client information and confidences. It is not unethical to store such electronic information on computer systems whether or not those same systems are used to connect to the internet. However, to comply with these ethical rules as they relate to the client's electronic files or communications, an attorney or law firm is obligated to take competent and reasonable steps to assure that the client's confidences are not disclosed to third parties through theft or inadvertence. In addition, an attorney or law firm is obligated to take reasonable and competent steps to assure that the client's electronic information is not lost or destroyed. In order to do that, an attorney must either have the competence to evaluate the nature of the potential threat to the client's electronic files and to evaluate and deploy appropriate computer hardware and software to accomplish that end, or if the attorney lacks or cannot reasonably obtain that competence, to retain an expert consultant who does have such competence.

Questions and Comments

1. The bar opinion analyzes the attorney's duty to safeguard client data by citing cases dealing with the scope of the attorney-client privilege and attorney work-product doctrine. To what extent are these bodies of law relevant to the question at hand?

2. The bar opinion requires the attorney to undertake "reasonable and competent steps" to safeguard client information stored in electronic form. The opinion suggests, for example, that the attorney can satisfy her duty to safeguard client data by using the services of companies like Microsoft, Symantec, or McAfee. Does this standard provide sufficient protection for sensitive client information?

3. Do you detect a concern not to overburden law firms, especially small practitioners, with unwieldy information security requirements?

4. How much sophistication does the author of this opinion display about information security issues?

5. Would the opinion have been written this way if the context was not that of a law firm responsibly inquiring as to the scope of its ethical duties, but rather some data breach that had imposed substantial costs on a client?

6. As of the date of publication of this book, there were few, if any cases, in which attorneys were sanctioned for failing to secure client files against hacking or the equivalent. However, news reports indicate that cyber-attacks on law firms have increased at an alarming rate. Bar association meetings regularly feature discussions of cybersecurity; and it seems to be only a matter of time before a serious breach occurs.

7. Is the security of client information sufficiently protected by the threat that a law firm — at least a large law firm — will suffer a loss of reputation if it experiences a large security breach?

8. What due diligence obligations should banks or other highly regulated clients have to investigate a law firm's data security measures before retaining it for a substantial project?

9. What training should law firms provide to lawyers, paralegals, secretaries, IT personnel, and others who might have access to sensitive information? How deeply should the firm inquire into an employee's or partner's work habits (do they go online at Starbucks?) or the data security measures they employ at home (how secure is their home network?).

Note on Cloud Computing

Data and applications are increasingly moving to the "cloud" — to remote servers and other machines not hosted or maintained by the proprietor or original custodian of the data. Cloud computing creates ethical problems for attorneys that bar associations would not even have imagined a generation ago.

There are many advantages of cloud computing, as reported in the Pennsylvania Bar Association opinion excerpted below, including:

- Reduced infrastructure and management;
- Cost identification and effectiveness;
- Improved work production;
- Quick, efficient communication;

- Reduction in routine tasks, enabling staff to elevate work level;
- Constant service;
- Ease of use;
- Mobility;
- Immediate access to updates; and
- Possible enhanced security.

But attorney use of cloud computing also presents significant problems of privacy and data security. A working group of the ABA Commission on Ethics 20/20 identified the following:

- Storage in countries with less legal protection for data;
- Unclear policies regarding data ownership;
- Failure to adequately back up data;
- Unclear policies for data breach notice;
- Insufficient encryption;
- Unclear data destruction policies;
- Bankruptcy;
- Protocol for a change of cloud providers;
- Disgruntled/dishonest insiders;
- Hackers;
- Technical failures;
- Server crashes;
- Viruses;
- Data corruption;
- Data destruction;
- Business interruption (e.g., weather, accident, terrorism); and
- Absolute loss (i.e., natural or man-made disasters that destroy everything).

Obviously, the stakes are high on both sides. To what extent, if at all, should attorneys be allowed to use cloud computing in such a way as to place confidential client information in potential jeopardy of being lost or stolen? Consider the following excerpt, which contains one of the most complete explorations of the problem to date:

Pennsylvania Bar Association Committee on Legal Ethics and Professional Responsibility Ethical Obligations for Attorneys Using Cloud Computing/Software as a Service While Fulfilling the Duties of Confidentiality and Preservation of Client Property

Formal Opinion 2011-200

. . . In recent years, technological advances have occurred that have dramatically changed the way attorneys and law firms store, retrieve and access client information. Many law firms view these technological advances as an opportunity to reduce costs, improve efficiency and provide better client service. Perhaps no area has seen greater changes than "cloud computing," which refers to software and related services that store information on a remote computer, i.e., a computer or server that is not located at the law office's physical location. Rather, the information is stored on another company's server, or many servers, possibly all over the world, and the user's computer becomes just a way of accessing the information. The advent of "cloud computing," as well as the use of electronic devices such as cell phones that take advantage of cloud services, has raised serious questions concerning the manner in which lawyers and law firms handle client information, and has been the subject of numerous ethical inquiries in Pennsylvania and throughout the country. . . .

Recent "cloud" data breaches from multiple companies, causing millions of dollars in penalties and consumer redress, have increased concerns about data security for cloud services. The Federal Trade Commission ("FTC") has received complaints that inadequate cloud security is placing consumer data at risk, and it is currently studying the security of "cloud computing" and the efficacy of increased regulation. Moreover, the Federal Bureau of Investigations ("FBI") warned law firms in 2010 that they were being specifically targeted by hackers who have designs on accessing the firms' databases.

This Committee has also considered the client confidentiality implications for electronic document transmission and storage in Formal Opinions 2009-100 ("Metadata") and 2010-200 ("Virtual Law Offices"), and an informal Opinion directly addressing "cloud computing." Because of the importance of "cloud computing" to attorneys — and the potential impact that this technological advance may have on the practice of law — this Committee believes that it is appropriate to issue this Formal Opinion to provide guidance to Pennsylvania attorneys concerning their ethical obligations when utilizing "cloud computing." . . .

For lawyers, "cloud computing" may be desirable because it can provide costs savings and increased efficiency in handling voluminous data. Better still, cloud service is elastic, and users can have as much or as little of a service as they want at any given time. The service is sold on demand, typically by the minute, hour or other increment. Thus, for example, with "cloud computing," an attorney can simplify document management and control costs. . . .

Because "cloud computing" refers to "offsite" storage of client data, much of the control over that data and its security is left with the service provider. Further, data may be stored in other jurisdictions that have different laws and procedures concerning access to or destruction of electronic data. Lawyers using cloud services must therefore be aware of potential risks and take appropriate precautions to prevent compromising client confidentiality, i.e., attorneys must take great care to assure that any data stored offsite remains confidential and not accessible to anyone other than those persons authorized by their firms. They must also assure that the jurisdictions in which the data are physical stored do not have laws or rules that would permit a breach of confidentiality in violation of the Rules of Professional Conduct.

. . . Absent a client's informed consent, as stated in Rule 1.6(a), confidential client information cannot be disclosed unless either it is "impliedly authorized" for the representation or enumerated among the limited exceptions in Rule 1.6(b) or Rule 1.6(c). This may mean that a third party vendor, as with "cloud computing," could be "impliedly authorized" to handle client data provided that the information remains confidential, is kept secure, and any disclosure is confined only to necessary personnel. It also means that various safeguards should be in place so that an attorney can be reasonably certain to protect any information that is transmitted, stored, accessed, or otherwise processed through cloud services. . . .

At its essence, "cloud computing" can be seen as an online form of outsourcing subject to Rule 5.1 and Rule 5.3 governing the supervision of those who are associated with an attorney. Therefore, a lawyer must ensure that tasks are delegated to competent people and organizations. This means that any service provider who handles client information needs to be able to limit authorized access to the data to only necessary personnel, ensure that the information is backed up, reasonably available to the attorney, and reasonably safe from unauthorized intrusion. It is also important that the vendor understands, embraces, and is obligated to conform to the professional responsibilities required of lawyers, including a specific agreement to comply with all ethical guidelines, as outlined below. Attorneys may also need a written service agreement that can be enforced on the provider to protect the client's interests. In some circumstances, a client may need to be advised of the outsourcing or use of a service provider and the identification of the provider. A lawyer may also need an agreement or written disclosure with the client to outline the nature of the cloud services used, and its impact upon the client's matter. . . .

In the context of "cloud computing," an attorney must take reasonable care to make sure that the conduct of the cloud computing service provider conforms to the rules to which the attorney himself is subject. Because the operation is outside of an attorney's direct control, some of the steps taken to ensure reasonable care are different from those applicable to traditional information storage. While the measures necessary to protect confidential information will vary based upon the technology and infrastructure of each office — and this Committee acknowledges that the advances in technology make it difficult, if not impossible to provide specific standards that will apply to every attorney — there are common procedures and safeguards that attorneys should employ.

These various safeguards also apply to traditional law offices. Competency extends beyond protecting client information and confidentiality; it also includes a lawyer's ability to reliably access and provide information relevant to a client's case when needed. This is essential for attorneys regardless of whether data is stored onsite or offsite with a cloud service provider. However, since cloud services are under the provider's control, using "the cloud" to store data electronically could have unwanted consequences, such as interruptions in service or data loss. There are numerous examples of these types of events. Amazon EC2 has experienced outages in the past few years, leaving a portion of users without service for hours at a time. Google has also had multiple service outages, as have other providers. Digital Railroad, a photo archiving service, collapsed financially and simply shut down. These types of risks should alert anyone contemplating using cloud services to select a suitable provider, take reasonable precautions to back up data and ensure its accessibility when the user needs it.

Thus, the standard of reasonable care for "cloud computing" may include:

- Backing up data to allow the firm to restore data that has been lost, corrupted, or accidentally deleted;
- Installing a firewall to limit access to the firm's network;
- Limiting information that is provided to others to what is required, needed, or requested;
- Avoiding inadvertent disclosure of information;
- Verifying the identity of individuals to whom the attorney provides confidential information;
- Refusing to disclose confidential information to unauthorized individuals (including family members and friends) without client permission;

- Protecting electronic records containing confidential data, including back-ups, by encrypting the confidential data;
- Implementing electronic audit trail procedures to monitor who is accessing the data;
- Creating plans to address security breaches, including the identification of persons to be notified about any known or suspected security breach involving confidential data;
- Ensuring the provider:
  - explicitly agrees that it has no ownership or security interest in the data;
  - has an enforceable obligation to preserve security;
  - will notify the lawyer if requested to produce data to a third party, and provide the lawyer with the ability to respond to the request before the provider produces the requested information;
  - has technology built to withstand a reasonably foreseeable attempt to infiltrate data, including penetration testing;
  - includes in its "Terms of Service" or "Service Level Agreement" an agreement about how confidential client information will be handled;
  - provides the firm with right to audit the provider's security procedures and to obtain copies of any security audits performed;
  - will host the firm's data only within a specified geographic area. If by agreement, the data are hosted outside of the United States, the law firm must determine that the hosting jurisdiction has privacy laws, data security laws, and protections against unlawful search and seizure that are as rigorous as those of the United States and Pennsylvania;
  - provides a method of retrieving data if the lawyer terminates use of the SaaS product, the SaaS vendor goes out of business, or the service otherwise has a break in continuity; and,
  - provides the ability for the law firm to get data "off" of the vendor's or third party data hosting company's servers for the firm's own use or in-house backup offline.
- Investigating the provider's:
  - security measures, policies and recovery methods;
  - system for backing up data;
  - security of data centers and whether the storage is in multiple centers;
  - safeguards against disasters, including different server locations;
  - history, including how long the provider has been in business;
  - funding and stability;
  - policies for data retrieval upon termination of the relationship and any related charges; and,
  - process to comply with data that is subject to a litigation hold.
- Determining whether:
  - data is in non-proprietary format;
  - the Service Level Agreement clearly states that the attorney owns the data;
  - there is a 3rd party audit of security; and,
  - there is an uptime guarantee and whether failure results in service credits.
- Employees of the firm who use the SaaS must receive training on and are required to abide by all end-user security measures, including, but not limited to, the creation of strong passwords and the regular replacement of passwords.

- Protecting the ability to represent the client reliably by ensuring that a copy of digital data is stored onsite.
- Having an alternate way to connect to the internet, since cloud service is accessed through the internet.

The terms and conditions under which the "cloud computing" services are offered, i.e., Service Level Agreements ("SLAs"), may also present obstacles to reasonable care efforts. Most SLAs are essentially "take it or leave it," and often users, including lawyers, do not read the terms closely or at all. As a result, compliance with ethical mandates can be difficult. However, new competition in the "cloud computing" field is now causing vendors to consider altering terms. This can help attorneys meet their ethical obligations by facilitating an agreement with a vendor that adequately safeguards security and reliability. . . .

One caveat in an increasing field of vendors is that some upstart providers may not have staying power. Attorneys are well advised to consider the stability of any company that may handle sensitive information and the ramifications for the data in the event of bankruptcy, disruption in service or potential data breaches.

The use of "cloud computing," and electronic devices such as cell phones that take advantage of cloud services, is a growing trend in many industries, including law. Firms may be eager to capitalize on cloud services in an effort to promote mobility, flexibility, organization and efficiency, reduce costs, and enable lawyers to focus more on legal, rather than technical and administrative, issues. However, lawyers must be conscientious about maintaining traditional confidentiality, competence, and supervisory standards.

This Committee concludes that the Pennsylvania Rules of Professional Conduct require attorneys to make reasonable efforts to meet their obligations to ensure client confidentiality, and confirm that any third-party service provider is likewise obligated. Accordingly, as outlined above, this Committee concludes that, under the Pennsylvania Rules of Professional Conduct an attorney may store confidential material in "the cloud." Because the need to maintain confidentiality is crucial to the attorney-client relationship, attorneys using "cloud" software or services must take appropriate measures to protect confidential electronic communications and information. In addition, attorneys may use email but must, under appropriate circumstances, take additional precautions to assure client confidentiality.

Questions and Comments

1. As of 2014, the excerpted opinion was one of more than a dozen bar association opinions in various states that address the issue of cloud computing. All approved the practice, so long as the attorney uses reasonable care to employ proper data security safeguards along the way.

2. The opinion mentions Model Rules 5.1 and 5.3. Rule 5.1(a) provides that "[a] partner in a law firm, and a lawyer who individually or together with other lawyers possesses comparable managerial authority in a law firm, shall make reasonable efforts to ensure that the firm has in effect measures giving reasonable assurance that all lawyers in the firm conform to the Rules of Professional Conduct." Perhaps more pertinently, as regards cloud computing issues, Rule 5.3 provides as follows: "With respect to a non-lawyer employed or retained by or associated with a lawyer: (a) a partner, and a lawyer who individually or together with other lawyers possesses

comparable managerial authority in a law firm shall make reasonable efforts to ensure that the firm has in effect measures giving reasonable assurance that the person's conduct is compatible with the professional obligations of the lawyer; (b) a lawyer having direct supervisory authority over the non-lawyer shall make reasonable efforts to ensure that the person's conduct is compatible with the professional obligations of the lawyer; and (c) a lawyer shall be responsible for conduct of such a person that would be a violation of the Rules of Professional Conduct if engaged in by a lawyer if: (1) the lawyer orders or, with the knowledge of the specific conduct, ratifies the conduct involved; or (2) the lawyer is a partner or has comparable managerial authority in the law firm in which the person is employed, or has direct supervisory authority over the person, and knows of the conduct at a time when its consequences can be avoided or mitigated but fails to take reasonable remedial action." By their own terms, as opposed to how they are interpreted, how much guidance do these provisions offer on questions of cloud computing?

3. Cloud computing issues are, in large measure, matters pertaining to the management of vendors—a pervasive theme of this book. What guidance does the opinion provide for how attorneys should manage vendors? Are the oversight measures contained in the opinion realistically achievable, especially for smaller law firms or solo practitioners? Is there some way that vendor contracting or management could be centralized so as to overcome the inefficiencies and information asymmetries associated with non-expert law firms reviewing the controls in place for outsourced cloud computing services?

PROBLEM 11-4

You are managing partner of Storm & Kang, a 1,100-lawyer firm specializing in corporate and securities law. You recently authorized an initiative to digitalize all of your client files and move them to the "cloud" where they can more easily be accessed by attorneys working from remote locations. At your insistence, the firm's IT department has taken precautions to ensure that malefactors cannot access these files, and also has implemented security measures restricting access to lawyers and support staff who have been issued special privileges. Unfortunately, criminals operating out of Eastern Europe bypass these controls, invade your server, and download millions of pages of client files. You receive a message from the criminals threatening to make all of this information available on the Internet unless you pay a ransom of $30 million in Bitcoin. What should you do?

12

Off-Label Drugs

In this chapter we consider a leading compliance issue for the health care industry: the promotion of "off-label" drug use by pharmaceutical manufacturers. An off-label drug use occurs when a medication approved by the FDA to treat one condition is used to treat a different condition for which it is not approved. Off-label drug sales have been a major profit center for pharmaceutical companies but also a source of spectacular liability. In this chapter we examine the law pertaining to off-label drugs and the strategies used to ensure that drug companies comply with their legal obligations.

A. BACKGROUND

The federal Food, Drug and Cosmetic Act (FDCA) provides that the Food and Drug Administration (FDA) must approve a new drug for specific uses before it can be sold in interstate commerce. In order to obtain FDA approval, the manufacturer must demonstrate, through clinical trials, that the medication is safe and efficacious for its intended use. Once the drug is approved as safe and efficacious, the manufacturer and the FDA agree on the contents of the label, which includes both the text attached to the drug container as well as the patient package insert. Among other things, the label identifies the medication and its manufacturer, states its expiration date, sets forth directions for use, and lists its ingredients. Drug manufacturers are not permitted to promote their products for non FDA-approved uses.

The decision whether to prescribe a given drug is up to the treating physician. The problem with off-label uses arises because treating physicians are not limited to prescribing the drug for the FDA-approved use. It is permissible for the doctor to prescribe the drug for related conditions — or even for an entirely different purpose, if the doctor believes that the drug may help. When a doctor prescribes for an off-label use, the profits go to the pharmaceutical company; and the company earns the money without having to incur the cost and risk of putting the medication through clinical trials to demonstrate its safety and efficacy. It is not surprising, therefore, that drug companies have often attempted to influence physicians to prescribe their medications for unapproved uses.

Questions and Comments

1. Why are doctors allowed to prescribe drugs for uses unapproved by the FDA? Consider the following possibilities:

   a. Allowing a physician to prescribe drugs can advance medical science because if the drug proves efficacious, the physician can report this fact in medical journals and stimulate further research.

   b. Because the FDA approval process is time-consuming, allowing physicians to prescribe for unapproved uses allows valuable therapies to be provided to patients whose medical conditions will not wait on the FDA.

   c. Because the clinical trial process is costly, the drug manufacturer may elect not to obtain FDA approval for rare conditions on the ground that the cost of obtaining approval exceed any profit that the manufacturer can expect to earn from the new approved use. Allowing physicians to prescribe for these rare conditions allows needed medications to get to patients.

   d. Perhaps the political power of the medical profession has something to do with it. Doctors don't like to be bossed around by the government on treatment decisions. Because physicians have a potent lobby in Washington, lawmakers and regulators have not attempted to limit their clinical judgment.

2. If you have recently received prescription medication, did you read the package label and package insert? Was it helpful? Did it influence whether you would take the medication or not?

3. The FDA's rationale for banning promotions of drugs for unapproved uses is grounded in compelling reasons of policy: If drug companies could willy-nilly promote medications in this way, they could circumvent much of the regulatory scheme that requires clinical trials in order to demonstrate a medication's safety and efficacy before it is marketed.

Some "don'ts" of off-label marketing are described in the following press release:

U.S. Department of Justice Press Release, Pharmaceutical Company Eli Lilly to Pay Record $1.415 Billion for Off-Label Drug Marketing: Criminal Penalty Is Largest Individual Corporate Criminal Fine

Jan. 15, 2009

[The FDA had approved Zyprexa for use by adults for treatment of schizophrenia and certain types of bipolar disorder.] In September 1999, Eli Lilly began encouraging doctors to prescribe the drug for the treatment of dementia, Alzheimer's, agitation, aggression, hostility, depression, and generalized sleep disorder. Zyprexa was not approved for use for any of these disorders, which, unlike schizophrenia, are prevalent in the elderly population. Nevertheless, Eli Lilly's long-term care sales force promoted the use of Zyprexa in elderly populations for these symptoms.

Because one of Zyprexa's side effects is sedation, Eli Lilly directed its long-term care sales force to tell doctors that Zyprexa would help patients with sleep problems, behavioral issues, and dementia. They claimed this side effect was a therapeutic benefit, not an adverse event, with the sales slogan "5 at 5," that five milligrams of Zyprexa at 5 P.M. would help their patients sleep. Then in 2000, Eli Lilly expanded its illegal marketing to primary care physicians with its primary care sales force in the "Viva Zyprexa" campaign, adding even more sales representatives. The goal of the campaign was to make Zyprexa an "everyday agent in primary care" even though the company recognized that schizophrenia and bipolar disorder were not viewed as conditions typically treated by primary care physicians. Lilly instructed the sales force to recommend Zyprexa for all adult patients with behavioral symptoms like agitation, aggression, hostility, mood and sleep disturbances, and depression.

The information alleges that Eli Lilly's illegal off-label marketing campaign raised safety issues and posed potential risk to patients. Eli Lilly knew that significant weight gain and obesity were adverse side effects of Zyprexa and that weight gain and obesity were factors in causing hyperglycemia and diabetes. Yet despite written caution from the FDA, Eli Lilly continued to promote these adverse events as therapeutic benefits of Zyprexa use, particularly in the elderly.

Eli Lilly's management created marketing materials promoting Zyprexa for off-label uses, trained its sales force to disregard the law, and directed its sales personnel to promote Zyprexa for off-label uses. Anticipating the possibility of resistance from primary care physicians to prescribing Zyprexa, defendant Eli Lilly specifically trained its sales representatives on how to respond to doctors' concerns about off-label uses of Zyprexa, and how to continue to promote Zyprexa for off-label conditions. Eli Lilly retained medical professionals to speak to doctors during peer-to-peer sessions about off-label uses of Zyprexa. When promoting Zyprexa to health care providers, Lilly emphasized that the weight gain side effect of the drug was a therapeutic benefit for patients who had trouble maintaining their weight. . . .

Questions and Comments

1. Eli Lilly comes across rather poorly in the excerpted text. It seems intent on hawking its product by all means fair and foul — even going so far as turning the side effect of weight gain, which might be considered a negative, into yet another reason to prescribe the drug. Remember, however, that this is a press release issued by the prosecutors. Eli Lilly undoubtedly presented a different picture of its motivations and of the conduct of its marketing department.

2. What was the problem with Eli Lilly's behavior? The press release suggests that the company was completely irresponsible, promoting its drugs as magic treatments for all human ailments. However, the case against Eli Lilly was not primarily based on the allegation that Eli Lilly had engaging in false and deceptive marketing. Would it affect your view of the morality or social utility of Eli Lilly's conduct if it turned out there was nothing untruthful about the company's claims?

3. The government apparently did not allege that Eli Lilly was actively paying for off-label prescriptions — that is, paying explicit or implicit kickbacks to physicians who cooperated either by writing prescriptions or by helping to persuade other doctors to do so. At one time these kickbacks were common in the pharmaceutical industry. Today, as a result of lawsuits brought under the federal anti-kickback

statute (described below), the practice is much less common, and where it occurs it is likely to be carefully disguised.

What happens when a manufacturer receives inquiries from physicians, patients, medical researchers, or others about off-label uses? Often the manufacturer has scientific studies and other information in its files pertinent to the efficacy and safety of its medication for these uses. Should it be allowed to share this information with others? Should researchers affiliated with the company be allowed to publish the results of their clinical studies of off-label uses?

Consider the policy tradeoff. On the one hand, the progress of medical science could be hampered if valuable information of this sort could not be shared. Further, given that physicians are allowed to prescribe for off-label uses, it would seem nearly irresponsible to deny them or their patients access to the information needed to determine if the treatment holds promise to be efficacious.

On the other hand, drug companies could easily use requests from others as a "back door" to off-label marketing; they can simply enlist friendly doctors to obtain the information and publicize it independently. These risks are magnified by the growth of the Internet and social media. Many diseases and conditions are associated with organizations that host websites, bulletin boards, chat rooms or other media by which information about off-label uses can be rapidly and quickly shared. What sorts of information may a drug manufacturer supply for publication on these media?

In 2011, the FDA issued provisional policy guidance about this difficult issue:

Food and Drug Administration, Guidance for Industry: Responding to Unsolicited Requests for Off-Label Information About Prescription Drugs and Medical Devices

December 2011

1. Information distributed in response to an unsolicited request should be provided only to the individual making the request directly to the firm as a private, one-on-one communication.
2. Information distributed in response to an unsolicited request should be tailored to answer only the specific question(s) asked.
3. Information distributed in response to an unsolicited request should be truthful, non-misleading, accurate, and balanced.
4. Information distributed in response to an unsolicited request should be scientific in nature.
5. Responses to unsolicited requests for information should be generated by medical or scientific personnel independent from sales or marketing departments.
6. Information distributed in response to an unsolicited request should be accompanied by [the product label, scientific references, warnings, and other information].
7. A firm should maintain [records on all requests for information pertaining to off-label uses].

If a firm responds to non-public unsolicited requests for off-label information in the manner described above, FDA does not intend to use such responses as evidence of the firm's intent that its product be used for an unapproved or un-cleared use. Such responses also would not be expected to comply with the disclosure requirements related to promotional labeling and advertising.

Questions and Comments

1. The advice excerpted above concerns only unsolicited requests for information. All bets are off if the manufacturer responds to a *solicited* request. For example, if a sales representative invites a health care professional to request information about an off-label use, the resulting request would be considered to be solicited.

2. The advice also applies only to "non-public" requests: cases where the firm is responding to request for off-label information that was specifically directed to the firm privately through a one-on-one communication. As to public requests, the FDA recommends that the firm's response should be limited to providing the firm's contact information and should not include any off-label information.

Medical researchers publish many studies examining the effects of drugs for off-label uses. Some of these studies are conducted by the company's own scientists; others are carried out by outside researchers. Some are funded by the manufacturer; others are independent. To what extent should manufacturers be allowed to publish or otherwise distribute the results of research which supports an off-label use of a manufacturer's drug? Here, again, we see a clash of social policies. On the one hand, it is in the interest of scientific progress, as well as of society generally, that the results of scientific research be widely shared. On the other hand, if manufacturers could promote their studies of off-label effects too widely, the consequence would be to undermine the requirements of clinical trials and safety and efficacy testing.

In 2009, the Department of Health and Human Services and the FDA issued guidance to industry about these practices:

Food and Drug Administration, Good Reprint Practices for the Distribution of Medical Journal Articles and Medical or Scientific Reference Publications on Unapproved New Uses of Approved Drugs and Approved or Cleared Medical Devices

January 2009

. . . A scientific or medical journal article that is distributed [by a manufacturer] should:

- be published by an organization that has an editorial board that uses experts who have demonstrated expertise in the subject of the article under review by the organization and who are independent of the organization to review and objectively select, reject, or provide comments about proposed articles; and that has a publicly stated policy, to which the organization adheres, of full disclosure of any conflict of interest or biases for all authors, contributors, or editors associated with the journal or organization;
- be peer-reviewed and published in accordance with the peer-review procedures of the organization; and

- not be in the form of a special supplement or publication that has been funded in whole or in part by one or more of the manufacturers of the product that is the subject of the article.

A scientific or medical reference publication that is distributed should not be:

- primarily distributed by a drug or device manufacturer, but should be generally available in bookstores or other independent distribution channels (e.g. subscription, Internet) where medical textbooks or periodicals are sold;
- written, edited, excerpted, or published specifically for, or at the request of, a drug or device manufacturer; or
- edited or significantly influenced by a drug or device manufacturer or any individuals having a financial relationship with the manufacturer.

The information contained in the scientific or medical journal article or reference publication should address adequate and well-controlled clinical investigations that are considered scientifically sound by experts with scientific training and experience to evaluate the safety or effectiveness of the drug or device. . . .

The following publications are examples of publications that would not be considered consistent with the "Good Reprint Practices" outlined in this guidance:

- letters to the editor;
- abstracts of a publication;
- reports of Phase 1 trials in healthy subjects; or
- reference publications that contain little or no substantive discussion of the relevant investigation or data. . . .

The journal reprint or reference publication should be accompanied by a prominently displayed and permanently affixed statement disclosing:

- that the uses described in the information have not been approved or cleared by FDA, as applicable to the described drug or medical device;
- the manufacturer's interest in the drug or medical device that is the subject of the journal reprint or reference text;
- any author known to the manufacturer as having a financial interest in the product or manufacturer or who is receiving compensation from the manufacturer, along with the affiliation of the author, to the extent known by the manufacturer, and the nature and amount of any such financial interest of the author or compensation received by the author from the manufacturer;
- any person known to the manufacturer who has provided funding for the study; and
- all significant risks or safety concerns known to the manufacturer concerning the unapproved use that are not discussed in the journal article or reference text.

Questions and Comments

1. What policies do you detect at play in this statement? Does the FDA make the appropriate tradeoffs?

2. Why should we allow manufacturers to selectively distribute journal articles that provide support for off-label uses of the manufacturer's products?

3. What is wrong with a manufacturer distributing truthful reports on the results of Phase 1 clinical trials with healthy subjects?

4. What is wrong with distributing an abstract of a peer-reviewed medical journal article?

5. Should the policy statement evaluate the credibility of the journal in which the article is published? Is it a sufficient protection to demand that the journal be peer-reviewed? What if the journal requires that the author pay for the privilege of publishing there?

6. Do you see a potential trap in the requirement that the manufacturer must prominently disclose "all significant risks or safety concerns known to the manufacturer concerning the unapproved use that are not discussed in the journal article or reference text"? What if there's a "smoking gun" in the files?

Pharmaceutical companies that promote off-label uses are, in essence, engaging in speech: For example, their sales representatives are talking to doctors and encouraging them to prescribe the medication in question for an unapproved purpose. Speech is protected under the First Amendment, but not wholly so. In commercial contexts, a sufficiently cogent government interest can justify restrictions on what people can say. Do you think the activities of drug companies in marketing their products for unapproved uses should qualify for protection under the First Amendment, so that the government is disabled from prosecuting them? Consider the following case:

United States v. Caronia

703 F.3d 149 (2d Cir. 2012)

CHIN, Circuit Judge:

[Alfred] Caronia was found guilty of conspiracy to introduce a misbranded drug into interstate commerce . . . . Specifically, Caronia, a pharmaceutical sales representative, promoted the drug Xyrem for "off-label use," that is, for a purpose not approved by the U.S. Food and Drug Administration (the "FDA"). Caronia argues that he was convicted for his speech — for promoting an FDA-approved drug for off-label use — in violation of his right of free speech under the First Amendment. We agree. Accordingly, we vacate the judgment of conviction and remand the case to the district court.

Orphan Medical, Inc. ("Orphan"), now known as Jazz Pharmaceutical, was a Delaware-incorporated pharmaceutical company that primarily developed drugs to treat pain, sleep disorders, and central nervous system disorders. Orphan manufactured the drug Xyrem, a powerful central nervous system depressant. In 2005, after Jazz Pharmaceuticals acquired Orphan, Jazz continued to manufacture and sell Xyrem, grossing $20 million in combined Xyrem sales in 2005.

Xyrem can cause serious side effects, including difficulty breathing while asleep, confusion, abnormal thinking, depression, nausea, vomiting, dizziness, headache, bedwetting, and sleepwalking. If abused, Xyrem can cause additional medical problems, including seizures, dependence, severe withdrawal, coma, and death. Xyrem's active ingredient is gamma-hydroxybutryate ("GHB"). GHB has been federally classified as the "date rape drug" for its use in the commission of sexual assaults.

Despite the risks associated with Xyrem and GHB, the FDA approved Xyrem for two medical indications. In July 2002, the FDA approved Xyrem to treat narcolepsy patients who experience cataplexy, a condition associated with weak or paralyzed muscles. In November 2005, the FDA approved Xyrem to treat narcolepsy patients with excessive daytime sleepiness ("EDS"), a neurological disorder caused by the brain's inability to regulate sleep-wake cycles.

To protect against its serious safety concerns, in 2002, the FDA required a "black box" warning to accompany Xyrem. The black box warning is the most serious warning placed on prescription medication labels. Xyrem's black box labeling stated, among other things, that the drug's safety and efficacy were not established in patients under 16 years of age, and the drug had "very limited" experience among elderly patients. To identify patients suffering side effects from the drug, the FDA also regulated Xyrem distribution, allowing only one centralized Missouri pharmacy to distribute Xyrem nationally.

In March 2005, Orphan hired Caronia as a Specialty Sales Consultant to promote Xyrem. Caronia primarily worked in Queens, Nassau, and Suffolk counties. Caronia's salary was based on his individual sales. In July 2005, Caronia started Orphan's "speaker programs" for Xyrem. Speaker programs enlist physicians, for pay, to speak to other physicians about FDA-approved drug use. Orphan's speaker programs for Xyrem presented the benefits of the drug among patients with cataplexy and narcolepsy. Orphan hired Dr. Peter Gleason to promote Xyrem through its speaker programs.

Under Orphan's procedures, if Caronia, as a sales consultant for Xyrem, was asked about the off-label use of Xyrem, he was not permitted to answer; instead, when such questions were posed, Orphan sales consultants would fill out "medical information request forms" and send them to Orphan, and Orphan would send information to the inquiring physician. In contrast, physicians employed by Orphan as promotional speakers for Xyrem were permitted to answer off-label use questions; their responses were often informed by their own experiences with Xyrem.

In the spring of 2005, the federal government launched an investigation of Orphan and Gleason. The investigation focused on the off-label promotion of Xyrem. Caronia and Gleason were audio-recorded on two occasions as they promoted Xyrem for unapproved uses, including unapproved indications and unapproved subpopulations. . . .

[Orphan and Gleason pleaded guilty to criminal charges of misbranding. Caronia pleaded innocent and was convicted at trial. He was sentenced to one year of probation, 100 hours of community service, and a $25 special assessment. He appealed his conviction to the United States Court of Appeals for the Second Circuit.

[The court concluded that the government had prosecuted Caronia for statements made in promoting the medication for an off-label use. It rejected the government's argument that evidence of Caronia's statements was used only to establish that the intended use of the drug included off-label applications.]

[W]e decline the government's invitation to construe the FDCA's misbranding provisions to criminalize the simple promotion of a drug's off-label use by pharmaceutical manufacturers and their representatives because such a construction — and a conviction obtained under the government's application of the FDCA — would run afoul of the First Amendment. . . .

Debra Ann Livingston, Circuit Judge, dissenting:

Alfred Caronia was convicted of conspiring to introduce a prescription drug into interstate commerce with the intent that it be used in ways its labeling neither disclosed nor described. This intent was revealed, inter alia, through his speech. Because the First Amendment has never prohibited the government from using speech as evidence of motive or intent, I would affirm Caronia's conviction. By holding, instead, that Caronia's conviction must be vacated—and on the theory that whatever the elements of the crime for which he was duly tried, he was in fact convicted for promoting a drug for unapproved uses, in supposed violation of the First Amendment—the majority calls into question the very foundations of our century-old system of drug regulation. I do not believe that the Supreme Court's precedents compel such a result. I therefore respectfully dissent.

Questions and Comments

1. Xyrem, the medication at issue in the excerpted case, is a Schedule III controlled substance. Among other street names, the drug is known as "lollipop," "Georgia Home Boy," "Liquid Ecstasy," and "G." It is popular among clubgoers because of its tendency to produce euphoria; it is also reportedly used as a date rape drug. It is sometimes abused by athletes who believe that it may enhance the effect of human growth hormones. Could the fact that this drug is susceptible to abuse have influenced the government in its decision to pursue the manufacturer for off-label marketing?

2. The excerpted case involved only a prosecution of Alfred Caronia, a salesman employed by Orphan, the drug manufacturer. As Judge Chin notes in his opinion, Orphan pleaded guilty to criminal charges. The company paid a $20 million fine to resolve the claims against it. It must have been obvious to Orphan's counsel—as it was to Caronia's—that the prosecution raised First Amendment issues. Why did the company plead guilty rather than defend on First Amendment grounds?

3. How persuasive do you find the majority's conclusion that the prosecution of Caronia for promoting Xyrem violated his constitutional rights?

4. Read broadly, the majority opinion might be taken to insulate all truthful off-label promotional activity from criminal liability, on the ground that such activity is speech protected under the First Amendment. Judge Livingston, who wrote the dissenting opinion, certainly sees this as a possible consequence of the decision. Yet the scope of the majority opinion is not entirely clear. Judge Chin stressed that the government had prosecuted Caronia for his speech alone, and had not relied on his speech only as evidence of the drug's intended off-label use. In future cases, prosecutors might skirt the First Amendment problem by being more cautious in their arguments and in the jury charges that they recommend to the judge.

5. In the wake of the *Caronia* case, the government subtly changed the terminology it uses in describing off-label prosecutions. A press release describing the settlement of a misbranding case against GlaxoSmithKline, issued before the *Caronia* decision, stated that "promotion by the manufacturer of . . . 'off-label uses' renders the product 'misbranded.'" In a post-*Caronia* press release announcing a settlement against Amgen, the government stated that "it is illegal for drug companies to introduce into the marketplace drugs that the company intends will be used 'off-label,' i.e., for uses or at doses not approved by the FDA." Do you see the difference?

6. Reconsider the FDA's policy statement on distribution of medical journal articles (excerpted above). If implemented and enforced, could it stand up to the constitutional standard articulated in the *Caronia* case? Is it immunized from constitutional scrutiny on the ground that the policy represents only the agency's "current thinking" about the issue and does not create legally enforceable rights and responsibilities?

The discussion above deals with a drug company's possible criminal liability for selling misbranded drugs. Off-label marketing presents another major risk of liability under the False Claims Act (FCA) (see Chapter 8, where we addressed the use of this statute in *qui tam* actions). Section 3729(a) of Title 31 imposes treble damages liability on any person who knowingly causes a false or fraudulent claim to be presented to the United States for payment. The government's Medicaid program generally does not provide for reimbursement for off-label drug uses. Accordingly, when a pharmaceutical company promotes off-label drug use to physicians, knowing that the off-label prescriptions the physicians write will be filled and then submitted to Medicaid for reimbursement, the company arguably "causes" a false claim to be submitted to the federal government. Because the Medicaid program is gigantic and damages from a false claim are tripled, a drug manufacturer's liability exposure under the false claims statute can be huge.

A closely related basis of liability is the anti-kickback statute, a law that prohibits payments to induce or reward the referral of federal health care program business. 42 U.S.C. §1320a-7b. Drug companies can violate this statute when they reward doctors for writing off-level prescriptions. The anti-kickback statute is enforced by both criminal and civil damage penalties.

B. THE COMPLIANCE RESPONSE

As is evident from the previous section, the issue of off-label marketing presents an exquisite problem for drug companies. On the one hand the profits from off-label uses can be large. On the other hand the legal exposure is mind-boggling. Companies have paid enormous sums in fines and penalties for their off-label marketing activities. In 2013, Johnson & Johnson paid more than $2.2 billion to settle criminal and civil charges arising out of its marketing of the anti-psychotic drug Risperdal; in 2009 Pfizer paid $2.3 billion to settle charges of off-label marketing for its antibiotic agent Zyvox; and in 2009 Eli Lilly paid a $1.4 billion fine in connection with Zyprexa, an antipsychotic. The penalties for off-label marketing activities are not limited to fines: Some employees of pharmaceutical firms have faced criminal sentences.

The confluence of these two factors — the significant temptation to engage in off-label marketing and the equally significant risk associated with this activity — creates the ideal environment for the compliance function. An effective and well-designed compliance program can guide those charged with marketing drugs into engaging in legal activities and avoiding illegal ones. It can also serve a useful purpose if the company is charged with illegal conduct: The presence of a well-designed and well-funded compliance operation tends to negative criminal intent on the part of the company and to induce a more charitable attitude on the part of the FDA, prosecutors, judges and juries.

Companies can adopt off-label drug promotion compliance programs on their own. Often, however, the program is shaped by the settlement of an enforcement action in which the regulated firm agrees to enhance its compliance operations. The following excerpt is an illustration:

Corporate Integrity Agreement Between the Office of Inspector General of the Department of Health and Human Services and Cephalon, Inc.

Sept. 24, 2008

Cephalon, Inc. (Cephalon) hereby enters into this Corporate Integrity Agreement (CIA) with the Office of Inspector General (OIG) of the United States Department of Health and Human Services (HHS) . . . . Contemporaneously with this CIA, Cephalon is entering into a Settlement Agreement with the United States. Cephalon will also enter into settlement agreements with various States . . . and Cephalon's agreement to this CIA is a condition precedent to those agreements.

Prior to the Effective Date of this CIA . . . , Cephalon established a voluntary compliance program (known as "Global Compliance" or "Global Compliance Program") applicable to all Cephalon employees . . . . Cephalon's Global Compliance Program includes an Executive Vice President, [a] Chief Compliance Officer who reports directly to the Audit Committee of the Board of Directors and to the CEO, and a Compliance Committee. The Global Compliance Program also includes a Code of Conduct applicable to all employees that is regularly reviewed and disseminated, written policies and procedures that, as represented by Cephalon, promote high ethical standards, educational and training initiatives that, as represented by Cephalon, help to ensure compliance with applicable laws and regulations, a Disclosure Program that allows for the confidential disclosure and investigation of potential compliance violations and appropriate disciplinary procedures, screening measures . . . , and regular internal auditing procedures.

Cephalon shall continue its Compliance Program throughout the term of this CIA and shall do so in accordance with the terms set forth below. Cephalon may modify its Corporate Integrity Agreement Compliance Program as appropriate, but, at a minimum, Cephalon shall ensure that during the term of this CIA, it shall comply with the obligations set forth herein. . . .

TERM AND SCOPE OF THE CIA

The period of the compliance obligations assumed by Cephalon under this CIA shall be five years from the effective date of this CIA, unless otherwise specified. . . .

CORPORATE INTEGRITY OBLIGATIONS

Cephalon shall establish and maintain a Compliance Program throughout the term of this CIA that includes the following elements:

COMPLIANCE RESPONSIBILITIES OF CHIEF COMPLIANCE OFFICER, COMPLIANCE COMMITTEE, THE BOARD OF DIRECTORS, AND MANAGEMENT CERTIFICATIONS.

Chief Compliance Officer

Prior to the Effective Date, Cephalon appointed a Chief Compliance Officer, and Cephalon shall maintain a Chief Compliance Officer during the term of the CIA.

The Chief Compliance Officer shall be responsible for developing and implementing policies, procedures, and practices designed to ensure compliance with the requirements set forth in this CIA and with Federal health care program requirements and FDA requirements. The Chief Compliance Officer is and shall continue to be a member of executive management of Cephalon, shall make periodic (at least quarterly) reports regarding compliance matters directly to the Audit Committee of the Board of Directors of Cephalon, and shall be authorized to report on such matters to the Board of Directors at any time. The Chief Compliance Officer shall not be or be subordinate to the General Counsel or Chief Financial Officer. The Chief Compliance Officer shall be responsible for monitoring the day-to-day compliance activities engaged in by Cephalon as well as for any reporting obligations created under this CIA. . . .

Compliance Committee

Prior to the Effective Date, Cephalon established a Compliance Committee, and Cephalon shall maintain a Compliance Committee during the term of this CIA. The Compliance Committee shall, at a minimum, include the Chief Compliance Officer and other members of senior management necessary to meet the requirements of this CIA (e.g., senior managers of relevant departments, such as legal, medical affairs, sales, marketing, human resources, and internal audit). The Chief Compliance Officer shall chair the Compliance Committee and the Committee shall support the Chief Compliance Officer in fulfilling his/her responsibilities. . . .

Board of Directors

The Board of Directors (Board) or a Committee of the Board, if applicable, shall be responsible for the review and oversight of matters related to compliance with Federal health care program requirements, FDA requirements, and the obligations of this CIA. The Board, or a Committee of the Board, shall, at a minimum, be responsible for the following:

- Meeting at least quarterly to review and oversee Cephalon's Global Compliance Program, including but not limited to the performance of the Chief Compliance Officer and Global Compliance Department.
- For each Reporting Period of the CIA, adopting a resolution (pursuant to the process outlined in the bylaws for adopting resolutions) summarizing its official review and oversight of Cephalon's compliance with Federal health care program requirements, FDA requirements, and the obligations of this CIA. Each individual member of the Board or, if applicable, each member of the Committee of the Board having responsibility for compliance, shall sign a statement indicating that he or she agrees with the resolution.

At minimum, the resolution shall include the following language:

"The Board of Directors [or a Committee of the Board] has made a reasonable inquiry into the operations of Cephalon's Global Compliance Program, including the performance of the Chief Compliance Officer and the Global Compliance department. Based on its inquiry, the Board [or Committee] has concluded that, to the best of its knowledge, Cephalon has implemented an effective Global Compliance Program to meet the Federal health care program requirements, FDA requirements, and the obligations of the CIA."

If the Board [or the Board Committee] is unable to provide such a conclusion in the resolution, the Board [or Committee] shall include in the resolution a written explanation of the reasons why it is unable to provide the conclusion and the steps it is taking to implement an effective Compliance Program at Cephalon.

Cephalon shall report to OIG, in writing, any changes in the composition of the Board, or any actions or changes that would affect the Board's ability to perform the duties necessary to fulfill the obligations in this CIA, within 15 days after such a change.

MANAGEMENT ACCOUNTABILITY AND CERTIFICATIONS

Cephalon represents that compliance is a component of each employee's performance objectives. In addition to the responsibilities set forth in this CIA for all Covered Persons [major shareholders, officers, directors, employees and contractors working more than 160 hours per year], certain Cephalon employees ("Certifying Employees") are specifically expected to monitor and oversee activities within their areas of authority and shall annually certify in writing or electronically that the applicable area of authority is compliant with Federal health care program requirements, FDA requirements, and the obligations of this CIA. The Certifying Employees include, at a minimum, the following: Chairman and Chief Executive Officer, Executive Vice President of Worldwide Medical and Regulatory Operations, Executive Vice President of Worldwide Pharmaceutical Operations, all business unit sales vice presidents, all business unit marketing vice presidents, all business unit sales directors, all business unit marketing directors, the Vice President of Worldwide Medical Affairs, and all medical directors of communications and medical science liaisons (MSLs).

For each Reporting Period, each Certifying Employee shall certify in writing or electronically that:

"I have been trained on and understand the compliance requirements and responsibilities as they relate to [department or functional area], an area under my supervision . . . . To the best of my knowledge, except as otherwise described herein, the [department] of Cephalon is in compliance with all applicable Federal health care program requirements, FDA requirements, and the obligations of the CIA."

WRITTEN STANDARDS

Code of Conduct

Prior to the Effective Date, Cephalon developed, implemented, and distributed a written Code of Conduct to all Covered Persons.

Cephalon currently requires all newly employed persons to certify in writing or electronically that they have received, read, understood, and shall abide by Cephalon's Code of Conduct. Cephalon shall continue to make the promotion of, and adherence to, the Code of Conduct an element in evaluating the performance of all employees.

The Code of Conduct sets forth and shall continue to set forth, at a minimum, the following:

- Cephalon's commitment to full compliance with all Federal healthcare program and FDA requirements, including its commitment to market, sell, promote, research, develop, provide information about, and advertise its products in accordance with Federal health program requirements and FDA requirements;

- Cephalon's requirement that all of its Covered Persons shall be expected to comply with all Federal health care program and FDA requirements and with Cephalon's own Policies and Procedures . . . ;
- The requirement that all of Cephalon's Covered Persons shall be expected to report to the Chief Compliance Officer, or other appropriate individual designated by Cephalon, suspected violations of any Federal health care program and FDA requirements or of Cephalon's own Policies and Procedures;
- The possible consequences to both Cephalon and Covered Persons of failure to comply with Federal health care program and FDA requirements and with Cephalon's own Policies and Procedures and the failure to report such noncompliance; and
- The right of all individuals to use the Disclosure Program . . . and Cephalon's commitment to maintain, as appropriate, confidentiality and anonymity with respect to such disclosures.

To the extent not already accomplished, within 120 days after the Effective Date, the Code of Conduct shall be distributed to each Covered Person and each Covered Person shall certify, in writing or electronically, that he or she has received, read, understood, and shall abide by Cephalon's Code of Conduct. New Covered Persons shall receive the Code of Conduct and shall complete the required certification within 30 days after becoming a Covered Person or within 120 days after the Effective Date, whichever is later. . . .

THIRD PARTY PERSONNEL

Within 90 days after the Effective Date, and annually thereafter . . . , Cephalon shall send a letter to each entity employing Third Party Personnel. The letter shall outline Cephalon's obligations under the CIA and its commitment to full compliance with all Federal health care program and FDA requirements. The letter shall include a description of Cephalon's Compliance Program. Cephalon shall attach a copy of its Code of Conduct to the letter and shall request the employing Third Party Personnel to either: (a) make a copy of Cephalon's Code of Conduct and a description of Cephalon's Compliance Program available to its Third Party Personnel; or (b) represent to Cephalon that it has and enforces a substantially comparable code of conduct and compliance program for its Third Part Personnel.

POLICIES AND PROCEDURES

Prior to the Effective Date, Cephalon implemented written Policies and Procedures regarding the operation of the Compliance Program and Cephalon's compliance with Federal health care program and FDA requirements (Policies and Procedures). To the extent not already accomplished, within 120 days after the Effective Date, Cephalon shall ensure that the Policies and Procedures address or shall continue to address:

- the subjects relating to the Code of Conduct;
- appropriate ways to conduct Promotional and Product Services Related Functions in compliance with all applicable Federal healthcare program requirements . . . ;
- appropriate ways to conduct Promotional and Product Services Related Functions in compliance with all applicable FDA requirements;

- the mechanisms through, and manner in which, Cephalon receives and responds to requests for information about non-FDA approved (or "off-label") uses of Cephalon's products; . . .
- development of call plans for field sales representatives who promote Government Reimbursed Products; . . .
- consultant or other fee-for-service arrangements entered into with [health care providers and health care institutions];
- programs to educate field representatives, including preceptorships . . . ;
- sponsorship or funding of grants (including educational grants) or charitable contributions . . . ;
- funding of, or participation in, any Third Party Educational Activity;
- review of promotional materials by appropriate qualified personnel (such as regulatory, medical, and/or legal personnel) . . . ;
- sponsorship or funding of research or related activities . . . ;
- compensation (including salaries and bonuses) for Relevant Covered Persons . . . ;
- disciplinary policies and procedures for violations of Cephalon's Policies and Procedures. . . .

TRAINING AND EDUCATION

Cephalon represents that it provides training to its employees on a regular basis concerning a variety of topics. The training required by this CIA need not be separate and distinct from the regular training provided by Cephalon, but instead may be integrated fully into such regular training so long as the training covers the areas specified below. . . .

REVIEW PROCEDURES

General Description

- Engagement of Independent Review Organization. Within 90 days after the Effective Date, Cephalon shall engage an entity (or entities), such as an accounting, auditing, or consulting firm (hereinafter "Independent Review Organization" or "IRO"), to perform reviews to assist Cephalon in assessing and evaluating its Promotional and Product Services Related Functions . . . . Each IRO engaged by Cephalon shall have expertise in applicable Federal health care program and FDA requirements as may be appropriate to the Review for which the IRO is retained. Each IRO shall assess, along with Cephalon, whether it can perform the engagement in a professionally independent and objective fashion, as appropriate to the nature of the review, taking into account any other business relationships or other engagements that may exist. . . .

IRO REVIEW REPORTS

The IRO(s) shall prepare a report (or reports) based upon each Review performed. . . .

VALIDATION REVIEW

In the event OIG has reason to believe that: (a) any IRO Review fails to conform to the requirements of this CIA; or (b) the IRO's findings or Review results are inaccurate, OIG may, at its sole discretion, conduct its own review to determine whether the applicable IRO Review complied with the requirements of the CIA and/or the findings or Review results are inaccurate (Validation Review).

DISCLOSURE PROGRAM

Cephalon represents that it has a disclosure program designed to facilitate communications relating to compliance with Federal health care program and FDA requirements and Cephalon's policies (the "Disclosure Program"). During the term of the CIA, Cephalon shall maintain a Disclosure Program that includes a mechanism (a toll-free compliance telephone line) to enable individuals to disclose, to the Compliance Officer or some other person who is not in the disclosing individual's chain of command, any identified issues or questions associated with Cephalon's policies, conduct, practices, or procedures with respect to a Federal health care program or FDA requirement believed by the individual to be a potential violation of criminal, civil, or administrative law. . . .

The Disclosure Program shall emphasize a non-retaliation policy, and shall include a reporting mechanism for anonymous communications for which appropriate confidentiality shall be maintained. . . .

Questions and Comments

1. The excerpted order is termed a "corporate integrity agreement" (CIA). This is the name the FDA uses to describe what are in essence consent decrees that settle regulatory enforcement proceedings. A CIA typically includes requirements to hire a compliance officer; appoint a compliance committee; develop written standards and policies; implement a comprehensive employee training program; retain an independent organization to conduct annual reviews; establish a confidential disclosure program; restrict employment of ineligible persons; report overpayments, reportable events, and ongoing investigations and legal proceedings; and provide an implementation report and annual reports on the status of the entity's compliance activities.

2. In connection with the CIA excerpted above, Cephalon agreed, among other things, to pay $425 million to settle charges that it had improperly marketed several of its prescription medications for unapproved uses.

3. Cephalon's situation illustrates the pack of trouble a company can experience as a result of a serious compliance breakdown. At the time it entered this settlement agreement with HHS, the company was also being pursued by the U.S. Department of Justice, various state attorneys general, and (undoubtedly) many plaintiffs' attorneys. Part of the task of counsel, in a crisis such as this, is to find a path to a comprehensive settlement that allows the company to go forward free of the burden of its past conduct.

4. The compliance program and other obligations set forth in the excerpted agreement are at the high end of the level of detail one finds in cases of this sort. Regardless of the defendant's underlying conduct, is it appropriate for the government to intrude this minutely into a company's internal operations?

5. Were most of the terms excerpted above dictated by the government? The agreement recites that Cephalon had already implemented extensive compliance reforms prior to the settlement. For the most part, the excerpted terms merely require the company to continue to follow procedures and programs which the company had already put in place. Still, the reforms in question were almost

certainly adopted in the "shadow" of government enforcement. It is, accordingly, difficult to sort out what in this agreement is truly voluntary and what is the product of government pressure.

6. This agreement specifies that Cephalon must appoint a chief compliance officer, who "shall not be or be subordinate to the General Counsel or Chief Financial Officer." Why did HHS believe this to be important? Why didn't it go further and require that the chief compliance officer must report only to the chief executive officer — or even that she must report substantively only to the board of directors or a committee of the board?

7. The agreement contemplates that the company's audit committee is responsible for overseeing compliance, although it seemingly leaves open the possibility that a different committee (presumably a compliance committee) would exercise this responsibility. Why didn't HHS go further and require Cephalon to establish a specialized board-level compliance committee?

8. The agreement requires that responsible board members sign a statement in each reporting period that "Cephalon has implemented an effective Global Compliance Program," or explain to the government why they cannot sign such a statement. What is this requirement intended to accomplish?

9. What about the requirement that executive officials certify that the department under their supervision is "in compliance with all applicable Federal health care program requirements, FDA requirements, and the obligations of the CIA." What is this requirement intended to accomplish?

10. As is increasingly common in compliance consent agreements, the Cephalon CIA requires the company to retain an outside consultant to "perform reviews to assist Cephalon in assessing and evaluating its Promotional and Product Services Related Functions." What function is served by this outside review? Can a third-party vendor retained and compensated by Cephalon be trusted to provide an objective assessment of the company's compliance efforts?

11. Corporations are fluid organizations. What happens if, during the five years of this agreement, Cephalon finds it necessary or convenient to change some of the compliance-based procedures contained in this document? Is there a way for it to do so? The agreement provides that "Cephalon shall continue its Compliance Program throughout the term of this CIA and shall do so in accordance with the terms set forth below. Cephalon may modify its Corporate Integrity Agreement Compliance Program as appropriate, but, at a minimum, Cephalon shall ensure that during the term of this CIA, it shall comply with the obligations set forth herein." Can those two sentences be reconciled?

12. Did the agreement in the excerpted matter impose new obligations on Cephalon's board of directors? *See* In re Pfizer, 722 F. Supp. 2d 453, 461 (S.D.N.Y. 2010) (although corporate integrity agreement did not create new fiduciary duties, it "imposed affirmative obligations on Pfizer's board that went well beyond the basic fiduciary duties required by Delaware law"). For discussion, see Wulf A. Kaal & Elizabeth R. Malay, *The Role of Corporate Integrity Agreements in the Expansion of Fiduciary Duties*, U. St. Thomas (Minn.) Legal Studies Research Paper No. 13-25 (2013), available at http://papers.ssrn.com/sol3/papers.cfm?abstract_id=2317580.

13. In 2010, a purported whistleblower filed a lawsuit alleging that Cephalon was again promoting a product for off-label uses — this time pushing its leukemia drug Treanda as a treatment for lymphoma. What does this say about programs such as the one contained in the agreement excerpted above?

13

Foreign Corrupt Practices

As noted briefly in Chapter 4, the current U.S. regulation of foreign corrupt practices grew out of revelations in the 1970s that hundreds of American companies were bribing foreign officials to secure contracts overseas, and were falsifying their financial records to conceal the activity. The public outrage that followed these disclosures — heightened by the context of the Watergate scandal that had eroded faith in the legitimacy of American institutions — sparked Congress into action.

The spirit of the Foreign Corrupt Practices Act (FCPA) is reflected in the Senate report on the measure, which proclaimed as follows: "Corporate bribery is bad business. In our free market system it is basic that the sale of products should take place on the basis of price, quality, and service. Corporate bribery is fundamentally destructive of this basic tenet. Corporate bribery of foreign officials takes place primarily to assist corporations in gaining business. Thus foreign corporate bribery affects the very stability of overseas business. Foreign corporate bribes also affect our domestic competitive climate when domestic firms engage in such practices as a substitute for healthy competition for foreign business." S. Rep. No. 95-114 (1977), at 3-4.

A. BASICS

1. Elements of the Statute

There are two essential requirements of the FCPA: the anti-bribery provisions and the accounting provisions. The first of these, the anti-bribery provision, makes it an illegal practice, "in order to assist . . . in obtaining or retaining business," for a covered person corruptly to give or offer "anything of value" to any foreign official, politician, political party, or agent for the purpose of influencing an official act or omission, inducing such a person to influence a foreign government decision, or to secure "any improper advantage." 15 U.S.C. §78dd-1(a)(3). A "foreign official" is "any officer or employee of a foreign government or any department, agency, or instrumentality thereof." Id. §78dd-2(h)(2)(A)

Much is packed into this language. Consider the following:

- Who is a foreign official? Often the answer to this question is clear, but significant uncertainty arises when the person is employed by an entity that, although not officially part of the government, nevertheless is affiliated with the government by ownership or contractual ties and carries out activities that may be associated with governmental functions. Is such an entity an "instrumentality" of a foreign government?
- What nexus with the United States is required to trigger the statute? The required connections are not demanding. Essentially all U.S. entities and individuals are covered, as are foreign nationals or entities that, directly or through an agent, engage in any act in furtherance of a corrupt payment while in the territory of the United States. The jurisdictional sweep is extraordinarily broad. Any telephone call, email, or fax made from, to, or through the United States could qualify, as would acts to facilitate the wire transfer of funds, which often pass through the United States *en route* to their corrupt destination. And conspiracy liability can extend even further, since each conspirator is brought within the statute if any of their co-conspirators engaged in the requisite acts.
- What acts qualify as having a business purpose? Sending a wedding gift to a personal friend who happens to be a foreign government official might fall outside the statute, but only if there is no connection between the gift and the acquisition or retention of business. If any such connection exists, however, the business purpose requirement is likely to be satisfied — at least in the eyes of the enforcement agencies. *See* United States v. Kay, 359 F.3d 738 (5th Cir. 2004) (bribes paid to secure tax reductions fell within the statute).
- When is a payment "corrupt"? The legislative history of the FCPA explains that the term refers to the idea that the payment must be made to induce the recipient to misuse her official position. What, then, about payments made in response to extortion? Often, American businesspeople complain that they don't want to pay bribes, but that they are held up by foreign officials who give them no choice but to do so if they want to do business in the jurisdiction. Does the language requiring a corrupt purpose apply when the foreign official is extorting the payment? U.S. regulators recognize that instances of true extortion will not generate enforcement actions under the statute if the payment is made under "imminent threat of physical harm." But they won't extend this exception further, even when the payment is necessary as the price for gaining access to the market. *See* United States v. Kozeny, 582 F. Supp. 2d 535, 540 (S.D.N.Y. 2008).
- What is necessary to complete the offense? Suppose, for example, that a U.S. firm offered a bribe to a foreign official, but the official was removed from office before the bribe was paid. Is the offense completed with the mere offering of an inducement that was never paid? Answer: Yes, the offense is complete when a bribe is offered, regardless of whether it is actually paid.
- What sorts of consideration constitute "anything of value"? The statute means what it says. Cash, payment of personal expenses, and gifts of personal property all meet the statutory definition. So are personal favors such as conferring a benefit on a child or spouse of an official. There is, moreover, no *de minimis* exception: Any item, no matter how inexpensive, potentially triggers liability under the statute provided it has some value. To prevent the statute from deteriorating into farce, the regulators offer the comfort that things like

purchasing a cup of coffee or paying for a shared taxi will not trigger liability, on the theory that payment of items of merely nominal value probably will not reflect a corrupt intent. But, in theory at least, even such small matters could in appropriate circumstances provide a basis for liability. What about gifts of the type that are conventionally exchanged in business relationships? These are probably permitted so long as they are appropriate in type and amount, and that they are given openly and transparently, properly recorded on a reporting firm's books, and compliant with local law.

- What is an "improper advantage" — and how is it different from the other benefits specifically named? There is little guidance on this issue, but the regulators have not developed the idea into any sort of safety value for limiting U.S. firms' liability.
- What culpable mental state is required to establish liability under the FCPA? Often U.S. enterprises don't actually *know* that bribes are being paid: They don't approve the expenditures or sign off on a program of greasing the palms of foreign officials. Even so, they may have good reason to believe that bribes are being distributed. If lack of actual knowledge were a defense, then it would be relatively easy for U.S. enterprises and individuals to avoid exposure. The government's approach is to assert that liability can be founded on "willful blindness" or "conscious disregard" of facts that anyone in the defendant's position would believe to be the case.

As the foregoing discussion makes clear, courts and the regulators (the FCPA is enforced by the Department of Justice and, for listed firms, also by the Securities and Exchange Commission) have usually interpreted the FCPA anti-bribery rules broadly and have given little leeway for defendants to avoid liability by relying on potential statutory limitations. There are, however, certain safety valves:

- Regulators recognize an exception for facilitating or expediting payments in connection with "routine" government actions. Suppose, for example, that an American company needs a certificate of occupancy under foreign law to move into a building, and, even though all preconditions to the permit are satisfied, the building inspector refuses to grant the permit unless she receives a small gratuity. If the action in question is essentially ministerial, the FCPA allows American businesses to pay small bribes to facilitate their ability to do business. However, "routine" actions are narrowly defined to include only actions such as granting permits; processing papers such as visas or work permits; providing police, telephone, power, water, or mail services; performing inspections; paying to load or unload cargo (a major headache for importers and exporters); or protecting perishable products from deterioration. Specifically excluded from the category of "routine" government action are any decisions to award new business or to continue an existing business.
- The statute also recognizes two affirmative defenses. One covers situations where the payment in question was lawful under the written laws of the foreign country. In a sense, this defense might be considered to be unnecessary because, if the payment is legal under foreign law, it might not qualify as "corrupt." Nevertheless, the defense is important because it makes clear that the legality of a practice under foreign law protects a covered party only in limited circumstances. Suppose that the payment of gratuities to

foreign officials is part of the ordinary and accepted business practices of a foreign country. Would an American firm be exonerated if it made such payments? The answer is, not necessarily. The defense exists only if the payment is legal under the *written* law of the country; informal but widely observed practices are not enough.

- The other affirmative defense concerns "reasonable and bona fide" expenditures, such as travel and lodging expenses, incurred by or on behalf of a covered foreign person, which are directly related either to the promotion, demonstration, or explanation of products or services; or to the execution or performance of a contract with a foreign government or agency. For example, it might not be a corrupt practice for a U.S. firm to pay the hotel expense of a foreign official who is attending a sales meeting at which the American firm is seeking to persuade a foreign government to purchase its products, at least if the expense is reasonable (a seven-star hotel might not qualify).

As can be seen from the foregoing, the coverage of the anti-bribery provisions is broad, and only limited protections are available to avoid liability if the basic elements of the statute are met. But the challenge for U.S. businesses doesn't stop there, because there is still the potential for liability under the accounting provisions of the statute (these provisions were adopted as part of the FCPA but apply broadly to many forms of transactions not otherwise subject to that statute).

The accounting rules have two subparts. The "books and records" rule requires SEC-reporting firms to make and keep books, records, and accounts that, in reasonable detail, accurately and fairly reflect an issuer's transactions and dispositions of the issuer's assets. 15 U.S.C. §78m(b)(2)(A). The "internal controls" provision requires issuers to devise and maintain a system of internal accounting controls sufficient to assure management's control, authority, and responsibility over the firm's assets. 15 U.S.C. §78m(b)(2)(B).

Unlike the anti-bribery provision, which applies to all sorts of firms, the accounting provisions apply only to public companies. This limitation provides some degree of protection from exposure, but the protection may be illusory if the private firm accused of violations is a subsidiary of a public company. The government is likely to argue in such a case that the subsidiary acted as an agent of the public parent company, making the parent company liable under the accounting provisions for the subsidiary's improper conduct. At the same time, the accounting provisions are broader than the anti-bribery rule because they apply even when no foreign corrupt practice is involved.

The accounting provisions pose many unanswered questions.

- When are books and records inadequate? When is the level of detail "reasonable," and how much deviation from the true state of affairs is permitted before they are considered to be inaccurate or unfair?
- What evidence establishes a violation of the internal controls rule? The government has interpreted this provision very broadly—in the view of some commentators, too broadly—by taking the fact that a violation of the anti-bribery rule occurred as nearly conclusive evidence that internal controls were inadequate.

Penalties for violations of the FCPA can be severe. Consider first the criminal penalties (enforced by the Department of Justice). Corporations and other entities are liable for criminal fines up to $2 million for each violation of the anti-bribery provisions; individuals are subject to fines of up to $250,000 and imprisonment for up to five years.

As for the accounting provisions, business entities are liable for fines up to $25 million and individuals for fines up to $5 million and imprisonment for up to 20 years. Under the Alternative Fines Act, 18 U.S.C. §3571(d), courts may impose even higher penalties, up to twice the benefit that the defendant obtained from the corrupt payment; and companies may not indemnify individual defendants for fines under this statute.

Both the Department of Justice and the Securities and Exchange Commission can also seek civil penalties for FCPA violations — fines of up to $16,000 per violation for violations of the anti-bribery provisions and, for violations of the accounting provisions, a penalty not to exceed the defendant's pecuniary gain (a form of disgorgement), or specified dollar penalties ranging from $7,500 to $725,000 depending on the circumstances and the identity of the violator.

In addition, the government may seek orders requiring defendants to forfeit U.S. assets. Sometimes the assets under forfeiture can be quirky. In one 2014 case involving the son of the ruler of the Republic of Equatorial Guinea, the Justice Department sought forfeiture of a $30 million mansion in Malibu, a Ferrari, and hundreds of thousands of dollars' worth of Michael Jackson memorabilia, including the pop icon's famous glove. The latter case had the entertaining caption United States v. One White Crystal-Covered Bad Tour Glove.

And these are only the direct consequences.

Violators of the FCPA may also suffer debarment (loss of rights to do business with the government); cross-debarment (loss of rights to do business with multinational development banks); loss of export licenses; potential exposure to class action and shareholder derivative lawsuits; loss of the value of the contract that forms a basis for the FCPA charges; professional fees and expenses; loss of share market value and increased cost of capital; loss of competitive position vis-à-vis rivals; reputational costs, and potential civil or criminal liability under the laws of the country whose officials were involved or any other country that has an arguable nexus with the transaction. For discussion, see Mark Koehler, *Foreign Corrupt Practices Act Ripples*, 3 Am. U. Bus. L. Rev. 291 (2014).

For a sense of the extent of potential liability, consider the following table of leading FCPA settlements:

Company	Country	Total Resolution	Date
Siemens AG	Germany	$800,000,000	2008
Alstrom	France	$772,000,000	2014
KBR/Halliburton	USA	$579,000,000	2009
BAE Systems	UK	$400,000,000	2010
Total, S.A.	France	$398,200,000	2013
Alcoa	USA	$384,000,000	2014
Snamprogetti/ENI	Holland/Italy	$365,000,000	2010
Technip S.A.	France	$338,000,000	2010
JGC Corp.	Japan	$218,000,000	2011
Daimler AG	Germany	$185,000,000	2010

No wonder FCPA problems keep senior managers up at night!

Questions and Comments

1. What is the purpose of the FCPA?

2. Notice the nationality of the firms involved: Only two of the top ten largest fines involved U.S. companies. What explains this pattern? Does this reflect bias by U.S. regulators? A greater propensity for wrongdoing on the part of foreign firms? Chance?

3. Given that the liability exposure for FCPA violations is so large, why do U.S. companies continue to violate the statute?

4. A problem with the FCPA is that competitors to U.S. corporations may not be subject to the same onerous sanctions, so they may obtain a competitive advantage in doing business in certain countries. The FCPA reaches foreign corporations that are listed in the United States and any foreign firm, even though not listed, that causes an act to occur in the United States as part of the corrupt practice. In effect, this rule extends the net of the FCPA to cover many of the larger foreign firms. Even so, many foreign firms are outside the reach of U.S. law. Arguably, these firms have a competitive advantage over U.S. firms if they are allowed to pay bribes and U.S. firms are not.

5. A partial remedy to the problem of unfair competition is to press for international agreements that commit many countries to similar enforcement policies. The OECD's Anti-Bribery Convention, which requires signatory countries to make it a crime to bribe foreign officials, is a step in that direction. Approximately three dozen countries have signed on, including (in addition to the United States) all member states of the European Union, plus Australia, Brazil, Canada, Chile, Japan, Korea, Mexico, New Zealand, and Turkey. In addition to the OECD agreement, the United Nations Convention Against Corruption (UNCAC), adopted in 2003 and ratified by the United States in 2006 and now ratified by more than 160 countries, embodies a broad international consensus—at least at the level of official rhetoric—against bribery and other improper payments. The UNCAC requires signatory countries to enact legislation criminalizing acts such as domestic or foreign bribery and related offenses such as money laundering or obstruction of justice. The convention also establishes guidelines governing the creation and makeup of anti-corruption bodies, codes of conduct, procurement protocols, and enhanced accounting and auditing standards for private firms. A peer review mechanism operates to ensure that countries actually perform their commitments under the convention—although so far the process has been largely limited to ensuring that they actually pass the required legislation, not necessarily that they implement it effectively. Other important international anti-bribery standards are the Inter-American Convention Against Corruption (IACAC), adopted by members of the Organization of American States, with more than 30 signatories, and the Council of Europe's Criminal Law Convention on Corruption, as implemented by the Group of States Against Corruption (GRECO). At the country level, one of the most stringent of all anti-bribery statutes is the U.K. Bribery Act of 2010, which carries onerous sanctions such as imprisonment, large fines, potential confiscation of property, and disqualification of directors.

6. In 2012, JPMorgan Chase and other firms were accused of hiring the sons and daughters of Chinese politicians in an effort to curry favor with the government. Does it violate the FCPA to hire the child of a politician? What if the new employee attended a first-class university?

7. Was it a corrupt practice for NBC News to hire Chelsea Clinton as a special correspondent at the time her mother was serving as Secretary of State?

8. What happens if a campaign to root out corruption is itself corrupt? Anti-corruption rules can provide a handy weapon for politicians to use against their adversaries. Critics have charged that biased prosecutions for official corruption are common in important countries such as Russia and China. Even in the United States, government officials have been accused of using the powers of office as weapons against their rivals. In 2014, Texas Republicans alleged that Rosemary Lehmberg, a district attorney from Democratic-leaning Travis County, had abused her position as head of the state's public integrity unit by selectively bringing charges against Republican officials. When Lehmberg was arrested for drunk driving, Governor Rick Perry, a Republican and possible candidate for president, threatened to veto funding for the unit unless Lehmberg resigned. In response, a Travis County grand jury indicted the governor for felony abuse of power. Once again, Republicans cried "foul!" In 2016, the Texas Court of Criminal Appeals dismissed all charges against Perry on the ground that the prosecution violated the separation of powers and infringed Perry's right to freedom of speech. Dust-ups of this intensity might be particularly characteristic of bare-knuckles Texas politics, but the use of legal process against political rivals is not unknown elsewhere.

9. Although the FCPA is the most important domestic U.S. statute governing corrupt payments abroad, it is far from the only weapon in the regulatory arsenal. Prosecutors who go after an American company for paying foreign bribes are likely to charge not only criminal violations of the FCPA, but also offenses such as mail fraud, wire fraud, and violations of the Travel Act, 18 U.S.C. §1952 (the latter statute makes it an offense to engage in interstate or foreign travel or use the mails or "any facility in interstate or foreign commerce" for the purpose of distributing the proceeds of an unlawful activity, committing a crime of violence in furtherance of an unlawful activity, or to promote, manage, establish, or carry on an unlawful activity).

10. You may be wondering about the fact that the FCPA applies only to *foreign* corrupt practices. It might seem that while bribing a foreign official is bad, bribing an official of your own country is even worse. In fact, bribery of domestic officials has long been a crime, and although domestic bribery cases have not generated the same spectacular publicity as the international cases, these cases are frequently brought by federal and state prosecutors. Consider the government's case against Quality Eggs, LLC, a large egg production company with operations in Wright County, Iowa. A massive salmonella outbreak in 2010 made thousands of people sick and lead to the recall of more than 500 million eggs. The outbreak was traced to eggs produced and distributed by Quality Eggs. The government's subsequent investigation revealed that the company systematically misbranded its eggs by misrepresenting their freshness and quality. When inspectors from the U.S. Department of Agriculture caught some of the violations, company officials bribed them to release the pallets for sale. The Justice Department prosecuted the company and several of its senior officials and obtained guilty pleas in 2014. In 2016, the Supreme Court substantially restricted the scope of federal bribery statutes by adopting a narrow construction of the statutory requirement that an official must commit an "official act" in exchange for money or gifts. McDonnell v. United States, 136 S. Ct. 2355 (2016).

11. Bribery, almost by definition, is something that happens in secret. People know it is wrong, and therefore they take steps to conceal it. An important challenge for enforcement is to devise mechanisms to smoke out bribes and other corrupt practices. How, then, do foreign corrupt practices become known to the regulators? The following pathways are most salient:

- Sometimes a foreign government itself catches the responsible official and traces her back to the bribe. In such a case, the foreign government may inform the U.S. regulators, or the regulators may learn of the foreign enforcement action through the media or other sources.
- Increasingly, people use social media to express anger about corruption in government. U.S. regulators track social media posts from around the world and follow up on bona fide leads indicating possible violations of the FCPA.
- The Sarbanes-Oxley Act requires the CEO and CFO of public companies to certify the financial statements. To avoid the liability accompanying a false certification, these officials are demanding greater assurances that the statements are accurate — assurances that sometimes result in the disclosure of FCPA problems.
- The FCPA is subject to the SEC's whistleblower program. Given the large fines that have been assessed in some FCPA cases, a whistleblower could potentially enrich herself by reporting FCPA violations by her company and its officials.

2. What Is an "Instrumentality" of a Foreign Government?

United States v. Esquenazi

752 F.3d 912 (11th Cir.), *cert. denied*, 135 S. Ct. 293 (2014)

[Defendant co-owned Terra Communications Corp., which purchased and resold cell phone minutes. One of its principal customers was Telecommunications D'Haiti, S.A.M. (Teleco), an enterprise located in Haiti. Originally a government monopoly, Teleco was essentially wholly owned by the Haitian central bank until it was privatized in 2009-2010. A witness testified that in order to reduce the amount of its debt to Teleco, Terra paid money to Teleco's Director of International Relations, Robert Antoine, in order to induce Teleco to reduce the bill; when Antoine left the job, Terra allegedly paid his replacement to do the same thing.]

The FCPA prohibits "any domestic concern" from "mak[ing] use of the mails or any means . . . of interstate commerce corruptly in furtherance of" a bribe to "any foreign official," or to "any person, while knowing that all or a portion of such money or thing of value will be offered, given, or promised, directly or indirectly, to any foreign official," for the purpose of "influencing any act or decision of such foreign official . . . in order to assist such domestic concern in obtaining or retaining business for or with, or directing business to, any person." 15 U.S.C. §§78dd-2(a)(1), (3). A "foreign official" is "any officer or employee of a foreign government or any department, agency, or instrumentality thereof." Id. §78dd-2(h)(2)(A). The central question before us, and the principal source of disagreement between the parties, is what "instrumentality" means (and whether Teleco qualifies as one).

The FCPA does not define the term "instrumentality," and this Court has not either. For that matter, we know of no other court of appeals who has. The definition matters in this case, in light of the challenges to the district court's jury instructions on "instrumentality"; to the sufficiency of the evidence that Teleco qualified as an instrumentality of the Haitian government; and to Mr. Esquenazi's contention that the statute is unconstitutionally vague. Before we address these challenges, however, we must define "instrumentality" for purposes of the FCPA.

We begin, as we always do when construing statutory text, with the plain meaning of the word at issue. According to Black's Law Dictionary, an instrumentality is "[a] means or agency through which a function of another entity is accomplished, such as a branch of a governing body." Webster's Third New International Dictionary says the word means "something that serves as an intermediary or agent through which one or more functions of a controlling force are carried out: a part, organ, or subsidiary branch esp. of a governing body." These dictionary definitions foreclose Mr. Rodriguez's contention that only an actual part of the government would qualify as an instrumentality—that contention is too cramped and would impede the "wide net over foreign bribery" Congress sought to cast in enacting the FCPA. Beyond that argument, the parties do not quibble over the phrasing of these definitions, and they agree an instrumentality must perform a government function at the government's behest. The parties also agree, however, and we have noted in other cases interpreting similar provisions, that the dictionary definitions get us only part of the way there. Thus, we turn to other tools to decide what "instrumentality" means in the FCPA.

To interpret "instrumentality" as used in the Americans with Disabilities Act, we relied upon what the Supreme Court has called the "commonsense cannon of noscitur a sociis," —that is, "'a word is known by the company it keeps.' In the FCPA, the company "instrumentality" keeps is "agency" and "department," entities through which the government performs its functions and that are controlled by the government. We therefore glean from that context that an entity must be under the control or dominion of the government to qualify as an "instrumentality" within the FCPA's meaning. And we can also surmise from the other words in the series along with "instrumentality" that an instrumentality must be doing the business of the government. What the defendants and the government disagree about, however, is what functions count as the government's business.

To answer that question, we examine the broader statutory context in which the word is used. In this respect, we find one other provision of the FCPA and Congress's relatively recent amendment of the statute particularly illustrative. First, the so-called "grease payment" provision establishes an "exception" to FCPA liability for "any facilitating or expediting payment to a foreign official . . . the purpose of which is to expedite or to secure the performance of a routine governmental action by a foreign official." 15 U.S.C. §78dd-2(b). "Routine governmental action" is defined as "an action . . . ordinarily and commonly performed by a foreign official in," among other things, "providing phone service." Id. §78dd-2(h)(4)(A). If an entity involved in providing phone service could never be a foreign official so as to fall under the FCPA's substantive prohibition, there would be no need to provide an express exclusion for payments to such an entity. In other words, if we read "instrumentality," as the defendants urge, to categorically exclude government-controlled entities that provide telephone service, like Teleco, then we would render meaningless a portion of the definition of "routine governmental action" in section 78dd-2(b). "It is a cardinal rule of statutory construction that significance and effect shall, if possible, be accorded to every word." Thus, that a government-controlled entity provides a commercial service does not automatically mean it is not an instrumentality. In fact, the statute expressly contemplates that in some instances it would.

Next, we turn to Congress's 1998 amendment of the FCPA, enacted to ensure the United States was in compliance with its treaty obligations [under the bribery convention of the Organization for Economic Coordination and Development, which defines a "public function" as "any activity in the public interest, delegated by a foreign country." Based upon this reading, we decline] to limit the term only to entities that perform traditional, core government functions. Nothing in the statute imposes this limitation. And were we to limit "instrumentality" in the FCPA in that way, we would put the United States out of compliance with its international obligations.

The Supreme Court has cautioned that "the concept of a 'usual' or a 'proper' governmental function changes over time and varies from nation to nation." That principle guides our construction of the term "instrumentality." Specifically, to decide in a given case whether a foreign entity to which a domestic concern makes a payment is an instrumentality of that foreign government, we ought to look to whether that foreign government considers the entity to be performing a governmental function. And the most objective way to make that decision is to examine the foreign sovereign's actions, namely, whether it treats the function the foreign entity performs as its own. Presumably, governments that mutually agree to quell bribes flowing between nations intend to prevent distortion of the business they conduct on behalf of their people. We ought to respect a foreign sovereign's definition of what that business is. Thus, for the United States government to hold up its end of the bargain under the OECD Convention, we ought to follow the lead of the foreign government itself in terms of which functions it treats as its own.

Although we believe Teleco would qualify as a Haitian instrumentality under almost any definition we could craft, we are mindful of the needs of both corporations and the government for ex ante direction about what an instrumentality is. With this guidance, we define instrumentality as follows. An "instrumentality" under section 78dd-2(h)(2)(A) of the FCPA is an entity controlled by the government of a foreign country that performs a function the controlling government treats as its own. Certainly, what constitutes control and what constitutes a function the government treats as its own are fact-bound questions. It would be unwise and likely impossible to exhaustively answer them in the abstract. Because we only have this case before us, we do not purport to list all of the factors that might prove relevant to deciding whether an entity is an instrumentality of a foreign government. For today, we provide a list of some factors that may be relevant to deciding the issue.

To decide if the government "controls" an entity, courts and juries should look to the foreign government's formal designation of that entity; whether the government has a majority interest in the entity; the government's ability to hire and fire the entity's principals; the extent to which the entity's profits, if any, go directly into the governmental fisc, and, by the same token, the extent to which the government funds the entity if it fails to break even; and the length of time these indicia have existed. We do not cut these factors from whole cloth. Rather, they are informed by the commentary to the OECD Convention the United States ratified. They are also consistent with the approach the Supreme Court has taken to decide if an entity is an agent or instrumentality of the government in analogous contexts.

We then turn to the second element relevant to deciding if an entity is an instrumentality of a foreign government under the FCPA—deciding if the entity performs a function the government treats as its own. Courts and juries should examine whether the entity has a monopoly over the function it exists to carry out; whether the government subsidizes the costs associated with the entity providing services; whether the entity provides services to the public at large in the foreign country; and whether the public and the government of that foreign country generally perceive the entity to be performing a governmental function. Just as with the factors indicating control, we draw these in part from the OECD Convention. And we draw them from Supreme Court cases discussing what entities properly can be considered carrying out governmental functions.

Questions and Comments

1. This important decision offers a two-step analysis for whether an entity is a "foreign instrumentality." What are the steps, and what purposes do they serve?

2. How much guidance does this opinion provide for parties, enforcement agencies, and courts? The lists of factors to be considered in applying each of the steps in the analysis are extensive and inherently fact-specific. Much would appear to depend on the particular facts of the institution as well as the political and legal framework within which it operates. On the other hand, how could the court have provided greater clarity?

3. Given the inherent uncertainty in the analysis, perhaps a company faced with a FCPA problem should simply presume that the foreign party receiving the payment is covered by the statute. After all, bribery of any sort would appear to be problematic, even when the recipient is not associated with the government. Or is there a difference in policy when the bribe is paid to a private party?

4. This case involves telecoms, a field of commerce in which governments are often involved. What if the entity in question was in a more traditional commercial field — say, exporting wheat? How would the court's analysis play out then?

5. The court in the excerpted case relied heavily on the OECD bribery convention, a treaty that the United States ratified after the enactment of the original FCPA, which included the term "instrumentality." How much weight (if any) should a U.S. court give to a subsequently ratified foreign treaty, even if on the subject matter, when interpreting a U.S. statute?

6. The court also relied on the official commentary to the OECD treaty. Is mere commentary, even if "official," an appropriate source of interpretation?

3. Consultants and Business Partners

A particular concern in FCPA compliance is the use of local agents to develop business. As a practical matter, a company wishing to enter a foreign market often has little choice but to employ locals who are familiar with the language, customs, laws, and government of the country in question. But these agents may not always scrupulously observe U.S. rules on foreign corrupt practices. If the country itself has a culture of corruption, someone who is familiar with the culture, and who is capable of making the necessary introductions and arrangements, may not herself display the most ethical business practices.

It is difficult for U.S. firms to know whether their agents or intermediaries are greasing the palms of foreign officials in order to facilitate sales. Worse yet, some U.S. companies might chose to "wink" at the activities of foreign representatives; they know or suspect that their agents are giving bribes, but close their eyes to the conduct because the bribes generate lucrative contracts. Typically, companies claim they thought they were paying for legitimate consulting services, and they are are "shocked, shocked" to learn that money or favors have passed under the table. The following case illustrates the SEC's approach to the use of consultants:

Securities and Exchange Commission
In the Matter of Alcoa, Inc.

File No. 3-15673

Jan. 9, 2014

These proceedings arise from violations of the Foreign Corrupt Practices Act of 1977 (the "FCPA") by Respondent Alcoa Inc. ("Alcoa") concerning alumina sales to Aluminium Bahrain B.S.C. ("Alba"), an aluminum manufacturer owned primarily by the Kingdom of Bahrain.

Between 1989 and 2009, Alcoa of Australia ("AofA") and Alcoa World Alumina LLC ("AWA") (collectively, the "AWAC Subsidiaries") retained a consultant to act as their middleman in connection with sales of alumina to Alba and knew or consciously disregarded the fact that the relationship with the consultant was designed to generate funds that facilitated corrupt payments to Bahraini officials. The consultant was paid a commission on sales where he acted as an agent and received a markup on sales where he acted as a purported distributor. On sales where the consultant acted as a purported distributor, no legitimate services were provided to justify the role of the consultant as a distributor. The consultant used these funds to enrich himself and pay bribes to senior government officials of Bahrain.

The commission payments to the consultant and the alumina sales to the consultant made pursuant to the distribution agreements were improperly recorded in Alcoa's books and records as legitimate commissions or sales to a distributor and did not accurately reflect the transactions. The false entries were initially recorded by the AWAC Subsidiaries which were then consolidated into Alcoa's books and records. During the relevant period, Alcoa also lacked sufficient internal controls to prevent and detect the improper payments. . . .

Consultant A is an international middleman who resides in London and is a citizen of Canada, Jordan, and the United Kingdom. Consultant A had close contacts with certain members of Bahrain's Royal Family, some of whom were senior officials in the Government of Bahrain. Consultant A met with Alcoa executives to discuss matters relating to the relationship with Alba. Consultant A operates through many shell companies. . . .

Aluminium Bahrain B.S.C. ("Alba") is an aluminum smelter operating in Bahrain. At the relevant times, the state holding company of the Kingdom of Bahrain, the Mumtalakat, which was controlled by the Bahrain Ministry of Finance, held 77 percent of the shares of Alba. The Saudi Basic Industries Corporation ("SABIC"), which is majority-owned and controlled by the government of the Kingdom of Saudi Arabia, held a twenty percent minority stake in Alba, and three percent of Alba's shares were held by a German investment group. The majority of profits earned by Alba belonged to the Mumtalakat, though part of the profit was permitted to be used by Alba for its operations. The Bahrain Ministry of Finance had to approve any change in Alba's capital structure and had to be consulted on any major capital projects or contracts material to Alba's operations. Members of the Royal Family of Bahrain and representatives of the government sat on the Board of Directors of

Alba, controlled its Board, and had primary authority in selecting its chief executive officer and chief financial officer.

Alcoa's global bauxite and alumina refining business (the "Alumina Segment") is part of the Global Primary Products group, one of Alcoa's three business lines. The Alumina Segment operationally consists of multiple subsidiaries. During the relevant time period, the Alumina Segment reported to the global head of the Global Primary Products group, who was an executive of Alcoa and reported directly to Alcoa's CEO.

Alcoa exercised control over the Alumina Segment, including the AWAC Subsidiaries. Alcoa appointed the majority of seats on the AWAC Strategic Council, and the head of Global Primary Products served as its chair. Alcoa and AofA transferred personnel between them, including alumina sales staff; Alcoa set the business and financial goals for AWAC and coordinated the legal, audit, and compliance functions of AWAC; and the AWAC Subsidiaries' employees managing the Alba alumina business reported functionally to the global head of the Alumina Segment.

Alba was a significant alumina customer for Alcoa's Alumina Segment and during the relevant period, members of Alcoa senior management met both with Alba officials and Consultant A to discuss matters related to the Alba relationship, including a proposed joint venture between Alcoa and Alba. During this time, Alcoa was aware that Consultant A was an agent and distributor with respect to AofA's sales of alumina to Alba and that terms of related contracts were reviewed and approved by senior managers of Alcoa's Alumina Segment in the United States.

From at least 1989 to 2009, AofA supplied alumina to Alba through a series of multi-year contracts. During this period, Alba was one of Alcoa's largest alumina customers purchasing a total of nearly 19 million metric tons beginning with an annual volume of 300,000 metric tons increasing to 1.6 million metric tons.

Beginning in approximately 1989, AofA retained Consultant A to assist in long-term contract negotiations with Alba and Bahraini government officials, including the negotiation and execution of a new long-term alumina supply agreement in 1990 (the "1990 Supply agreement").

By 1996, Consultant A was playing a significant role in the relationship between the AWAC Subsidiaries and Alba. Around this time, Alba complained to the AWAC Subsidiaries that it was paying an above-market price for alumina. AofA learned that Alba was seeking to increase its alumina supply requirements from 600,000 metric tons a year up to 970,000 metric tons a year, and that other major global suppliers of alumina were seeking to capture these additional requirements. The AWAC Subsidiaries' sales team decided that, to "comply with business norms in the Middle East[,]" the AWAC Subsidiaries would propose supplying some of Alba's alumina through Alumet, which was one of Consultant A's shell companies, which would pay the "required commission." An AofA manager proposed using Consultant A as the intermediary because Consultant A was "well versed in the normal ways of Middle East business" and "will keep the various stakeholders in the Alba smelter happy. . . ."

Despite the red flags inherent in this arrangement, AofA's in-house counsel approved the arrangement without conducting any due diligence or otherwise determining whether there was a legitimate business purpose for the use of a third party intermediary.

The AWAC Subsidiaries' sales managers traveled to London in August 1996 to meet with Consultant A to discuss this proposal to route some of AofA's alumina through Consultant A's company for resale to Alba. Upon their return to Australia, an AWA manager told other members of the AWAC Subsidiaries sales team that: "It feels like we subsidize the Sheiks and end up with a 5 year outcome that is about $10-15/t lower than the average of the rest of our business."

In September 1996, the AWAC Subsidiaries' sales managers traveled to London to meet with Alba and Consultant A and agreed to an addendum to the 1990 Supply Agreement ("1996 Addendum"). Under the 1990 Agreement, AofA was supplying 600,000 metric tons per year to Alba under a formula pricing structure (as opposed to a "market"-based price). Under the 1996 Addendum, AofA agreed to supply Alba with an additional 285,000 metric tons per year through one of Consultant A's shell companies using a "market"-based price that resulted in pricing that was, at times, actually below market and allowed Consultant A to mark up his sales of alumina to Alba.

Employees at AWA and AofA either knew or were willfully blind to the high probability that Consultant A would use his commissions and markup to pay bribes. For example, in an internal document memorializing the negotiations surrounding the 1996 Addendum, a member of AofA's alumina sales staff wrote: "The methodology of business in the Middle East is a complex web of interactions that are necessarily difficult to understand to disguise the payment of commissions. We have in the past maintained a position of paying our agent a 1% commission on the basis of the agent work that he has done for us. We have also, however, been asked by Alba to supply some cargoes through other intermediaries, including our agent, on various occasions and we can only assume at the purpose this serves. . . ."

In 2001, with the coming expiration of the 1990 Supply Agreement and 1996 Addendum, AWA approached Alba to extend and expand the alumina supply relationship. Alba agreed to extend the existing supply relationship ("2001 Extension"). Following the 2001 Extension, AofA stopped selling alumina directly to Alba; all AofA alumina destined for Alba was instead routed through AAAC, which was one of Consultant A's shell companies.

In 2004, AofA entered into another distribution agreement with Consultant A that involved the sale of up to 1.6 million metric tons of alumina to Alba every year through AAAC, which was a shell company of Consultant A. This arrangement lasted until approximately December 31, 2009.

The 2001 Extension and 2004 purported distributorship agreements facilitated the corrupt payments by allowing Consultant A to impose an inflated markup on his purported sales of alumina to Alba and used the markup from those sales to enrich himself and pay bribes to senior government officials of Bahrain. . . .

By the summer of 2004, AofA was supplying approximately one million metric tons of alumina annually to Alba, but Consultant A's companies were invoicing Alba for the shipments. Unlike a true distributorship, Consultant A's companies never took possession of the alumina, assisted with the shipping arrangements, or otherwise performed any legitimate services for either the AWAC Subsidiaries or Alba. The only function the shell companies provided was to invoice Alba for the shipments at a significant markup.

Alba's obligations under pre-existing supply arrangements with AofA were set to expire at the end of 2004. In the summer of 2004, AWA sought to secure a new long term alumina supply agreement with Alba. On or around August 5, 2004, Alcoa management was advised by a former senior Alcoa executive who had a relationship with Consultant A that if they attempted to negotiate a direct contractual relationship between AofA and Alba, rather than negotiate a supply arrangement through

Consultant A and one of his companies, some or all of Alba's business could be lost
to another alumina supplier. . . .

On or around September 29, 2004, AWA facilitated Consultant A's tendering a
bid to supply Alba up to 1.6 million metric tons of alumina for ten years commencing in 2005. On or about October 8, 2004, the in-house attorney responsible for
supporting the alumina business suggested terminating the consulting agreement
that Alcoa had entered with Consultant A in connection with the proposed joint
venture, as "the terms of [Consultant A's] current engagement created a lot of
anxiety in the organization." However, an AWA executive decided that the consul-
tancy agreement should not be terminated until AofA had secured a new long-term
alumina supply agreement with Alba. . . .

For sales of alumina to Alba, Consultant A did not receive payment until after
Consultant A was bound to pay AofA. Given the discrepancy in the timing of payment, Consultant A sought a line of credit from Alcoa to cover the cost of alumina
shipments to Alba until Alba remitted payment to Consultant A. Alcoa's policies and
procedures required its customers to submit financial statements for an extension of
credit. Consultant A, however, refused to provide financial statements to Alcoa's
credit department. Nevertheless, in or around December 2004, senior management
of AWA invoked an override procedure that resulted in an Alcoa executive approving a $23 million line of credit to Consultant A's companies.

Thereafter, in each of contract years 2005 through 2009, Alcoa continued to
grant overrides to extend increasing credit lines to Consultant A's purported dis-
tributorships. By 2007, Alcoa was extending a credit line of $58 million. During this
period, Alcoa granted Consultant A credit lines that were significantly greater than
those granted by Alcoa to any other third party. By facilitating the extension of credit
to Consultant A, AWA enabled the purported distributorship scheme by allowing
Consultant A to defer paying AofA for the multi-million dollar shipments of alumina
to Alba until Consultant A received payment from Alba.

From 2005 through 2009, AWA caused Consultant A to receive in excess of $188
million on the markup of alumina sales to Alba. This money was transferred from
the initial accounts in which payment from Alba was received through various bank
accounts controlled by Consultant A, including accounts in the name of shell
companies.

The AWAC Subsidiaries knew or consciously disregarded the fact that Consultant
A was inserted into the Alba sales supply chain to generate funds to pay bribes to
Bahraini officials. Ultimately, these funds facilitated at least $110 million in corrupt
payments to Bahraini officials. The vast majority of those funds were generated from
the markup between the price Consultant A sold to Alba and the price that
AofA sold to Consultant A. Those funds were also generated from the commissions
that AofA paid to Consultant A.

The recipients of the corrupt payments included a senior Bahraini official, members of the board of directors of Alba, and senior management of Alba. Examples of
the corrupt payments include:

- In August 2003, Consultant A's shell companies made 2 payments totaling $7
  million to accounts for the benefit of a Bahraini government official who
  Consultant A had been retained to lobby. Two weeks later, Alcoa and Alba
  signed an agreement in principle to have Alcoa participate in Alba's plant
  expansion.

- In October 2004, Consultant A's shell company paid $1 million to an account for the benefit of that same government official. Shortly thereafter, Alba agreed in principle to Alcoa's offer for the 2005 Alba Supply Agreement.
- In or around the time of the execution of the final 2005 Alba Supply Agreement, Consultant A-controlled companies paid another Bahraini government official and/or his beneficiaries $41 million in three payments. . . .

This Order contains no findings that an officer, director or employee of Alcoa knowingly engaged in the bribe scheme. As described above, Alcoa violated Section 30A of the Exchange Act by reason of its agents, including subsidiaries AWA and AofA, indirectly paying bribes to foreign officials in Bahrain in order to obtain or retain business. AWA, AofA, and their employees all acted as "agents" of Alcoa during the relevant time, and were acting within the scope of their authority when participating in the bribe scheme. . . .

It is hereby ordered that Respondent shall pay disgorgement of $175,000,000.

Questions and Comments

1. This order concerns the FCPA liability of Alcoa, the parent corporation. In a related matter, an Alcoa subsidiary pled guilty to criminal charges brought by the Department of Justice and agreed to pay $223 million in fines and penalties. After deducting $14 million in credits for tax payments in the DOJ proceeding, the total cost of the settlement to Alcoa entities was $384 million. And this was not all: Previously, in 2012, Alcoa paid $85 million to settle a civil RICO lawsuit brought against it by Alba arising out of the same transactions.

2. Can you see how Alcoa's arrangement with Consultant A facilitated the payment of bribes?

3. Given that no officer of Alcoa knowingly engaged in a bribery scheme, how does the SEC justify imposing a $175 million fine?

4. What were the "red flags" that, in the view of the SEC, should have alerted Alcoa that Consultant A was bribing Bahraini officials?

5. Why didn't the SEC name the consultant who paid or the officials who accepted the bribes?

6. News reports identified the consultant as Victor Dahdaleh, a businessman with connections in Canada, Jordan, and Great Britain; the senior Bahraini official was Sheikh Isa Bin Ali al Khalifa, a member of the Bahraini royal family. The U.K. Serious Fraud Office charged Dahdeleh with paying $63 million in bribes to al Khalifa and former Alba CEO Bruce Hall, but the case was dismissed in 2013 for lack of evidence.

7. If you were in charge of compliance at Alcoa, what procedures would you implement to prevent this sort of problem from occurring again?

8. The government noted that it had exercised a certain amount of leniency in the penalties it demanded because Alcoa had cooperated fully with the government's investigation. Was leniency warranted, given that red flags of improper payments had been waving for many years and the company had failed to act?

9. The government allowed Alcoa to pay the penalties over a period of years, apparently due to concerns that the company would not survive financially if it were required to pay everything at once. Is it appropriate for the government to allow deferred payments when a violator is in financial distress? What factors should be

taken into consideration when determining whether and how long an extension should be granted?

10. In 2013, a scandal erupted about marketing activities in China conducted by GlaxoSmithKline, a big U.K. drug company. Chinese officials alleged that GSK used a network of travel agents to distribute as much as $489 million to doctors and purchasing agents in order to facilitate the sales of its products there. In some cases, according to press accounts, representatives of GSK went so far as to gratify physicians' "sexual desires" in order to induce them to prescribe GSK medications.

4. Successor Liability

What happens when a company or a division of a company is acquired by another firm, and later it turns out that before the acquisition, the former company or division engaged in violations of the FCPA? Does the acquiring firm assume the liabilities associated with the violations?

DOJ Opinion Procedure Release No. 14-02

Nov. 7, 2014

. . . Requestor intends to acquire 100% of the Target Company's shares beginning in 2015. The Target Company's shares are currently held almost exclusively by another foreign corporation ("Seller"), which is listed on the stock exchange of Foreign Country. Seller is a prominent consumer products manufacturer and distributor in Foreign Country, with more than 5,000 full-time employees and annual gross sales in excess of $100 million. The Target Company represents part of Seller's consumer products business in Foreign Country and sells its products through several related brands.

Seller and the Target Company largely confine their operations to Foreign Country, have never been issuers of securities in the United States, and have had negligible business contacts, including no direct sale or distribution of their products, in the United States.

In preparing for the acquisition, Requestor undertook due diligence aimed at identifying, among other things, potential legal and compliance concerns at the Target Company. Requestor retained an experienced forensic accounting firm ("the Accounting Firm") to carry out the due diligence review. This review brought to light evidence of apparent improper payments, as well as substantial accounting weaknesses and poor recordkeeping. On the basis of a risk profile analysis of the Target Company, the Accounting Firm reviewed approximately 1,300 transactions with a total value of approximately $12.9 million. The Accounting Firm identified over $100,000 in transactions that raised compliance issues. The vast majority of these transactions involved payments to government officials related to obtaining permits and licenses. Other transactions involved gifts and cash donations to government officials, charitable contributions and sponsorships, and payments to members of the state-controlled media to minimize negative publicity. None of the payments, gifts, donations, contributions, or sponsorships occurred in the United States and none was made by or through a U.S. person or issuer.

The due diligence showed that the Target Company has significant recordkeeping deficiencies. The vast majority of the cash payments and gifts to government officials and the charitable contributions were not supported by documentary records. Expenses were improperly and inaccurately classified in the Target Company's books. In fact, the Target Company's accounting records were so disorganized that the Accounting Firm was unable to physically locate or identify many of the underlying records for the tested transactions. Finally, the Target Company has not developed or implemented a written code of conduct or other compliance policies and procedures, nor have the Target Company's employees, according to the Accounting Firm, shown adequate understanding or awareness of anti-bribery laws and regulations.

In light of the Target Company's glaring compliance, accounting, and record-keeping deficiencies, Requestor has taken several pre-closing steps to begin to remediate the Target Company's weaknesses prior to the planned closing in 2015. Requestor anticipates completing the full integration of the Target Company into Requestor's compliance and reporting structure within one year of the closing. Requestor has set forth an integration schedule of the Target Company that encompasses risk mitigation, dissemination and training with regard to compliance procedures and policies, standardization of business relationships with third parties, and formalization of the Target Company's accounting and recordkeeping in accordance with Requestor's policies and applicable law.

Based upon all of the facts and circumstances, as represented by Requestor, the Department does not presently intend to take any enforcement action with respect to pre-acquisition bribery Seller or the Target Company may have committed. It is a basic principle of corporate law that a company assumes certain liabilities when merging with or acquiring another company. In a situation such as this, where a purchaser acquires the stock of a seller and integrates the target into its operations, successor liability may be conferred upon the purchaser for the acquired entity's pre-existing criminal and civil liabilities, including, for example, for FCPA violations of the target. "Successor liability does not, however, create liability where none existed before. For example, if an issuer were to acquire a foreign company that was not previously subject to the FCPA's jurisdiction, the mere acquisition of that foreign company would not retroactively create FCPA liability for the acquiring issuer."

This principle . . . squarely addresses the situation at hand. Assuming the accuracy of Requestor's representations, none of the potentially improper pre-acquisition payments by Seller or the Target Company was subject to the jurisdiction of the United States. For example, none of the payments occurred in the United States, and Requestor has not identified participation by any U.S. person or issuer in the payments. Requestor also represents that, based on its due diligence, no contracts or other assets were determined to have been acquired through bribery that would remain in operation and from which Requestor would derive financial benefit following the acquisition.

The Department would thus lack jurisdiction under the FCPA to prosecute Requestor (or for that matter, Seller or the Target Company) for improper payments made by Seller or the Target Company prior to the acquisition. The Department expresses no view as to the adequacy or reasonableness of Requestor's integration of the Target Company.

The circumstances of each corporate merger or acquisition are unique and require specifically tailored due diligence and integration processes. Hence, the exact timeline and appropriateness of particular aspects of Requestor's integration of the Target Company are not necessarily suitable to other situations. To be sure, the Department encourages companies engaging in mergers and acquisitions to (1) conduct thorough risk-based FCPA and anti-corruption due diligence; (2) implement the acquiring company's code of conduct and anti-corruption policies as quickly as practicable; (3) conduct FCPA and other relevant training for the acquired entity's directors and employees, as well as third-party agents and partners; (4) conduct an FCPA-specific audit of the acquired entity.

Questions and Comments

1. It is clear that successor liability can occur in the FCPA context, and that the consequences can be large. But when successor liability applies is not well defined. Does it matter, for example, if only a division of a company is acquired, rather than an entire firm? Does the nature of the acquisition make a difference—stock for stock, all-cash, or some other form? Should a sale of all the assets be distinguished from a merger? What about the diligence that the acquiring firm displays in vetting possible FCPA violations before completing the acquisition?

2. Would the Department have displayed as charitable attitude if the requesting party had displayed less diligence or been less forthright in dealing with the problem?

3. What about the FCPA liability of a parent corporation for the actions of a subsidiary company? It may be difficult to charge the parent under the anti-bribery provisions if no one at the parent knew of the misconduct at the subsidiary. But the parent may still face exposure under the books and records provisions. In the Matter of Bruker Corporation, SEC Securities Act Release No. 73835 (Dec. 15, 2014), involved an American corporation with Chinese subsidiaries. Apparently unbeknownst to the parent, employees of the subsidiaries paid substantial bribes to Chinese officials. In the ensuing administrative proceeding, the SEC did not charge the parent under the anti-bribery provisions. But it did charge violations of the books and records and internal controls rules. The reason: The payments to the Chinese government officials were recorded as legitimate business and marketing expenses in the Bruker China Offices' books and records, when in fact they were improper payments designed to personally benefit the officials. The Bruker China Offices' books and records were consolidated into Bruker's (the parent's) books and records, thereby causing Bruker's books and records to be inaccurate. Bruker failed to devise and maintain an adequate system of internal accounting controls sufficient to prevent and detect the improper payments.

4. For discussion of some of these issues, see Daniel J. Grimm, *The Foreign Corrupt Practices Act in Merger and Acquisition Transactions: Successor Liability and Its Consequences*, 7 N.Y.U. J.L. & Bus. 247 (2010); Daniel J. Grimm & Taylor J. Phillips, *The Federal Common Law of Successor Liability and the Foreign Corrupt Practices Act*, 6 Wm. & Mary Bus. L. Rev. 89 (2015).

5. Problems

To test your intuitions about the scope and meaning of the FCPA, consider whether the conduct described in the following problems violates the statute. What compliance measures should the involved companies institute to ensure that violations, if any, do not occur, and what measures should they take once any violations have come to light?

PROBLEM 13-1

Armco, a U.S. manufacturer of armor for automobiles, participates in a trade show in a foreign country. It operates a booth at which it gives away pens, teeshirts, and other promotional items displaying the Armco logo; it also serves free beverages and snacks. Given the nature of its product, many of the visitors to the booth are foreign officials, and Armco knows this fact. In itself, does this conduct violate the FCPA? What if as the day is ending, a foreign official approaches the Armco representative, explains that he has lost his wallet, and requests the equivalent of $100 for cab fare to the airport? What if, instead, the Armco representative takes a group of foreign officials out to an expensive restaurant for dinner at a cost of $100 per person? Do any of these behaviors violate the FCPA?

PROBLEM 13-2

Flowerland, an American producer of orchids and bromeliads, operates a factory in China that produces ceramic pots in which its products are shipped. Recognizing the value of maintaining good relationships with the residents of the town, Flowerland donates several thousand dollars to a local children's hospital each year, and is proud to have a wing of the facility named in its honor. Does the donation violate the FCPA? What if the director of the hospital is the wife of a local official who has the power to inspect — and potentially shut down — the factory for unsafe working conditions? What if that official had been the one to suggest the donation?

PROBLEM 13-3

Engineering Solutions is competing for a contract to supply baggage-handling systems to a new airport being built in a developing nation. While the tender for bids is underway, the company flies the official charged with awarding the contract to the United States for a tour of some of the company's systems installed at U.S. airports. The official flies business class and, while in the United States, is chauffeured by an executive limousine company. The company pays for all the official's food and lodging expenses. Because the official is in the United States for a full week, the company pays for a $1,000/night suite at a Las Vegas casino over the weekend, justified by the fact that the Las Vegas airport uses the company's system. Among other items from that weekend, the company pays a $2,000 tab that the official submits for dinner and drinks at Samantha's Ranch Brothel, a legal house of prostitution located near Las Vegas. Has Engineering Solutions violated the FCPA?

PROBLEM 13-4

Jockeycraft, an Irish company, manufactures sulkies — carts used in harness racing. Because the design is unconventional — the cart has a single shaft extending over the horse's back instead of one on each side — the item needs approval from racing commissions of every track where it is used. The racing commission of Plattemata, a Latin American country, is comprised of five officials, three appointed by the president of the country and two by a confederation of private race tracks. The commission is authorized under law to establish regulations for competition and safety conditions at all racetracks in the country. The commission's members are not paid for their services and continue to work in their day jobs. One day Ricardo Richards, the head of Plattemata's racing commission, reaches Brendan Boyle, Jockeycraft's CEO, on Boyle's cellphone while Boyle is making an international connection at JFK Airport on a trip from Dublin to Mexico City. Richards lets it be known that the sulky will not receive approval in Plattemata unless Jockeycraft contributes to a charitable foundation that Richards has established for retired jockeys. Boyle tells the official that he will "see what we can do." When he arrives in Mexico City, Boyle arranges for a wire transfer in the amount of $50,000 from Jockeycraft's account at an Irish subsidiary of JPMorgan Chase bank, payable to Ricardo Richards' personal bank account in Plattemata. The transfer carries the notation "charitable contribution." Has Jockeycraft violated the FCPA?

PROBLEM 13-5

Jenny Jones is a U.S. lawyer with the 400-lawyer firm Bigger & Best. Jones represents the government of the Republic of Sparta, a foreign country, in connection with foreign arbitrations, earning approximately $2 million per year in fees for her firm. Over the course of her work for this client, Jones has become friendly with a senior attorney in Sparta's attorney general's office. This attorney's daughter suffers from a serious illness that cannot be treated in Sparta. To have a chance at a cure, the daughter will have to travel to Switzerland for treatment at a specialized clinic at a cost of $20,000. Knowing that the official doesn't have the means to pay for the treatment, Jones wishes to pick up the tab. Her only goal is the wish to help a friend, and she will pay for the treatment entirely out of her personal funds. Both the government of Sparta and the leadership of Bigger & Best have expressly indicated that they have no objection to the proposed payment of medical expenses. Additionally, Jones has provided a certified letter from the Attorney General of Sparta, representing that Jones' payment will have no impact on any future decisions about hiring outside counsel and that payment of these expenses would not violate any of the laws of Sparta. May Jones make this payment without running afoul of the FCPA?

PROBLEM 13-6

Smith Industries, a U.S. company, is involved in a long-term contract with a foreign counterparty. An investigation in the counterparty's home country reveals that the counterparty may have engaged in systematic bribery of officials there. As yet, the investigation has not been concluded, and Smith Industries has not been able to verify whether or not the allegations are true. Smith Industries worries that it will face potential FCPA liability if it continues to perform its obligations under the contract. On the other hand, ceasing to perform its obligations will expose it to potential liability for breach of contract. Is there a way out of this dilemma? Would it matter if the contract contained a "force majeure" clause, under which either party can suspend performance after the occurrence of an extraordinary event or circumstance that prevents the party from performing?

B. ELEMENTS OF EFFECTIVE FCPA COMPLIANCE

1. FCPA Compliance Programs

Suppose you were appointed as chief compliance officer for a company that is just entering foreign markets. Given what you know of the FCPA, how would you structure a compliance program? To make things more concrete, consider the following scenario:

PROBLEM 13-7

Drilltech, Inc., is a manufacturer of specialty drill bits. It is publicly traded on the NASDAQ. In the past it has limited its market to the United States and Canada, but recently it has decided to enter markets in China, India, Australia, Singapore, Brazil, Kazakhstan, Uzbekistan, Mexico, Indonesia, and several countries in Africa. Because Drilltech has no established distribution network in these countries, it plans to hire a few salespeople for each country and then to allow these people to retain consultants from the local markets to make introductions and negotiate contracts. Most of the employees Drilltech plans to send abroad are Americans without extensive international experience. The company hopes to sell its drills to governments, government-sponsored entities, and government-owned oil and gas companies doing business in the target countries. Contracts for sale will be subject to negotiation and could be denominated in the local currency. In several of the countries where the company plans to do business, small bribes are necessary if one is to do business at all — for example, to get a permit to operate a motor vehicle. Several countries, moreover, have a tradition of gift-giving in which business relationships are sealed by the exchange of favors, such as bottles of Scotch. In some of these markets, senior government officials regularly demand bribes or other favors (such as hiring their children) for the placement of any government contract. If you were designing Drilltech's compliance program, what elements would you include and what steps, if any, would you demand of senior management in fulfillment of this task?

Guidance on effective FCPA compliance can be found in the text of the FCPA, in SEC/DOJ guidance, and in decisions the government has taken in enforcement actions. The FCPA requires that the company

devise and maintain a system of internal accounting controls sufficient to provide reasonable assurances that—

(i) transactions are executed in accordance with management's general or specific authorization;

(ii) transactions are recorded as necessary (I) to permit preparation of financial statements in conformity with generally accepted accounting principles or any other criteria applicable to such statements, and (II) to maintain accountability for assets;

(iii) access to assets is permitted only in accordance with management's general or specific authorization; and

(iv) the recorded accountability for assets is compared with the existing assets at reasonable intervals and appropriate action is taken with respect to any differences. . . .

Section 13(b)(2)(B) of the Exchange Act, 15 U.S.C. §78m(b)(2)(B).

Much depends on how these general requirements are interpreted and implemented. The Department of Justice and the Securities and Exchange Commission, which jointly enforce the FCPA, have the following advice to covered entities and their advisers:

U.S. Department of Justice and Securities and Exchange Commission, A Resource Guide to the U.S. Foreign Corrupt Practices Act

November 2012

HALLMARKS OF EFFECTIVE COMPLIANCE PROGRAMS

Individual companies may have different compliance needs depending on their size and the particular risks associated with their businesses, among other factors. When it comes to compliance, there is no one-size-fits-all program. Thus, the discussion below is meant to provide insight into the aspects of compliance programs that DOJ and SEC assess, recognizing that companies may consider a variety of factors when making their own determination of what is appropriate for their specific business needs. Indeed, small- and medium-size enterprises likely will have different compliance programs from large multi-national corporations, a fact DOJ and SEC take into account when evaluating companies' compliance programs.

Compliance programs that employ a "check-the-box" approach may be inefficient and, more importantly, ineffective. Because each compliance program should be tailored to an organization's specific needs, risks, and challenges, the information provided below should not be considered a substitute for a company's own assessment of the corporate compliance program most appropriate for that particular business organization. In the end, if designed carefully, implemented earnestly, and enforced fairly, a company's compliance program — no matter how large or small the organization — will allow the company generally to prevent violations, detect those that do occur, and remediate them promptly and appropriately.

COMMITMENT FROM SENIOR MANAGEMENT AND A CLEARLY ARTICULATED POLICY AGAINST CORRUPTION

Within a business organization, compliance begins with the board of directors and senior executives setting the proper tone for the rest of the company. Managers and employees take their cues from these corporate leaders. Thus, DOJ and SEC consider the commitment of corporate leaders to a "culture of compliance" and look to see if this high-level commitment is also reinforced and implemented by middle managers and employees at all levels of a business. A well-designed compliance program that is not enforced in good faith, such as when corporate management explicitly or implicitly encourages employees to engage in misconduct to achieve business objectives, will be ineffective. DOJ and SEC have often encountered companies with compliance programs that are strong on paper but that nevertheless have significant FCPA violations because management has failed to effectively implement the program even in the face of obvious signs of corruption. This may be the result of aggressive sales staff preventing compliance personnel from doing their jobs effectively and of senior management, more concerned with securing a valuable business opportunity than enforcing a culture of compliance, siding with the sales team. The higher the financial stakes of the transaction, the greater the temptation for management to choose profit over compliance. A strong ethical culture directly supports a strong compliance program. By adhering to ethical standards, senior managers will inspire middle managers to reinforce those standards. Compliant middle managers, in turn, will encourage employees to strive to attain those standards throughout the organizational structure. In short, compliance with the FCPA and ethical rules must start at the top. DOJ and SEC thus evaluate whether senior management has clearly articulated company standards, communicated them in unambiguous terms, adhered to them scrupulously, and disseminated them throughout the organization.

CODE OF CONDUCT AND COMPLIANCE POLICIES AND PROCEDURES

A company's code of conduct is often the foundation upon which an effective compliance program is built. As DOJ has repeatedly noted in its charging documents, the most effective codes are clear, concise, and accessible to all employees and to those conducting business on the company's behalf. Indeed, it would be difficult to effectively implement a compliance program if it was not available in the local language so that employees in foreign subsidiaries can access and understand it. When assessing a compliance program, DOJ and SEC will review whether the company has taken steps to make certain that the code of conduct remains current and effective and whether a company has periodically reviewed and updated its code.

Whether a company has policies and procedures that outline responsibilities for compliance within the company, detail proper internal controls, auditing practices, and documentation policies, and set forth disciplinary procedures will also be considered by DOJ and SEC. These types of policies and procedures will depend on the size and nature of the business and the risks associated with the business.

Effective policies and procedures require an in-depth understanding of the company's business model, including its products and services, third-party agents, customers, government interactions, and industry and geographic risks. Among the risks that a company may need to address include the nature and extent of transactions with foreign governments, including payments to foreign officials; use of third parties; gifts, travel, and entertainment expenses; charitable and political donations; and facilitating and expediting payments. For example, some companies with global operations have created web-based approval processes to review and approve routine gifts, travel, and entertainment involving foreign officials and private customers with clear monetary limits and annual limitations. Many of these systems have built-in flexibility so that senior management, or in-house legal counsel, can be apprised of and, in appropriate circumstances, approve unique requests. These types of systems can be a good way to conserve corporate resources while, if properly implemented, preventing and detecting potential FCPA violations. Regardless of the specific policies and procedures implemented, these standards should apply to personnel at all levels of the company.

OVERSIGHT, AUTONOMY, AND RESOURCES

In appraising a compliance program, DOJ and SEC also consider whether a company has assigned responsibility for the oversight and implementation of a company's compliance program to one or more specific senior executives within an organization. Those individuals must have appropriate authority within the organization, adequate autonomy from management, and sufficient resources to ensure that the company's compliance program is implemented effectively. Adequate autonomy generally includes direct access to an organization's governing authority, such as the board of directors and committees of the board of directors (e.g., the audit committee).

Depending on the size and structure of an organization, it may be appropriate for day-to-day operational responsibility to be delegated to other specific individuals within a company. DOJ and SEC recognize that the reporting structure will depend on the size and complexity of an organization. Moreover, the amount of resources devoted to compliance will depend on the company's size, complexity, industry, geographical reach, and risks associated with the business. In assessing whether a company has reasonable internal controls, DOJ and SEC typically consider whether the company devoted adequate staffing and resources to the compliance program given the size, structure, and risk profile of the business.

RISK ASSESSMENT

Assessment of risk is fundamental to developing a strong compliance program, and is another factor DOJ and SEC evaluate when assessing a company's compliance program. One-size-fits-all compliance programs are generally ill-conceived and ineffective because resources inevitably are spread too thin, with too much focus on low risk markets and transactions to the detriment of high-risk areas. Devoting a disproportionate amount of time policing modest entertainment and gift-giving instead of focusing on large government bids, questionable payments to third-party consultants, or excessive discounts to resellers and distributors may indicate that a company's compliance program is ineffective. A $50 million contract with a government agency in a high-risk country warrants greater scrutiny than modest and routine gifts and entertainment. Similarly, performing identical due diligence on all third party agents, irrespective of risk factors, is often counterproductive, diverting attention and resources away from those third parties that pose the most significant risks.

DOJ and SEC will give meaningful credit to a company that implements in good faith a comprehensive, risk-based compliance program, even if that program does not prevent an infraction in a low risk area because greater attention and resources had been devoted to a higher risk area. Conversely, a company that fails to prevent an FCPA violation on an economically significant, high-risk transaction because it failed to perform a level of due diligence commensurate with the size and risk of the transaction is likely to receive reduced credit based on the quality and effectiveness of its compliance program.

As a company's risk for FCPA violations increases, that business should consider increasing its compliance procedures, including due diligence and periodic internal audits. The degree of appropriate due diligence is fact-specific and should vary based on industry, country, size, and nature of the transaction, and the method and amount of third-party compensation. Factors to consider, for instance, include risks presented by: the country and industry sector, the business opportunity, potential business partners, level of involvement with governments, amount of government regulation and oversight, and exposure to customs and immigration in conducting business affairs. When assessing a company's compliance program, DOJ and SEC take into account whether and to what degree a company analyzes and addresses the particular risks it faces.

TRAINING AND CONTINUING ADVICE

Compliance policies cannot work unless effectively communicated throughout a company. Accordingly, DOJ and SEC will evaluate whether a company has taken steps to ensure that relevant policies and procedures have been communicated throughout the organization, including through periodic training and certification for all directors, officers, relevant employees, and, where appropriate, agents and business partners. For example, many larger companies have implemented a mix of web-based and in-person training conducted at varying intervals. Such training typically covers company policies and procedures, instruction on applicable laws, practical advice to address real-life scenarios, and case studies. Regardless of how a company chooses to conduct its training, however, the information should be presented in a manner appropriate for the targeted audience, including providing training and training materials in the local language. For example, companies may want to consider providing different types of training to their sales personnel and accounting personnel with hypotheticals or sample situations that are similar to the situations they might encounter. In addition to the existence and scope of a company's training program, a company should develop appropriate measures, depending on the size and sophistication of the particular company, to provide guidance and advice on complying with the company's ethics and compliance program, including when such advice is needed urgently. Such measures will help ensure that the compliance program is understood and followed appropriately at all levels of the company.

INCENTIVES AND DISCIPLINARY MEASURES

In addition to evaluating the design and implementation of a compliance program throughout an organization, enforcement of that program is fundamental to its effectiveness. A compliance program should apply from the board room to the supply room — no one should be beyond its reach. DOJ and SEC will thus consider whether, when enforcing a compliance program, a company has appropriate and clear disciplinary procedures, whether those procedures are applied reliably and promptly, and whether they are commensurate with the violation. Many companies have found that publicizing disciplinary actions internally, where appropriate under local law, can have an important deterrent effect, demonstrating that unethical and unlawful actions have swift and sure consequences.

DOJ and SEC recognize that positive incentives can also drive compliant behavior. These incentives can take many forms such as personnel evaluations and promotions, rewards for improving and developing a company's compliance program, and rewards for ethics and compliance leadership. Some organizations, for example, have made adherence to compliance a significant metric for management's bonuses so that compliance becomes an integral part of management's everyday concern. Beyond financial incentives, some companies have highlighted compliance within their organizations by recognizing compliance professionals and internal audit staff. Others have made working in the company's compliance organization a way to advance an employee's career.

SEC, for instance, has encouraged companies to embrace methods to incentivize ethical and lawful behavior:

> [M]ake integrity, ethics and compliance part of the promotion, compensation and evaluation processes as well. For at the end of the day, the most effective way to communicate that "doing the right thing" is a priority, is to reward it. Conversely, if employees are led to believe that, when it comes to compensation and career advancement, all that counts is short-term profitability, and that cutting ethical corners is an acceptable way of getting there, they'll perform to that measure. To cite an example from a different walk of life: a college football coach can be told that the graduation rates of his players are what matters, but he'll know differently if the sole focus of his contract extension talks or the decision to fire him is his win-loss record.

No matter what the disciplinary scheme or potential incentives a company decides to adopt, DOJ and SEC will consider whether they are fairly and consistently applied across the organization. No executive should be above compliance, no employee below compliance, and no person within an organization deemed too valuable to be disciplined, if warranted. Rewarding good behavior and sanctioning bad behavior reinforces a culture of compliance and ethics throughout an organization.

THIRD-PARTY DUE DILIGENCE AND PAYMENTS

DOJ's and SEC's FCPA enforcement actions demonstrate that third parties, including agents, consultants, and distributors, are commonly used to conceal the payment of bribes to foreign officials in international business transactions. Risk-based due diligence is particularly important with third parties and will also be considered by DOJ and SEC in assessing the effectiveness of a company's compliance program. Although the degree of appropriate due diligence may vary based on industry, country, size and nature of the transaction, and historical relationship with the third-party, some guiding principles always apply.

First, as part of risk-based due diligence, companies should understand the qualifications and associations of its third-party partners, including its business reputation, and relationship, if any, with foreign officials. The degree of scrutiny should increase as red flags surface.

Second, companies should have an understanding of the business rationale for including the third party in the transaction. Among other things, the company should understand the role of and need for the third party and ensure that the contract terms specifically describe the services to be performed. Additional considerations include payment terms and how those payment terms compare to typical terms in that industry and country, as well as the timing of the third party's introduction to the business. Moreover, companies may want to confirm and document that the third party is actually performing the work for which it is being paid and that its compensation is commensurate with the work being provided.

Third, companies should undertake some form of ongoing monitoring of third-party relationships. Where appropriate, this may include updating due diligence periodically, exercising audit rights, providing periodic training, and requesting annual compliance certifications by the third party. In addition to considering a company's due diligence on third parties, DOJ and SEC also assess whether the company has informed third parties of the company's compliance program and commitment to ethical and lawful business practices and, where appropriate, whether it has sought assurances from third parties, through certifications and otherwise, of reciprocal commitments. These can be meaningful ways to mitigate third-party risk.

CONFIDENTIAL REPORTING AND INTERNAL INVESTIGATION

An effective compliance program should include a mechanism for an organization's employees and others to report suspected or actual misconduct or violations of the company's policies on a confidential basis and without fear of retaliation. Companies may employ, for example, anonymous hotlines or ombudsmen. Moreover, once an allegation is made, companies should have in place an efficient, reliable, and properly funded process for investigating the allegation and documenting the company's response, including any disciplinary or remediation measures taken. Companies will want to consider taking "lessons learned" from any reported violations and the outcome of any resulting investigation to update their internal controls and compliance program and focus future training on such issues, as appropriate.

CONTINUOUS IMPROVEMENT: PERIODIC TESTING AND REVIEW

Finally, a good compliance program should constantly evolve. A company's business changes over time, as do the environments in which it operates, the nature of its customers, the laws that govern its actions, and the standards of its industry. In addition, compliance programs that do not just exist on paper but are followed in practice will inevitably uncover compliance weaknesses and require enhancements. Consequently, DOJ and SEC evaluate whether companies regularly review and improve their compliance programs and not allow them to become stale.

According to one survey, 64% of general counsel whose companies are subject to the FCPA say there is room for improvement in their FCPA training and compliance programs. An organization should take the time to review and test its controls, and it should think critically about its potential weaknesses and risk areas. For example, some companies have undertaken employee surveys to measure their compliance culture and strength of internal controls, identify best practices, and detect new risk areas. Other companies periodically test their internal controls with targeted audits to make certain that controls on paper are working in practice. DOJ and SEC will give meaningful credit to thoughtful efforts to create a sustainable compliance program if a problem is later discovered. Similarly, undertaking proactive evaluations before a problem strikes can lower the applicable penalty range under the U.S. Sentencing Guidelines. Although the nature and the frequency of proactive evaluations may vary depending on the size and complexity of an organization, the idea behind such efforts is the same: continuous improvement and sustainability.

MERGERS AND ACQUISITIONS: PRE-ACQUISITION DUE AND POST-ACQUISITION INTEGRATION

In the context of the FCPA, mergers and acquisitions present both risks and opportunities. A company that does not perform adequate FCPA due diligence prior to a merger or acquisition may face both legal and business risks. Perhaps most commonly, inadequate due diligence can allow a course of bribery to continue — with all the attendant harms to a business's profitability and reputation, as well as potential civil and criminal liability. In contrast, companies that conduct effective FCPA due diligence on their acquisition targets are able to evaluate more accurately each target's value and negotiate for the costs of the bribery to be borne by the target. In addition such actions demonstrate to DOJ and SEC a company's commitment to compliance and are taken into account when evaluating any potential enforcement action. For example, DOJ and SEC declined to take enforcement action against an acquiring issuer when the issuer, among other things, uncovered the corruption at the company being acquired as part of due diligence, ensured that the corruption was voluntarily disclosed to the government, cooperated with the investigation, and incorporated the acquired company into its compliance program and internal controls. On the other hand, SEC took action against the acquired company, and DOJ took action against a subsidiary of the acquired company. When pre-acquisition due diligence is not possible, DOJ has described procedures . . . pursuant to which companies can nevertheless be rewarded if they choose to conduct thorough post-acquisition FCPA due diligence. FCPA due diligence, however, is normally only a portion of the compliance process for mergers and acquisitions. DOJ and SEC evaluate whether the acquiring company promptly incorporated the acquired company into all of its internal controls, including its compliance program. Companies should consider training new employees, reevaluating third parties under company standards, and, where appropriate, conducting audits on new business units. . . .

Questions and Comments

1. The Resource Guide sets forth a shorthand version of the agencies' views in ten "hallmarks" of an effective compliance program:

   a. Commitment from senior management and a clearly articulated policy against corruption;
   b. Code of conduct and compliance policies and procedures;
   c. Oversight, autonomy, and resources;
   d. Risk assessment;
   e. Training and continuing advice;
   f. Incentives and disciplinary measures;
   g. Third-party due diligence and payments;
   h. Confidential reporting and internal investigation;
   i. Continuous improvement: periodic testing and review;
   j. Mergers and acquisitions: pre-acquisition due diligence and post-acquisition integration.

Which of these is the most important? Can a company have an effective FCPA compliance program that doesn't include all of these elements?

2. If the company does maintain such a program, and a violation occurs, will it receive any credit during subsequent enforcement proceedings?

3. This guidance refers in derogatory fashion to "check-the-box" compliance programs. Mechanical approaches to compliance, which depend on the compliance officer or investigator ascertaining that certain conditions or factors are met, are decidedly in eclipse in modern "best practices" thinking. What is so objectionable about "check-the-box" approaches to compliance? Can anything good be said about them?

4. This guidance alludes to another common theme of contemporary compliance thinking: the idea that there is no one-size-fits-all compliance program, and that the nature of an effective program may appropriately be adjusted to the size of the operation. This is undoubtedly true in the abstract, but how straightforward is the process of sealing the compliance program so as to maintain effectiveness while an institution changes size?

5. The guidance states that "devoting a disproportionate amount of time policing modest entertainment and gift-giving instead of focusing on large government bids, questionable payments to third-party consultants, or excessive discounts to resellers and distributors may indicate that a company's compliance program is ineffective." Maybe, but if employees know that modest entertainment and minor gifts will escape scrutiny, could many small offenses arise to replace a few major ones?

6. In place of "check-the-box" approaches to compliance, the guidance follows contemporary thinking in recommending a "risk-based" approach that tailors the intensity of the compliance inquiry to the estimated risk of the activity in question. Do you agree with the risk-based focus of contemporary compliance practice? It seems clear that the approach offers significant benefits if the company's risk assessment is accurate, but how can we be sure that the assessment isn't off-base?

7. Could the risk-based approach wind up creating a different type of "check-the-box" mentality, in which the company develops for regulatory purposes an elaborate documentation of risks that bears little resemblance to the actual situation on the ground?

8. The guidance calls out third-party due diligence as a special problem in FCPA compliance. Why is this such a difficult problem area?

9. The guidance cites a poll finding that 64 percent of general counsel whose companies are subject to the FCPA say there is room for improvement in their FCPA training and compliance programs. How meaningful is this poll result? Would it be a bit arrogant to claim that there is no room for improvement in one's compliance program?

10. FCPA compliance is increasingly calling on the capabilities of "big data." Sophisticated compliance programs today gather information from many data sources — text mining, social media, email, news stories, blogs, government reports, and much more. Sophisticated programs for detection of "red flags" allow compliance officials to zero in on areas calling for further investigation. For example, vendors may be identified as "high risk" if fraud indicators show up in the company's financial transactions or if these companies show up in international sanctions or adverse media databases. Unusual patterns of travel and entertainment expenses can be flagged for investigation; and emails can be scanned for appearances of sensitive words or phrases. Big data analytics also plays a role in the allocation of compliance resources, since it can not only identify potential violations, but also mark out regions or business units deemed to pose the greatest risk — and

therefore that require the greatest allocation of scarce compliance resources. All this information can be compiled, analyzed, and presented to internal audit or to the audit committee for their evaluation.

11. In 2016, the Fraud Section of the United States Department of Justice announced a FCPA "pilot" program designed to encourage firms to voluntarily self-report FCPA violations, cooperate with government investigators, and remediate flaws in their internal compliance programs. The pilot program specifies the enforcement credit that Fraud Section attorneys are expected to give to companies that voluntarily self-disclose, fully cooperate, and remediate. What, in your opinion, are the pros and cons of this approach to FCPA enforcement? Should the government go further and provide an affirmative defense if a company has an effective compliance program in place? *See* United States Department of Justice, Criminal Division, The Fraud Section's Foreign Corrupt Practices Act Enforcement Plan and Guidance (April 5, 2016).

Further guidance on effective FCPA compliance may be gleaned from a careful review of government enforcement decisions. In April 2012, the Department of Justice announced that a former Morgan Stanley executive, Garth Peterson, had pleaded guilty to conspiring to evade internal controls that the firm was required to maintain under the FCPA. Specifically, Mr. Peterson was accused of conspiring with others to circumvent Morgan Stanley's internal controls in order to transfer a multi-million-dollar ownership interest in a Shanghai building to himself and a Chinese public official with whom he had a personal friendship. The DOJ had this to say about the plea agreement:

> According to court documents, Morgan Stanley maintained a system of internal controls meant to ensure accountability for its assets and to prevent employees from offering, promising or paying anything of value to foreign government officials. Morgan Stanley's internal policies, which were updated regularly to reflect regulatory developments and specific risks, prohibited bribery and addressed corruption risks associated with the giving of gifts, business entertainment, travel, lodging, meals, charitable contributions and employment. Morgan Stanley frequently trained its employees on its internal policies, the FCPA and other anti-corruption laws. Between 2002 and 2008, Morgan Stanley trained various groups of Asia-based personnel on anti-corruption policies 54 times. During the same period, Morgan Stanley trained Peterson on the FCPA seven times and reminded him to comply with the FCPA at least 35 times. Morgan Stanley's compliance personnel regularly monitored transactions, randomly audited particular employees, transactions and business units, and tested to identify illicit payments. Moreover, Morgan Stanley conducted extensive due diligence on all new business partners and imposed stringent controls on payments made to business partners. . . . After considering all the available facts and circumstances, including that Morgan Stanley constructed and maintained a system of internal controls, which provided reasonable assurances that its employees were not bribing government officials, the Department of Justice declined to bring any enforcement action against Morgan Stanley related to Peterson's conduct. The company voluntarily disclosed this matter and has cooperated throughout the department's investigation.

This language, coupled with the fact that DOJ conspicuously did not charge Morgan Stanley with any offenses, suggests that regardless of the lack of a statutory compliance defense under the FCPA, the Justice Department will weigh the presence of a robust FCPA compliance program as a factor counseling against charging a company for FCPA violations by employees. Also of interest is the implication of the charge, namely that conspiring to circumvent a compliance program is itself a violation of the FCPA.

In the Matter of Bruker Corporation, SEC Securities Act Release No. 73835 (Dec. 15, 2014), involved Bruker Corp., a manufacturer of analytical tools and life science and materials research systems. When the parent company discovered that employees at the company's Chinese subsidiaries had been bribing Chinese government officials, it undertook a number of corrective actions to its system of internal controls that the SEC release describes as praiseworthy. These steps included (1) instituting preapproval processes for nonemployee travel and significant changes to contracts; (2) establishing a new internal audit function and hiring a new director of internal audit who was charged with oversight over Bruker's global compliance program, including FCPA compliance; (3) adopting an amended FCPA policy translated into local languages; (4) implementing an enhanced FCPA training program, which included training programs in local languages as well as mandatory online employee training programs regarding ethics and FCPA compliance; (5) enhancing due diligence procedures for third parties; and (6) implementing a new global whistleblower hotline.

The SEC's release praised the company for proactively undertaking these steps. The agency also lauded the fact that the company had cooperated fully with the government once it discovered the misconduct:

> Throughout the process, Bruker provided extensive, thorough, and real-time cooperation with the Commission. In addition to self-reporting to the Commission shortly after discovering the FCPA violations, Bruker voluntarily provided the Commission with real-time reports of its investigative findings; shared its analysis of important documents and summaries of witness interviews; expanded the scope of the investigation at the Commission's request; and responded to the Commission's requests for documents and information in a timely manner. These actions assisted the Commission in efficiently collecting valuable evidence, including information that may not have been otherwise available to the staff.

The SEC suggested that it would have come down much harder had the company not taken these steps: "In determining to accept the Offer, the Commission considered remedial acts promptly undertaken by Bruker and the significant cooperation it afforded to the Commission staff." Even so, the company did not escape punishment: It agreed to pay $2,399,969 to the United States Treasury, including $1,714,852 in disgorgement, $310,117 in prejudgment interest, and a civil monetary penalty of $375,000.

2. FCPA Investigations

What happens if a company uncovers red flags of potential FCPA violations? At this point it may need to start an internal investigation; and if the red flags point to serious violations, the company probably will need to engage outside counsel (see Chapter 5 for discussion of internal investigations generally).

FCPA investigations can be extraordinarily complex and sensitive: complex because the activity in question — bribery — is almost always disguised and hidden from public view; sensitive because the counterparties to the bribes are often high-ranking officials of foreign governments. Because these investigations involve activities conducted overseas, moreover, the company will need to consider the application of each jurisdiction's privacy laws or other rules that may limit its ability to ferret out information.

The company will also need to consider whether the investigation needs to be disclosed to investors. The tradeoffs here are challenging. Disclosing the investigation may harm the company's reputation and may spook investors who fear that the investigation will uncover serious violations and lead to punitive fines. Not disclosing the investigation may constitute a failure to properly inform investors of material events, as required under the securities laws. Consider in this regard the following disclosure contained in Avon Products Inc.'s 2010 annual report:

Avon Products, Inc., 2010 Form 10K

. . . As previously reported, we have engaged outside counsel to conduct an internal investigation and compliance reviews focused on compliance with the Foreign Corrupt Practices Act ("FCPA") and related U.S. and foreign laws in China and additional countries. The internal investigation, which is being conducted under the oversight of our Audit Committee, began in June 2008. As we reported in October 2008, we voluntarily contacted the United States Securities and Exchange Commission and the United States Department of Justice to advise both agencies of our internal investigation. We are continuing to cooperate with both agencies and inquiries by them, including but not limited to, signing tolling agreements, translating and producing documents and assisting with interviews.

As previously reported in July 2009, in connection with the internal investigation, we commenced compliance reviews regarding the FCPA and related U.S. and foreign laws in additional countries in order to evaluate our compliance efforts. We are conducting these compliance reviews in a number of other countries selected to represent each of the Company's four other international geographic segments. The internal investigation and compliance reviews are focused on reviewing certain expenses and books and records processes, including, but not limited to, travel, entertainment, gifts, use of third-party vendors and consultants and related due diligence, joint ventures and acquisitions, and payments to third-party agents and others, in connection with our business dealings, directly or indirectly, with foreign governments and their employees. The internal investigation and compliance reviews of these matters are ongoing, and we continue to cooperate with both agencies with respect to these matters. At this point we are unable to predict the duration, scope, developments in, results of, or consequences of the internal investigation and compliance reviews.

Beginning in July and August 2010, several derivative actions were filed against certain present or former officers and/or directors of the Company that allege breach of fiduciary duty, and, in certain complaints, abuse of control, waste of corporate assets, unjust enrichment and/or proxy disclosure violations, relating to the Company's compliance with the FCPA. The relief sought in one or more of the derivative complaints includes certain declaratory and equitable relief, restitution, unspecified damages, exemplary damages and interest. The Company is named as a nominal defendant. . . . We are unable to predict the outcome of these matters. . . .

Questions and Comments

1. Reading the description excerpted above, one might think that the issue was not overly important; the information reported in the excerpt was previously known.

Yet the dollars involved were very large. The same filing disclosed that Avon had incurred "significant professional and related fees associated with the FCPA investigation and compliance reviews" amounting to approximately $95 million in the reporting year (up approximately $59 million from the previous year).

2. Avon and related entities finally resolved their FCPA exposure in 2014, after years of additional investigation. The settlement committed the firms to pay fines of $135 million to settle the SEC's charges and a parallel criminal case brought by the United States Department of Justice.

3. These substantial fines reflected the government's belief that, while Avon had done the right thing and commenced a bona fide internal investigation in 2009, it had previously failed to act with sufficient vigor in response to known FCPA violations. The government claimed that Avon first learned about potential FCPA problems at its Chinese subsidiary through an internal audit report in late 2005. Although the company consulted a law firm about the issue and directed that reforms be instituted, it allegedly failed to follow up to make sure that the proper remedial actions had been undertaken — allowing the bribery scheme to continue for another three years. Avon didn't begin a full-scale investigation until 2008, when it received a letter from a whistleblower revealing the continuing illegal conduct.

4. In addition to paying substantial fines, Avon consented to the appointment of an independent compliance monitor for a period of 18 months, followed by an 18-month period of self-reporting on its compliance efforts.

14

Anti-Money Laundering, the Bank Secrecy Act, and OFAC

Criminals, terrorists, and rogue states need financial services to carry out their activities.

A drug cartel, for example, is mostly a cash business; dealers on the street aren't keen on taking checks or credit cards. It's fine to have a few twenty-dollar bills on hand, but when you have a few thousand, things get complicated. Storing that much money is risky. It could be lost or stolen. And often the senior people live in different cities or countries. Transporting large amounts of cash is a problem for criminal organizations, both because of the issue of security and also because if cash in transit is discovered by the authorities, it might tip them off as to the underlying criminal conduct. The cartel would work more smoothly if the cash could be deposited in a bank and drawn on when and where it is needed.

There is also the investment problem. Although crime may not pay in the long run, it can be lucrative for a while — so lucrative that the leaders of the enterprise have more wealth on hand than they can profitably put back into the criminal enterprise. They may want to invest their ill-gotten gains some legitimate or ostensibly legitimate enterprise. To make such an investment, the criminal needs to use the services of a broker or other financial services firm.

Terrorists also use the financial system. Although terror is not a particularly expensive business — the Boston Marathon bombers spent only a few hundred dollars on their homemade devices — it does involve some outlays of funds. Terrorist organizations, moreover, don't simply commit acts of terror. They support a network of people who work for the organization and expect to be compensated. Sometimes, they also function as de facto governments, and in that capacity they need financing to fund the activities — military and civilian — associated with their quasi-governmental role. This means that terror organizations also have a need to use the financial system in order to raise and transfer funds.

Governments, too, need access to the financial system. Even closed countries like North Korea need a means to transfer payments and access funds for international transactions. Governments also need to use the financial system in order to trade for goods that cannot be produced efficiently in the domestic market.

The financial services sector therefore is a key battleground in the fight against crime, terror, and state violators of human rights or international law. The problem, from the standpoint of the financial sector, is that banks and other financial firms have traditionally not concerned themselves very much with the nature of their clients' business. When someone shows up at the bank and wishes to make a wire transfer, the bank ordinarily is not motivated to ask where the money came from. Its job starts and ends with carrying out the transfer: If the money came from illegal sources, that is someone else's problem. Likewise banks have always tended to maintain their customer's confidences. People often have good reasons to keep their financial activities private. Bankers cooperated by remaining tight-lipped about the private financial lives of their clients. It is not that banks are fond of criminals or terrorists — usually they aren't — but it is just not in their nature to partner with the government on clamping down on such people.

Sometimes, moreover, banks do become more than passive participants in illegal activities. One notorious example was the Bank for Credit and Commerce International (BCCI). BCCI's founder, Agha Hasan Abedi, was a Pakistani financier with brilliant talents for both good and evil. He persuaded several wealthy Middle-Eastern investors — most notably the Sheikh of Abu Dhabi — to entrust him with huge amounts of money. Operating simultaneously in many different countries, Abedi promoted BCCI as a model for financial innovation in the developing world. By splitting the operation into two groups, one regulated by Luxembourg and one by the Cayman Islands, Abedi avoided effective regulation by either. Many of BCCI's customers were legitimate; but some were not. BCCI's clients included dictators such as Manuel Noriega of Panama, violent drug lords, money launderers, and notorious terrorists. BCCI's model was successful for a long time. At its peak it had more than $20 billion in assets and was one of the largest private banking organizations in the world. The bank was shut down in 1991 and most of its misdeeds were brought to light, but not before it had caused serious harm. The operation of the organization was so opaque that some of its activities have never been fully understood.

Governments, therefore, cannot count on banks voluntarily and enthusiastically participating in law enforcement, anti-terror, and international human rights activities. It is necessary to require them to cooperate. In this chapter we consider the compliance implications of important bodies of law that impose obligations on financial institutions and others.

A. ANTI-MONEY LAUNDERING/BANK SECRECY

The Bank Secrecy Act was the first U.S. statute specifically aimed at enlisting banks in the fight against criminality. The principal concern of the statute was money laundering by organized crime organizations. The Act and its implementing regulations require banks to file "Suspicious Activity Reports" ("SARs") with the Financial Crimes Enforcement Network, a bureau of the U.S. Department of the Treasury known as "FinCEN." These reports are required whenever a transaction involves at least $5,000 "and the bank knows, suspects, or has reason to suspect" that the "transaction involves funds derived from illegal activities or is intended or conducted in order to hide or disguise funds or assets derived from illegal activities. . . ." 31 U.S.C. §5318(g) (2006); 31 C.F.R. §103.18(a)(2) (2006). In addition, a bank may also file a report of any other suspicious transaction that it believes is relevant to the possible violation of any law or regulation.

As noted in Chapter 6, the Bank Secrecy Act is unusual in that it requires private firms to implement compliance programs. 31 U.S.C. §5318(h) provides that "[i]n order to guard against money laundering through financial institutions, each financial institution shall establish anti-money laundering programs, including, at a minimum — (A) the development of internal policies, procedures, and controls; (B) the designation of a compliance officer; (C) an ongoing employee training program; and (D) an independent audit function to test programs." Congress paid special attention to transactions involving foreign nationals with bank accounts in the United States: 31 U.S.C. §5318(i)(1) provides that "[e]ach financial institution that establishes, maintains, administers, or manages a private banking account or a correspondent account in the United States for a non-United States person, including a foreign individual visiting the United States, or a representative of a non-United States person shall establish appropriate, specific, and, where necessary, enhanced, due diligence policies, procedures, and controls that are reasonably designed to detect and report instances of money laundering through those accounts."

The requirement of filing SARs presents unusually daunting compliance problems. Banks conduct millions of transactions every day, and often those transactions involve amounts greater than $5,000. It is feasible for a bank to keep track of transactions that exceed the size threshold, through the use of appropriate computer systems. But how is it to determine which of these transactions might involve illegal activities?

Many forms of financial activity may give rise to suspicions of illegal activity, but some occur on a frequent enough basis to warrant being called out by the regulators. FinCEN's list includes the following:

FinCEN Guidance on Preparing a Complete and Sufficient Suspicious Activity Report Narrative

November 2003

. . . Examples of some common patterns of suspicious activity are:

- a lack of evidence of legitimate business activity, or any business operations at all, undertaken by many of the parties to the transaction(s);
- unusual financial nexuses and transactions occurring among certain business types (e.g., food importer dealing with an auto parts exporter);
- transactions that are not commensurate with the stated business type and/or that are unusual and unexpected in comparison with the volumes of similar businesses operating in the same locale;
- unusually large numbers and/or volumes of wire transfers and/or repetitive wire transfer patterns;
- unusually complex series of transactions indicative of layering activity involving multiple accounts, banks, parties, jurisdictions;
- suspected shell entities;
- bulk cash and monetary instrument transactions;

- unusual mixed deposits of money orders, third party checks, payroll checks, etc., into a business account;
- transactions being conducted in bursts of activities within a short period of time, especially in previously dormant accounts;
- transactions and/or volumes of aggregate activity inconsistent with the expected purpose of the account and expected levels and types of account activity conveyed to the financial institution by the accountholder at the time of the account opening;
- beneficiaries maintaining accounts at foreign banks that have been subjects of previous SAR filings;
- parties and businesses that do not meet the standards of routinely initiated due diligence and anti-money laundering oversight programs (e.g., unregistered/unlicensed businesses);
- transactions seemingly designed to, or attempting to avoid reporting and recordkeeping requirements; and
- correspondent accounts being utilized as "pass-through" points by foreign jurisdictions with subsequent outgoing funds to another foreign jurisdiction.

Once a bank has identified a suspicious activity, the next step is to report the matter to FinCEN. The agency facilitates the reporting task (as well as its task of analyzing the reports received) by providing an online filing system. The SAR form is rather extensive, containing numerous fields for specific information about the filing institution, the institution where the activity occurred, the subject of the suspicious activity, the nature of the suspicious activity, and a narrative of the events giving rise to suspicion. The most challenging of these requirements is the narrative, since this requires the exercise of judgment and cannot be automated. FinCEN makes it clear, however, that the narrative is also the most important part of the SAR. It is only here that the government can get a full picture of the nature of the bank's concerns.

FinCEN instructs banks to use the narrative section as a means for describing the "modus operandi" of the subject committing the suspicious activity, and to do so in a "concise, accurate, and logical manner" containing the "five W's": Who? What? When? Where? and Why? Bankers are not journalists, however; not all have well-developed skills at expository writing. To assist banks in the process, FinCEN provides examples of good and bad narratives. Here is a sample:

FinCEN Guidance on Preparing a Complete and Sufficient Suspicious Activity Report Narrative

November 2003

Sufficient and Complete Depository Institution SAR Narratives:

> Investigation case number: A5678910. The customer, a grocery store and its owner, are suspected of intentionally structuring cash deposits to circumvent federal reporting requirements. The customer is also engaged in activity indicative of an informal value transfer operation: deposits of bulk cash, third party out of state personal checks and money orders, and engaging in aggregate wire transfers to Dubai, UAE. The type and volume of activity observed is non-commensurate with the customer's expected

business volume and deviates from the normal volume of similar types of businesses located in the same area as the customer. Investigative activities are continuing. Our bank has elected to directly contact law enforcement concerning this matter along with filing this SAR.

John Doe opened a personal checking account, #12345-6789, in March of 1994. Doe indicated that he was born in Yemen, presented a Virginia driver's license as identification, and claimed he was the self-employed owner of a grocery store identified as Acme, Inc. A business checking account, #23456-7891, was opened in January of 1998 for Acme, Inc. Between January 17, 2003, and March 21, 2003, John Doe was the originator of nine wires totaling $225,000. The wire transfers were always conducted at the end of each week in the amount of $25,000. All of the wires were remitted to the Bank of Anan in Dubai, UAE, to benefit Kulkutta Building Supply Company, account #3489728.

Reviews covering the period between January 2 and March 17, 2003, revealed that 13 deposits (consisting of cash, checks, money orders) totaling approximately $50,000 posted to the personal account. Individual amounts ranged between $1,500 and $9,500 and occurred on consecutive business days in several instances. A number of third-party out of state checks and money orders were also deposited into the account.

A review of deposit activity on the Acme, Inc. account covering the same period revealed 33 deposits (consisting of cash, checks, money orders) totaling approximately $275,000. Individual amounts ranged between $4,446 and $9,729; however 22 of 33 deposits ranged between $9,150 and $9,980. It was further noted that in nine of 13 instances in which cash deposits were made to both accounts on the same day, the combined deposits of cash exceeded $10,000. The bank filed currency transaction reports to the IRS for all aggregate daily transactions exceeding $10,000.

A search of the world wide web identified a website for Acme, Inc., which identified the company as a grocery store that provides remittance services to countries in the Middle East that includes Iran (an OFAC blocked country). Contact with the Virginia State Department of Banking indicates Acme, Inc. is not a licensed money wire transfer business. The bank will close this account because of the suspect nature of the transactions being conducted by John Doe.

[FinCEN] Comments:

This narrative is a well-written summary of all the suspicious activity and supports the stated purpose for filing the SAR. Furthermore, the narrative provides an internal bank reference number for the SAR that can be used by law enforcement should investigators wish to contact the bank to discuss pertinent facts presented in the narrative. Specific information is also provided in the narrative that details the source and application of suspect funds. The SAR also identifies other actions taken by the financial institution as part of its internal due diligence program and its efforts in detecting possible illegal activity being facilitated by the suspect. . . .

Insufficient or Incomplete Depository Institutions SAR Narratives:

John Doe was the originator of nine wires totaling $225,000. All of the wires were remitted to a Dubai based company. During the same period of time John Doe deposited cash, money orders, and checks into his account. . . .

[FinCEN] Comments:

This SAR fails to provide specific details on the application of the suspect funds (the name, bank, and account number of the beneficiary, if identifiable). . . . The depository institution fails to provide any information concerning the relationship, if any, between the institution and the customer. Also, no specific transaction data is provided that identifies the dates and amounts of each wire transfer.

Questions and Comments

1. If you were the regulator, how would you specify what sorts of considerations a financial institution should take into account in connection with AML/BSA requirements? The size of the transaction? How long the party has been a customer of the bank? The citizenship of the customer? The location where the money came from or is going? The frequency and timing of transactions? Whether the transaction was in cash? Whether the transaction was for an amount in excess of what the customer would be expected to conduct? Whether the transaction had a plausible business purpose?

2. Why might banks not want to comply with the SAR process?

3. Should banks be required to aid law enforcement in this way—without compensation?

4. Should banks be required to do more — perhaps going "undercover" to assist in covert operations designed to ferret out drug cartel or other organized crime activities?

5. Vendors play an important role in bank compliance with BSA/AML requirements. A number of companies offer sophisticated software designed to identify and report on suspicious transactions, without requiring costly evaluations by human beings in each case. The presence of vendors in this space raises the obvious problem — pervasive in the law of compliance — as to who monitors the vendors.

United States v. Wachovia Bank
No. 1:10-cr-20165-JAL

S.D. Fla. 2010

[The following facts are taken from an exhibit to the agreement entitled "Factual Statement."] . . . Beginning in June 2005, the United States Attorney's Office for the Southern District of Florida, the Drug Enforcement Administration ("DEA"), and the Internal Revenue Service-Criminal Investigation Division ("IRS") began investigating certain wire transfers that were sent to the United States from Mexico. The wired funds were being used for the purchase of aircraft in the United States. Those aircraft were then being used to move illegal narcotics from narcotics-producing countries for ultimate distribution in the United States.

The wire transfers were traced back to correspondent bank accounts held by certain Mexican currency exchange houses (commonly referred to as "casas de cambio" or "CDCs") at Wachovia in the United States. The CDC correspondent bank accounts were supervised and managed by a business unit of Wachovia that was located in Wachovia's offices in Miami, Florida.

On numerous occasions, monies were deposited into a CDC by a drug trafficking organization. Using false identities, the CDC then wired that money through its Wachovia correspondent bank accounts for the purchase of airplanes for drug trafficking organizations. On various dates between 2004 and 2007, a least four of those airplanes were seized by foreign law enforcement agencies cooperating with the United States and were found to contain large quantities of cocaine.

In total, nearly $13 million dollars went through correspondent bank accounts at Wachovia for the purchase of aircraft to be used in the illegal narcotics trade. From these aircraft, more than twenty thousand kilograms of cocaine were seized. . . .

Wachovia maintained correspondent bank accounts for a number of Mexican CDCs. The Wachovia business unit that managed and oversaw the CDC business was located in Miami, Florida. Miami has been designated as both a High Intensity Money Laundering and Related Financial Crime Area and a High Intensity Drug Trafficking Area. In 2005 Mexico also was designated as a high-risk source of money laundering activity, particularly the financial activities through CDCs. The CDCs involved in the movement of drug monies in this investigation were all based in Mexico.

As early as 1996, the DEA . . . warned that Mexican drug trafficking organizations were increasingly using CDCs to place drug proceeds into the U.S. financial system by smuggling the drug proceeds out of the United States to Mexico and selling those dollars to Mexican CDCs for pesos. The placement of drug proceeds with Mexican CDCs is beneficial to both sides of the transaction: the drug trafficking organization is able to obtain local currency (pesos) to continue its illicit activities without having to risk structuring drug proceeds into the banking system, and the CDCs, which have a significant need for U.S. dollars in the ordinary course of their currency exchange activities, obtain a valuable source of discounted U.S. dollars. . . .

From September 2005 to December 2007, Wachovia provided correspondent banking services to 22 CDCs, including Casa de Cambio Puebla. Wachovia offered the CDCs at least three services. First, Wachovia allowed CDCs to conduct wires through Wachovia. These wires were sent by the CDC on behalf of its third-party customers, who were in Mexico, to recipients throughout the world. Second, Wachovia offered "bulk cash" service to CDCs. Using this service, CDCs collected large amounts of U.S. dollars in Mexico. These dollars, or "bulk cash," would then be physically transported to the United States from the CDC either through an armored car service or through a means designated by the CDC. Once in the United States, the money would ultimately be deposited at the Federal Reserve. Through this method, CDCs could repatriate U.S. dollar into the U.S. market. Third, Wachovia offered a pouch deposit service to the CDCs. The CDCs would accept deposit items drawn on U.S. banks, e.g., checks and traveler's checks presented by their customers. Those items would then be aggregated and placed into a "pouch" that would be forwarded to Wachovia in the United States for deposit. In or around May 2005, Wachovia introduced a new delivery method for international check deposits called "remote deposit capture" ("RDC"). The scanned files would be forwarded electronically to Wachovia for credit.

The CDCs that banked at Wachovia conducted significant wire, bulk cash, and "pouch" or "RDC" activity through Wachovia. For the time period of May 1, 2004 through May 31, 2007, Wachovia processed at least $373,630,892,102 in wire activity on behalf of the CDCs. During that same time period, Wachovia processed at least $4,728,626,300 in bulk cash for the CDCs. For the same time period, Wachovia processed approximately $47,000,000,000 in RDC deposits for all its correspondent banking customers, which included the Mexican CDCs.

During the investigation, law enforcement reviewed the CDC banking activity that occurred at Wachovia and found readily identifiable evidence and red flags of large-scale drug money laundering. [These included "structured wire transactions" by multiple people operating under false identities into the same account over a brief time period, for purposes of acquiring an aircraft that was subsequently seized with 2,000 kilos of cocaine aboard; deposits of sequentially numbered travelers checks with unusual markings; and significant bulk cash transactions in great excess of a customer's self-identified expectations. The investigation found that at least $110 million in drug proceeds were filtered through CDC accounts held at Wachovia.] . . .

Since the beginning of the BSA investigation, Wachovia has fully cooperated and has provided valuable assistance to law enforcement. Wachovia has retained an outside law firm to assist in investigating the facts relevant to the United States' investigation. With the assistance of outside counsel, Wachovia has made numerous detailed periodic reports to the United States concerning those facts.

Wachovia has devoted substantial resources to that investigation and to responding to the United States' requests for information. To date, Wachovia has produced more than 8 million pages of documents. Wachovia has organized its document productions as requested by the United States and has provided summaries, indices, and explanations of relevant documents to assist the United States in its understanding of the facts relevant to its investigation. Wachovia has also made employees available to be interviewed by the United States as requested.

Wachovia has also taken extensive remedial measures to assess any shortcomings in its BSA/AML programs.

(a) In June 2007, Wachovia hired a new Chief Compliance Officer. In April 2008, Wachovia also hired a new BSA/AML Officer.

(b) Under the leadership of the new Chief Compliance Office and the new BSA/AML Officer, Wachovia undertook a substantial remediation of its AML and compliance functions.

(c) Wachovia has enhanced its manual transactional party monitoring, with focuses on high-risk countries and financial institution risk.

(d) Wachovia developed and provided enhanced AML training for employees, including AML Investigative Services staff. Topics of training have included regulatory responsibility, red flag detection, the black market peso exchange, large cash transactions, wires to high-risk countries, and activity inconsistent with an account's stated purpose.

Wachovia voluntarily conducted a detailed "look-back" of Wachovia's transactions with thirteen Mexican CDCs during a three-year period. Wachovia has provided the results of the look-back, which was conducted by an independent consultant, to the United States and its banking regulators. As a result of the "look-back" program, Wachovia has filed SARS for conduct related to the CDCs.

(a) Wachovia filed more than 4200 SARs relating to wire transactions conducted by the CDCs, which included $4.3 billion in total dollars;

(b) Wachovia filed 8 SARs relating to bulk cash transactions conducted by the CDCs, which included $4,011,256,648 in total dollars;

(c) Wachovia filed 18 SARs relating to sequentially numbered traveler's check transactions conducted by the CDCs, which included $25,155,000 in total dollars.

Since Wachovia's acquisition by Wells Fargo, Wachovia has been subject to Wells Fargo's BSA/AML Compliance Program and compliance and operational risk management, oversight, and independent testing. Wells Fargo's policies and procedures, including those relating to escalating and exiting of customer relations, now apply to Wachovia. As the integration progresses, Wells Fargo's transaction monitoring system, a more advanced version of the system used by Wachovia will be used to monitor Wachovia's transactions.

[The following text is from the Deferred Prosecution Agreement:]

THE CHARGES

Wachovia shall waive indictment and agree to the filing of a one (1) count information in the United States District Court for the Southern District of Florida charging it with failing to maintain an effective anti-money laundering program, in violation of Title 31, United States Code, Sections 5318(h)(1) and 5322(a).

ACCEPTANCE OF RESPONSIBILITY

Wachovia accepts and acknowledges responsibility for its conduct and that of its employees as set forth in the Factual Statement attached hereto. . . . If the United States . . . initiates a prosecution that is deferred by this Agreement against Wachovia, Wachovia agrees that it will neither contest the admissibility of the Factual Statement or any other documents provided by Wachovia to the United States, nor contract in any such proceeding the facts contained within the Factual Statement.

FORFEITURE AND FINE

. . . Wachovia agrees to settle and does settle any and all civil and criminal forfeiture claims presently held by the United States . . . for the sum of $110,000,000. . . . The parties agree that in addition to the above forfeiture, Wachovia shall pay a fine of $50,000,000. . . . The United States has considered a number of factors in determining the appropriate fine in this matter. The parties agree that a $50,000,000 fine is appropriate in this case because (i) of Wachovia's considerable remedial actions specified within the factual statement; (ii) the legal entity that will pay the fine is Wells Fargo Bank [which acquired Wachovia during the financial crisis of 2007-2009], while the failures occurred at Wachovia; and (iii) there is no evidence or allegation that Wells Fargo Bank's anti-money laundering program is deficient.

Questions and Comments

1. Are you surprised by the recitation of facts? It makes Wachovia's Miami office seem all too eager to offer its services to violent Mexican drug cartels. Is this what you would expect from what was (at the time) one of the best-known financial institutions in the United States?

2. There's no evidence that the government would proceed personally against any employees at Wachovia. Could the bank have cooperated for so long and so extensively with illegal money laundering activities without someone at the bank knowing about it?

3. As this case illustrates, AML/BSA cases can be — and often are — brought by several different government agencies at once. At the same time as it settled the criminal case, Wachovia also resolved civil actions by FinCEN and the Office of Comptroller of the Currency, Wachovia's principal regulator.

4. The Wachovia deal presaged several other huge AML/BSA settlements, including ING's $619 million agreement with state and federal regulators in 2012 and HSBC's $1.92 billion settlement in 2013.

5. State regulators have also entered the picture to enforce their own rules on money laundering. Benjamin Lawsky, New York's then chief financial regulator, were particularly active. In 2013, he embarrassed federal officials by obtaining a $250 million settlement from Bank of Tokyo-Mitsubishi UFJ over charges related to matters that federal regulators had settled the previous year for $8.57 million.

6. How important was it that Wachovia had been acquired by Wells Fargo? Did the government pull its punches because the costs of the settlement would be principally borne by Wells and its shareholders, who had nothing to do with the wrongdoing?

The except above regarding Wachovia was from a deferred prosecution agreement in a criminal case. AML/BSA enforcement with compliance elements is also frequently observed in civil administrative proceedings. The following excerpt provides an example:

Board of Governors of the Federal Reserve System, Written Agreement by and Among M&T Bank Corporation, Manufacturers & Traders Trust Company and Federal Reserve Bank of New York

June 11, 2013

. . . Whereas, the most recent inspection of M&T conducted by the Federal Reserve Bank of New York (the "Reserve Bank") identified deficiencies in M&T's firm-wide compliance risk management program with respect to compliance with BSA/AML Requirements; the Bank's internal controls, customer due diligence procedures, and transaction monitoring processes with respect to compliance with BSA/AML Requirements; and [Wilmington Trust Corporation's (WTC)] due diligence practices for foreign correspondent accounts; . . .

Now, therefore, the Reserve Bank, M&T, and the Bank hereby agree as follows:

FIRM-WIDE BSA/AML COMPLIANCE PROGRAM

Within 60 days of this Agreement, M&T shall submit to the Reserve Bank an acceptable revised written firm-wide BSA/AML compliance program that describes the specific actions that will be taken, including timelines for completion, to ensure compliance with applicable BSA/AML Requirements. The revised program shall, at a minimum, include:

(a) reporting to and oversight by senior management of M&T's firm-wide BSA/AML compliance controls and processes, including, but not limited to, procedures to ensure oversight of a firm-wide customer due diligence program;

(b) written policies, procedures, and compliance risk management standards;

(c) a comprehensive BSA/AML risk assessment process;

(d) measures to ensure that BSA/AML compliance functions outsourced by subsidiaries to third-parties, including affiliates, are performed to meet regulatory requirements;

(e) measures to ensure compliance and improve accountability within all business lines and legal entities and their respective compliance functions;

(f) procedures to require the escalation of significant matters related to compliance risks to appropriate senior officers and the board of directors; and

(g) the findings and recommendations of the consultant recently engaged by M&T to assist in matters related to compliance with the BSA/AML Requirements.

BSA/AML COMPLIANCE

Within 60 days of this Agreement, the Bank shall submit to the Reserve Bank an acceptable written revised BSA/AML compliance program. The program shall include provisions for updates on an ongoing basis, as necessary, to incorporate amendments to the BSA and the rules and regulations issued thereunder. At a minimum, the revised program shall include:

(a) Internal controls to ensure compliance by the Bank and any non-bank subsidiaries with applicable BSA/AML Requirements; and

(b) policies and procedures designed to ensure identification and verification of the identity of account holders in accordance with applicable regulations.

CUSTOMER DUE DILIGENCE

Within 60 days of this Agreement, the Bank shall submit to the Reserve Bank an acceptable written revised program for conducting appropriate levels of customer due diligence by the Bank, WTC, and as applicable, other subsidiaries. At a minimum, the program shall include:

(a) Policies, procedures, and controls to ensure that the Bank and WTC collect, analyze, and retain complete and accurate customer information for all account holders;

(b) a plan, with timelines, to remediate deficient due diligence for existing customer accounts; and

(c) a methodology for assigning risk ratings to account holders that considers factors such as type of customer, type of products and services, and geographic location;

(d) a risk-focused assessment of the Bank's and WTC's customer base to:

(i) identify the categories of customers whose transactions and banking activities are routine and usual; and

(ii) determine the appropriate level of enhanced due diligence necessary for those categories of customers that pose a heightened risk of conducting potentially illicit activities at or through the Bank or WTC;

(e) for each customer whose transactions require enhanced due diligence, procedures to:

(i) determine the appropriate documentation necessary to verify the identity and business activities of the customer; and

(ii) understand the normal and expected transactions of the customer;

(f) policies and procedures, including appropriate documentation, for identification and due diligence with regard to politically exposed persons;

(g) policies, procedures, and controls to ensure that foreign correspondent accounts are properly identified and accorded the appropriate due diligence and, where necessary, enhanced due diligence; and

(h) procedures to ensure [that] periodic reviews and evaluations are conducted and documented for all account holders.

SUSPICIOUS ACTIVITY MONITORING AND REPORTING

Within 60 days of the Agreement, M&T and the Bank shall jointly submit to the Reserve Bank an acceptable written program to reasonably ensure the identification and timely, accurate, and complete reporting by M&T, the Bank, and WTC, as applicable, of all known or suspected violations of law or suspicious transactions to law enforcement and supervisory authorities, as required by applicable suspicious activity reporting laws and regulations. At a minimum, the program shall include:

(a) Monitoring and investigation criteria and procedures to ensure the timely detection, investigation, and reporting of all known or suspected violations of law and suspicious transactions;

(b) policies regarding the level and type of due diligence required when reviewing suspicious account activity; and

(c) measures to ensure escalation to, and documented oversight by, senior management of significant matters, including, but not limited to repetitive suspicious activity reporting and suspected structuring activities.

TRANSACTION REVIEW

(a) Within 60 days of this Agreement, the Bank shall engage an independent consultant, acceptable to the Reserve Bank, to conduct a review of account and transaction activity associated with any high risk customer accounts conducted at, by, or through the Bank and WTC from July 1, 2012 to December 31, 2012 to determine whether suspicious activity involving high risk customer accounts or transactions at, by, or through the Bank or WTC was properly identified and reported in accordance with applicable suspicious activity reporting regulations (the "Transaction Review") and to prepare a written report detailing the consultant's findings (the "Transaction Review Report"). For each covered customer, the Transaction Review may commence as soon as the Bank has completed the remediation of the covered customer's account in accordance with the revised remediation program required by paragraph 3 of this Agreement.

(b) Based on the Reserve Bank's evaluation of the results of the Transaction Review, the Reserve Bank may direct the Bank to engage the independent consultant to conduct a review of the types of transactions described in paragraph 5(a) for additional time periods.

Within 10 days of the engagement of the independent consultant, but prior to the commencement of the Transaction Review, the Bank shall submit to the Reserve Bank for approval an engagement letter that sets forth:

(a) the scope of the Transaction Review;

(b) the methodology for conducting the Transaction Review;

(c) the expertise and resources to be dedicated to the Transaction Review;

(d) the anticipated date of completion of the Transaction Review and the Transaction Review Report; and

(e) a commitment that supporting material associated with the Transaction Review will be made available to the Reserve Bank upon request.

The Bank shall provide to the Reserve Bank a copy of the Transaction Review Report at the same time that the report is provided to the Bank.

Throughout the Transaction Review, the Bank shall ensure that all matters or transactions required to be reported that have not previously been reported are reported in accordance with applicable rules and regulations. . . .

Questions and Comments

1. The agreement refers to the "findings and recommendations of the consultant recently engaged by M&T." What do you think is the background to this comment?

2. Paragraph 5 of the agreement requires the regulated parties to engage an "independent consultant" to review transactions associated with "high risk customer accounts" for the period July 1, 2012 to December 31, 2012. Usually, vendors are tolerated but not required. Is it a good idea to demand that a regulated entity employ a vendor?

B. SANCTIONS

The Office of Foreign Assets Control (OFAC) administers and enforces economic and trade sanctions against entities such as targeted foreign countries, terrorists, international narcotics traffickers, and those engaged in activities related to the proliferation of weapons of mass destruction. OFAC regulations require banks to block accounts and other property and to prohibit or reject unlicensed trade and financial transactions with specified countries, entities, and individuals.

Both OFAC and AML/BSA require financial institutions to keep detailed records of their transactions for purposes of policing against the use of the financial system by bad actors; a difference is that in the case of BSA/AML it is up to the bank to identify the suspicious party, and in the case of OFAC the bad actor is already identified, giving the bank the task of making sure it doesn't engage in a prohibited transaction with that person or entity. Because the requirements are to some extent parallel, BSA/AML and OFAC compliance issues are often grouped together.

United States v. Barclays Bank
Deferred Prosecution Agreement
1:10-cr-00218-EGS
D.D.C.,

Aug. 16, 2010

[Based on the facts admitted to in the Factual Statement set forth below, Barclays agreed to pay a fine of $149 million, to cooperate with the authorities in the investigation of other entities, and to upgrade its OFAC compliance program. In exchange, the government agreed to defer any prosecution for two years and, if Barclays remained in compliance with the commitments contained in the agreement, to recommend dismissal of the charges at the close of the deferral period.]

This Factual Statement is made pursuant to, and is part of, the Deferred Prosecution Agreements dated August 16, 2010, between the United States Department of Justice ("DOJ") and Barclays Bank PLC ("Barclays"), a financial institution registered and organized under the laws of England and Wales, and between the New York County District Attorney's Office ("DANY") and Barclays.

From the mid-1990s through September 2006, Barclays violated both U.S. and New York State criminal laws by knowingly and willfully moving or permitting to be moved hundreds of millions of dollars through the U.S. financial system on behalf of banks from Cuba, Iran, Libya, Sudan, and Burma, and persons listed as parties or jurisdictions sanctioned by the Office of Foreign Assets Control of the United States Department of the Treasury ("OFAC") (collectively, the "Sanctioned Entities") in violation of U.S. economic sanctions.

Barclays engaged in this criminal conduct by: (a) following instructions, principally from banks from Cuba, Iran, Libya, Sudan, and Burma not to mention their names in U.S. dollar ("USD") payment messages sent to Barclays' branch in New York, New York (the "New York Branch") and to other financial institutions located in the United States; (b) routing USD payments through an internal Barclays sundry account to hide the payments' connection to Sanctioned Entities; (c) amending and reformatting USD payment messages to remove information identifying Sanctioned Entities; and (d) deliberately using a less transparent method of payment messages, known as cover payments.

Barclays' conduct, which occurred outside the United States, caused its New York Branch, and other financial institutions located in the United States, to process payments that otherwise should have been held for investigation, rejected, or blocked pursuant to U.S. sanctions regulations administered by OFAC.

Additionally, by its conduct, Barclays: (a) prevented its New York Branch and other financial institutions in the United States from filing required Bank Secrecy Act ("BSA") and OFAC-related reports with the U.S. government; (b) caused false information to be recorded in the records of U.S. financial institutions; and (c) caused U.S. financial institutions not to make records that they otherwise would have been required by law to make.

In May 2006, Barclays voluntarily disclosed to OFAC four transactions that were made in violation of U.S. sanctions. At that time, Barclays commenced a limited internal investigation into the operation and limitations of its automated filtering system and Barclays' USD transactions involving U.S. sanctioned countries and persons. Thereafter, in November 2006, Barclays exited all USD correspondent relationships with banks subject to U.S. economic sanctions, banks headquartered in sanctioned countries, and the subsidiaries of such banks (the "Sanctioned Banks"). In 2007, after being contacted by federal and state prosecutors, Barclays agreed to cooperate fully, and broadened its review to conduct a comprehensive internal investigation and historical payment analysis covering activity and transactions from January 1, 2000 to July 31, 2007.

Barclays has provided prompt and substantial cooperation by sharing the results of its internal investigation with DOJ and DANY, as well as with OFAC, and Barclays' U.S. banking regulators, the Board of Governors of the Federal Reserve System and the New York State Banking Department. From the beginning of the investigation, Barclays has taken full responsibility for its conduct.

Barclays is a global financial services provider headquartered in London, United Kingdom, and is one of the largest banks in the world. Barclays employs more than 144,000 people, has more than 48 million customers, and operates in more than 50 countries. At all times relevant to this matter, Barclays was a wholly-owned subsidiary of Barclays PLC, a public limited liability company organized under the laws of England and Wales. Barclays' home country regulator is the United Kingdom's Financial Services Authority ("FSA"). The New York Branch functioned as the primary USD clearer for all of Barclays, its affiliates, and its customers.

Until November 2006, Barclays maintained correspondent banking relationships with several Sanctioned Banks. Barclays did not, however, maintain physical branches or representative offices in Cuba, Iran, Libya, Sudan, Burma, or other countries subject to OFAC sanctions.

Barclays' December 31, 2009 annual report listed its annual audited consolidated net income attributable to shareholders as equaling $14.31 billion USD; and $6.76 billon USD as of December 31, 2008. Total audited consolidated assets as of the same dates equaled $1.97 trillion USD and $2.86 trillion USD, respectively.

At all times relevant to this matter, various U.S. economic sanctions laws regulating financial and other transactions involving sanctioned countries, entities, and persons were in existence. Those laws applied to transactions occurring within U.S. territorial jurisdiction. OFAC promulgated regulations to administer and enforce the economic sanctions laws, including regulations for economic sanctions against specific countries, entities, and individuals, including Specially Designated Nationals ("SDNs"). . . .

DOJ alleges, and Barclays admits, that Barclays' conduct, as described herein, violated [the Trading with the Enemy Act]. Specifically, Barclays violated 50 U.S.C. app. §§5 and 16, which makes it a crime to willfully violate or attempt to violate any regulation issued under TWEA, including regulations restricting transactions with Cuba. DOJ further alleges, and Barclays admits, that Barclays' conduct, as described herein, violated the International Emergency Economic Powers Act ("IEEPA"). Specifically, Barclays violated 50 U.S.C. §1705, which makes it a crime to willfully violate or attempt to violate any regulation issued under IEEPA, including regulations restricting transactions with Iran, Libya, Sudan, and Burma.

DANY alleges, and Barclays admits, that Barclays' conduct, as described herein, violated New York State Penal Law Sections 175.05 and 175.10, Falsifying Business Records in the First Degree and Second Degree, which make it a crime to: "with intent to defraud . . . (i) make or cause a false entry in the business records of an enterprise . . . or (iv) prevent the making of a true entry or cause the omission thereof in the business records of an enterprise." Under the Penal Law, it is a felony when, as here, a person or entity commits Falsifying Business Records in the Second Degree and the person's or entity's "intent to defraud includes an intent to commit another crime or to aid or conceal the commission of a crime."

For more than a decade, Barclays knowingly and willfully engaged in conduct and practices outside the United States that caused its New York Branch and other financial institutions located in the United States to process payments in violation of U.S. sanctions. To hide these illegal transactions, Barclays altered and routed payment messages to ensure that payments violating IEEPA, TWEA, and OFAC regulations cleared without difficulty though its New York Branch and other U.S. financial institutions. The total value of prohibited transactions for the period of Barclays' review was approximately $500 million. . . .

During the relevant time period, Barclays knowingly and willfully engaged in conduct that caused its New York Branch and other financial institutions in the United States to process payments in violation of U.S. sanctions. As part of this effort to evade U.S. sanctions, Barclays: (a) followed instructions from certain Sanctioned Entities not to mention their names in USD payment messages sent to the New York Branch and to other financial institutions located in the United States; (b) routed USD payments through an internal Barclays sundry account, thereby hiding the payments' connection to Sanctioned Entities; (c) amended or reformatted USD payment messages to remove information identifying Sanctioned Entities; and (d) re-sent messages as cover payments to take advantage of cover payments' lack of transparency. . . .

After passage of the Patriot Act in 2001, Barclays reviewed its correspondent banking practices and identified certain of its practices as problematic. Despite this review, Barclays did not begin to take effective action until 2006. Further, prior to mid-2006, Barclays did not train its non-U.S. employees regarding Barclays' obligations under U.S. sanctions law and did not formulate or circulate any meaningful policy regarding the OFAC regulations and their requirements.

The List of Correspondents ("LOC") was a Barclays' payment operations manual containing instructions on how to process payments for both sanctioned and non-sanctioned banks with which Barclays had correspondent relationships. As early as November 1987, Barclays received instructions from Sanctioned Banks directing Barclays not to mention their names on payment messages sent to the United States. . . .

A sundry account is a bank's internal suspense account typically used for the legitimate purpose of recording miscellaneous items until an appropriate account entry is determined. Barclays, however, knowingly routed sanctioned payments though Barclays' own sundry accounts, thereby disguising the true originator of USD payments. The effect of using the sundry account was that the New York Branch would believe a payment was originating from Barclays when in reality it was from a sanctioned entity. This ensured that the transaction would evade detection and would be processed by the New York Branch without question or scrutiny.

The New York Branch maintained an automated filter that screened incoming payment messages against an OFAC list of sanctioned countries, entities, and individuals. This software was designed to identify potential positive matches to OFAC–sanctioned entities in USD payment messages being routed through the New York Branch. Payments received by the New York Branch involving Sanctioned Entities would have been subject to investigation by the bank and then, depending on the results of the investigation, permitted, rejected, or blocked. . . .

Barclays' standard operating procedures allowed and even educated its employees how to bypass . . . the U.S. financial institution's OFAC filters to permit illegal payments. Pursuant to these procedures, when the Poole filter identified a payment message that contained a reference to an OFAC-sanctioned entity, that payment message was stopped for further review by Barclays' employees at Poole. If those employees found that the payment message contained a reference to a sanctioned entity, they would follow one of the following procedures: (i) return the payment message to the remitting area via a pre-formatted fax cover sheet; (ii) alter or delete fields in the SWIFT message; or (iii) change the routing of the payment message from a serial payment to a cover payment in order to hide any connection to the sanctioned entity.

Consistent with bank procedure when a payment was flagged by the . . . OFAC filter, Barclays' employees would generally return the flagged payment message to the original remitting bank. Barclays' employees would use a specific fax cover sheet to advise the remitting area of Barclays that the payment message had been cancelled and would further identify the specific words in the payment message that had caused the message to be stopped by the . . . filter. The fax cover sheet contained the following:

OFAC ITEM: Wording below is contained in the message and does not comply with the Office of Foreign Assets Control regulations applicable to all payments sent via the U.S.A. Payments to U.S.A. must NOT contain the word listed below.

Subsequently, because Barclays was advising the remitting bank of the prohibited language, some of these payment messages would be re-sent by the remitting bank without the offending language. This enabled the payment message to now pass cleanly through the . . . filter and then be processed by the New York Branch and other unwitting U.S. financial institutions.

In November 2001, the use of the fax cover sheet was identified by internal audit as problematic because "without adequate guidance the recipient of the fax advice may not be aware of the implications and may merely remove the offending text and re-submit the payment without any wider consideration." In early 2002, as a result of this audit report, the language of the fax template was re-worded in an attempt to mitigate these issues. The fax language was changed to:

OFAC ITEM: Wording below is contained in the message and does not comply with the U.S.A. / U.K. / E.C. / U.N. Sanctions.

Despite the altered wording in the fax cover sheet, no implementing guidance was circulated, and the practice of stating the offending text nevertheless continued, as did the resubmission of prohibited OFAC-sanctioned transactions with the offending text removed.

Barclays intentionally altered SWIFT messages when a sanctioned entity was named in the payment message and when the payment message contained an explicit instruction not to mention the name of the Sanctioned Bank when making the USD payment via the United States. In both of these instances, Barclays' employees knew that if these payment messages were sent in an unaltered form, they would be stopped and potentially blocked or rejected in the United States because of the information contained in the message. The employees removed the problematic references and the altered payment messages were sent to U.S. financial institutions.

Another practice Barclays developed to ensure that sanctioned transactions would be processed through the United States was to change the routing of the payment. Barclays routinely cancelled serial payment messages being routed through the United States that contained references to a sanctioned entity, knowing that the message could be blocked or rejected in the United States. These cancelled payment messages were resubmitted using the cover payment method. By using this bifurcated payment method, Barclays was able to disguise the beneficiary and ordering customer information from the New York Branch and other U.S. correspondent banks. Barclays would thereby successfully route prohibited transactions through the United States. . . .

In the spring of 2006, Barclays' senior management learned that four cover payments involving sanctioned parties had been routed through the New York Branch and were processed because the cover payments did not mention the sanctioned beneficiary or originator. Barclays' current management immediately made a voluntary disclosure regarding these payments to OFAC and to its banking regulators. Soon thereafter, Barclays was contacted by DOJ and DANY.

Barclays has fully acknowledged and accepted responsibility for its conduct. Barclays undertook a voluntary and comprehensive internal review of its historical payment-processing and sanctions compliance practices. As part of its review, Barclays interviewed more than 175 current and former employees and reviewed more than one hundred million records, including hard copy and electronic documents. The review identified the practices described above, including the use of the LOC, the practice of altering payment instructions and omitting the names of Sanctioned

Entities from payment messages, and the use of the sundry account. Barclays reported all of its findings in a timely manner to DOJ, DANY, and to the regulatory authorities in the United States and the United Kingdom. During the course of investigations by DOJ, DANY, and other authorities, Barclays has provided prompt and substantial cooperation including the following:

a. Committing substantial resources, including, but not limited to, external consultants, numerous high level Barclays' employees, and an extensive document retention program, in order to conduct a thorough investigation;

b. Providing timely and detailed reports of the Bank's investigation;

c. Conducting an extensive review of customer records and SWIFT transactions, including the review of incoming and outgoing USD payments and trade finance transactions processed by Barclays between January 1, 2000 and July 31, 2007, to identify transactions that may have violated U.S. sanctions laws;

d. Conducting extensive data analysis, document review, and interviews to identify the practices discussed above;

e. Agreeing to toll any applicable statutes of limitation; and

f. Making current and former Barclays' employees available for interviews by DOJ and DANY.

Barclays has taken voluntary steps to enhance and optimize its sanctions compliance programs by:

a. Voluntarily terminating relationships with Sanctioned Bancs and entities;

b. Committing substantial personnel and resources to sanctions compliance programs, including appointing a senior employee to oversee sanctions screening processes and to ensure operational compliance with applicable sanctions laws;

c. Enhancing its USD payment filtering systems;

d. Designing and providing sanctions training to more than 130,000 employees, including intensive training to more than 800 specialist employees, and ensuring that sanctions training is incorporated in training for new employees;

e. Creating a new enhanced sanctions compliance policy that includes a general prohibition of transactions on behalf of SDNs in all currencies;

f. Undertaking an extensive internal audit of its sanctions compliance programs in 2008 and reporting the results to interested authorities, including DOJ and DANY;

g. Committing to conduct regular further audits of sanctions compliance issues; and

h. Ensuring that U.S. sanctions compliance is reported to the most senior executives of the Bank.

Questions and Comments

1. Suppose a company on a blocked list enters into a joint venture with a company that is not on the blocked list. May a U.S. firm transact business with the joint venture? What if the blocked company has a minority stock interest in a company

that is not subject to sanctions? OFAC guidance provides that any entity is blocked if one or more blocked persons own a total of 50 percent or more of the entity. Consider the due diligence problems this rule poses for U.S. firms: It is one thing to identify entities on the blocked list, but how is a U.S. firm going to know what other entities the blocked firm may have invested in? On the other hand, if the regulation did not extend to affiliates of blocked firms, how could it be effectively enforced?

2. Suppose a blocked entity enters into a contract to act as an agent of a firm that is not subject to sanctions. Can a U.S. firm negotiate or conduct business with the blocked firm solely in its capacity as agent? OFAC says "no": U.S. firms may not deal with the blocked entity in any capacity. What is the rationale for this rule?

3. For a detailed description of recent OFAC cases, some of which generated very large fines, see Paul Lee, *Compliance Lessons from OFAC Case Studies — Part I*, 131 Banking L.J. 657 (2014); Paul Lee, *Compliance Lessons from OFAC Case Studies — Part II*, 131 Banking L.J. 717 (2014).

Department of Justice Office of Public Affairs
BNP Paribas Agrees to Plead Guilty and to Pay $8.9 Billion for Illegally Processing Financial Transactions for Countries Subject to U.S. Economic Sanctions

June 30, 2014

BNP Paribas S.A. (BNPP), a global financial institution headquartered in Paris, [has] agreed to enter a guilty plea to conspiring to violate the International Emergency Economic Powers Act (IEEPA) and the Trading with the Enemy Act (TWEA) by processing billions of dollars of transactions through the U.S. financial system on behalf of Sudanese, Iranian, and Cuban entities subject to U.S. economic sanctions. The agreement by the French bank to plead guilty is the first time a global bank has agreed to plead guilty to large-scale, systematic violations of U.S. economic sanctions. . . .

[O]ver the course of eight years, BNPP knowingly and willfully moved more than $8.8 billion through the U.S. financial system on behalf of sanctioned entities, including more than $4.3 billion in transactions involving entities that were specifically designated by the U.S. Government as being cut off from the U.S. financial system. BNPP engaged in this criminal conduct through various sophisticated schemes designed to conceal from U.S. regulators the true nature of the illicit transactions. BNPP routed illegal payments through third party financial institutions to conceal not only the involvement of the sanctioned entities but also BNPP's role in facilitating the transactions. BNPP instructed other financial institutions not to mention the names of sanctioned entities in payments sent through the United States and removed references to sanctioned entities from payment messages to enable the funds to pass through the U.S. financial system undetected. . . .

BNPP processed approximately $6.4 billion through the United States on behalf of Sudanese sanctioned entities from July 2006 through June 2007, including approximately $4 billion on behalf of a financial institution owned by the government of Sudan, even as internal emails showed BNPP employees expressing concern about the bank's assisting the Sudanese government in light of its role in supporting international terrorism and committing human rights abuses during the same time period. Indeed, in March 2007, a senior compliance officer at BNPP wrote to other high-level BNPP compliance and legal employees reminding them that certain Sudanese banks with which BNPP dealt "play a pivotal part in the support of the Sudanese government which . . . has hosted Osama Bin Laden and refuses the United Nations intervention in Darfur."

One way in which BNPP processed illegal transactions on behalf of Sudanese sanctioned entities was through a sophisticated system of "satellite banks" set up to disguise both BNPP's and the sanctioned entities' roles in the payments to and from financial institutions in the United States. As early as August 2005, a senior compliance officer at BNPP warned several legal, business and compliance personnel at BNPP's subsidiary in Geneva that the satellite bank system was being used to evade U.S. sanctions: "As I understand it, we have a number of Arab Banks (nine identified) on our books that only carry out clearing transactions for Sudanese banks in dollars. . . . This practice effectively means that we are circumventing the US embargo on transactions in USD by Sudan."

Similarly, BNPP provided Cuban sanctioned entities with access to the U.S. financial system by hiding the Cuban sanctioned entities' involvement in payment messages. From October 2004 through early 2010, BNPP knowingly and willfully processed approximately $1.747 billion on behalf of Cuban sanctioned entities. In the statement of facts, BNPP admitted that it continued to do U.S. dollar business with Cuba long after it was clear that such business was illegal in order to preserve BNPP's business relationships with Cuban entities. BNPP further admitted that its conduct with regard to the Cuban embargo was both "cavalier" and "criminal," as evidenced by the bank's 2006 decision, after certain Cuban payments were blocked when they reached the United States, to strip the wire messages for those payments of references to Cuban entities and resubmit them as a lump sum in order to conceal from U.S. regulators the bank's longstanding, and illicit, Cuban business.

Further according to court documents, BNPP engaged in more than $650 million of transactions involving entities tied to Iran, and this conduct continued into 2012—nearly two years after the bank had commenced an internal investigation into its sanctions compliance and had pledged to cooperate with the Government. The illicit Iranian transactions were done on behalf of BNPP clients, including a petroleum company based in Dubai that was effectively a front for an Iranian petroleum company, and an Iranian oil company. . . .

BNPP will waive indictment and be charged in a one-count felony criminal information, filed in federal court in the Southern District of New York, charging BNPP with knowingly and willfully conspiring to commit violations of IEEPA and TWEA, from 2004 through 2012. BNPP has agreed to plead guilty to the information, has entered into a written plea agreement, and has accepted responsibility for its criminal conduct. . . . The plea agreement, subject to approval by the court, provides that BNPP will pay total financial penalties of $8.9736 billion, including forfeiture of $8.8336 billion and a fine of $140 million.

In addition to the joint forfeiture judgment, the New York County District Attorney's Office is also announcing today that BNPP has pleaded guilty in New York State Supreme Court to falsifying business records and conspiring to falsify business records. In addition, the Board of Governors of the Federal Reserve System is announcing that BNPP has agreed to a cease and desist order, to take certain remedial steps to ensure its compliance with U.S. law in its ongoing operations, and to pay a civil monetary penalty of $508 million. The New York State Department of Financial Services (DFS) is announcing BNPP has agreed to, among other things, terminate or separate from the bank 13 employees, including the Group Chief Operating Officer and other senior executives; suspend U.S. dollar clearing operations through its New York Branch and other affiliates for one year for business lines on which the misconduct centered; extend for two years the term of a monitorship put in place in 2013, and pay a monetary penalty to DFS of $2.2434 billion. In satisfying its criminal forfeiture penalty, BNPP will receive credit for payments it is making in connection with its resolution of these related state and regulatory matters. The Treasury Department's Office of Foreign Assets Control has also levied a fine of $963 million, which will be satisfied by payments made to the Department of Justice. . . .

Questions and Comments

1. As the case against BNP progressed toward resolution — and it became clear that the bank was facing massive fines for its past conduct — the matter became an affair of state. In April 2014, French President François Hollande wrote to U.S. President Barak Obama demanding that any penalty assessed against the bank should not be "unfair and disproportionate." Other French officials were not so measured in tone: Finance Minister Michel Sapin warned that "if all the U.S. authorities involved in this case d[o] not treat BNP Paribas fairly, France will respond firmly to protect its fundamental interests."

2. Was it significant that BNP was a foreign bank? Would the U.S. regulators have behaved in a similarly punitive way if the bank was chartered in the United States?

3. Why was there such a massive compliance breakdown at BNP? Was the compliance function disabled, coopted, corrupt, or deprived of the information or resources needed to perform its job effectively?

4. What in your opinion was the influence of corporate culture on BNP's actions in response to U.S. sanctions regulations?

C. ATTORNEYS

Ill-gotten gains can be laundered through various means ranging from very simple (actually running a laundry!) to the very complex. Terrorist activities can be financed by straightforward means (such as wiring money to a bank account maintained by a terrorist organization), or by more indirect methods. Complex arrangements are more insidious because they are difficult to detect and punish. These are also arrangements that, because of their complexity, often call for the services of attorneys. Thus lawyers play an important role, for good or bad, in the area of money laundering and terrorist finance. They can facilitate these activities by providing services to bad actors; they can also help prevent or deter these activities by refusing to provide services or by cooperating in government law enforcement efforts. The following excerpt contains advice on the topic from the American Bar Association.

American Bar Association Task Force on Gatekeeper Regulation and the Profession, Voluntary Good Practices Guidance for Lawyers to Detect and Combat Money Laundering and Terrorist Financing

Apr. 23, 2010

[T]he purpose of this paper is to assist members of the legal profession in the United States in designing and implementing effective risk-based approaches [to money laundering or terrorist financing]. It is not intended to be, nor should it be construed as, a statement of the standard of care governing the activities of lawyers in implementing a risk-based approach to combat money laundering and terrorist financing. Rather, given the vast differences in practices, firms, and lawyers throughout the United States, this paper seeks only to serve as a resource that lawyers can use in developing their own voluntary risk-based approaches.

[A]n overarching purpose of this paper is to encourage lawyers to develop and implement voluntary, but effective, risk-based approaches consistent with the Lawyer Guidance, thereby negating the need for federal regulation of the legal profession. . . .

WHAT IS THE RISK-BASED APPROACH?

The risk-based approach is grounded in the premise that the limited resources (both governmental and private sector) available to combat money laundering and terrorist financing should be employed and allocated in the most efficient manner possible so that the sources of the greatest risks receive the most attention. A risk-based approach is intended to ensure that measures to prevent or mitigate money laundering and terrorist financing are commensurate with the risks identified, thereby facilitating an efficient allocation of this limited pool of resources.

The proportionate nature of the risk-based approach means that higher risk areas should be subject to enhanced procedures, such as enhanced client due diligence ("CDD") and enhanced transaction monitoring. By contrast, simplified, modified, or reduced controls may apply in lower risk areas. . . . In no case [will] the risk may ever be so low as to eliminate any form or level of CDD. An effective risk-based approach involves identifying and categorizing money laundering and terrorist financing risks and establishing reasonable controls based on the risks identified. . . .

WHAT ARE THE RISK CATEGORIES?

The Lawyer Guidance identifies three major risk categories with regard to legal engagements: (a) country/geographic risk, (b) service risk, and (c) client risk. Lawyers need to determine their exposure to each of these risk categories. The relative weight to be given to each risk category in assessing the overall risk of money laundering and terrorist financing will vary from one lawyer or firm to another because of the size, sophistication, location, and nature and scope of services offered by the lawyer or the firm. Based on their individual practices and judgments, lawyers will need to assess independently the weight to be given to each risk factor. These risk factors are subject to variables that may increase or decrease the perceived risk posed by a particular client or type of work. . . .

Country/Geographic Risk

[There is no] universally adopted listing of countries or geographic areas that are deemed to present a lower or higher risk. The client's domicile, the location of the transaction, and the source of the funding are but a few sources from which a money laundering risk can arise. . . . These higher risk countries include those that are subject to sanctions, embargoes, or similar measures issued by certain bodies, such as the United Nations and those identified by credible sources as having significant levels of corruption or other criminal activity or a location from which funds or support are provided to terrorist organizations. Countries are also considered to pose a higher risk of money laundering when credible sources identify those countries as generally lacking appropriate [anti-money laundering] laws, regulations, and other measures. . . .

Client Risk

A critical component to the development and implementation of an overall risk-based framework is determining the potential money laundering or terrorist financing risk posed by a client. Clients range from individuals, partnerships and limited liability companies with dozens of partners or members to multinational corporations. Given this spectrum of clients, a lawyer will be challenged to determine whether a particular client poses a higher risk and, if so, the level of that risk and whether the application of any mitigating factors influences that assessment. The Lawyer Guidance identifies various categories of higher risk clients. If a client falls into one of these categories, the lawyer is then required to apply a set of risk variables that may mitigate or exacerbate the risk assessment the lawyer is required to make to determine the necessary level of [client due diligence].

The Lawyer Guidance identifies nearly a dozen categories of potentially higher risk clients. Lawyers need to determine whether any of their clients fall into one or more of these categories and therefore warrant an evaluation of any mitigating circumstances and increased risk assessment. [These categories include:]

- Politically exposed persons ("PEPs") are individuals who are or have been entrusted with prominent functions in a foreign country. . . .
- Unusual Activity. Clients conducting their relationship or requesting services in unusual or unconventional circumstances (as evaluated in light of all the circumstances of the representation). . . .
- Masking of Beneficial Ownership. Where the structure or nature of the client entity or relationship makes it difficult to identify in a timely manner the true beneficial owner or controlling interests. . . .
- Cash Intensive Businesses. Clients that are cash (and cash equivalent) intensive businesses. . . .
- Charities and NPOs. Charities and other NPOs that are not subject to monitoring or supervision. . . .
- Financial Intermediaries Not Subject to Adequate [Money Laundering] Laws. . . .
- Clients with Certain Criminal Convictions. Clients having convictions for proceeds generating crimes who instruct the lawyer (who has actual knowledge of

such convictions) to undertake specified activities on their behalf are potentially higher risk clients. . . .

- Clients with No Address/Multiple Addresses. Clients who have no address, or multiple addresses without legitimate reasons. . . .
- Unexplained Change in Instructions. Clients who change their settlement or execution instructions without appropriate explanation are potentially higher risk clients. . . .
- Structures With No Legal Purpose. The use of legal persons and arrangements without any apparent legal or legitimate tax, business, economic or other reason are potentially higher risk situations. . . .

Service Risk

[S]ome services are at higher risk for money laundering and terrorist financing. Typically those services involve the movement of funds and/or the concealment of beneficial ownership. . . .

Questions and Comments

1. Why did a committee of the American Bar Association issue this guidance?

2. The U.S. Department of the Treasury added the following endorsement of the recommendations of this report: "The Treasury Department welcomes this Good Practices paper as a useful step in protecting the legal profession as well as the broader financial system from the risks of money laundering and terrorist financing. Treasury looks forward to continuing engagement with the ABA to facilitate implementation of effective policies and procedures to protect against money laundering and terrorist financing."

3. The report refers to the concept of "gatekeepers," a topic that we studied in Chapter 9. "Gatekeepers" in the context of this report include lawyers, notaries, trust and company service providers, real estate agents, accountants, and auditors who assist with transactions involving the movement of money in the domestic and international financial systems. To what extent, if any, does this guidance endorse a gatekeeper role for attorneys? To what extend does it endorse the model of attorney as public servant?

4. Sanctions programs administered by OFAC prohibit a U.S. person from engaging in transactions with persons in certain countries. In such cases an attorney may be prohibited by law from engaging in the representation at all even if it was otherwise not problematic.

5. The guidelines excerpted above present a risk-based approach to the attorney's role in preventing money laundering and terrorist financing. This approach involves an initial risk assessment that influences the intensity of compliance activities that follow: more comprehensive vetting and scrutiny for persons or transactions deemed to present a higher risk, less comprehensive vetting and scrutiny for persons and transactions deemed to present lower risk.

6. The leading authority on risk-based approach in this area is Financial Association Task Force, *Guidance on the Risk-Based Approach to Combating Money Laundering and Terrorist Financing for Legal Professionals* (Oct. 23, 2008).

American Bar Association Standing Committee on Ethics and Professional Responsibility, Formal Opinion 463: Client Due Diligence, Money Laundering, and Terrorist Financing

May 23, 2013

The Model Rules of Professional Conduct and the ABA Voluntary Good Practices Guidance for Lawyers to Detect and Combat Money Laundering and Terrorist Financing ("Good Practices Guidance") are consistent in their ethical principles, including loyalty and confidentiality. The Good Practices Guidance provides information to help lawyers recognize and evaluate situations where providing legal services may assist in money laundering and terrorist financing.

By implementing the risk-based control measures detailed in the Good Practices Guidance where appropriate, lawyers can avoid aiding illegal activities in a manner consistent with the Model Rules. In an effort to combat money laundering and terrorist financing, intergovernmental standards-setting organizations and government agencies have suggested that lawyers should be "gatekeepers" to the financial system.

The underlying theory behind the "lawyer-as-gatekeeper" idea is that the lawyer has the capacity to monitor and to control, or at least to influence, the conduct of his or her clients and prospective clients in order to deter wrongdoing. Many have taken issue with this theory and with the word "gatekeeper." The Rules do not mandate that a lawyer perform a "gatekeeper" role in this context.

More importantly, mandatory reporting of suspicion about a client is in conflict with Rules 1.6 and 1.18, and reporting without informing the client is in conflict with Rule 1.4(a)(5). In this opinion we examine the contours of a lawyer's ethical obligations under the Model Rules of Professional Conduct with regard to efforts to deter and combat money laundering.

In August 2010 the ABA's policymaking House of Delegates adopted the Voluntary Good Practices Guidance for Lawyers to Detect and Combat Money Laundering and Terrorist Financing ("Good Practices Guidance"), along with a resolution stating that the Association "acknowledges and supports the United States Government's efforts to combat money laundering and terrorist financing." The approved Good Practices Guidance states that it is not intended to be, nor should it be construed as, a statement of the standard of care governing the activities of lawyers in implementing a risk-based approach to combat money laundering and terrorist financing, but rather is intended to serve as a resource that lawyers can use in developing their own voluntary approaches.

Good Practices Guidance policy supports a "risk-based" approach in accord with guidelines developed by the Financial Action Task Force on Money Laundering ("FATF") created by the U.S. and other leading industrialized nations.

This approach differs from a rules based approach that requires compliance with every element of detailed laws, rules, or regulations irrespective of the underlying quantum or degree of risk. The Good Practices Guidance urges lawyers to assess money-laundering and terrorist financing risks by examining the nature of the legal work involved, and where the business is taking place.

The Model Rules neither require a lawyer to fulfill a gatekeeper role, nor do they permit a lawyer to engage in the reporting that such a role could entail. It would be prudent for lawyers to undertake Client Due Diligence ("CDD") in appropriate circumstances to avoid facilitating illegal activity or being drawn unwittingly into a criminal activity. This admonition is consistent with Informal Opinion 1470 (1981), where we stated that "[a] lawyer cannot escape responsibility by avoiding inquiry. A lawyer must be satisfied, on the facts before him and readily available to him, that he can perform the requested services without abetting fraudulent or criminal conduct and without relying on past client crime or fraud to achieve results the client now wants." Further in that opinion we stated that, pursuant to a lawyer's ethical obligation to act competently, a duty to inquire further may also arise.

An appropriate assessment of the client and the client's objectives, and the means for obtaining those objectives, are essential prerequisites for accepting a new matter or continuing a representation as new facts unfold. Rule 1.2(d) prohibits a lawyer from knowingly counseling or assisting a client to commit a crime or fraud. A lawyer also is subject to federal laws prohibiting conduct that aids, abets, or commits a violation of U.S. anti-money laundering laws . . . or counter-terrorist financing laws. Thus, for example, lawyers should be mindful of legal restrictions applicable to all persons in the U.S. to avoid providing certain legal services to, and receiving money from, individuals or entities publicly identified by the U.S. Department of the Treasury on its Specially Designated Nationals List ("SDN List"). In certain circumstances, checking a client's identity internally within the firm against the SDN List can avoid the risk of unlawful conduct by the lawyer. . . .

The level of appropriate CDD varies depending on the risk profile of the client, the country or geographic area of origin, or the legal services involved. For example, the fact that clients are deemed to be "Politically Exposed Persons," (e.g., domestic or foreign senior government, judicial, or military officials) may justify enhanced due diligence on the part of the lawyer because of the potential for corruption. Clients or legal matters associated with countries that are subject to sanctions or embargoes issued by the United Nations, or those identified by credible sources as having significant levels of corruption or other criminal activity or that provide funds or support to terrorist organizations, may require greater examination. Furthermore, clients who ask that the lawyer handle actual receipt and transmission of funds or those who request accelerated real estate transfers for no apparent reason may also require an extra level of scrutiny.

Once a representation has commenced, a lawyer may terminate it in a number of circumstances in which the lawyer does not know for certain the client's plans or whether the client is engaged in criminal or fraudulent activities, but the lawyer has reason to believe that the client is engaging, or plans to engage, in such improper activities. Rule 1.16(b)(2) (Declining or Terminating Representation) states that a lawyer may withdraw from representing a client if "the client persists in a course of action involving the lawyer's services that the lawyer reasonably believes is criminal or fraudulent."

The Committee believes that the advice derived from the Good Practices Guidance is consistent, and not in conflict, with the ethical obligations of lawyers under the Model Rules. Indeed, the Good Practices Guidance states that "when faced with a situation where the lawyer is compelled to decline or terminate the relationship, the lawyer should comply with the requirements of the applicable rules of professional conduct." Accordingly, lawyers should be conversant with the risk-based measures and controls for clients and legal matters with an identified risk profile and use them for guidance as they develop their own client intake and ongoing client monitoring processes. When in a lawyer's professional judgment aspects of the contemplated representation raise suspicions about its propriety, that lawyer's familiarity with risk-based measures and controls will assist in avoiding unwitting assistance to unlawful activities. Indeed, the usefulness of the Good Practices Guidance is an example of the declaration in the Model Rules that "[t]he Rules do not . . . exhaust the moral and ethical considerations that should inform a lawyer. . . ."

Questions and Comments

1. Why did the ABA Standing Committee on Ethics and Professional Responsibility feel it was necessary to add this footnote to the guidance issued in 2010? To what extent does it back away from the previous guidance?

2. Attorneys are encouraged, in every case, to conduct "due diligence" to assess the risk posed by a potential client in the areas of money laundering and terrorist financing. What should a law firm do when it is asked to represent a client from, say, Kazakhstan on a transaction involving an American corporation? If Kazakhstan is considered to be a high-risk country, must the attorney refuse the representation? If the attorney wants to accept the representation notwithstanding the client's location, what must she do in order to justify going forward?

3. Must an attorney inform the client that she is conducting client due diligence in connection with concerns about money laundering and terrorist financing?

4. Do constraints on legal representation of persons suspected of money laundering or terrorist financing activities impair the constitutional right to counsel?

PROBLEM 14-1

You are a junior partner in the tax department at Bobkis and Zilch, a 20-lawyer general practice firm in Atlanta, Georgia. Your brother-in-law calls you one day to ask if you would be willing to meet with one of his friends, Sasha Aliyev, whom he knows from a powerboat racing event on a lake in Wisconsin. Your brother-in-law explains that Aliyev is a wealthy contractor and real estate investor who is also the cousin of a four-star general in his native country of Kornastan. Kornastan is apparently privatizing undeveloped land by auctioning it off at a fraction of its true value. Aliyev wishes to liquidate his American assets, including his contracting business, in order to raise the capital to bid at the auction. He has already found a buyer for his contracting business and negotiated the essential deal terms. He needs an attorney to represent him in this transaction. Because the land auction is due to be held in two weeks, Aliyev wants the closing on the sale of his business to occur very quickly. He is willing to pay you double your usual hourly rate, in cash, if you can drop what you are doing in order to help him. A little investigation discloses that Kornastan is one of the most corrupt countries on the planet and that it is a hotbed for Islamic radicalism — directed, until now, principally at Russia. You also find that Aliyev is a naturalized American citizen and uncover nothing to indicate concerns about his bona fides other than a recent arrest for driving a boat while impaired. You need the money. Should you take on the matter?

15

Sexual Harassment

A. INTRODUCTION

Sexual harassment in the workplace is prohibited under both state and federal law. At the federal level, 42 U.S.C. §2000e-2(a) makes it illegal for an employer "to fail or refuse to hire or to discharge any individual, or otherwise to discriminate against any individual with respect to his compensation, terms, conditions or privileges of employment, because of such individual's race, color, religion, sex, or national origin." In Meritor Savings Bank, FSB v. Vinson, 477 U.S. 57, 67 (1986), the Supreme Court held that this language encompasses cases in which an employer subjects employees to a hostile work environment by acts of sexual harassment.

The Equal Employment Opportunity Commission (EEOC), defines sexual harassment as follows: "[u]nwelcome sexual advances, requests for sexual favors, and other verbal or physical conduct of a sexual nature constitute sexual harassment when (1) submission to such conduct is made either explicitly or implicitly a term or condition of an individual's employment, (2) submission to or rejection of such conduct by an individual is used as the basis for employment decisions affecting such individual, or (3) such conduct has the purpose or effect of unreasonably interfering with an individual's work performance or creating an intimidating, hostile, or offensive working environment." 29 C.F.R. §1604.11(a).

The implementation of these standards is complicated by the fact that employers subject to the rules are usually corporations. The corporation can only act through it agents — the people who work for it. Under traditional principles of *respondeat superior*, an employer is liable for the wrongful conduct of an employee only when the employee is acting within the scope of her employment or acting to serve the interests of her employer. If the employee commits a wrongful act while on a "frolic and detour" outside the scope of employment, the employee is liable but the employer is not. The problem as far as sexual harassment is concerned is that no employer will say publicly that harassing behavior is part of an employee's job description. Nor is it easy to establish that such behavior in any way serves the interests of the employer. Accordingly, it becomes difficult to fit employer liability for sexual harassment within the framework of traditional doctrine. In 1998, the Supreme Court clarified the scope of the employer's liability in several cases, including the following:

Faragher v. City of Boca Raton

524 U.S. 775 (1998)

Justice SOUTER delivered the opinion of the Court.

Between 1985 and 1990, while attending college, petitioner Beth Ann Faragher worked part time and during the summers as an ocean lifeguard for the Marine Safety Section of the Parks and Recreation Department of respondent, the City of Boca Raton, Florida (City). During this period, Faragher's immediate supervisors were Bill Terry, David Silverman, and Robert Gordon. . . .

From time to time over the course of Faragher's tenure at the Marine Safety Section, between 4 and 6 of the 40 to 50 lifeguards were women. During that 5-year period, Terry repeatedly touched the bodies of female employees without invitation, would put his arm around Faragher, with his hand on her buttocks, and once made contact with another female lifeguard in a motion of sexual simulation. He made crudely demeaning references to women generally, and once commented disparagingly on Faragher's shape. During a job interview with a woman he hired as a lifeguard, Terry said that the female lifeguards had sex with their male counterparts and asked whether she would do the same.

Silverman behaved in similar ways. He once tackled Faragher and remarked that, but for a physical characteristic he found unattractive, he would readily have had sexual relations with her. Another time, he pantomimed an act of oral sex. Within earshot of the female lifeguards, Silverman made frequent, vulgar references to women and sexual matters, commented on the bodies of female lifeguards and beachgoers, and at least twice told female lifeguards that he would like to engage in sex with them.

Faragher did not complain to higher management about Terry or Silverman. Although she spoke of their behavior to Gordon, she did not regard these discussions as formal complaints to a supervisor but as conversations with a person she held in high esteem. Other female lifeguards had similarly informal talks with Gordon, but because Gordon did not feel that it was his place to do so, he did not report these complaints to Terry, his own supervisor, or to any other city official. Gordon responded to the complaints of one lifeguard by saying that "the City just [doesn't] care."

In April 1990, however, two months before Faragher's resignation, Nancy Ewanchew, a former lifeguard, wrote to Richard Bender, the City's Personnel Director, complaining that Terry and Silverman had harassed her and other female lifeguards. Following investigation of this complaint, the City found that Terry and Silverman had behaved improperly, reprimanded them, and required them to choose between a suspension without pay or the forfeiture of annual leave. . . .

In February 1986, the City adopted a sexual harassment policy, which it stated in a memorandum from the City Manager addressed to all employees. In May 1990, the City revised the policy and reissued a statement of it. Although the City may actually have circulated the memos and statements to some employees, it completely failed to disseminate its policy among employees of the Marine Safety Section, with the result that Terry, Silverman, Gordon, and many lifeguards were unaware of it. . . .

[I]n implementing Title VII it makes sense to hold an employer vicariously liable for some tortious conduct of a supervisor made possible by abuse of his supervisory authority. . . . The agency relationship affords contact with an employee subjected to a supervisor's sexual harassment, and the victim may well be reluctant to accept the risks of blowing the whistle on a superior. When a person with supervisory authority discriminates in the terms and conditions of subordinates' employment, his actions necessarily draw upon his superior position over the people who report to him, or those under them, whereas an employee generally cannot check a supervisor's abusive conduct the same way that she might deal with abuse from a co-worker. . . . Recognition of employer liability when discriminatory misuse of supervisory authority alters the terms and conditions of a victim's employment is underscored by the fact that the employer has a greater opportunity to guard against misconduct by supervisors than by common workers; employers have greater opportunity and incentive to screen them, train them, and monitor their performance.

In sum, there are good reasons for vicarious liability for misuse of supervisory authority. That rationale must, however, satisfy one more condition. . . . [The employer must be allowed to] show as an affirmative defense to liability that the employer had exercised reasonable care to avoid harassment and to eliminate it when it might occur, and that the complaining employee had failed to act with like reasonable care to take advantage of the employer's safeguards and otherwise to prevent harm that could have been avoided. . . . This composite defense would, we think, implement the statute sensibly, for reasons that are not hard to fathom.

An employer is subject to vicarious liability to a victimized employee for an actionable hostile environment created by a supervisor with immediate (or successively higher) authority over the employee. When no tangible employment action is taken, a defending employer may raise an affirmative defense to liability or damages, subject to proof by a preponderance of the evidence. The defense comprises two necessary elements: (a) that the employer exercised reasonable care to prevent and correct promptly any sexually harassing behavior, and (b) that the plaintiff employee unreasonably failed to take advantage of any preventive or corrective opportunities provided by the employer or to avoid harm otherwise. While proof that an employer had promulgated an anti-harassment policy with complaint procedure is not necessary in every instance as a matter of law, the need for a stated policy suitable to the employment circumstances may appropriately be addressed in any case when litigating the first element of the defense. And while proof that an employee failed to fulfill the corresponding obligation of reasonable care to avoid harm is not limited to showing an unreasonable failure to use any complaint procedure provided by the employer, a demonstration of such failure will normally suffice to satisfy the employer's burden under the second element of the defense. No affirmative defense is available, however, when the supervisor's harassment culminates in a tangible employment action, such as discharge, demotion, or undesirable reassignment.

Applying these rules here, we believe that the judgment of the Court of Appeals must be reversed. The District Court found that the degree of hostility in the work environment rose to the actionable level and was attributable to Silverman and Terry. It is undisputed that these supervisors "were granted virtually unchecked authority" over their subordinates, "directly controll[ing] and supervis[ing] all aspects of [Faragher's] day-to-day activities." It is also clear that Faragher and her colleagues were "completely isolated from the City's higher management." . . .

While the City would have an opportunity to raise an affirmative defense if there were any serious prospect of its presenting one, it appears from the record that any such avenue is closed. The District Court found that the City had entirely failed to disseminate its policy against sexual harassment among the beach employees and that its officials made no attempt to keep track of the conduct of supervisors like Terry and Silverman. The record also makes clear that the City's policy did not include any assurance that the harassing supervisors could be bypassed in registering complaints. Under such circumstances, we hold as a matter of law that the City could not be found to have exercised reasonable care to prevent the supervisors' harassing conduct. Unlike the employer of a small workforce, who might expect that sufficient care to prevent tortious behavior could be exercised informally, those responsible for city operations could not reasonably have thought that precautions against hostile environments in any one of many departments in far-flung locations could be effective without communicating some formal policy against harassment, with a sensible complaint procedure.

Questions and Comments

1. The Court recognizes that employers can be liable for the sexually harassing acts of city officials. The liability, however, is hedged by significant limitations:

   a. The conduct in question must be relatively severe: "[T]he ordinary tribulations of the workplace, such as the sporadic use of abusive language, gender-related jokes, and occasional teasing" do not create a basis for liability.
   b. If no tangible employment action has occurred, the employer can assert an affirmative defense that it exercised reasonable care to prevent and promptly correct any sexually harassing behavior, and that the plaintiff employee unreasonably failed to take advantage of any preventive or corrective opportunities provided.

Do you agree with these restrictions on the remedy?

2. The excerpted case involves a case of harassment by a supervisor. What if — as is often the case — the hostile work environment is created by co-workers rather than supervisors? The rationale that the wrongdoer is leveraging a position of power at the employer doesn't work here. Perhaps for this reason, the employer is allowed to defend on the ground that it did not know or have reason to know of the misconduct. However, this defense is available only if the employer made clear that complaints could be brought to the attention of management and that such complaints would be addressed.

3. The rule of the excerpted case is an open invitation to adopt and administer sexual harassment compliance programs. If employers undertake such actions, and if they thereafter implement the policies in an effective manner, they can insulate themselves from liability for harassing actions of supervisory employees that do not result in tangible employment actions. Is this an appropriate strategy for balancing the competing social policies?

4. The affirmative defense applies only if the employee has not suffered a tangible employment action (such as being fired, demoted, or reassigned). When such action has occurred, compliance strategies will not preclude liability. Do you agree

with this limitation? What if the offending supervisor disguises the reason for the action and the employer has no reason to know of the harassment? Does strict liability make sense in context?

B. SEXUAL HARASSMENT PROGRAMS

Left open is the question of what sorts of compliance programs satisfy the requirements for the affirmative defense. The EEOC has the following advice:

U.S. Equal Employment Opportunity Commission, Vicarious Employer Liability for Unlawful Harassment by Supervisors

Mar. 29, 2010

... The first prong of the affirmative defense requires a showing by the employer that it undertook reasonable care to prevent and promptly correct harassment. Such reasonable care generally requires an employer to establish, disseminate, and enforce an anti-harassment policy and complaint procedure and to take other reasonable steps to prevent and correct harassment. The steps described below are not mandatory requirements — whether or not an employer can prove that it exercised reasonable care depends on the particular factual circumstances and, in some cases, the nature of the employer's workforce. Small employers may be able to effectively prevent and correct harassment through informal means, while larger employers may have to institute more formal mechanisms.

There are no "safe harbors" for employers based on the written content of policies and procedures. Even the best policy and complaint procedure will not alone satisfy the burden of proving reasonable care if, in the particular circumstances of a claim, the employer failed to implement its process effectively. If, for example, the employer has an adequate policy and complaint procedure and properly responded to an employee's complaint of harassment, but management ignored previous complaints by other employees about the same harasser, then the employer has not exercised reasonable care in preventing the harassment.

Similarly, if the employer has an adequate policy and complaint procedure but an official failed to carry out his or her responsibility to conduct an effective investigation of a harassment complaint, the employer has not discharged its duty to exercise reasonable care. Alternatively, lack of a formal policy and complaint procedure will not defeat the defense if the employer exercised sufficient care through other means.

1. POLICY AND COMPLAINT PROCEDURE

It generally is necessary for employers to establish, publicize, and enforce anti-harassment policies and complaint procedures. ... An employer should provide every employee with a copy of the policy and complaint procedure, and redistribute it periodically. The policy and complaint procedure should be written in a way that will be understood by all employees in the employer's workforce. Other measures to ensure effective dissemination of the policy and complaint procedure include posting them in central locations and incorporating them into employee handbooks.

If feasible, the employer should provide training to all employees to ensure that they understand their rights and responsibilities.

An anti-harassment policy and complaint procedure should contain, at a minimum, the following elements:

- A clear explanation of prohibited conduct;
- Assurance that employees who make complaints of harassment or provide information related to such complaints will be protected against retaliation;
- A clearly described complaint process that provides accessible avenues of complaint;
- Assurance that the employer will protect the confidentiality of harassment complaints to the extent possible;
- A complaint process that provides a prompt, thorough, and impartial investigation; and
- Assurance that the employer will take immediate and appropriate corrective action when it determines that harassment has occurred.

Questions and Comments

1. Complaints of sexual harassment can be embarrassing. To what extent must the employer keep these matters confidential? To conduct an investigation, the employer may need to speak, not only to the complaining party, but also to others who may have witnessed the harassment. But if others are brought in, confidentiality is likely to disappear. EEOC guidelines recognize that confidentiality often cannot be guaranteed, but limit the extent of disclosure: The allegations are to be shared on a need-to-know basis and records relating to the harassment complaints are required to be held on a confidential basis.

2. Sometimes employees who report misconduct request that the employer take no action. Can or should an employer satisfy this request? The EEOC's answer is that once a complaint is made, the victim cannot control what is done about it: The employer must discharge its duty to prevent and correct harassment. But if victims know that they cannot limit the actions that follow from their complaints, will they be less likely to come forward in the first place?

3. While an investigation into a complaint of harassment is underway, what should the employer do about the supervisory relationship? It seems that the complainant cannot remain under the supervisor's direct control. But what is the alternative? Should the supervisor be temporarily relieved of her duties? What if it turns out that she is innocent of misconduct? Should the complainant be reassigned to another supervisor or another department? How can this be done without prejudicing the employees' situation?

4. What if after an investigation the employer concludes that it is a case of "he said, she said." The complainant and the supervisor tell two different stories, each of them plausible and neither of them confirmed or refuted by witnesses, documents, or other evidence. Should the employer conclude that because people who complain about harassment face costs from doing so (retaliation, embarrassment), the complaint if otherwise credible should be accepted over the supervisor's denial? Alternatively, should the employer conclude that because there is a harassment policy in place and because there is no evidence of harassment other than the complaint's allegations, the supervisor's account of events should be accepted?

Would it be relevant if the complainant had made previous allegations of harassment? If the supervisor had previously been accused of harassment?

5. What are an employer's obligations if it concludes after investigation that the allegations of harassment are substantially true? Must the offending supervisor be terminated? Would disciplinary sanctions short of termination be appropriate? What if the misconduct, while sufficient to amount to an offense, was limited in scope and followed by genuine indications of remorse? In determining on a course of action, is it appropriate for the employer to mitigate the seriousness of the punishment out of concern for its own liability — say because it fears being sued for wrongful termination? The EEOC indicates that the employer has substantial discretion in determining the sanction, and that penalties can include termination, reassignment, reprimands, demotion, reduction in pay, and other measures.

6. If the offender is terminated, may the employer agree to keep the reason for the termination confidential, including in communications to potential future employers? What are the pros and cons?

7. Penalizing the offender will not necessarily rectify the harm to the complainant. What can or should the employer do to make amends? In some cases, the matter may be resolved with an apology by the offender. Is this an effective way to remediate the harm?

8. What if the employer investigates a complaint of harassment and concludes that it is unsubstantiated? May or must the employer undertake remedial actions to protect or restore the reputation of the wrongfully accused supervisor, if word of the investigation has gotten out? May the employer fire or otherwise discipline the employee who made the false allegations?

PROBLEM 15-1

Bob's Best Bread is a family-owned and operated bakery founded in 1956 by Robert Brecca. It is now managed by Roberta Brecca, Robert's granddaughter. About half of the company's 50 employees are members of the Brecca family. The company has no formal sexual harassment program. Every August the company holds a barbecue for employees and their families at the Brecca estate. One of the activities is a "best body" contest held at the pool, where male and female contestants clad only in bathing suits are judged for their pulchritude and musculature. Jim Johnson is a baker at the company and not a member of the Brecca clan. Although he is an excellent baker, he is also known as having a bad attitude and as someone who is often late for work. A few weeks after the barbecue he comes to see Roberta in her office to complain about the best body event. He says that it degrades both women and men, and that people without athletic builds are made to feel ashamed and unappreciated. Roberta thanks him for his feedback and sends an announcement to the employees that the best body event is canceled for next year, to be replaced by a "best dressed" competition. Several months later Roberta fires Jim based on his unacceptable record of tardiness and his "poor attitude" about his job. Jim files a complaint with the EEOC. What result?

Merely distributing and administering a sexual harassment policy and complaint procedure may not be a fully effective strategy to minimize the risk of harassment. Employees receive a regular flow of official memoranda and official documents during the course of their employment. If the document has no immediate relevance to the performance of their jobs, they may put the paper in the "to read" file and move on to more pressing tasks. Often the documents that pile up in the "to read" file are eventually transferred to the "circular" file — the wastebasket — without ever being read. If this fate awaits sexual harassment policies, they may not deter supervisors from engaging in inappropriate behavior — even if the company effectively administers the policy when complaints arise.

A possible strategy to supplement a policy and complaint procedure is to require supervisory employees to undergo training designed to sensitize them to the requirements and the risks of harassing behavior. The EEOC doesn't require formal training, but does suggest that a company that implements such programs will be viewed in a favorable light: "An employer should ensure that its supervisors and managers understand their responsibilities under the organization's anti-harassment policy and complaint procedure. Periodic training of those individuals can help achieve that result. Such training should explain the types of conduct that violate the employer's anti-harassment policy; the seriousness of the policy; the responsibilities of supervisors and managers when they learn of alleged harassment; and the prohibition against retaliation."

Many companies — and most small firms — are not equipped to run their own training programs. Unless they have hired an officer specializing in sexual harassment policy, firms are likely to lack the personnel to lead these programs. Even if they have personnel on staff that could teach the program, the officer may not have access to written or audiovisual materials or a course of study. Moreover, programs conducted in-house may not be viewed as credible as programs offered by independent human resources consultants, employment discrimination attorneys, or other professionals — and certainly not as credible as the instruction offered by the EEOC's own Training Institute.

What is the content of sexual harassment training by third-party vendors? A typical curriculum includes:

- Laws that prohibit unlawful harassment in the workplace;
- Specific forms of harassment;
- How to prevent harassment and hostile environments;
- How to identify and prevent retaliation;
- The rights and responsibilities of staff members;
- Consequences of harassment suits;
- What to do in the event a harassment complaint is filed; and
- How to conduct an investigation.

PROBLEM 15-2

Gamestat owns a website that compiles sports statistics from other websites and provides them to subscribers in a single integrated platform. Users of Gamestat can quickly find up-to-date information about many different sports — tennis, football, horse racing, soccer, basketball, golf, even curling and polo. The site has become popular with sports enthusiasts and gamblers. Gamestat has adopted and widely circulates a state-of-the-art sexual harassment policy; it requires all new hires to sign a statement that they have read and accept the policy. All supervisors are also required to undergo a half-day training in sexual harassment avoidance once every three years. Most of Gamestat's 275 employees are former "jocks" and the company's culture is a bit boisterous — practical jokes and teasing are a normal part of the work day, even for senior managers. The sexual harassment training is conducted in the afternoon by the company's in-house human resources department; it includes a boring lecture on legal requirements and a poorly acted video displaying types of behavior that are prohibited. Gamestat supervisors, most of whom have attended multiple training sessions, have developed the tradition of a pre-training lunch well lubricated by martinis, followed by humorous banter during the training video. In one scene, where an actor playing a supervisor is about to place his hand on a female employee's buttocks, attendees yell out, "no, no, don't do it!" — and "oh no, you blew it!" when he does. If asked, the participants would say they get the message and that the joking attitude is just part of the company's culture. Does Gamestat have an effective anti-sexual harassment program?

C. ENFORCEMENT

EEOC v. Carrols Corp.

Consent Decree (Jan. 10, 2013)

This cause of action was initiated on November 17, 1998 by the Equal Employment Opportunity Commission ("EEOC"), an agency of the United States Government, to correct unlawful employment practices on the basis of sex. EEOC alleges that Defendant Carrols Corporation ("Carrols") subjected Charging Party Wendy McFarlan and other female employees to sexual harassment, retaliation, and/or constructive discharge in violation of Title VII of the Civil Rights Act of 1964, as amended ("Title VII"). Carrols denies having engaged in any unlawful discrimination, harassment, or retaliation, and denies all of the allegations of the complaint. . . .

MONETARY RELIEF

Carrols will pay monetary relief in the total sum of two and one-half million dollars and no cents ($2,500,000.00) (the "Claim Fund"). . . . Monetary relief will include payments in the nature of back pay and compensatory damages. EEOC has allocated two hundred five thousand eight hundred seventy-six dollars and no cents ($205,876.00) of the Claim Fund to claims for lost earnings to Claimants. . . . EEOC has allocated two million two hundred ninety-four thousand one hundred twenty-four dollars and no cents ($2,294,124.00) to Claimants as compensatory damages. . . .

INJUNCTIONS

Carrols and its managers, supervisors, officers and agents are enjoined from harassment toward any of the Claimants or any other female because of her sex. Carrols and its managers, supervisors, officers and agents are also enjoined from retaliating against any of the Claimants or any other female who has complained of sexual harassment, opposed discrimination, filed a charge of discrimination, or who gives testimony or assistance concerning the investigation or litigation of sexual harassment charges or lawsuits filed under Title VII. . . .

TRAINING

... Carrols will provide all new employees, within their first three (3) days at work, an E-learning training program that includes a module on recognizing, preventing, and eliminating sexual harassment in the workplace. This training program will be done on a computer at the work location provided by Carrols. The E-learning material will clearly make known that all employees have the right to work in an atmosphere which is free from sexual harassment, and that harassment in any form will not be tolerated. It will also include instruction on how to lodge a harassment complaint, including a list of personnel, by title and phone number, to whom such complaints may be addressed. In the event that a harassment complaint arising out of the employees' restaurant is substantiated, the employee and his or her co-workers will receive group retraining in these topics, such training to be provided in person by the Regional Human Resources Manager ("Regional HR Manager") or his or her designee within thirty (30) days of the conclusion of the investigation. ...

Carrols will provide all Restaurant Managers, Assistant Managers, and Shift Supervisors, within four (4) weeks of hire or promotion, a unit of no fewer than two (2) hours of formal in-person training on Human Resources issues, including training on anti-discrimination, anti-harassment, and anti-retaliation laws. If trainers are not available during the four (4) week period, this unit will be provided as early as is reasonably practicable within the training program required for each of these managers and supervisors. The training sessions will be conducted by the Training Manager or the Regional HR Manager during the existing management certification program. This training unit will emphasize managerial employees' obligation not only to refrain from harassment of and retaliation against any employee, but to report any harassment that they observe or that is reported to them. Carrols will also incorporate into the training of shift supervisors and managers material addressing the special needs of teenaged workers with respect to preventing and remedying sexual harassment. The training further will inform managerial employees that their annual appraisal will include review of their performance in these areas, ... and will explain to them how they will evaluate, and be evaluated, on compliance with Carrols' policies. Written materials on these topics will be provided to all managerial employees.

[A]ll Regional Vice-Presidents, Regional HR Managers, District Supervisors, Restaurant Managers, Assistant Managers, and Shift Supervisors, within six (6) months of hire or promotion, also will attend an approximately five (5)-hour training course, "Shades of Harassment," unless they have already taken that course prior to promotion.

[A]t each Annual Supervisors' Conference all Regional Vice-Presidents, Regional HR Managers and District Supervisors will attend a training module of at least one (1) hour concerning Carrols' policies and procedures and federal laws against harassment, discrimination, and retaliation, and on how to investigate complaints of sexual harassment.

[A]t each Annual Regional HR Managers' Meeting, all Regional HR Managers will attend a multi-day corporate-level seminar which will include training in on laws against discrimination; managing diverse workforce, including teenaged workers; how to investigate complaints of sexual harassment, consistent with the company's guidelines; and legal developments with respect to harassment. The training sessions will be conducted by Carrols' General Counsel. This training will include the use of videos and other written materials concerning sexual harassment, and tests to confirm managers' knowledge at the seminar's conclusion.

. . . Carrols will pay for Regional HR Managers' membership in SHRM [the Society for Human Resource Management] and offer Regional HR Managers the opportunity to attend periodic HR seminars and programs.

ANTI-DISCRIMINATION POLICIES

Commencing within ten (10) days of entry of this Decree, at the time Carrols provides the E-learning training . . . , Carrols will provide and review with all new employees a pamphlet entitled "Recognizing, Preventing and Eliminating Sexual Harassment," which includes a copy of Carrols' policy, "Preventing and Eliminating Sexual Harassment." That pamphlet has a tear-out form which states "the Carrols Corporation Sexual Harassment policy has been explained and reviewed with me and I understand its contents. I have received a copy of the Carrols Corporation Sexual Harassment Booklet." Managers will be instructed that it is their responsibility and obligation to secure a signed acknowledgement form from each new hire provided with these materials, and that their annual performance appraisals . . . will include evaluation of their compliance with this responsibility and obligation. . . . Within ninety (90) days of entry of this Decree: (a) Carrols' anti-harassment policies and complaint reporting contact information will be made available on Carrols .com, with a hyperlink to Carrolsethics.com; and (b) Carrols anti-harassment policies and complaint reporting contact information available on Carrols.com will be made available on Carrolsethics.com with an on-line reporting feature for employees to file complaints of sexual harassment, including anonymously. The anti-harassment policies and complaint reporting contact information also will be made available in Carrols restaurants in a three-ring binder near the bulletin board where all employee notices and policies are regularly displayed. Finally, Carrols will provide Restaurant Managers with additional copies of the policies and will inform employees of the policies' availability by notice in all of the locations described above.

Within one hundred and twenty (120) days of entry of this Decree, Carrols will delete any and all language in its policy, "Preventing and Reporting Sexual Harassment," and its PowerPoint training program, "Sexual Harassment Training," that references "false" and/or "malicious" harassment complaints or potential sanctions for such complaints. Carrols will not include the deleted language in any policies, procedures, or training related to sexual harassment. Within one hundred and twenty (120) days of entry of this Decree, Carrols will delete any and language in its pamphlet, "Recognizing, Preventing and Eliminating Sexual Harassment," its policy "Preventing and Reporting Sexual Harassment," and its E-learning training program indicating that non-supervisory employees are "obligated" or otherwise required to report all harassment, including any and all language indicating that employees are obligated to confront the harasser(s) before invoking Carrols' complaint procedure. Carrols will include in written materials and in training a statement that advises non-management employees that one of the steps they can take if harassed is to tell the harasser to stop and that sexual harassment should be reported promptly. Carrols will not include any of the deleted language in any policies, procedures, or training relating to sexual harassment. . . .

Carrols will offer all voluntarily departing hourly employees the opportunity to fill out a written exit interview form for submission to the Regional HR

Manager. . . . Carrols will offer all voluntarily departing managers the opportunity to fill out a written exit interview form for submission to the Regional HR Manager. . . . The notice received by the departing employee will contain his or her unique password-protected log-in code by which he or she can access Grapevine for the purpose of responding to the interview form these written exit interviews will specifically ask whether sexual harassment occurred at the restaurant where the employee worked, whether Carrols made the employee aware of how and to whom to report any kind of sexual harassment, and whether the employee ever complained of sexual harassment or participated in an investigation of a sexual harassment complaint. The exit interview also will afford an opportunity to provide a narrative response to these questions.

. . . Carrols' Vice President for Human Resources will receive immediate alerts when he or she receives negative responses to any of the sexual harassment-related exit interview questions. Carrols will investigate any complaint of sexual harassment uncovered in the course of an exit interview in accordance with its regular procedures for investigation of such complaints. Exit interviews including a complaint of sexual harassment will be shared with the appropriate District Supervisor(s) if the District Supervisor will be involved in the investigation of the complaint or if the complaint is determined to be substantiated however, an exit interview will not be provided prior to investigation to a district supervisor who is the object of a complaint contained in it. Additionally, all responses to the exit interviews will be provided to the appropriate District Supervisor(s) on a semi-annual basis.

COMPLAINT HOTLINE AND DEDICATED EMAIL ADDRESS

. . . Carrols will maintain a toll free Hotline telephone number run by outside provider EthicsPoint and an email address (the "dedicated email address") for employees to file complaints of sexual harassment, including anonymously. . . .

[C]omplaints of sexual harassment made through the Hotline or dedicated email, or made to the District Supervisor, the Vice President for Human Resources, or any manager at Carrols, will be referred to the relevant Regional HR Manager or his or her designee, or the designee of Corporate Human Resources for prompt and through investigation. The relevant District Supervisor also will be informed that a complaint has been received, unless the District Supervisor is the object of the complaint or to do so would compromise Carrols' ability to investigate pursuant to its anti-discrimination policy. Carrols will maintain guidelines for investigation of complaints of sexual harassment complaints, including the importance of considering demeanor of complainants and witnesses and the existence of prior complaints the maintenance of consistency in complaint resolution, and the importance and manner of informing complainant of investigation outcomes. . . . Individuals filing complaints of harassment or interviewed in the course of the investigation will be compensated for their time and given the option to conduct interviews (1) by phone; (2) by interview at the restaurant; or (3) in a meeting outside of their work location if they indicate they do not want to meet at the restaurant. . . .

AUDITS

. . . Carrols' Regional HR managers will conduct audits of HR practices in Carrols' restaurants as part of the biennial audit of each restaurant . . . and will provide the results to outside counsel of record of Carrols. . . . The audit will include question about whether any employee has been the victim of, or observed sexual harassment of another employee at their restaurant. . . .

MANAGER EVALUATION FORMS

[E]valuation forms for all Restaurant Managers, Assistant Managers and District Supervisors will include a criterion of adherence to EEO policies of Carrols. In particular, the Checklist of appraisal Characteristics for Managers for will include the following question: "To what extent does the individual take measures to prevent sexual harassment and discrimination and comply with federal, state and local employment law?" Reviewing managers will be requested to explain, in the comments portion of the review form, the basis for the rating assigned in this category . . .

DURATION OF DECREE AND RETENTION OF JURISDICTION

This Decree will remain in effect for two (2) years from the date of entry. . . .

Questions and Comments

1. Carrols, the defendant in this matter, was in 2013 the largest Burger King franchise in the world, operating more than 500 restaurants in 20 states.

2. This action was triggered when an employee of a Carrols' restaurant filed a complaint with the EEOC. The EEOC's subsequent investigation found evidence that female employees were sexually harassed in numerous Carrols restaurants in various states. Acts of harassment, according to the EEOC, included obscene comments, jokes, propositions, unwanted touching, exposure of genitalia, strip searches, stalking, and even rape — perpetrated by managers in the majority of cases. The EEOC also charged that Carrols retaliated against some of the victims by cutting their hours, concocting disciplinary charges against them, and even firing them, while it forced more women to quit because the harassment made their working conditions intolerable. The EEOC brought an action against Carrols' claiming that, by tolerating a pervasive environment of sexual harassment, it had engaged in a pattern or practice of discrimination based on sex.

3. Carrols denied the EEOC's allegations. It claimed that it had adopted a policy against sexual harassment in 1991, long before the EEOC's complaint was filed, that it had a zero tolerance policy towards harassment, and that it had vigorously enforced its anti-harassment policy, including termination of numerous employees. As for the instances of harassment cited by the EEOC, Carrols argued that most were unsubstantiated and that many of the complaints cited by the EEOC were lodged after the filing of this lawsuit and in response to the EEOC's solicitations.

4. Was Carrols wise to fight the EEOC so tenaciously? Did it have other options? What would you have advised if the senior managers presented their version of the case to you in 1998 after the EEOC had started its investigation?

5. The complaint in this action was filed in 1998; the case finally settled in 2013. Some of the employees whose claims were resolved in the settlement, teenagers at the time of the alleged infractions, were in their thirties by the time they received any compensation. Why was the litigation so protracted? Could it be that both sides were fighting for what they believed was a matter of principle? Who benefited most from the delay?

6. This consent decree is long and complicated, but the key elements are indicated by the headings. Which are the most important parts of the decree? Which are likely to be most effective at preventing a repeat of the alleged misconduct? Is anything left out that should have been included?

7. The monetary relief — $2.5 million — was one of the largest ever achieved by the EEOC in a sexual harassment case. It was distributed to 89 women who had filed claims against Carrols, for an average of approximately $28,000 per claimant. Assuming an interest rate of 5 percent, the present value of this relief in 1998 was approximately $14,000.

8. EEOC takes exception to certain language contained in Carrols' policy and training program relating to false reports of harassment. What was objectionable about the language? What could Carrols' have been trying to accomplish with the former language?

9. The EEOC's press release on the settlement stated that Carrols' would undertake "significant remedial steps." Carrols' press release on the settlement described the remedial portions as follows: "Carrols agreed to continue to uphold its obligations under Title VII and continue to maintain its existing and comprehensive anti-harassment policies and procedures and training programs" while making "certain enhancements" to such existing policies and procedures. Do you detect a difference in tone?

10. Most of the employees of Carrols' restaurants are in their teens or early twenties, and many do not have much education. What accommodations does the consent decree make for this circumstance? How effective do you think exposure to the e-learning material will be at informing new employees of their rights and duties under the law of sexual harassment? Presumably, the store manager puts the new employee in a back room at the restaurant in front of a computer, powers up the e-learning program, and tells the employee to review the materials. Will this have much of an effect? On the other hand, what else could the company (and the EEOC) do?

11. Another way of preventing harassment is to foster a culture that views preventing sexual harassment as an important priority of the company. This requires that people in management be involved. What does the decree do to enlist the cooperation and "buy in" of managers? Will these steps be effective?

12. This decree expires after two years. Given that the litigation had already dragged out for fifteen years, is two years enough? After the expiration of the decree, what would you advise the management of Carrols regarding whether to continue the provisions of the decree in effect?

13. What happens if Carrols is acquired by another company and its stores and management are consolidated into the acquirer's operation? Does the consent decree remain effective? How can it continue in effect if the identity of the defendant is extinguished by the acquisition? The consent decree addresses this issue as follows: "Carrols . . . will provide written notice and a copy of this Decree to any prospective successors or assigns and will simultaneously inform EEOC of the same . . ." What is the effect of this requirement? Could EEOC seek to prevent the merger if the acquiring firm doesn't have an equally effective sexual harassment policy in effect?

14. Was this case a victory for the EEOC, a defeat, or something in between? What significance do you give to the fact that after 15 years of litigation Carrols never admitted any fault?

16

Ethics, Social Responsibility, and Culture

So far we have addressed the issue of legal compliance — making sure that organizations abide under the law. But compliance may not be all we would wish of a company. Perhaps, in addition to following the rules and making a profit for shareholders, organizations should be encouraged to go beyond their formal obligations in the service of the public interest. This chapter deals with the issue of ethical or moral responsibilities of complex organizations and with the question of how these responsibilities can be enforced within a system of internal controls.

A. CHARITABLE GIFTS

A.P. Smith Mfg. Co. v. Barlow

13 N.J. 145, 98 A.2d 581 (1953)

The Chancery Division, in a well-reasoned opinion by Judge Stein, determined that a donation by the plaintiff The A.P. Smith Manufacturing Company to Princeton University was intra vires. Because of the public importance of the issues presented, the appeal duly taken to the Appellate Division has been certified directly to this court. . . .

   The company was incorporated in 1896 and is engaged in the manufacture and sale of valves, fire hydrants and special equipment, mainly for water and gas industries. Its plant is located in East Orange and Bloomfield and it has approximately 300 employees. Over the years the company has contributed regularly to the local community chest and on occasions to Upsala College in East Orange and Newark University, now part of Rutgers, the State University. On July 24, 1951 the board of directors adopted a resolution which set forth that it was in the corporation's best interests to join with others in the 1951 Annual Giving to Princeton University, and appropriated the sum of $1,500 to be transferred by the corporation's treasurer to the university as a contribution towards its maintenance. When this action was questioned by stockholders the corporation instituted a declaratory judgment action in the Chancery Division and trial was had in due course.

Mr. Hubert F. O'Brien, the president of the company, testified that he considered the contribution to be a sound investment, that the public expects corporations to aid philanthropic and benevolent institutions, that they obtain good will in the community by so doing, and that their charitable donations create favorable environment for their business operations. In addition, he expressed the thought that in contributing to liberal arts institutions, corporations were furthering their self-interest in assuring the free flow of properly trained personnel for administrative and other corporate employment. Mr. Frank W. Abrams, chairman of the board of the Standard Oil Company of New Jersey, testified that corporations are expected to acknowledge their public responsibilities in support of the essential elements of our free enterprise system. He indicated that it was not "good business" to disappoint "this reasonable and justified public expectation," nor was it good business for corporations "to take substantial benefits from their membership in the economic community while avoiding the normally accepted obligations of citizenship in the social community." Mr. Irving S. Olds, former chairman of the board of the United States Steel Corporation, pointed out that corporations have a self-interest in the maintenance of liberal education as the bulwark of good government. He stated that "Capitalism and free enterprise owe their survival in no small degree to the existence of our private, independent universities" and that if American business does not aid in their maintenance it is not "properly protecting the long-range interest of its stockholders, its employees and its customers." Similarly, Dr. Harold W. Dodds, President of Princeton University, suggested that if private institutions of higher learning were replaced by governmental institutions our society would be vastly different and private enterprise in other fields would fade out rather promptly. Further on he stated that "democratic society will not long endure if it does not nourish within itself strong centers of non-governmental fountains of knowledge, opinions of all sorts not governmentally or politically originated. If the time comes when all these centers are absorbed into government, then freedom as we know it, I submit, is at an end."

The objecting stockholders have not disputed any of the foregoing testimony nor the showing of great need by Princeton and other private institutions of higher learning and the important public service being rendered by them for democratic government and industry alike. Similarly, they have acknowledged that for over two decades there has been state legislation on our books which expresses a strong public policy in favor of corporate contributions such as that being questioned by them. Nevertheless, they have taken the position that (1) the plaintiff's certificate of incorporation does not expressly authorize the contribution and under common-law principles the company does not possess any implied or incidental power to make it, and (2) the New Jersey statutes which expressly authorize the contribution may not constitutionally be applied to the plaintiff, a corporation created long before their enactment. . . .

When the wealth of the nation was primarily in the hands of individuals they discharged their responsibilities as citizens by donating freely for charitable purposes. With the transfer of most of the wealth to corporate hands and the imposition of heavy burdens of individual taxation, they have been unable to keep pace with increased philanthropic needs. They have therefore, with justification, turned to corporations to assume the modern obligations of good citizenship in the same manner as humans do. Congress and state legislatures have enacted laws which encourage corporate contributions, and much has recently been written to indicate the crying need and adequate legal basis therefor. In actual practice corporate giving has correspondingly increased. Thus, it is estimated that annual corporate contributions throughout the nation aggregate over 300 million dollars, with over 60 million dollars thereof going to universities and other educational institutions. Similarly, it is estimated that local community chests receive well over 40% of their contributions from corporations; these contributions and those made by corporations to the American Red Cross, to Boy Scouts and Girl Scouts, to 4-H Clubs and similar organizations have almost invariably been unquestioned.

During the First World War corporations loaned their personnel and contributed substantial corporate funds in order to insure survival; during the depression of the '30s they made contributions to alleviate the desperate hardships of the millions of unemployed; and during the Second World War they again contributed to insure survival. They now recognize that we are faced with other, though nonetheless vicious, threats from abroad which must be withstood without impairing the vigor of our democratic institutions at home and that otherwise victory will be pyrrhic indeed. More and more they have come to recognize that their salvation rests upon sound economic and social environment which in turn rests in no insignificant part upon free and vigorous nongovernmental institutions of learning. It seems to us that just as the conditions prevailing when corporations were originally created required that they serve public as well as private interests, modern conditions require that corporations acknowledge and discharge social as well as private responsibilities as members of the communities within which they operate. Within this broad concept there is no difficulty in sustaining, as incidental to their proper objects and in aid of the public welfare, the power of corporations to contribute corporate funds within reasonable limits in support of academic institutions. But even if we confine ourselves to the terms of the common-law rule in its application to current conditions, such expenditures may likewise readily be justified as being for the benefit of the corporation; indeed, if need be the matter may be viewed strictly in terms of actual survival of the corporation in a free enterprise system. The genius of our common law has been its capacity for growth and its adaptability to the needs of the times. Generally courts have accomplished the desired result indirectly through the molding of old forms. Occasionally they have done it directly through frank rejection of the old and recognition of the new. But whichever path the common law has taken it has not been found wanting as the proper tool for the advancement of the general good. . . .

In encouraging and expressly authorizing reasonable charitable contributions by corporations, our State has not only joined with other states in advancing the national interest but has also specially furthered the interests of its own people who must bear the burdens of taxation resulting from increased state and federal aid upon default in voluntary giving. It is significant that in its enactments the State has not in anywise sought to impose any compulsory obligations or alter the corporate objectives. And since in our view the corporate power to make reasonable charitable contributions exists under modern conditions, even apart from express statutory provision, its enactments simply constitute helpful and confirmatory declarations of such power, accompanied by limiting safeguards.

In the light of all of the foregoing we have no hesitancy in sustaining the validity of the donation by the plaintiff. There is no suggestion that it was made indiscriminately or to a pet charity of the corporate directors in furtherance of personal rather than corporate ends. On the contrary, it was made to a preeminent institution of higher learning, was modest in amount and well within the limitations imposed by the statutory enactments, and was voluntarily made in the reasonable belief that it would aid the public welfare and advance the interests of the plaintiff as a private corporation and as part of the community in which it operates. We find that it was a lawful exercise of the corporation's implied and incidental powers under common-law principles and that it came within the express authority of the pertinent state legislation. As has been indicated, there is now widespread belief throughout the nation that free and vigorous non-governmental institutions of learning are vital to our democracy and the system of free enterprise and that withdrawal of corporate authority to make such contributions within reasonable limits would seriously threaten their continuance. Corporations have come to recognize this and with their enlightenment have sought in varying measures, as has the plaintiff by its contribution, to insure and strengthen the society which gives them existence and the means of aiding themselves and their fellow citizens. Clearly then, the appellants, as individual stockholders whose private interests rest entirely upon the well-being of the plaintiff corporation, ought not be permitted to close their eyes to present-day realities and thwart the long-visioned corporate action in recognizing and voluntarily discharging its high obligations as a constituent of our modern social structure.

The judgment entered in the Chancery Division is in all respects affirmed.

Questions and Comments

1. This is an important precedent in the development of the modern legal attitude toward corporate charitable giving. Early cases were reluctant to allow corporations to make charitable gifts on the theory that support for the welfare of society was *ultra vires*—outside the scope of corporate powers. Here, the New Jersey court boldly rejects that approach and endorses liberal corporate charitable giving.

2. What limits does the court recognize in how much a corporation may give to charity, or what kinds of charity it may favor with its largesse?

3. Do you agree that corporations should be given wide latitude to support charitable causes? Could a shareholder complain that she invested in the company to make a profit, not to support charity? Could a shareholder complain that even if she supports charity, she should be allowed to make the decision about what charity to support and how much to give?

4. What if a shareholder in the A.P. Smith Company had a grudge against Princeton University? Is there anything she can do, after this decision, if the company makes a gift to that school?

5. The gift in question was for a relatively small amount of money ($1,500), and the company had without controversy made gifts to other charitable causes. Why did the shareholder in the excerpted case care so much?

6. The complaining shareholder conceded that that educational institutions perform an important public service, that such institutions have a compelling need for private financial support, that the New Jersey legislature had encouraged charitable donations by corporations, and so on. Why give these points away?

7. How was the A.P. Smith Company able to enlist the assistance of luminaries such as Frank W. Abrams, chairman of the board of the Standard Oil Company of New Jersey, or Irving S. Olds, former chairman of the board of the United States Steel Corporation, in a petty squabble over a $1,500 gift?

8. The court, in effect, accepted expert testimony from the president of A.P. Smith and also the president of Princeton University. Was this appropriate, given that these people had a personal interest in the case?

9. The court says that "we are faced with other, though nonetheless vicious, threats from abroad which must be withstood without impairing the vigor of our democratic institutions at home and that otherwise victory will be pyrrhic indeed." The opinion was written in 1953, at the height of the Red Scare. What does a charitable gift to Princeton University have to do with the fear that communists were infiltrating U.S. institutions?

10. For an analysis concluding that the excerpted opinion was the product of collusive litigation, see Geoffrey Miller, *Narrative and Truth in Judicial Opinions: Corporate Charitable Giving Cases*, 2009 Mich. St. L. Rev. 831 ("As would be expected in such a situation, the parties selected for the roles were out of central casting: the old-line, traditional manufacturing firm, paragon of integrity and virtue, wishing to make a small contribution to a valuable cause, motivated by a benign mix of idealism, patriotism, and enlightened self-interest, and, in the co-starring role, the state's most elite university, founded before the Declaration of Independence, framer and shaper of the leaders of tomorrow—all played out against the backdrop of an insidious threat of subversion at home and danger abroad. In this posture, the matter was presented to New Jersey judges who were more than willing to wink at the collusion, provide the necessary legal authorization, and, for good measure, deliver a heartfelt encomium to the virtues of corporate charitable giving.").

11. For general commentary on corporate charitable giving, see Faith Stevelman Kahn, *Pandora's Box: Managerial Discretion and the Problem of Corporate Philanthropy*, 44 UCLA L. Rev. 579 (1997); Nancy J. Knauer, *The Paradox of Corporate Giving: Tax Expenditures, the Nature of the Corporation, and the Social Construction of Charity*, 44 DePaul L. Rev. 1 (1994).

PROBLEM 16-1

Flush-n-Go Corp. manufactures toilets for airplanes and buses. The company's product is more environmentally friendly than its competitors because it uses fewer toxic chemicals; for the same reason, the product is also more expensive. Since going public three years ago, the company has barely turned a profit. Sumit Khana, the chief executive officer, believes that the company's best hope is to promote itself with opinion leaders and senior managers of companies with large travel budgets. Accordingly, she proposes that the company become a "sponsor" of the city's symphony orchestra, at a cost of $300,000. The names of sponsors are prominently displayed in all symphony programs and publications, and sponsoring organizations are given free tickets to all symphony performances. Sumit proposes this gift to her board of directors with the argument that it will help the company achieve name recognition and create a favorable impression with people who can help promote its product. She knows this, she says, because she and her husband are classical music fans and because her husband's brother is under consideration for the position of conductor. The board approves the gift even though it will reduce the annual dividend from $5/share to $4/share. The resolution of approval states that "the board finds that the gift will materially enhance the company's strategy of increasing market penetration." You are a corporate attorney with a small firm in town. A dissident shareholder asks you to represent him, on a contingency fee basis, in a lawsuit challenging the Flush-n-Go gift. Should you take the case?

B. PUBLIC BENEFIT COMPANIES

The past decade has witnessed the rise of state statutes that authorize the creation of special business entities that are allowed to seek both profitable and charitable goals. Variously dubbed "benefit corporations," "low-profit limited liability companies," "flexible purpose corporations," or other names, the distinguishing mark of these firms is that charitable or public interest activities are not merely a sideline to a profit-making business, but rather a central focus of the organization. Part of the justification for these entities is that people who invest in them do so knowing that the entity will be devoted in part to charitable causes; investors cannot then object when the company behaves in eleemosynary ways. These organizations may also capture certain tax benefits because they offer charitable foundations a way to invest funds that they would otherwise be required to distribute.

It is too early yet to assess whether these entities will become a significant part of the business landscape. States incur few costs authorizing their creation, but that does not mean that many such entities will be established, or if established, that they will flourish. Nevertheless, the speed with which states have fallen into line in enacting social benefit corporation statutes illustrates that there is considerable enthusiasm for the idea.

Questions and Comments

1. Is there a need for public benefit corporations, given that for-profit companies have wide latitude these days to make gifts to charity and that not-for-profit corporations serve some of the same purposes?

2. If created, will these organizations be able to compete with for-profit corporations in the private benefit side of their operation?

3. For a suggestion that the nature of the organization can form part of a firm's "brand," see Matthew C. Hutchens, *Beneficial Branding: Will Benefit Corporations Promote Environmental Interests More Effectively than the Traditional Corporate Form?* (Oct. 24, 2013), available at SSRN: http://ssrn.com/abstract=2344896 or http://dx.doi .org/10.2139/ssrn.2344896.

4. For discussion of the rise of these firms, see Lyman Johnson, *Pluralism in Corporate Form: Corporate Law and Benefit Corps.*, 25 Regent U. L. Rev. 269 (2012-2013). For skeptical analysis, see Brian Galle, *Social Enterprise— Who Needs It?*, 54 B.C. L. Rev. 2025 (2013); Kent Greenfield, *A Skeptic's View of Benefit Corporations*, 1 Emory Corp. Governance & Accountability Rev. 17 (2015).

5. What are the fiduciary duties of directors at public benefit corporations? The Model Act directs that "[i]n discharging the duties of their respective positions and in considering the best interests of the benefit corporation, the . . . directors . . . (1) shall consider the effects of any action or inaction upon" a list of persons including the shareholders, employees, customers, "community and societal factors," the environment, long-term interests, and "the ability of the benefit corporation to accomplish its general public benefit purpose and any specific public benefit purpose." Model Act §301(a). Should the conventional duties of care and loyalty change when the company's objectives include activities serving the broader social welfare? For example, given that one of the purposes of these firms is to serve public goals, should members of the public have standing to enforce the director's

fiduciary duty to serve the company's objectives? Most state public benefit statutes, as well as the Model Act, provide broad protections for directors against the threat of having to pay damages for failing to pursue public benefits. Those protections, however, may not be a complete shield to damages liability. For discussion, see Brett McDonnell, Committing to Doing Good and Doing Well: Fiduciary Duty in Benefit Corporations, 20 Ford. J. Corp. & Fin. L. 19 (2014).

C. CODES OF ETHICS

Many companies have adopted codes of ethics that call on their employees and others to abide by high standards of behavior. The general theme of these ethics codes is that the company is encouraging or demanding that anyone affiliated with the firm go beyond what is merely required by law or regulation and display a higher level of socially conscious business conduct.

Ethics codes have a hortatory element: They admonish people to act in commendable ways. Judge Cardozo's description of the duties partners owe to one another, in Meinhard v. Salmon, 164 N.E. 545 (N.Y. 1928) (discussed in Chapter 2), is a classic example; although he was describing the nature of a fiduciary duty enforceable in law, it is clear that his language was intended

> A code of ethics is a formal statement, endorsed by the highest authority in the organization, of the organization's expectations regarding the conduct of employees and other constituents.

to encourage managers to do the right thing on their own, even without the lash of legal compulsion. Joint co-adventurers, Cardozo announced, are "held to something stricter than the morals of the market place. Not honesty alone, but the punctilio of an honor the most sensitive, is then the standard of behavior . . . the level of conduct for fiduciaries [has] been kept at a level higher than that trodden by the crowd." Id. at 546.

Questions and Comments

1. What is the purpose of hortatory rhetoric such as that quoted from Meinhard v. Salmon? Is it to induce a moral sense in people who might otherwise act in a self-interested way? To mark out a standard of fair dealing that goes beyond what is ordinarily required, so that people don't accidentally transgress the boundaries of the law? To claim a moral high ground for the courts and thus deflect criticism of the law's failure to insist on better behavior?

2. To what extent is an organization's ethics code legally binding? This question comes up in the context of securities fraud lawsuits where company executives simultaneously promulgate and violate a corporate code of ethics. Plaintiffs in such cases may claim that the company's statements regarding its commitment to the code of ethics are false and misleading given that senior executives were flouting the rules. In general, these lawsuits have not succeeded: The courts view ethics codes as "puffery" that cannot support a claim of reliance. *See* Andropolis v. Red Robin Gourmet Burgers, Inc., 505 F. Supp. 2d 662, 685-686 (D. Colo. 2007) ("[A] code of ethics is inherently aspirational; it simply cannot be that every time a violation of that

code occurs, a company is liable under federal law for having chosen to adopt the code at all. . . ."). Do you agree that investors should not be entitled to rely on corporate codes of ethics? If these codes can't be relied on, what credibility do they have?

3. Even if a securities fraud action cannot be maintained against a company that violates its own ethics code, could shareholders successfully prosecute a derivative action based on the same conduct, on the theory that if a company defines standards of corporate ethics, those standards become obligations binding on the company's directors and executives?

What provisions are typically found in a corporate code of ethics? Consider the following ethics codes of Mike's Bagels, a (fictional) manufacturer of baked bread products.

Mike's Bagels, Code of Ethics and Professional Conduct

Mike's Bagels conducts its business ethically, honestly, and in full compliance with all laws and regulations. This policy applies to employees, independent contractors, consultants, and others who do business with the company.

All persons who are subject to this policy are expected to observe the following principles:

- Compliance: Comply with all applicable laws and regulations.
- Honesty: Demonstrate truthfulness in all business dealings.
- Confidentiality: Protect the confidentiality of Mike's Bagel's recipes, production methods, and business practices, as well as non-public information provided by our customers, suppliers, and employees.
- Respect: Treat others with respect and courtesy.

Persons subject to this policy shall engage in the following conduct:

- Follow the policy: If you are unable to comply with this policy, you should terminate your affiliation with the company.
- Notify appropriate officers if you know of possible violations of the policy or of legal or regulatory requirements.
- Use good judgment: Every case is different, and must be evaluated according to its unique facts and circumstances.
- When in doubt, ask questions about what to do. Don't rely on your own interpretation if you are not sure about your obligations. Mike's Bagels' human resources department, General Counsel's office, or other senior management officers will be glad to be of assistance.

Mike's Bagels will not retaliate — and will not tolerate retaliation — against any individual for filing a good faith complaint.

Questions and Comments

1. Should corporate ethics codes apply to the personal lives of senior managers, even if they have done nothing at all wrong on the job?

2. Section 406 of the Sarbanes-Oxley Act gives a nudge in favor of corporate codes of ethics by requiring public companies to disclose to shareholders whether

they have adopted a code of ethics for senior managers — and, if they have not done so, explain why not.

3. What is accomplished by declaring in a formal document that employers should be courteous and respectful?

4. Would you favor a code of ethics that requires employees of a company to contribute at least 5 percent of their incomes to charity?

PROBLEM 16-2

You are head of human resources for Albion, a publisher of Christian-themed books. The senior managers are evangelical Christians; they view their work life as an extension of their faith. The chief executive officer hands you a draft "code of company ethics" for your review. The code states, in part, "All employees of Albion are expected to manifest in their professional and their personal lives a commitment to basic Christian values: humility, kindness, patience, respect, responsibility, truthfulness, loyalty, and compassion for others." How should you respond?

D. SOCIAL RESPONSIBILITY

Corporate social responsibility (CSR) has been a leading theme for activists in the corporate governance area for generations. The basic motivation behind the CSR movement is to push corporations away from an exclusive focus on earning a profit for shareholders and more in the direction of providing value for society as a whole. The social values promoted by CSR are something of a grab bag; they include, among others, human rights, animal rights, workplace safety, environmental protection, "unfair" business practices, worker's rights, community development, and consumer protection. There are many definitions of CSR; the one set forth in the text box, although undoubtedly under-inclusive, is sufficient for our purposes.

A key to corporate social responsibility is that the desired conduct is not forced (or not explicitly forced) on corporations. Firms are expected to adopt socially responsible policies and goals on their own and thereafter to work to achieve those objectives through ordinary mechanisms of corporate governance. Part of the argument for CSR is that adopting socially responsible policies is not only good for society but also good for

> "Corporate social responsibility" refers to the concept that corporations should seek to advance broader social objectives rather than focus exclusively on earning a profit for shareholders.

business and for shareholders: Companies that adopt enlightened CSR policies, it is said, will perform as well or better than companies that do not.

Of course, corporate boards of directors may have different ideas, as might shareholders who wish to leave the achievement of broader social objectives to the government or other private actors. The CSR movement therefore has sought to bring the power of public opinion to bear on corporate managers and directors, shaming them if they fail to implement good CSR policies and lauding them if they do. CSR also seeks to change corporate values from within, by encouraging the election of directors who are committed to a socially progressive agenda.

Questions and Comments

1. Is there coherence to the idea of CSR other than that corporations should be good?

2. Proponents of CSR tend to make two general arguments: (a) CSR is beneficial for companies, so managers should adopt it even if their sole objective is to maximize shareholder returns; and (b) even if CSR does not maximize shareholder returns, it should be adopted because it is better for society. For the first argument, CSR proponents sometimes claim that shareholder returns are improved by socially responsible activities due to the fact that customers will reward companies for good behavior and punish them for bad behavior; they also argue that even without consequences of being known as a "good guy" or a "bad guy," companies can improve shareholder returns by adopting socially responsible activities simply because these activities are themselves good business.

3. Do you agree with these arguments? If CSR is good for shareholders, why is a CSR movement needed — why don't managers adopt socially responsible policies on their own? Is it of interest that corporate social responsibility initiatives tend to be defeated by wide margins when included in shareholder resolutions in company proxy statements? Could it be that managers and shareholders have an excessively narrow or short-term perspective on corporate decisions?

4. Do you agree that even if CSR doesn't enhance shareholder value, it should be adopted because of the benefits it affords to society as a whole? Granting that social benefits are desirable, are profit-oriented companies the best vehicles to achieve those results?

5. CSR is promoted by international standard-setting bodies. The most important of these is the International Organization for Standardization (ISO). ISO standard 26000, introduced in 2010, contains advice and guidance on socially responsible behavior and best practices, but is not intended as a set of mandatory requirements.

6. CSR initiatives have progressed further outside the United States. India may be the most stringent of all: That country mandates that all large companies spend a share of their profits on qualifying social responsibility investments.

7. What motivates the groups that promote social responsibility agendas? Idealism is a fundamental factor, but social responsibility organizations may also provide private benefits to participants. For discussion, see Donald J. Kochan, *Corporate Social Responsibility in a Remedy-Seeking Society: A Public Choice Perspective*, 17 Chap. L. Rev. 413 (2014) (identifying objectives such as maximizing budgets, obtaining influence, increasing membership, securing jobs, and promoting wealth transfers into their organizations or constituencies). What is your sense of the motivating factors?

Companies often advertise their commitment to socially responsible values and projects. Look at the website of nearly any large company and you will find information on this topic.

To take one of hundreds of examples, consider the website of Chiquita Brands International, one of the world's leading producers and distributors of bananas and other produce. Chiquita's site declared in 2013 that "[w]e're dedicated and committed on a daily basis to be responsible citizens of the world in which we live." As to labor relations, the site noted that the company had adopted a labor rights standard, developed by Social Accountability International, which addressed issues such as child labor, forced or compulsory labor, working hours, workplace health and safety, discriminatory practices, and the right to collective bargaining. On environmental issues, the site mentioned Chiquita's engagement with Rainforest Alliance, an organization that "works to conserve biodiversity and ensure sustainable livelihoods by transforming land-use practices, business practices and consumer behavior." On community development and involvement, the site declared that "[f]or more than 100 years, Chiquita has been committed to improving the communities where we do business." Chiquita Brands International, in other words, is a "good guy" — aware of its moral obligation to serve the broader good, eager to work with members of the advocacy community, concerned about the welfare of its communities and its employees, and dedicated generally to improving the quality of life on the planet.

Questions and Comments

1. The company's literature promoting Chiquita's corporate social responsibility activities suggests that these are a "win" for everyone — workers, the environment, women, shareholders, local communities, employees, and the public at large. Could things be this easy?

2. Chiquita Brands' socially responsible policies and actions have no doubt contributed to the public betterment both in the United States and around the world. Yet despite the references to a long history of concern for employees, communities, and the environment, the company has not always received accolades from others. Chiquita, its subsidiaries or predecessors have been accused of a litany of bad acts including making payoffs to terrorists, intimidating workers, exposing employees to unsafe conditions, harming the environment, and facilitating human rights violations. Critiques of United Brands, a predecessor firm, appear in works by Latin American Nobel laureates Gabriel García Márquez, Pablo Neruda, and Miguel Ángel Asturias. In 2011, a federal district court denied motions to dismiss a class action lawsuit alleging that the company had aided and abetted acts of torture, extrajudicial killing, war crimes, and crimes against humanity. In re Chiquita Brands Int'l, Inc. Alien Tort Statute and Shareholder Derivative Litigation, 792 F. Supp. 2d 1301, 1317 (S.D. Fla. 2011). Could Chiquita's enthusiasm for CSR be, in part, a response to allegations of past misconduct?

3. In 2014, Chiquita agreed to be acquired by the Brazilian orange juice supplier Cutrale Group and private bank Safra Group for $681 million.

4. For an empirical analysis finding that companies with strong CSR activities also tend to provide good governance in other respects, see Allen Ferrell, Hao Liang & Luc Renneboog, Socially Responsible Firms, CentER Discussion Paper Series No. 2014-043, July 29, 2014 (cross-country finding that CSR ratings are higher for companies with fewer agency problems and that certain aspects of CSR (e.g., environmental, labor, and social protection) are associated with increased executive pay-for-performance sensitivity and the maximization of shareholder value).

5. Developments in the area of corporate social responsibility have been occurring outside the United States at an even faster pace. In April 2014, the European Parliament adopted a Directive on Disclosure of Non-Financial and Diversity Information by Certain Large Companies and Groups. This wide-ranging directive requires covered companies to disclose information regarding environmental concerns, diversity on their boards of directors, social and employee-related matters, human rights, and anti-corruption and bribery issues. The directive, which must be implemented by domestic legislation in member states, applies to firms with more

than 500 employees and exceeding certain minimum levels of financial activity, to their parent companies, and to publicly traded firms. *See* http://ec.europa.eu/internal_market/accounting/non-financial_reporting/index_en.htm.

E. HUMAN RIGHTS

To what extent should a company located in the United States concern itself with possible human rights abuses committed by states or state-affiliated actors in other countries where the U.S. company does business? The issue is one of fundamental importance given that, with ever increasing globalization, American business organizations are active in certain countries where the behaviors of governments fall short of what would be expected of a decent and civilized society.

The focus of human rights activism has traditionally been on state actors. In recent years, however, that focus has expanded to include corporations and other organizations whose activities influence abusive states and state-affiliated parties. Much attention has focused on the Alien Tort Claims Act, 28 U.S.C. §1350, which establishes federal court jurisdiction over "any civil action by an alien for a tort only, committed in violation of the law of nations or a treaty of the United States." If the law of nations is deemed to include principles of human rights—embodied, say, in international treaties or other legal documents—and if the statute applies to acts of corporations committed overseas, then federal courts could police against certain human rights violations committed in other countries. In 2011, however, the Supreme Court ruled that the presumption against extraterritorial application applies to the Alien Tort Claims Act—meaning that in many cases, the statute will not reach actions committed overseas, even if those actions are in violation of international law. Kiobel v. Royal Dutch Petroleum Co., 133 S. Ct. 1659 (2013).

Kiobel limited one possible mechanism for enforcing human rights requirements, but it also focused enhanced attention on the possible utility of others. Among the most important of these alternative mechanisms is human rights enforcement through corporate governance standards. Consider in this respect the following excerpt, from a publication of the United Nations High Commissioner for Human Rights, setting forth principles that had been endorsed by the United Nations Human Rights Council in 2011.

United Nations High Commissioner on Human Rights, Guiding Principles on Business and Human Rights

2011

. . . Business enterprises should respect human rights. This means that they should avoid infringing on the human rights of others and should address adverse human rights impacts with which they are involved.

The responsibility to respect human rights is a global standard of expected conduct for all business enterprises wherever they operate. It exists independently of States' abilities and/or willingness to fulfill their own human rights obligations, and does not diminish those obligations. And it exists over and above compliance with national laws and regulations protecting human rights.

Addressing adverse human rights impacts requires taking adequate measures for their prevention, mitigation and, where appropriate, remediation. Business enterprises may undertake other commitments or activities to support and promote human rights, which may contribute to the enjoyment of rights. But this does not offset a failure to respect human rights throughout their operations. . . .

The responsibility of business enterprises to respect human rights refers to internationally recognized human rights—understood, at a minimum, as those expressed in the International Bill of Human Rights and the principles concerning fundamental rights set out in the International Labor Organization's Declaration on Fundamental Principles and Rights at Work. . . .

The responsibility to respect human rights requires that business enterprises:

- Avoid causing or contributing to adverse human rights impacts through their own activities, and address such impacts when they occur;
- Seek to prevent or mitigate adverse human rights impacts that are directly linked to their operations, products or services by their business relationships, even if they have not contributed to those impacts. . . .

The responsibility of business enterprises to respect human rights applies to all enterprises regardless of their size, sector, operational context, ownership and structure. Nevertheless, the scale and complexity of the means through which enterprises meet that responsibility may vary according to these factors and with the severity of the enterprise's adverse human rights impacts. . . .

In order to meet their responsibility to respect human rights, business enterprises should have in place policies and processes appropriate to their size and circumstances, including:

- A policy commitment to meet their responsibility to respect human rights;
- A human rights due diligence process to identify, prevent, mitigate and account for how they address their impacts on human rights;
- Processes to enable the remediation of any adverse human rights impacts they cause or to which they contribute. . . .

As the basis for embedding their responsibility to respect human rights, business enterprises should express their commitment to meet this responsibility through a statement of policy that:

- Is approved at the most senior level of the business enterprise;
- Is informed by relevant internal and/or external expertise;
- Stipulates the enterprise's human rights expectations of personnel, business partners and other parties directly linked to its operations, products or services;
- Is publicly available and communicated internally and externally to all personnel, business partners and other relevant parties;
- Is reflected in operational policies and procedures necessary to embed it throughout the business enterprise. . . .

In order to identify, prevent, mitigate and account for how they address their adverse human rights impacts, business enterprises should carry out human rights due diligence. The process should include assessing actual and potential human rights impacts, integrating and acting upon the findings, tracking responses, and communicating how impacts are addressed. Human rights due diligence:

- Should cover adverse human rights impacts that the business enterprise may cause or contribute to through its own activities, or which may be directly linked to its operations, products or services by its business relationships;

- Will vary in complexity with the size of the business enterprise, the risk of severe human rights impacts, and the nature and context of its operations;
- Should be ongoing, recognizing that the human rights risks may change over time as the business enterprise's operations and operating context evolve. . . .

Questions and Comments

1. To what extent does this statement govern corporate policy in the United States?

2. Given this policy statement, should states of the United States revise their corporation codes to require companies chartered under their law to adopt written human rights policies? Should states require corporations to engage in human rights due diligence? Should due diligence of this sort be considered to be a part of a corporate director's fiduciary obligation?

3. What is the content of the "human rights" that the excerpted document calls on corporate boards to protect? The document refers to the International Labor Organization's Declaration on Fundamental Principles and Rights at Work, which in turn declares that "effective recognition of the right to collective bargaining" is a fundamental employment right. Should U.S. corporations be required to promote collective bargaining campaigns abroad when they may be actively (and legally) involved in resisting efforts to organize their own workers in the United States?

4. To what extent should attorneys take human rights issues into account when representing clients in international business transactions? Consider:

   a. Should contracts with firms in high-risk areas be drafted to include representations and warranties regarding the counterparty's human rights policies?
   b. Should contracts include specific provisions requiring the counterparty to undertake affirmative actions to combat human rights violations in its home country?
   c. What if the counterparty resists or refuses to include such terms — should the client do business with the firm?
   d. What if the client is party to a long-term supply contract with a foreign supplier, the contract doesn't contain any terms relevant to human rights, and the client finds out that the counterparty has engaged in human rights abuses?
   e. What if the lawyer is hired to do the technical legal tasks associated with a contract, but believes that the client should as a matter of ethics and good conscience take a stronger human rights stance with its business partners?
   f. Under what circumstances would a lawyer be required to withdraw from the representation if the client persistently fails to undertake actions to combat human rights violations by its counterparties?

5. Other international bodies that have endorsed an expanded role for private companies in enforcing human rights norms include the European Commission's "A Renewed EU Strategy for Corporate Social Responsibility" and the Organization for Economic Cooperation and Development's "Guidelines for Multinational Enterprises."

6. For commentary on some of these issues, see Faith Stevelman, *Global Finance, Multinationals and Human Rights: With Commentary on Backer's Critique of the 2008 Report by John Ruggie,* 9 Santa Clara J. Int'l L. 101 (2011); Jena Martin, *Business*

and Human Rights: What's the Board Got to Do with It?, 2013 U. Ill. L. Rev. 101; David Kinley & Junko Tadaki, *From Talk to Walk: The Emergence of Human Rights Responsibilities for Corporations at International Law*, 44 Va. J. Int'l L. 931 (2004).

Business today is international in scope; few companies obtain all their goods from domestic sources or market their products only within their own country. The internationalization of business raises the question of human rights violations by participants in their supply and distribution chains. Does a company have a legal or ethical obligation to insist on ethical behavior by counterparties?

In general, the answer has been "no": Human rights and other matters of corporate ethics have been enforced directly against the offending party, but that party's business partners do not have an enforceable obligation arising out of the problematic conduct. That general rule is beginning to erode at the edges, however.

Perhaps the most important move in the direction of imposing enhanced duties on counterparties is §1502 of the Dodd-Frank Act and accompanying SEC Rule 13p-1 and Form SD. These rules require SEC reporting firms to engage in due diligence and make disclosures in connection with their use of "conflict minerals" — defined to include cassiterite, columbite-tantalite, wolframite, gold, and other minerals designated by the SEC to be financing conflict in the Democratic Republic of the Congo and adjoining countries ("DRC countries"). Conflict minerals find their way into many products; they are common in automobile parts, electronic devices, and jewelry, among other items. If an issuer knows or has reason to believe that its conflict minerals may have originated in DRC countries (and may not have come from recycled or scrap sources), it is then required to prepare an audited "conflict minerals report" describing matters such as the products the issuer produces with conflict minerals, the facilities used to process conflict minerals, the country of origin of the minerals, and what efforts the issuer has made to determine the location of origin of the materials. As for what qualifies as supply chain due diligence, the SEC references the OECD's "Due Diligence Guidance for Responsible Supply Chains of Minerals from Conflict-Affected and High-Risk Areas."

Questions and Comments

1. The National Association of Manufacturers challenged the SEC's conflict minerals rule on the ground that the agency had failed adequately to consider the costs and benefits. A federal district court rejected the challenge in 2013. National Association of Manufacturers v. Securities and Exchange Commission, 2013 WL 3803918 (D.D.C. 2013). The National Association of Manufacturers and other business interests appealed the grant of summary judgment to the United States Court of Appeals. In April 2014, the court issued an opinion upholding the conflict minerals rule in most respects, but striking down on First Amendment grounds a provision of the statute and rule that required an issuer to describe its products as "not found to be 'DRC conflict free'" in the report it files with the Commission and must post on its website. 15 U.S.C. §78m(p)(1)(A)(ii) & (E). National Association of Manufacturers v. SEC, 748 F.3d 359 (D.C. Cir. 2014). The D.C. Circuit reaffirmed its constitutional ruling the following year. National Association of Manufacturers v. SEC, No. 13-5252 (D.C. Cir. 2015). In the wake of the appeals court decision, the SEC declared that an issuer is not required to identify its products as "DRC conflict free," "DRC conflict undeterminable," or "not found to be 'DRC conflict free.'" Issues may, however, voluntarily elect to do so. Issuers are

required to make all other disclosures required under the rule, including — for products that an issuer finds to be "DRC conflict undeterminable" or "not found to be 'DRC conflict free'" — disclosure of the facilities used to produce the minerals, the country of origin, and a description of the efforts the issuer has made to determine the location of origin.

2. Rule 13p-1 applies only to public companies. As a practical matter, however, the rule imposes a due diligence requirement on private suppliers to public firms, since they will be required to make conflict minerals disclosures to their purchasers.

3. What is the purpose of conflict minerals disclosure? To inform investors about the value of the company in which they invest? To inform investors about non-economic facts that might affect a person's investment decision? To shame companies into not using conflict minerals? To influence the outcome of civil strife in the DRC? All of the above?

4. What factors should companies take into consideration when preparing conflict minerals disclosures? Clearly, they need to comply with the SEC's regulation, but that document leaves many questions unanswered. Meanwhile human rights activists are warning companies that they expect more comprehensive disclosures than is required by the SEC. Should a company disclose more?

5. States are also beginning to take an interest in human rights enforcement through supply chain management. In 2011, California enacted legislation barring companies found to be in violation of the federal conflict minerals rule from participating in state contracts.

6. The task of compliance with the conflict minerals rule is daunting, because the issuer must inquire not only into its direct sources of minerals, but also into sources of its suppliers. A substantial number of vendors have entered the market to offer conflict minerals software compliance platforms that simplify and automate the process of supplier due diligence.

7. A principal purpose of the conflict minerals rule is to staunch the supply of money that is believed to be fueling and prolonging a conflict that has involved rape, gender-based violence, and other human rights violations. Is the conflict minerals policy likely to achieve this goal? If firms in some countries stop purchasing conflict minerals, will sellers turn to purchasers in other countries who are less scrupulous? Will the price of minerals rise in those countries that do regulate supply chains, thus increasing domestic costs? If a policy is successful at crimping off conflict minerals, moreover, might some of the losses fall on civilians who are the principal victims of the violence? If militias cease to pose a viable threat, would the central government celebrate victory with atrocities of its own?

8. If you agree with the policy underlying the conflict minerals rule, why stop there? It is not hard, looking around the world, to find markets where materials are produced in deplorable working conditions, or where funds from the sale of materials have fueled violence. What about "blood diamonds" mined in conflict zones in Angola, Sierra Leone, or Cote d'Ivoire? What about Indonesian "death metal" — tin mined on the island of Bangka under conditions that are alleged to be both unsafe for workers and harmful to the environment? What about garments manufactured in factories in Bangladesh, such as the Rana Plaza complex in Savar, where a building collapse cost nearly a thousand lives? What about coconuts, or bananas, or a host of other products that may be produced in poor countries under unsafe and inhumane working conditions?

9. For more on corporate responsibility for human rights violations in the global supply chain, see, e.g., Meredith R. Miller, *Corporate Codes of Conduct and Working*

Conditions in the Global Supply Chain: Accountability Through Transparency in Private Ordering (Oct. 20, 2013), available at SSRN: http://ssrn.com/abstract=2342756.

10. In addition to the conflict minerals rule, the Dodd-Frank Act mandated disclosure of "resource extraction" payments. The SEC summarized the purpose of this rule as being to help combat corruption and to empower citizens of resource-rich countries to hold their governments accountable. The Act requires the SEC to adopt rules under which any reporting company engaged in the commercial development of oil, natural gas, or minerals must provide annual disclosure of the amounts it pays to governments for that purpose. A proposed rule implementing this mandate failed to survive a court challenge in 2012. API v. SEC, No. 12-1668 (D.D.C. Oct. 10, 2012). In 2015, the SEC issued a revised rule. *See* SEC Release No. 34-76620 (Dec. 11, 2015).

Complex organizations have hundreds or thousands of suppliers, and suppliers can have hundreds or thousands of customers. The task of monitoring the supply chain could be unmanageable if every customer had to monitor every supplier. What alternatives can you imagine that might perform the job at lower cost? Consider the following:

1. What about an external audit of a supplier by an independent firm charged with evaluating its adherence to human rights and other norms? The results of the audit could be made available to the industry and, if the company receives a clean audit, could substitute for individual customer due diligence. Can you see advantages or disadvantages of this approach?

2. Alternatively, organizations might outsource their supply chain monitoring tasks to a professional monitor that is experienced in the monitoring task (and that, accordingly, can perform the job better and at lower expense). Is this preferable to the external audit approach?

3. Much depends on the attitudes, tolerances, and perceptions of the third party, whether in the role of external supply chain auditor or outsourced monitor. For discussion of how the characteristics of the party performing the assessment can affect the results obtained, see Jodi L. Short, Michael W. Toffel & Andrea Hugill, *Monitoring the Monitors: How Social Factors Influence Supply Chain Auditors* (2014), available at http://papers.ssrn.com/sol3/papers.cfm?abstract_id=2343802.

PROBLEM 16-3

Pomfruit Corporation, a Delaware company listed on the New York Stock Exchange, is in the business of importing tropical fruits for sale in gourmet groceries throughout the United States. One of its most profitable items is the fafaraway, a citrus fruit that is purported to have anti-oxidant and anti-aging properties. Pomfruit purchases fafaraways from a company operating in the West African nation of Gormanda, the only place where the fruit is currently produced. Pomfruit's supplier is a government-owned enterprise; the sales revenues are contributed to Gormanda's general budget account. Recently, reports have appeared in the news media that the government of Gormanda is brutally suppressing a rebellion in the tribal area where fafaraway is grown. You are an independent member of the board of directors of Pomfruit. What are your obligations upon hearing these reports?

PROBLEM 16-4

Same as above, but instead of the government suppressing a rebellion, Pomfruit's supplier is resisting efforts to unionize the workforce by importing "scab" labor from other parts of the country and firing workers suspected of harboring union sympathies.

PROBLEM 16-5

Same as above, but assume that shareholder proposals asking the company to evaluate possible responses to these issues have been defeated in each of the past two years by overwhelming margins.

PROBLEM 16-6

You are chief ethics officer at Sweetcheeks, a manufacturer of naturally sweetened beverages. Your company obtains its sugar under a long-term supply contract with Bangor Brands, an international commodities firm based in Thailand. Bangor Brands, in turn, obtains its sugar in Cambodia from Khmerco, a company half-owned by Bangor Brands and half-owned by the Cambodian government. Landsaver Foundation, a well-known human rights organization, brings to your attention an allegation that Khmerco has obtained the land for its plantations by evicting the local population. Claiming that Khmerco has engaged in an illegal "land grab," Landsaver demands that your company immediately cease doing business with Sweetcheeks or it will launch a publicity campaign against you. You raise the issue with your company's CEO, who observes that because of commodity price increases, Sweetcheeks is obtaining its sugar from Bangor Brands at 25 percent below the market price. What should you do?

F. SUSTAINABILITY

While the notion of corporate social responsibility has been a leading theme in corporate governance debates for generations, the notion of sustainability is a more recent entrant onto the scene. Sustainability is a concept borrowed from the field of ecology; the idea is that a corporation should operate in such a manner that the environment would support its continuing to do so indefinitely. The notion of sustainability is an aspect of corporate social responsibility but one that has been

> An activity is sustainable if it is consistent with the needs and interests of future generations.

separated out from other social responsibility concepts in order to focus attention (and pressure) on this issue in particular.

Judd F. Sneirson, Green Is Good: Sustainability, Profitability, and a New Paradigm for Corporate Governance

94 Iowa L. Rev. 987 (2009)

Sustainable businesses aspire to [tread] as lightly as possible on the earth and its natural resources. . . . This sort of business model may include behaviors — such as being more than minimally compliant with environmental regulations, being more than minimally generous towards employees, or paying more for goods and services that are sustainably harvested or humanely produced — that sacrifice profits in the short run. Studies have shown, however, that these practices on the whole pay for themselves and sometimes even enhance profitability. As many firms have shown and seem to believe, it is quite possible, and profitable, to "do well by doing good."

Two complementary ways of operationalizing sustainability in business have emerged in the management literature: one that applies a "triple bottom line" approach to measuring corporate performance and success, and a second method that calls for businesses to "gear up" through increasingly pervasive levels of sustainability.

The triple-bottom-line approach to sustainable business views corporate performance and success in three separate dimensions: "economic prosperity, environmental quality, and social justice." That is, in addition to "the traditional bottom line of financial performance . . . sustainable firms must also mind "their impact on the broader economy, the environment, and on the society in which they operate." By using this approach in its accounting, a firm can measure its financial success as well as the extent to which it is "reducing (or increasing) the options available to future generations" during a particular reporting period.

Triple-bottom-line adherents argue that a sustainable mindset not only helps the environment and society, it can also help firms' financial bottom lines. For example, efforts to reduce waste and pollution often result in greater efficiency and the discovery of innovative techniques and materials, all of which in turn can benefit the firm, its workforce, and the environment in both the short and the long runs. Such opportunities often lurk in the zones where business interests and stakeholder interests overlap, "where the pursuit of profit blends seamlessly with the pursuit of the common good." Thus, an energy company's triple-bottom-line efforts might focus on renewable-energy sources, an automobile company's efforts might focus on fuel efficiency and hybrid and fuel-cell technologies, and a food company's efforts might focus on healthful options and reduced packaging. In each of these examples, a company can better its financial bottom line while also bettering its social and environmental bottom lines.

A second strategy for incorporating sustainability principles into a business is the "gearing up" framework. Like a manual transmission, the framework is designed to take a company from a level of bare compliance with applicable law to a place where sustainability is a systemic, integrated part of its strategy that transforms its business model and markets. Viewed in this way, sustainability is not just a kinder, gentler way of conducting business; it is a "catalyst for growth and innovation" that can transform an entire industry, with committed, sustainable companies at the leading edge.

The framework's first gear denotes compliance. In this first stage, a firm views the business case for sustainability with skepticism and, aside from generic corporate philanthropy, does little beyond comply with applicable labor and environmental regulations. In second gear, firms voluntarily move beyond mere compliance, view sustainability as legitimate though mostly a public-relations matter, and focus their efforts on "eco-efficiency" and "measuring, managing, and reducing" the direct impact of their operations. Companies that shift into third gear are more proactive in their efforts, often partnering with the government as well as "suppliers, customers, and others in their industry" to innovate sustainable solutions together. By fourth gear, a firm has integrated sustainability principles into its strategy and business processes (starting with product or service development), putting the firm at a competitive advantage in its sector and at the same time creating value for all of its stakeholder groups. In the fifth and highest gear, companies redesign or "reengineer" their business models, financial institutions, and markets to root out underlying causes of non-sustainability at "macro" (planetary ecological limits), "meso" (human-consumption demands), and "micro" (industry and company) levels. To be sure, "for many people, most of the time, four gears is enough, [b]ut there are times when it is necessary to shift into fifth gear, or overdrive."

Nike, the familiar sportswear and equipment company, explicitly follows the gearing-up framework. According to a recent corporate-responsibility report, most of its current efforts lie in the fourth, or redesign, gear. The company has deliberately rethought its entire design and production processes to reduce waste; to utilize improved, sustainable, and even reusable materials; and in some cases to eliminate the use of harmful materials altogether. Specifically, the company has, among other efforts, instituted recycling programs that turn used athletic shoes into playing-field surfaces and replaced adhesives with stitching on some of its footwear lines. Nike's efforts at "considered design" present an "enormous opportunity for innovation that can benefit [its] business and society," its supply chain and, one assumes, Nike's entire industry.

Questions and Comments

1. What do you think of the idea of corporate sustainability? Is it an excellent way to enlist the private sector in the important task of environmental protection and climate change management?

2. The author of this excerpt makes both of the standard arguments in favor of sustainability: Sustainable initiatives can be profitable for companies using conventional measures, and even if they are not, they are still desirable. On the latter point, the author notes that "[green] business practices can sometimes entail profit sacrifices, particularly in the short term. A conflict thus arises with the commonly held view that corporate directors and officers must strive to maximize shareholder wealth and affirmatively neglect other corporate constituencies like labor, creditors, suppliers, customers, the public, and the environment. This perceived duty to maximize shareholder profits lies at the heart of the conventional law-and-economics-laced view of corporate governance, thus imposing a formidable obstacle to corporations wishing to become more sustainable." In parts of the article not excerpted here, the author seeks to refute the conventional law-and-economics theory of shareholder dominance over corporate objectives.

3. How does "being more than minimally generous towards employees" contribute to environmental sustainability?

4. More generally, what does "social justice" have to do with sustainability? Suppose that a company employs a labor force in a developing country. Principles of social justice might dictate that the company pay its workers more than the prevailing wage. But then the increased wealth might allow these employees to purchase automobiles, air conditioners, and other items that consume fossil fuels and detract from sustainability. Can these be reconciled?

5. What is conveyed by the "gearing" metaphor referred to in this article? The image conveys the idea of a car speeding up. Aside from concern about the fossil fuels that might be consumed in this rapid acceleration, the image is one of progressive improvement. When it comes to fifth gear, some drivers prefer to stop accelerating — there is no need to go this fast. The author indicates, accordingly, that while going into the fifth gear on sustainability is to be commended, it is ethically permissible to stop at four.

6. Another part of the "gearing" metaphor has to do with attitudes toward environmental issues. The idea is that corporate managers — being perhaps not as advanced in their environmental thinking as the proponents of sustainability initiatives might wish — are not to be blamed for their initial reticence. They are allowed to proceed by baby steps on the theory that when they get used to thinking along environmental lines they will become more comfortable with the ideas and come to want more of them. Or is it that as the industry as a whole gears up, those who do not follow suit will be embarrassed at being left behind, much as drivers don't like to be the slowest car on the road?

7. The other metaphor endorsed by the author is the "triple-bottom-line" approach to accounting. How is this different than using creative accounting to manipulate financial results?

8. The "gearing" and "triple bottom line" metaphors capture a notion of progressive improvement and incentivize corporate managers to move in the direction of sustainable policies. Do they have any other intellectual content?

9. It is impossible as a practical matter for corporations to be completely sustainable: Their "carbon footprint" can be shrunk but it cannot be erased. How much "sustainability" is enough?

10. Is there a danger that in the name of sustainability, companies will engage in projects that enrich special interests rather than benefiting the public as a whole?

Sustainability policies, being drafted within organizations, tend to have idiosyncratic features that make them difficult to compare. The same is true for reporting on compliance with these policies. Some companies don't report their compliance performance at all; others do so in varying ways. Should sustainability policies and sustainability reporting be standardized, so company managers, investors, and members of the public can obtain the benefits of greater transparency and improved understanding of what the company is actually doing relative to its peers?

Several organizations are seeking to introduce a degree of standardization into this area. One, the Sustainability Accounting Standards Board (SASB), describes itself as an "independent 501(c)(3) non-profit" organization whose mission "is to develop and disseminate sustainability accounting standards that help publicly-listed corporations disclose material factors in compliance with SEC requirements. Through these standards, along with associated education and outreach, SASB is working to increase the usefulness of information available to investors, and improve corporate performance on the environmental, social, and governance issues most likely to impact value." The organization sees sustainability reporting as a natural and logical development and hopes that its proposed reporting standards for ten industry segments will achieve the level of acceptance currently given to standards issued by the Financial Accounting Standards Board.

To date, the SASB's standards have achieved "buy-in" from important industry and regulatory parties (New York's former mayor Michael Bloomberg and former SEC Chairwoman Mary Schapiro serve respectively as chairman and vice chair of the organization). However, it remains to be seen whether a large majority of public companies will voluntarily adopt the SASB's approach.

Questions and Comments

1. How would you design a standardized system of reporting on sustainability issues, if you were drafting the rules?

2. Is standardization realistically possible in this area? If so, is it desirable?

3. If public companies do not fall into line voluntarily, should regulators or legislators force them to do so?

How should the concept of sustainability be implemented? Increasingly, companies are adopting sustainability policies that articulate the organization's attitude toward environmental issues, such as global warming. Issuing such a policy has several advantages. It can express the company's genuine commitment to the cause of environmental protection. It can display a "tone at the top" that encourages employees throughout the organization to show greater respect for the environment. It can also support the

> A sustainability policy is a statement, adopted by the highest authority in the organization, setting forth the organization's commitment to engaging in sustainable projects.

company's claim to be a "good guy" on environmental issues, thus improving its public image and reducing the chance that it will be targeted by activists.

The following excerpt is from the sustainability policy of Plexus, Inc., a (fictional) wood products company with operations throughout the world.

Plexus Inc. Sustainability Policy

As a global business, we recognize that a changing climate will increasingly affect our customers, the communities in which we operate, and the world's economy. This statement sets out our approach to managing the environmental impacts of our operations.

The company is committed to seeking continual improvement in mitigating our direct environmental impacts by reducing our use of natural resources, implementing sustainable logging techniques, and minimizing pollution of our waters, lands, and atmosphere.

The company will work with clients, customers, and other stakeholders to identify ways of managing our indirect impacts and to develop approaches that promote environmental sustainability.

Specifically, it is the company's policy:

- To comply fully with all applicable environmental regulations and other requirements in each of the countries in which we operate.
- To reduce our direct environmental impacts through implementing environmental management systems.
- To reduce indirect impacts through implementation of the company's environmental and social risk assessment policy.
- To integrate environmental considerations into business decisions at every level of responsibility in the company.
- To reduce emissions from our operations.
- To encourage the development of products and services that enable the transition to a lower carbon economy.
- To manage indirect impacts in the supply chain by collaborating with key suppliers to secure improved environmental performance.
- To use sustainable practices in property design and property management.
- To raise employees' awareness of environmental issues.
- To engage with industry groups and non-governmental organizations in order to contribute to increased environmental awareness.
- To communicate proactively and openly about our environmental commitments and performance.

Questions and Comments

1. In the past, some wood products companies have been notorious polluters and have contributed to environmental degradation by engaging in poor logging practices. Do they owe special obligations of sustainability going forward?

2. To what extent does this policy manifest a genuine commitment to sustainability, as opposed to a willingness to mouth the words when it is convenient to do so?

3. How many concrete, externally observable commitments are contained in this policy?

4. How can anyone determine whether or not the company complies with its own policy?

5. Is it enough to comply with the environmental laws of the countries where the company does business? What if a particular country has excessively lax regulations?

17

When Compliance Fails

A. INTRODUCTION

No compliance program is foolproof. State-of-the art programs can fail; notorious failures have occurred even though the organizations involved operated what appeared to be excellent compliance operations. In this chapter we examine cases of compliance breakdown. We consider two issues: (a) what was the cause of the breakdown? and (b) what should the managers of the organization have done once the breakdown occurred?

B. ENRON

Enron started as a sleepy natural gas pipeline firm located in Texas. In the 1990s, Kenneth Lay, the company's charismatic chairman, moved the company into a diversified group of activities, including broadband services and online commodities trading. The initial results were spectacular; by 2000 Enron was the seventh-largest company on the Fortune 500 and the sixth-largest energy company in the world, with reported annual revenues of $100 billion. Fortune Magazine named Enron "America's Most Innovative Company" for six consecutive years.

Unfortunately, the company's profits were inflated and its financing structures were rife with fraud and conflicts of interest. The company's stock collapsed, the SEC launched an investigation, and by year-end 2001 Enron was in bankruptcy. Several Enron officials went to prison; Lay himself was found guilty of crimes associated with Enron's collapse but died before serving time.

Report of Investigation by the Special Investigative Committee of the Board of Directors of Enron Corp.

On October 16, 2001, Enron announced that it was taking a $544 million alter-tax charge against earnings related to transactions with LJM2 Co-Investment, L.P.

("LJM2"), a partnership created and managed by [Andrew Fastow, Enron's former Executive Vice President and Chief Financial Officer]. It also announced a reduction of shareholders' equity of $1.2 billion related to transactions with that same entity.

Less than one month later, Enron announced that it was restating its financial statements for the period from 1997 through 2001 because of accounting errors relating to transactions with a different Fastow partnership, LJM Cayman, L.P. ("LJMI"), and an additional related-party entity, Chewco Investments, L.P. ("Chewco"). Chewco was managed by an Enron Global Finance employee, Kopper, who reported to Fastow.

The LJM1- and Chewco-related restatement . . . was very large. It reduced Enron's reported net income by $28 million in 1997 (of $105 million total), by $133 million in 1998 (of $703 million total), by $248 million in 1999 (of $893 million total), and by $99 million in 2000 (of $979 million total). The restatement reduced reported shareholders' equity by $258 million in 1997, by $391 million in 1998, by $710 million in 1999, and by $754 million in 2000. It increased reported debt by $711 million in 1997, by $561 million in 1998, by $685 million in 1999, and by $628 million in 2000. Enron also revealed, for the first time, that . . . Fastow received more than $30 million from LJM1 and LJM2. These announcements destroyed market confidence and investor trust in Enron. Less than one month later, Enron filed for bankruptcy.

SUMMARY OF FINDINGS

. . . Our investigation identified significant problems beyond those Enron has already disclosed. Enron employees involved in the partnerships were enriched, in the aggregate, by tens of millions of dollars they should never have received — Fastow by at least $30 million, Kopper by at least $10 million, two others by $1 million each, and still two more by amounts we believe were at least in the hundreds of thousands of dollars. We have seen no evidence that any of these employees, except Fastow, obtained the permission required by Enron's Code of Conduct of Business Affairs to own interests in the partnerships. Moreover, the extent of Fastow's ownership and financial windfall was inconsistent with his representations to Enron's Board of Directors.

This personal enrichment of Enron employees, however, was merely one aspect of a deeper and more serious problem. These partnerships — Chewco, LJM1, and LJM2 — were used by Enron Management to enter into transactions that it could not, or would not, do with unrelated commercial entities. Many of the most significant transactions apparently were designed to accomplish favorable financial statement results, not to achieve bona fide economic objectives or to transfer risk. Some transactions were designed so that, had they followed applicable accounting rules, Enron could have kept assets and liabilities (especially debt) off of its balance sheet; but the transactions did not follow those rules.

Other transactions were implemented — improperly, we are informed by our accounting advisors — to offset losses. They allowed Enron to conceal from the market very large losses resulting from Enron's merchant investments by creating an appearance that those investments were hedged — that is, that a third party was obligated to pay Enron the amount of those losses — when in fact that third party was simply an entity in which only Enron had a substantial economic stake. We believe these transactions resulted in Enron reporting earnings from the third quarter of 2000 through the third quarter of 2001 that were almost $1 billion higher than should have been reported.

Enron's original accounting treatment of the Chewco and LJM1 transactions that led to Enron's November 2001 restatement was clearly wrong, apparently the result of mistakes either in structuring the transactions or in basic accounting. In other cases, the accounting treatment was likely wrong, notwithstanding creative efforts to circumvent accounting principles through the complex structuring of transactions that lacked fundamental economic substance. In virtually all of the transactions, Enron's accounting treatment was determined with extensive participation and structuring advice from [Arthur Andersen, a big accounting firm], which Management reported to the Board. Enron's records show that Andersen billed Enron $5.7 million for advice in connection with the LJM and Chewco transactions alone, above and beyond its regular audit fees.

Many of the transactions involve an accounting structure known as a "special purpose entity" or "special purpose vehicle" (referred to as an "SPE" in this Summary and in the Report). A company that does business with an SPE may treat that SPE as if it were an independent, outside entity for accounting purposes if two conditions are met: (1) an owner independent of the company must make a substantive equity investment of at least 3% of the SPE's assets, and that 3% must remain at risk throughout the transaction; and (2) the independent owner must exercise control of the SPE. In those circumstances, the company may record gains and losses on transactions with the SPE, and the assets and liabilities of the SPE are not included in the company's balance sheet, even though the company and the SPE are closely related. It was the technical failure of some of the structures with which Enron did business to satisfy these requirements that led to Enron's restatement. . . .

The Board of Directors

With respect to the issues that are the subject of this investigation, the Board of Directors failed, in our judgment, in its oversight duties. This had serious consequences for Enron, its employees, and its shareholders.

The Board of Directors approved the arrangements that allowed the Company's CFO to serve as general partner in partnerships that participated in significant financial transactions with Enron. As noted earlier, the two members of the Special Investigative Committee who have participated in this review of the Board's actions believe this decision was fundamentally flawed. The Board substantially underestimated the severity of the conflict and overestimated the degree to which management controls and procedures could contain the problem.

After having authorized a conflict of interest creating as much risk as this one, the Board had an obligation to give careful attention to the transactions that followed. It failed to do this. It cannot be faulted for the various instances in which it was apparently denied important information concerning certain of the transactions in question. However, it can and should be faulted for failing to demand more information, and for failing to probe and understand the information that did come to it. The Board authorized the Rhythms transaction and three of the Raptor transactions. It appears that many of its members did not understand those transactions — the economic rationale, the consequences, and the risks. Nor does it appear that they reacted to warning signs in those transactions as they were presented, including the statement to the Finance Committee in May 2000 that the proposed Raptor transaction raised a risk of "accounting scrutiny." We do note, however, that the Committee was told that Andersen was "comfortable" with the transaction. As complex as the transactions were, the existence of Fastow's conflict of interest demanded that the Board gain a better understanding of the LJM transactions that came before it, and ensure (whether through one of its Committees or through use of outside consultants) that they were fair to Enron.

The Audit and Compliance Committee, and later the Finance Committee, took on a specific role in the control structure by carrying out periodic reviews of the LJM transactions. This was an opportunity to probe the transactions thoroughly, and to seek outside advice as to any issues outside the Board members' expertise. Instead, these reviews appear to have been too brief, too limited in scope, and too superficial to serve their intended function. The Compensation Committee was given the role of reviewing Fastow's compensation from the LJM entities, and did not carry out this review. This remained the case even after the Committees were on notice that the LJM transactions were contributing very large percentages of Enron's earnings. In sum, the Board did not effectively meet its obligation with respect to the LJM transactions.

The Board, and in particular the Audit and Compliance Committee, has the duty of ultimate oversight over the Company's financial reporting. While the primary responsibility for the financial reporting abuses discussed in the Report lies with Management, the participating members of this Committee believe those abuses could and should have been prevented or detected at an earlier time had the Board been more aggressive and vigilant.

OUTSIDE PROFESSIONAL ADVISORS

The evidence available to us suggests that Andersen did not fulfill its professional responsibilities in connection with its audits of Enron's financial statements, or its obligation to bring to the attention of Enron's Board (or the Audit and Compliance Committee) concerns about Enron's internal controls over the related-party transactions. Andersen has admitted that it erred in concluding that the Rhythms transaction was structured properly under the SPE non-consolidation rules.

Enron was required to restate its financial results for 1999 and 2000 as a result. Andersen participated in the structuring and accounting treatment of the Raptor transactions, and charged over $1 million for its services, yet it apparently failed to provide the objective accounting judgment that should have prevented these transactions from going forward. . . . Andersen apparently failed to note or take action with respect to the deficiencies in Enron's public disclosure documents.

According to recent public disclosures, Andersen also failed to bring to the attention of Enron's Audit and Compliance Committee serious reservations Andersen partners voiced internally about the related-party transactions. . . . The Board appears to have reasonably relied upon the professional judgment of Andersen concerning Enron's financial statements and the adequacy of controls for the related party transactions. Our review indicates that Andersen failed to meet its responsibilities in both respects.

Vinson & Elkins, as Enron's longstanding outside counsel, provided advice and prepared documentation in connection with many of the transactions discussed in the Report. It also assisted Enron with the preparation of its disclosures of related-party transactions in the proxy statements and the footnotes to the financial statements in Enron's periodic SEC filings. [Because of the relationship between Vinson & Elkins and the University of Texas School of Law, the portions of the Report describing and evaluating actions of Vinson & Elkins are solely the views of Troubh and Winokur.] Management and the Board relied heavily on the perceived approval by Vinson & Elkins of the structure and disclosure of the transactions.

Enron's Audit and Compliance Committee, as well as in-house counsel, looked to it for assurance that Enron's public disclosures were legally sufficient. It would be inappropriate to fault Vinson & Elkins for accounting matters, which are not within its expertise. However, Vinson & Elkins should have brought a stronger, more objective and more critical voice to the disclosure process. . . .

The tragic consequences of the related-party transactions and accounting errors were the result of failures at many levels and by many people: a flawed idea, self-enrichment by employees, inadequately-designed controls, poor implementation, inattentive oversight, simple (and not-so-simple) accounting mistakes, and over-reaching in a culture that appears to have encouraged pushing the limits. Our review indicates that many of those consequences could and should have been avoided.

Questions and Comments

1. This excerpt is from the Powers Report, previously discussed in Chapter 8. Based on this report, what if anything could have been done to prevent the catastrophe at Enron? Were red flags in evidence that should have alerted responsible parties that something was much amiss? Why didn't anyone stop the madness?

2. In its heyday, Enron was assiduous in courting favor from powerful politicians. According to a 2000 survey of business executives, its chairman, Kenneth Lay, was one of the top 50 individual donors of soft money, with contributions totaling more than $361,000. Lay was a big donor to President George W. Bush's campaigns, and he was at one time a candidate for Secretary of the Treasury in the George W. Bush administration. Enron's political largesse was not limited to Republicans: The company sponsored events at the 2000 Democratic National Convention. Enron was also savvy at hiring politically connected individuals including former Secretary of State James Baker and former Secretary of Commerce Robert Mosbacher. There was nothing inherently wrongful or illegal about these activities, but taken together could they raise concerns?

3. Enron operated what appeared to be a cutting-edge compliance shop. Most of the members of its board of directors were independent of management; they included a former chairwoman of the Commodities Futures Trading Commission and a former dean of Stanford University's Graduate School of Business. Enron's "Code of Conduct of Business Affairs" set forth high ethical obligations for senior management. The company established procedures for review of related-party transactions at the highest corporate levels and required its Audit and Compliance Committee to conduct annual reviews of such transactions. It operated a whistleblower program with mechanisms for anonymous reporting. It retained reputable independent professionals — Arthur Andersen for accounting and Vinson & Elkins for law. Yet all these safeguards failed to detect or prevent a colossal fraud. How was this possible, and what does this say about the value of compliance programs? Could Enron's compliance program have made matters worse by inducing complacency and a lack of independent judgment on the part of others who relied on the

effectiveness of its internal controls? For discussion, see Geoffrey Miller, *Catastrophic Financial Failures: Enron and More*, 89 Cornell L. Rev. 423 (2004).

C. WORLDCOM

WorldCom started in 1983 in the business of re-selling long distance capacity that it purchased on a wholesale basis from the major carriers. The company went public in 1989 and immediately experienced a meteoric stock price increase; at the same time it grew aggressively through acquisitions of other companies, often using its own shares for the purchases. The following years were difficult for the telecommunications industry because of increased competition, but WorldCom continued to post impressive revenue numbers and strong growth. It turned out, however, that the company's reported good performance was largely achieved through accounting fraud. WorldCom filed for bankruptcy in July 2002.

The following excerpt is from a special report prepared by three independent members of WorldCom's board, each of whom was appointed after the frauds had come to light.

Report of Investigation by the Special Investigative Committee of the Board of Directors of WorldCom, Inc.

Mar. 31, 2003

. . . From 1999 until 2002, WorldCom suffered one of the largest public company accounting frauds in history. As enormous as the fraud was, it was accomplished in a relatively mundane way: more than $9 billion in false or unsupported accounting entries were made in WorldCom's financial systems in order to achieve desired reported financial results. The fraud did not involve WorldCom's network, its technology, or its engineering. Most of WorldCom's people did not know it was occurring. Rather, the fraud occurred as a result of knowing misconduct directed by a few senior executives centered in its Clinton, Mississippi headquarters, and implemented by personnel in its financial and accounting departments in several locations. The fraud was the consequence of the way WorldCom's Chief Executive Officer, Bernard J. Ebbers, ran the Company. Though much of this Report details the implementation of the fraud by others, he was the source of the culture, as well as much of the pressure, that gave birth to this fraud. That the fraud continued as long as it did was due to a lack of courage to blow the whistle on the part of others in WorldCom's financial and accounting departments; inadequate audits by Arthur Andersen; and a financial system whose controls were sorely deficient. The setting in which it occurred was marked by a serious corporate governance failure. . . .

In the 1990s, the principal business strategy of WorldCom's Chief Executive Officer, Bernard J. Ebbers, was growth through acquisitions. The currency for much of that strategy was WorldCom stock, and the success of the strategy depended on a consistently increasing stock price. WorldCom pursued scores of increasingly large acquisitions. The strategy reached its apex with WorldCom's acquisition in 1998 of MCI Communications Corporation ("MCI"), a company more than two-and-a-half times WorldCom's size (by revenues). Ebbers' acquisition strategy largely came to an end by early 2000 when WorldCom was forced to abandon a proposed merger with Sprint Corporation because of antitrust objections.

At that point, WorldCom's continued success became dependent on Ebbers' ability to manage the internal operations of what was then an immense company, and to do so in an industry-wide downturn. He was spectacularly unsuccessful in this endeavor. He continued to feed Wall Street's expectations of double-digit growth, and he demanded that his subordinates meet those expectations. But he did not provide the leadership or managerial attention that would enable WorldCom to meet those expectations legitimately.

Ebbers presented a substantially false picture to the market, to the Board of Directors, and to most of the Company's own employees. At the same time he was projecting, and then reporting, continued vigorous growth, he was receiving internal information that was increasingly inconsistent with those projections and reports. Moreover, he did not disclose the persistent use of non-recurring items to boost reported revenues. Ebbers was aware, at a minimum, that WorldCom was meeting revenue expectations through financial gimmickry. Yet he kept making unrealistic promises, and failed to disclose the existence of these devices or their magnitude.

Ebbers directed significant energy to building and protecting his own personal financial empire, with little attention to the risks these distractions and financial obligations placed on the Company that was making him one of the highest paid executives in the country. It was when his personal financial empire was under the greatest pressure — when he had the greatest need to keep WorldCom's stock price up in order to avoid margin calls that he could not meet — that the largest part of the fraud occurred. And it was shortly after he left that it was discovered and disclosed.

The fraud was implemented by and under the direction of WorldCom's Chief Financial Officer, Scott Sullivan. As business operations fell further and further short of financial targets announced by Ebbers, Sullivan directed the making of accounting entries that had no basis in generally accepted accounting principles in order to create the false appearance that WorldCom had achieved those targets. In doing so he was assisted by WorldCom's Controller, David Myers, who in turn directed the making of entries he knew were not supported. This was easily accomplished, because it was apparently considered acceptable for the General Accounting group to make entries of hundreds of millions of dollars with little or no documentation beyond a verbal or an e-mail directive from senior personnel. . . .

Awareness of this financial fraud was not confined to just two or three people. Others at WorldCom either knew or suspected that senior financial management was engaged in improper accounting. These included not only people in the General Accounting group (generally located at the Clinton, Mississippi corporate headquarters) who ordered or implemented the entries, but people in other financial reporting and accounting groups whose responsibilities were affected by them. Employees in several such groups suggested, made or knew of entries that were not supportable, or prepared reports that were false or misleading as a consequence. Remarkably, these employees frequently did not raise any objections despite their awareness or suspicions that the accounting was wrong, and simply followed directions or even enlisted the assistance of others. Some of them complained to their supervisors or, in a handful of cases, refused to take actions they considered inappropriate. However, none took effective action to try to halt or expose these practices until the Spring of 2002. Employees in the financial and accounting groups believed that forcefully objecting to conduct that they knew was being directed by Sullivan would cost them their jobs; few of them were prepared to take that risk.

The Board of Directors does not appear to have known of the fraud, nor did it receive information we believe should have put it on notice. However, the Board was so passive and reliant on Ebbers and Sullivan that it had little opportunity to learn of the fraud. Moreover, by authorizing WorldCom to lend Ebbers hundreds of millions of dollars so he could meet margin calls without selling his stock, and by creating a bonus plan that rewarded short-term revenue growth, the Board—and more specifically the Compensation and Stock Option Committee (the "Compensation Committee")—created incentives that may have played a role in motivating the misconduct that occurred at WorldCom.

In the Spring of 2002—within two months after Ebbers' resignation as Chief Executive Officer in April 2002—Internal Audit undertook a review of the capital expenditures, and persisted in the face of discouragement by Sullivan (to whom Internal Audit reported in part) and Myers. Personnel in other areas of WorldCom also questioned Sullivan or Myers about the entries. Myers ultimately acknowledged to internal auditors that he could not support the capitalization of line costs. The Audit Committee of WorldCom's Board of Directors, once advised of the issue, took it seriously and directed prompt attention to it. After providing Sullivan an opportunity to justify the accounting, WorldCom and its new outside auditors (who had replaced Andersen, the auditors during the period of the fraud) concluded that the capitalization entries were improper. The Board immediately terminated Sullivan and obtained Myers' resignation, and WorldCom disclosed the improper capitalization to the SEC and the public. . . .

Numerous individuals—most of them in financial and accounting departments, at many levels of the Company and in different locations around the world—became aware in varying degrees of senior management's misconduct. Had one or more of these individuals come forward earlier and raised their complaints with Human Resources, Internal Audit, the Law and Public Policy Department, Andersen, the Audit Committee, individual Directors and/or federal or state government regulators, perhaps the fraud would not have gone on for so long. Why didn't they? The answer seems to lie partly in a culture emanating from corporate headquarters that emphasized making the numbers above all else; kept financial information hidden from those who needed to know; blindly trusted senior officers even in the face of evidence that they were acting improperly; discouraged dissent; and left few, if any, outlets through which employees believed they could safely raise their objections. This culture began at the top. Ebbers created the pressure that led to the fraud. He demanded the results he had promised, and he appeared to scorn the procedures (and people) that should have been a check on misreporting. When efforts were made to establish a corporate Code of Conduct, Ebbers reportedly described it as a "colossal waste of time." He showed little respect for the role lawyers played with respect to corporate governance matters within the Company. While we have heard numerous accounts of Ebbers' demand for results—on occasion emotional, insulting, and with express reference to the personal financial harm he faced if the stock price declined—we have heard none in which he demanded or rewarded ethical business practices. . . .

Based on the materials available to us, the blame for Andersen's failure to detect the fraud appears to lie with personnel both at Andersen and at WorldCom. There were apparent flaws in Andersen's audit approach, which limited the likelihood it would detect the accounting irregularities. Moreover, Andersen appears to have missed several opportunities that might have led to the discovery of management's misuse of accruals, the capitalization of line costs, and the improper recognition of revenue items. For their part, certain WorldCom personnel maintained inappropriately tight control over information that Andersen needed, altered documents with the apparent purpose of concealing from Andersen items that might have raised questions, and were not forthcoming in other respects. Andersen, knowing in some instances that it was receiving less than full cooperation on critical aspects of its work, failed to bring this to the attention of WorldCom's Audit Committee.

Andersen employed an approach to its audit that it itself characterized as different from the "traditional audit approach." It focused heavily on identifying risks and assessing whether the Company had adequate controls in place to mitigate those risks, rather than emphasizing the traditional substantive testing of information maintained in accounting records and financial statements. This approach is not unique to Andersen, and it was disclosed to the Audit Committee. But a consequence of this approach was that if Andersen failed to identify a significant risk, or relied on Company controls without adequately determining that they were worthy of reliance, there would be insufficient testing to make detection of fraud likely.

Andersen does not appear to have performed adequate testing to justify reliance on WorldCom's controls. We found hundreds of huge, round-dollar journal entries made by the staff of the General Accounting group without proper support; examples include unsupported journal entries of $334,000,000 and $560,000,000 on July 21, 2000, and July 17, 2001, respectively. We also found accrual reversals were made with little or no support. And where we did find documentary support it was frequently disorganized and maintained haphazardly. These deficiencies made reliance on controls impossible. We do not understand how they escaped Andersen's notice.

Andersen concluded year after year that the risk of fraud was no greater than a moderate risk, and thus it never devised sufficient auditing procedures to address this risk. It did so despite rating WorldCom a "maximum risk" client—an assessment Andersen never disclosed to the Audit Committee—and having given management less than favorable ratings in a few areas (such as accounting and disclosure practices, behavior toward Andersen's work, and policies to prevent or detect fraud) in Andersen internal documents. Andersen relied heavily on senior management and did not conduct tests to corroborate the information it received in many areas. It assumed incorrectly that the absence of variances in the financial statements and schedules—in a highly volatile business environment—indicated there was no cause for heightened scrutiny. As a result, Andersen conducted only very limited audit procedures in many areas where we found accounting irregularities. . . .

WorldCom, for its part, exerted excessive control over Andersen's access to information, and was not candid in at least some of its dealings with Andersen. The WorldCom personnel who dealt most often with Andersen controlled Andersen's access to information in several respects. They denied Andersen's requests to speak with some employees. They "struck" Andersen's requests for detailed information, supporting documentation, or material that they felt was overly burdensome. WorldCom personnel also repeatedly rejected Andersen's requests for access to the computerized General Ledger through which Internal Audit and others discovered the capitalization of line costs. And they fostered an attitude in which questions from Andersen were to be parried, rather than answered openly. Of course, it was Andersen's responsibility to overcome those obstacles to perform an appropriate audit, and to inform the Audit Committee of the difficulties it faced, but it did not do so. . . .

We found no evidence that members of the Board of Directors, other than Ebbers and Sullivan, were aware of the improper accounting practices at the time they occurred. We have reviewed materials (including slide presentations) the Board received and have not found information that should reasonably have led it to detect the practices or to believe that further specific inquiry into the accounting practices at issue was necessary.

The Board received regular financial and operational presentations that included a level of detail consistent with what we believe most properly run Boards received during that period. The reduced levels of line costs that resulted from release of accruals and improper capitalization did not appear unusual, in part because the entire purpose of the improper accounting exercise was to hold line costs at a level consistent with earlier periods. It is possible, however, that a Board more closely familiar with what was happening operationally in the Company might have questioned financial trends and comparisons with competitors, including the level of reported capital expenditures: the Board received reports that capital expenditures were declining—as the Board had directed—but in fact capital spending was being slashed much more heavily. There was a disparity between the large cuts that were actually taking place and the reported numbers, which were being pushed back up by the improperly added capitalized line costs.

The Board and its Committees did not function in a way that made it likely that they would notice red flags. The outside Directors had little or no involvement in the Company's business other than through attendance at Board meetings. Nearly all of the Directors were legacies of companies that WorldCom, under Ebbers' leadership, had acquired. They had ceded leadership to Ebbers when their companies were acquired, and in some cases viewed their role as diminished. Ebbers controlled the Board's agenda, its discussions, and its decisions. He created, and the Board permitted, a corporate environment in which the pressure to meet the numbers was high, the departments that served as controls were weak, and the word of senior management was final and not to be challenged.

The Audit Committee in particular needed an understanding of the Company it oversaw in order to be effective. However, the Audit Committee members do not appear to have had a sufficient understanding of the Company's internal financial workings or its culture, and they devoted strikingly little time to their role, meeting as little as three to five hours per year. WorldCom was a complicated Company in a fast-evolving industry. It had expanded quickly, through a series of large acquisitions, and there had been virtually no integration of the acquisitions. WorldCom had accounting-related operations scattered in a variety of locations around the country. These facts raised significant accounting, internal control and systems concerns that required Audit Committee knowledge and attention, and that should also have elicited direct warnings from Andersen. However, the Audit Committee members apparently did not even understand—though the evidence indicates that Andersen disclosed—the non-traditional audit approach Andersen employed. To gain the knowledge necessary to function effectively as an Audit Committee would have required a very substantial amount of energy, expertise by at least some of its members, and a greater commitment of time.

Neither WorldCom's legal department nor Internal Audit was structured to maximize its effectiveness as a control structure upon which the Board could depend. At Ebbers' direction, the Company's lawyers were in fragmented groups, several of which had General Counsels who did not report to WorldCom's General Counsel for portions of the relevant period; they were not located geographically near senior management or involved in its inner workings; and they had inadequate support from senior management. Internal Audit — though eventually successful in revealing the fraud — had been structured in ways that made this accomplishment more difficult: it reported in most respects to Sullivan, and until 2002 its duties generally did not include financial reporting matters.

The outside Directors had virtually no interaction with Company operational or financial employees other than during the presentations they heard at meetings. While in this respect the Directors were far from unique among directors of large corporations, this lack of contact meant that they had little sense of the culture within the Company, or awareness of issues other than those brought to them by a few senior managers. They were not themselves visible to employees, and there were no systems in place that could have encouraged employees to contact them with concerns about either the accounting entries or operational matters. In short, the Board was removed and detached from the operations of WorldCom to the extent that its members had little sense of what was really going on within the Company. Ebbers was autocratic in his dealings with the Board, and the Board permitted it. With limited exceptions, the members of the Board were reluctant to challenge Ebbers even when they disagreed with him. They, like most observers, were impressed with the Company's growth and Ebbers' reputation, although they were in some cases mystified or perplexed by his style. This was Ebbers' company. Several members of the Board were sophisticated, yet the members of the Board were deferential to Ebbers and passive in their oversight until April 2002.

The deference of the Compensation Committee and the Board to Ebbers is illustrated by their decisions beginning in September 2000 to authorize corporate loans and guaranties that grew to over $400 million, so that Ebbers could avoid selling WorldCom stock to meet his personal financial obligations. This was not the first occasion on which Ebbers had overextended himself financially and borrowed from the Company: he had done so in 1994 as well. On neither occasion did anyone on the Board challenge Ebbers with respect to his use of WorldCom stock to extend his personal financial empire to the point that it threatened to cause involuntary liquidation of his stock. The approach of the Board, as one member characterized his own view, was to say nothing to Ebbers because they thought Ebbers was a grownup and could manage his own affairs — even though Ebbers' management of his own affairs involved the use of Company funds, eventually to the tune of hundreds of millions of dollars.

We believe that the extension of these loans and guaranties was a 19-month sequence of terrible decisions — badly conceived, and antithetical to shareholder interests — and a major failure of corporate governance. Indeed, we do not understand how the Compensation Committee or the Board could have concluded that these loans were an acceptable use of more than $400 million of the shareholders' money. These decisions reflected an uncritical solicitude for Ebbers' financial interests, a disregard of the incentives the situation created for Ebbers' management of the Company, and a willingness to subordinate shareholders' interests to Ebbers' financial wellbeing.

A second example of the Board's deference is its failure to challenge Ebbers on the extent of his substantial outside business interests (and the resulting claim on his time and energies). Those interests included a Louisiana rice farm, a luxury yacht building company, a lumber mill, a country club, a trucking company, a minor league hockey team, an operating marina, and a building in downtown Chicago. We do not believe most properly-run Boards of Directors would permit a Chief

Executive Officer to pursue an array of interests such as these, certainly not without careful examination of the time and energy commitments they would require. Yet we have seen no evidence of any such challenge. . . .

Auditing standards warn that domineering management behavior in dealing with auditors, being denied access to records or employees, and unusual delays in providing requested information may be indicative of fraudulent financial reporting practices. When WorldCom's management exhibited similar behavior, it appears that Andersen found ways to accommodate the behavior instead of raising the issue with the Audit Committee. . . . WorldCom's management withheld information from Andersen with the apparent purpose of hampering Andersen's ability to identify problems at the Company. . . .

We have carefully examined the available information pertinent to the Board's activities from 1999 until 2002, to answer two basic questions: Did the Board or the Audit Committee know of the improper accounting? If not, should they have detected it? We have found no evidence that the Board or Audit Committee in fact knew of the accounting improprieties. Nor have we found any glaring red flags that should have led the Board or Audit Committee to become aware of it. The Board and the Audit Committee were given information that was both false and plausible. . . . However, we believe the Board — and in particular the Audit Committee — played so limited a role in the oversight of WorldCom that it is unlikely that any but the most flagrant and open financial fraud *could* have come to their attention. Until April 2002, the Board and the Audit Committee did not exert independent leadership. . . .

The events we have described involved misconduct by a few dozen out of approximately 75,000 employees at WorldCom. Those involved in the misconduct, those who failed to blow the whistle, and those who did not adequately oversee are gone. The Company's systems, networks, and technical capabilities and the vast majority of its employees were not part of the fraud, and they remain. . . .

The Company and the Corporate Monitor have not waited for this formal process. They have taken substantial steps to put in place a governance process designed to cure the principal failing that gave rise to the fraud: a lack of effective checks and balances on the power of senior management. The general concepts to be implemented through concrete remedial steps include:

- An active and independent Board of Directors and Committees.
- A corporate culture of candor, in which ethical conduct is encouraged and expected, as exemplified by the ethics pledge that the Company and the Corporate Monitor have developed and that senior management has signed.
- A corporate culture in which the advice of lawyers is sought and respected.
- Formalized and well-documented policies and procedures, including a clear and effective channel through which employees can raise concerns or report acts of misconduct.
- Compensation policies and practices that create incentives consistent with the interests of the Company's shareholders.
- An expanded role for Internal Audit, with commensurate resources and expertise.
- Integrated financial accounting and reporting systems, to which all appropriate personnel have access.
- Formalized and well-documented accounting policies and procedures, including robust internal controls surrounding the capture and reporting of financial data.

- Open and candid dealings with the Company's outside auditors, reflecting the critical role they play in the ability of the markets, shareholders, the Board, and senior management to perform their functions.
- Whenever feasible, housing significant corporate organizations or groups that perform similar or related functions (such as finance, accounting, and internal audit) in the same location.
- Use of budgets and financial targets as benchmarks, rather than as drivers of reported financial results or influencing the accounting treatment of transactions.

With these steps and many others to be developed the Company will complete the process it began when it disclosed the fraud and commissioned this investigation: to ensure insofar as possible that what went wrong at WorldCom will not be repeated.

Questions and Comments

1. The authors of this report were a distinguished trio: Dennis R. Beresford, former chairman of the Financial Accounting Standards Board; Nicholas deB. Katzenbach, former Attorney General of the United States; and C.B. Rogers Jr., former chairman and chief executive officer of Equifax. Assisting the special committee were two of the top firms in their respective industries: the law firm Wilmer, Cutler & Pickering (now WilmerHale), and PricewaterhouseCoopers LLP, the largest of the "big four" accounting firms.

2. Ebbers was convicted of fraud and conspiracy and, as of 2016, was serving a 25-year prison term at Oakdale Federal Correctional Complex in Louisiana. Scott Sullivan pleaded guilty to conspiracy, securities fraud, and making false financial filings; cooperated with the government by testifying against Ebbers; and received a five-year sentence (completed in 2009). David Myers pleaded guilty, cooperated with prosecutors, and served nine months in prison; he later became an executive in the health care industry.

3. The problems at WorldCom had several features in common with other corporate frauds (such as Enron): a "high-flying" company that seemed to go from success to success; excellent public relations; assiduous efforts to cultivate politicians; extraordinary stock price performance; rapid expansion through mergers rather than internal growth; lavish compensation of senior managers; ostentatious spending; domination by a single individual or small group; and a complex corporate structure that made it difficult to understand the entire enterprise. *See* Geoffrey Miller, *Catastrophic Financial Failures: Enron and More*, 89 Cornell L. Rev. 423 (2004). On the other hand, several of these features could also describe Berkshire Hathaway, Warren Buffet's investment vehicle and one of the most successful companies in history. How can one sort out the good, the bad, and the ugly?

4. Reputation seems to have played a role in the perpetuation of the WorldCom fraud. For example, the excerpted report noted that Scott Sullivan was trusted and well-respected in the industry. In 1998, CFO Magazine called Sullivan a "whiz kid" and awarded him a CFO Excellence Award. To many, Sullivan had a reputation of impeccable integrity. Some who learned about the capitalization of line costs rationalized that Sullivan must have found an accounting loophole or legitimate way to justify these entries. While reputation is extremely valuable as a guide to quality in human beings, it can also be a trap, leading to excessive deference to people who are not in fact worthy of the reputations associated with their names.

5. WorldCom's board of directors or board audit committee only saw information provided to them by management—information that during the period of the fraud had been carefully massaged. Moreover, as the report observes, the information they reviewed didn't contain obvious "red flags" because it was essentially a continuation of the same performance they had come to expect from WorldCom. On the other hand, if they were aware of trends in the telecommunications industry, they could have known that other firms were experiencing financial stress at this time. Should the lack of problems at WorldCom have put them on notice that something was afoot?

6. A financial fraud of this magnitude cannot be carried out without many people either knowing about it or at least turning a blind eye to obvious warning signs. Not a single whistleblower came forward during most of the period when this fraud was underway. The report suggests that many people feared that they would lose their jobs if they made a fuss. But was this a sufficient answer? Could they have quit and found another job?

7. The report bows to lawyers by saying that one problem at WorldCom was that the lawyers were not given full information, and also noting that the new WorldCom had a culture in which lawyers were consulted. Is bringing lawyers into the picture a desirable safeguard against accounting fraud?

8. Members of the Compensation Committee knew of large loans that World-Com had made to Ebbers; they also knew that Ebbers would be in financial distress if WorldCom's stock decreased in value. Were they at fault for not recognizing that an over-spending, hyper-aggressive, over-optimistic, financially stressed CEO would not necessarily be the most reliable person to entrust with the company's future?

9. Had you been an independent member of WorldCom's board of directors, and been presented for years with wonderful revenue and profit figures, would you have had the gumption to challenge Ebbers' domineering management style or to insist on better documentation of financial results?

10. What was with Arthur Andersen? Why did this firm—one of the most successful accounting firms in the country at that time—seem so supine and so willing to accept abuse and lack of cooperation from its client?

D. SEXUAL ABUSE BY PRIESTS

Compliance breakdowns can occur at any complex organization, not just publicly traded companies. One of the most complex organizations in the world is the Roman Catholic Church. During the decade of the 2000s, reports of sexual abuse by priests surfaced in the United States and elsewhere. Investigative reports by the *Boston Globe* and the *Dallas Morning News* heightened concerns about the problem. Critics claimed that abusive priests were often moved to other positions without punishment, and that the Church did little either to investigate the problem or to take effective actions to stop it. A flood of lawsuits followed the reports of abuse, resulting in more than one billion dollars in settlement payments. Several dioceses sought bankruptcy protection and the Church itself suffered significant reputational harm.

To address and provide perspective on these problems, the United States Conference of Catholic Bishops commissioned a study by a research team from the John Jay College of Criminal Justice. The report, entitled "The Causes and Context of

Sexual Abuse of Minors by Catholic Priests in the United States, 1950-2010," was submitted in May 2011 and received wide publicity.

Among the conclusions of this report were the following:

- Sexual abuse by priests increased from the 1960s through the late 1970s and then sharply declined by 1985, and "continues to remain low."
- No single cause of sexual abuse of minors by priests could be identified.
- Priests were affected by the "increased levels of deviant behavior" that occurred throughout American culture in the 1960s and 1970s. As examples of deviant behavior, the report cited "drug use and crime, as well as changes in social behavior, such as an increase in premarital sexual behavior and divorce."
- Priests who abused minors could not readily be distinguished from others who did not abuse minors.
- Because priests had been exclusively male and committed to celibacy throughout the period in question, these factors "are not causes of the 'crisis.'"
- Priests ordained in the 1930s, 1940s and 1950s did not usually abuse before the 1960s or 1970s; those ordained in the 1960s and the early 1970s engaged in abusive behavior more quickly after their entrance into ministry.
- Priests who studied "human formation" in seminary were less likely to engage in abusive behavior. The "human formation" curriculum deals explicitly with the problem of sexual abuse.
- Many accused priests were experiencing increased job stress and social isolation at the time they committed acts of abuse, and did not have ready access to psychological or professional counseling.
- Less than 5 percent of alleged abusers exhibited behavior consistent with pedophilia. Thus, "it is inaccurate to refer to abusers as 'pedophile priests.'"
- Priests who had homosexual experiences either before or in seminary were more likely to manifest sexual behavior after ordination, but were not more likely to abuse minors.
- Priests who were sexually abused as children were more likely to commit abuse.
- Church leaders preferred to deal with the problem in-house rather than referring cases to prosecutors. This "is not an atypical response to deviant behavior by members of an institution."
- Procedures for defrocking priests were often avoided because they were time-consuming and complicated.
- The media focused on bishops who were slow to act, thus "further perpetuating the image that the bishops as a group were not responding to the problem of sexual abuse of minors."

Questions and Comments

1. The report finds that episodes of sexual abuse principally occurred between the mid-1960s and the mid-1980s. It suggests that cases of abuse were uncommon before that time and tailed off significantly thereafter. The report backs these findings with statistics. Why would sexual abuse occur in this time period but not others? The report supplies a reason: Priests were influenced by the "deviant" behavior characteristic of the period, such as "drug use and crime, as well as changes in social

behavior, such as an increase in premarital sexual behavior and divorce." Do you find this convincing?

2. Do you think that premarital sex and divorce are forms of deviant behavior?

3. The report rejects the stereotype of "pedophile priests"; it blames the media for focusing on priests who were slow to respond; and it suggests that recent abuse claims are the product of lawyers who encourage clients to file complaints based on events that happened decades ago. To what extent does the report also blame the Church or its senior officials?

4. What seems to have been the purpose of this report?

5. If you were a Church official, what changes might you institute based on this report?

Commonwealth of Pennsylvania
Office of the Attorney General
A Report of the Thirty-Seventh Statewide Investigating
Grand Jury

2015

The following report is based upon information which has been developed by the Office of Attorney General (OAG) . . . in conjunction with the efforts of the 37th Statewide Investigating Grand Jury and its inherent powers. In issuing this report the Grand Jury reviewed over 200 Grand Jury exhibits, took witness testimony and generated thousands of pages of Grand Jury testimony transcripts. . . .

This report contains the findings of the Grand Jury as they relate to the Diocese of Altoona-Johnstown. These findings are both staggering and sobering. Over many years hundreds of children have fallen victim to child predators wrapped in the authority and integrity of an honorable faith. As wolves disguised as the shepherds themselves—these men stole the innocence of children by sexually preying upon the most innocent and vulnerable members of our society and of the Catholic faith.

If these discoveries were not dreadful enough, this Grand Jury further found that the actions of Bishops James Hogan and Joseph Adamec failed to protect children entrusted to their care and guidance. Worse yet, these men took actions that further endangered children as they placed their desire to avoid public scandal over the wellbeing of innocent children. Priests were returned to ministry with full knowledge they were child predators.

This is not an indictment of the Catholic religion or the Catholic Church. Many who testified and spoke out regarding the horror of this abominable malfeasance are devout Catholics; as are members of this Grand Jury and OAG investigative personnel. This is a finding of fact and an effort at transparency—not to slander a religion but to expose the truth about the men who hijacked it for their own grotesque desires.

An Overview of the Diocese of Altoona-Johnstown

As of July 31, 2015, the public website of the Diocese of Altoona-Johnstown stated the following information as it pertains to the history of that institution:

> The Diocese of [Altoona-Johnstown] . . . is divided into eight Deaneries, or geographic administrative units. As of 2010, the total Catholic population of the eight-county area

was 94,284. The Church of Altoona-Johnstown is home to 89 parishes, 74 active Diocesan priests and 36 permanent deacons. Two men are enrolled in seminaries in preparation for Ordination to the Diocesan Priesthood. The Diocese is further served by priests from various Religious orders, including the Third Order Regular Franciscans, the Conventual Franciscans, and the Order of Saint Benedict. . . . Since its establishment in 1901, eight Bishops have led the Diocese of Altoona-Johnstown. The current Bishop, the Most Reverend Mark L. Bartchak, was ordained a Bishop on April 19, 2011, at the Cathedral of the Blessed Sacrament in Altoona, and installed as the eighth Bishop of the Diocese on that day. . . . The Church of Altoona-Johnstown boasts a proud education tradition with 20 Catholic elementary schools and three independent Catholic high schools. A fourth high school is scheduled to open in State College in Fall 2011. Enrollment in the elementary schools for the 2010-2011 academic year is 2,978. There are 963 students enrolled in the three high schools this year. Religious Education programs at each parish serve approximately 9,800 students not enrolled in Catholic schools. There are two Catholic colleges/universities located in the Diocese and Diocesan-sponsored Catholic Campus Ministry at all colleges/universities in the Diocese.

EXPLOITATION AND ABUSE OF CHILDREN BY DIOCESAN PRIESTS

The Grand Jury was able to document child sexual abuse by at least 50 different priests or religious leaders within the Diocese of Altoona-Johnstown. The evidence also demonstrated that hundreds of children have been victimized by religious leaders operating within the Diocese; and that the mere presence of these child predators endangered thousands of children by exposure to potential sexual abuse. Predator after predator came before the Grand Jury. Each indicated that it was the first time any law enforcement official had questioned them.

The nature of this child sexual abuse took on many forms. Children reported having their genitals fondled; being forced to participate in, watch, or permit masturbation; being forced to perform or receive oral sex on and/or from priests, and being anally raped. In addition to this vile criminal behavior, the Grand Jury saw evidence of both alcohol and pornography being provided to children by Catholic priests.

Bishops James Hogan and Joseph Adamec could have reported these matters to the police. Those same Bishops could have removed these child molesting priests from any and all ministry. Hogan and Adamec could have encouraged the fellow priests of these child molesters to report what they saw or heard of this sexual behavior involving children. The Bishops did nothing of the sort. Instead Bishop James Hogan and Bishop Joseph Adamec chose to shield the institution and themselves from "scandal." Because of their choices and failed leadership hundreds of children suffered.

The Grand Jury has learned that euphemisms like "sick leave" and "nervous exhaustion" were code for moving offending priests to another location while possible attention to a recent claim of child molestation "cooled off." Diocese approved treatment centers like Saint Luke's Institute in Maryland or Saint John Vianney Center in Downingtown, Pennsylvania were used to provide cover for the Bishops as they left child predators in ministry. Reliant entirely on the cooperation and self-reporting of the sexual offender, these "treatment" facilities would often note that they had not diagnosed the offender as a "pedophile." But when dealing with the safety of children, this language matters. The accused priest had not been *cleared* of being a child predator. A simplistic diagnosis had been offered that insufficient evidence existed to say that the accused was a sex offender; which was based almost entirely upon the self-reporting of the accused. Hiding behind that tissue thin layer of justification, the Bishops returned these monsters to ministry.

Challenging the Bishop: A Layperson

In the earliest stages of the Grand Jury's investigation, the Grand Jury heard from Mr. George Foster. Foster is a businessman in the billboard advertising business and a devout Catholic who attends a church within the Diocese of Altoona-Johnstown. George is a proud father and concerned Catholic. His efforts to expose the conspiracy of silence within the Diocese are nothing short of heroic.

Foster explained that he was initially concerned about what he saw as immorality occurring amongst the priests. Foster felt that rather than being good examples to the congregations they served, they were public embarrassments to an ancient and sacred religion. Foster was aware of reports of sexual activity, alcoholism, embezzlement and other types of misconduct that caused him concern for the wellbeing of the Church. Foster's mantra was simple[:] if a priest was unfit for ministry [he] should not be permitted to minister.

Over time Foster's concerns narrowed to a specific issue. Foster's discussion with other concerned Catholics and his brother in the clergy led him to conclude that there was a shocking secret sitting in broad daylight but hidden by the shadow of the Bishops. Foster discovered that priests were molesting children and the Bishops were doing nothing, or worse yet, hiding the conduct from exposure.

After writing an editorial in a local paper Foster began to receive telephone calls stating that certain priests in the Diocese were pedophiles. One victim of sexual child abuse perpetrated by a priest even came to see George personally to report his abuse at the hands of Father Bernard Grattan. Other family members and victims soon followed. George found himself in an avalanche of humanity all claiming that priests were molesting young boys in the Diocese.

George asked one victim "why are people coming to me?" The victim explained that people had read George's editorial and that he had stood up to the Bishop in public. George's fellow Catholics had decided he wasn't afraid of the Bishop. Foster explained to the Grand Jury that at that time he couldn't understand why people would think that. George noted, "I only answer to God. . . . Bishops don't bother me." Victims provided Foster with letters they had written the Diocese year after year reporting child abuse or requesting that an offending priest be removed from ministry. Foster even went to the Blair County Courthouse and reviewed the documents admitted in the Luddy case. Foster told the Grand Jury they were "eye-opening." Yet, nothing was done. . . .

Foster again and again found evidence that jarred him. When reviewing the letters of victims, as well as the courthouse's Luddy files, he found clear and credible allegations of sexual child abuse were made against various priests. Foster couldn't believe no one had done anything. Foster wondered, "Where were the police and the Bishops?" He noted the files were accessible to the authorities, "they're unsealed." Foster became aware that the Bishop even attended the trial. Luddy's civil trial happened in the open and in daylight. Foster was baffled as to why no one acted. Foster testified that he read Luddy's confession to molesting numerous boys and saying one in particular he didn't molest because he was "too ugly." George Foster complained that he couldn't imagine why the Diocese was fighting so hard for a priest that had admitted to molesting children. Foster concluded something was terribly and dangerously wrong. . . .

George Foster slowly became a novice detective. He decided he wasn't going to make a claim to the Bishop if it wasn't true. Citing scripture, George told the Grand Jury he wasn't going to "bear false witness." George took more calls. He interviewed more people. Over time Foster began keeping files on individual priests. As word got out that George Foster, the man that has billboards, was investigating some Diocesan leaders and priests began to get nervous. As Foster testified, they "thought I was crazy" and explained that they believed he might just start putting what he knew on billboards.

Things took a strange turn for Foster the more he investigated. He began to get calls from police officers providing him information. The officers told him he was on the right track. The officers said that people knew, but it was being covered-up. . . . The Grand Jury finds George Foster was right. A concerned Catholic businessman had done what so many hadn't; he built cases against monsters to protect children. Foster's efforts came at a price. He was told his family might be in danger. He knew that Adamec had threatened others with excommunication to silence them. But George was undeterred.

On or about June 21, 2002, Foster took his concerns to Bishop Joseph Adamec. Adamec acknowledged that he knew of the allegations and priests Foster named. Foster laid out the admissions of the priests, the letters of the victims, and accused priests that were still in ministry. Foster specifically noted accounts that priests had gone on trips with children and had slept in the same bed as the child. Adamec remarked, "Haven't you ever slept in a bed with your child?" Following the meeting Foster sent Adamec a letter memorializing their conversation. Line by line George Foster explains that there have been and may be child predators in the Diocese of Altoona-Johnstown. He invited the Bishop to "correct any inconsistencies." The Bishop responded in his own letter but he neither acknowledged nor denied the contents of Foster's letter. He corrected minor and irrelevant details. One error was that Foster had said the Bishop had called the priests his "boys." Adamec believed he had said "my guys." George Foster had made his great push with the victims' support at his back. Adamec didn't budge. Nothing changed. . . .

George Foster came to the Bishop to seek redress for what he saw as an epidemic within the Church. The Bishop chose to respond with threats and attempted to silence a critic. However, behind closed doors Adamec took steps that showed the widespread nature of the problem. Adamec created a pay-out chart guide used to direct the judgments of the Diocese in the payment of claims and in the purchase of silence. The chart appears as follows:

LEVEL OF ABUSE	RANGE OF PAYMENT
I. Above clothing, genital fondling	$10,000-$25,000
II. Fondling under clothes; masturbation	$15,000-$40,000
III. Oral Sex	$25,000-$75,000
IV. Sodomy; Intercourse	$50,000-$175,000

The chart is footnoted with "Factors to consider for valuation within a range." Those "factors" are: number of occurrences; duration of abuse over time; age of victim; use of alcohol or drugs; apparent effect of abuse on victims (psychosis); and other aggravating circumstances.

The Grand Jury notes the cold bureaucracy of this chart. The problem Bishop Adamec denied in public was a problem he secretly acknowledged to himself and the Diocesan insurance. The epidemic of priests offending on children was so significant that the Bishop privately perceived a need for a scale of "payments" to the victims of child sexual abuse.

The Grand Jury predicts that interested parties to whom this report is adverse will claim that many times payments occurred after the civil statute for suit had expired. The Diocese will likely claim this is demonstrative of their goodwill to those who were abused by their priests. The Grand Jury has observed another function. With these payouts came an onslaught of confidentiality agreements or waivers of liability releases. Those who find themselves exposed by this report were not gifting money to the abused; they were buying silence and protection from public scrutiny. The Grand Jury finds this was the primary interest of Bishop Joseph Adamec. . . .

Bishop Joseph Adamec was given the opportunity to explain his actions to the Grand Jury on November 18, 2015. The following exchange occurred:

Mr. Dye: Now I see that you're here in the trappings of a priest, and I would just ask, are you now or have you ever been a Bishop of the Roman Catholic Diocese of Altoona-Johnstown?
Bishop Adamec: Yes, I—

The Bishop's counsel conferred with the Bishop. The Bishop Emeritus of the Diocese of Altoona-Johnstown exercised his right to refuse to answer questions on the grounds of incriminating himself.

BISHOP MARK BARTCHAK

Bishop Mark Bartchak's term as Bishop of the Diocese of Altoona-Johnstown is relatively young. The power of the Bishop in the Diocese is nearly absolute. Bishop Bartchak acknowledged the responsibility of any Bishop to protect the welfare of the public. The Grand Jury commends Bishop Bartchak for the cases in which it has identified action in reporting allegations of child molestation to authorities and removing accused child predators from ministry. Bartchak's removals of [certain offending priests] were positive steps. . . .

The Grand Jury is concerned the purge of predators is taking too long. However, Bishop Bartchak explained he has attempted to prioritize his review of Diocese materials and remove active or current priests. He was unaware of the number of historical predators in the Diocese when he appeared before the Grand Jury. Bartchak explained that this was due to an ongoing review in which he has involved legal counsel in the review of Diocesan files. We conditionally accept this explanation in hopes that an earnest review prioritizing protecting the children over the institution is in effect.

Bishop Bartchak is not Bishop Hogan or Adamec. Those men wrote their legacy in the tears of children. The Bishop must continue, as he says he is, reporting allegations of child abuse to law enforcement immediately. We encourage the current Bishop to create a real and meaningful victim assistance program [and] [p]rovide real confidentiality and involve qualified experts in the review of allegations.

The legacy of Bishop Bartchak has yet to be written. The onslaught of attorneys the Grand Jury had to wade through in obtaining its evidence is concerning. There are certainly signs that the institution could revert to the protection of image over truth. The Grand Jury encourages Bishop Mark Bartchak to take bold action in correcting and rectifying the wrongs exposed in this report. The current Bishop has a choice. We pray he chooses wisely. . . .

THE ALLEGATION REVIEW BOARD

The Grand Jury report has already touched upon the payouts devised by Bishop Adamec to quiet the outrage of the abused. Bishop Adamec created an additional protocol within the Diocese [—] [a] board of hand selected operatives who answer to the Bishop. This group is called the Allegation Review Board.

The Allegation Review Board was launched in an effort to convince the public and sexual child abuse victims that the days of a mysterious Bishop deciding how to handle a scandalous and heinous report of child molestation and sodomy were over. The Allegation Review Board claims to determine the credibility of an "allegation of abuse." In reality, the Bishop still exclusively makes the decision how or what to do with a report of child molestation. Nothing has changed but the trappings of how a report is procedurally made.

Victims of child sexual abuse who believe they are reporting to a board of unbiased or neutral observers would be sadly mistaken. Investigations into victims are commonplace. Unbeknownst to the victim the investigation is often initiated by the "victim advocate" whose reports read more like police reports than the compassionate aid of anything that would remotely resemble advocacy. Victims must endure questions as to whether there are witnesses, mental health problems, or other personal issues. Additionally, the priest's assignments are investigated by the "advocate" once she gleans details of the assault from the victim. If the victim reported an assault in a particular year at a particular parish, the "advocate" will then look to see if the priest was assigned to that parish in that year. The "advocate" points any error out in her report — even in cases where the discrepancy is mere months. These investigations also seek personal or compromising or damaging information on victims. In one case the Allegation Review Board sought the gynecological records of a victim following the victim's testimony.

If the intrusion into privacy wasn't enough to deter a victim from reporting, one only needs to consider the so-called process of verbal reports followed by written reports followed by whatever additional inquiry the Board sees fit. A victim of sexual abuse or sexual violence may recount the traumatic events to a panel of unqualified fellow Catholics as many times as this Board or the Bishop feels is appropriate. If the victim fails to do so, compensation and a finding of "credibility" can be withheld. By contrast the accused priest need only deny the events and have a glance taken at his personnel file. The imbalance in favor of the Diocese and the accused priest is total.

The Board members are selected on ambiguous "qualifications." The Grand Jury learned they are often selected on who the Bishop "likes" or if they are "good Catholics." Medical background might be a basis for appointment. However no specific qualifications are required other than the presence of a member-priest. The Grand Jury learned that one member must be an active priest, and the Bishop may sit in to observe. In fact, the Allegation Review Board never met without Bishop Adamec personally present.

The Diocese will not apologize or take responsibility for its dark history. The Diocese blames the men and avoids institutional responsibility for a failure to act and protect. When darkest moments of a victim's life are laid bare before the Allegation Review Board those details are forwarded to lawyers whose interest is solely protecting the Diocese. Exact details are sought from victims, sometimes details from decades prior to the appearance before the Board. And while that Board's record for recommending payments to victims is robust, the alternative for the Diocese is public exposure of yet another predator priest or possibly the attention of additional victims coming forward.

In reality the Allegation Review Board is only as real as any Bishop may want it to be. There is no confidentiality or privacy and no right to see what documentation the Diocese may have in support of the allegation. The Diocese takes significant direction from attorneys retained to protect the Diocese from criminal and civil liability. Reporting to police in the modern Diocese may occur, but rest assured Diocese attorneys have vetted any Diocese action first. In the course of this investigation, witness after witness appeared with a Diocese approved attorney. One witness had an attorney appear to "represent" him before the Grand Jury, over his own objection. That matter had to be resolved by the Supervising Judge.

The Grand Jury credits the Diocese for offering $10,000.00 in counseling for victims with that cap possibly removed in certain circumstances. However, numerous Diocesan records show that the Diocese encourages the use of Diocese approved counselors. Secular counselors are not preferred.

Real change will come to the Diocese when the institution engages in transparency and acknowledges its failure. The victims of sexual child abuse need to hear the Diocese apologize, admit to the past, and confess it was wrong. Only then can true healing begin. The Diocese's response to this report will be a telling moment in whether the Diocese is moving in the right direction. . . .

The Bishops

Supervisory Special Agent Isom, of the FBI's Behavioral Analysis Unit, analyzed the conduct of Bishops James Hogan and Joseph Adamec of the Diocese of Altoona-Johnstown. Her conclusions were blunt but exact. James Hogan and Joseph Adamec enabled the priests of the Diocese to sexually abuse children. . . . Isom also spoke to the continued statements regarding scandal, publicity, public scrutiny, and the lack of police reporting. In fact, where police did appear deals were brokered to avoid prosecution. Taken in total, Isom noted that such a constellation of reckless behaviors directed at protecting public perception rather than protecting children diminishes the seriousness of the offense to the offender and endangers children.

In regards to Bishop James Hogan, Isom noted that Hogan's interference with police investigations to the benefit of predators like Father Gaborek certainly supported conclusions by Gaborek and potentially other offenders or victims that the most powerful official in the Diocese condoned or tolerated the sexual abuse of children.

The Behavioral Assessment Unit characterized Bishop Joseph Adamec's approach to sexual child abuse as "laissez-faire." Isom and the group noted in particular that Adamec was mailed an anonymous letter stating that Joseph Bender had sexually abused children. When Adamec interviewed Father Bender he stated he hadn't done anything like that for 20 years. Adamec's bold effort to protect the children of the Diocese was to return Bender to ministry reasoning that if it had been serious the writer would have signed the letter. The FBI noted other incidents where even the accused priests were alarmed that Adamec wasn't taking notes when interviewing them regarding the allegations. Adamec's statement that he would "write down what he needed to remember" would have only furthered the accused's belief that the allegation alone must be insufficient or not important.

While the Grand Jury found it was not Bishop Joseph Adamec's practice to call the police when dealing with allegations of sexual child abuse, the FBI noted a damning example of just how little Adamec seemed to be concerned with the well-being of the children of his Diocese. SSA Isom noted the case of Mark Powdermaker. Powdermaker was not a priest but a lay person working as a librarian at Bishop Guilfoyle High School from 1994 to 2002. On December 19, 2002 school officials began an investigation into a questionable internet story that had been printed by a school employee. In the course of their investigation they came to learn that Mark Powdermaker was using school library computers to download graphic stories of the rape and torture of female children as young as 13 years-of-age. Chat logs also showed that Powdermaker was actively discussing his desire to sexually assault and to lure a child with other men online. The Grand Jury suffered through a reading of a portion of the writings Mark Powdermaker obtained sexual gratification from. To call the stories sadistic is an understatement.

Before the end of December 2002 the school had notified Bishop Joseph Adamec via email of the investigation and its outcome. Powdermaker was resultantly dismissed from the school. However, the Diocese knew how deplorable Powdermaker's interests were. . . . Mark Powdermaker had spent eight years amongst the teenage girls he dreamed of raping. Bishop Guilfoyle High School and the Diocese of Altoona-Johnstown helped him keep his secret. As FBI Special Agent Isom noted, no one, including Bishop Joseph Adamec, called the police. . . .

Questions and Comments

1. It is impossible to miss the difference in tone of this report from the Catholic Bishops' report excerpted above. Which do you feel presents a more reliable picture of the issue? Are they inconsistent?

2. It appears that bishops have a high level of autonomy in the management of their dioceses. Did the bishops of the Altoona-Johnstown diocese exercise too much authority? Should their activities be more closely supervised by higher authority?

3. The grand jury report asserts that it is not intended as an indictment of the Church. Does the Church itself, as opposed to the individual priests and bishops mentioned in this report, bear some of the blame?

4. Do you agree with the grand jury's criticism of Bishop Adamec's schedule of payments to abuse victims?

5. The grand jury report criticizes the diocese for relying on attorneys. Is there anything objectionable about seeking the advice of counsel when faced with serious accusations of misconduct?

6. Why did the bishops tolerate a system that allowed priests to serially abuse children, given the harm inflicted on victims, the financial costs, and the risk to the reputation of the Church?

7. Suppose the current bishop of Altoona-Johnstown appoints you to a new position with the authority of a chief compliance officer of the diocese. You believe

that the bishop sincerely wants to institute reforms and that he will back your efforts to prevent the problem from recurring. What steps should you take?

8. Suppose a parishioner comes to see you in your new position with a report of ongoing abuse by a priest. Aside from this report, you have no evidence that the priest has committed misconduct. You know that the complaining party is a troubled young man with serious emotional problems but you also find his allegations to be plausible. What steps would you take? At what point would you involve the civil or criminal authorities?

In response to criticisms of the Church hierarchy's response to sex abuse scandals in various parts of the world, the Vatican press office issued the following statement:

Protecting Minors: Declaration by the Director of the Holy See Press Office on Response to Sexual Abuse

2016

March 4, 2016

The depositions of Cardinal Pell before the Royal Commission as part of its inquiry carried out by live connection between Australia and Rome, and the contemporary presentation of the Oscar award for best film to "Spotlight," on the role of the Boston Globe in denouncing the cover-up of crimes by numerous pedophile priests in Boston (especially during the years 1960 to 1980) have been accompanied by a new wave of attention from the media and public opinion on the dramatic issue of sexual abuse of minors, especially by members of the clergy.

The sensationalist presentation of these two events has ensured that, for a significant part of the public, especially those who are least informed or have a short memory, it is thought that the Church has done nothing, or very little, to respond to these terrible problems, and that it is necessary to start anew. Objective consideration shows that this is not the case. The previous archbishop of Boston resigned in 2002 following the events considered in "Spotlight" (and after a famous meeting of American cardinals convoked in Rome by Pope John Paul II in April 2002), and since 2003 (that is, for 13 years) the archdiocese has been governed by Cardinal Sean O'Malley, universally known for his rigor and wisdom in confronting the issue of sexual abuse, to the extent of being appointed by the Pope as one of his advisers and as president of the Commission instituted by the Holy Father for the protection of minors.

The tragic events of sexual abuse in Australia, too, have been the subject of inquiries and legal and canonical procedures for many years. When Pope Benedict XVI visited Sydney for World Youth Day in 2008 (eight years ago), he met with a small group of victims at the seat of the archdiocese governed by Cardinal Pell, since the issue was also of great importance at the time and the archbishop considered a meeting of this type to be very timely.

Merely to offer an idea of the attention with which these problems have been followed, the section of the Vatican website dedicated to "Abuse of minors: the Church's response," established around ten years ago, contains over 60 documents and interventions.

The courageous commitment of the Popes to facing the crises that subsequently emerged in various situations and countries — such as the United States, Ireland, Germany, Belgium and Holland, and in the Legionaries of Christ — has been neither limited nor indifferent. The universal procedures and canonical norms have been renewed; guidelines have been required and drawn up by the Episcopal

Conferences, not only to respond to abuses committed but also to ensure adequate prevention measures; apostolic visitations have taken place to intervene in the most serious situations; and the Congregation of the Legionaries has been radically reformed. These are all actions intended to respond fully and with far-sightedness to a wound that has manifested itself with surprising and devastating gravity, especially in certain regions and certain periods. Benedict XVI's Letter to the Irish faithful in March 2010 probably remains the most eloquent document of reference, relevant beyond Ireland, for understanding the attitude and the legal, pastoral and spiritual response of the Popes to these upheavals in the Church in our time; recognition of the grave errors committed and a request for forgiveness, priority action and justice for victims, conversion and purification, commitment to prevention and renewed human and spiritual formation.

The encounters held by Benedict XVI and Francis with groups of victims have accompanied this by now long road with the example of listening, the request for forgiveness, consolation and the direct involvement of the Popes.

In many countries the results of this commitment to renewal are comforting; cases of abuse have become very rare and therefore the majority of those considered nowadays and which continue to come to light belong to a relatively distant past of several decades ago. In other countries, usually due to very different cultural contexts that are still characterized by silence, much remains to be done and there is no lack of resistance and difficulties, but the road to follow has become clearer.

The constitution of the Commission for the protection of minors announced by Pope Francis in December 2013, made up of members from every continent, indicates how the path of the Catholic Church has matured. After establishing and developing internally a decisive response to the problems of sexual abuse of minors (by priests or other ecclesial workers), it is necessary to face systematically the problem of how to respond not only to the problem in every part of the Church, but also more broadly how to help the society in which the Church lives to face the problems of abuse of minors, given that — as we should all be aware, even though there is still a significant reluctance to admit this — in every part of the world the overwhelming majority of cases of abuse take place not in ecclesiastical contexts, but rather outside them (in Asia, for instance, tens of millions of minors are abused, certainly not in a Catholic context).

In summary, the Church, wounded and humiliated by the wound of abuse, intends to react not only to heal herself, but also to make her difficult experience in this field available to others, to enrich her educational and pastoral service to society as a whole, which generally still has a long path to take to realize the seriousness of these problems and to deal with them.

From this perspective the events in Rome of the last few days may be interpreted in a positive light. Cardinal Pell must be accorded the appropriate acknowledgement for his dignified and coherent personal testimony (twenty hours of dialogue with the Royal Commission), from which yet again there emerges an objective and lucid picture of the errors committed in many ecclesial environments (this time in Australia) during the past decades. This is certainly useful with a view to a common "purification of memory."

Recognition is also due to many members of the group of victims who came from Australia for demonstrating their willingness to establish constructive dialogue with Cardinal Pell and with the representative of the Commission for the protection of minors, Fr. Hans Zollner S.J., of the Pontifical Gregorian University, with whom they further developed prospects for effective commitment to the prevention of abuse.

If the appeals subsequent to *Spotlight* and the mobilization of victims and organizations on the occasion of the depositions of Cardinal Pell are able to contribute to supporting and intensifying the long march in the battle against abuse of minors in the universal Catholic Church and in today's world (where the dimensions of these tragedies are endless), then they are welcome.

Questions and Comments

1. To what extent does this document acknowledge responsibility for the misconduct?

2. How significant were the various measures recounted in this document? Were they an appropriate response to the problems that had been uncovered?

3. What do you make of the observation that most cases of sexual abuse of children occur outside of the Church?

4. Do you detect a wish to take credit for contributing to a broader social recognition of the problem of sexual abuse of children?

5. Does the excerpted statement see positive value in the accounts of sexual abuse, such as those contained in the *Boston Globe* investigation and portrayed in the movie *Spotlight?*

6. The statement provides assurances that, even though the process of reform is not yet complete, the Catholic Church has addressed and continues to address these problems in a robust and effective manner. Do you find the statement convincing?

E. GENERAL MOTORS IGNITION SWITCH SCANDAL

An excellent example of a compliance breakdown is the 2014 revelations regarding how General Motors dealt with information in its possession that ignition switches on several of its models would sometimes turn off while the automobile was in motion, disabling airbags and causing other dangerous conditions for passengers in the vehicle. The following excerpts provide some background on the events:

**Written Testimony of General Motors Chief Executive
Officer Mary Barra
Before the House Committee on Energy and Commerce
Subcommittee on Oversight and Investigations**

Apr. 1, 2014

[In 2014, General Motors was overwhelmed with a crisis sparked by revelations that many of its automobiles had safety issues involving faulty ignition switches that the company neither redressed nor made known to the government—issues that allegedly had caused dozens of fatalities over the preceding years. By April 2014, GM had recalled more than six million vehicles for emergency repairs. In testimony before a committee of the House of Representatives, submitted on April Fools' Day, Mary Barra, GM's new CEO, apologized to the victims and others in the following testimony.]

More than a decade ago, GM embarked on a small car program. Sitting here today, I cannot tell you why it took years for a safety defect to be announced in that program, but I can tell you that we will find out. When we have answers, we will be fully transparent with you, with our regulators, and with our customers.

As soon as l learned about the problem, we acted without hesitation. We told the world we had a problem that needed to be fixed. We did so because whatever mistakes were made in the past, we will not shirk from our responsibilities now and in the future. Today's GM will do the right thing.

That begins with my sincere apologies to everyone who has been affected by this recall — especially to the families and friends of those who lost their lives or were injured. I am deeply sorry.

I've asked former U.S. Attorney Anton Valukas to conduct a thorough and unimpeded investigation of the actions of General Motors. He has free rein to go where the facts take him, regardless of the outcome. The facts will be the facts. Once they are in, my management team and I will use his findings to help assure this does not happen again. We will hold ourselves fully accountable.

Our customers who have been affected by this recall are getting our full and undivided attention. We're talking directly to them through a dedicated website, with constantly updated information, and through social media platforms. We've trained and assigned more people to our customer call centers, and wait times are down to seconds. And, of course, we're sending customers written information through the mail.

We've empowered our dealers to take extraordinary measures and to treat each case specifically — and they are doing a great job taking care of our customers. Here's what we are doing with our dealers: if people do not want to drive a recalled vehicle before it is repaired, dealers can provide them a loaner or rental car — free of charge. If a customer is already looking for another car, dealers can provide an additional cash allowance for the purchase or lease of a new vehicle.

Our supplier is manufacturing new replacement parts for the vehicles that are no longer in production. We have commissioned two and asked for a third production line, and those parts will start to be delivered to dealers as soon as possible.

These measures are only the first in making things right and rebuilding trust with our customers. As I've reminded our employees, getting the cars repaired is only the first step. Giving customers the best support possible throughout this process is how we will be judged. I would like this committee to know that all of our GM employees and I are determined to set a new standard. And I am encouraged to say that everyone at GM — up to and including our Board of Directors — supports this.

I'm a second-generation GM employee and I'm here as the CEO, but I'm also here representing the men and women who are part of today's GM and are dedicated to putting the highest-quality and safest vehicles on the road.

I recently held a town hall meeting to formally introduce our new VP of global vehicle safety to the company. We met at our Technical Center, one of the places where the men and women who engineer our vehicles work. They are the brains behind our cars, but they are also the heart of GM.

It was a tough meeting. Like me, they are disappointed and upset. I could see it in their faces, and could hear it in their voices. They had many of the same questions that I suspect are on your minds. They want to make things better for our customers, and in the process, make GM better.

That's what I'm committed to doing.

GM Announces New Vehicle Safety Chief
Jeff Boyer Named Vice President, Global Vehicle Safety

DETROIT — General Motors CEO Mary Barra today named a new vehicle safety leader whose first priority will be to quickly identify and resolve product safety issues.

Jeff Boyer has been named to the newly created position of Vice President, Global Vehicle Safety, effective immediately. Boyer, who has spent nearly 40 years in a wide range of engineering and safety positions at GM, will have global responsibility for the safety development of GM vehicle systems, confirmation and validation of safety performance, as well as post-sale safety activities, including recalls.

Boyer will provide regular and frequent updates on vehicle safety to Barra, senior management and the GM Board of Directors.

"Jeff's appointment provides direct and ongoing access to GM leadership and the Board of Directors on critical customer safety issues," said Barra. "This new role elevates and integrates our safety process under a single leader so we can set a new standard for customer safety with more rigorous accountability. If there are any obstacles in his way, Jeff has the authority to clear them. If he needs any additional resources, he will get them."

"Nothing is more important than the safety of our customers in the vehicles they drive," said Boyer. "Today's GM is committed to this, and I'm ready to take on this assignment."

Boyer, 58, will report to John Calabrese, Vice President of Global Vehicle Engineering and become a member of Global Product Development staff, led by Mark Reuss, Executive Vice President, Global Product Development, Purchasing and Supply Chain.

Boyer began his GM career in 1974, as a co-op student and has held several senior engineering, safety and process leadership positions, including the role of a total vehicle integration engineer. His most recent position since 2011 was Executive Director of Engineering Operations and Systems Development. Before that, Boyer served as Executive Director of Global Interior Engineering and Safety Performance where he was responsible for the performance and certification of GM vehicle safety and crashworthiness. He holds a Bachelor of Science in Electrical Engineering from Kettering University and a Masters of Business Administration from Michigan State University.

Statement of the Honorable David Friedman
Acting Administrator, National Highway Traffic Safety Administration
Before the Committee on Energy and Commerce
Subcommittee on Oversight and Investigations
U.S. House of Representatives

Apr. 1, 2014

Thank you for the opportunity to appear before you today to discuss the recall process of the National Highway Traffic Safety Administration (NHTSA) and the General Motors (GM) ignition switch recall.

Let me begin my testimony by saying, on behalf of everyone at NHTSA, that we are deeply saddened by the loss of life in vehicle crashes involving the GM ignition switch defect. Our deepest sympathies are with the families and friends.

It is this kind of tragedy that our defects investigation team works long hours trying to prevent. Our core mission to save lives and prevent injuries on America's roadways is something we take very seriously, whether we are trying to curb dangerous driver behavior, improve the safety of vehicles, or find safety defects and ensure that automakers correct them.

Our first priority is the recall; we need to ensure that GM gets the vehicles fixed quickly and that it is doing all it can to keep consumers at risk informed and to identify all vehicles that may have a defective ignition switch. Second, we are pursuing an investigation of whether GM met its timeliness responsibilities to report and address this defect under Federal law — an investigation that will end with holding GM accountable if it failed in those responsibilities. Third, we are examining the new facts and our efforts in this case to understand what took place and to determine how to continue to improve our efforts.

NHTSA has an aggressive and effective defects investigation program with staff who is deeply and personally dedicated to their mission, often working nights and weekends in pursuit of potential defects. That work has resulted in thousands of recalls involving hundreds of millions of vehicles and items of motor vehicle equipment, which have helped to protect millions of consumers from unanticipated safety hazards in their vehicles. . . .

NHTSA and DOT's Office of General Counsel (OGC) are currently engaged in a continuous improvement and due diligence process regarding past efforts on airbag non-deployments in GM vehicles under its ignition switch defect recall. Secretary Foxx recently requested the Department of Transportation Inspector General to initiate an agency audit in connection with the GM recall. These efforts will ensure that DOT and NHTSA have a full understanding of the facts regarding the GM recall and can take corrective actions to enhance NHTSA's safety function to the extent necessary and appropriate. These processes will also benefit from any findings from NHTSA's timeliness investigation, which may shed light on what additional information NHTSA could have had in evaluating airbag non-deployments in this case.

Questions and Comments

1. Barra was treading carefully. Given the public anger at GM — concern about the defect, which apparently could have been corrected by a part costing less than a dollar, outrage at GM's prior failure to acknowledge or address the issue, and resentment at GM's recent history of bankruptcy and bailout — she could not really offer a stout defense without getting shouted down in the court of public opinion. She had to accept blame. On the other hand, she herself was newly appointed and was not responsible for the problems she had inherited. So she also attempts to avoid acknowledging personal responsibility for the failures. Who else, then, could be blamed? Obviously, GM's former managers. Barra could have cast the blame on them directly, but to do so could have been seen as disloyal and could also have been demoralizing within the company. How well does she do at managing the competing considerations?

2. At the time Barra made this statement, GM was facing millions or billions of dollars of potential liability in connection with the safety problems and apparent cover-up, including damages to persons injured as a result of ignition switch malfunctions as well as potential class action liability to purchasers of GM vehicles — not to mention fines by the federal safety regulator, the National Highway Traffic Safety

Administration. An apology is one thing; an admission of legal liability is another. Does Barra manage to do one without the other?

3. Barra's reason for failing to provide more information was that the company was conducting an internal investigation. It retained a noted law firm, Jenner & Block LLP, whose Chairman Anton Valukas served as a government-appointed examiner of the failure of Lehman Brothers. (Valukas' investigation was just getting started at the time of Barra's testimony; it is excerpted below). Is this persuasive?

4. A particularly sensitive matter concerns the effect of GM's bankruptcy in 2009, which apparently wiped out claims for injuries that occurred earlier. People injured prior to that date, or the representatives of people who were killed, may claim with some justification that they had no knowledge of the defect and therefore no ability to bring a lawsuit or file a claim in the bankruptcy proceeding. At about the same time as Barra's statement, the company announced that it had retained Kenneth Feinberg, noted (among other things) as the administrator of the 9/11 victim compensation and BP oil spill funds; the purpose was to compensate victims whose claims were extinguished in the bankruptcy.

5. What steps does Barra take to maintain morale in her organization while at the same time acknowledging serious shortcomings in the past? Are they likely to be effective?

6. Why hadn't Barra fired the responsible officials at the time she made this statement?

7. One of the remedial steps Barra announced was the appointment of a new vice president for global vehicle safety. Why didn't such a position exist already? Was GM trying to downplay the dangers posed by its automobiles? Recall the history here: One of the convulsive events in the history of the American automobile industry was the publication of Ralph Nader's *Unsafe at Any Speed* in 1965, a muckraking attack on the industry in general, and GM in particular, for failing to ensure the safety of its vehicles. Perhaps GM wanted to forget about that period of its history. On the other hand, the company failed to bury the ghost: The more recent scandal revived memories of the old troubles, and with a vengeance.

8. Note the qualifications of the new product safety officer, Jeff Boyer. He was a career GM executive and former executive director of a GM office concerned with safety performance. Was he the right person to appoint to the job, given that GM's failures seemed to arise from inherited attitudes in the company's leadership team? What about the fact that he had a background in safety performance? On the one hand, this is a plus because it appears to qualify him for the position; on the other, it suggests, rightly or wrongly, that he may have been part of the problem rather than being part of the solution. Was Barra — herself a longtime GM veteran — really just circling the wagons?

9. When it comes to apologies, what do you think of the statement by the head of the NHTSA? Like Barra, Administrator Friedman professes "deepest" emotions about the losses suffered by victims of the defect. But unlike Barra, he doesn't apologize. Far from it: He notes that his team "works long hours" trying to prevent such tragedies, and — repeating himself — asserts that the agency houses an "aggressive and effective defects investigation program with staff who is deeply and personally dedicated to their mission, often working nights and weekends in pursuit of potential defects." Fine: No doubt there are many dedicated public servants and capable people at the agency. But the bottom line is that their job is

to prevent problems such as the one that manifested itself in GM cars, and they failed to do so. Should Friedman have apologized for the agency's shortcomings?

10. A memorandum released by the House Committee prior to Friedman's testimony alleged that the NHTSA had been alerted to the GM ignition switch problem — not once but twice. As early as 2007, NHTSA's Defects Assessment Division reviewed 29 complaints and four fatal crashes involving failed air-bag deployments in Chevrolet Cobalts and Saturn Ions, but the NHTSA didn't even open an investigation. Likewise in 2010 an investigator provided a report on a 2005 crash involving a Cobalt in which the airbags failed to deploy and the ignition switch was found to be in an improper position. Again the agency failed to act. Given what appears to be a pattern of serial failures by the agency, should Friedman have done more than profess his deepest concern for the victims?

11. The defensiveness evident in Friedman's comments might have been due, in part, to the fact that his agency was in the cross hairs of criticism. The Transportation Department's Inspector General was conducting an audit of the agency's performance in connection with the defect. Friedman sugar-coats the news by placing it in the context of what he describes as his agency's "continuous improvement and due diligence process," characterizing the goal of the investigation as being to "enhance" NHTSA's safety function, and blaming GM for failing to provide "additional information" in connection with the airbag non-deployments. Is he successful at deflecting blame?

12. GM's problems continued to mount, as more and more models turned out to have ignition switch defects requiring recalls. In June 2014, GM added 8.2 million vehicles to its recall list, bringing the total for the year to 29 million.

Anton R. Valukas
Report to the Board of Directors of General Motors Company Regarding Ignition Switch Recalls

May 29, 2014

. . . [T]he tone at the top is relevant background for assessing GM's approach to the issues discussed in this report. Repeated throughout the interview process we heard from GM personnel two somewhat different directives — "when safety is at issue, cost is irrelevant" and "cost is everything." It is worth examining how those two messages collided.

GM personnel were quite consistent in saying that they understood that safety was a critical priority and that, if they identified a safety problem, cost should not be a factor in deciding whether and how to address the safety problem. . . . That said, the 2000s was a time of extraordinary cost-cutting at GM. The messages from top leadership at GM — both to employees and to the outside world — as well as their actions were focused on the need to control costs. We heard repeatedly from GM personnel about the focus on cost-cutting and the problems it caused. For example, an engineer stated that an emphasis on cost control at GM "permeates the fabric of the whole culture."

Cost-cutting impacted all aspects of the business. Keeping projects on time — because of impact on cost — became a paramount concern. . . . Those responsible for a vehicle were responsible for its cost, but if they wanted to make a change th[at] incurred cost and affected other vehicles, they also became responsible for the costs incurred in the other vehicles. For example, if the Cobalt team wanted an ignition switch replaced, the other vehicle lines that used the ignition switch would request that the cost for their new switches be paid for by the Cobalt team because the Cobalt team requested the change.

Reductions in staff, especially in Engineering, meant that employees were forced to do more with less. In the time leading up to the bankruptcy, one cost-cutting measure was to decrease the Engineering headcount by adding to responsibilities of the Design Release Engineer. . . . Witnesses stated that the reduction in force created a difficult environment in which people were overworked and the quality of work suffered. . . .

We have uncovered no evidence that any employee made an explicit trade-off between safety and cost in the investigation of the Cobalt. To be sure, the Cobalt engineers working in the 2004-2006 timeframe rejected various fixes to the moving stall issue because there was "no acceptable business case," but those engineers' error was that they failed to understand the connection to airbags and the safety issue that they were facing. Having wrongly identified the issue as a consumer convenience issue, cost considerations that would otherwise have been immaterial became part of their calculus.

That noted, we cannot conclude that the atmosphere of cost-cutting had no impact on the failure of GM to resolve these issues earlier. . . . Engineers did not believe that they had extra funds to spend on product improvements. Staff was cut dramatically. It is not feasible for three to do a job as effectively as eight, . . . and there were specific impacts. . . .

Some witnesses said that there was resistance or reluctance to raise issues or concerns in the GM culture. . . . A small number of participants also suggested a fear of retaliation. . . . Some witnesses provided examples where culture, atmosphere, and the response of supervisors may have discouraged individuals from raising safety concerns, including, in a different context than the Cobalt, supervisors warning employees to "never put anything above the company" and "never put the company at risk." . . .

Whether general "cultural" issues are to blame is difficult to ascertain, but the story of the Cobalt is one in which GM personnel failed to raise significant issues to key decision-makers. Senior attorneys did not elevate the issue within the Legal chain of command to the General Counsel—even after receiving the [deleted] evaluation the summer of 2013 that warned of the risk of punitive damages because of a "compelling[]" argument that GM had "essentially done nothing to correct the problem for the last nine years." Engineers, too, failed to elevate the issues. Starting in mid-2012, there were three high-level managers brought in as "champions"— Woychowski, Federico, and Kent. The very reason they were brought in was to help resolve an unexplained pattern of airbag non-deployments in an expeditious manner. But they did not elevate the issue to their superiors, and the common thread was to hold more meetings and refer the matter to additional groups or committees.

Similarly on the issue of culture, GM employees received formal training as to how to write about safety issues. A PowerPoint presentation from 2008 warned employees to write "smart," and not to use "judgmental adjectives and speculation." Employees were given a number of words to avoid, with suggested replacements:

- "Problem = Issue, Condition, Matter"
- "Safety = Has Potential Safety Implications"
- "Defect = Does Not Perform to Design"

Employees were also given examples of sentences not to use, including "Dangerous . . . almost caused accident" and "This is a safety and security issue. . . ." And they were told, in what the author described as an attempt at humor, not to use phrases such as "Kevorkianesque," "tomblike," or "maniacal," or "rolling sarcophagus." The "actual examples" provided in the presentation described how a plaintiff's lawyer had used a memo from a senior manager at another automaker warning that a risk of documenting a survey about a problem was that it could provide "product liability credence to a hypothesis we have long ignored."

In addition to being trained on how to write, a number of GM employees reported that they did not take notes at all at critical safety meetings because they believed GM lawyers did not want such notes taken. . . . The no-notes direction . . . reached the status of an urban myth that was followed, an instruction passed from GM employee to GM employee over the years. Thus, as we learned in our investigation, for many meetings . . . there are no clear records of attendance or of what was discussed or decided.

Leadership at GM has tried to counter this culture with clear messages that employees should raise issues. "Winning with Integrity" (the code of conduct) instructs employees to raise problems (although it does not explicitly reference vehicle safety) and ensure they receive proper attention, and to conduct themselves with the highest ethical standards. . . .

A cultural issue repeatedly described to us and borne out by the evidence is a proliferation of committees and a lack of accountability.

The Cobalt Ignition Switch issue passed through an astonishing number of committees. We repeatedly heard from witnesses that they flagged the issue, proposed a solution, and the solution died in a committee or with some other *ad hoc* group exploring the issue. But determining the identity of any actual decision-maker was impenetrable. No single person owned any decision. Indeed it was often difficult to determine who sat on the committees or what they considered, as there are rarely minutes of meetings.

One witness described the GM phenomenon of avoiding responsibility as the "GM salute," a crossing of the arms and pointing outward towards others, indicating that the responsibility belongs to someone else, not me. It is this same cabining of responsibility, the sense that someone else is responsible, that permeated the Cobalt investigation for years.

Similarly, Mary Barra described a phenomenon known as the "GM nod." The GM nod, Barra described, is when everyone nods in agreement to a proposed plan of action, but then leaves the room with no intention to follow through, and the nod is an empty gesture. It is an idiomatic recognition of a culture that does not move issues forward quickly, as the story of the Cobalt demonstrates.

Repeatedly, over a decade, GM personnel failed to search for, share or gather knowledge, and that failure had serious consequences. There are multiple components to these failures, involving individual mistakes, organizational dysfunction and systems inaccessible to some and impenetrable to many.

In 2004 and 2005, when complaints of moving stalls came in, the engineers who considered the issue did not know that the vehicle was designed so that the airbags would not deploy when the ignition switch was in Accessory. As a consequence, the engineers failed to recognize the stalls as a safety issue and resolve the problem quickly. Even the committees . . . that were designed to have cross-disciplinary members did not connect the dots. . . .

There are two dates at which critical information resided in a single place, and yet action was not taken. Witnesses state that the reason for this lack of action at either time was that the "root cause" was not known with certainty or that a full solution had not been devised.

- In 2011, [GM investigators knew that] any time a MY 2005 or 2006 Ignition Switch was inadvertently turned to Accessory, the airbags were turned off. Instead of addressing this repeating problem, the investigators worked to find an ultimate solution that would solve the problem for all years and for every permutation of the Ignition Switch. The consequence was a two-and-a-half year delay.
- In late April 2013 . . . engineers and GM Legal Staff knew [that the Ignition Switch had changed for the MY 2008 Cobalts]. In other words, even the difference between the early Cobalts and the MY 2008 Cobalts was now explained. The recall did not occur until February 2014, approximately nine months later. . . .

At both of the times described above, there was a view that no action should be taken until the "root cause" of the problem was fully understood and a solution developed. To be sure, GM needed to investigate to understand the problem in the Cobalt. But the search for root cause became a basis for doing nothing to resolve the problem for years. The lengthy search for root cause thus diverted GM from its obligations and failed to produce the required urgency to bring to matter to fast closure. . . .

RECOMMENDATIONS

Organizational Structure . . .

- Ensure that the responsibilities of the Vice President of Global Vehicle Safety are appropriately defined to comprehensively cover safety and compliance issues, and ensure that sufficient resources are made available to allow this executive to comprehensively address safety and compliance issues. Ensure that this executive has direct access to the CEO and the Board and is required to make reports to the Bard at least quarterly. [The Vice President of Global Vehicle Safety is a new position created in the wake of the ignition switch recall.]
- Ensure that all departments, divisions, or groups that have substantial responsibilities concerning the identification, investigation or remediation of safety issues have a direct or indirect reporting line that leads up to the Vice President of Global Vehicle Safety. . . .
- Review the activities of all organizational departments, division or groups that have safety-related responsibilities . . . for the purpose of identifying any areas where multiple groups have similar or overlapping functions such as investigating or resolving safety issues. Where overlap is identified, consolidate or coordinate those functions to ensure, for example, that [groups] do not have independent and parallel responsibility for identifying and resolving a safety defect but rather that each group is aware of, and not duplicating, the other's activities. To the extent that areas of overlap remain, ensure that a clear owner is identified.

Cultural Emphasis on Safety . . .

- Implement regular communications with employees about safety to raise awareness and reinforce the tone at the top, for example by issuing periodic bulletins from the Vice President of Global Vehicle Safety and/or the CEO that include updates or reminders on safety issues, or including a column on safety in an employee newsletter. Ensure that employees understand that they have an obligation to raise any concerns they have about safety or compliance, and to continue to raise those concerns if they do not believe those concerns have been resolved.

- We understand that GM has created a new "Speak Up For Safety" program to encourage employees to raise safety issues, and we recommend that GM promote that program through visible communications, such as posters on employee bulletin boards. Bulletins or newsletters could include features recognizing employees who have raised safety issues and highlight the significance of the potential safety problem averted by the escalation of the issue.

- [V]isibly promote and rigorously enforce the non-retaliation policy, including for employees who report concerns regarding actual or potential safety-related defects or potential no-compliance with the Federal Motor Vehicle Safety Standards.

- Regularly communicate to suppliers the importance of safety and GM's expectation that suppliers will promptly and accurately identify any potential safety issues. . . .

- [E]xplicitly communicate to employees that they should not be reluctant to classify issues as safety issues or potential safety issues, including in written work, and eliminate any language in any guidelines, training decks, or policies that suggest otherwise or that caution against using specific words or phrases that might be deemed too sensitive or inflammatory. Communications to employees on safety policy issues like this should come from the level of the Vice President of Global Vehicle Safety or higher. . . .

Individual Accountability

All employees have responsibility for raising safety issues, and many employees have responsibility for addressing safety issues once they have been identified. The Company should take steps to ensure that employees are aware of their safety-related responsibilities and that individuals are accountable for addressing the safety issues for which they are given responsibility. . . .

Communications Between and Within Groups

Breakdowns in communications between and within groups were a critical part of the failures described in this report. Specific . . . recommendations are:

- Provide regular written or oral updates by the Legal Staff for relevant engineering groups on alleged or potential defects.
- Formalize coordination between and among [relevant teams and groups]. . . .
- Conduct an assessment of the adequacy of mechanisms for ensuring coordination between groups handling different subsystems of the same vehicle regarding safety-related information and items that may affect safety performance, and implement improvements as necessary. . . .

- Assign the Global Ethics and Compliance Center ("GECC") to oversee the review of issues raised through the new Speak Up For Safety program. This will have the benefit of ensuring that review of issues raised through the . . . program is coordinated with review of issues raised to the compliance organization, and to ensure that internal inquiries and investigations prompted by the . . . program are appropriately tracked and handled consistent with GECC procedures. . . .

Communication with [the National Highway Traffic Safety Administration (NHTSA)]

NHTSA should be viewed not only as a regulator but also as an ally in the effort to ensure that the Company's vehicles are as safe as they can be. Interactions with NHTSA should be consistent with that type of relationship. . . .

Role of Lawyers

The Legal Staff can and should play a critical and unique role in assisting with the identification, analysis, and resolution of safety issues that have given rise to customer claims. To ensure that Legal Staff play this critical role effectively, we recommend the following steps:

- Hold regular discussions between each product litigation attorney and [senior managers in the Legal Department] regarding whether the attorney has observed trends of potential safety issues in lawsuits or not-in-suit matters ("NISMs").
- Designate a member of the Legal Staff as a liaison to provide regular reports . . . to the Global Vehicle Safety organization on safety-related issues identified in matters handled by Legal Staff. . . .
- Hold monthly meetings between the GM Legal Staff and [engineers] responsible for each specialty to discuss observed trends and potential safety issues in that specialty area. . . . If any trends or safety issues are identified, ensure that . . . the trends or safety issues are . . . elevated as appropriate.
- Ensure that at the outset of litigation, the Legal Staff . . . generate a list of all [recalls, product investigations, and other issues] for the subject vehicle make and model. Include this information in the new suit package provided to outside counsel at the onset of litigation. . . .
- Provide specific guidance concerning the type of issues that should be elevated to the General Counsel. Those issues should include serious safety issues and safety issues that are not being resolved expeditiously, and more broadly, any concerns that could have a significant impact on the Company, its customers, or its shareholders. Explain in this guidance that lawyers should request the General Counsel's assistance when important processes are not progressing with appropriate speed. Include such guidance in the orientation program for all new hires to the Legal Staff.
- [E]nsure that in-house counsel are aware of the expectation that they will respond appropriately if they become aware of any threatened, on-going, or past violation of any federal, state or local law or regulation, a breach of fiduciary duty, or violation of GM policy, including the expectation that if they raise such an issue and believe it has not been addressed appropriately, they will bring the situation to the attention of their supervisors, and if they believe their supervisors have not addressed it appropriately, to higher levels

including the General Counsel if necessary. Ensure that this expectation extends to issues of safety. Communicate similar expectations to outside counsel in written guidelines.

- Provide guidance for product liability attorneys on how to recognize and communicate safety issues to ensure that they are properly addressed notwithstanding ongoing litigation or claims activity, while fulfilling their obligations to defend the Company in litigation and appropriately protect attorney-client privilege. . . .

Questions and Comments

1. The report suggests that employees at GM were given a mixed message about product safety — on the one hand, they were informed that safety was non-negotiable; on the other hand, they were told to ruthlessly cut costs. These two factors — safety and cost — play a role in all business organizations. Is it ever appropriate to trade them off? Surely at some point a tradeoff is unavoidable: What if a super-safe car cost ten million dollars? But if a company must compromise between safety and cost, how can it send the right message?

2. GM was obsessed with finding the "root cause" of the ignition switch problem. Because it was for some reason unable to identify the root cause for many years, it failed to undertake readily available measures — such as a product recall — that would have addressed at least the part of the problem that was understood. Meanwhile people were being injured or killed. Why was the company so concerned with identifying the root cause? Was this an excuse for delay, or did the company really believe that a more fundamental understanding of the issue was a necessary precursor to any action?

3. Was there anything wrong with the reported practice of warning employees against using "loaded" terms that could be exploited by plaintiffs' attorneys when bringing lawsuits against the company?

4. Some of the practices reported in this excerpt seem dysfunctional — for example, the culture in which problems were endlessly vetted in committees with no apparent intention to do anything about them. How could an industrial giant like GM — historically one of the most successful companies ever — have fallen into practices that rival for ineffectiveness the management habits of university departments?

5. Do you find it mind-boggling that GM's teams of engineers and investigators apparently failed for years to realize that when the ignition switch was inadvertently turned to Accessory, the airbags were turned off — and that this could pose a safety hazard for occupants of the vehicle? How could they have failed to connect the dots?

6. What implicit judgments does this study make about the role of lawyers within GM prior to the ignition switch crisis? Do you get the sense that the company was a bit paranoid about attorneys (possibly because it was often sued) and that it failed to give its in-house and outside counsel a sufficient degree of credibility and authority? Or was it that the company didn't want to hear the information about product safety defects that the attorneys would have brought to the attention of senior management, if asked?

7. If you were an attorney on GM's legal staff and you observed a raft of ignition switch lawsuits being brought against the company, what would your obligations

have been to make an inquiry or to elevate the issue within the organization if you observed that nothing was being done to deal with an apparent safety hazard?

8. What do you think of the recommendations in this report? The report relies rather heavily on the fact that the company had appointed a vice president of global vehicle safety with significant authority within the company and a clear mandate to monitor for safety problems. Do you think this move is likely to be effective — or are the cultural problems within the company so pervasive that no amount of juggling job descriptions is likely to change practices at a fundamental level?

9. How realistic is the recommendation that the company embrace the NHTSA as an ally and partner in the job of achieving a safe product?

10. What do you think of the report's recommendations regarding the tone at the top of the organization? Are they likely to be effective?

11. Could GM really change the tone at the top when its new CEO, Mary Barra, worked at GM since age 18 and once served in the position of vice president of global manufacturing? Even though Barra was not charged with misconduct or negligence in connection with the ignition switch fiasco, she is publicly identified as a "GM person" and has been thoroughly socialized into the company's culture and mind-set. Did her appointment send the message that things would fundamentally change — or is it a case of *plus ça change, plus c'est la même chose?*

12. If you were magically given complete power to make changes within GM, what would you do, based on the information contained in this report?

Part III

Risk Management

18

Introduction to Risk Management

A. WHAT IS RISK?

Before venturing into the issue of risk management, it is important to understand the basic concept of risk. Risk-management professionals employ two definitions of risk, often without clearly distinguishing between them.

The first idea is that risk is the *chance of something bad happening*. It seems normal to say "there's a risk of showers," but odd to say "there's a risk of sunshine" (unless you are a farmer in the midst of a drought). Risk in this sense is something to be avoided.

The second idea of risk is not limited to a danger of something bad happening. Rather, this idea understands risk as the *dispersion* of possible future events — bad or good. Take two situations: In the first you get \$1 for sure; in the second you flip a coin and get \$0 if the coin flips to "heads" and \$2 if the coin flips to "tails." Statistically, you get the same expected return in both situations (\$1). But the second is more risky: The reason is that the outcomes (\$0 or \$2) are more dispersed than a certainty of getting \$1.

> **Definition 1: Risk is the chance of something bad happening.**

> **Definition 2: Risk is the dispersal of possible outcomes.**

For an introduction to the concept of risk and how it has evolved over time, see Peter L. Bernstein, *Against the Gods: The Remarkable Story of Risk* (1996).

B. WHAT IS RISK MANAGEMENT?

Risk management, broadly understood, has been around as long as there has been risk. When an ancient city surrounded itself by a defensive wall, this was a form of risk management; it dealt with the risk that a hostile power would attack and loot the town. When (according to the Bible) Pharaoh followed Joseph's advice to store up grain in anticipation of famine, this was a form of risk management. In the Renaissance, merchants engaged in risk management when they took out policies of insurance on their vessels. What do these activities have in common? All are responses to the fact that people can make themselves better off when they plan for the future.

It may have already occurred to you that the risk management function seems to have substantial overlap with compliance. It should be evident that the threat of legal liability, a principal topic of Part II of this book, is for most purposes simply another aspect of risk;

> Risk management, broadly understood, is any activity that an organization undertakes to deal with future uncertainties.

the compliance function is a form of risk management. As the Basel Committee on Banking Supervision remarked in a consultative document, "[t]he purpose of the compliance function is to assist the bank in managing its compliance risk, which can be defined as the risk of legal or regulatory sanctions, financial loss, or loss to reputation a bank may suffer as a result of its failure to comply with all applicable laws, regulations, codes of conduct and standards of good practice. . . . Compliance risk is sometimes also referred to as integrity risk, because a bank's reputation is closely connected with its adherence to principles of integrity and fair dealing."

How should organizations respond to the fact that risk management and compliance appear to be essentially two sides of the same coin? Three models are possible. In one, compliance and risk management operate in essentially discrete "silos," each with its own policies, procedures, and management. This has largely been the practice to date. This approach, however, is problematic: It ignores the essential similarities in the functions, sacrifices potential economies of scale and scope, and generates inconsistencies or conflicts in expectations.

A second approach is to simply acknowledge that compliance is part of risk management and place the compliance function squarely within the risk management operation. Several companies have reportedly adopted this approach by merging their compliance and risk management operations within the overall framework of risk. This approach has the virtue of integrating risk and compliance and also achieving better economies of scale and scope (for example, by cross-training employees in both disciplines). But it also has drawbacks. An obvious, although surmountable problem is that any attempt to merge the operations is going to be controversial. The result can be conflict over turf, since the chief compliance officer is unlikely to want the chief risk officer snooping under her doorstep. A deeper problem is that, whether for appearances' sake or in reality, risk management and compliance have different philosophical premises. Risk management recognizes that all business activities carry risk and seeks to ensure that the company's operations remain within the parameters of a risk appetite defined by the board of directors. Compliance, on the other hand, cannot easily admit that the company has any "appetite" for non-compliance; this could offend the regulators and the public as well, even if in fact it is an accurate description of how the company carries out the compliance function. For compliance purposes, the prevailing ideology is one of "zero tolerance" — the view that no level of compliance violations is acceptable. Combining risk management and compliance must overcome the hurdle of these fundamentally inconsistent attitudes.

The third model is that the risk-management and compliance functions should be coordinated but not combined. Considerations of risk management are integrated into the compliance function by allocating compliance resources on a risk-based model (more compliance resources devoted to areas of greater risk). Compliance, along with internal audit, can also assist in implementing the organization's risk appetite both by reporting perceived compliance risk to the risk-management department and by responding to findings of non-compliance in a way that takes account of risk (for example, by requiring the head of a business line to explicitly accept the risk of violations). Conversely, the results of the compliance operation are integrated into risk management because the risk operation takes explicit account of legal and regulatory risk as one element of the spectrum of risks facing the organization at any given moment. Advantages of the coordination approach are that it reduces (although does not eliminate) turf battles over efforts to reorganize departments, that it does not require the organization to reconcile inconsistent philosophies, and that it achieves some (but not all) of the potentially available economies of scale and scope.

Questions and Comments

1. Which of the above models, in your opinion, best takes account of both the similarities and differences between risk management and compliance?

2. Are there other possible approaches that might be better?

C. THE PUBLIC INTEREST IN RISK MANAGEMENT

It might seem that the task of risk management is solely of interest to the organization, and therefore not a good candidate for regulation. A little reflection, however, reveals that this is not necessarily the case. The reason is that the costs and benefits of risks assumed by firms are not fully internalized by the organization: Third parties gain or lose from what the firm does. These third-party effects are known as "externalities"; they play a key role in the economic analysis of social welfare. Because third parties are affected by the risks that organizations take on, there is a public interest in risk management that transcends the particular concerns of the organization or its owners.

The public interest in risk management was demonstrated in spectacular fashion during the financial crisis of 2007-2009. Many banks and "shadow banks" undertook large risks during the 2000s by investing in subprime mortgage-backed securities. These securities seemed to offer the best of all possible worlds: They were relatively high-yield, but also highly rated (and therefore, in the view of the rating agencies, unlikely to default). It turned out that all was not for the best in the best of all possible worlds. The subprime mortgage-backed securities were not, in fact, low-risk; many of the mortgages that had been originated and placed into these asset pools were issued to borrowers who could not repay the loans unless the values of their houses continued to rise at unrealistically elevated rates. When the housing bubble collapsed in 2007, these borrowers began to default at alarming rates. The value of the subprime mortgage-backed securities plummeted accordingly. Huge losses in these investments or in financial commitments tied to these investments were precipitating causes of the failures of Bear Stearns, Lehman Brothers, AIG, and Indymac Financial; the financial distress experienced by major institutions such as Citigroup, Bank of America, and Merrill Lynch; and the freezing of credit markets, the government takeovers of Fannie Mae and Freddie Mac, the stock market collapse, and the downturn in the real economy that accompanied these events. In retrospect, many analysts have concluded that excessive risk taking by financial institutions was a cause of the financial market turmoil. Risky behavior represented an externality because the costs of the behavior, while incurred partly by shareholders and creditors of the firms that undertook the risks, also extended to the general public.

External effects of risky behavior are not limited to financial institutions. Consider the power industry. A nuclear power plant might decide to cut corners on safety in order to save money, thus increasing the risk of an accident. If a serious accident occurs, the shareholders and creditors of the utility company will suffer, but so will many others — as Japanese citizens who resided near the Fukushima nuclear power plant in 2011 can attest. Or consider the pharmaceutical industry. A drug company might stint on clinical trials of a new medication, either to save money or because it doesn't want to know about health downsides. If the drug turns out to be dangerous, many who took the medication will suffer; and although they might be able to bring lawsuits for money damages against the manufacturer, the suits may fail or settle for less than the full amount of the harms incurred, or the company may declare bankruptcy and avoid paying the people it harmed.

One might think that, in consequence of these external effects, the regulators would take it on themselves to dictate the terms of a company's risk appetite. In general, regulators do not do this. However, they find other means to make their influence felt. A company's risk appetite will be reviewed by the regulator, and if anything sparks concern, the regulator is likely to raise the problem with management. Beyond this, regulators and legislators impose substantive controls that bear on risk — prohibiting or limiting activities, requiring disclosure of key policies, imposing risk-adjusted capital regulations, mandating provisions for managerial compensation to discourage risk taking, and so on.

In practice, therefore, the process of risk management, at least for highly regulated industries, is effectively a partnership between the government and the private sector. For some managers, it may even feel as if they have been relegated to a figurehead role: They are officially in charge, but if they take on risks the regulators don't like, they face the consequences.

Questions and Comments

1. Do you agree that risk in large organizations is a pressing matter of public concern and a suitable subject for regulation?

2. Can we trust regulators to regulate risk appropriately? Regulators are unlikely to be criticized harshly if they *over-regulate* risk taking and thereby prevent companies from operating as efficiently or profitably as the could otherwise do; but they are

likely to be blamed, even if they regulate risk appropriately, if something bad does happen. Do regulators have an inherent bias towards over-regulating risk?

3. What about the political economy of risk regulation? Stephen Bainbridge argues that risk was not effectively regulated in the lead-up to the financial crisis because the political constituency to lobby for such regulation was lacking: "[R]isk management was not on the agenda of any organized interest group. In particular, the unions, institutional investors, and their academic allies that were so influential on other corporate governance issues were largely indifferent to risk management. . . . Real problems thus go unaddressed while the business community is saddled with new obligations unrelated to the crisis that supposedly motivated them." Stephen Bainbridge, *Corporate Governance After the Financial Crisis* (2012). Do you agree?

4. Is it a good idea for the government to require private institutions to implement risk-management policies and programs? What might the dangers be? *See* Luca Enriques & Dirk A. Zetzsche, *The Risky Business of Regulating Risk Management in Listed Companies*, 103 European Company & Fin. L. Rev. 271 (2013).

D. ENTERPRISE RISK MANAGEMENT

Although organizational risk management has an ancient pedigree, it is also a live topic of controversy and debate. More changes have occurred in the theory and practice of risk management over the past three decades than in any similar time period over the entire history of complex organizations. Many features of traditional risk management have undergone substantial transformation. Let's consider the traditional approach to risk management and then compare it with the more modern approach.

1. Definition of Risk

We noted above that risk-management professionals employ two different ideas of risk. The traditional notion conceives of risk as the chance of something bad happening. This notion retains a great deal of influence, in part because of its intuitive character. The more modern approach, however, sees the chance of something bad happening as only one aspect of risk. A more general understanding would also include the chance of something good happening. Risk in this sense is measured by the dispersal of outcomes rather than simply the chance of a bad one.

These two concepts of risk generate different philosophies of risk management. If the first idea is used, the objective of risk management is to minimize risk. If the second concept is used, the focus shifts slightly. Since risk in this second sense involves both positive and negative outcomes, the goal of minimizing risk is not necessarily paramount. Rather, the focus is on *determining how much risk the organization is willing to take on.* Modern approaches to risk management generally use this second, more encompassing definition of risk. However, as a practical matter, the principal focus is still on adverse events rather than good ones.

2. Distribution of Responsibility for Managing Risk

Historically, the risk-management function was distributed across business lines. The consumer products division might manage the risk inherent in that unit (for example, risk of product liability, risk of supply chain disruptions, etc.); the leasing division might manage the risk of that unit (interest rate risk, foreign exchange risk, counterparty risk, etc.), and so on across all business lines. Among the virtues of this system were the following: (a) responsibility was given to an officer who "owned" the risk in question; (b) the task of risk management was allocated to persons who knew the most about the operation; and (c) the lack of division between risk management and operations meant that the risk function could be thoroughly integrated into day-to-day activities.

This approach to risk management, in which the responsibility for controlling risk is widely distributed to siloes within the organization, has fallen out of fashion. The reason is that dividing the task of risk management came to be seen as sacrificing more than it gains. When risk is combined with operations, the official charged with both responsibilities might be more attentive to the latter, either because operational issues require an immediate response or because the manager lacks an appreciation or understanding of how to conceptualize and manage risk. Further, allocating risk management to operating divisions does not necessarily generate optimal results because the incentives and philosophy of the line managers may not align reliably with the interests of the organization. For example, a manager whose compensation is tied to the performance of her division might elect to have that division take on more risk than would be preferred by the board of directors. People who rotate across divisions, moreover, might not worry very much about "long-tail" risks whose bad outcomes would be realized only at some time in the future.

Even more importantly, dividing the tasks of risk management ignores correlations across different parts of the company. A risk that might seem acceptable in one division (because it is not material to the division's performance) could be seen as unacceptable if similar risks pervade the organization as a whole. Conversely, a risk that might seem unacceptable to the manager of a division might cease to be material when viewed in light of the company's overall operations (for example, because the risk is not present in other divisions or, if present, is offset by good outcomes elsewhere if the event in question occurs). Risk-management strategies that make sense for the division might not make sense for the enterprise.

Risks can also "fall through the cracks" when managed on a siloed basis, because no one takes responsibility for ensuring that the separate operations are coordinating their activities. A classic example is the case of NASA's Mars Planet Orbiter. Launched from Cape Canaveral with great expectations in 1998, this spacecraft reached Mars in September 1999. It orbited behind the planet and went out of radio contact, never to return. An investigation revealed that one of the two navigation teams assigned to the mission used the metric system (meters, kilograms, and so on) and the other used the imperial system (pounds, feet, etc.). No adjustment was made when the two software programs were combined. In consequence, the spacecraft entered orbit at too low an altitude and failed due to atmospheric stress and friction.

The modern approach seeks to centralize the task of risk management and to provide greater analytical focus by defining a risk appetite applicable to the organization as a whole. This more integrated approach to risk management is intended to deal with the problems of insufficient or skewed incentives, conflicts in goals, and problems of coordination that had afflicted the silo approach.

3. Risk Mitigation Strategies

Risk managers traditionally viewed the purchase of insurance as the preferred strategy for mitigating risk. If the firm faced some risk of loss — say, the chance that the factory would be destroyed by a fire — the best approach was to purchase an appropriate policy of insurance in order to shift that risk to a third party. The idea of insurance was generalized to include, for example, hedging strategies in financial markets or the purchase of credit default swaps; but in essence the idea remained the same: The company would pay a third party to take on some of its risk.

Modern risk-management programs do not focus so intensively on insurance. Insurance sometimes may not be needed because activities in other parts of the enterprise offset the risks; in other cases, the company may be better off bearing the risk itself (effectively, self-insuring) rather than purchasing a policy of insurance. Alternatives to insurance are also given greater weight in the analysis, such as implementing systems of internal controls that reduce the chance of an adverse event occurring. Beyond this, the concept of insurance as the preferred device for mitigating risk grows out of the first definition of risk — the chance of something bad happening; it doesn't take account of the upside of risk that is included in the newer definition of the concept.

4. Priority of the Topic

Risk management, while never viewed as unimportant, was once given a modest priority in the hierarchy of issues facing the board of directors and senior management. It was viewed as largely a technical issue that would ordinarily be handled by professional managers without substantial board or chief executive officer attention. This is no longer the case. As we saw in Part I of this book, risk is today a central focus of board deliberations — so central that many companies have instituted specialized board-level risk committees, created positions for chief risk officers, and devoted substantial resources to the task of managing risk across the organization.

5. Focus of Risk Assessment

Traditionally, the risk-management function looked at financial risks to the organization — contingencies that, if they occurred, would result in an immediate hit to earnings and profits. Risks that took longer to develop, including a variety of non-financial risks, were not given as much importance. The more modern approach to risk management focuses on non-financial as well as financial risks. This change in focus is based on the perception that while all risks affect an organization's bottom line, not all risks are easily quantified in financial terms. Consider, for example, the issue of succession risk: Who will take over leadership in the organization if the chief executive officer is killed in an automobile accident? The skills and talents of the top executive have a major impact on a company's performance — in the long run. But because the risk is not immediate or easily quantified, it might receive less attention than other risks that are more tractable from a financial point of view. The newer approach to risk management seeks to take account of these long-tail or inherently unquantifiable risks.

6. Transparency of Risk and Risk Management

Traditionally, neither risk nor risk management were transparent, either to the investing public, the regulators, or even the company's board of directors and senior management. The lack of transparency was due, in part, to the fact that the risk management function was distributed widely within an organization; it also arose from the fact that risk itself was not systematically understood or analyzed. The financial crisis of 2007-2009 demonstrated that risks were not in fact transparent in many financial organizations. A poster child is American International Group (AIG), a huge and profitable insurance company that experienced catastrophic financial distress in 2008 as a result of poorly understood bets made by a London office that wrote credit default swaps. It appears that AIG's senior managers did not fully grasp the extent of risk to the organization posed by the London office's operating strategies.

Today, risk at many institutions is treated in a much more transparent manner. The rationale for this change is straightforward: Given that a company's risk management activities have important consequences for future performance, it is desirable that the process be open and well understood, at least to the senior managers who direct the organization's strategic decisions. Contemporary risk-management operations seek to avoid unpleasant surprises such as the one that descended on AIG.

These and other changes in practices and outlook in the field of risk management are captured in the concept of "enterprise risk management" (ERM). The term is always used in a positive sense, conveying an idea of progress and subtly denigrating the approaches to risk management used in the past.

Commonly included in the notion of ERM are the following ideas:

- Risk is conceptualized as dispersal or variance of results, not the chance of something bad happening.
- Risk management is carried out on an enterprise-wide basis rather than being distributed within the organization.
- Risk includes any contingency that may affect the organization's performance; it is not limited to financial risks or to risks that will have an immediate effect on earnings or profits.
- Approved risk-management strategies are broader than the purchase of insurance, and include changes in the underlying business operations as well as a deliberate decision, made at an appropriate level of seniority within the organization, to accept the risk.
- The risk-management function is elevated in importance within the organization through institutional changes such as the creation of board risk committees or chief risk officers.
- The organization's policies toward risk and risk management are more transparent both internally and for purposes of regulatory review.

ERM is heavily promoted by opinion leaders in the field of corporate governance. ERM guidelines issued in 2004 by the Committee of Sponsoring Organizations of the Treadway Commission were an important step; another was a white paper on risk management published in 2009 by the International Organization for Standardization (ISO 31000). Regulators jumped on to the ERM juggernaut and began to push organizations under their supervision to move to an enterprise-based risk management approach; as we have seen, they also encourage organizations to incorporate a risk assessment as a central feature in the design and implementation of other systems of internal control. Purveyors of software have facilitated the process of converting to ERM by offering sophisticated packages that can be tailored to the needs, conditions, and preferences of many different clients. Almost all large organizations today endorse the principles of enterprise risk management; it could be foolish not to do so given the overwhelming consensus in the corporate governance community that ERM is the way to go.

> Enterprise risk management is a set of policies and procedures under which upside and downside risks are analyzed systematically, comprehensively managed, and treated as central aspects of an organization's strategic plans.

E. TYPES OF RISK

ERM calls on an organization's managers to assess all material risks to the organization. The first step in the process is to compile an inventory of risks with a view to assessing both the probability they will occur as well as the costs that the organization will experience if they do. The following list outlines a number of the leading risks that regulators and others have identified over the past few decades. A word of caution: The categories on this list are not precisely defined; in some cases a problem that fits within one category of risk fits in another category as well.

- Credit risk: Credit risk is the risk that borrowers will not repay the principal or interest on loans in a timely fashion. Much ingenuity has been expended by finance economists in an effort to develop reliable indicators of default risk. Credit rating agencies offer their opinions on the subject; and for banks, the Basel capital adequacy guidelines implement a sophisticated methodology for assessing the risk posed by loan customers drawing on the bank's own internal risk assessments.
- Liquidity risk: Liquidity risk is the risk that an organization will not have access to the funds it needs to pay its obligations. Liquidity risk was on display in spectacular fashion during the peak of the financial crisis of 2007-2009, when credit markets around the world "froze up" and it became nearly impossible, for a brief period, for firms to borrow the money they needed to pay their debts and carry out operations. All organizations manage their liquidity positions (or attempt to do so) by finding means to ensure that they will have funds on hand to pay off their debts as they mature. Liquidity risk for banks is regulated by reserve ratios and also by the Basel III liquidity provisions (when they become effective).
- Market risk: Market risk is the risk of price fluctuations in assets that are actively bought and sold by an organization. If, for example, an organization such as a hedge fund goes "long" on the euro, then it faces market risk in fluctuations of the price of the euro relative to other currencies.
- Strategic risk: Strategic risk is the risk posed by business decisions. If a company decides to open a factory in China, the performance of the factory represents a strategic risk for the company. As a practical matter, the company is likely to view this risk more in terms of the chance that the factory will fail rather than the chance it will exceed expectations. The risk of the decision for

ERM purposes, however, technically includes both the risk of failure and the risk of success.

- Competitive risk: Competitive risk is the risk that other companies offering competitive products or services will erode an organization's profits or market share by engaging in aggressive marketing or lowering prices.

- Regulatory risk: Regulatory risk is the risk that laws or regulations will change in a way that will impact the organization's operations or results. For example, in the wake of the financial crisis of 2007-2009, European countries explored the idea of imposing a tax on bank transactions (the stated purpose was to discourage excessive speculation). Such a tax could suppress bank profits — a regulatory risk. Regulatory risk can also work in a positive direction; suppose for example that the government decides to open offshore oil reserves to drilling; the consequence could be to increase profits of energy companies with licenses to operate in the newly opened areas.

- Reputation risk: Reputation risk is the risk that news about an organization will increase or decrease the esteem in which the organization is held by constituencies or the public at large. For example, suppose that a pharmaceutical company is found to have conducted clinical trials on people from a developing country without adequately disclosing the health risks. This news could trigger proxy campaigns by activist investors, public hearings by congressmen, boycotts by customers, and unwanted scrutiny by regulatory agencies. Damage to reputation can be particularly dangerous because it takes a long time to repair; a company tarred with the label of "bad guy" can't become a "good guy" overnight. Reputational risk can be positive as well as negative; a company might earn kudos in the public eye for conspicuously good behavior (as illustrated by efforts many companies are making to portray themselves as committed to "green" or "sustainable" activities).

- Asymmetric information risk: "Asymmetric information risk" is a fancy way of referring to the fact that the board of directors and even senior executives may not fully understand what is going on in the companies they manage. The information is "asymmetric" because the information exists, but not necessarily in the hands of those who need it in order to make decisions. A conspicuous example of asymmetric information risk is JPMorgan Chase's "London Whale" trading fiasco, discussed in Chapter 20. For discussion, see generally Nicola Faith Sharpe, *Informational Autonomy in the Boardroom*, 2013 U. Ill. L. Rev. 1089.

- Operational risk: Operational risk is one of the most frequently mentioned but also most mysterious types of risk. The phrase suggests that the risk is from operations; but this interpretation would be far too broad because many of the other risks discussed above are also the result of operations. The Basel Committee defines operational risk as follows: the "risk of losses resulting from inadequate or failed internal processes, people and systems, or external events."

> Operational risk is the "risk of losses resulting from inadequate or failed internal processes, people and systems, or external events."

Questions and Comments

1. An important strategic risk for many companies is transformation risk — the risks associated with changes in the organization's business model. Surveys of risk managers often place the topic of change management — that is, the management of transformation risk — among the biggest worries that keep them up at night. It is easy to see why: Big changes bring big headaches; and even the best-laid plans of corporate directors often go awry.

Consider the following events, all of which occur on a regular basis among American corporations:

    a. The company merges with another firm, gets a new board of directors, and seeks to fold its business operations into those of the merger partner.

    b. The company runs out of money, goes into bankruptcy reorganization, and is brought under the control of a creditors' committee.

    c. The company decides to close its existing network of stores and to move to a purely online sales operation.

    d. The company jettisons its data management system and substitutes a new and incompatible system.

    e. The company decides to move its IT operations to the "cloud."

    f. The company's chairman and chief executive officer is killed in a plane crash without designating a successor.

It requires only a little imagination to appreciate that much can go wrong in any of these situations. Change can often be good, but it is not always good; and even when the final result is positive there are often bumps along the road.

2. Managing the risk of corporate change is challenging, not only because of the magnitude of the potential problems, but also because in many cases the infrastructure used to manage change is itself disrupted by the change. If the board of directors changes, what happens to the risk committee? If the company falls under the control of its creditors, what happens to the executive risk manager and her department? Moreover, because fundamental change disrupts the entire environment in which a company operates, the task of analysis and quantification can be complicated. Ordinary risk management deals with "known unknowns": The company knows that it faces foreign exchange risk, for example, although it doesn't know what will happen to exchange rates. Corporate changes, in contrast, often involve "unknown unknowns": The company has no firm basis for understanding, much less quantifying, the risks it will face in the post-change environment.

3. Let's turn to operational risk. In the first place, note that operational risk, as the Basel Committee uses the term, is defined in the traditional, loss-focused sense; it does not address the risk of gains from above-average internal processes, systems, or people or fortunate external events. The loss-focused definition of operational risk may reflect the fact that the Basel guidelines were adopted before the enterprise risk management movement came into full flower.

4. Operational risk, in this definition, is intended to exclude strategic or competitive risks. If a company's board of directors makes a bad business decision — say, to overpay for an asset that turns out to offer less value than anticipated — this is strategic risk, not operational risk. The board of directors has not failed or shown itself to be inadequate merely because it made a decision that did not pan out well. Similarly, and for the same reason, if the company finds that it is unable to meet competition from cheap imports, this is not operational but rather competitive risk.

5. Included in operational risk are cases of compliance failures or other violations of the law. These are operational risks because they represent a failure of people or systems of internal control. In a sense, the entire area of compliance that we studied in the previous section of this book is simply one aspect of operational risk. The devices a company uses to ensure compliance can be understood as ways to mitigate this form of risk.

6. Operational risk includes systems breakdowns. Suppose, for example, that an organization implements a "cloud-based" data storage and retrieval system, but that due to a glitch or programming error non-public customer information leaks out into the public arena. We saw from the chapter on data security that this can be a serious problem. The risk of such a system breakdown is operational risk. Operational risk also includes harmful external events. The utility company that owned the Fukushima nuclear power plant faced operational risk from an earthquake or tsunami, although it didn't appreciate the gravity of the threat. Proper operational risk management might have called for the company to install more reliable backup generators or coolant systems that could have withstood the event that crippled the facility in 2011.

7. You may be asking what these various types of operational risk have in common. If you are wondering this, you are not alone. Critics complain that the only thing that unites the various forms of operational risk is the fact that they are not within the other risk categories. In other words, perhaps operational risk is a residual category that covers things not covered elsewhere. However, the concept then becomes difficult to handle: If operational risks are essentially independent and *sui generis*, then no single strategy or policy can possibly manage them all. Specialists in operational risk management deny that the concept lacks coherence; they see fundamental similarities in all the examples of operational risk mentioned above.

8. How is a company to perform the task of risk management after having identified the category of operational risk? The range of operational risks is so enormous that it may be impossible to inventory all cases.

9. Even if particular operational risks are identified, how can they be analyzed? In the case of some other types of risk, quantitative methodologies exist to give substance to the analysis. But no similar methodologies exist for most categories of operational risk. The risk manager is essentially left to make an educated guess.

10. A problematic aspect of operational risk concerns the risk associated with vendors. Organizations these days place trust and confidence in third parties who perform essential services—including assisting in compliance and risk management, among other tasks. This practice exposes the organization to risk from an operational risk failure at a vendor. In the case of vendors, the usual techniques for mitigating operational risk are not particularly effective. Because the client doesn't perform the service, the client can't directly change the way the service is conducted. Nor, generally, can the client monitor the vendor on a day-to-day basis. The client is typically left with little recourse other than insisting on contractual terms that commit the vendor to employing safeguards. But these terms are difficult to draft, may not address key issues, and provide little protection against a catastrophic failure at the vendor.

11. An example of vendor risk occurred in 2011 at Fidelity National Information Services (FIS), the world's largest global provider of banking and payments technologies. Although not itself a household word, FIS is an important cog in the banking infrastructure: It serves more than 14,000 institutions in over 100 countries and employs more than 35,000 people worldwide. Especially for smaller banks, FIS is

an essential business partner; without its help they would be unable to process their checking accounts, prepare required reports to regulators, or perform many other important functions. In 2011, criminal elements broke into FIS's network and stole ATM cards and passwords. They then altered the cards to remove controls on the amount of cash that could be withdrawn and shipped the cards to confederates around the world who proceeded to withdraw $13 million in cash in the space of 24 hours. The fraud itself was unusually large, but not devastating; what was more worrisome is that the crime itself might have indicated that FIS had a point of weakness in its operations. In a case such as this, how is a client to assess its vendor risk going forward?

F. GOVERNANCE OF RISK

We investigated governance in Chapters 1 through 3. We saw that the job of overseeing risk management, like other key management responsibilities, is ultimately reserved for the board of directors. Boards, however, often delegate risk management to committees. Sometimes the audit committee assumes this response; more frequently, these days, a special risk committee of the board is constituted and assigned the responsibility.

1. Corporate Law Approaches

At the executive level, the task of risk management is carried out by a suitably designated officer, who may have a title such as "chief risk officer" or "CRO." The CRO reports to the risk committee, the full board, or the chief executive officer, or some combination of these. Some companies also maintain executive-level risk committees that facilitate the management of risk across business lines and areas of responsibility.

Recall the *Caremark* opinion from Chapter 2. The Delaware Chancellor there held (in an opinion subsequently endorsed by the Delaware Supreme Court) that directors owe a fiduciary duty to ensure that reporting systems are in place for detecting legal violations by corporate agents. Does *Caremark* liability extend to risk management? Do directors owe a non-delegable duty to ensure that the board of directors exercises affirmative oversight over the risk inherent in a company's operations? If so, what is the scope of that obligation?

Wachtell, Lipton, Rosen & Katz, Risk Management and the Board of Directors

2013

The risk oversight function of the board of directors has never been more critical and challenging than it is today. In the context of the current global financial crisis and the swooning global economy, companies now face risks that are more complex, interconnected and potentially devastating than ever before. Risk from the financial services sector has contributed to large-scale bankruptcies, bank failures, government intervention and rapid consolidation. And the repercussions have spread to the broader economy, as companies in nearly every industry have suffered from the effects of a global paralysis in the credit markets, sharply reduced consumer demand and extremely volatile commodity, currency and stock markets. In addition, the public and political perception that undue risk-taking has been central to the breakdown of the financial and credit markets is leading to an increased legislative and regulatory focus on risk management and risk prevention. In this environment, boards and companies must be mindful of the possibility that courts will apply new standards, or interpret existing standards, to increase board responsibility for risk management.

But what exactly is the proper role of the board in corporate risk management? The board cannot and should not be involved in actual day-to-day risk management. Directors should instead, through their risk oversight role, satisfy themselves that the risk management processes designed and implemented by executives and risk managers are adapted to the board's corporate strategy and are functioning as directed, and that necessary steps are taken to foster a culture of risk-adjusted decision-making throughout the organization. Through its oversight role, the board can send a message to the company's management and employees that corporate risk management is not an impediment to the conduct of business nor a mere supplement to a firm's overall compliance program but is instead an integral component of the firm's corporate strategy, culture and value generation process.

Given the increased significance of the risk oversight role in the current risk environment, a company's risk management system should function to bring to the board's attention the company's most material risks and permit the board to understand and evaluate how these risks interrelate, how they affect the company, and how management addresses these risks. It is important for directors to have the experience, training and knowledge of the business necessary for making a meaningful assessment of the risks that the company faces, however complicated they may be. The board should also consider the best organizational structure to give risk oversight sufficient attention at the board level. In some companies, this may include creating a separate risk management committee or subcommittee. In others, it may be sufficient to have the review of risk management as a dedicated, periodic agenda item for an existing committee such as the audit committee, in addition to periodic review at the full board level. While no "one size fits all," it is important that risk management be a priority and that a system for risk oversight appropriate to the company be put in place. . . .

The Delaware courts have developed a framework for the board oversight of risk management in a line of cases dealing with alleged violations of fiduciary duty. . . . In light of the focus on risk oversight in the current environment, however, boards should recognize the possibility that what constitutes a red flag and what constitutes conscious disregard may be evaluated in the future with heightened focus. Moreover, it is important to note that the courts have taken the view that a breach of duty for failure to exercise oversight would be a breach of the duty of loyalty, which is not subject to exculpation or indemnification by the company. Accordingly, a board is best advised to act well above the minimal standards established by *Caremark* and its progeny.

To avoid risk of *Caremark* liability, boards should ensure that the company implements appropriate monitoring systems tailored to each type of risk. The board should periodically review these monitoring systems and ask management and/ or outside consultants for an assessment of the systems' adequacy. Directors should also involve the company's general counsel as appropriate with respect to fulfilling the board's duty to have effective monitoring systems. The board should be sensitive to "red flags" or "yellow flags," investigating them or causing them to be investigated as necessary, and should document its monitoring and investigatory activities in minutes that accurately convey the time and effort spent by the board. The monitoring system should include reports on material regulatory proceedings, or material regulatory fines or censures, that may be used by plaintiffs to allege knowledge of non-compliance. The board should treat material proceedings of this kind as a red flag and investigate appropriately.

Questions and Comments

1. One of the authors of the excerpted report is Martin Lipton, widely considered to be the "dean" of the corporate law bar. His opinions are influential with corporate managers and lawyers, especially those affiliated with large public companies.

2. Under what circumstances, if any, would a board's oversight of risk management be so deficient as to give rise to liability under *Caremark*?

3. Suppose the risk committee displays conscious indifference to its responsibilities — an indifference so extreme as to create liability under *Caremark*. Should that liability extend to other board members not on the risk committee? If so, in what circumstances?

Unwritten Rules: The Importance of a Strong Risk Culture
Thomas J. Curry, Comptroller of the Currency

The Clearing House Banking Perspective (Third Quarter 2014)

. . . The problems that have come to light in the years since the financial crisis may not have been the result of conscious decisions on the part of senior management. I doubt, for example, that any large bank chief executive officer called together his senior executives and said, "Foreclosure paperwork is too time-consuming. Let's start robo-signing the documents." Yet it happened, and for reasons that in some ways are even more worrisome than if they were the deliberate decisions of senior management.

What troubles me is not that some individuals made bad decisions, but that the business practices that have caused problems were made possible by weaknesses in the organization's risk management and risk culture. Senior management bears responsibility for the problems that occurred in the years leading up to and following the financial crisis, but the nature of that responsibility is not necessarily in specific business decisions that senior executives made. Rather, management's responsibility lies in its failure to set an appropriate tone at the top and to build a strong organizational culture that promotes responsible business practices and guards against excessive or improper risk-taking. . . .

[It] seems reasonable to ask why some large banks allowed themselves to stray from the principles of sound business practices that have differentiated successful banks from unsuccessful ones over many years. Was it the conscious decision of management to flout laws, regulations, and basic precepts of business ethics? Or was it something more subtle, less visibly apparent, and more difficult to measure, that caused them to lose their way? . . .

Every organization has a unique risk culture that consists of the core values that drive business practices and shape executive decision making and employee actions. A strong risk culture consists of more than written policies. It's the tone set by top management, the expectation that everyone, from senior executives on down, will conduct themselves in a way that will protect the bank from credit losses as well as injury to the organization's reputation.

A strong risk culture is really the beacon that guides employees to behave responsibly, knowing that they will have the support and approval of their superiors and the organization as a whole. When that beacon goes dark, an organization can lose direction, entering markets or introducing new products without proper due diligence, or aggressively pursuing earnings and growth at any cost.

The strength of an organization's risk culture is not easy for regulators to measure. It's not like credit quality or earnings strength. But it's important because it has an incredibly powerful influence on the risk decisions and behaviors at all levels of an organization. We at the OCC are looking to boards of directors and the senior management of our large banks to set the tone at the top that leads to a healthy organizational culture that abhors improper practices and excessive risk taking.

At the end of the day, . . . regulations only go so far, and systems of internal control are no stronger than the culture that surrounds them. We can't write rules to cover every conceivable situation that might come up, and risk officers are only as effective as the support they receive from top management, which is another way of saying that they can only be as effective as their bank's culture will permit.

Maintaining a healthy organizational culture . . . should be the objective of every bank in the country, especially the large institutions that have the capacity to affect the lives and livelihood of so many people around the globe. Meeting this challenge won't be easy, but we've seen progress already at the large banks we supervise, and I have every confidence that the men and women who lead our banking system are more than up to the task.

Questions and Comments

1. The author of the excerpted text, Thomas Curry, was the Comptroller of the Currency, and in that capacity was the principal regulator for nationally chartered depository institutions.

2. Mr. Curry acknowledges that it is "not easy" for regulators to measure the strength of an institution's risk culture. How could this factor be measured, if at all?

3. Mr. Curry seems to equate a strong risk culture, in the sense of dislike of risk, with a strong compliance culture, in the sense of a dislike for engaging in legal violations. Are these the same? If not, what is their relationship?

4. Can the idea of "strong risk culture" be reconciled with the idea of enterprise risk management? The former, as Mr. Curry conceives it, appears to represent an abhorrence of risk taking; the latter represents a commitment to the effective management of risks. Does Mr. Curry really want banks to avoid all risks? If not, what is he asking bankers to do?

5. Could the Comptroller of the Currency bring and win an enforcement action against a national bank on the ground that the bank lacks a sufficiently strong risk culture?

PROBLEM 18-1

Your company does 30 percent of its business in Europe, and many of its contracts are denominated in euros rather than dollars. You have been following news reports indicating that fiscal problems in European countries may presage the possible breakup of the Eurozone and the demise of the euro as an international currency. Is this something that you, as chief risk officer, should take into account?

2. Regulatory Approaches

In the wake of the financial crisis of 2007-2009, the OCC developed a set of "heightened expectations" for risk management at large banks:

- Preserving the "sanctity of the charter" — making sure that a bank subsidiary of a bank holding company is operated as a separate institution and that the safety and soundness of the bank, rather than the corporate group, is the objective of the bank's directors and senior executives.
- Engaging in compensation and personnel management policies that ensure appropriate staffing, provide for orderly transition, and discourage excessive risk taking.
- Defining and communicating an acceptable risk appetite across the organization.
- Developing and maintaining strong internal audit and risk-management functions.
- Ensuring that directors provide a "credible challenge" to bank managers' decision making on risk-related issues.

After several years of informal "jawboning," the OCC in January 2014 proposed a formal, enforceable framework for administering this new risk-management approach for large banks (more than $50 billion in assets): the OCC Guidelines Establishing Heightened Standards for Certain Large Insured National Banks, Insured Federal Savings Associations, and Insured Federal Branches. The new OCC guidelines require banks to quantify and describe their risk appetite in writing and to set out a three-year strategic plan. A company that fails to comply with the OCC's guidelines will have to submit a remediation plan.

Questions and Comments

1. This administrative initiative took the form of "guidelines" rather than "regulations." The difference, under §39 of the Federal Deposit Insurance Act, 12 U.S.C. §1831p-1, is that a bank that fails to meet the requirements of a *regulation* must submit a remediation plan, whereas if the bank fails to comply with *guidance*, the OCC has discretion whether or not to require a remediation plan. Why do you think the agency opted for the more lenient approach? The OCC explains that by retaining discretion, it leaves room for self-corrective or remedial actions undertaken by banks in the absence of more formal compliance requirements.

2. Most banks — and essentially all large banks — are wholly-owned subsidiaries of holding companies that also own other institutions. The idea of the "sanctity of the charter" suggests that the board of directors of the bank must act in the best interests of the bank — even, apparently, if the bank's interests are in tension with those of the parent or the corporate group. What does this imply about the fiduciary obligations of a bank's board of directors?

3. Is it realistic to expect that bank boards will heed the OCC's sermon about the sanctity of the charter when the sole shareholder — and the institution that determines whether they are appointed or remain in office — is an institution whose interests may be damaged if the board member follows the OCC's instructions?

4. It is obviously an awkward situation if a bank's risk governance framework is different from the risk appetite of the parent. One of the reasons for having subsidiaries and parents is to achieve the economies of scale and scope that flow from combining operations and business strategies. Would those benefits be imperiled if the bank's risk-management framework is required to deviate substantially from the framework employed by the parent? In many cases, this problem doesn't arise because the bank dominates the corporate group, thus making the risk profiles of the parent and bank essentially the same. But some corporate groups involve banks that are only part of a much larger organization. Is the OCC wise to require that the bank operate under a stand-alone risk-management framework in such cases?

5. The guidelines require that covered banks employ both a chief audit executive and a chief risk executive, each operating with substantial independence from line managers and senior executives and each reporting directly to the chief executive officer. Is it appropriate or wise for the government to intrude this deeply into the internal governance of private business organizations?

6. The guidelines identify and require a covered bank to take account of the following eight categories of risk: credit risk, interest rate risk, liquidity risk, price risk, operational risk, compliance risk, strategic risk, and reputation risk. Are these a full inventory of risks facing an institution? What about regulatory risk — the risk that regulators will impose new and unforeseen requirements on financial institutions that may erode profitability or interfere with flexibility of operations?

7. As for internal audit, the guidelines require the department to test for risks, including the evaluation of reputational and strategic risks. Are these issues within internal audit's pay grade? Are they better characterized as issues that should be evaluated and managed by the board of directors or its risk committee?

8. Each covered bank is required to develop a multi-year "strategic plan," which must "contain a comprehensive assessment of risks that currently impact the Bank or that could impact the Bank during this period, articulate an overall mission statement and strategic objectives for the Bank, and include an explanation of how the Bank will achieve those objectives." What is the purpose of this requirement?

9. Boards of directors of covered banks must approve a risk appetite statement containing both quantitative and qualitative elements. What is the reason for requiring both sorts of elements? The OCC explains that the qualitative elements of the statement are intended, in part, to demonstrate that the board of the directors and the banks they supervise should have a "sound risk culture." As for the quantitative elements, the OCC requires covered banks to incorporate stress testing processes for earnings, capital, and liquidity.

10. What about the compilation and analysis of data pertinent to risk? The OCC offers the opinion that many big banks had inadequate data acquisition and analytic

processes in place at the time of the financial crisis of 2007-2009: "[I]t became apparent that many banks' IT and data architectures were inadequate to support the broad management of financial risks. Many banks lacked the ability to aggregate risk exposures and identify concentrations quickly and accurately at the bank level, across business lines, and among legal entities." The OCC's guidelines address this problem by requiring covered banks to have "risk aggregation and reporting capabilities that meet the Board's and management's needs for proactively managing risk and ensuring the Bank's risk profile remains consistent with its risk appetite."

11. The guidelines do not exempt bank directors from enhanced risk-management requirements. They explicitly recognize that the directors must pose a credible challenge to management on risk-related issues. And they seek to ensure that board members possess sufficient knowledge and expertise to deal with risk issues, requiring training of independent board members and annual board self-assessments. Are there appropriate responsibilities to impose on boards of directors?

In the wake of the financial crisis of 2007-2009, federal banking agencies significantly ramped up their expectations regarding the risk-management programs in systemically important banks:

1. In February 2014, the Federal Reserve promulgated a set of Enhanced Prudential Standards for Foreign Banking Organizations. Among other things, this rule requires large foreign banks operating in the United States to do the following:

   • Establish a U.S. risk committee of the board of directors. This committee can be structured in several ways, for example, as part of the bank's global risk committee or as a separate, stand-alone committee for U.S. operations. However structured, the U.S. risk committee must include at least one member with experience in identifying, assessing, and managing risk exposures of large, complex firms, and — for the largest firms — at least one independent member. The U.S. risk committee is charged with responsibility for monitoring all the U.S. activities of the foreign banking organization, including risk-management policies. For the largest institutions, the U.S. risk committee has more specific responsibilities: It must review and approve all risk-management policies; approve liquidity risk limits; review whether the institution's U.S. operations operate within the prescribed liquidity risk tolerance; and review and approve the contingency funding plan for the bank's U.S. operations.

   • The largest foreign banking organizations must have a U.S. chief risk officer, designed to be the "single point of contact within a foreign banking organization that is required to oversee the management of risks within the organization's combined U.S. operations." The U.S. chief risk officer must have experience in identifying, assessing, and managing risk exposure at large, complex financial institutions; be an employee of U.S. branch or subsidiary (i.e., not be an employee of a foreign parent); be physically located in the United States; and report directly to the U.S. risk committee and to the foreign banking organization's global chief risk officer. The U.S. chief risk officer is given an extensive set of responsibilities to design, oversee, and monitor the U.S. risk-management framework.

   • The largest foreign banking organizations must institute a risk-management framework for their U.S. operations that is appropriate in light of the risk profile, complexity, activities, and size of the organization's U.S. operations. This framework must include policies and procedures for the framework, processes, and systems to identify and report deficiencies and emerging risks; processes and systems to establish the responsibilities and duties of managers and employees to implement the framework; and processes and systems to ensure the independence of the risk-management function.

2. The Federal Reserve also instituted a program called the Comprehensive Capital Analysis and Review (CCAR), an intensive assessment of the capital adequacy and capital management policies of large U.S. bank holding companies. Part of this process involves "quantitative" assessments conducted by means of stress tests; another part consists of "qualitative" evaluations of the institution's processes and procedures for ensuring capital adequacy. One bank (Zions Bancorporation) failed the quantitative part of the analysis in 2014 but four failed the qualitative part (Citigroup, HSBC North America, RBS Citizens Financial Group, and Santander Holdings). Central to the Fed's qualitative analysis is a focus on risk and enterprise risk management: Large banking institutions, according to the Fed, should operate "effective firm-wide risk-identification, . . . and risk-management practices and ongoing consideration of the potential for stressful outcomes, with strong oversight by boards of directors and senior management." Board of Governors of the Federal Reserve System, Comprehensive Capital Analysis and Review 2014: Assessment Framework and Results (March 2014). Reading between the lines, it is apparent that the Fed was using this program as a lever to encourage big banking institutions to upgrade their enterprise risk-management systems.

3. European regulators also have greatly upgraded their focus on risk management within banking organizations. Capital Requirements Directive IV (CRD IV), the EU legislation implementing the Basel III standards on bank capital and liquidity, came into force on January 1, 2014. CRD IV requires all banks to institute robust risk-management operations. Large banks are required to create a position of chief risk officer (or equivalent) who enjoys substantial protections against removal from office. Supervisors are directed to "introduce principles and standards to . . . promote a sound risk culture . . . and enable competent authorities to monitor the adequacy of internal governance arrangements." Directors play an important role implementing the risk culture contemplated by CRD IV. They are expected to devote the time necessary to understand the implications of the institution's risk strategy. Independent directors should exercise a "credible challenge" to management in order to satisfy themselves that "systems of risk management are robust and defensible." The risk-related requirements for large banks are even more exacting. Significant institutions must maintain board-level risk committees composed of independent directors, and must give these committees access to (a) information about the risks facing the institution, (b) executive risk managers, and (c) external expert advice. Large banks are also required to operate an executive-level risk function headed by a senior officer (e.g., a chief risk officer), who may report to the board or a board committee and who may not be summarily removed by other executives.

4. The European Central Bank (ECB) plays a role in enhancing regulation of risk management in Europe. Principle 6 of the ECB's "Guide to Banking

Supervision" explicitly adopts a risk-based approach to bank regulation: taking into account both "the degree of damage which the failure of an institution could cause to financial stability" and "the possibility of such a failure occurring." Risks are assessed using both "qualitative and quantitative approaches" as well as the exercise of "judgment and forward-looking critical assessment." In carrying out their supervisory responsibilities, regulators are directed to evaluate risks to which the institutions are exposed, risks that an institution poses to the financial system in general, and risks revealed by stress tests. European bank regulators are also instructed to employ a risk-based approach when assessing an institution's compliance with regulatory requirements. In addition to integrating risk considerations throughout the supervisory process, the ECB operates a risk analytics division that reviews the overall risk environment and performs risk analyses across institutions.

5. Enhanced focus on risk and compliance is manifest in the technical standards and rules developed by the European Banking Authority (EBA), which is charged with developing rules to implement European banking regulation. The EBA publishes a semi-annual Risk Assessment Report and an associated risk dashboard that summarizes the main risks and vulnerabilities in the banking sector. The EBA also deals extensively with internal controls. Its High Level Principles of Risk Management, published in 2010, sets forth best practices for financial institutions in the risk-management area, and its Guidelines on Internal Governance deal extensively with issues in risk management such as risk culture, alignment of remuneration with risk appetite, risk management framework, board-level risk committees, and management-level risk control activities. The Guidelines also encourage banks to institute robust compliance functions, headed by "a person responsible for this function across the entire institution and group (the Compliance Officer or Head of Compliance)."

6. Rating agencies have jumped on the enterprise risk-management bandwagon, and in a significant way. Standard & Poor's, for example, has included ERM assessments for financial institutions since 2005 and for rated companies generally since 2009. These involve "holistic assessment of enterprise risk management of corporations and financial institutions," which include an expanded review including risk-management culture and strategic risk-management practices. S&P assigns rated companies a five-level ERM score, ranging from "excellent" to "weak." Risk-management practices also play a role in S&P's evaluation of management and corporate governance, which takes account of factors such as risk-management standards and tolerances and comprehensiveness of financial standards and risk tolerances. These ratings are influential: A poor rating can increase a company's borrowing cost and impair its reputation, whereas a strong rating can have the opposite effect.

G. DISCLOSURE OF RISK

How much risk-related information must an SEC-reporting company provide to investors in annual reports or other disclosure documents? The risk of an enterprise is one of the most important factors investors consider when they decide on what securities to buy or sell. One might expect, therefore, that the SEC would mandate fulsome disclosure of risk factors. In practice, however, risk disclosures are considerably less substantial. The reasons for allowing management considerable flexibility in disclosing risk factors include the following:

- Risk is not quantifiable in the same sense as, say, the profit and loss figures for the previous year. It is a projection into the future and inevitably involves a range of possible outcomes — a range that increases, moreover, as the projection moves into the future.
- Risk, because it is about the future, involves business decisions that, if disclosed, would reveal strategic plans and provide rivals with a potential competitive advantage.
- Because projections into the future might be wrong, the company and its senior officials face potential securities fraud exposure in the event that things do not turn out as anticipated.
- Statements of risk can also be used for touting the company's prospects and driving up its stock price — if, for example, the company predicts excellent future results (recall that risk in the modern sense includes good as well as bad outcomes). But there is a danger that, allowed full range to engage in such statements, companies will offer overly rosy projections about their future performance, distorting capital markets and potentially harming investors.

Notwithstanding these limitations, certain disclosures of risk factors are required. Item 303 of Regulation S-K, governing management's discussion and analysis of financial condition and results of operations, requires the registrant to identify "any known trends or any known demands, commitments, events or uncertainties that will result in or that are reasonably likely to result in the registrant's liquidity increasing or decreasing in any material way"; to describe "any known material trends, favorable or unfavorable, in the registrant's capital resources"; and disclose "any known trends or uncertainties . . . that the registrant reasonably expects will have a material . . . unfavorable impact on . . . revenues or income from continuing operations." Item 503(c) of Regulation S-K requires, in connection with a prospectus for a new issue of securities, that the registrant discuss the most significant factors that make the offering speculative or risky. Risk factors include the registrant's lack of an operating history; lack of profitable operations in recent periods; financial position; business or proposed business; or lack of a market for the company's securities or securities. Item 1A to Form 10-K, applicable to larger companies, mandates annual disclosure of significant factors that may adversely affect the issuer's business, operations, industry, financial position, or future financial performance.

The Private Securities Litigation Reform Act of 1995 (PSLRA) undertook to encourage companies to be more forthcoming about risk factors. The "safe harbor" provision of that statute shields parties from liability for "forward-looking statements" — i.e., projections or evaluations about future performance — provided these statements are accompanied by "meaningful cautionary statements identifying important factors that could cause actual results to differ materially from those in the forward looking statement."

The key to the safe harbor provision of the PSLRA is the presence of "meaningful cautionary statements." A "cautionary" statement is clearly one that warns about the dangers of relying too heavily on a forward-looking statement. But when is such a statement "meaningful"? The Conference Committee Report on the PSLRA stated that "cautionary statements must convey substantive information about factors that realistically could cause results to differ materially from those projected in the forward-looking statements." In other words, the statements should not be phrased at such a general level as to lack real content, and should offer information sufficient to enable the reader to make an informed assessment of how much he or she should rely on the projection in question.

When is a cautionary statement inadequate? It must not be so cryptic that it is not meaningful to the average investor. In re Nike, Inc. Securities Litigation, 181 F. Supp. 2d 1160, 1172 (D. Or. 2002). Presumably, also, the cautionary statement must not be phrased in technical terms, requiring a degree in finance to understand it. The statement should also not be mere "boilerplate," inserted without much thought in each successive disclosure statement. Where the risks facing a reporting company change materially, the cautionary statement should reflect that fact; if it does not, the protection of the safe harbor may be lost. *See* Asher v. Baxter International, Inc., 377 F.3d 727 (7th Cir. 2004).

Consider the following excerpt, which reproduces the risk factors announced by Target, a major retailer, in its 2012 annual report:

Target Corporation
2012 Form 10-K Item 1A

Our business is subject to many risks. Set forth below are the most significant risks that we face.

If we are unable to positively differentiate ourselves from other retailers, our results of operations could be adversely affected.

The retail business is highly competitive. In the past we have been able to compete successfully by differentiating our guests' shopping experience by creating an attractive value proposition through a careful combination of price, merchandise assortment, convenience, guest service, loyalty programs and marketing efforts. Guest perceptions regarding the cleanliness and safety of our stores, our in-stock levels and other factors also affect our ability to compete. No single competitive factor is dominant, and actions by our competitors on any of these factors could have an adverse effect on our sales, gross margins and expenses.

We sell many products under our owned and exclusive brands. . . . These brands are an important part of our business because they differentiate us from other retailers, generally carry higher margins than national brand products and represent a significant portion of our overall sales. If one or more of these brands experiences a loss of consumer acceptance or confidence, our sales and gross margins could be adversely affected.

The continuing migration and evolution of retailing to online and mobile channels has increased our challenges in differentiating ourselves from other retailers. In particular, consumers are able to quickly and conveniently comparison shop with digital tools, which can lead to decisions based solely on price. We have been working with our vendors to offer unique and distinctive merchandise, and encouraging our guests to shop with confidence with our price match policy. Failure to effectively execute in these efforts, actions by our competitors in response to these efforts or failure of our vendors to manage their own channels and content could hurt our ability to differentiate ourselves from other retailers and, as a result, have an adverse effect on sales, gross margins and expenses.

Our continued success is substantially dependent on positive perceptions of Target which, if eroded, could adversely affect our business and our relationships with our guests and team members.

We believe that one of the reasons our guests prefer to shop at Target and our team members choose Target as a place of employment is the reputation we have built over many years for serving our four primary constituencies: guests, team members, the communities in which we operate and shareholders. To be successful in the future, we must continue to preserve, grow and leverage the value of Target's reputation. Reputational value is based in large part on perceptions of subjective qualities. While reputations may take decades to build, even isolated incidents can erode trust and confidence, particularly if they result in adverse mainstream and social media publicity, governmental investigations or litigation. Those types of incidents could have an adverse impact on perceptions and lead to tangible adverse effects on our business, including consumer boycotts, lost sales, loss of new store development opportunities, or team member retention and recruiting difficulties.

If we are unable to successfully develop and maintain a relevant and reliable multichannel experience for our guests, our reputation and results of operations could be adversely affected.

Our business has evolved from an in-store experience to interaction with guests across multiple channels (in-store, online, mobile and social media, among others). Our guests are using computers, tablets, mobile phones and other devices to shop in our stores and online and provide feedback and public commentary about all aspects of our business. We currently provide full and mobile versions of our website (Target.com), applications for mobile phones and tablets and interact with our guests through social media. Multichannel retailing is rapidly evolving and we must keep pace with changing guest expectations, and new developments and technology investments by our competitors. If we are unable to attract and retain team members or contract with third parties having the specialized skills needed to support our multichannel efforts, implement improvements to our guest-facing technology in a timely manner, or provide a convenient and consistent experience for our guests regardless of the ultimate sales channel, our ability to compete and our results of operations could be adversely affected. In addition, if Target.com and our other guest-facing technology systems do not reliably function as designed, we may experience a loss of guest confidence, data security breaches, lost sales or be exposed to fraudulent purchases, which, if significant, could adversely affect our reputation and results of operations.

If we fail to anticipate and respond quickly to changing consumer preferences, our sales, gross margins and profitability could suffer.

A substantial part of our business is dependent on our ability to make trend-right decisions and effectively manage our inventory in a broad range of merchandise categories, including apparel, home décor, seasonal offerings, food and other merchandise. Failure to accurately predict constantly changing consumer tastes, preferences, spending patterns and other lifestyle decisions may result in lost sales, spoilage and increased inventory markdowns, which would lead to a deterioration in our results of operations by hurting our sales, gross margins and profitability.

Our earnings are highly susceptible to the state of macroeconomic conditions and consumer confidence in the United States.

Most of our stores and all of our digital sales are in the United States, making our results highly dependent on U.S. consumer confidence and the health of the U.S. economy. In addition, a significant portion of our total sales is derived from stores located in five states: California, Texas, Florida, Minnesota and Illinois, resulting in further dependence on local economic conditions in these states. Deterioration in macroeconomic conditions, consumer confidence and guest financial situations could negatively affect our business in many ways, including slowing sales growth or reduction in overall sales, and reducing gross margins. These same considerations impact the success of our credit card program. Even though we no longer own a consumer credit card receivables portfolio, we share in the economic performance of the credit card program with TD Bank Group (TD). Deterioration in macroeconomic conditions could adversely affect the volume of new credit accounts, the amount of credit card program balances and the ability of credit card holders to pay their balances. These conditions could result in us receiving lower profit-sharing payments.

If we do not effectively manage our large and growing workforce, our labor costs and results of operations could be adversely affected.

With approximately 361,000 team members, our workforce costs represent our largest operating expense, and our business is dependent on our ability to attract, train and retain qualified team members. Many of those team members are in entry-level or part-time positions with historically high turnover rates. Our ability to meet our labor needs while controlling our costs is subject to external factors such as unemployment levels, prevailing wage rates, collective bargaining efforts, health care and other benefit costs and changing demographics. If we are unable to attract and retain adequate numbers of qualified team members, our operations, guest service levels and support functions could suffer. Those factors, together with increasing wage and benefit costs, could adversely affect our results of operations. As of March 20, 2013, none of our team members were working under collective bargaining agreements. We are periodically subject to labor organizing efforts. If we become subject to one or more collective bargaining agreements in the future, it could adversely affect our labor costs and how we operate our business.

Lack of availability of suitable locations in which to build new stores could slow our growth, and difficulty in executing plans for new stores, expansions and remodels could increase our costs and capital requirements.

Our future growth is dependent, in part, on our ability to build new stores and expand and remodel existing stores in a manner that achieves appropriate returns on our capital investment. We compete with other retailers and businesses for suitable locations for our stores. In addition, for many sites we are dependent on a third party developer's ability to acquire land, obtain financing and secure the necessary zoning changes and permits for a larger project, of which our store may be one component. Turmoil in the financial markets may make it difficult for third party developers to obtain financing for new projects. Local land use and other regulations applicable to the types of stores we desire to construct may affect our ability to find suitable locations and also influence the cost of constructing, expanding and remodeling our stores. A significant portion of our expected new store sites is located in fully developed markets, which is generally a more time-consuming and expensive undertaking than expansion into undeveloped suburban and ex-urban markets.

Interruptions in our supply chain or increased commodity prices and supply chain costs could adversely affect our gross margins, expenses and results of operations.

We are dependent on our vendors to supply merchandise in a timely and efficient manner. If a vendor fails to deliver on its commitments, whether due to financial difficulties or other reasons, we could experience merchandise out-of-stocks that could lead to lost sales. In addition, a large portion of our merchandise is sourced, directly or indirectly, from outside the United States, with China as our single largest source. Political or financial instability, trade restrictions, the outbreak of pandemics, labor unrest, transport capacity and costs, port security, weather conditions, natural disasters or other events that could slow port activities and affect foreign trade are beyond our control and could disrupt our supply of merchandise and/or adversely affect our results of operations. In addition, changes in the costs of procuring commodities used in our merchandise or the costs related to our supply chain, including labor, fuel, tariffs, and currency exchange rates could have an adverse effect on gross margins, expenses and results of operations.

Failure to address product safety concerns could adversely affect our sales and results of operations.

If our merchandise offerings, including food, drug and children's products, do not meet applicable safety standards or our guests' expectations regarding safety, we could experience lost sales and increased costs and be exposed to legal and reputational risk. All of our vendors must comply with applicable product safety laws, and we are dependent on them to ensure that the products we buy comply with all safety standards. Events that give rise to actual, potential or perceived product safety concerns, including food or drug contamination, could expose us to government enforcement action or private litigation and result in costly product recalls and other liabilities. In addition, negative guest perceptions regarding the safety of the products we sell could cause our guests to seek alternative sources for their needs, resulting in lost sales. In those circumstances, it may be difficult and costly for us to regain the confidence of our guests.

If our efforts to protect the security of personal information about our guests and team members are unsuccessful, we could be subject to costly government enforcement actions and private litigation and our reputation could suffer.

The nature of our business involves the receipt and storage of personal information about our guests and team members. We have a program in place to detect and respond to data security incidents. To date, all incidents we have experienced have been insignificant. If we experience a significant data security breach or fail to detect and appropriately respond to a significant data security breach, we could be exposed to government enforcement actions and private litigation. In addition, our guests could lose confidence in our ability to protect their personal information, which could cause them to discontinue usage of REDcards, decline to use our pharmacy services, or stop shopping with us altogether. The loss of confidence from a significant data security breach involving team members could hurt our reputation, cause team member recruiting and retention challenges, increase our labor costs and affect how we operate our business.

Our failure to comply with federal, state or local laws, or changes in these laws could increase our costs, reduce our margins and lower our sales.

Our business is subject to a wide array of laws and regulations. Significant legislative changes that affect our relationship with our workforce could increase our expenses and adversely affect our operations. Examples of possible legislative changes affecting our relationship with our workforce include changes to an employer's obligation to recognize collective bargaining units, the process by which collective bargaining agreements are negotiated or imposed, minimum wage requirements, and health care mandates. In addition, changes in the regulatory environment regarding topics such as banking and consumer credit, Medicare reimbursements, privacy and information security, product safety, supply chain transparency or environmental protection, among others, could cause our expenses to increase without an ability to pass through any increased expenses through higher prices. In addition, if we fail to comply with applicable laws and regulations, particularly wage and hour laws, we could be subject to legal risk, including government enforcement action and class action civil litigation, which could adversely affect our results of operations by increasing our costs, reducing our margins and lowering our sales.

Weather conditions where our stores are located may impact consumer shopping patterns, which alone or together with natural disasters, particularly in areas where our sales are concentrated, could adversely affect our results of operations.

Uncharacteristic or significant weather conditions can affect consumer shopping patterns, particularly in apparel and seasonal items, which could lead to lost sales or greater than expected markdowns and adversely affect our short-term results of operations. In addition, our three largest states, by total sales, are California, Texas and Florida, areas where hurricanes and earthquakes are more prevalent. Natural disasters in those states or in other areas where our sales are concentrated could result in significant physical damage to or closure of one or more of our stores or distribution centers, and cause delays in the distribution of merchandise from our vendors to our distribution centers and stores, which could adversely affect our results of operations by increasing our costs and lowering our sales.

Changes in our effective income tax rate could adversely affect our profitability and results of operations.

Our effective income tax rate is influenced by a number of factors, including changes in tax law, tax treaties, interpretation of existing laws, and our ability to sustain our reporting positions on examination. Changes in any of those factors could change our effective tax rate, which could adversely affect our profitability and results of operations. In addition, the expansion of our retail store operations outside of the United States may cause greater volatility in our effective tax rate.

If we are unable to access the capital markets or obtain bank credit, our financial position, growth plans, liquidity and results of operations could suffer.

We are dependent on a stable, liquid and well-functioning financial system to fund our operations and growth plans. In particular, we have historically relied on the public debt markets to raise capital for new store development and other capital expenditures and the commercial paper market and bank credit facilities to fund seasonal needs for working capital. Our continued access to these markets depends on multiple factors including the condition of debt capital markets, our operating performance and maintaining strong debt ratings. If our credit ratings were lowered, our ability to access the debt markets, our cost of funds and other terms for new debt issuances could be adversely impacted. Each of the credit rating agencies reviews its rating periodically, and there is no guarantee our current credit rating will remain the same. In addition, we use a variety of derivative products to manage our exposure to market risk, principally interest rate and equity price fluctuations. Disruptions or turmoil in the financial markets could reduce our ability to meet our capital requirements or fund our working capital needs, and lead to losses on derivative positions resulting from counterparty failures, which could adversely affect our financial position and results of operations.

A significant disruption in our computer systems could adversely affect our operations.

We rely extensively on our computer systems to manage inventory, process guest transactions, service REDcard accounts and summarize and analyze results. Our systems are subject to damage or interruption from power outages, telecommunications failures, computer viruses and malicious attacks, security breaches and catastrophic events. If our systems are damaged or fail to function properly, we may incur substantial costs to repair or replace them, experience loss of critical data and interruptions or delays in our ability to manage inventories or process guest transactions, and encounter a loss of guest confidence which could adversely affect our results of operations.

If we do not effectively execute our plan to expand retail store operations into Canada, our financial results could be adversely affected.

Our 2013 entry into the Canadian retail market is our first retail store expansion outside of the United States. Our ability to successfully open the expected number of Canadian Target stores on schedule depends, in large measure, upon our ability to remodel existing assets, build our supply chain capabilities and technology systems and recruit, hire and retain qualified team members. In addition, our ability to offer the expected assortment of merchandise in certain markets may be impacted by the availability of local vendors of certain types of goods. The effective execution of our Canadian retail store expansion is also contingent on our ability to design new marketing programs that positively differentiate us from other retailers in Canada, and achieve market acceptance by Canadian guests. If we do not effectively execute our expansion plan in Canada, our financial performance could be adversely affected.

A disruption in relationships with third parties who provide us services in connection with certain aspects of our business could adversely affect our operations.

We rely on third parties to support a variety of business functions, including our Canadian supply chain, portions of our technology systems, multichannel platforms and distribution network, and extensions of credit for our 5% REDcard Rewards loyalty program. If we are unable to contract with third parties having the specialized skills needed to support those strategies or integrate their products and services with our business, or if those third parties fail to meet our performance standards and expectations, our reputation, sales and results of operations could be adversely affected. In addition, we could face increased costs associated with finding replacement providers or hiring new team members to provide these services in-house.

Questions and Comments

1. After reading the excerpt, do you feel better informed about whether Target Corporation is a good investment?

2. Which of the risk factors identified in the excerpt apply to virtually any American retail business? Which apply to Target specifically?

3. What attempt, if any, does Target make to identify either the probability or the magnitude of any of these risk factors? Without such information, can an investor make a realistic assessment of risks?

4. Target discloses a risk of data breaches, noting that a major breach could expose it to government enforcement actions, consumer litigation, and loss of reputation. On the other hand, Target suggests — in 2012 — that the risk may not be a cause for excessive concern because "we have a program in place to detect and respond to data security incidents" and "to date, all incidents we have experienced have been insignificant." In 2013, Target experienced a huge breach involving theft of 40 million credit and debit card numbers and 70 million names, addresses, phone numbers, and email addresses. Between one and three million cards were sold on the black market and used for fraudulent transactions. Target suffered a major loss of reputation and a 46 percent drop in profits. In light of these events, did Target adequately disclose the risk of a security breach?

5. The excerpt discloses certain risks associated with Target's entry into the Canadian market. In January 2015, the company acknowledged that its Canadian venture had failed (at a cost of $2.5 billion), announced that it was closing all 133 Canadian stores, and terminated more than 17,000 employees. Given this outcome, did the 2012 document accurately report the risk factors involved in the Canadian operation?

6. What are the consequences if a registrant fails to disclose a material risk as required under SEC regulations? The SEC can bring an enforcement proceeding, but can private parties sue? The SEC's Rule 10b-5, which is privately enforceable, makes it illegal for any person to "omit to state a material fact necessary in order to make the statements made, in the light of the circumstances under which they were made, not misleading." Is a material omission under Item 303 actionable under this rule? *Compare* Stratte-McClure v. Morgan Stanley, 598 Fed. Appx. 25 (2d Cir. 2015) (yes) *with* In re NVIDIA Corp. Securities Litigation, 768 F.3d 146 (9th Cir. 2014) (no).

19

Approaches to Risk Management

So far we have discussed general issues related to risk management: how risk is defined; how the task of risk management is conceptualized; what sorts of risks need to be managed; and how within complex organizations the risk management task is carried out. We have not, however, touched on the details of the risk-management process. We take up that topic in the present chapter.

No single approach to risk management dominates analysis in organizations today. Even within organizations, there is often no consensus. Instead, the risk-management techniques in common usage are adapted to, and sometimes grow out of, specific business lines or areas. That said, some approaches are observed commonly enough that they can be considered to be more or less "state of the art."

A. DATA

All risk management techniques depend crucially on the acquisition, analysis, and presentation of information. Each of these steps is crucial. If the relevant decision maker has no access to key information, she will, nearly by definition, be hamstrung in her ability to arrive at sound judgments about risk. If she cannot analyze the information she will be unable to make effective use of data once acquired. If the analysis of information is not effectively communicated to the relevant decision-makers, the organization will be unable to incorporate the results of the analysis in effective strategic decisions.

For the decision maker to have the necessary information, the data must first be compiled. The decision maker is not going to be able or willing to sort through or understand the raw data. Someone must categorize and analyze the information so it can be presented to the decision maker in summary form.

The presentation of data, moreover, must be embodied in a medium and a form that allows the decision maker to focus on the important patterns and screen out the noise. The importance of this information processing function can hardly be over-stated. If done well, the function can be a key to wise and farsighted decisions by corporate managers. If done poorly, the function can generate bad or even catastrophic mistakes.

A classic example of the importance of information analysis and presentation is the case of the NASA Challenger space shuttle disaster. It was unusually cold on the day of the scheduled launch, and NASA's mission control team had to decide whether to go forward or delay the mission. In prior shuttle launches, NASA had recovered the booster rockets (in all but one case) and was able to analyze whether the O-ring seals had experienced incidents of thermal distress. NASA also had information on weather conditions for each of these launches. Putting this data together, the information looked as follows:

Table 19-1: Incidents of Thermal Distress

Flight	Temp	Incidents	Flight	Temp	Incidents	Flight	Temp	Incidents
STS 1	66	0	STS 9	70	0	STS 51-B	75	0
STS 2	70	1	STS 41-B	57	1	STS 51-G	70	0
STS 3	69	0	STS 41-C	63	1	STS 51-F	81	0
STS 4	80	?	STS 41-D	70	1	STS 51-I	76	0
STS 5	68	0	STS 41-G	78	0	STS 51-J	79	0
STS 6	67	0	STS 51-A	67	0	STS 61-A	75	2
STS 7	72	0	STS 51-C	53	3	STS 61-B	76	0
STS 8	73	0	STS 51-D	67	0	STS 61-C	58	1

Drawing on this data, someone associated with the mission prepared a chart that correlated temperature with incidents of structural stress for all previous missions where structural stress had been detected.

There appears to be no pattern correlating O-ring thermal distress and temperature: While distress occurred when the outside temperature was 53°, it also occurred

Figure 19-1: Incidents of Thermal Distress

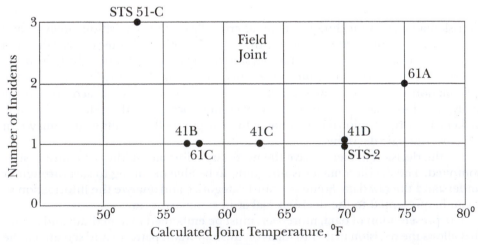

Plot of flights with incidents of O-ring thermal distress as function of temperature

Report of the Presidential Commission on the Space Shuttle Challenger Accident, 1986 (Vol. 1, p. 145)

at 75° and 70°. This chart would give no particular reason for concern about O-ring failure in cold-weather launches (although the weather on the Challenger's launch date was 31°, colder than any of the data points on the chart).

After the disaster, NASA scientists and others realized that the O-rings had failed because they could not stand up to the cold weather at the time of the launch. Why was this problem not detected in time to avoid the catastrophe? When investigators re-analyzed the data, they realized that key information had been omitted. The chart reproduced above reports only on launches where thermal distress to O-rings was detected. It doesn't report on cases where no thermal distress was discovered. When those launches were included, the pattern looks different:

Figure 19-2: Evidence from All Launches

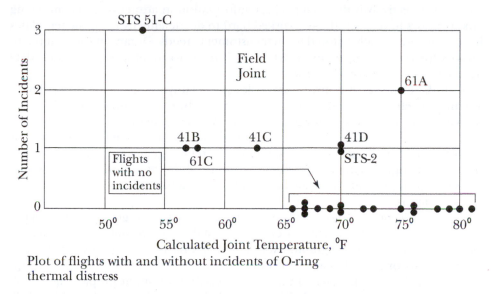

Plot of flights with and without incidents of O-ring thermal distress

Report of the Presidential Commission on the Space Shuttle Challenger Accident, 1986 (Vol. 1, p. 145)

As can be seen, every one of the launches with no thermal distress occurred when the temperature was above 65°. Just eyeballing the data, it now appears that O-ring thermal distress *was* correlated with temperature at launch. A statistical analysis confirms the intuition. The proper analysis, known as a "logistic regression" (used when the dependent variable is binary and qualitative—here, "incident" or "no incident"), indicated that the probability of O-ring distress was exceptionally elevated at a launch temperature of 31°. Although the lack of observations at low temperature launches gave the analysis a large margin of error, it would have been clear that the risk of failure was too high to justify a launch.

The Challenger disaster illustrates two points about the role of information in risk management. First, the proper information must be used if the analysis is to be valid. In the case of the Challenger, the relevant information had been compiled, but it was not used: Launches without thermal distress were excluded on the erroneous assumption that they were not relevant. Second, the Challenger disaster illustrates the power — and also the perils — of graphic presentation of data. Graphic presentations are powerful because they allow the brain to process key information and focus attention on important features. Compare the table of raw data with the figures above: Much more of the crucial information appears from the latter. On the other hand, because it *is* a powerful way of conveying information, graphic presentation can mislead as well as enlighten. The figure that the NASA mission team examined led them astray, possibly because the pattern seemed so clear that they were not inspired to inquire further.

Graphic or tabular presentation of data is a key element of contemporary risk management. The nearly universal use of this form of presentation is driven by two developments. First, vendors of analytic risk-management products sell their services most effectively if they can package information in attractive and compelling ways. Vendors have, accordingly, worked hard to devise effective graphic templates that can be individually tailored to their customers' needs. Organizations that retain vendors for risk management analytics don't need to develop sophisticated data presentation formats on their own.

Second, attractive and inexpensive color photocopying has made it possible to enhance the effectiveness of graphic presentations by coding information in color. The key colors in the risk management palate are red, green, and yellow. Think of these as traffic light colors. A red signal generally means that something is wrong, or at least that something requires attention. A green signal generally means that something is right, or that something does not require attention. A yellow signal is a warning; it generally indicates that indices are approaching their established tolerance levels.

The graphic presentation of data is often known by the generic term "dashboard." A dashboard is a suite of charts or a slide deck containing information displayed in a variety of graphic formats (bar charts, histograms, pie charts, maps, and so on). Dashboards are often organized in hierarchical fashion; for example, in the risk-management area, an organization might prepare an overall enterprise risk management dashboard, and then supplement this with "drill-down" graphics at various level of detail. In this way senior managers or directors can get the big picture but also have the ability, if they wish to do so, to take a deep dive into particular areas of concern (for example, the items in a particular portfolio that have been performing below expectations).

Tables are important elements of virtually any dashboard. Usually, the rows contain variables that require review. The columns typically represent time, but may stand for other variables as well. When time is the column variable, management can investigate the chronological performance of key risk metrics. The following is a crude example of a table from a risk dashboard for a financial institution, showing key performance metrics and evaluating their trend over time:

If this chart had been set in color, as would be the case in any corporate dashboard, the values that are out of range would show up in red — here they are displayed with the darkest gray. Would these jump out at you? What picture does this table provide about the health of the company? Based on this table, are you comfortable with the company and its performance? If you were on the risk committee of

Figure 19-3: First Fidelity Bank: Key Metrics

Metric	Tolerance	Jan	Feb	Mar	Apr	May	YTD
Risk-Adjusted Capital	12%-15%	13.2%	13.5%	12.9%	13.0%	13.3%	13.2%
Net Interest Margin	9%-11%	10.1%	9.8%	9.3%	9.0%	8.8%	9.4%
Return on Assets	1.5%-2%	1.8%	1.9%	1.8%	1.8%	1.5%	1.8%
Return on Equity	13%-15%	14.5%	14.6%	13.0%	12.8%	13.0%	13.6%

the board of directors, what questions would you want to direct to senior management at the current meeting? Notice that the information conveyed by the table is heavily influenced by the choice of tolerance ranges. If the tolerance ranges were set differently, all of the cells might switch to red — or green. How should the tolerances be set, and what role should the board of directors play in setting them?

"Heat maps" are also in common usage, both in the risk management field and in many other settings calling for the graphic presentation of data (see Figure 19-4 below for an example). A heat map is a matrix that displays how one variable varies across two others. For example, a heat map might consist of a map of the United States with average summer temperatures at each location on the map shown by a color (usually, red will indicate hotter temperatures). Viewing this chart, one can see how average summer temperature varies with latitude and longitude within the United States. In the case of risk management, a typical heat map might locate different functions on a grid formed by the variables "likelihood" and "impact": The area of greatest impact and greatest likelihood would be shown in red and the area of lowest impact and lowest likelihood shown in green, with intermediate values shown in yellow. The attention of the decision maker is then drawn to the functions that fall in the red areas of the chart. The heat map has the virtue that it can accommodate continuous as well as discrete variables; computer graphics can generate variations of colors that reflect gradual changes in values. Many software packages (including Excel) offer heat map functionality today.

Complex organizations these days spend time thinking about optimal dashboard design — and for good reason, since the dashboard is a key instrument for tracking performance, identifying risks, and formulating policy. Unfortunately, interest in design does not necessarily translate into effective performance. Officials tasked with creating the dashboards tend to fall into three traps.

First, they may confuse quantity with quality, with the result that the decision maker is overwhelmed with detail. Just as in cooking, where more of an ingredient is not necessarily better, too much information can impair the analytic process just as much as too little. A dashboard with 200 key performance indicators misunderstands the concept of what a key performance indicator is all about.

Why is so much information so often stuffed into the dashboard? Sometimes the reason is that the designers of the tool give too much credit to the intelligence and perspicacity of the audience for whom it was designed. Members of the board of directors are often insightful and wise, but they are not omniscient (if they were, we wouldn't need dashboards). They need to have the information simplified and boiled down to the essentials if they are to exercise their judgment in the most effective way. Another reason for overfilling the dashboard is the worry that the staff person preparing the dashboard will be criticized if she leaves something out: It is safer to include more rather than less because you are less likely to be blamed for the former if things go awry.

Second, dashboard designers, like architects, sometimes fall for what seems sexy or clever, without attending sufficiently to whether the information being provided will serve its purpose. Dials and gauges, charts and maps, and elaborate schemes for color coding do not substitute for sound analysis. Why do dashboard designers overdo the flash? Sometimes, they fall in love with the technology and simply enjoy playing with the options that the dashboard software allows. They may also hope to call attention to themselves and thereby improve their visibility in the organization. Generally, simpler is better, even if it is not sexy.

Third, ownership over discrete dashboard elements should, if possible, be assigned to definite individuals within the organization and should be based on objective metrics. Ownership information is often omitted from dashboards for several reasons. Sometimes it is politically awkward to designate an owner of the element because several employees are vying for the honor and management doesn't want to choose between them. Sometimes the dashboard element is truly a team production, so it might be considered a bit of a distortion to assign ownership to one individual. Finally, sometimes an organization may resist assigning ownership when doing so will embarrass those whose results are not up to expectations. Although these are cogent considerations, consultants on dashboard design advise that all key dashboard elements should designate an executive owner — the person on the management team who is held responsible for the results. Identifying the owner clearly assigns responsibility for the function involved and builds accountability for performance.

Questions and Comments

1. Risk analysis at complex organizations is typically treated as a technical subject and analyzed with the infrastructure of logic, rationality, and (often) mathematics. Should the more subjective or emotional factors be taken into account as well? For an argument that contemporary risk analytics needs to account more explicitly for the role of emotions in decision making, see Susan A. Bandes, Emotions and Risk Regulation, in Bettina Lange, Dania Thomas & Austin Sarat eds., *From Economy to Society? Perspectives on Transnational Risk Regulation*, 62 Stud. in L. Pol. & Soc'y 219-238 (2013).

2. Taking issue both with neoclassical and behavioral economics, Bandes argues that "[f]raming normatively complex problems like immigration, terrorism, or monetary crisis as risks that require regulating suggests that . . . the problems are measurable or quantifiable, that they lend themselves to utilitarian calculus, and that they have ascertainably correct solutions that require no value judgments." She critiques this view on the ground that an "interdisciplinary inquiry into the role of emotion in human behavior sheds light on how risks are assessed, prioritized, and ameliorated, on how the category of risk is constructed, and on how that categorization affects the cognitive tools and approaches we bring to normatively complex problems."

3. Given that emotions are not well understood and hard to control, does it make sense to consider their role when constructing a theory of decision making under uncertainty, or when actually making decisions in risky and pressured situations?

B. RISK APPETITE

A key step in modern risk management the selection of a "risk appetite."

The risk appetite is approved by the board of directors, and thus represents a policy implemented on an enterprise-wide basis and adopted at the highest corporate level. In these respects the risk appetite approach reflects core objectives of enterprise risk management.

The term "risk appetite" is important. Why would an organization have an "appetite" for risk? The metaphor is slightly inexact because we do not ordinarily think of firms as seeking out risk for risk's sake. It is not risk per se that firms desire, but rather the return that cannot be achieved without accepting a certain level of risk. An investment in a U.S.

> A "risk appetite" is a formal statement of the amount of risk that the board of directors is willing to take on.

Treasury security carries little risk — the United States is very unlikely to default on its debt. But this investment also offers little in the way of return. If an investor is willing to purchase junk bonds — debt issued by low-rated corporations — then if things go well the investor can earn a much larger return. On the other hand, investments in junk bonds also carry a substantial risk of default. An investment in a junk bond isn't necessarily a bad investment; much depends on the investor's willingness to tolerate risk. The risk appetite captures this idea of tolerance for risk.

The idea of a risk "appetite" is appropriate in yet another sense. An appetite is a desire, but usually not one that is unlimited. When we are hungry a slice of pizza seems delicious and much to be desired. After wolfing down the first slice, we may still be hungry, but probably less so. The second slice may seem attractive but not necessarily our heart's desire. If we give in to temptation and consume the second slice, our hunger is likely to be sated; from then on the idea of eating additional slices becomes unpleasant. Similarly, a risk appetite suggests that while an organization is willing to take on a certain level of risk (in order to achieve a given level of return), its appetite for risk is not unlimited; there are some strategies that simply carry too much risk to be accepted.

C. IMPLEMENTING THE RISK APPETITE

If the risk appetite works properly, the organization's managers respond by undertaking strategic decisions that implement the basic policy. Five steps are involved (risk-management professionals use a number of approaches and, accordingly, might define the problem somewhat differently than the methodology presented here, but the essential analytic steps are the same).

1. Compiling a Risk Inventory

The first step in implementing the risk appetite — actually one that should be undertaken even before the risk appetite is established — is to take an inventory of the risks facing the organization. The list of types of risk set forth in the previous chapter can be useful for compiling a risk inventory, but each organization is likely to define its risk inventory in such a way as to be most relevant to its own business and strategic focus.

Many of the risks in the inventory are well known and require little effort to identify. A bank understands that one of its key challenges is to deal with the risk of borrower default; a food company understands that it must address the risk of spoilage.

In addition to risks that chronically impact an organization's operations, there are always incipient or emerging risks — dangers that loom on the horizon. These are important to identify for planning purposes. If risks are not recognized in advance, it may not be possible to prevent their occurrence or to mitigate their impact when and if they arrive. With advance warning of the approach of a tornado, one might be able to get to a shelter; but if the only warning is the appearance of a funnel cloud, it may be too late. The challenge, with respect to emerging risks, is that they are not immediately salient. The organization's managers, who are (appropriately) focused on the challenges of today, may lack the ability to recognize emerging risks before they materialize.

Organizations can use various strategies in responding to the challenge of identifying emerging risks. The CRO or others can encourage staff to "think outside the box" in evaluating potential risks. Management consultants bring fresh insights and a broader perspective to bear on the questions. Independent directors can be helpful in asking probing questions and offering the insights of their own business or professional experience. Regulators can also be of service, because their unique perspective and broad overview can give them a perspective on industry trends that is lacking within any particular organization.

2. Assessing Inherent Risk

Once a risk inventory is compiled, the organization can quantify the inherent risk of each given activity. The inherent risk of an activity is simply the risk that the activity would pose for the organization if no efforts were undertaken to prevent or mitigate the risk.

Inherent risk is measured by evaluating two variables: the probability that the event will occur, and the magnitude of the event if it does occur. The reason for including the latter factor should be obvious: Since the risk is not certain to occur, the harm (or benefit) that the organization will experience from the event in question must be discounted by the chance that the event will never occur.

Technically, this calculation should be performed by multiplying the probability times the magnitude in order to estimate the expected value. For example, if we are flipping a fair coin, on the understanding that we will lose a dollar if it comes out tails, then the inherent risk of losing a dollar has a value of 50 cents — one dollar multiplied by a probability of 0.5.

In practice, risk managers often use a somewhat more qualitative approach. Instead of calculating precise values, they plot possible events on a heat map that relates probability and magnitude — sometimes referred to as "likelihood" and "impact." Consider Figure 19-4:

The event marked "3" in the top right hand cell has a high likelihood of occurring and a large impact if it does. This would be

> Inherent risk is the risk associated with an activity if the organization undertakes no efforts to prevent or mitigate the risk.

Figure 19-4: Likelihood and Impact

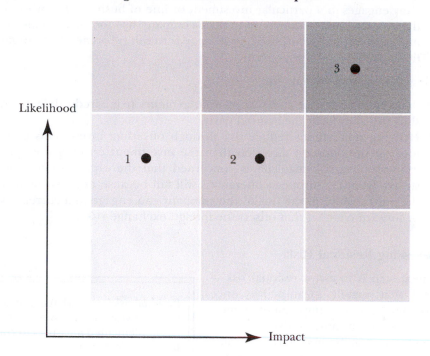

characterized as high risk. In contrast, the event marked "2" has both a lower likelihood of occurring and a lower impact if it occurs, but still seems to have a significant amount of both; this might be characterized as medium risk. The event marked "1" has the same likelihood of occurring but a lower impact if it does; this might be characterized as low risk. An event that is placed in the lower left hand cell would be less risky still.

3. Assessing Controls and Mitigation Options

A next task in implementing the risk appetite is to assess control strategies and mitigation options. Controls are things an organization can do to prevent the risky event from happening in the first place; they reduce the likelihood of a bad event occurring. Mitigation options are things the organization can do to limit the costs if the risky event does occur; they reduce the magnitude of the event if it does take place. Suppose the risk in question is the risk of loss to a homeowner as a result of storm damage. A control strategy would be some measure that the homeowner uses to prevent damage if a storm occurs—for example, installing hurricane windows. A mitigation option would be to purchase insurance that covers storm damage to the home.

In the case of complex organizations, leading control strategies include the following:

- Internal controls reduce risk by creating lines of defense against mistakes or violations of policy that could harm the organization. For example, a robust internal audit function can help ensure that the business lines do not engage in risky behaviors that violate company policies or procedures.

- Activity level management reduces risk by reducing the amount that a company engages in a particular investment or line of business. If, for example, the risk manager is concerned that a company has too much exposure to mortgage-backed securities, one strategy is to sell off some of the organization's portfolio of these products.

Mitigation options include the following:

- Policies of insurance and related arrangements (e.g., credit default swaps) shift risk away from the insured party.
- Hedging transactions reduce risk through offsetting investments that perform in the opposite direction than the investment creating the risk. For example, if a risk manager is concerned that the organization's income stream from its European operations will fall because of a loss in value of the euro relative to the dollar, the company can engage in a currency swap or forward contract that offsets the foreign exchange risk.

4. Assessing Residual Risk

The next step is to assess residual risk — the risk that remains in an activity once the organization has implemented measures to control or mitigate risk.

Residual risk can be modeled on the same heat map that the risk manager uses to evaluate inherent risk. Returning to the example above, an analysis of residual risk might look like Figure 19-5:

> Residual risk is the risk that remains in an activity once the organization has implemented measures to control or mitigate risk.

Figure 19-5: Effects of Controls and Mitigation

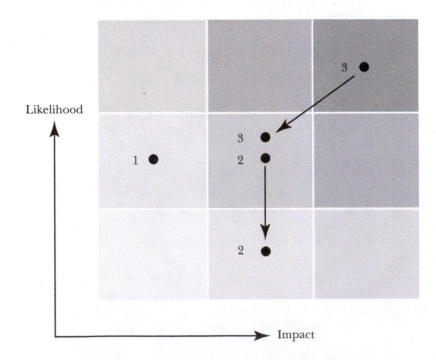

For the high risk event marked 3, the organization has implemented both control strategies and mitigation options. The control strategies reduce the probability the event will occur; the mitigation options reduce the impact of the event if it does. As a result, residual risk has moved from the top left cell to the middle cell. As for the event marked 2, the organization has implemented control strategies that reduce the probability the event will occur, but has not attempted to mitigate the impact of the event if it does occur. The organization has done nothing either to control the likelihood or mitigate the impact of event 1, presumably because the threat that it poses to the organization is considered to be so minor as not to warrant intervention.

A concrete example might help explain these concepts. One important risk for drug manufacturers is the risk that they will be found liable for "off-label" marketing of its products. There is an "inherent" element of this risk — the chance that if the company does nothing to stop it, its sales force will commit regulatory violations. Then there are control strategies — such as the company's compliance program — and mitigation options — the measures that may be available to mitigate the expected costs of violations by performing an internal investigation, upgrading compliance operations, and cooperating with the regulators. The residual risk is the risk of off-label marketing violations after the risk management measures have been implemented.

5. Accepting Residual Risk

Once she has determined a given level of residual risk based on a mix of control strategies and mitigation options, the decision maker can evaluate whether, all things considered and in light of the enterprise's risk appetite, the risk is something the company is willing to accept in order to achieve the benefits of the activity with which the risk is associated. The acceptance of risk is a key step in the process. It is a step that ideally should be undertaken deliberately, by persons with appropriate levels of responsibility within the organization. The idea of accepting residual risk is central to the concept of enterprise risk management, which views risk as reflecting good as well as bad outcomes and which insists that risk be intelligently and comprehensively managed on an enterprise-wide basis.

These five steps — identifying risks, assessing inherent risk, assessing control strategies and mitigation options, estimating residual risk, and determining whether to accept the residual risk — do not occur one after the other. Instead they occur more or less simultaneously, and are performed on an ongoing basis.

There are several points of leverage in this process. Given the analysis of costs and benefits, the organization can (a) cut back (or increase) the level of the proposed activity; (b) increase (or cut back) on the strategies and options used to control or mitigate risk; or (c) accept or not accept the level of inherent risk that remains given choices (a) and (b). Ideally, the process would be iterative, in the sense that the organization would search for the option that offers the greatest value to the company in light of its risk appetite. Senior managers can (and should) assess the full range of options before presenting questions to the board of directors for decision.

D. BLACK SWANS, FAT TAILS, AND STRESS TESTS

Most organizations have in place a plan for dealing with normal times; the plan is usually simply to keep on doing what they are already doing. Effective risk management, however, requires that organizations also plan for unusual times and circumstances. The importance of such contingency planning became all too clear during the financial crisis of 2007-2009, when governments and private institutions turned out to have made inadequate provisions for the unanticipated but severe market turmoil that occurred during those years.

In the course of discussion about the financial crisis, you have probably heard talk of "black swans" and "fat tails." The reference is not to a flying animal with over-sized feathers, but rather to probability theory. A black swan event is one that is unanticipated and unexpected but which has major consequences. The metaphor is drawn from the Latin poet Juvenal, who spoke of a *"rara avis"* — a rare bird — " much like a black swan."

Events can be unexpected in two ways. First, the event in question, while rare, may be predicted to happen according to a well-understood pattern. For example, people's IQs are (or are supposed to be) distributed according to a normal probability distribution. Suppose someone has an IQ of 137. This is uncommon — the person is very bright — but predictably one out of every 100 people will score this high or higher. People this intelligent are remarkable, but it is not surprising that they are around.

When the underlying probability distribution is known, risk managers should be able to plan for and predict uncommon events in a rational way. The strategy is to evaluate the impact of the event weighted by its probability in order to estimate the expected loss. Some events are so uncommon that a rational risk manager would do nothing to cope with them — for example, the probability that the factory will be hit by a meteor may be so low that no precautions need to be taken (although a meteor did damage a Russian city in 2013). In other cases, the probability distribution may be such that it would be worth expending resources to prevent the event from happening or to mitigate its costs.

However, people do not always behave rationally; they have limited imagination and their analytical capacities tend to be biased by a propensity to overvalue recent events and excessively discount older ones. The probability that a storm of the magnitude of Hurricane Sandy would strike the Northeastern seaboard was fairly well understood; but because no such events had occurred for decades, people excessively discounted the risk and failed to take appropriate precautions before the storm struck in 2012. Thus unexpected events pose challenges for risk management even when the probability of the event can be determined.

The other and more troubling way an event can be unexpected is that we do not even understand the probability distribution from which the event is drawn. A "fat tail" distribution is one where the probabilities of the tails — the extreme events — are higher than under the normal "bell curve" distribution. In the wake of the financial crisis of 2007-2009 many have argued that financial markets obey a fat-tail distribution, meaning that extreme financial events — bubbles and panics — happen more often than would be expected under the normal distribution. A problem here is that when it comes to financial panics, we have insufficient information to model the underlying probabilities with any confidence. Yet we must make important and costly decisions about risk management despite the fact we lack this key information.

Stress testing is the most effective way devised so far to deal with the risk of unexpected, high-cost contingencies. Stress tests are useful tools for identifying organizations' vulnerabilities and for developing effective strategies for managing the risks so identified. They do not predict the underlying probability of the stressors — and so are not a complete solution to the black swan problem — but at least they help organizations plan for adverse contingencies.

A stress test encompasses two key elements. First, there must be a model of the organization. Because the stress test is by definition a hypothetical scenario, it is impossible to subject the actual organization to stressed conditions. Nor would one wish to do so, since these conditions, being stressed, are dangerous and costly. The engineer doesn't determine the load-bearing capacity of a bridge by putting weights on it until it collapses. Instead, the decision maker must prepare a *model* of the organization that will respond in predictable ways to the chosen stressors. The model may be and often is quantitative; it will be embodied in computer code and stressed by quantitative inputs. The model may also be partly or wholly qualitative; here the effect of the stress is evaluated through the exercise of judgment by people with expertise and experience in the area.

> A stress test is a scenario in which a model of an organization is subjected to unusual and challenging conditions and then evaluated for its performance.

The use of models for stress tests is a strength of the technique, but also a weakness. The strength of the technique is its ability to test the effects of stressed conditions before they occur. The weakness is that the results of the test are only as good as the model. If the model incorporates accurate assumptions about how the organization will behave under the circumstances, then the stress test will provide information that will be useful in the risk-management process. If the model contains inaccurate or outdated assumptions, then the stress test will be of less use. In the worst case, failures in the model could lead to bad decisions that increase costs or exacerbate rather than mitigate the risks facing the organization. An important part of contemporary risk management is to develop and maintain an appropriate model of the organization's functioning under different stressed conditions.

The second key component of a stress test is the stressors chosen. Although the institution should have only one model that is consistently applied, many different stress scenarios may be chosen. For example, the organization may run stress tests for mild, moderate, or severe conditions. Each set of stressors will generate different performance by the model. A company that can withstand a mild or moderate stress scenario may not be able to survive a severe set of conditions.

What stressors are commonly chosen for stress tests? The answer depends, in part, on the reason why the test is run. A financial institution that wants to understand risks to its capital or liquidity will look at one set of conditions; a mining company that wants to understand the risks of a workplace accident will look at another set of conditions; an aircraft manufacturer that wants to understand the risks of an equipment malfunction will look at yet another set of conditions.

The most fully developed set of stress scenarios are in the area of financial institutions — in part because these institutions have recently undergone severe stress and in part because the conditions of 2007-2009 provide a fruitful example of the relevant components of stress. An example of a financial institution stress scenario is found in the Basel III recommendations for bank liquidity regulation. The concern of this scenario is to stress a bank's access to liquidity — cash — in severe market conditions that can generate a potentially destabilizing run on the bank. The designated stressors are as follows:

- A three-notch downgrade in the institution's public credit rating.
- Run-off of a proportion of retail deposits.
- A loss of unsecured wholesale funding capacity and reductions of potential sources of secured funding on a term basis.
- Loss of secured, short-term financing transactions for all but high quality liquid assets.
- Increases in market volatilities that impact the quality of collateral or potential future exposure of derivatives positions and thus requiring larger collateral haircuts or additional collateral.
- Unscheduled draws on all of the institution's committed but unused credit and liquidity facilities.
- The need for the institution to fund balance sheet growth arising from non-contractual obligations honored in the interest of mitigating reputational risk.

Although some of these stressors may sound unfamiliar, it should be evident from even a casual inspection that this scenario is very bad indeed. Most banks would blanch at the prospect of even a one-notch downgrade of their public credit rating; a three-notch downgrade is little short of a catastrophe. The losses of sources of financing assumed in the scenario mean that the bank will be searching for cash; and given that these different components are unlikely to arise in a single bank, many other institutions will probably be scouring credit markets for liquidity at the same time. In fact, the scenario presented above is more or less an accurate description of the conditions in financial markets in September 2008 when, in the wake of the failure of Lehman Brothers, credit markets around the world fell into a disastrous tailspin. The liquidity stress test essentially asks: If September 2008 were to happen again, would your institution be able to withstand the strains until market conditions ease?

One danger, evident in the above example is that the designers of the stress scenario will end up "fighting the last war" — modeling events that have already happened and not taking into account the dynamic forces that may create new risks and new stresses in the future. Another danger is the possibility that the stress test will be rigged to generate an intended result. Critics charged that stress tests conducted in Europe in the wake of the financial crisis of 2007-2009 did exactly that: The stressors were allegedly selected so as to declare most banks safe.

It should be evident from the foregoing discussion that the selection of stressors is fraught with difficulty. Ideally, designers of the test should have a sense of the probability of the events in question. It is impossible, however, to confidently assign probabilities to most stress scenarios, simply because we lack reliable models of overall economic functioning. What are the chances that a market breakdown as severe as the events of 2008 will recur in the next 50 years? To know the answer to that question, we would have to understand the probability distribution of market conditions in the economy, and we don't have this knowledge. We have only a rudimentary sense of how often and in what form market disruptions occur. Lacking such a probability distribution, we must operate on the basis of assumptions. The risk is that our assumptions will be wrong. There is also the natural tendency to assign inflated probabilities to recent events. Many people become worried about air travel in the weeks after a crash, even though the fact a crash occurred has little bearing on the likelihood of another. The Basel III liquidity stress scenario may reflect this sort of "recency bias": It is surely no accident that the stressors chosen happened to be ones that had just occurred. But what does the fact they occurred once indicate about the likelihood they will happen again?

An additional problem arises from the fact that most stress tests are performed by the regulated institution. This is necessary because only the institution has access to the detailed internal information needed to run the analysis. How can the regulator be sure that the institution is not intentionally or unintentionally jiggering the results?

The problem is exacerbated by the fact that stress tests are complicated exercises in which mistakes are likely to happen. And mistakes have been made. In 2014, RBS, one of Britain's largest banks, reported that it had easily passed the European Banking Authority's stress test: Even under adverse economic conditions, its core capital ratio remained at 6.7 percent, well above the minimum of 5.5 percent. Later RBS admitted that it had overstated capital in this scenario by more than $6 billion, and that its core capital in this scenario would fall to only 5.7 percent — still a passing grade, but only barely.

It turned out that the mistake had to do with accounting technicalities. The stress scenario would have generated losses for the bank. As a result of those losses, the bank would have obtained a tax relief, which was accounted for as a "deferred tax asset." The bank mistakenly included a large amount of this tax relief in its calculation of core capital and had to deduct the amount when the mistake came to light. That explains the error but leaves open the more fundamental question: How could the bank have made such a colossal mistake? The error was especially embarrassing for the British government because RBS was at the time 81 percent government owned.

RBS is far from the only bank to make errors on stress test results. In April 2014, Bank of America admitted it had botched a stress test required by the Federal Reserve Board. The size of the mistake was far less than RBS's. For example, the bank had reported Tier 1 capital of 12.1 percent when the actual figure was 11.9 percent, a change that did not affect the bank's status as "well capitalized." Nonetheless, the market's response was swift and punitive: Bank of America's stock dropped 6.3 percent on the news, erasing all its gains for the year, and the bank was forced to cancel a long-anticipated dividend increase.

In addition to stress tests, a related approach to risk identification and management is the use of "crisis simulation" scenarios in which management and/or the board of directors is confronted with a hypothetical stressor and asked to play out the events in real time as if they were actually happening. An example might be a cyber-breach situation in which management is alerted to a potential intrusion into the company's systems and then asked to investigate, identify, and manage all dimensions of the problem.

Another example: "dawn raid" exercises involving a simulated unannounced regulatory inspection and investigation into serious allegations of misconduct. Participants in these exercises often report that the company's carefully developed crisis management plan often went out the window in the first hour of the simulation; after that the managers were writing the script as they went along.

Kevin Dowd, Math Gone Mad: Regulatory Risk Modeling by the Federal Reserve

Cato Institute Policy Analysis, Sept. 3, 2014

The U.S. financial system faces a major, growing, and much under-appreciated threat from the Federal Reserve's risk modeling agenda — the "Fed stress tests." These were intended to make the financial system safe but instead create the potential for a new systemic financial crisis.

The principal purpose of these models is to determine banks' regulatory capital requirements — the capital "buffers" to be set aside so banks can withstand adverse events and remain solvent. Risk models are subject to a number of major weaknesses. They are usually based on poor assumptions and inadequate data, are vulnerable to gaming and often blind to major risks. They have difficulty handling market instability and tend to generate risk forecasts that fall as true risks build up. Most of all, they are based on the naïve belief that markets are mathematizable.

The fed's regulatory stress tests are subject to all these problems and more. They:

- Ignore well-established weaknesses in risk modeling and violate the core principles of good stress testing;
- Are overly prescriptive and suppress innovation and diversity in bank risk management; in so doing, they expose the whole financial system to the weaknesses in the Fed's models and greatly increase systemic risk;
- Impose a huge and growing regulatory burden;
- Are undermined by political factors;
- Fail to address major risks identified by independent experts; and
- Fail to embody lessons to be learned from the failures of other regulatory stress tests.

The solution to these problems is legislation to prohibit risk modeling by financial regulators and establish a simple, conservative capital standard for banks based on reliable capital ratios instead of unreliable models. The idea that the Fed, with no credible track record at forecasting, can be entrusted with the task of telling banks how to forecast their own financial risks, displacing banks' own risk systems in the process, is the ultimate in fatal conceits. Unless Congress intervenes, the United States is heading for a new systemic banking crisis. . . .

Questions and Comments

1. Do you agree that the government's attempt to make banks safer through the use of stress tests could backfire by making the financial system more rather than less risky?

2. Other than stress tests, what else are banking agencies going to do in order to assess the risks posed by large financial institutions?

3. Assuming the author is correct about the problems in stress testing, could the process be improved rather than abandoned?

E. DRILLING DOWN: SPECIFIC RISK-MANAGEMENT STRATEGIES

The process described above occurs at the level of senior management, and often involves qualitative factors that cannot easily be reduced to numeric form. In several areas, however, particularly in financial firms, quantified risk-management strategies are utilized to control particular forms of risk. What these techniques have in common is that they rely on mathematical models: simplified versions of reality that seek to emulate, in tractable form, some features of the institutions being managed or evaluated.

The models with the greatest impact combine several features:

- They must be quantitatively precise: Given certain numerical inputs, the output of the model must be exact.
- The inputs to the models must be limited in number and readily available.
- The models must be supported by intellectual credentials.
- The models must generate output that can easily be used in defined strategies for action and employed by people who don't necessarily understand the underlying theory (e.g., traders).

Let's look at a few of these approaches.

1. Corporate Default Estimation Methods

How can one determine the default probability of a corporate bond or loan or account receivable? This problem is fundamental to any firm that invests in corporate debt—banks, insurance companies, pension funds, mutual funds, hedge funds, and other counterparties. Default probabilities are obviously also central to the operations of credit rating agencies.

These days there are many candidates for measuring default probabilities. One of the earliest and best-known is Altman's Z score, a model published in 1968 by Edward Altman, an economist at New York University's Stern School of Business. Based on a study of matched public manufacturing firms, half of which had declared bankruptcy and half of which had not, Altman devised an estimate of the risk of default based on five readily available inputs.

Altman's original formula (which has subsequently been tweaked based on additional data) was as follows:

$$Z = 1.2X_1 + 1.4X_2 + 3.3X_3 + 0.6X_4 + 0.999X_5.$$

This looks complicated but in fact is simple. To calculate the Z score for a particular firm, you simply needed to find out the values of the variables (X_1 through X_5) and plug the numbers in to the equation. The variables themselves are easy to find from published financial data:

X_1 = Working Capital/Total Assets
X_2 = Retained Earnings/Total Assets
X_3 = Earnings Before Interest and Taxes/Total Assets
X_4 = Market Value of Equity/Book Value of Total Liabilities
X_5 = Sales/Total Assets

Once calculated, the Z score is also easy to interpret: The score can be sorted into relatively simple categories that provide an estimate of default probability.

Altman's Z turned out to be effective at predicting bankruptcy of industrial firms in the short and medium terms (in 1995, Altman published another version of the Z score that is considered more appropriate for firms in industries such as retailing or services). The Z score approach was adopted by regulators, credit rating agencies, securities firms, banks, and many others in the financial services industry. The success of the methodology was due to several factors: its proven track record; the fact that it was one of the first available techniques; its distinguished intellectual pedigree; its ease of use, requiring only widely available data as inputs; and its ease of interpretation. Other candidates for calculating bankruptcy risk have now entered the market, but a version of Altman's Z is still in widespread use.

2. Black-Scholes Option Pricing Formula

The option pricing approach associated with the Black-Scholes formula is one of the most successful economic innovations of all time, generating several Nobel prizes and providing the foundation stone for an entire industry. An option is a financial instrument that confers a right but not obligation to purchase or sell a security at a given price ("exercise price") at a given time in the future (the "strike date"). The right to purchase is called a "call" option; the right to sell is called a "put" option.

Options have value because in certain future states of the world the holder of the option will make a profit by exercising the underlying right. Specifically, if the market price of a security at the strike date exceeds the exercise price, then the holder of a call option can capture the price difference by exercising the call; conversely, if the market price of the security at the strike date is below the exercise price, then the holder of a put option can earn a profit by exercising her rights to sell the security at a higher price.

The question that the inventors of the option pricing approach (Fisher Black, Myron Scholes, and Robert Merton) addressed in 1969-1970 was this: How much is the option worth? Given that options are important in modern finance, this was and is a fundamental question. It is highly relevant to risk management because it concerns the value of a risky asset. The Black-Scholes equation is one answer to the question. It is commonly expressed as follows:

$$\frac{\partial_w}{\partial_t} = rw - rx\frac{\partial_w}{\partial_x} - \frac{1}{2}\sigma^2 x^2 \frac{\partial^2 w}{\partial x^2}$$

Don't worry about the technical details; it is enough to note that the formula can easily be embodied in a computer program that will spit out results after input of some fairly simple information.

The Black-Scholes formula enjoyed a spectacular success. It was so successful, in fact, that when market prices for options began to conform more accurately to the formula in later years, some theorized that prices were being set through application of the formula rather than on the basis of economic fundamentals.

Why was the Black-Scholes formula so popular? Several features similar to the factors at play in Altman's Z appear important: The authors were distinguished financial economists; the formula and the information needed to generate results were widely available; and the formula generated results that could readily be used by market traders even if they did not understand the underlying theory.

The Black-Scholes formula provided a foundation for the options trading industry. Prior to the publication of the formula, options traders were viewed essentially as gamblers. Options exchanges were threatened with regulation and many investors shied away from entering the market. The Black-Scholes model conferred legitimacy on the options trading market and squelched attempts to tar the activity of options trading with the epithet of "gambling" (although nothing in the formula prevents a trader from using options trading for speculative purposes).

3. Value-at-Risk Models

Many financial institutions use of "value-at-risk" or "VaR" methodologies for assessing the risk inherent in their investments. Value at risk is a broad metric of the market risk of assets. It is used to prevent portfolio managers from exceeding risk tolerances established in conformity with the organization's risk appetite. Unlike Altman's Z or the Black-Scholes Option Pricing Model, VaR cannot be calculated by inputting parameters readily available from public sources. Instead, the user must develop a model of the probability distribution of the portfolio being modeled. The probability distribution models the performance of the portfolio at a defined time in the future.

While VaR models require work, they generate useful outputs once they are in place. The VaR model can answer the following question: What is the worst expected loss of a given portfolio over a given time horizon at a given confidence level under normal market conditions? Suppose a $10 million portfolio is said to have a 30-day VaR of $1.3 million with a 99 percent confidence level. This means that the model estimates a 1 percent chance that the portfolio will experience losses of $1.3 million or more in a 30-day period under normal market conditions. Those who set risk policy for the portfolio can determine the maximum allowable VaR. If the portfolio comes to exceed the allowable VaR, the manager can adjust it by reducing the risk of assets in the portfolio.

VaR has been a spectacularly successful innovation. It is widely used across the financial sector. Its prestige is so great that the Basel Committee on Banking Supervision, when it established capital standards for market risk in banks, required that they employ this methodology to determine the risk of their trading portfolios.

What explains the success of VaR? It has many of the same features of Altman's Z and the Black-Scholes option pricing model: It is backed by prestigious authority and, in general, has been validated by experience. Most importantly, VaR succinctly summarizes the risk exposure of a portfolio. Portfolio managers, traders, and others who are busy and not concerned with theory need a simple metric to guide their decisions; VaR fits the bill.

At the same time, value at risk, like the other metrics discussed already, is perilous as well as potent. People who implement trading policies based on VaR have a natural inclination to accord too much authority to the magic number that VaR generates for the portfolio at any given time. VaR is not the Holy Grail. It is only an analytic tool, and like all tools it must be used for the right purposes and with due regard for its limitations.

Several limitations of VaR should be obvious from the description above. VaR analysis depends on the construction of a probability distribution of future portfolio performance. The probability distribution is an estimate based on past performance coupled with assumptions about how prices behave. Past performance, however, may not necessarily be a good guide to the future, and assumptions about price behavior may be incorrect.

Critics of VaR have argued, in particular, that the VaR models used at the time of the financial crisis of 2007-2009 were subject to a black swan problem, in that the "tail risk" of unusual market conditions was far higher than the risk that was incorporated in financial institutions' VaR models. These critics note that financial markets during this period displayed behavior that would be exceedingly unlikely under the normal probability distribution that these models assumed. One may infer either that the normal distribution was correct, and an extremely unusual event took place, or alternatively that the normal distribution was not correct because it understated the probability of extreme events.

In the wake of the crisis of 2007-2009, proponents of VaR are careful to qualify that the model provides an estimate of losses under normal market conditions. This qualification, while appropriate, may also be a bit of an evasion. Risk planners have to consider not only normal conditions, but also the risk of extreme events. How can one confidently rely on VaR if it only provides information about price behavior under normal conditions?

On the other hand, without VaR, portfolio risk management would be even less well controlled. At present banks, regulators and financial economists are sorting through the question of how to properly utilize VaR if one abandons the assumption that it can provide reliable information about portfolio performance under abnormal conditions.

F. MODEL RISK

Each of the three risk-control methodologies just discussed depends on a mathematical model. Mathematical models have power because they generate controlled and theoretically justified quantitative results that can be of immediate use to decision makers. But mathematical models also have shortcomings. The financial crisis of 2007-2009 brought some of these shortcomings into sharp relief and stimulated thinking about the use and abuse of modeling methodologies. The following excerpt provides an example of bank regulators' thinking on the topic:

Board of Governors of the Federal Reserve System, Supervisory Guidance on Model Risk Management

Apr. 4, 2011

Banks rely heavily on quantitative analysis and models in most aspects of financial decision making. They routinely use models for a broad range of activities, including underwriting credits; valuing exposures, instruments, and positions; measuring risk; managing and safeguarding client assets; determining capital and reserve adequacy; and many other activities. In recent years, banks have applied models to more complex products and with more ambitious scope, such as enterprise-wide risk measurement, while the markets in which they are used have also broadened and changed. Changes in regulation have spurred some of the recent developments, particularly the U.S. regulatory capital rules for market, credit, and operational risk based on the framework developed by the Basel Committee on Banking

Supervision. Even apart from these regulatory considerations, however, banks have been increasing the use of data-driven, quantitative decision-making tools for a number of years.

The expanding use of models in all aspects of banking reflects the extent to which models can improve business decisions, but models also come with costs. There is the direct cost of devoting resources to develop and implement models properly. There are also the potential indirect costs of relying on models, such as the possible adverse consequences (including financial loss) of decisions based on models that are incorrect or misused. Those consequences should be addressed by active management of model risk. . . .

The purpose of this document is to provide comprehensive guidance for banks on effective model risk management. Rigorous model validation plays a critical role in model risk management; however, sound development, implementation, and use of models are also vital elements. Furthermore, model risk management encompasses governance and control mechanisms such as board and senior management oversight, policies and procedures, controls and compliance, and an appropriate incentive and organizational structure. . . .

Models are simplified representations of real-world relationships among observed characteristics, values, and events. Simplification is inevitable, due to the inherent complexity of those relationships, but also intentional, to focus attention on particular aspects considered to be most important for a given model application. Model quality can be measured in many ways: precision, accuracy, discriminatory power, robustness, stability, and reliability, to name a few. Models are never perfect, and the appropriate metrics of quality, and the effort that should be put into improving quality, depend on the situation. . . . In all situations, it is important to understand a model's capabilities and limitations given its simplifications and assumptions.

The use of models invariably presents model risk, which is the potential for adverse consequences from decisions based on incorrect or misused model outputs and reports. Model risk can lead to financial loss, poor business and strategic decision making, or damage to a bank's reputation. Model risk occurs primarily for two reasons:

- The model may have fundamental errors and may produce inaccurate outputs when viewed against the design objective and intended business uses. The mathematical calculation and quantification exercise underlying any model generally involves application of theory, choice of sample design and numerical routines, selection of inputs and estimation, and implementation in information systems. Errors can occur at any point from design through implementation. In addition, shortcuts, simplifications, or approximations used to manage complicated problems could compromise the integrity and reliability of outputs from those calculations. Finally, the quality of model outputs depends on the quality of input data and assumptions, and errors in inputs or incorrect assumptions will lead to inaccurate outputs.

- The model may be used incorrectly or inappropriately. Even a fundamentally sound model producing accurate outputs consistent with the design objective of the model may exhibit high model risk if it is misapplied or misused. Models by their nature are simplifications of reality, and real-world events may prove those simplifications inappropriate. This is even more of a concern if a model is used outside the environment for which it was designed. Banks may do this intentionally as they apply existing models to new products or markets, or inadvertently as market conditions or customer behavior changes. Decision makers need to understand the limitations of a model to avoid using it in ways that are not consistent with the original intent. Limitations come in part from weaknesses in the model due to its various shortcomings, approximations, and uncertainties. Limitations are also a consequence of assumptions underlying a model that may restrict the scope to a limited set of specific circumstances and situations. . . .

A guiding principle for managing model risk is "effective challenge" of models, that is, critical analysis by objective, informed parties who can identify model limitations and assumptions and produce appropriate changes. Effective challenge depends on a combination of incentives, competence, and influence. Incentives to provide effective challenge to models are stronger when there is greater separation of that challenge from the model development process and when challenge is supported by well-designed compensation practices and corporate culture. Competence is a key to effectiveness since technical knowledge and modeling skills are necessary to conduct appropriate analysis and critique. Finally, challenge may fail to be effective without the influence to ensure that actions are taken to address model issues. Such influence comes from a combination of explicit authority, stature within the organization, and commitment and support from higher levels of management.

Even with skilled modeling and robust validation, model risk cannot be eliminated, so other tools should be used to manage model risk effectively. Among these are establishing limits on model use, monitoring model performance, adjusting or revising models over time, and supplementing model results with other analysis and information. Informed conservatism, in either the inputs or the design of a model or through explicit adjustments to outputs, can be an effective tool, though not an excuse to avoid improving models. . . .

Model risk management should include disciplined and knowledgeable development and implementation processes that are consistent with the situation and goals of the model user and with bank policy. Model development is not a straightforward or routine technical process. The experience and judgment of developers, as much as their technical knowledge, greatly influence the appropriate selection of inputs and processing components. The training and experience of developers exercising such judgment affects the extent of model risk. Moreover, the modeling exercise is often a multidisciplinary activity drawing on economics, finance, statistics, mathematics, and other fields. Models are employed in real-world markets and events and therefore should be tailored for specific applications and informed by business uses. In addition, a considerable amount of subjective judgment is exercised at various stages of model development, implementation, use, and validation. It is important for decision makers to recognize that this subjectivity elevates the importance of sound and comprehensive model risk management processes. . . .

The widespread use of vendor and other third-party products — including data, parameter values, and complete models — poses unique challenges for validation and other model risk management activities because the modeling expertise is external to the user and because some components are considered proprietary. Vendor products should nevertheless be incorporated into a bank's broader model risk management framework following the same principles as applied to in-house models, although the process may be somewhat modified.

[B]anks should ensure that there are appropriate processes in place for selecting vendor models. Banks should require the vendor to provide developmental evidence explaining the product components, design, and intended use, to determine whether the model is appropriate for the bank's products, exposures, and risks. Vendors should provide appropriate testing results that show their product works as expected. They should also clearly indicate the model's limitations and assumptions and where the product's use may be problematic. Banks should expect vendors to conduct ongoing performance monitoring and outcomes analysis, with disclosure to their clients, and to make appropriate modifications and updates over time.

Banks are expected to validate their own use of vendor products. External models may not allow full access to computer coding and implementation details, so the bank may have to rely more on sensitivity analysis and benchmarking. Vendor models are often designed to provide a range of capabilities and so may need to be customized by a bank for its particular circumstances. A bank's customization choices should be documented and justified as part of validation. If vendors provide input data or assumptions, or use them to build models, their relevance for the bank's situation should be investigated. Banks should obtain information regarding the data used to develop the model and assess the extent to which that data is representative of the bank's situation. The bank also should conduct ongoing monitoring and outcomes analysis of vendor model performance using the bank's own outcomes. . . .

Developing and maintaining strong governance, policies, and controls over the model risk management framework is fundamentally important to its effectiveness. Even if model development, implementation, use, and validation are satisfactory, a weak governance function will reduce the effectiveness of overall model risk management. A strong governance framework provides explicit support and structure to risk management functions through policies defining relevant risk management activities, procedures that implement those policies, allocation of resources, and mechanisms for evaluating whether policies and procedures are being carried out as specified. Notably, the extent and sophistication of a bank's governance function is expected to align with the extent and sophistication of model usage.

Model risk governance is provided at the highest level by the board of directors and senior management when they establish a bank-wide approach to model risk management. As part of their overall responsibilities, a bank's board and senior management should establish a strong model risk management framework that fits into the broader risk management of the organization. That framework should be grounded in an understanding of model risk—not just for individual models but also in the aggregate. The framework should include standards for model development, implementation, use, and validation.

While the board is ultimately responsible, it generally delegates to senior management the responsibility for executing and maintaining an effective model risk management framework. . . . Board members should ensure that the level of model risk is within their tolerance and direct changes where appropriate. These actions will set the tone for the whole organization about the importance of model risk and the need for active model risk management. . . .

A bank's internal audit function should assess the overall effectiveness of the model risk management framework. . . . Findings from internal audit related to models should be documented and reported to the board or its appropriately delegated agent. Banks should ensure that internal audit operates with the proper incentives, has appropriate skills, and has adequate stature in the organization to assist in model risk management. Internal audit's role is not to duplicate model risk management activities. Instead, its role is to evaluate whether model risk management is comprehensive, rigorous, and effective. To accomplish this evaluation, internal audit staff should possess sufficient expertise in relevant modeling concepts as well as their use in particular business lines. . . .

Although model risk management is an internal process, a bank may decide to engage external resources to help execute certain activities related to the model risk management framework. These activities could include model validation and review, compliance functions, or other activities in support of internal audit. These resources may provide added knowledge and another level of critical and effective challenge, which may improve the internal model development and risk management processes. However, this potential benefit should be weighed against the added costs for such resources and the added time that external parties require to understand internal data, systems, and other relevant bank-specific circumstances. . . .

Questions and Comments

1. Many of the models utilized by large organizations are too complicated or too sophisticated for the average board member to understand. Given this fact, how can a board member responsibly do her job of supervising the management of the company?

2. As noted in the excerpt, many models are supplied by vendors. For obvious reasons, vendors are usually unwilling to share details of the inner workings of their models. The customer is asked to take the model on faith. Given this, how can the customer validate that the model is appropriate?

3. Should the board of directors meet with vendors to assess the reliability of their models?

4. The excerpt from the Fed's supervisory guidance suggests several strategies for avoiding over-reliance on models: "establishing limits on model use, monitoring model performance, adjusting or revising models over time, and supplementing model results with other analysis and information." These sound good, but are they realistic?

5. If a company relies heavily on models to manage risks, should it be encouraged or required to include among its board members someone with the mathematical sophistication to understand the model, to appreciate its limitations and to ask intelligent questions of those who have created or who run the model on a day-to-day basis?

Department of the Treasury
Comptroller of the Currency
January 14, 2013

In the Matter of:	)
JPMorgan Chase Bank, N.A.	)
Columbus, Ohio	)

. . . [T]he Bank shall submit an acceptable written plan to ensure appropriate control over the market risk and price risk models of the Bank ("Model Risk Management Plan"). . . .

The Model Risk Management Plan shall ensure adequate standards for model development, implementation and use, and shall at a minimum:
Ensure compliance with:

- Model-related standards set forth in . . . applicable laws and regulations;
- [A]pplicable supervisory guidance; and
- Bank policies, procedures and directives;

Ensure the identification and tracking of all models requiring regulatory or Bank approval and all models subject to supervisory guidance;
Require the adoption of templates to ensure that all material aspects of a model are sufficiently documented prior to submission to the model review group;
Prevent the inappropriate use of un-reviewed or unapproved models;
Prevent the implementation of disapproved models, unless use of the model is authorized in writing by a senior management official pursuant to a documented exception process;
Ensure that for all un-reviewed or unapproved models, the Bank:

- Identifies the un-reviewed or unapproved model on a comprehensive list;
- Develops an associated action plan to address issues associated with using such models in a timely manner; and
- Where appropriate, applies a conservative capital treatment approved by the OCC until validation is completed and issues associated with using such models are addressed;

Prevent the implementation, modification or use of an approved model in a manner materially inconsistent with the approval and ensure that a qualified individual is responsible for compliance, unless use of the model in a manner materially inconsistent with its approval is authorized in writing by a senior management official pursuant to a documented exception process;
Require periodic gap analyses, not less frequently than annually, to identify any model not in conformance with this Article and ensure prompt corrective action;
Ensure that the VaR model development process is adequate, which shall at a minimum:

- Provide for adequate and well-qualified staff with clearly defined mandates, roles and responsibilities and application of a consistent approach;
- Require complete documentation, including but not limited to, evaluation and discussion of conceptual soundness, assumptions and limitations, and adequate support for testing and analysis; and
- Require a VaR model inventory that includes details regarding technology employed, data feeds, implementation procedures and operational controls;

Ensure that the model review process includes an independent review of all models used in measuring market risk and price risk, which shall at a minimum:

- Require model tiering that specifically considers model complexity and all material associated risks due to the quantity of inputs, inputs derived from other models, implementation methods and operational risk;
- Require a rigorous assessment of the quality and suitability of all material model components including inputs from other models and data feeds;
- Prevent undue reliance on the model developer's input;

- Provide model review staff with explicit authority and the ability to provide credible challenges to model developers;
- Ensure that any material issues or deficiencies are appropriately documented and addressed in a timely and substantive manner; and
- Require a documented update or an independent model review when a model's methodology is materially changed sufficient to permit auditing of the changes;

Integrate and enhance the VaR model technology framework, which shall at a minimum:

- Ensure that the model infrastructure provides flexibility and scalability with appropriate governance, controls and change control management;
- Ensure that the Bank's technology framework includes appropriate controls and detailed reporting capabilities that takes into account legal entities, lines of business and the Bank's consolidated holding company; and
- Ensure that the Bank has documented mitigating controls for those components of VaR and data feeds that are not part of the Bank's Market Risk Infrastructure framework and related repositories; and

Ensure that VaR model implementation and governance processes are adequate, which shall at a minimum:

- Ensure that all material operational risks associated with model usage are addressed and that documentation details the methods employed to minimize these risks;
- Implement procedures and compensating controls to ensure that proper safeguards are in place prior to production release including, but not limited to, situations where manual intervention is necessary to invoke a model including, but not limited to, spreadsheet based models or spreadsheet based data feeds;
- Ensure that documentation fully addresses technology change control requirements and information security concerns;
- Require model approval sign-off by the appropriate model control officer attesting to the controls in this paragraph and include such attestation in the control self-assessment for the line of business;
- Require model performance testing that considers the control processes in this paragraph including documented reviews during post implementation monitoring; and
- Implement standardized governance processes for VaR model implementation and controls that includes, but is not limited to, processes for data soundness. . . .

Questions and Comments

1. This is an effort to implement the guidance on model risk management. Overall, do you think that compliance with this order will improve the bank's use of models and its management of model risk?

2. One problem dealt with in this order is the risk associated with nascent or outmoded models. When a model is abandoned, it doesn't just go away on its own. It remains in place, probably installed in many computer systems. In a vast

organization like JPMorgan Chase, there is always the chance that outmoded models will continue to be utilized. Conversely, as a new model is developed it may come to be used by some in the organization before it has received an official sign-off from the appropriate manager. How does the consent decree deal with these problems?

3. Models, like drugs, can have approved uses and unapproved uses. For example, a model that generates loss probabilities for portfolios of mortgage-backed securities might (or might not) be useful in predicting loss probabilities of securities backed by portfolios of consumer credit card debt. If no model for the latter is available in an organization, traders and others may have an impulse to use the former in lieu of anything better. But doing this may be dangerous because the model is designed for a different type of instrument. What safeguards does the consent decree require to prevent use of authorized models for unapproved uses?

4. Sometimes models require as input data generated by other models. In this way the reliability of one model depends on one or more others. What safeguards does the consent decree have in place for this situation of overlapping models?

G. RATING AGENCIES

Another approach to risk management is to "outsource" part of the function to external evaluation and analysis. Among the most important sources of risk analytics are the rating agencies that assess the chances that debtors will default on bonds. Three rating agencies dominate the market: Moody's, Standard & Poor's, and the Fitch Group.

Rating agencies long enjoyed a high level of prestige. They were viewed as so credible, in fact, that the framers of the Basel II capital adequacy standards encouraged banks to rely on public credit ratings as a method for calculating the capital they held against risky assets. The financial crisis of 2007-2009, however, severely damaged the prestige of these institutions.

In the aftermath of that disaster, lawmakers took steps to reduce reliance on the opinions of the rating agencies. The Basel III guidelines, designed to regulate banks around the world, encourage large banks to "develop internal credit risk assessment capacity and to increase use of the internal ratings based approach for calculating their own-funds requirements for credit risk" — in other words, to use their own risk assessments rather than relying on rating agencies. In the United States, the Dodd-Frank Act directs federal regulators to reduce their reliance on credit ratings as inputs into regulatory action. The statute deleted assorted statutory references to credit ratings, ordered regulators to replace references to credit ratings with alternative standards of creditworthiness, and required each agency to report how it carried out this mandate. The Dodd-Frank Act also contains rules designed to reduce rating agency conflicts of interest and to improve the quality of rating agency evaluations.

European regulators have also taken steps to reduce reliance on credit ratings. CRA III, the basic regulation of credit rating agencies, now requires financial institutions to "make their own credit risk assessment and not solely and mechanistically rely on credit ratings for assessing the creditworthiness of an entity or financial instrument." The same general principle is found in regulations governing particular industrial sectors. For example, the Capital Requirements Directive (CRD IV) and the Capital Requirements Regulation (CRR) encourage "sophisticated" credit institutions to have their own procedures for credit risk assessment and, tracking the CRA rule, require domestic regulators to ensure that financial institutions do not rely solely and mechanistically on external credit ratings for the purpose of calculating regulatory capital requirements.

H. GOVERNMENT RISK ASSESSMENT

So far we have discussed the use of private parties to identify, measure, and manage risk. The government also has a role to play in these processes. Among other things, the government plays an active role in risk assessment—both for purposes of designing risk-based regulatory strategies and for providing guidance to private firms carrying out their enterprise risk-management function.

The Comptroller of the Currency (OCC), which regulates nationally chartered banks and savings institutions, has been at the forefront of these efforts. It sponsors conferences for bank directors that focus on best practices to identify, measure, monitor, and control risk. The OCC also operates a "National Risk Committee," which "monitors the condition of the federal banking system and emerging threats to the system's safety and soundness." The NRC issues quarterly guidance to examiners identifying risk trends in the industry, as well as a publicly available "Semi-annual Risk Perspective" offering the OCC's views on the risk facing the banking industry as a whole. The agency also provides banks with its assessment of their individual risk profiles as part of the bank examination process. In 2015, the OCC went further and appointed a chief risk officer charged with managing a risk department and evaluating whether the agency was staying within its risk appetite statement.

Risk is also central to the activities of the Financial Stability Oversight Council (FSOC), an entity created by the Dodd-Frank Act consisting of federal financial regulators, state regulators, and an independent insurance expert appointed by the President. FSOC provides "comprehensive monitoring of the stability of our nation's financial system." The Council is charged with "identifying risks to the financial stability of the United States; promoting market discipline; and responding to emerging risks to the stability of the United States' financial system." The Council issues an annual report assessing matters such as the macroeconomic environment, regulatory developments, financial developments, and "potential emerging threats" to financial system stability. Identified threats include items such as risk of reliance upon short-term wholesale funding, developments in financial products, services and business practices, risk-taking incentives of large, complex, interconnected financial institutions, financial system vulnerability to interest rate volatility, operational risks, foreign economic and financial developments, and data gaps and data quality. Other federal and state agencies offer different sorts of risk assessments for matters under their supervision.

Questions and Comments

1. What are the benefits of regulatory involvement in risk assessment? Consider the fact that regulators have broader access to information and a systemic overview

that private institutions lack, and so may be able to offer a more balanced and informed analysis. Private sector firms may have an incentive to understate risk in order to justify profitable but hazardous ventures. Arguably, banks could only gain from having access to an independent analysis.

2. On the other hand, are there perils in government risk assessments? Is it healthy, for example, for an agency such as the OCC to be offering banks its assessment of their risk profile? Given that the OCC is a powerful agency with enormous powers over the banks it supervises, will this practice inhibit banks from undertaking independent assessments of their own risks?

3. Do regulators have appropriate incentives to assess risk accurately? If the regulator assesses a risk as high and the bad event in question does not come to pass, few will notice; but if the regulator assesses a risk as low and event does come to pass, the regulator is likely to be blamed. Given these incentives, are regulatory risk assessments trustworthy?

4. Does FSOC offer a truly independent analysis? Consider its makeup: The voting members are the Secretary of the Treasury, the Chairman of the Fed; the Comptroller of the Currency; the Director of the Bureau of Consumer Financial Protection, the Chairman of the SEC, the Chairperson of the FDIC, the Chairperson of the Commodity Futures Trading Commission, the Director of the Federal Housing Finance Agency, the Chairman of the National Credit Union Administration, and an independent member with insurance expertise (de facto representing state insurance regulators). Is this group of recycled bureaucrats likely to do anything more than advocate for their agencies' positions when acting as members of the council? Is there a danger that the perception of an independent assessment will lead to complacency when that assessment turns out to dovetail with the views already entertained by federal regulators?

5. Are regulators good at assessing risk? Consider the following remarks from Ben Bernanke, then the Chairman of the Fed:

- 2005: A decline in housing prices is "pretty unlikely." Beginning in 2007, the nation experienced a catastrophic decline in housing prices with values plummeting more than 30 percent in some markets.

- 2005: "I don't think [problems in the housing sector are going] to drive the economy too far from its full employment path." In 2008 and 2009, as a result of problems in housing markets and other issues, the U.S. labor market lost more than eight million jobs, with the unemployment rate peaking at around 10 percent.

- 2007: "[T]he effect of the troubles in the subprime sector on the broader housing market will likely be limited, and we do not expect significant spillovers from the subprime market to the rest of the economy or to the financial system." Beginning in 2007, problems in the subprime market spilled over into the rest of the economy and the financial system, leading to one of the most traumatic financial crises in American history.

- 2008: "The Federal Reserve is not currently forecasting a recession." The country had already fallen into a recession.

- 2008: Fannie Mae and Freddie Mac "are in no danger of failing." Two months later both institutions were placed in receivership.

Bernanke is a respected economist who, as Chairman of the Fed, had access to the world's best statistics, highly sophisticated financial models, and a legion of PhDs. If he and his colleagues could get things so wrong, can any government agency do better?

I. BEHAVIORAL-ECONOMIC APPROACHES TO RISK MANAGEMENT

Classical economic theory assumes that economic agents act rationally in pursuit of their objectives. This doesn't mean that people are necessarily selfish; they may be altruists. But the models of classical economics assume that regardless of their goals and purposes, people will generally act in such a way as to maximize whatever objectives they seek to achieve. Behavioral economics challenges this assumption. Foundational work by Daniel Kahneman and Amos Tversky claims that people don't always act in the ways modeled by classical economics and that behavior deviates from rationality in predictable ways. Kahneman and Tversky claim that human decision making is subject to systemic biases or tendencies toward irrationality. Important among these biases are the following:

- People tend to value things they have more than things that they don't have but could acquire — the "endowment effect."
- People tend to focus more on changes in their welfare than they focus on the absolute level of welfare; thus regardless of their wealth, they tend to think they would be happy if they could only get a little more.
- People's estimates of economic information is biased by anchoring — by attraction to some preexisting norm.
- People tend to assign too high a probability to recent events and too low a probability to events that have not occurred for a long time.

Behavioral economics is the application of these and similar ideas to economic phenomena. The literature in this area is somewhat chaotic — as might be expected in an area that is still developing — characterized by inexactly defined terms and competing theoretical claims. But the core premise of behavioral-economic work of any sort is the idea, drawn from Kahneman and Tversky, that people tend to behave in predictable but irrational ways.

The modern discipline of risk management, in general, endorses the classical economic view that — at least in the context of decision making within complex organizations — people generally make rational choices. Yet the behavior displayed by financial institutions and their regulators in the lead-up to the financial crisis of 2007-2009 might give reason to doubt that premise. Were banks really behaving rationally when they became so heavily invested in mortgage-backed securities? Was the Federal Reserve Board behaving rationally when it observed a housing bubble in the United States (and elsewhere in the world) and did nothing to stop it? Were insurance regulators behaving rationally when they allowed AIG to conduct a massive credit default swap operation out of an unregulated office in London? For that matter, are regulators and financial institutions behaving rationally today?

Consider in this respect the following excerpt, which argues that financial markets and financial market regulation are subject to pervasive and systematically significant conceptual biases and that those biases played a role in the financial crisis of 2007-2009.

Geoffrey Miller & Gerald Rosenfeld, Intellectual Hazard: How Conceptual Biases in Complex Organizations Contributed to the Crisis of 2008

33 Harv. J.L. & Pub. Pol'y 807 (2010)

. . . This Article identifies an important but previously unrecognized systemic risk in financial markets: intellectual hazard. Intellectual hazard, as we define it, is the tendency of behavioral biases to interfere with accurate thought and analysis within complex organizations. Intellectual hazard impairs the acquisition, analysis, communication, and implementation of information within an organization and the communication of such information between an organization and external parties. We argue that intellectual hazard was a cause of the Crisis of 2008 and suggest that this risk may be an important factor in all financial crises. . . .

Financial markets today are among the most sophisticated, well-funded, well-informed, and technologically advanced institutions in the world. They process trillions of dollars in transactions each year. Many highly trained, hard-working, brilliant people work in the industry. Yet these markets and their regulators suffered an astonishing breakdown in 2008. Few people fully appreciated the implications of the housing market bubble or understood the risk that the burgeoning market in subprime mortgage-backed securities posed for the world's financial system. Those who did understand were unable to make their voices heard. When the storm made landfall, in September 2008, financial markets and their regulators were as woefully unprepared as the City of New Orleans in the face of Hurricane Katrina. What went wrong?

The thesis of this Article is that the Crisis of 2008 was partially caused by a problem with the processing of risk-related information in complex organizations. [A]ctors in complex organizations failed to properly acquire, process, transmit, and implement key information pertinent to risk. We call this problem "intellectual hazard." . . .

Intellectual hazard is similar to moral hazard in the following respects. Moral hazard is a problem that results from a structural feature of markets that is in other respects highly beneficial: the shifting of risk to more efficient risk-bearers. Similarly, intellectual hazard results from the otherwise beneficial division of responsibility among specialized instrumentalities. Like moral hazard, intellectual hazard is pervasive. Just as moral hazard exists whenever risk is shifted away from an actor whose actions may cause harm, intellectual hazard exists whenever production becomes segmented into complex organizational forms. And like moral hazard, intellectual hazard can present systemic risks: Because it affects organizations that are large, interconnected, or linked to many other similarly situated organizations, intellectual hazard can pose a threat to the stability of an entire system of markets or institutions. In particular, intellectual hazard poses a threat to the smooth, orderly, and efficient functioning of the world's financial markets.

[The authors go on to argue that a variety of intellectual biases contributed to excessive risk taking by financial institutions, poor performance by bank regulators, and severe policy mistakes by the Federal Reserve, all of which contributed to the financial crisis of 2007-2009.]

Questions and Comments

1. On the application of behavioral-economic principles to legal questions, see Christine Jolls et al., *A Behavioral Approach to Law and Economics*, 50 Stan. L. Rev. 1471 (1998); Ryan Bubb & Richard Pildes, *How Behavioral Economics Trims Its Sails and Why*, 127 Harv. L. Rev. 1593 (2014). On the implications of behavioral law and economics for legal policy, see, e.g., Richard H. Thaler & Cass R. Sunstein, *Nudge: Improving Decisions About Health, Wealth, and Happiness* (2008). For criticism of behavioral economic approaches to legal issues, see, e.g., Jennifer Arlen, *The Future of Behavioral Economic Analysis of Law*, 51 Vand. L. Rev. 1765 (1998); Gregory Mitchell, *Why Law and Economics' Perfect Rationality Should Not Be Traded for Behavioral Law and Economics' Equal Incompetence*, 91 Geo. L.J. 67 (2002). For an application of behavioral law and economics to risk-management processes in financial institutions, see Nizan Geslevich Packin, *It's (Not) All About the Money: Using Behavioral Economics to Improve Regulation of Risk Management in Financial Institutions*, 15 U. Pa. J. Bus. L. 419 (2013).

20

When Risk Management Fails

In this final chapter we consider cases where risk management failed. We look at two general issues: (a) what factors cause the risk-management function to break down? and (b) what steps could or should have been undertaken to ward the disaster before it occurred?

A. UBS AND THE FINANCIAL CRISIS

The financial crisis of 2007-2009 swept up many firms in its tentacles, both in the United States and around the world. UBS, a large Swiss bank, took huge losses at the outset of the crisis as a result of improvident investments in subprime mortgage-backed securities; assistance by the Swiss National Bank was required to tide the bank through its troubles. Nearly at the same time, it came out that employees of UBS had been soliciting American wealth management customers with promises that they could avoid U.S. taxes by entrusting their money to the bank. Perhaps not surprisingly, the U.S. tax authorities did not react favorably to this news.

In 2010, UBS issued a "transparency report" to its shareholders that — commendably, in the view of many observers — frankly examined the bank's failures leading up to the crisis. The report identified the following causes.

UBS, Transparency Report to the Shareholders of UBS AG: Financial Market Crisis, Cross-Border Wealth Management Business, Liability Issues and Internal Reviews*

2010

GROWTH STRATEGY

UBS had an internal corporate objective of becoming one of the top banks in the world in a variety of financial sectors. After it spun off its subsidiary Dillon Read

---

*The following is the author's summary of the main findings in this report.

Capital Management in 2005, it sought to quickly develop the same sort of business in-house. The growth strategy was not systematically planned or implemented and was not integrated with UBS's traditional strategy of investing only in high-quality investment products.

No Balance Sheet Limits

UBS did not have any limits in place for how large it could grow. In consequence, it grew too fast, and did so by accumulating a huge portfolio of U.S. mortgage securities, which caused equally huge losses when these securities lost value.

Low Refinancing Rates

UBS had an excellent reputation in financial markets prior to the crisis, and thus its investment bank was able to able to obtain low short-term financing to support its investment in U.S. mortgage-backed securities. This strategy backfired when credit markets froze during the crisis, since UBS was not able to refinance these investments on favorable terms.

Complacency

UBS was aware that the American housing market bubble was beginning to burst as early as 2006, but remained confident that it would not be badly affected. It falsely believed that its investments in subprime mortgage-backed securities were safe, based on their high credit rating and the fact that they were often backed by bond insurers. It also believed that its holdings could be sold at any time in the market. Because it nurtured an overconfident attitude about its risks, UBS neglected to limit its exposure in the U.S. housing market.

No Overall Assessment of Risk Positions

UBS's investment bank failed to make any overall assessment of the entirety of the bank's credit and default risks associated with its portfolio of mortgage backed securities.

Reliance on Information from Business Units

UBS's senior management relied on the heads of the business units who assured them that risk in the U.S. housing market was under control. Senior management of the investment bank only learned of the extent of the problem in July 2007, too late to do much about it.

Overreliance on Statistical Models

UBS risk control specialists relied too heavily on statistical models and paid too little attention to the fundamental risks underlying the U.S. housing market.

Remuneration

Compensation practices at UBS did not distinguish good performance from income "generated by exploiting market advantages, such as low funding costs." This incentive structure "encouraged the generation of revenues without adequately considering the associated risks."

Questions and Comments

1. This report was prepared by a company that experienced a breakdown in risk management. One might expect, in this circumstance, to see the report being essentially a whitewash exonerating the firm of any mistakes. The tone of the UBS report, however, is different: One sees here an apparently candid effort to address issues in a straightforward and realistic fashion, without notable attempts to skew conclusions in any particular direction. What explains this sudden outbreak of honesty? Could it be significant that the bank's former chief executive officer had resigned the previous year?

2. One of UBS's self-criticisms is that the bank failed to impose limits on growth. Why is it a *desideratum* of sound banking to restrain balance sheet growth? Put another way, what problems might arise if a bank grows exceptionally rapidly?

3. The report faults the bank for complacency and overconfidence — complacency in believing that it could obtain cheap financing indefinitely, regardless of the risk of its portfolio, and overconfidence in believing that its portfolio was sound despite early warning signs that it was not. Why did the sophisticated managers at UBS fall prey to these errors? Is this another example of "intellectual hazard"? Was the fact that the bank was Swiss — and that it had previously enjoyed a reputation for "Swiss" conservatism in its banking practices — a factor that contributed to its problems?

4. One of the most insidious risks facing complex organizations is that associated with fundamental change. In the analysis of the company's report, change was part of UBS's problems. UBS had spun off Dillon Read Capital Management and was seeking to develop its own in-house book of business, in an effort to become one of the world's premier investment banks. The report suggests that ordinary standards of business prudence were cast by the wayside in the company's impetuous push for growth.

5. The study concludes that UBS relied too heavily on statistical models — thus confirming observations made in the previous chapter about the risks of these techniques. What, however, should the bank do differently next time around, given that statistical models are essential to the conduct of its business?

6. Is asymmetric information risk reflected in this report? When was the bank's most senior management alerted to the fact that the bank's positions in the U.S. mortgage market were not properly controlled?

7. This study involves breakdowns both in risk management and compliance. The risk management breakdown occurred when the bank maintained a large, unhedged portfolio of mortgage-backed securities. The compliance breakdown occurred when representatives of UBS's wealth management department solicited business of American citizens on promises to help them avoid U.S. taxes. Where these breakdowns coincidental, or was there a deeper underlying cause?

B. THE LONDON WHALE

The next example of risk management breakdown is JPMorgan Chase's "London Whale" fiasco.

Permanent Subcommittee on Investigations, United States Senate, JPMorgan Chase Whale Trades: A Case History of Derivatives Risks and Abuses

Mar. 15, 2013

In 2005, JPMorgan Chase spun off as a separate unit within the bank its Chief Investment Office (CIO), which was charged with investing the bank's excess deposits, and named as its head Ina Drew who served as the bank's Chief Investment Officer. In 2006, the CIO approved a proposal to trade in synthetic credit derivatives, a new trading activity. In 2008, the CIO began calling its credit trading activity the Synthetic Credit Portfolio ["SCP"]. Three years later, in 2011, the SCP's net notional size jumped from $4 billion to $51 billion, a more than tenfold increase. In late 2011, the SCP bankrolled a $1 billion credit derivatives trading bet that produced a gain of approximately $400 million.

In December 2011, JPMorgan Chase instructed the CIO to reduce its Risk Weighted Assets (RWA) to enable the bank, as a whole, to reduce its regulatory capital requirements. In response, in January 2012, rather than dispose of the high risk assets in the SCP — the most typical way to reduce RWA — the CIO launched a trading strategy that called for purchasing additional long credit derivatives to offset its short derivative positions and lower the CIO's RWA that way. That trading strategy not only ended up increasing the portfolio's size, risk, and RWA, but also, by taking the portfolio into a net long position, eliminated the hedging protections the SCP was originally supposed to provide.

In the first quarter of 2012, the CIO traders went on a sustained trading spree, eventually increasing the net notional size of the SCP threefold from $51 billion to $157 billion. By March, the SCP included at least $62 billion in holdings in a U.S. credit index for investment grade companies; $71 billion in holdings in a credit index for European investment grade companies; and $22 billion in holdings in a U.S. credit index for high yield (non-investment grade) companies. Those holdings were created, in part, by an enormous series of trades in March, in which the CIO bought $40 billion in notional long positions which the OCC later characterized as "doubling down" on a failed trading strategy. By the end of March 2012, the SCP held over 100 different credit derivative instruments, with a high risk mix of short and long positions, referencing both investment grade and non-investment grade corporations, and including both shorter and longer term maturities. JPMorgan Chase personnel described the resulting SCP as "huge" and of "a perilous size" since a small drop in price could quickly translate into massive losses.

At the same time the CIO traders were increasing the SCP's holdings, the portfolio was losing value. The SCP reported losses of $100 million in January, another $69 million in February, and another $550 million in March, totaling at quarter-end nearly $719 million. A week before the quarter ended, on March 23, 2012, CIO head Ina Drew ordered the SCP traders to "put phones down" and stop trading. In early April, the press began speculating about the identity of the "London Whale" behind the huge trades roiling the credit markets, eventually unmasking JPMorgan Chase's Chief Investment Office. Over the next three months, the CIO's credit derivatives continued to lose money. By May, the Synthetic Credit Portfolio reported losing $2 billion; by the end of June, the losses jumped to $4.4 billion; and by the end of the year, the total reached at least $6.2 billion.

The excerpt reproduced immediately above was from a congressional committee which may have seen political value in highlighting management failures at the bank. A few months earlier, in January 2013, JPMorgan Chase had released its own report entitled "Report of JPMorgan Chase & Co. Management Task Force Regarding 2012 CIO Losses." Not surprisingly, the bank's report adopted a somewhat less inflammatory tone. But in its own way the bank's report was also critical of the mistakes that had been made.

The JPMorgan Task Force criticized both those who designed and implemented the flawed trading strategy and also those in management, including top bank officers, for having allowed the losses to occur. In its view:

- Ina Drew, the bank's Chief Investment Officer, failed to ensure that the CIO management understood and properly monitored the trades, failed to ensure that internal controls functioned as intended, and failed to understand or appreciate the changes that occurred to the Synthetic Credit Portfolio in 2012.
- Barry Zubrow, head of the enterprise's risk management operation at the time of the trades, failed to properly control risk in the CIO operation.
- Douglas Braunstein, the enterprise's chief financial officer, did not correct weaknesses in financial controls applicable to the Synthetic Credit Portfolio, failed to question the changes displayed by the portfolio in 2012, and believed that the problems were primarily the responsibility of risk management rather than finance.
- As for Chairman and Chief Executive Officer Jamie Dimon, the Task Force diplomatically quoted the boss's self-criticism: "CIO, particularly the Synthetic Credit Portfolio, should have gotten more scrutiny from both senior management, and I include myself in that, and the firm-wide risk control function. These were egregious mistakes. They were self-inflicted, we were accountable and what happened violates our own standards and principles by how we want to operate the company. This is not how we want to run a business." However, the Task Force also defended Dimon by noting that he responded forcefully when he became aware of the seriousness of the issue.

Questions and Comments

1. JPMorgan Chase is an enormous company, with assets of more than $2.4 trillion. A $6 billion trading loss is a very large amount of money, but in the context of the bank's overall operations, is it that significant?

2. Several people lost their scalps as result of the London Whale fiasco, among them Ina Drew, the head of the CIO, as well as all of the traders who were directly involved in implementing the catastrophic strategy. In August 2013, two traders who worked in the CIO department were indicted for allegedly falsifying records and hiding losses from regulators.

3. In 2013, JPMorgan Chase entered into a $920 million agreement with multiple regulators to settle charges arising out of the fiasco (the regulators were the Comptroller of the Currency, the Board of Governors of the Federal Reserve System, the Securities and Exchange Commission, and the U.K. Financial Conduct Authority). A few weeks later the bank agreed to a $100 million settlement with the

Commodities Futures Trading Commission — and acknowledged that it bore some degree of blame for the fiasco.

4. It appears from published reports that JPMorgan Chase's Chief Investment Office had only an indistinct idea of the purposes to be served by the Synthetic Credit Portfolio. This portfolio was officially a hedging instrument, yet it had earned excellent profits in previous years — profits that did not go unrewarded. Were the traders given mixed messages — hedge, even if it means taking a loss on the portfolio, and also make a profit, even if it means giving up the hedge?

5. In the end, the portfolio generated the worst possible outcome: It neither hedged anything in particular and it made spectacular losses rather than profits. Could this have been a consequence, in part, of the lack of clarity about what the operation was supposed to achieve in the first place?

6. Ina Drew, the head of the CIO office, alerted her superiors of the problem when news reports were about to appear in the financial press. Reading between the lines, it appears that she may have hesitated to come forward earlier in hopes that market conditions would turn around and the problem would go away. Drew is faulted for tardiness, but might the report also reflect badly on her superiors to the extent that it indicates that she may have feared being punished if she reported the losses sooner?

7. Should Jamie Dimon have resigned in recognition of the fact that a serious failure occurred on his watch?

8. The London Whale fiasco blew through the lines of defense we discussed in Chapter 2: The traders and their supervisors failed to implement the correct strategy or apply proper controls; compliance and risk management did not detect the problem; and internal audit didn't notice anything amiss. Why didn't internal controls work?

9. Notice that change risk is manifested in this account: The role of the CIO had evolved in the recent past and internal controls had not kept pace to deal with the new reality.

10. What about intellectual hazard? JPMorgan Chase's senior management appears to have had a pre-formed idea of the CIO as a stodgy, conservatively managed fixed income operation that did not pose significant risks and did not require much of their attention. In fact, by 2012 the reality was quite the opposite.

11. JPMorgan Chase's Risk Policy Committee met eight times a year for approximately three hours per meeting. Was it active enough?

12. How could a reputedly well-managed bank like JPMorgan Chase have allowed this situation to evolve?

C. BENGHAZI

Not all risk management breakdowns occur in the private sector. The government is also a complex organization subject to many risks. The following excerpt contains a report by a State Department review board of the events surrounding the terror attacks in Benghazi, Libya on September 11-12, 2012 that cost the lives of Ambassador Chris Stevens and three other U.S. government personnel, as well as seriously wounding several others.

Report of the State Department Accountability Review Board

Dec. 19, 2012

. . . Four Board members were selected by the Secretary of State and one member from the intelligence community (IC) was selected by the Director for National Intelligence. Ambassador Thomas R. Pickering served as Chairman, with Admiral Michael Mullen as Vice Chairman. Additional members were Catherine Bertini, Richard Shinnick, and Hugh Turner, who represented the IC. . . .

[T]his report examines: whether the attacks were security related; whether security systems and procedures were adequate and implemented properly; the impact of intelligence and information availability; whether any other facts or circumstances in these cases may be relevant to appropriate security management of U.S. missions worldwide; and, finally, whether any U.S. government employee or contractor, as defined by the Act, breached her or his duty. . . .

The Benghazi attacks took place against a backdrop of significantly increased demands on U.S. diplomats to be present in the world's most dangerous places to advance American interests and connect with populations beyond capitals, and beyond host governments' reach. With State Department civilians at the forefront of U.S. efforts to stabilize and build capacity in Iraq, as the U.S. military draws down in Afghanistan, and with security threats growing in volatile environments where the U.S. military is not present — from Peshawar to Bamako — the Bureau of Diplomatic Security (DS) is being stretched to the limit as never before. DS overall has done a fine job protecting thousands of employees in some 273 U.S. diplomatic missions around the world. No diplomatic presence is without risk, given past attempts by terrorists to pursue U.S. targets worldwide. And the total elimination of risk is a non-starter for U.S. diplomacy, given the need for the U.S. government to be present in places where stability and security are often most profoundly lacking and host government support is sometimes minimal to nonexistent.

The Benghazi attacks also took place in a context in which the global terrorism threat as most often represented by al Qaeda (AQ) is fragmenting and increasingly devolving to local affiliates and other actors who share many of AQ's aims, including violent anti-Americanism, without necessarily being organized or operated under direct AQ command and control. This growing, diffuse range of terrorist and hostile actors poses an additional challenge to American security officers, diplomats, development professionals and decision-makers seeking to mitigate risk and remain active in high threat environments without resorting to an unacceptable total fortress and stay-at-home approach to U.S. diplomacy.

For many years the State Department has been engaged in a struggle to obtain the resources necessary to carry out its work, with varying degrees of success. This has brought about a deep sense of the importance of husbanding resources to meet the highest priorities, laudable in the extreme in any government department. But it has also had the effect of conditioning a few State Department managers to favor restricting the use of resources as a general orientation. There is no easy way to cut through this Gordian knot, all the more so as budgetary austerity looms large ahead. At the same time, it is imperative for the State Department to be mission-driven, rather than resource-constrained — particularly when being present in increasingly risky areas of the world is integral to U.S. national security. The recommendations in this report attempt to grapple with these issues and err on the side of increased attention to prioritization and to fuller support for people and facilities engaged in working in high risk, high threat areas. The solution requires a more serious and sustained commitment from Congress to support State Department needs, which, in total, constitute a small percentage both of the full national budget and that spent for national security. One overall conclusion in this report is that Congress must do its part to meet this challenge and provide necessary resources to the State Department to address security risks and meet mission imperatives.

Mindful of these considerations, the ARB has examined the terrorist attacks in Benghazi with an eye towards how we can better advance American interests and protect our personnel in an increasingly complex and dangerous world. This Board presents its findings and recommendations with the unanimous conclusion that while the United States cannot retreat in the face of such challenges, we must work more rigorously and adeptly to address them, and that American diplomats and security professionals, like their military colleagues, serve the nation in an inherently risky profession. Risk mitigation involves two imperatives — engagement and security — which require wise leadership, good intelligence and evaluation, proper defense and strong preparedness and, at times, downsizing, indirect access and even withdrawal. There is no one paradigm. Experienced leadership, close coordination and agility, timely informed decision making, and adequate funding and personnel resources are essential. The selfless courage of the four Americans who died in the line of duty in Benghazi on September 11-12, 2012, as well as those who were injured and all those who valiantly fought to save their colleagues, inspires all of us as we seek to draw the right lessons from that tragic night. . . .

In examining the circumstances of these attacks, the Accountability Review Board for Benghazi determined that:

1. The attacks were security related, involving arson, small arms and machine gun fire, and the use of RPGs, grenades, and mortars against U.S. personnel at two separate facilities — the SMC and the Annex — and en route between them. Responsibility for the tragic loss of life, injuries, and damage to U.S. facilities and property rests solely and completely with the terrorists who perpetrated the attacks. The Board concluded that there was no protest prior to the attacks, which were unanticipated in their scale and intensity.

2. Systemic failures and leadership and management deficiencies at senior levels within two bureaus of the State Department (the "Department") resulted in a Special Mission security posture that was inadequate for Benghazi and grossly inadequate to deal with the attack that took place.

   Security in Benghazi was not recognized and implemented as a "shared responsibility" by the bureaus in Washington charged with supporting the post, resulting in stove-piped discussions and decisions on policy and security. That said, Embassy Tripoli did not demonstrate strong and sustained advocacy with Washington for increased security for Special Mission Benghazi. The short-term, transitory nature of Special Mission Benghazi's staffing, with talented and committed, but relatively inexperienced, American personnel often on temporary assignments of 40 days or less, resulted in diminished institutional knowledge, continuity, and mission capacity.

   Overall, the number of Bureau of Diplomatic Security (DS) security staff in Benghazi on the day of the attack and in the months and weeks leading up to it was inadequate, despite repeated requests from Special Mission Benghazi and Embassy Tripoli for additional staffing. Board members found a pervasive realization among personnel who served in Benghazi that the Special Mission was not a high priority for Washington when it came to security-related requests, especially those relating to staffing.

The insufficient Special Mission security platform was at variance with the appropriate Overseas Security Policy Board (OSPB) standards with respect to perimeter and interior security. Benghazi was also severely under-resourced with regard to certain needed security equipment, although DS funded and installed in 2012 a number of physical security upgrades. These included heightening the outer perimeter wall, safety grills on safe area egress windows, concrete jersey barriers, manual drop-arm vehicle barriers, a steel gate for the Villa C safe area, some locally manufactured steel doors, sandbag fortifications, security cameras, some additional security lighting, guard booths, and an Internal Defense Notification System.

Special Mission Benghazi's uncertain future after 2012 and its "non-status" as a temporary, residential facility made allocation of resources for security and personnel more difficult, and left responsibility to meet security standards to the working-level in the field, with very limited resources. In the weeks and months leading up to the attacks, the response from post, Embassy Tripoli, and Washington to a deteriorating security situation was inadequate. At the same time, the SMC's dependence on the armed but poorly skilled Libyan February 17 Martyrs' Brigade (February 17) militia members and unarmed, locally contracted Blue Mountain Libya (BML) guards for security support was misplaced.

Although the February 17 militia had proven effective in responding to improvised explosive device (IED) attacks on the Special Mission in April and June 2012, there were some troubling indicators of its reliability in the months and weeks preceding the September attacks. At the time of Ambassador Stevens' visit, February 17 militia members had stopped accompanying Special Mission vehicle movements in protest over salary and working hours.

Post and the Department were well aware of the anniversary of the September 11, 2001 terrorist attacks but at no time were there ever any specific, credible threats against the mission in Benghazi related to the September 11 anniversary. Ambassador Stevens and Benghazi-based DS agents had taken the anniversary into account and decided to hold all meetings on-compound on September 11.

The Board found that Ambassador Stevens made the decision to travel to Benghazi independently of Washington, per standard practice. Timing for his trip was driven in part by commitments in Tripoli, as well as a staffing gap between principal officers in Benghazi. Plans for the Ambassador's trip provided for minimal close protection security support and were not shared thoroughly with the Embassy's country team, who were not fully aware of planned movements off compound. The Ambassador did not see a direct threat of an attack of this nature and scale on the U.S. Mission in the overall negative trend line of security incidents from spring to summer 2012. His status as the leading U.S. government advocate on Libya policy, and his expertise on Benghazi in particular, caused Washington to give unusual deference to his judgments.

Communication, cooperation, and coordination among Washington, Tripoli, and Benghazi functioned collegially at the working-level but were constrained by a lack of transparency, responsiveness, and leadership at the senior levels. Among various Department bureaus and personnel in the field, there appeared to be very real confusion over who, ultimately, was responsible and empowered to make decisions based on both policy and security considerations.

3. Notwithstanding the proper implementation of security systems and procedures and remarkable heroism shown by American personnel, those systems and the Libyan response fell short in the face of a series of attacks that began with the sudden penetration of the Special Mission compound by dozens of armed attackers.

The Board found the responses by both the BML guards and February 17 to be inadequate. The Board's inquiry found little evidence that the armed February 17 guards offered any meaningful defense of the SMC, or succeeded in summoning a February 17 militia presence to assist expeditiously. The Board found the Libyan government's response to be profoundly lacking on the night of the attacks, reflecting both weak capacity and near absence of central government influence and control in Benghazi. The Libyan government did facilitate assistance from a quasi-governmental militia that supported the evacuation of U.S. government personnel to Benghazi airport. The Libyan government also provided a military C-130 aircraft which was used to evacuate remaining U.S. personnel and the bodies of the deceased from Benghazi to Tripoli on September 12.

The Board determined that U.S. personnel on the ground in Benghazi performed with courage and readiness to risk their lives to protect their colleagues, in a near impossible situation. The Board members believe every possible effort was made to rescue and recover Ambassador Stevens and Sean Smith. The interagency response was timely and appropriate, but there simply was not enough time for armed U.S. military assets to have made a difference.

4. The Board found that intelligence provided no immediate, specific tactical warning of the September 11 attacks. Known gaps existed in the intelligence community's understanding of extremist militias in Libya and the potential threat they posed to U.S. interests, although some threats were known to exist.

5. The Board found that certain senior State Department officials within two bureaus demonstrated a lack of proactive leadership and management ability in their responses to security concerns posed by Special Mission Benghazi, given the deteriorating threat environment and the lack of reliable host government protection. However, the Board did not find reasonable cause to determine that any individual U.S. government employee breached his or her duty.

Questions and Comments

1. What, in the committee's view, were the breakdowns of risk management that allowed the attack at Benghazi to happen? How can they be corrected to prevent similar disasters (if at all)?

2. Four members of the committee were picked by the Department of State and one came from the intelligence community. Given that the State Department selected a majority of the committee, how credible are its findings effectively exonerating senior State Department officials?

3. The committee members were persons of distinction and excellent reputations. Thomas Pickering, the committee chairman, is a distinguished career diplomat; he was United States Ambassador to the United Nations from 1989-1992 and Under Secretary of State for Political Affairs from 1997 to 2000. Michael Mullen, the vice-chairman, had an equally illustrious career in the military, rising to Chairman of the Joint Chiefs of Staff — the highest ranking officer in the United States military — from 2007-2011. Both of these men had retired from their positions and had no reason to fear retaliation for anything they said. Is it likely they were browbeaten? On the other hand, could their version of events have been colored, perhaps unconsciously, by a wish to protect their former offices — the Department of State and the U.S. military — from criticism for possibly mishandling the situation?

4. The committee declared that they had full and complete access to every source of information which they deemed relevant to their investigation. However, the committee never interviewed Hillary Clinton, the Secretary of State. What do you make of the committee's claim to have conducted a full and complete investigation given the fact that they never spoke with the government official with overall responsibility for the matter?

5. In 2013, a junior staffer at the U.S. National Security Agency (NSA), claiming to be a whistleblower, revealed that the agency had been engaged in extensive surveillance involving American citizens. It later came out that the agency had also been listening to telephone conversations involving leaders of friendly countries, including German Chancellor Angela Merkel. The result was a loss of face for the United States, an embarrassing diplomatic imbroglio, and significant damage to the effectiveness of an important government agency. People have different opinions about whether the supposed whistleblower, Edward Snowden, was acting for or against the best interests of the United States. Putting that judgment aside, how could the national security establishment have been so sloppy as to allow this sort of thing to happen?

D. ROYAL BANK OF SCOTLAND

U.K. Financial Conduct Authority
Final Notice to Royal Bank of Scotland Plc. et al.

Nov. 19, 2014

On Wednesday 20 June 2012 customers of the [Royal Bank of Scotland and affiliates] found that they could not use all of the banks' online banking facilities to access their accounts or obtain accurate account balances from ATM machines. The events which would develop throughout the day are referred to in this notice as the "IT Incident." Customers learned that the problems were not isolated to these facilities, but they discovered that they were unable to drawdown loans, transfer payments to external creditors including credit card companies and mortgage providers or transfer monies using SWIFT payment methods.

Customers would later find that the Banks had applied incorrect credit and debit interest to their accounts, duplicated entries on their statements and failed to accurately record transactions on their accounts. Customers also learned that the Banks had not processed their standing orders on time. The problems affected not only the Banks' customers in the UK. They also affected customers who were abroad. The

Banks declined their credit card purchases leaving customers unable to pay bills and make purchases. Some customers found themselves without access to cash in foreign countries.

The IT Incident also affected individuals who were not customers of the Banks. They were unable to receive monies from the Banks' customers and this prevented them from honoring their own financial commitments. The effect on commercial customers included the inability to use Bankline, an internet banking service. This meant that commercial customers were unable to manage payments, verify checks or make international cash transfers. Other commercial customers were unable to finalize their audited accounts and meet payroll commitments. At a broader level, this affected the Banks' ability to fully participate in clearing.

Clearing is a system established to settle payments among banks and is the process by which banks ensure that a payee receives the full value of a check or standing order. An efficient clearing system is fundamental to the efficient operation of the financial markets. The IT Incident affected at least 6.5 million customers in the UK (92% of whom were UK retail customers). This was 10% of the population. Disruptions to the majority of RBS's and NatWest's systems lasted until 26 June 2012, and the disruptions to the majority of Ulster Bank's systems continued until 10 July 2012. Disruptions to other systems . . . affected all the Banks and those disruptions lasted until July 2012.

The actual cause of the IT Incident was a software compatibility issue between the upgraded software and the previous version of the software. The compatibility issue occurred when Technology Services (the centralized Group IT function which provides IT services to the Banks) backed out a software upgrade that they had installed on Sunday, 17 June 2012. To "back out" a software upgrade means to uninstall the current version of the software and go back to a previous version of software. The underlying cause of the IT Incident was the failure of the Banks to meet their obligations to have adequate systems and controls to identify and manage their exposure to IT risks. The Banks' IT risk arrangements were provided at Group level through a number of support and control functions. At the Group level there were failings in Technology Services, in the Three Lines of Defense and in the Group's approach to IT operational risk.

[Government regulations require] a firm to take reasonable care to organize and control its affairs responsibly and effectively with adequate risk management systems. On the basis of the facts and matters described in more detail below, the banks breached [this requirement] because they failed to have adequate systems and controls in place to identify and manage their exposure to IT risks. In particular: Technology Services did not take reasonable steps to ensure that changes to the Banks' IT systems were carried out in a carefully planned and consistent manner. It did not manage and plan those changes adequately because it did not devise and implement adequate: processes for identifying, analyzing and resolving IT incidents; and policies for testing software.

The Three Lines of Defense did not carry out their responsibilities adequately:

Technology Services Risk, (the risk function within Technology Services), the First Line of Defense, was responsible for identifying and managing IT risks. It did not carry out its duties adequately because it had a culture of reacting to events and a team with insufficient experience and skills. Business Services Risk, the Second Line of Defense, was responsible for reviewing Technology Service's view of risks and identifying gaps in the Group's view of risk. It did not carry out these duties adequately because it had limited IT skills and it did not sufficiently challenge

Technology Services Risk's view of IT risk. Group Internal Audit, the Third Line of Defense, was responsible for providing independent assurance on the design and operation of risk management and internal control processes. There were weaknesses in the communications between Group Internal Audit and the First and Second Line of Defense.

The Banks failed to adequately inform themselves about the nature and effect of IT operational risk. The operational risk appetite relevant to IT was the "Business Continuity & IT Continuity" risk appetite ("IT Continuity Risk Appetite"). This was too limited because, in addition to Business Continuity (recovering from an incident), it should have included a much greater focus on IT Resilience (designing IT systems to withstand or minimize the risks of disruptive events). This appetite directly informed the Group's IT Continuity Policy Standard which had the same limitations. . . .

A retail bank's core business function is the provision of financial services. This includes making deposit accounts and loans available to its customers, updating customer balances, giving customers access to their accounts through online banking and ATM machines, processing customers' and third parties' payments.

The IT Incident [failed to provide] an appropriate degree of protection for customers because [it] prevented the Banks' customers from engaging in basic banking functions. . . . It . . . could have affected financial stability because the high tiering of UK payment systems means that an operational failure in one settlement bank can lead to intraday credit and liquidity exposures between settlement banks and the indirect participants that use their services and this can lead to contagion and disruption in the financial system; and depositors' inability to access their funds prevents them from undertaking economic activity. . . .

Questions and Comments

1. This case illustrates the risks banks and many other institutions face in managing their information technology systems. RBS was attempting to replace an outmoded system. During the upgrade, the technicians detected problems with the new software and tried to revert to the older system. But the damage had been done: The upgrade had created incompatibilities that interfered with the banks' ability to process consumer transactions.

2. The incident at RBS was described as a "glitch." It was an expensive glitch. The banks were assessed fines of $88 million and paid approximately $111 million in redress to affected customers.

3. As of 2014, RBS was 81 percent owned by the U.K. government as a result of a bailout stemming from the financial crisis of 2007-2009. Thus, as a result of this order, one arm of the British government was effectively fining another.

4. What was the root cause of this fiasco, in the view of the regulator? The problem was not a lack of financial commitment: The RBS Group was spending more than $1.5 billion each year to maintain IT infrastructure. What, then, was the problem?

5. The regulator indicated that this action was part of a campaign to encourage cultural changes in bank IT departments: "Today's decision reflects the [regulator's] commitment to ensuring that banks make the cultural shift away from 'business continuity' (recovering from disruptive events) to 'resilience' (ensuring that the banking activities most critical to customers can withstand the effect of

disruptive events like software and other IT failures)." The implication is that bank IT departments have a "culture" that focuses excessively on dealing with the consequences of a breakdown and pays insufficient attention to preventing breakdowns in the first place. Why would IT departments have a dysfunctional culture? If the culture was dysfunctional, do you think a regulator can change it?

6. The incident sparked a management crisis. Customers lost access to their checking accounts, failed to pay their mortgages, were unable to close on house sales, and faced potential downgrades in credit ratings. Some were stranded abroad without access to cash; one was reportedly kept in prison because he could not make bail. The public outrage was magnified by lingering anger about the earlier bailout and rumors that the glitch was due to outsourced operations in India. Politicians threatened punitive actions. Thousands complained to watchdog agencies. Meanwhile the bank itself was struggling to correct the problem, understand its consequences, and communicate effectively with the public and the regulators. How would you respond if you were in charge?

7. A few days after the breach, while disruptions were still occurring, the bank canceled a scheduled corporate hospitality function at the Wimbledon tennis tournament and the CEO of the bank's Irish affiliate waived his annual bonus. Were these responses appropriate?

Table of Cases

Table of Authorities, Statutes, and Other Materials

& Employment Policy Journal 325 (2010), 353

Green, Bruce A. and Ellen S. Podgor, Unregulated Internal Investigations: Achieving Fairness for Corporate Constituents, 54 B.C. L. Rev. 73 (2013), 221

Greenberg, Michael D., Culture, Compliance and the C-Suite: How Executives, Boards, and Policymakers Can Better Safeguard Against Misconduct at the Top (Rand 2013), 122

Greenfield, Kent, A Skeptic's View of Benefit Corporations, 1 Emory Corp. Governance & Accountability Rev. 17 (2015), 650

Groff, Lynndon, Is Too Big to Fail Too Big to Confess? Scrutinizing the SEC's "No-Admit" Consent Judgment Proposals, 54 B.C. L. Rev. 1727 (2013), 303

Group of Thirty, Toward Effective Governance of Financial Institutions (2012), 152

Hazard, Geoffrey C. Jr., The Meaning of the Kaye Scholer Case, 26 Akron L. Rev. 395 (1992-1993), 384

Hermalin, Benjamin and Michael Weisbach, Boards of Directors as an Endogenously Determined Institution: A Survey of the Economic Literature, 9 Fed. Reserve Bank of N.Y. Econ. Pol'y Rev. 7 (2003), 44

Hess Corporation 2013 Proxy Statement, 77

Hill, Claire A. & Brett H. McDonnell, Stone v. Ritter and the Expanding Duty of Loyalty, 76 Fordham L. Rev. 1769 (2007), 68

Hines, Christopher T., Returning to First Principles of Privilege Law: Focusing on the Facts in Internal Corporate Investigations, 60 U. Kan. L. Rev. 33 (2011), 423

Holy See Press Office, Protecting Minors, Declaration by the Director of the Holy See Press Office on Response to Sexual Abuse, March 4, 2016, 692-694

Hutchens, Matthew C., Beneficial Branding: Will Benefit Corporations Promote Environmental Interests More Effectively than the Traditional Corporate Form? (October 24, 2013), available at SSRN: http://ssrn.com/abstract=2344896 or http://dx.doi.org/10.2139/ssrn.23448, 650.

Jackson, Howell, Reflections on Kaye, Scholer: Enlisting Lawyers to Improve the Regulation of the Financial System, 66 S. Cal. L. Rev. 1019 (1993), 384

Jacobs, James B., Mobsters, Unions and Feds: The Mafia and the American Labor Movement (2007), 257-258

Jacobs, James B. and Kerry T. Cooperman, Breaking the Devil's Pact: The Battle to Free the Teamsters from the Mob (2011), 257

Jacobs, James B. and Ronald Goldstock, Monitors & IPSIGS: Emergence of a New Criminal Justice Role. 43 Crim. L. Bull. 217 (2007), 449

John Jay College Research Team, The Causes and Context of Sexual Abuse of Minors by Catholic Priests in the United States, 1950-2010, May 2011, 682-684

Johnson, Lyman, Pluralism in Corporate Form: Corporate Law and Benefit Corps., 25 Regent U. L. Rev. 269 (2012-2013), 650

Jolls, Christine et al., A Behavioral Approach to Law and Economics, 50 Stan. L. Rev. 1471 (1998), 770

Kaal, Wulf A. and Elizabeth R. Malay, The Role of Corporate Integrity Agreements in the Expansion of Fiduciary Duties, U. St. Thomas (Minn.) Legal Studies Research Paper No.13-25, (2013), available at http://papers.ssrn.com/sol3/papers.cfm?abstract_id=2317580, 567

Kahn, Faith Stevelman, Pandora's Box: Managerial Discretion and the Problem of Corporate Philanthropy, 44 UCLA L. Rev. 579 (1997), 649

Kaplan, Robert S., et al., Managing Risk in the New World, 87 Harv. Bus. Rev., 68 (October 2009), 152

Khanna, Vikramaditya and Timothy L. Dickinson, The Corporate Monitor: The New Corporate Czar?, 105 Mich. L. Rev. 1713 (2007), 449

Killingsworth, Scott, The Privatization of Compliance, RAND Center for Corporate Ethics and Governance Symposium White Paper Series, Symposium on Transforming Compliance: Emerging Paradigms for Boards, Management, Compliance Officers, and Government (2014), 205

STATUTES

Index